York Deeds Volume 8

You are holding a reproduction of an original work that is in the public domain in the United States of America, and possibly other countries. You may freely copy and distribute this work as no entity (individual or corporate) has a copyright on the body of the work. This book may contain prior copyright references, and library stamps (as most of these works were scanned from library copies). These have been scanned and retained as part of the historical artifact.

This book may have occasional imperfections such as missing or blurred pages, poor pictures, errant marks, etc. that were either part of the original artifact, or were introduced by the scanning process. We believe this work is culturally important, and despite the imperfections, have elected to bring it back into print as part of our continuing commitment to the preservation of printed works worldwide. We appreciate your understanding of the imperfections in the preservation process, and hope you enjoy this valuable book.

YORK DEEDS

BOOK VIII

PORTLAND
BROWN THURSTON COMPANY
1892

CONTENTS.

Preface . . . . Page 5
Register's Certificate . . . . Page 7
Errata . . . . Page 8

York Deeds . . . . Folios 1—268

Index
    I. Grantors . . . . . . Pages 1— 75
    II. Grantees . . . . . Pages 76—153
    III. Other Persons, ... Pages 154—166
    IV. Places . . . . . . Pages 167—170
    V. General . . . . . . Pages 171—186

PREFACE.

VOLUME VIII of the series of manuscript books of public records deposited in the state archives at Alfred is of the same quality in manufacture as those used next preceding, and it was opened July 7, 1713—the same day volume VII was closed. A very few of its first leaves are detached and the bottom ends considerably worn. Folios numbered fifty-six, seven, eight and nine, furnish an evidence of much study of the record thereon contained, relating to land titles at the place now known as Brunswick and vicinity; otherwise the volume is in an excellent state of preservation, considering the long time it has been in use. The first page is inscribed thus:

>The Eight Book of Deeds &c' for
>The County of York—
>1713
>JOSEPH HAMMOND, Register.
>cost 40^d || $6.66 cents.

The Joseph Hammond here represented was the immediate successor as register and only son at the time of the death of his father, Joseph Hammond, of whose personal history considerable has been recorded in the Introduction to a former book of the copies of the Deeds. The Probate Court records show that he was possessed of a comparatively large worldly estate considering the time in which he lived, and on one of the pages of the probate records I find an entry of which the following is a copy:

Joseph Hammond, Esq., Judge of Probate of Wills and granting administration within the County of York, died Feb. 20, 1709-10.

And

Joseph Hammond, late of Kittery, letter of adm granted his son, 24 July, 1710.

The will of Charles Frost represents him as his son-in-law, and other records as well as the York Deeds make a similar exhibit. From the inventory on file at Alfred of his estate may be obtained the number of rooms of his dwelling, their furnishings and value placed upon each article thereof.

PREFACE.

The pages of volume VIII of the Deeds, copied, printed and herewith presented to the public were inscribed by the hand of Joseph Hammond, who succeeded his father Joseph, and the book closed January 7, 1717, he continuing in office as register till 1721, making his last entry April 3, of that year. On the 17th of April, 1739, Joseph Hammond was appointed to administer on the estate of his mother, deceased, and on April 2, 1753, his own will was probated, a copy of which appears in the book entitled "Maine Wills," published by Sargent in 1887, which shows he had four sons all domiciled on his landed estate in Kittery, and three daughters, all of whom had married. One provision of the will reads:

> I give and bequeath unto Six Bearers, two Overseers, and the Rev. Mr. Josiah Chase each a Ring of Gold and a pair of Gloves, and to the Bearers of Mr. Chase's Wives.

Nine rings were purchased by the administrator for which £6 : 1 : 1½ was paid.

The work of copying the original manuscript for the typesetter, the proof-reader and indexer, has been performed with a determination equal to if not in excess of all former efforts to make this volume of the series as correct in every particular as the volumes preceding it. I visited Alfred while the work of copying was going on and failed to find anything needing correction or suggestive of change in adopted methods of procedure, and have examined from time to time the operations at the printing house of the Brown Thurston Company, and in no instance have I discovered the slightest inclination by any one to shrink from rigid and persistent demands for the most perfect correctness obtainable.

The historical information this volume contains appears to me to be in excess of all others of the series. Covering as it does, a larger field of territory, the information volume VIII contains is of a more general character.

A record of the authorizing of the publication hereof and my connection with the matter may be found in the Preface to the printed volume numbered VII.

LEONARD B. CHAPMAN.

DEERING, AUGUST 8, 1892.

REGISTER'S CERTIFICATE.

State of Maine.

COUNTY OF YORK, ss:

This may certify that the following printed volume is a true copy of the eighth book of records of the Registry of Deeds for this County; that I have read and compared the same with the original records; and that all accidental variations that have been detected are noted in the table of errata on the following page.

Attest:

Justin M. Leavitt

Register of Deeds for York County.

ERRATA.

Fol. 47 line 84 *for* Calfe *read* Calef
    58   72   " pmises   "   pmisses
    67 on margin " All ex and " Allexand
   146 line 59   " neither   " Meither

   170 Mark of Sarah Gurney

   172 line 34 *for* Premised *read* Demised

   199 Mark of John Davis jun *for*   *read*

   259 line 105 *for* by *read* ly
For omissions in indexes see p. 152.

YORK DEEDS.

This Indenture made the Second of January one thousand Six hundred Eighty & five & in ye first year of ye Reign of our Soveraign James ye Second King of England Scotland France & Ireland &c^t Between These partyes That is to Say that I Henry Donnel of York in ye Province of Maine have Sold & delivered & by these presents do Sell Alienate Effife & deliver over unto John Stover of Cape Nuddack to him & his heirs forever apcell of Land lying & being at ye further end of ye long Sands Comonly So called going to ye Cape-neck that is to Say a parcel of land that lyeth above ye path that goeth to ye aboves^d Cape Nuddack from ye end of ye long Sands afores^d also all ye barbery marsh That Lyeth on ye Eastward Side of ye Great Island in ye barbery marsh runing from ye bredth Northwest & by west by ye Eastward Side of ye Great Island afores^d over to ye upland

Donnell: to Stover

all which Land & marsh was granted to me Henry Donnel by a General Town meeting held at york & Lyeth in ye old book of Town grants as may appear by that old book all which Lands & marsh with all ye priviledges & Imunitys thereunto belonging I ye s^d Henry Donnel do by these presents Sell Alienate Effife & Deliver over unto, ye aboves^d John Stover To have & To hold to him his heirs Execut^{rs} Adm^{rs} & Assigns forever for which s^d Land & marsh I ye afores^d Henry Donnel do Confess my Selfe fully Satisfyed & I ye aboves^d Henry Donnel do promiss & bind my Selfe my heirs Execut^{rs} Adm^{rs} & Assignes to defend ye Sale of ye aboves^d pmises & that ye aboves^d Land & marsh above Expressed is free from all Mortgages or any Mollestations whatsoever unto all which I ye s^d Henry Donnel have hereunto Set my hand & Seal the day & year above written

Signed Sealed & Delivered   Henry *his HD mark* Donnel (a Seale)
In ye psence of us
Francis Johnson

Mary *her M mark* Davis

Henry Donnel Came befor me this Second day of January 1685 & acknowledged this Instrum^t or bill of Sale to be his act & deed   John Davis Dep^{ty} presid^t
A True Copie of ye Orignal Recorded July 7° 1713/
                      p Jos: Hamond Reg^r

BOOK VIII, FOL. 1.

To all People to whom these presents Shall come Greeting Know yee that I Joseph Weare of ye Town & County of York within ye Province of Maine yeoman for & in Consideration of a Walluable Sum to me in hand paid before ye Ensealing hereof well & Truely paid by Cap^{tn} Abraham Preble Junr of ye Town County & province afores^d Gent ye Reciept where of I do hereby Acknowledge & my Selfe therewith fully Satisfyed & Contented & thereof & of Every part & pcell thereof do Exonerate Acquitt & discharge ye s^d Abraham Preble his heirs Executors Adm^{rs} forever by these psents have given granted bargained Sold Aliened Conveyed & Confirmed & by these psents do freely fully & Absolutely give grant bargaine Sell alien Convey & Confirm unto him ye s^d Preble his heirs & Assignes forever one Messuage or Tract of Land Scittuate lying & being in ye Town of York being one quarter of an Acre of upland at ye place where ye old warehouse Stood [1] Built by Major Davis Taking in s^d point on both Sides butted on York River on ye South west in bredth by s^d river Sixteen pole & bounded by ye land s^d Preble bought of Cap^{tn} James Plaisted otherwise Northeastward To have & To hold ye s^d granted & bargained pmisses with all ye Appurtenances priviledges & Comoditys to ye Same belonging or in any wise Appurtaining to him ye s^d Preble his heirs & Assignes forever to his and their only propper use benefit & behalfe forever & I ye s^d Weare for me my heirs Execut^{rs} Adm^{rs} do Covenant promiss & grant to & with ye s^d Preble his heirs & Assignes that before ye Ensealing hereof I am ye True & Sole & Lawfull owner of ye above bargained pmisses & am Lawfully Siez^d & possessed of ye same in my own propper right as a good perfect & absolute Estate of Inheritance in fee Simple & have in my Selfe good right full power & Lawfull Authority to grant bargain Sell Convey & Confirm ye s^d bargained premisses in manner as afores^d & that ye s^d Preble his heirs & Assignes shall & may from time to time & at all times forever hereafter by force & vertue of these presents Lawfully peaceably & Quietly have hold use occupy possess & Enjoy ye s^d demised & bargained premisses with ye Appurtenances free & clear & freely & Clearly Acquitted & Exonerated & discharged of & from all maner of former & other gifts grant barguins Sales Leases Mortgages wills Entails Joynturs Dowrys Judgments Executions & Extents, Furthermore I ye s^d Joseph Weare for my Selfe my heirs Execut^{rs} Adm^{rs} do Covenant & Engage ye above demised premisses to him ye s^d Abraham Preble his heirs & Assignes against ye Lawfull claims & demands of any person or p^{r}sons whatso-

Weare to Preble

Book VIII, Fol. 1.

ever hereafter to warrant & Secure & Defend In Witness hereof I have hereunto Set my hand & Affixed my Seal this Twentyeth day of June in y[e] year of our Lord one Thousand Seven hundred & Tenn & in y[e] ninth year of y[e] Reign of our Soveraign Lady Anne by y[e] grace of God of Great Brittaine France & Ireland Queen &c[t]

Signed Sealed & Delivered
 I y[e] psence of us   Joseph X Weare (a Seale)
 Sarah Black   his mark
 Job P Young
   his mark
York July y[e] s 15th 1713

York ss/ The above named Joseph Weare psonally Appeared before me y[e] Subscriber one of her Maj[tys] Justices of y[e] peace within s[d] County of york & Acknowledged y[e] above written Instrum[t] to be his act & deed

             Abra[x] Preble
A True Coppy of y[e] Original Recorded July 16° 1713/
            p Jos Hamond Reg[r]

I Robert Elliot of Newcastle in y[e] Province of New Hampsh[r] in New Engl[d] do hereby acknowledge to have received of M[r] Samuel Penhallow of Portsm° in s[d] Province y[e] Sum of fifty Six pounds money in full Satisfaction of y[e] above Instrum[t] both as to principle & Interest and do hereby Assign & make over all my right Title & Interest in & to y[e] Same & all things mentioned from me my heirs Execut[rs] & Adm[rs] To have & To hold unto him y[e] s[d] Sam[ll] Penhallow his heirs &c[t] forever Witness my hand March 4th 1712/

Signed Sealed & Delivered   Rob[t] Elliot (a Seale)
 in psence off
 Tho: Pierce
   mark
 Sarah X Thomas

Prov of New Hampsh[r] Portsm° May 9. 1713 Robert Elliot Esq[r] psonally Appeared and Acknowledged y[e] above Instrum[t] to be his act & Deed

      Coram me Ala Hunking Justices ps

Memor The Deed above mentioned unto which this assignm[t] is Añexed is recorded in Lib[r] VI Folio 165

A True Coppy of ye Original Assignm[t] Recorded Aug[st] 7° 1713   p Jos Hamond Reg[r]

BOOK VIII, FOL. 2.

This Indenture made ye fourteenth day of Octob[r] Anno Dom one thousand Seve hundred & one Annoq[r] R R[o] Gullielmi Tertii Anglia &c[t] Decimo Tertio Between Samuel Allen Esq[r] Proprietor of y[e] province of New Hampshire in New England on y[e] one part & John Usher of Charles Town in y[e] County of Middlesex within y[e] province of y[e] Massachusets Bay in New England afores[d] Esq[r] on y[e] other part Witnesseth That y[e] s[d] Sam[ll] Allen for & in Consideration of y[e] Sum of one Thousand five hundred pounds Currant money of New England to him in hand well & Truely paid at & before y[e] Ensealing & Delivery of these psents by y[e] s[d] John Usher y[e] receipt whereof to full Content and Satisfaction y[e] s[d] Sam[ll] Allen doth hereby Acknowledge & thereof & of Every part & pcell thereof doth Acquitt Exonerate & discharge y[e] s[d] John Usher his heirs Execut[rs] Adm[rs] & Assigns & Every of them for ever by these psents as also for diverse other good causes & Considerations him thereunto moveing he y[e] s[d] Sam[ll] Allen hath given granted bargained Sold Aliened Enfeoffed Conveyed & Confirmed & by these psents for himselfe & his heirs doth fully freely clearly & Absolutely give grant bargain Sell Aliene Enfeoffe Convey & Confirm unto y[e] s[d] John Usher his heirs & Assignes all that part purpart & portion of y[e] Maine Land of & in New England in America begining from y[e] Middle part of Neumkeek river & from thence to proceed along y[e] Sea Coast to Cape Ann & round about y[e] Same to piscattaqua harbour & So forwards up with in y[e] river of Nechawanack & to y[e] further head of s[d] river & from Thence Northwestward untill Sixty Miles be finished from y[e] first Entrance of piscattaqua harbour & also from Neumkeek Thr[o)] y[e] river thereof up into y[e] land west

. . . .

[2] From piscattaqua Thro[o] Nichewanack river to y[e] Land Northwestward aboves[d] & also all that y[e] South halfe of y[e] Isles of Shoals Together with all other lands & Islets as well Imbayed as Adjoyning lying or abutting upon or near pmisses or any part or pcell thereof within five Leagues distance not other wise granted to any by Special name at any Time before y[e] Eighteenth day of Aprill 1635 all which part & portions of land Islands & pmisses are . alled by y[e] Name of New Hampsh[r] or y[e] Province of New Hampsh[r] & also all That other parcell or portion of lands woods & wood grounds lying on y[e] Southeast part of y[e] river of Sagadehock in y[e] Northeast part of New Engl[d] afores[d] at y[e] mouth or Entrance thereof Containing there Ten Thousand Acres which s[d] other pcell of lands is Called & known by y[e] Name of Massonia & also all that part or portion of land in y[e] province of Maine

Book VIII, Fol. 2.

in New Engl^d afores^d begining at ye Entrance of Newchewanack river & So upwards along ye s^d river & to ye furthest head thereof & to Contain in bredth Thro' all ye length Afores^d Three miles within ye Lands from Every part of ye s^d river & halfe way over ye s^d river and also all Towns Villages & habitable places Scittuate Standing or being in ye s^d Province of New Hampsh^r pcells of land wood & wood grounds called Massonia part of ye s^d Province of Maine or any of them & also all ye firm lands Soyles & grounds as well under water as above water & Every Shoars Creeks havens harbours bayes ports rivers Lakes floods waters mines & minerals as well royal mines & mineralls of gold & Silver as other mines & minerals be they such mines & minerals or veins of Mettiel as are close hidden in ye Earth or openly Seen in or upon ye Earth Saving only ye fifth part of all ye Ore of gold & Silver to remain to his Maj^{ty} his heirs & Successo^{rs} all Quarries of preceous Stones pearles Ambergrease pine Trees firr Trees oak & all other Timber Trees woods under woods & all fishing of what kind or kinds of fish Soever wheth^r Royall fishes as whales Sturgions or any other fishs by whatsoever Name or Names they or any of Them are or shall be called or known hunting hawking fowling & all & Singular other prorogatives rights Comoditys Jurisdictions Royaltys priviledges franchises Libertys preeminencies Marrine power in & upon ye Seas Lakes & rivers within ye s^d Province & other pmisses & Also all Escheats Casualtyes Flottzom Jetzam Lagan Anchorage & other Such dutys all Imunitys Leets Islets Perquesits and profits of Courts Deo dands waines & Stray goods of Fellonies & Fugitives Escheats Casual profits heriditaments & Appurtenances whatsoever Scittuate Lying being Ariseing happening Occuring or to be had Taken or Enjoyed or any wayes Appurtaining or belonging upon within or of ye s^d Province of New Hampsh^r parcells of Land wood & woodgrounds . . . . ed Massonia part of s^d pr . . . . of Maine or any of Them of what . . . or Nature Sovever in N . . . . and Afores^d whereof . . . . . Whereinto ye s^d Sam^{ll} Allen is Siezed possessed or have any Estate right Title Interest Equity of Redemption claime or demand whatsoever also all ye revertion & revertions remaind^r & remainders of and in all Every ye heriditaments & pmisses in & by these presents granted or mentio to be granted & all ye rents of ye rates of Six pence or any other Sum by ye Acre And all other chief rents Quitt rents or other rents reservations Services Issues & profits reserved due payable Issueing or arising out of all & Every or any of ye s^d heriditam^{ts} & pmisses & by these psents

Book VIII, Fol. 3.

granted or Mentioned to be granted & all royal & other rights powers Libertys Authoritys Jurisdicetion royaltys bennefits Advantage & other Matters & things whatsoever & all ye Estate right Title Interest power Authority claime & demand whatsoever of ye s^d Sam^{ll} Allen of into or out of all & Every ye s^d Province Tracts of land Towns Villages habitable places heriditam^{ts} & premisses in & by These psents granted or Mentioned to be granted or any of Them & also all deeds writings rentals Accounysts papers & Evidences whatsoever any ways relating unto Touching or Concerning ye s^d heriditam^{ts} & pmisses To have & To hold ye s^d Province of New Hampsh^r parcells of Land wood & woodgrounds Called Massonia & all other ye above granted & bargained pmisses with their and Every of their rights members & Appurtenances & Every part and parcel thereof unto ye s^d John Usher his heirs & Assignes forever to his & their own Sole & proper use beñefit & behoofe forever Provided Always & upon Condition Nevertheless being ye True Intent & meaning of these p^{r}sents And partyes to ye Same any thing herein to ye Contrary Notwithstanding That if ye s^d Sam^{ll} Allen his heirs Execut^{rs} Adm^{rs} or assignes Shall & do well & Truely pay or Cause to be paid unto ye above named John Usher his heirs Execut^{rs} Adm^{rs} or Assignes at or in ye Dwelling house of ye s^d John Usher Scittuate on his farm in Charles Town where he now Liveth in Currant money of New England as it now passeth in ye Massachusets province afores^d ye Sum of one Thousand five hundred pounds in manner and According to ye Articles & Agreements Signed by ye Above Named Sam^{ll} Allen & John Usher bareing date with These psents & that on or before the fourteenth of day of October which will be in ye year of our Lord 1703 without Fraud Coven or further delay That Then This psent Indenture Sale Mortgage & grant & Every Clause & Article herein Contained Shall Cease determine be utterly voyd & of none Effects or Else to abide & remaine in full force Strength & vertue to all Intents & purposes in y^e Law whatsoever In Witness whereof y^e s^d partyes have Interchangeably Set their hands & Seals y^e day & year first above written   Samuel Allen ($_{Seale}^{a}$)
Signed Sealed & Delivered
. . . . . in psence of us
. . . .

[3] Boston February 16th 170 3/4 Benj^a Eliot of full age psonally Appearing before me y^e Subscriber one of her

Book VIII, Fol. 3.

Maj^{tys} Justices of y^e peace within y^e Province of y^e Massa Bay in New England made oath that he Saw ye within named Samuel Allen Esqr Sign Seal & Deliver ye within written Instrum^t as his Act & deed & that he ye Depona^t Together with James Minzies Set to their names as Witnesses of ye Execution Thereof. Jurat Coram

Isaac Addington

Entered & Recorded According to ye Original March ye 14th 1703/4   p Samuel Penhallow Record^r

Portsm^o 26th of Augst 1713

A True Copia from ye Records of ye Province of New Hampsh^r as it stands there recorded in Book N° 7 Fol^o 60 61 & 62 & Examined   p Wm Vaughan Record^r

Exam^d & Compared with ye Coppy above written & foregoing & Recorded September ye 6th 1713

p Jos. Hammond Reg^r

Prov^{ce} of New Hampsh^r in New England   John Abbot of Portsm^o in ye Province of New Hampsh^r in New England aged about Sixty four years Master of ye Sloop Seaflower & John Doer of ye Same place aged about Twenty nine years Deposeth & Saith that John Usher of Charles Town in ye County of Middlesex in ye Province of ye Massachusets bay Esqr on ye first day of this Insta^t month of Septr 1713 he calling us for witnesses did Enter upon & take possession of an Island lying to ye Eastward of Piscattaqua river about Thirty Leagues formerly called Sackadehock Island & named it Allens Island & marked a Stump of a Tree with ye following letters vizt *I. V.* & then went upon great Island & There marked a pitch pine Tree with These Letters following vizt *I. V* and Laid a heap of Stones in ye form following vizt *V* on ye back Side of a Chimney where there had been a house Standing Some years agoe which was built or Caused to be built by Samuel Allen Esqr dec^d in which house one John Hornibrook lived to ye knowledge of ye Deponant Abbot & as ye Deponant Doer hath been Informed upon which Island of Sackadehock & Great Island Al^s Massonia ye s^d John Usher Esqr declared he read an Instrum^t in writing or deed of Mortgage from s^d Sam^{ll} Allen to him dated ye 14th of Octob^r 1701 that by Vertue hereof he

Book VIII, Fol. 3.

took possession in part for ye whole Contained in s^d Instrum^t or deed of Mortgage which was forfeited to him for ye Non paym^t of fifteen hundred pounds & also declared he did demand from ye Estate of ye s^d Samuel Allen with ye forfieture of ye Mortgage ye Sum of four Thousand one hundred & forty five pounds Two shilling & Tennpence all which wee See & heard read on ye places Taken possession of & further Saith not
            John Abbot
             his
          John X Doer
             mark

Pro^{ce} of N Hampsh^r Second day of Septr 1713

John Abbot & John Doer ye Above depona^{ts} psonally Appearing made oath to ye Truth of ye above deposition
     Coram Theo: Atkinson Jus^t ps unus Quor^x
         Cha: Story Just^s p^a

A True Coppy of ye Original Recorded Septr ye 6th 1713/
        p Jos Hamond Reg^r

To All People to whom these presents shall come Jeremiah Dummer of Boston in ye County of Suffolk within her Majestyes Province of ye Massachusets bay in New England Esqr only brother & heir of ye late Revd Mr Shubael Dummer Deceased Sendeth Greeting Know yee that 'ye s^d Jeremiah Dummer for & in Consideration of ye Sum of Twelve pounds in Currant money of ye aboves^d Province to me in hand before ye Ensealing hereof well & Truely paid by Abra^m Preble Junr of york in ye County of york in ye Province of Maine in New England afores^d yeomans The receipt whereof I do hereby Acknowledge and thereof & of Every part & parcell thereof do Exonerate Acquitt and discharge ye s^d Abraham Preble his heirs & Assignes forever have given granted bargained Sold remised released Conveyed & Confirmed and by these psents do fully freely & Absolutely give grant Bargaine Sell remise release Transferr convey and confirm unto ye s^d Abraham preble & to his heirs and Assignes forever all ye Estate Right Title Interest Inheritance use propperty possession Claime and demand whatsoever which I ye s^d Jeremiah Dummer Ever had now have or which I my heirs Execut^{rs} Adm^{rs} in Time to Come may might Should or in any wise ought to have of in or to all That one piece or parcel of upland & Swampy ground Scittuate Lying & being within ye bounds and Limits of ye Township of York afores^d at a place known

Dumer To Preble

Book VIII, Fol. 4.

by ye Name of ye Ridge of land Containing by Estimation fourteen acres butted & bounded on ye South west Side by Land formerly granted to Majr John Davis on ye Southeast End partly by ye Land of Hopewell Weare & partly by ye Land of Abraham Preble Esqr & runing on ye Northeast Side by s^d Prebles bounds northwest to a Small freshet river known by ye name of ye Little river & on ye northwest Side is bounded by a Town way leading from s^d Town of York into ye woods as also all that Smal Ashen Swamp Containing by Estimation Two Acres Lying & being in ye Township of York afores^d near a Cove known by ye Name of paimers Cove which s^d Land & Swamp Containing in ye whole Sixteen Acres by Estimation be ye Same more or Less was formerly granted to ye s^d Late Reverend Mr Shubael Dummer Then minister at York afores^d by s^d Town of York as by s^d Town of Yorks book of Records & Returns of lands may more fully Appear To Have & To Hold ye s^d Granted & Released pmisses & Every part thereof to him ye s^d Abraham Preble Junr & to his heirs and Assignes forever to his & their only propper use bennefit & behooffe forever more So that neither I ye s^d Jeremiah Dummer my heirs or Assignes nor any other pson or psons by from or under me them or any of them Shall or will by any meanes hereafter have Claime Challenge or demand any Estate right Title or Interest of in or to all or any part of ye s^d Granted & released pmisses But of & from Every Action of Rights Estate Title Interest Claime & Demand of in & to ye pmisses & Every part and parcell thereof I my Selfe & Every of them Shall be utterly Excluded and forever Debarred [4] By these psents & further I ye s^d Jeremiah Dummer for my Selfe my heirs Execut^{rs} Adm^{rs} do hereby Covenant grant and agee ye above granted & released pmisses with ye Appurtenances & Every part thereof unto ye s^d Abraham Preble Junr his heirs & Assignes against ye Lawfull Claims & Demands of all & Every pson & psons any wayes Claiming or demanding ye Same or any part thereof by from or und^r me forever hereafter to Warrant and Defend/

In Witness whereof I have hereunto Set my hand & Seal ye Ninth day of June Anno Domini one Thousand, Seven hundred & Thirteen Annoq, Regni Reginee Anna nunc Magna Brittana &c^t Duodecimo/   Jer: Dummer (a. Seal)
Signed Sealed & Delivered
  In ye psence of
  Joseph Storer
  Edwd Goddard

BOOK VIII, FOL. 4.

Suffolk ss/ Boston June 9th 1713/
The above named Jeremiah Dummer Esq[r] psonally Appeared before me y[e] Subscriber one of her Maj[tys] Justices of y[e] peace within s[d] County of Suffolk & Acknowledged y[e] above written Instrument to be his Act & Deed
Addington Davenport

Boston June 9th 1713/
Rec[d] of y[e] within Named Abraham preble Jun[r] y[e] Sum of Twelve pounds money in full payment of y[e] purchase Consideration within Mentioned.   p me Jer: Dummer./
Recorded According to y Original July y[e] 16th 1713/
p Jos Hamond Reg[r]

Preble
to
Weare

To All Christian People to whom These presents Shall come Greeting Know yee that I Abraham Preble Jun[r] of y[o] Town & County of york in y[e] province of Maine Gent for & in Consideration of a valuable Sum to me in hand paid before y[e] Ensealing hereof well and Truely paid by Joseph Weare of y[e] Town County & Province afores[d] yeoman y[e] reciept whereof I do hereby Acknowledge and my Selfe therewith fully Satisfyed Contented & thereof & of every part and parcel thereof do Exonerate Acquit & discharge y[e] s[d] Joseph Weare his heirs Execut[rs] Administrators for ever by these presents Have given granted bargained Sold Aliened Conveyed & Confirmed & by These psents do freely fully & Absolutely give grant bargaine Sell Aliene Convey & Confirm to him y[e] s[d] Weare his heirs & Assignes for ever Two Acres of land Scittuate Lying & being in y[e] Town of york at y[e] head of y[e] burnt plaine be y[e] Same more or Less as it is bounded at y[e] Northeast by my own Swampy Land on y[e] Northwest by my own Land & on y[e] Southwest by s[d] Prebles fence new built by s[d] Weare as Stakes drove into y[e] ground & markt Trees & on y[e] South East by Daniel Blacks land To have & To hold y[e] s[d] granted & bargained pmises with all y[e] Appurtenances priviledges & Comoditys to y[e] Same belonging or in any wise Appertaining to him y[e] s[d] Weare his heirs & Assignes for ever to his & their only propper use benefit And behalf for ever & I y[e] s[d] Preble for me my heirs Execut[rs] Adm[rs] do Covenant promiss & grant to & with y[e] s[d] Weare his heirs & Assignes that before y[e] Ensealing hereof that I am y[e] True & Sole & Lawfull owner of y[e] above bargained pmises & am Lawfully Siezed & possessed of y[e] Same in my own propper right as a good perfect & Absolute Estate of Inheritance in Fee

Book VIII, Fol. 4.

Simple & have in my Selfe good right full power & Lawfull Authority to grant bargaine Sell Convey & Confirm y⁰ sᵈ bargained pmises in manner as abovesᵈ & that y⁰ sᵈ Weare his heirs & Assignes Shall & may from Time to Time & at all Times for ever hereafter by force & vertue of These pmises Lawfully & peaceably & Quietly have hold use Occupy possess & Enjoy y⁰ sᵈ demised & bargained pmises with y⁰ Appurtenances free & clear & freely & clearly Acquitted and Exonerated & Discharged of & from all maner of former & other gifts grants bargains Sales Leases Mortgages wills Entails Joyntures Dowrys Judgmᵗˢ Executions & Extents./ Furthermore I y⁰ sᵈ Preble for my Selfe my heirs Executʳˢ Admʳˢ do Covenant & Ingage y⁰ above Demised pmises to him y⁰ sᵈ Weare his heirs & Assignes against y⁰ Lawfull claims & demands of any pson or psons whatsoever hereafter to Warrant & Secure & Defend In Witness hereof I have hereunto Set my hand & Affixed my Seale this Twentyeth day of June in y⁰ year of our Lord one Thousand Seven hundred & Teñ. And in y⁰ Ninth year of the Reign of our Soveraign Lady Anne of Great Brittaine ffrance & Ireland Queen &cᵗ/   Abraᵐ Preble Junʳ (ₛₑₐₗa)
Signed Sealed & Delivered
   In y⁰ psents of us
   Sarah Black
                his
   Job   ⟋   Young
              mark
         York ss/   York July y⁰ 13ᵗʰ 1713/

The above named Abraᵐ Preble Junʳ psonally Appeared before me y⁰ Subscriber one of her Maᵗʸᵃ Justice of y⁰ peace within sᵈ County of York & Acknowledged y⁰ Above written Instrumt to be his Act & Deed./   Abraˣ Preble
   Recorded According to y⁰ Original July 16ᵗʰ 1713./
                              p Jos Hañiond Regʳ

To All Christian People to whom this psent deed of Sale Shall Come I Richard Walker of Ipswich in y⁰ County of Essex in y⁰ province of y⁰ Massachusets Bay in New Eng-
<small>Walker to Harris</small> land husbandman Sendeth Greeting/ Know Yee that y⁰ sᵈ Richard Walker for & in Consideration of five pound passable money to him in hand paid to Satisfaction before y⁰ Ensealing & Delivery of These psents by John Harris of y⁰ Town aforesᵈ in y⁰ Coun-

ty afores^d Gunsmith ye rec^t whereof ye s^d Richard Walker doth Acknowledge himselfe therewith all fully Satisfyed Contented & paid & in Consideration whereof he hath Given granted bargained Sold Aliened Assigned Enfeoffed & Confirmed and by these psents he doth fully & Absolutely Give grant bargaine Sell Aliene Assigne Enfeoffe Convey & Confirm [5] Unto ye s^d John Harris his heirs Execut^rs Adm^rs & Assignes for ever one parcell or Tract of land Lying & being at Cocks Hall in ye County of york in ye Province of The Massachusets Bay in New England about Eight miles from ye Town of Wells Near Cape porpoise river & Kennebunk which s^d Tract of land ye s^d Richard Walker purchased of Mr Harlackinton Simonds of Ipswich afores^d in ye province afores^d ye Quantity whereof was & is Three hundred Acres as p Deed from s^d Simonds to s^d Walker may Appear & ye afores^d land Lyeth or Adjoyneth upon Cape porpoise river & Lyeth on ye East Side of ye s^d river To have & To hold ye s^d parcell or Tract of land before mentioned with ye woods under woods Standing Lying or Growing on ye Same & all & Singular ye rights Libertyes profits priviledges & Appurtenances to ye Same belonging or in Any wayes Appurtaining to him ye s^d John Harris his heirs Execut^rs Adm^rs & Assignes for ever & to his & their Sole & only propper use benefit & behoofe for ever and ye s^d Richard Walker for himselfe his heirs Execut^rs and Adm^rs doth Covenant promiss & grant to & with ye s^d John Harris his heirs Execut^rs Adm^rs & Assignes by these psents That he ye s^d Richard Walker is Imediately before ye Ensealing & delivery of These psents ye True & rightfull Owner of ye above granted & bargained premises & Every part thereof & hath in himself good right full power & Lawfull Authority ye Same to Sell Convey & Assure as is above Expressed & That ye Same is free & clear & clearly acquitted & discharged of & from all other Bargains Sales Alienations Titles Troubles Charges & Incumbrances in what Nature or kind So ever & that ye s^d John Harris his heirs & Assignes Shall & may Every part thereof have a full & firm right thereunto and further ye s^d Richard Walker doth Covenant & Ingage that he will warrant & defend ye Same to him ye s^d John Harris his heirs & Assignes against all & Every pson or psons claiming any right or Title or Interest therein from by or under him/ In Witness whereof ye s^d Richard Walker hath hereunto Set his hand & Seal This Seventeenth day of Septemb^r Anno Domini one Thousand Seven hundred & Thirteen/ The words Enterlined at Cocks hall in ye County of York in ye province of y^e

Massachusets Bay in New England was before Signing & Sealing between y⁰ 15ᵗʰ & 32 line./ Richard Walker (a seal)
Signed Sealed & Delivered
In psence of us
Sam¹¹ Appleton
John Dane
  Essex ss Ipswich Sepʳ 15ᵗʰ 1713
Richard Walker psonally Appeared & Acknowledged this Instrument to be his Act & deed, Before me
      Sam¹¹ Appleton Justˢ peace
Recorded According to yᵉ Original Septembʳ yᵉ 23ᵗʰ 1713/.
      p Jos : Hamond Regʳ

Cole to Allen

Know All men by these presents that I John Cole of Kittery in yᵉ County of york Miller for & in Consideration of a valluable Sum of money to me in hand paid by my brother Frances Allen of yᵉ Same place yeoman the recᵗ thereof I do Confess & my Selfe therewith fully Satisfyed Content & paid have given granted bargained & Sold and do by these prsents give grant bargaine & Sell & forever Set over unto yᵉ sᵈ Francis Allen his heirs & Assignes forever all that my Thirty Acres of Land that was granted by yᵉ Town of Kittery may yᵉ 10ᵗʰ 1703 and Layd out unto me by Capᵗⁿ John Smith then Surveyʳ of sᵈ Town yᵉ 5ᵗʰ day of August 1703 and is on record in Kittery Town book as Appears undʳ yᵉ hand of yᵉ Late Major Joseph Hamond Esqʳ Town Clerk referrence thereunto being had respecting yᵉ place where & boundarys thereof Together with all yᵉ wood & Timber under woods Standing or lying on sᵈ land with all yᵉ Appurtenances & priviledges whatsoever belonging to sᵈ land & pmises To have & To hold all yᵉ abovesᵈ land with yᵉ Appurtenances and priviledges thereunto belonging or in any wise Appurtaining unto yᵉ only & Sole use benefit & behoofe of him yᵉ sᵈ Francis Allen his heirs Execuᵗʳˢ Admʳˢ or Assignes for ever against me yᵉ sᵈ John Cole or my heirs for ever & I yᵉ sᵈ John Cole do hereby Covenant for my Selfe & my heirs with yᵉ sᵈ Francis Allen his heirs & Assignes for ever that yᵉ pmises are free from all Incumbrances whatsoever as gifts Sales grants Mortgages Joyntures or Dowryes and that I am yᵉ True & Lawfull owner thereof at & before yᵉ Signing & Sealing hereof the peaceable possession thereof to Warrant & forever defend against all psons Laying a Lawfull Claime

BOOK VIII, FOL. 6.

thereunto In Witness whereof I have hereunto Set my hand & Seal this Twenty Seventh day of March one Thousand Seven hundred & Eleven./ 1711./   John Cole ($_{Seale}^{a}$)
Signed Sealed & Delivered in y^e
psence of us y^e Subscribers
  Peter Staple
  Margriet Paul
  William Godsoe
  York ss/
The within named John Cole psonally Appeared before me y^e Subscrib^r one of her Maj^{tys} Justices of y^e peace for aboves^d County & Acknowledged This Instrum^t to be his free Act & deed May 12 : 1712   John Hill
  Recorded According to ye Original September ye 28th 1713./   p Jos: Hamond Reg^r

[6] This Indenture made ye Seventeenth day of February in ye year one Thous^d Seven hundred & Twelve Thirteen between Reinold Jenkins of Kittery in ye County of york in New England yeoman on ye one part & francis Allen of ye Same place yeoman on ye other part Witnesseth that ye s^d Reinold Jenkins in Consideration of a valluable Sum of money to him in hand paid by Francis Allen as Also for diverse other Considerations herein after Exprest to ye full Satisfaction of him ye s^d Reinold Jenkins Doth by these psents give grant bargain Sell & for— Set over unto ye s^d ffrancis Allen his heirs & Assignes for ever all that Tract or pcell of Land lying in Kittery Near Dover river & Sturgeon Creek by Estimation fifteen Acres or thereabouts be it more or Less & Takes its begining at a white oak at ye Corner of W^m ffryes land which was agreed upon between Jabuz Jenkins & W^m ffry for a bound mark & from thence

Allen
&
Jenkins
Exchange

East to a Stone by Frosts Land, North Fifty pole by Frosts land Then on a Straight line to a Stone at ye Northeast corner of Francis Allens land & from thence Southerly on a Straight line to ye afores^d white Oak where ye land first began To have & To hold all ye s^d Tract of land as it is bounded & Set forth by these psents Together with all ye priviledges & Appurtenances thereto belonging whatsoever unto ye only & Sole use & behoofe of him ye s^d Francis Allen his heirs & Assignes for ever ye peaceable possession thereof to Warrant and Defend against all psons Laying Claime thereunto from by or und^r him ye s^d Reinold Jenkins or his heirs forevermore./ And y^e

s^d ffrancis Allen on ye other part & in Consideration & by way of Exchange for & in full Satisfaction for ye aboves^d lands herein Mentioned hath & doth by these psents Give grant bargaine Sell & forever Set over unto ye s^d Reinold Jenkins his heirs & Assignes for ever Two Small Tracts of land lying in Kittery aboves^d Near Dover river ye first Tract is bounded by John Morrell Senr on ye South & on ye west with ye land that was Poundings & on ye North wth ye land that was formerly John Whites to a Stone at ye Northeast Corner of s^d land & on ye East with ye land of ffrancis Allen & W^m ffry ye Second Tract of land lyes by ye highway that goes from John Morrills Junr to Kittery Mill being that Tract of land that Reinold Jenkins his barn Stands upon being Seven pole East & west & Six pole North & South To have & To hold all ye Two aboves^d Tracts of land as they are described Set forth & bounded unto ye only use benefit & behoofe of him ye s^d Reinold Jenkins his heirs & Assignes forever against ye s^d Francis Allen or his heirs ye Peaceable possession thereof to Warrant & forever defend against all psons whatsoever Laying Claime thereunto from by or under him y^e s^d ffrancis Allen or his heirs for ever or any other pson Claiming from by or under them In Witness whereof both partyes above Named Viz^t Reinold Jenkins & ffrancis Allen have Set to their hands & Seals y^e day & year first above written   Francis Allen (${}_{Seal}^{a}$)
Signed Sealed & Delivered   Reinold Jenkins (${}_{Seal}^{a}$)
In y^e p^{r}sence of us y^e Subscrib^{rs}
James Chadborn
James Warren
John Shapleigh

   york ss/ Kittery : 16th Marsh : 1712
             $\overline{3}$

Francis Allen & Hannah his wife Reinold Jenkins & Elizabeth his wife psonally Appeared before me & Acknowledged this Instrum^t to be their act & deed
            Wm Pepperrell
Recorded According to y^e Original Sept. 28th 1713
          p Jos : Hammond Reg^r

To All Christian People to whom this Bill of Sale Shall come & Appear Now Know yee that I Stephen Jenkins of ye Township of Dover & province of New Hampshire in New England./ Send Greeting Now Know Yee that I ye s^d Stephen Jenkins for Diverse good Causes me thereunto

Book VIII, Fol. 7.

moveing Especially for & Consideration of Six pounds money Curra[t] of New England to me in hand paid & Delivered by Reinold Jenkins of y[e] Town of Kittery in y[e] province of Maine have for my Selfe my heirs Execut[rs] Adm[rs] & Assignes do acquit & discharge y[e] fores[d] Reinold Jenkins him his heirs Execut[rs] Adm[rs] & Assignes for ever y[e] fores[d] Sum of Six pounds & that of Every part & parcell thereof have given granted bargained Sold Aliened Confirmed unto y[e] s[d] Reinold Jenkins his heirs Executors Adm[rs] & Assignes & by these psents do freely Clearly & Absolutely give grant bargaine Sell Aliene & Confirm unto him y[e] s[d] Jenkins him his heirs Execut[rs] Adm[rs] & Assignes forever all & whole an parcell of land Scittuate & being in Cold harbour in y[e] s[d] Town of Kittery Containing fourteen Acres Land as it is bounded between y[e] land of John Morrell on y[e] South & on y[e] North to y[e] Land formerly Poundings To have & To hold y[e] above given & granted pmises with all y[e] priviledges thereunto belonging or any wayes Appurtaining to y[e] s[d] Reinold Jenkins to him his heirs Execut[rs] Adm[rs] or Assignes for ever from me y[e] s[d] Stephen Jenkins me my heirs Execut[rs] Adm[rs] or Assignes & that free & Clear & free from all other former Gifts grants Mortgages Legacyes powers of Thirds & that wth y[e] free Consent & Advise of Anne Kincaid y[e] relict of Stephen Jenkins dec[d] & all other Incumbrance whatsoever against all psons from by or und[r] us our means or procurem[t]./ In Confirmation hereof wee have hereunto Set our hands & Seals this Second day of June one Thousand Seven hundred & three./ Stephen Jenkins (a Seal)

In psence of us Witnesses   Anne Kincaid (a Seale)

David Kincaid
his mark   her Σ mark

Francis ⟩ Pitman

June y[e] Seventh day 1703./ Stephen Jenkins psonally Appeared before me y[e] Subscrib[r] & Acknowledged this Bill of Sale to be his Act & Deed   John Woodman
     Justice of peace for y[e] province of New Hampsh[r]
Recorded According to y[e] Original Sept[r] 28[th] 1713./
         p Jos: Hamond Reg[r]

Mendum
to
Skillin

To All Christian People to whom These p[r]sents Shall Come Nathaniel Mendum of Portsmouth within her Maj[tys] Province of New Hampshire in New England Joyner Sends Greeting. Know Yee that y[e] s[d] Nathaniel Mendum for & in Consideration of y[e] Sum of Thirty four pounds Currant [7] Money of New Eng-

Book VIII, Fol. 7.

land to him in hand paid before y[e] Ensealing & Delivery of These presents by Sam[ll] Skillin of Exetor in y[e] afores[d] province Shipwright y[e] rec[t] whereof to full Content & Satisfaction he y[e] s[d] Nathaniel Mendum doth by these p[r]sents Acknowledge & thereof & of Every part thereof for himselfe his heirs Execut[rs] & Adm[rs] doth acquit Exonerate & discharge y[e] s[d] Samuel Skillin his heirs Execut[rs] Adm[rs] & Assignes & Every of them for ever by These psents he y[e] s[d] Nathaniel Mendum Hath given granted bargained Sold Aliened Enfeoffed Conveyed & Confirmed & by these psents doth fully freely Clearly & Absolutely give grant bargaine Sell Aliene Enfeoffe Convey & Confirm unto y[e] s[d] Samuel Skillin his heirs & Assignes for ever y[e] one full quarter part of a Certaine Tract of upland & Swamp Scittuate Lying & being in y[e] Township of Kittery in y[e] County of york in y[e] Province of y[e] Massachusets bay in New England on y[e] Eastern Side of y[e] place Comonly known by y[e] Name of Spruce creek which upland & Swamp was given to his brother Robert Mendum late of Kittery dec[d] by his Grandfather Rob[t] Mendum of Kittery dec[d] as by his Last will & Testament may Appear referrence thereunto being had & is butted & bounded on y[e] Southwest by y[e] aboves[d] Spruce Creek & on y[e] Northwest by Joseph Weeks his land on y[e] Northeast by y[e] woods & on y[e] Southeast by Andrew Halys Land or howsoever otherwise bounded or reputed to be bounded Together with all Such rights Libertys Imunitys profits Priviledges Comoditys Imolluments & Appurtenances as in any kind Apurtaine thereunto with y[e] reverĉon & remainder thereof and all y[e] Estate Right Title Interest Inheritance propperty Possession Claime & demand whatsoever of him y[e] s[d] Nathaniel Mendum of in & to y[e] one quarter part of y[e] aboves[d] whole Tract of upland & Swamp & Every part thereof To have & To hold y[e] one full Quarter part of y[e] aboves[d] whole Tract of upland & Swamp with all & Singular y[e] Appurtenances Thereof unto y[e] s[d] Samuel Skillin his heirs & Assignes & to his & their own Sole and propper use benefit & behoofe from henceforth for ever and y[e] s[d] Nathaniel Mendum for himselfe his heirs Execut[rs] & Adm[rs] doth hereby Covenant promiss grant & Agree to & with y[e] s[d] Samuel Skillin his heirs & Assignes in mañer & form following) That Is To Say That at y[e] time of y[e] Ensealing & Delivery hereof he y[e] s[d] Nath[ll] Mendum is y[e] True & Lawfull owner of y[e] above bargained & Sold premises & hath in himselfe good right full power & Lawfull Authority to Sell & dispose of y[e] Same in maner as afores[d] & that y[e] s[d] Samuel Skillin his heirs & Assignes Shall & may henceforth forever Lawfully peaceably and Quietly have hold use Occupy possess & Enjoy ye above granted pmises with ye Appurtenances thereof free & Clear & Clearly Acquitted & discharged of & from all & all mañer of former & other gifts grants bargains Sales Leases Mortgages Joyntures Dowers Judgments Executions Entails forfeitures & of & from all other Titles Troubles Charges & Incumbrances whatsoever had made Cōmitted done or Suffered to be done by ye s^d Nathaniel Mendun his heirs or Assignes at any time or times before ye Ensealing & Delivery of these psents./ And further ye s^d Nath^{ll} Mendun doth hereby Covenant promiss bind and Oblige himselfe his heirs Execut^{rs} & Adm^{rs} from henceforth & forever hereafter to Warrant & Defend all ye above granted pmises & ye Appurtenances thereof unto ye s^d Sam^{ll} Skillin his heirs & Assignes against ye Lawfull Claims & Demands of all & Every person or persons whomsoever & at any time or times hereafter on demand to give & pass Such farther & Ample Assurence & Confirmations of ye pmises unto ye s^d Sam^{ll} Skillin as in Law or Equity Can be reasonably devised Advised or required In Witness whereof y^e s^d Nathaniel Mendun hath hereunto Set his hand & Seal y^e fourteenth day of Aprill in y^e year of our Lord 1713./ & in y^e Twelfth year of y^e Reign of our Soveraign Lady Anne Queen of Great Brittaine &c^t—

Signed Sealed & Delivered   Nath^{ll} Mendun ($_{Seal}^a$)
   In psence of   Frances Mendun ($_{Seal}^a$)
   John Newmarch
   Jonathan Mendun
       her
.Joan   Denefor
      mark

Pro^{ce} of New Hampsh^r Portsm^o June 20th 1713

Nath^{ll} Mendum & Frances Mendum psonally Appeared & Acknowledged y^e above Instrument to be their Act & Deed./
                  Before me Sam^{ll} Penhallow Just^s p^{ce}

Recorded According to ye Original Octob^r ye 6th 1713./
                       p Jos: Hamond Reg^r

To All Christian People to whom these presents shall Come Nicholas Frost of Portsmouth within her Maj^{tys} Province of New Hampshire in New England Marrin^r & Dorothy his wife Sends Greeting Know yee that ye s^d Nicholas Frost

& Dorothy his wife for & in Consideration of y{e} Sum of Twenty nine pounds Currant money of New England to them in hand paid before y{e} Ensealing & Delivery of these psents by Samuel Skillin of Kittery in y{e} County of York within y{e} province of y{e} Massachusets Bay in New England Shipwright y{e} receipt whereof to full content & Satisfaction they y{e} s{d} Nicholas Frost & Dorothy his wife do by these psents Acknowledge & thereof & of Every part thereof for themselves their heirs Execut{rs} & Adm{rs} do Acquitt Exonerate & Discharge y{e} s{d} Samuel Skillin his heirs Execut{rs} Adm{rs} & Assignes & Every of Them for ever by these [S] Presents They y{e} s{d} Nicholas Frost & Dorothy his wife Have given granted bargained Sold Aliened Enfeoffed conveyed & Confirmed and by these presents do fully freely clearly & Absolutely give grant bargain Sell Aliene Enfeoffe convey & confirm unto y{e} s{d} Samuel Skillin his heirs & Assignes for ever y{e} one full Quarter or fourth part of a Certain Tract of upland & Swamp Scittuate Lying & being in y{e} Township of Kittery in y{e} County of york in y{e} province of y{e} Massachusets Bay in New England on y{e} Eastern Side of y{e} place comonly known by y{e} Name of Spruce Creek which upland & Swamp was given to their brother Robert Mendum late of Kittery deceased by their Grandfather Robert Mendum of Kittery deceased as by his last will & Testament may Appear referrence thereunto being had & is butted & bounded on y{e} Southwest by y{e} Aboves{d} Spruce creek & on y{e} Northwest by y{e} woods & on y{e} Southeast by Andrew Haleys land or howsoever otherwise bounded or reputed to be bounded Together with all Such rights Libertys Imunitys profits priviledges Commoditys Imoluments & Appurtenances as in any kind App{r}tain thereunto with y{e} revercõns & remainders thereof & all y{e} Estate right Title Interest Inheritance propperty possession Claime & Demand whatsoever of them y{e} s{d} Nicholas Frost & Dorothy of in & to y{e} one fourth part of y{e} aboves{d} whole Tract of upland & Swamp & Every part thereof To have & To hold y{e} one full Quarter part of y{e} aboves{d} whole Tract of upland & Swamp with all & Singular y{e} Appurtenances thereof unto y{e} s{d} Sam{ll} Skillin his heirs & Assignes & to his & their own Sole & propper use benefit & behoofe from henceforth forever And y{e} s{d} Nicholas Frost & Dorothy his wife for y{m}selves their heirs Execut{rs} & Adm{rs} do hereby Covenant promiss grant & agree to & with y{e} s{d} Sam{ll} Skillin his heirs & Assignes in mañer & form following (that is to Say) that at y{e} Time of y{e} ensealing & delivery hereof They y{e} s{d} Nicholas ffrost & Dorothy his wife are y{e} True & Law-

Frost to Skillin

Book VIII, Fol. 8.

full owners of ye above bargained & Sold pmises & have in y^mselves good right full power & Lawfull Authority to Sell & dispose of ye Same in mañer as afores^d & that ye s^d Sam^{ll} Skillin his heirs & Assigns shall & may henceforth forever Lawfully peaceably & Quietly have hold use Occupy possess & Enjoy ye above granted pmises with ye Appurtenances thereof free & clear & clearly Acquitted & discharged of & from all & all maner of former & other gifts grants bargains Sales Leases Mortgages Joyntures Dowers Judgm^{ts} Executions Entails forfieturs & of & from all other Titles Troubles charges & Incumbrances w^tsoever had made Comitted done or Suffered to be done by ye s^d Nicholas ffrost & Dorothy his wife their heirs or assignes at any time or times before ye Ensealing & Delivery of These presents And further ye s^d Nicholas ffrost & Dorothy do hereby Covenant promiss bind & Oblige Themselves their heirs Execut^{rs} and Adm^{rs} from hence forth & forever hereafter to Warrant & Defend all ye above granted pmises & ye Appurtenances thereof unto ye s^d Sam^{ll} Skillin his heirs & Assignes against ye Lawfull claims & demands of all & Every pson or psons whomsoever & at any time or times hereafter on demand to give & pass Such farther & Ample Assurence & confirmation of ye pmises unto ye s^d Sam^{ll} Skillin as in Law or Equity can be reasonably devised Advised or required./ In Witness whereof ye s^d Nicholas ffrost & Dorothy his wife have hereunto Set y^r hands & Seals ye Twentyeth day of June in ye year of our Lord one thousand Seven hundred & Thirteen & in ye Twelfth year of ye Reign of our Soveraign Lady Anne Queen of Great Brittain &c^t

Signed Sealed & Delivered   Nicholas ◯ Frost (a Seal)
   his
In psence of   mark
  Sam^{ll} Penhallow Junr   Dorothy Frost (a Seal)
  Wm Cotton Junr

Province of New Hampsh^r Portsm^o June 20th 1713

Nicholas Frost & Dorothy Frost psonally Appeared & Acknowledged ye above Instrument to be y^r Act & Deed

                   Before me Sam^{ll} Penhallow Just^s p^{ce}

Recorded According to ye Original October ye 6th 1713

                   p Jos. Hamond Reg^r

To All Christian people to whom these psents come Greeting Now Know yee that I Richard Bonighton formerly Apprentis to James Waymouth of New Castle in ye province of New Hampshire in New England Cordwainer Son & heir

BOOK VIII, FOL. 9.

Bonighton to Weare

to ye Estate of Mr John Bonighton of Saco for Diverse good & Lawfull considerations moveing me hereunto & in Special for a Mare & a guñ & money in hand paid & by me recieved of Liev^t Peter Weare of Hampton in ye Province of New Hampshire whereby I Acknowledge my Selfe Contented & Sattisfied & do Acquit ye s^d Weare his heirs & Adm^{rs} or Assignes from any further demand have given granted Sold & Confirmed & do by these psents give grant bargaine Sell make over Alienate convey & confirm unto ye s^d Peter Weare his heirs Execut^{rs} Adm^{rs} & Assignes for ever a Certaine Tract of land Containing Six Score Acres lying & being on ye Northerly or Northeast Side of Saco river in ye pattent granted to his honoured Grandfather Mr Richard Bonighton & Thomas Lewis in ye Division made to his father John Bonighton ye s^d Weare to have & Take one hundred Acres of upland & Twenty Acres of Marsh or Meadow where he ye s^d Weare Shall See Cause in his father ye s^d John [9] Bonightons lands but if ye s^d Weare Shall not Se cause to take ye Twenty Acres of Marsh or Meadow Then to take ye Six Score acres of Land Together and Also all my right in ye Island Lying against Saco Fort Called Bonithons or Indian Island with all wood Timber trees under wood Stones Springs Water Courses Streams belonging or Adjoyning thereunto with all priviledges & Appurtenances whatsoever thereunto belonging forever & Further I ye s^d Richd Bonighton do Avouch my Selfe to be ye True & Lawfull owner of ye bargained pmises & do for my Selfe my heirs Execut^{rs} & Adm^{rs} Warrantize ye s^d pmises to be free & clear from all former gifts grants Sales Judgm^{ts} Executions Entailes Dowryes or Title of Dowrys or any Legall Incumbrance whatsoever had made or done by me or any person or psons whatsoever laying Lawfull claime Thereunto but that ye s^d Peter Weare his heirs Execut^{rs} Adm^{rs} & Assignes Shall from Time to time & at all Times use Occupy possess & Enjoy ye s^d pmises to their own bennefit & behoofe for ever./ In Confirmation hereof I Set my hand & fix my Seal this Sixteenth day of Novemb^r one Thousand Seven hundred & Thirteen & in ye Twelfth year of our Soveraign Queen Anne Over Great Brittaine France & Irel^d Queen Defender of ye faith

The mark & Seal

Signed Sealed & Delivered   Richard Bonighton (a Seal)
In ye psents of us
Nath^{ll} Weare Junr
Thomas Waite
Daniel Weare

Book VIII, Fol. 9.

Hampton in New Hampsh[r]
Rich[d] Bonighton psonally Appeared this Seventeenth day of Nov[r] 1713 : & Acknowledged this Instrum[t] to be his free & voluntary Act & Deed Before me
       Nath[ll] Weare Just[s] peace
Recorded According to y[e] Original Novemb[r] y[e] 18th 1713./
       p Jos : Hamond Reg[r]

To All Christian People to whom these presents Shall Come I James Gooch of Boston Send Greeting./ Whereas I y[e] aboves[d] James Gooch of Boston in y[e] County of Suffolk in y[e] province of y[e] Massachusets Bay in New England did by deed of Sale make over & Convey to Joseph Hill of Wells in y[e] County of york province afores[d] one Quarter part of a Saw mill & Iron work belonging to s[d] Quarter part of s[d] mill & also one Quarter part of land granted with s[d] priviledge of y[e] Stream on which s[d] Mill Stands Viz[t] on y[e] river Called Merryland river Near y[e] Marsh called by that name which bill of Sale bare date June Eighteenth one Thousand Seven hundred & Two & it being defaced by y[e] Indian Enemy before the Acknowledgm[t] & recording thereof./ Now Know yee that I James Gooch aboves[d] in Consideration of y[e] full & Just Sum of forty Two pounds & Tenn Shillings to me in hand paid by Joseph Hill of Wells afores[d] & for other good Considerations me thereunto Moveing do by these psents give grant bargaine Sell Alienate Enfeoffe make over & Confirm unto Joseph Hill afores[d] one Quarter part of y[e] mill above Expressed Together with one Quarter part of y[e] Iron work which belonged to s[d] Mill when I made him y[e] Deed of Sale before mentioned As also one Quarter part of y[e] land & priviledge of Stream & Timb[r] mentioned in y[e] grant it lying & being in y[e] Township of Wells near y[e] marsh Comonly Called Merryland marsh It was granted by y[e] Town of Wells to Sam[ll] Hatch William ffrost & David Littlefield & purchased of them by me y[e] aboves[d] James Gooch y[e] which fourth part of s[d] Mill & priviledge of Stream Iron work & Lands as above Specifyed I y[e] aboves[d] James Gooch do Confirm & make over from me my heirs Execut[rs] Adm[rs] Together with all y[e] priviledges rights & Appurtenances thereto belonging or any wise Appurtaining to him ye aboves[d] Joseph Hill his heirs Execut[rs] Adm[rs] or assignes only he or they p forming y[e] Conditions in proportion with y[e] other partners upon which it was granted by y[e] Town of Wells to

Book VIII, Fol. 10.

them To have & To hold as a free & clear Estate in fee Simple for ever More over I ye aboves^d James Gooch do for my Selfe my heirs Execut^{rs} Adm^{rs} Covenant & promiss to & with ye aboves^d Joseph Hill his heirs Execut^{rs} Adm^{rs} or Assignes That it Shall & may be Lawfull for them from Time to time & at all times to use occupy possess & Enjoy ye above granted premises without any Let Suit hinderance or Mollestation w^{t}soever upon any Acco^t of gift grant Sale dowry Mortgage or any other Acco^t from any pson or psons in by from or under me y^e aboves^d James Gooch or my heirs Execut^{rs} or Adm^{rs} In Witness whereof I y^e aboves^d James Gooch have hereunto put my hand & Seale This Twenty first day or may Annoq$_3$ Domini one Thousand Seven hundred & Eleven & in y^e Tenth year of y^e Reign of our Soveraign Lady Anne by y^e grace of God of Great Brittain France & Ireland Queen Fid: Deff./   James Gooch ($_{Seal}^{a}$)
Signed Sealed & Delivered   Sarah Gooch ($_{Seal}^{a}$)
  In prsence of
Mary Hubart
John Hubart
          Suffolk ss/ Boston 22^d may 1711./
  The above James Gooch & Sarah his wife Acknowledged y^e above Instrum^t to be their free Act & Deed Before me
                    Jer: Dummer J. peace
Recorded According to y^e Original October y^e 6th 1713./
                    p Jos: Hammond Reg^r

[10] To All Christian people to whom these psents shall come William Sawyer of ye Town of Wells in ye County of York in ye province of ye Massachusets bay in New England yeoman Send Greeting./ Now Know all men by These presents that I William Sawyer Several good causes & well grounded considerations me thereunto moveing & more Especially that Feliel Love & Natural Affection which I do bare unto my Dear & Welbeloved Sonn Francis Sawyer have freely given granted Aliened Enfeoffed released Assigned & Confirmed and by these psents doe fully freely & Absolutely give grant release Aliene Assigne Enfeoffe & Confirm unto my s^d Son Francis Sawyer all That Tract &
Wm Sawyer   & parcell of land & Marsh which I bought of
   To   Peter ffolsham of Exeter which Tract of land &
Fran Sawy^r marsh is Lying & being in ye Town of Wells &
formerly in ye possession of John Wadleigh of s^d Wells deceased which halfe part granted to my s^d Son ffrancis

Book VIII, Fol. 10.

Sawyer is to Ly on ye East Side of s^d Land next to ye brook or ruñ of water also I have given unto my s^d Son ye one Quarter part of a Saw mill now built & Standing on s^d brook to him ye s^d Francis Sawyer his heirs Execut^rs Adm^rs & Assignes for ever all ye above mentioned granted premises buildings housing woods under woods Comõns & all other profits priviledges rights Comoditys heriditaments Imolluments & Appurtenances to ye Same belonging or in any kind Appurtaining & also all ye Estate right Title Interest use possession Dower Thirds claims revertion remainder propperty Claims & Demand whatso ever of me ye s^d William Sawyer my heirs & Assignes of in & to ye Same & Every part thereof To have & To hold all ye before mentioned granted Enfeoffed confirmed pmises with ye Appurtenances unto ye s^d Francis Sawyer his heirs & Assignes for ever it is hereto — That ye s^d William Sawyer hath reserved free Liberty for him Selfe & his Successors for ye Carting or Sleding of Timber or bords or any other Accasion over ye Land here granted to ye mill on ye fores^d brook all ye above granted premises are free & clear unto ye aboves^d Francis Sawyer & his heirs Lawfully begotton of his body & for want of Such Issue to ye next of kiñ of my family to his & Their own propper use bennefit & behoofe from henceforth & forever freely peaceably & Quietly without any maner of reclaim challenge or Contradiction of me ye s^d William Sawyer my heirs Execut^rs or assignes or of any other p^rson or p^rsons whatso ever by their or any of their means Title or procurement in any maner or wise or without any Acco^t or reconing or answer therefore to them or Any in their names to be given rendered or done in Times to come So that Neither I ye s^d William Sawyer my heirs Execut^rs or Assignes or any other pson or psons whatsoever by them for them or in ye Names of any of them at any Time or Times hereafter may Ask claime Challenge or demand in or to the premises or any part thereof any right Title Interest use possession or Dower butt from all & Every Action of right Title Interest use possession & demand thereof They & Every of Them to be utterly Excluded & for Ever by These psents debarred./ In Testimony where of I ye above named William Sawyer have Set my hand & Seal this 22^cond day of march Anno Domini 1704/5 & in ye fifth year of ye Reign of our Soveraign Lady Anne Over England Queen &c^t./ I do upon further Consideration give & grant that if in Case ye s^d

Book VIII, Fol. 10.

Francis Sawyer die without Issue & Leave a widdow ye Lands Shall be hers dureing her widdowhood
Signed Sealed & Delivered   William Sawyer (Seal)
  In psence of./   Sarah Sawyer (Seal)
  Nathaniel Clark
  Jona^n Hamond
   Province of ye Massachusets Bay in New Engl^d &c^t
   York ss Wells Septr ye 7th Anno Domini 1706./
Then ye above named William Sawyer & Sarah Sawyer psonally Appeared before me ye Subscrib^r one of her Maj^tys Justices of ye peace within s^d County & freely Acknowledged This above written deed of Gift or Instrum^t to be their Act & Deed & ye s^d Sarah Sawyer did at ye Same Time freely Surrender her right of Dower or Thirds in whatsoever is Contained in ye above written deed or Instrum^t
          John Wheelwright
Recorded According to ye Original Octob^r ye 6th 1713./
          p Jos : Hamond Reg^r

Province of Maine in New England
  Coll. Shadrach Walton of Newcastle in province New Hampsh^r in New Engl^d aged about fifty years & John Hall of s^d place Aged about Seventeen years & Wm Grant of Berwick in Province Maine aged about forty five years Deposeth & Saith That John Vsher of Charles Town in County Middlesex in Province Massachusets Bay Esqr on ye 9th day of This Insta^t Septr 1713 he Calling us for Witnesses did enter upon & Take possession of Wast lands in Berwick above a brook near & above a place Called Dover bounds did mark a white Oak Tree with ye following Letters IV did Take Turfe Twigg and ye s^d John Vsher declared he reading a writing by Vertue of Deed Mortgage from Sam^ll Allen Esqr to him Dated 14th Octob^r 1701/ That by vertue thereof he did take possession in part for ye whole contained in s^d Mortgage which was forfieted to him for ye non paym^t of ffifteen hundred pounds & also declared he did demand from ye Estate of s^d Sam^ll Allen with ye fforfeiture of ye Mortgage ye Sum four Thousand one hundred & forty five pounds Two Shill & Ten pence all which wee See & heard read on y^e

place Taken possession & further Saith not ye s^d bounds being as Informed & to best of their knowledge

Sha^d Walton
Wm Grant
John ✕ Hall
his / mark

York ss Berwick Sep^t 9th 1713/ Conal Shadrach Walton Wm Grant John Hall psonally Appeared & made oath : to ye above before me./   Ichabod Plaisted J peace :

Recorded According to ye original Novr 16th 1713

p Jos. Hamond Reg^r

[11] To All Christian people to whom this present Deed of Sale may Come or doth concern Johnson Harmon of york in ye County of york in ye Late province of Maine now of ye Massachusets Bay in New England Gent Sendeth Greeting Know yee that ye s^d Johnson Harmon & Mary his wife for & in consideration of a Certaine Sum of money to them in hand well & Truely paid or Satisfactorily Secured to be paid by Samuel Came of s^d York Mill wright ye reciept thereof ye s^d Johnson & Mary doth Acknowledge themselves Therewth fully Satisfyed & Contented & do for themselves their heirs Execut^{rs} & Admin^{rs} Discharge & Acquitt ye s^d Samuel Came his heirs or Assignes of all & Every part & pcell of Lands or Meadow ground hereafter Mentioned & Set forth ye which ye s^d Johnson & Mary hath given granted bargained Sold Aliened Enfeoffed & Conveyed & doth by these presents give grant bargaine Sell Aliene Enfeoffe & Convey & fully freely & absolutely make Over & Confirm unto ye s^d Samuel Came his heirs & Assignes for ever a Certain piece or pcell of land being Sixty three Acres Scittuated between ye branches of York river & Lyeth on ye north East Side of ye cove of Marsh belonging to ye Ministry of s^d york & is bounded as followeth begining at a pine tree markt on four Sides Standing at ye Southward Corner of a Lott of land laid out to Peter Nowell & is ye Eastward corner of a Lot of land of Mackintires & runs from s^d Tree South & by west by s^d Mackintires land Sixty four poles to afores^d Cove of Marsh & So is bounded by s^d Cove of Marsh as it lyeth down to ye Southwest branch of s^d York river & then down ye river as ye upland Lyeth to a red Oak Tree Standing near ye Middle of a piece of Salt Marsh known by ye Name of Harmons Midle Marsh which s^d

Harmon To Came

Book VIII, Fol. 11.

Oak is Markt on four Sides There being reserved one acre of land by s^d Harmon Adjoyning to s^d Marsh for his Conveniency of fencing his s^d Marsh Together with all ye right priviledges Advantages both of land Meadow ground wood under wood Timber Timber Trees Standing Lying or remaining Thereupon with all its Appurtenances thereunto belonging or any wayes at any Time redownding to ye Same or any part thereof unto ye s^d Samuel Came his heirs & Assignes for ever To have & To hold & Quietly & peaceably to possess Occupy & Enjoy as a Sure Estate in Fee Simple Moreover ye s^d Johnson & Mary do for themselves their heirs Execut^{rs} & Adm^{rs} to & with ye s^d Sam^{ll} Came his heirs & Assignes do Covenant Ingage & promiss ye aboves^d land and all its priviledges to be free & clear from all former gifts grants bargains Sales deeds Mortgages Sales rents rates dowers deeds or any other Incumberments whatsoever as also from all future claims Challenges Law suits Judgm^{ts} Executions or any Interruptions whatsoever to be had or Comenced by them ye s^d Johnson or Mary their heirs or Assigns or any other p^{r}son or p^{r}sons whatsoever upon any grounds of Law or Title but that for ever after ye date hereof ye s^d Johnson & Mary their heirs Execut^{rs} & Adm^{rs} will Warrentize defend & Avouch & make good ye Sale of ye above bargained premises with all its priviledges unto ye s^d Samuel Came his heirs & Assignes./ In Witness hereof ye Above named Johnson Harmon & Mary his wife have hereunto Set to their hands & Seals this Tenth day of August in ye year of our Lord one thousand Seven hundred & Twelve & in y^o Eleventh year of ye Reign of our Soveraign Lady Anne Queen of Great Brittain &c^t/

Before Signing it is to be understood ye bounds of aboves^d Land runs from aboves^d red oak Tree North one hundred & Eight poles to a Lot of s^d Cames Land bought by him of s^d Harmon & is bounded by s^d Land & Nowells Land to ye pine first mentioned./   Johnson Harmon (seal)
Signed Sealed & Delivered   (seal)
   In psence of us Witnesses
   Joseph Moulton
   Abra^m Preble Junr
     York ss/ Octob^r 6. 1713./

The within Named Johnson Harmon psonally Appearing Acknowledged this Instrum^t to be his Act & Deed Before me   Abra^m Preble Justice peace

Recorded According to ye Original Octob^r ye 6th 1713./
                  p Jos Hamond Reg^r

Book VIII, Fol. 12.

Know All men by these psents wee who Sign to this Instrument as I Anne Spiller widdow & Relict of one Richard Roe once of Kittery in province of Maine in New England & wee daughters of s^d Roe & Sons in Law as James Cocks & wife Mary Cocks & John= Dorothy & wife Elizabeth Dorothy now of Boston in New England Have for & in Consideration of Twenty pounds of Currant money of New England to us in hand paid by Diamond Sargent of Kittery in Province of Maine in New England Tayler./ for which Sum of Twenty pounds wee do Acknowledge our Selfe fully Satisfyed & Contented have therefore Consented given granted & Sold and do by these presents Clearly & Absolutely give grant bargain and Sell Set over & Confirm unto ye aboves^d Diamond Sargent & his heirs Execut^{rs} Adm^{rs} & Assignes forever all that parcell of grants & granted Land Lying in ye Township of Kittery in New England it Lying now in wood which was Land granted by Town of Kittery in New England unto my husband & our father it being a Tracts of Land granted & Laid out by John Wincoll Surveyer for Town of Kittery by vertue of Two grants one Containing fifteen Acres & Twenty five Acres Laid out as followeth Eighty poles in bredth & runs Norwest by York line Near ye head of ye old mill creek of york & Eighty poles in Length Southwest bounded on ye South east Side of & with Digery Jefferys Land & ye rest with psent Comons as may appear by returns on Record in all Lying & being in ye Town of Kittery afores^d To have & To hold Quietly to Enjoy & possess all ye afores^d [12] Land Containing Forty Acres with all ye rights Titles priviledges & Appurtenances thereunto belonging as wood & under wood & all Things thereunto belonging./ And wee ye aboves^d Anne Spiller & James Cocks & Mary Cocks & John Dorothy & Elizabeth Dorothy do by these presents bind our Selfs our heirs Execut^{rs} Adm^{rs} & Assignes forever unto ye s^d Diamond Sargent his heirs Execut^{rs} Adm^{rs} & Assignes that ye s^d land is free & Clear from all gifts grants bargains Sales Mortgages Joyntures Dowrys or any Titles what Sumever & that wee & they Shall from Time to Time Save & keep harmless ye s^d Diamond Sargent or his heirs or Assignes for ever from any pson or mañer of psons that Shall Lay any claime right or Title to any of ye s^d Land afores^d or to any part or parcell thereof & that it Shall be Lawfull to s^d Diamond Sargent to Improve ye s^d Land afores^d from Time to Time & at all Times what Sum Ever & that this Shall be & Stand firm as ye True Intent & meaning of a firm Bill of Sale in all points in Law as witness whereof wee ye afores^d

Ann Spiller to D Sergeant

Book VIII, Fol. 12.

Anne Spiller & James Cocks & Mary Cocks & John Dorothy & Elizabeth Dorothy my wife have hereunto Set our hands & Seals Dated in Boston this yͤ 26 day of October 1713./

Signed Sealed & Delivered
In psence of us
Wᵐ Hamlyn
Anne Harris

Anne *Uₐn* Spiller (ₛₑₐₗᵃ)
    mark

James ⌐ Cocks (ₛₑₐₗᵃ)
   her mark

John Dorothy (ₛₑₐₗᵃ)
   his

Mary *CM* Cocks (ₛₑₐₗᵃ)
   her mark

Elizabeth ⊥ Dorothy (ₛₑₐₗᵃ)
   her mark

Suffolk ss Boston Oct 26ᵗʰ 1713./ The above named Anne Spiller James Cocks John Dorothy Mary Cocks & Eliz Dorothy Each & Every of them Acknowledged this Instrument to be their free Act & Deed

    Before me Jer: Dummer J peace
Recorded According to yᵉ Original Novembʳ yᵉ 9ᵗʰ 1713./
    p Jos: Hamond Regʳ

T. Rice to his Father

Know All men by These presents That I Thomas Rice Junʳ of Kittery in yᵉ County of York for yᵉ Consideration of a Tract of land Sold & Exchanged wᵗʰ me by my father Thomas Rice Senʳ bareing Date with these presents as appears by his deed of Exchange to me & for other good & valluable Considerations me hereunto moveing have given granted bargained & Sold & do by these psents give grant bargaine & Sell & for ever Confirm all that Teñ Acres of land Lying at yᵉ Southwest end of my Thity Acre Lot given me by my father abovesᵈ as appears by his deed of Gift to me bareing date October yᵉ 19ᵗʰ 1700 Together with all yᵉ Appurtenances & priviledges whatsoever thereunto belonging unto him yᵉ sᵈ Thomas Rice Senʳ his heirs Executʳˢ Admʳˢ or Assignes for ever yᵉ sᵈ Ten Acres of land being in Length Northwest & Southeast forty Three pole And in bredth Southwest & Northeast Thirty Seven pole as its Specified in yᵉ abovesᵈ Deed of Gift To have & To hold all yᵉ abovesᵈ Teñ acres of land wᵗʰ yᵉ Appurtenances thereunto belonging unto yᵉ sᵈ Thomas Rice Senʳ his heirs Executʳˢ Admʳˢ or Assignes forever to their own propper use bennefit & behoofe hereby warranting y⁰ above Tract of Land to be free & Clear from all Incumbrances by me made y⁰ peaceable possession thereof to defend & maintaine against all psons laying claime thereunto from by or under me Witness my hand & Seal this 29 : Decemb⁰ 1705./

 one word Interlined between Line y⁰ 12 & 13 Rice
Signed Sealed & D D⁰⁰   Thomas Rice Jun⁰ (ᵃSeal)
 In psence of us y⁰ Subscrib⁰ˢ
 Richard Rice
  The mark of
 Elizab E Surplice
 W⁰⁰ Godsoe
  York ss. March y⁰ 18ᵗʰ 1711/12
 Thomas Rice psonally appearing Acknowledged y⁰ above Instrum⁰ in writing to be his free Act & Deed
      Coram Ichabod Plaisted J : P
Recorded According to y⁰ Original Novemb⁰ 24ᵗʰ 1713./
       p Jos Hamond Reg⁰

Aaron Ferris to Tho⁰ Huff

Know All men by these presents that I Aaron Ferris of Kittery in y⁰ County of york in New England fisherman & Grace my wife for and in Consideration of y⁰ Love & resp⁰ that wee beare unto Thomas Huff of y⁰ Town & County afores⁰ who marryed our Daughter Grace but more Especially for a Certain Instrument of Even date with these psents whereby he Ingageth himselfe his heirs Execut⁰ˢ & Adm⁰ˢ to maintain me & my wife dureing our Natural Lives in Sickness & in health with all things Necessary & Convenient Also to Take care & provide for our decent funeralls when ever it Shall please god to call us hence./ That wee y⁰ s⁰ Aaron Ferris & Grace Ferris have given & granted & by these presents do freely fully & Absolutely give grant Aliene Convey Confirm & make over unto y⁰ s⁰ Thomas Huff & Grace Huff their heirs Execut⁰ˢ Adm⁰ˢ & Assignes for ever all our Moveables & Im˟oveables whatsoever which wee or Either of us at y⁰ Signing hereof are owners of or in any way doth of Right belong or Appertaine to us : to Say all our Land on Spruce creek which wee bought of Elihue Crocket with all y⁰ housing Orchards building & Every thing Else thereunto belonging with our Quarter part of y⁰ Sloop whereof y⁰ s⁰ Thomas Huff is now Mast⁰ with all & Singular all our other goods & Chattells whether money cloathing Cattle Debts house hold goods

Book VIII, Fol. 13.

&c^t of any nature or kind whatsoever unto him ye s^d Thomas Huff & Grace his wife to be unto them their heirs Execut^{rs} Adm^{rs} & Assignes Imediately & Absolutely at ye Signing hereof without any Let hinderence or Controal whatsoever from us or Either of us hence forward he ye s^d Huff & his wife their heirs &c^t [13] Still doing & providing for us dureing our Natural lives As by an Instrum^t of Even date as afores^d more particularly doth Appear./ In Testimony w^{r}of wee ye s^d Aaron Ferris & Grace Ferris have hereunto Set our hands & Seals this fourteenth day of February in ye year of our Lord 1708./

Signed Sealed & Delivered
  In ye psence of
  Henry Barter
  James Hall

The mark of
Aaron Ferris (a Seal)

The mark of
Grace Ferris (a Seal)

20 June 1711/
Then Aaron Ferris psonally Appeared before me ye Subscrib^r hereof one of her Majsetys Justices of ye County of york & did Acknowledge this above Instrum^t to be his free Act & deed./   Wm Pepperrell
  Recorded According to ye Original Decemb^r ye 11th 1713./
                      p Jos Hamond Reg^r

Wm Frost
to
Sam^{ll} Emery

To All People to whom these psents Shall Come Greeting Now Know Yee that I William Frost of Salem in ye County of Essex in ye province of ye Massachusets Bay in New England planter divers good & Lawfull Causes but more Especially for & in Consideration of ye full & Just Sum of Ten pounds in good Lawfull money of New England to me partly in hand paid & partly by bill Obligatory Secured to be paid by Samuel Emery of Wells in ye County of york & in ye province afores^d Clerk have given and granted & do by these psents fully clearly & Absolutely give grant bargaine Sell alienate Enfeoffe Set over & Confirm unto Sam^{ll} Emery afores^d his heirs Execut^{rs} Adm^{rs} & Assignes a Certain Tract of Land & Meadow Lying & being in ye Township of Wells afores^d Containing by Estimation one hundred of Land & Ten Acres of Meadow be it more or Less that is to Say one hundred Acres of Land more or Less Bounded as followeth./ By Samuel Hatch his land Southwesterly upon a highway at ye head of ye old Lotts South Easterly & So to runn upon s^d highway fifty rods or poles more or Less & thence to run up by Eliab Littlefields land to a pitchpine before his house where it Stood & thence on a Straight line to ye road that leads to Merryland Mills to a Stump of An Applepine that was formerly broken down & So up into ye Country on that course untill ye hundred Acres be Accomplished as Also Ten Acres of Marish or Meadow ground partly laid out vizt five acres lying near ye pond marsh & bounded on Joseph Hills Meadow Southwesterly or thereabouts & Sam^{ll} Hatch his Meadow Northeasterly or thereabouts as also ye other five acres not yet laid out The which hundred Acres of land & Ten Acres of Meadow was granted to me by ye Town of Wells & which land & meadow bounded & Estimated & part to be laid out as afores^d I ye aboves^d William Frost for my Selfe my heirs Execut^{rs} Adm^{rs} do Confirm & Set over to Samuel Emery afores^d his heirs Execut^{rs} Adm^{rs} or Assignes Together with all and Singular ye priviledges rights & Appurtenances thereto belonging or any wise Appurtaining To have & To hold as a free & clear Estate in fee Simple for ever And I ye aboves^d William Frost for my Selfe my heirs Execut^{rs} Adm^{rs} Covenat^t & promiss to & with ye aboves^d Samuel Emery his heirs Execut^{rs} Adm^{rs} & Assignes that I am ye True & rightfull owner of ye above granted pmises & that I have full power right & Authority to Sell & Dispose of ye Same as afores^d as Also that it is free & cleare & fully & clearly Acquitted & Discharged of & from all other & former gifts grants bargains Sales Mortgages Dowerys or Incumbrances whatsoever Moreover that I will Warrant & Defend ye Same from all p^{r}sons whatsoever in by from or under me my heirs Execut^{rs} or Adm^{rs} Laying any Legall claime thereto or any part or parcell thereof./ In witness whereof I ye aboves^d William Frost have hereto Set my hand & Seale this Seventh day of Novemb^r in ye year of our Lord one Thousand Seven hundred & Thirteen & in ye Twelfth year of ye Reign of our Soveraign Lady Anne by ye grace of God of Great Brittaine France & Ireland Queen &c^t

Signed Sealed & Delivered   William Frost (a seal)

 In psence of us
 Benj^a Ropes
 John Sawyer
 William Frost Acknowledged ye above written Instrum^t to be his Act & Deed
  Salem Novemb^r ye 7th 1713./ Before me
          John Hathorne Just^s pc
 Recorded According to ye Original Decr 31st 1713./
         p Jos. Hamond Reg^r

Book VIII, Fol. 14.

Jno Libbey
To
his Son Jno

Know all men by these psents that I John Libbey Senr of Portsmo in New Hampshr formerly of Scarborough or Black point in ye County of york for ye Love and Affection I bare & for other good Causes have given granted bargained & Sold & do by These psents give grant bargaine & Sell Aliene Enfeoffe deliver & Confirm unto my Son John Libbey That my Tract & farm of Land & Marsh Scittuate Lying & being at Black point Alias Scarborough whereon my father John Libbey decd formerly Lived with all ye priviledges & Accomodations Thereunto belonging & is ye Same land & Marsh wch my sd father Obtained of Mr Henry Joslyn by vertue of a deed or Lease baring date Janry ye first 1663./ in ye 15 : year of King Charles 2d to be to him my sd Son John Libbey his heirs or assignes forever To have & To hold ye sd Neck of land & marsh As above with all priviledges [14] without any Mollestation Let hinderence or denial & which Shall Continue to him ye sd John Libby Junr his heirs or Assigns free & clear from all Incumbrances whatsoever In Testimony & for Confirmation of which I have hereunto put my hand & Seal this first of Novembr 1713./

Signed Sealed & Delivered   John $\frac{his}{\text{H}}$ Libbey Senr ($^a_{seal}$)
In psence of
Geo : Vaughan
James Gray

No : 9th 1713./ John Libby Senr Acknowledged ye above Instrumt to be his Act & Deed Before

Geo : Vaughan Justs peace
Recorded According to ye Original Janry 5th 1713/4

p Jos : Hammond Regr

Jno Cole
To
Ramsdal

To All Christian people to whom These psents may Come or do Concern Know yee that I John Cole of york in ye County of york in ye Province of Maine in New England Fisherman Send Greeting for & in Consideration of a Certain Sum of money to me in hand paid by Nathll Ramsdell of sd york weaver ye Receipt I do Acknowledg & my Selfe therewith fully Satisfied & Contented and do by this writing Acquit ye sd Nathaniel his heirs & Executrs & Admrs for ever for a Thirty Acre grant granted to my father Joseph Cole by ye Town of York in ye year 1679 Augst 25th as in York Town book doth more fully Appear & I ye sd John Cole do by these psents give

grant bargaine Sell Aliene & make over unto y⁰ sᵈ Nathˡˡ Ramsdell yᵉ full right Title & Interest of Aboveˢᵈ grant of land to Say Thirty Acres Clear of former grants if he can find it unto him yᵉ sᵈ Nathˡˡ Ramsdell his heirs & Assignes for ever To have & To hold & Quietly to Occupy & Enjoy yᵉ Same as a Sure Estate in Fee Simple./ In Witness hereof I have hereunto Set my hand & Seal Septʳ yᵉ Sixth one Thousand Seven hundred & Twelve & in yᵉ Eleventh year of yᵉ Reign of our Soveraign Lady Anne Queen of Great Brittaine &cᵗ./   John : Cole — (ₛₑₐₗₑᵃ)
Signed Sealed & Delivered
 In psence of
 Geo : Jackson
 Abraˣ Preble Junʳ
  York ss/
At an Inferioʳ Court of Comon pleas holden at york for yᵉ County of York Janʳʸ 5ᵗʰ 1713 Capᵗⁿ Abraˣ Preble & Mʳ George Jackson witnesses to yᵉ within deed psonally Appearing made Oath that they Saw yᵉ within named John Cole yᵉ Granter Sign Seal & Deliver yᵉ within written Instrumᵗ as his Act & Deed./   Attestʳ Jos. Hamond Clerᵈ
Recorded According to yᵉ Original Janʳʸ yᵉ 5ᵗʰ 1713./
        p Jos : Hamond Regʳ

 Katherine Nanney Alias Nayler aged Eighty four years or Thereabouts Testifyeth & Saith that She yᵉ Deponant doth very well remember that Sixty Six years Agoe or upwards my father yᵉ Reverend Mʳ John Wheelwright Minister Then Lived in yᵉ Town of Wells in yᵉ County of york on a farm at yᵉ Easterly End of yᵉ Town above yᵉ harbour or Barr from whence Comes up a Creek near where his house Then Stood & that Then he possessed yᵉ sᵈ ffarm or Tract of Land as his own propper right as I understood & that I yᵉ Deponaᵗ then Lived with my sᵈ ffather on sᵈ farm about three or four years./
 Midlesˣ Charles Town Novembʳ 2ᵈ 1713.// Katherine Nanney Alˢ Nayler The above named Deponant made Oath to yᵉ Truth of yᵉ above written Deposition in Perpetuam Rei Memoriam, Before us this 2ᵈ day of 9bʳ 1713 : Justices of peace./   Joseph Lynde Quoram me
      Nathˡˡ Cary Justˢ peace
 The above Deposition Came Sealed to my hand and is here Recorded According to yᵉ Original Janʳʸ yᵉ 5ᵗʰ 1713/4/
        p Jos : Hamond Regʳ

BOOK VIII, FOL. 15.

James Smith
&
Lewis Bane

This Indenture made ye Sixteenth day of Septemb^r Annoq, Domini one Thousand Seven hundred & Thirteen & in ye Twelfth year of ye Reign of our Soveraign Lady Anne Queen of England &c^ra between James Smith of york in ye County of York in her Majestys Province of ye Massachusetts Bay in New England Blacksmith of ye one party And Lewis Bane of ye Same Town Gent of ye other party Witnesseth that ye s^d James Smith for & in Consideration of ye Sum of fforty Three pounds Ten Shillings Cura^t money of N. E to him in hand paid before ye Ensealing & Delivery of these psents by Lewis Bane afores^d The rec^t whereof to full Satisfaction he ye s^d James Smith doth by These psents Acknowledge & thereof & of Every part thereof for himselfe his heirs Execut^rs & Adm^rs doth Acquitt Exonerate And Discharge ye s^d Lewis Bane his heirs Execut^rs & Adm^rs Every of Them for ever by These psents and for Diverse good Causes & Considerations him thereunto moveing he ye s^d James Smith hath given granted bargained Sold Aliened Enfeoffed Conveyed & Confirmed & by these psents doth fully freely clearly & Absolutely give grant bargaine Sell Aliene Enfeoffe Convey & Confirm unto ye s^d Lewis Bane his heirs & Assignes for ever a Certaine Tract of Land Containing Eighty Acres be it more or Less Scittuate Lying & being in york afores^d bounded on ye N: W Side of ye Land of Wm Shaws on ye S. W by ye Country road that leads to Nechewanack on ye S: E by ye Land of Dan^ll Junkins & N. E by ye Towns Comons Together with ye orchards houses barns on s^d land & all Such rights Libertys & Imunitys profits priviledges Comoditys [15] Emoluments & Appurtenances as in any kind Appurtain thereunto with ye Revertions & Remainders thereof & all ye Estate right Interest Title Inheritance propperty possession claim & demand whatsoever of him ye s^d James Smith of in & to ye Same & Every part thereof To have & To hold all ye above granted premises with all & Singular ye Appurtenances thereof unto him ye s^d Lewis Bane his heirs & Assigns to his & their own Sole & propper use benefit & behoofe from henceforth & for ever & ye s^d James Smith for himselfe his heirs Execut^rs & Adm^rs doth hereby Covena^t promiss grant & agree to & with ye s^d Lewis Bane his heirs & Assignes in manner & form following./ That is to Say/ That at ye time of ye Ensealing & Delivery of These presents he ye s^d James Smith is ye True Sole & Lawfull owner of all ye afores^d bargained premises & Stands Lawfully Siezed thereof in his own propper right & good perfect & indefeazable Estate of

This Mortgage Discharged in Fol^o 127

Book VIII, Fol. 15.

Inheritance in fee Simple having in himselfe full power good right and Lawfull Authority to Sell & dispose of ye Same in maner as afores^d and that ye s^d Lewis Bane his heirs & Assignes shall & may henceforth for ever lawfully peaceably & Quietly have hold use Occupy possess & Enjoy ye above granted pmises with ye Appurtenances thereof free & clear & clearly Acquitted & discharged of & from all & all manner of former & other gifts grants bargains Sales Leases Mortgages Joyntures Powers Judgm^ts Executions Entails forfeitures & of & from all other Titles Troubles charges & Incumbrances whatsoever had made Comitted done or Suffered to be done by ye s^d James Smith his heirs or Assignes At any time or times before ye Ensealing & Delivery hereof And further ye s^d James Smith doth hereby Covenant promiss bind & Oblige himselfe his heirs Execut^rs & Adm^rs from henceforth & for ever hereafter to warrant & Defend all ye above granted pmises & ye Appurtenances thereof unto ye s^d Lewis Bane his heirs & Assignes against ye Lawfull claims & Demands of All & Every pson & psons whomsoever & at any time & Times hereafter on demand and pass Such further & Ample Assurence & Confirmation of ye premises unto ye s^d Lewis Bane his heirs & Assignes for ever as in Law or Equity Can be reasonably Devised Advised or required./

Provided Always & These p^rsents are upon Conditions Nevertheless that if ye above named James Smith his heirs Execut^rs Adm^rs shall & do well & Truely pay or cause to be paid unto ye afore named Lewis Bane or his Certain Attorney heirs Execut^rs Adm^rs or Assignes at york afores^d in ye present Currant money of ye afores^d province as it now passeth ye Sum of forty Three pounds Ten Shillings at or upon ye Thirteenth day of Septemb^r which will be in ye year of our Lord one Thousand Seven hundred & fourteen Just Eleven month four dayes after ye date of This Instrum^t without fraud Coven or further delay that then this present deed of bargaine & Sale & Every Clause & Article therein Contained Shall Cease determine be null voyd & of non Effect but if Default happen to be made in ye afores^d payment Contrary to ye True Intent thereof Then to abide remaine in full force Strength & vertue to all Intents & purposes in ye Law whatsoever./ In Witness whereof ye s^d James Smith hath hereunto Set his hand & Seal ye Day & year first above written./ James Smith (Seale^a)
Signed Sealed & Delivered
  In p^rsence of./
  Joseph Brown
  Jonathan Bane
  Nath^ll Freeman

Book VIII, Fol. 15.

York ss/ James Smith above named psonally Appearing Acknowledged this Instrum^t to be his Act & Deed./
York Jan^ry 5th 1713/4 Before me Abra^x Preble Just^e peace Recorded According to ye Original Jan^ry 5th 1713/4

p J. Hamond Reg^r

Blagdon &c^t
To
Lewis Bane

To All People to whom these psents shall come Greetings &c^t Know yee that Mary Blagdon Widdow Hannah Blagdon Nicholas Follet & Mary his wife all of Portsmouth in ye Province of New Hampsh^r in New England for & in Consideration of ye Sum of fifteen pounds Currant money of New England to them in hand before ye Ensealing hereof well & Truely paid by Lewis Bane of york in ye County of york in New England afores^d ye rec^t whereof they do hereby Acknowledge & themselves therewith fully Satisfied & Contented & thereof & of Every part thereof do Exonerate Acquit & Discharge ye s^d Lewis Bane his heirs Execut^rs Adm^rs for ever by these presents./ Have given granted bargained Sold Aliened Conveyed & Confirmed & Do by These presents freely fully and Absolutely give grant bargaine Sell Aliene Convey & Confirm unto him ye s^d Lewis Bane a Certaine lot or parcel of land Scittuate lying & being in york in ye County of York afores^d Containing by Estimation ffifteen Acres of land more or less lying in ye new mill creek that Henry Saywards Mill Stood in & bounded on ye one Side by Abraham Prebles lot lying North & by East Twenty five rods & in length one hundred rods East & by South Adjoining upon lands of ye s^d Lewis Bane To have & To hold ye s^d granted & bargained premises wth all ye priviledges & Appurtenances to ye Same in any wise belonging or Appurtaining to him ye s^d Lewis Bane his heirs & Assignes for ever to his & their only propper use benefit & behalfe for ever & ye s^d Mary Blagdon Hannah Blagdon Nicholas Follet & Mary his wife for Them Their heirs Execut^rs & Adm^rs do Covenant promiss & grant to & with ye s^d Lewis Bane his heirs & Assignes that before ye Ensealing hereof they are ye True & Lawfull owners of ye above granted premises & have in themselves good right & Lawfull Authority to Sell & Convey ye above granted pmises in mañer as afores^d & That ye s^d Lewis Bane his heirs & Assignes Shall & may at all Times for ever hereafter by vertue of These presents peaceably & Quietly have hold use Occupie possess & Enjoy ye s^d Demised pmises with the Appurtenances freely & Clearly Acquitted Exonerated & Discharged of & from all maner of former & other gifts grants bargains Sales leases Mortgages Wills Entails Joyntures Dowrys Judgm[ts] Executions Incumbrances & Extents Furthermore y[e] s[d] Mary Blagdon Hannah Blagdon Nicholas Follet & Mary his wife for themselves their heirs Execut[rs] Adm[rs] do Covenant and Engage y[e] above demised pmises to him y[e] s[d] Lewis Bane his heirs & Assigns against y[e] Lawfull claims & Demands of any person or persons whatsoever for ever hereafter to Warrant Secure & Defend./ In Witness whereof they have hereunto Set their hands & Seals y[e] 25th day of Octob[r] in y[e] Twelfth year of y[e] Reign of our Soveraign Lady Anne by y[e] Grace of God Queen of Great Brittaine &c[t] Annoq, Domini one Thousand Seven hundred & Thirteen

Signed Sealed & Delivered
In y[e] psence of us
Benj[a] Gambling
Robert Almery

Mary Blagdon (Seal)
Hannah Blagdon (Seal)
Nicholas Follet (Seal)
Mary Follet (Seal)

Mary Blagdon Hannah Blagdon Nicholas Follet & Mary Follet psonally appeared before me y[e] Subscrib[r] one of her Maj[tys] Just[s] of peace at Portsm[o] in y[e] Province of New Hampsh[r] & Member of Council within y[e] Same & Acknowledged The above Instrum[t] to be their Act & Deed Octob[r] 25th 1713./

4
Sam[ll] Penhallow

Recorded According to y[e] Original Jan[ry] 5th 1713./

p Jos: Hamond Reg[r]

[16] Whereas wee y[e] Sagamors of Penecook Pentucket Squomsquot & and Nuchawanack are Inclined to have y[e] English Inhabit amongst us as they are amongst our Countrymen in y[e] Massachusets bay by which means we hope in time to be Strengthened against our Enemys y[e] Tareteens who yearly doth us Damage Likewise being purswaded that it will be for y[e] good of us & our Posterity &c[t]

Sagamores
To
Jn[o] Wheelw[t]
&c[s]

To that end have at a General meeting at Squomsqot on Piscattaqua river wee y[e] afores[d] Sagamores with a Universal consent of our Subjects do Covenant & agree with y[e] English as followeth Now Know all men by these psents that wee Passaconawaye Sagamore of Penecook. Runaawitt Sagamore of Pentuckit Wahangnonawitt Sagamore of Squomsquot & Rowls Sagamore of Nuchawanack for a Competent Valluation in goods Already recieved in Coats shirts & victuals and also for ye Considerations afores^d do According to ye Limits & bounds hereafter granted Give grant bargain Sell release ratifie & Confirm unto John Wheelwright of ye Massachusets Bay late of England a minister of ye gospel Agustine Story Thomas White William Wentworth and Thomas Levet all of ye Massachusets Bay in New England to them their heirs and Assignes for ever all that part of ye Maine land bounded by ye river of Piscattaqua & ye River of Meremak./ That is Say to begin at Nuchawanack falls in piscattaqua river afores^d & So down s^d river to ye Sea & So alongst ye Sea Shore to Meramack river and So up along s^d river to ye falls at pentuckit afores^d & from s^d pentucket falls upon a Northwest line Twenty English miles into ye woods and from thence to run upon a Straight line Northeast & Southwest Till meet with ye Maine rivers that ruñs down to Pentuckett falls & Nuchawanack falls & ye s^d rivers to be ye bounds of ye s^d lands from ye Thwart line or head line to ye afores^d falls & ye maine chanell of Each river from Pentuckitt & Nuchawanack falls to ye Maine Sea to be ye Side bounds & ye Maine Sea between Piscattaqua river and Meramack river to be ye Lower bounds & ye Thwart line that ruñs from river to river to be ye upper bounds Together with all Islands within s^d bounds As Also ye Isles of Shoals So called by ye English Together with all profits Advantages & Appurtenances whatsoever to ye s^d Tract of Land belonging or in Any wayes Appurtaining reserving to our Selves liberty of makeing use of our own planting land as also free Liberty of hunting fishing & fowling & it is likewise with these provisors following vizt/ First that ye s^d John Wheelwright Shall within Ten years after ye date hereof Set down with a Company of English & begin a plantation At Squomsquot falls in Piscattaqua river afores^d

Secondly that what other Inhabitants shall come & live on s^d Tract of land amongst them from time to time and at all times shall have & Enjoy the Same benefits as ye s^d Wheelwright afores^d

Thirdly that if at any time there be a number of people amongst them that have a mind to begin a new plantation that they be Encouraged So to do & that no plantation Exceed in lands above Ten English Miles Square or Such a proportion as Amounts to Ten miles Square

Fourthly that ye afores^d granted lands are to be divided into Townships as people Increase & Appear to Inhabit them & that no lands shall be granted to any particular psons but what shall be for a Township & what lands within a Township is granted to Any particular persons to be by vote of ye Major paft of ye Inhabitants Legally & orderly Settled in s^d Township

Fifthly for managing & regulating and to avoyd Contentions Amongst them they are to be under ye Governm^t of ye Collony of ye Massachusets their Neighbors & to Observe their Laws & Orders untill they have a Settled Governm^t amongst themselves./

Sixthly Wee ye afores^d Sagamores and our Subjects are to have free liberty wthin ye afores^d granted Tract of land of fishing fowling hunting & planting &c^t

Seventhly & Lastly Every Township within ye afores^d Limitts or Tract of land that hereafter shall pay to Passaconaway our Chief Sagamore that now is & to his Siccessors for ever if Lawfully Demanded one Coat of Trucking cloth a year & Every year for an Acknowledgm^t and also shall pay to Mr John Wheelwright afores^d his heirs & Successors forever if Lawfully Demanded Two bushells of Indian Corn a year for & in Consideration of s^d Wheelwrights great pains and Care as also for ye Charges he hath been at to obtaine this our grant for himselfe & those aforementioned and ye Inhabitants that shall hereafter Settle in Townships on ye afores^d Granted pmises./ And wee ye Afores^d Sagamores Passaconaway Sagamore of Penecook Runaawitt Sagamore of Pentuckitt wahangnanawitt Sagamore of Squomsquot & Rowles Sagamore of Nuchawanack do by these p^{r}sents ratifie & Confirme all ye afore granted & bargained pmises & Tract of land afores^d Excepting & reserving as afores Excepted & reserved and ye provisors afores^d fullfilled with all ye Meadow & Marsh ground therein Together with all ye mines minerals of what Kind or Nature Soever with all ye woods Timb^r & Timb^r trees ponds rivers lakes runs of water or water courses thereunto belonging with all ye fredom of fishing fowling & hunting as our Selves with all other benefits proftis priviledges & Appurtenances whatsoever thereunto of all & Any part of ye s^d Tract of land belonging or in any wayes Appurtaining unto him ye s^d John Wheelwright Augustine Storer Thomas Wight Wm Wentworth & Thomas Levet & their heirs forever as afores^d To have & To hold ye Same as their own [17] Propper right & Interest without ye Least Disturbance mollestation or Trouble of us our heirs Execut^{rs} & Adm^{rs} to & with ye s^d John Wheelwright Augustine Storer Thomas Wight Wm Wentworth & Thomas Levet their heirs Execut^{rs} Adm^{rs} & Assignes & other ye English that Shall Inhabit there & their heirs & Assignes forever Shall Warrant maintaine and Defend./ In Witness whereof wee have hereunto Set our hands & Seals ye Seventeenth day of may 1629 and in ye fifth year of King Charles his Reign over England &c

Passaconaway	mark./	Runaawitt	mark (a Seal)
(a Seal)
	Wahangnonawitt	mark (a Seal)

Signed Sealed & Delivered
In psence of us	Rowles	mark (a Seal)

Wadargascom	mark

Mistonobite	mark

John Oldham
Sam^ll Sharpe

Memorandum on ye Seventeenth day of may one Thousand Six hundred Twenty & nine in ye fifth year of ye Reign of our Soveraign lord Charles King of England Scotland france & Ireland Defender of ye faith &c^t/ Wahangnonawitt Sagamore of Squomsquot in Piscattaqua river did in behalfe of himselfe & ye other Sagamores afore mentioned then psent deliver Quiet & peaceable possession of all ye Lands mentioned in ye within written deed unto ye within Named John Wheelwright for ye Ends within Mentioned In psence of us./ Walter Neale Governour George Vaughan factor and Ambrose Gibbins Trader for ye Company of Laconia Richd Vines Govern^r & Richd Bonighton Assistant of ye plantation at Saco Thomas Wiging Agent & Edwd Hilton Steward of ye plantation of Hiltons point and was Signed Sealed & Delivered in our psence In Witness whereof wee have hereunto Set our hands ye Day & year above written./

Rich: Vines	Tho: Wiggin	W^a Neale
Rich: Bonighton	Edward Hilton	George Vaughan
		Ambrose Gibbins

Recorded According to ye Original found on ye Antient files for ye County of york this 28th day of Jan^ry 1713/4

p Jos: Hamond Reg^r

Book VIII, Fol. 17.

F. Champernown
To
Jnᵒ Billin

To All to whom these psents shall come I Francis Champernown of Kittery in ye province of Maine in New England Gent Send Greeting &cᵗ Know yee that I yᵉ sᵈ Francis Champernown for & in Consideration of yᵉ Sum of Thirteen pounds Curraᵗ pay of New England to me in hand paid by John Billin of Kittery in New England in yᵉ Province of Maine husbandman before yᵉ Ensealing & Delivery hereof yᵉ recᵗ whereof I yᵉ sᵈ Francis Champernown do hereby Acknowledge & my Selfe therewith to be fully Satisfyed Contented & paid have for my Selfe my heirs Executʳˢ Admʳˢ & Assignes given granted bargained Sold Delivered & Confirmed unto yᵉ sᵈ John Billin his heirs Executʳˢ Admʳˢ & Assignes a Certain pcell of land Containing Twenty Acres Lying & being on yᵉ North west Side of Capᵗⁿ Champernowns Island in yᵉ aforesᵈ Province & bounded as followeth./ by Christopher Mitchell on yᵉ East & So runs Eighty pole North by west westerly from yᵉ Marsh Side a white oak Tree Marked four Square to a Smal pine Marked four Square and from thence forty pole to a beach tree marked four Square west & by South & from thence South by East E: ly four score pole to a pine tree in yᵉ highway marked four Square & from thence to a brook or runn of water by yᵉ creek Side on yᵉ South Side of James Foys Marsh & one piece of Marsh Containing Three Acres more or Less bounded by James Foy on yᵉ South by a rock near yᵉ Creek & by Capᵗⁿ Champernowns Marsh on yᵉ North East to yᵉ foresᵈ white oak tree Marked four Square

To have & To hold yᵉ sᵈ land Marsh & pmises as above bounded with all Timber Timber Trees woods & underwoods profits priviledges Comoditys & all other Appurtenances whatsoever thereunto belonging from me my heirs Executʳˢ Admʳˢ & Assignes unto yᵉ sᵈ John Billin his heir Executʳˢ Admʳˢ & Assignes as his & their own propper goods & Estate for ever & to his & their own propper use & behoofe for ever more & I yᵉ sᵈ Francis Champernown for my Selfe my heirs Executʳˢ Admʳˢ and Assignes do Covenant promiss & grant to & with yᵉ sᵈ John Billin his heirs Executʳˢ Admʳˢ & Assignes by these psents that I yᵉ sᵈ Francis Champernown on yᵉ day of yᵉ Date hereof & at yᵉ time of yᵉ Ensealing & Delivery hereof have in my Selfe full power good right & Lawfull Authority to give grant bargaine Deliver & Confirm yᵉ sᵈ land marsh & pmises hereby bargained & Sold unto yᵉ sᵈ John Billin his heirs Executʳˢ Admʳˢ & Assignes for ever more in Manner & form aforesᵈ & Also that he yᵉ sᵈ John Billin his Executʳˢ Admʳˢ & Assignes or any of them Shall or Lawfully may from Time to time & at all times here-

BOOK VIII, FOL. 18.

after peaceably & Quietly have hold use & Enjoy ye s^d land Marsh & pmises hereby bargained & Sold without any Mañer of let suit Trouble Eviction Ejection Mollestation disturbance challenge claime Denial or demand whatsoever of or by me ye s^d Francis Champernown my Execut^{rs} Adm^{rs} & Assignes or any of them or of or by any [18] Other pson or psons whatsoever Lawfully claiming or to claime from by or und^r me my Act or Title he ye s^d John Tillin his heirs Execut^{rs} Adm^{rs} or Assignes paying unto ye s^d Francis Champernown his heirs Execut^{rs} Adm^{rs} or assignes Two Shillings & Six pence in money p Annum In Witness whereof I have hereunto put my hand & Seal this 17th day of May 1686

Signed Sealed & Delivered   Fran : Champernown (a Seal)
In ye psence of us   Mary Champernown (a Seal)
Edmund Gach

Christoph^r ◯ Mitchell
      his mark
John Penwill

19th day Feb^{ry} 1713/4/ then Edmund Gach psonally Appeared besore me ye Subscrib^r one of her Maj^{tys} Justices of ye peace for ye County of york & Made Oath that he Saw this psent Instrum^t Signed Sealed & Delivered & Saw Christopher Mitchell & John Penwill Sign as wittnesses

                      Wm Pepperrell Js peace
Recorded According to ye Original Feb^{ry} 23 : 1713/4
                    p. Jos : Hamond Reg^r

Mo. Worster to Ri. Gowele

Kittery July ye 22^d 1713/ To All Christian people to whom these psents shall come Greeting Know yee that for asmuch as there has been a long controversy or difference between us ye Subscribers hereunto vizt Moses Worster and Richd Gowell Senr relating to a dividing line between their respective lots of land fronting ye great Cove Vulgarly called Spinneys creek and for ye final Ending of s^d Difference and for ye Concluding of all Controversies between both partys & their heirs forever hereafter & for ye Makeing of peace & Maintaining of love & Amity. It is agreed between ye s^d Moses Worster & Richard Gowell Senr and Samuel Ham & Richard Gowell Junr as followeth that ye Dividing line between their respective lots of land Shall begin at an old hemlock turn^d up by ye root at ye head of s^d Worsters lot or ye lot that formerly belonged to

Book VIII, Fol. 18.

John Soaper dec^d and to run from s^d Hemlock on a Straight line to a Stake Set up between both partys as a bound Mark in ye Lane about four or five rods above ye Country road and from that Stake on a Straight line to a red oak tree Standing in ye fence by the great Cove Antiently Marked on four Sides all which s^d bounds or land marks Shall Stand and remaine as y^e undoubted & known land marks between us y^e Subscrib^rs hereunto forever hereafter In Witness whereof wee have hereunto Set our hands & Seals y^e Day & year Above written

Signed & Sealed   y^e mark of
In psence of us   Moses ⊘ Woster (ₛ^a_eal)

                his mark
Rich^d R King   Richard R Gowell (ₛ^a_eal)
John Dennet   Sam^ll Ham (ₛ^a_eal)
Wm Godsoe   Richd Gowell Junr (ₛ^a_eal)

The 25 Aug^st 1713 Mr John Dennet & Mr Richd King doth Attest upon oath that they was p^rsent when these p^rsons whose hands & Seals are Affixt to y^e agreem^t above written and that they Saw these partys Sign Seal & deliver in y^e psence of us Taken upon oath before me Wm Pepperrell J. peace   It is agreed by & between Richard Gowell Senr Richd Gowell Junr And Samuel Ham three of ye partys Signing ye within Instrum^t that ye bounds begin at ye hemlock within Mentioned & from thence Straight to a beach Tree Standing in ye lane Eastward from Richard Gowell Junr his barn & from ye s^d beach Straight to a rock Set in ye ground in ye lane near ye Dwelling house of Richard Gowell Senr and from s^d rock Straight to ye red oak at ye water Side within mentioned to which Agreem^t ye partys aboves^d have Set their hands & Seal this 4th day of February 1713/ any thing Contained in y^e within Agreem^t to the Contrary hereof in Any wise Notwithstanding y^e aboves^d bounds to be y^e Stated bounds for ever

                                 his
Signed Sealed & Delivered   Richard X Gowell (ₛ^a_eal)
                                mark
In psence of us   Richd Gowell Junr (ₛ^a_eal)
John Pickerin   Samuel Ham (ₛ^a_eal)
Jos: Hamond

York ss Feb: 4th 1713/4
The partys above Named psonally Appearing Acknowledged y^e above Instrum^t to be their act & Deed before me
                                  Wm Pepperrell Js peace

Recorded According to y^e Original Feb: 4th 1713/4/
                                  p Jos Hamond Reg^r

Book VIII, Fol. 19.

Sam{{ll}} Came
To
R. Oliver

To all Christian People to whom this Deed of Sale may Come Samuel Came of york in y{{e}} County of york of y{{e}} province of y{{e}} Massachusets bay in New England Sendeth Greeting Know yee y{{e}} s{{d}} Samuel for & in Consideration of fifteen pounds money well & Truely paid or other wise Satisfactorily Secured to be paid by Robert Oliver of s{{d}} york y{{e}} s{{d}} Sam{{ll}} hath given granted bargained Sold Aliened Enfeoffed & Conveyed and doth by these presents give grant bargaine Sell Aliene Enfeoffe & Convey & fully freely & Absolutely Confirm unto y{{e}} s{{d}} Robert his heirs & Assignes for ever a Certain piece or parcell of land lying & being within y{{e}} Township or precinct of s{{d}} York upon ye Southwest Side of y{{e}} Northwest branch of s{{d}} york river And Adjoining to a pcell of land Sold by Jeremiah Moulton to Allexander Tompson & is on y{{e}} South Side of y{{e}} Cove of Marsh known by y{{e}} Name of Frethys cove which is in Quantity Twenty Acres & is butted & bounded as followeth viz{{t}} begining at a great white oak Tree old marked four Sides & now new markt Standing by s{{d}} branch of s{{d}} york river which Tree is a bound marked Tree between s{{d}} Tompson & a lot or Tract of land s{{d}} Came bought of Cap{{tn}} Johnson Harmon & runs from s{{d}} tree Southwest & by South Twenty four pole or rod to a white oak Stake drove into y{{e}} ground marked on four Sides & runs from Thence by s{{d}} Tompsons land Northwest & by west one hundred & Twenty & five poles to a white oak Tree marked on four Sides and runs from thence South west & by South nineteen pole to a white oak Tree marked on four Sides and runs from thence South East & by East unto y{{e}} Aboves{{d}} branch of s{{d}} York river to a Small white oak Tree marked on four Sides & runs thence North East Nineteen pole to a white oak Then on a Straight line over a little point of upland to a [19] Smal red oak markt on four Sides Standing by s{{d}} river branch & thence on a northwestward point to y{{e}} great white oak first above mentioned Together with all y{{e}} rights benefits priviledges unto s{{d}} Land belonging both upland Swampy land wood under wood Timb{{r}} Timb{{r}} trees Standing lying being remaining & belonging unto s{{d}} land above bounded & Stated or any part thereof or any way at any Time redounding to y{{e}} Same unto him y{{e}} s{{d}} Robert Oliver his heirs & Assignes for ever To have & To hold and Quietly & peaceably to Occupy possess & Enjoy as a Sure Estate in Fee Simple, Moreover y{{e}} s{{d}} Sam{{ll}} doth for him selfe his heirs Execut{{rs}} and Adm{{rs}} Covenant Ingage & promiss to & with y{{e}} s{{d}} Robert his heirs and assigns y{{e}} aboves{{d}} land with all its priviledges to be free & clear from all former

Book VIII, Fol. 19.

gifts grants bargains Sales rents rates dowers or any Incumberments whatsoever as also from all future claims challenges lawsuits or any Interruptions to be had or Comenced by him ye s^d Samuel his heirs Execut^{rs} Adm^{rs} or Assignes or any other pson or psons upon grounds or Title of law after ye Date of this deed of Sale but will Defend & do warrantise y^e Same./ In Witness hereof y^e s^d Samuel Came hath hereunto Set his hand and Seal this Tenth day of Decemb^r in y^e year of our lord one Thousand Seven hundred & Twelve & in y^e Eleventh year of y^e Reign of our Soveraign Lady Anne Queen of Great Brittaine &c^t Samuel Came ($_{Seal}^a$)
Signed Sealed & Delivered
 In psence of
  Daniel Simpson
  Robert Pike
York April y^e 1st 1713

Sam^{ll} Came above named psonally Appeared & Acknowledged y^e Above written deed of Sale to be his Act & Deed before me   Abra^x Preble Justice peace
 Recorded According to y^e Original Feb^{ry} y^e 1st 1713 :
                                           4
                          p Jos. Hamond Reg^r

To All People to whom these presents shall come Greeting Know Yee that I Roger Dearing Senr of Kittery in ye County of york in New England Shipwright for & in Consideration of a valluable Sum of money to me in hand before ye Ensealing hereof well & Truely paid by Roger Couch of ye Same place & Occupation ye reciept whereof I do hereby Acknowledge & my Selfe therewith fully Satisfied & Contented & thereof & of Every part & parcell thereof do Exonerate Acquitt & Discharge ye s^d Roger Couch his heirs Execut^{rs} & Adm^{rs} forever by these psents have given granted bargained Sold Aliened Conveyed & Confirmed and by these psents do freely fully & Absolutely give grant bargaine Sell Aliene Convey & Confirm unto him ye s^d Roger Couch his heirs & Assignes forever one Messuage or Tract of land Scittuate lying & being in Kittery within ye County afores^d Containing by Estimation Three Acres be it more or Less which is all That Tract of land where his late fathers dwelling house now Stands Together with all ye houses barns Orchards & gardens & ye rest of ye land belonging thereunto & long in ye possession of his s^d Father & also one Acre of Salt Marsh at brave boat harb^r

R. Dearing
  To
R. Couch

Book VIII, Fol. 19.

Lying between ye Marsh of Edmond Gage & Joseph Mitchell To have & To hold all ye s^d three acres of land be it more or Less Together with ye aboves^d Acre of Salt marsh wth all ye houses barns Orchards &c^t with all ye Appurtenances priviledges and Comoditys to ye Same belonging or in any way Appurtaining to him ye s^d Roger Couch his heirs & Assignes forever to his & their only proper use benefit & behalfe forever and I ye s^d Roger Dearing Senr for me my heirs Execut^{rs} Adm^{rs} do Covena^t promiss & grant to & with ye s^d Roger Couch his heirs & Assignes that before ye Ensealing hereof I am ye True Sole & Lawfull owner of ye above bargained premises and am Lawfully Siezed & possessed of ye Same in mine own propper right as a good perfect & Absolute Estate of Inheritance in Fee Simple & have in my Selfe good right full power & lawfull Authority to grant bargaine Sell Convey & Confirm s^d bargained pmises in maner as aboves^d & that ye s^d Roger Couch his heirs & Assigns shall & may from Time to Time & at all Times forever hereafter by force & vertue of These psents Lawfully peaceably & Quietly have hold use Occupy possess & Enjoy ye s^d demised & bargained premises with ye Appurtenances free & clear & freely & clearly Exonerated Acquitted & Discharged of from all & all maner of former & other gifts grants bargains Sales leases Mortgages wills Entails Joyntures Dowrys Judgments Executions Incumbrances & Extents Furthermore I ye s^d Roger Dearing for my Selfe my heirs Execut^{rs} Adm^{rs} do Covenant & Engage ye above demised pmises to him ye s^d Roger Couch his heirs & Assignes against ye Lawfull claims or Demands of any pson or psons whatsoever forever hereafter to warra^t Secure & Defend And Mary Dearing ye wife of me ye s^d Roger Dearing doth by these presents freely willingly give yield up & Surrend^r all her right of Dowry & power of thirds of in & unto ye above demised pmises unto him ye s^d Roger Couch his heirs and Assignes./ In Witness whereof I have hereunto Set my hand & Seal ye fifth day of February Anno Domini 1713/4./   Roger Dearing (a Seale)

Signed Sealed & Delivered
  In ye psence of
  Theo: Atkinson
  Eliz: Pike
    Pro. N Hamp^r./
  Mr Roger Dearing Acknowledged ye above Instrum^t to be his Act & Deed this 6th of Feb: in ye Twelfth year of her Maj^{tys} Reign Anno Dom. 1713/4 before
                    Theo: Atkinson J peace
  Recorded According to ye Original Feb^{ry} 22^d 1713/4
                    p Jos Hamond Reg^r

BOOK VIII, FOL. 20.

M. Austin
To
W{m} Pepper{ll}

[20] To All People to whom these p{s}ents shall come Greeting Know yee that I Mathew Austine of york in y{e} County of york within her Maj{tys} province of y{e} Massachusets Bay in New England Gentleman for & in Consideration of Sixty five pounds in good & Lawfull money of y{e} province Afores{d} to me in hand before y{e} Ensealing hereof well & Truely paid by W{m} Pepperrell of Kittery in y{e} s{d} County Merchant y{e} rec{t} whereof I do hereby Acknowledge & my Selfe therewith fully Satisfyed & Contented & thereof & of Every part & parcel thereof do Exonerate Acquitt & Discharge y{e} s{d} William Pepperrell his heirs Execut{rs} Adm{rs} & Assigns forever by these p{s}ents have given granted bargained Sold Aliened Conveyed & Confirmed & by these p{s}ents do freely fully & Absolutely give grant bargaine Sell Aliene Convey and Confirm unto him y{e} s{d} W{m} Pepperrell his heirs & Assignes for ever One Messuage or Tract of land all that my house & land which was formerly my father Mathew Austines Scittuate lying & being in y{e} Townsh{p} of york afores{d} & on y{e} western Side of y{e} New mill Creek Joyning to y{e} bridge that is over s{d} creek runing upon a Nortwest line one hundred & Sixty pole in length & forty pole in bredth South west & north East Together with all other y{e} houses barns out houses Edefices & buildings gardens orchards pastures & fences thereon To have & To hold y{e} above given granted p{r}mises with all & Singular y{e} priviledges Appurtenances and Comoditys thereunto belonging or any wise Appurtaining with all y{e} woods und{r} woods Timber trees waters water Courses & all y{e} priviledges whatsoever to him y{e} s{d} W{m} Pepperrell his heirs & Assigns for Ever to his & their only propper use benefit & behalfe for ever & I y{e} s{d} Mathew Austine for me my heirs Execut{rs} Adm{rs} do Covenant promiss and grant to and with y{e} s{d} W{m} Pepperrell his heirs and Assignes that before y{e} Ensealing hereof I am y{e} True Sole & Lawfull owner of y{e} Above bargained p{r}mises and am lawfully Siezed & possessed of y{e} Same in mine own propper right as a good perfect & Absolute Estate of Inheritance in Fee Simple and have in my Selfe good right full power & Lawfull Authority to grant bargaine Sell Convey & Confirm s{d} bargained premises in maner as aboves{d} and that y{e} s{d} W{m} Pepperrell his heirs & Assignes Shall & may from time to time & at all Times for ever hereafter by force & vertue of these p{r}sents Lawfully peaceably and Quietly have hold use Occupie possess & Enjoy y{e} s{d} Demised & bargained p{r}mises with y{e} Appurtenances free & clear & freely & clearly Acquitted Exonerated & discharged of from all & all manner of

former and other gifts grants bargains Sales leases Mortgages Wills Entails Joyntures dowrys Judgm^{ts} Executions Incumbrances & Extents

Furthermore I ye s^d Mathew Austine for my Selfe my heirs Execut^{rs} Adm^{rs} do Covenant and Engage ye above demised premises to him ye s^d Wm Pepperrell his heirs & Assignes against ye Lawfull claims Demands of any pson or psons whatsoever for Ever hereafter to Warrant Secure & Defend ye Same & Mary Austine ye wife of me ye s^d Mathew Austine doth by these psents freely willingly give yield up & Surrender all her right of Dowry & power of Thirds of in and unto ye Above Demised premises unto him ye s^d Wm Pepperrell his heirs & Assignes In Witness whereof I have hereunto Set my hand & Seal this Twentyeth day of June in ye Twelfth year of the Reign of our Soveraign Lady Anne by ye grace of God Queen of Great Brittain France & Ireland & in ye year of our Lord one Thousand Seven hundred Thirteen   Mathew Austine (a Seal)

Signed Sealed & Delivered   her
In psence of   Mary M Austine (a Seal)
Jos: Hamond
Jno Frost
Hannah Hamond

York ss/ July 7° 1713

Mathew Austine above named psonally Appearing before me ye Subscrib^r one of her Maj^{tys} Justices of ye peace for ye County of york and Acknowledged this Instrum^t to be his Act & Deed./   Ichabod Plaisted

Recorded According to ye Original Feb: 27th 1713/4./
     p Jos: Hamond Reg^r

This Indenture made ye Twenty third day of Novemb^r in ye year of our Lord Seventeen hundred & Thirteen Anno Regni Anna Regina Duodecimo./

Jno Leighton & Joseph Ham^d
Chas Frost
Jno Frost & R Cutt

Between John Leighton Charles Frost Robert Cutt & Joseph Hamond of Kittery in ye County of york within her Maj^{tys} province of ye Massachusets Bay in New England yeoman & John Frost of New Castle in ye province of New Hampsh^r in New Engl^d afores^d Marrin^r/ Witnesseth that ye s^d John Leighton Charles Frost Robert Cutt Joseph Hamond & John Frost are & do now Stand Siezed in Comon & undivided of & in Sundry Tracts & parcells of land & priviledges thereunto belonging late Appurtaining to Nicholas Frost Junr Late of Kittery in y^e

County of york afores[d] Marrin[r] dec[d] which lands are Scittuate in Kittery afores[d] lying & being as followeth viz[t] Thirty Acres or Thereabouts part thereof lying between y[e] land of y[e] s[d] Leighton and y[e] Land of y[e] Late Maj[r] Nicholas Shapleigh dec[d] bounded Southwestward by y[e] river of Piscattaqua and running back into y[e] woods as Set forth in y[e] grants & return thereof on Record in Kittery afores[d] reference thereunto being had more at large doth & may Appear./ five acres other part thereof lying at and Abutting upon Sturgeon Creek./ Thirty four Acres an halfe other part thereof lying a little distance North East from y[e] head of Maj[r] Clarks pattent land & Joshua Downings out lot laid out June 21st 1682 As by y[e] return thereof on record as afores[d] Appears./ Thirty Acres [21] Other part thereof begining at y[e] South End of Katherin Leightons land near y[e] highway that goes from Sturgeon Creek to y[e] head of Spruce creek and was laid out and bounded Jan[ry] y[e] 17th 1687/8 as by y[e] return thereof on record As Afores[d] Appears./ Sixty Acres other part thereof being an hundred Twenty four rod in length & Eighty rods in bredth bounded with John Frosts land on y[e] North & on y[e] East with robert Knights Marsh and comon land & on y[e] South with Comon land & on y[e] west with y[e] land of Katherine Leighton and was laid out and bounded February y[e] 29th 1671 as by y[e] return thereof on record as afores[d] Appears It is now to y[e] End a perpetual Division shall be had and made between y[e] aboves[d] partyes of and in y[e] aboves[d] Several Tracts or parcells of lands & priviledges as afores[d] Covenanted Concluded & agreed by & between y[e] s[d] partys to these psents in Manner & form following That is to Say That y[e] s[d] Charles Frost Joseph Hamond & John Frost for themselves their heirs Execut[rs] & Adm[rs] Covenant & agree that y[e] s[d] John Leighton & Robert Cutt their heirs and Assignes shall from hence forth have hold & peaceably Enjoy in Severalty for ever to their own propper use & behoofe all y[e] above Thirty Acres of land first Mentioned in These presents Abutting upon Piscattaqua river & y[e] five Acres Abutting on Sturgeon creek with y[e] Appurtenances and priviledges thereunto belonging and that y[e] s[d] Charles Frost Joseph Hamond & John Frost nor their heirs shall from henceforth claime or demand any right Title use or possession in or to y[e] Same or any part thereof but that y[e] s[d] Charles Frost Joseph Hamond & John Frost shall at all times for ever hereafter from all actions rights and demands thereof be utterly Excluded & for ever debarred by these psents./ And y[e] s[d] John Leighton Robert Cutt Joseph Hamond for themselves their heirs Execut^{rs} & Adm^{rs} Covenant and agree that ye s^d Charles Frost & John Frost their heirs and Assignes shall from henceforth have hold and peaceably Enjoy in Severalty for ever to their own propper use & behoofe all ye above mentioned Two tracts or parcells of land ye one of Thirty Acres laid out Jan^{ry} ye 17th 1687/8 & ye other of Thirty four Acres & an halfe laid out June ye 21st 1682 with ye Appurtenances & priviledges thereunto belonging (That is to Say five Sixth parts thereof to ye s^d Charles Frost & ye other Sixth part to ye s^d John Frost and that ye s^d John Leighton Robert Cutt & Joseph Hamond nor their heirs Shall from hence forth claime or demand any right Title use or possession in or to ye Same or any part thereof Butt that ye s^d John Leighton Robert Cutt & Joseph Hamond Shall at all Times for ever hereafter from all Actions rights and Demands thereof be utterly Excluded & for ev^r debarred by these presents./ And ye s^d John Leighton Charles Frost Robert Cutt & John Frost for themselves their heirs Execut^{rs} & Adm^{rs} Covenant & agree that ye s^d Joseph Hamond Adm^r to ye Estate of Joseph Hamond Esqr dec^d his heirs and Assignes Shall from henceforth have hold and peaceably Enjoy in Severalty for ever to his & their own propper use & behoofe all ye above mentioned Sixty acres of land being an hundred Twenty four rods in length & Eighty rods in bredth bounded with John Frosts land on ye North & on ye East with Robert Knights marsh & Comon Lands & on ye South with Comon land and on ye west with the land of Katherine Leighton and was laid out & bounded Feb: 29 1671. And that ye s^d John Leighton Charles Frost Robert Cutt and John Frost nor their heirs shall from henceforth claime or Demand any right Title use or possession in or to ye Same or any part thereof but that ye s^d John Leighton Charles Frost Robert Cutt & John Frost Shall at all Times for ever hereafter from all Actions rights & Demands thereof be utterly Excluded & for ever Debarred by these presents./ And forasmuch as the Sixty Acres by these psents Alotted & Asigned unto ye s^d Joseph Hamond was at ye Ensealing hereof of more & greater Vallue than the other parts before Allotted & Assigned to ye s^d Charles & John Frost he ye s^d Joseph Hamond at ye Ensealing hereof well & Truly paid to ye s^d Charles Frost & John Frost ye Sum of five pounds Curra^t money of New England afores^d ye reciept whereof ye s^d Charles Frost & John Frost do hereby Acknowledge.

In Witness whereof ye partyes to these psents have hereunto Set their hands & Affixed their Seals ye day & Date first above written (after Enterlining ye words (Joseph

Haṁond) between yᵉ Eighth & ninth line) & yᵉ word Haṁond towards yᵉ bottom

John Leighton (₍ₛₑₐₗ₎ᵃ)
Charles Frost (₍ₛₑₐₗ₎ᵃ)

Signed Sealed & Delivered
In the psence of us
Joseph Young
Daniel Emery
Sylvanus Wentworth

Robert Cutt (₍ₛₑₐₗ₎ᵃ)
Jos Haṁond (₍ₛₑₐₗ₎ᵃ)
Jnᵒ Frost (₍ₛₑₐₗ₎ᵃ)

York ss Janʳʸ 26ᵗʰ 1713/4./ The psons Subscribing yᵉ above Instrumᵗ & Every of Them psonally Appearing Acknowledged this Instrumᵗ to be their Act & Deed Before me/

Wᵐ Pepperrell Js peace

Recorded According to yᵉ Original Janʳʸ 26 : 1713/4./

p Jos : Haṁond Regʳ

[22] To All Christian People to whom these psents shall Come Dodavah Curtis of Kittery Sendeth Greeting./ Know yee that I yᵉ sᵈ Dodevah Curtis of Kittery in yᵉ County of york in her Majesties Province of yᵉ Massachusets Bay in New England yeoman for & in Consideration of love good will & Affection which I have & bare towards my Two Loving Sonns in law Withers Berry and Benjamin Berry both of yᵉ Same place Batchellors have given & granted & by these pʳsents do freely clearly & Absolutely give & grant unto yᵉ sᵈ Withers Berry & Benjamin Berry their heirs & Assignes forever after my Decease & yᵉ Decease of Elizabeth Curtis my Now wife all & Singular my houseing & lands wherein I now Dwell & Occupy & possess lying in yᵉ Township of Kittery Together with my part of yᵉ Sawmill lying near Adjacent to my Dwelling house that I purchased of Mʳˢ Sarah Shapleigh & Mʳ Nicholas Shapleigh with all yᵉ priviledges & Appurtenances thereunto belonging or in any wise Appurtaining Together with all & Singular my psonal Estate of what kind or Quallity Soever it may be as Cattle household goods Tools for husbandry or belonging to yᵉ abovesᵈ Sawmill./ To have & To hold all & Singular yᵉ sᵈ land houseing & part of Sawmill with their Appurtenances and priviledges thereunto belonging whatsoever with all & Singular yᵉ psonal Estate above mentioned as household good Cattle Implements for husbandry unto yᵉ only & Sole use of them yᵉ sᵈ Withers Berry & Benjamin Berry their heirs & Assignes forever to be by them possessed & Enjoyed Imediately after yᵉ Decease of me yᵉ sᵈ Dodavah Curtis & Elizabeth my wife from thence forth as their own propper Estate of Inheritance

Book VIII, Fol. 22.

Absolutely without any mañer of Conditions whatsoever./ In Witness whereof I have hereunto Set my hand & Seal this Twenty first day of Decemb{r} in y{e} twelfth year of y{e} Reign of our Soveraign Lady Anne by y{e} grace of god Queen of Great Brittaine France & Ireland and in y{e} year of our lord one Thousand Seven hundred & Thirteen 1713./

Signed & Sealed & Delivered   Dodavah Curtis (${}^a_{Seal}$)
 In y{e} psence of us y{e} Subscribers
William Godsoe
              The Sign of
Elizabeth E Godsoe
      Province of New Hampsh{r} 22{d} Dec{r} 1713

Dodavah Curtis psonally Appearing Acknowledged this Deed or Instrum{t} in writing to be his Volluntary Act & Deed./   Coram Cha: Story Jus. ps

Recorded According to y{e} Original March 17{th} 1713/4./
                              p Jos: Hamond Reg{r}

Know all men by these p{r}sents that I Job Hanscom of Kittery in y{e} County of york in y{e} province of y{e} Massachu-

J{b} Hanscom
   To
T. Hanscom

sets bay in New England weaver for a valluable Consideration to me in hand paid by my Kinsman Thomas Hanscom Eldest Son of my Brother Thomas Hanscom late of Kittery afores{d} dec{d} have given granted bargined & Sold and by these p{r}sents for me my heirs Execut{rs} Admin{rs} & Assigns do freely Clearly & Absolutely give grant bargaine Sell Aliene Enfeoffe make over & Confirm unto him y{e} s{d} Thomas Hanscom his heirs Execut{rs} Admin{rs} & Assigns forever all my right & Interest which I have Ever had or ought to have or which I y{e} s{d} Job Hanscom my heirs Execut{rs} Admin{rs} & Assigns in time to come May might Should or in any wise ought to have of in or unto y{e} house & lands of Thomas Hanscom my father Late of s{d} Kittery dec{d} with all y{e} priviledges & appurtenances thereunto belonging with y{e} revercōn & revercōns remainder and remainders rents Issues & profits there of To have & To hold unto him y{e} s{d} Thomas Hanscom his heirs and Assigns for ever to his & there own propper use bennefit & behoofe forevermore and I y{e} s{d} Job Hanscom do by these p{r}sents Covena{t} promiss & grant to & with y{e} s{d} Thomas Hanscom his heirs & Assigns that y{e} p{r}mises are free from all former & other gifts grants bargains Sales leases Mortgages or any other Incumbrances

BOOK VIII, FOL. 23.

whatsoever by me made done or Suffered ye peaceable possession thereof to Warrant & forever Defend by these p^{r}sents from all & every p^{r}son or persons Claiming any right title or Interest there unto from by or und^r me In Witness whereof I y^e s^d Job Hanscom have hereunto Set my hand & Seal this Thirteenth day of February Seventeen hundred & Twelve Thirteen in y^e Eleventh year of y^e Reign of our Soveraign Lady Anne of Great Brittain &c^t Queen

Signed Sealed & Delivered   Job: Hanscom ($^a_{Seal}$)
  In p^{r}sents of us
  John Rogers
  Peter Staple
  Jos: Hamond
    York ss Feb^{ry} 22^d 1713/4

Job Hanscom above named psonally appearing acknowledged this Instrument to be his act & Deed

                               Charles ffrost J peace

Recorded According to y^e Original Feb^{ry} 22^d 1713/4
                               p Jos Hamond Reg^r

Mo Hanscom
To
T. Hanscom

Know. All men by these p^{r}sents that I Moses Hanscom of Kittery in ye County of york in ye province of ye Massachusets Bay in New England husbandman for a valluable Consideration to me in hand paid by my kinsman Thomas Hanscom Eldest Son of my brother Thomas Hanscom late of Kittery afores^d dec^d have given granted bargained & Sold unto him ye s^d Thomas Hanscon his heirs & assigns forever all my right & Interest which I have Ever had or ought to have or which I my heirs Execut^{rs} or Admin^{rs} in time to Come may might Should or in any wise ought to have of in or unto ye houses & land of my father Thomas Hanscom Late of s^d Kittery dec^d with all ye priviledges & Appurtenances thereunto belonging with ye reverc̃ons & reverc̃ons remaind^r & remainders rents Issues & profits thereof To have & To hold unto him ye s^d Thomas Hanscom his heirs & Assigns forever to his & their own propper use beñefit & behoof forever More and I ye s^d Moses Hanscom [23] do by these presents Covena^t & promiss & grant to & with ye s^d Thomas Hamscom his heirs & Assigns that ye p^{r}miss as are free from all former & other gifts grants bargains Sales Leases Mortgages or any other Incumbrance whatsoever by me made done or Suffered ye peaceable possession thereof to warrant & forever Defend by these presents from all & every p^{r}son & p^{r}sons Claiming any

right title or Interest thereunto from by or und^r me In Witness whereof I ye s^d Moses Hanscom have hereunto Set my hand & Seal this Seventeenth day of Feb^ry Seventeen hundred & Twelve thirteen in ye Eleventh year of ye Reign of our Soveraign Lady Anne of Great Brittain &c^t Queen
Signed Sealed & Delivered
  In presents of us   Moses ⁕his⁕ M ⁕mark⁕ Hanscom (a Seal)
  Jos: Hamond
  Jos: Curtis
  James Chadborn
        York ss Feb^ry 22^d 1713/4
Moses Hanscom within named psonally Appearing Acknowledged this Instrum^t to be his Act & Deed
                        Charles Frost J. Peace
Recorded According to ye Original Feb^ry 22^d 1713/4
                          p Jos: Hamond Reg^r

Mo. Worster To His Son Thos

To all People to whom these psents Shall come Know Yee that I Moses Worster of Kittery in ye County of york within her Maj^tys Province of ye Massachusets Bay in New England yeoman for Diverse good causes & considerations me thereunto Moveing & More Especially for ye Natural Love & affection which I bear toward my Wellbeloved Son Thomas Worster of ye Same place Yeoman have given & granted & by these presents do give & grant unto him ye s^d Thomas Worster his heirs & Assigns for ever all That my Certain Tract piece or parcell of land Lying & being within ye Township of Berwick in ye County afores^d being pcell of That Two hundred Acres of land which I purchased of Captn John Wincoll and is within ye Limite & bounds of That Deed or Instrum^t I made to my s^d Son Thomas Worster bareing Date Novemb^r ye 30th 1711 which s^d piece or pcell of land I Excepted & reserved to my disposal for ever as by ye s^d Deed or Instrum^t referrence thereunto being had more at Large doth appear which s^d Tract of land with all & Singular ye profits & Advantages thereunto belonging or in any wise Appurtainiag I do for my Selfe my heirs Execut^rs Adm^rs & Assigns give grant Set over & for ever Confirm unto him ye s^d Thomas Worster his heirs and Assigns for ever, and further I doe by these presents give & grant unto my s^d Son Thomas Worster & to his heirs & Assigns forEver all my household Stuf Cattle and all other my psonall Estate of what kind or Nature Soever To have & To hold unto him ye s^d

Thomas Worster his heir Execut[rs] Adm[rs] and assignes for evermore/ and I y[e] s[d] Moses Worster for my Selfe my heirs Execut[rs] and Admin[rs] to & with y[e] s[d] Thomas Worster his heirs & Assigns do Covenant & promiss in Manner & form following That is to Say that at y[e] time of y[e] Ensealing & Delivery hereof I am y[e] true & Lawfull owner of y[e] above granted pmises with y[e] Appurtenances and that I have in my Selfe good right full power & Lawfull Authority to dispose of y[e] Same in Manner as aboves[d] The Quiet & peaceable possession thereof & of Every part & parcell thereof against my Selfe my heirs Execut[rs] Adm[rs] & Assigns unto him y[e] s[d] Thomas Worster his heirs and Assignes to Warrant Maintain & Defend In Witness whereof I y[e] s[d] Moses Worster have hereunto Set my hand & Affixed my Seal this Twenty fourth day of February Annoq Domini One Thousand Seven hundred & Thirteen fourteen/ Anno Reignie Anna Regina Duodecimo

Signed Sealed & Delivered   Moses his mark Worster (a Seal)
In y[e] psence of us
Charles ffrost
Jos: Hamond

    york ss Kittery March 8th 1713/14
The above named Moses Woster psonally Appearing Acknowledged this Instrument to be his act & Deed Before me
                            Charles ffrost J Peace
Recorded According to y[e] Original March y[e] 8th 1713/4
                          p Jos Hamond Reg[r]

James Emery
To
Jn[o] Morrell

To All People to whom this present Instrument in writing Shall Come James Emery Sen[r] of Berwick in y[e] County of york within her Maj[tys] Province of y[e] Massachusets Bay in New England Sends Greeting Know Yee that whereas on y[e] 3[d] day of March 1651/ There was granted unto Anthony Emery and Nicholas Frost a Tract of land on y[e] South Side of Sturgeon Creek from y[e] Mouth of y[e] Creek forty four rods by y[e] water Side untill Two hundred acres ware Accomplished and whereas y[e] s[d] Anthony Emery by his Deed or Instrument in writing under his hand & Seal bearing Date y[e] 12th day of may 1660/ did Alienate & make over y[e] Same or his Interest therein unto y[e] s[d] James Emery and afterwards by y[e] s[d] James Emery Sold & Conveyed unto one Phillip Benmore & by by y[e] heirs of s[d] Benmore was Sold unto John Morrell of Kittery afores[d] as by a Certain Deed or Instrument in writing under ye hand & Seal of Charles Addams bearing Date ye 26th day of March 1692/ and by s^d John Morrell was given to his Son John Morrell Junr as by ye Several deeds above recited refference being thereunto had more at large doth Appear Now for as much as ye Deed or Conveyance from ye s^d James Emery to Phillip Benmore is not to be found and was Neglected in ye day thereof to be recorded Know yee that I ye s^d James Emery haveing received full Satisfaction formerly of ye s^d Phillip Benmore do by these psents for my Selfe my heirs Execut^{rs} & Adm^{rs} relinquish Quitt claime & Sur Surrender up unto ye s^d John Morrell Junr his heirs & assigns for ever all ye right Title or Interest which I have or Ever had unto ye above mentioned grant of land And I ye s^d James Emery & my heirs to him ye s^d John Morrell Junr and his heirs Shall & will warrant Maintaine & Defend ye Title thereof [24] against all & Every pson & psons Claiming any right Title or Interest thereunto from by or under mee them or any of them In Witness whereof I y^e s^d James Emery have hereunto Set my hand and Affixed my Seal this Twelfth day of march in y^e Thirteenth year of y^e Reign of our Soveraign Lady Anne of Great Brittain &c^t Queen/ annoq, Domini Seventeen hundred & Thirteen Fourteen/ 1713/4   James Emery ($_{Seale}^{a}$)

Signed Sealed & Delivered   Daniel Emery
   In psence of us
   Bial Hambleton
   Mary Plaisted
     York ss Berwich March : 17 : 1713/4
   Mr James Emery Senr pasnally appeared and acknowledged the above Instrument to be his act and deed before me   Ichabod Plaisted J peace
   Recorded According to ye Original April ye 5th 1714./
                       p Jos. Hamond Reg^r

Jno Parker
To
T. Kemble

To All Christian People to whom this present Deed Shall come Know yee that whereas I John Parker of Kenebeck river in New Engl^d fisherman for & in Consideration of ye Sum of Sixty pounds in Curra^t money of New England for me in hand well & Truely p^d by Thomas Kemble of Boston in New England afores^d Merchant ye rec^t whereof I do hereby Acknowledge & my Selfe therewith to be fully Satisfyed & Contented did give grant bargaine Sell Aliene & Confirm unto ye s^d Thomas Kimble his heirs & Assigns forever a Certain Tract of land lying & being in Kenebeck river ye Contents & boundarys whereof is in & by this presents after Expressed ye which Deed of grant ye s^d Kimble doth Affirm was burned in ye fire that happened in Boston in ye year of our Lord 1676

Now Know All men by this presents that as a Supplem^t to ye s^d Deed and for ye better Confirmation of ye s^d Tract of land to ye s^d Thomas Kimble his heirs & Assignes I ye s^d John Parker for ye Considiracõn above Mentioned have & hereby do freely clearly & Absolutely give grant Bargaine Sell Aliene Convey & Confirm unto ye s^d Thomas Kimble his heirs Execut^rs & Assignes ye afores^d Tract land Scittuate in Kenebeck river afores^d & is Next Adjoyning to ye land of John Vering of Kenebeck afores^d & all ye wood Timber & Timber Trees upon ye s^d Tract of land Standing growing & being & all ye Meadow ground & upland within ye s^d Tract of land Contained & also ye Creek or creeks as well Salt as fresh waters rivers water Courses or ruñs of water & all ye Marshes as well Salt as fresh & also all mines mineralls profits priviledges & Appur^ces w^tsoev^r to ye s^d Tract of land belonging or in Any wise Appurtaining Excepting a Small piece of Marsh belonging to Hosea Mallet ffisherman The which tract of land is butting & bounded in Maner following that is to Say) by ye land of ye s^d John Vering on ye Northern Side begining at a pine tree Standing at ye mouth of ye Salt water Creek & So runing from thence upon a northwest line or Course over to ye Estern Side of Casco bay & is bounded on ye Southward Side by ye s^d Salt water Creek and runing up from ye mouth thereof up by ye Southward Side of ye s^d Creek up to ye fresh water falls & is then bounded by ye s^d fresh Creek or river on ye Southerly Side & Extends its Selfe home to ye Eastw^d Side of ye s^d Casco bay all which tract of land & all ye profits priviledges and Imunitys within ye s^d bounds & Limits contained ye s^d Thomas Kimble is to Have and to Hold & peaceably to possess & Enjoy to him his heirs Execut^rs Adm^rs & Assignes forever./ & to his & their Sole & propper use & behoofe from henceforth forever. And ye s^d John Parker and Margriet his wife for themselves, their heirs Execut^rs & Adm^rs do Covenant promiss & grant to & with ye s^d Thomas Kimble his heirs Execut^rs Adm^rs and Assignes that ye s^d tract of land & all ye bargained pmises & Appur^ces are at ye Sealing & Delivery hereof free & clear Acquitted & discharged of & from all former and other gifts grants bargains Sales Leases Mortgages Titles troubles Acts Alienations & Incumbrences whatsoev^r and ye pmises against themselves unto ye s^d Thomas Kimble his heirs & Assignes & against Every other pson lawfully Claiming any right thereto

Book VIII, Fol. 25.

or Interest therein from by or under them Shall Warrant & forever Defend by these psents./ And y[e] s[d] John Parker & Margriet his wife do further promiss to do & pform any other Act or thing that may be for y[e] more Ample Secureing & Sure making y[e] s[d] tract of land and all y[e] Appurtenances thereto belonging to y[e] s[d] Thomas Kimble his heirs Execut[rs] & Assignes forever by these psents and Such as by men Expercenced in y[e] law Shall be Adjudged to be necessary requisite or Expedient, In Witness w[r]of y[e] s[d] John Parker & Margriet his wife have hereunto Set their hands and Seals y[e] Seven & twentyeth day of April Anno Dom one Thous[d] Six hundred & Eighty Eight Annoq, Regni Regis Jacobi Secundi Anglia &c[t] Quarto 1688

Signed Sealed & Delivered
  In y[e] psence of us   John : J. P. Parker (Seal)
  Abraham Erington   his / mark
      his   Margriet Parker (Seal)
  John ✝ Pennell   her name
      mark

John Parker Appeared y[e] 30th of April 1688 Before me & owned & Acknowledged this Instrum[t] to be his Act & Deed & that he & his wife Set y[r] hands & Seals thereto y[e] day & year above written   Larens Jones Jus of peace

Recorded According to y[e] Original April 15th 1714.

                            p Jos. Hamond Reg[r]

[25] Reconed 2[d] Aug[st] 1688 with M[r] Robert Eliot on y[e] Great Island and then rest due to him from me Thomas Hanscom Sen[r] y[e] Sum of Seventeen pounds Twelve Shillings
                     Test   Nich[o] Heskins

There is also due to M[r] Eliot on my Son Thomas Hanscom Jun[r] his Acco[t] y[e] Sum of four pounds Seven Shillings

Recorded According to y[e] Original April 16th 1714/

                          p Jos : Hamond Reg[r]

Thomas Hanscom Sen[r] hath Credit on M[r] Robert Eliots Book for 30 p[s] of Timb[r] fetcht by M[r] Nathan[ll] Fryer about Novemb[r] 1688 Contents Twenty Eight Tunns of pine Timb[r]
                         Test Nich[o] Heskins

Recorded According to y[e] Original April 16th 1714/

                          p Jos. Hamond Reg[r]

BOOK VIII, FOL. 25.

Jno Chapman
To
Ab Morrell

To all Christian People To whom these presents Shall come John Chapman of Kittery in ye County of York within her Maj^{tys} Province of ye Massachusets Bay in New England Carpenter Sends Greeting Know Yee that the Said John Chapman for & in Consideration of ye Sum of Seventy two pounds Currant money of New England to him in hand paid before ye ensealing and delivering of these presents by Abraham Morrill of Kittery in ye County afores^d Black Smith ye Receipt whereof to full content and Satisfaction he ye s^d John Chapman doth by these presents acknowledge and thereof & of Every part thereof for him Selfes his Heirs Executors and administrators doth acquit Exonerate & discharge ye s^d Abraham morrell his Heirs Executors and and admin^{rs} every of them for ever doth by these p^{r}sents & for diverse other good causes and Considerations him hereunto moveing he ye s^d John Chapman hath given granted bargained Sold Aliened Enfeoffed Conveyed and Confirmed And by these presents doth fully freely Clearly and absolutely give grant bargain Sell Aliene enfeoffe convey and Confirm unto ye s^d Abraham Morrell his Heirs & Assigns for ever a Certain Tract of Land Containing Twenty two Acres and halfe Scituate in ye Township of Kittery afores^d being bounded as followeth to witt Fifteen acres of ye afores^d Twenty—two and halfe Begining at the East end of Samuel Hills Home Lott next to John Morrills Fifteen pole in breadth North and South from thence it runs Eighty two poles East the Same bredth and then it extends North in bredth Thirtythree poles more to a highway of three poles wide betwene the said Lands and William Frys Land and So ye Same bredth till Fifteen acres be accomplished as may appear by a deed or Instrument under the hand and Seal of Adrian Fry bearing date the first day of July anno annoq Dom: 1709 the other Seven acres and halfe being bounded on the west by the afores^d Fifteen acres on the North by a highway of John Morrell on the South by the aforesaid Fifteen acres twenty four poles then East the Same bredth till Seven acres and halfe be accomplished as may appear by another Deed under the hand and Seal of the aforesaid Adryan Fry Dated the twenty Sixth day of September anno Dom 1711 Reference being had thereunto may more at large appear Together with all Such Rights Libertys Immunities profits priviledges Commodities Emoluments and appurtenances as in any kind appertain thereunto with ye Reversions and Remainders thereof and all the Estate Right title Interest Inheritance possession Claime and demand whatsoever of him the said John Chapman of in and to

the Same and Every part thereof To Have and To Hold all ye above Granted Premises with all and Singular ye Appurtenances thereof unto ye s^d Abraham Morrell his Heirs & Assignes To his and their one Sole and proper Use benefit & behoof from henceforth for ever And the s^d John Chapman for him Selfe his Heirs Execut^{rs} and Admin^{rs} Doth hereby Covenant promise Grant & agree to and with ye s^d Abraham Morrell his heirs and Assignes in manner & form following y^t is to Say y^t att ye time of ye Ensealing and delivering of these presents he ye s^d John Chapman is ye true Sole & Lawfull owner of all ye afore bargained premises & Stands Lawfully Seized thereof in his own propper Right of a good perfect & Indefeazable Estate of inheritance in fee Simple having in him Salfe full power good Right and Lawfull Authority to Sell and dispose of ye Same in manner as afores^d and y^t ye Said Abraham Morrill his Heirs and Assignes Shall and may henceforth forever Lawfully peaceably & quietly have hold use occupie possess & Enjoy ye abouv Granted premises with ye appurtinences thereof and further ye s^d John Chapman doth hereby Covenant promiss bind & oblige himSelfe his Heirs Execut^{rs} & Admin^{rs} from henceforth & forever hereafter to warrant and defend all ye above Granted premises unto ye s^d Abraham Morrell his heirs & Assigns against y^e Lawfull Claims & Demands of all persons whomsoever In Witness whereof the s^d John Chapman hath hereunto Set his hand and Seal the Twenty Seventh day of march anno Dom One Thousand Seven hundred and fourteen Annque Regni Anne Regina Decimo Tertio
Signed Sealed and delivered   John Chapman ($_{Seal}^a$)
 in Presences of us
 Elisha Ingersill
 James Chadbourne
 Samuel Shory
    york ss/ Kittery march 27th 1714
The above named John Chapman appearing acknowledged the above written Instrument to be his free act and Deed Rachael the wife of the above named Chapman also appearing and Surrendered up her right of Dower to the above granted premises   Before me. Charles ffrost J peace
 Recorded According to ye Original Aprill ye 20th 1714/
            p Jos. Hamond Reg^r

Book VIII, Fol. 26.

T. Greely
To
Ti Waymonth

To All People to whom this present Deed or Instrument in wrighting Shall Come Know y^{ee} that I Thomas Greeley of Portsmouth in the Province of New Hampsh^r in New England Tanner for and in Consideration of ye Sum of one hundred pounds Lawfull money of New England to me in hand before ye Ensealing & Delivery of these presents well & Truly paid by Timothy Waymouth of Kittery in ye County of york in ye Province of ye Massachusets Bay in New England afores^d yeoman Have given granted bargained Sold released Enfeoffed & Confirmed And by these psents for my Selfe my heirs Execut^{rs} and Admin^{rs} do freely clearly & Absolutely give grant bargaine Sell release Assigne Enfeoffe Convey & Confirm unto him ye s^d Timothy Waymouth his heirs and Assigns for ever all Those my Several Tracts or parcells of land lying and being within ye Township of Kittery afores^d viz all that Tract of land which was granted by ye town of Kittery unto John Ross late of s^d Kittery Dec^d on ye 23^d of November 1665 bounded on ye west Side by Edward Waymouths Lott and on ye South Side by a fresh brook of water and it is bounded on ye North Side by Thomas Ethingtons lot and Severall Marked Trees & on ye East Side or head by Jeremiah Hodsden which s^d lot Contains Twenty Acres be it more or less Lying Near unto a place called Mast Cove Also all that Tract of Land which was laid out and bounded unto John Bready on ye 30th of Decemb^r 1674 by John Wincoll & Roger Plaisted Survey^{rs} for Kittery Containing Sixty one Acres being one hundred & Two poles in length East north Easts from ye ledge of Rocks and one hundred poles in breadth South South East bounded on ye north with the land of Israel Hodsden and on ye East with ye Comons at ye third hills and on ye South & west with ye other Comons which s^d Several Tracts of Lands I purchased of James Treworgie Late of s^d Town of Kittery Containing in ye whole about Eighty one Acres of land be ye Same More or Less as by ye Severall Deeds and returns on Record in ye Town of Kittery [26] And County of York respectively referrence thereunto being had more at large doth and may Appear Together with all and Singular ye houses buildings Edefices fences orchards gardens Trees woods und^r woods waters water Courses Swamps Meadows Meadow grounds rights Memb^{rs} profits priviledges Comoditys Advantages heredittam^{ts} Comon rights & Appurtenances upon belonging or in any wise appurtaining unto ye above granted & bargained premises or any part there of and ye reversion & reversions remaind^r & remainders rents Issues & profits therof

Book VIII, Fol. 26.

And all yᵉ Estate right Title Interest use propperty Inheritance Claime & Demand of me yᵉ sᵈ Thomas Greely my heirs Executʳˢ Adminʳˢ & Assigns of in & to yᵉ Same To have & To hold yᵉ sᵈ Several Tracts of land & pmises & Every part & parcell thereof and all & Singular yᵉ pmises herein before granted bargained & Sold unto him yᵉ sᵈ Timothy Waymouth his heirs & Assigns to his and their own Sole & propper use bennefit and behoofe for ever & I yᵉ sᵈ Thomas Greely for my Selfe my heirs &cᵗ do hereby Covenant & agree to & with him yᵉ sᵈ Timothy Waymouth his heirs & Assignes in Manner Following (That is to Say That at and untill yᵉ Ensealing & Delivery hereof I am yᵉ True and lawfull Owner of yᵉ pmises herein before granted And Stand Lawfully Siezed thereof in my own propper right as a good perfect & absolute Estate or Inheritance in Fee Simple without any Maner of Condition reversion or Limitation of use or uses whatsoever So as to alter Change Defeat or make voyd the Same & have in my Selfe full power good right and Lawfull Authority to grant Sell & Assure yᵉ sᵈ land and pmises in manner as aforesᵈ & that yᵉ Same Are free & clear & clearly Acquitted & Discharged of & from all formʳ & other gifts grants Bargins Sales leases Morgages Wills Entails Judgmᵗˢ Executions Titles Troubles Charges & Incumbrances whatsoever And Further that I yᵉ sᵈ Thomas Greely my heirs &cᵗ Shall & will for Ever Save harmless warraᵗ & Defend yᵉ sᵈ Timothy Waymouth his heirs &cᵗ against yᵉ Claims & Demand of all & Every pson & psons whatsoever Claiming any right Title or Interest Thereunto from by or under me In Witness whereof I yᵉ sᵈ Thomas Greely and Rebecah my wife have hereunto Set our hands & Seals yᵉ thirteenth day of march Annoq Domini Seventeen hundred and Thirteen Fourteen 1713/4

anno Regni Anna Regnia Decimo Tertio

Signed Sealed & Delivered
In psence of
John Gowen
Clement Hughs
Mary Polley

Thomas ✗ Greely (Seal)
his
mark
Rebecah Greeley (Seal)

Province of New Hampshʳ 16ᵗʰ March 1713/4

Thomas Greely & Rebecah his wife psonally Appearing acknowledged this Instrument in writing to be yʳ acts and Deed   Coram Charles Story Jus : peace

Recorded According to yᵉ Original March 16 : 1714/3

p Jos. Hamond Regʳ

Book VIII, Fol. 27.

To All to whom these presents shall Come Nathaniel Winslow of Shawamett in ye Town of Swanzey in ye County of Bristoll yeoman Sendeth Greeting &c^t Know Yee that I ye s^d Nathan^{ll} Winslow for & in Consideration of ye full & Just Sum of Twenty Six pounds Ten shillings in Currant money of New England by Job Otis of Sittuate in ye County of Plymouth Cordwainer well & Truely paid wherewith I do Acknowledge my Selfe to be fully Satisfyed Contented & paid & thereof do Acquitt & Discharge ye s^d Job Otis his heirs Execut^{rs} Adm^{rs} & Assignes forever by these psents have given granted bargained Aliened Sold Enfeoffed and Confirmed and by these psents for me & my heirs do hereby fully & Absolutely give grant bargain Sell Aliene Enfeoffe & Confirm unto ye s^d Job Otis his heirs and Assignes forever ye one Moiety or halfe part of a Certain Tract or pcell of upland and Meadow Scittuate lying & being at Casco Bay in ye Province of Maine in ye Province of ye Massachusetts Bay in New England which s^d Tract & parcell of upland and meadow I ye s^d Nathaniel Winslow Purchased of Enoch Wiswal who purchised ye Same of Joseph Nash & were form^{r}ly ye Lands of John Mosure which s^d upland in ye whole Contains Three hundred Acres bounded & Runing by ye Side of Arisicket river runing from ye Second Gutt northwesterly untill ye full Contents & Measure of Three hundred Acres be Meeted out wth all ye Meadow thereunto belonging the first parcel of Meadow haveing a pond in ye Middle of it and Three parcells more by ye Side of ye uper part of ye river Containing in all about Twenty or Thirty Acres be it more or Less together with all houses out houses Edefices & buildings thereon To have & To hold ye one halfe part or Moiety of ye afores^d Three hundred Acres of upland and ye Moiety or half part of all ye s^d Tracts & parcels of Meadow with all & Singular ye Rights memb^{rs} profits priviledges wayes Easm^{ts} Comons & Comon Rights fishing & fowling and heriditaments whatsoever thereunto belonging or in any wise Appertaining to him ye s^d Job Otis his heirs & Assignes forever to ye only propper use & behoofe of him ye s^d Job Otis his heirs & Assignes for ever./ And I ye s^d Nathaniel Winslow for me my heirs Execut^{rs} and Adm^{rs} to and with ye s^d Job Otis his heirs and Assignes do promiss Covenant & grant in Maner & form following That is to Say) that I ye s^d Nath^{ll} Winslow At ye Time of ye Ensealing & Delivery of these psents have good right full power & Lawfull Authority to grant & Confirm all & Singular the [27] Above granted & bargained premises & thereof to make a pure & perfect Estate of Inheritance in ffee Simple in maner & form above Expressed & that ye Same are free & Clear & Clearly Acquitted of & from all other &

former gifts grants bargains Sales Titles Troubles Charges and Incumbrences whatsoever heretofore by me made had Suffered or done and that I y^e s^d Nathaniell Winlsow & my heirs Execut^{rs} & Adm^{rs} to him y^e s^d Job Otis his heirs & Assignes Shall & will Warrant & forever Confirm y^e Same by these psents In Witness whereof I y^e s^d Nathaniell Winslow have hereunto Set my hand & Seal y^e Seventeenth day of February Anno$_q$ Dom. 1702/
Signed Sealed & Delivered Nathaniel Winslow ($_{Seale}^{a}$)
In psence of us
Elizabeth Thomas
Caleb Thomas
Memorandum that I Lydia Winslow wife of y^e aboves^d Nath^{ll} Winslow have & by these psents do Agree and Consent to y^e above mentioned bargain & Sale and by these psents release and grant all my right Title Claime & Demand which I now have or hereafter may befall & Accrew to me in y^e above mentioned lands unto him y^e s^d Job Otis his heirs & Assignes In Witness whereof I have hereunto Set my hand & Seal y^e day & year aboves^d Lydia Winslow ($_{Seale}^{a}$)
Memorandum that on y^e 17th day of February 1702./ The above named Nath^{ll} Winslow & Lydia his wife before me y^e Subscriber one of her Maj^{tys} Justices did Acknowledge y^e above written Instrum^t to be their Acts & Deeds./
Nathaniel Thomas
Recorded According to y^e Original April 28th 1714
p Jos: Hamond Reg^r

•

To All Christian People to whom this Deed of Sale Shall Come Gilbert Winslow of Shawamett in ye Town of Swanzy in ye County of Bristoll yeomand Sendeth Greeting &c^t Know yee that I ye s^d Gilbert Winslow for and in Consideration of ye full & Just Sum of Twenty & Six pounds & Ten Shillings of Currant Silver money of New England to me in hand at or before ye Ensealing & Delivery of these psents by Job Otis of Scittuate in ye County of Plymouth in ye Province of ye Massachusetts Bay in New England Cordwainer well & Truely paid the receipt whereof I ye s^d Gilbert Winslow do hereby Acknowledge & my Selfe fully Satisfyed Contented & paid & thereof & of Every part & parcell thereof for my Selfe & my heirs do freely & Clearly Exonerate Acquitt & Discharge him ye s^d Job Otis hee his heirs Execut^{rs} Adm^{rs} & Assignes for ever by these psents have given granted bargained & Sold & by these Presents do freely fully & Absolutely give grant bargaine Sell Aliene

Book VIII, Fol. 28.

Enfeoffe & Confirm from me ye s^d Gilbert Winslow & my heirs unto him ye s^d Job Otis he his heirs and Assignes for ever ye one Moiety or halfe Endeale of Certain Tracts or parcells of upland and Meadow lands Scittuate lying & being at Casco bay in ye Province of Maine in ye Province of ye Massachusets bay in s^d New England which s^d Tracts & parcells of upland & Meadow I ye s^d Gilbert Winslow & Nathaniel Winslow purchased of Enoch Wiswall who purchased ye Same of Joseph Nash and were formerly ye lands of John Mosure which s^d upland in ye whole Containeth Three hundred Acres bounded & runing by ye Side of Aresiket river runing from ye Second Gutt Northwesterly untill ye full Contents and Measure of Three hundred Acres be Meeted out wth all ye Meadow thereunto belonging, The first parcell of Meadow haveing a pond in ye Middle of it and three parcells more by ye side of ye uper part of ye river Containing in all About Twenty or Thirty Acres be it more or Less Together with all houses out houses Edefices & buildings thereon To have & To hold ye one halfe part or Moiety of ye Afores^d Three hundred Acres of upland & ye Moiety or halfe part of all ye s^d Tracts & parcells of Meadow lands with all & Singular ye rights members benefits profits priviledges wayes Easments Comons & Comon rights fishings & foulings & heridittaments whatsoever thereunto belonging or in any wise appertaining to all & Every part & parcell thereof unto him ye s^d Job Otis he his heirs & Assignes for ever & to y^e only propper use bennefit & behoofe of himselfe his heirs and Assignes for ever./ And I y^e s^d Gilbert Winslow for my Selfe my heirs Execut^r & Adm^{r}s to & with y^e s^d Job Otis he his heirs & Assignes do grant promiss & Covenant in maner & form following=That is Say) that I y^e s^d Gilbert Winslow at y^e Time of y^e Ensealing & Delivery of these psents have good right full power & Lawfull Authority to grant & Confirm all & Singular y^e above granted & bargained pmises & thereof to make a pure & perfect Estate of Inheritance in ffee Simple in maner & form above Expressed and that ye s^d three hundred Acres of upland and ye s^d Tracts & pcells of Meadow land The Moiety or halfe part thereof which is now Sold by me ye s^d Gilbert Winslow is free & Clearly Acquitted & Every way Sufficiently Discharged of & from all & all maner of gifts grants bargains Sales Titles Troubles Charges & Incumbrances whatsoever had made Comitted done or Suffered to be done by me ye s^d Gilbert Winslow or my Assignes or any other pson or psons by my Means Consent privity or procurem^t at any time or times before y^e [28] Ensealing & Delivery of these psents and that I ye s^d Gilbert Winslow & my heirs Execut^{rs} & Ad-

ministrat[rs] to him y[e] s[d] Job Otis he his heirs & Assigns Shall & will warrant & for ever Confirm y[e] Same by these presents To and for pformance of all & Every y[e] above granted & bargained pmises I y[e] s[d] Gilbert Winslow bind my Selfe my heirs Execut[rs] Adm[rs] & Assignes firmly by these psents In Witness whereof I have hereunto Set my hand and Seale Dated y[e] first day of may Anno Dom. one Thousand Seven hundred & Three 1703./ Memor[x] ye words (pformance of) were Enterlined before Ensealing   Gilbert Winslow (a Seale) Signed Sealed & Delivered
In y[e] psence of us Witnesses
Ephraim Little
Charles Little
Memorandum that on y[e] 3[d] day of may Annoq, Dom 1703 The above Named Gilbert Winslow before me y[e] Subscriber one of her Maj[tys] Justices Acknowledged y[e] Above written Instrum[t] to be his Act & Deed./   Nathaniel Thomas
Recorded According to y[e] Original April 28th 1714./
p Jos: Hammond Reg[r]

To All People to whom these psents Shall Come Jonathan Mendum of Kittery in y[e] County of york within her Ma[tys] Province of the Massachusets Bay in New England Shipwright Sends Greeting./ Know yee that y[e] s[d] Jonathan Mendum for & in Consideration of y[e] Sum of Sixty pounds Currant money of New England to him in hand paid before y[e] Ensealing and Delivery of these psents by Samuel Skillin of Exeter in y[e] Province of New Hampshire Shipwright y[e] receipt whereof to full Content & Satisfaction he y[e] s[d] Jonathan Mendum doth by these psents Acknowledge & thereof & of Every part thereof for himselfe his heirs Execut[rs] & Adm[rs] doth Acquitt Exonerate and Discharge y[e]s[d] Samuel Skillin his heirs Execut[rs] & Adm[rs] & Every of them forever by these psents he y[e] s[d] Jonathan Mendum hath given granted bargained Sold Aliened Enfeoffed Conveyed & Confirmed & by these psents doth freely fully Clearly & absolutely give grant bargaine Sell Aliene Enfeoffe Convey & Confirm unto y[e] s[d] Samuel Skillion his heirs & Assignes forever y[e] Moiety or one halfe part of a Certaine Tract of land & Swamp Scittuate Lying & being in y[e] Township of Kittery afores[d] which was given unto my brother Robert Mendum late of Kittery dec[d] by my Grandfather Robert Mendum of Kittery dec[d] as by his last will & Testam[t] may Appear butted & bounded on. y[e] Southwest by y[e] river Comonly Called Spruce Creek & on y[e] Northwest by y[e] land of Joseph Weekes on y[e] northeast by yᵉ woods & on yᵉ Southeast by Andrew Haleys land or howsoever Otherwise bounded or reputed to be bounded Together with all Such rights Libertys Imunitys profits priviledges Comoditys Emolluments & Appurtenances as in any kind Appertaine thereunto with yᵉ Reverc̃ons & remainders thereof and all yᵉ Estate right Title Interest Inheritance propperty possession Claime & Demand whatsoever of him yᵉ sᵈ Jonathan Mendum of in & to yᵉ one halfe part of yᵉ abovesᵈ whole parcell of upland & Swamp & Every part thereof Excepting and always Saveing out of yᵉ whole Tract that part which yᵉ sᵈ Jonathan Mendum hath heretofore Alienated & Sold unto Joseph Weeks and also that part which John Fennike & Deberoh his wife now possess & Dwell on which is Excepted dureing yᵉ Term of their Natural lives & After their decease yᵉ sᵈ Samuel Skillion his heirs & Assignes to be possest of yᵉ one halfe part of that as of yᵉ other or in lieu thereof As much of yᵉ other halfe As Shall be to yᵉ sᵈ Skillion his Satisfaction To have & To hold yᵉ one full Moiety or halfe part of yᵉ Abovesᵈ whole Tract of upland & Swamp Excepting what is before Excepted with all & Singular yᵉ Appurtenances thereof unto yᵉ sᵈ Samˡˡ Skillion his heirs & Assignes & to his & their own Sole & propper use benefit & behoofe from henceforth forever and yᵉ sᵈ Jonathan Mendum for himselfe his heirs Executʳˢ & Admʳˢ doth thereby Covenant promiss grant & agree to & with yᵉ sᵈ Samˡˡ Skillion his heirs & Assignes in maner & form following That is to Say) that at yᵉ time of yᵉ Ensealing & Delivery of these psents he yᵉ sᵈ Jonathan Mendum is yᵉ True & Lawfull owner of yᵉ above bargained & Sold pmises & hath in himselfe good right full power & Lawfull Authority to Sell & Dispose of yᵉ Same in maner as aforesᵈ & that yᵉ sᵈ Samˡˡ Skillion his heirs & Assignes Shall & may henceforth forever Lawfully peaceably & Quietly have hold use Occupy possess & Enjoy yᵉ above granted pmises with yᵉ Appurtenances thereof free & Clear & Clearly Acquitted & Discharged of & from all & all maner of former & other gifts grants bargains Sales Leases Mortgages Joyntures Dowers Judgmᵗˢ Executions Entails forfeitures & of & from all other Titles Troubles Charges and Incumbrances whatsoever had made Comitted done or Suffered to be done by yᵉˢᵈ Jonathan Mendum his heirs or Assignes at any time or times before yᵉ Ensealing & Delivery hereof And further yᵉ sᵈ Jonaⁿ Mendum doth hereby Covenant promiss bind & Oblige himselfe his heirs Executʳˢ & Admʳˢ from henceforth & forever hereafter to Warrant & Defend all yᵉ above granted pmises & yᵉ Appurtenances thereof unto yᵉ sᵈ Samˡˡ Skillion his heirs & Assignes against yᵉ Lawfull Claims & Demands of

of all & Every pson or psons whomsoever and at any [29] Time or times hereafter on demand to give & pass Such further and Ample Assurence & Confirmation of ye pmises unto ye s^d Sam^{ll} Skillion his heirs and Assignes forever as in Law or Equity Can be reasonably Devised Advised or required./ In Witness whereof y^e s^d Jonathan Mendum hath hereunto Set his hand & Seal y^e fourteenth day of April in y^e year of our lord 1713./ and in y^e Twelfth year of y^e Reign of our Soveraign Lady Anne Queen of Great Brittaine &c^t
Signed Sealed & Delivered   Jonathan Mendum (s$_{Seal}^a$)
In psence of
John Newmarch   Sarah Mendum her mark ($_{Seal}^a$)
Nath^{ll} Mendum
Dorothy Frost

The 6 March 1713/4/ Then Mr Jonathan Mendum & Sarah his wife both psonall Appeared before me & did Acknowledge this above Instrum^t to be their ffree Act & Deed   Wm Pepperrell Js peace
Recorded According to y^e Original April 7th 1714/
                          p. Jos Hamond Reg^r

To All People to whom this present deed or Instrum^t in writing Shall Come Know yee that I Sam^{ll} Spinney of Kittery in ye County of york within her Maj^{tys} Province of ye Massachusets Bay in New England yeoman for & in Consideration of ye Sum of forty pounds Curra^t money of New England Afores^d which I ye s^d Samuel Spinney do Justly owe and Am Truly Indebted under John Woodman of Kittery afores^d fferryman And for Security to him ye s^d John Woodman ye s^d forty pounds well & Truely to be paid I ye s^d Samuel Spinney have given granted bargained & Sold released Eufeoffed & Confirmed and by these presents do give grant bargaine Sell release Eufeoffe Convey & Confirmed unto ye s^d John Woodman his heirs & Assignes for ever all that my Messuage or Tennem^t and land thereto belonging lying & being in ye Township of Kittery afores^d & is that land on which I now Dwell with ye houses buildings Orchards fences & Appurtenances thereon Together with all my other lands which now of Right doth belong to me within ye Township of Kittery Afores^d with all & Singular ye rights memb^{rs} profits Advantages heriditaments priviledges & Appurtenances thereunto belonging with all ye Estate right Title Interest Inheritance use property possession Claime & Demand

This Mortgage is discharged by an Instrum^t und^r ye hand & Seal of ye Mortgagee recorded in this book folio 161 —— Att^t Jos. Hamond Reg^r

Book VIII, Fol. 29.

of me y[e] s[d] Samuel Spinney of in & unto y[e] s[d] lands & pmises with y[e] revertion & revertions Remaind[r] and remaind[rs] rents Issues & profits thereof to Have & to Hold unto him y[e] s[d] John Woodman his heirs Execut[rs] Adm[rs] & Assigns for ever more

Provided Alwayes and upon Condition Nevertheless anything herein Contented Notwithstanding that if y[e] s[d] Samuel Spinney his heirs Execut[rs] Adm[rs] or Assignes at any Time or Times before y[e] Tenth day of March which will be in y[e] year of our Lord Seventeen hundred & Eighteen or Nineteen Shall & do well & Truely pay or Cause to be p[d] unto y[e] s[d] John Woodman his heirs Execut[rs] Adm[rs] or Assignes in Kittery afores[d] y[e] full & Just Sum of forty pounds Lawfull money of New England without fraud or delay./ Then this present deed & Every grant Article & Thing therein Contained to Cease determin be voyd and of non Effect but in default thereof to Abide & remaine in full force & vertue with good Effect in y[e] Law./. And I y[e] s[d] Sam[ll] Spinney do Avouch my Selfe at y[e] Time of this bargaine & Sale & untill y[e] Ensealing & Executing of these psents to be y[e] True Sole & lawfull owner of all y[e] within mentioned lands & premises & Am Lawfully Siezed thereof in my own propper right as a Sure & Absolute Estate of Inheritance in ffee Simple having in my Selfe good right full power & Lawfull Authority to grant Sell & Assure y[e] Same As Afores[d] & I do for me my heirs Execut[rs] & Adm[rs] Covena[t] grant and agree to & with y[e] s[d] John Woodman his heirs Execut[rs] Adm[rs] and Assignes from Time to Time & at all Times for ever hereafter to warra[t] maintaine & Defend y[e] Title of y[e] above granted & bargained pmises with y[e] Appurtenances Against y[e] Lawfull Claims & demands of all & Every pson & psons whatsoever

In Witness whereof I y[e] s[d] Samuel Spinney have hereunto Set my hand & Affixed my Seal this first day of March Annoq, Domini Seventeen hundred & thirteen or fourteen Anno Regni Anna Regina Duodecimo

Signed Sealed & Delivered   Samuel Spinney (a Seale)
   In psence of
   Jos. Hamond
   John Morrell
   Joseph Hamond Jun[r]

Province of New Hampsh[r] 3rd of April 1714

The above named Sam[ll] Spinney psonally Appearing before me y[e] Subscrib[r] one of her Maj[tys] Justices of y[e] peace

Book VIII, Fol. 30.

in y{e} s{d} Province & Acknowledged this Instrum{t} in writing to be his Act & Deed　　　　　　　　　　Cha./ Story
　Recorded According to y{e} Original April y{e} 14{th} 1714
　　　　　　　　　　p Jos Hamond Reg{r}

[30] To All Christian people to whom these presents Shall Come or deed of Sale doth Concern Daniel Black weaver & Sarah his wife of york in y{e} County of york of y{e} province of y{e} Massachusetts Bay in New England Sendeth Greeting Know yee that y{e} s{d} Daniel & Sarah for & in Consideration of a Certain Sum of money to them in hand well & Truely paid by Peter Nowell of s{d} York yeoman have Given granted Bargained Aliened Enfeoffed & Confirmed and do by these p{r}sents give grant bargaine Sell Aliene Enfeoffe Convey and Confirm & fully freely & Absolutely make Over unto y{e} s{d} Peter Nowell his heirs & Assignes for ever a Certaine piece or parcel of Salt marsh & Thatch banks Containing by Estimation Two Acres be it More or Less lying & being within y{e} Township or precinct of s{d} York to Say y{e} one halfe of that piece of Salt marsh & Thatch banks that lyeth on y{e} northeast Side of y{e} Creek that runs through y{e} Cove of Marsh belonging to y{e} Ministry known by y{e} Name of Hulls Creek formerly but now by y{e} Name of M{r} Moodeys Cove which piece or parcell of Marsh & Thatch bankes was formerly in y{e} possession of Phillip Addams & William More Late of s{d} York dec{d} & Since disposed of to their Execut{rs} or Childer : y{e} s{d} Sarah now wife of s{d} Daniel Black being a daught{r} of y{e} s{d} Phillip Addams dec{d} y{e} s{d} Marsh & Thatch ground being Still undivided y{e} piece or parcell being alwayes Accounted four Acres y{e} one halfe of s{d} Marsh & Thatch ground or bancks for Quantity & Quality as it now lyeth & remaineth in Copartnership with Thomas Addams is that y{e} s{d} Daniel & Sarah have now Sold to Aboves{d} Peter Nowell as is Above Specified Together with all y{e} Priviledges Advantages Thereunto belonging both of wayes river & landing place or places or any wayes at any Time redownding to y{e} Same or any part Thereof unto him y{e} s{d} Peter Nowell his heirs Execut{rs} Adm{rs} & Assignes for ever to Have & to Hold and Quietly & peaceably possess Occupy & Enjoy y{e} s{d} Marsh & Thatch ground or banckes that is to Say y{e} one halfe of y{e} whole four Acres As it is by Estimation undivided with all its priviledges as a Sure Estate in ffee Simple forever And further y{e} s{d} Daniel Black doth for himselfe his heirs Execut{rs} Adm{rs} & Assignes to &

with yͤ sᵈ Peter Nowell his heirs Executrs Admrs & Assigns Covenant Engage and promiss yͤ above mentioned halfe part of yͤ Marsh & Thatch ground or bancks above bargained for & Sold to be free & Clear from all former gifts grants bargains Sales Conveyences deeds Mortgages rents rates dowrys or any other Incumberments whatsoEver as Also from all future Claime Challenges Suits or demands or Interuptions whatsoever to be had or Comenced by Them yͤ sᵈ Daniel or Sarah their heirs Executrs Admrs or Assignes or Any other pson or psons whatsoever upon Title of law but that yͤ sᵈ Daniel & Sarah do Ingage both for them Selves their heirs & Assignes to Warrantize & Defend yͤ sᵈ Marsh wᵗʰ all its Priviledges as fully as is above Specifyed unto & for yͤ sᵈ Peter Nowell his heirs Executrs & Admrs & Assignes declareing themselves to be yͤ whole Sole & propper owners of yͤ Abovesᵈ premises untill the Ensealing of this Instrument In Witness hereof yͤ sᵈ Daniel Black & Sarah his wife have hereunto Set their hands & Seals this Twenty fourth day of August in yͤ year of our Lord one Thousand Seven hundred & Nine and in yͤ Ninth year of yͤ Reign of our Soveraign Lady Anne Queen of Great Brittain &cᵗ

Signed Sealed & Delivered   Daniel Black (ᵃ Seal)
  In psence of us Witnesses   Sarah Black (ᵃ Seal)
  Johnson Harmon
  Abram Preble Junr

York Janʳʸ 28ᵗʰ 1711/2. Then Johnson Harmon & Abram Preble Junr psonally Appeared & made Oath That they Saw yͤ Signer Daniel Black Sign Seal & Deliver yₑ Above written Instrumᵗ to Mʳ Peter Nowell as his Act & Deed./. Before me   Abram Preble Justice peace

May 22ᵈ 1713/ Sarah Black above named psonally Appeared and Acknowleged yͤ Above written deed of Sale to be her Act & deed./.
  Before me   Abram Preble Justice peace
Recorded According to yͤ Original April 6ᵗʰ 1714.
         p J. Hamond Regʳ

To All Christian People to whom these presents Shall Come Greeting Now Know yee that I Lieut Joseph Banckes & Elizabeth my wife of york in yͤ Province of yͤ Mathuses in New England for diverse good & Lawfull Considerations us hereunto moveing & in Special for & in Consideration of yͤ Sum of Sixty pounds of money in hand paid or Security given whereby wee Acknowledge our Selves Contented &

Satisfied have given granted bargained & Sold unto Lieut Peter Weare of Hampton in ye province of New Hampshiere & Decon Richard Milbery & Mr Peter Nowell of york in ye province [31] of ye Mathuses and do by these psents give grant bargaine Sell Alienate Enfeofe & Confirm unto ye sd Weare Milbery & Nowell Them their heirs Execut rs Admrs & Assignes forever ye one halfe of all our Lands & Marsh or Meadow ground lying & being on Northerly or Northeast Side of Saco river & in particular one halfe of all that which belongeth to ye right of Richard Cumins & his wife lying & being in ye Township of Saco it being part of ye Pattent granted to Mr Thomas Lewis & Mr Richard Bonighton by ye right Honble ye Precident & Councill for New England all that land given or Sold by ye sd Mr Bonighton to his daughter Elizabeth ye wife of Richard Cumins & her heirs as it was afterwards divided to her Second husband John Harmon & Phillip Foxell for their part of ye Pattent bounded from Thomas Rogers his garden by ye Sea runing Two miles & fifty rod Northwest & So Northeast to ye line of ye Pattent next blue point which is ye first division & also one halfe of ye land in ye Second division Two miles Square as it is Exprest in ye Division ye one halfe of these Two Divisions laid out to ye sd Harmon & Foxell belongeth to me Joseph Banckes & Elizabeth my wife as ye Sole heir thereof & have good right to dispose of Any part thereof and do for ye Consideration before Exprest give grant Sell make Over Alienate & Convey & Confirm unto ye sd Peter Weare Richard Milbery & Peter Nowell one halfe of our part of sd Pattent as above bounded to sd Harmon & Foxell to Have & to Hold to them their heirs Execut rs Admrs & Assignes forever with all rights royaltys Priviledges and Appurtenances as it was granted to our Hond Grandfather Mr Richard Bonighton & Mr Thomas Lewis as a good & Sure Title of Inheritance in fee Simple forever./ And further I ye sd Joseph Banckes & Eliza my wife do for our Selves our heirs Execut rs Admrs & Assignes Warrantize ye sd bargained Premises to be free from all former gifts grants Sales Mortgages Judgmts Executions Dowryes or Title of Dowryes or any lawfull Incumbrence whatsoever from by or undr us or any other pson whatsoever laying lawfull Claime Thereunto but will maintaine & Defend ye Same So that ye sd Weare Milbery & Nowell their heir heirs & Successors Shall from Time to Time & at all Times use Ocupy possess & Enjoy ye Same to their own benefit & behoofe forever wee also agree that ye first Division by ye Sea be Equally divided in Quantity & Quallity & ye Second division in like mañer ye sd Banckes haveing ye first Choyce

BOOK VIII, FOL. 32.

as also if there be found any Convenient place for a Mill or Mills Then Every one of ye Afore Mentioned men Viz^t Banckes Weare Milbery & Nowell to have an Equall benefit Each of them a Quarter./. In Witness & Confirmation of All above written wee have hereunto Set our hands & fixed our Seals The 22^d day of February and in y^e 12th year of y^e Reign of our Soveraign Lady Queen Anne over Great Brittaine De^r of y^e faith 1713/14   Joseph Banks ($_{seal}^a$)
Signed Sealed & Delivered   Elizabeth Banks ($_{seal}^a$)
  In y^e psence of us
  Dependence Littlefield
  John Parsons
  York March y^e 30th 1714./ Lieu^t Joseph Banks & Eliz^a his wife psonally Appeared before me & Acknowledged this Instrum^t to be their Volluntary Act & Deed Before me./
                      Abra^m Preble Justice peace
Recorded According to ye Original April ye 6th 1714./
                      p Jos. Hamond Reg^r

    To All Christian People to whom this psent Deed of Sale may Come or Concern William Shaw & Annis his wife of york in ye County of York in ye Province of ye Massachusets Bay in New England Sendeth Greeting Know Yee that ye s^d William & Annis for & in Consideration of a Certain Sum of money or other Comiditys well & Truely paid in hand to Them by Peter Nowell of s^d york have given granted bargained Sold Aliened Enfeoffed & Conveyed & do by these psents give grant bargaine Sell Aliene Enfeoffe & Convey and fully freely & Absolutely make over unto ye s^d Peter Nowell his heirs Execut^{rs} Adm^{rs} & Asssignes a Certaine piece or parcell of upland & Swampy land Containing Twenty Acres more or Less within ye Town ship of s^d york lying & being Scittuated upon both Sides of ye highway where Phillip Frost did live the which land was Sold by Arthur Bragdon dec^d unto Phillip ffrost dec^d lying between ye land of Arthur Bragdon Junr and ye land of Constant Rainking and is bounded as followeth Ten poles in bredth along by s^d york river Side between the lots above mentioned and So runs back upon ye Same [32] Point ye other lotts do till they Come back to Bass Cove river or brook Together with all ye rights bennefits priviledges & Appurtenances thereunto belonging or to any part or parcell thereof both of upland Swampy land Trees Timber Trees wood und^r wood Standing lying or remaining on s^d land as also all

Book VIII, Fol. 32.

fruit trees Spring or Springs of water or whatever Else doth now belong to ye s^d lands or ever hereafter doth redound to ye Same unto ye s^d Peter Nowell his heirs Execut^{rs} Adm^{rs} & Assignes to Have & to Hold & Quietly & peaceably to possess Occupie and Enjoy as a sure Estate in fee Simple for ever Moreover ye s^d William & Annis do for themselvs their heirs Execut^{rs} & Adm^{rs} Covena^t Engage & promiss to & with ye s^d Peter Nowell ye aboves^d land with all its priviledges to be free & Clear from all former gifts grants Bargains Sales Mortgages rents rates dowrys or Incumberments whatsoever as also from all future Claims Challenges writs or Interuptions whatsoever & that they ye s^d William & Annis do for themselves their heirs Execut^{rs} for ever after ye date of this deed Ingage & promiss to warrantize ye aboves^d land with all its priviledges upon any Claime of Title of Law to be had or Comenced by them their heirs Execut^{rs} Adm^{rs} or Assignes or any other pson or psons whatsoever./ In Witness hereof ye s^d William Shaw and Annis his wife have hereunto put their hands & Seals this first day of march one Thousand Seven hundred & Nine Ten./. 1709/10

Signed Sealed & Delivered   William Shaw (a Seal)
In ye psence of us Witnesses   her
Henry Lyon   Annis a Shaw (a Seal)
Abra^m Preble Junr mark

William Shaw Annis his wife psonally Appeared & Acknowledged ye Above written deed of Sale to be their Act & deed this 22^d day of May 1713./

     Before me Abra^m Preble Justice peace.
Recorded According to ye Original April 6th 1714
     p Jos : Hamond Reg^r

Know All men to whome this deed of Sale may Come that I Mary Weare of York in ye province of Maine for & in Consideration of four pounds Annually to be paid me by ye psons hereafter Mentioned dureing my Natural life and for diverse good & Lawfull Considerations me thereunto moveing have given granted bargained Sold made over Aliened Enfeoffed ratified and Confirmed & do by these psents fully freely Absolutely & for Ever give grant bargaine Sell make over Aliene Enfeoffe Confirm & ratify from me my heirs Execut^{rs} Adm^{rs} Assignes & from all maner of psons for from by or und^r me to Peter Nowell & Hopewell Weare of york aboves^d their heirs Execut^{rs} Adm^{rs} & Assignes a Certain parcell of Salt Marsh Containing 8 Acres more of Less lying & being in yᵉ Township of york Aboveˢᵈ on yᵉ Northwest branch of york river Adjoining to the Marish of Samuel Bragdon To have & To hold Improve Occupy possess & Enjoy to yᵉ sᵈ Nowell & Weare & their heirs &cᵗ forever without any Lett hinderence disturbence or Mollestation from me or any pson for from by or undʳ me yᵉ sᵈ Mary Weare, I thesᵈ Mary Weare do further Acknowledge my Selfe fully Satisfyed with yᵉ Security I have recieved for yᵉ four pounds Above Mentioned to be Annually paid as if it were in hand Already paid./ In Witness to all & Singular yᵉ pmises Above written I yᵉ sᵈ Mary Weare have Set to my hand & Seale this Twenty Sixth of Novembʳ one Thousand Seven hundred & Eight

Signed Sealed & Delivered   Mary   *MW*   Weare (seal)

In yᵉ psence of us —   her mark

Witness   Joseph Heath

          Caleb Preble

Nov Twenty Sixth one Thousand Seven hundred & Eight Mʳˢ Mary Weare psonally Appeared before me yᵉ Subscriber & Acknowledged yᵉ above written Instrumᵗ to be her Act & Deed   Abraˣ Preble Justice peace

Recorded According to yᵉ Original April 6ᵗʰ 1714./

                   p Jos. Hamond Regʳ

[33] To All People to whom these presents shall Come Greeting Know yee that I Arthur Bragdon Senʳ of york in yᵉ County of york within yᵉ Province of yᵉ Massachusets Bay in New England for & in Consideration of yᵉ Sum of Eight pounds Currant money of yᵉ Province afores to me in hand before yᵉ Ensealing hereof well & Truely paid by Peter Nowell of yᵉ Town & County aforesᵈ the reciept whereof I do hereby Acknowledge & my Selfe therewᵗʰ fully Satisfyed & Contented and thereof do Exonerate Acquit & discharge yᵉ sᵈ Peter Nowell his heirs Executʳˢ Admʳˢ forever by these presents have given granted bargained Sold Aliened Conveyed and Confirmed unto him yᵉ sᵈ yᵉ sᵈ Peter Nowell his heirs and Assigns forever one Tract of land Scittuate lying & being in york in yᵉ County Aforesᵈ Containing by Estimation Thirty Seven acres be it more or Less bounded at a white oake marked on four Sides Standing below yᵉ Beaver dam At yᵉ Marsh known by yᵉ Name of yᵉ Bell Marsh and runeth from sᵈ tree North Northwest point one hundred Seventy Two pole to a white Oake marked & then North yᵉ East forty Six pole to a white Oake Marked & then South

Book VIII, Fol. 33.

Southeast Ninty Two pole to a white Oake Marked Standing by ye Side of ye bell Marsh and is bounded by s^d Marsh & brook to Have & to Hold this s^d granted & bargained pmises with all ye Appurtenances & priviledges to ye Same belonging or in any wayes Appurtaining to him ye s^d Nowell his heirs & Assignes forever to his & their only propper use bennefit & behalfe forever & I ye s^d Arthur Bragdon for me my heirs Execut^{rs} Adm^{rs} do Covenant promiss & grant to & with ye s^d Peter Nowell his heirs & Assignes that before ye Ensealing hereof I am ye True Sole & Lawfull owner of ye Above granted pmises and am Lawfully Siezed & possessed of ye Same in my own propper right as a good pfect Absolute Estate in fee Simple & have in my Selfe good right full power & Authority to grant and Confirm s^d pmises in Maner as aboves^d & ye s^d Nowell his heirs & Assignes Shall & may from time to time and at all Times forever hereafter by force & vertue of These psents Lawfully peaceably have hold use possess & Enjoy ye s^d bargained premises with ye Appurtenances free & Clear & freely & Clearly Acquitted & discharged of from all maner of former gifts grants Bargains Sales and Incumbrances whatsoever Furthermore I the s^d Arthur Bragdon for my Selfe my heirs Execut^{rs} Adm^{rs}s do Covenant and Engage ye above pmises to him ye s^d Peter Nowell his heirs & Assignes against ye Lawfull Claims or Demands of Any pson or psons whatsoever forever hereafter to warrant Secure & Defend forever In Witness whereof I have hereunto Set my hand & Seal this Twelfth day of Decemb^r in y^e Ninth year of our Soveraign Lady Anne by y^e Grace of God Queen of Great Brittain ffrance & Irel^d and in y^e year of our lord one Thousand Seven hundred & Ten./
Signed Sealed & Delivered   Arthur Bragdon (${}_{\text{Seal}}^{\text{a}}$)
  In y^e psence of
  John Dill
  Josiah Bridges
  Lewis Bane
    York Aprill y^e 5th 1711—

Arthur Bragdon Above Named psonnally Appeared & Acknowledged y^e above written Instrum^t to be his Act & Deed. Before me   Abrã Preble Justice peace
Recorded According to y^e Original April 6th 1714
                       p Jos: Hamond Reg^r

Know All men by these presents that I Humphrey Spencer of Kittery in ye Parrish of Berwick in ye County of york in

Book VIII, Fol. 34.

ye Province of ye Massachusets Bay in New England yeoman for & in Consideration of ye Sum of Thirty Shillings Curra^t money of ye Province afores^d to me in hand well & Truely paid by Daniel Goodwin Senr of ye Same Town County & Province afores^d yeoman The receipt whereof I ye s^d Humphrey Spencer do hereby Acknowledge & my Selfe therewith fully Satisfyed Contented & paid have bargained Sold Aliened Assigned Enfeoffed Set over & Confirmed and do by these psents Bargaine Sell Aliene Assigne Enfeoffe Set over and Confirm unto ye s^d Daniel Goodwin Senr his heirs & Assignes for ever a Certaine piece or pcell of land Scittuate lying and being in ye Parrish of Berwick afores^d At a place known by ye Name of ye out let Containing about one Acre bounded to s^d Daniel Goodwins land that he had of his father Spencer on the highway & on land of s^d Spencer on other Sides [34] To have & To hold ye s^d one Acre of land unto him ye s^d Daniel Goodwin Senr his heirs & Assignes for ever free & clear & is freely & Clearly Acquitted of & from all former & other gifts grants Bargains Sales Mortgages Judgments Executions Extents & from all other Incumbrance or Incumbrances whatsoever & I ye s^d Humphrey Spencer at ye Time of ye Ensealing & Delivery hereof am ye Lawfull owner of ye granted & bargained pmises and have good right full power & Lawfull Authority to grant bargaine Sell & Convey ye Same as afores^d & that it Shall & may be lawfull to & for ye s^d Daniel Goodwin Senr his heirs & Assignes to have hold use Occupy possess & Enjoy ye Same & Every part thereof with all ye rights profits priviledges & Appurtenances & Accomodations thereto in any wayes belonging without any let hinderence Mollestation or Interruption from me the s^d Humphrey Spencer my heirs Execut^rs or Adm^rs from henceforth & for Ever and from all other psons Shall & will Warrant ye Same unto ye s^d Daniel Goodwin Senr his heirs & Assignes for ever more In Witness whereof I ye s^d Humphrey Spencer have hereunto Set my hand & Seal this 22^d day of Jan^ry Anno Domini 1711/12

Signed Sealed & Delivered
  In ye psence of   Humphrey his H. mark Spencer (a Seal)
  us Jeremiah Wise
      John Croade
      York ss/

Humphrey Spencer Acknowledged ye above written Instrum^t to be his Act & Deed at Kittery ye 22th Jan^ry 1711/12 and Mary his wife relinquished her right of Dowry therein Before me   John Hill J peace

Recorded According to ye Original June 25th 1714./.

                p. Jos: Hamond Reg^r

To All People to whom this psent Deed of Sale Shall Come Greeting Know yee that Thomas Goodwin of ye parrish of Berwick in Kittery in ye County of york & within her Maj^{tys} Province of ye Massachusets Bay in New England Husbandman for & in Consideration of ye Sum̃ of forty Shillings in Curra^t passable money to him in hand well & Truely paid at and before ye Ensealing & Delivery of These p^{r}sents by Daniel Goodwin of ye Parrish County & province afores^d husbandman ye rec^t w^r of ye s^d Thomas Goodwin doth hereby Acknowledge to his full Content & Satisfaction and doth hereby Acquitt and forever discharge ye s^d Daniel Goodwin his heirs Execut^{rs} Adm^{rs} & Assignes of Every part & parcell thereof by these psents hath fully freely clearly & Absolutely Sold And Confirmed unto ye s^d Daniel Goodwin and to his heirs & Assignes forever Sundry pieces & parcells of upland & Meadow Viz^t a Certain piece of Meadow & upland Scittuate Lying & being in s^d Berwick at a place Comonly Called & known by ye Name of Slutts Corner Containing Two Acres more or Less bounded Eastwardly on Meadow of Richard Lord Southerly on ye road Leading to Wells Westerly on land of ye s^d Daniel Goodwin & Northeasterly on ye land of s^d Thomas Goodwin./ Also Three Quarters of an acre of Meadow be ye Same more or Less runing Two rod in bredth Northward from a pitch pine Tree Joyning to that formerly purchased of Daniel Goodwin Senr dec^d and bounded Northerly on Meadow of s^d Thomas Goodwin Southwardly on Meadow of Moses Spencer & westerly on s^d Thomas Goodwin & halfe an Acre of Meadow ground bounded on Meadow of Richd Lord afores^d ye s^d pieces or parcells of upland & Meadow So bounded or reputed to be bounded Together with all & Singular ye wayes profits priviledges rights Comoditys heridittam^{ts} & Appurtenances and whatsoever thereunto belonging or in any kind way or Manner Appurtaining to Have & to Hold all ye above pieces & parcells of upland & Meadow with all other ye above granted & bargained pmises with their Appurten^{ces} unto him y^{e}s^d Daniel Goodwin his heirs Execut^{rs} Adm^{rs} & Assigns to his & their own only propper use benefit & behoofe for ever And ye s^d Daniel Goodwin his heirs & Assignes Shall & may Lawfully peaceably & Quietly have hold used Occupy & uninteruptedly possess & Enjoy all ye above granted & bargained pmises with their Appurtenances without ye Let hinderence or denial of y^{e}s^d Thomas Goodwin his heirs Execut^{rs} or Adm^{rs} ye pmises being freely Clearly & Absolutely Acquitted Exonerated and discharged of & from all former & other gifts grants bargains Sales Leases Mortgages Titles Thirds dowrys claims & demands whatsoever & Further y[e]s[d] Thomas Goodwin his heirs Execut[rs] & Adm[rs] Shall & will from hence forth & forever hereafter warrant & Defend all y[e] above granted & bargained pmises with their Appurtenances unto him y[e] s[d] Daniel Goodwin & unto his heirs Execut[rs] Adm[rs] & Assignes against y[e] Lawfull Claims & Demands of all & Every pson or psons whatsoever Laying any Claime or Title Thereunto from by or under him his heirs and Assignes

[35] In witness whereof y[e] above named Thomas Goodwin & Mehittable Goodwin his wife in Testimony of her relinquishing her thirds of right & Dowry have hereunto Set their hands & Seals y[e] Twentyeth day of may Anno Domini Seventeen hundred & Thirteen In y[e] Twelfth year of her Majestys Reign &c[t]

Note before Subscription that y[e] Three quarters of An Acre of Meadow ruñing Two rod in bredth Northwardly from a pitch pine Tree as aboves[d] was formerly given to y[e]s[d] Daniel Goodwin by his father M[r] Daniel Goodwin dec[d] Entered before Signing & Sealing./. The words from by or und[r] him his heirs or Assignes Enterlined before Subscription/   Thomas Goodwin (Seal)
Signed Sealed & Delivered   Mehittable Goodwin (Seale)
In y[e] psence of us
John Bradstreet
Mary Spencer
William W Wadlin
    his mark
Berwick March 26 : 1714

Mehittable Goodin psonally Appeared & Acknowledged y[e] within Instrument to be her Act & Deed
    Ichabod Plaisted J. peace

M[r] John Bradstreet & W[m] Wadlin within Named psonally Appeared before me y[e] Subscrib[r] one of her Maj[tys] Justices of peace for y[e] County of Yorkshire and made Oath that they Saw Thomas Goodwin & Mehittable his wife Sign Seal & Deliver y[e] within deed As their Volluntary Act this 3[d] of June 1714   John Plaisted

Recorded According to y[e] Original June 7[th] 1714/
    p Jos. Hañond Reg[r]

Know All men by these p[r]sents that I Allexander Grant of Berwick Al[s] Kittery in y[e] County of york in y[e] Province of y[e] Massachusets Bay in New England Labourer for & in Consideration of y[e] Suñ of Three pounds in Curra[t] money of y{e} Province afores{d} to me in hand well & Truely paid by Byal Hambleton of y{e} Same Town County & Province afores{d} Labourer y{e} rec{t} whereof I do hereby Acknowledge and my Selfe therewith fully Satisfied Contented & paid have therfore given granted bargained Sold Aliened Assigned Enfeoffed Set over & Confirmed and do by these psents give grant bargaine Sell Aliene Assigne Enfeoffe Set over & Confirm unto him y{e} s{d} Byal Hambleton his heirs & Assignes forever Eight Acres & Twenty rod of Land being part of a Grant of Fifteen Acres that was granted to his father Peter Grant Bounded as followeth Viz{t} Begining At y{e} west End of Bever dam that is on Loves Brook About a quarter of a mile Above y{e} way that Leads to A Marsh Called Humphreys Marsh & Twenty poles broad East by North & Sixty five poles long North by west & is bounded on y{e} west Side with y{e} bank of s{d} Brook & on all other Sides with Marked Trees as p y{e} return thereof Aug{st} y{e} Twenty Eighth day Seventeen hundr{d} & one At large may Appear to have & to hold y{e} s{d} Eight Acres of land with all y{e} rights profits priviledges & Appurtenances thereunto belonging unto him y{e} s{d} Byal Hambleton his heirs & Assignes forever free & clear & freely & clearly Acquitted Exonerated & Discharged of & from all other & former grants Bargains Sales Mortgages Judgm{ts} Executions & all other Incumbrance or Incumbrances whatsoever & that it Shall & may be Lawfull to & for y{e} s{d} Byal Hambleton his heirs & Assignes to have hold use Occupy possess & Enjoy y{e} Same & Every part thereof from henceforth & forever and I y{e} s{d} Allexander Grant for my Selfe my heirs Execut{rs} & Adm{rs} do hereby Covena{t} to & with y{e} s{d} Byal Hambleton that'at y{e} time of y{e} Ensealing & Delivery hereof I am y{e} True & Lawfull owner of y{e} granted & bargained pmises & have good right full power & Lawfull Authority to grant Bargaine Sell & Convey y{e} Same as afores{d} and I y{e}s{d} Allexander Grant do further Oblige my Selfe my heirs Execut{rs} & Adm{rs} To Warrant Acquitt & Defend y{e} Same against all & all manner of pson or psons whatsoever laying Legall Claime thereunto unto him y{e}s{d} Byal Hambleton his heirs & Assignes forever in y{e} Quiet & peaceable possession thereof./ In Witness whereof I y{e}s{d} Allexander Grant have hereunto Set my hand & Seale y{e} first day of June Annoq Domini 1710/

Signed Sealed & Delivered   Allexander Grant (a Seal)
In y{e} psence of

Timothy Wentworth his / mark

John Croade

Book VIII, Fol. 36.

York ss/ Memorandum that on ye 18th day of June 1710/ ye Above Named Allexander Grant Acknowledged ye Above written Instrument to be his Act and Deed Before me ye Subscriber one of her Maj^tys Justices of ye peace for Said County
          Ichabod Plaisted
 Recorded According to ye Original June 14th 1714./
       p Jos. Hamond Reg^r

[36] Know All men by These psents that I James Emery of Kittery in ye County of york in ye Province of ye Massachusets Bay in New Engl^d planter for & in Consideration of ye Sum of Three pounds Currant money of ye Province afores^d to me in hand well & Truely paid by Byal Hambleton of s^d Kittery in ye County & Province afores^d planter ye rec^t whereof I ye s^d James Emery do hereby Acknowledge and my Selfe therewith fully Satisfied Contented & paid have given granted bargained Sold Aliened Assigned Enfeoffed Set over & Confirmed & do by these psents give grant bargaine Sell Aliene Assigne Enfeoffe Set over & Confirm unto ye s^d Byal Hambleton his heirs and Assignes forever one Third part of Eighteen Acres of land part of a grant of forty Acres granted by s^d Town of Kittery to William Grant ye Twenty fourth day of may Sixteen hundred Ninety Nine & Takes its begining at a pitch pine Tree Standing about Sixteen poles above a pair of falls Called Doutyes falls & on ye west Side of ye river which tree is marked with J. E. W. Thence South west Seventy Six pole to a parcell of Birches marked on four Sides which is about Twelve poles on ye Southwest Side of Neguttaquid river Thence South East Seventy Six poles to ye river at a parcell of Basswood Trees & may be Something more or Less by reason of ye Crookedness of ye river & is bounded by ye afore mentioned Courses & ye river that runs over s^d falls as by ye return thereof Appears to Have & to hold ye s^d one Third part of s^d Eighteen Acres as bounded with one Third part of all ye rights profits priviledges Appurtenances Accomodations brooks Streams Water Courses falls & whatsoever Else thereunto belongs unto him ye s^d Bial Hambleton his heirs & Assignes for ever to ye only propper use & behoofe of him ye s^d Byal Hambleton his heirs & Assignes for ever free & Clear & Clearly Acquitted of & from all other & former gifts grants bargains Sales Titles Troubles Charges & Incumbrances whatsoever & That I y^e s^d James Emery & my heirs to him y^e s^d Bial Hambleton his heirs &

Book VIII, Fol. 36.

Assignes Shall & will warrant & for ever Confirme y^e Same./
In Witness whereof I y^e s^d James Emery have hereunto Set my hand & Seal y^e 21st day of April 1713/

Signed Sealed & Delivered   James Emery ($_{Seal}^{a}$)
 In y^e p^{r}sence of
Samuel Smith
John Hains
  York ss/ June 18th 1714/

James Emery above written Acknowledged y^e above written Instrum^t to be his Volluntary Act & Deed before me y^e Subscriber one of her Maj^{tys} Justices of y^e peace for s^d County./.   Ichabod Plaisted

Recorded According to ye Original June 14th 1714
          p Jos Hamond Reg^r

To All People to whom these psents shall Come Greeting Know yee that I William Bracey of York in ye County of york within ye Late province of Maine Weaver for & in Consideration of ye Sum of Twenty pounds Currant passable money of New England to me In hand before ye Ensealing hereof well & Truely paid by Daniel Junkins of The Town County & province afores^d yeoman ye rec^t whereof I do hereby Acknowledge & my Selfe therewith fully Satisfyed Contented & thereof & of Every part & parcell thereof do Exonerate Acquit & discharge ye s^d Daniel Junkins his heirs Execut^{rs} Adm^{rs} for ever by these psents do freely fully and Absolutely Give grant Bargaine Sell Aliene Convey & Confirm unto him ye s^d Daniel Junkins his heirs & Assignes a Certain Tract of land Containing Twenty Acres be ye Same more or Less Scittuate lying & being on ye Southwest Side of york river by Lieu^t James Plaisteds Marsh & begining at a black birch Tree marked on four Sides which is ye Northward Corner bounds mark of a lot of land of Micum Mackintiers & runeth from thence Northwest Twenty pole to a beach Tree marked four Sides & from Thence South west an hundred & Sixty pole to a hemlock Tree marked on Three Sides with a letter B on ye Northeast Side and from Thence by a lot of land formerly Given to John Pierce & Southeast Twenty pole to ye land of Micum Mackintier afores^d and is bounded by his land to ye black birch Tree first mentioned and also ye one halfe of a Lot of land formerly Given to John Pierce as Appeareth in york Town book being in All forty Acres and is bounded as followeth. Ten acres of s^d land lyeth on ye Northwest Side of s^d William

York ss/ Memorandum that on ye 18th day of June 1710/ ye Above Named Allexander Grant Acknowledged ye Above written Instrument to be his Act and Deed Before me ye Subscriber one of her Maj^tys Justices of ye peace for Said County   Ichabod Plaisted

Recorded According to ye Original June 14th 1714./

p Jos. Hamond Reg^r

[36] Know All men by These psents that I James Emery of Kittery in ye County of york in ye Province of ye Massachusets Bay in New Engl^d planter for & in Consideration of ye Sum of Three pounds Currant money of ye Province afores^d to me in hand well & Truely paid by Byal Hambleton of s^d Kittery in ye County & Province afores^d planter ye rec^t whereof I ye s^d James Emery do hereby Acknowledge and my Selfe therewith fully Satisfied Contented & paid have given granted bargained Sold Aliened Assigned Enfeoffed Set over & Confirmed & do by these psents give grant bargaine Sell Aliene Assigne Enfeoffe Set over & Confirm unto ye s^d Byal Hambleton his heirs and Assignes forever one Third part of Eighteen Acres of land part of a grant of forty Acres granted by s^d Town of Kittery to William Grant ye Twenty fourth day of may Sixteen hundred Ninety Nine & Takes its begining at a pitch pine Tree Standing about Sixteen poles above a pair of falls Called Doutyes falls & on ye west Side of ye river which tree is marked with J. E. W. Thence South west Seventy Six pole to a parcell of Birches marked on four Sides which is about Twelve poles on ye Southwest Side of Neguttaquid river Thence South East Seventy Six poles to ye river at a parcell of Basswood Trees & may be Something more or Less by reason of ye Crookedness of ye river & is bounded by ye afore mentioned Courses & ye river that runs over s^d falls as by ye return thereof Appears to Have & to hold ye s^d one Third part of s^d Eighteen Acres as bounded with one Third part of all ye rights profits priviledges Appurtenances Accomodations brooks Streams Water Courses falls & whatsoever Else thereunto belongs unto him ye s^d Bial Hambleton his heirs & Assignes for ever to ye only propper use & behoofe of him ye s^d Byal Hambleton his heirs & Assignes for ever free & Clear & Clearly Acquitted of & from all other & former gifts grants bargains Sales Titles Troubles Charges & Incumbrances whatsoever & That I ye s^d James Emery & my heirs to him ye s^d Bial Hambleton his heirs &

Book VIII, Fol. 36.

Assignes Shall & will warrant & for ever Confirme yᵉ Same./
In Witness whereof I yᵉ sᵈ James Emery have hereunto Set
my hand & Seal yᵉ 21ˢᵗ day of April 1713/

Signed Sealed & Delivered   James Emery (ₛₑₐₗᵃ)
  In yᵉ pʳsence of
Samuel Smith
John Hains
    York ss/ June 18ᵗʰ 1714/

James Emery above written Acknowledged yᵉ above
written Instrumᵗ to be his Volluntary Act & Deed before
me yᵉ Subscriber one of her Majᵗʸˢ Justices of yᵉ peace for
sᵈ County./.   Ichabod Plaisted
  Recorded According to yᵉ Original June 14ᵗʰ 1714
                            p Jos Hamond Regʳ

To All People to whom these psents shall Come Greeting
Know yee that I William Bracey of York in yᵉ County of
york within yᵉ Late province of Maine Weaver for & in Con-
sideration of yᵉ Sum of Twenty pounds Currant passable
money of New England to me In hand before yᵉ Ensealing
hereof well & Truely paid by Daniel Junkins of The Town
County & province aforesᵈ yeoman ye recᵗ whereof I do
hereby Acknowledge & my Selfe therewith fully Satisfyed
Contented & thereof & of Every part & parcell thereof do
Exonerate Acquit & discharge yᵉ sᵈ Daniel Junkins his heirs
Executʳˢ Admʳˢ for ever by these psents do freely fully and
Absolutely Give grant Bargaine Sell Aliene Convey & Confirm unto him yᵉ sᵈ Daniel Junkins his heirs & Assignes a
Certain Tract of land Containing Twenty Acres be yᵉ Same
more or Less Scittuate lying & being on yᵉ Southwest Side
of york river by Lieuᵗ James Plaisteds Marsh & begining
at a black birch Tree marked on four Sides which is yᵉ
Northward Corner bounds mark of a lot of land of Micum
Mackintiers & runeth from thence Northwest Twenty pole
to a beach Tree marked four Sides & from Thence South
west an hundred & Sixty pole to a hemlock Tree marked
on Three Sides with a letter B on yᵉ Northeast Side and from
Thence by a lot of land formerly Given to John Pierce &
Southeast Twenty pole to yᵉ land of Micum Mackintier
aforesᵈ and is bounded by his land to yᵉ black birch Tree
first mentioned and also yᵉ one halfe of a Lot of land formerly Given to John Pierce as Appeareth in york Town book
being in All forty Acres and is bounded as followeth. Ten
acres of sᵈ land lyeth on yᵉ Northwest Side of sᵈ William

Braceys land there & runeth from Thence in bredth Ten pole Northwest from s^d Braceys land and back Southwest one hundred & Sixty pole ye Same bredth only what land lyeth within Henry Donnels fence Above his Cove of Marsh he is not to Medde with and ye other Thirty Acres at ye head of ye aboves^d Ten acres and ye head of William Braceys Lot and micum Mackintiers lot begining at a beach Tree marked on four Sides Standing about Three pole Northwest from ye head of ye afores^d Ten Acres & Then in bredth to a beach Tree Marked on four Sides and then back Southwest Eighty pole bounded on ye Southward Corner with a green pine Tree Marked on four Sides and an hemlock Marked four Sides on ye Southward Corner ye aboves^d Ten Acres and Ten of ye Thirty [37] Is hereby bargained & Sold to s^d Daniel Junkins & his heirs & Assigns for ever To have & To hold ye s^d bargained pmises with all ye Appurtenances priviledges & Comoditys to ye Same belonging or in any wise Appurtaining to him ye s^d Daniel Junkins his heirs & Assignes for ever to his & their only propper use benefit & behalfe for ever And I ye s^d William Bracey for me my heirs Execut^{rs} Adm^{rs} do Covenant promiss & Grant to & with ye s^d Daniel Junkins his heirs & Assignes that before ye Ensealing hereof I am ye True Sole & Lawfull owner of ye above bargained pmises and am Lawfully Seized & possessed of ye Same in my own propper right as a good p fect & Absolute Estate of Inheritance in Fee Simple And have in my Selfe good right full power & Lawfull Authority to grant bargaine Sell Aliene Convey & Confirm s^d Bargaind premisses in maner as aboves^d And that ye s^d Daniel Junkins his heirs & Assigns Shall & may from time to time & at all Times for ever hereafter by force & Vertue of These psents Lawfully peaceably & Quietly have hold Occupy use possess & Enjoy ye aboves^d Bargained pmises with ye Appurtenances free & Clear and freely & Clearly Acquited Exonerated & Discharged of from all & all manner of former and other gifts grants Bargains Sales leases Mortgages wills Entails Joyntures dowrys Judgm^{ts} Executions Incumbrances & Extents Furthermore I ye s^d William Bracey for my Selfe my heirs Execut^{rs} Adm^{rs} do Covenant & Engage ye above demized pmises to him ye s^d Daniel Junkins his heirs and Assignes against ye Lawfull Claims and demands of any p^{r}son or p^{r}sons whatsoever hereafter to warrant Secure & Defend and ye wife of me ye s^d William Bracey doth by these psents freely & willingly give yield up & Surrend^r all her right of Dowry & power of Thirds of in & unto ye Above demised pmises./ In Witness whereof wee have hereunto

Set our hands & Affixed our Seals this Twenty Eighth Day of Novemb^r in y^e year of our Lord one Thousand Seven hundred & Ten And in y^e Ninth year of y^e Reign of our Soveraign Lady Anne of Great Brittaine France & Ireland Queen &c^t William Bracey ($_{Seale}^{a}$)
Signed Sealed & Delivered
 In y^e presence of
Daniel Mackintire
Hephzibah Preble

         her mark
        Mary ✗ Bracey

York Jan^{ry} 6 : 1710/11

Wm Bracey above named psonally Appeared & Acknowledged y^e above written deed of Sale to be his act & deed Before me   Abr$\bar{a}$ Preble Justice peace
 Recorded According to y^e Original April 6th 1714./
         p Jos : Ha$\overline{m}$ond Reg^r

 Memorandum Also That y^e Deponant William Hains Aged about fifty years Testifyeth upon Oath that at Sundry Times when Thomas Rice was wont to Signifie Spleene & Mallace Rancor & Enmety against y^e old Mr Withers Comitting & useing unlawfull practices I asked him at Some Times being Together upon Accations in ye woods wherefore there was Such proceedings & Troubles between them & ye s^d Thomas Rice told me it was because his fath^r Law had made him a deed of land that he had given away & Shewing me at another time a deed fairly wrote I Imagined by Sam^{ll} Knight with witnesses & Signed & Sealed by Mr Withers and Mr Rishworth Named & Acted Cunningly I Judged it forged in this maner. Acknowledged or Recorded Named Edwd Rishworth Record^r but I Advised him to have a Care of whom he Shewed Such a deed unto but he Said he had Shewed ye Same before to Cap^{tn} Wincoll Moreover I ye Depona^t Saith Also that I afterward heard Mary Rice found her Selfe agrieved and Complained that her father had not given Nor Ensured them of Somuch Land as to plant a few Trees upon Towards an Orchard haveing an Nursery at home that their Children might be ye better for it hereafter but only Twenty Acres at a Spruce Creek which he had bought by his work & Service when he lived with his father Withers & I Heynes afores^d ye Depona^t well rememb^{rs} that Mr Withers a little before his death Sent me ye Depona^t to York to a Court to know & Enquire of Mr Rishworth ye Record^r whether Thomas Rice had recorded or Shewed him a deed or not & he ye s^d

Recorder Said he Saw none nor knew none & Mʳ Withers ordʳᵈ me to desire him & yᵉ Court to Take Notis that he Never Allowed Neither Ever did or would Ever own but disown any deed to his dying hour to Thomas Rice or to his wife & further Saith not

 Province William Hayns Took Oath to yᵉ Truth of yᵉ of Maine within written Testimony this 7ᵗʰ day of August 1690 Before me   John Wincoll Justˢ peac

Recorded According to yᵉ Original June 28ᵗʰ 1714 which Came open to my hand. p Jos. Hamoud Regʳ

[38] Know All men to whom this pʳsents may Come that I James Smith & Martha his wife of york in yᵉ County of York in yᵉ Province of yᵉ Massachusets Bay in New England for & in Consideration of A valluable Sum to them in hand paid by Daniel Junkins of yᵉ Town & County Abovesᵈ yᵉ recᵗ whereof they do hereby Acknowledge & themselves therewith to be fully Satisfyed Contented & paid & thereof & from Every part & parcell thereof for themselves their heirs Executʳˢ Administratʳˢ & Assignes do Exonerate Acquitt a discharge yᵉ sᵈ Junkins his heirs Executʳˢ Admʳˢ & Assigns for ever have bargained Sold Aliened Conveyed & Confirmed & by these psents do freely fully & Absolutely give grant bargaine Sell Aliene Convey & Confirm unto him yᵉ Said Daniel Junkins his heirs & Assignes for ever a Small Tract of upland Containing Twelve Acres on yᵉ South Side of Bass Cove Marsh formerly granted to Joseph Pray by yᵉ Town of york bounded as followeth begining at a white Oake Marked on four Sides at yᵉ Southermost End of sᵈ Marsh & runneth from sᵈ Oak East by & Adjoyning to Sᵈ Marsh Twenty four poles to a white Oak Marked on four Sides Then South Eighty pole to A Oak Marked on four Sides then west Twenty four poles to a white Oake marked on four Sides Then north to yᵉ white Oak first mentioned this land thus bounded to Have & to Hold this granted & bargained pmises with all the Appurtenances to yᵉ Same belong or in any wayes Appurtaining to him yᵉ sᵈ Daniel Junkins his heirs & Assignes for ever to his & their only propper use benefit & behalfe for ever. And I yᵉ sᵈ James Smith for me my heirs Executʳˢ Admʳˢ do Covenant promiss & grant to & with yᵉ sᵈ Daniel Junkins his heirs & Assignes that before Ensealing hereof I am yᵉ True Sole & Lawfull owner of yᵉ Above bargained pmises and have in my Selfe good right full power & Lawfull Authority

BOOK VIII, FOL. 38.

to Sell Convey & Confirm ye above granted pmises & ye s^d Junkins his heirs & Assignes Shall by force & vertue of These p^rsents Lawfully & peaceably possess & Enjoy ye s^d bargained pmises for ever & I ye s^d Smith for my Selfe my heirs & Assignes do Covenant & Engage ye above granted premises to him ye s^d Daniel Junkins his heirs and Assignes

Against ye Lawfull Claims & demãnds of any pson or psons whatsoever for ever to Warrant Secure & defend In Witness whereof I have hereunto Set my hand & Seal this   day of   one Thousand Seven hundred & Twelve/
Signed Sealed & Delivered   James Smith (_{Seal}^a)
   In psence of
                his
   Mark   M   Round
                mark
   Mary Plaisted
   York June ye 30th 1713/

James Smith above named psonally Appeared & Acknowledged ye Above written deed of Sale to be his Act & deed,
Before me/   Abrã Preble Justice peace
   Recorded According to ye Original April ye 6th 1714
                                p J^s Hamõnd Reg^r

To All People to whom these psents Shall Come Greeting Know Yee that I Daniel Mackintire of york in ye County of york in ye Province of ye Massachusets Bay in New England Cordwainer for & in Consideration of ye Sum of Ten pounds of Good & Lawfull money or Land Equivolent thereto to me in hand paid before ye Ensealing hereof well & Truly paid by John Mackintire of ye Same County afores^d ye rec^t whereof I do hereby Acknowledge & my Selfe therewith fully Satisfied & Contented & paid And thereof & Every part & parcell thereof do Acquitt & discharge ye s^d John Mackintire his heirs Execut^{rs} Adm^{rs} forever by these p^rsents have given granted Bargained Sold Aliened Conveyed & Confirmed and by these psents do freely fully & Absolutely give grant Bargaine Sell Aliene Convey unto him y^es^d John Mackintire his heirs & Assignes forever a Certaine piece of land lying & being on ye Northwest Side of ye land of Micum Mackintire where s^d Mackintire now Liveth on ye west Side of york river & is bounded by s^d land & is Seventeen Acres in Quantity & begins near Mackintires Marsh and is Seventeen pole in bredth & So ruñs by s^d Mackintires land Till

Seventeen Acres be Compleated this land thus bounded is ye Land that was given to Daniel Mackintire by his father as more fully will Appear by his fathers Will to have & to hold ye s^d piece or parcell of Land & priviledges to ye Same belonging or in any wayes Appurtaining to him ye s^d John Mackintire his heirs or Assignes forever to his & their only propper use benefit forever and I this s^d Daniel Mackintire for me my heirs Execut^rs Adm^rs & Assigns do Covenant promiss & grant to with ye s^d John Mackintire his heirs & Assigns that before ye Ensealing hereof I am ye True Sole & Lawfull owner of ye Above bargained pmises & am Lawfully Siezed & possessed of ye Same in mine own propper right as a good pfect & Absolute Estate of Inheritance in Fee Simple and have in my Selfe good right full power & Lawfull Authority to grant bargaine Sell Convey & Confirm s^d bargained pmises in maner as aboves^d Furthermore I ye s^d Daniel Mackentire for my Selfe my heirs Execut^rs Adm^rs & Assignes do Covenant & Engage ye Above demised pmises to him ye s^d John Mackintire his heirs & Assignes against ye Lawfull Claimes or demands of Any pson or psons whatsoever forever hereafter to Warra^t Secure & Defend, In Witness w^rof I have hereunto Set my hand & Seal this 16 day of March. 1713./   Daniel Mackintire (Seal)

Signed Sealed & Delivered
 In ye psence of
 John Kater
 Arthur Bragdon
 York ss/ April 6th 1714.   Daniel Mackintire psoually Appearing Acknowledged this Instrum^t to be his Act & Deed Before me   Abra Preble Just^s peace
 Recorded According to ye Original April 6th 1714/
         p Jos: Hamond Reg^r

[39] Bee it Known unto all men by these psents that wee Daniel Littlefield and Mehittable Littlefield of ye Town of Wells in ye County of york in ye Province of ye Massachusets Bay in New England Several good Causes & Considerations us thereunto Inducing & more Especially for & in Consideration of ye Sum of four pounds & five Shillings to us in hand paid by Daniel Junkins of y^e Town of york in y^e Province of y^e Massachusets bay afores^d by which paym^t we do Acknowledge our Selves to be fully Satisfyed & Contented have bargained & Sold and by these psents do bar-

BOOK VIII, FOL. 39.

gaine & Sell make over Infeoffe and Confirm unto y\e above named Daniel Junkins a Certaine parcell of Marsh Lying Scittuated & being in y\e Town of York Containing y\e Quantity of Two Acres being y\e one halfe of a Certain pcell of Marsh formerly Given to my above named wife Mehittable with Some other of her Sisters by their Grandfather Nicholas Davis of York dec^d y^e s^d Marish is bounded as followeth lying on y^e Southwest branch of York river butting upon y^e upland & So to run down to y^e river & Lying between & bounded by a parcel of Marsh of John Parker Sen^{rs} on ye Southwest Side & a parcell of Marsh of John Braun Sen^{rs} on ye Northeast Side all which Two Acres of Marsh thus bounded be it more or Less wee have given granted Enfeoffed released Assigned & Confirmed & by these psents do fully freely & Absolutely give grant release Aliene Enfeoffe Assigne & Confirm unto ye aboves^d Daniel Junkins his heirs Execut^{rs} & Assignes with all ye priviledges right Comodityes Emolluments & Appurtenances to ye Same belonging or in any kind Appurtaining & Also all ye Estate right Title Interest use possession dower Thirds Claims revercōns remaind^{rs} propperty Claime & demand whatsoever of us ye s^d Daniel & Mehittable Littlefield our heirs & Assignes of in & to ye Same & Every part thereof To have & To hold all ye before mentioned granted Enfeoffed Confirmed pmises with ye Appurtenances unto ye s^d Daniel Junkins his heirs & Successors for ever to his & their own Sole & propper use benefit & behoofe from henceforth & forever freely peaceably & Quietly without any Mañer of reclaime Challenge or Contradiction of us ye s^d Daniel & Mehittable Littlefield our heirs Execut^{rs} or Assignes or of any other pson or psons w^{t}soever by their or any of their means Title or procurem^t in any Mañer or wise or without any Account or reconing or Answer therefore to them or any in their Names to be given rendred or done in Time to Come So that Neither ye s^d Daniel Littlefield His heirs Execut^{rs} Adm^{rs} or Assignes or any other pson or psons whatsoever by them for them or in their Names or in the Names of Any of them any time or times hereafter may Ask Claime Challenge or demand in or to ye pmises or any part thereof Any right Title Interest use possession or dower but from all & Every Action of right Title use Interest Claime possession & Demand thereof they & Every of them to be utterly Excluded & by these p^{r}sents forever debarred In Witness whereunto wee ye Aboves^d Daniel & Mehittable Littlefield have Set our hands & Seals this 7th day of August in ye year of our Ld Anno Domini

Book VIII, Fol. 40.

1701 & in ye 13th year of our Soveraign Lord William ye Third over England King &c^t   Daniel Littlefield (_{Seale}^a)
Signed Sealed & Delivered   Mehittable Littlefield (_{Seale}^a)
 In presence of
 Jonaⁿ Hamond
 Mary Hamond
 Elizabeth Hamond
  County of York/
Daniel Littlefield & Mehittable his wife psonally Appeared before me one of his Maj^{tys} Justices of ye peace of this County & Acknowledged this above written Instrum^t to be their Act & deed this 7th day of Augst 1701
       John Wheelwright
 Recorded According to ye Original April 6th 1714./
      p Jos: Hamond Reg^r

To All Christian People to whom these psents Shall Come Greeting Know yee that I Robert Eliot of New Castle in ye Province of New Hampsh^r in New Engl^d Gentleman for & in Consideration of fifteen pounds money to him in hand paid before the Ensealing hereof by Benjamin Hilton of York in New Engl^d yeoman ye receipt whereof he ye s^d Robert Eliot doth hereby Acknowledge himselfe therewith to be fully Satisfyed & Contented & thereof & of Every part & parcell thereof doth Exonerate Acquitt & Discharge ye said Benjamin Hilton his heirs Execut^{rs} & Adm^{rs} for ever by these psents have given granted Bargained Sold Aliened Conveyed & Confirmed & doth by these psents fully freely & Absolutely give grant Bargaine Sell Aliene Convey and Confirm unto him ye s^d Benjamin Hilton his heirs and Assignes for ever one Messuage or Tract of land Scittuate lying & being within ye Town of york on ye Southwest Side of s^d York rivers in Quantity Twenty Six acres being one [40] Part of that Tract of land laid out by ye Request of Aboves^d Eliot March 16: 1703 in Two lots as Appears in York Town book page 204 & page 205 To Say part of That Lot that lyeth on ye Southeast Side & begins at the river & So runs back into ye woods & Joyns with ye widdow Coles land Southwest a little westward to ye head of ye back lotts and on ye North west Side bounded by Samuel Sewal which is Just one Quarter of ye whole of ye Two lotts Above Mentioned. To have & To hold ye s^d granted & bargained pmises with all ye Appurtenances priviledges & Comoditys to ye Same belonging or in Any wise Appurtaining to ye Same to him ye s^d

Book VIII, Fol. 40.

Benjamin Hilton his heirs Execut^{rs} Adm^{rs} or Assignes forever to his & their own proper use benefit & behalfe forever and ye s^d Robert Eliot doth for him Selfe his heirs Execut^{rs} And Admin^{rs} or Assignes doth Covenant grant & promiss to & with ye s^d Hilton his heirs & Assignes that before ye Ensealing hereof he is ye True Sole & propper owner of ye Above bargained pmises and is Lawfully in possession of ye Same as a Sure Estate of Inheritance & hath in himselfe full power & Lawfull Authority to grant bargaine Sell & Confirm ye above bargained pmises in Maner as afores^d & That y^{e}s^d Hilton his heirs & Assigns Shall & may from time to time and at all Times forever hereafter by force and vertue of these psents Lawfully peaceably & Quietly have hold use Occupy & Enjoy As a Sure Estate in fee Simple forever & Clearly Acquitted & Exonerated & Discharged of & from all form^r gifts grants bargains Sales Mortgages or Incumberments or Interruptions whatsoever as Also from all future Claims or Interuptions upon grounds of Law proceeding ye date of this Instrum^t & ye said Robert Eliot doth Covenant & promiss for himselfe his heirs Execut^{rs} & Admin^{rs} To & with ye s^d Hilton his heirs and Assignes To warrant & Defend ye Above bargained Land & All its priviledges Against all pson or psons whatsoever Laying Lawfull Claime thereunto or any part thereof./ In Witness hereof y^e Aboves^d Robert Eliot hath hereunto Set his hand & Seale this fourth day of Decemb^r in y^e 12th year of her Majestyes Reign Anno Domini 1713 Robt Eliot ($_{Seale}^a$)

Signed Sealed & Delivered
 In psence of
 The mark of Black ✗ Bess
 The mark of Mary ✗ Cosso

Pro New Hamp^r
Robert Eliot Esqr Acknowledged y^e above Instrum^t to be his Act & Deed y^e 26th March 1714./ Before
 Theo: Atkinson J: peace
Recorded According to y^e Original April y^e 6th 1714/
 p Jos. Hamond Reg^r

To All Christian People to whom these psents shall Come Greeting Know Yee That Mr Robert Eliot of New Castle in the Province of New Hampshire in New England Gentleman for & in Consideration of fifteen pounds money to him in hand paid before ye Ensealing hereof by Hannah Cole of

York in y{e} County of York in New England Widdow y{e} rec{t} whereof he y{e} s{d} Eliot doth hereby Acknowledge himselfe therew{th} to be fully Satisfyed & Contented & Thereof & Every part and parcell thereof doth Exonerate Acquitt & Discharge y{e} s{d} Hannah Cole her heirs Execut{rs} & Adm{rs} forever by These psents Have given granted bargained Sold Aliened Conveyed & Confirmed & Doth by These psents fully freely & Absolutely give grant Bargaine Sell Aliene Convey & Confirm unto her y{e} s{d} Hannah Cole her heirs & Assigns forever one Messuage or Tract of Land Scittuate lying & being within y{e} Town of York on y{e} Southwest Side of York river in Quantity Twenty Six Acres being y{e} one Quarter that Tract of land Laid out by y{e} request of Aboves{d} Eliot March y{e} 16 : 1703 in Two Lotts as appears in York Town book page 204 & page 205 to Say that quart{r} that lyeth on y{e} Southeast Side begining at y{e} head of A Little Cove Next to A parcell of land Sold by Johnson Harmon to Nathaniel Whitney and runeth into y{e} woods by s{d} Whitneys bounds Southwest a little westward Ninety Two poles the home lot & Sixty pole Southwest & by west to y{e} head of the back lott and Quarter y{e} bredth of s{d} back lot & y{e} front lot by y{e} river & is bounded by y{e} river on y{e} Northeast & So by y{e} Cove above mentioned & So is to devide by a just Quarter of y{e} whole of y{e} Two Lotts above Sighted begining at y{e} river Side and to run y{e} whole length into y{e} woods To have & To hold y{e} s{d} Granted & bargained pmises with all y{e} Appurtenances priviledges & Comoditys to y{e} Same belonging or in any wayes Appurtenaning to y{e} Same to her y{e} s{d} Hannah Cole her heirs Execut{rs} Adm{rs} or Assigns forever to her & their own propper use benuefit & behoofe for ever & y{e} s{d} Eliot doth for himselfe his heirs Execut{rs} & Adm{rs} doth Covenant grant & promiss to & with y{e} s{d} Cole her heirs & Assignes that before y{e} Ensealing hereof he is y{e} True Sole & propper owner of y{e} Above bargained pmises & is Lawfully in possession of y{e} Same as a firm Estate of Inheritance & hath in himselfe full power & Lawfull Authority to grant bargaine Sell & Confirm y{e} Above bargained in Maner as afores{d} & that y{e} s{d} Cole her heirs & Assignes Shall & may from Time to Time & at all Times for ever [41] Hereafter by force & vertue of these psents Lawfully & peaceably have hold use Occupy & Enjoy as a Sure Estate in Fee Simple forever & Clearly Acquitted & Exonerated & Discharged of & from all maner of former gifts grants bargains Sales Mortgages or Incumbrances or Interuptions whatsoever As Also from all future Claims or Interuptions upon grounds of Law proceeding y{e} date of this Instrum{t}./ And y{e} s{d}

Book VIII, Fol. 41.

Eliot doth Covenant & promiss for himselfe his heirs Executt[rs] & Adm[rs] to & with y[e] s[d] Cole her heirs and Assignes To Warrantize and Defend y[e] Above bargained Land & all y[e] priviledges against all psons & psons whatsoev[r] laying Lawfull Claime thereunto or Any part thereof

In Witness whereof y[e] Aboves[d] Robert Eliot hath hereunto Set to his hand & Seal this Eighteenth day of February in y[e] year of our Lord God one Thousand Seven hundred & Thirteen & in y[e] —— year of her Maj[tys] Reigne Anne by y[e] Grace of God Queen of Great Brittain &c[t]

Signed Sealed and   Rob[t] Eliot — (a Seale)
  Delivered in psence
  John Elenwod
  Abraham Croket
    Pro. N. Hamp[r]./
Robert Eliot Esq[r] Acknowledged y[e] Above Instrum[t] to be his Act & deed y[e] 26 march 1714./
              Before Theo: Atkinson J peace
Recorded According to y[e] Original April 6th 1714/
                  p Jos. Hamond Reg[r]

To all People to whom this present writing shall Come Greeting Know yee that I William Pepperrell of Kittery in y[e] County of York in New England Merchant as well for & in Consideration of y[e] Natural Affection & love which I have & bear unto my welbeloved Son William Pepperrell of s[d] Town & County As Also for diverse other good Causes & Considerations me at this present Especially Moveing have given & Granted & by These psents do give grant & Confirm unto my s[d] Son W[m] Pepperrell his heirs Execut[rs] Adm[rs] or Assigns one Messuage or Tract of Land Scittuate lying & being in y[e] Town of Kittery within y[e] s[d] County which is now known & Called by y[e] Name of y[e] New farm which Sixty Acres of it was granted me by a Town grant & forty five acres more w[ch] Joyns with y[e] Land which was John Dearings now dec[d] which I bought of Joseph Crocket & all y[e] Land which was layd out by a Town grant upon y[e] land which was Called Farmoths & Thirty Acres which I purchased of Coll[el] Edmund Gosse which was Called by y[e] Name of Lockwoods as by draughts Laid out und[r] y[e] Scrveyers hand As Shall more Largely Appear with Also a Tract of land which was purchased of M[rs] Mary Hook deceased which lyes in y[e] Township of York which Appears by a deed of Sale und[r] s[d] Hooks hand which land was formerly

Book VIII. Fol. 41.

purchased of Abraham Parker with also a piece of Land which lyes to ye Norward of Richard Mitchells which Tract of land Containeth Ninety five Acres or Thereabouts be the Same More or Less which was laid out by vertue of a Town grant As more Largely Appears As a draught und^r ye Surveyers hand with all ye Marsh Timber Trees woods houses Orchards water & water & water Courses whatsoever To have & To hold all ye aboves^d granted & bargained pmises with all ye Appurtenauces Priviledges & Comoditys to ye Same belonging or in any wayes Appurtaining to him ye s^d Wm Pepperrell his heirs & Assignes forever. to him & their own propper use & behoofe forever freely & Quietly without Any matter of Challenge Claime or demand of me ye s^d Wm Pepperrell or of Any pson whatsoever for me in my Name means or procurem^t And without Any money or other Thing therefore to be yielded paid or done unto me ye s^d Wm Pepperrell my heirs Execut^{rs} Adm^{rs} or Assignes And I ye s^d Wm Pepperrell all & Singular ye afores^d Land with all ye pmises & Appurtenances Thereunto belonging To Warrant my Afores^d Son William Pepperrell his heirs Execut^{rs} Adm^{rs} or Assignes to ye use Afores^d Against all People to warrant & forever Defend by these psents In Witness whereof I have hereunto Set my hand & Seal ye Six day of June in ye year of our Lord one Thousand Seven hundred and Thirteen
Signed Sealed & Delivered   Wm Pepperrell (Seal)

In ye Presence of
William Phillips
John Veñard
Miriam Pepperrell
Arthur Haiding
Mary Dearing

It is further to be understood before ye Signed & Sealed of This Instrum^t that if I ye Above Named Wm Pepperrell Should die before I make any will That this Deed of Gift Shall not hinder my afores^d Son Wm Pepperrell Junr to have a double Share of ye remaind^r of my Estate or if there Should be any Objection made in ye will which I have Already drawn Ruff in my Chest but it is my desire that that will may Stand as I have Declared it before These Witnesses./   Wm Pepperrell

York ss April 6th 1714/ William Pepperrell Esqr Appearing Acknowledged ye above written Instrum^t with ye postscript Annexed to be his free Act & deed./
Before me   John Wheelwright Jus^t peac
Recorded According to ye Original April 6th 1714./
     p Jos: Hamond Reg^r

Book VIII, Fol. 42.

[42] To All People to whom these psents Shall Come Greeting &c Know yee that I Henry Barter of Kittery in ye County of York in her Maj^{tys} Province of ye Massachusets bay in New England Fisherman for & in Consideration of ye Sum of one hundred pounds Currant Money of New England to me in hand well & Truely paid by William Pepperrell jun^r of Kittery on Piscattaqua river Merchant ye reciept w^{r}of I do hereby Acknowledge & my Selfe therewith fully Sattisfyed & Contented & thereof and of Every part & parcell Thercof do Acquitt & Discharge ye s^d Wm Pepperrell jun^r his heirs Execut^{rs} & Adm^{rs} forever by These psents have given granted bargained Sold Aliened Conveyed & Confirmed And by These psents do fully freely & Absolutely give grant bargaine Sell Aliene Convey & Confirm unto him ye s^d Wm Pepperrell Junr his heirs & Assigns forever one Certain parcel of upland & Marish Scittuate Lying & being in ye Township of Kittery afores^d Containing by Estimation Sixteen Acres be ye Same more or Less whereon s^d Henry Barter Now lives with all ye houses Orchards fences Timb^r Trees & water & water Courses whatsoever & priviledges & Appurten^{ces} to ye Same belonging or in any wise Appurtaining which s^d land lyes on Crocketts Neck & joyns with ye land which was Aaron Ferris^s on ye Eastern Side & on ye western Side ye land which was form^{rly} Richard Crockets and a Certaine parcel of land which is known & Called by ye Name of Crockets Neck Scittuate Lying & being in ye Township of Kittery afores^d Containing by Estimation forty Acres be ye Same more or Less bounded on ye Eastern Side of s^d Barters home Lott & ye Southward Side ye Land of Robing & ye Souse & bee west Side ye land Parret & was formerly in ye Possession of Richard Crocket To have & To hold ye s^d granted & bargained pmises wth all ye Appurtenances priviledges & Comoditys to ye Same belonging or in any wayes Appurtaining to him ye s^d William Pepperrell jun^r his heirs & Assigns forever to his & their own propper use befiefit & behoofe & I ye s^d Henry Barter for me my heirs Execut^{rs} & Adm^{rs} do Covenant promiss & grant to & with ye s^d Wm Pepperrell jun^r his heirs & Assignes that before ye Ensealing hereof I am ye True Sole & Lawfull owner of ye Above bargained pmises & have in my Selfe good right full power & Lawfull Authority to grant bargain Sell Convey & Confirm s^d bargained premises in Maner As Aboves^d and that ye s^d Wm Pepperrell jun^r his heirs & Assignes Shall & May from time to time & At All times forever hereafter by force & Vertue of these psents Lawfully peaceably & Quietly have hold use Occupy possess & jnjoy ye s^d demised & bargained

pmises with yᵉ Appurtenances free & Clear & Clearly Acquitted & Discharged of & from all and all maner of former & other gifts grants Bargains Sales Titles Troubles & Incumbrances whatsoever./ Furthermore I yᵉ sᵈ Henry Barter for my Selfe my heirs Execut^{rs} & Admin^{rs} do Covenant and Engage yᵉ Above Demised pmises to him yᵉ sᵈ William Pepperrell jun^r his heirs & Assignes against yᵉ Lawfull Claims & demands of Any pson or psons whatsoever forever hereafter to Warrant Secure & Defend./ But it is further to be understood that if yᵉ aboves^d Henry Barter or his heirs or Assigns Shall well & Truely pay or Cause to be paid unto yᵉ Aboves^d Wᵐ Pepperrell jun^r his heirs or Assignes yᵉ full & Just Sum of one hundred pounds Currant money As Afores^d and yᵉ Interest According to Law which is Six pounds A year dureing yᵉ sᵈ Term of Six years at or before yᵉ sᵈ Term which will be in yᵉ Year of our Lord Anno: Domini 1719: & sᵈ Interest to be paid yearly dureing sᵈ Term of Six years that then this psent Obligation to be voyd & of Non Effect otherwise to be & Remaine in full force & Vertue In Witness whereof I have hereunto Set my hand & Seale this 28th day may in yᵉ Twelfth year of her Majesties Reigne Anno Domini one Thousand Seven hundred and Thirteen   Henry Barter (Seal)

Signed Sealed & Delivered
  In yᵉ psence of
  Diamond Sargent
  Richard Crocket
  Wᵐ Pepperrell
  28th may 1713

    Then Henry Barter personally Appeared before me yᵉ Subscriber one of her Maj^{tys} Justices for yᵉ County of York and Acknowledged this above written Instrument to be his free Act & deed/   Wᵐ Pepperrell Js peace

    Recorded According to yᵉ Original April 6th 1714/

                             p Jos. Hamond Reg^r

    This Indenture made yᵉ Sixth day of March in yᵉ year of our Lord one Thousand Seven hundred & Thirteen fourteen between Samuel Skillion of Kittery in yᵉ County of York in New England Shipwright on yᵉ one part & William Pepperrell jun^r of Afores^d Town & County Merch^t on yᵉ other part Witnesseth that I yᵉ sᵈ Samuel Skillion for diverse good Causes & Considerations me thereunto moveing have given granted bargained Sold Aliened Conveyed & Confirmed &

BOOK VIII, FOL. 43.

by these psents do freely fully & Absolutely give grant Bargaine Sell Aliene Convey & Confirm unto him ye s^d Wm Pepperrell his heirs Execut^{rs} Adm^{rs} & Assignes forever one Messuage or Tract of land & Swamp Scittuate lying and being in ye Township of Kittery afores^d Containing by Estimation [43] Eighty Acres be it more or Less which was that Tract of land which I ye s^d Skillion purchased of Jonathan Mendum of Kittery afores^d County butted & bounded on ye Southwest by ye river Comouly Called Spruce Creek and on ye Northwest by ye land of Joseph Weeks and on ye Northeast by ye woods & on ye Southeast by Andrew Haleys land or howsoever otherwise bounded or reputed to be bounded Together with all Such rights libertys profits priviledges Comoditys & Appurtenances As in Any kind Appertaine thereunto with Every part & parcell thereof belonging to ye afores^d land To have & To hold ye s^d granted & bargained pmises with all ye Appurtenances priviledges & Comoditys to ye Same belonging or in any wayes Appurtaining To him ye s^d William Pepperrell his heirs & Assignes forever to his & their own propper use benefit and behalfe for ever & I ye s^d Sam^{ll} Skillion for me my heirs Execut^{rs} Adm^{rs} do Covenant promiss & grant to & with ye s^d Wm Pepperrell his heirs and Assignes That before ye Ensealing hereof I am ye True Sole & Lawfull owner of ye Above bargained pmises and am Lawfully Siezed & possessed of ye Same in mine own propper right as a good perfect & Absolute Estate of Inheritance in fee Simple & have in my Selfe good right full power and Lawfull Authority to grant Bargaine Sell Convey & Confirm s^d Bargained pmises in Maner as aboves^d & that ye s^d William Pepperrell his heirs & Assignes Shall & may from time to time & at all times forever hereafter by force & Vertue of these psents Lawfully peaceably & Quietly have hold use Occupy possess & Enjoy ye s^d Demised & bargained p^{r}mises with ye Appurtenances free & Clear and freely & Clearly Acquitted Exonerated & Discharged of & from all & all maner of former & other gifts grants bargains Sales leases Mortgages Wills & Encumbrances whatsoever Furthermore I ye s^d Sam^{ll} Skillion for my Selfe my heirs Execut^{rs} Adm^{rs} do Covenant & promiss at & upon ye reasonable request & at ye propper Costs and Charges in ye Law of ye s^d Wm Pepperrell his heirs Execut^{rs} Adm^{rs} or Assignes to make do pform & Execute Any further or other Lawfull & reasonable Act or Acts thing or things devise or Devices in ye Law Needfull or requisite for

(margin: 1st day of Octob^r: 1728 : Receiv^d in full Sattisfaction of this Mortgage p Wm Pepperrell Junr Witness Abra^m Preble Reg^r)

BOOK VIII, FOL. 43.

ye More perfect Assurence Settleing & Sure makeing of ye pmises as aboves^d

Provided Nevertheless & it is ye True Intent & meaning of Grant^r and Grantee in these psents Any thing herein Contained to ye Contrary Notwithstanding That if ye above named Samuel Skillion his heirs Execut^{rs} Adm^{rs} or Assigns do well & Truely pay unto ye Above named Wm Pepperrell jun^r his heirs Execut^{rs} Adm^{rs} or Assignes ye full & whole Sum of fifty Three pounds Currant Money of New England At on or before this day Twelve months which will be on ye Sixth day of March & in ye year of our Lord one Thousand Seven hundred & fourteen fifteen Then this Above written deed or Obligation and Every Cause & Article Therein Contained Shall be Null Voyd & of Non Effect or Else Shall in full force & Vertue. Sealed with my Seale Dated in Kittery y^e Day & year first above written

Signed Sealed & Delivered . Sam^{ll} Skillion ($_{Seale}^{a}$)

In psence of
Joseph Simpson
James Foy
Dorothy Pepperell

Kittery 5th day April 1714

This day Sam^{ll} Skillion psonally Appeared before me y^e Subscrib^r one of her Maj^{tys} Justices for y^e County of York & Acknowledged This above written Instrum^t to be his free Act & Deed./. Wm Pepperell Js peace

Recorded According to ye Original April 6th 1714./
p Jos : Hamond Reg^r

Know All men by These psents that I Margriet Addams of Kittery in ye County of York and Administratrix to ye Estate of Isaac Gudrig late of Kittery in ye County of York dec^d for a valluable Consideration to me in hand paid by Phillip Carpenter of ye Same place Marrin^r have given granted bargained & Sold and do by these p^{r}sents give grant bargain & Sell & for ever Set over all that Tract or pcell of Land Lying in ye Township of Kittery in ye County of york Containing by Estimation Ten Acres lying between ye Lands of Nicholas Tucker on ye Northwest & Henry Barter on ye Southeast within Spruce Creek & is that tract of land that was Sold by Nicholas Tucker to his brother Richard Tuck as Appears by his Conveyence bareing date ye Second day of January one Thousand Six hundred Ninty Eight nine and Sold to ye Aboves^d Isaac Gudrig by ye within Named Richard

Tucker as Appears by his Conveyance bareing date ye Twenty Seventh day of Octob^r one Thousand Six hundred Ninety & nine Together with all ye priviledges & profits w^{t}soever Thereunto belonging as is in ye above Specifyed deeds Mentioned & at large Set forth reference thereunto being had to have & to hold all ye s^d Tract of land As its bounded & Set forth by ye Aboves^d Conveyences as is Mentioned in this psent writing with ye Dwelling house thereon and all ye Appurtenances thereunto belonging unto ye s^d Phillip Carpenter his heirs Execut^{rs} Adm^{rs} or Assigns for ever more An Furthermore [44] I ye s^d Margriet Addams As Administratrix afores^d do Covenant to and with y^{e}s^d Phillip Carpenter his heirs & Assignes y^e peaceable & Quiet possession thereof to warra^t and for ever defend Against all psons laying a Lawfull Claime Thereunto./ In Witness whereof I have hereunto Set my hand & Seal this fifth day of Novemb^r one Thousand Seven hundred & Six 1706/

Signed Sealed & Delivered　　　Margriet Addams ($_\text{Seal}^\text{a}$)

In y^e psence of y^e Subscrib^{rs}
Mark Addams
Henry Esmon
William Godsoe
the 21st of April 1710./

Then Mrs Margriet Addams psonally Appeared before me the Subscrib^r Wm Pepperrell one of her Maj^{tys} Justices for y^e County of York & Acknowledged this Instrum^t to be her free Act & Deed　　　Wm Pepperrell J^s peace

Recorded According to ye Original April 6th 1714./

　　　　　　　　　　p Jos: Hamond Reg^r

To All Christian People to whom This present writing Shall Come Know yee that I Richard White of Kittery in ye Province of Maine in New England do for diverse good Causes & valluable Considerations me hereunto moveing and for & in Consideration of ye Sum of forty Two pounds money in Hand rec^d of Henry Dering of Boston Shopkeeper do Acknowledge & Confess my Selfe to be fully Satisfied & paid for a parcell of land houseing & Marsh And Accordingly do give grant bargaine & Sell unto ye afores^d Henry Dering his heirs Execut^{rs} Adm^{rs} & Assigns Ninety Acres of upland beginning at ye bridge At ye head of brave boat harb^r & runing from thence Along by York line one hundred & Sixty poles into ye woods and ninety poles in bredth Southwest being bounded on yᵉ Southeast with a Smal piece of Salt Marsh which Ephraim Crocketts father did usually mow leaving out yᵉ places where John Billin & Ja Wiggin built their houses And further Know yee that I yᵉ sᵈ Richard White do by these psents Give grant Aliene Sell Enfeoff and Confirm unto yᵉ abovesᵈ Henry Dering all yᵉ Marsh begining at yᵉ bridge aforesᵈ & runing in yᵉ bredth of fifty acres of yᵉ abovesᵈ upland on yᵉ Southeast of it which marsh is bounded with yᵉsᵈ upland on yᵉ one Side and broad berd harbour Creek on yᵉ other Side As Also a Small Strip of Marsh lying on yᵉ North East Side of yᵉ Neck Above yᵉ bridge aforesᵈ To have & To hold all yᵉ above bargained pmises both upland & Marsh and houseing now Standing upon sᵈ Land and all undʳ wood Trees Timber & fences with all & Singular Appurtenances And Priviledges thereunto belonging or in Any wise Appurtaining to him yᵉ sᵈ Henry Dering his heirs & Assignes for ever Further I thesᵈ Richard White do for my Selfe my heirs Executʳˢ & Admʳˢ Promiss & Engage for ever to Warrant & Defend yᵉ abovesᵈ Title of upland & Marsh &cᵗ unto yᵉ sᵈ Henry Dering his heirs & Assignes forever against yᵉ Lawfull Claims and demands of all & Every pson & psons whatsoever & yᵉ sᵈ Richard White for himselfe his heirs Executʳˢ and Admʳˢ do hereby Covenant promiss grant & agree to & with yᵉ sᵈ Henry Dering his heirs & Assignes that at yᵉ Time of this psent grant & Sale & unto theusealing & Delivery of These pʳsents he yᵉsᵈ Richard White is yᵉ True Sole & Lawfull owner and Stand Lawfully Seized of & in all yᵉ above bargained & granted pmises in his own propper right of a good perfect & Absolute Estate of Inheritance in Fee Simple without any maner of Condition reverc̃on or Limitation whatsoever So as to Alter change defeat or make Voyd yᵉ Same Haveing in my Selfe full power good right & Lawfull Authority to grant Sell Convey & Assure yᵉ Same in manner as aforesᵈ & that yᵉ sᵈ Henry Dering his heirs & Assigns Shall & may by force & vertue of these psents from henceforth & forever hereafter Lawfully peaceably & Quietly have hold use Occupy possess & Enjoy yᵉ above granted pmises with yᵉ Appurtenances thereof free & Clear & Clearly Acquitted and discharged of & from all & all maner of former & other gifts grants bargains Sales leases Mortgages Joyntures Dowers Judgmᵗˢ Excutions Entails forfeitures & of & from all other Titles Troubles Charges & Incumbrances whatsoever./ In Witness whereof yᵉ sᵈ Richard White have hereunto Set his hand and Seal yᵉ Twenty Seventh day of Sepᵗ Anno Domini

one Thousand Six hundred Ninety Two Annoq, RR[s] et Regina Gulielmi et Maria Nunc Anglia &c[t] Quarto
Signed Sealed & Delivered
   In psence of us
Sam[ll] Wentworth
John Wentworth

Richard White (Seal[a])
his mark

Boston in New England Sep[tr] 28th 1692./ Richard White Came & Acknowledged y[e] above deed of Sale to be his Act & Deed./   Before me Sam Sewall Justice of peace

[45] By Vertue of a Letter of Attorney from y[e] within Mentioned Richard White unto my Selfe bareing date y[e] 27th day of Sep[t] last past I have given by Turfe & Twigg possession of y[e] within mentioned pmises unto y[e] within mentioned Henry Dering As Witness my hand this 5th day of Octob[r] 1692./   Francis Hooke

     The mark of
Witness John ✗ More
     Eliz[a] Parsons
Recorded According to y[e] Original May y[e] 10th 1714/
     p Jos: Hamond Reg[r]

This Indenture made y[e] fifteenth day of January 1698 Between Henry Dering of y[e] province of y[e] Massachusets Bay in New England Shopkeeper on y[e] one part & Roger Dering of Kittery in y[e] province of Maine on y[e] other part Witnesseth that whereas in Consideration of y[e] Sum of Sixty pounds part whereof rec[d] & the other part Secured by Two Obligations to be paid do by these psents demise grant Bargaine Sell & Especially Assign over unto y[e] s[d] Roger Dearing all my right Title & Interest of y[e] within written deed of Sale and y[e] Houses and land therein mentioned with the rights members & Appurtenances thereof from me my heirs Execut[rs] & Adm[rs] unto y[e] s[d] Roger Dearing his heirs Execut[rs] Adm[rs] and Assignes forever./ Provided Alwayes that if y[e] s[d] Roger Dering his his heirs Execut[rs] Adm[rs] or Assignes or Some of them do not well & Truly pay or Cause to be paid unto y[e] s[d] Henry Dering his heirs Execut[rs] Adm[rs] or Assignes y[e] Sum & Sums of forty pounds as is Expressed in his Two Obligations bareing date y[e] 25th March 1699 without fraud that Then this psent Indenture & Assignm[t] and all & Every Covenant grant bargaine Sale & Article therein Contained Shall be utterly Voyd frustrate & of non Effect any thing herein before Specified to y[e] Contrary thereof in any wise

BOOK VIII, FOL. 45.

notwithstanding./ In Witness whereof I have hereunto Set my hand & Seal y^e day Above written./
Signed Sealed & Delivered   Henry Dering·($_{Seal}^{a}$)
　In y^e psence of
Samuel Gaskell
Samuel Gaskell jun^r
　The above named Henry Dering psonally Appearing before me y^e Subscrib^r one of their Maj^{tys} Councill of their province of y^e Massachusets Bay & Justice of y^e peace with y^e Same Acknowledged y^e Above written Assignment to be his Act & Deed At Boston Jan^{ry} 20th 1698

　　　　　　　　　　　　Sam^{ll} Wheelwright
　By Vertue of a Letter of Attorney from ye Above mentioned Henry Dering Possession of ye above granted pmises was given to ye aboves^d Roger Dering by Turfe & Twigg
　Kittery ye 25th March 1699/　　p Theodore Atkinson
　In psence of
　　　The Sign of
　John More ✗
　Joseph Couch
　Richard . R . Mitchel
　Recorded According to ye Original May ye 10th 1714/
　　　　　　　　　　　　p Jos: Hamond Reg^r

　Know All men by these psents that I Roger Dearing of Kittery in ye Province of Maine in New England Shipwright for & in Consederation of Sixty pounds in Currant money to me in hand paid by Richard Mitchell of ye Same Town & province ye rec^t whereof I do Acknowledge & my Selfe fully Satisfied Contented & paid have given granted bargained & Especially Assigned over unto ye s^d Richard Mitchell & unto his heirs Execut^{rs} & Assigns all my right Title & Interest of in & to ye within written bill of Sale & ye houses lands & p^{r}mises therein Mentioned with all ye rights priviledges & Appurtenances unto ye Same belonging or in Any kind Appurtaining from me my heirs Execut^{rs} Adm^{rs} & Assignes unto ye s^d Richard Mitchell his heirs Execut^{rs} Adm^{rs} & Assignes forever as fully & Amply in Every respect as it was Conveyed & Assigned unto me &c^t In Witness hereof I ye s^d Roger Dearing have hereunto Set my hand & Seal this fourth day of Aprill Anno Dom^i Seventeen hundred & Eleven

Book VIII, Fol. 46.

in y{e} Tenth year of Queen Ann her Reign over Great Brittaine &c{t}   Roger Dearing (Seal{a})
Signed Sealed & Delivered
  In psence of us Witness
  Edward Hazen
    The mark of
Mary *M* Couch
        Pro New Hamp{r} 8{th} may 1714
  M{r} Roger Dearing Acknowledged the above Instrum{t} to be his Act & Deed Before   Theo: Atkinson J Peace
Recorded According to y{e} Original May 10{th} 1714./
                    p Jos: Hamond Reg{r}

[46] Know All men by these presence that I Joseph Bolls Gent in y{e} County of york for diverse Causes and Considerations thereunto me Moveing do give & grant unto my Daughter Lock her heirs Execut{rs} & Adm{rs} a Certain Tract of upland & Ten Acres of Marsh Lying & being in Wells At y{e} three mile brook being a hundred Acres more or Less which Land I bought of Goodman Baker which Land I do Confirm unto my daughter Elizabeth Lock./ In Witness whereunto I have Set my hand & Seale this 25{th} of Octob{r} 1678/ The words Ten Acres of Marsh was Enterlined between y{e} Third & fourth lines before y{e} Signing hereof./
  Witness Sam{ll} Wheelwright
      Sam: Austin   Joseph his mark Bolls (Seal{a})
  M{r} Joseph Bolls Acknowledged This Instrum{t} to be his Act & Deed this 25{th} of Octob{r} 1678
        Before me   Sam{ll} Wheelwright Assotiate
Recorded According to y{e} Original July 14{th} 1714./
                    p Jos: Hamond Reg{r}

To All Christian People to whome these presents Shall come Elisha Ingersol of Kittery in the County of York within her Majesties Province of the Massachusets Bay in New England Yeoman Sends Greeting Know Ye That y{e} Said Elisha Ingersol for and in Consideration of the Sum of Forty pounds Currant money of New England to him in hand paid before the enSealing and Delivery of these pres-

Book VIII, Fol. 46.

ents by John Chapman of Kittery afores^d Yeoman the Receipt whereof to full content and Satisfaction He ye s^d Elisha Ingersol doth by these presents acknowledg and thereof and of Every part thereof for himselfe, his Heirs executors and Administrators, Doth acquit Exonerate and discharge the Said John Chapman his Heirs Executors and Administrators every of them forever by these presents: He ye s^d Elisha Ingersol hath given granted bargained Sold aliened Enfeoffed Conveyed and Confirmed and by these presents doth fully freely Clearly and absolutely give grant bargain Sell aliene enfeoffe Convey and confirm unto the Said John Chapman his Heirs and assignes forever A Certain Tract of land Containing Thirty one acres and halfe be it more or less Scituate lying and being in Kittery aforeSaid on the Eastern Side of Spruce Creek Thirty acres of which was a grant of the Town of Kittery made unto John Ingersol the 16th May 1694, and laid out to Said Ingersol The 8th day of March 1696/7: And is bounded as followeth Lying on the northeast End of Mr Elihu Gunisons land at Brians Point and is in length North East one Hundred and twenty poles and is in breadth Northwest and SouthEast forty poles, of which the Said Elisha Ingersol is assignee as may appear by Several deeds or Instruments on record Reference thereunto being had the other acre and halfe was purchased by Said Elisha Ingersol of Richard Endle of Kittery afores^d as may Appear by deed or Instrument under ye hand & Seale of the Said Endle bearing date the Eighteenth day of July Anno, Dom: 1707, being bounded as by Said deed is Set forth referance being had thereunto or how so ever other wise bounded, or reputed to be bounded Together with all Such Rights Liberties Immunities Profits Priviledges Commodities Emolument & appurtenances as in any kind appertain thereunto with the Reversions and remainders thereof and all the Estate Right Title Interest Inheritance property possession Claim & demand, whatsoever of him the s^d Elisha Ingersol of in & to the Same and every part thereof To Have and To Hold all the above granted Premises with all and Singular the appurtenances thereof unto the Said John Chapman his Heirs and assigns to his and their own Sole & proper use benefit and behoof from, henceforth forever: and the Said Elisha Ingersol for himselfe his Heirs Execut^{rs} Adm^{rs} doth hereby Covenant promiss grant & agree to & with the Said John Chapman his Heirs and Assignes in manner and form following: (that is to Say:) that at the time of the ensealing and delivery of these presents he the s^d Elisha Ingersol is the true Sole and lawfull owner of all the afore bargained Premises

Book VIII, Fol. 47.

and Stand lawfully Seized thereof in his own proper Right of a good perfect & Indefeazeable Estate of Inheritance in Fee Simple; haveing in himselfe full power good Right and lawfull Authority to Sell and dispose of the Same in manner as afores Said and that the s^d John Chapman his heirs & Assigns Shall & may henceforth forever Lawfully Peaceably & Quietly: Have hold use occupie possess and enjoy the above granted premises with the Appurtenances thereof Free and Clear and Clearly acquitted & discharged of and from all and all manner of former and other gifts grants bargains Sales Leases Mortgages Joyntures dowers Judgments Executions Entailes Forfeitures and of and from all other Titles Troubles Charges and Encumbrances whatsoever had made comitted Done or Suffered to be, done by the s^d Elisha Ingersol his heirs or assigns at any time or times before the Ensealing and delivery hereof and farther ye s^d Elisha Ingersol doth hereby Covenant promise bind and oblige himselfe his heirs Execut^{rs} & adm^{rs} from henceforth and forever hereafter to warrant and defend all ye above granted premises and ye appurtenances thereof: unto ye s^d John Chapman his heirs & assigns against ye Lawfull Claims & demands of all and every person or persons whatsoever: In Witness whereof y^e s^d Elisha Ingersol hath hereunto Set his [47] hand and Seal y^e twentieth day of May in y^e year of our Lord 1714 and in y^e thirteenth year of the Reign of our Soveraign Lady anne Queen of great Brittain France & Ireland defender of y^e Faith &c   Elisha Ingersol ($_{Seal}^{a}$)
Signed Sealed and delivered
in presence of
Geo: Jackson
John: Wainwright:
John Belcher

York ss Kittery may y^e 20th 1714
The within named Elisha Ingersol Acknowledged y^e within written Instrument to be his free Act & Deed Before me
     Charles ffrost J peace
Recorded According to y^e Original July ye 12th 1714./
     p Jos: Hamond Reg^r—

Know All men by these presents that I John Heard of Kittery in the County of york in ye Province of ye Massachusets Bay in New England yeoman for diverse valluable Considerations me hereunto Moveing do hereby by way of Deed of Gift give grant Aliene Assigne Enfeoffe Set Over

& Confirm And do by these psents give grant Aliene Assigne Enfeoffe Set over & Confirm unto Nathan Bartlet late of Newbery now of Kittery in ye County & Province afores^d Tanner Two Certaine pieces of land Scittuate lying & being in Kittery Afores^d out of ye homestead land of s^d Heard Viz^t/ one piece Containing ninty one Rods bounded from ye Beach Tree Northwestwardly Thirteen rod Then west Southward Eight rods Then Straight to ye highway & Six rod to ye Southward of ye Afores^d beach tree ye other piece Containing one hundred & fifty rod bounded from ye Corner of ye Sellar Northwardly Seven rods Then westwardly Twenty rods Then Southwardly Eight rods to ye Country road To ye first begining Twenty rods To have & To hold ye Two afores^d pieces of land as they are butted & bounded with all ye rights profits priviledges Accomodations waters Courses Streams & All other priviledges & Appurtenances of what nature kind or Quality so Ev^r unto ye Same & unto Each & every part & parcell thereof belonging unto him ye s^d Nathan Bartlet his heirs and Assigns for Ever & I ye s^d John Heard for my Selfe my heirs Execut^{rs} & Adm^{rs} do hereby Covenant to & with ye s^d Nathan Bartlet his heirs Execut^{rs} Adm^{rs} or Assignes that at ye Time of ye Ensealing and delivery hereof I am ye rightfull owner of ye hereby given and granted pmises & that ye Same & Each & Every part thereof is free & clear from all Incumbrances whatsoever & that it is Shall & may be Lawfull to & for ye s^d Nathan Bartlet his heirs & Assignes to have hold use Occupy possess & Enjoy y^e Same & Every part thereof Quietly & peaceably without any let hinderence Mollestation or Interruption from me y^e s^d John Heard my heirs Execut^{rs} or Adm^{rs} from henceforth & forever In Witness where of I have hereunto Set my hand & Seal y^e 27th day of February Annoq$_{,}$ Domini 1713/4./   John Heard (a Seal)

Signed Sealed & Delivered
  In psence of
  Benjamin Lord
  John Croade
        Berwick March 2^d 1713/4

York ss/ Cap^{tn} John Heard Appeared & Acknowledged y^e above written Instrum^t or deed of gift to be his Act & Deed & Jane his wife Also Appeared & relinquished her right of Dower or Thirds to ye lands above mentioned
                Before me   Ichabod Plaisted
Recorded According to y^e Original June 3^d 1714/
                p Jos. Hamond Reg^r

Book VIII, Fol. 48.

To All Christian people to whom these presen s Shall Come Know Ye that I Jeremiah Calef of Pourtsmouth in y^e Province of New=New Hampsh^r in=England for diverse good Causes and Considerations me thereunto Moveing more Especially for the Sum of Eighty Six pounds Curent Money of New England to me in hand well & truly paid by James Chadbourne of Kittery in the Province of Main Son and heir of James Chadbourne deceased hath Remised Released and for Ever quited Claimed & by these presents for my Selfe & my heirs do fully Clearly & absolutely Remise Release & for Ever quitt Claime unto James Chadbourne afores^d unto a Tract of land lying & being in ye Town of Kittery at a place Caled Sturgeon Creek part of which land ye s^d James Chadourns Grandfather bought of Major Nicolas Shapleigh also a Town grant To s^d Chadbourns Father adjoyning to ye Same Now in s^d Chadbournes possession unto his heirs and Assignes for ever all Such rights Estate Title Interest & demand whatsoever which I ye s^d Jeremiah Calfe have or ought to have of in and to ye above Mentioned premises In or by any Means whatsoever To Have and to Hold all ye s^d Tract of Land unto ye s^d James Chadbourne his Heirs and assignes for Ever So that Nither I ye s^d Jeremiah Calfe nor my Heirs Nor any other person or persons for me or them or in mine or their Steeds Shall or will by any way or meanes hereafter have Claime Chalenge or demand any Estate Right Title or Interest of in and to ye premises afores^d or any part or parcell thereof and every of them Shall, be uterly Excluded and barred for Ever by these presents and also ye s^d Jeremiah Calef and his heirs ye s^d tract of Land unto ye s^d James Chadbourne : his heirs and assignes with all the priviledge & appurtenances to the Same belonging to his & their owne proper use and uses in Manner and forme afore Specified against their, heirs and assignes & Every of them Shall warrant and for ever defend by these presents : In Witness whereof I have Set to my hand & Seal this twentyninth day of July one thousand Seven hundred and thirteen and in the thirteenth year of the Reigne of Soveraign Lady Anne over England Queen   Jeremiah Calef ($_{Seal}^{a}$)
Signed Sealed a Delivered   Luce Calef ($_{Seal}^{a}$)
   In presence of us
   Solomon Hewes
   Martha Hewes

[48] Jeremiah Calfe above named psonally Appeared before me the Subscriber one of her Majestyes Justices & Ac-

Book VIII, Fol. 48.

knowledged this Instrument to be his free Act and deed this 30th of July 1713 & in ye 13 year of Queen Anne over Great Brittain &. C   John Plaisted
 Recorded According to ye Original June 24th 1714:
        p Jos: Hamond Regr

 The Deposition of Joseph Crocket aged about Sixty years Testifyeth & Saith that in or about yⁿ year of our Lord god 1686 he ye Deponant was with Nathaniel Fryer Esqr of New Castle in ye province of New Hampshr & Captⁿ Elias Styleman of sd place & Island Called and known by ye name of Champernouns Island on ye Easterly Side of Piscattaqua river harbours mouth at which Time I heard ye sd Fryer order ye sd Styleman to lay out a Tract or parcell of land for John Hinckes Esqr of ye aforesd New Castle & Accordingly sd Styleman did./ sd Fryer Ordered him to begin at a great rock on ye Southerly or Southeast Side of a parcell of Marsh Called by ye name of Waltons Marsh & from sd rock ye bounds then Set was to a red oak Tree Standing on ye Inside of ye beach which sd red oak is there Standing & as I understood ye land was to run into ye Island from ye aforesd Bounds & the Deponat further Testifyeth that Samll Jordan lyveth on part of yesd lands between ye Two aforesd bounds   The Sign of

      Joseph ✝ : Crocket

 April 21. 1713/ Joseph Crocket within named psonally Appeared & made oath to ye Truth within written before me
      Abraˣ Preble Justice peace
 Recorded According to ye Original Augst 23d 1714:
        p Jos Hamond Regr

 John Graves Aged about Sixty years or therebout Testifyeth & Saith that I have known & been well Acquainted with ye Island Comonly Called Captn Champernouns Island & lived on sd Island when it was in ye possession of Captn Nathll Fryer Esqr in Sixteen hundred, & Eighty & lived upon ye sd Island aforesd untill ye year of our lord god Sixteen hundred Eighty & Seven in which time I heard Captn Nathll Fryer Esqr Say he had given unto Mr John Hinckes & Daughter Elizabeth a Certain parcell of land on sd Island wch pcell of land I alwayes understood by Cap^{tn} Fryer & Sundry others that s^d land Takes its begining at ye rock near ye mouth of ye Creek or pond on ye Southwest Side of ye rock near ye Marsh Comonly Called Waltons marsh & I do further Testify that this day being ye 15th day of May 1712 I have been upon s^d Island & Viewed s^d land & Say that there was formerly a pond on ye Southwest Side of ye Rock where s^d land took its begining ye pond being filled up with Stones dirt & Sand ye s^d highway Comes by s^d rock as formerly belonging to s^d Hinckes as I often heard Cap^{tn} Fryer Say ye bounds began at ye rock near Waltons marsh & Thence to a red oak Tree which I have Viewed & I understand that ye red Oak is Set forth in ye plot that Mr Wm Godsoe Surveyed & laid out is ye True bound marks

Jno Graves

Mr John Graves above named Appeared before me ye Subscrib^r one of her Maj^{tys} Council & Justice of peace for ye Province of New Hampsh^r & made Oath to: ye Truth above

John Plaisted

Recorded According to ye Original Augst 23^d 1714:

p Jos. Hamond Reg^r

[49] Know all men by these presents that I Jonathan Hutchins of Kittery in ye County of York husbandman for a valluable Consideration to me in hand paid by my brother Benjamin Hutchins of ye Same place yeoman & do by these p^{r}sents Acquitt ye s^d Benj^a Hutchins for ye Same & Every part thereof have given granted bargained & Sold & do by these psents fully and Absolutely give Grant Bargaine & Sell & for ever Confirm unto him ye s^d Benj^a Hutchins all that my right Title Interest in and unto that Estate of my Hon^d father Enoch Hutchins dec^d lying near ye head of ye Eastern Creek in Kittery whereof I ye s^d Jonathan Hutchins have good right & full power to Sell & dispose of my Interest in ye Same & do by these psents fully Absolutely Sell Alienate & Convey all that my Interest in ye s^d Estate that now is & may Accrew unto me hereafter from ye Estate of my deceased father Mr Enoch Hutchins lying at ye Eastern Creek by Any Maner of Means w^{t}soever unto my brother Benjamin Hutchins Afores^d to him & his heirs Execut^{rs} Adm^{rs} for ever hereby giving him full power to Ask re Cover & recieve ye Same in what hands So ever it may be found To have & To hold all my s^d Interest in s^d Estate unto ye only and Sole use of my brother Benjamin Hutchins

afores⁴ his heirs or Assignes for ever more hereby renounceing all my right Title and Interest in & to yᵉ Same & do by these psents make it Lawfull for him yᵉ s⁴ Benjᵃ Hutchins to Take use & Occupy & Dispose yᵉ Same to his own propper use for ever./ and for yᵉ True pformance of yᵉ Above premises I bind my Selfe my heirs Executʳˢ Admʳˢ & Assignes unto yᵉ s⁴ Benjamin Hutchins him his heirs Executʳˢ Admʳˢ & Assigns yᵉ peaceable & Quiet possession to Warrant & Defend from all mañer of psons laying claime thereunto./ In Witness hereof I Set to my hand & Seal this Eleventh day of Janʳʸ & in yᵉ year of our Lord one Thousand Seven hundred & Thirteen fourteen./

Signed Sealed & Delivered
   In psence of   Jonathan ✗ Hutchins (ₛₑₐₗᵃ)
Benjᵃ Hañion ⚏   ʰⁱˢ   mark
Stephen Ross
Jos Curtis

Kittery June 23⁴ 1714./ This day Jonathan Hutchins psonally Appeared before me yᵉ Subscribʳ one of her Majᵗʸˢ Justices of yᵉ peace for yᵉ County of York & Acknowledged this above written deed to be his free Act & Deed
                                   Wᵐ Pepperrell

Recorded According to yᵉ Original Septʳ 22⁴ 1714./
                             p Jos: Hañiond Regʳ

Know All men by these pʳsents that I Samuel Hutchins of Kittery in yᵉ County of york in New England Husbandman for a valluable consideration to me in hand paid by my brother Benjamin Hutchins of yᵉ afores⁴ Town & County yeoman and do by these psents Acquitt yᵉ s⁴ Benjamin Hutchins for yᵉ Same & Every part thereof have given granted Bargained & Sold & do by these psents fully & Absolutely give grant Bargaine & Sell & forever Confirm unto him yᵉ s⁴ Benjamin Hutchins all that my right Title Interest in & unto that Estate of my father Enoch Hutchins dec⁴ Lying near yᵉ head of yᵉ Eastern Creek in Kittery whereof I yᵉ s⁴ Samˡˡ Hutchins have good right & full power to Sell & dispose of my Interest in yᵉ Same and do by these psents fully Absolutely Sell Alienate & Convey all my Interest in yᵉ s⁴ Estate that now is & may Accrew unto me hereafter from yᵉ Estate of my deceased father Mʳ Enoch Hutchins lying at yᵉ Eastern Creek by Any manner of means whatsoever unto my Brother Benjᵃ Hutchins afores⁴ to him

& his heirs Execut^rs Admin^rs forever hereby giving him full power to Ask recov^r & recieve ye Same in what hands Soever it may be found To have & To hold all my s^d Interest in s^d Estate unto ye only & Sole use of my Brother Benj^a Hutchins afores^d his heirs or Assigns forevermore hereby renounceing all my right Title & Interest in & to ye Same and do by these psents make it Lawfull for him ye s^d Benj^a Hutchins to Take use & Occupy & Dispose ye Same to his own propper use forever & for ye True pformance of ye above pmises I bind my Selfe my heirs Execut^rs Adm^rs & Assigns unto ye s^d Benj^a Hutchins his heirs Execut^rs Adm^rs or Assignes ye peaceable & Quiet possession to Warrant & Defend from all manner of persons laying Claime Thereunto./ In Witness whereof I have hereunto Set my hand and Seal this Twenty Ninth day of June & in ye year of our Lord one Thousand Seven hundred & fourteen./

Signed Sealed & Delivered
  In psence of   Samuel H Hutchins (a Seal)
  Joseph Simpson   his mark
  Miriam Pepperrell
  Wm Pepperrell Junr
  Kittery June 29th 1714./

This day Sam^ll Hutchins psonally Appeared before me ye Subscrib^r one of her Ma^tys Justices of ye peace for ye County of york & Acknowledged this above written Deed to be his ffree Act & Deed./   Wm Pepperrell./

Recorded According to ye Original Septr 22^d 1714./

           p Jos: Hamond Reg^r

---

[50] To All Christian People to whom these psents may Come or doth Concern Johnson Harmon & Mary his wife of york in ye County of york in ye Province of Maine in New England Sendeth Greeting Know yee thes^d Johnson & Mary for & in Consideration of fifty pounds money to them well & Truely paid or otherwise Satisfactorily Secured to be paid by Sam^ll Came ofs^d York the rec^t thereof ye s^d Johnson & Mary do Acknowledge themselves therewith fully paid Satisfyed & Contented and Every part & parcel thereof and do by these psents Acquit Exonerate & Discharge ye s^d Sam^ll Came his heirs Execut^rs and Adm^rs for ye Land & priviledges hereafter Mentioned ye which they ye s^d Johnson & Mary have given granted bargained Sold Aliened Enfeoffed & Conveyed And do by these psents give grant bargaine Sell Aliene Enfeoffe

Harmon T Came

Book VIII, Fol. 50.

& Convey & fully freely & Absolutely make over & Confirm unto ye s^d Samuel Came his heirs & Assigns forever one Tract Tennement or parcell of land Lying and being within ye Township of s^d york Scittuated between ye Two branches of s^d York river Comonly Called ye partings which Tract or parcell of land Containeth fffty Acres be it more or Less and is butted & bounded As followeth Viz^t begining At a red oak Tree Standing about Six poles Northwestward from John Harmons Marsh which Tree is ye Eastward bound Marked Tree of a Tract or lot of land s^d Came bought of s^d Harmon above Mentioned & runns from Thence East Twenty five poles to a white oak Tree Markt on four Sides Standing by the Southwest branch of s^d York river & bounded by s^d river Northeast Eleven pole to Another white Oak markt on four Sides & runs from thence North East & by North forty pole to A little red Oak Tree Standing by ye Northwest branch of s^d York river & is bounded by s^d branch & as ye upland lyeth up s^d branch of s^d river one hundred poles then west Northwest Thirty Seven pole to a leaning red Oak marked on four Sides being ye Eastward Corner bounds Marked Tree of a Sixty Acre Lot s^d Sam^{ll} Came bought of s^d Johnson Harmon And from Thence is bounded by s^d Sixty Acre Lot on a Southwest point ye bredth thereof & on ye westward Side is bounded by s^d Samuel Cames Land bought of s^d Harmon above Mentioned Together with all ye rights benefits priviledges & Appurtenances thereunto belonging or any wise Appurtaining or at any time redownding unto ye s^d land or any part or parcell thereof unto him ye s^d Sam^{ll} Came his heirs & Assigns forever/

To have & To hold & Quietly & peaceably to possess Occupy & Enjoy ye s^d Land & all its priviledges as a Sure Estate in fee Simple Moreover ye s^d Johnson & Mary do for themselves their heirs Execut^{rs} & Adm^{rs} Covenant bargaine Ingage & promiss to & with ye s^d Samuel his heirs & Assigns ye above bargained premisses with all ye priviledges to be ffree & Cleare from all former gifts grants bargaines Sales rents rates Mortgages Wills Joyntures or any other Incumberments whatsoever./ As Also from all future claims Challenges writs or Executions or any other Incumberments whatsoever to be had or Comenced by them ye s^d Johnson or Mary their heirs Execut^{rs} Adm^{rs} or Assignes or any other pson or psons whatsoever after ye date of this Instrument the s^d Johnson & Mary do warrantize & will Defend ye Same

In Witness hereof ye above Named Johnson Harmon & Mary his wife have hereunto Set their hands & Seals ye Twenty Seventh day of Aprill in ye year of our Lord one Thousand

Seven hundred & fourteen & in y⁰ Thirteenth year of y⁰ Reign of our Soveraign Lady Anne Queen of Great Brittaine &c¹ It is agreed before Signing y⁰ s⁴ Harmon doth reserve for himSelfe & his heirs priviledge to ffell Cut & Carry off from y⁰ aboves⁴ land firewood for his own family as long as s⁴ wood Shall Last./ Johnson Harmon (ᵘ Seal)
Signed Sealed & Delivered
  In psence of us Witnesses
  Wᵐ Walters
  Abraᵐ Preble junʳ
    York ss/
York April y⁰ 27ᵗʰ 1714 The above Named Johnson Harmon Appeared before me y⁰ Subscribʳ one of her Maᵗʸˢ Justices of s⁴ County & Acknowledged this Instrumᵗ to be his free Act & Deed   Abrã Preble
Recorded According to the Original July y⁰ 7ᵗʰ 1714 —
                    p. Jos: Hamond Regʳ

  To All Christian People to whom these presents may Come Samuel Webber Senʳ of york in y⁰ County of york in y⁰ Province of maine in New England Sendeth Greeting Know Yee that y⁰ s⁴ Samuel Webber for & in Consideration of ffifty pounds money to him in hand paid or otherwayes Satisfactorily Secured to be paid by Richard Milberry of s⁴ york at y⁰ recᵗ thereof y⁰ s⁴ Samuel Webber doth therewith Acknowledge himselfe fully paid Satisfyed & Contented & of & for Every [**51**] part or parcel thereof & doth by these psents Exonerate Acquitt & Discharge y⁰ s⁴ Richard Milbury his heirs & Assigns forever for that y⁰ s⁴ Samˡˡ Webber Senʳ hath given granted bargained Sold Aliened Enfeoffed & made over and doth by these psents give grant bargaine Sell Aliene Enfeoffe & make Over & fully freely and Absolutely Convey and Confirm unto y⁰ s⁴ Richᵈ Milbury his heirs or Assigns forever one fourth or quarter part of a Saw Mill & one fourth part of y⁰ priviledge of y⁰ Streem of water where y⁰ s⁴ Mill now Standeth is Erected and built within y⁰ Township or precinct of s⁴ York Comonly Called & known by y⁰ Name of Cape nuddick mill being y⁰ Lower mill Next to y⁰ Salt water or Sea with one Acre of land Joyning unto y⁰ s⁴ Mill being y⁰ one Quarter part of four Acres of land lying & being and Adjoyning unto y⁰ Mill & Streem Called by y⁰ Name of Cape nuddick river s⁴ Mill & Streem (entered where s⁴ Mill now Standeth) with s⁴ four Acres of land

being in Copartnership wth Mr James Saywood Dependence Stover & ye heirs & Execut^{rs} of Mr John Sayword late of s^d York deceased with ye one Quarter part of ye Damm Saws Doggs Crows & Iron work & wooden work & Timber thereunto belonging to s^d Quarter part or priviledge that doth of right or Shall hereafter thereunto Appurtaine unto him ye s^d Richard Milbury his heirs & Assigns forever To have & To hold & Quietly & peaceably to Occupie and Enjoy ye Same as a Sure Estate in ffee Simple Moreover ye s^d Samuel Webber doth for himselfe his heirs Execut^{rs} & Adm^{rs} Covena^t Ingage & promiss to & with ye s^d Richard Milbury his heirs & Assigns ye Above bargained premises to be free & Clear from all former gifts grants bargains Sales deeds Mortgages rents rates dowrys or any other Incumberments whatsoever As Also from all future Claims Challenges Judgm^{ts} Executions or any other Law Suits or Interruptions to be had or Comenced by him ye s^d Webber his heirs or Assigns or any other p^{r}son or psons whatsoever upon any grounds or Title of Law after the Date of this Instrum^t will Defend & by these p^{r}sents do Warrantize ye Same./ In Witness hereof ye s^d Sam^{ll} Webber hath hereunto Set his hand & Seal this Twenty fourth day of June in ye year of our lord one Thousand Seven hundred & fourteen & in ye Thirteenth year of ye reign of our Soveraign Lady Anne Queen of Great Brittaine &c^t Samuel Webber (a)
Signed Sealed & Delivered   Deberoh Webber (Seal)
   In ye psence of us Witnesses   her mark
   Johnson Harmon
   Sam^{ll} Came
   Abra Preble jun^r
        County of york ss/ July ye 7th 1714/
   The within Named Sam^{ll} Webber p^{r}sonally Appeared before me ye Subscrib^r one of her Ma^{tys} Justices of ye peace within s^d County of York & Acknowledged this wthin written Instrum^t to be his free Act & Deed   Abra Preble
   Recorded According to ye Original July ye 7th 1714./
                      p Jos: Hamond Reg^r

To All Christian People to whom this present deed of Sale may Come Samuel Webber & Deberoh his wife of york in ye County of york in the Province of Maine in New England Sendeth Greeting Know Yee: thes^d Samuel & Deberoh for & in Consideration of a Certain Sum of money to them in hand paid before y[e] Signing of this Instrument by Richard Milbury of s[d] York y[e] Receipt thereof y[e] s[d] Samuel & Deberoh doth Acknowledge & declare themselves therewith fully Satisfyed & Contented & do by these psents Exonerate discharge & Acquitt y[e] s[d] Richard his heirs Execut[rs] & Adm[rs] And have given granted bargained Sold Aliened Enfeoffed & Conveyed and do by these psents give grant bargaine Sell Aliene Enfeoffe & Convey & fully freely & Absolutely make over & Confirm unto y[e] s[d] Richard Milbury a Tract parcell Lott or piece of land Containing by Estimation Sixteen Acres be it more or Less lying & being within y[e] Township of s[d] york on y[e] Northeast Side of y[e] Little river near y[e] Rockey ground and is butted & bounded as followeth viz[t] begining at an ash Tree marked on four Sides Standing on y[e] Eastward Corner of a Lot of land of s[d] Milburys & runns Northeast Sixteen pole to a beach Tree marked on four Sides then Northwest one hundred & forty pole to A pine Tree marked on four Sides & Then Southwest to aboves[d] Milburys land & is bounded by s[d] Milburys land to y[e] Ash Tree above mentioned Together with all y[e] rights Titles Interest Advantages and priviledges thereunto belonging or any wayes at any time Appurtaining or redownding unto y[e] s[d] land or any part or parcell thereof unto him y[e] s[d] Richard Milbury his heirs and Assignes forever To have & To hold & Quietly & peaceably to use Occupie & Enjoy y[e] s[d] land and all its priviledges as a Sure Estate in ffee Simple Moreover y[e] s[d] Sam[ll] & Deberoh do for Themselves their heirs Execut[rs] & Adm[rs] to & with y[e] s[d] Richard Milbury his heirs & Assignes Covenant Ingage and promiss y[e] aboves[d] premises with all its priviledges & Appurtenances to be free & clear from all former gifts grants bargains Sales deeds Mortgages rents rates dowryes or any other Incumberments whatsoever as Also from all future claims Challenges Executions Lawsuits or Interruptions whatsoever to be had or to be had or Comenced by them y[e] s[d] Sam[ll] or Deberoh their heirs Execut[rs] Adm[rs] or assignes or any other pson or psons upon grounds or Title of Law and after y[e] Date of this [52] Instrument they will defend y[e] s[d] bargained land & do by these psents warrantize y[e] Same./ In Witness hereof y[e] s[d] Sam[ll] Webber & Deberoh his wife have hereunto Set their hands & Seals this first day of April in. y[e] year of our Lord one Thousand Seven hundred & fourteen.

Signed Sealed & Delivered   Samuel Webber (a Seale)
   In psence of us Witnesses   Deberoh Webber (a Seal)
   Samuel Webber
   Peter Nowel   her mark ℂ —

Book VIII, Fol. 52.

York ss/ July y{e} 7{th} 1714./ The above named Sam{ll} Webber psonally Appeared before me one of her Ma{tys} Justices of y{e} peace in y{e} County of York & Acknowledged this above written to be his free Act & Deed   Abra{x} Preble

Recorded According to y{e} Original July y{e} 7{th} 1714./

p Jos: Hamond Reg{r}

To All Christian people to whom these presents Shall Come Greeting Know yee that I Job Emery now resident in Berwick in y{e} County of york in y{e} province of y{e} Massachusets Bay in New England husbandman for & in Consideration of ffifty pounds to me in hand paid by Daniel Emery my brother of Kittery in y{e} County & Province above mentioned y{e} receipts whereof I own my selfe Satisfied Contented and paid & of Every part & parcell thereof do Acquit & for ever discharge Have given granted bargained & Sold and do by these presents give grant bargaine Sell release Alienate Enfeoffe pass over & Confirm unto Daniel Emery Aboves{d} all my right Title Interest propperty Claime or demand in or two a Certaine piece or parcell of land & Meadow Swamp & heath Scittuate & in y{e} Township of Kittery & bounded As followeth Viz{t} on the East & Southeast by y{e} Land of John Tompson & a pond Called york pond & Peter Grants land & on y{e} North with s{d} Peter Grants formerly & Comons which line runns northeast & Southwest and on y{e} west by Edward Hayes or Comons & on y{e} Southwest by Edward Waymouth or Comons & Contains Two hundred Acres more or Less as it was granted to my father & Grandfather y{e} one halfe of y{e} above mentioned land & Meadow being my own propper right I now make over as aboves{d} to my brother Daniel Emery To have & To hold y{e} afores{d} Tract of.land Together with all & Singular y{e} Appurtenances priviledges & Comoditys of woods Timb{r} Trees und{r} woods waters Water Courses &c{t} to him y{e} s{d} Daniel Emery his heirs & Assigns for ever without Let Interruption or Mollestation of me y{e} s{d} Job Emery or any other pson or psons by from or und{r} me or by my procurem{t} my heirs or Assigns for ever only I reserve to my Selfe my heirs or Assigns Twenty Acres of my part which is agreed to be Measured at y{e} Northeast Corner of s{d} land begining at the great hill & So runn North to y{e} Corner bounds Then Southwest Till it is Accomplished./ And for Confirmation of y{e} pmises I y{e} s{d} Job Emery hereunto Set my hand & Seal this Twelfth day of March Anno Dom: one Thousand Seven hundred &

BOOK VIII, FOL. 53.

Thirteen fourteen 1713/4 & in y[e] Thirteenth year of her
Ma[tys] Reign of Great Brittaine &c[t]   Job Emery— (a Seal)
Signed Sealed & Delivered
 In psence of us
 John Gowen
 John Beltcher
 John Gowen jun[r]
  York ss Kittery March 12th 1713/4
 The above named Job Emery psonally Appearing Acknowledged y[e] above written Instrum[t] to be his free Act & Deed./ Before me   Charles ffrost J peace
 Recorded According to y[e] Original June 4th 1714
                            p Jos Hamond Reg[r]

 This Indenture made the   day of Decemb[r] in y[e] first year of y[e] Reign of our Soveraign Lady Anne by the grace of God of England Scotland ffrance and Ireland Queen Defend[r] of y[e] faith &c[t] & in y[e] year of our Lord one Thousand Seven hundred & Two/ Between John Plaisted of Portsmouth in y[e] Province of New Hampshire Esq[r] and Capt[n] John Hill of Kittery in y[e] County of York in y[e] Province of y[e] Massachusets Bay of y[e] one part & Abraham Lord of y[e] Same Kittery husbandman on y[e] other part Witnesseth that y[e] s[d] John Plaisted & John Hill for & in Consideration of - pounds Currant money of New England to them in hand well & Truely paid at & before the sealing & Delivery of these psence by y[e] s[d] Abraham Lord to y[e] full Content & Satisfaction of y[e] s[d] John Plaisted & John Hill as for & under y[e] yearly rents payments & reservacons hereafter menconed to be yielded rendered & paid by y[e] s[d] Abra Lord his heirs or Assignes Have given granted bargained Sold Aliened Enfeoffed & Confirmed & by These psence do freely fully & Absolutely give grant bargaine Sell Aliene Enfeoffe release Convey & Confirm unto y[e] s[d] Abraham Lord his heirs & Assignes for ever a Certaine piece or pcell of land Lying & being Scittuate in y[e] Township of Kittery afores[d] and is part of that land which y[e] s[d] John Plaisted purchased of./ [53] Eliakim Hutchinson of Boston Esq[r] as by deed bareing date Jan[ry] 10th 1699 doth and may Appear bounded as followeth Viz[t] begining at y[e] outmost Corner marked tree Northerly Joyning to Humphrey Chadbourns Land & from s[d] Trea Northeast halfe a point Easterly by s[d] Chadbourns land Ninety Six pole and from s[d] Tree Southerly Joyning to s[d]

Book VIII, Fol. 53.

Chadbourns land fifty poles & from ye Extent of ye s^d Ninety Six pole to ruñ Eastwardly by s^d Lords own Land forty Nine pole & from ye Extent of ye s^d ffifty poles to ye s^d fforty nine poles upon a Straight line Containing Twenty Nine Acres or Thereabouts be ye Same more or Less with all & Singular ye priviledges profits Comoditys & Appurtenances thereunto belonging or in any wise Appurtaining To have & To hold ye s^d piece or parcel of land with all right Title Interest Claime & Demand which they ye s^d John Plaisted & John Hill now have or in time past have had or which they their heirs Execut^{rs} Adm^{rs} or Assigns in time to come may might or in any wise ought to have of in or to ye above granted pmises or in any part thereof & that ye same is free & clear Acquitted & Discharged of & from all former & other gifts grants bargains Sales Mortgages Titles Troubles & Incumbrances whatsoever had made done Comitted or Suffered to be done or Comitted by them ye s^d John Plaisted & John Hill or either of them or their or Either Assigns and they ye s^d John Plaisted & John Hill do Covenant promiss & grant to & with him ye s^d Abraham Lord his heirs & Assigns that at & untill thensealing & Delivery of these presence they are ye True right & propper owners of ye pmises & Every part thereof & have in themselves good right full power & Lawfull Authority ye Same to Sell & Convey unto him ye s^d Abraham Lord his heirs & Assigns And that ye s^d Abraham Lord his heirs or Assigns Shall & may from time to time & At all times for ever hereafter have hold Occupie Improve possess & Enjoy ye Same & Every part thereof without any Mollestacõn let denial hinderence or disturbence whatsoever of or by them ye s^d John Plaisted & John Hill or Either of them their heirs Execut^{rs} Adm^{rs} or Assignes And that ye Sale thereof Against Themselves their heirs & Assignes & against all other psons whatsoever Lawfully Claiming ye Same or any part thereof from by or under them or either of them their or Eother heirs Execut^{rs} or Assignes they ye s^d John Plaisted & John Hill shall & will for ever Save harmless warrant & Defend by these psents And Also that they ye s^d John Plaisted & John Hill their heirs Execut^{rs} & Adm^{rs} at any time hereafter At ye request Cost & Charge of ye s^d Abraham Lord his heirs or Assignes shall & will make Seal & Execute Such further Instruments writings Acts & things for ye Confirmacõn & more Sure makeing of ye s^d bargained pmises unto ye s^d Abraham Lord his heirs & Assignes As by his or their Councill Learned in ye Law shall be Lawfully or reasonably devised Advised or required So that ye Same Contain no other or Larger Warranty than what is

Book VIII, Fol. 53.

above written And he y{e} s{d} Abraham Lord for himselfe heirs Exect{rs} and Assigns doth Covenant & agree to & with y{e} s{d} John Plaisted & John Hill Their heirs & Assigns by these p{s}ents that he y{e} s{d} Abraham Lord his heirs & Assignes shall & will well & Truely pay or Caused to be paid unto Robert Tufton Mason who was y{e} Grandson & heir to Capt{n} John Mason of London Esq{r} dec{d} or to y{e} Lawfull heirs or Assigns of s{d} Robert Tufton Mason if Demanded or required thereunto upon y{e} five & Twentyeth day of Decem{r} yearly & in Every year Successively for ever hereafter y{e} full & just Sum or Quitt rent of one Shilling & Eight pence Currant money of New England p Annum for part & parcell of y{e} Land above mentioned which y{e} s{d} Eliakim Hutchinson purchased formerly of y{e} s{d} Tufton Mason & all other paym{ts} & Quitrents reserved by and payable unto y{e} s{d} Robert Tufton Mason his heirs or Assigns According to y{e} Ten{r} true Intent & meaning of a Covenant grant & agreem{t} on y{e} part & behalfe of y{e} s{d} Eliakim Hutchinson in a Certaine Indenture bareing date ye 16{th} of Decemb{r} 1687 made between y{e} s{d} Robert Tufton Mason of y{e} one part & y{e} s{d} Eliakim Hutchinson on y{e} other part in & by which Indenture y{e} s{d} Robert Tufton Mason hath bargained & Sold unto y{e} s{d} Eliakim Hutchinson his heirs & Assigns Certain tracts & parcells of land and are part of y{e} premises herein before granted unto y{e} s{d} Abraham Lord & further y{e} s{d} Abra{x} Lord doth for himselfe his heirs Execut{rs} & Adm{rs} Covenant promiss & grant to & with y{e} s{d} John Plaisted & John Hill their heirs & Assignes that he y{e} s{d} Abraham Lord his heirs &c{t} Shall & will well & Truely pay or cause to be paid unto y{e} s{d} Rob{t} Tufton Mason his heirs &c{t} if demanded All Such Sum & Sums of money as have already grown due unto y{e} s{d} Rob{t} Tufton Mason or his heirs for rent or Quitt rent of y{e} p{r}mises & y{e} Arrearages thereof According to y{e} s{d} Indenture Since y{e} Date thereof & Shall & will at all times hereafter well & Sufficiently defend keep harmless & Indempnify y{e} s{d} John Plaisted & John Hill their heirs Execut{rs} & Adm{rs} of & from y{e} Same & all actions Suits to be therefore brought & prosicuted against them by y{e} s{d} Robert Tufton Mason his heirs or Assignes & y{e} paym{t} above Menc̃oned to be made by & on y{e} part of y{e} s{d} Abra{m} Lord to be in full of all rents Acknowledgm{ts} Dutys & Services for y{e} above granted premises & Every part thereof: to any pson or p{r}sons whatsoever Excepting & reserving his Majesty heirs & Successors all pine Trees upon s{d} land of four & Twenty Inches Deamit{r} fit to make masts for his Maj{tys} ships./ In Witness whereof y{e} partys aboves{d} to These p{r}sents Enter-

changeably have Set their hands & Seals y̖ᵉ day & year aboves ͩ./ Mary Plaisted John Plaisted (ₛₑₐₗᵃ)
Signed Sealed & Delivered Mary Hill John Hill (ₛₑₐₗᵃ)
In yᵉ pʳsences of us
John Leighton
Daniel Goodin
York ss/ Aug ͤͭ 13 : 1703. The within Named John Plaisted & John Hill psonally Appearing before me yᵉ Subscribʳ one of her Maᵗʸˢ Justices of yᵉ peace within s ͩ County of york Acknowledged this Instrumᵗ to be their act & deed
Ichabod Plaisted
Recorded According to yᵉ Original Sepᵗʳ yᵉ 11ᵗʰ 1714 :/
p Jos. Hamond Regʳ

[54] To All Christian People to whom these presents shall Come Know yee that wee Martha Lord & Nathan Lord Senʳ Benjamin Lord John Cooper of yᵉ Town of Kittery in yᵉ County of york in yᵉ province of yᵉ Massachusets Bay in New England & Moses Littlefield of yᵉ Town of Wells in yᵉ County aforesᵈ & Thomas Downs William ffrost Tobias Hanson of yᵉ Town of Dover in yᵉ province of New Hampshʳ in yᵉ County aforesᵈ for a Valluable Sum of money to us in hand paid by William Lord of yᵉ Town of Kittery aforesᵈ yᵉ Son of Abraham Lord yᵉ receipt whereof wee Acknowledge our Selves to be fully Satisfyed for a Certaine parcell of land with a house & barn Standing thereon & for one Yoke of Oxen one Cow Two hiefers Two Calves & five pounds worth of cloathing & for yᵉ one halfe of a grindstone all which Lands goods & Cattle was our brother Samuel Lords Son of yᵉ aforesᵈ Martha Lord That Lot or Tract of land that he bought of Henry Child being forty Acres or thereabouts lying and Scittuate in yᵉ Township of Kittery aforesᵈ & Adjoyning to yᵉ East Side of sᵈ William Lords land which land good & Cattle & Grindstone wee yᵉ foresᵈ Martha Lord Nathan Lord Benjᵃ Lord John Cooper Moses Littlefield Thomas Downs William ffrost & Tobias Hanson Have Absolutely & free given granted bargained Sold Alienate Enfeoffed & Confirmed & do by these psents for our Selves our heirs Execut ͬˢ Adm ͬˢ & Assigns give grant bargaine Sell Alienate Enfeoffe pass over & Confirm unto yᵉ foresᵈ William Lord yᵉ foresᵈ Tract of Land with yᵉ goods & Cattle that was our brother Samuel Lords To have & To hold all & Singular yᵉ Above granted premises with all & Singular yᵉ Appurtenances & priviledges & Comoditys there-

Book VIII, Fol. 54.

unto belonging to him y{e} s{d} William Lord his heirs Execut{rs} Adm{rs} & Assigns forever freely & Clearly Exonerated & Discharged from all former Sales gifts grants Mortgages or any other Incumbrances whatsoever had made done or Suffered to be done by us y{e} fores{d} Martha Lord Nathan Lord Benj{a} Lord John Cooper Moses Littlefield Thomas Downs William ffrost & Tobias Hanson whereby y{e} s{d} William Lord his heirs Execut{rs} Adm{rs} or Assignes may be in any wayes Mollested or disturbed in their Quiet & peaceable Injoyment & Improvem{t} of y{e} Abovegranted pmises or of Any part or parcell thereof & for Confirmation of y{e} pmises wee y{e} fores{d} Martha Lord Nathan Lord Sen{r} Benj{a} Lord John Cooper Moses Littlefield Thomas Downs William ffrost & Tobias Hanson have hereunto Set our hands & Seals this Twenty Second day of March Anno Domini one Thousand Seven hundred Six Seven and in y{e} Sixth year of her Maj{tys} Reign Anne by y{e} grace of God of England Scotland ffrance & Ireland Queen Defender of y{e} faith &c{t}

Signed Sealed & Delivered
In y{e} psence of us
Humphrey Chadbourne
James Warren   Witnesses
Moses Littlefield Signed &c{t}
In y{e} psence of
Samuel ffrench
Joshua Finney

Martha her mark Lord (a Seal)
Nathan his mark Lord (a Seal)
John Cooper (a Seal)
Tobis Hanson (a Seal)
William ffrost (a Seal)
Benjamin Lord (a Seal)
Moses Littlefield (a Seal)

York ss Berwick march y{e} 22{d} 1706/7 John Cooper Tobias Hansom William ffrost Benjamin Lord psonally Appeared before me y{e} Subscriber one of her Maj{tys} Justices in s{d} County and Acknowledged y{e} above Instrum{t} to be their Act & Deed//   Ichabod Plaisted J peace.

Martha Lord & Nathan Lord within mentioned psonally Appeared before my Selfe y{e} Subscrib{r} one of her Maj{tys} Justices for y{e} County of York S{r} this 12{th} of April 1707 & Acknowledged the within Instrum{t} to be their free Act & Deed./   John Plaisted./

York ss/ Moses Littlefield psonally Appeared before me y{e} Subscriber one of her Ma{tys} Justices of y{e} peace within this County & ffreely Acknowledged this within written In-

BOOK VIII, FOL. 55.

strum^t or deed of Sale with his hand & Seal Affixed thereunto to be his Act & Deed this 26th day of March 1708./
John Wheelwright

Recorded According to ye Original Sep^{tr} ye 11th 1714./
p Jos : Hamond Reg^r

To All People unto whom this present Deed of Sale Shall Come William Haley of Boston in the County of Suffolk in ye Province of the Massachusets Bay in New England Shipwrite Sends Greeting Know Yee That I the s^d William Haley for and in Consideration of the Sum of Fourty pounds money to me in hand paid and secured to be paid at and before the ensealing & delivery hereof by Andrew Haley of Kittery in the County of York in New England Husbandman The receipt whereof to fully content and Satisfaction I do hereby acknowledge and thereof & from every part and parcell thereof ye Said Andrew Haley his heirs Execut^{rs} Adm^{rs} assignes & every of them do acquit and fully discharge for ever by these presents Have Given granted Bargained Sold Set over assigned conveyd and confirmed, and by these presents Do fully freely clearlie and absolutely Give grant Bargained Sell Setover convey & confirme unto the sd Andrew Haley his heirs and Assignes [55] forever All that My Peice or Parcell of Land Situate Lying and being in Kittery afores^d Laid out unto me by Vertue of a Town grant Sep^t 8^{ts} one thousand Six hundred & Ninety nine, Bounded South East by the s^d Andrew Haley on the North East by John Muggeridge on the Northwest by ye Land of Henry Barns And on the South west with the Land of Nicholas Weeks being by Estimation Thirty Acres as it lies in one peice with ye s^d Andrew's Land as by ye s^d Town grant and Record of the Same may Appear Together with all the Trees wood timber Stones Water wayes profitts priviledges & appurtenances whatsoever to ye Same belonging and appurtaining and all the Right title Interest claime and demand whatsoever of me the S^d William Haley and my heirs of in & to the same and every part and parcell thereof To have and to hold the aforegranted Peice or parcell of Land Together with all & every the appurc̃es thereof & of every part and Parcell thereof unto the Set Andrew Haley his heirs Executors Adm^{rs} and Assignes forever To his & their Own Sole & proper use bennifitt & behoofe from henceforth forever// And I the s^d William Haley do

Book VIII, Fol. 55.

hereby Covenant promise & grant unto & with the s^d Andrew Haley his heirs & assignes in manner & form following that is to Say That at the time of ye Ensealing and delivery hereof I am the true Sole and Lawfull Owner of all & Singular ye herein before granted premises with the Appur^{ces} and have in my Selfe full power good right & Lawfull Authority the same to grant Sell & assure in manner as afores^d And that the s^d premises Are Free & Clear & Clearly acquited exonerated & fully discharged of and from all & all manner of former & other Gifts Grants Bargaines Sales titles troubles acts Alienations & incumbrances whatsoever And Further I do hereby Bind and oblige my Selfe & my heirs the Said granted premises with the appurtenances thereof and every part & parcell thereof unto the s^d Andrew Haley his heirs Execut^{rs} Admin^{rs} Assignes & every of them Against the Lawfull Claims & demands of all & every person & persons whomsoever to Warrant and forever defend by these presents: In Witness whereof I ye said William Haley and Sarah my wife who hereby also Resignes all her Right of thirds in the premises have here unto Set our hands & Seales the third day of August Anno Domi One thousand Seven hundred & fourteen In the Thirteenth year of her Maj^{ts} Reigne Over Great Brittain &c./ Mem^o the words (do acquit & fully discharge forever) interlined between the fifth & Sixth line before Sealing
Signed Sealed and delivered
  in presence of
  Nicholas Dun
  Robert Gibbs
      Suffolk ss Boston August th3^d 1714
William Haley & Sarah his wife psonally appeared and Acknowledged this Instrument to be their act & Deed,
              Before me   John Clark Justs Peace
                      William Haley ($_{Seal}^{a}$)
                      Sarah: Haley ($_{Seal}^{a}$)
Recorded According to y^e Original Octob^r 19th 1714
                    p Jos: Hamond Reg^r

At a Legal Town meeting held at Kittery May 10th 1703—
Granted to John ffollet his heirs & Assigns forever fifty Acres of Land
  A True Coppy as Appears of Record in Kittery Exam^d—
                p Jos: Hamond Town Cler:

Book VIII, Fol. 56.

Know All men by these psents that I John ffollet of Kittery in ye County of York within her Ma^{tys} Province of ye Massachusets Bay in New England for my Selfe my heirs Execut^{rs} Adm^{rs} & Assigns for & in Consideration of ye Suṁ of fifty Shillings to me in hand paid by Diamond Sargent of Kittery in ye County & Province afores^d Tayler have given granted bargained and Sold ye aboves^d Grant of Land unto him ye s^d Diamond Sargent his heirs & Assigns forever To have & To hold y^e s^d grant of ffifty Acres of Land unto y^e s^d Diamond Sargent his heirs &c^t forevermore./ In Witness whereof I have hereunto Set my hand & Seal this Twenty Ninth day of Septr Seventeen hundred & Twelve 1712./

Signed Sealed & Delivered   John $\overset{\text{mark}}{FF}$ ffollet ($_{\text{Seale}}^{\text{a}}$)
In pscnce of us   his
Joseph Gunnison
John Walker jun^r

York ss/ 15th of Octob^r 1714. this day John ffollet psonally Appeared before me y^e Subscrib^r one of his Maj^{tys} Justices of y^e peace & Acknowledged this Above written deed or Obligation to be his ffree Act & Deed./   Wm Pepperrell

Recorded According to ye Original Octob^r 25th 1714/

p Jos: Haṁond Reg^r

To all people to whom these Presents Shall come Samuel Spiney & Nathaniel Kene both of ye town of Kittery in ye County of york in ye Province of ye Massachusets Bay in New England yeomen Send Greeting Know ye that whereas there hath been in time past a Differance & controverSie between ye S^d Samuel Spinney & Nathaniel Kene concerning the Lines Courses or bounds between their Lands Scituate Lying & being in the Township of Kittery afores^d and for the making of a final Issue periods & End of all the differance Law Suits Actions Quarrels & controversies whatsoever that have arose between: y^m relating to their above Said Lands & for ye fixing & Stating of bounds between their Lands aboveS^d the aboveS^d Samuel Spinney & Nathaniel Kene do by these Presents for themselves their Heirs Execut^{rs} Administrators [**56**] and Assignes mutually agree consent & conclude that henceforth and forever ye Courses or lines on which the Land of the Said Nathaniel Kene Shall run are as followeth that is to Say begining at ye Gutter in ye head of ye western Creeck in Spruce Creek near John Shepards Land whereon he now dwells & to run from thence

one hundred & Sixteen poles North north West & then west
& by South one hundred & thirty poles & then South which
two last Courses or Lines Shall be & remain ye Stated fixed
& determined bounds between their Lands for them their
Heirs Executors Amin^{rs} & Assigns from this time forward &
forever and that all actions Suits & controversies whatsoever
that have arison about their bounds Shall from this time forever hereafter determine & cease And for the faithfull & true
observing Keeping & performing all and every of ye Articles
& clauses in these Presents exprest the perSons above named
Sam^{ll} Spinney & Nathaniel Kene do bind themSelves their
Heirs Executors & admin^{rs} each to other in ye Penal Sum of
fifty :—: Pounds of good Currant money of New England
to be paid by ye failing to ye observing party :—: In : witness : whereof they have hereunto Set their hands & Seals
this Seventh day of may Anno Domini : 1714/ in ye thirteenth year of the Reign of Queen Anne

Signed & Sealed   Sam^{ll} Spinney (Seal)
   in ye presence of   Nathaniel Kene (Seal)
John Shepherd
Jonathan Kene

/ it is agreed that ye gore of land Lying between John
Shapleighs land & Sam^{ll} Spinneys land be nath^{ll} Kene
                                     Sam^{ll} Spinney

York ss/ The 18th day of October 1714./ This day
Samuel Spinney & nathaniel Kene Personally appeared before me ye Subscriber One of his Majesties Justices of y^e
peace for ye County of york afores^d & Acknowledged this
within written deed or obligation to be their Free Act &
Deed   Wm Pepperrell

Recorded According to y^e Original Octob^r 30th 1714./
                     p Jos Hamond Reg^r—

This Indenture made y^e fifth day of Novemb^r Anno Domini one Thousand Seven hundred & fourteen Annoq$_e$ RR^s
Georgii Magna Brittannia &c^t Primo. Between Ephraim
Savage of Boston in y^e County of Suffolk within his Maj^{tys}
province of y^e Massachusets Bay in New England Gent Ad-
ministrat^r to y^e Estate of Richard Wharton Late of Boston
afores^d Esqr deceased of y^e one part And Cap^{tn} Thomas
Hutchinson of ye Same place Esqr John Wentworth of Portsmouth in ye province of New Hampshire Esqr Addam
Winthrope John Watts David Jeffries Stephen Minot Oliver
Noyes & John Ruck all of s^d Boston Merchants on ye other

part./ Whereas Eliezer Way of Hartford in y Collony of Connecticut Merchant Son & heir of George Way Late of Dorchester in ye County of Dorset within ye Kingdom of England dec^d in & by a good deed und^r his hand & Seal bareing date ye Tenth day of Octob^r Anno Domini 1683 duly Executed & Recorded with ye Records of Deeds &c^t for ye County of york Lib^o 4to folio 18 & 19 for ye Considerations therein Mentioned did give grant Bargaine Sell Aliene Enfeoffe & Confirm unto ye s^d Richard Wharton his heirs & Assignes for ever one Moiety or halfe part or whatsoever Share part or proportion ye s^d Eliezer Way then had or in any wise ought to have or Claime of in or to a Certain tract or parcell of land Comonly Called or known by ye Name of Pejepscott Scituate Lying & being within ye Province of Maine in New Engl^d afores^d Together with one Moyety or halfe part of whatsoever other Share or part or portion be ye Same more or Less which he ye s^d Eliezer Way Then had might Should or in any wise ought to have or Claime of in or to All & Singular ye uplands Meadow lands Arrable Land Marishes Swamps Trees woods underwoods waters water Courses rivers fishing fouling Mines Mineralls Royaltys profits priviledges beaches flats rights Comoditys heridittaments Emolluments & Appurtenances whatsoever to ye pmises or any part or pcell thereof belonging or in any wise Appurtaining which s^d Tract of Land & premises for ye Space of forty years or thereabouts before ye Warr with ye Indians was in ye Actuall possession & Improvem^t of Mr Thomas Purchase dec^d and was Antiently given by Pattent from ye Councill of Plymouth within ye Kingdom of England to ye s^d George Way & Thomas Purchase deceased— And whereas John Blaney of Lynn in ye Collony of ye Massachusets & Elizabeth his wife ye Late relict widdow & Administratrix to ye Estate of Thomas Purchase aforenamed in & by a Certaine Deed of Sale und^r their hands & Seals dated ye Twenty fifth day of Octob^r 1683 Acknowledged & Recorded in ye Same book ffol^o 17 for ye Considerations therein also Expressed & with ye full & free Consent of all ye Children of ye s^d Thomas Purchase & in Order for Some further Settlem^t [57] And provision for their Subsistance & livelyhood did give grant Bargaine Sell Aliene Enfeoffe & Confirm unto ye s^d Richard Wharton his heirs & Assignes for ever all that Moyety or halfe deal & remaining Share whatsoever ye Same is or may be of ye s^d Lands Late belonging to the s^d Thomas Purchase by Vertue of ye s^d pattent or any other right in partnership with ye s^d George or Eliezer Way & all ye right

& Title propriety & Interest which ye s^d Thomas Purchase dyed Siezed of or that he might Should or Ought to have had in ye s^d province of Maine./ Together with all & Singular the uplands Arrable lands Meadow Lands Marshes Swamps Trees woods underwoods waters water courses rivers fishing fouling Mines Mineralls royaltys profits priviledges Beach flats rights Comoditys heriditaments Emolluments and Appurtenances whatsoever to ye s^d Premises or any part or parcell thereof belonging or in Any wise Appurtaining or therewith now or heretofore used Occupied or Enjoyed./ And Whereas John Shapleigh of Kittery in ye s^d Province of Maine in New England Gent heir to Major Nicholas Shapleigh late of Kittery afores^d dec^d in & by a deed of Sale und^r his hand and Seal bareing date ye fourth day of July Anno Domini 1683./ well Executed in ye Law & Recorded in the third book of Records for ye province of Maine page 127 &c^t for & in Consideration of Two hundred & Eighty pounds & other good Considerations Mentioned therein gave granted bargained Sold Demised Aliened Enfeoffed & Confirmed unto ye s^d Richard Wharton all that Tract or neck of land Called Merryconeeg lying over Against an Island Called Sebasco Alias Sequasco Diggin in Casco Bay in ye province of Maine & is bounded At ye head or uper End with the plains of pejepscot or Lands late belonging to or Claimed by Mr Purchase and on all other parts & Sides is Encompassed & bounded with & by ye Salt water and Also all that ye afores^d Island Called Sebasco Alias Sequasco Diggin Together with all rocks Shoars Beaches havens Creeks Coves & all Trees woods underwoods pools ponds waters water courses & all Minerals and Mines & all other profits priviledges Advantages & Emolluments to ye premises or any part thereof belonging or in Any wise Appurtaining To have & To hold to him ye s^d Richard Wharton his heirs & Assignes for ever as by ye s^d Deed (relation being thereunto had) will more fully Appear./ And whereas Also Warrumbee Darramkine Wihikermet Weeden Domhegon Neonongasset and Nimbanewit Sagamores of ye afores^d rivers & Land Adjacent in and by a Certaine Deed und^r their hands & Seals bareing date ye Seventh day of July Anno Domini 1684 duely proved & Enroled in ye s^d fourth Book of Records Fol^o 15 & 16—for Sundry Considerations therein Enumerated & in Confirmation of s^d Richard Whartons Title & propriety did fully freely & Absolutely give grant ratify & Confirm unto him ye s^d Richard Wharton All ye afores^d Lands from ye uppermost part of Androscoggan falls four miles westward & So down to Maycoit by ye s^d river of Pejepscot and from ye other Side of Androscoggan falls All ye Land from ye falls to Pejepscot & Merrymeeting Bay to Kennebeck & Towards ye wilderness to be bounded by a Southwest & Northeast line to Extend from ye upper part of ye s^d Androscoggan upermost falls to ye s^d river of Kennebec & all ye Land from Maycoit to Pejepscot & to run & hold ye Same Bredth where ye Land will bare it unto Atkins^s Bay in Kennebeck river & Smal point harbo^r in Casco Bay & all Island in Kennebeck & Pejepscot rivers & Merrymeeting Bay & wthin ye afores^d bounds Especially ye afores^d Neck of Land Called Merryconeeg & Island Called Sebasco Diggin Together with all rivers rivolets Brooks ponds pools waters water courses all wood Trees Timber & all Mines Minerals Quarries & Especially ye Sole & Absolute use & bennefit of Salmon & Sturgeon fishing in all ye rivers rivolets & bayes afores^d & in all rivers brooks creeks or ponds within any of ye bounds afores^d & further ye s^d Sagamores in & by ye s^d Deed gave granted bargained Sold & Confirmed unto him ye s^d Rich^d. Wharton all ye Land Lying five miles above ye upermost of ye s^d Androscoggan falls in bredth & Length holding ye Same bredth from Androscoggan falls to Kennebeck river & to be bounded by ye afores^d Southwest & Northeast line and a parcell of land at five miles distance to run from Androscoggan to Kennebeck river as afores^d Together with all ye profits priviledges Comoditys bennefits Advantages & particularly ye Sole propriety bennefit & Advantage of ye Salmon & Sturgeon fishing within ye bounds & Limits afores^d To have & To hold ye Same & Every part thereof unto ye s^d Richard Wharton his heirs & Assignes forever as in & by ye s^d Deed or ye record thereof (relation being thereunto had will among other things Appear of all which Lands & pmises ye s^d Richard Wharton dyed Siezed in his own right As a good Estate of Inheritance in ffee Simple./ Now This Indenture Witnesseth that ye Afore named Ephraim Savage pursuant to A power & Authority from ye Superio^r Court of Judicature At their Session in Boston on ye Last Tuesday of Octob^r Anno Domini 1697 to him given to make Sale of ye real Estate of ye s^d Richard Wharton dec^d Insolvent for ye Enabling him ye s^d Savage to pay ye Several Creditors to ye s^d Richard Whartons Estate their respective proportions thereof So farr as ye Same will Extend for & in Consideration of ye Sum of one hundred & fforty pounds Currant money of New England to him in hand paid at before ye delivery hereof [58] By ye s^d Thomas Hutchinson John Wentworth Adam Winthrop John Watts David Jeffries Stephen Minot Oliver Noyes & John Ruck ye receipt where-

BOOK VIII, FOL. 58.

of yᵉ sᵈ Ephraim Savage doth hereby Acknowledge & yᵉ Same to be Applyed towards payment of yᵉ Creditors of yᵉ sᵈ Richard Wharton & thereof doth Acquit & discharge yᵉ sᵈ Thomas Hutchinson John Wentworth Adam Winthrop John Watts David Jeffries Stephen Minot Oliver Noyes and John Ruck their heirs Execut^rˢ & Admrs for ever by these psents hath given granted bargained Sold released Enfeoffed & Confirmed & by these psents by Vertue of yᵉ Ordʳ of yᵉ sᵈ Superior Court doth fully freely & Absolutely give grant bargaine Sell release Enfeoffe Convey & Confirm unto them yᵉ sᵈ Thomas Hutchinson John Wentworth Adam Winthrop John Watts David Jeffries Stephen Minot Oliver Noyes & John Ruck their heirs & Assignes for ever all yᵉ afore mentioned Tract or parcel or parcels of land Called Pejepscot purchased of yᵉ sᵈ Eliezer Way & John Blaney & Elizabeth his wife Administratrix to yᵉ Estate of yᵉ sᵈ Thomas Purchase Togethʳ with all other Lands & pmises above mentioned to be by them granted & Sold to yᵉ sᵈ Richard Wharton And Also all that Tract or Neck of Land Called Merryconeeg and also all that Island Called Sebasco Alias Sequasco Digin with all other yᵉ pmises above mentioned to be bought & purchased by yᵉ sᵈ Richard Wharton of John Shapleigh & Also All yᵉ land lying five miles above yᵉ uppermost of yᵉ sᵈ Androscoggan falls & all other yᵉ Lands & premises which yᵉ sᵈ Indian Sagamores Sold Conveyed and Confirmed to yᵉ sᵈ Richard Wharton in & by yᵉ Above recited deed Togethʳ with all rivers fishing fouling mines Minerals royaltys Beaches flats Meadows Trees Cops fencing waters water courses profits priviledges & Appurᶜᵉˢ to yᵉ Same granted Lands & pmises belonging & all the Estate right Title Interest Inheritances Claime & demand whatsoever of him yᵉ sᵈ Richard Wharton & his heirs of in & to yᵉ sᵈ Lands & pmises or any part or parcell thereof with all deeds writings Evidences relating thereunto Saving & reserving out of this grant unto yᵉ sᵈ Ephraim Savage Lawsons plantation of Weskege Alias Whigby of one Thousand Acres To have & To hold yᵉ sᵈ Tract of Land Called pejepscot yᵉ neck of land Called Merryconeeg & yᵉ Island Called Sebasco Alias Sequasco Diggin & also all yᵉ land Lying five miles Above yᵉ upermost of yᵉ sᵈ Androscoggan falls & all other yᵉ above given & granted or Mentioned or Intended to be granted pmisses with their Appurtenances & Every part & parcell thereof unto them yᵉ sᵈ Thomas Hutchinson John Wentworth Adam Winthrop John Watts David Jeffries Stephen Minot Oliver Noyes & John Ruck their Severall and respective heirs & Assignes for ever Equally to be divided between them & not to hold by Survivorship to their Sole propper use bennefit

& behoofe from henceforth & for evermore reserving only as above reserved free & Clear & fully Acquitted Exonerated & Discharged of & from all & all maner of Gifts grants bargains Sales mortgages leases Wills Entails Joyntures Dowers Titles Troubles Debts Charges & Incumbrances whatsoever had made done Comitted or Suffered to be done by ye s^d Richard Wharton in his Lifetime or done Comitted or Suffered to be done Since his decease and ye s^d Ephraim Savage doth hereby Covenant promiss grant & agree to & with ye s^d Thomas Hutchinson John Wentworth Adam Winthrop John Watts David Jeffries Stephen Minot Oliver Noyes & John Ruck their Several & respective heirs & Assignes that he ye s^d Ephraim Savage in his Capacity of Adm^r as afores^d & by Vertue of ye power & Ord^r from ye s^d Superior Court of Judicature hath in himselfe full power & Lawfull Authority to grant bargaine Sell & Convey ye s^d Tracts or parcells of land Islands and Premisses with their Appurtenances & Every part thereof in manner & form as afores^d And ffurther ye s^d Ephraim Savage for himselfe his heirs Execut^{rs} & Adm^{rs} doth hereby Covenant grant & agree to Warrant & Defend all ye above given granted & bargained Lands & pmises with ye Memb^{rs} & Appurtenances belonging thereunto or to any part or parcell thereof unto them thes^d Thomas Hutchinson John Wentworth Adam Winthrop John Watts David Jeffries Stephen Minot Oliver Noyes and John Ruck their Several & respective heirs & Assignes in Severalty for ever against ye Lawfull Claims & Demands of the heirs of ye s^d Richard Wharton or of any other pson or psons from by or under him them or any or Either of them in any manner of wise./ & At any time or times hereafter at & upon ye reasonable request or demand of ye s^d Grantees their heirs or Assignes and At their Cost & Charge to do p forme & Execute Any further Act or Deed Device or Devices in ye Law for ye better Assureing Confirming & more Sure making of ye s^d bargained pmisses to them or Any of them respectively for ever as Shall or may be Lawfully Advised Devised or required So as such Assureance or Assurances Containe no other or further Warranty than As afores^d./ In Witness whereof ye s^d parties to these p^{r}sents have hereunto Interchangeably Set their hands & Seals the day & year herein first above written./   Ephraim Savage (a Seal)
Signed Sealed & Delivered in ye psence:
of us./. John Watts being Interlined in Six Severall places he being a purchaser with ye rest of ye Grantees within Named before Signing & Sealing—   John Greenough
      Thom^s Gross
      Samuel Tyley jun^r

BOOK VIII, FOL. 59.

Rec^d ye day & year first within written of ye Grantees within Named ye Sum of one hundred & forty pounds being ye full Consideration within Expressed

p Ephraim Savage

[59] Suffolk ss/ Boston Novr 6th 1714./ The within Named Ephraim Savage psonally Appearing before me under written one of his Maj^{tys} Justices of ye peace for ye County afores^d Acknowledged ye within Instrument to be his Act & Deed./ John Clark

Recorded According to ye Original Novr ye 18th 1714./

p Jos: Hamond Reg^r

Be it known unto all Christian People to whom these Presents Shall Come Greeting Know Yee that I Joshua Downing of Kittery in ye County of York within his Maj^{tys} Province of ye Massachusets Bay in New England Yeoman for and in Consideration of ye Sum of Sixty ffive pounds in Good and Currant money of the Province afores^d to me in hand Before the Ensealing hereof well and truly Paid By James Furnald of ye Same Place Afores^d yeoman ye Receipt whereof I Do hereby acknowledge and my Selfe therewith fully Satisfied Contented and paid and Doe By these Presents acquitt and Discharge ye S^d James Furnald his heirs Execut^{rs} admin^{rs} forever By these Presents have Granted Bargained Sold aliened Conveyed and Confirmed and By these presents Do freely fully and absolutely give Grant Bargain Sell alien Convey & Confirm unto him ye S^d James Furnald his heirs & assignes forever a Certain Tract of Land Scituate lying & being in Kittery in ye County afores^d Containing fforty acree of land & is that forty acres of Land that was Granted unto me by ye Town of Kittery the 20th of March in ye year 1678/9 & Laid out unto me by Capt John wincol the 28th of March 1679 : begining att ye East Side of a Brook known By ye name of Simons his Brook & Runs from thence two hundred and Sixteen poles north East and be East in Length and thirty Pole in Breadth South East and be South bounded with ye land of Major Joseph Hamond Esqr on ye South East and ye two Eands and ye north west Side with Comons To Have To Hold ye S^d granted & Bargained Premeses with all ye appurtenances Priviledges and Commodities to the Same Belonging or or in any wayes Appurtaining as Timber wood underwood Standing or lying on ye s^d land to him ye s^d James Furnald his heirs & Assigns forever to his and their Only proper use benefit & behalfe

Book VIII, Fol. 59.

forever & I y[e] s[d] Joshua Downing for me my heirs Execut[rs] Administrat[rs] doe Covenant promise and Grant to & with y[e] s[d] James ffurnald his heirs & assignes that before y[e] EnSealing hereof I am y[e] true Sole & Lawfull owner of y[e] above Bargained pmises & am lawfully Seized & posesed of y[e] Same in mine own proper Right as a good perfect & absolute Estate of inheritance in fee Simple & have in my Selfe Good Right full power & lawfull authority to grant bargain Sell & Convey Said bargained pmises in manner as aboves[d] & that the S[d] James Fernald his heirs or assignes forever hereafter by fforce & vertue of these Presents Lawfully Peaceably & Quietly have hold use Occupie poses & Injoy y[e] s[d] demised pmises with y[e] appurtenances free & Clear & freely & Clearly acquited & discharged of from all & all manner of fformer & other gifts grants bargains Sales Leases Mortgages wills Entails Jointurs & dowers Judgments Executions Incumbrances and Extents further more I y[e] s[d] Joshua Downing for my Selfe my heires Execut[rs] Administrat[rs] do Covenant & Engage y[e] above demised pmises to him y[e] s[d] James Furnald his heires & asignes against the Lawfull Claimes or demands of any person or persons whatsoever forever hereafter to warrant Secure & defend In Witness whereof I have hereunto Set my hand & Seal this Seventeenth day of November in y[e] y[e] year of our Lord one thousand Seven hundred & ffourteen   Joshua Downing (Seal)
Signed Sealed & Delivered
In y[e] Presents of y[e] Subscriber
William Jones
William Godsoe
      the mark of
Elizabeth F Godsoe

Prov: of New hampsh[r] Novbr: 18[th] 1714
Joshua downing this day personally appearing before me y[e] Subscriber acknowledged the above Instrument to be his act and Deed and Rebeccah his wife being att Same time p[r]sent resigned up her thirds of dowery &·
    Sam[ll] Penhallow Just
Recorded According to y[e] Original Novemb[r] y[e] 20[th] 1714./
    p Jos: Hamond Reg[r]

To All Christian People to whom this psent deed of Sale may Come or Concern Micom Mackentier of york in y[e] County of york in y[e] Province of y[e] Massachusets Bay in New England Sendeth Greeting Know Yce y[t] for & in Considera-

Book VIII, Fol. 60.

tion of a Sertain Peace of Salt marsh & thatch banck on ye South West Side of s^d york River delivered by a deed & Confirmed by lie^{tt} James Plaisted of afores^d york s^d micom hath given granted bargained Sold alienated Enfeoffed & Confirmed and doth by these Presents give grant bargain Sell alienate Enfeoffe & Confirm & fully freely & absolutely make over unto ye S^d Plaisteed a Sertain pease or perSell of upland Swampy land & Meadow Containing by Estemation ten acres be it more or less Lying & being within ye township or pSing^{tt} of afores^d york & Scittuate upon ye Northeast Side of S^d york River on the South East Side of bass Cove Crick which land & meddow was formerly in ye possession of Wm Pearce but of late years in ye Possession of s^d micoms Fathers But Sence his fathers deseas in S^d micoms Possession & is bounded as followeth Viz^t by ye Mash of bass Cove on ye Northwest Side & from a Small gusell or Cove to a wallnut tree markt fore Sides & So is Divided by a Strait line down to york river Joining to Willm Bracys Land on ye South East Side which was laid out wth it Septr ye 16: 1701. Together with all the Rights benifits Emoliments advantages & Priviledges their: unto belonging or any ways at any times Redowning to ye Same or any part or parcell thereof To have and to hold & quietly & Peasably to Posses Occupy & Injoy as a sure Estate in fee Simple unto him ye s^d James Plaisted his heires Execut^{rs} administrat^{rs} & assignes forever: more over ye s^d Micom [60] Doth for him Selfe his heires Execut^{rs} & admin^{rs} to & with ye S^d James his heires Executors administrators & assignes Covenant Ingage & Promiss the aboveS^d land and Meadow or Mash to be free and Clear from all former gifts gants Sales Suits Mortgages Sales and Incumberments whatsoever as also from all future Claims or Suits to be had or Comenced by him ye s^d Micum or any other from by or under him or any other person or persons WhatSoever Proseeding the date of this Instrument and that he ye S^d Micom doth warrantise the S^d Land & Mash with all their Priviledges unto y^e s^d James Plaisteed as aboves^d: In Witness whereof y^e above S^d Micom Mackintier hath hereto Set tu his hand & Seal this Seventh day of January in the year of our Lord one thousand Seven hundred and Eight & C   Micom :: Mackintier ($_{Seal}^a$)
Signed Sealed &
   Delivered in Presents of
   Joseph : Banks
   Abraham Preble Junr
   Micom : Mackintier above S^d Parsonaly appeared before

BOOK VIII, FOL. 60.

me y^e Subscriber & acknowledged y^e above written Deed of Sale to be his act and Deed this 26th day of february 1707/8
       Abra^m Preble Justis a peac
Recorded According to the Original Novr 22^d 1714./
       p Jos : Hammond Reg^r/

 To All Christian people to whom these psents may Come or doth concern George Stover of york in ye County of york in ye Province of Maine in New England yeoman Send Greeting Know Yee ye s^d George Stover for & in Consideration of a Deed of quit Claim given to him the s^d George by his brother John Stover of ye Town & County aboves^d for a parcill or Percells of land & Meadow within ye Township of s^d york as by s^d Deed doth at large appear at ye resait whereof ye s^d George doth Acknowledge himSelfe therewith to be fully : paid Sattisfyed and Contented for & of all & every part & Parcill of ye Estate of Inheritance raile & Personal which he ye s^d George Should or oft of right to have or Receave by will deed Joynture land or Equitie which did of late belong to ye s^d Stovers father Late of s^d york Deceased whose name was Silvester Stover & he ye s^d George doth by these Presents both for him Selfe his heires Execut^{rs} & admin^{rs} & assignes acquit discharge & Exonerate & forever remis & releace his above Said brother John Stover His heires & Assignes forever for & of ye whole of the pmisses hereafter Set forth & Expreed the which he hath given granted bargained Sold aliened Enfeoffed & assigned & doth by these Presents give grant bargain Sell alien Enfeoffe & assigne & fully freely & absolutely make over & confirm unto his s^d Brother John Stover his heires & assignes forever his whole Right Title & Interest which he ye s^d George Now hath or ever ought to have unto any part or percill of land Meadow orchard house or housing or any Priviledg thing or things Belonging to ye place or Inheritance where his s^d Brother John Stover Now liveth & hath lately Erected & built a new house with : out houes Scituated upon ye South west Side of Cape neddick River in Said york ye which was ye homesteed of his above s^d father Silvester Stover where he formerly dwelt the bounds & quantity thereof by deed or deeds & Town grant on Record Reference there unto being had may att large appear together with all ye right Title Interest Priviledges advantages & appurtenances thereunto belonging or any part or parcill thereof unto him ye s^d John Stover his heires & Assignes forever

Book VIII, Fol. 61.

To have and To hold & quiately & peaceably to posses occupie & Injoy as asure Estate in fee Simple more over ye s^d George doth for him Selfe his heirs Execut^rs & administrat^rs as also from all persons from by and under him Covenant Ingage and Promise to and with the s^d John his heires & assignes that from & after the date hereof he doth warrantise & will defend ye above bargained pmisses with all its Priviledges according to ye Tonor hereof In witness hereof ye above s^d George Stover & abagail his wife have hereunto Set their hands & Seals this fifteenth day of November in ye year of our Lord one thousand Seven hundred and fourteen & in ye first year of ye Raign of our Soveraign Lord George King of grate Brittain & : C //

Signed Sealed & delivered   George Stover (Seal)
  in Presence of us wittnesses
  Lues Bane   Abagail <u>her</u> Stover (Seal)
  Abra^m Preble   mark
  Samuel Steuart

York ss Memorandom york November the 16th 1714./ ye within named George Stover & abagail Stover Personaly appeared before me ye Subscriber one of his Maj^tys Justices of ye Peace within s^d County & freely acknowledged ye within quitclaime or Instrument to be their free act & deed with their hands & Seals affixed their unto
                                        John Wheelwright
Recorded According to ye Original Novr 24th 1714./
                                          p Jos : Hamond Reg^r

[61] To All Christian People to whom this psent deed of Sale shall Come Greeting Know yee that I Allexander Tompson of york in ye County of York in his Maj^tys Province of ye Massachusets Bay in New England Shumaker with Consent of Anne my wife for & in Consideration of a Considerable Sum of money to me in hand paid by Wm Rogers of Kittery in ye County aboves^d yeoman have given granted Sold and Confirmed & do by these presents give grant bargaine Sell Alienate & Confirm unto William Rogers aboves^d his heirs or Assigns forever a piece or parcell of Land Containing Twenty Acres which Land was granted by ye Town of Kittery May Sixteenth one Thousand Six hundred Ninty four & was laid out by Mr Wm Godsoe Decemb^r Twenty Seventh 1698 & Lyes near Spruce Creek road bounded by Thomas Rice his land on ye North & is one hundred &

Twenty poles in Length East & is Twenty Seven poles in bredth North & South referrence Thereunto being had on Kittery Record./ To have & To hold all & Singular ye aboves^d piece or parcell of land with all priviledges of Timber Trees woods water Courses./ And I ye s^d Allexander Tompson do for my Selfe my heirs Execut^{rs} & Adm^{rs} Covena^t & promiss to & with ye s^d William Rogers his heirs Execut^{rs} Adm^{rs} and Assignes that I have in my Selfe good right full power & Lawfull Authority to Sell ye pmisses & that it is free & clear from all former gifts grants Leases Mortgages Wills Entailments or any Incumbor whatsoever./ And further I ye s^d Allexander Tompson do for my Selfe my heirs Execut^{rs} Adm^{rs} & Assignes do Covenant and promiss to & with ye aboves^d William Rogers his heirs Execut^{rs} Adm^{rs} or Assigns that I will forever Save harmless warrant & Defend as by this psents & Acknowledge my Selfe Satisfied Contented & paid all ye aboves^d Sum of money & Every part thereof In Witness hereunto I have Set to my hand & Seal y^e Sixth day of November in y^e year of our lord one Thousand Seven hundred and ffourteen & in y^e first year of y^e Reign of our Soveraign Lord George of Great Brittaine ffrance & Ireland King Defend^r of y^e faith &c^t./

Signed, Sealed & Delivered   Allexander Thompson.(s$_{eale}^a$)
In psence of
William 𝔔 Beale (his mark)   Anne 𝔔 Thompson (s$_{eale}^a$) (her mark)
Sarah C Pope (her mark)
Daniel Emery

York Allexand^r Thompson psonally appeared before me one of his Maj^{tys} Justices of y^e peace & Acknowledged this Instrument to be his Volluntary Act & Deed this 15th of Novr one Thousand Seven hundred & fourteen & in y^e first year of King George Over Great Brittaine &c^t

                         John Plaisted Justice peace
Recorded According to ye Original Decemb^r ye 1st 1714
                         p Jos Hamond Reg^r

Know All men by these psents that I Samuel Skillion of Kittery in the County of York in New England Shipwright for ye Consideration of forty Shillings Curra^t money of New England paid before ye Signing & Sealing hereof have given

granted bargained Sold Aliened made over & Confirmed unto William Wilson of y[e] afores[d] Town & County Thirty Acres of a grant which is part of A ffifty Acre grant granted to s[d] Skillion by y[e] Town of Kittery in y[e] year 1703./ And for y[e] True pformance whereof I y[e] s[d] Sam[ll] Skillion do bind my Selfe my heirs Execut[rs] & Adm[rs] that he y[e] s[d] W[m] Wilson his heirs Execut[rs] Adm[rs] or Assignes Shall forever have y[e] Thirty Acres of the grant As Afores[d] to his or his heirs or Assigns disposeing of as they Se fitting./ In Witness whereof I have hereunto Set my hand & Seale this first day of July Anno Domini 1714 Sam[ll] Skillion (Seal[a])
Signed Sealed & Delivered
  In psence of
  Diggery his Robins
   mark ⋎)
  W[m] Pepperrell jun[r]
The 3[d] day of July 1714 This day Sam[ll] Skillion psonally Appeared before me y[e] Subscrib[r] one of her Maj[tys] Justices of y[e] peace & Acknowledged this above written Deed or Obligation to be his free Act & Deed./   W[m] Pepperrell
  Recorded According to y[e] Original July 10th 1714./
                    p Jos. Hamond Reg[r]

Know all men by these presents that wee John Tompson & John Paul both of Kittery in y[e] County of york for a valluable Consideration to us in hand paid by Thomas Knight of y[e] Same place Cordwainer y[e] receipt thereof we do Confess & our Selves there with Contented & fully paid have Given granted bargained & Sold unto y[e] abous named Thomas Knight his heires or assignes forever all that tract or parcell of land lying in y[e] township of Kittery Joining To our house lotts being by Eastemation about ffive acres & a halfe of Land being bounded & Takes its begining att a red birtch Tree joining unto Richard Kings land & from thence right athirt John Tompsons lott to a rock Seet up for a bound mark between them in y[e] line that was laid out to go to y[e] Town Comons & from thence about twenty Eight rod down y[e] s[d] lane to two beach trees Standing together att y[e] foot of John Tompsons lott & from thence to Kittery road on a Straight line about twenty Eight rod to a Stake Sett up by Kittery road for a land mark & from that Stake by Richard Kings [62] Land To the afore s[d] Red birtch y[e]

lower part of s^d land lyes in form of a Triangle./ To have & To hold all ye aboves^d Tract of land as it is deScribed & Sett forth unto ye ondly & Sole use of him the Said Thomas Knight his heires or assignes forever more & further more we ye Said John Tompson & John Paul doe for our Selves & our heires Covenant to & with ye s^d Thomas Knight & his heires that we are the True & proper owners thereof & have within our Selves full power to Sell & dispose of ye Same ye peaceable & Quiate possession thereof to warrand & forever defend against all parsons laying a lawfull Claime thereunto Wittness our hands & Seales this Sixth day of October one thousand Seven hundred & Seven : : 1707
Signed Sealed & delivered   John Tompson (seal)
   in ye presents of us ye Subscriber John Paul (seal)
Elezer Coleman
John Morgeredg
William Godsoe
York ss march : 8th 1713/14. the above named John Tompson & John Paul Personally appearing Acknowledged ye above written Instrument to be their free act & deed before me :   Charles ffrost J peace
   Recorded According to ye Original March 8th 1713/4
                        p Jos : Hamond Reg^r

    To All People to whom these psents shall Come Greeting & Know yee that I Richard Crocket of Exeter in ye County of Portsmouth in her Maj^{tys} Province of New Hampshire in New England husbandman for & in Consideration of ye Sum of a hundred pounds money to me in hand well & Truely paid by Henry Barter of Kittery on Piscattaqua river ffisherman ye rec^t whereof I do hereby Acknowledge & my Selfe therewith fully Satisfied & Contented & thereof & of Every part and parcell thereof do Acquit & discharge ye s^d Henry Barter his heirs Execut^{rs} & Adm^{rs} forever by these psents Have given granted bargained Sold Aliened Conveyed & Confirmed And by these psents do fully freely & Absolutely give grant Bargaine Sell Aliene Convey & Confirm unto him ye s^d Henry Barter his heirs & Assignes forever one Certaine pcell of upland & Marsh Scittuate Lying & being in ye Township of Kittery Afores^d Containing by Estamation forty Acres be ye Same more or Less bounded with ye Eastward Side of s^d Richard Crockets Orchard & on ye westw^d Side Spruse Creek & on ye Northw^d Side Tuckers Creek which land is known & Called by ye Name of Crockets neck & was formerly in ye possession of Thomas Crocket dec^d & Then in ye possession of Ephraim Crocket dec^d And Now Was in ye Possession of ye Aboves^d Richard Crocket To have & To hold y^es^d granted & bargained pmises with all ye Appurtenances priviledges and Comoditys to ye Same belonging or in any wayes Appurtaining to him ye s^d Henry Barter his heirs & Assignes forever to his and their only proper use bennefit & behoofe./ And I ye s^d Richard Crocket for me my heirs Execut^rs & Adm^rs do Covenant promiss & grant to & with ye s^d Henry Barter his heirs & Assignes that before The Ensealing hereof I am ye True Sole & Lawfull owner of ye above bargained pmises & have in my Selfe good right full power & Lawfull Authority to grant bargaine Sell Convey & Confirm s^d Bargained pmises in maner as aboves^d & that ye s^d Henry Barter his heirs & Assignes Shall & may from Time to Time & at all Times forever hereafter by force & vertue of these psents Lawfully peaceably & Quietly have hold use Occupy possess & Enjoy ye s^d Demised & bargained pmises with the Appurtenances free & clear & clearly Acquitted & discharged of & from all & all maner of former & other gifts grants bargains Sales Titles Troubles & Incumbrances whatsoever ffurthermore I ye s^d Richard Crocket for my Selfe my heirs Execut^rs Adm^rs do Covenant & Ingage ye above demised pmises to him ye s^d Henry Barter his heirs & Assignes against ye Lawfull Claims or demands of Any pson or psons whatsoever forever hereafter to Warrant Secure and defend, And Deberoh Crocket wife of me ye s^d Richard Crocket doth by these psents freely and Willingly give yield up & Surrend^r all her right of Dowry & power of Thirds of in & unto ye above demised pmises unto him ye s^d Henry Barter his heirs & Assignes forever

In Witness whereof wee have hereunto Set our hands & Sealls ye Twenty Sixth day in ye Twelfth year of her Maj^tys Reign Anno Domini 1713./ It is further to be understood that ye bounds of ye aboves^d land is As followeth begining at ye well Cove & So runing back North the East half Easterly on ye Eastward Side of s^d Richard Crockets Orchard by ye Side of s^d Parrets land Thirty Six pole & from Thence East North ye East halfe Northerly to An old bass Stump Sixteen pole & from Thence by ye North Side of Anne Robings land running South west a Little westerly Twenty four pole & halfe to a heap of Stones & from Thence upon a South & by East Course to a bound Stone by ye Easterd Side of s^d Robings lands Sixteen pole & halfe & then runing upon a north ye East and be East Course Seventeen pole Towards Henry Barters house to another bound Stone &

Book VIII, Fol. 63.

from Thence up to a Spruce Tree Standing near y‍e Spring Cove Called y‍e back Spring by y‍e s‍d Barters [63] Land upon a North Course a little Easterly Sixty four pole & halfe　　　　　　　　　　　　Richard Crocket (a Seale)

Signed Sealed & Delivered
 In presents of   Deberoh 〇 Crocket (a Seal)
 Diamond Sargent   mark
 William Pepperrel jun‍r
 W‍m Pepperrell

Kittery 5‍th day of July 1714./ Then Richard Crocket & his wife Deberoh Crocket both psonally Appeared before me y‍e Subscriber one of her Maj‍tys Justices of y‍e peace & Acknowledged y‍e above written deed to be their free Act & deed　　　　　　　　　　　　　　W‍m Pepperrell

Recorded According to y‍e Original Decemb‍r y‍e 1‍st 1714./
        p Jos: Hamond Reg‍r

Know All men by these psents that I John Skriggin of Kittery in y‍e County of york in y‍e Province of y‍e Massachusets Bay in New England am holden & Stand firmly bound unto John Paul of y‍e Same Town and Province in y‍e Sum of Twenty pounds Curra‍t money of New England to be paid to y‍e s‍d John Paul his heirs Execut‍rs & Adm‍rs to y‍e True paym‍t of which I bind my Selfe my heirs Execut‍rs or Adm‍rs firmly by these psents Sealed with my Seal./ Dated this 17‍th day of Novemb‍r 1714 Annoq‍ Regni Georgii Regis Primo./

The Condition of this Obligation is Such that whereas there is a Controversie between y‍e s‍d John Skriggin & y‍e s‍d John Paul relating to y‍e Estate of Stephen Paul dec‍d They haveing chosen M‍r Joseph Hamond and M‍r John Woodman to Arbitrate & decide y‍e s‍d Controversie and all other differences that are now between them with pow‍r to choose A Third pson as Umpire in Case y‍e s‍d Hamond & Woodman Cannot agree Now if y‍e aboves‍d John Skriggin Shall Stand and abide by y‍e Award or decision that Shall be made by y‍e s‍d Hamond & Woodman or if they chose a Third pson then by y‍e Major part of y‍e s‍d Three psons then this Obligation is to be voyd otherwise to remain in full force & Vertue

 Witnessed by us   John Skriggin (a Seale)
 John Tompson
 Benj‍a Gambling

Recorded According to y‍e Original Dec‍r 6‍th 1714./
        p Jos: Hamond Reg‍r—

Book VIII, Fol. 63.

Whereas wee y® Subscrib™ being Chosen & Appointed by John Paul & John Skriggin of Kittery in y® County of york to Arbitrate & decide all differences between them relating to y® Estate of Stephen Paul Late of s^d Kittery dec^d & all other Controversies now between them &c^t wee haveing this day mett & heard y® debates of both partyes & their Evidences & pleas of both Sides and upon mature Consideration of y® Same have Awarded that y® s^d John Skriggin do forever hereafter rest Satisfied & Contented with what he has rec^d of y® Estate of y® s^d Stephen Paul dec^d & for all other Accot^s & reconings between them from y® begining of y® world to y® day of y® date hereof

2dly That y® s^d John Paul do rest Satisfied & Contented with what he has rec^d of y® s^d John Skriggin on any Acco^t whatsoever And that they be hereby debarred for ever hereafter from any Action or Suit whatsoever to be brought Each against other for or Conserning y® Estate of Stephen Paul dec^d or for any other Acco^t or Controversie whatsoever from y® begining of y® world to this day

3dly Wee Award that y® s^d Paul & Skriggin pay us y® Arbitrat^rs 5/ Each and that all other Charges & Expences of this day be Equally born by them./ In Witness whereof wee have Set our hands & Seals this Sixth day of December 1714./

Annoq Regni Georgii Regis Primo   Jos: Hamond (a seal)
                                   John Woodman (a Seal)

Recorded According to y® Original Decr 6th 1714./

p Jos: Hamond Reg^r

Know All men by these psents that I Richard Randol of Dover in the province of New Hampshire in New England for and in Consideration of y® Natural Love & Affection which I bear to my Two Soñs Richard Randol & William Randol do by these presents by way of Deed of Gift give grant Aliene Assigne Enfeoffe Set over & Confirm and have hereby given granted Aliened Assigned Enfeoffed Set over & Confirmed unto my Two Soñs Richard Randol & Wm Randol their heirs & Assigns for ev^r Thirty Acres of Land Viz^t fifteen Acres to Each Scittuate lying & being in y® Town of Kittery in y® County of York in y® Province of y® Massachusets Bay in New England which Thirty Acres was given to me y® doner hereof by y® s^d Town of Kittery May y® Tenth Seventeen hundred & three & lyeth on y® North west

Book VIII, Fol. 64.

Side within ye bounds of Richard Toziars hundred Acres//
[64] as by ye returne of Daniel Emery Surveyer dated March 27th 1712 At large may Appear To have & To hold ye s^d Thirty Acres of land Viz^t fifteen Acres each with all ye rights profits priviledges & Appurtenances thereunto belonging to them ye s^d Richd Randol & Wm Randol their and Each of their heirs & Assignes for ever & it Shall & may be Lawfull to & for ye s^d Richard Randol & William Randol my Two Soñs to have hold use Occupy possess & Enjoy ye Same them their heirs and Assigns for ever Quietly & peaceably without Any manner of Reclaim Challenge or demand from me ye s^d Richard Randol ye father my heirs Execut^{rs} or Adm^{rs} & from all other pson or psons whatsoever laying Legall Claime thereunto Shall & will warrant Acquit and Defend them my Two Soñs in ye Quiate & peaceable possession thereof from henceforth & for ever./ In Witness whereof I ye s^d Richard Randol have hereunto Set my hand & Seal ye 21st day of Jan^{ry} Annoq, Domini 1712/3

Signed Sealed & Deliver^d   his mark
 In ye psence of   Richard R Randol (_{Seale}^a)
 James ffrost.
 Love Roberts
 York ss/ Richard Randol Senr psonally Appeared & Acknowledged the Above written Instrum^t to be his Act & deed at Kittery y^e   Jan^{ry} 1712/3
        Before me   Ichabod Plaisted Just^s Peace
 Recorded According to ye Original Decr 16 : 1714./
                    p Jos: Hamond Reg^r

Know All men by these psents that I Richard Toziar of Kittery in ye County of york in ye Province of Massachusets bay in New England for and in Consideration of ye Natural love & Affection which I bear to my Two Nephews Richard Randol & William Randol do by these psents by way of Deed of Gift give grant Aliene Assigne Enfeoffe Set over and Confirm And have hereby given granted Aliened Assigned Enfeoffed Set over & Confirmed unto my Two Nephews Richard Randol & Wm Randol their heirs & Assigns forever. Ten acres of Land Viz^t five Acres to Each Scittuate lying & being in Kittery afores^d which Ten Acres Land was given to me ye Doner hereof by ye s^d Town of Kittery may Tenth Seventeen hundred & Three & lyeth on the Northwest Side within ye bounds of s^d Toziars hundred

Book VIII, Fol. 64.

Acres As by ye returne of Daniel Emery Surveyer dated March 27th 1712. At Large may Appear To have & To hold ye s^d Ten Acres of land Viz^t five acres to Each with all ye rights profits priviledges & Appurtenances thereunto belonging to them ye s^d Richard Randol and William Randol their and Each of their heirs & Assigns forever And it Shall & may be lawfull to & for ye s^d Richard Randol & William Randol to have hold use Occupie possess & Enjoy ye Same Them their heirs & Assigns forever Quiatly & peaceably without any Mañer of reclaime Challenge or demand from me ye s^d Richard Toziar my heirs Execut^{rs} or Adm^{rs} and from all other pson or psons whatsoever laying legal claime thereunto Shall & will Warrant Acquitt & defend them y^e s^d Richard Randol & William Randol in y^e Quiet & peaceable possession thereof from henceforth & forever./ In Witness whereof I y^e s^d Richard Toziar have hereunto Set my hand & Seal y^e 21th day of January Annoq, Domini : 1712/13./
Signed Sealed & Delivered   Richard Toziar (s$_{eal}^a$)
In the presence of
James Frost
Love Roberts
 York ss/
Richard Toziar psonally Appeared and Acknowledged y^e above written Instrum^t to be his Act & Deed at Kittery the — January 1712/13./
    Before me   Ichabod Plaisted Justice of peace
Recorded According to y^e Original Decr 16th 1714./
          p Jos : Hamond Reg^r

Know All men by these psents that I John Gowen of Kittery in the County of york within her Maj^{tys} Province of ye Massachusets Bay in New England Marrin^r for & in Consideration of ye Sum of Ten pounds Currant money of New England Afores^d to me in hand well & Truely paid by John ffrost of New Castle within her Maj^{tys} Province of New Hampshire Marrin^r the receipt whereof I do hereby Acknowledge & my Selfe therewith fully Satisfied Contented & paid have given granted bargained & Sold and do by these psents give grant bargaine Sell & for ever Set over unto ye s^d John Frost his heirs & Assignes for ever a Certaine Tract or plat of land Containing ffifty Acres Lying within ye Township of Kittery formerly So Called & now Berwick & is ye fifty Acres that was given unto ye s^d Gowen by ye Town

Book VIII, Fol. 65.

of Kittery At a Town Meeting held on May ye Tenth 1703 : & laid out unto ye s^d Gowen Novemb^r ye fourteenth one Thousand Seven hundred & Nine and lyes ffifty poles in bredth East & west & one hundred & Sixty poles in Length North & South & bounded on ye East by Daniel Emerys land & Comons & on ye South by Wm Grants Meadow & on west y^e & North [65] with Comons as may more at Large Appear by ye returne on Record All ye s^d ffifty acres of Land with all ye Trees Timber wood und^r wood water & water Courses mines mineralls profits and priviledges & Appurtenances thereunto belonging or Appurtaining To have & To hold all ye aboves^d Land woods & pmises herein before mentioned & Granted bargained & Sold unto him ye s^d John ffrost his heirs & Assignes to his & their own proper use bennefit & behoofe for ever And I ye s^d John Gowen my heirs Execut^{rs} & Adm^{rs} to him y^e s^d John ffrost his heirs & Assignes Shall & will Warrant & for ever defend and Confirm y^e Title of y^e afores^d Land & pmises unto y^e s^d John ffrost his heirs & Assignes./. In Witness whereof I y^e s^d John Gowen & Mercy my wife have hereunto Set our hands & Seals this first day of June Annoq$_s$ Domini 1714./

Signed Sealed & Delivered   John Gowen ($_{Seale}^{a}$)
  In presence of us   Mercy Gowen ($_{Seale}^{a}$)
  Daniel Emery
  Tim^o Waymouth
  John Morriss
    York ss/ Decr 7 : 1714.

The within named John Gowen and Mercy Gowen Acknowledged the within written Instrum^t to be their ffree Act & Deed   Before me   Charles ffrost J peace
   Recorded According to y^e Original Decr 10th 1714./
                         p Jos: Hamond Reg^r

Burrell
To
Came

To All People to whom these presents Shall Come Greeting that I John Burrell & Hannah my wife of york in ye County of York wthin his Ma^{tys} Province of ye Massachusets Bay in New England for and in Consideration of a valluable Sum to uss in hand before: ye Ensealing: hereof well & truly paid by Samuel Came: of: y^e: aboveS^d: place County & Province Receipt whereof wee do: hereby acknowledge: &: our: Selves therewith: fully Satisfied & Contented & thereof and; of every part & parcel thereof do Exonerate Acquit & Discharge the S^d Sam^{ll}

Book VIII, Fol. 65.

Came his heires Executors Administrat[rs] forever by these Presents have given granted bargained Sold aliened Conveyed & Confirmed & by these Presents do freely fully & absolutely give grant bargain Sell Aliene convey & Confirm unto him y[e] S[d] Samuel Came his heirs & Assignes forever all y[e] marsh & Thatch banks be it more or less Scituated : & lying upon the South East Side of bass Cove in york which leads up to y[e] Country Road that goes to Scotland : To have and To Hold y[e] s[d] granted and bargained Premises with all the Appurtenances Priviledges & Commdites To the Same belonging or in any wise appertaining to him y[e] s[d] Sam[ll] Came his heirs & assigns forever To his and their own proper use benifit and behoof forever and wee the Said John Burrel & Hannah his wife for our Selves our heires Executors Admin[r] do Covenant promise grant to and with the Said Samuel Came his heires & assignes that before y[e] Ensealing hereof wee are y[e] true Sole and lawfull owner of y[e] above bargained pmises and are Lawfully Seized & : possessed of y[e] Same in : our : own proper Right as a good perfect & absolute Estate of Inheritance in Fee Simple & have in our Selves good Right full power & Lawfull Authority to grant bargain Sell Convey & Confirm S[d] bargained pmises in manner As above s[d] and that the s[d] Sam[ll] Came his heires and assignes Shall & may from time to time : and : at : all : times forever hereafter by force & virtue of these Presents lawfully peaceably & quietly have hold use occupie possess and injoy y[e] s[d] Demised and bargained pmises with y[e] appurtenances free & and clear and freely & Clearly acquitted Exonerated Discharged of from all and all manner of former & other other gifts grants bargaines Sales Leases Mortgages wills Entails joyntures Dowries judgments Executions : Incumbrances & Extents Furthermore : Wee the s[d] John : Barrel : & : hannah for our : Selves Our Heires Executors administrators do Covenant and Ingage y[e] above Demised pmises to him y[e] s[d] Sam[ll] Came his Heires & assignes against y[e] lawfull Claimes or demands of any person or persons whatsoever forever hereafter to Warrant Secure & defend in Witness whereof wee have hereunto Set to our hands and Seales this fourth day of January in y[e] year of our Lord God One Thousand Seven hundred and ffourteen & in y[e] first year of Our Soveraigne Lord George by y[e] grace of God King King of great Brittain &c[t]

Signed Sealed and   John Burrell (a Seal)
   Delivered in presence of   mark
   Joseph Moulton   Hannah X Burrell (a Seal)
   Nathaniel Freeman
   James Grant

York ss Jan^ry 5 : 1714/5./ The above named John Burrill acknowledged the above written Instrument to be his free Act and Deed Before me :   Charles ffrost J : Peace
Recorded According to ye Original Jan^ry 5th 1714/5
           p Jos : Hamond Reg^r

That Whereas I Edward Rishworth of York in New England do Stand Indebted to my uncle Mr Richard Hutchinson of London Merch^t for Several pcells of goods rec^d of his Agents to ye Vallue of Thee hundred fifty Nine pounds 8^s 10^d which at psent I am uncapeable to discharge but very willing to Secure by ye greatest part of what Estate I have in my hands & to reserve ye Same free from all future [66] Alienations & Intanglements unto any pson whatsoever in Signification whereof I ye s^d Rishworth by this Obligation doe bind over unto Mr Eliakim Hutchinson Agent & Attorney for ye afores^d Mr Richard Hutchinson & Assigne my Sole Interest & right in a Certaine pcell of upland lying & being next unto Tho : Moultons & Nath^ll Maystersons lands to ye Quantity of 70 Acres & Likewise all & Every part of my Meadow lying & being upon ye Northwest Side of ye old mill creek from ye first Cove above ye old mill unto ye head of ye s^d Creek with all ye priviledges & Appurtenances thereof And Also I make over Two thirds of what Cattle I have in ye hands of Tho : Bragdon when divided & in Case of my Mortallity & in ye mean Time if I live & provided that after Seven years be Expired & in that time no better way by ye s^d Rishworth Can be propounded to Satisfie his s^d Debt Then he hereby promisses to own a Judgment upon ye s^d lands & Cattle mentioned unto ye s^d Eliakim Hutchinson which Shall be without any trouble or delay Legally and Indifferently Apprized by Two Equall minded psons & delivered into his hands in his fathers behalfe to make Satisfaction for y^e Same./ In Testimony whereof I have hereunto Affixed my hand & Seal y^e 9th day of Octob^r 1668/   Edw : Rishworth (Se^a_ale)

In psence of
Sa : Hutchinson
Wm Hutchinson

The within mentioned Seventy Acres of land I Acknowledge to have Sold unto James Plaisted of York As Witness my hand this Eleventh of Aug^st 1699.   E^m Hutchinson

I Eliakim Hutchinson do Assigne over unto James Plaisted of York all my right Title & Interest of All y^e

within mentioned lands & Stock to him & his heirs for ever this 8th of July 1707 as well for my father Richard Hutchinson as my Selfe As Witness my hand Em Hutchinson
Sealed & Delivered
  In psence of us
  Benja Bromsdon
  Nathaniel Balston junr .
    Suff: ss: Boston 8th July 1707
  Eliakim Hutchinson psonally Appeared before me ye Subscribr Acknowledged ye Above Instrumt or Assignment to be his Act & Deed Tho: Palmer Justice peace
  Recorded According to ye Original Janry ye 18th 1714/5
                    p Jos: Hamond Regr

Memorandum ffolo 176. This Deed of Mortgage is discharged in this book Att Jos Hamond Regr

This Indenture made ye 27th day of Decembr Anno Domini one Thousand Seven hundred & fourteen Annoq, Ri Ris Georgii Mags Brittania &ct Primo Between Peter Nowell of York within ye County of York & Province of ye Massachusets Bay in New England Yeoman of ye one part And Ebenezar Pemberton of Boston in ye County of Suffolk & Province aforesd Clerk on ye other part Witnesseth that ye sd Peter Nowell by & with ye free & full Consent of Sarah his wife Testified by her Signing & Sealing of these psents for & in Consideration of ye Sum of One hundred & fifty pounds in good & Lawfulll Publick Bills of Cridit on the Province abovesd to him in hand at & before ye Ensealing & Delivery hereof well & Truely paid by ye sd Ebenezer Pemberton The receipt whereof he hereby Acknowledgeth & himSelfe therewith fully Satisfied & Contented and thereof Doth fully Acquitt & discharge ye sd Ebenezar Pemberton his heirs & Assigns for ever hath given granted bargained Sold released Enfeoffed Conveyed & Confirmed & by these presents doth give grant bargaine Sell release Enfeoffe Convey & Confirm unto ye sd Ebenezer Pemberton his heirs & Assignes forever All that his full Three Quarters or fourth parts of a Certain ffarm Tract or parcell of Land Scittuate Lying & being at a place Called Scotland in ye Town of York aforesd ye whole Containing One hundred & Thirty Acres more or Less butted & bounded Southerly upon york river Easterly upon land of Allexander Maxwell & Micum Mackintire Westerly upon Curtis' Cove how ever otherwise ye Same is butted & bounded or reputed to be bounded Together with all and Singular

Book VIII, Fol. 67.

woods underwoods waters pastures feedings fences profits priviledges hereditaments & Appurtenances whatsoever unto ye s^d Three Quarter parts of ye s^d Tract or parcell of land belonging or in any wise Appurtaining & ye revercon & revercons remainder & remainders Also all ye Estate right Title Dower Interest Inheritance use propperty possession Claime & demand whatsoever of ye s^d Peter Nowell & Sarah his wife & Each of them of in & to ye s^d granted premises & Every part & parcell thereof./ To have & To hold ye s^d Three quarters or fourth parts of ye s^d ffarm Tract or parcel of Land & all other ye premises aforementioned unto ye s^d Ebenezer Pemberton his heirs & Assigns to his & their only proper use benefit & behoofe forever

Provided Always and upon Condition Nevertheless that if ye s^d Peter Nowell his heirs Execut^{rs} or Admin^{rs} Shall & [67] Do well & Truely pay or Cause to be paid unto ye s^d Ebenezer Pemberton his heirs Execut^{rs} Adm^{rs} or Assigns ye full & Just Sum of One hundred and fifty pound in good & Lawfull Publick bills of Credit on ye Province afores^d with Lawfull Interest for ye Same in like good & Lawfull Bills of publick Credit or in Lawfull money of ye s^d Province At on or before ye Twenty Seventh day of December next Ensuing which will be in ye year of our Lord one Thousand Seven hundred and ffifteen which payment of principle & Interest is to be made in Time as before Limited without Coven fraud or delay then this present Deed & Every grant & Article therein Contained to Cease determine be Voyd & of Non Effect but if Default happen to be made in ye s^d payment in maner as afores^d Then to Abide & remaine in full force Strength & Vertue./ And thes^d Peter Nowell for himselfe his heirs Execut^{rs} & Adm^{rs} doth by these presents Covenant grant & agree to & with ye s^d Ebenezer Pemberton his heirs Execut^{rs} Adm^{rs} & Assignes from time to time and at all Times forever to Warrant & Defend all ye s^d Three Quarters or fourth parts of ye s^d farm Tract or parcel of land wth other ye premises & Appurtenances unto him ye s^d Ebenezer Pemberton his heirs & Assigns against ye Lawfull Claims & demand of all & Every p^{r}son & p^{r}sons whomsoever and that ye s^d bargained pmises At ye Time of ye Ensealing & Executing of these psents are free & Clear & fully Acquitted & discharged of & from all former & other gifts grants bargains Sales Mortgages Titles Troubles Charges & Incumbrances whatsoever And ye s^d Peter Nowell for himselfe his heirs Execut^{rs} & Adm^{rs} doth further Covenant grant & agree to & with ye s^d Ebenezar Pemberton his heirs Execut^{rs} Adm^{rs} & Assignes upon default made of ye afore mentioned payment or payments to deliver Quiet & peaceable possession of all ye s^d granted pmises unto

BOOK VIII, FOL. 67.

yᵉ sᵈ Ebenezar Pemberton his heirs or assigns & to do Execute & pform any other Act or thing Device or devices in yᵉ Law for further Confirmation & more Sure makeing of yᵉ sᵈ Bargained pmises unto yᵉ sᵈ Ebenezar Pemberton as a good perfect Absolute & Indefeazable Estate of Inheritance for Ever as by his Councill in yᵉ Law Shall Lawfull & reasonably be Devised Advised or required In Witness whereof yᵉ sᵈ Peter Nowell & Sarah his wife have hereunto Set their hands & Seals yᵉ day & year first within written
Signed Sealed & Delivered by Peter Nowell

In yᵉ presence of us   Peter Nowell ($_{Seal}^{a}$)
Hannah Sewal junʳ   Sarah Nowell ($_{Seal}^{a}$)
Relience Mayhew

Boston Decembʳ 28 1714./ The above named Peter Nowell psonally Appearing Acknowledged yᵉ afore within Instrument to be his free Act & Deed./

      Before me   Samuel Sewal J Pac
York ss/ Janʳʸ 20 1714./

The Above Named Sarah Nowell Acknowledged yᵉ Above written Instrument to be her free Act & Deed Coram:
       Charles ffrost J peace
Recorded According to yᵉ Original Janʳʸ 20ᵗʰ 1714/5./
       p Jos: Hamond Regʳ

April 29th 1716. Mr Peter Nowell yᵉ Mortgagee Came this day into yᵉ Registrs office and did Acknowledge to have receivᵈ full Satisfaction for yᵉ Sum Mentioned in this Mortgage & both Discharge All exand Thompson yᵉ Mortgagee Attests Jos Hamond Regʳ Witness my hand Peter Nowel

This Indenture made yᵉ third day of January Annoq, Domini one thousand Seven hundred & fourteen fifteen & in yᵉ first year of yᵉ Reign of our Soveraign Lord George King of Engᵈ &cᵗ between Allexander Tompson of York in yᵉ County of York in his Majᵗʸˢ Province of yᵉ Massachusets Bay in New England yeoman of yᵉ one party & Peter Nowell of yᵉ Same Town Yeoman of yᵉ other party Witnesseth that yᵉ sᵈ Allexander Tompson and Anne his wife for & in Consideration of yᵉ Sum of Twenty Nine pounds Curant money of N E to him in hand paid before yᵉ Ensealing & Delivery of these psents by Peter Nowell aforesᵈ yᵉ recᵗ whereof to full Satisfaction he yᵉ sᵈ Allexander Tompson doth by these psents Acknowledgee & thereof & of Every part thereof for himselfe his heirs Executʳˢ & Admʳˢ doth Acquitt Exonerate & discharge yᵉ sᵈ Peter Nowell his heirs Executʳˢ & Admʳˢ & Every of them for ever by these psents & for diverse good causes & Considerations him thereunto moveing he yᵉ sᵈ Allexandʳ Tompson hath given and granted bargained Sold Aliened Enfeoffed & Conveyed & Confirmed & by these p’sents doth fully freely Clearly & Absolutely give grant bargaine Sell Aliene Enfeoffe Convey & Confirm unto y̨ᵉ sᵈ Peter Nowell his heirs & Assignes for ever a Certaine Tract of Land Containing forty or fifty Acres be it more or Less Scittuate lying & being in york afores⁽ᵈ⁾ bounded by John Hoy on yᵉ one Side & on yᵉ other Side old ffrethys & on yᵉ head with Wᵐ Youngs & John ffrosts & at yᵉ other End with Salt marsh & is that Tract of land Benjᵃ Curtis bought of old Master Everet Together with yᵉ houses barns on sᵈ land & all Such rights Libertys & Imunitys profits priviledges Comoditys Emoluments & Appurtenances as in any kind Appurtaine thereunto with yᵉ revercoñs & remainders thereof & all yᵉ Estate right Interest Title Inheritance propperty possession Claime & Demand whatsoever of him yᵉ sᵈ [68] Allexander Tompson of in & to yᵉ Same & Every part thereof To have & To hold all yᵉ above granted pmises with all & Singular the Appurᶜᵉˢ thereof unto yᵉ sᵈ Peter Nowell his heirs & Assignes to his & their own Sole & propper use benefit & behoofe from hence forth & for ever & yᵉ sᵈ Allexᵃʳ Tompson for himselfe his heirs Executʳˢ Admʳˢ doth hereby Covenant promiss grant and Agree to & with yᵉ sᵈ Peter Nowell his heirs & Assignes in manner & form following That is to Say that at yᵉ time of the Ensealing & Delivery of these p’sents he yᵉ sᵈ Allexander Tompson is yᵉ True Sole & Lawfull owner of All yᵉ abovesᵈ bargained premises & Stands Lawfully Siezed thereof in his own propper right & good perfect & Indefeazable Estate of Inheritance in ffee Simple haveing in himselfe full power good right & Lawfull Authority to Sell & dispose of yᵉ Same in manner as aforesᵈ and that yᵉ sᵈ Peter Nowell his heirs & Assignes Shall & may henceforth for ever lawfully peaceably & Quietly have hold use Occupie possess & Enjoy yᵉ above granted pmises with yᵉ Appurtenances thereof free & Clear & Clearly Acquitted & Discharged of & from all & all manner of former & other gifts grants bargains Sales leases Mortgages Joyntures powers Judgmᵗˢ Executions Entails forfietures & of & from all other Titles Troubles Charges & Incumbrances whatsoever had made Comitted done or forfietures & of & from all other Titles Troubles Charges & Incumbrances what Soever had made Comitted done or Suffered by yᵉ Same Allexʳ Tompson his heirs or Assigns At any Time or Times before yᵉ Ensealing & Delivery hereof and further yᵉ sᵈ Allexandʳ Tompson doth Covenant promiss bind & Oblige himselfe his heirs Executʳˢ & Admʳˢ from henceforth & for ever hereafter to Warrant & Defend all yᵉ above granted pmises & yᵉ Appurᶜᵉˢ thereof unto yᵉ sᵈ Peter Nowell his

Book VIII, Fol. 68.

heirs & Assigns against ye Lawfull Claims & Demands of all & Every pson & psons whomsoever & At any Time & Times hereafter on demand and pass Such further & Ample Assureance & Confirmation of ye premises unto ye s^d Peter Nowell his heirs & Assignes for ever as in Law or Equity Can be reasonably devised Advised or required

Provided alwayes & these presents are upon Condition Nevertheless that if ye above bounden Allexand^r Tompson his heirs Execut^rs Adm^rs Shall do well & Truely pay or Cause to be paid unto the Afore Named Peter Nowell or his Certaine Attorney heirs Execut^rs Adm^rs or Assigns at York afores^d in ye present Currant money of ye afores^d province as it now passeth ye Sum of Twenty Nine pounds at or upon ye Third day of Jan^ry which will be in ye Year of our Lord one Thousand Seven hundred ffifteen Sixteen just one year after ye Date of this Instrum^t without fraud Coven or further delay that then this psent deed of Bargain & Sale & Every Clause & Article Therein Contained Shall Cease Determine be Null Voyd & of Non Effect but if Default happen to be made in ye afores^d payment Contrary to the true Intent thereof Then to Abide remaine in full force Strength & Vertue to all Intents & purposes in ye Law whatsoever./ In Witness whereof ye s^d Allexand^r Tompson hath hereunto Set his hand & Seale ye day & year first above written

Signed Sealed and   Allexander Tompson (Seal)
Delivered in psence
William Bracey
Nathaniel ffreeman

York ss Jan^ry 4 : 1714/5
The above Named Allexand^r Tompson Acknowledged ye above written Instrum^t to be his free Act & deed
         Before me   Charles ffrost J : Peace
Recorded According to ye Original Jan^ry 4 : 1714/5/
         p Jos Hamond Reg^r

To All Christian people to whom this psent Deed of Gift may Come Jeremiah Moulton of york in ye County of york in ye province of maine in New England Yeoman & Mary his wife Send Greeting Know Yee ye s^d Jeremiah & Mary for & in Consideration of ye Natural Affection & real Love & good will they have and alwayes Carry on ye Spirits of their minds unto their one & only Son Joseph Moulton of s^d York have given granted Bargained Sold Aliened Enfeoffed & do by these p^rsents give grant Aliene Enfeoffe & make Over unto ye s^d Joseph Moulton his heirs & Assigns forever a

Certaine piece pcell or Tract of Land Lying & being within ye Township of s^d York & is Scittuated upon ye North west Side of ye Creek Comonly known by ye Name of ye new mill Creek ye New dwelling house lately Erected by ye s^d Joseph Moulton Standing on s^d Lott ye bounds thereof are as followeth Vizt on ye South East by ye s^d New Mill Creek & on ye North East Side by ye Land of John Sayword Late of s^d York deceas^d & by ye Land now in ye possession of Mrs Mary Plaisted or otherwayes by a Town way between s^d Lotts and doth Extend to ye Northwest of s^d New house Twenty [69] Poles or perch and is in bredth from s^d way Thirty poles or perch and So runeth ye Same bredth South East or there Abouts down to aboves^d Mill Creek ye which s^d piece or parcell of Land as it now Stand bounded Containeth Six acres be it more or Less Together with all ye rights priviledges Appurtenances & Advantages thereunto belonging or any wayes at any Time redownding to ye Same or any part or parcell thereof unto him ye s^d Joseph Moulton his heirs & Assignes forever./ To have & To hold and Quietly & peaceably to possess Occupie & Enjoy as A Sure Estate in ffee Simple Moreover ye s^d Jeremiah & Mary do for them Selves their heirs Execut^rs & Adm^rs to & with ye s^d Joseph his heirs & Assignes Covenant Ingage & promiss ye above granted p^rmises with all its priviledges to be free & Clear from all former gifts grants bargains Sales rents rates Mortgages or any Incumberments whatsoever or any future Claims Challenges Titles or Lawsuits to be had or Comenced by them their heirs or Assignes or any pson or psons whatsoever from by or und^r them their heirs or Assignes but from ye date of this Instrum^t will Warrantise ye Same./ In Witness hereof ye s^d Jeremiah Moulton & Mary his wife have hereunto Set their hands & Seals this Seventeenth day of Decemb^r one Thousand Seven hundred & fourteen & in ye first year of ye Reign of our Soveraign Lord George King of Great Brittaine &c^t

Signed Sealed & Delivered   Jeremiah ^{his} ⁘ Moulton (a seal)
  In psence of
  Arthur Bragdon   mark
  William Grow   her
  Abra^m Preble   Mary ⁘ Moulton (a Seal)
                              mark

York ss/ Jan^ry 5th 1714/5./ Mr Jeremiah Moulton psonally Appearing before me ye Subscrib^r one of his Maj^tys Justices of ye peace for ye County of York Acknowledged this Instrum^t to be his Act & Deed   John Wheelwright

  Recorded According to ye Original Jan^ry ye 5th 1714/5.

                          p Jos: Hammond Reg^r

Book VIII, Fol. 69.

This Indenture made this Twenty third day of Decemb[r] in the year of our Lord one Thousand Seven hundred & fourteen between Edward Beal of york in y[e] County of york in New England Marrin[r] on y[e] one part & William Pepperrell of Kittery in y[e] County afores[d] Merch[t] on y[e] other part Witnesseth that I y[e] s[d] Edw[d] Beal for diverse good Causes and Considerations me thereunto moving as also for y[e] Sum of Two hundred pounds in good & Lawfull money of y[e] County afores[d] to me in hand before the Ensealing hereof well & Truely paid by W[m] Pepperrell Afores[d] the rec[t] whereof I do hereby Acknowledge & my Selfe therewith fully Satisfied & Contented & thereof & of Every part & parcel thereof do Exonerate Acquit & discharge y[e] s[d] W[m] Pepperrell his heirs Execut[rs] Adm[rs] forever by these psents have given granted bargained Sold Aliened Conveyed & Confirmed & by these psents do freely fully & Absolutely give grant bargain Sell Aliene Convey & Confirm unto him y[e] s[d] W[m] Pepperrell his heirs & Assignes forever one Messuage or Tract of land & Meadow Scittuate lying & being in York in y[e] County afores[d] Containing by Estimation Two hundred Acres be it more or Less Butted & bounded on y[e] Northwest by William Pepperrell Land & on y[e] North East by y[e] river & on y[e] Southwest by M[r] Raynes[s] land & on y[e] South East by y[e] Sea which is y[e] Land where I now Live on & now possess As also all my lands which lyes on y[e] South Side of York river with all y[e] houses barns Orchards Trees Timb[r] wood water Courses thereunto belonging To have & To hold y[e] s[d] granted & bargained premises with all y[e] Appurtenances priviledges & Comoditys to y[e] Same belonging or in any wayes Appurtaining to him y[e] s[d] W[m] Pepperrell his heirs & Assigns forever to his & their own propper use benefit & behoofe forever & I y[e] s[d] Edward Beal for me my heirs Execut[rs] Adm[rs] do Covenant promiss & grant to & with y[e] s[d] W[m] Pepperrell his heirs & Assignes that before y[e] Ensealing hereof I am y[e] True Sole & Lawfull owner of y[e] above bargained premises & Am Lawfully Siez[d] & possesst of y[e] Same in mine own propper right as a good perfect & Absolute Estate of Inherritance in ffee Simple & have in my Selfe good right full power and Lawfull Authority to grant bargaine Sell Convey & Confirm s[d] bargained pmises in manner as aboves[d] & that y[e] s[d] W[m] Pepperrell his heirs & Assigns

April 2[d] 1718. Rec[d] of Edw[d] Beal the Sum of Two hundred pound y[e] Sum Mentioned in this Mortgage & do hereby discharge him of y[e] Same York ss April 2[d] 1718. W[m] Pepperrell Esq[r] psonally Appearing Acknowledged y[e] above discharge
to be his Act & Deed Witness my hand W[m] Pepperrell

Cor[t] Jos Hamond J. peace
Recorded According to y[e] Original April 2[d] 1718.
p Jos. Hamond Reg[r]

Shall & may from Time to Time & at all Times forever hereafter by force & Vertue of [70] These presents Lawfully peaceably & Quietly have hold use Occupie possess & Enjoy ye s^d Demised & bargained premises with ye Appurtenances free & Clear & freely & Clearly Acquited Exonerated & discharged of & from all & all manner of former & other gifts grants bargains Sales Leases Mortgages wills Entails Joyntures Dowryes Judgm^{ts} Executions Incumbrances & Extents. ffurthermore I ye s^d Edward Beal for my Selfe my heirs Executᵣˢ Adm^{rs} do Covenant & promiss At and upon ye reasonable request & at ye propper Cost & Charges in ye Law of ye s^d Wm Pepperrell his heirs Execut^{rs} Adm^{rs} or Assignes to Make do perform & Execute any further or other Lawfull or reasonable Act or Acts thing or thing device or devices in ye Law Needfull or requisite for ye more perfect Asurence Setling & Sure making of ye premises as Abovesᵈ And Eliz^a Beal ye wife of me ye s^d Edward Beal doth by these presence freely Willingly give Yield up & Surrend^r all her right of Dowry & power of Thirds of in & unto ye Above demised pmises unto him ye s^d Wm Pepperrell his heirs & Assignes forever Provided Nevertheless & it is ye True Intent & Meaning of grantor and grantee in these presents any thing herein Contained to the Contrary Notwithstanding that if ye above Named Edward Beal his heirs Execut^{rs} Adm^{rs} or Assigns do well & Truely pay or Cause to be paid unto ye above named Wm Pepperrell his heirs Execut^{rs} Adm^{rs} or Assigns the full & whole Sum of Two hundred pounds good & Lawfull money of New England with ye Interest yearly According to Law At on or before this day Three years which will be in ye year of our Lord One Thousand Seven hundred and Seventeen Then this above written deed or Obligation & Every Clause & Article therein Contained Shall be Null Voyd & of Non Effect or Else Shall abide in full force & Vertue

 Sealed with my Seal Dated in Kittery ye day & year first Above written   Edward Beale (Seal)
Signed Sealed & Delivered
 In Presence of   Elizabeth her Beale (Seal)
 James ffoy
 Thomas Ball   mark
 William Pepperrell jun^r
  York ss Jan^{ry} 6th 1714/5

The above named Edward Beal & Elizabeth Beal Acknowledged ye above written Instrum^t to be their free Act & Deed.   Before me./ Charles ffrost J : Peace

Recorded According to ye Original Jan^{ry} 7 : 1714/5
       p Jos. Hamond Reg^r

Book VIII, Fol. 70.

Know All men by these presents that I Timothy Wentworth of Kittery Alias Berwick in y[e] County of York in y[e] Province of y[e] Massachusets Bay in New England husbandman for & in Consideration of y[e] Sum of one hundred pounds Currant money of y[e] Province afores[d] to me in hand well & Truely paid by Nicholas Morrell of y[e] Same Town County & province afores[d] husbandman y[e] rec[t] whereof I y[e] s[d] Timothy Wentworth do hereby Acknowledge & my Selfe therewith fully Satisfied Contented & paid have given granted bargained Sold Aliened Assigned Enfeoffed Set over & Confirmed and do by these psents give grant bargaine Sell Aliene Assign Enfeoffe Set over & Confirm unto him y[e] s[d] Nicholas Morrell his heirs & Assigns for ever the one halfe part of all my right Title Interest Claime & Demand in a Certaine water Course known by y[e] Name of Worsters river that runs into Salmon fall river s[d] Worsters land being on both Sides of s[d] river above y[e] s[d] Salmon falls To have & To hold y[e] one halfe part of my part which is one fourth part of y[e] whole of s[d] Water Course Stream or river with y[e] one fourth part of y[e] Saw mill thereon Erected Together with y[e] one fourth part of all y[e] rights profits priviledges Appurtenances & Accomodations in any wise whatsoever belonging or Appurtaining unto y[e] s[d] Water Course & Saw mill Iron work &c[t] Together with y[e] halfe of Two Acres of Land to be laid out for y[e] Most & best benefit & Advantage of s[d] Saw mill with y[e] highwayes on Each Side of y[e] river According to s[d] Worsters Obligation to me y[e] s[d] Timothy Wentworth referrence whereto being had my other halfe part which is a fourth part of y[e] whole after s[d] Worsters time is Come to recieve one Saw I have before Alienated to John Croade as by his deed Appears So now I y[e] s[d] Timothy Wentworth have Employed & quitted my whole & Sole right & Interest therein & of Every part & parcell thereof to him y[e] s[d] Nicholas Morrell his heirs & Assigns for Ever y[e] one halfe of my part or fourth part free & clear & is freely & Clearly Acquitted from all other or former bargains Sales Mortgages Judgments Executions & from any & all other Incumbrance or Incumbrances whatsoever & that it Shall & may be Lawfull to & for y[e] s[d] Nicholas Morrell his heirs Execut[rs] Adm[rs] or Assigns to have hold use Occupie possess & Enjoy y[e] Same quietly & peaceably without any Let hinderence Mollestation or Interuption from me y[e] s[d] Timothy Wentworth my heirs Execut[rs] or Adm[rs] y[e] s[d] Morrell his heirs Execut[rs] Adm[rs] or Assignes maintaining his s[d] part of Charge for repairs &c[t] at all times for ever hereafter as I y[e] s[d] Timothy Wentworth am Obliged to s[d] Worster &

Book VIII, Fol. 71.

Croade So to do & I ye s^d Timothy Wentworth for my Selfe my heirs [71] Execut^rs & Adm^rs do hereby promiss & Engage to Warrant Acquit & defend him ye s^d Nicholas Morrell his heirs Execut^rs Adm^rs or Assigns in ye quiet & peaceable possession of ye hereby granted & bargained premises against all & all maner of pson or psons Laying Legall Claime thereto or any part thereof from henceforth & for ever

In Witness whereof I ye s^d Timothy Wentworth have hereunto Set my hand & Seale this 22^d day of Novemb^r Annoq, Domini : 1710

Signed Sealed & Delivered   Timothy ⟨his mark⟩ Wentworth (a seal)
In ye psence of
Jeremian Wise
John Croade

York ss/
Timothy Wentworth psonally Appeared & Acknowledged ye within written Instrum^t to be his free Act & Deed & Sarah his wife did at the Same Time relinquish & Surrender up her right of Dowry or thirds in ye Estate Conveyed in s^d Instrum^t at Berwick Alias Kittery ye 23^d day of ffebruary 1710/11

Before me.   Ichabod Plaisted J : P
Recorded According to ye Original ffebruary 3^d 1714/5.
p Jos : Hamond Reg^r

To All Christian People to whom these presents shall Come John Fennix of Kittery in ye County of York within her Majesties Province of ye Massachusets Bay in New England (yeoman) Sends Greeting Know Yee that ye s^d John Fennicks for & in Consideration of a Certain Sum of money to him in hand paid before ye Ensealing & Delivery of these p^rsents by Charles ffrost of ye Same. Kittery Esqr the receipt whereof to full Content & Satisfaction he ye s^d John Fennicks doth by These p^rsents Acknowledged & thereof & of Every part thereof for him Selfe his heirs Execut^rs & Adm^rs doth Acquitt Exonerate & Discharge ye s^d Charles ffrost his heirs Execut^rs And Adm^rs Every of them forever by these presents & for diverse other good Causes & Considerations him hereunto moveing, he ye s^d John Fennicks hath given granted bargained Sold Aliened Enfeoffed Conveyed & Confirmed and by these presents doth fully freely Clearly & Absolutely give grant bargaine Sell Aliene Enfeoffe Convey & Confirm unto him ye s^d Charles ffrost his heirs and Assignes forever all his part portion or proportion of in & unto y^e

Book VIII, Fol. 71.

Comon & undivided lands within ye Township of Kittery & Berwick as ye Same has been heretofore Stated & proportioned or how ever otherwise ye Same may hereafter be Stated or proportioned Together with all Such rights Libertys Imunitys profits priviledges Comoditys Imolluments and Appurtenances as in Any kind Appurtaine thereunto with ye reversions & remaind^{rs} thereof and all ye Estate right Title Interest Inheritance propperty possession Claime & demand whatsoever of him Thes^d John Fennicks of in & to ye Same and Every part thereof To have & To hold all ye above granted premises with all & Singular ye Appurtenances thereof unto ye s^d Charles ffrost his heirs and Assigns to his & their own Sole & propper use bennetit and behoofe from hence forth forever & that ye s^d Charles ffrost his his heirs Execut^{rs} or Assignes Shall Act & have ye Voyce of ye s^d John Fennicks in ye ordering Setleing & Dividing of s^d Comon rights As he ye s^d John Fennicks might himselfe have done before ye Sale thereof & ye s^d John Fennicks doth hereby Covenant promiss bind & oblige himselfe his heirs Execut^{rs} & Adm^{rs} from henceforth & forever hereafter to Warrant & defend all ye above granted premises & ye Appurtenances thereof unto ye s^d Charles ffrost his heirs & Assignes against ye Lawfull Claims & Demands of all & Every pson or psons whomsoever & at any Time or Times hereafter on demand to give & pass Such farther & Ample Assurence & Confirmation of ye premises unto thes^d Charles ffrost his heirs & Assignes forever as in Law or Equity Can be reasonably devised Advised or required./ In Witness whereof ye s^d John Fennickes hath hereunto Set his hand & Seal y^e Second day of August in y^e year of our Lord One Thousand Seven hundred and fourteen & in y^e Thirteenth year of y^e Reign of our Soveraign Lady Anne Queen of Great Brittaine ffrance & Ireland Defender of y^e faith &c^t./
Signed Sealed & Delivered   John Fennicks ($^n_{seal}$)
  In presence of
  John Belcher
  Abigail ffryer
      her
  Abigail A Hoopper
     mark
    York ss Kittery Septr 30th 1714

The above Named John Fennicks psonally Appearing before me the Subscrib^r one of his Maj^{tys} Justices of y^e peace for y^e County of York Acknowledg^d the above written Instrum^t to be his ffree Act & Deed./   Wm Pepperrell
Recorded According to ye Original Jan^{ry} 24th 1714/5
                                      p Jos: Hamond Reg^r

BOOK VIII, FOL. 72.

To All Christian People to whom these presents Shall Come James Chadbourne of Kittery in ye County of York within her Majesties province of ye Massachusets Bay in New England yeoman Sends Greeting./ Know Yee that y^{e}s^d James Chadbourne for & in Consideration of ye Sum of fifteen pounds Curra^t money of New England to him in hand paid before ye Ensealing [72] And Delivery of these psents by Charles ffrost of ye Same Kittery Esqr the rec^t whereof to full Consent & Satisfaction he ye s^d James Chadbourne doth by these presents Acknowledge & thereof & of Every part thereof for himselfe his heirs Execut^{rs} & Adm^{rs} doth Acquit Exonerate & discharge ye s^d Charles ffrost his heirs Execut^{rs} & Adm^{rs} Every of them for ever by these presents & for diverse other good Causes & Considerations him thereunto Moving he ye s^d James Chadbourne hath given granted bargained Sold Aliened Enfeoffed Conveyed & Confirmed and by these psents doth fully freely Clearly & Absolutely give grant bargaine Sell Aliene Enfeoffe Convey & Confirm unto ye s^d Charles ffrost his heirs & Assignes for ever a Certain Strip or Tract of Land Containing in the whole Three Acres be it more or Less Scittuate lying & being in Kittery afores^d & is part of ye farm whereon ye s^d James Chadbourne now dwells Adjoining on ye South: Southeast: East & Northeast Sides thereof to ye farm whereon ye s^d Charles ffrost now dwells & on ye other Sides thereof partly by s^d Chadbournes own Land & partly by ye highway which Leads from s^d Charles ffrosts dwelling house Towards Kittery. bebegining at a Certaine Stake distant Sixteen poles west from a walnut Tree Standing at ye Northwest Corn^r of s^d Charles ffrosts old Orchard ye s^d Stake being ye Antient bounds between ye Afores^d ffarmes & from s^d Stake runing Northeast a little Easterly Thirty four poles & quarter to a Stone Set up at the Northwest Corner of s^d James Chadbournes Nursery being west Eight poles distant from ye brook & from s^d Stone Crossing ye highway to Another Stone distant four poles west from s^d brook Standing in ye Turn of ye way & from thence runing North by west halfe west Thirty three poles & quarter to a red oak tree Standing on ye Northward Side of ye pound & from s^d red oak tree runing Thirty four poles & Three quarters Northwest a little westerly to ye southwest Corner of s^d Charles ffrosts Ox pasture fence at ye Turn of ye way which leads to Cap^{tn} Heards Together with all Such rights Libertys Imunitys profits priviledges Comoditys Emolluments & Appurtenances as in any kind Appurtaine thereunto with ye reversions & remainders thereof & all ye Estate right Title Interest Inheritance propperty possession Claime

Book VIII, Fol. 72.

& Demand whatsoever of him y{e} s{d} James Chadbourne of in & to y{e} Same & Every part thereof to have & to hold all y{e} above granted premises with all & Singular the Appurtenances thereof unto the s{d} Charles ffrost his heirs & Assignes to his & their own Sole & propper use bennefit and behoofe from henceforth for ever & y{e} s{d} James Chadbourne ffor himselfe his heirs Execut{rs} & Adm{rs} doth hereby Covenaut promiss grant & agree to & with y{e} s{d} Charles ffrost his heirs & Assigns in Manner & form following (That is to Say) that at y{e} time of the Ensealing & Delivery of these presents he y{e} s{d} James Chadbourn is the true Sole & Lawfull owner of all y{e} afore bargained premises & Stands Lawfully Siezed thereof in his own propper right as a good perfect & Indefeazable Estate of Inheritance in ffee Simple haveing in himselfe full power good right & Lawfull Authority to Sell & dispose of y{e} Same in manner as afores{d} and that y{e} s{d} Charles ffrost his heirs & Assignes shall & may hence forth for ever Lawfully peaceably & quietly have hold use Occupy possess & Enjoy y{e} above granted premises with y{e} Appurtenances thereof ffree & Clear & Clearly Acquitted & discharged of & from all & all manner of former & other gifts grants bargains Sales Leases Mortgages Joyntures Dowers judgments Executions Entails forfeitures & of & from all other Titles troubles Charges & Incumbrances whatsoever had made Comitted done or Suffered to be done by y{e} s{d} James Chadbourne his heirs or Assigns at any time or times before y{e} Ensealing & Delivery hereof and further y{e} s{d} James Chadbourne doth hereby Covenant promiss bind & Oblige himselfe his heirs Execut{rs} & Administrat{rs} from hence forth & for ever hereafter to Warrant & defend all the above granted pmises & y{e} Appurtenances thereof unto y{e} s{d} Charles ffrost his heirs & Assignes against y{e} Lawfull Claims & Demands of all & Every pson or psons whomsoever & Sarah y{e} wife of y{e} s{d} James Chadbourne doth fully & freely give & yield up unto y{e} s{d} Charles ffrost his heirs & Assignes All her right & Title of Dower & Interest of in or to y{e} premisses respectively for ever by these presents In Witness whereof y{e} s{d} James Chadbourne & Sarah his wife have hereunto set their hands & Seals the Twenty first day of April in y{e} year of our Lord One thousand seven hundred & fourteen & in y{e} thirteenth year of y{e} reign of our Soveraign Lady Anne

Book VIII, Fol. 73.

Queen of Great Brittaine ffrance & Ireland Defender of y⁶ faith &c^t
Signed Sealed & Delivered
in presence of
John Belcher
John Buship
Sarah X Nason
  her.
  mark

James Chadbourne (ₛₑₐₗ ᵃ)
Sarah Chadbourne (ₛₑₐₗ ᵃ)

York ss March 29ᵗʰ 1715/.
The within Subscribed James Chadbourne & Sarah Chadbourn psonally Appearing before me yᵉ Subscriber one of her Maj^tys Justices of yᵉ peace for yᵉ County of York & Acknowledged yᵉ within written Instrum^t to be their ffree Act & Deed./   Lewis Bane Justice
Recorded According to yᵉ Original April yᵉ 30ᵗʰ 1715/
                    p Jos: Hamond Reg^r

[73] Know all men by these presents that I Moses Spencer of Barwick Alies Kittery in the County of York in the Province of the Massachusets Bay in New England labourer for & in Consideration of yᵉ Sum of Nine pounds to me in hand well & truly paid before the Ensealing and Delivery hereof by John Croade of yᵉ Same town County & Province afores^d Merchant the receipt whereof I do hereby acknowledge and my Selfe therewith fully Satisfied Contented and paid have bargained Sold aliened Enfeoffed Set over & Confirmed and do by these presents bargaine Sell aliene Enfeoffe Set over & Confirm unto him yᵉ s^d John Croade his heirs and Assignes forever Twenty Seven acres of land Sittuate lying and being in the Town of Barwick Alies Kittery afores^d and is part of the fifty acres given & bequeathed unto me the s^d Moses Spencer in yᵉ last will and Testement of William Spencer late of S^d Barwick Alies Kittery dec^d To have and To hold the S^d Twenty Seven acres of land with all yᵉ rights proffits priviledges and appurtenances thereunto belonging and in any wayes appertaining unto him yᵉ s^d John Croade his Heires & assigns for ever free & Clear and freely and Clearly acquited exonerated and discharged of and from all and all maner of other & former grants bargaines Sales Mortgages Judgments Executions Extents and all other Incumbrance or Incumbrances whatsoever & Also I yᵉ s^d Moses Spencer for my Selfe my Heires Executors and Admin^rs do further Covenant

to and with the s⁴ John Croade his Heires and Assignes that at & before the Ensealing & delivery of these presents I am yᵉ true & Lawfull owner of yᵉ hereby granted and bargained premises & have good right full power & lawfull Authority to grant bargain Sell & Convey the Same as aforesᵈ and that it Shall & may be Lawfull to & for the Said John Croade his Heires & Assignes forever to have hold use Occupie possess & Injoy the Same & every part thereof without any let hindrance Mollestation or Interuption from me yᵉ sᵈ Moses Spencer my Heirs Execut^rs or admin^rs and do further Covenant To Warrant acquit & defend yᵉ sᵈ John Croade his Heirs and Assignes forever in the quiate and peaceable possession thereof against all and all mañer of person or persons whatsoever from henceforth & forever In Witness Whereof I yᵉ Said Moses Spencer have hereunto Set my hand & Seal yᵉ 23ᵈ day of Janʳʸ Annoq̣ Domini 1710/11./

Signed Sealed & Delivered   Moses Spencer (a Seal)
in presence of ———
Eleazer ⊂ (his mark) Ward ———
Thomas Croade ———
York ss/

Moses Spencer parSonally appeared and Acknowledged the within Written Instrument to be his Voluntary act & deed & Elizabeth his wife did at yᵉ Same time relinquish & Surrender up her right of thirds or dowry in the land conveyed in Sᵈ Instrument at Barwick alies Kittery the 23ᵈ day of January 1710/11   Before me./   John Hill J Peace
Recorded According to yᵉ Original Janʳʸ 24ᵗʰ 1714/5./
                         p Jos. Hañond Regʳ

Know All men by these presents that I John Croade of Berwick in the County of York in yᵉ Province of Massachusets Bay in New England Merchant for and in Consideration of the Sum of fifteen Pounds Currant money of the province aforesᵈ to me in hand well & Truely paid by Nathan Lord Senʳ of the Same towne County and & Province aforesᵈ Yeoman the receipt whereof I do hereby Acknowledge my Selfe therewith fully Satisfied Contented and paid/ have given granted bargained Sold aliened assigned Enfeoffed Set Over and Confirmed and do by these presents give grant bargain Sell aliene assigne Enfeoffe Set over & Confirm unto him the Said Nathan Lord Senʳ his Heires and assignes forever Twenty Seven Acres of land Sittuate lying & being in

Barwick afores{d} & is part of the fifty acres given & bequeathed unto Moses Spncer in the last will and testement of William Spencer late of Barwick dec{d} as by Said Moses Spencers Deed to me the S{d} Croade appears To have and To hold the S{d} Twenty Seven acres of land with all the right proffits priviledges and appurtenances whatsoever thereto belonging unto him the S{d} Nathan Lord Sen{r} his Heires & Assignes forever to y{e} only proper Use & behoof of him the S{d} Nathan Lord his Heirs & assignes forever free & clear & clearly Acquitted of and from all other and former Gifts grants bargains Sales Titles troubles charges & Incumbrances whatsoever & that I the S{d} John Croade & my Heirs to him y{e} s{d} Nathan Lord Sen{r} his Heirs and assignes Shall & will Warrant & forever Confirm the Same In Witness whereof I y{e} s{d} John Croade have hereunto Scet my hand & Seal the 24{th} day of January Annoq, Domini 1714/

Signed Sealed & delivered   John Croade (Seal)
in y{e} Presents of
John Bradstreet
Mary Spencer

York ss

John Croade psonally appeared & acknowledged y{e} above written Instrument to be his act & deed & Deborah his wife did at y{e} Same time relinquish & Surrender up her: right of thirds or dowry in y{e} land Conveyed in Said Instrument Barwick y{e} 24{th} day of Jan{ry} 1714/   Before me
        Charles Frost J peace

Recorded According to y{e} Original January y{e} 24{th} 1714/5
        p Jos: Hamond Reg{r}

This Deed Above written is Assigned by Nathan Lord to Moses Spencer in Lib{o} X Folio 15 Att{r}
        Jos Hamond Reg{r}

[74] To All People to whome these presents Shall Come or Concern// Know Yee that Samuel Hill of portsmouth in the province of New: Hampshire in New England Gentleman Son of William Hill of Boston in New England Gentleman for and in Consideration of the Sum of Twenty Five pounds Currant money of New England to him in hand before the Ensealing and delivery hereof well & Truly paid by John Frink of the Town of Kittery in the County of York Yeoman the receipt whereof he y{e} s{d} Samuel Hill doth hereby acknowledge & therrof & of every part & parcel

thereof doth acquit Exonerat & Discharge him ye s^d John Frink his Heirs Execut^{rs} Admin^{rs} & Assignes & every of them forever by these Presents Hath given granted Bargained Sold Remised Released and forEver quitt Claimed and by these for himSelfe & his Heirs doth give grant Bargain Sell Remise Release & forever quitt Claime Unto ye s^d John Frink in his full & peaceable possession & Sezin and to his Heirs and assignes forEver all Such Right Estate Title interest & demand whatsoever as he ye S^d Samuel Hill had or ought to have of in or to a certaine percil of Land Scituate lying & being in Kittery in the County of york in Newengland at a place called or Known by ye Name of Spruce Creek Containing Fifty Acres be it more or less and is that Land or Farme which he ye Said John Frink Now Dwelleth Upon & is bounded as followeth (to witt) begining at ye Norwest End of Nicholas Tuckers House Lott & runneth from thence in Breadth Fifty Four poles Northwest & South East and in Length one Hundred & fforty Eight poles North East & South west bounded by Mr Gunnisons Land on ye Northwest & Nicholas Tuckers Land on ye Southwest or with what other Meets or bounds ye Same is bounded All which above Said parcel of land ye S^d Sam^{ll} Hill Recovered Judgment for his Title & Possession off before her Majesties Justices of her Majesties Superior Court of Judicature holden for and within the County of Soffolk at Boston in New England ye first Tuesday oin may)1709(To have and To hold all ye Said Tract or parcil of land Unto the Said John Frink his heires or assigns to the only Use & behoof of him ye S^d John Frink his heirs & assignes for Ever So that nither he ye Said Samuel Hill nor his heirs nor any other person or persons for him or them or in his or their Names or in ye Name Right or Stead of Any of them Shall or will by any wayes or Meanes hereafter have Claime Challenge or demand any Estate Right title or interest of in or to ye premises or any part or percill Thereof but from all & every action Right Estate Title interest & demand of in or to ye premisses or any part or perill Thereof They & Every of Them Shall be Utterly Excluded & barred forEver by these presents and also ye Said Samuel Hill and his heirs ye Said percill of land & other ye premises with ye Appurtenances to ye Said John Frink his heirs & Assignes to His & Their own proper Use and Uses in manner & forme Afore specified against their theires and Assignes & Every of them Shall warrant & for Ever defend by these presents) In Witness whereof y^e Said Samuel Hill hath hereunto Sett his hand & Seale y^e Twenty first day of September in y^e Eighth

Book VIII, Fol. 74.

year of her present Majesties Reigne that now is over Great Brittain &c^t Anno$_q$ Domini)1709)   Sam^{ll} Hill ($_{\text{Seal}}^{\text{a}}$)
Sealed & delivered
  In the presence of
  Mem^d y^e words y^e first
  Tuesday in may 1709/ was/
  first interlined before Sealing
  William Briar
  Cha: Story
  Province of New Hampshier 21st September 1709 Samuel Hill psonally appearing Acknowledged y^e above Release or Instrument in writting to be his free & volluntary Act & deed
                        Coram Cha: Story Jus: p$^{\circ}$
  January y^e 1st 1714/5./ Recorded According to y^e Original
                        p Jos: Hammond Reg^r

To All People to whom these Presents Shall Come or Concern Know Yee that John ffrink of Kittery in y^e County of York in y^e Province of y^e Massachuscts Bay in New Eng= land Yeoman for and in Consideration of the Summe of twenty and Eight pounds Currant money of New=England to him in hand before the Ensealing and delivery hereof well & truely paid by William Briar of y^e Same place aboves^d Ferry-man the receipt whereof he y^e Said John ffrink doth hereby acknowledge and thereof & of every part and parcel thereof doth acquit exonerate & discharge him y^e Said William Briar his heirs Executors Administrators and assignes and every of them forever by these Presents hath given granted Bargained Sold Remised Released and for: ever Quitt Claimed & by these Presents for himself and his Heires doth give Grant Bargaine Sell Remise Release and for: ever Quitt Claime unto the said William Briar in the full and peaceable possession & Seizen & to his heirs & Assignes forever All such right Estate Title interest & demand w^{t}soever as he ye said John ffrink had or ought to have off in or to a Certain parcel of Land Scittuate Lying & being in Kittery aforeSaid att a place called or Known by ye name of Spruce Creek Containing twenty five acres or one Moiety or half of that Land or ffarm which ye said John ffrink now possesseth & purchased of Sam^{ll} Hill of Portsmouth in New: hampshire in New England as by a Deed of Sale from the Said Hill to ye Said ffrink bareing Date the 21st day of Septemb^r in ye year of our Lord (1709) May more at Large Appear & is 'bounded as followeth (to witt) begining at ye North west end of Nicholas Tuckers house Lott and runs from thence [75] in breadth Twenty seven poles Northwest and South East & in Length one hundred & forty eight poles North East and South west bounded by ye Said ffrinks land on the Northwest and Nicholas Tuckers Land on the South West or with what other Meets or bounds the Same is bounded To have and to hold all the Said Tract or Parcel of Land unto ye Said William Briar his Heirs or assignes to the only use and behoof of him the S^d William Briar his heirs & Assignes for ever So that neither he the Said John ffrink nor his Heires nor any other person or persons for him or them or in his or their names or in the Name right or stead of any of them shall or will by any wayes or means hereafter have claim Challeng or demand any Estate Right title or interest of in or to ye premises or any part or parcil thereof but from all and every action Right Estate Title interest and demand of in or to ye premises or any part or parcel thereof they and every of them Shall be utterly Excluded & Barred for : ever by these Presents and also ye s^d John ffrink & his Heirs the S^d parcel of land and other ye premises with ye Appurtenances To ye said William Bryar his Heirs & Assignes to his And their own proper use & Uses in : manner and form afore specified against their Heirs & Assignes & every of them Shall warrant and for ever defend by these presents) In witness whereof the Said John ffrink hath hereunto set his hand & Seal y^e twenty third day of may in y^e year of our Lord one thousand Seven hundred and ten

Signed Sealed & delivered
  In y^e presence of us   Sign
  John New=march   John ffrinks (a Seal)
  george Frink
                          her Sign
  Sarah Mendam   Hannah ffrink X (a Seal)

  her mark
York ss/
John ffrink parsonally Appeared before y^e Subscriber this twenty Eighth day of Decemb^r anno domi : 1714 : And acknowledged this above and this within written deed or Obligation to be his ffree act & deed   Wm Pepperrell Js : pease
  Recorded According to ye Original Jan^{ry} 1st 1714/5./
                       p Jos : Hamond Reg^r

Know All men by these presents that I Mary Spencer of Barwick in ye County of York in ye province of the Massa-

Book VIII, Fol. 75.

chusets Bay in New England widow for & in Consideration of the Sum of ten pound Currant money of ye province afores^d to me in hand paid or Secured to be paid by John Bradstreet of ye Same town County & Province afores^d Clothier the receipt Whereof I do hereby acknowledge and my Self therewith fully Satisfied Contented & paid have given granted bargained Sold aliened assigned Set over and Confirmed and do by these presents give grant bargain Sell alliene assigne Set Over and Confirm unto him the S^d John Bradstreet his heires & assignes for ever A certain peice of Land Scittuate lying & being in Barwick afores^d Containing One acre & half bounded North Westerly on y^e great=works river s^d line measures twelve pole on y^e country roade leading from Stirgion Creek to Salmon falls North Easterly wch line measures Twenty rod and Easterly and Southwesterly on land of S^d Mary Spencer the easterly line Measures twelve rod the South westerly line twenty rods and is bounded at the Sotherly corner with a Stake & heap of Stones Together with all & Singular the rights proffits priviledges & appurtenances in any wise whatsoever thereto belonging To have and To hold ye s^d piece of land as bounded with ye rights & priviledges as afores^d unto him the said John Bradstreet his heirs & Assignes for ever to ye only proper use & behoof of him the s^d John Bradstreet his heirs & Assignes for Ever free & Clear and Clearly acquitted of and from all other & former gifts grants bargains Sales titles Troubles charges and Incumbrances Claims & demands whatsoever and That I y^e s^d Mary Spencer and my heirs Execu^{rs} & Admin^{rs} to him the Said John Bradstreet his Heirs and Assignes Shall & will Warrant and for ever Confirm the Same against all persons whatsoever In Witness whereof I have hereunto Set: my hand & Seal the Seventh day of January Annoq$_,$ Domini 1714 In y^e first year of y^e Reign of our Soveraign Lord King George of Great Brittain &c   Mary Spencer ($_{Seal}^{a}$)
Signed Sealed & Delivered
  In the Presents of
  Sarah Cutt
  Benjamin Lord
  ye words against all persons whatsoever Entered before Signing & Sealing as also y^e words clames and demands and Executors and Administrators
    York ss/ ffebruary the 11th: 1714/5
  Then Mrs Mary Spencer appeared before me ye Subscriber one of his maj^{tys} Justices of ye place for s^d county and acknowledged the above written Instrument to be her voluntary act and deed   John Plaisted

Book VIII, Fol. 76.

Recorded According to ye Original ffebruary ye 15th
1714/5— p Jos: Hamond Reg^r

Know All men by these presents that I John Bradstreet of Barwick in ye County of York in the province of the Massachusets Bay in New: England Clothier for and in consideration of ye Sum of Thirty Three pounds currant money of ye province afores^d to me in hand well and Truly paid by Mary Spencer of the Same Town county and province afores^d widdow the receipt whereof I do hereby acknowledge and my Selfe therewith fully Satisfied contented and paid have given granted bargained Sold aliened assigned Enfeoffed Set over and Confirmed and Do by these presents give grant bargain Sell aliene Assigne Enfeoffe Set over and confirme unto her the S^d Mary Spencer her heirs and assigne forever a certain peice of land Scittuate lying & being in Barwick afores^d containing one acre & half bounded north westerly on the graeit works river S^d [76] Line measuring Twelve pole on ye Country rode leading from Sturgeon Creek to Salmonfalls northeasterly which line Measures Twenty rod and Easterly and Southwesterly on land of said Mary Spencer the Easterly line measures Twelve rod ye South westerly line Twentey rod and is bounded at ye Southerly Corner with a Stake and heape of Stones Together with all and Singular ye rights proffits priviledges and appurtenances thereto in any wise belonging with ye new Shop erected thereon Copper press and all working gears whatsoever To have & To hold ye s^d land as bounded with all ye rights & priviledges Shop Copper press working gears &c^a as afores^d unto her ye s^d Mary Spencer her heirs and assignes forever to ye only proper use and behoof of her ye s^d Mary Spencer her heirs and assignes forever free and Clear and Clearly acquitted of and from all other and former gifts grants bargains Sales Titles Troubles charges & Incumbrances whatsoever and that I ye s^d John Bradstreet and my heirs to her ye s^d Mary Spencer her heires and assignes Shall and will Warrant and forever Confirm ye Same Now Know Yee that if ye s^d John Bradstreet do well & truely pay the full & whole Sum of Thirty Three pound in currant money of ye province afores^d at or before ye first day of may which will be in ye year of our Lord one Thousand Seven hundred and Sixteen according to and at ye times Set in Three Severall bonds unto ye s^d Mary Spencer her heirs Executors administrators or assignes without fraud or further delay then this present Deed of Mortgage to be void and of none efect anything herein contained to y^e contrary notwithStanding Otherwise to abide and remain full force Strength and virtue In Witness Whereof I have hereunto Set my hand and Seal y^e Seventh day of January annoq$_e$ Domini 1714/ In y^e first year of his Maj^{tys} Reign   Jno Bradstreet (a Seal)

Signed Sealed & Delivered
  In presence of us
  Sarah Cutt
  Benjamin Lord
  York ss/ 11th feb : 1714/5

  y^n Jno Bradstreet appeared before me y^e Subscriber one of his Maj^{tys} Justices of y^e peace for : s^d County and acknowledged ye above written Instrument to be his Voluntary act and Deed   John Plaisteed

  Recorded According to the Original ffeb^{ry} 15th 1714/5./
                             p. Jos : Hamond Reg^r

  This Indenture made ye tenth day of February Annoque Domini one Thousand Seven Hundred & fourteen fifteen and and in ye first year of ye Reign of our Soveraign Lord Georg King of Great Brittain France & Ireland Defender of ye faith &c^t Between John Gowen of Kittery in ye County of York in his Maj^{tys} Provinces of ye Massachusets Bay in New England (yeoman) of ye one party & Charles ffrost of Kittery in ye County afores^d Esqr of ye other party Witnesseth That ye Said John Gowen for and in Consideration of ye Sum of Seventy four pounds Currant money Of ye Province of ye Massachusets Bay Hath given granted bargained Sold aliened Enfeoffed Conveyed & Confirmed And by these presents doth fully freely Clearly & absolutely give grant bargain Sell Alliene Enfeoffe convey & Confirm unto ye Said Charles ffrost his Heirs & Assignes forever A Certain messuage with a Tract of land adjoyning thereunto Containing in ye whole one hundred & Eight acres Scituate lying & being in ye Township of Kittery afores^d & is ye Plantation or Farm whereon ye Said John Gowen now the Said John Gowen now dwells being butted & bounded as following begining at a Small white oak tree on ye Northwest Corner thereof which tree is ye bounds betweene the Said

Book VIII, Fol. 76.

John Gowen & Nicholas Gowen and from Said tree running
South by East halfe South one hundred &
Eleven poles to a certain red oak tree marked
on four Sides and from thence runing west
halfe north two hundred & fourteen poles to a
Small black burch marked on four Sides and
from thence northwest by north Sixty eight
pole and from thence by Nicholas Gowens land
to y[e] first begining or howsoever otherwise
bounded or reputed to be bounded Together
will all Such rights Liberties Immunities Profits
Priviledges Commodities Emoluments & Appurtenances as in any kind appertain thereunto
with the reversions & remainders thereof and
all the Estate Right Title Interest Inharitance
property possession Claim & demand whatsoever of him the Said John Gowen of in and To
the Same and Every part thereof To Have and
To Hold all y[e] above granted premises with all
& Singular the appurtenances thereof unto y[e]
s[d] Charles Frost his Heirs & Assignes to his
and their own Sole and proper Use benifit and
behoof from hence forth forever: and y[e] Said
John Gowen for him Selfe his Heirs Executors
and Administrators doth hereby Covenant promise grant and
agree to & with y[e] s[d] Charles ffrost his Heirs & and assignes
in manner & form following (That is to Say) that at y[e] time
of the Ensealing & delivery of these Presents, he the Said
John Gowen is y[e] true Sole & Lawfull owner of all y[e] afore
bargained premises and Stands Lawfully Seized thereof in
his own propper right of a good perfect & Indefeazable
Estate of Inheritance in fee Simple Haveing in him Selfe
full power good right & Lawfull Authority to Sell and dispose of the Same in manner as aforesaid & that the Said
Chaarles Frost his, Heirs and assignes Shall & may hence
forth for Ever Lawfully Peaceably and Quietly Have hold
use occupie possess & Enjoy the above granted premises
with the appurtenances thereof Free & Clear & & Clearly
Acquitted & discharge of & from all & all manner of former
& other gifts grants bargains Sales Leases Mortgages Joyntures Dowers Judgments Executions Entailes forfeitures &
of & from all other Titles Troubles Charges & Encumbrances
whatsoever had made committed done or Suffered to be done
by the said John Gowen his Heirs or Assignes at any time
or times before the Ensealing & Delivery hereof & further
the Said John Gowen doth hereby Covenant promiss bind &

oblige himselfe his Heirs Executors and [77] Administors from hence forth & forever hereafter to warrant & defend all the above granted premises & ye appurtenances thereof: unto the Said Charles ffrost his Heirs & assignes against the Lawfull Claims & demands of all & every person or persons whomsoever and Mercy ye wife of the Said John Gowen Doth fully & freely give & Yield up unto the Said Charles ffrost his Heirs & assignes all her Right & Title of Dower & Interest of in or to ye premises Respectively forever by these Presents

Provided Alwayes & These presents are upon Condition Nevertheless That if ye above named John Gowen his Heirs &c^t Shall & do well and truly pay or Cause to be paid unto ye afore named Charles ffrost or his Certain Attorney Heirs Executors Administrators or Assignes at Kittery aforeSaid In Currant money of ye aforesaid Province as it Shall then pass the Sum of Seventy four pounds at or before the Tenth day of February which will be in the Year of our Lord God one Thousand Seven Hundred & Nineteen/ twenty without fraud Coven or further delay That then this present deed of Bargain and Sale/ And every clause & article therein contained Shall Cease determine be null void & of none affect but if default happen to be made in ye afores^d payment contrary to the true Intent hereof then to abide & remain in full force Strength & virtue to all Intents & purposes in y^e Law whatsoever: In Witness whereof y^e s^d John Gowen & Marcy his wife hath hereunto Set Their hands & Seals y^e day & year/ first above written   John Gowen ($_{Seal}^a$)
Signed Sealed & Delivered   Mercy Gowen ($_{Seal}^a$)
in y^e Presents of
John Belcher
Peter Whittom jun^r
Samuel Smalley

York ss/ Feb: y^e 15th 1714/5

The above named John Gowen & Mercy his wife Appeared before me y^e Subscribar one of his Ma^{tys} Justices of y^e peace for y^e County afores^d Acknowledged y^e within written Instrum^t to be their ffree Act & Deed./   John Plaisted

Recorded According to ye Original ffeb^{ry} 22nd 1714/5

p Jos: Hamond Reg^r

This Indenture made ye Twenty Sixth day of March in ye Eighth year of ye Reigne of our Soveraigne Lady Anne by the Grace of god of Greate Brittaine ffrance and Ireland

Book VIII, Fol. 77.

Queen dafender of y{e} faith &c{t} Between John Wincoll of Portsmouth in y{e} Province of New Hampshire in New England Marriner & Deborah his wife of y{e} one part And John Smith of Selmon ffalls in y{e} Town of Barwick in the County of York in New England yeoman Son of James Smith late of Salmon ffalls afore Said Yeoman Deceased of y{e} other part Witnesseth that y{e} Said John wincol and Deborah his wife for and in Consideration of y{e} Sum of Eighty pounds Currant mony of New England to him y{e} S{d} John Wincol at and before y{e} Ensealing and Delivery hereof well and Truly paid by y{e} Seid John Smith y{e} receipt whereof he y{e} s{d} John Smith doth hereby accknowledge & thereof & of Every part and parcell thereof doth acquitt Exonerate and Discharge y{e} S{d} John Smith his Heirs Execut{rs} Administrat{rs} and Assignes and every of them for ever by these psents Hath Given granted Bargained Sold Aliened Enfeoffed Conveyed & Confirmed and by these Presents doth fully ffreely Clearly and absolutely Give grant Bargaine Sale Aliene Enfeoffe Convey and Confirme Unto the Said John Smith his Heirs and assignes for ever Ninety acres of upland be it more or Less Scitate Lying & being at Newichawanock in y{e} Township of Berwick Afores{d} between y{e} land formerly Clement Shorts on y{e} North west & y{e} land formerly Benony Hodsden on y{e} Southeast Upon y{e} Commons on y{e} Northeast and y{e} Highway on y{e} Southwest being part of That Land which was granted unto M{r} John Wincol dec{d} and George Veazy by y{e} Town of Kittery y{e} Eleventh day of December one Thousand Six hundred Sixty & Two Together with all Houses Buildings woods Under woods wayes passages profits advantages and appurtenances whatsoever to y{e} S{d} Ninety acres of Land belonging or in any wise appetaining as also all y{e} Estate Right Title propperty Dowry Claime and demand whatsoever of Them y{e} S{d} John Wincol and Deborah his wife of in or to y{e} pmises or any part or parcell thereof To have and to hold y{e}s{d} Ninety Acres of upland be it more or Less and all and Singular other y{e} before granted and Bargained pmises with Their and Every of their appurtenances and Every part and parcil thereof unto y{e} s{d} John Smith his heirs and assignes for ever to y{e} only propper use and behoof of him y{e} s{d} John Smith his heirs and Assigns for Ever And the Said John Wincol and Deborah his wife Doth for Themselves their heirs Execut{rs} and Administ{rs} Covenant promise grant and agree to and with The s{d} John Smith his Heirs and and assignes in manner and form following (that is to Say) that it Shall and may be Lawfull to and for y{e} s{d} John Smith his Heirs and assignes from time to time and at all Times for

Ever here after peaceably and Quietly to have hold Use occupie possess and Enjoy ye s^d Ninety acres of upland and all and Singular other : the before granted & bargained p^{r}mises with their and Every of their appurtenances and Every part and parcel thereof without ye Least lett Suite Trouble denial Molestation Interruption Expulsion or Eviction of them ye S^d John Wincol & Deborah his wife their heirs Execut^{rs} Administrat^{rs} or assignes or any of them or of any other person or persons whatsoever Claiming by from or under him her them or any of them & that ffree and Clear & freely and Clearly acquitted Exonerated & Discharged of and from all and all Manner of former and other gifts grants bargaines Sales Titles Troubles Dowers Judgments Executions Charges and Incumbrances whatsoever had made comitted [78] Done or Suffered by them ye S^d John Wincol and Deborah his wife Their heirs or assignes or by any : other person or persons Claiming by from or under him her them or any of Them And further ye S^d John Wincol for himselfe and his heirs ye S^d Ninety acres of upland be it more or Less and all and Singular other the pmises before granted Bargained and Sold with their and Every of their appurtenances Unto ye s^d John Smith and his heirs to ye only proper use and behoof of the Said John Smith his heirs and assignes for Ever against him the Said John Wincol his heirs and assignes and all and every other person and persons whatsoever Shall and will warrant and for ever Defend by these psents (ye Lord of ye ffee or ffees only Excepted) In Witness whereof ye s^d John Wincol and Deborah his wife hath hereunto Set their hands & Seals ye day & year first above written Annoq, Domini : 1709/ John Wincol (Seal)
Sealed and Delivered Deborah Wincol (Seal)
   In ye presents off
   Benj^a Gambling
   Cha : Story
     Province of New Hampsh^r 26th of march/ 1709
John wincoll and Deborah his wife psonally appearing acknowledged this Indenture of Bargaine and Sale to be their voluntary Act & deed Coram : Cha Story Jus ps
  Recorded According to ye Original ffeb^{ry} 28th 1714/5/
                     p Jos : Hamond Reg^r

To All Christian People to whom these presents Shall Come Nicholas Morrell of Kittery in ye County of york within his Maj^{ts} Province of ye Massachusets Bay in New

England (Yeoman) Sends Greeting Know Yee that ye Said Nicholas Morrell for & in Consideration of ye Sum of one Hundred and Twenty Pounds Currant money of New England to him in hand paid before the Ensealing and Delivery of these presents by James Davis of Kittery in the County afore Said (Yeoman) the Receipt whereof to full Content and Satisfaction he ye Said Nicholas Morrell doth by these Presents acknowledge and thereof and of Every part thereof for him Selfe his Heirs Executors and Administrators Doth Acquitt Exonerate & Discharge ye S^d James Davis his Heirs Executors & Administrators every of them forever Doth by These presents and for divers other Good Causes and Considerations him hereunto moveing He the Said nicholas Morrell hath given granted bargained Sold Aliened Enfeoffed Conveyed and Confirmed and by these preSents doth fully freely Clearly and absolutely give grant bargaine Sell Aliene Enfeoffe Convey and Confirm unto ye s^d James Davis his Heirs & assignes forever A Certain Tract of Land Containing Thirty five Acres be it more or Less Scituate in Kittery afore Said and is part of ye Land which Said Morrell purchased of Richard Estes as may appear by his Deed of Sale bareing Date the Eighth day of February annoq, Domini 1692/3 : referance : being : had thereunto Begining on ye Northwest Corner at a Stone Standing in ye Corner of ye highway that leads from Cold harbour to Kittery Mill Dam and from s^d Stone bounded by s^d highway from Sturgeon Creek north East by East halfe Northerly one hundred & ninty poles five feet & halfe to another Stone and from thence runing Southeast & by South halfe Easterly Twenty Nine poles four feet & halfe by the propriaters of ye land formerly Mr Mavericks to another Stone Set up and from thence Southwest by west halfe Southerly by the lands belonging to Samuel Hill Junr & Sam^{ll} Hill Senr till it Comes to ye highway at ye northwest corner of Thomas Coxes house and from thence by ye Roade to ye first begining reserving to ye s^d Nicholas Morrell one acre of Land at ye lower Corner next to s^d Coxes house Together with all Such Rights Liberties Immunities Profits priviledges Commodities Emoluments and appurtenances as in any Kind appertain thereunto with ye reversions and remainders thereof and all ye Estate Right Title Interest Inheritance possession Claim and Demand whatsoever of him ye Said nicholas Morrell of in and to the Same and every part thereof To Have and To Hold all the above granted pmises with all & Singular ye appurtenances thereof unto ye s^d James Davis his His Heirs & assignes to His and their one Sole & proper use benefit and behoof from henceforth forever And ye S^d Nicholas Morrell for him Selfe his Heirs Executors and Administrators Doth hereby Covenant promiss Grant & agree to & with the Said James Davis His Heirs & assignes in manner and form following (that is to Say) that at ye time of ye Ensealing and Delivery of these presents he ye S^d Nicholas Morrell is ye true Sole and Lawfull owner of all ye Afore bargained pmises & Stands Lawfully Seized thereof in his own proper Right of a good perfect & Indefeazable Estate of Inheritance in fee Simple having in himSelfe full power good Right & Lawfull Authority to Sell and dispose of the Same in manner as afores^d and that the S^d James Davis his Heirs & assignes Shall and may henceforth forever Lawfully Peaceably & Quietly have hold use occupie possess and Enjoy the above granted premises with ye appurtenances thereof and futher the s^d Nicholas Morrell doth hereby Covenant promiss bind and oblige himSelfe his Heirs Executors and Administrators from henceforth and forever heseafter to warrant and Defend all ye above granted premises unto the Said James Davis his Heires and assignes against ye Lawfull Claimes & demand of all persons whomsoever In Witness whereof the Said Nicholas Morrell hath hereunto Sett his hand and Seal ye Seventh day of march anno Dom one [79] Thousand Seven Hundred and fourteen fifteen 1714/5 annoq, Regni Georgii Regis Primo/ and the above named Nicholas Morrell before the Signing and Sealing of these presents do hereby oblige him Selfe to allow unto y^e s^d James Davis his Heirs Executors administrators & assignes forever a highway of Two poles wide from the river runing by y^e north Side of Adryan Frys dwelling house to y^e Countery Roade

Signed Sealed & Delivered   Nicholas Morrell (s$_e^a$al)
In presents of
Nathan Bartlett
John Gowen
John Gowen Junr
York ss/ march : 7th 1714/5

y^e above named Nicholas morrell acknowledged y^e within written Instrument to be his free act & deed and Sarah his wife also appearing & Delivered up to y^e within named James Davis all her Right Title & Interest of Dower to ye above granted premises   Before me   Charles ffrost Js Peace

Recorded According to ye Original March ye 7th 1714/5/
p Jos : Hamond Reg^r

Book VIII, Fol. 79.

To All Christian People to whom these presents Shall Come John Ingersol of Kittery in y[e] County of york within his Maj[tys] Province of y[e] Massachusets Bay in New England Yeoman Sends Greeting Know Yee that y[e] s[d] John Ingersol for and in Consideration of y[e] Parental love & affection which he hath and dos bare towards his well beloved Son Elisha Ingersol & Son In Law John Chapman both of Kittery In y[e] County afores[d] Yeomen have given & granted & by these presents do freely Clearly and absolutely give and grant to y[e] S[d] Elisha Ingersol and John Chapman their Several Respectives Heirs In Fee Tail all y[e] Estate Right Title Interest Inheritance property possession Claim & demand whatsoever of him y[e] S[d] John IngerSol of in and to all his Land & Tenements within the Township of Falmouth Alias Casco in y[e] County of York aforeSaid Excepting & reserving A Certain Tract or percell of Land which the Said John Ingersol bought of M[r] George Montjoy (That is to Say) y[e] Farm whereon y[e] S[d] John Ingersol formerly dwelt He y[e] S[d] John Ingersol Doth hereby give & grant to y[e] s[d] Elisha Ingersol the Southermost part thereof and to the Said John Chapman y[e] Northermost part thereof to be Equally Divided between them y[e] S[d] Elisha Ingersol & John Chapman & So to Descend to their Several respective Heirs in Tail for ever and all other the Land & Tenements belonging or any wayes appurtaining to the Said John Ingersol Excepting the above mentioned Land bought of M[r] Montjoy He y[e] s[d] John Ingersol doth hereby give & grant to y[e] S[d] Elisha Ingersol & John Chapman their Several Respective Heires forever To be Equally divided between them y[e] s[d] Elisha Ingersol and John Chapman & their Several Respective Heirs as afores[d] forever: To Have & To Hold all the above granted pmises Together with all & Singular the appurtenances thereof unto y[e] S[d] Elisha Ingersol & John Chapman their Several Respective Heirs as aforeSaid To their own Sole & proper use benifit & behoof henceforth & forever more

In Witness whereof The Said John Ingersol hath hereunto Set his hand & Seal the fourteenth day of march In y[e] year of our Lord one Thousand Seven hundred & fifteen & in the first Year of y[e] Reign of our Lord George King of England &c[t]

Signed Sealed & Delivered
  In presents of
Charles ffrost
John Belcher
Charles ffrost jun[r]

John his Ingersol (Seal[a])
mark

Book VIII, Fol. 80.

York ss/ March 14th 1715/
the above named John Ingersol acknowledged the within written Instrument to be his free act and Deed
      Before me Charles ffrost J peace
Recorded According to ye Original March ye 15th 1714/5
       p Jos: Hamohd Reg^r

To All People unto whom this present Deed of Sale Shall come John Heard of Kittery in ye County of york in ye Province of ye Massachusets Bay in New England Yeoman Sendeth Greeting Know Yee that for and in Consideration of ye Sum of Thirty three pounds Currant money of New England to me in hand paid at and before the enSealing & Delivery of these presents by Nicholas Morrell of ye Same Kittery afores^d Bricklayer the Receipt whereof He Doth hereby acknowledge and himselfe therewith to be fully Satisfyed & paid and thereof & of & from every part & parcell thereof for him his Heirs Executors & Administrators Doth Exonerate acquitt and fully discharge ye s^d Nicholas Morrell his Heirs Execut^{rs} and Administrat^{rs} by these presents forever ye s^d John Heard hath Given granted bargained Sold Aliened Conveyed Enfeoffed Delivered & Confirmed and by these p^{r}sents Doth for Himselfe his Heirs Executors and Administrators fully freely and absolutely give grant bargaine Sell aliene Enfeoffe Deliver and Confirm unto thes^d Nicholas Morrell his heirs and Assigns a Certaine Tract or parcell of Land Scittuate & being in ye Township of Kittery afores^d Containing Thirty acres Bounded on ye west End by a line going South from Sturgion Creek on ye South Side over against a point of marsh called the round about marsh Belonging to Reinold Jinkins and So To run upon s^d South line to Emerys way which goes from Sturgeon Creek to Cold Harbour & So to run East up by ye s^d Creek and all ye breadth to ye s^d Emerys way till Thirty acres be accomplished which s^d Thirty acres of Land was [80] Given and granted unto John Heard Grandfather to John Heard ye grantor by ye Town of Kittery on ye twenty fourth day of June 1662/ as p the grant recorded in the Records of s^d Town more at Large Doth appear Together with all ye Several Bennefits priviledges rights Liberties and appurtenances to ye s^d Land belonging or in any wise appurtaining To Have & To Hold ye s^d Tract or parcell of Land wth all its priviledges and appurtenances to ye afores^d Nicholas Morrell his Heirs and assignes and to his and their Sole and

Book VIII, Fol. 80.

proper use benefit & behoof forever and ye s^d John Heard Doth for himselfe his Heirs Executors & Administrators Covena^t promiss and grant to & with ye s^d Nicholas Morrell his Heirs Executors administrators & assignes that at and before ye ensealing & Delivery hereof he is ye true right and propper owner of ye above bargained p^rmises and their appurtenances and that he is Legally posest thereof and have good right full power and Lawfull authority in my own name to give to give grant Sell and convey ye Same as afores^d unto ye s^d Nicholas Morrell his Heirs & assignes & that ye Same and Every part thereof is free & Clear & clearly acquitted and Discharged off and from all former and other gifts grants Sales Leases Mortgages Dowryes Titles Troubles alienations and Incumbrances whatsoever and that it Shall and may be Lawfull to & for him ye s^d Nicholas Morrell his Heirs & assignes forever hereafter to have hold use Occupie possess & Enjoy peaceably and Quietly to his and Their use & uses all ye Demised pmises and their appurtenances and that ye Sale thereof against my Selfe my Heirs Execut^{rs} & Administrat^{rs} & against all other p^rsons whatsoever Lawfully Claiming ye Same or any part thereof from by or und^r me or my s^d Grandfather John Heard Dec^d I will for ever Save harmless Warrant & Defend by these p^rsents In Witness whereof I ye s^d John Heard have hereunto Set my hand & affixed my Seal this Seventeenth day of Decemb^r in ye Tenth year of ye Reign of our Soveraign Lady Anne of Great Brittain &c^a Queen Annoq, Domini One Thousand Seven Hundred & Eleven./ 1711/   John Heard (Seal)

Signed Sealed & Delivered
  In the presents of us
  Joseph Smith
  Nicholas Cole
  Joseph Hamond
    York ss/ March 7th 1714/5

The above named John Heard acknowledged the above written InStrument to be his free act and Deed
                Before me   Charles ffrost J Peace
Recorded According to ye Original March 9th 1714/5
                      p Jos∴Hamond Reg^r

  To All People to whom these Presents Shall Come Greeting Viz: Know Yee that I Thomas Huff of Kittery in the County of York within her Majesties Province of ye Massachusets Bay in New England House Carpenter for & in Consideration of yᵉ Sum of fifty pounds in good & Lawfull money of yᵉ Province aforesᵈ to me in hand before yᵉ Enscaling hereof well & Truly paid by William Pepperell junʳ of sᵈ Town and County aforesᵈ Merchant yᵉ receipt whereof I Do hereby acknowledge & my Selfe therewith fully Satisfied and Contented & thereof & of Every part & parcell thereof Do Exonerate acquit & Discharge yᵉ sᵈ William Pepperell junʳ his Heirs Executʳˢ & Administratʳˢ for ever by these psents have Given Granted Bargained Sold Aliened Conveyed & Confirmed & by these psents D freely fully & absolutely give grant bargaine Sell aliene Convey & Confirm unto him yᵉ sᵈ Wᵐ Pepperrell junʳ his Heirs & assignes for ever one Messuage or Tract of uplpand & meadow Scittuate lying & being in Kittery in yᵉ County aforesᵈ Containing by Estemation Eighteen acres be it more or Less wᶜʰ is yᵉ Land where I formerly Dwelt & Lyes between Henry Barter & Joseph Crockits Land where yᵉ sᵈ Barter & Crockit now Dwells wᶜʰ Land was given to me yᵉ sᵈ Thomas Huff by my father In Law Aaron Farris as will more at Large appear by a Deed of Gift undʳ Said Aaron Ferrises hands Together with all yᵉ houses barns Orchards Timber trees wood waters & water Courses wᵗˢoever To have & To hold yᵉ sᵈ granted & bargained Premises with all yᵉ appurtenances Priviledges and Comodities to yᵉ Same belonging or in any ways appurtaining to him yᵉ sᵈ Wᵐ Pepperrell junʳ his Heirs & assignes for Ever to his & their only proper use benefit & behalfe for Ever & I yᵉ sᵈ Thomas Huff for mee my Heirs Executors Administrators Do Covenant promiss & grant to & with yᵉ sᵈ Wᵐ Pepperrell junʳ his Heirs and assignes that before yᵉ Enseaing hereof I am yᵉ True Sole and Lawfull Owner of yᵉ above Bargained premises & am Lawfully seized and possessed of yᵉ Same in mine own proper right as a good perfect & Absolute Estate of Inheritance in ffee Simple and have in my Selfe good right full power & Lawfull authority to Grant bargaine Sell convey & Confirm Said bargained pmises in manner as aforesᵈ & That yᵉ sᵈ Wᵐ Pepperrell junʳ his Heirs & assignes Shall and may from Time to Time & at all Times for Ever hereafter by fforce & Virtue of these presents Lawfully peaceably & Quietly have hold use Occupie possess & Enjoy yᵉ sᵈ Demised & bargained Premises with yᵉ appurtenances ffree and Clear and ffreely and Clearly acquitted Exonerated and Discharged of from all & all manner of former & other Gifts grants bargaines Sales Leases Mortgages Wills Entails [81]

Joyntures Dowers Judgments Executions Incumbrances & Extents Further more I ye s^d Thomas Huff for my Selfe my Heirs Execut^{rs} Administrators Do Covenant & Engage the above Demised Premises To him ye s^d Wm Pepperrell jun^r his Heirs & assignes against the Lawfull Claimes or Demands of any perSon or perSons w^{t}soever For ever hereafter to warrant Secure & Defend & Grace Huff The wife of mee the s^d Thomas Huff Doth by these Presents ffreely Willingly Give yeald up and Surrender all her right of Dowry And power of Thirds of in & unto ye above Demised premises unto him ye s^d Wm Pepperrell jun^r his Heirs & assignes In Witness whereof I hereunto Set my hand & Seal the Tenth Day of March in ye first Year of ye Reign of our SoverAign King George by ye Grace of God King of Great Brittaine ffrance & Ireland and in ye year of our Lord one Thousand Seven Hundred & fourteen fifteen   Thomas Huff (Seal)
Signed Sealed & Delivered   (Seal)
In the Presents of
Sarah Dearing

Meriam Pepperrell
Dorithy Pepperrell
    Kittery 10th day of March 1714/5
This Day Thomas Huff Parsonaly appeared before me ye Subscriber one of his Maj^{tys} justices for ye County of York & acknowledged this above written Deed or Obligation to be his free act & Deed   Wm Pepperrell
Recorded According to ye Original March ye 10th 1714/5./
                p Jos Hamond Reg^r

    Know All persons Concerned that I Thomas Huff within & this deed above & within Named have for ye vallue of forty one pounds 18^s to me in hand paid by Sam^{ll} Penhallow Esqr of Portsm^o in the Province of New Hampshire ye rec^t whereof I do hereby Acknowledged and my Selfe to be fully Satisfied Contented & paid have bargained Sold Enfeoffed released & Confirmed & by these presents do freely firmly and Absolutely bargaine Sell release Enfeoffe & Confirm unto him ye s^d Penhallow his heirs Execut^{rs} Adm^{rs} & Assignes forever all ye right Title Claime & Interest that I have to all & Every part & parcell of ye within Mentioned houses Lands Stock & Every particular thing & things as they Stand Mentioned in ye above & within Deed made to me & my wife the Same & Every part thereof To have & To hold unto him ye s^d Penhallow his heirs Executors

Book VIII, Fol. 81.

Adm[rs] and Assignes forever without y[e] least Lett Trouble hinderence Interuption of me y[e] s[d] Huff my heirs Execut[rs] or Adm[rs] or any other person or persons whatsoever Claiming any right Title or Interest To the Same or any part thereof forever./ Alwayes provided & it is to be understood that if I y[e] s[d] Huff my heirs Execut[rs] Adm[rs]. Assigns or Order do well & Truely pay or Cause to be paid unto y[e] s[d] Penhallow his heirs Assigns or ord[r] y[e] full Sum of forty one pounds Eighteen Shillings Together with Lawfull Interest in Merchantable fish at Money price At or before y[e] first day of Decemb[r] in y[e] year one Thousand Seven hundred & Sixteen Then y[e] Above deed to be Voyd otherwayes to Stand in full force & vertue as Witness my hand & Seal this 15th day of Decemb[r] 1713./ the words Lawfull Interest So Interlined before Signing —   Thomas Huff (Seal)
Signed Sealed & Delivered
  In psence of
  John Pickerin
  John Hoard

Tho: Huff psonally Appeared before me y[e] Subscrib[r] hereof one of her Maj[tys] Justices of y[e] peace for y[e] province of New Hampsh[r] this 15th day Dec[r] 1713./ and Acknowledged y[e] Indenture of Bargain & Sale on y[e] other Side to be his free Act & Deed   Richard Gerrish

This above & on y[e] other Side was written on y[e] back side of a deed given by Aaron fferris & Grace his wife to Thomas Huff y[e] Granter bareing Date y[e] 14th of ffeb[ry] 1708 & recorded in this book Folio 13th is here recorded According to y[e] Original this 17th of March 1714/5./
                                p Jos Hamond Reg[r]

Know all men by these presents that I Sam[ll] Penhallow of Portsmouth in y[e] Province of New Hampsh[r] In New England for & in Consideration of y[e] Sum of forty four pounds Ninteen Shillings and Three pence to me this day in hand paid by William Pepperrell jun[r] of Kittery in y[e] County of York Gentleman have Sold and made Over & these p[r]sents do Sell Aliene Enfeoffe Convey make Over & Confirm all my right Title and Interest to y[e] within Mortgage of Thomas Huff from me my Heirs & Assignes in as full &   manner to all Intents & purposes unto y[e] s[d] W[m] Pepperrell jun[r] as I y[e] s[d] Sam[ll] Penhallow have y[e] Same from y[e] s[d] Huff To have & To hold unto him y[e] s[d] Pepperrell his Heirs & Assignes for ever In Testimony whereof I Have hereunto Set my hand & Seale this 10th of march 1714/5

Signed Sealed & Delivered   Sam^ll Penhallow ($_{Seal}^{a}$)
In y^e Presence of
Theo Atkinson
Lydia Penhallow

Pro N Hamp^r 10 march 1714/5

Sam^ll Penhallow Esqr Acknowledged y^e above to be his Act Before: Theo: Atkinson J peas.

Recorded According to y^e Original March 17th 1714/5/
         p Jos: Hamond Reg^r

[82] This Indenture Witnesseth a bargaine of Exchange Between John Heard of Kittery in ye County of york in New England yeoman on ye one part & Nicholas Morrell of ye Same town & County Brick Layer on ye other part wch is as followeth vizt Thes^d John Heard Doth by these p^rsents Give Grant bargaine Sell release Allien Convey & Confirm unto ye s^d Nicholas Morrell a Certaine Tract of Land in ye Township of Kittery afores^d Begining at ye highway Leading from Sturgeon Creek Bridge to ye Ceders Joyning to ye Land of Nicholas ffrosts dec^d thence North East Six pole thence North Northwest four poles thence North East Twenty five pole thence South East to ye Rode Twenty Eight pole together with all & Singular ye profits priviledges & appurtenances thereunto belonging or in any wise Apperttaining with all Right title Interest Claime & Demand of him ye s^d John Heard heirs Executors Administrators & assignes of in & to ye Same to have & to hold ye s^d Tract of Land & Every part & p^rcell thereof with all ye priviledges & appur^ces herein before Granted Bargained & Sold unto him ye s^d Nicholas Morrell his Heirs & assignes for Ever./, And ye s^d Nicholas Morrell doth by these p^rsents Give grant Bargain Sell Release Aliene Convey & Confirm unto ye s^d John Heard a Certain tract of Land in ye Township of Kittery afores^d Bounded on ye Northwest by ye Country Road Leading from Sturgeon Creek bridge Toward Newchewanack & on ye South by Sturgeon Creek & on all other Sides by ye Lands of ye s^d John Heard it being part of ye Antient Possession of Abra^m Conley dec^d which ye s^d Nicholas Morrell purchased of William Lord of Kittery afores^d as p his Deed Bareing Date with these p^rsents Doth more at Large Appear together with all & Singular ye profits Priviledges & Appurtenances thereunto belonging or in any wise appertain-

BOOK VIII, FOL. 82.

ing with all Right Title Interest Claime and demand of him y[e] s[d] Nicholas Morrell his heirs Execut[rs] Adm[rs] & Assignes of in & to y[e] Same To have & To hold y[e] s[d] Tract of Land & Every part & parcell thereof with all the priviledges & appur[ces] herein before Granted bargained & Sold unto him y[e] s[d] John Heard his Heirs & assignes forever In Confirmation of all above written wee y[e] s[d] John Heard & Nicholas Morrell have hereunto Set our hands & Seals this Second day of March in y[e] Eighth year of y[e] Reign of our Soveraign Lady Anne of Great Brittaine &c[a] Queen Annoq, Domini one thousand Seven Hundred & Nine Tenn/ 1709/10
Signed Sealed & D[d]   John Heard (Seal)
In Presents of us   Nicholas Morrell (Seal)
      his
John ✝ Brooks
     mark
Nicholas Gowen
          York ss/ March : 7th 1714/5

The within named John Heard & Nicholas Morrel Acknowledged y[e] within written Instrument to be their free Act & Deed.   Before me   Charles ffrost J : Peace :
Recorded According to y[e] Original March y[e] 9th 1714/5
                  p Jos : Hamond R[e]g[r]

To All People to whom this present Deed or Instrument in writing Shall Come Moses Woster of Kittery in y[e] County of york within his Maj[tys] Province of y[e] Massachusets Bay in New England Sends Greeting Know yee that y[e] s[d] Moses Worster for and in Consideration of y[e] Natural Affection which I Have & bear towards my Well beloved Sonn Thomas Worster of y[e] Same place yeoman & More Especially for y[e] Consideration of Sixty pounds Currant money of y[e] Province afores[d] to be paid by y[e] s[d] Thomas Worster his Heirs Execut[rs.] or Admin[rs] As hereafter in this Instrum[t] is Expressed I y[e] s[d] Moses Worster have Given Granted Bargained Sold Aliened Enfeoffed Conveyed & Confirmed & by these presents Do fully freely Clearly & Absolutely give grant bargaine Sell Aliene Enfeoffe Convey & Confirm unto y[e] s[d] Thomas Worster his Heirs & Assignes forever all that my remaining part of Two Hundred Acres of Land purchased of Cap[tn] John Wincoll with y[e] remaining part of An Addition of Sixty rods back from y[e] head thereof & also his whole remaining part of Two Town grants of Land Laid out and bounded To him Selfe with y[e] remaining part of a

Saw mill wth Utencills and Implem^{ts} thereto belonging Standing on ye river known by ye name of Worsters river Above ye Sallmonfalls with his whole Right and Interest in s^d river being ye whole remaining part of s^d Worsters Land & p^{r}mises as afores^d which are particularly Discribed & Set forth in a certaine Instrument or Indenture between the Said Moses Worster And his s^d Son under their hands & Seals bareing Date y^e thirtyeth day of Novemb^r in y^e year of our Lord Seventeen Hundred & Eleven & Recorded at Length wth the Records of Deeds for y^e County of york/ Lib^r 7th ffol^o 163 = Reference thereunto being had more at Large Doth appeare wch Said Tract or remaining part of Land is bounded by Sallmonfalls river Southwestward by y^e Land before given to y^e s^d Thomas Worster Southeastward George Broughtons Land Northwestward & running back North East & by North to y^e furthest Extent of s^d Worsters Land Together with all ye Trees woods und^r woods waters water Courses Swamps Meadows rights members profits priviledges Comoditys Advantages heridittaments And appurtenances whatsoever upon belonging or in Any wise Appertaining unto ye granted p^{r}mises or any part or parcell thereof belonging And all ye Estates right title Interest use property possession Claime & Demand whatso ever of Him ye s^d Moses Worster his Heirs Execut^{rs} Administrat^{rs} and Assignes of in & to ye Same & Every part thereof To have & To hold ye s^d Tract of Land river Sawmill Saws Doggs Crows Dams ruñing Gear & all & Singular ye p^{r}mises & Appurtenances before Mentioned unto him y^{e}s^d Thomas Worster his Heirs Execut^{rs} Administrat^{rs} & Assignes forever more & to his & their own propper use benefit & behoofe free from all manner of Incumbrances) w^{t}soever [83] And ye s^d Moses Worster for him Selfe his Heirs Exut^{rs} & Admin^{rs} To & with him ye s^d Thomas Worster his Heirs & assignes Doth by these Presents Covenant & Promiss to warrãnt & Defend ye Title & possession thereof unto him ye s^d Thomas Worster his Heirs & assignes against the Lawfull Claims & Demands of all Persons whatsoever Claiming ye Same or any Part Thereof

And ye s^d Moses Worster before ye Ensealing hereof Doth order and appoint ye s^d Thomas Worster to pay ye aboves^d Suñ of Sixty pounds the Purchase Consideration of ye above granted p^{r}mises in maner following (that is to Say) Thirty pounds ye Moiety thereof unto his Brother William Worster & Thirty pounds ye other Moiety thereof unto his Sister Elizabeth Worster ye Son & Daughter of ye s^d Moses Worster at or before y^e first day of March which Shall be in y^e year of our Lord Seventeen Hundred & Twenty five any

thing herein Contained to y^e Contrary hereof in any wise NotwithStanding In Witness whereof y^e s^d Moses Worster Hath hereunto Set his hand & Seal y^e Twenty first Day of March annoq$_a$ Domini Seventeen Hundred & fourteen fifteen Annoq$_a$ RR^s Georgii Magna Brittania &c^t Primo
Signed Sealed & Delivered
 In Presents of us   Moses $\underset{\text{mark}}{L}$ Worster ($\underset{\text{Seal}}{\text{a}}$)
 Charles ffrost
 Richd Rice
 Joseph Hamond
 York ss/ Kittery y^e 21st of March/ 1714/5
Moses Worster above Named psonally appearing Acknowledged y^e above written Instrum^t to be his free act & Deed
    Coram Charles ffrost J : Peace
Recorded According to y^e Original March 21st 1714/5./
     p Jos : Hamond Reg^r

To All People to whom these presents Shall Come Nicholas Morrell of Kittery in ye County of York within his Maj^{tys} Province of the Massachusets Bay in New England Brick layer Sends Greeting Know Yee that ye s^d Nicholas Morrell for and in Consideration of ye Sum of Twenty four pounds Currant money of New England to him in hand at & before ye Ensealing & Delivery of these presents well & Truly paid by Nathan Bartlett of ye Same Kittery afores^d Tanner the receipt whereof to full Content & Satisfaction he ye s^d Nicholas Morrell Doth by these p^{r}sents Acknowledge & thereof & of Every part thereof for himselfe His Heirs Executors & Administrat^{rs} Doth acquit Exonerate & Discharge the Said Nathan Bartlet his Heirs Executors & Admin^{rs} for ever by these Presents He ye s^d Nicholas Morrell Hath given granted bargained Sold aliened Enfeoffed Conveyed & Confirmed & by these p^{r}sents Doth fully freely Clearly & absolutely give grant bargaine Sell aliene Enfeoffe Convey & Confirm unto him ye s^d Nathan Bartlet his Heirs & Assignes for ever a Certaine Tract of Land Containing four acres Be ye Same more or Less Setttuate Lying & being in Kittery afores^d on ye North Side of a place Called Sturgeon Creek begining at ye Highway that Leads
From Sturgeon Creek bridge to ye Ceaders from Thence Joyning to ye Land of Nicholas ffrosts Deceas^d Northeast Six poles Thence north Northwest four pole Thence North East Twenty five pole Thence South east to ye Road leading from s^d Bridge Towards Newchewanack Twenty Eight pole Thence

Southwest a Little westward Twenty Six pole & from Thence by y̑ᵉ path from y̑ᵉ bridge to y̑ᵉ Cedars to y̑ᵉ first Station Twenty Six pole which piece of Land sᵈ Morrell purchased in part of William Lord and in part of John Heard as by Certaine Deeds undʳ their hands & Seals bareing Date y̑ᵉ Second Day of March Annoq̑ Domini Seventeen Hundred & Nine Teñ or however otherwise bounded or reputed to be bounded Together with all Such rights Liberties Imunities profits priviledges Comodityes Emolumᵗˢ & Appurtenances As in any kind Appurtaine Thereunto with y̑ᵉ reversions & remainders thereof & all y̑ᵉ Estate right Title Interest Inheritance propperty possession Claime & Demand whatsoever of him y̑ᵉ sᵈ Nicholas Morrell of in & to y̑ᵉ Same & Every part thereof To have & To hold all y̑ᵉ above granted pʳmises with all & Singular y̑ᵉ Appurtenances thereof unto y̑ᵉ sᵈ Nathan Bartlet his Heirs & assignes to his & their own Sole & propper use benefit and behoofe from hence forth for ever And y̑ᵉ sᵈ Nicholas Morrell for himselfe his Heirs Execuᵗʳˢ & Administrators Doth hereby Covenant Promiss grant & agree to & with y̑ᵉ sᵈ Nathan Bartlet his Heirs & Assignes in manner & form following (That is To Say) That At y̑ᵉ Time of y̑ᵉ Ensealing & Delivery of these pʳsents he y̑ᵉ sᵈ Nicholas Morrell is y̑ᵉ true Sole & Lawfull owner of all Afore bargained premises & Stands Lawfully Seized thereof in his own propper right as a good perfect & Indefeazable Estate of Inheritance In ffee Simple having in him Selfe full power good Right & Lawfull Authority to Sell & Dispose of y̑ᵉ Same in manner as aforesᵈ & that y̑ᵉ sᵈ Nathan Bartlet his Heirs & Assignes Shall & may henceforth for ever Lawfully peaceably & quietly have Hold use Occupie possess & Enjoy y̑ᵉ Above granted premises with y̑ᵉ Appurtenances thereof free & Clear & Clearly acquitted & Discharged of & from all & all mañer of former & other gifts grants bargains Sales Leases Mortgages Joyntures Dowers Judgments Executions Entails forfitures & of & from all other Titles Troubles Charges & Incumbrances whatsoever & further y̑ᵉ sᵈ Nicholas Morrell Doth hereby Covenant promiss bind & oblige himselfe his Heirs Executors & Administratʳˢ from henceforth & for ever hereafter to Warrant & Defend all y̑ᵉ above granted premises & y̑ᵉ appurtenances thereof unto y̑ᵉ sᵈ Nathan Bartlet his heirs & assignes against y̑ᵉ Lawfull Claimes & Demands of all & Every pson or psons whomsoever In Witness whereof y̑ᵉ sᵈ Nicholas Morrell hath hereunto Set his Hand & Seal y̑ᵉ Tenth day of March in y̑ᵉ year

BOOK VIII, FOL. 84.

of our Lord Seventeen Hundred & fourteen fifteen Annoq̨
Regni Georgii Regis Primo   Nicholas Morrell ($_{Seal}^{a}$)
Signed Sealed & Delivered
 In y^e PreSents of us
 John Bellcher
 James Davis
 Charles ffrost Junr
    York ss/ March 22^d 1714/5
 y^e within Named Nicholas Morrell acknowledged y^e within
written Instrum^t to be his free act & deed & Sarah y^e wife of
y^e s^d Morrell also appearing & Surrendered up her right of
Dower to ye within granted p^{r}mises
              before me Charles ffrost J peace
 Recorded According to ye Original March 23^d 1714/5.
            p Jos: Ham̃ond Reg^r

[84] Know All men by these presents that I Thomas
Spinney of Kittery In ye County of york In New England
Cordwainer for & in ConSideration of ye Sum of Six pounds
in money to me in hand paid before the Ensealing hereof
by my Cuzen James ffernald of ye Same place Yeoman y^e
receipt whereof I Do Acknowledge and my Self therewith
fully Satisfied Contented & paid Have Given Granted bargained & Sold & Confirmed & by these presents do ffreely
fully & Absolutely give grant bargaine Sell Convey & Confirm unto him ye s^d James ffernald his Heirs & Assignes forever all that tract of Land Lying & being in Kittery afores^d
by Estemation two acres be it more or Less butted & bounded
on ye South with ye s^d James ffernalds own Land Eleven
pole in Breadth & by a brook of water on ye East twenty
four pole & John Spinneys Land on ye west in length Twenty
four pole & on ye North with my own land ye whole breadth
thereof To have & To hold all ye s^d Granted & bargained
premises with all ye appurtenances priviledges & Commodities
to ye Same belonging or appertaining to him ye s^d James
ffernald his Heirs or assignes forever to his & their proper
use benefit & & behoof for Ever And I ye s^d Thomas Spinney Do for my Selfe & my Heirs Covenant To & with ye s^d
James ffernald & his & assignes that ye s^d land & p^{r}mises are
free from all Incumbrances whatsoever & that I am ye True
& Lawfull owner thereof at & before ye Signing & Sealing
hereof & have within my Selfe full power & Lawfull authority
to Sell & Dispose of ye Same & that it Shall be Lawfull for
ye s^d James ffernald his Heirs & assignes to use Occupie &

Book VIII, Fol. 84.

possess y° Same freely & Clearly acquitted & Discharged from all manner of former & other gifts grants bargains Sales wills or joinntures y° peaceable Possession thereof To Warrant and for Ever Defend against all persons whatsoever Laying Lawfull Claime thereunto In Witness whereof I have hereunto Set my hand & Seal this Twenty first day of march one Thousand Seven hundred & fifteen
Signed Sealed & Delivered   y° Sign of
  In y° p^r sents of us y°   Thomas ⌠ Spinney (Seal)
Subscriber
    y° Sign of   y° Sign of
John ◯ Gilden
                     Christain ⟨ Spinney
William Godsoe
    y° Sign of
Elizabeth E Godsoe

I Christain Spinney Do Render up all my Right of Dowery in y° aboves^d land to my Cuzen James ffernald witness my hand & Seal y° day & year aboves^d York ss/ March 21st 1714/5

   the within named Thomas Spinney acknowledged y° within written Instrum^t to be his free act & Deed Before me
                           Charles ffrost J peace
Recorded According to y° Original March 21st 1714/5.
                              p Jos: Hamond Reg^r

   To All People to whom these psents Shall Come Edmund Gage of the Town of Kittery in the County of York in the Province of Maine in New England Yeoman Sendeth Greeting Know Yee that y° s^d Edmund Gage For & in consideration of the Sum of fifty Pounds Currant money of New England to him in hand before the Ensealing and Delivery hereof well and truly paid By Ebenezar More of the Same place Shipwright the receipt whereof he the S^d Edmand Gage Doth hereby acknowledge & himselfe therewith fully Satisfyed and Contented and thereof and of Every part and pcell thereof Do Exonerate Acquit & Discharge the S^d Ebenezar More his Heirs Ex^rs adm^rs & Assignes forever By these psents have given granted Bargained Sold aliened Enfeoffed Conveyed & Confirmed and by these psents Doe fully freely Clearly & Absolutely Give grant Bargaine Sell Aliene Enfeoffe Convey & Confirm unto him the Said Ebenezar More his Heirs & Assignes for Ever A Certaine tract or pcell of upland Containing twenty two acres & three acres of Marsh Adjoyning to it Scittuate lying & being on the

Northwest Side of Broadbut: Harbour In ye County affores^d & bounded as followeth (that is to Say) by a pine tree marked four Square being on a Little Hummock in ye Marsh on ye East End & So Northwest by ye Land of Henry Brown & James Oare to ye head of Andrews line one Hundred & Sixty Pole & from the S^d Pine tree on ye humock twenty Eight Pole to a maple tree marked four Square Near a Little run of water for his braadth to ye Marsh & from thence North west to ye s^d Andrews line together with all woods underwoods Standing Lying & being on ye Same with all other p^{r}viledges & appurtenances to ye Same p^{r}mises belonging or in any wise appertaining To have & To hold all & Singular the above granted & bargained p^{r}mises together with ye priviledges & Appurtenances unto him ye s^d Ebenezer More his Heirs & assignes forever ffree & Cleare from all Titles Troubles charges & Incumbrances had made Comitted or done or Suffered To be done by me ye s^d Edmund Gage my heirs Ex^{rs} Adm^{rs} or assignes or by any other pson by from or under me them or any of them and that ye s^d Ebenezar More his heirs & assignes Shall and may for Ever hereafter Lawfully peaceably & Quietly have hold use occupie possess & Injoy all ye above granted & bargained pmises without the Least Hurt trouble Deniall or Mollestation of me ye s^d Edmund Gage My Heirs Execut^{rs} Adm^{rs} or Assignes or any other pson or psons by from or und^r me them or any of them Furthermore I ye s^d Edmund Gage for me my Heirs Ex^{rs} & Adm^{rs} Doe Covenant Promise And Engage from hence forth & for Ever hereafter to warrant Secure & Defend all ye before granted & bargained p^{r}mises & ye appurtenances thereof unto ye s^d Ebenezer More his Heirs & assignes against the Lawfull Claimes & Demands of all & Every pson & psons whomsoever To warrant Secure and Defend Alsoe Johanah the wife of me ye s^d

[85] Edmund Gage Doth by these presents freely & Willingly Give Yeald up and Surrender All her right of Dowry & power of thirds of in & unto All ye Above granted & bargained p^{r}mises unto him ye s^d Ebenezar More his Heirs and Assignes for Ever In Witness whereof they ye s^d Edmund Gage & Johannah his wife Have Hereunto Set their hands & Seals this Twenty Eighth Day of ffebruary In ye year of our Lord one Thousand Seven Hundred & fourteen fifteen) Whereas the Dwelling House Barn & Orchards are Not pticularly Exprest before I ye s^d Edmund Gage & Johannah my wife for our Selves our heirs Ex^{rs} Adm^{rs} & assignes Doe by these psents alsoe Intend No other but that they are

absolutely y̆ᵉ sᵈ Ebenezer Mores His Heirs & assignes for Ever as all yᵉ other bargained premises are
Signed Sealed & Delivered
    In psents of us
    Robert Lang
    James Jeffry

yᵉ mark of
Edmund E Gage (ₛₑₐₗ ᵃ)

her
Johanah ⟂ Gage (ₛₑₐₗ ᵃ)
mark

Kittery march 3ᵈ Day 1714/5
This Day Edmund Gage & Johanah his wife both personally appeared before me yᵉ Subscriber & acknowledged this above written Deed or Obligation to their ffree act & Deed
                    Wᵐ Pepperrell J Pes
Recorded According to yᵉ Original March 21ˢᵗ 1714/5.
                    p Jos: Hamond Regʳ

To All People to whom these presents Shall Come Greeting Know Yee that I Hannah Willson of Kittery In yᵉ County of York in New England widdow for and in Consideration of yᵉ Sum of thirty Six pounds good & Lawfull money of aforesᵈ to me in hand before yᵉ Ensealing hereof well and Truly paid by Ebenezer More of sᵈ town & County Shipwright yᵉ receipt whereof I Doe hereby acknowledge & my Selfe therewith fully & Entierly Satisfied & contented & thereof & of Every part & parcell thereof Do Exonerate acquit & Discharge yᵉ sᵈ Ebenezʳ More his Heirs Executors Admʳˢ for Ever by these presents Have given granted Bargained Sold aliened Conveyᵈ and confirmed & by these presents Do freely fully & Absolutely Give grant Bargaine Sell aliene Convey & Confirm unto him yᵉ sᵈ Ebenezʳ More his Heirs and assignes for Ever one Quartʳ part of a Sawmill Scittuate Lying & being on yᵉ East Side of Spruce Creek it being part of yᵉ Mill which my Husband Joseph Willson Now Deceasᵈ was formerly possest of wᵗʰ one quarter Part of yᵉ Stream belonging to yᵉ aforesᵈ mill with one quartʳ of all Saws Crows of Iron and all her appurtenances & priviledges to her belonging or in any ways appertaining wᶜʰ are Mentioned or not mentioned in this Said Deed To have and To hold the Said pʳmises as aforesᵈ wᵗʰ all yᵉ appurtenances & Priviledges to her belonging or in any wais appertaining to him yᵉ sᵈ Ebenezar More his Heirs & Assignes forever to his & their only propper use benefit & behalfe forEver & I yᵉ sᵈ Hannah Willson for me my Heirs Exʳˢ Admʳˢ Do Covenant promiss & grant to and with yᵉ sᵈ Ebenezar More his Heirs and assignes   That before yᵉ Ensealing Hereof I am yᵉ True Sole & Lawfull Owner of yᵉ above Bargained Premises & am Lawfully Seized and Possessed of yᵉ Same in mine own propper right as a good perfect & Absolute Estate of Inheritance In ffee Simple & Have in my Selfe good right full Power & Lawfull Authority to grant bargaine Sell Convey & Confirm Said Bargained Premises in Maner as abovesᵈ and that he yᵉ sᵈ Ebenezar More his Heirs & assignes Shall & may from time to time & at all Times forever Hereafter by force & vertue of these presents Lawfully Peaceably & Quietly Have Hold use occupie possess & Enjoy yᵉ sᵈ Demised & bargained Premises as abovesᵈ & that it is free & Clear of all Incumbrances whatsoever & that I yᵉ sᵈ Hannah Willson will forever Defend yᵉ aforesᵈ premises to him yᵉ sᵈ Ebenezer More against any person or psons lying any Lawfull Claimes thereunto In Witness whereof I have hereunto Set my hand & Seal this 26ᵗʰ Day of ffebruary anno Dom 1714/5

Signed Sealed & Delivered
  In Presence of   Hannah :N: Willson (seal)
  Andrew Tyler   her mark
  Elihu Parsons
  Wᵐ Pepperrell junʳ
    Kittery ffebʳ 26ᵗʰ 1714/5

This Day Hannah Wilson parsonally appeared before me yᵉ Subscribʳ one of his Majᵗʸˢ Justices for yᵉ County of york and acknowledged this within written Deed of Sale to be her free act & Deed/   Wᵐ Pepperrell
  Recorded According to yᵉ Original March 21ˢᵗ 1714/5./
                p Jos: Hamond Regʳ

  To All People to whom this present Deed or Instrument in writing Shall Come Know Yee that I John Tompson of Kittery in yᵉ County of York within his Majestyes Province of the Nassachusets Bay in New England yeoman for & in Consideration of yᵉ Sum of Twelve pounds Curraᵗ money of New England to me in hand paid or Secured in yᵉ Law to be paid at & before the Ensealing & Delivery of these presents by Thomas ffernald of Kittery in yᵉ County & Province aforesᵈ Cordwainer the receipt whereof I Do hereby Acknowledge & my Selfe therewith fully Satisfied Contented & paid Have given granted bargained & Sold and by these

Book VIII, Fol. 86.

presents for my Selfe my heirs Executors Admin[rs] & Assignes Do give grant bargain Sell aliene Enfeoffe Convey & Confirm unto him y[e] s[d] Thomas ffernald his heirs & assignes for ever a Certaine Tract or parcell of Land Scittuate lying & being in Kittery afores[d] Containing Ten acres & one Quarter of an acre of Land Three acres & Three quarters of an acre whereof was laid out & bounded unto y[e] s[d] John Tompson by Daniel Emery Surveyer for s[d] Town of Kittery on y[e] Twentyeth Day of December in y[e] year of our Lord Seventeen hundred & ten Recorded with y[e] Records of s[d] Town Lib[r] 1st ffolio 132 The other Six acres & an halfe was laid out & bounded unto y[e] s[d] Tompson by y[e] afores[d] Surveyer on y[e] Twenty first Day of Octob[r] Seventeen hundred & fourteen Recorded with y[e] Records of s[d] Town Lib[r] 2[d] ffolio 28th As by y[e] s[d] Respective returnes referrence being there unto had more At Large Doth Appear To have and To hold y[e] s[d] Ten acres & Three quarters of An acre of land with all & Singular y[e] priviledges [86] And appurtenances thereunto belonging or in any wise appertaining unto Him y[e] s[d] Thomas ffernald his Heirs & assignes for Ever to his and their own propper use benefit & behoofe for Ever more/ And further I y[e] s[d] John Tompson for my Selfe my Heirs Execut[rs] & Adm[rs] to & with Him y[e] s[d] Thomas ffernald his Heirs & Assignes Do Covenant in manner following That is to Say/ that at & untill y[e] Ensealing & Delivery of these p[r]sents I am the True Sole & Lawfull owner of y[e] above bargained Land & Premises & have in my Selfe full power good right & Lawfull Authority y[e] Same to Convey as afores[d] and that y[e] Same & Every part thereof is free & Clear & Clearly Acquited & Discharged of & from all & all maner of former & other gifts grants bargaines Sales Leases Mortgages & all other Incumbrances whatso Ever by me made Done or Suffered, And I y[e] s[d] John Tompson & my Heirs to Him y[e] s[d] Thomas ffernald his Heirs & Assignes the Quiet & Peaceable possession thereof Shall & will Warrant and for ever Confirm by these psents In Witness whereof I y[e] s[d] John Tompson & Elizabeth my wife have hereunto Set our hands & Affixed our Seals this twenty Second Day of January annoq, Domini Seventeen Hundred fourteen fifteen 1714/5
Annoq, Regni Georgii Regis Primo
Signed Sealed & Delivered   John Thompson ($_{Seal}^{a}$)
   In the Presence of us   her
   John Staple   Elizabeth —— Tompson ($_{Seal}^{a}$)
   Thomas Knight   mark

BOOK VIII, FOL. 86.

York ss/ March 21st 1714/5
The above named John Tompson acknowledged y^e above written Instrument to be his free act & Deed before me
                                    Charles ffrost J peace
Recorded According to y^e Original March 21st 1714/5
                        p Jos : Hamond Reg^r

This Indenture made this first of May 1675./ Between George Munjoy of falmouth of ye one party & John Ingersol of ffalmouth of ye other p^{r}ty Witnesseth that whereas ffrancis Smale did grant Bargain & Sell unto Mr John Phillips of Boston a Certain Tract of Land lying at Cape pissack which he purchased of Sattery Gusset deceas^d & Since hath given it to me by deed of Gift Now this Indenture Witnesseth that I ye s^d George Munjoy do Acknowledge to have recieved Ten pounds to Content of John Ingersol of which Sum I do acknowledge my Selfe fully Satisfied & paid by these presents have given granted bargained & Sold Assigned & Set over & by these presents do give grant bargaine & Sell unto John Ingersol all that Tract & Parcell of land Lying & bounded as followeth begining at ye bounds of Thomas Clayce on ye East being on ye Gulley runing down on ye back Side of s^d Clace^{es} house bounded on ye South by that s^d Gulley As it Turneth & bounded on ye west by ye old path near Cape pissack ffalls that went down to ye back Cove begining At ye Cross path for its breadth & So to run an Equal breadth to ye water Side & So in An Equal breadth into ye woods, proportionably as far as ye Original grant doth goe To have & To hold all ye Estate right Title Claime Interest that I have may or ought to have of in or to ye s^d land & Every & any part thereof with all ye woods underwoods & Appurtenances Thereunto belonging unto ye s^d John Ingersol his heirs Execut^{rs} Adm^{rs} & Assignes forever peaceably to have hold Occupy & Injoy ye s^d parcell of land with all ye Appurtenances & Every part & parcel thereof without ye Let Trouble Contradiction or Interruption of him ye s^d George Munjoy or of any other pson or psons whatsoever Lawfully Claiming from by or und^r him or by his means Act Title or

Book VIII, Fol. 87.

procurem^t whatsoever./ In Witness whereof I have hereunto Set my hand & Seal ye day & year above written./
Signed Sealed & Delivered   George Munjoy (Seale)
   In ye presence of us
   John Munjoy
   Thomas ┬ Hues
       his mark
Recorded According to ye Original March 14th 1714/5./
                    p Jos : Hamond Reg^r

Know All men by these psents that I William Wadley of Kittery Alias Berwick in ye County of York in Province of Massachusets Bay in New England Labourer for & in Consideration of ye Sum of five pounds to me in hand well & Truely paid by John Croad of ye Same Town County & Province afores^d Merch^t ye rec^t whereof I do hereby Acknowledge & my Selfe therewith fully Satisfied Contented & paid have bargained Sold Aliened Assigned Enfeoffed Set over & Confirm^d and do by these psents Bargaine Sell Aliene Assigne Enfeoffe Set over & Confirm unto ye s^d John Croade his heirs & Assignes forever All my right Title propperty & Interest in ye river pond Stream Water or water Courses brook or brookes Next Adjoyning & is on one Side of that which s^d Croad bought of Benj^a Lord on a brook runing out of William Cocks pond As by s^d Lords deed to s^d Croade bearing date fourteenth March Seventeen hundred Eighty nine may Appear Together with one Acre Land next Adjoyning to ye pond river brook or Stream to be laid out for ye best Advantage [87] And Convenience of A Saw mill Intended to be Erected & built by s^d Croade & Improved by him his heirs & Assignes forever to Come & go Carry & recarry by Cart Sled or otherwise as he or they Shall See Cause ye s^d Acre of Land to be laid out So as to Admitt of a road way Twelve foot wide at ye Least To have & To hold./ ye bargained pmises with their Appurtenances unto him ye s^d John Croade his heirs & Assignes forever free & Clear & is frely & Clearly Acquitted from all Incumbrance or Incumbrances w^{t}soever And I ye s^d Wm Wadley at & before ye Ensealing & Delivery hereof am ye true & Lawfull owner of ye bargained pmises & that it Shall & May be Lawfull to & for ye s^d John Croad his heirs & Assignes forever to have hold use Occupie possess & Quietly to Enjoy ye Same without any Mollestation hinderence or Interruption from me ye s^d William Wadley my heirs Ex^{rs} Adm^{rs} or Assignes and do further Covenant finally to Warrant Acquit & Defend him yᵉ sᵈ John Croade his heirs & Assigns in yᵉ Quiet and peaceable possession thereof against all & all manner of pson or psons whatsoever from henceforth and forever./ In Witness whereof I have hereunto Set my hand & Seal yᵉ Tenth day of Septembʳ Annoq, Domini 1709

Signed Sealed & Delivered   William Wadley (ₛₑₐₗᵃ)
In psence of
Samuel Bracket
     his
Edward ≻ Walker
     mark

York ss/ William Wadley psonally Appeared & Acknowledged yᵉ above written Instrumᵗ to be his Act & Deed Berwick yᵉ 13ᵗʰ April 1715./
                Before me   Ichabod Plaisted J. peace
Recorded According to yᵉ Original Aprill 15ᵗʰ 1715/
                         p Jos : Hamond Regʳ

Know All men by these presents that I John Croade of Berwick in yᵉ County of york in yᵉ Province of yᵉ Massachusets Bay in New England Merchant for & in Consideration of yᵉ Sum of Seventy pounds in Currant money of yᵉ Province aforesᵈ to me in hand wᶜʰ Capᵗⁿ Joseph Boynton of Rowley in yᵉ County of Essex in yᵉ Province aforesᵈ yeoman is bound as Surety for me yᵉ sᵈ Croade to Mʳ ffrancis Wainwright of Boston in yᵉ County of Suffolk in yᵉ Province aforesᵈ Merchant & for yᵉ better Security of yᵉ sᵈ Boynton on yᵉ Consideration aforesᵈ have given granted bargained Sold Aliened Assigned Enfeoffed Set over & Confirmed and do by these pʳsents give grant bargaine Sell Aliene Assigne Enfeoffe Set over & Confirm unto him yᵉ sᵈ Joseph Boynton his heirs & Assignes fforever my now Dwelling house Scittuate in Berwick aforesᵈ Also All my right Title & Interest in yᵉ Saw mill at Worsters in Berwick aforesᵈ Vizᵗ halfe a Saw with all yᵉ appurᶜᵉˢ and priviledges thereto belonging Stream water water Courses & land Each Side yᵉ Stream and all other Accomodations wᵗsoever Also three Acres land in Berwick aforesᵈ At yᵉ Eastward end of Cocks pond So Called bounded As by Benjamin Lords deed to me yᵉ sᵈ Croad Dated yᵉ 14ᵗʰ March 1708/9./ Appears referrence thereto being had with all yᵉ rights profits priviledges & Appurtenances thereto belonging being on yᵉ Southward Side of sᵈ pond Also all my right & Interest on ye Northward Side of s^d pond in Berwick afores^d which I bought of Wm Wadley as by s^d Wadleys deed to me s^d Croade dated ye Tenth Septr 1709 referrence whereto being had At Large Appears which makes An Accomodation & priviledge on both sides ye head of s^d pond for pitching a dam & Errecting a Saw mill Also Twenty four Acres Land Scittuate in Berwick afores^d Near ye great falls Sixty poles in Length Sixty poles north East by North & Sixty four poles in bredth Northwest by west at ye Northeast End of John Broughtons Lot as by ye return of Daniel Emery Surveyer 19th Decr 1711. To have & To hold all ye aboves^d to him ye s^d Joseph Boynton his heirs & Assignes for ever./ Now Know yee that if ye s^d Croade his Ex^{rs} or Adm^{rs} Shall & do well & Truely pay & discharge ye s^d Obligation unto ye s^d ffrancis Wainwright or unto ye s^d Joseph Boynton his Ex^{rs} or Adm^{rs} At or before ye Last day of June next whereby he or they are kept harmless & Indempnified then ye above written deed of Sale or Mortgage to be voyd & of non Effect or Else to abide & remaine in full force & Vertue

In Witness whereof I have hereunto Set my hand & Seal ye 13th day of April Annoq Domini 1715/ in ye first year of his Maj^{tys} Reign/   John Croade (s^{a}eal)
Signed Sealed & D^d
In ye psence of
John Boynton
William |/| Newton
     mark
York ss/
John Croade psonally Appeared and Ackowledged ye above written Instrum^t to be his Act & Deed, Berwick ye 13th April 1715,

      Before me Ichabod Plaisted Justice peace
Recorded According to ye Original April ye 15 : 1715
              p Jos: Hamond Reg^r

[88]   Octob^r ye 8 day 1675
Bee it known unto all men that I Simon Booth of Saco in ye County of york & Colloney of ye Massachusets for & in Consideration of a Certaine Sum of money to me in hand at & before ye Ensealing & Delivery of these p^{r}sents by ye s^d Bryam Pendleton well & Truely paid ye Rec^t whereof I

yᵉ sᵈ Simon Booth do hereby Acknowledge my Selfe therewith fully Satisfied and pᵈ and thereof & of Every pᵗ & parcel thereof do Clearly Acquit Exonerate & discharge yᵉ sᵈ Bryan Pendleton his heirs Exʳˢ & Admʳˢ forever have by these psents given granted Aliened bargained Sold Enfeoffed & Confirmed & by these pʳsents do fully clearly & Absolutely give grant bargaine Sell Aliene Enfeoffe and Confirm unto yᵉ sᵈ Bryan Pendleton his heirs & Assigns yᵗ Tract of upland & Marsh that I lately inhabited upon Occupied & Improved being & lying below yᵉ grist mill (of my Mother Booths At Winter harbour with all & Singular their rights Appurᶜᵉˢ & priviledges Any way Appurtaining or belonging to Any part or parcell of yᵉ aforesᵈ Tract Together with all fences buildings wᵗsoever To have & To hold yᵉ sᵈ tract of Land & all before Expressed to him yᵉ sᵈ Bryan Pendleton him his heirs & Assigns & that all & Every of them Shall or may by force & vertue of these psents from Time to Time & At all Times forever hereafter Lawfully peaceably & Quietly have hold use Occupie possess & Enjoy yᵉ Same with all yᵉ rights membʳˢ Appurᶜᵉˢ & have & receive & Take yᵉ Issues and profits to his yᵉ sᵈ Bryan Pendleton his heirs & Assignes propper use and behoofe without any let Suit Trouble denial Interruption Eviction or disturbence of yᵉ sᵈ Bryan Pendleton his heirs or Assignes by me yᵉ sᵈ Simon Booth or any by from or undʳ me In Witness wʳof I hereby bind my Selfe my heirs & Exʳˢ & Admʳˢ in all that Concerns yᵉ premises firmly by these psents Set my hand & Seal hereunto yᵉ day & year above written with yᵉ free & full Consent of my wife
Signed Sealed & Deᵈ   Simon Booth (Seal)
 In psence of   Rebecca ⸱O⸱ Booth (Seale)
James Gibbens Senʳ

his ℰ mark

Juedeth ⸱ɿ᛫ɠ᛫ Gibbens

This Instrumᵗ Acknowledged yᵉ day & year above written by simon Booth to be his Act & Deed Before me/
      Brian Pendleton Assotiate

Mʳˢ Elinoʳ Pendleton Executrix & Capᵗⁿ James Pendleton Executʳ to yᵉ Estate of Majʳ Bryan Pendleton decᵈ do resign up their right in this deed above written unto Pendleton ffletcher as a gift by what we undʳstand was given unto him by his Grandfather Bryan Pendleton wʳby wee do Confirm ye pmises to him & his heirs In Testimony whereof wee have hereunto Set our hands this 22th June '81/

her
Elinor Pendleton ʃ
mark
James Pendleton

Mrs Elner Pendleton & Cap^{tn} James Pendleton owneth this Confirmation to be their Act & deed this 22th of June 1681./
Before me Edw : Rishworth Just^s pc
Recorded According to ye Original May ye 2^d 1715/

p Jos. Hamond Reg^r

These may Signifie whom it may Concern that Mr Peter Nowell hath Satisfied a Judgm^t of Court which I Obtained Against Cap^{tn} Harmon Amounting to in ye whole ye Sum of Thirty Three pounds Seventeen Shillings)that is to Say) The Original Debt Interest & Costs of Suit./ Kittery Feb^{ry} 16th 1714/5./ Charles ffrost

Recorded According to ye Original April 7th 1715

p Jos Hamond Reg^r

To All People these p^{r}sents shall Come Greeting Know yee that I Richd Stimpson of Saco in ye County of york within his Ma^{tys} Province of ye Massachusets Bay in New England planter for & in Consideration of ye Sum of Ten pounds in good Curra^t money of New England Secured to be paid to me by bill Obligatory under the hand & Seal of Samuel Emery of Wells in ye County afores^d Clerk & bearing Equal date with these presents have given & granted & do hereby give grant bargaine Sell Alienate Enfeoffe & Confirm unto Samuel Emery afores^d a Certain Tract of Land & marsh or meadow ground Lying & being in ye Township of Wells Containing one hundred & Ten Acres be it more or Less & bounded as followeth The Tract of land is bounded Southwesterly by a pitch pine Tree marked on four sides with an H on ye Southwest side thereof about Twenty Rods from ye Old Chimney back where I formely dwelt that tree being ye bounds between Said land & Eliab Littlefields lot Northeasterly by a red oak Marked on four sides about Ten rod Westerly from ye back of a Chimney belonging formerly to Thomas Wilson dec^d it being ye bounds between my land & Thomas Wilsons afores^d & to ruñ on that breadth on Each side East South East to ye highway at ye head of ye Old Lotts & west North west from s^d bound trees till ye hundred Acres be fully Compleated ye Ten Acres of Marsh not yet laid out which hundred Acres of Land & Ten acres of Meadow was formerly granted by ye Town of Wells to William Venney & by s^d Venney Sold to me ye which s^d land & meadow bounded & Specified as afores^d I ye aboves^d Richard Stimpson do for my Selfe my heirs Execut^{rs} & Adm^{rs} Convey & Confirm unto Sam^{ll} Emery Afores^d his heirs Ex^{rs} Adm^{rs} or Assigns Together with all & Singular ye priviledges my rights in Comon & ye Appurtenances thereto belonging or Any wise Appurtaining To have & To hold as a free & Clear Estate in [89] ffee Simple forever And I ye Aboves^d Richard Stimpson for me my heirs Ex^{rs} & Adm^{rs} do Covena^t & promiss that I am at ye Ensealing hereof ye True & rightfull owner of ye Above granted pmises & that I have full power right & Authority to dispose of ye Same as afores^d As Also that ye above demised & bargained premises are free & Clear & freely & Clearly Acquitted & Discharged off & from all other & former gifts grants Sales bargains Mortgages Executions & Incumbrances w^{t}soever Moreover that I will Warra^t & Defend ye Same from all or any pson or psons in by from or und^r me laying any Legall Claime thereunto./ In Witness whereof I ye Aboves^d Richard Stimpson have hereto put my hand & Seal this Twenty fifth day of Decemb^r Anno Domini One Thousand Seven hundred & fourteen in ye first year of ye Reign of our Soveraign Lord George by ye grace of god of great Brittaine ffrance & Ireland King Defend^r of ye faith &c^t

Signed Sealed & Delivered   Richard Stimpson (a Seal)
  In psence of us   his X mark
  Jona^n Hamond
  Caleb Kimbal
  George Jacobs
  April 4th 1715

Then Richard Stimpson Appeared & Acknowledged ye Above written Instrum^t to be his Act & Deed Before me
                   John Wheelwright Just^s peace

Recorded According to ye Original April ye 6ta 1715./
                  p Jos Hamond Reg^r/

To All Christian People to whom this present deed of Sale shall Come or doth Concern John Mackintire of York

Book VIII, Fol. 89.

in y[e] County of York in y[e] Province of y[e] Massachusets Bay in New England Sendeth Greeting Know yee y[e] s[d] John Mackintire for & in Consideration of a Certaine Sum of money to him in hand well & Truely paid by his brother Micum Mackintire of s[d] york y[e] receipt thereof y[e] s[d] John Mackintire doth Acknowledge himselfe therewith to be paid fully Sastisfied & Contented & of Every part thereof and doth by these psents Acquit & discharge of y[e] paym[t] of Twenty Acres of Land being y[e] one halfe of a forty acre Lot formerly Laid out unto their father Micum Mackintire late of york dec[d] & y[e] one halfe of a forty Acre Lot formerly laid out to their Grandfather John Pierce late of s[d] York dec[d] As in York Town records will more fully Appear & is hereafter Set forth more at Large and y[e] s[d] John Mackintire hath Given granted bargained Sold Aliened Enfeoffed & Conveyed & doth by these psents Give grant bargaine Sell Aliene Enfeoffe & Convey & fully freely & Absolutely make over & Confirm unto y[e] s[d] Micum Mackintire his heirs & Assignes for Ever forty Acres of upland & Swampy Land Lying & being within y[e] Township of aboves[d] York & is Scittuated upon y[e] Southwest Side of s[d] York river & is bounded as followeth Viz[t]/ Twenty Acres Adjoyning to s[d] York river or to y[e] Salt marsh by s[d] river being y[e] one halfe of y[e] forty Acres first Above mentioned granted unto their father Micum Mackintire above mentioned Marsh y[e] 15th 1668./ and being bounded by y[e] s[d] Micums house Lot on y[e] South East Side & is in breadth Twenty poles runing back Southwest one hundred Sixty poles from s[d] river y[e] other Twenty Acres is y[e] one halfe of a forty Acre grant of Land Given unto Grandfather John Pierce above Mentioned at a Town Meeting in s[d] York April y[e] 22[d] 1686 & laid out by y[e] Selectmen of s[d] york June y[e] 4th 1686/ as Appears on Record in s[d] York Town book a part thereof on y[e] Northwest Side of afores[d] Micum Mackintires Land Above Mentioned & y[e] other part on y[e] Southwest of s[d] Mackintires land as by s[d] return reference thereunto being had will more fully Appear y[e] s[d] Micum Mackintire being Lawfully in the possession of y[e] other half of y[e] Above Mentioned Lots or Tracts of Land & now y[e] other halfe As is above Set forth or ought to be bounded & Set forth Together with all y[e] rights priviledges Appur[ces]/ & Advantages thereunto belonging or unto any part or parcell thereof or any wise At any time Redownding to y[e] Same unto him y[e] s[d] Micum Mackintire his heirs & Assignes forever To have & To hold & Quietly & peaceably to Occupie & Enjoy y[e] aboves[d] Land & all its Priviledges as a Sure Estate in fee Simple Moreover

BOOK VIII, FOL. 90.

yᵉ sᵈ John Mackintire doth for himselfe his heirs Executʳˢ Admʳˢ & Assignes Covenant Ingage & promiss to & with yᵉ sᵈ Micum Mackintire his heirs Executʳˢ Admʳˢ & Assignes yᵉ above bargained premises with all its Priviledges to be free and Clear from all former gifts grants bargains Sales rents rates dowry or any Incumberments wᵗsoever as also from all future Claims Challenges Lawsuits or any other Interuptions to be had or Comenced by him yᵉ sᵈ Mackintire his heirs [90] Executʳˢ Admʳˢ or any other pson or psons upon grounds or Title of Law After yᵉ Date of these psents but do Warrantise & will Defend yᵉ Same in Witness hereof yᵉ Abovesᵈ John Mackintire hath hereunto Set his hand & Seal this Twenty fourth day of May in yᵉ year of our Lord One Thousand Seven hundred & fourteen & in yᵉ Thirteenth year of yᵉ Reign of our Soveraign Lady Anne Queen of Great Brittaine &cᵗ

It is to be understood before Signing that Three Acres of abovesᵈ Land Sold by John Mackintire is only Excepted which doth belong unto his Brother Daniel Mackintire

Signed Sealed & Delivered
  In psence of us Witnesses   John Mackintire ✝ his mark (seale a)
  Abrᵐ Preble
  Joseph Bankes

York ss/ Janʳʸ 5ᵗʰ 1714/5./ The within Named Jnᵒ Mackintire Acknowledged yᵉ within written Instrumᵗ to be his free Act & Deed   Before me   Charles ffrost J. Peace

Recorded According to yᵉ Original Janʳʸ yᵉ 5ᵗʰ 1714/5
                          p Jos: Hamond Regʳ

To All Christian People to whom these presents may come or doth Concern Abrᵐ Preble Junʳ of york in yᵉ County of york in yᵉ Province of Maine in New England Sendeth Greeting./ Know yee yᵉ sᵈ Abrᵐ for & in Consideration of a Certaine Sum of fifteen pounds money to him in hand well & Truely paid or otherwise Satisfactorily Secured to be paid At yᵉ Signing of this Instrumᵗ by Nathaniel Donnell of Aforesᵈ york have Given Granted bargained Sold Aliened Enfeoffed & Conveyed & doth by these psents give grant bargaine Sell Aliene Enfeoffe & Convey & fully freely & Absolutely make over & Confirm unto yᵉ sᵈ Nathˡˡ Donnell a piece or parcell of Swamp or Meadow ground being by Estimation Three Acres be it more or Less Lying & being within yᵉ Township of sᵈ York Scituated near yᵉ Sea Wall or beach by a Cove of yᵉ Sea formerly known by the name of Palmers

Book VIII, Fol. 90.

Cove & s^d Swamp by ye name of ye Mirey Ashen Swamp being formerly given by ye Town of york to Mr Shubal Dumer late of s^d york dec^d & since sold by Jeremiah Dumer of Boston Esqr unto Abra^m Preble jun^r as by Record doth Appeare which s^d Swamp or Meadow ground is bounded As followeth Viz^t on ye Southwest side by ye fence of Mr Richard Millbery & on ye North west & on ye North East by ye Land of Mr Samuel Donnell & on ye South East by a Strip of upland lying between s^d Swamp & the Sea wall Together with all ye rights priviledges Appurten^{ces} & Advantages thereunto belonging or any wayes At any time redounding unto ye Same or any part or parcell thereof unto him ye s^d Nathaniel Donnel his heirs & Assignes for ever To have & To hold & Quietly & Peaceably to possess & Enjoy ye s^d Swamp with all its priviledges as a Sure Estate in fee Simple./ Moreover ye s^d Abra^m Preble doth for himSelfe his heirs Execut^{rs} Adm^{rs} & Assignes Covenant Engage & promiss to & with ye s^d Nath^{ll} Donnell his heirs Execut^{rs} Adm^{rs} & Assignes ye above bargained premises with all its priviledges to be free & clear from all former gifts grants bargains Sales rents rates Dowrys Deeds or Mortgages As Also from all future Claims Challenges or Law Suits to be had or Comenced by him his heirs or Assignes or Any other pson or psons whatsoever upon grounds or Title of Law from by & und^r him do Warrantise & will Defend y^e Same In Witness hereof y^e aboves^d Abra^m Preble jun^r hath hereunto Set his hand & Seal this Twentyfourth day of May one Thousand Seven hundred & fourteen & in y^e Thirteenth year of y^e Reign of our Soveraign Lady Anne Queen of Great Brittaine &c^t

Signed Sealed & Delivered   Abra^m Preble ($_{Seal}^a$)
  In psence of us Witnesses
  John Woodbridge
  Thomas Card
  Sam^{ll} Donnell jun^r
    York ss/ Jan^{ry} 5th 1714/5./—

The above named Abra^m Preble Acknowledged y^e Above written Instrum^t to be his free Act & deed
                     Before me   Charles ffrost J : peace
Recorded According to ye Original Jan^{ry} 5th 1714/5
                          p Jos : Hamond Reg^r

To All Christian People to whom this p^{r}sent deed of Gift may Come or doth Concern./ Cap^{tn} Lewis Bane of york in ye County of york in ye Province of maine in New England & Mary his wife

for & in good Consideration of their Love & Natural Affection unto their Dutyfull & welbeloved Son Jonathan Bane have given granted bargained Aliened Enfeoffed & Conveyed and do by these p^{r}sents give grant bargaine Aliene Enfeoffe & Convey & fully freely & Absolutely make over & Confirm unto their s^d Son Jonathan Bane his heirs & Assigns forever [91] One Certain piece parcell or Tenem^t of upland & Swampy Land Containing by Estimation Thirty Acres be it more or Less lying & being within ye Township of s^d york & is Scituated upon ye Northeast Side of ye highway or Country Road that Leads from ye Meeting house to ye Corn mill between ye Land that was formerly in ye possession of John Preble Late of s^d york dec^d & ye s^d Cap^{tn} Banes now dwelling house and is butted & bounded As followeth Viz^t on ye South East Side of ye Land of Nathaniel Donnell formerly of Aboves^d John Prebles Dec^d & on ye Southward by ye Country road or highway above mentioned & is in breadth on a Square Sixteen pole from s^d Donnells bounds & runneth backward on both Sides on ye Same point of ye Compass that s^d Nathl Donnells Lot doth & as far backward into ye Country as ye Adjacent lots run being bound by s^d Cap^{tn} Lewis Banes Land on ye northwest Side Together with all ye rights priviledges Appurtenances & Advantages Thereunto belonging or any ways at any time redownding to ye Same or any part or pcell thereof unto him ye s^d Jonathan Bane his heirs & Assignes forever To have & To hold & Quietly & peaceably to pessess Occupy and Enjoy as a Sure Estate in Fee Simple for Ever: Moreover ye s^d Cap^{tn} Lewis Bane doth for himselfe his heirs Execut^{rs} & Adm^{rs} to & with his s^d Son Jonathan Bane his heirs and Assignes Warrantise & will defend ye aboves^d Land & priviledges in all & Every part & Parragraph thereof unto his s^d Son Jonath^x his heirs & Assigns after ye Assigning & Delivery of this deed of gift or Instrum^t as a part of his portion or Inheritance as from by & under him ye s^d Cap^{tn} Bane his heirs or Assignes In Witness hereof ye above named Cap^{tn} Lewis Bane & his wife hath hereunto Set their hands & Seals this Eleventh day of Octob^r in ye year of our Lord one Thousand Seven hundred & fourteen and in ye first year of ye Reign of our Soveraign Lord George King of Great Brittaine &c^t/
Signed Sealed & Delivered   Lewis Bane (a Seal)
   In ye psence of   (a Seal)
   Johnson Harmon
   Abra^m Preble
   York sc/
   York Lewis Bane psonally Appeared before me one of his

BOOK VIII, FOL. 91.

Maj^tys Justices of peace & Acknowledged this within written Instrum^t to be his Act & deed April: 5: 1715./
                    Before me Charles ffrost J. peace
Recorded According to ye Original April ye 5th 1715
                              p Jos: Hamond Reg^r

*May ye 23^d 1718 Rec^d of John Harmon on Acco^t of Johnson Harmon ye Mortgager ye Sum of thirty four pounds & Seven Shillings being in full for principle & Interest on ye within Mortgage
                    p me Peter Nowel*

This Indenture ye 15th day of January Annoq, Domini 1714/15./ and in ye first year of ye our Soveraign Lord George King of Great Brittaine &c^t Between Johnson Harmon of york in ye County of York in his Maj^tys Province of ye Massachusets Bay in New England Gentleman of ye one party & Peter Nowell of ye Same Town County & Province of ye other party Witnesseth that ye s^d Johnson Harmon for & in Consideration of ye Sum of Thirty pounds Curra^t money of New England to him in hand paid before ye Ensealing & Delivery of these psents by Peter Nowell Afores^d the rec^t whereof to full Satisfaction he ye s^d Johnson Harmon doth by these psents Acknowledge & thereof & of Every part thereof for himselfe his heirs Execut^rs & Adm^rs doth Acquit Exonerate & discharge ye s^d Peter Nowell his heirs Execut^rs & Adm^rs Every of them for ever by these p^rsents & for divers other good Causes & Considerations him thereunto moveing he ye s^d Johnson Harmon hath given granted bargained Sold Alliened Enfeoffed Conveyed & Confirmed & by these psents doth fully freely clearly & absolutely give grant bargaine Sell Aliene Enfeoffe Convey & Confirm unto ye s^d Peter Nowel his heirs and Assignes forever a piece or parcell of Salt Marsh lying & being within ye Township of York Containing Eight Acres more or Less & About Ten or Twelve Acres of upland Adjoyning thereunto being Scittuated between ye Two Branches of York river ye Marsh Comonly Called Harmons Lower Marsh & ye upland is bounded on ye westward & northwest by Mr Cames Land ye other Side by ye Marsh & branches of s^d river To have & To hold all ye above granted pmises with all & Singular ye Appurtenances thereof unto ye s^d Peter Nowell his heirs & Assigns to his & their own Sole & propper use bennefit & behoofe from hence forth forever, And ye s^d Johnson Harmon for himselfe his heirs Execut^rs Adm^rs doth hereby Covenant promiss grant & agree to & with ye s^d Peter Nowell his heirs

& Assignes in maner & form following./ That is To Say that at ye time of the Ensealing & Delivery of these psents he ye s^d Johnson Harmon is ye True Sole & Lawfull owner of all ye above bargained pmises & Stands Lawfully Seez^d thereof in his own propper right of good perfect & Indefeazeable Estate of Inheritance in fee Simple haveing in himselfe full power good right & Lawfull Authority to Sell & dispose of ye Same in maner as afores^d & that ye s^d Peter Nowell his heirs & Assigns Shall & may henceforth for ever Lawfully peaceably & Quietly hold use Occupie possess & Enjoy ye above granted pmises with ye Appurtenances [92] Thereof free & clear and clearly Acquitted and discharged of and from all & all maner of former and other gifts grants bargains Sales Leases Mortgages Joyntures dowrys Judgm^{ts} Executions forfietures & of & from all other Titles Troubles Charges and Incumbrances whatsoever had made Comitted done or Suffered to be done by ye s^d Johnson Harmon his heirs or Assignes At any time or times before ye Ensealing & Delivery hereof & further ye s^d Johnson Harmon doth hereby Covenant promiss bind & oblige himselfe his heirs Execut^{rs} & Adm^{rs} from hence forth & for Ever hereafter to Warra^t & Defend all ye Above granted premises and ye Appurtenances thereof unto ye s^d Peter Nowell his heirs and Assigns against ye Lawfull Claims & Demands of All & Every pson & psons whomsoever And at any Time & Times hereafter on demand to give & pass Such further Ample Assurences & Confirmations of ye pmises unto ye s^d Peter Nowell his heirs & Assignes for ever as in Law or Equity Can be reasonably Devised Advised or required Provided Always & these p^{r}sents are upon Condition Nevertheless that if ye above named Johnson Harmon his heirs Ex^{rs} Adm^{rs} Shall & do well & Truely pay or cause to be paid unto ye Afore named Peter Nowell or his Certaine Attorney heirs Ex^{rs} Adm^{rs} or Assignes At york afores^d in ye psent Currant money of ye Afores^d Province as it now passeth ye Sum of Thirty pounds At or upon ye Twenty Seaventh of Decemb^r which will be in ye year of our Lord one Thousand 7 hundred & fifteen Just Eleven Months Twelve dayes After ye Date of this Instrum^t without fraud Coven or further Delay that then this psent deed of Bargaine & Sale & Every Clause & Article therein Contained Shall Cease determine be null Voyd & of non Effect but if Defauld happen to be made in ye Afores^d paym^t Contrary to y^e true Intent thereof then to Abide and remaine in full force Strength & Vertue to all Intents & purposes in y^e Law whatsoever./ In Witness whereof y^e s^d Johnson Har-

Book VIII, Fol. 92.

mon hath hereunto Set his hand & Seal y^e day & year first above written   Johnson Harmon (${}_\text{Seale}^\text{a}$)
Signed Sealed & Delivered
In psence of
Abra^m Preble
Nath^{ll} ffreeman
  Cap^{tn} Johnson Harmon came before me this 8th day of March 1714/5 And Acknowledged this within written Instrum^t to be his Act & Deed
                Before me   Lewis Bane Jus peace
Recorded According to y^e Original April 5th 1715/
                       p Jos : Hamond Reg^r

  Whereas there has been a long Controversie & difference between Richard Tozer & Joseph Pray both of ye Town of Berwick in ye County of york relating to ye Dividing line between their Lotts above the Salmonfalls in Berwick afores^d./ And whereas ye s^d Line heretofore has been Somewhat Irregularly Settled which has proved to ye Dissatisfaction of both partyes upon which Sundry Actions were depending./ Now Know All men by these psents that Wee ye above named Richard Tozer & Joseph Pray have agreed to put a final Issue & Period to All those Controversies in Manner following Viz^t/ That ye s^d Prays Land Extend on a Northwest & by west Line from Collonel Plaisteds line Towards s^d Tozers Land Thirty & Eight rods & from that Extent northeast & by North into ye woods to ye utmost Extent of his Lot & ye s^d Richaard Tozer is to have & Enjoy to him his heirs & Assignes for ever all ye s^d Prays right in all ye land to ye Northwestward of ye line last above mentioned Alwayes Provided ye s^d Tozer Allow A highway of Two rods wide on ye Northwest Side of s^d line for ye Equall use & bennefit of ye s^d Tozer & Pray their heirs Ex^{rs} Adm^{rs} & Assignes for ever./ Provided also that ye Lands between ye Oak Tree Last mentioned in ye Award of Cap^{tn} John Hill & Mr James Emery & Salmonfall river be & remaine to ye use & benefit of ye s^d Tozer & Pray their heirs &c^t for ever as it was & might have been before this Agreem^t to y^e True pformance of all above./ Wee y^e s^d Tozer & Pray do bind and Oblige our Selves our heirs Ex^{rs} Adm^{rs} & Assignes firmly by

these psents Sealed with our Seals./ Dated in Berwick Afores^d y^e 29th day of March Seventeen hundred & fifteen
Signed Sealed & Delivered Richard Tozer ($_{Seal}^a$)
In psence of us Joseph Pray ($_{Seal}^a$)
Tho: Packer
Jeremiah Wise
Jos: Hamond.

York sc/ Richard Tozer & Joseph Pray both psonally Appeared before me y^e Subscrib^r one of his Maj^{tys} Justices for s^d County and Acknowledged y^e within written Instrum^t with their hands & Seales thereto Affixed to be their & Each of their Act & Deed At Berwick ye 30th March 1715
  Before me Ichabod Plaisted
Recorded According to ye Original May 5th 1715./
  p Jos: Hamond Reg^r

[93] Know All men by these psents that Wee Samuel Bracket & Eliz^a his wife of Berwick in ye County of York in ye Province of ye Massachusets Bay in New England ye s^d Eliz^a being ye only Child and heiris of Isaac Botts Late of s^d Berwick dec^d Now Know yee that I ye s^d Samuel Bracket & Eliz^a my wife for & in Consideration of ye Sum of Six pounds Curra^t money of ye Province afores^d to us in hand well & Truely paid by Richard Tozer of s^d Berwick in ye County & Province afores^d husbandman ye Rec^t whereof wee do hereby Acknowledge & our Selves therewith fully Satisfied Contented & paid have given granted bargained Sold Aliened Assigned Enfeoffed Set over & Confirmed and do by these presents give grant bargaine Sell Aliene Assigne Enfeoffe Set over & Confirm unto ye s^d Richard Tozer his heirs & Assignes forever a Certaine piece or parcell of Land Scittuate lying & being in Berwick afores^d Containing Twenty Acres being part of a Sixty acre grant granted to Isaac Botts by ye parrish Unity in ye Town of Kittery Aprill 13th 1671. & Measured & laid out to Samuel Bracket & Eliz^a his wife May ye 1th 1715 as by ye return thereof Appears being at ye head of s^d Tozers Land At Salmonfalls & At ye head of Abell Hambletons ye whole Sixty acres being Seventy poles in bredth North west by west & one hundred & Thirty Eight pole Northeast & by North bounded in part by Joseph Pray on ye Southeast Side and ye Two other Sides by Comons To have & To hold ye s^d Twenty Acres part of ye Sixty unto him ye s^d Richard Tozer his heirs & Assigns

Book VIII, Fol. 93.

forever with all y[e] rights profits priviledges & Appurtenances unto y[e] Same in any wayes belonging to y[e] only propper use & behoofe of him y[e] s[d] Richard Tozer his heirs & Assignes forever free & Clear & Clearly Acquitted of & from all other & former gifts grants bargains Sales Titles Troubles charges & Incumbrences w[t] soever and that it Shall & may be Lawfull to & for y[e] s[d] Richard Tozer his heirs & Assignes to have hold use Occupie possess & Enjoy y[e] Same Quietly & peaceably from hence forth & forever & that Wee y[e] s[d] Sam[ll] Bracket & Eliz[a] his wife & our heirs to him y[e] s[d] Richard Tozer his heirs & Assignes Shall & will Warrant & forever Confirm y[e] Same./ In Witness whereof wee have hereunto Set our hands and Seals y[e] 13th day May in y[e] first year of his Maj[tys] Reign Annoq Domini 1715

Signed Sealed & Delivered   Samuel Bracket (Seal)
   In y[e] psence of   her
   Jeremiah Wise   Eliz[a] X Bracket (Seal)
   John Croade   mark
     York sc/

Sam[ll] Bracket & Eliz[a] his wife both of Berwick in y[e] County of York psonally Appear[d] before me y[e] Subscriber & owned y[e] within written Instrum[t] to be their Act & Deed at Berwick this 14th day of May Anno Domini 1715

                      Ichabod Plaisted J. peace

Recorded According to y[e] Original May y[e] 14th 1715./
                      p Jos: Hammond Reg[r]

To All Christian People to whom these psents Shall Come John Snell of Portsm[o] in y[e] Province of New Hampsh[r] in New Engl[d] Cooper & Elizabeth his wife Send Greeting Know yee that y[e] s[d] John Snell & Elizabeth his wife for & in Consideration of Twenty & five pounds Lawfull money of New England to them in hand paid before y[e] Delivery of these psents by Richard Milbery of york in y[e] County of york in y[e] Province of y[e] Massachusets Bay in New England planter y[e] rec[t] whereof is hereby Acknowledged to full Satisfaction by s[d] John Snell & Eliz[a] his wife & for divers other good Causes & Considerations them thereunto moveing they y[e] s[d] John Snell & Eliz[a] his wife have bargained Sold Conveyed & Confirmed & do by these psents bargaine Sell Convey & Confirm unto y[e] s[d] Richard Milbery his heirs & Assignes forever one Third part of a Certaine farm or Tract of Land Containing by Estimation fifty Acres be it more or Less which farm was given by Captn Job Alcock late of Portsm^o. dec^d in his Last will & Testam^t to Joseph Banckes John Banckes & ye Aboves^d John Snell Scittuate Lying & being in York Afores^d on Mr Dummers Neck bounded partly by ye Sea & partly by s^d Milberys land Together with all Such rights priviledges & Appurtenances as in Any kind do or may hereafter Appurtaine thereunto To have & To hold all ye above granted primises wth all & Singular ye Appurtenances thereof Even the full Third part of ye whole farm or Tract of Land which was possessed by Cap^{tn} Alcock aboves^d unto ye s^d Richd Milbery his his heirs & Assignes to his & their own Sole & propper use bennefit & behoofe from henceforth for ever & ye s^d John Snell and Elizabeth his wife for themselves their heirs Ex^{rs} & Adm^{rs} do hereby Covena^t promiss grant & Agree to & with ye s^d Richd Milbery his heirs & Assignes in manner & form following That is to Say that at ye time of ye Ensealing & Delivery of these psents ye s^d John Snell & Eliz^a his wife are ye True Sole & Lawfull owners of all ye Afore bargained pmises haveing in themselves full power to Sell & Dispose of ye Same in Manner as afores^d & that ye s^d Richd Milbery his heirs & Assignes Shall henceforth Lawfully & Quietly have hold Occupie possess & Enjoy ye Above granted pmisses with ye Appurtenances thereof Clearly Acquitted & discharged from all maner of other & former gifts grants bargains Sales or Incumbrances whatsoever & further ye s^d John Snell & Eliz^a his wife do hereby Covenant Promiss bind & oblige themselves their heirs Execut^{rs} & Adm^{rs} from henceforth & forever hereafter to Warrant & Defend all ye above granted pmises & Appurtenances thereof unto the aboves^d Richard Milbery his heirs & Assigns against ye Lawfull Claime & Demands of all psons whatsoever & at any time or Times hereafter on demand to give & pass Such further & Ample Assurance & Confirmation of ye Premises unto ye s^d Richard Milbery his heirs & Assigns forever as in Law or Equity Can be reasonably Devised [94] Advised or required./ In Witness whereof ye s^d John Snell & Elizabeth his wife have hereunto Set their hands & Seals this 4th day of Aprill Anno Domini 1715./ and in ye first year of ye Reign of our Soveraign Lord George King of Great Brittaine &c^t/   Jno Snell (a Seal)

Signed Sealed & Delivered   Elizabeth Snell (a Seale)
  In presence of

James Pitman E P (his mark)

Abra^m Sentle
Eliz^a Snell

BOOK VIII, FOL. 94.

John Snell & Eliz^a his wife psonally appeared before me ye Subscrib^r one of his Maj^{tys} Justices of peace at portsm^o in ye Province of New Hampsh^r in New England & memb^r of Councill within ye Same this 4th of April 1715. & Acknowledged ye Above Instrum^t to be their Act & Deed

Sam^{ll} Penhallow

Recorded According to ye Original April ye 5th 1715./

p Jos : Hamond Reg^r

At a Legal Town meeting held at Kittery may 24th 1699./
Granted unto James ffernald his heirs & Assignes forever Thirty Acres of Land if he Can find it Clear of former grants. Att^r Jos. Hamond Clerk

Know All men by these psents that I James ffernald above Named for & in Consideration of a Valluable Sum of money to me in hand paid by Nicholas Morrell of Kittery in ye County of York in ye Province of ye Massachusets Bay have given granted Assigned & Set over and by these psents do freely & Absolutely give grant Sell Assign Set over & Confirm unto him ye s^d Nicholas Morrell his heirs & Assignes forever Twenty Acres part of ye Above grant of Thirty Acres of Land To have & To hold to him ye s^d Nicholas Morrell his heirs and Assignes as afores^d peaceably to Enjoy y^e Same without Mollestation of or by me y^e s^d James ffernald my heirs Ex^{rs} Adm^{rs} or Assignes &c^t In Witness whereof I have hereunto Set my hand and Seal this Seventh day of December Annoq, Dom. 1711

Signed Sealed & Delivered   James $\overset{his}{H}$ Fernald. (^a_{Seal})
In the psence of us   mark
John Dennet
John Tompson

York sc/ May 9th 1715./ The within Named James Fernald Acknowledged y^e within written Instrum^t to be his free Act & Deed   Before me   Charles Frost J peace
Recorded According to y^e Original May y^e 9th 1715

p. Jos : Hamond. Reg^r

Know All men by these psents that I John Croade of Berwick in ye County of York in ye Province of ye Massachusets Bay in New England Merchant for & in Consideration

of ye Sum of Eight pounds to me in hand Truely paid by Joseph Wood of ye Same Town County & Province afores^d Labourer the receipt whereof I do hereby Acknowledge & my Selfe therewith fully Satisfied Contented & paid have bargained Sold Aliened Assigned Enfeoffed Set over & Confirmed and do by these psents bargaine Sell Aliene Assign Enfeoffe Set over & Confirm unto him ye s^d Joseph Wood his heirs & Assignes forever four Acres of Land Scittuate Lying & being in ye Town of Berwick afores^d At ye foot of ye rockey hills next Adjoyning to ye Comons road bounded Easterly with three Spotted pines Southerly with lands Said to be John Abbots Westerly wth land Baker Nason Northerly by land of James Warren To have & To hold ye s^d four Acres land with all ye rights profits priviledges & Appurtenances unto ye Same belonging unto him ye s^d Joseph Wood his heirs & Assignes for ever to ye only propper use & bennefit of him ye s^d Joseph Wood his heirs & Assignes forever free & Clear & Clearly Acquitted of & from all other & former gifts grants Bargains Sales Titles Troubles Charges & Incumbrances whatsoever And that I y^e s^d John Croad & my heirs to him y^e s^d Joseph Wood his heirs & Assignes Shall & will Warrant & forever Confirm y^e Same in Witness whereof I have hereunto Set my hand and Seal y^e 17th June Annoq, Domini 1714./   John Croade ($_{Seal}^a$)
Signed Sealed & D^d/
  In presence of
  John Bradstreet
      her
  Abigail X Blacstone
      mark
  York sc/
John Croade psonally appeared and Acknowledged y^e above written Instrum^t to be his Act & Deed Berwick y^e 23^d day may 1715./ Before me Ichabod Plaisted Jus^t peace
Recorded According to ye Original June 17th 1715./
                              p Jos: Hamond Reg^r

  To All People to whom these psents Shall Come I John Ingersol of Kittery in ye County of York in ye Province of ye Massachusets Bay in New England Carpenter Send Greeting Know yee that I John Ingersol for diverse Causes me hereunto moveing but more Especially for & in Consideration of ye Love & Tender Affection which I have & do bear Toward my Son Nathaniel Ingersol & Also in Consideration of my s^d Son his Takeing Care of & providing Suitable Subsistance for me & my wife during our Natural Lives have given granted Enfeoffed & Confirmed & by these presents do fully freely & Absolutely give grant & Confirm unto my s^d Son Nathaniel Ingersol his heirs & Assignes forever all that my whole plantation Messuage [95] Or Tenement whereon I now live Scittuate in Kittery afores^d on ye Eastern Side of ye river Comonly Called Spruce Creek Containing about Thirty Six Acres be it more or Less butted & bounded on ye Northern Side by ye land that was formerly Richard Endles on ye Eastern End by Elisha Ingersol his land or John Chapmans land on ye Southern Side by John Ingersol jun^r on ye western End by Elisha Ingersoll or John Chapmans land & ye aboves^d Creek or however otherwise butted and bounded Together with all housing lands garden orchard pasture meadow ground & all other Appurtenances & priviledges whatsoever thereunto belonging To have & To hold ye s^d Plantation Together with all ye houseing Barns Orchards gardens meadows pastures & all other Appurtenances profits & heriditam^{ts} to ye s^d plantation belonging or in any wise Appurtaining unto my s^d Son Nath^{ll} Ingersol his heirs Ex^{rs} Adm^{rs} and Assignes forover after ye decease of mee & my wife & to ye Sole use bennefit & behoofe of my s^d Son his heirs & Assignes forever ye Aboves^d given & granted premises my s^d Son may Lawfully Enter into possess have hold & Improve As he Shall Se Cause Imediately after ye death of me & my wife & not before without our leave or Consent./ In Testimony whereof I have hereunto Set my hand & Seal y^e Nineteenth day of May in y^e year of our Lord One Thousand Seven hundred & fifteen & in y^e first year of y^e Reign of our Soveraign Lord George King of Great Brittaine &c^t

Signed Sealed & D^d
In y^e psence of   John   his   Ingersol ($^a_{Seal}$)
John Newmarch   mark
George King

Joaña   her X   Pope
   mark

Province of Massachusets Bay
York sc/ June y^e 23 1715/ John Ingersol psonally Appeared & Acknowledged y^e Above written Instrum^t to be his free Act & Deed   Before me   Wm Pepperrell Js. peace
Recorded According to y^e Original June 23^d 1715./
        p Jos. Hamond Reg^r

Book VIII, Fol. 95.

To All People unto whom this present deed of Sale Sha'l Come Elisha Hutchinson of Boston in y[e] County of Suffolk within his Ma:[tys] Province of y[e] Massachusets Bay in New England Esq[r] & Elizabeth his wife y[e] only Surviving child heir & Executrix of y[e] Last will & Testam[t] of Major Thomas Clark Late of s[d] Boston Merch[t] dec[d] Send Greeting Know Yee that y[e] s[d] Elisha Hutchinson & y[e] s[d] Eliz[a] his wife for and in Consideration of y[e] Sum of one hundred Twenty five pounds Currant money in New England to them in hand at & before the Ensealing & Delivery of these psents well & Truely paid & Secured in y[e] Law to be paid by Nathaniel Harris of Rowley in y[e] County of Essex within y[e] Province Afores[d] Yeoman to y[e] full Content & Satisfaction of y[e] s[d] Elisha Hutchinson & y[e] s[d] Eliz[a] his wife have Given granted bargained Sold Aliened Enfeoffed released Conveyed & Confirmed & by these presents do fully freely clearly & Absolutely give grant bargaine Sell Aliene Enfeoffe release Convey & Confirm unto y[e] s[d] Nath[ll] Harris his heirs & Assignes forever all that their Certain Tract or parcell of land Containing one hundred & Thirty Two Acres Twelve whereof Are Meadow Scittuate Lying & being in y[e] Town of York within y[e] County of York in y[e] Province aboves[d] & butted & bounded Easterly by y[e] land of Allexand[r] Maxwell & Micum Mackintire Southerly by York river to a Cove Comonly Called Curtis[s] Cove & Extending from s[d] York river Northerly As other Lots in y[e] Town of york afores[d] Adjoyning to y[e] s[d] river do run untill y[e] Afores[d] Quantity of one hundred & Thirty two Acres be fully Compleated which s[d] land was formerly part of y[e] Estate of y[e] s[d] Major Thomas Clarke and was by him purchased in Several parcells of Elenor Hook widdow Margriet Norton & George Norton Richard Banckes & John Twisden./ Together with all the Trees Timb[r] Woods underwoods waters water Courses Stones herbage pasturage rights members profits priviledges Comodityes Advantages heriditam[ts] Emollum[ts] & Appurtenances whatsoever upon or in Any wise belonging or Appurtaining to y[e] s[d] Tract or parcell of land herein before granted or any part or parcell thereof & All y[e] Estate right Title Interest Inheritance use propperty possession Claime & Demand whatsoever of them y[e] s[d] Elisha Hutchinson & y[e] s[d] Eliz[a] his wife & of Each of them their & Each of their heirs of in or to y[e] Same & y[e] revercōn & revercōns remaind[r] & remainders thereof To have & To hold y[e] before mentioned Tract or pcell of Land with all & Singular y[e] pmises And Appurtenances thereof herein & hereby before granted & Sold unto y[e] s[d] Nathaniel Harris his heirs & Assignes to his & their only propper use bennefit & behoofe forever,/ And the s^d Elisha Hutchinson & Eliz^a his s^d wife for themselves their heirs Execut^{rs} & Adm^{rs} do hereby Covenant grant & agree to & wth ye s^d Nath^{ll} Harris his heirs & Assignes in Manner & form following. (That Is To Say) that they ye s^d Elisha Hutchinson & Elizabeth his s^d Wife are At & untill ye Ensealing & delivery of these psents ye True & Lawfull owners of All ye s^d land & premises herein before granted & Sold & Stand Lawfully Siez^d thereof in their own propper right as of a good perfect and Indefeasible Estate of Inheritance in fee Simple without any mañer of Condition reversion or Limitation of use or uses whatsoever So as to Alter change defeat or make Voyd ye Same & have in themselves full power good right & Lawfull Authority to grant Sell Convey & Assure ye s^d granted & bargained pmises in maner As Afores^d & that ye Same are free & Clear & Clearly Acquitted & Discharged of & from all & all [96] Manner of former & other gifts grants bargains Sales Leases releases Mortgages Alienations Joyntures Dowers Wills Entails Titles Troubles Charges & Incumbrances whatsoever And further that they ye s^d Elisha Hutchinson & Eliz^a his s^d wife their heirs Exec^{rs} & Adm^{rs} Shall & will Warrant & Defend all ye s^d Land & pmises hereby granted & Sold unto ye s^d Nathaniel Harris his heirs & Assigns forever against ye Lawfull Claimes & Demands of all & Every pson & psons whomso ever,/ And at any time hereafter upon ye reasonable request & at ye Cost & Charges of ye s^d Nathaniel Harris his heirs or Assignes Shall & will give & pass unto him or them Such further Confirmation & Assurence of ye s^d granted & bargained premises As by their Councill Learned in y^e Law Shall be Lawfully or reasonably Devised Advised or required./ In Witness whereof y^e s^d Elisha Hutchinson and Elizabeth his s^d wife have hereunto Set their hands and Seals the fourteenth day of March Anno Domini 1701 Annoq, RR^s Gulielmi Tertii Anglia &c^t Decmo Quarto   Elisha Hutchinson ($_{Seal}^a$)

Signed Sealed & Delivered by   Elizabeth Hutchinson ($_{Seal}^a$)
y^e Above named Elisha
Hutchinson & Elizabeth his
wife in psence of us
Edw: Hutchinson
Elizabeth Hutchinson
   Boston March 14. 1701

The above Named Elisha Hutchinson & Elizabeth his wife psonally Appearing before me y^e Subscriber one of y^e Councill & Justice of Peace within his Maj^{tys} Province of ye Mas-

sachusets Bay in New England Acknowledged y⁰ Above written Instrumᵗ to be their Act & Deed./
                                    Peter Sergeant
Recorded According to yᵉ Original May 28ᵗʰ 1715./
                                    p Jos. Ham̄ond Regʳ

To All People unto whom this present deed of Sale shall Come Eliakim Hutchinson of Boston in yᵉ County of Suffolk within yᵉ Province of yᵉ Massachusets Bay in New England Merchanᵗ Sendeth Greeting./ Know Yee that I yᵉ sᵈ Eliakim Hutchinson for & in Consideration of yᵉ Sum̄ of Thirty Seven pounds Curraᵗ money of New England to me Secured to be well & Truely paid at & before yᵉ Ensealing & Delivery of these presents by Nathaniel Harris of York in yᵉ County of york in yᵉ Province aforesᵈ Husbandman have given granted bargained Sold released Enfeoffed & Confirmed and by these presents do give grant bargaine Sell release Enfeoffe & Confirm unto yᵉ sᵈ Nathaniel Harris his heirs & Assigns forever all those my Two Several pieces or parcells of land Herein after Mentioned Scittnate Lying & being within yᵉ Township of York aforesᵈ (That is To Say) one parcel of Twenty five acres on part whereof Stood yᵉ Dwelling house of yᵉ Late Edward Rishworth Now or Late in yᵉ Tenaʳ & Occupation of Jeremiah Moulton. The other parcell Containing Ten Acres being part of a Tract of Land Com̄only Called & known by yᵉ name of burnt plaine both which pcells of Land above mentioned were formerly belonging to yᵉ afore named Edward Rishworth To have & To hold. yᵉ sᵈ Two Severall parcells of land with yᵉ rights Members priviledges & Appurtenances to them & Every of them belonging unto yᵉ sᵈ Nathaniel Harris his heirs & Assignes to his & their only propper use bennefit & behoofe forever./ And I yᵉ sᵈ Eliakim Hutchinson for me my heirs Exʳˢ & Admʳˢ do Covenant grant & Agree to & with yᵉ sᵈ Nathˡ Harris his heirs Executʳˢ Admʳˢ & Assignes that at yᵉ time of this bargaine & Sale & untill yᵉ Ensealing & Delivery of these presents I yᵉ sᵈ Eliakim Hutchinson am yᵉ True Sole & Lawfull owner of yᵉ sᵈ Two Several parcells of land above mentioned & have in my Selfe full power good right & Lawfull Authority to grant bargain Sell & Confirm yᵉ Same as aforesᵈ & Shall & will Warrant & Defend yᵉ sᵈ Bargained pmises unto yᵉ sᵈ Nathaniel Harris his heirs & Assignes forever against my Selfe & my heirs & all & Every other pson & psons haveing claiming or pretending to have:

Book VIII, Fol. 97.

or Claim any right Title or Interest thereinto or into any part thereof from by or und^r me./ In Witness whereof I ye s^d Eliakim Hutchinson & Sarah my wife in Testimony of her free Consent to ye Sale of ye pmises & releice of all right of Dower or Thirds to be by her had or claimed thereto have hereunto Set our hands & Seals ye Twenty fourth day of Aprill Anno Domini 1703./ Annoq, RR^a Anna Anglia &c^t Secundo   E^m Hutchinson (Seal)
Signed Sealed & Delivered   Sarah Hutchinson (Seal)
  In psence of us
  John Hubbard
  Wm Hutchinson
    Province of ye Massachusets Bay Boston Apr^l 27 1703
    The within Named Eliakim Hutchinson Esqr & Sarah his wife Acknowledged ye within written Instrum^t to be their Act & Deed   Before me./   Js. Addington J pac̃.//
  Recorded According to ye Original May 28th 1715
                   p Jos : Ham̃ond Reg^r

[97] Know All men to whom these p^rsents Shall Come that I Nathan^l Harris of Pembrook in ye County of Plymouth Late of Rowley in New England Yeoman Send Greeting Know Yee that I ye s^d Nath^ll Harris for & — Consideration of ye Love good will & Affection which I bear and do bear towards my Loving friend & Son in Law John Prichard of Boston in ye County of Suffolk of New England Joyner have given & granted & by these presents do freely clearly & Absolutely give and grant to ye s^d John Pricherd his heirs Exec^rs Admin^rs a Certain parcel of land being & lying Scittuate in Cockshall bounding upon Wells Saco & Cape porpoise in ye County of york in New England being land which I ye s^d Harris bought with John Harris John Stanford & others of Mr Harlackinden Simonds it being Still undivided fifty Acres of which I do freely grant make Over & forever Confirm unto my Son in Law John Pricherd his heirs Ex^rs &c^t from henceforth as his & their propper Estate in fee Simple without any Let hinderence or Mollestation by from or und^r me ye s^d Harris my heirs Exec^rs Admin^rs forever Absolutely without any maner of Condition./ In Witness whereof I have Set to my hand and Seal this Second day of March one Thousand Seven

sachusets Bay in New England Acknowledged y'e Above written Instrum't to be their Act & Deed./
Peter Sergeant
Recorded According to y'e Original May 28th 1715./
p Jos. Hamond Reg'r

To All People unto whom this present deed of Sale shall Come Eliakim Hutchinson of Boston in y'e County of Suffolk within y'e Province of y'e Massachusets Bay in New England Merchan't Sendeth Greeting./ Know Yee that I y'e s'd Eliakim Hutchinson for & in Consideration of y'e Sum of Thirty Seven pounds Curra't money of New England to me Secured to be well & Truely paid at & before y'e Ensealing & Delivery of these presents by Nathaniel Harris of York in y'e County of york in y'e Province afores'd Husbandman have given granted bargained Sold released Enfeoffed & Confirmed and by these presents do give grant bargaine Sell release Enfeoffe & Confirm unto y'e s'd Nathaniel Harris his heirs & Assigns forever all those my Two Several pieces or parcells of land Herein after Mentioned Scittnate Lying & being within y'e Township of York afores'd (That is To Say) one parcel of Twenty five acres on part whereof Stood y'e Dwelling house of y'e Late Edward Rishworth Now or Late in y'e Tena'r & Occupation of Jeremiah Moulton. The other parcell Containing Ten Acres being part of a Tract of Land Comonly Called & known by y'e name of burnt plaine both which pcells of Land above mentioned were formerly belonging to y'e afore named Edward Rishworth To have & To hold. y'e s'd Two Severall parcells of land with y'e rights Members priviledges & Appurtenances to them & Every of them belonging unto y'e s'd Nathaniel Harris his heirs & Assignes to his & their only propper use bennefit & behoofe forever./ And I y'e s'd Eliakim Hutchinson for me my heirs Ex'rs & Adm'rs do Covenant grant & Agree to & with y'e s'd Nath'l Harris his heirs Execut'rs Adm'rs & Assignes that at y'e time of this bargaine & Sale & untill y'e Ensealing & Delivery of these presents I y'e s'd Eliakim Hutchinson am y'e True Sole & Lawfull owner of y'e s'd Two Several parcells of land above mentioned & have in my Selfe full power good right & Lawfull Authority to grant bargain Sell & Confirm y'e Same as afores'd & Shall & will Warrant & Defend y'e s'd Bargained pmises unto y'e s'd Nathaniel Harris his heirs & Assignes forever against my Selfe & my heirs & all & Every other pson & psons haveing claiming or pretending to have :

or Claim any right Title or Interest thereinto or into any part thereof from by or und{r} me./ In Witness whereof I y{e} s{d} Eliakim Hutchinson & Sarah my wife in Testimony of her free Consent to y{e} Sale of y{e} pmises & releice of all right of Dower or Thirds to be by her had or claimed thereto have hereunto Set our hands & Seals y{e} Twenty fourth day of Aprill Anno Domini 1703./ Annoq RR{a} Anna Anglia &c{t} Secundo   E{m} Hutchinson (Seal)
Signed Sealed & Delivered   Sarah Hutchinson (Seal)
In psence of us
John Hubbard
W{m} Hutchinson

   Province of y{e} Massachusets Bay Boston Apr{l} 27 1703
The within Named Eliakim Hutchinson Esq{r} & Sarah his wife Acknowledged y{e} within written Instrum{t} to be their Act & Deed   Before me./ Js. Addington J pac.//
Recorded According to y{e} Original May 28{th} 1715
                        p Jos: Hamond Reg{r}

[97] Know All men to whom these p{r}sents Shall Come that I Nathan{l} Harris of Pembrook in y{e} County of Plymouth Late of Rowley in New England Yeoman Send Greeting Know Yee that I y{e} s{d} Nath{ll} Harris for & — Consideration of y{e} Love good will & Affection which I bear and do bear towards my Loving friend & Son in Law John Prichard of Boston in y{e} County of Suffolk of New England Joyner have given & granted & by these presents do freely clearly & Absolutely give and grant to y{e} s{d} John Pricherd his heirs Exec{rs} Admin{rs} a Certain parcel of land being & lying Scittuate in Cockshall bounding upon Wells Saco & Cape porpoise in y{e} County of york in New England being land which I y{e} s{d} Harris bought with John Harris John Stanford & others of M{r} Harlackinden Simonds it being Still undivided fifty Acres of which I do freely grant make Over & forever Confirm unto my Son in Law John Pricherd his heirs Ex{rs} &c{t} from henceforth as his & their propper Estate in fee Simple without any Let hinderence or Mollestation by from or und{r} me y{e} s{d} Harris my heirs Exec{rs} Admin{rs} forever Absolutely without any maner of Condition./ In Witness whereof I have Set to my hand and Seal this Second day of March one Thousand Seven

Book VIII, Fol. 97.

hundred & fourteen & in ye Twelfth year of our Soveraign Lady Anne Queen of Great Brittaine./
Signed Sealed & Delivered   Nath^ll Harris (_{Seal}^a)
 In ye psence of us
 John Leathe
 Nathaniel Boynton
    Suffolk ss Boston may ye 12th 1715
 Nathaniel Harris ye Subscriber psonally Appeared & Acknowledged this Instrum^t to be his Act & Deed Before me
       John Clark Just^s peace
Recorded According to ye Original may 28th 1715.
      p Jos: Hamond Reg^r

  To All Christian People to whom these psents shal Come Nathan^l Harris of York in ye County of York within his Maj^tys Province of ye Massachusets Bay in New England yeoman Sends Greeting Know Yee that Nathaniel Harris for & in Consideration of ye Sum of one hundred & forty pound Curra^t money to him in hand paid before the Enseuling & Delivery of these psents by John Pricherd of Boston in ye County of Suffolk ye Rec^t whereof to full Content & Satisfaction & for divers other good Causes and Considerations him hereunto moveing he ye s^d Nathaniel Harris hath given granted Bargained Sold Aliened Conveyed and Confirmed & by these psents doth fully freely Clearly and Absolutely give grant bargaine Sell alliene Enfeoffe Convey and Confirm unto ye s^d John Pricherd his heirs & Assignes forever a Certain Tract or parcell of land Containing as by Estimation one hundred & Thirty Two Acres be it more or less Scittuate lying in ye bounds of York afores^d butted And bounded as followeth Easterly by land of Allexand^r Maxwell & Micum Mackintire Southerly by York river to a Cove Comonly called Curtis^es Cove & Extending from ye s^d York river Northerly as other Lotts in ye Town of York afores^d Adjoyning to ye s^d river do run until ye afores^d Quantity of one hundred & Thirty Two Acres be Compleated it being land which was formerly Colonell Elisha Hutchinsons of Boston & s^d Harris purchased it of him ye s^d Hutchinson as by s^d Harris^es deed Shall being had may Appear & Also Another Tract or parcel of land which him ye s^d Harris bought of Sam^ll Webber of York afores^d As is Contained in a deed from s^d Webber to s^d Harris with all ye buildings on s^d land & all his right Interest & Estate At York afores^d whatsoever or any wayes Appurtaining to him ye s^d Nath^ll Harris To have & To hold

all y̛ᵉ Above granted p̛mises with all & Singular yᵉ Appurtenᶜᵉˢ thereof unto yᵉ sᵈ John Pricherd his heirs & Assignes to his & their own Sole & propper use bennefit & behoofe from henceforth forever & yᵉ sᵈ Nathˡˡ Harris for himselfe his heirs Exʳˢ & Admʳˢ doth hereby Covenant promiss grant and agree to & with yᵉ sᵈ John Prichard his heirs & Assignes in mañer & form following/ That is To Say/ that at yᵉ time of yᵉ Ensealing & Delivery of these psents he yᵉ sᵈ Nathˡˡ Harris is yᵉ True Sole & Lawfull owner of all yᵉ Above bargained p̛mises having in himselfe full Power good right & Lawfull Authority to Sell & dispose of yᵉ Same in mañer as aforesᵈ & that sᵈ John Pricherd his heirs Exʳˢ Admʳˢ or Assignes may henceforth forever Lawfully peaceably and Quietly have hold use Occupy possess & Enjoy all yᵉ afore bargained p̛mises with yᵉ Appurtenances thereof wᵗʰout any Let hinderence Mollestation or disturbence by from or under me my heirs or Assignes forever or any other pson or psons laying any Lawfull Claims thereunto or any part thereof & at any time or Times hereafter on demand to give & pass Such further & Ample Assurence & Confirmation of yᵉ p̛mises unto yᵉ sᵈ John Pricherd his heirs or Assignes forever as in law or Equity can be reasonably devised Advised or required./ In Witness whereof yᵉ sᵈ Nathˡ Harris hath hereunto Set to his hand & Seal yᵉ Tenth day of May & in yᵉ year of our lord one Thousand Seven hundred and fifteen & in yᵉ first year of yᵉ Reign of our Soveraign King George
Signed Sealed & Dᵈ   Nathˡˡ Harris (ˢᵉᵃₐₗ)
In yᵉ psence of
John Drew
John Leathe

        Suffolk sc/ Boston may yᵉ 12ᵗʰ 1715

Nathˡˡ Harris yᵉ Subscribʳ psonally Appeared & Acknowledged yᵉ Instrumᵗ before written to be his Act & Deed
         Before me./   John Clarke Just peace
Recorded According to yᵉ Original May 28ᵗʰ 1715./
                       p Jos: Hañond Regʳ

[98] To All Christian People to whom these p̛ʳsents shall Come Nathaniel Harris of york in yᵉ County of York within his Maᵗʸˢ Province of yᵉ Massachusets Bay in New England yeoman Sends Greeting Know yee that yᵉ sᵈ Nathˡˡ Harris for and in Consideration of yᵉ Suñ of forty pounds in Curraᵗ money of New England to him in hand paid before yᵉ Ensealing & Delivery of these psents by John Pricherd

of Boston in ye County of Suffolk in New Engl^d Joyner ye receipt whereof to full Content & Satisfaction he ye s^d Nath^ll Harris doth by these presents Acknowledge thereof and Every part thereof for himselfe heirs Execut^rs & Adm^rs doth Acquitt Exonerate & Discharge ye s^d John Pricherd his heirs Ex^rs Adm^rs Every of them forever by these psents & for diverse other good Causes hereunto moveing he ye s^d Nathaniel Harris hath given granted bargained Sold Aliened Enfeoffed Conveyed & Confirmed and by these psents doth fully freely Clearly & Absolutely give grant Bargaine Sell Aliene Enfeoffe Convey & Confirm unto ye s^d John Pricherd his heirs & Assignes forever a Certain Tract or pcell of land Containing about Thirty five acres be it more or Less it being all that Tract of Land which s^d Harris bought of Mr Eliakim Hutchinson of Boston Merch^t Scittuate & lying in ye bounds of York afores^d butted & bounded as in s^d Harris^s deed from Hutchinson or however otherwise bounded or repuied to be bounded Together with all Such rights Libertys Imunitys profits priviledges Comodityes Emollum^ts & Appur^ces as in any kind Appurtaine thereunto with ye reverc̃ons & remaind^rs thereof & all ye Estate right Title Interest Inheritance propperty possesion Claime & Demand whatsoever of him ye s^d Nathan^ll Harris of in & to ye Same & Every part thereof To have & To hold all ye above granted pmises with all & Singular ye Appurten^ces thereof unto ye s^d John Pricherd his heirs & Assignes to his & their own Sole & propper use bennefit & behoofe from henceforth forever And ye s^d Nathaniel Harris for himselfe his heirs Ex^rs & Adm^re doth hereby Covenant promiss grant & agree to & with y^s s^d John Pricherd his heirs & Assignes in mañer & form following./ That is To Say that at ye Ensealing and delivery of these psents he ye s^d Nath^ll Harris is ye True and Lawfull owner of all ye afore bargained pmises having in himselfe full power good right & Lawfull Authority to Sell and dispose of ye Same in maner as afores^d & that ye s^d John Pricherd his heirs & Assignes Shall & may henceforth forever Lawfully peaceably & Quietly have hold use Occupy & Enjoy The above granted pmises with ye Appurtenances thereof without any Let hinderence or Mollestation by from or under me my heirs Execut^rs or Admin^rs or any other pson or psons forever after ye Date of these psents & At any time or Times hereafter on demand to give & pass Such further & Ample Assurences & Confirmation of ye premises unto ye s^d John Pricherd his heirs or Assignes forever as in Law or Equity can be reasonably Devised Advised or required./ In Witness whereof y^e s^d Nathl Harris hath Set to his hand &

Seal this Tenth day of May in y^e year of our Lord one Thousand Seven hundred & fifteen & in y^e first year of y^e Reign of our Sdveraign King George
Signed Sealed & Delivered   Nathaniel Harris ($^a_{seal}$)
  In the psence of
  John Drew
  John Leathe
        Suffolk sc Boston may y^e 12th 1715.//

Nathan^l Harris y^e Subscriber psonally Appeared & Acknowledged y^e above written Instrum^t to be his Act & Deed./
Before me   John Clark Just peace
  Recorded According to y^e Original May 28th 1715./
                p Jos : Hamond Reg^r

To All Christian People to whom these presents Shall come Nathaniel Harris of York in ye County of york in his Maj^{tys} Province of ye Massachusets Bay in New England Yeoman Sends Greeting Know Yee that ye s^d Nathaniel Harris for & in Consideration of Thirty Two pounds Curra^t money of New England to him in hand paid before ye Ensealing of these psents by John Pricherd of Boston in ye County of Suffolk Joyn^r ye rec^t whereof to full Content & Satisfaction he ye s^d Nathan^l Harris doth by these psents Acknowledge thereof & of Every part thereof for himselfe his heirs Execut^{rs} & Adm^{rs} full Satisfaction & discharge ye s^d John Pricherd his heirs Ex^{rs} & Adm^{rs} Every of y^m by these psents & for divers other good Causes & Considerations moving ye s^d Nathaniel Harris thereunto hath given granted bargained Sold Aliened Enfeoffed Conveyed & Confirmed & by these psents doth fully freely clearly & absolutely give grant Bargaine Sell Aliene Enfeoffe Convey & forever Confirm unto him ye s^d John Pricherd his heirs & Assignes forever a Certaine Tract or pcell of land Scittuate Lying & being in ye bounds of york afores^d it being all that Tract of Land which s^d Harris bought of Samuel Webber of York afores^d butted & bounded As followeth it being by Estimation about Twenty Acres be it more or less begining [99] At a heap of Stones by ye Side of ye highway Adjoyning to ye Land that formerly was Edward Rishworth^s on ye Southeast Side & So runing one hundred & Eight rods upon a Northeast line & from thence Thirty & Two rods upon a northwest line & from thence Ninety & Six rods upon a Southwest line & from thence Twenty rods upon a Southeast line & from thence Twelve rods upon a Southwest line to ye heap of Stones by ye way

Book VIII, Fol. 99.

Side where wee began or any other wayes bounded or reputed to be bounded Together with all Such rights Libertyes Imunityes profits priviledges Comodities Emollum^{ts} & Appurtenances as in any kind Appurtaine thereunto Together with all ye buildings on s^d land To have & To hold all ye above granted premisses with all & Singular ye Appurtenances thereof unto ye s^d John Pricherd his heirs & Assignes to his & their own propper use benefit and behoofe from henceforth forever And ye s^d Nathl Harris for himselfe his heirs Ex^{rs} Adm^{rs} & Assignes doth Covenant promiss grant and agree to & with ye s^d John Prichard his heirs & Assignes in mañer and form following./ That is to Say./ that at ye Time of ye Ensealing and delivery of these psents he ye s^d Nathaniel Harris is ye True and Sole & Lawfull owner of all ye Afore bargained pmises having in himselfe full power good right & Lawfull Authority to Sell and dispose of ye Same in Maner afores^d/ And ye s^d John Prichard his heirs Ex^{rs} Adm^{rs} & Assignes shall & may henceforth forever Lawfully peaceably and Quietly have hold use Occupy possess & Enjoy ye Above granted pmises with ye Appurtenances thereof free & Clear without and Let hinderence disturbence or Mollestation by from or und^r me my heirs Ex^{rs} Adm^{rs} or Assignes or any other pson or psons laying any Lawfull claime thereunto or any part thereof & at any time or times hereafter on demand to give & pass Such further & Ample Assurence & Confirmation of ye pmises unto ye s^d John Pricherd his heirs Ex^{rs} Adm^{rs} or Assignes forever as in Law or Equity can be reasonably Advised devised or required In Witness w^{r}of ye s^d Nathaniel Harris hath Set to his hand & Seal this Twelfth day of May in ye year of our Lord one Thousand Seven hundred & fifteen and in ye first year of ye Reign of our Soveraign Lord George King of Great Brittaine &c^t

Signed Sealed & Delivered   Nathaniel Harris (a Seal)
In ye psence of us Witnesses
John Drew
John Leathe

        Suffolk ss/ Boston may 12th 1715

Nathl Harris ye Subscrib^r psonally Appeared & Acknowledged ye above Instrument to be his Act & Deed./ Before me   John Clark Just^s peace

Recorded According to ye Original May 28th 1715./

               p Jos. Hañond Reg^r

To All People to whom These presents shall Come I Mar^{tl} John Harris of Ipswich in ye County of Essex in ye Province of ye Massachusets Bay in New England America Send Greeting —

Know Yee that I ye s^d John Harris for diverse good Causes & Considerations me thereunto moveing but Especially for & in Consideration of a Valluable Sum in hand paid unto me by Mr Jonathan Woodman of Newbury in ye County and Province afores^d to my full Satisfaction & Content & I do Accordingly for my Selfe my heirs Execut^rs & Adm^rs Acquit Exonerate & Discharge ye s^d Jonathan Woodman his heirs Ex^rs & Adm^rs by these psents Have given granted bargained & Sold Enfeoffed & Confirmed & do by these psents fully freely clearly & absolutely give grant Bargaine Sell Enfeoffe & Confirm unto ye s^d Mr Jonathan Woodman Two hundred Acres of Land being part of a Tract of Land which I ye s^d John Harris have purchased ye s^d Tract of land formerly belonging to Mr Harlackenden Symonds of Ipswich in ye County afores^d which s^d Tract of land diverse joynt purchasers had purchased of him ye s^d Symonds & it is Six miles in length & four miles in Breadth known by ye Name of Cockshall in ye County of Yorkshire in ye Province of Maine & is bounded as followeth Viz^t At ye Southeast End partly by ye Line of ye Township of Wells & partly upon ye line of ye Township of Capeporpoise & on ye northeast Side partly bounded by ye line of ye Land formerly Maj^r William Phillips his land & partly on ye Comon land & on ye Northwest End ye land is bounded on ye Comon land & on ye Southwest Side bounded with ye land of ye s^d Symonds as by a deed of Sale under ye hand & Seal of Mr Harlackenden Symonds bareing Date June ye 12. An: Dom: 1688/ & by him Acknowledged June 22^d 1688 before John Vsher Esqr and Entred with ye Records of ye County of York Octob^r 12: 1693: in Fol. 84. more at large may Appear & I ye s^d John Harris for my Selfe my heirs Ex^rs & Adm^rs do Covenant & promiss to & with ye s^d Mr Jonathan Woodman his heirs Ex^rs & Adm^rs & Assignes that ye s^d Two hundred Acres of land & Every part & parcell thereof is free & clear & freely & Clearly Exonerated & discharged & Acquitted of & from all former gifts grants bargains Sales Alienations Charges Mortgages Dowers Joyntures Extents Judgm^ts Executions & all other Incumbrances w^tsoever [100] And I ye s^d John Harris for my Selfe my heirs Execut^rs & Adm^rs do & Shall from Time to Time & At all Times warrantize & Maintaine ye s^d bargained premises with all & Singular ye priviledges & Appurtenances and Comodities to ye s^d Two hundred Acres of land herein Mentioned belonging as Viz^t The Trees woods under wood Stand-

ing or lying on s^d land with all ye Meadows Swamps waters Water Courses Mines or Minerals in or upon ye s^d land Whatsoever or Wheresoever it be against all manner of psons whatsoever from by or under me ye Aboves^d Harris Claiming or pretending to have any Just and Lawfull right & Title or Interest to ye s^d Bargained pmises or any part or pcell thereof To have & To hold ye s^d bargained pmises and Every part & parcell thereof to him ye s^d Mr Jonathan Woodman his heirs Ex^{rs} Adm^{rs} & Assignes forever./ In Witness & Confirmation of all ye above written pmisses I ye s^d John Harris have hereunto Set my hand & Seal this Eighth day of June one Thousand Six hundred Ninety Seven & in ye Ninth year of his Ma^{tys} Reign   John Harris (a Seal)
Signed Sealed & Delivered
By Mr John Harris to M^r
Jonathan Woodman in
presence of us

John [his mark] Bare

Witnesses   John Dickingson
The words between ye fifth & Sixth lines were written before Signing & Sealing

Mr John Harris psonally Appeared and Acknowledged this above written Instrum^t to be his Volluntary Act & Deed
Newbury Septr 30th 1713./ Before me

Steph. Sewall Just peace
Recorded According to ye Original July 7th 1715./

p Jos : Hamond Reg^r

To All to whom these psents shall Come Know yee that I the within named Joseph Otis for Several good Causes & Considerations me thereunto moveing do by these psents Assigne Set ov^r Convey & Confirm ye within mentioned dwelling house wth ye Appurtenances unto Cap^{tn} Joseph Boynton of Rowley in ye County of Essex & to his heirs & Assignes forever To have & To hold ye s^d Dwelling house with all ye priviledges & Appur^{ces} thereunto belonging unto him ye s^d Joseph Boynton & to his heirs & Assignes forever free & Clear & Clearly Acquitted and discharged of & from all Claims & Demands of me y^e s^d Joseph Otis & my heirs & Assigns forever & for y^e Confirmation hereof I y^e s^d Joseph

Book VIII, Fol. 100.

Otis have hereunto Set my hand & Seal this Seventh day of July Anno Domini 1715/   Joseph Otis ($_\text{Seal}^\text{a}$)
Signed Sealed & Delivered
   In y^e psence of
   Nathaniel Otis
   James Ludden
         Plym^o ss Scittuate July y^e 7th 1715
   The above named Joseph Otis Appear^d & Acknowledged y^e Above written Instrum^t to be his Act & Deed Before me
                 John Cushing Just peace
   Recorded According to y^e Original y^e 27th July 1715
   The Instrum^t it refers unto being recorded in $\overline{\text{Lib}^r}$ 7 Fol^o
226   p Jos : Ham̃ond Reg^r

   To All People to whome this present deed of Sale Shall Come John Parsons of York in y^e County of York & province of y^e Massachusets Bay in New England Cordwainer Sendeth Greeting Know yee that y^e s^d John Parsons for & in Consideration of y^e Sum̃ of Twenty Two pounds Lawfull money of New England to him in hand paid well & Truely at & before ye Ensealing & Delivery of these psents by Elihue Parsons of ye aboves^d County & Province ye rec^t w^{r}of ye aboves^d John Parsons doth hereby Acknowledge & Every part & parcell thereof & doth Acquit Exonerate & discharge ye s^d Elihue Parsons his heirs & Assignes forever by these presents Have given granted bargained Sold Aliened Enfeoffed & Confirmed & by these presents do fully freely & clearly & Absolutely give grant bargaine Sell Aliene Enfeoffe & Confirm unto him ye s^d Elihue Parsons his heirs Execut^{rs} Adm^{rs} & Assignes forever a Certaine Tract of Land containing Twenty & Two Acres be it more or Less Scittuate Lying & being in york afores^d Between ye Land of Daniel Simpson formerly Henry Simpson & ye land of John Preble late of York dec^d Com̃only known by ye Name of Parson^s place butted & bounded by ye s^d Land of Simpsons & Prebles & by ye highway & So ruñing into ye Woods or however otherwise bounded or reputed to be bounded Together with ye Orchard on s^d Land & All Such rights Libertyes & Imunityes profits priviledges Commodityes Imollum^{ts} & Appurtenances or in any kind Appurtaining Thereunto with ye Reversions & remainders thereof & all ye Estate Right Interest Title Inheritance propperty possession Claime & Demand whatsoever of him ye s^d John Parsons of in & to the

Same & Every part thereof To have & To hold all ye Above
[101] granted premises with all & Singular ye Appurtenances thereof unto him ye s^d Elihue Parsons his heirs & Assignes to his & their own Sole & propper use benefit & behoofe from henceforth forever & ye s^d John Parsons for himselfe his heirs Execut^rs Adm^rs doth hereby Covenants promiss grant & agree to & with ye s^d Elihue parsons his heirs & Assignes in manner & form following that is to Say) that at ye Time of ye Ensealing & delivery of these presents he ye s^d John Parsons is ye True Sole & Lawfull owner of all ye aboves^d bargained premises & Stands Lawfully Siez^d thereof in his own propper right of good perfect & Indefeazeable Estate of Inheritance in Fee Simple haveing in himselfe full power good Right & Lawfull Authority to Sell & dispose of ye Same in Manner as afores^d & that ye s^d Elihue Parsons his heirs & Assignes Shall & may henceforth forever Lawfully peaceably & Quietly have hold use Occupie possess & enjoy ye above granted pmises with ye Appurtenances thereof free & Clear & Clearly Acquitted & discharged off & from all Maner of former & other gifts grants bargains Sales leases Mortgages Joyntures Dowries Judgm^ts Executions Entails forfeitures & of & from all other Titles Troubles Charges & Incumbrances whatsoever have made Comitted done or Suffered to be done by ye s^d John Parsons his heirs or Assigns at any Time or Times before ye Ensealing & Delivery hereof & further ye s^d John Parsons doth hereby Covenant promiss bind & Oblige himselfe his heirs Execut^rs & Adm^rs from henceforth & forever hereafter to Warrant & Defend all ye Above granted premises and Appurtenances thereof unto ye s^d Elihue Parsons his heirs and Assignes Against ye Lawfull Claims & Demands of all & Every pson & psons whomsoever & at any Time & Times hereafter on demand to give & pass Such further & Ample Assurence & Confirmation of ye Premises unto ye s^d Elihue Parsons his heirs & Assignes forever as in Law or Equity Cañ be reasonably devised Advised or Required As Given und^r my hand & Seal this first day of March in ye year of our Lord God One Thousand Seven hundred & fourteen fifteen & in ye first year of ye Reign of our Soveraign Lord George by the Grace of God King of Great Brittaine france & Irel^d &c^t/   John Parsons (Seal a)
Signed Sealed & Delivered
  In ye p^rsence
  John Kingsbury
  Nath^ll ffreeman
  Jos Wilson

Book VIII, Fol. 101.

Essex ss/ Salem Aprⁱ 30 : 1715
Then John Parsons yᵉ Conveyer pſonally Appearing Acknowledged yᵉ Above written to be his free & Volluntary Act & Deed./   Coram. Stephⁿ Sewal Just. peac
Recorded According to yᵉ Original July. 15ᵗʰ 1715/
p Jos : Hammond Regʳ

To All Christian People to whom these presents shall Come I Baker Nason of yᵉ Town of Berwick in yᵉ County of York in his Majᵗʸˢ Province of yᵉ Massachusets Bay in New England Carpentʳ & Elizabeth his wife Sendeth Greeting./ Know Yee that for & in Consideration of a Valluable Summ of money to us in hand paid by one John Hooper of yᵉ Town aforesᵈ Cordwainʳ yᵉ receipt hereof I do hereby Acknowledge my Selfe to be fully Satisfied & am therewith Contented & paid. Have bargained Sold Alienated Assigned Enfeoffed Set over & Confirmed & do by these pſents for mySelfe my heirs Executʳˢ Admʳˢ & Assignes forever freely Clearly & Absolutely give grant bargaine Sell Alienate Enfeoffe Set over & Confirm unto yᵉ foresᵈ John Hooper & to his heirs Exʳˢ Admʳˢ & Assignes forever a Certaine parcell or Tract of Land Containing Six Acres or thereabouts Scittuate Lying & being in yᵉ Town of Berwick aforesᵈ bounded as followeth Vizᵗ/ Takeing its begining at yᵉ Northermost Corner of Benjamin Nasons Twenty Acres of Land that Lyeth at yᵉ head of his home Lot & from thence runing Southeast by East halfe a point Easterly Sixteen pole by James Warrens land & from that Extent Southwest by South halfe a point Southerly forty Eight poles then west by north. Sixteen poles Then northeast by North halfe a point Northerly fifty Two poles being partly bounded by yᵉ foresᵈ Benjamin Nason his Twenty Acres of Land aforesᵈ Till it Comes to our first Station to a Smal hemlock Tree marked four Square which bounds Includes five Acres of yᵉ foresᵈ Six acres of land & yᵉ other acre Lyeth At yᵉ Southwest & west Corner of yᵉ foresᵈ five Acres & Joyning to it & to be four poles & one halfe wide & from thence runing & Containing yᵉ Same breadth Thirty Six poles more or Less till it Comes Square with yᵉ Land that yᵉ foresᵈ John Hooper bought of John Abbot./ To have & To hold the foresᵈ Six Acres of land with all & Singular yᵉ rights profits priviledges & Appurtenances thereunto belonging to him yᵉ aforesᵈ John. Hooper & to his heirs Exʳˢ Admʳˢ & Assigns forever frely & clearly Exonerated & diccharged of & from all maner of former Deed Sales Wills Dowries Mortgages or any other Incumbrances whatsoever had made done or Suffered to be done by me ye fores^d Baker Nason whereby ye fores^d John Hooper his heirs Execut^{rs} Adm^{rs} or Assignes may be in Any wise Mollested or disturbed in their Quiet & peaceable Injoyment & Improvem^t of ye above granted premises or any part thereof & further I ye fores^d Baker Nason do by these presents for my [102] Selfe my heirs Ex^{rs} Adm^{rs} & Assignes Covenant & promiss to & with ye fores^d John Hooper his heirs Ex^{rs} Adm^{rs} & Assignes for Ever to Save them harmless & to Warrant & Defend ye Title of ye above granted premises Against any person or persons whatsoever that may or Shall hereafter Claime any lawfull right Title or propriety to ye above granted premises or any part thereof whereby ye fores^d John Hooper his heirs Ex^{rs} Adm^{rs} or Assigns may be in any way Mollested or disturbed in their Quiet & peaceable Injoym^t & Improvem^t of ye above granted premises or any part thereof./ In Witness hereof I ye fores^d Baker Nason & Elizabeth his wife have hereunto Set our hands & Seals this Twenty Eight day of ffebruary Anno Domini one Thousand Seven hundred & fourteen fifteen & in ye first year of his Maj^{tys} Reign./ George by ye grace of God over great Brittaine ffrance & Ireland King Defender of ye faith &c^t

Signed Sealed & Delivered   Baker X (his mark) Nason (a Seal)
In the presence of us
Margret Warren   Elizabeth Nason (a Seal)
Joseph Wood
James Warren
York sc/
Baker Nason & Elizabeth his wife both psonally Appeared & Acknowledged ye Above written Instrum^t to be their Act & Deed./ Berwick ye 23^d day of May 1715 —

       Before me./   Ichabod Plaisted Just. peace
Recorded According to ye Original Augst 2nd 1715.

                       p Jos. Hamond Reg^r

To All Christian People to whom these p^{r}sents Shall come I Joseph Wood of ye Town of Berwick in ye County of York in his Maj^{tys} Province of ye Massachusets Bay in New England Weaver and Patience his wife Sendeth Greeting./ Know yee that for & in Consideration of a valluable Sum of money to us in hand paid by one John Hooper of ye Town afores^d Cordwainer ye rec^t thereof I do hereby Acknowledge

[BOOK VIII, FOL. 102.

my Selfe to be fully Satisfied therewith Contented & paid have given granted bargained Sold Aliened Enfeoffed Assigned Set over & Confirmed & do by these presents for my Selfe my heirs Ex^{rs} Adm^{rs} & Assignes forever give grant Bargaine Sell Aliene Enfeoffe Set over Assign & Confirm freely clearly & Absolutely unto ye fores^d John Hooper his heirs Ex^{rs} Adm^{rs} & Assigns forever a Certaine parcell or Tract of Land Containing about Three Acres & one halfe or thereabouts which I ye fores^d Joseph Wood bought of Mr John Croade As Appears by a deed under his hand & Seal bareing date The 17th day of June 1714./ bounded as followeth Viz^t Scittuate being & Lying in ye Town of Berwick afores^d & Taking its begining at ye Northeast Corner of a piece of land which ye fores^d John Hooper bought of Baker Nason As Appears by a deed of Sale bearing date herewith & runing Southeast & by East halfe a point Easterly Sixteen poles by James Warrens Land & from thence forty Seven poles by ye Comons Towards John Abbots Land & from thence to ye fores^d land that was ye fores^d Baker Nasons & runing to s^d land & Joyning To it forty Eight poles Northeast & by North halfe a point Northerly where it took its begining to a black ash Tree Mark^t on Three Sides all which Three Acres & one halfe or thereabouts more or Less as it is herein Bounded To have & To hold to him ye fores^d John Hooper & to his heirs & Execut^{rs} Adm^{rs} & Assigns forever with all & Singular ye rights profits priviledges & Appurtenances thereunto belonging freely & Clearly Exonerated & Discharged of & from all former deeds Sales wills dowryes Mortgages or any other Incumbrances whatsoever had made done or Suffered to be done by me ye fores^d Joseph Wood whereby ye fores^d John Hooper his heirs Ex^{rs} Adm^{rs} or Assigns may be in Any wise Mollested or disturbed in their Quiet & peaceable Injoym^t & Improvem^t of ye Above granted pmises or any part thereof & further I the fores^d Joseph Wood do by these presents for my Selfe my heirs Ex^{rs} Adm^{rs} & Assigns forever Covenant & promiss to & with ye fores^d John Hooper his heirs Ex^{rs} Adm^{rs} & Assignes forever to Save them harmless & to Warrant & Defend ye Title of ye above granted premisses against any pson or psons w^{t}soever that may or Shall hereafter claime any lawfull right or propriety to ye above granted premisses whereby ye fores^d John Hooper his heirs Ex^{rs} Adm^{rs} or Assignes may be in any wayes Mollested or disturbed in their peaceable Injoym^t & Improvem^t of ye above granted premisses or any part thereof./ In Witness hereof I ye fores^d Joseph Wood & Patience his wife have hereunto Set our hands & Seals this Twenty Eight day

BOOK VIII, FOL. 103.

of ffebruary Annoq, Domini one Thousand Seven hundred & fourteen fifteen & in ye first year of his Maj^tys Reign George by ye grace of God Over Great Brittaine ffrance & Ireland King Defend^r of ye faith &c^t/ Joseph Wood (a Seal)
Signed Sealed & Delivered
 In ye Presence of us   Patience X Wood (her Seal)
 Baker Nason ✗   mark
    mark
James Warren   Witnesses
Margriet Warren
York ss/
Joseph Wood & Patience his wife both psonally Appeared & Acknowledged ye above written Instrum^t to be their Act & deed./ Berwick ye 23^d day of May 1715./
     Before me Ichabod Plaisted J. peace
Recorded According to ye Original Aug^st ye 2^d 1715./
       p Jos. Hamond Reg^r

[103] Know All men by these presents that I ffrancis Raynes of York in ye County of york in New England for divers good causes & Considerations me thereunto moveing have given granted bargained Sold Aliened Conveyed & Confirmed & by these presents do freely fully and Absolutely give grant bargaine Sell Aliene Convey & Confirm unto my Uncle Mr John Woodman of ye Same place his heirs & Assignes forever five Acres of Salt Marsh lying & being at Brabut harbour in ye Township of york lying near Adjoyning to ye Lands Vulgarly Called Hodsdens where ye s^d Woodman Now dwells To have & To hold ye s^d granted & bargained pmises with all ye Appurtenances priviledges & Comoditys to ye Same belonging or in any wayes Appertaining to him ye s^d John Woodman his heirs & Assigns forever to his & their own proper use benefit & behalfe forever and I ye s^d Francis Raynes for me my heirs Ex^rs Adm^rs do Covena^t promiss & grant to & with ye s^d John Woodman his heirs & Assigns that at & before ye Ensealing hereof I am ye True Sole & Lawfull owner of ye above bargained premises & am Lawfully Siezed & possessed of ye Same in my own proper right as a good perfect & Absolute Estate of Inheritance in fee Simple & have in my Selfe good right full power & Lawfull Authority to grant & Convey ye Same as

York April 6. 1726. I have received the full Sum of twenty pounds within mentioned of Mr Francis Raynes I say received p me John woodman.
Witness Jos: Moodey Reg^r

aboves^d & that ye s^d John Woodman his heirs & Assigns Shall & may from Time to Time & at all Times hereafter by force of these presents lawfully peaceably & Quietly have hold use & Occupy & Enjoy ye s^d demised pmises free & Clearly discharged of and from all former & other gifts grants bargains Sales Leases Mortgages Wills Entails Joyntures Dowers Judgm^{ts} Executions Incumbrances & Extents./ Provided Nevertheless & it is ye True Intent and meaning of ye s^d Grantor & Grantee in these presents any thing herein Contained to ye Contrary Notwithstanding that if ye above Named ffrancis Raynes his heirs Execut^{rs} Adm^{rs} or Assigns do well & Truely pay unto ye Above Named John Woodman his heirs Ex^{rs} or Adm^{rs} or Assignes ye full & whole Sum of Twenty pounds in money ye Lawfull Coyn of this Province with ye Lawfull Interest at or before ye fifteenth day of Aprill next Coming which will be in ye year 1716./ then ye above written deed or Obligation & Every Clause & Article therein Contained Shall be null Voyd and of non Effect or Else Shall abide in full force & vertue. Sealed wth my Seal this fifteenth day of April one Thousand Seven hundred & fifteen   Interlined four words between lines y^e Thirty Second & line y^e Thirty Third with y^e Lawfull Interest before Sealing & Signing   Francis Rayns ($_{Seal}^a$)
Signed Sealed & Delivered
 In psence of us y^e Subscrib^{rs}
 William Godsoe
 Richd Rice
                her
 Eliz^a E Godsoe
         mark
 York ss/ y^e 20th June./ Anno Dom: 1715./ Francis Raynes psonally Appearing before me y^e Subscrib^r one of his Ma^{tys} Justices for y^e County afores^d & Acknowledged this within written deed or Obligation to be his free Act & deed./   Wm Pepperrell Js peace
 Recorded According to ye Original July 2^d 1715
                            p Jos: Hamond Reg^r

To All Christian People to whom this p'sent deed of Gift may Come Arthur Beal of York in ye County of york in ye province of ye Massachusets Bay in New England Sendeth Greeting./ Know Yee that ye s^d Arthur & Anna his wife for diverse good Causes & Considerations them thereunto moveing but more Especially ye Love they bear & have to their

Book VIII, Fol. 103.

Son in Law Wm Pearse & Mary his wife their own daughter have given granted made Over & Confirmed & do by these psents give grant make over & Convey & fully freely & Absolutely Confirm a Certaine piece or parcell of land by Estimation Ten acres be it more or Less Scittuate within this Town of york upon ye Neck of land where ye s^d Beal now Liveth on ye Southwest Side of s^d york river and upon ye northwest or west Side of a lot of land given by s^d Beal to his son in law Joshua Knap The bounds are as followeth Viz^t begining by ye river Side Joyning to s^d Knaps bounds & ruñs by s^d Knaps bounds South Eighty four poles & then ruñs west Twenty poles to a great hemlock Tree markt on four Sides then ruñs North to ye Aboves^d river & So is bounded by s^d river to ye place first began at ye s^d Beal only doth Except a way of Two poles Wide for a priviledge to pass & repass to ye neck of land next to ye Sea but for all ye rest or remaind^r of s^d Lot or Tract of land as is above bounded ye s^d Arthur Beal & Anna his wife do give & grant unto ye aboves^d Wm Pearce & to Mary his wife & their heirs & forever with all ye priviledges Advantages thereunto belonging or any wayes At any Time Redounding To have & To hold & Quietly & peaceably to possess Occupie & Enjoy & ye s^d Arthur & Anna do by these psents after ye date hereof release & Acquit their Claime unto ye aboves^d land & all its priviledges After ye Ensealing of this Instrum^t unto ye s^d Wm Pearce & Mary his wife & their heirs forever According to what right & Title they ye s^d Arthur & Anna have or Ever Shall Appear to have unto ye s^d land above Specified & bounded In Witness Hereof ye s^d Arthur Beal & Anna his wife have hereunto Set to their hands & Seals this Eighteenth day of Jan^ry in ye year of our Lord one Thousand Seven hundred & Eleven & in ye ninth year of ye Reign of our Soveraign Lady Anne Queen of Great Brittaine &c^t

Signed Sealed & Delivered
  In psence of us   Arthur   his AB mark   Beal (a Seal) (a Seal)
  Sam^ll Webber
  Sam^ll Donnell Junr
  Abra^m Preble Junr
  April ye 16th 1711

Arthur Beal above named psonally Appeared & Acknowledged ye above written deed of Gift to be his Act & deed Before me   Abra^x Preble Justice peace

Recorded According to ye Original July ye 6th 1715./

          p Jos Hamond Reg^r

Book VIII, Fol. 104.

[104] To All People to whom this present deed of Sale Shall Come Greeting./ Know yee that wee Daniel Mackintire & Micum Mackintire of york in ye County of york within his Maj^{tys} Province of ye Massachusets bay in New England Yeoman for & in Consideration of ye Sum of Twelve pounds Curra^t money of ye s^d Province to us in hand before ye Ensealing & Delivery hereof well & Truely paid by John Newmarch of Kittery in ye afores^d County & Province Clerk ye receipt thereof & of Every part & parcell thereof do Exonerate Acquit & fully discharge ye s^d John Newmarch his heirs Execut^{rs} and Adm^{rs} forever by these presents have given granted bargained Sold Aliened Enfeoffed Conveyed & Confirmed & by these presents do freely fully & absolutely give grant bargaine Sell Aliene Enfeoffe Convey & Confirm unto him ye s^d John Newmarch his heirs Execut^{rs} Adm^{rs} & Assignes forever Two third parts of a Certaine Tract of land Scittuate lying & being in ye Township of york afores^d on ye Southwest Side of ye Southwest branch of york river ye whole Tract Containing by Estimation Thirty Acres & is that Tract of land which was granted to our honoured father dec^d by ye Town of york on ye 18th of march 1671 & was Measured out to him by ye Selectmen of s^d york on ye 15th of Novemb^r 1679. As p ye Records of s^d York may Appear & is butted and bounded As followeth that is to Say by a great hemlock Tree by a Little Cove of Marsh that is between John Mackintires and John Cards Marsh & from that hemlock Tree Along by his Marsh Southwest Seventy Six rods to Kittery bounds & Sixty four rods by Kittery bounds upon a Southeast line a little Southerly unto a Maple Tree & from thence Northeast Seventy & Six rods unto a little pine Tree Markt & from thence Sixty four rods upon a northwest line a little Northerly unto ye hemlock Tree first Mentioned Together with all woods underwoods water Courses rivulets Appurtenances & priviledges unto ye Two thirds parts of ye s^d Tract of land belonging or in any wise Appurtaining: To have & To hold ye s^d granted & bargained premises with all ye Appurtenances priviledges & Comodityes to ye Same belonging or in Any wise Appurtaining to him ye s^d John Newmarch his heirs Ex^{rs} Adm^{rs} or assignes forever to his & their only proper use benefit & behoofe forever./ And wee ye s^d Daniel Mackintire and Micum Mackintire for our Selves our heirs Execut^{rs} & Adm^{rs} do Joyntly & Severally Covenant promiss & grant to & wth ye s^d John Newmarch his heirs Execut^{rs} Adm^{rs} & Assignes that before ye Ensealing & Delivery hereof wee are ye True Sole

Book VIII, Fol. 104.

and Lawfull owners of ye above bargained premises & are Lawfully Siezed & possessed of ye Same in our own propper right as a good Perfect & Absolute Estate of Inheritance in fee Simple & have in our Selves good right full power & Lawfull Authority to grant bargaine Sell Convey & Confirm s^d bargained pmises in maner as aboves^d & that ye s^d John Newmarch his heirs Execut^{rs} Adm^{rs} & Assignes Shall & may from time to Time & At all times for Ever hereafter by force & Vertue of these presence Lawfully peaceably & Quietly have hold Occupie possess & Enjoy ye s^d demised & bargained pmises with ye Appurtenances free & Clear & freely & Clearly Acquitted Exonerated & Discharged of from all & all maner of former or other gifts grants bargains Sales leases Mortgages Wills Entailes Joyntures dowries Judgm^{ts} Executions & Incumbrances whatsoever./ Furthermore Wee ye s^d Daniel & Micum Mackintire Joyntly & Severally for our Selves our heirs Execut^{rs} & Adm^{rs} do Covenant & Engage ye above demised & Sold premises to him ye s^d John Newmarch his heirs Execut^{rs} Adm^{rs} and Assignes against ye Lawfull claims & Demands of any pson or psons whatsoever forever hereafter to Warrant Secure and Defend./ In Witness whereof wee have hereunto Set our hands & Seals this Twenty Seventh day of June in ye year of our Lord one Thousand Seven hundred & fifteen & in ye first year of ye Reign of our Soveraign Lord George of Great Brittaine &c^t King./ The words/ in Curra^t money of this province between ye Third & fourth lines./ & ye words. on ye Southwest Side of ye Southwest branch of York river between ye Eleventh & Twelfth lines were Interlined before Signing & Sealing hereof

Signed Sealed & Delivered   Daniel Mackintire (Seal)
   In ye psence of   Micum Mackintire (Seal)
   John Mackintire
   Jonathan Mendum
           his
   Joseph C Crocket jun^r
       mark

York sc July 6: 1715./

The above named Daniel Mackintire & Micum Mackintire Acknowledged ye above written Instrum^t to be their free Act & Deed   Before me Charles ffrost J. Peace

Recorded According to ye Original July 6th 1715.
                 p Jos Hamond Reg^r

BOOK VIII, FOL. 105.

To All People to whom these presents Shall Come Greeting &c[t] Know Yee that I Timothy Waymouth of Kittery in y[e] County of york within his Maj[tys] Province of y[e] Massachusets Bay in New England Yeoman for & in Consideration of y[e] Sum of Ten pounds Currant money of new England Afores[d] to me in hand before y[e] Ensealing hereof well & Truely [105] paid by John Frost of New Castle within his Maj[tys] Province of New Hampshire in New England afores[d] Marrin[r] y[e] receipt whereof I do hereby acknowledge and my Selfe therewith fully Satisfied Contented & paid & thereof and of Every part and parcell thereof do Exonerate acquit and discharge y[e] s[d] John ffrost his heirs Ex[rs] & Adm[rs] forever by these presents Have given granted bargained Sold Aliened Conveyed & Confirmed & by these presents do freely fully & Absolutely give grant bargaine Sell Aliene Convey & Confirm unto him y[e] s[d] John ffrost his heirs & Assignes forever one Certaine Tract of land Scittuate Lying & being in Kittery or Berwick in y[e] County afores[d] Containing fifty four acres of land butted and bounded as followeth Viz[t]/ Adjoyning on Neguttaquid river & on y[e] South Side of it begining at s[d] river by y[e] Mast way then Ninety Two poles Southwest Then Seventy poles South Then one hundred and Eight poles East Northeast Then Sixty poles Northwest Then Thirty two poles Northeast then Thirty poles North Northwest to y[e] first Station & is bounded Northwest by a mast way which is between Jonathan Nasons land & s[d] Waymouths land, on y[e] west by W[m] Lord and on y[e] Southeast by M[r] Charles ffrosts land & on y[e] Eastern Two Sides by James Grant & north by s[d] river & is a grant granted to Edw[d] Waymouth by y[e] Parrish of unity in Kittery afores[d] y[e] thirteenth day of April Sixteen hundred Seventy one of ffifty Acres y[e] other four Acres is part of a grant of Ten acres granted to s[d] Edward Waymouth by y[e] Town of Kittery y[e] Sixteenth day of May Sixteen hundred Ninety Nine both which were given me by my father Edw[d] Waymouth afores[d] which s[d] Tract of land was laid out & bounded by Daniel Emery Survey[r] for s[d] Town of Kittery on y[e] fourth day of february Seventeen hundred & Nine Ten & Stands Recorded in y[e] Second book of records for s[d] Town of Kittery folio y[e] Ninth as p y[e] records Appears referrence being thereunto had./ To have & To hold y[e] s[d] granted & bargained premises with all y[e] Appurtenances priviledges & Comodityes to y[e] Same belonging or in Any wise Appurtaining to him y[e] s[d] John ffrost his heirs & Assignes forever to his & their only proper use benefit & behoofe forever & I y[e] s[d] Timothy Waymouth for me my heirs Ex[rs] and Adm[rs] do

BOOK VIII, FOL. 105.

Covenant promiss & grant to & with ye s^d John ffrost his heirs & Assignes that before ye Ensealing hereof I am ye True Sole & Lawfull owner of ye above bargained premises & am Lawfully Seized & possessed of ye Same in mine own propper right as a good perfect & absolute Estate of Inheritance in fee Simple & have in my Selfe good right full power & Lawfull Authority to grant bargaine Sell Convey & Confirm s^d bargained premises in manner as above s^d and that ye s^d John ffrost his heirs & Assignes Shall & may from Time To Time & at all Times forever hereafter by force and Vertue of these psents Lawfully peaceably & Quietly have hold use Occupie possess & Enjoy ye s^d demised & bargained pmises with ye Appurtenances free & Clear & freely & Clearly Acquitted Exonerated And discharged of & from all & all maner of former & other gifts grants bargains Sales Leases Mortgages Wills Entails Joyntures dowrys Judgm^{ts} Executions Incumbrances & Extents Furthermore I ye s^d Timothy Waymouth for my Selfe my heirs Execut^{rs} & Adm^{rs} do Covena^t and Engage ye above demised premises to him ye s^d John ffrost his heirs and Assignes against ye Lawfull Claims & demands of any pson or psons whatsoever forever hereafter to Warra^t Secure & defend In Witness whereof I ye s^d Timothy Waymouth have hereunto Set my hand and Seal ye Third day of June Annoq, Domini Seventeen hundred & fifteen Annoq, Regni Regis Georgii Magna Brittania &c^t Primo./   Tim^o Waymouth (Seal)

Signed Sealed & Delivered   her
  In ye psence of us   Patience X Waymouth (Seal)
  Charles ffrost   mark
  John Belcher
  Ebenezer Emons
  York sc June 3^d 1715./

The above named Timothy Waymouth & Patience Waymouth Acknowledged ye above written Instrum^t to be their free Act & deed   Before Charles ffrost. J. peace

Recorded According to ye Original August ye 8th 1715.

        p Jos. Hamond Reg^r

This Indenture made this 29th of June Annoq, Domini 1715. &/ in ye first year of ye Reign of George King of Great Brittaine &c^t between Wm Pearse Weaver of ye one party & Joseph Harris Joyner of ye other party both of york in ye County of york in ye Province of Maine in N : E Witnesseth that ye s^d Wm Pearse for & in Consideration of y^e

BOOK VIII, FOL. 106.

Sum of Eight pounds money Curra^t in N : E to him in hand paid before ye Ensealing of these psents by Joseph Harris aboves^d & for divers other good Causes & Considerations him hereunto moveing he ye s^d Wm Pearse hath given granted bargained Sold Aliened Enfeoffed & Confirmed & by these presents doth fully freely clearly & Absolutely give grant bargaine Sell aliene Enfeoffe Convey & Confirm unto ye s^d Joseph Harris his heirs & Assigns forever a Certaine piece or parcell of land by Estimation Ten Acres be it more or Less as it Expressed in a deed of Gift from Arthur Beal of york Afores^d to Wm Pearse aboves^d Scittuate within this Town of york upon the Neck of land formerly Arthur Beals aboves^d on ye Southwest Side of York river & upon ye Northwest or west Side of a lot of land given by Arthur Beal aboves^d to his Son in Law Joshua Knap further bounded as is Expressed in ye deed aboves^d from Arthur Beal aboves^d to his Son in Law Wm Pearse aboves^d & his daughter Mary Pearse wife of s^d Wm Pearse as may Appear referrence [106] being herein had to s^d deed of Gift which Ten Acres of land s^d Joseph Harris Shall have & hold to himselfe his heirs & Assignes forever for him and them to use Occupie & Enjoy without any Mollestation from hence forth & forever & s^d Pearse doth further bind himselfe Execut^{rs} Adm^{rs} heirs &c^t to Defend s^d Harris in ye peaceable possession of s^d land from all persons whatsoever laying any Lawfull Claime thereunto & Mary ye wife of s^d Pearse doth fully & freely give & Yield up unto ye s^d Joseph Harris his heirs & Assigns all ye right & Title of Dower or Interest of in or to the ye premises respectively forever by these presents & at any time on demand they ye s^d W^m & Mary Pearse Shall give & pass Such further and more Ample Confirmation of ye premises to s^d Joseph Harris his heirs or Assignes forever as in Law ,or Equity Can be reasonably devised Ad-,vised or required./ Provided Alwayes & these p^{r}sents are upon Condition Nevertheless that if ye above named Wm Pearse his heirs &c^t do well & Truely pay or Cause to be paid unto ye above named Joseph Harris or his Certaine Attorney heirs Ex^{rs} Adm^{rs} or Assigns at york afores^d within three months from ye Date of these presents Nine pounds in ye present Currant money of ye afores^d Province without fraud Coven or further delay that then this present deed of Bargaine and Sale Shall Cease determine be null voyd & of non Effect but if defauld hapen to be made in ye afores^d paym^t Contrary to ye True Intent hereof Then to Abide & remaine in full force & Vertue to all Intents & purposes in ye Law whatsoever

BOOK VIII, FOL. 106.

Furthermore inasmuch as Joseph Harris above[d] doth Scruple W[m] Pearses Title to y[e] land above[d] Said W[m] Pearse with y[e] full Consent of Mary his wife doth hereby fully freely & Absolutely make over Sell & Convey unto y[e] s[d] Joseph Harris y[e] Two Milch Cows which they s[d] W[m] & Mary Pearse have now in possession to be delivered to s[d] Harris his heirs or Execut[rs] or administrat[rs] or assigns at y[e] End of three months after y[e] Date of these p[r]sents in Case s[d] W[m] Pearse doth fayle of paying s[d] Nine pounds within three months as above[d] In Witness whereof y[e] s[d] W[m] Pearse & Mary his wife have hereunto Set their hands & Seals y[e] year month & day first above written   William Pearse (a Seal)
Signed Seal[d] & Delivered   her
    In psence of these Witnesses   Mary ⟨ Pearse (a Seal)
    Lewis Bane
    Henry Gibbs   mark
    Samuel Moodey
York sc/
York June 30. 1715 W[m] Pearse & Mary his wife psonally Appeared before me y[e] Subscrib[r] one of his Maj[tys] Justices for y[e] County of York & Acknowledged y[e] within written Instrum[t] to be their Act & Deed   Lewis Bane
    Recorded According to y[e] Original Aug[st] 8th 1715./
                                p Jos. Hamond Reg[r]

To All People to whom these presents shall Come Greeting &c[t] Know Yee that I Job Otis of Scittuate in y[e] County of Plymouth in New England Shopkeeper for & in Consideration of y[e] full & Just Sum of one hundred & Thirty pounds in Curra[t] money of New England to mee in hand paid by William Thomas of Boston in y[e] County of Suffolk in New England Merch[t] y[e] Receipt whereof I do hereby acknowledge & my Selfe therewith to be fully Satisfied Contented & paid & thereof & of every part thereof do Acquitt and discharge him y[e] s[d] William Thomas his heirs Execut[rs] Adm[rs] & Assigns & Every of them forever by these presents have given granted bargained Sold Aliened Enfeoffed & Confirmed & by these presents do fully freely & Absolutely give grant bargaine Sell Aliene Enfeoffe & Confirm unto him y[e] s[d] W[m] Thomas his heirs & Assigns forever all those my Certaine Tracts or parcells of uplands & Meadows Scittuate Lying & being at Casco Bay in y[e] Province of Maine in the Province of y[e] Massachusets Bay in New England which s[d] Tracts & parcells of upland & Meadow I y[e] s[d] Job Otis bought and purchased of Nathaniel &

Gilbert Winslow which s^d Nathaniel & Gilbert Winslow bought & purchased of Enoch Wiswall who purchased ye Same of Joseph Nash & were formerly ye lands of John Mosure which s^d upland Contains Three hundred Acres bounded & runing by ye Side of Aresiket river runing from ye Second Gutt Northwesterly untill ye full Contents & Measure of Three hundred Acres be Meeted out with all ye Meadow thereto belonging ye first parcell of Meadow haveing a pond in ye Middle of it & three parcells more by ye Side of ye uper part of ye river Containing in all about Twenty or thirty Acres be ye Same more or Less./ To have & To hold all ye above granted and bargained premises Together with all ye rights Priviledges & Appurtenances thereunto belonging unto him ye s^d Wm Thomas his heirs Execut^{rs} Adm^{rs} & Assignes to his & their own proper use benefit & behoofe forever./ And ye s^d Job Otis for himSelfe his heirs Ex^{rs} & Adm^{rs} doth Covena^t with him ye s^d William Thomas his heirs & Assignes that at & untill ye Ensealing & Delivery of these presents he ye s^d Job Otis hath in himselfe good right full power & Lawfull Authority to give grant bargaine. Sell Convey & Confirm all ye above granted and bargained premises in maner & form as is above Expressed free & clear freely & Clearly Acquitted & discharged of & from all other Titles Troubles charges & Incumbrances whatso Ever And ye s^d Job Otis doth by these presents further Covena^t [107] Promiss & bind himSelfe his heirs Ex^{rs} Adm^{rs} & Assignes from henceforth & at all Times hereafter to Warrant & Defend all & Singular ye above granted & bargained premises with ye Appurtenances thereof unto him ye s^d Wm Thomas his heirs & Assignes for ever against ye Lawfull Claims & Demands of All & Every pson or psons whatsoever./ In Witness whereof y^e s^d Job Otis hath hereunto Set his hand & Seal this Ninth day of Novemb^r in y^e year of our Lord One Thousand Seven hundred & fourteen./ In y^e first year of y^e Reign of our Soveraign Lord George by y^e Grace of God of Great Brittaine ffrance & Ireland King Defend^r of y^e faith &c^t Job Otis ($_{Seal}^a$)
Signed Sealed & Delivered
  In psence of
  John Cushing jun^r
  Nathaniel Pitcher
  Plym^o sc/ Novr y^e 11th 1714 : Job Otis above named Appeared & Acknowledged y^e above written Instrum^t to be his Act and Deed & At y^e Same time Mercy y^e wife of s^d Otis

Book VIII, Fol. 107.

did freely give up all right & Interest in ye above Granted premises   Before mee   Joseph Otis Justice of peace
Recorded Accorded to ye Original July ye 2^d 1715.

p Jos: Hammond Reg^r

To All People to whom this present deed of Sale Shall Come John Morrell jun^r of Kittery in ye County of york & within her maj^tys Province of ye Massachusets Bay in New England Mason Sendeth Greeting Know yee that ye s^d John Morrell for & in Consideration of ye Sum of Thirty pounds Curra^t money of New England to him in hand well & truely paid at ye Ensealing & Delivery of these presents by John Tidy of ye same Town County & Province afores^d ye receipt whereof ye s^d Morrell doth hereby Acknowledge to his full Content & Satisfaction and doth Acquit and discharge ye s^d John Tidy his heirs & Assigns of ye same forever by these presents hath given granted bargained & Absolutely Sold Enfeoffed & Confirmed unto him ye s^d John Tidy & to his heirs & Assigns forever Thirty acres of land be ye Same more or Less it being a Town grant of land & Laid out to s^d John Morrell March ye fifth Sixteen hundred ninty nine. 10 As Appears by ye Surveyers return on record in Kittery Town book & s^d land lyes on ye North Side of Sturgeon Creek at ye North East End of Christopher Banfields land & fronts Dover river & bounds by a white oak Tree mark^t runing by ye river Side from ye head of Banfields Seventeen pole or there abouts & from that on an East line Northerly Eighty five pole into ye woods & Next Christopher Banfields Eighty poles Southeast & from that Extent by John Hoitt Northeast Seventy Two pole & from that Extent ye s^d Tract goes over ye head of s^d Hoitts Twenty Two poles South East & then Norteast Forty pole then northwest Twenty two pole & from thence to ye above mentioned East line as Appears by Markt Trees To have & To hold ye s^d land & all ye rights propertys & priviledges & Appurtenances unto him ye s^d John Tidy his heirs Ex^rs Adm^rs & Assignes to his & their own only proper use benefit & behoofe forever And ye s^d John Tidy & his heirs & Assignes Shall & may from hence forth and forever hereafter Lawfully peaceably & Quietly have hold use Occupie possess & Enjoy all ye Above granted pmises without let hinderence denial or Mollestation from s^d Morrell or his heirs Ex^rs or Adm^rs ye premises being free & clearly Acquitted Exonerated & discharged of & from all former & other gifts grants bargaines Sales Leases Mort-

gages Titles Troubles Charges Claims & demands whatsoever./ And further ye s^d John Morrell his heirs Ex^{rs} & Adm^{rs} Shall & will from henceforth & forever hereafter Warrant and defend all ye Above granted & bargained premisses with their Appurtenances unto him ye s^d John Tidy & to his heirs and Assignes forever against ye Lawfull claims of all & Every pson whatsoever from by or und^r him ye s^d John Morrell his heirs Execut^{rs} or Adm^{rs} or by their procurem^t/ In Witness whereof the above named John Morrell hath hereunto Set his hand and Seal ye Nineteenth day of June Annoq, Domini Seventeen hundred & Ten in ye Ninth year of ye Reign of our Soveraign Lady Anne Queen of Great Brittaine &c^t John Morrell jun^r (a Seal)
Signed Sealed & Delivered
  In ye p^{r}sence of us
  Katherine Neal
  Joseph Gould
  John Bradstreet
York sc July ye 7th 1710 John Morrell personally Appeared before me ye Subscrib^r one of her Maj^{tys} Justices of ye peace for s^d County & Acknowledged ye above written Instrum^t to be his Volluntary Act & Deed./
                                          Ichabod Plaisted
Recorded According to ye Original Septr 23^d : 1715.
                                        p Jos : Hamond Reg^r

  Know All People to whom these p^{r}sents shall Come Greeting Know yee that I John Linscot in york in ye County of york & in ye Province of ye Massachusets Bay in New England yeoman for & in Consideration of a parcell of land at Birch hill as Appears by a deed of Sale the receipt whereof I do hereby Acknowledge my Selfe therewth fully Satisfied & Contented & thereof & of Every part & parcell thereof do Exonerate Acquit & discharge ye s^d Peter Nowell his heirs Execut^{rs} Administrat^{rs} forever by these presents have given granted bargained & by these presents do fully & Absolutely give grant [108] Bargaine Sell Aliene Convey & Confirm unto him ye s^d Peter Nowell his heirs & Assigns forever one Messuage or Tract of Land Scittuate Lying and being in york and Containing Thirty one Acres & one halfe Lying on ye Northwest Side of ye brook that runeth down to york bridge on ye N^o East Side of Mr Sam^{ll} Donnells land Toward ye bell marsh begining at a Small pitch pine Tree Mark^t on four Sides and runeth back Northwest from

BOOK VIII, FOL. 108.

ye Square of it one hundred & Sixty poles to a Small tree marked on four Sides & then South South East to three Small birch Trees marked on Two Sides apiece bounded by ye brook that runeth out of ye bell marsh and is by s^d brook down to ye pine where wee began To have & To hold ye s^d Granted and bargained premisses with all ye Appurtenances priviledges and Comodityes to ye Same belonging or in Any wise Appurtaining to him ye s^d Peter Nowell his heirs & Assigns forever to his and their only propper use benefit and behoofe forever and I ye s^d John Linscot for me my heirs Ex^{rs} Adm^{rs} do Covenant promiss and grant to & with ye s^d Peter Nowell his heirs & Assignes that before ye Ensealing hereof I am ye True Sole & Lawfull owner of ye above bargained premises & am Lawfully Seized & possessed of ye Same in my own proper right as a good perfect & Absolute Estate of Inheritance in Fee Simple & have in my Selfe good right full power & Lawfull Authority to grant Bargaine Sell Convey and Confirm s^d bargained premisses in Maner as afores^d & that ye s^d Peter Nowell his heirs & Assignes Shall & may from time to Time & at all Times forever hereafter by force & Vertue of these p^{r}sents Lawfully peaceably & Quietly have hold use Occupie possess & Enjoy ye s^d Demised & bargained pmises with the Appurtenances free & clear & clearly Acquitted Exonerated and Discharged of from all & all maner of former & other Gifts grants bargains Sales Leases Mortgages Wills Entails Joyntures Dowries Judgm^{ts} Executions Incumbrances & Extents./ Furthermore I ye s^d John Linscot for my Selfe my heirs Execut^{rs} Adm^{rs} do Covena^t and Engage ye Above demised pmisses to him ye s^d Peter Nowell his heirs & Assignes Against y^e Lawfull Claims or demands of Any pson or psons whatsoever forever hereafter to Warrant Secure & Defend./ In Witness whereof I have hereunto Set my hand & Seal y^e Eighteenth day of Septr in y^e year of our Lord god Seventeen hundred fourteen./

Signed Sealed & Delivered   John $\cancel{P}$ Linscot (Seale)
   In presence   mark
   James Smith
   Joseph Smith

John Linscot psonally Appeared before me one of his Maj^{tys} Justices of y^e peace for y^e County of york & Acknowledged this Instrum^t to be his Act & Deed./ York July 3 : 1715
                                              Lewis Bane

Recorded According to ye Original Augst 24th 1715/
                         p Jos. Hamond Reg^r

BOOK VIII, FOL. 108.

To All People to whom these Presents shall Come Greeting Know Yee that I James Smith of york in ye County of york within his Maj^{tys} Province of ye Massachusets Bay in New England Smith for and in Consideration of ye Sum of One hundred pounds to me in hand before ye Ensealing hereof well & Truely paid by Peter Nowell of ye aboves^d place County & Province Yeoman the rec^t whereof I do hereby Acknowledge & my Selfe therewth fully Satisfied and Contented & thereof & of Every part & parcell thereof do Exonerate Acquit & discharge ye s^d Peter Nowel his heirs Execut^{rs} Adm^{rs} forever by these psents Have given granted bargained Sold Aliened Conveyed & Confirmed by these psents do freely fully & Absolutely Give Grant Bargaine Sell Aliene Convey & Confirm unto him ye s^d Peter Nowell his heirs & Assignes forever one Messuage or Tract of land Scittuate Lying & being in York in ye s^d County of York Containing by Estimation forty Six Acres bounded Southwesterly by ye way Leading from York to Berwick Northwesterly by land formerly Cap^{tn} Job Alcocks Southeasterly by land formerly Robert Junkins & Northeasterly by York Town Comons To have & To hold ye s^d granted & bargained premises with all ye Appurten^{ces} priviledges & Comodityes to ye Same belonging or in any wise Appurtaining to him ye s^d Peter Nowell his heirs & Assigns forever to his & their only proper use benefit & behoofe forever & I ye s^d James Smith for me my heirs Execut^{rs} Adm^{rs} do Covena^t promiss & grant to & with ye s^d Peter Nowell his heirs & Assignes that before ye Ensealing hereof I am ye True Sole & Lawfull owner of ye above bargained premises & Am Lawfully Seized & possessed of ye Same in mine own proper right As a good perfect and Absolute Estate of Inheritance in Fee Simple & have in my Selfe good right full power & Lawfull Authority to grant bargain Sell Convey & Confirm s^d bargained premisses in maner as aboves^d And that ye s^d Peter Nowell his heirs & Assignes Shall & may from time to time & at all times forever hereafter by force & vertue of these p^{r}sents Lawfully peaceably & Quietly have hold use Occupy possess & Enjoy ye s^d Demises & bargained pmises with ye Appur^{ces} free & Clear & freely & Clearly Acquited Exonerated & discharged of from all & all maner of former & other Gifts grants bargains Sales Leases Mortgages wills Entails Joyntures Dowries Judgm^{ts} Executions Incumbrances & Extents./ furthermore I ye s^d James Smith for my Selfe my heirs Execut^{rs} Adm^{rs} do Covenant and Ingage ye above demised premisses to him ye s^d Peter Nowell his heirs & Assigns against ye Lawfull Claims or demands of any person or persons whatsoever forever hereafter to [109] Warrant Secure & Defend In Witness whereof I have hereunto Set my hand & Seal this Twenty third day of may in y[e] year of our Lord God One Thousand Seven hundred & fffifteen./ And in y[e] first year of y[e] Reign of our Soveraign Lord George by y[e] Grace of God King of Great Brittaine &c[t]/

Signed Sealed & Delivered   James Smith (seal)
  In y[e] Presence
  W[m] Shaw   Martha Smith (seal)
        mark
  Annis ⟨C⟩ Shaw
  Nath[ll] Freeman

   York sc. York in y[e] County of york July : 3 : 1715
   James Smith & Martha his wife psonally Appeared before me one of his Ma[tys] Justices of y[e] peace for y[e] County of York & Acknowledged this within written Instrum[t] to be their Act & Deed   Lewis Bane
   Recorded According to y[e] Original Aug[st] 24th 1715./

                            p Jos. Hamond Reg[r]

     To All Christian People to whom these presents Shall Come Greeting Whereas Nathaniel Masters of Manchester in y[e] County of Essex in New England housecarpenter Addministrat[rs] of y[e] Estate of Nath[ll] Masters his Grandfather Late of Wells in y[e] County of york in New England deceased hath had power & Authority granted him from y[e] Superio[r] Court of Judicature held at Kittery for y[e] s[d] County of York by Adjournm[t] y[e] 24th of Aug[st] 1715 to make Sale of y[e] real Estate of y[e] s[d] deceased As by y[e] Order of y[e] s[d] Court & y[e] Inventory of y[e] s[d] Real Estate of y[e] s[d] dec[d] may Appear Now Know Yee that y[e] s[d] Nathaniel Masters Adm[rs] as afores[d] for & in Consideration of y[e] Sum of Eighty pounds in Currant money to him in hand paid At y[e] Ensealing & Delivery of these presents by Samuel Brown of Salem in y[e] County of Essex in New England Afores[d] Esq[r] y[e] rec[t] whereof y[e] s[d] Nath[ll] Masters y[e] Grandson doth Acknowledge & thereof Doth Acquit & discharge y[e] s[d] Samuel Brown his heirs Execut[rs] & Adm[rs] by these presents Hath given granted bargained & Sold Enfeoffed Conveyed & Confirmed & by these psents doth give grant bargaine Sell Enfeoffe Convey & Confirm unto y[e] s[d] Samuel Brown his heirs & Assignes forever a Certaine farm with a dwelling house & Orchard lying & being in y[e] Township of Wells afores[d] on Ogunquit Side Containing one hundred Acres as Appears by Wells Town

Book VIII, Fol. 109.

Records granted to ye s^d Nathaniel Masters ye Grandfather Anno: 1666 & also ffifty Acres more granted him by ye s^d Town Anno: 1669 to Contain Thirty poles in Breadth & to run up into ye Country as other Lots do also a Certaine parcell of Salt Marsh Creek & Thatch banckes lying & being near ye harbours Mouth in ye Town of Wells afores^d bounded As followeth Viz^t the uper End of s^d Marsh by a parcell of Marsh belonging to Joseph Littlefield & So to run down to s^d harbours Mouth & lying between two parcells of Marsh Lately belonging to Mr Thomas Wells the s^d Marsh in ye Middle being Eighteen poles or thereabouts in breadth ye whole parcell of Marsh Creeks & Thatch banks Containing Eight Acres or more bounded by ye s^d Joseph Littlefield at one End & So between ye s^d Mr Wells Marsh down to ye river Called Webhaunt river Also an Island of Thatch being in ye s^d Town of Wells butting on ye river & bounded on ye Northeast Side and Southwest Side by Marsh formerly Ezekiel Knights And Also Ten Acres of fresh meadow in ye s^d Township of Wells Comonly Called by ye name of Masters Meadow Granted to ye s^d Nath^{ll} Masters ye Grandfather by ye s^d Town of wells ye whole of which s^d farm with ye Dwelling house & Orchard & all & Singular ye Aboves^d parcells of land Marsh Creek Thatch banks Island of Thatch & fresh Meadow belonged unto & was ye Estate of s^d Nath^{ll} Masters ye Grandfather in fee as by ye Several grants from ye Town of wells afores^d & good purchases from other persons to him may more fully Appear The whole of which s^d farm with all & Singular ye premises & their & Every of their Appurtenances ye s^d Nathaniel Masters ye Adm^r as afores^d to his s^d Grandfather & by Vertue of his power & Authority as above Expressed hath hereby bargained & Sold unto ye s^d Samuel Brown his heirs & Assigns forever To have & To hold ye s^d farm and premisses with all & Singular & Every part & parcell thereof Together with all & Every their Severall rights Comons priviledges & Appurtenances whatsoever to all or any of them belonging or Appurtaining to ye s^d Samuel Brown his heirs & Assignes to his & their only proper use & behoofe forever And ye s^d Nath^{ll} Masters ye Grandson for himSelfe his heirs Execut^{rs} & Adm^{rs} doth hereby Covenant Promiss grant & Agree to & with ye s^d Sam^{ll} Brown his heirs & Assignes that he hath Just & Lawfull right Power & Authority to Sell & Convey All & Every ye s^d bargained premisses & Appurtenances unto ye s^d Sam^{ll} Brown as Afores^d & that ye premisses & Every part & parcell thereof are free & Clear of & from All & all maner of former Gifts Grants bargains Sales Executions Joyntures Dowers & Incumbrances whatsoever & that he & his heirs Shall & will at all times forever hereafter make do & Execute All & any Act writing or thing in ye Law whatsoever for ye further & more Sure makeing & Confirming ye s^d bargained premisses & Every part & parcell thereof unto ye s^d Sam^{ll} Brown his heirs & Assigns forever As by him or them Shall be Legally Advised & required And farther that he ye s^d Nath^{ll} Masters ye Grandson his heirs Execut^{rs} & Adm^{rs} Shall & will at all Times forever hereafter Warrant & Defend ye s^d Samuel Brown his heirs & Assigns forever in ye Quiet & peaceable Seizen [110] possession & Enjoym^t of all & Singular ye s^d bargained premisses & Appurten^{ces} from & Against all & any pson or psons Lawfully Claiming ye Same or any part or parcell thereof whatsoever./ In Witness whereof y^e s^d Nathaniel Masters y^e Grand Son hath hereunto Set his hand & Seal y^e Seventh day of Sep^{tr} in y^e Second year of his Majesty King George of Great Brittaine &c^t Annoq Domini 1715./

Signed Sealed & Delivered   Nathaniel Marsters ($_{Seal}^a$)
In p^{r}sence of us
Richard Bethel
Daniel Sherman

    Essex ss/ Salem y^e 9th of Septemb^r 1715.— Nathaniel Masters y^e feoffer aboves^d psonally Appearing before me y^e Subscrib^r one of his Maj^{ths} Justices of y^e peace & Council Acknowledged The above Instrum^t in writing to be his free Act & Deed   Benj^a Lynde
Recorded According to ye Original Sep^t 30 1715./

           p Jos Hamond Reg^r/

    To All Christian People to whom these p^{r}sents shall Come Greeting Know Yee that I Nathaniel Ramsdell of York in ye Province of ye Massachusets Bay in New England for & in Consideration of ye Sum of four pounds Curra^t money of ye Province afores^d in hand paid before ye Ensealing hereof well & Truely paid by Peter Nowell of ye Town & Province afores^d there with I do hereby Acknowledge my Selfe therewith fully Satisfied and Contented & thereof do Acquit & discharge ye s^d Peter Nowell his heirs Execut^{rs} & Adm^{rs} forever by these presents have given granted bargained Sold Aliened Conveyed & Confirmed unto him ye s^d Peter Nowell his heirs and Assignes forever One Quarter part of my halfe of that Marsh or fresh Meadow which I ye s^d Ramsdell bought of Arthur Bragdon Senr ye whole being by Estimation Eight Acres be it more or less ye s^d Nowell Shall have

Book VIII, Fol. 110.

one whole quarter part of s^d Meadow both for Quantity & Quallity The meadow lyes near Agamenticus hills & was formerly granted to Thomas Bragdon & Arthur Bragdon ye s^d Nowell is To have & To hold ye s^d quarter part of s^d Ramsdells right of ye above mentioned Meadow with all ye Appurtenances & priviledges to ye Same belonging or in Any wayes Appurtaining to him ye s^d Nowell his heirs & Assigns forever to his & their only proper use benefit & behoofe forever And I ye s^d Nathaniel Ramsdell for my heirs Ex^{rs} Adm^{rs} & Assignes do Covenant promiss & grant to & with ye s^d Peter Nowell his heirs Ex^{rs} Adm^{rs} & Assignes that before the Ensealing hereof I am ye True Sole & Lawfull owner of ye above granted pmises & am lawfully Seized & possesst of ye Same as my own proper right as a good perfect & Absolute Estate in Fee Simple and have in my Selfe good right full power & Authority to grant & Confirm s^d Premisses in mañer as aboves^d And ye s^d Nowell his Heirs & Assignes Shall & may from time to time & at all times forever hereafter by force & Vertue of these p^{r}sents Lawfully Peaceably have hold use possess & Enjoy s^d bargained premisses with ye Appurtenances free & Clear & freely & Clearly Acquitted & discharged of from all maner former grants gifts bargains Sales & Incumbrances whatsoever Furthermore I ye s^d Ramsdell for my Selfe my heirs Ex^{rs} Adm^{rs} do Covenant & Engage ye above premises to him ye s^d Peter Nowell his heirs & Assigns against ye Claims or demands of Any pson or psons whatsoever forever hereafter to Warrant & Defend forever In Witness whereof I have hereunto Set my hand & Seal this Twelfth day of Jan^{ry} in y^e Twelfth year of our Soveraign Lady Anne by y^e grace of God Queen of Great Brittaine &c^t in y^e year of our lord God One Thousand Seven hundred & Thirteen fourteen
Signed Sealed & Delivered   Nathaniel Ramsdell ($_{Seal}^a$)
In y^e psence of

Allexander Junkins (mark)

Phillip Welch (mark)

Nath^{ll} ffreeman

York July 5th 1715./ Nath^{ll} Ramsdell Appeared before me y^e Subscriber one of his Ma^{tys} Justices of y^e peace & Acknowledged this within written Instrum^t to be his Act & Deed./   Lewis Bane

Recorded According to ye Original August 24th 1715./
      p Jos. Hamond Reg^r

Book VIII, Fol. 111.

To All People to whom these presents Shall Come Greeting Know yee that I Hannah Sayward of York in ye County of York & Province of the Massachusets Bay in New England for & in Consideration of ye Sum of Twenty pounds in good & Lawfull money of ye Province afores^d to me in hand before ye Ensealing hereof well & truely paid by my brother John Sayward of ye Same County & Province afores^d Yeoman ye rec^t whereof I do hereby Acknowledge & my Selfe therewith fully Satisfied & Contented & thereof & of Every part & parcell thereof do Exonerate Acquit & discharge ye s^d Jno Sayward his heirs Ex^{rs} Adm^{rs} forever by these presents have given granted bargained Sold Aliened Conveyed and Confirmed & by these presents do freely fully & Absolutely give grant Bargaine Sell Aliene Convey & Confirm unto him ye s^d John Sayward his heirs & Assignes forever All my right Title Claime or Interest to Any parts or parts of Any of ye Estate that was my father John Saywards To have and To hold ye s^d granted & bargained premises with all ye Appurtenances priviledges & Comoditÿes to ye Same belonging or in any wayes Appurtaining to him ye s^d John Sayward his heirs & Assigns forever to his & their only proper use benefit & behalfe forever & I ye s^d Hannah Sayward for me my heirs Execut^{rs} Adm^{rs} do Covenant promiss & grant to & with ye s^d John Sayward his heirs & Assigns that before ye Ensealing hereof I am ye True Sole & Lawfull owner of ye above bargained premisses & am [111] Lawfully Seiz^d & possess^d of ye Same in mine own proper right as a good perfect and Absolute Estate of Inheritance in fee Simple & have in my Selfe good right full power & Lawfull Authority to grant bargaine Sell Convey & Confirm s^d bargained premisses in maner as aboves^d & that ye s^d John Sayward his heirs & Assignes Shall & may from time to time & at all times forever hereafter by force & Vertue of these presents Lawfully peaceably & Quietly have hold use Occupie possess & Enjoy ye s^d Demised & bargained premisses with ye Appurtenances free & clear & freely & Clearly Acquitted Exonerated & discharged of from all & all maner of former & other gifts grants bargains Sales lenses Mortgages Wills Entails Joyntures Dowries Judgm^{ts} Executions Incumbrances & Extents./ In Witness whereof I have hereunto Set my hand & Seal this first day of may in ye year of our Lord God one Thousand Seven hundred & Twelve./

Signed Sealed & Delivered   Hannah Sayward (a Seal)
   In ye psence of us
   Abraham Batting
   Nath^{ll} ffreeman

Book VIII, Fol. 111.

May ye 8th day 1712 Hannah Sayward above named psonally Appeared & Acknowledged ye Above written deed of Sale to be her Voluntary Act & Deed./ Before me
Abra^x Preble Justice peace.
Recorded According to ye Original Septemb^r 29th 1715./
p Jos : Hamond Reg^r

To All Christian People to whom this present Shall Come that I John Pickerin Senr of portsm° in ye province of New Hampsh^r many good Causes and Considerations me hereto moveing but more in Special for ye Consideration of thirty pounds Currant money to me in hand paid by John Sayward of york in ye province of Maine ye rec^t thereof & Every part thereof I do hereby Acknowledge & my Selfe to be fully Satisfied Contented & paid and thereof & of Every part parcell & peny thereof do by these presents Acquit & discharge him ye s^d Sayward his heirs Ex^rs Adm^rs forever have bargained Sold Enfeoffed released delivered & Confirmed & by this present deed do freely firmly & Absolutely grant bargaine Sell Enfeoffed released delivered & Confirmed unto him ye s^d Sayward, To Say one Certaine parcell of Salt marsh lying & being in afores^d york on ye north Side of ye mill Creek begining At ye place where ye old mill Stood on ye East Side of York river that was built by one Elingham & Gale I Say all ye marsh on ye North Side of s^d Mill Creek from ye place where s^d Mill Stood up to ye head of s^d Mill Creek being about Two Acres more or Less To have & to hold all s^d Marsh from s^d Creek to ye upland up to ye head of s^d Mill pond with all ye profits priviledges & Advantages to ye Same belonging or in any wayes Appurtaining unto him ye s^d Sayward his heirs & Assignes forever without ye least trouble Interuption or Mollestation of me ye s^d Pickerin my heirs Ex^rs or Adm^rs or any other pson or psons whatsoever laying any Lawfull Claime to all or any part of s^d bargained & Sold Marsh from by or und^r me them or any of them forever but that it is & Shall be Lawfull for him ye s^d Sayward his heirs Ex^rs Adm^rs or Assignes ye s^d Marsh & Every part thereof to Enter into have hold Improve & Enjoy as a free & perfect Estate in fee Simple freed Saved & kept harmless of & from all & all maner of former & other bargains Sales Joyntures mortgages Judgmt^s Executions & all maner of Incumbrances of what nature & kind soever had made Suffered or done or to be had made Suffered or done by me ye s^d Pickerin my heirs Execut^rs Adm^rs &c^t forever

BOOK VIII, FOL. 112.

In Confirmation hereof I have hereunto Set my hand and Seal this 17th day of Octobr 1712./   John Pickerin (a Seal)
Signed Sealed & Delivered
In psence of
Samuel Came
Nathll ffreeman
Captn John Pickerin above named as by his hand & Seal psonally Appeared before my Selfe & Acknowledged the above Instrumt to be his free Act & Deed this 27th of Octobr 1714 & in ye first year of King George Over Great Brittain france & Ireland Defendr of ye faith
John Plaisted Justs peace
Recorded According to ye Original Sept 29th 1715./
p Jos : Hamond Regr

This Indenture made & Concluded between Elisha Kelly of ye Isle of Smuttinose in his Majtys Province of Maine fisherman & Susanah his wife on ye one part & John Ellis of Boston in ye County of Suffolk within his Majtys Province of Massachusets Bay in New England Mercht on ye other part Witnesseth that ye sd Elisha Kelley & Susannah his wife for & in ye Consideration of ye Sum of Three hundred pounds in Currat Lawfull money of new England in hand paid unto them ye sd Elisha Kelley & Susannah his wife ye rect whereof ye sd Elisha Kelley & Susannah his wife doth hereby Acknowledge & thereof & Every part thereof doth hereby Also Clearly Acquitt & discharge ye sd John Ellis his heirs Executrs &ct & for diverse other Caused & Considerations they ye sd Elisha Kelley & Susannah his wife thereunto moveing hath demised granted bargained & Sold & by these presents do demise grant bargaine & Sell unto ye sd John Ellis his heirs Executrs Admrs &c all that Land Dwelling houses buildings Edefices Trees & fences at a place Called Crooked lane in Kittery in ye Province of Maine aforesd which houses & lands are in ye present [112] possession of my Brother Charles Kelley To have & To hold ye sd land houses buildings & Every part & parcell thereof unto him ye sd John Ellis his Exrs Admrs &ct from ye day of ye Date hereof & forever & it is hereby agreed & Concluded by & between ye sd partyes to these presents & ye sd Elisha Kelley doth for himselfe & Susannah his wife their Executrs Admrs &c Covenant promiss & agree to & with ye sd John Ellis his heirs Exrs &ct that it Shall & may be lawfull for ye sd John Ellis his heirs Exrs Admrs and Assignes Quietly & peaceably to have hold Occupy possess & Enjoy all and Singular ye s^d Land houses buildings & Edefices whatsoever from Time to time & at all times hereafter without any Lawfull Let or hinderence of him ye s^d Elisha Kelley & Susannah his wife their and Either of their heirs Ex^{rs} Adm^{rs} or Assignes or of any other pson or psons whatsoever Lawfully claiming from by or under them or Either of them & Also freed from & discharged of & from all & All mañer of former Sales gifts grants & Judgm^{ts} Executions & all other Charges of Incumbrances whatsoever had made done or Suffered by them or Either of them./ Provided Alwayes & it is nevertheless Agreed & Concluded by & between ye s^d parties to these presents and it is ye True Meaning & intent thereof that if ye s^d Elisha Kelley his heirs Execut^{rs} Adm^{rs} or assignes Shall well & truely pay or Cause to be paid unto ye s^d John Ellis ye Suñ of one hundred & fifty pounds Curra^t Lawfull money New England his heirs Ex^{rs} Adm^{rs} or Assignes on or before ye Thirtyeth day of Aprill now next Ensueing ye Date hereof that then this present Indenture demise and grant & Every Clause & Article herein Contained Shall Cease be Voyd & of none Effect & Else remaine & abide in full force Strength & Vertue./ In Witness whereof wee have hereunto Set our hands & Seals this Eleventh day of Aprill Anno Domini One Thousand Seven hundred & fifteen and in y^e first year of y^e reign of our Soveraign Lord George King of Great Brittaine ffrance & Ireland Defend^r of y^e faith &c^t

Signed Sealed & Delivered   Elisha Kelley ($_{Seal}^a$)
  In y^e psence of   Susannah Kelley ($_{Seale}^a$)
  George Blackdon
  William Sanderson
  Walter Mathews

Elisha Kelley psonally Appeared before my Selfe y^e Subscriber & Acknowledged y^e within Instrum^t to be his Volluntary Act & Deed this 6th day of Septemb^r 1715./ & in y^e Second year of his maj^{tys} Reign Over Great Brittaine ffrance & Irel^d &c^t John Plaisted Just^s peace

Recorded According to ye Original Octob^r 8th 1715./

                      p Jos. Hamond Reg^r

To All Christian People to whom this present deed of Gift Shall Come George Norton of Manchester in ye County of Essex in ye Province of ye Masachusets Bay in New England formerly of ye Town of york in ye Province of Maine in New England Shipwright Sendeth Greeting &c^t Know Yee

Book VIII, Fol. 113.

that I ye s^d George Norton for good Causes me thereunto moveing & Especially in Consideration of that Natural love and parental Affection which I bear to my daughter Elizabeth Woodbridge ye wife of John Woodbridge of Newbury in ye County afores^d Joyner I have given granted Aliened Assigned Enfeoffed and Confirmed & by these presents I do fully clearly & Absolutely give grant Aliene Assigne Enfeoffe Convey & Confirm unto ye s^d John Woodbridge my Son in law & Elizabeth his now wife my daughter their heirs Ex^{rs} Adm^{rs} & Assigns forever all those my Severall parcells of land Scittuate in ye s^d Township of York in ye province of maine afores^d be ye Same upland Meadow ground Swampland or salt marsh being all ye lands belonging to me ye s^d George Norton in ye afores^d Township of York at ye day of ye Date hereof Together with all ye houseing buildings & Edefices fences & fruit Trees woods & underwoods Standing on ye whole or any part or parcell of ye afores^d lands or lying or growing on ye Same To have & To hold all ye afores^d lands be ye Same more or less & According to ye Several bounds marks as any of them are bounded or reputed to be bounded & all & Singular ye rights Libertys profits priviledges & Appurtenances to s^d lands & Any & Every part or parcell of ye same Together with any Comonage or Comon right or rights that doth belong or Appurtaine to me ye s^d George Norton in ye afores^d Township of york & all grants or divisions of land that doth or may belong to me by vertue of ye afores^d Comonage or Comon right or rights with ye priviledges & appurtenances to ye same & Every part & parcel thereof belonging or in any wayes Appurtaining to him ye s^d John Woodbridge & Elizabeth his wife their heirs Ex^{rs} Adm^{rs} & Assigns forever & to his & their Sole & only propper use benefit & behoofe forever Imediately after my decease & ye decease of Mary my now wife & to be Accounted as part of their Share or portion in my Estate./ & ye s^d John Woodbridge his Ex^{rs} & Assignes to have ye use & Improvem^t of All ye above granted & Demised premises from ye day of ye date hereof he ye s^d John Woodbridge & Elizabeth his wife or Either of them or their heirs or Assignes or Either or any of them Allowing Yielding & Annually paying or Causeing to be paid to me ye s^d George Norton & Mary my now wife dureing ye Term of our Natural lives ye yearly rent of five pounds in Currant passable money of New England or good Currant bills of Cridit for ye use & Improvem^t of ye afores^d lands & premises s^d yearly rent to be paid At or before ye Twenty fifth [113] Day of march Annually yearly & Every year in Case ye Same

Book VIII, Fol. 113.

Called for or demanded by me ye s^d George Norton or Mary my now wife and ye s^d George Norton for himselfe & ye rest of his heirs Execut^{rs} and Adm^{rs} doth Covenant promiss & grant to & with ye s^d John Woodbridge and Elizabeth his now wife their heirs Execut^{rs} & Assignes by these presents that he ye s^d George Norton is Imediately before ye Ensealing & delivery of these psents ye True & rightfull owner of ye above granted & demised premisses & Every part & parcell thereof & hath in himSelfe good right full power & Lawfull Authority ye Same to give grant & Confirm as above Expressed & that ye Same is free & Clear from all former & other bargains Sales Alienations Titles Troubles charges & Incumbrances of what nature and kind So ever & that ye s^d John Woodbridge & Elizabeth his wife and their heirs Ex^{rs} Adm^{rs} & Assignes Shall & may from Time to Time & at all Times forever hereafter Quietly & peaceably possess and Enjoy ye Same as a good & Indefeazable Estate of Inheritance in fee Simple forever Imediately after my decease & decease of Mary my Now wife./ And I ye s^d George Norton do further Covenant & Ingage that I will warrant & Defend ye above granted & Demised premises to him ye s^d John Woodbridge & Eliz^a his wife their heirs Ex^{rs} Adm^{rs} & Assigns agast all & Every person or persons Legally Claiming any right Title or Interest therein Excepting only that whereas I ye s^d George Norton have Two Sons that are gone abroad to Sea & it is uncertain whether they or Either of them be liveing if in Case Either of them Shall Live & return againe to New England then he to have an Equal Share or part of ye one halfe of all ye Above granted & Demised premises both for quantity & quallity and ye s^d John Woodbridge and Eliz^a his wife & their heirs Execut^{rs} & Assigns to have only y^e other halfe of y^e above granted & Demised premises & In Witness whereof I y^e s^d George Norton & Mary wife in Testimony of her full Consent have Mutually Set to our hands & Seals this Sixth day of July Anno Dom: Seventeen hundred & fourteen 1714

Signed Sealed & Delivered George Norton ($_{Seale}^a$)
 In y^e presence of   The mark of
 John Newman   Mary ⁄⁄⁄ Norton ($_{Seale}^a$)
  The mark of
 John ⟨⟩ Pearce Essex ss/ Manchester July y^e 6th 1714
      Mr George Norton & Mary his
 Aaron Bennet wife above Named psonally
Appeared & Achnowledged y^e Above written Instrum^t to be their free Act & Deed Before John Newman Jus^t peace
Recorded According to y^e Original Oct y^e 5th 1715
     p Jos. Hamond R$_e$g^r

BOOK VIII, FOL. 113.

To All People to whom these presents Shall Come Greeting Know Yee that I Nathaniel ffreeman of york in y^e County of york & in y^e Province of y^e Massachusets Bay in New England Schoolmaster for & in Consideration of a Valluable Sum to me in hand paid before y^e Ensealing hereof well & Truely paid by John Woodbridge of Newbury in ye County of Essex in ye Province of ye Massachusets Bay in New England Joyner the receipt whereof I do hereby Acknowledge & my Selfe therewith fully Satisfied & Contented & thereof & of Every part & parcell thereof do Exonerate Acquit & discharge ye s^d John Woodbridge his Execut^rs Adm^rs forever by these presents have given granted bargained Sold Aliened Conveyed & Confirmed unto him & by these presents do freely fully & Absolutely give grant bargain Sell Aliene Convey & Confirm unto him ye s^d John Woodbridge his heirs & Assigns forever Twenty Acres of land where he can find it clear of all former grants given unto me ye s^d ffreeman At a Legall Town Meeting in york May ye fifth 1714/ To have & To hold ye s^d granted & bargained premisses with all ye Appurtenances priviledges & Comoditys to ye Same belonging or in any wise Appurtaining to him ye s^d John Woodbridge his heirs & Assigns forever to his & their own proper use benefit & behoofe forever & I ye s^d Nath^ll ffreeman for me my heirs Execut^rs Adm^rs do Covenant promiss & grant to & with ye s^d John Woodbridge his heirs and Assignes that before ye Ensealing hereof I am ye True Sole and lawfull owner of ye above bargained premisses & am Lawfully Seized & possessed of ye Same in mine own proper right as a good perfect & Absolute Estate of Inheritance in fee Simple & have in my Selfe good right full power & Lawfull Authority to grant bargain Sell Convey & Confirm s^d bargained pmises in maner as above s^d & that ye s^d John Woodbridge his heirs and Assignes Shall & may from time to time & at all times forEver hereafter by force & vertue of these p^rsents Lawfully peaceably & Quietly have hold use Occupie possess & Enjoy ye s^d Demised & bargained premises with ye Appurtenances free & Clear & freely & Clearly Acquitted Exonerated & Discharged of from all & all maner of former & other gifts grants bargaines Sales Leases Mortgages wills Entailes Joyntures Dowries Judgm^ts Executions Incumbrances & Extents Furthermore I ye s^d Nath^ll ffreeman for my Selfe my heirs Ex^rs Adm^rs do Covena^t & Engage ye above demised pmises to him ye s^d John Woodbridge his heirs & Assigns against ye Lawfull Claims & demands of any

[margin: Novr ye 16th 1714 Rec^d ye full Contents of ye within mentioned deed p Nath^ll Freeman]

BOOK VIII, FOL. 114.

p'son or persons whatsoever forever hereafter to Warrant Secure & Defend

In Witness whereof I have hereunto Set my hand and [114] Seale this Tenth day of Novemb' in y^e year of our Lord God one Thous^d Seven hundred fourteen in y^e first year of y^e Reign of our Soveraign Lord King George of Great Brittaine &c^t./   Nathaniel Freeman ($_{Seal}^a$)
Signed Scaled & Delivered
In psence of
Thomas Card
Abra^m Preble
York ss/ Novr 14: 1714

The above Named Nath^{ll} ffreeman Acknowledged y^e above written Instrum^t to be his ffree Act & Deed
    Before me./ Charles ffrost J: Peace
Recorded According to y^e Original Octr y^e 5th 1715./
    p Jos: Hamond Reg^r

To All People to whom these presents Shall Come Greeting Know yee that I Jo: Bragdon of york in ye County of york & in ye Province of ye Massachusets Bay in New England Labourer for & in Consideration of a valluable Sum to me in hand paid before ye Ensealing hereof well & Truely paid by John Woodbridge of Newbury in ye County of Essex in ye Province of ye Massachusets Bay in New England Joyner ye receipt whereof I do hereby Acknowledge and my Selfe therewith fully Satisfied & Contented and thereof & of Every part and parcel thereof do Exonerate Acquit & Discharge ye s^d John Woodbridge his Ex^{rs} Adm^{rs} forever by these presents have Given granted bargained Sold Aliened Conveyed & Confirmed unto him, And by these p'sents do freely fully Absolutely give grant bargaine Sell Aliene Convey & Confirm unto him ye s^d John Woodbridge his heirs & Assignes forever Twenty Acres of land where he Can find it clear of all former grants given unto me ye s^d Bragdon At a Legal Town meeting in york March ye 23^d 1712/3 to have & to hold ye s^d granted & bargained pmises with all ye Appurtenances priviledges & Comodityes to ye Same belonging or in any wayes Appurtaining to him ye s^d John Woodbridge his heirs & Assigns forever to his & their own proper use benefit & behoofe forever & I ye s^d Joseph Bragdon for me my heirs Ex^{rs} Adm^{rs} do Covenant promiss & grant to & with ye s^d John Woodbridge his heirs & Assignes that before ye Ensealing hereof I am ye True Sole &

Book VIII, Fol. 114.

Lawfull owner of ye above bargained premises & am Lawfully Siezed & possessed of ye Same in my own proper right as a good perfect & Absolute Estate of Inheritance in fee Simple & have in my Selfe good right full power & Lawfull Authority to grant bargaine Sell Convey & Confirm s^d bargained premises in maner as above s^d and that ye s^d John Woodbridge his heirs & Assignes Shall & may from Time To Time & at all Times forever hereafter by force & vertue of these psents Lawfully & peaceably & Quietly have hold use Occupie possess & Enjoy The s^d Demised & bargained premises with ye Appurtenances free and Clear & freely & Clearly Acquitted Exonerated & discharged of from all & all manner of former & other gifts grants bargains Sales leases Mortgages Wills Entails Joyntures Dowries Judgm^{ts} Executions Incumbrances & Extents Furthermore I ye s^d Joseph Bragdon for my Selfe my heirs Ex^{rs} Adm^{rs} do Covenant & Ingage ye Above demised pmises to him ye s^d John Woodbridge his heirs & Assignes against ye Lawfull Claims & Demands of Any person or persons whatsoever for ever hereafter to warrant Secure & Defend In Witness w^ro^f I have hereunto Set my hand & Seal this Sixteenth day of Novemb^r in ye year of our Lord God Seventeen hundred fourteen And in The first year of ye Reign of our Soveraign Lord George King of Great Brittaine &c^t

Signed Sealed & D^d   Joseph Bragdon (_{Seal}^a)
In p^rsence
Abra^m Preble
John Kingsbury
Nath^{ll} Freeman
York sc Novr 16th 1714

The above Named Joseph Bragdon Acknowledged ye above written Instrum^t to be his free Act & Deed. before me
                        Charles ffrost J peace

York Novr ye 16th 1714 Then rec^d ye full of ye within Specified forty Shillings or otherwayes Secured to be paid Witness my hand   Joseph Bragdon

Recorded According to ye Original Octr 5th 1715.
                        p Jos. Hamond Reg^r

To All Christian People to whom this present deed of Sale may Come John Harmon of york in ye County of York in ye Province of Maine in New England Sendeth Greeting Know Yee ye s^d John Harmon for & in Consideration of Eight pounds money to him in hand well & Truely paid before y^e

Book VIII, Fol. 115.

Signing of this Instrum^t by Mr John Woodbridge of Newbury in ye County of Essex in ye Province of ye Massachusets Bay in New England Joyner ye rec^t whereof ye s^d John Harmon doth Acknowledge himselfe fully paid Satisfied & Contented and doth hereby Acquit & discharge ye s^d John Woodbridge for & of Every part & parcell of Two Twenty Acre grants of land as is hereafter Set forth ye which ye s^d John Harmon hath given granted bargained Sold Aliened Conveyed & made over and doth by these presents give grant bargaine Sell Aliene Convey and make over & fully freely & Absolutely Confirm unto ye s^d John Woodbridge forty Acres of land where he ye s^d John Woodbridge Can find it Clear of All former grants within [115] This precinct or Township of s^d York ye which s^d forty Acres of land was granted unto ye s^d John Harmon At Two Several Town meetings in s^d york as by york Town records referrence thereunto being had may more fully Appear./ The first Twenty Acres was at a Legal Town Meeting holden in s^d york March ye 6th 1710/11./ The Later Twenty Acres was granted unto him ye s^d Harmon at a Legal Town meeting holden in s^d York March ye Seventeenth 1711/12. Together with all ye rights priviledges Advantages & Appurtenances thereunto belonging or any wayes at any Time redownding to ye s^d grant or grants or any part or parcell thereof unto him ye s^d John Woodbridge his heirs & Assignes for ever to. have. &. to. hold & quietly & peaceably to possess Occupie and Enjoy As a free & Clear Estate in fee Simple Moreover ye s^d John Harmon doth for himselfe his heirs Execut^{rs} & Adm^{rs} to & with ye s^d John Woodbridge his heirs & Assignes Covena^t Ingage & promiss ye Above bargained grants of Land to be free & Clear from all former gifts grants bargains Sales or any Incumberments whatsoever as also from all future Claimes Challenges or Interuptions to be had or Comenced by him ye s^d John Harmon his heirs or Assignes but doth untill ye Signing Sealing & Delivery of this Instrum^t Avouch himselfe ye True & proper owner of ye above bargained premisses or grants According to ye Tenour thereof & will warrantise & Defend ye Same In Witness hereof ye Aboves^d John Harmon hath hereunto Set his hand & Seale this Second day of Novemb^r in ye year of our Lord one Thousand Seven hundred and fourteen & in ye first year of

Book VIII, Fol. 115.

yᵉ Reign of our Soveraign Lord George King of Great Brittaine &cᵗ   John Harmon (ₛₑₐₗₑ ᵃ)
Signed Sealed & Delivered
 In psence of us Witnesses
 Nathˡˡ Freeman
 Abraᵐ Preble
 York sc Octʳ 5ᵗʰ 1715

John Harmon above named Acknowledged yᵉ above written Instrumᵗ to be his free Act & Deed./
        Before Charles ffrost J peace
York Novʳ yᵉ 5ᵗʰ 1714. Then recᵈ yᵉ full of yᵉ within
         p me John Harmon
Recorded According to yᵉ Original Octʳ 5ᵗʰ 1715./
         p Jos. Hammond Regʳ

To All Christian People to whom these presents may Come Nathaniel Ramsdell and mary his wife of york in yᵉ County of york in the Province of Maine in New England Sendeth Greeting Know yee yᵉ sᵈ Nathaniel & Mary for & in Consideration of yᵉ Sum of four pounds in money to them in hand well & Truely paid by Caleb Preble of sᵈ York before yᵉ Signing hereof yᵉ recᵗ whereof yᵉ sᵈ Nathaniel & Mary doth Acknowledge themselves Therewith fully paid Satisfied & Contented & for Every part thereof & do Exonerate Acquit & discharge yᵉ sᵈ Caleb Preble his heirs & Assigns for Ever by these presents have given granted bargained Sold Alienated Enfeoffed and made over & do by these presents give grant Bargaine Sell Aliene Enfeoffe & make over & fully freely & Absolutely Convey and Confirm unto him yᵉ sᵈ Caleb Preble his heirs & Assignes forever One Messuage piece or parcel of fresh Marsh or Meadow Lying & being within yᵉ Township or precinct of sᵈ York lying & being upon yᵉ Northwestward of Agamenticus great hill being yᵉ Eighth part of yᵉ fresh marsh or Meadow that was formerly granted unto Thomas Bragdon & Arthur Bragdon late of sᵈ York decᵈ At a Town meeting in sᵈ York August yᵉ 30ᵗʰ 1666 as by York Town records may more fully Appear and Since Purchased by sᵈ Nathaniel Ramsdell Together with all yᵉ rights Priviledges Appurtenances or Advantages of yᵉ one Eighth part of sᵈ Meadow or Swamp marsh as it is undivided that doth belong to yᵉ Same or any wayes at any time may redownd unto yᵉ Same unto him yᵉ sᵈ Caleb

Book VIII, Fol. 116.

Preble his heirs & Assignes forever To have & To hold and quietly to possess Occupie & Enjoy ye Same with all its priviledges as a Sure Estate in Fee Simple Moreover ye s^d Nathaniel & Mary do for themSelves their heirs Ex^{rs} & Adm^{rs} Covenant to & with ye s^d Caleb Preble his heirs & Assignes as also promiss & Engage ye above bargained premises with all its priviledges to be free & Clear from all former gifts grants bargains Sales rents rates Dowries or any incumbrances whatsoever as also from all future Claims Challenges demands LawSuits or Interuptions whatsoever to be had or Comenced by them ye s^d Nathaniel or Mary their heirs Ex^{rs} Adm^{rs} or assignes or any other person or persons whatsoever after ye Date of this Instrum^t but that they ye s^d Nath^{ll} & Mary their heirs Ex^{rs} Adm^{rs} do Warrantise & will defend ye above bargained premises & all y^n priviledges thereof unto ye s^d Caleb Preble his heirs & Assignes In Witness hereof ye s^d Nath^{ll} Ramsdell & Mary his wife have hereunto Set their hands & Seals this Sixteenth day of February in y^e year of our Lord one Thousand Seven hundred Thirteen. 14. in y^e Twelfth year of the Reign of our Soveraign Lady Queen Anne of Great Brittaine &c^t
Signed Sealed & Delivered   Nathaniel Ramsdel ($_{Seal}^a$)
   In psence of us Witnesses
Lewis Bane
Peter Nowell
Novr 21 : 1715/
   York in y^e County of york Nath^{ll} Ramsdel psonally Appeared before me y^e Subscrib^r & Acknowledged this within written Instrum^t to be his Act & Deed Before me
                                 Lewis Bane Just p^s
   Recorded According to ye Original Octob^r 3^d 1715/
                                 p Jos Hamond Reg^r

[116] To All Christian People to whom this present writing Shall Come Know yee that I Richard White of ye Township of york near braveboat harbour in ye Province of Maine in New England planter for & in Consideration of ye Sum of Twenty pounds in goods At price Curra^t & Two pounds in Curra^t money of New England afores^d to me in hand paid & Secured by John More of the Same place Shipwright wherewth I am well Satisfied & Contented at & before ye Ensealing and delivery of these p^{r}sents have bargained & Sold & by these presents do fully freely & Absolutely bargaine & Sell unto ye s^d John More Shipwright and Inhabitant at

brave boat harbour in ye Township of york afores^d one Certaine Tract or parcell of land Scittuate Lying & being at ye bridge foot at brave boat harb^r afores^d & from thence runing up into ye woods North East between ye Land of ye s^d John More & Major Nicholas Shapleigh dec^d Containing one hundred & Seventy rods in length & Twenty five rods in breadth being Thirty Acres more or less & which land is a Town grant & recorded to ye s^d Richard White in ye Township of York afores^d To have & To hold ye s^d Thirty Acres of land bounded and Laid out as above Mentioned unto ye s^d John More his heirs Ex^{rs} Adm^{rs} & Assignes to his & their proper uses & behoofes forever and I ye s^d Richd White my heirs Ex^{rs} & Adm^{rs} & Every of us Shall & will Warrant and forever defend ye Sale of ye s^d Thirty acres of land Together with all ye Appurtenances & priviledges thereunto belonging unto ye s^d John More his heirs Ex^{rs} Adm^{rs} or Assigns against all maner of persons w^{t}soever In Witness whereof I ye s^d Richard White & ffrancis White my wife have hereunto put our hands & Seals without fraud this twenty Second day of Octr in ye year of our Lord one Thousand Six hundred Eighty and Seaven./ Annoq, Regni Regis Jacobi Secundi Anglia Scota ffrancie & Hiburni Rex Tertio./

Signed Sealed & Delivered   mark of

   In presence of   Richard ⊗ White (a Seale)
   Job. Alcock
   W Barefoot
   Robt Eliot
   Nicholas Heskins

   Portsm^o Province of New Hampsh^r July ye 15ta 1713

Robt Eliot Esqr & Cap^{tn} Job Alcock psonally Appeared before me ye Subscrib^r & Acknowledged that they did sign their Names as witnesses to ye Above Instrum^t of writing & did Se Richard White Signe Seal & Deliver ye Same Instrum^t or deed of Sale as his Act & Deed

                       Ata^h Hunking Justice peace

Recorded According to ye Original Augst 24th 1715./

                       p Jos: Hammond Reg^r

To All Christian People to whom this deed of Sale Shall Come and Concern that I John Pickerin Senr of Portsm^o in ye Province of New Hampsh^r Some Time resident in York for ye Consideration of one hundred pounds to me in hand paid by Ebenezer Blasdel and Ralph ffarnum both of york n ye Province of Maine ye reo^t whereof I do hereby Acknowledge & my Selfe to be fully Satisfied Content & paid and thereof & of Every part & peney thereof do by these presents Acquit and discharge them the Said Blasdell & ffarnum their heirs Execut[rs] and Administrators forever have bargained Sold Enfeoffed released delivered & Confirmed and by this my present deed do freely firmly & Absolutely grant bargaine sell release deliver & Confirm unto them the Said Blasdel & ffarnum their heirs & Assigns forever To say one parcel of land Timber Trees wood &c[t] lying and being in y[e] Town of York on y[e] southwest Side of said york river butted and bounded as followeth./ begining at y[e] Northeast Corner of Elihue Parsons' lot of land thence along y[e] upland near said river up to y[e] Next Cove below goose cove So runing y[e] same breadth from said Parsons' land to y[e] s[d] Cove clear back to Kittery bounds with all y[e] profits priviledges to y[e] said land belonging or in any wise Appurtaining y[e] said land Timber Trees woods underwood Together with all profits priviledges & Advantages to y[e] same belonging or in any wise Appurtaining To have & To hold unto them y[e] s[d] Blasdel & ffarnum their heirs Executors Administrators and Assignes forever without y[e] least let trouble Interuption or Mollestation of me y[e] said Pickerin my heirs Executor or Admin[rs] or any other person or persons whatsoever Claiming y[e] s[d] land or any part thereof from by or under me them or any of them and that forever but that it is & shall be lawfull for them y[e] said Blasdell & ffarnum their heirs Executors Administrator Assigns or order The said bargained & sold land & priviledges to Enter into have hold possess & Enjoy as a free & perfect Estate without any Trouble or Mollestation of me y[e] s[d] Pickerin my heirs Execut[rs] Adm[rs] or any from by or under me them or any of them forever In Confirmation hereof I have hereunto set my hand and seal this 27th day of August 1713./ in y[e] Twelfth year of her Majestys Reign Over great Brittaine ffrance & Ireland Queen Defender of y[e] faith &c[t]/ It is to be understood & it is the true Intent and meaning that y[e] above bargained land is to Containe y[e] full third part of all y[e] land from y[e] old mill Creek to y[e] s[d] Cove Next below goose Cove Clear over to Kittery bounds

Signed Sealed & Delivered   John Pickerin (a Seale)
In presence of
Samuel Came
James Allen

   Portsm[o] in New Hampsh[r] May y[e] 26th 1715
Cap[tn] John Pickerin Appeared before me the Subscrib[r]

Book VIII, Fol. 117.

hereof & Acknowledged this deed to be his free Act & Deed y[e] day & year aboves[d]   John Plaisted Just[s] peace
Recorded According to y[e] Original Oct[r] 5th 1715./
        p Jos. Hamond Reg[r]

[117] Know All men by these presents that wee Martha Lord widow of Benjamin Lord husbandman both of Berwick alias Kittery in y[e] County of York in y[e] Province of y[e] Massachusets Bay in New Engl[d] for & in Consideration of y[e] Sum of Thirty pounds in Currant money of y[e] province afores[d] to us in hand well & Truely paid by Richard Lord of y[e] same Town County & Province afores[d] husbandman y[e] receipt whereof wee do hereby Acknowledge & our selves therewith fully Satisfied Contented and paid have therefore given granted bargained & sold Aliened Assigned Enfeoffed set over & Confirmed & do by these presents give grant bargaine sell Aliene Assigne Enfeoffe set over & Confirm unto thes[d] Richard Lord his heirs & assignes forever a Certaine piece of Meadow or fresh marsh ground lying & being near a place Comonly Called by y[e] Name of Whites Marsh Containing five acres more or less and is bounded by John Coopers land on y[e] Northwest side James Warrens land East Benjamin Lords land North and south by a brook & on all y[e] Marsh & Marsh ground that goes by y[e] name of Nathan Lords sen[rs] Island to have & to hold y[e] s[d] five acres of Marsh more or less as bounded unto him y[e] s[d] Richard lord his heirs and Assignes forever free & clear & is freely & Clearly Acquited Exonerated and discharged of & from all former & other gifts grants bargains sales Mortgages Judgm[ts] Executions and all other Incumbrance or Incumbrances whatsoever & that it Shall & may be lawfull to & for y[e] s[d] Richard Lord his heirs or assignes to have hold use Occupie possess & Enjoy y[e] same from henceforth forever without any let hinderence mollestation or Interruption from us y[e] said Martha Lord & Benjamin Lord our heirs Ex[rs] or Adm[rs] and wee y[e] s[d] Martha Lord & Benjamin Lord do further Covenant for ourselves our heirs Ex[rs] and Adm[rs] to Warrant Acquit and Defend him y[e] s[d] Richard Lord his heirs & Assignes in y[e] quiet and peaceable possession of y[e] premisses against all person & persons w[t]soever from henceforth & forever./ In

Book VIII, Fol. 117.

Witness whereof wee y̆ᵉ s̆ᵈ Martha Lord & Benjamin Lord have hereunto set our hands & seals the 11ᵗʰ day of August Annoq̨ Domini 1712./
Signed Sealed & Delivered   Martha her L̸ Lord (ₛₑₐₗ ᵃ)
 In the psence of
 Thomas Goodwin   Benjamin mark Lord (ₛₑₐₗ ᵃ)
 John Croade
York sc/ Martha Lord & Benjᵃ Lord both psonally appearᵈ & acknowledged yᵉ above written Instrumᵗ to be their act & Deed Kittery yᵉ 11ᵗʰ Augˢᵗ 1712./
         John Hill J. peace
Recorded According to yᵉ Original Sepᵗʳ 14 : 1715./
        p Jos. Hañiond Regʳ

To All Christian People to whom these Shall Come Greeting Know Yee that I Benjamin Nason Senʳ now resident in Berwick in yᵉ County of york in her Maᵗʸˢ Province of yᵉ Massachusets bay in New England yeoman for & in Consideration of a valluable Suɱ of money to me in hand paid by Richard Lord of yᵉ same Town County & Province abovesᵈ yᵉ receipt whereof I own and my selfe satisfied Contented & paid & of Every part & parcell thereof Do Acquit & forever discharge have granted bargained & sold and do by these presents grant bargaine sell release Alienate Enfeoffe pass over & Confirm unto Richard Lord his heirs and Assignes forever a piece or parcell of land Scittuate and lying in Berwick abovesᵈ Containing Two acres & a quarter be it more or Less as it is bounded Vizᵗ begining at a heap of Stones by yᵉ Town highway on yᵉ south side of sᵈ way against Herlows uper corner bounds and from sᵈ heap of stones west southwest by yᵉ road Twenty one pole & one Third of a pole : then south southeast Twelve poles Then East northEast about Twelve poles to yᵉ Top of a hill Then East Northerly Till it Comes to Two birches & so to said. Richard Lords land yᵉ same Course & by sᵈ Lords land Northwest by west to sᵈ heap of stones which piece or parcell is part of my home lot that was given to my father Richard Nason by yᵉ Town of Kittery and was purchased by me Benjamin Nason from my father & now sold by me to yᵉ abovesᵈ Richard Lord to have & to hold yᵉ aforesᵈ Tract of land Together with all & singular yᵉ Appurtenances priviledges & Comodityes of wood Timbʳ Trees undʳ wood water water Courses to him yᵉ sᵈ Richard Lord his heirs or Assignes forever without Let Interruption or Mollestation of me y̆ᵉ sᵈ

Book VIII, Fol. 118.

Benjamin Nason or any other pson or persons from by or under me or by my procurem^t my heirs or Assignes & further do Covenant that I have in my selfe good right full power & Lawfull Authority to ye Disposeing of ye pmisses & that it is free of & from all maner of former gifts grants Mortgages wills Entailments Judgm^{ts} Executions power of thirds or any other Incumbrance w^{t}soever And I ye s^d Benjamin Nason do bind my selfe my heirs Ex^{rs} Adm^{rs} & Assignes to ye aboves^d Richard Lord his heirs Execut^{rs} Adm^{rs} & Assigns to save harmless warrant & Defend from all persons Excepting ye Crown or high Land lord In Witness whereof I have hereunto Set my hand & seal this Twenty fifth day of June Anno Dom One Thousand seven hundred & Thirteen and in y^e Twelfth year of y^e reign of our Soveraign Lady Anne by the Grace of God of Great Brittaine ffrance & Ireland Queen Defend^r of y^e faith &c^t Benjamin Nason ($_{Seal}^a$)
Signed Sealed & Deliver^d Elisha Plaisted
  In presence of us   Samuel Gatchel
  [118] Benjamin Nason within Named Acknowledged y^e above Instrum^t to be his free Act & Deed this 25th June 1713/ Before me   John Plaisted Just^e peace
  Recorded According to y^e Original Sept 14th 1715./
                              p Jos. Hamond Reg^r

To All Christian People to whom these presents shall come I Moses Spencer of ye Town of Kittery in ye County of york in her Maj^{tys} Province of ye Massachusets Bay in New England husbandman and Elizabeth his wife Sendeth Greeting./ Know Yee that for & in Consideration of a valluable Sum of money to us in hand paid by Richard Lord of ye Town & County afores^d husbandman The receipt whereof wee do Acknowledge our selves to be fully satisfied & therewith Contented have: given granted bargained sold Alienated Enfeoffed & Confirmed and do by these presents for my Selfe my heirs Ex^{rs} Adm^{rs} & Assignes fully freely and Absolutely give grant bargaine sell Alienate Enfeoffe Assigne pass over and Confirm Two Certain parcells or Tracts of land both Containing Eighteen Acres Lying & Scittuate in Town of Kittery aboves^d bounded as followeth ye one parcell or Tract Containing Six acres lyeth at ye East End of Francis Herlows land that he bought of Benjamin Nason and is bounded on ye South by ye highway that leads from s^d Herlows house to ye Comons at ye Rockey hills and Joyning to s^d highway and on ye north bounded partly by ye swamp Called Parkers

Marsh & partly by ye brook runing out of s^d Marsh begining at ye fores^d Herlows land & runing According to ye fores^d bounds Till the Six acres be Compleated & ye other parcell or Tract of land Containing Twelve Acres lyeth & is bounded on north by ye aforementioned highway Takeing it begining At Benj^a Nasons land & so runing by said land and by ye fores^d highway Eastward Till ye Twelve acres be Compleated all which Two parcells or Tracts of land to have & to hold to him ye afores^d Richard Lord and to his heirs Ex^rs Adm^rs & Assigns forever with all & singular ye Appurtenances priviledges and Comodityes thereunto belonging freely & clearly Exonerated & Discharged of & from all former wills Deeds leases dowries or any other Incumbrances whatsoever had made done or suffered to be done by me ye fores^d Moses Spencer whereby ye fores^d Richard Lord his heirs Ex^rs Adm^rs or Assignes may be in any wise Mollested in their peaceable & Quiet Injoym^t & Improvem^t of ye above granted premisses or any part thereof & furth I ye fores^d Moses Spencer do by these presents bind my selfe my heirs Ex^rs Adm^rs and Assignes unto ye afores^d Richard Lord his heirs Ex^rs Adm^rs & Assigns forever to warrant & Defend ye Title of ye above granted premisses & Every part thereof against any person or persons whatsoever that may or shall hereafter Claime or challenge any Legall or Lawfull right or propriety to ye above granted premisses

In Witness hereof I ye fores^d Moses Spencer & Elizabeth his wife have hereunto set our hands & seals this Thirtyeth day of March Anno Domini one Thousand Seven hundred & Thirteen & in ye Thirteenth year of her Maj^tys Reign Anne by ye grace of God Over Great Brittaine ffrance & Ireland Queen Defender of ye faith &c^t/

Signed Sealed & Delivered
In ye presence of us   Moses X (his mark) Spencer (a Seal)
Baker X (his mark) Nason
                          Elizabeth X (her mark) Spencer (a Seal)
James ᴧ (his mark) Gray
James Warren

York sc/
Moses Spencer psonally Appeared and Acknowledged ye Above written Instrum^t to be his Act & Deed & Elizabeth his wife relinquish^d her right of Dowry or thirds to ye Land or Estate as is above Conveyed./ Berw^k ye 5 Aug^st 1713./
              Before me Ichabod Plaisted J : P
Recorded According to ye Original Sep^t 14th 1715./
              p Jos : Hamond Reg^r

Book VIII, Fol. 119.

To All People to whom these presents Shall Come John Wincoll of yᵉ Town of Portsmᵒ in yᵉ Province of New Hampshʳ in New England Marriner sendeth Greeting Know Yee that I yᵉ sᵈ John Wincoll for & in Consideration of yᵉ sum̃ of Thirty pounds Curraᵗ money of New England to me in hand before yᵉ Ensealing & Délivery hereof well & Truely paid by Nathan Lord Senʳ & Richard Lord his son Both of yᵉ Town of Berwick in yᵉ Province of Maine in New England Husbandman yᵉ receipt whereof I do hereby Acknowledge & my Selfe therewith fully satisfied and Contented & thereof & of Every part and parcell thereof do Acquit Exonerate & Discharge yᵉ sᵈ Nathan and Richard Lord their heirs Execʳˢ Admʳˢ forever by these presents have given granted bargained sold Aliened Enfeoffed Conveyed & Confirmed and by these presents do freely fully and Absolutely Give grant bargaine sell Aliene Enfeoffe Convey and Confirm unto them yᵉ sᵈ Nathan & Richard Lord Their heirs & Assignes forever a smal Tract of Land Scittuate lying and being within yᵉ Township of Berwick aforesᵈ & is butted And bounded as followeth Vizᵗ on yᵉ south by yᵉ highway and by Will Cocks pond on yᵉ East side by yᵉ land that was Thomas Spencers Comonly Called yᵉ hundred Acre lot on yᵉ north side by yᵉ Great works river on yᵉ west side by yᵉ land that was laid out for yᵉ use of yᵉ Ministry being Sixty five Acres more or Less as it is so butted & bounded it being a grant of So much by sᵈ Town of Berwick to sᵈ Wincolls Mother. To have and To hold yᵉ sᵈ Granted & bargained premisses Together with all [119] The priviledges and Appurtenances to yᵉ same belonging or in any wise Appurtaining to them yᵉ sᵈ Nathan & Richard Lord their heirs and Assignes forever to their & Either of their only proper use benefit and behoofe forever And I yᵉ sᵈ John Wincoll for me my heirs Executʳˢ and Administrators do Covenant promiss and Grant to & with the said Nathan & Richard Lord their heirs and Assignes that before the Ensealing hereof I am the True sole & Lawfull owner of yᵉ above bargained pmisses and have in my Selfe good right full power and Lawfull Authority to Grant Bargaine Sell Convey and Confirm said Bargained premisses in Mañer as abovesᵈ and that yᵉ sᵈ Nathan & Richard Lord they their heirs or Assigns Shall & may from time to time & at all times forever hereafter by force and Vertue of these presents Lawfully peaceably & Quietly have Hold use Occupie possess & Enjoy yᵉ sᵈ Demised & bargained premisses with all yᵉ Appurtenances free and Clear and freely & Clearly Acquitted Exonerated & Discharged of from all & all maner of other

Book VIII, Fol. 119.

gifts Grants bargains sales Mortgages Wills Entailes Joyntures Dowries Thirds Judgm^{ts} Executions Extents or Incumbrances whatsoever had made done or suffered to be done by me ye s^d Johns Wincol my heirs or Assignes At any Time or times before ye Ensealing & Delivery hereof. Furthermore I ye s^d Johns Wincol for my Selfe my heirs Ex^{rs} & Adm^{rs} do Covenant and Engage ye above demised premisses to them ye s^d Nathan & Richard Lord their heirs & Assignes against ye Lawfull Claims or demands of Any person or persons whatsoever forever hereafter to Warrant & Defend. Also Deborah ye wife of ye s^d John Wincoll do by these presents freely & willingly Give yield up & surrender all her right of Dowry & power of thirds of in & unto ye above Demised pmisses unto them ye s^d Nathan & Richard Lord their heirs & Assignes forever. In Witness whereof they ye s^d John Wincoll & Deborah his wife have hereunto set their hands & Seals this Twentie Ninth day of July in ye year of our Lord one Thousand Seven hundred & Twelve.
1712/   John Wincoll (a Seal)
Sealed & Delivered   Deberoh Wincoll (a Seal)
   In presence of us
   Robert Rutherford
   James Jeffry
        Province of New Hampsh^r 30th July 1712
John Wincoll & Deberoh his wife psonally Appearing Acknowledged this deed or Instrum^t in writing to be their ffree and Volluntary Acts & Deeds
                    Coram me Cha: Story Jus. p^s
Recorded According to ye Original Sep^t 14th 1715./
                    p Jos. Hamond Reg^r

     To All People to whom these presents Shall Come Sam^{ll} Bolls of the town of Rochester in ye County of Plymouth & Province of ye Massachusets Bay in New England husbandman Sendeth Greeting Know yee that ye s^d sam^{ll} Bolls for & in Consideration of ye Just & full Sum of one hundred pounds Curra^t money of New England to him in hand paid or secured to be paid by samuel Hammond of Rochester in ye County afores^d doth therewith Acknowledge himselfe fully Satisfied Contented & paid and doth Acquit Exonerate & discharge ye s^d Sam^{ll} Hammond his heirs Ex^{rs} Adm^{rs} & Assignes & Every of them forever hath by these psents given granted bargained Sold Enfeoffed Aliened & Confirmed unto him ye s^d Sam^{ll} Hammond his heirs Ex^{rs} Adm^{rs} & Assignes forever one Messuage or Tract of land lying in yᵉ Township of Wells in yᵉ County of York & province of Maine Containing Three hundred Acres be it more or Less with Ten Acres of meadow or Marsh which is Called yᵉ pond marsh which yᵉ sᵈ Samˡˡ Boles had Given & granted to him by yᵉ Inhabitants of Wells as by their records do fully Appear with all yᵉ Trees Timbʳ herbage priviledges profits benefits & Appurtenances thereunto in any way Appurtaining to have & to hold yᵉ Abovesᵈ Three hundred Acres of Land & Ten Acres of Meadow with all & Singular yᵉ Trees Timbʳ herbage &cᵗ as aforᵉsᵈ unto him yᵉ sᵈ Samuel Hamond his heirs Executʳˢ Admʳˢ & Assignes forever to their propper use And benefit & behoofe forever & yᵉ sᵈ Samˡˡ Bolls doth Covenant and promiss for himselfe his heirs Exʳˢ Admʳˢ & Assigns to & with yᵉ sᵈ Samˡˡ Hammond that he yᵉ sᵈ Samˡˡ Bolls is yᵉ True & propper owner of yᵉ above bargained & granted premisses before & at yᵉ Signing Ensealing & Delivery of these pʳsents & hath of himselfe good right & Lawfull Authority to Sell & Convey yᵉ same & that it is clear & free & Clearly & freely Acquitted & discharged of & from all other gifts grants bargains sales & all other Acts of Incumbrence whatsoever and that yᵉ sᵈ Samˡˡ Hamond shall or may peaceably & Quietly Enjoy & possess As also his heirs Exʳˢ Admʳˢ or Assignes yᵉ same as a good Estate of Inheritance in fee Simple without any let suit or Mollestation from yᵉ sᵈ Samˡˡ Bolls his heirs Exʳˢ Admʳˢ or assignes or from any pʳson or pʳsons whatsoever And yᵉ sᵈ Samˡˡ Boles will Warraᵗ and defend yᵉ same from any Lawfull Claims of any pʳson or pʳsons whatsoever unto yᵉ sᵈ Samˡˡ Hamond his heirs Exʳˢ Admʳˢ Assignes forever In Witness whereof yᵉ sᵈ Samˡˡ Bolls hath hereunto Set his hand & seal this first day of June in yᵉ Twelfth year of her Majᵗʸˢ Reign Annoq Domini one Thousand seven hundred & Thirteen

Signed Sealed & Delivered   Samˡˡ his B Bolls (a seal)
In pʳsence of/
Samˡˡ Hunt   mark
Wᵐ his X Parker
    mark

[120] June yᵉ 1ˢᵗ 1713/ The above named Samˡˡ Bolls psonally Appeared before me & Acknowledged yᵉ above written Instrumᵗ to be his Act and Deed

                 Seth Pope Justice of peace

Recorded According to yᵉ Original Novʳ 7ᵗʰ 1715./

                      p Jos Hamond Regʳ

Book VIII, Fol. 120.

This Indenture made ye fourth day of May in ye fourteenth year of ye Reign of our Soveraign Lord Charles by ye Grace of God King of England Scotland ffrance & Ireland Defend^r of ye faith &c^t

Between Sr Ferdinando Gorges of Long Ashton in ye County of Sumerset Knight of th' one p^{tie} And Edward Godfrey of Agamenticus of ye Province or reputed or intended Province of New Sumerset in New Engl^d in America Gent Oliver Godfrey of Seale in ye County of Kent Gent. And Richard Row of ye Citty of London Merchant of ye other party Witnesseth that ye s^d Sr Ferdinando Gorges for & in Consideration of ye yearly rent & rents of Two shillings for Every hundred Acres of Land that are or hereafter shall be Imployed Either for wood pasture Meadow or Tillage which shall from Time to Time be Inclosed and remaine so being part parcell or Member of ye Lands hereafter in and by these presents demised As Also for diverse other good causes and Considerations him thereunto Moveing hath demised granted and to farm Letten & by this p^rsents doth demise grant & to farm Let unto ye s^d Edwd Godfrey Oliver Godfrey & Richd Row all that part parcell portion or Tract of Land wood & woodgrounds in New England afores^d Lying & being within ye Province or reputed or Intended Province of New Sumerset Containing & to Containe one Thousand five hundred Acres to be had & Taken on ye Northeast side of a Certaine Creek or watercourse there Called by ye Name of Cape Nuddock Creek begining at ye Mouth or Entrance thereof and from thence to Extend & to be Extended along ye Sea shoare Northeastward by ye Space of Two English miles in ye breadth thereof and at both ends of ye s^d Space to Extend & be Extended up into the Inland parts along ye side of ye s^d Creek by a Northwest line so far as may Include ye s^d One Thousand & five hundred Acres Intirely Together as it were in Maner of a Square Together also with all ye Soyles woods and underwoods Mine Mines & Minerells as well Royall mines of Gold & Silver as other mines & minerells precious stones Quarries and all Royaltyes of hawking hunting fishing & fowling in and upon ye premisses or any part or parcell thereof Except & Alwayes reserved out of this present demise The fifth part of All ye Oare of such Royal Mines of Silver & gold as shall be found in & upon ye Premisses or any part or parcell thereof heretofore reserved to be due and payable unto his Ma^{ty} his heirs and successors out of the pmisses To have & To hold ye s^d Tract of Land woods & underwoods and all & singular other ye pmisses with their & Every of their Appur-

Book VIII, Fol. 120.

tenances Except before Excepted unto y̆e s̆d Edward Godfrey Oliver Godfrey & Richard Row their Exrs & Assignes from y̆e day of y̆e Date hereof for and Dureing y̆e Term of One Thousand years from thence Nex Ensueing & fully to be Compleat & Ended Yielding & paying therefore yearly from henceforth dureing y̆e s̆d Term unto y̆e s̆d S̆r fferdinando Gorges his heirs & Assignes y̆e yearly rent & rents sum̄ and sum̄s of Two shillings y̆e hundred for Every hundred Acres of y̆e premisses that are or shall be Imployed Either for wood pasture Meadow or Tillage which shall from time to time be Inclosed & remaine so or Converted to Tillage & so after that rate for Lesser Quantity or Quantitys of hundred or hundreds of acres At Two of the most usual feasts or Terms in y̆e year that is to say At y̆e feast of y̆e Anunciation of y̆e Blessed Virgin Mary And S̆t Michael y̆e Arch Angel by Even & Equal portions And If it shall hapen y̆e s̆d yearly rent & rents or any or Either of them to be behing & unpaid in part or in All by y̆e space of forty Dayes Next after any or Either of y̆e s̆d feasts or dayes of paymt in which as aforesd y̆e same is Limitted & Apointed to be paid that then & so often it shall & may be Lawfull to & for y̆e s̆d S̆r fferdinando Gorges his heirs or assignes or any of Them upon y̆e s̆d Demised premisses or any part thereof to Enter & distrein and y̆e distress or distresses Then & There so had & Taken to Leade drive have Take Carry away Impark & Impound & them in pound to Detaine & keep untill y̆e s̆d fferdinando Gorges his heirs or Assigns shall be of y̆e s̆d rent & rents & y̆e Arrearages of them & Every of them fully Satisfyed contented & paid & y̆e s̆d S̆r fferdinando Gorges for himselfe his heirs & Assignes doth Covenant promiss & grant to & with y̆e s̆d Edward Godfrey Oliver Godfrey & Richard Row their Exrs & Assigns by this prsents that they y̆e s̆d Edwd Godfrey Oliver Godfrey and Richard Row their Exrs or Assignes shall or Lawfully may from time to Time & At all Times hereafter dureing y̆e s̆d Term paying y̆e s̆d yearly rent & rents in & by these prsents reserved peaceably & Quietly have hold use Occupy possess & Enjoy all & singular y̆e s̆d Lands & pmisses Except before Excepted According to y̆e True Intent and meaning of these presents without y̆e Let mollestation or Eviction of him y̆e s̆d S̆r fferdinando Gorges his heirs or Assignes or of any other person or persons Lawfully claiming or Lawfully to Claime by from or under him them or Any of them And Also that he y̆e s̆d S̆r fferdinando Gorges his heirs & Assignes shall & will from Time to Time & At all Times hereafter dureing y̆e space of seven years upon y̆e reasonable request & at y̆e Cost & Charg of y̆e s̆d Edwd God-

frey Oliver Godfrey & Richard Row their Ex^{rs} or Assigns do make Acknowledge Execute & suffer all & Every such further & other Lawfull & reasonable Act & Acts thing & things device & devices [121] In ye Law for ye further & better Assurence & sure makeing of all and singular ye s^d demised premisses with their & Every of their Appurtenances unto ye s^d Edwd Godfrey Oliver Godfrey & Richd Row their Ex^{rs} or Assignes in maner and form afores^d as by them ye s^d Edwd Godfrey Oliver Godfrey & Richard Row their Ex^{rs} or Assignes or by their Every or any of their Council Learned in ye Law shall be reasonably devised or advised & required for ye doing whereof Neither ye s^d S^r fferdinando Gorges nor his heirs or assignes shall be Compelled to Travel above ye Space of five miles from ye place of his or their or any of their Abode or dwelling at ye time of such request to be made & ye s^d demised premisses to be made parcell or Memb^r of such Mañor as ye s^d S^r fferdinando Gorges his heirs or Assignes shall in his or their discreation think most meet & Expedient to Create in those parts./ In Witness whereof to this present Indentures have Interchangeably Set their hands & seals ye day & year first above written Annoq, Dñi 1638   fferde: Gorges
Sealed & Delivered
 In ye p^{r}sence of
 Theol: Gorges
 John Edwards
 William Satchfield
Copia vera concordans Cum Originali & Exaiat 26 Juny 1638./   p Nos. Fra Yeamans
           Watt: Yeamans
Recorded According to ye Original Coppy Septr 15th 1715./
         p Jos: Hañiond Reg^r

 This Indenture made the Seven & twentieth day of June In ye fourteenth year of the reign of our Soveraign Lord Charles by ye grace of god of England Scotland ffrance & Ireland King Defender of ye faith &c^t Between Edward Godfrye of Agamenticus of the Province or reputed or intended Province of New Somerset in New England in America gentleman of the one party And William Hook Citizen and Merchant of Bristoll and now of Agamenticus afores^d of ye other party Witnesseth that whereas S^r fferdinando Gorge of Long Ashton in ye County of Somerset Knight by his Indenture of Lease bearing date ye fourth day of may Last past before the date hereof for the Considerations thereof Expressed did

Book VIII, Fol. 121.

Demise grant and to farme Let unto yᵉ sᵈ Edward Godfrye and to Oliver Godfrye of Seale in yᵉ County of Kent Gent & to Richard Row of: yᵉ Sity of London Merchant All that part parcell portion or Tract of Land wood and wood grounds in New England aforesᵈ Lying and being within the Province or Reputed or Intended Province of New Somerset Containing and to Contain one Thousand five hundred Acres to be had & taken on yᵉ North East Side of a Certain Creek or water Course there Called by the name of Cape Neddock Creek begining at yᵉ Mouth or entrence thereof & from thence to Extend and be Extended along the Sea shore North East wards by yᵉ Space of Two English miles in yᵉ breadth thereof and at both Ends of the Said Space to Extend & be Extended up into the Inland Parts along the Side of yᵉ Said Creek by a Northwest line So far as may include yᵉ Said one Thousand & five hundred Acres Intirely together as it ware in manner of a Square together also with all yᵉ Soyles woods and underwoods Mine Mines and Mineralls as well Royal Mines of Gold and Silver as other mines & Mineralls Precious Stones quarries and all Royalties of Hauking hunting ffishing and fowling in or upon the pʳmises or any part or parcell thereof Except and all wayes reserved out of this pʳsent Demise the fifth part of all the oare of Such Royal mines of Silver & Gold as Shall be found in and upon the pmises or any part or parcell thereof heretofore reserved to be due & payable unto his Maᵗʸᵉ his heirs and Snckcessors out of yᵉ pmises To be Had and Holden unto yᵉ sᵈ Edward Godfrey Olliver Godfrey Richard Row their Executors and assignes from the day of yᵉ Date of yᵉ Same Indenture of Lease for & Dureing the term of one thousand years from thence next Ensueing and fully to be compleat and Ended Yielding & paying therefore Yearly from thenceforth Dureing the sᵈ Term unto the sᵈ Sʳ fferdinando Gorges his heirs & Assignes yᵉ yearly Rent & Rents Sum & Sums of Two Shillings the Hundred for Every Hundred Acres of the pmises that are or Shall be Imployed Either for wood pasture meadow or tillage which Shall from time to time be Inclosed and remain So or converted unto Tillage and So after that rate for lesser quantity or quantitys of Hundred or Hundreds of acres At Two of yᵉ most Usuall ffeasts or Terms in yᵉ year (that is to Say) At yᵉ feast of yᵉ Annunciation of yᵉ blessed vergen Mary and Sᵗ Michall the arch angel by Equal and Even payments as in & by yᵉ sᵈ Indenture of Lease amongst Divers other things therein Contained more plainly and at Large it doth & may appear Witnesseth now further this pʳsent Indenture That the sᵈ Edward Godfrye for divers good Causes

& Considerations him thereunto moveing Hath demised granted bargained Sould and to farm letten and by these presents Doth demise grant bargaine sell and to farme let and set to ye said William Hooke All That the one full Third part the whole into three Equal paarts to be devided of & in all ye s^d part parcell portion and Tract of land wood and wood ground and of all other the premises before mentioned to be Demissed or granted in and by ye s^d recited Indenture of lease and of Every part and parcell thereof with the appurtenances To Have and to hold ye s^d one full third part of all ye s^d part parcell portion & tract of land and of all other ye s^d pmises with ye Appurtenances to the Said William Hook his Executors administrators and Assignes from the day of ye date hereof for and dureing the term of nine hundred Ninty and nine years from thence next Ensewing fully to be compleat & Ended Yealding & paying therefore to ye s^d Edward Godfrey his Executors & Assignes the Yearly Rent of one Pepper Corn at ye feast of St Michall the arch angell and also yealding paying doeing and pforming one full Third part of all Rents & Reservations Reserved or payable for all ye s^d premisses by ye true Intent & meaning of the s^d Recited Indenture And ye s^d Edward Godfrey for himselfe his Ex^{rs} & Adm^{rs} doth Covena^t Promiss & grant to & with ye s^d William Hook his Executors Administrators & assignes by these p'sents that he ye s^d William [122] Hook his Executors administrators and assignes Shall or Lawfully may from time to time and at times hereafter Dureing the term hereby granted by and under the rents Conditions & Agreements afores^d & according to ye true meaning hereof peaceably & quietly Enter into have hold use occupie possess and Enjoy all ye s^d one full Third part of ye s^d Land and premisses & of Every part thereof without any Let Interuption Challenge claime disturbence or incumbrance of or by him ye s^d Edwd Godfrey or any other person or persons Lawfully Claiming or to Claime by or under him and that Clearly Acquitted and discharged of and from all other grants leases and Incumbrances made or done or to be made or done by him y^e s^d Edwd Godfrey In Witness whereof the partys first above named to these p'sent Indenture Interchangeably have

Book VIII, Fol. 122.

put their hands and Seals dated the day and year first above written 1638/ p me./   Edwd Godfrye (^a_Seal)
Sealed & Delivered
  In y^e presence of
  William Yeamans
  Jok. Haggatt
  ffrancis ffrenhawk
  ffra Yeamans

I Edward Godfrye do Acknowledge to have received of Humphrey Hook for part of y^e Charge in procureing a pattent for agamenticus wherein amongst others is named for planters & vndertakers the s^d Humphrey Hook as also William Hook Thomas Hook and Giles Elrige & as in ful of all their part of ye Charge in procuring — the grant for Cape nedock whereof one Third is assigned to Wm Hook by this writing as within mentioned I Say rec^d for full Satisfaction thereof ye Sum of Ten pounds witness my hand the 27th day of June 1638

These^d pattent & also of ye Charge in pcuring

                       p me Edwd Godfrey

I doe Assign all my Right & Interest in this pattent to m^r James Coffin of Newbury as Witness my hand ffebru^y 2nd 1693   William Hooke

Mr William Hooke of Salisbury Came & Acknowledged ye Above Assignation unto James Coffin to be his Act & Deed this Second of ffebruary 1693/4
                       Before me ffrancis Hooke Justice peace

James Coffin appeared before me ye Subscriber and Assigned ouer all his Right Title & Interest in this above written Instrum^t among his Daughters to Every Daughter an Equall Shear of s^d Estate June ye Twenty Third 1715/
         Thomas Noyes   Thomas Noyes Just^s peace
Witness Trustrum Coffin   James Coffin
         Daniel Coffin
Recorded According to ye Original Sep^tr 15 : 1715./
                       p Jos. Hamond Reg^r

To All Christian People to whom this present Deed of Sale Shall come Ephraim Savage of Boston in the County of Suffolk in ye Province of ye Massachusets Bay in New England Gent^l & Elizabeth his wife Send Greeting Know Yee that I ye Said Ephraim Savage & Elizabeth My wife For and in Consideration of ye Parentall Love Good Will &

Book VIII, Fol. 123.

Affection Wee oweor bare unto our Son & Daughter John & Hannah Butler & for the furthering their Comfortable Support and in part of her portion &c[t] and for divers other Good Causes & valuable Considerations hereunto Moveing Have given Granted bargained Sould Aliened conveyed & Confirmed & by these presents do give grant Bargaine Aliene Convey and Confirme unto y[e] Said John Butler & Hannah his Wife their heirs & Assignes forever All that our Farm Tract or parcell of Land Lying in Kenebeck River at a place caled Whigby alias Worsqueage Containing p Estemation one Thousand Acres be it more or Less formerly belonging to Christopher Lawson and purchased of him and though Included in y[e] Line of Purchases Pattent Yet is Excepted out of it, in y[e] Grand Deed of Sale thereof and is Butted & bounded on y[e] East: by Kenebeck River & Lyeth over against Purchases Island Southerly by a Creek that Runs out of Kenebeck River afores[d] up into a meadow And y[e] Suthermost Line of Said Land Runs from y[e] head of y[e] s[d] Creek to an Oake Tree Marked that Stands on y[e] South Side of a Meadow on y[e] West by the Land of Thomas Stevens and Northerly by a Certain bay there comonly Called & known by y[e] Name of Purchases bay or howsoever y[e] said Tract or parcell of Land or any part thereof is otherwise butted or bounded or Reputed to be butted or bounded Together with all proffits priviledges Rights Comodities & appurtenances Whatsoever to y[e] s[d] Messuage or Tenem[t] of Land belonging or in any wise appertaining To Have & to Hold, y[e] s[d] Messuage or Tenement & Land Being Butted & bounded as afores[d] with all other y[e] above granted pmises with all their rights pviledges and appurtenances whatsoever belonging to the Same Unto y[e] aboves[d] John & Hannah Butler their heirs Executors administrators & assigns forever: and y[e] s[d] Ephraim Savage & Elizabeth his wife do Covenant promiss Ingage & agree to & with y[e] s[d] John & Hannah Butler their heirs & assignes &c[t] That at y[e] time of y[e] Gift & Sale hereof and untill y[e] Delivery of these presents they are y[e] true Sole & Lawfull owners of y[e] above Granted premises and that no parson or persons Whatsoever hath any share part Title or Interest in y[e] y[e] Same & have in themselves full power just right & & Lawfull Authority to give grant bargaine Aliene Convey Confirm & dispose of y[e] Same and therefore will Warrant Defend & Secure y[e] Same from y[e] Legall Claimes or demands of any person or persons whatsoever In Witness whereof we have hereunto Set our hands & Seals this Sixth day of January One thousand Seven hundred & fourteen fifteen In y[e] first year of y[e] Reign

Book VIII, Fol. 123.

of our Soveraign Lord George by ye Grace of God of Great brittain France & Ireland &c^t
Signed Sealed & Delivered　　Ephraim Savage (Seal)
　in ye presence of us./　　Elizabeth Savage (Seal)
Peter Butler
Samuel Roch
　[123]　　　Boston January 6 1714/5
　Cap^tn Ephraim Savag & Elizabeth his wife psonally appeared and acknowledged this Instrument to be their Voluntary act & Deed　before me Penn Townsend Justis peace
Recorded According to ye Original Decemb^r ye 6th 1715./
　　　　　　　　　　　p Jos Hamond Reg^r

　To All Christian People to whome these Presents Shall come Arthur Bragdon Daniel Simpson Samuel Came Peter Nowel and Richard Milbery Selectmen for ye Town of York in ye County of York within his Maj^tys Province of ye Massachusets bay in N E do Send Greeting Know Ye that we ye fore named Selectmen being here unto improved for and in Consideration of ye Sum of Twenty pounds Current money of N E to us in hand paid before the Insealing & Delivery of these presents by Nicholas Sewall of ye town & County afores^d ye receipt whereof to full Content & Satisfaction we ye s^d Selectmen do by these presents acknowledge and thereof & of Every part thereof for our Selves for our Suckcessors & for ye Town of York do acquit Exonerate & Discharge ye s^d Nicholas Sewall his heirs Executors & Administrators Every of them forever by these presents and for Divers other good Causes & Considerations us hereunto moving we ye s^d Selectmen have given granted bargained Sold Aliened Enfeoffed Conveyed & Confirmed & by these presents do fully freely Clearly and absolutely give grant bargain Sell Aliene Enfeoffe Convey & Confirm unto ye s^d Nicholas Sewal his Heirs & assignes forever a Certain Tract or peice of land Containing two acres & fourteen poles be it more or Less Scituate Lying & being in york aforesaid buted & bounded as followeth vizt begining at a heap of Stones about four poles from ye Southwest Corner of ye old meeting house from thence runing East South East Fifteen poles & Half Some distance from Said meeting House on the South Side thereof & So Down to a white Oak Stake in ye brook by Johnsons bounds from thence on a North East line a little Northerly Twenty nine poles & half to a heap of Stones & then from Said Heap Last mentioned on a North

BOOK VIII, FOL. 123.

west Line five poles to ye aboves^d Nicholas Sewalls Land by his tanyard then from thence on a Southwest line by s^d Sewalls Land Eleven pole to his Southward Corner and from s^d Corner on a Northwest Line by s^d Suwalls bounds to y^e Town Highway & from thence by s^d Town Highway to y^e heap of Stones first Mentioned Together with all y^e Priviledges and appurtenances thereof that now do or Ever may belong to s^d Land To Have and To Hold all y$_i^e$ above Granted premisses with all & Singular y^e appurtenances thereof unto y^e s^d Nicholas Sewall His Heirs & assignes to his and their own Sole & propper use benefit and behoof from henceforth forever And further y^e s^d Selectmen Do bind them Selves & their Snckcessors in behalf of y^e Town of york afores^d from hence forth & forever hereafter to warrant and Defend all ye above granted premises & ye appurtenances thereof unto ye s^d Nicholas Sewall his Heirs & assignes against ye Lawfull Claimes & Demands of all & every person & persons whatsoever and at any Time or Times hereafter on Demand to give & pass Such further & ample assureance & Confirmation of ye premises unto ye s^d Nicholas Sewall his heirs & assigns forever as in Law or Equity Can be reasonably Devised Advised or Required In Witness whereof ye s^d Arthur Bragdon Daniel Simpson Samuel Came Peter Nowel and Richard Milbery have hereunto (as Selectmen for ye Town of york Empowered to make Sale as aboves^d Set their hands & Seals ye fifteenth Day of Febuary in ye year of our Lord 1714/5 and in ye first year of ye reign of our Soveraign lord George King of Eng:land &c^t Arthur Bragdon (Seal[a])
Signed Sealed & Delivered   Daniel Simpson (Seal[a])
  In presents of   Samuel Came (Seal[a])
  Mary Plaisteed   Peter Nowel (Seal[a])
  John Parsons   Richard Milbry (Seal[a])
  Samuel Moodey

Mr Arthur Bragdon Mr Peter Nowel Mr Daniel Simpson Mr Samuel Came Mr Richard Milbery Selectmen of ye town of York Came before me this 4th day of March 1714/5 and acknowledge this within written Instrument to be their Act & Deed   before me Lewis Bane Jus apeace
Recorded According to ye Original Octob^r 4th 1715./
         p Jos. Hamond Reg^r

To All People to whom these presents Shall Come Greeting Know ye that I Israel young of Eastham in the County of Bar:Stable in ye province of ye Massachusets Bay in New England yeoman and I Katherine Young the wife of ye s^d Israel young Being the Natural Daughter of Mr Nicholas ffrost of Newechawanock in y province afores^d Deceased for Several good Causes & Considerations us hereunto moveing & Especially for & in Consideration of Sixteen pounds to us in hand paid In Lawfull money of s^d Province by Thomas Cole of Eastham afores^d yeoman at and before ye Signing and Delivery hereof ye receipt whereof we ye s^d Israel young and Katherine young do hereby acknowledge & our Selves therewith fully Satisfied Contented and paid and tiereof & of Every part & pcell thereof Do Clearly acqui: exonerate and Discharge him ye s^d Thomas Cole his heirs and assignes forever by these presents have fully freely Clearly and absolutely given granted bargained Sold aliened Conveyed Enfeoffed and Confirmed & by these presents Do fully freely and Clearly give grant bargaine Sell Convey Confirm and Deliver unto him ye s^d Thomas Cole & to his heirs and assignes forever all and Singular our Rights Estate propperty Dowry legacie portion and proportion belonging or in any wise appertaining unto ye s^d Katherine young as one of ye heiresses to ye Estate of her Said father Nicholas ffrost Deceased it being ye one Sixth part [124] or moiety of all and Singular ye upland Meadow or marsh ground Swamp land or Messuage whatsoever that our s^d father ffrost dyed Seized of that doth of right belong & appertaine to ye aboves^d Estate lying & being in Newichawanock afores^d or else whereas may appear by ancient Deeds grant records or Claimes whatsoever to belong to ye aboves^d Estate (that is to Say) ye one Sixth part or moety of all & Singular ye real & personall Estate goods & Chattels Lands & tenement or tenements or messuage whatsoever & wheresoever that now Doth or hereafter Shall of right belong or any wise appertain unto ye aboves^d Estate of our s^d father Nicholas ffrost Deceased with all members rights priviledges & appurtences there unto belongin or In Any wise appertaining To Have and To Hold all & Singular ye before hereby granted premisses from us ye s^d Israel Young and Katherine young our heirs Executors & Admin^{rs} unto him ye s^d Thomas Cole & to heirs and assignes forever hereby declairing that before & untill ye time of granting these presents we ware ye Lawfull owners and proprietors of ye above Described and granted premisses and that ye s^d Thomas Cole may & Shall by force & vertue of these presents by him Selfe his heirs or assignes from time to time and at all times forever hereafter Have hold use Occupie possess & Enjoy ye Same without Suit lett or hindrance from us y® s^d Israel Young & Katherine young warranting y® Title & tennure thereof against any person or persons whatsoever Claimeing from by or under us or that by our right or title Shall Claime any right or title thereunto In Witness whereof we ye s^d Israel Young & Katherine young Do here unto Sett our hands & Seales ye Sixteenth Day of may and In ye first year of ye Reign our Soveraign Lord George by ye grace of God King of great Brittaine &c^t and In ye year of our Lord God one Thousand Seven Hundred & fifteen

Signed Sealed & delivered
 In presents of   Katherine her Y Young (a Seal)
 Nathan^ll ffreeman
 Mary ffreeman   mark
 Barstuble ss   Israel : Young (a Seal)

On ye Same day & year above written ye above Named Katherine young & Israel young her husband appearing before me ye Subscriber one of his Maj^trs Justices of ye peace for ye County aboves^d acknowledged ye above & within written Instrum^t to be their act and deed

           Nathaniel : ffreeman

Recorded According to ye Original June 29th 1715.

         p Jos. Hammond Reg^r

To All People to whom these presents Shall Come Greting Know ye that I William Merryfield of Cape Cod In ye County of BarStable in ye province of ye Massachusets Bay in New Engla^d yeoman and Margrett Merryfield ye wife of ye s^d William Merryfield Being ye Nattural Daughter of Mr Nicholas ffrost of Newichawanock in ye province afores^d Deceased for Several Good Causes & Considerations us hereunto moving and especially for and In Consideration of Sixteen pounds to us in hand paid In Lawfull money of s^d province by Thomas Cole of Eastham in ye County & province afores^d yeoman at & before ye Signing & Delivery hereof ye Receipt whereof we ye s^d William merryfield & margrett Merryfield Do hereby acknowledge and our Selves therewith fully Satisfied Contented & paid & thereof & of Every part and parcell thereof Do Clearly acquit Exonerate & discharge him ye Said Thomas Cole his Heirs and assignes forever by these presents have fully freely Clearly & absolutely given granted bargained Sold allinated Enfeoffed & Confirmed and by these presents D fully freely and Clearly give grant bargaine Sell Confeof & Confirm & Deliver unto him yᵉ Said Thomas Cole and to his heirs & assignes forever all & Singular on right Estate property Dowery legaly portion & proportion belonging or any wayes appertaining unto yᵉ sᵈ Margreett Merryfield as one of yᵉ heiressˢ to yᵉ Estate of her sᵈ father Nicholas ffrost Deceased it being yᵉ one Sixth part of all & Singular yᵉ upland meadow or marsh ground Swampland or Messuage whatsoever that our sᵈ father ffrost Dyed Seized of that doth of right belong & appertain to yᵉ abovesᵈ Estate Lying & being in Newichawanock aforesᵈ or Else where as may appear by ancient Deeds grants records or Claims whatsoever to belong to yᵉ abovesᵈ Estate (that is to Say) yᵉ one Sixth part or moiety of all & Singular yᵉ reall & personall Estate good Chattels Lands tenement or tenements or messuage whatsoever & wheresoever that now Doth or hereafter Shall of right belong or any wise appertaine unto yᵉ abovesᵈ Estate of our Said father Nicholas Frost Deceased with all members rights priviledges & appertences there unto belonging or in any wise appertaining To Have and To Hold all and Singular yᵉ before hereby granted premisses from us yᵉ sᵈ William Merryfield & Margriet Merryfield our our heirs Executors & adminʳˢ unto him yᵉ sᵈ Thomas Cole & to his heirs & to his assignes forever hereby Declaiming that before & untill yᵉ time of granting these presents we ware the Lawfull owners and proprietors of yᵉ above granted Bargained premisses & that yᵉ sᵈ Thomas Cole may & Shall by force & vertue of these presents by him Selfe his Heirs or assignes from time to time & at all times forever hereafter have hold use occupie possess & Injoy yᵉ Same without Suite lett hindrance from us yᵉ sᵈ William Merryfield Mergriet Merryfield warranting yᵉ title & tennure thereof against any person or persons whatsoever Claiming from by or under us or that by our right or title Shall Claime any right or title there unto In Witness whereof we yᵉ sᵈ William Merryfield Margriet Merryfield Do hereunto Sett to our hands & Seals yᵉ thirteenth Day of June & in yᵉ first year of yᵉ reign of our Soveraign Lord George by yᵉ grace of [125] God King of Great Brittaine &cᵗ and in yᵉ year of our Lord God One Thousand Seven Hundred fifteen   Margriet Merryfield (ₛₑₐₗᵃ)

Signed Sealed and Delivered
  In Presents of   her ⌡ mark
  Ruth Jackson   his
  Ralph Smith   William ƺ Merryfield (ₛₑₐₗᵃ)
  BarStuble ss   mark

On yᵉ Same Day & year above written yᵉ above named Margriet Merryfield & William Merryfield her husband

BOOK VIII, FOL. 125.

parsonally appeared before me ye SubScriber one of his Maj^{tys} Justices of ye peace for ye County aboves^d & acknowledged ye above written Instrument to be their act & Deed
John Doane

Recorded According to ye Original June 29th 1715./
p Jos. Hamond Reg^r

Bristol sc/ Anne by ye grace of god of England Scotland ffrance & Ireland Queen Defender of ye faith &c^t To ye Sheriff or marshall of ye County of york his under Sheriff or or Deputy Greeting Whereas Nicholas Morey of Taunton within our County of Bristol Carpenter by ye Consideration of our Justices of our Inferio^r Court of Common pleas holden at Bristol for & within Our County of Bristol afores^d on·ye Second Tuesday of Aprill Last past Recovereds Judgment against Joseph Bailey of: Cape porpoise in ye County of york Late of Newbery within our County of Essex yeoman for ye Sum of Thirty-three pounds Six Shillings & Eight pence Debt fifteen Shillings Six pence due for Interest & four pounds five Shillings Costs of Suite as to us Appears of record whereof Execution Remains to be done

Wee Comand you therefore that of ye goods Chatles or lands of ye Said Joseph Bailey within Your precinct you Cause to be paid & Satisfyed Unto ye s^d Nicholas Morey at ye vallue thereof in money ye afores^d Sumes being Thirty Eight pounds Seven Shillings & Two pence in ye whole with two Shillings more for this writt & thereof also to Satisfie for your own ffees and for want of goods Chattles or Lands of ye s^d Joseph Baley to be by him Shown unto you or found within your presinct to ye Acceptance of ye s^d Nicholas Morey to Sattisfie ye Sums aforeSaid We Comand to take ye body of ye s^d Joseph Bailey & him Commit unto our Goal in Kittery in our County of york afores^d & Detaine in yor Costodie with Our s^d Goal untill he pay ye Sums above mentioned with your ffees or that he be DisCharged by ye Said Nicholas Morey ye Crediter or otherwise by order of Law : Hereof fail not & make Return of this writ with your doings therein into our s^d Inferior Court of Comon pleas to be holden at Bristol within our County of Bristol afores^d upon ye Second Tuesday of July next Witness Nathan^{ll} Byfield Esqr at Bristol this Eighteenth Day of may In the Second year of our Reign Annoq Domini 1703
John Cary Clerk

A True Copie of y^e of this Execution Returned as on ye other Side of this paper Attest John Cary Cler for ye County of Bristol

Persuant to this writt to me Directed I have Levyed this Execution on a Certain parcell of Land and meadow at Capeporpoise in ye County of York of Joseph Bailey within mentioned & bounded Easterly by a Salt water Cove Northerly by land formerly in ye possession of Thomas Musey Dec^d Westerly by undivided land Sutherly by land formerly in ye Possession of John Sanders one Hundred acres more or Less which Land and Meadow was formerly Andrew Orgures & Sold to Joseph Bayley within mentioned by s^d Andrew Orgur The which land & Meadow I Delivered to ye Creaditer Nicholas Morey in part of this Execution at ye vallue of Twenty pounds in Money July ye 3^d 1703

A true Copie of ye Return .
      p Joseph Curtis jun^r Dep^{ty} Sheriff
A True Copie Recorded Augst ye 8th 1715
         p Jos: Hamond Reg^r

Bristol sc/ Anne by the Grace of God of England Scotland france & Ireland Queen Defender of ye faith (Seal) &c^t/ To ye Sheriff or marshall of our County of York his under Sheriff or Deputy Greeting Whereas Nicholas Morey of taunton within our County of Bristol Carpenter by ye Consideration of of our Justices of our Inferio^r Court of Comon pleas holden at Bristol for & within our County of Bristol afores^d on ye Second Tuesday of aprill Last past Recovered Judgment against Joseph Bailey of Capeporpoise in ye County of york lete of Newbury within our County of Essex Yeoman for ye Sum of Thirty three pounds Six Shillings Eight pence Dept four pounds twelve Shillings Interest & four pounds Six Shillings Cost of Suit as to us appears of Record whereof Execution Remains to be done We Comand you therefore of ye Goods Chattails of ye s^d Joseph Bayley within yor precinct you Cause to be paid & Satisfyed unto ye s^d Nicholas Morey at ye vallue thereof in money ye afores^d Sums being forty Two pounds four Shillings & Eight pence in ye whole with two Shilling more for this writt & thereof also to Satisfie yor own ffees And for want of goods Chattells or Lands of ye s^d Joseph Bailey to be by him Shown unto you or found within your precincts to ye Exceptance of ye s^d Nicholas

Book VIII, Fol. 126.

Morey to Satisfie ye Summs afores^d We Command you to take the body of the Said Joseph bailey & him Commit unto our Goal in Kittery in our County of york afores^d & Detain in yor Custodie within our Goal untill he pay ye full Sums above mentioned with [126] Your ffees or that he be Discharged by ye s^d Nicholas Morey ye Crediter or otherwise by order of Law hereof fail not and make return of this writt with yor doings therein into o^r Said Inferio^r Court of Comon to be holden at Bristol within our County of Bristol afores^d upon the Second Tuesday of July next Witness Nathaniel Byfield Esqr at Bristol ye Eighteenth day of may in ye Second year of our Reign Annoq, Domini 1703
 Bristol ss   John Cary Cler
a true Coppy of ye writt Returned Satisfied Attests
           John Cary Cler

 Pursuant to ye within written writt to me Directed I have Levyed ye Same on Certain Tracts of land & meadow at Capeporpoise in ye County of york of s^d Joseph Baileys Viz^t the bounds of s^d land & meadow is set forth in ye Deed Mr Nicholas Morey gave to Said Joseph Bailey of ye afores^d land and Meadow being one hundred & forty acres more or less Reference to ye s^d lands being had the afores^d Land and meadow Delivered to ye Creaditer Nicholas Morey in full of ye Execution forty Two pound four Shillings two pence with Two Shillings more for this Execution & my fees it being two pounds four Shillings & Six pence July ye 3^d 1703
 A True Coppy of the Return
Attest John Cary Cler./
      p Joseph Curtis jun^r Deputy Sheriff
 A True Copie Recorded Augst 8th 1715.
         p Jos. Hamond Reg^r

 To All Christian People to whom this present deed of Sale Shall come Nathaniel Whitney of york in ye County of york in ye Province of ye Massachusets Bay in New England Weaver with Sarah his wife Send Greeting Know Ye that ye s^d Nathaniel & Sarah for & in Consideration of fourscore pounds Money to them in hand as good as paid by Joseph Harris Joyner of ye Same Town County &c^t the Receipt whereof to full Content ye aboves^d Nathaniel & Sarah Whitney Do by these presents Acknowledg And for Divers other good Causes & Considerations them hereunto moving they ye s^d Nathaniel Whitney & Sarah his wife have given granted

BOOK VIII, FOL. 126.

bargained Sold Aliened Enfeoffed Conveyed & Confirmed & by these presents do fully freely clearly & absolutely give grant bargain Sell aliene Enfeoffe Convey & Confirm unto y^e s^d Joseph Harris his Heirs & assignes forever a Certain tract of Land & Sunken : Marsh (so Called) on y^e S W Side of york River over against y^e North of y^e old Meeting House Creek wch Land & Marsh is y^e one halfe of y^e 76 acres & $\frac{1}{2}$ wch s^d Whitney bought of Johnson Harmon of york he y^e s^d Whitney haveing Sold y^e other of s^d 76 acres & $\frac{1}{2}$ to John Stagpole and this half now by these presents Conveyed from Whitney aboves^d to y^e above Named harris is butted & bounded as is fully Expresed in Harmons Deed aboves^d to Nathaniel Whitney aboves^d & in s^d Whitneys Deed to Stagpole aboves^d Reservance being had to both Deeds wch 38 acres & $\frac{1}{4}$ of upland & Marsh be it more or less now in y^e possession of Nathaniel Whitney aboves^d Together with all Rights & priviledges any wise belonging thereunto Particularly all y^e houseing & fences & Standing Wood or Timber on y^e Same s^d Joseph Harris Shall Have & Hold to him self his Heirs & assignes to his and their own & sole use benifit and behoof from hence forth forever and ye s^d Nathaniel Whitney & Sarah his wife Do for them Selves their Heirs Executors & Admin^{rs} Covenant promiss grant & agree by these presents to and with ye s^d Joseph Harris his heirs & assignes in manner & form following (That is to Say that at ye time) of ye Ensealing & Delivery of these presents they ye s^d Nathaniel & Sarah Whitney have in them selves full Authority to Dispose of ye above bargained premises in manner as afores^d And further ye s^d Nathaniel & Sarah Whitney do hereby Covenant Promiss Bind & Oblige them Selves their Heirs Execut^{rs} & Admin^{rs} from hence forth and forever hereafter to warrant & Defend all ye above granted premisses & ye appurtenances thereof unto ye s^d Joseph Harris his heirs and Assignes against ye Lawfull Claims & Demands of all and Every person or persons whatsoever & at any Time or Times hereafter on Demand to give & pass such further & ample Assureance Confirmation of ye premisses unto ye Said Joseph Harris his Heirs and assignes forever as in Law or Equity Can be Reasonably Devised advised and required In Witness whereof ye s^d Nathaniel Whitney and Sarah his Wife have hereunto Set their hands & Seals ye first Day of Novemb^r 1715/ & in ye Second year of ye Reign of Our Soveraign Lord George King of England &c^t

Signed Sealed & Delivered   Nathaniel Whitney (Seal)
   In presents of   her
   John Kingsbury
   Samuel Donnel   Sarah ✝ Whitney (Seal)
                                  mark

Book VIII, Fol. 127.

Nathaniel Whitney & and Sarah his wife acknowledged this within written Instrum^t to be their act & deed before me this 1 day of Novr 1715   Lewis Bane Justice
Recorded According to ye Original Novr 7th 1715

                       p Jos. Hamond Reg^r

York ss   George by ye grace of God of Great Brittaine ffrance & Irel^d King Defender of ye faith &c^t
To ye Sheriff of our Court of york his und^r Sheriff or Deputy Greeting Whereas Wm Pepperrell of Kittery in our County of york Esqr by ye Consideration of our Justices of our Inferior Court of Comon pleas holden at york for & within our County of york afores^d on ye first Tuesday of July Last past recovered Judgm^t against ye Estate of Wm Roberts Late of s^d Kittery dec^d for ye Sum of fourteen pounds Thirteen Shillings & 5^d dept & one pound Eight Shillings & 4^d Cost of Suit as to us appears of record whereof Execution Remains to be done Wee Command you therefore that of ye goods [Chattells or Lands of ye s^d William Roberts dec^d within yor precinct you Cause to be paid & Satisfied unto ye s^d William Pepperrell At ye vallue thereof [127] In Money ye afore Said Sums being Sixteen pounds one Shilling and nine pence in ye whole with Two Shillings more for this writt & thereof Also to Satisfie yor Self for yor own fees hereof fayl not & make return of this writt with yor doings therein unto our s^d Inferior Court of Comon pleas to be holden at york within our County of york afores^d upon ye first Tuesday in Octob^r Next Witness John Wheelwright Esqr at wells ye 19th day of August in ye Second year of our Reign Annoq Domini 1715/   Joseph Hamond Clerk

York ss augst ye 30th 1715/
Then pursuant to ye within Execution made distress and Received of anne Roberts Widow & Relict unto ye Estate of ye within named Wm Roberts fourteen acres of Land and a Dwelling house Lying & being within the Township of Kittery within this County of york which Said Roberts died in possession of and as ye widow Saith always was Intended to Satisfie within Specyfied Debt which Land and house was accordingly Delivered to ye within Named Wm Pepperrell Esqr in full Satisfaction to him for ye whole of this Execution & Charges which Land is butted & boundes as followeth on ye South west by a Crik Cuming out of Spruce Creek in breadth fifty three poles & on ye South East by ye Land of

Book VIII, Fol. 127.

Henry Barter Running back North and by East thirty three poles to a heap of Stones and from thence North west twenty four Poles & then Southwest a little Southwardly to above s^d
Creek   p me Abraham Preble Sheriff
 Recorded According to ye Original Octob^r 4th 1715./
          p Jos Hamond Reg^r

      October ye 5th 1715/
 This may Certifie whom it may Concern that I Lewis Bane of york do acquitt & Discharge James Smith of s^d york of A Mortgage which Said Smith gave me bearing Date the 16th Day of Septr in ye year of our Lord God 1713/
   The deed   Thomas Hains   Lewis Bane
of Mortgage   Samuel Stewart
is in Fol^o 16.   York ss October 4th 1715/
 Cap^{tn} Lewis Bane above named acknowledged ye above written Instrum^t to be his free act and deed
        before Charles ffrost J peace
 Recorded According to ye Original Octob^r 4th 1715/
          p Jos. Hamond Reg^r

 To All Christian People to whom these presents Shall come John Frink of Kittery in the County of york within his Maj^{ts} Province of the Massachusets Bay in new England (Yeoman) Sends Greeting Know Yee That the Said John Frink for & in Consideration of a Certain Sum of Money To him in hand paid before the Ensealing & Delivery of these presents by Charles ffrost of ye Same Kittery Esqr the Receipt whereof to full content & Satisfaction He the Said John Frink doth by these presents Acknowledge & thereof and of Every part thereof for him Self his Heirs Executors and Administrators doth acquit exonerate & discharge the Said Charles ffrost his Heirs Executors & administrators Every of them forever by these presents And for divers other good Causes & Considerations him hereunto moving He the Said John Frink hath given granted bargained Sold Aliened Enfeoffed Conveyed & Confirmed & by these presents doth fully freely Clearly & Absolutely give grant bargain Sell Aliene Enfeoffe Convey & Confirm unto the Said Charles ffrost his Heirs & Assigns for Ever all his part portion or proportion of in or unto the Comon & undivided

Book VIII, Fol. 128.

lands within the Town Ship of Kittery & Barwick as ye Same hath bin heretofore Stands & proportioned or however otherwise the Same may hereafter be proportioned Together with all Such Rights liberties Immunities Profits Priviledges commodities Emoluments & Appurtenances as in any kind appertain thereunto with the reversions & Remainders thereof & all the Estate Right Title Interest Inheritance property possession claim & Demand whatsoever of him the Said John Frink of in & to the Same & Every part thereof To Have and To Hold all the above granted premisses with all & Singular the appurtenances thereof unto the Said Charles ffrost his Heirs & assignes To his & their own Sole proper use benefit & behoof from hence forth forever & that the Said Charles ffrost his Heirs Executors & Assigns Shall act & have the voice of ye s^d John Frink in the Ordering Settleing & Dividing of Said common rights as he the S^d John Frink might himSelfe have done before the Sale thereof & ye s^d John Frink doth hereby Covenant promiss bind & Oblige himSelfe his Heirs Executors & Administrators from hence forth and forever hereafter to warrant & Defend all the above granted premisses & the appurtenances thereof unto the Said Charles ffrost his Heirs & assignes against the Lawfull Claims & Demands of all and Every person or persons whomSoever & at any time or times hereafter on demand to give & pass Such farther & Ample assurance & Confirmation of the premisses unto the Said Charles ffrost his Heirs & assigns forever as in Law or equity can be Reasonably Devised advised or Required

In Witness whereof the Said John Frink hath hereunto Sett his hand & Seal the fourteenth day of March in ye year of our Lord One Thousand Seven Hundred and fifteen And in ye first year of the Reign of our Soveraign Lord George King of Great Brittaine France & Ireland Defend^r of ye faith &c^t

Signed Sealed & Delivered   John his ϟ2 Frink (Seal) in presents of   mark
John Belcher
Peter Whittum jun^r
Elizabeth her mark Breedeen

[128] The first of September 1715 Then John Frink parsonally appeared Before me the Subscriber one of his Maj^{ts} Justices for ye County of york & did acknowledge this above Instrument to be his free Act & Deed

                                    Wm Pepperrell

Recorded According to ye Original Decr 15th 1715.
                     p Jos. Hamond Reg^r

Book VIII, Fol. 128.

To All Christian People To whom these presents Shall Come John Ingersol of Kittery in the County of york within his Maj^{ts} Province of Massachusets Bay in Newengland Yeoman Sends Greeting Know Yee That the S^d John Ingersol for & in Consideration of a Certain Sum of Money to him in hand paid before the Ensealing & Delivery of these presents by Charles ffrost of the Same Kittery Esqr the Receipt whereof to full content & Satisfaction He the Said John Ingersol doth by these presents Acknowledge & thereof & of every part thereof for him Selfe his Heirs Executors and Administrators doth Acquit Exonerate & Discharg the Said Charles ffrost his Heirs Executors & Administrators every of them forever by these presents & for divers other good Causes & Consideration him hereunto Moving He ye s^d John Ingersol hath given granted bargained Sold Aliened Enfeoffed Conveyed & Confirmed And by these presents doth fully freely Clearly & absolutely give grant bargain Sell Aliene Enfeoffe Convey & Confirm unto the Said Charles ffrost his Heirs & assignes forever all his part portion or proportion of in or unto the Comon & undivided Land within the TownShip of Kittery & Barwick as ye Same hath bin heretofore Stated or proportioned or however otherwise the Same may hereafter be Stated or proportioned Together wth all Such Rights Liberties Immunities profits priviledges Comodities Emoluments & Appurtenances as in any kind appertaining thereunto wth ye Reversions & Remainders thereof & all the Estate Right Title Interest Inheritance property possession Claim & Demand whatsoever of him ye s^d John Ingersol of in & to ye Same and Every part thereof: To Have & To hold all ye above grant^d premisses with all and Singular the appurtenances thereof unto the Said Charles ffrost his Heirs & assigns to his & Their own Sole & proper Use benefit & behoof from hence forth & forever & that ye Said Charles ffrost his Heirs Executors Administrators or assignes Shall act and have the voice of ye Said John Ingersol in ye Ordering Setleing & Dividing of s^d Comon Right as he ye s^d John Ingersol might him Selfe have Done before the Sale thereof And ye Said John Ingersol doth hereby Covenant promiss bind & oblige himSelf his heirs Executors And Administrators henceforth & forever hereafter to warrant & Defend all ye Above granted premisses with The Appurtenances thereof unto ye s^d Charles ffrost his heirs & Assignes Against ye Lawfull Claimes & Demands of all & Every person or persons whomsoever./ And at any time or Times hereafter on demand to give & pass Such farther & ample assureance & Confirmation of ye premisses unto y̆ᵉ s̆ᵈ Charles ffrost his heirs & assignes forever as in Law or Equity can be reasonably Devised advised or Required In Witness whereof yᵉ Sᵈ John Ingersol hath hereunto Sett his hand and Seal the fourteenth day of March In yᵉ year of our Lord One Thousand Seven Hundred & fifteen & in yᵉ first year of the Reign of our Soveraign Lord George King of great Brittaine ffrance & Ireland Defendʳ of yᵉ faith &cᵗ

Signed Sealed & Delivered   Jonh _{his} ⏞ Ingersol (ˢᵉᵃˡ)
in Presents of   mark
John Belcher
John Chapman

Elizabeth ⏞ Breedeen
       mark

The 7 of Septembʳ 1715/

Then John Ingersol parsonally appeared before me one of his Majᵗˢ Justices for yᵉ County of york & Did Acknowledge this above InStrumᵗ to be his free act & Deed

                             Wᵐ Pepperrell Js peace

Recorded According to yᵉ Original Decʳ 15ᵗʰ 1715

                             p Jos Hamond Regʳ

To All Christian People to whom these presents Shall come Elihu Gunnison of Kittery in yᵉ County of york within his Majᵗʸˢ Province of yᵉ Massachusets Bay in New England (Shipwright) Sends Greeting Know Yee That yᵉ sᵈ Elihu Gunnison for and in Consideration of a Certain Sum of money to him in hand paid before yᵉ Ensealing & Delivery of these presents by Charles ffrost of yᵉ Same Kittery Esqʳ yᵉ Receipt whereof to full content & Satisfaction He the Said Elihu Gunnison Doth by these presents acknowledge & thereof & of Every part thereof for himself His heirs Executors & Administrators Doth acquit Exonerate & Discharge the Said Charles ffrost his Heirs Executors & Administrators Every of them forever by these presents And for Divers other Good Causes & ConSiderations him hereunto Moving He yᵉ Said Elihue Gunnison hath given granted bargained Sold Aliened Enfeoffed Conveyed & Confirmed And by these presents doth fully freely Clearly & Absolutely give grant bargaine Sell Aliene Enfeoffe Convey & Confirm unto the Said Charles ffrost his heirs & assignes forever all his part portion or proportion of in or unto the Comon and undivided Lands within yᵉ township of Kittery & Bar-

BOOK VIII, FOL. 129.

wick as ye Same hath bin heretofore Stated or proportioned or however other wise the Same may hereafter be stated or proportioned [129] Together with all Such Rights Liberties Immunities Profits Priviledges Commodities Emoluments & Appurtenances as in any kind appertaining thereunto wth the Reversions & Remainders thereof And all the Estate Right Title Interest Inheritance property possession Claim & Demand whatsoever of him the Said Elihu Gunnison of in & to the Same & Every part thereof To Have and To Hold all ye above granted premisses with all & Singular the Appurtenances thereof unto the Said Charles ffrost his Heirs & Assignes To his & their own Sole & proper use benefit & Behoof from henceforth forever And that the Said Charles ffrost his Heirs Execut^{rs} Administrators or assigns Shall act & have the voice of ye s^d Elihue Gunnison in y^d ordering Settleing & Dividing of s^d Comon Right as he ye s^d Elihu Gunnison might have himself Done before the Sail thereof and ye s^d Elihu Gunnison Doth hereby Covenant promiss bind & oblige himself his Heirs Execut^{rs} & Administrators from hence forth forever Hereafter To warrant & Defend all the above granted premisses wth ye appurtenances thereof unto the Said Charles ffrost his Heirs & assigns against the Lawfull Claimes & Demands of all & Every person or persons whomsoever at any time or times hereafter on Demand to give & pass Such farther & ample assureance & Confirmation of the premisses unto the Said Charles ffrost his Heirs & assignes forever as in Law or equity can be reasonably Devised Advised or Required

In Witness whereof ye s^d Elihu Gunnison hath hereunto Set his hand & Seal the twenty fifth Day of aprill In ye year of our Lord One Thousand Seven Hundred & fifteen And in ye first year of the Reign of our Soveraign Lord George King of Great Brittain France Ireland Defender of ye faith &c^t/   Elihu Gunnison (a Seal)

Signed Sealed & Delivered
  In presents of
  Jos : Curtis
         his
  John Ŏ Reed
      mark
  John Walker
  The first : Septemb^r 1715/

Then Mr Elihu Gunnison parsonally appeared before me ye Subscrib^r & did acknowledge this Instrum^t to be His free act & Deed   Wm Pepperrell Js peace

Recorded According to ye Original Decr 15th 1715./
                      p Jos Hamond Reg^r

Articles of Agreement made concluded & fully agreed upon ye Twenty eighth day of ffebruary in ye first year of ye reign of our Soveraign Lord George by ye grace of God of Great Brittaine ffrance & Ireland King Defend^r of the faith &c^t Between Charles ffrost of Kittery in ye County of york within his Maj^{tys} Province of ye Massachusets Bay in New England Esqr of ye one part And Josiah Maine of York in ye County of york afores^d yeoman on ye other part Witnesseth) Whereas there are Certaine Lands Lying Scittuate & being in ye Township of York afores^d formerly belonging to Henry Sayward Late of s^d York Milwright as may Appear by an Instrum^t bareing Date ye Second day of March in ye Seventeenth year of ye reign of King Charles ye Second Anno Domini 1665 And Whereas in ye Same Instrum^t amongst other things therein Contained there is granted unto ye s^d Henry Sayward of one Tract of Land Lying & being on ye furthermost Side of ye river Adjoining to that Tract & parcell of land which formerly was Thomas Bessons and now ye s^d Land is in ye Possession of Edward Rishworth which s^d grant Contained ye Quantity of Three hundred & fifty acres with Some giant of Swamps Appurtaining And whereas ye above mentioned Land which formerly was Thomas Bessons & afterward in ye possession of Edward Rishworth being Laid out & bounded to s^d Rishworth by ye selectmen & Survey^r of ye Town of York ye 16th of Jan^{ry} 1687./ being in breadth fifty poles & in Length one hundred & Sixty containing ye full Quantity of fifty Acres./ Now Know all men by these presents that Whereas ye Above Named Charles ffrost being in ye right & Possession of ye above mentioned Lands formerly belonging to Henry Sayward and ye Above named Josiah Maine being in ye right and possession of ye Above Mentioned Land formerly belonging to Edwd Rishworth as may Appear by ye Several Instruments on Record./ Now Know Yee that ye s^d Charles ffrost & Josiah Maine for & in Consideration of A better Conveniency to Each of their Lands do Mutually agree as followeth That is To Say: ye s^d Charles ffrost doth by these presents remitt release and forever Quitt claime to ye s^d Josiah Maine his heirs Ex^{rs} Adm^{rs} & Assigns forever ye breadth of Three poles on that side Joyning to s^d Maines Land To Have & To Hold ye s^d breadth of three poles from head to foot to ye s^d Josiah Maine his heirs Ex^{rs} Adm^{rs} & Assigns forever./ In Consideration & lieu whereof ye s^d Josiah Maine doth by these presents give & grant unto ye s^d Charles ffrost his heirs Ex^{rs} Adm^{rs} & assignes forever ye full Quantity of one Acre of Land on ye Northeast Corner of ye s^d Tract of land formerly Edwd Rishworths fronting Sixteen poles by York river and from s^d river runing Southwest into ye land Ten poles being bounded on ye Southeast side thereof by s^d ffrosts own land & on ye other Two sides by s^d Maines own Land To Have & To Hold ye s^d one acre of land with all & Singular ye priviledges & Appurtenances Thereunto belonging to [130] Him ye s^d Charles ffrost his heirs Ex^rs Adm^rs & Assignes forever And for ye True pformance hereof ye s^d Charles ffrost & Josiah Maine do bind Themselves Each to other their heirs Ex^rs Adm^rs & Assignes in ye Penal Sum of Ten pounds to be well & Truely paid by ye defective party to ye party Observing

In Witness whereof ye s^d Charles ffrost & Josiah Maine have hereunto Set their hands & Seals ye day & year first above written   Josiah Maine (a Seale)
Signed Sealed & Interchangeably   Charles ffrost (a Seale)
 Delivered In psence of us
   Daniel Emery
 Witness Sam^ll Addams
   Zacheus Trafton
York sc July 6th 1715./

The above named Josiah Maine and Charles ffrost psonally Appearing Acknowledged ye Above written Instrum^t to be their Volluntary Act & Deed./
   Before me John Wheelwright Jus^t peace
Recorded According to ye Original Decr 15th 1715./
     p Jos Hamond Reg^r

To All Christian People to whom this deed of Sale Come & Appear John Reed formerly of Berwick now of Lime in ye County of New London in ye Collony of Conecticut in New England planter Sendeth Greeting now Know yee that I ye aboves^d John Reed for divers Causes & good considerations me thereunto moveing & more especially for & in Consideration of ye Sum of forescore & five pounds in Curra^t passable money of New England to me in hand well & Truely paid by John Wentworth of ye Town of Dover in ye province of New Hampsh^r yeoman before ye ensealing & Delivery of these presents ye receipt thereof I do Acknowledge & my Selfe therewith to be fully Satisfied Contented paid & of Every part parcell & peney thereof do Exonerate Acquit & forever discharge ye afores^d John Wentworth him his heirs Ex^rs and Adm^rs by these presents have freely & Absolutely given granted bargained & sold & by these

BOOK VIII, FOL. 130.

presents do freely clearly & Absolutely give grant bargaine sell Enfeoffe Aliene Assigne Assure set over deliver & Confirm unto ye afores^d John Wentworth him his heirs Ex^{rs} Adm^{rs} & Assignes forever a Certain Tract or parcell of Land & Meadow Scittuated Lying & being in ye Town of Berwick in ye County of york Containing by Estimation fifty Acres more or Less Together with ye Addition granted thereunto by ye Town of Kittery as by their records it doth & may appear which s^d fifty Acres of Land afores^d is bounded as followeth on ye salmonfall river on ye Southwest James Barrys Land on ye Southeast and by Several Mark^t Trees on ye Northwest & is Thirty pole in breadth runing back upon a northeast & by north line Two hundred and Sixty Seven pole from s^d river all which s^d Tract of land & meadow within ye aboves^d bounds Together with ye Addition granted by ^{e} Town of Kittery as afores^d & all rights of Comonage wayes waters water Courses Timber Trees woods & underwoods and all other Imunityes Libertys priviledges Appurtenances profits & Advantages thereunto belonging or in any wise Appurtaining Shall be for & to ye whole & sole use benefit & behoofe of the afores^d John Wentworth To have & To hold all & Singular ye above bargained premisses & Every part and parcell thereof as above Expressed unto ye afores^d John Wentworth him his heirs Ex^{rs} Adm^{rs} & Assignes forever without any Mollestation Let Suit or denial of any pson or persons whatsoever The Royalty to ye Crown only Excepted & I ye afores^d John Reed do for my Selfe my heirs Ex^{rs} & Adm^{rs} Covena^t promiss agree & grant to & with ye afores^d John Wentworth that I have in my Selfe good right full power & Lawfull Anthority in & to ye above bargained premisses to sell & dispose of & that ye Same & Every part and parcell thereof are free & Clear & freely & Clearly Exonerated Acquited and discharged of & from all former & other gifts grants bargains Sales Leases wills Entailes Mortgages Judgm^{ts} Extents Executions power of thirds and all other Incumbrances of what nature or kind so ever whereby ye afores^d John Wentworth himselfe his heirs Ex^{rs} Adm^{rs} or assignes or any or Either of them Shall or may at any time hereafter any wayes be mollested in or Ejected out of ye afore bargained premisses or any part parcell or memb^r thereof by Any person or persons whatsoever Except before Excepted And further I ye afores^d John Reed do Covenant promiss Oblige & bind my Selfe my heirs Ex^{rs} & Adm^{rs} firmly by these presents ye afore bargained premisses Contained in this foregoing deed of Sale & Every part & parcell

Book VIII, Fol. 131.

thereof unto ye afores^d John Wentworth and to his heirs Execut^rs Adm^rs & Assignes to warrant & forever defend as a full free & Stable Estate of Inheritance in fee Simple forever against all psons whatsoever Except before Excepted./ In Witness whereof I have hereunto Set my hand & Seal this Twenty fifth day of Octob^r in ye year of Mans redemption one Thousand Seven hundred & fourteen Annoq, D̄m̄ 1714 Signed Sealed & Deliver^d and y^e
 Possession Given in psence of us   John O Reed (Seal)
Jno Tuttle   his mark
Richard Ockland
Howard Henderson
Dover 27th 8^br 1714./
John Reed Came & Acknowledged the foregoing Instrum^t to be his Act & Deed ye Day & year above written./
    Before me   Richard Waldron Just : peace
Recorded According to ye Originall Jan^ry 12th 1715./6
        p Jos Ham̄ond Reg^r

[131] Know all men by these presents that I John Croade of Berwick in ye County of york in ye Province of the Massachusets Bay in New England Merch^t do by these presents Confirm Assign & make Over unto ye within Named Joseph Boynton his heirs & Assignes forever and also do by these presents give him Possession of ye premisses Contained in ye deed within mentioned To have & To hold all contained therein to him and his heirs forever without any maner of reclaime Challenge or demand from me ye s^d John Croade my heirs Ex^rs or Adm^rs & from all other pson or psons Laying legall claime thereto from hence forth and forever./ & I ye s^d John Croade do also by these presents fully & Absolutely give unto ye s^d Joseph Boynton his heirs or Certain Attorney full power to make Sale of ye premisses contained in ye s^d Deed as ye proper Estate of ye s^d Joseph Boynton To have & To hold to him & his heirs forever as a good and Absolute Estate of Inheritance in fee Simple free & clear from any other or former Bargains Sales Mortgages and all other Incumbrances whatsoever./ And I ye s^d John Croade bind my Selfe my heirs Ex^rs & Adm^rs and against all other pson & psons unto ye s^d Joseph Boynton his heirs and assignes Shall and will Warrant Acquitt & Defend in y^e Quiet and

BOOK VIII, FOL. 131.

peaceable possession of y^e premisses from henceforth & forever

In Witness whereof I have hereunto Set my hand & Seal y^e 12th day of Decemb^r Annoq, Domini 1715./

Signed Sealed & D^d John Croade ($_{seal}^a$)
In p^{r}sence of
Wm Fellows   The word (Against) Interlined before
John Plumer   Signing and Sealing

Pro: N. Hampsh^r Jan^{ry} 13th 1715

Mr Jno Croade Acknowledged y^e above Instrum^t to be his Act & Deed./   Before me Jno ffrost J^t Peace

Recorded According to y^e Original Jan^{ry} 20th 1715/6
         p Jos. Hamond Reg^r

Memor^x The deed or Mortgage to which this Instrum^t has a Special referrence is recorded in this book folio: 87./
         Att^r J. Hamond Reg^r

To All Christian People to whom these presents Shall Come Greeting Know Y^e that for as much as there has been a Long difference & Controversie and diverse Lawsuits Between Nathl Raynes of york Gent and Mr John Woodman of ye Same place Concerning & relating to their Titles to a Certain Tract of Land Lying in ye Township of s^d York near a place Vulgarly Cal^d brave boat harbour which s^d Tract of Land was formerly granted to Cap^{tn} Francis Raynes dec^d by ye Town of York and by ye s^d Raynes Conveyed unto his Son in Law John Woodman as apears by An Instrum^t und^r his hand & Seal & recorded in ye records of ye County of York referrence thereunto being had may more at large Apear./ As also further Controversies relating to Several Acco^{ts} debts and reconings between ye above Nathl Raynes and John Woodman aboves^d and for ye Ending & Makeing of a final Issue of ye Above Controversies relating to their Titles to ye s^d Land and other debts & dues pretended to by ye s^d Nathl Raynes & John Woodman Aboves^d both partyes by ye good Advice of their friends that were willing to be peace makers (who are by our Savior pronounced blessed) and to the End that ye s^d psons might Live in peace Love & Unity as becomes all Christians Thes^d Nathaniel Raynes & ye s^d John Woodman have referr^d all their Differrence & Controversies to ye Arbitrament Award and Decision of Richard Cutt of Kittery Gent and Wm Godsoe of ye Same place as appears by An Obligation under ye hands & Seales of yᵉ sᵈ Nathaniel Raynes & John Woodman bareing Date yᵉ Twenty Seventh day of Janʳʸ in yᵉ year of our Lord One Thousand Seven hundred and fourteen fifteen in which obligation both partyes Stand bound Each to yᵉ other in yᵉ Penal Sum̅ of five hundred pounds Currant money of New England./ And yᵉ sᵈ Richard Cutt & William Godsoe the Subscribers hereunto do by these pʳsents Accept of yᵉ abovesᵈ request in makeing a final End of all yᵉ Controversies and differences between yᵉ sᵈ partyes from yᵉ begining of yᵉ world to yᵉ day of yᵉ Date hereof & in Order thereunto & in pursuance of yᵉ sᵈ Arbitration or Award as abovesᵈ We yᵉ sᵈ Richard Cutt & Wᵐ Godsoe haveing Examined into yᵉ Severall Controversies between both partyes do by these psents Enact Order Judge Sentence Determin Award & Decree./ Imprimis that yᵉ Above named John Woodman Shall pay or Cause to be paid unto yᵉ Above named Nathˡ Raynes or his Order Twenty pounds in Curraᵗ money of this Province at or before yᵉ Twenty Second day of July Next comeing./ Secondly that yᵉ sᵈ John Woodman his heirs & Assignes Shall from time to time & at all times forever hereafter Have Hold use Occupie possess & peaceably Enjoy all yᵉ Above mentioned Lands Contained in yᵉ above Specified deed from Capᵗⁿ Raynes to yᵉ sᵈ John Woodman referrence thereunto being had And do by these presents hereby declare & Decree that yᵉ sᵈ Nathaniel Raynsᵉˢ Claime Title & right to yᵉ abovesᵈ Land hereby intended to be Null Voyd and of non Effect and not to Mollest yᵉ sᵈ Woodman his heirs or Assigns in yᵉ Quiet Possession thereof./ Thirdly We do hereby declare Ordʳ and Decree that all Such matters as are now in Question and Controversie between yᵉ sᵈ Nathˡˡ Raynes & yᵉ sᵈ John Woodman & also for Touching & Concerning all and all maner of other Suits Quarrells Debts Debates dutyes bonds Speciallitys Controversies Transgressions Offences Strifes Contentions reconings Accoᵗˢ & Demands & all Judgmᵗˢ of Courts & Executions to be wholly Voyd ballenced and Totally Ended & of Non Effect from yᵉ begining of yᵉ world to yᵉ day of yᵉ Date hereof And that yᵉ sᵈ Nathˡ Raynes & yᵉ sᵈ John Woodman Shall not Mollest or Trouble Each other for any past matters or things from yᵉ begining of yᵉ world to yᵉ Day of yᵉ Date hereof./ And Fourthly we do hereby ordʳ and Decree that yᵉ sᵈ Nathaniel Raynes & John Woodman aforesᵈ Shall psonally Appear before yᵉ Worshipfull Wᵐ Pepperrell Esqʳ one of his Majᵗʸˢ Justices of yᵉ peace and Acknowledge their Consent to this Award or determinaion or Some other of his Majᵗʸˢ Justices and Cause These pʳsents

to be Registered in ye County Records of york [132] In Witness whereof We ye s^d Richard Cutt & Wm Godsoe have hereunto Set our hands & Seals this Tenth day of June one Thousand Seven hundred fifteen. 1715   Richard Cutt (Seal)
Wm Godsoe (Seal)

York sc/ July 19th 1715
This day Nathaniel Raynes & John Woodman both psonally appeared before me ye Subscrib^r one of his Maj^{tys} Justices for ye County of York afores^d and Acknowleeged this above Award or determination to be by both their free Consent
Wm Pepperrell
Recorded According to ye Original Septr 15th 1715./
p Jos : Hammond Reg^r

Know All men by these presents that I Thomas Wise of Georgeana Al^s york in ye Province of Maine in New England for diverse Considerations me hereunto moveing Have bargained Sold Assigned & Set over unto Isaac Guturidge now of Smuttinose Island one of ye Isles Shoales & in particular in Consideration of ye full Sum of fifteen pounds in money and fish already in hand recieved./ a Certaine Tract of Land or ground Lying on ye South Side of this river of Gorgeana/ bounded from the Cove Lying Opposite to ye house formerly known by ye name of Richard Ormsbyes house and ye afores^d Cove being called by ye name of Little cove up to ye point of Land Called Eddy point & So into ye Country South Southwest untill Twelve Acres of Land or ground be fullfilled or Compleated there is a Strip of Marsh be it more or Less within s^d bounds To Have & To Hold to him & to his heirs Execut^{rs} Adm^{rs} & Assignes forever with all ye Libertyes priviledges Imunityes thereunto belonging And do hereby for my Selfe Heirs Ex^{rs} Adm^{rs} Assignes Covenant and promiss to Warrant and defend ye Title of s^d land from all maner of persons whatsoever In Witness Whereunto I have hereto Affixed my hand & Seal this Sixth day of Decemb^r 1685.
All this being done by ye Consent of my wife
Signed Sealed & Delivered   Thomas Wise (Seal)
   In psence of us   Elizabeth Wise (Seal)
   Samuel Belcher   her T mark
   John Copleston
   John Harris
Essex sc/ Glocester Novr ye 8th 1715. Then Mr Thomas

Wise above named psonally Appeared and Acknowledged ye Above written Instrum^t with his Name & Seale Affixed thereunto to be his free act & Deed./
    Coram. John Newman Just^s peace
Recorded According to ye Original Decr 26th 1715./
       p Jos Hamond Reg^r

 Articles of Agreement between Olive Wincoll William Plaisted James Plaisted John Plaisted Elisha Plaisted Ichabod Plaisted Elizabeth Plaisted and Mehittable Plaisted as followeth Viz^t./
 That whereas there is an Estate in Lands Cattel Chattells & Moveables Left unto them by ye Late Mr Roger Plaisted of Kittery dec^d husband to ye s^d Olive & father to ye s^d Plaisteds which Estate Lyes part of it in Province of Maine and ye Rest of it in ye Colloney of Conecticut it is mutually agreed by ye psons aboves^d that all ye Lands Cattell Chattells and moveables whatsoever Lying & being within ye Province of Maine Together with one third part of ye debts which are now due to ye s^d Estate are to be and remaine to ye propper use & behoofe of ye fores^d Olive Wincoll ye Mother & Wm Plaisted James Plaisted & Elisha Plaisted her Sons forever they paying all debts that are due from ye s^d Estate of ye s^d Mr Roger Plaisted dec^d to Any person or persons w^t soever & that all other parts of ye fores^d Estate whether being & Lying in the Collony of Conecticot or else where in any other part of New England whether it be in Lands Cattell Chattells moveables &c^t Together with Two third parts of ye Debts now due to ye s^d Estate to be & remaine to ye propper use & behoofe of ye fores^d John Plaisted Ichabod Plaisted Eliz^a Plaisted & Mehittable Plaisted forever & this is our Mutual agreem^t und^r our hands & Seals this Sixteenth day of Septr in ye year of our Lord One Thousand Six hundred Eighty & Two./

Signed & Sealed   Olive 1 : 0 Wincall (Seal)
 In ye psence of us   her mark
  Daniel A Smith   Wm Plaisted (Seal)
   his mark   James Plaisted (Seal)
  Thomas Goodwin   John Plaisted (Seal)
   his / mark   . . . . . (Seal)
        Ichabod Plaisted (Seal)
        Eliz^a Plaisted (Seal)
        Mehittable A Plaisted (Seal)
          her mark

BOOK VIII, FOL. 133.

These may Certifie that w^t soever agreem^t my wife Olive hath or Shall hereafter make with her Sons & daughters concerning her Thirds or any other part of ye aboves^d Estate that may in any wise belong unto her I do hereby Allow of Ratify & Confirm as if I had done it my Selfe as Witness my hand./   John Wincoll
  Recorded According to ye Original Feb^ry 4th 1715/6.
           p Jos. Hamond Reg^r

  To All People to whom these p^rsents Shall Come Know Ye that I James Plaisted & Mary my wife of york in ye County of york in ye Province of ye Massachusets Bay in New England yeoman for & in Consideration of the Sum of one hundred pounds good & Lawfull money of New England to us in hand paid by Ichabod Plaisted of Kittery in ye County & Province afores^d Esqr the rec^t whereof I do hereby Acknowledge and my Selfe therewith fully Satisfied contented & paid have given granted bargained Sold Aliened Enfeoffed Assigned made over & Confirmed & by these psents do give grant bargaine Sell aliene Enfeoffe Assigne & make over & Confirm unto him [133] Thes^d Ichabod Plaishis heirs Ex^rs Adm^rs or Assignes for Ever all my Right Title or Interest which I have to any Lands Tennem^ts or heridita- m^t within ye Township of Kittery afores^d particularly all & Every those Tracts and parcells of Land or Meadow which of right doth or may belong unto me from ye Estate of my father Mr Roger Plaisted of Kittery afores^d Dec^d and also all other rights & proprietys within ye s^d Township of Kittery which doth of right belong unto me by any other way or means whatsoever unto him ye s^d Ichabod Plaisted his heirs Ex^rs Adm^rs or Assignes forever more To Have & To Hold ye s^d Tract or Tracts of Land and Every part and parcell there- of with all ye priviledges & Appurtenances thereunto be- longing or in any way appurtaining unto him ye s^d Ichabod Plaisted his heirs &c^t forever more And I ye s^d James Plaisted do hereby Covena^t promiss and agree to & with him ye s^d Ichabod Plaisted his heirs & Assignes to defend the Title & possession thereof against my selfe my heirs Ex^rs Adm^rs or Assignes forever and against all other persons whatsoever claiming ye Same or any part thereof from by or und^r me./ In Witness whereof I ye s^d James Plaisted and Mary my wife have hereunto Set our hands & Seals this third day of July one Thousand Seven hundred & Six and in ye fifth year

Book VIII, Fol. 133.

of yᵉ Reign of our Soveraign Lady Anne Over Engᵈ &cᵗ Queen./
Signed Sealed & Delivered
 In yᵉ presence of us
  Abrã Preble
  John Lane
  Mathew Austine

James Plaisted (ₛₑₐₗᵃ)
Mary Plaisted (ₛₑₐₗᵃ)

James Plaisted & Mary his wife Acknowledged yᵉ within written Instrumᵗ to be their Act & deed Dated at york yᵉ fifth day of July 1706 Before me Abraˣ Preble Jusᵗ peace
 Recorded Accorded to yᵉ Original Febʳʸ 4ᵗʰ 1715/6
    p Jos. Hamond Regʳ

This Indenture made yᵉ Twenty first day of May in yᵉ Sixth year of the reign of our Soveraign Lady Anne by yᵉ grace of god of England Scotland ffrance and Ireland Queen Defendʳ of yᵉ faith &cᵗ Between Edwᵈ Sargent of Newbury in yᵉ County of Essex in New England Vinter of yᵉ one part & Ichabod Plaisted of Newichawanack in yᵉ Township of Kittery in yᵉ province of Maine in New England Esqʳ on yᵉ other part Witnesseth that yᵉ sᵈ Edward Sargent for & in Consideration of yᵉ Sum of one hundred Ninety & Two pounds to him yᵉ sᵈ Edward Sargent well & Truely paid by yᵉ sᵈ Ichabod Plaisted before yᵉ ensealing & Delivery hereof yᵉ recᵗ whereof yᵉ sᵈ Edwᵈ Sargent doth hereby Acknowledge & Confess & thereof and of Every part thereof doth Acquit Exonerate & discharge yᵉ sᵈ Ichᵃ Plaisted his heirs Exʳˢ Admʳˢ or Assignes & Every of them by these pʳsents Hath granted Aliened bargained & Sold and by these pʳsents doth grant Aliene Bargaine & sell unto yᵉ sᵈ Ichabod Plaisted his heirs & assignes a Certaine Tract or parcell of Land Containing One hundred & Eighty Acres or thereabouts be it more or Less Scittuate Lying & being at a place called yᵉ Salmonfalls at Newichawanack atoresᵈ being that Land which was granted by yᵉ Town of Kittery to William Love decᵈ And is now in yᵉ Tenure or Occupation of him yᵉ sᵈ Ichabod Plaisted & is bounded upon yᵉ Land of Roger Plaisted Southerly upon yᵉ Land of Wᵐ Piles Northerly upon Salmonfalls river Westerly & upon the Comons or Comon feedings Easterly Together with all & Singular Trees Shrubs brushes woods underwoods Mines Minerals Quarries houses buildings Gardens Orchards Stables back sides Voyd grounds Yards Entries Lights Easmᵗˢ wayes Passages profits Advantages Heriditaments & Appurtenances whatsoever to ye s^d Tract of Land belonging or in any wise Appurtaining or to or with ye Same now or at any time heretofore Comonly held used Occupied or Enjoyed or Accepted reputed Taken or known to be as part parcell or memb^r thereof or Any part thereof And also all ye Estate right Title Interest use Trust possession property Claime challenge & Demand whatsoever which he ye s^d Edward Sargent now hath of in or unto ye before granted and bargained premisses with ye Appurtenances & Every or any part or parcell thereof and of in or unto all & Every other Lands whatsoever Scittuate Lying & being in ye Town or Township of Kittery afores^d To Have & To Hold ye s^d Tract of Land Containing one hundred & Eighty Acres be it more or Less and all & Singular other ye premisses before in & by these presents granted bargained & Sold or mentioned or Intended So to be with their & Every of their Appurtenances & Every part & parcell thereof unto 'ye s^d Ichabod Plaisted his heirs & assigns forever to ye only Sole propper use benefit and behoofe of him ye s^d Ichabod Plaisted his heirs & assignes forever And ye s^d Edward Sargent for himselfe his heirs Ex^{rs} & Adm^{rs} doth Covenant grant and Agree to & with ye s^d Ichabod Plaisted his heirs Ex^{rs} Adm^{rs} and Assignes & to & with every of them by these psents in maner and form following That is to Say that he ye s^d Edwd Sargent is now at ye Ensealing & Delivery hereof ye True Sole & Lawfull owner of all the before granted & bargained premisses And Stands Lawfully Siez^d thereof in his own propper right of an Absolute & Indefeaseable Estate of Inheritance in fee Simple and that he hath good right full power & Lawfull & absolute Authority to grant Convey & Assure ye s^d premisses with ye Appurtenances unto ye s^d Ichabod Plaisted his heirs & assigns in maner & form afores^d And ye s^d Edwd Sargent for himselfe his heirs Ex^{rs} & Adm^{rs} doth Covenant promiss & grant to & with ye s^d Ichabod Plaisted his heirs & assignes by these p^{r}sents that ye s^d Tract of Land & all & singular ye premisses before granted bargained & Sold & Every part & parcell thereof at ye Time of ye Ensealing & Delivery of These p^{r}sents are & be & at all Times hereafter Shall be remaine & Continue clearly Acquitted Exonerated & Discharged or otherwise upon request Sufficiently Saved & kept harmless of & from all & all maner of former bargains Sales gifts grants releases Mortgages Dowers Joyntures Judgm^{ts} Executions Entails fines forfeitures And of & from all other Titles Troubles Charges [134] And Incumbrances whatsoever had made Comitted done or Suffered by him yᵉ sᵈ Edwᵈ Sargent his heirs or assignes or by any other psou or psons Claiming by from or undᵣ him them or any of them & Also that he yᵉ sᵈ Ichabod Plaisted his heirs & Assignes shall & may at all Times forever hereafter peaceably Lawfully & Quietly have hold use Occupie possess & Enjoy all and Singular yᵉ sᵈ Tract of Land & all & Singular other yᵉ before granted & bargained pmisses with their & Every of their Appurtenances & Every part and parcell thereof without any maner of Let Suit Trouble Eviction or or disturbance of yᵉ sᵈ Edward Sargent his heirs or Assignes or of Any other pʳson or pʳsons whatsoever Claiming or to Claime by from or undᵣ him them or Any of them And yᵉ sᵈ Edward Sargent & his heirs yᵉ sᵈ Tract of Land & all & Singular yᵉ premisses in & by these pʳsents granted bargained & sold with their & Every of their Appurtenances unto yᵉ sᵈ Ichabod Plaisted his heirs & Assignes against him yᵉ sᵈ Edwᵈ Sargent his heirs & Assignes and against all & Every person & pʳsons whatsoever shall & will warrant & forever Defend by these psents the Chief Lord or Lords of yᵉ ffee or ffees only Excepted In Witness whereof yᵉ sᵈ Edwᵈ Sargent hath hereunto Set his hand & Seale yᵉ day & year first before written Annoq Domini 1707.

Sealed & Delivered in yᵉ psence of   Edward Sargent (Seal)
(The words (or Near) being first
interlined before Sealing
Wᵐ Williams
Cha: Story
Province of New Hampʳ
Edward Sargent psonally Appeared and Acknowledged yᵉ Above Instrumᵗ to be his free & Volluntary Act & Deed this Twenty first day of May in yᵉ Sixth year of yᵉ Queens Reign 1707.   Coram. Tho Phipps Jˢ Pacᵉ

Recorded According to yᵉ Original ffebʳʸ 4ᵗʰ 1715/6.
    p Jos Hamond Regʳ

Know All men by these presents that I John Rogers of Swanzey in yᵉ County of Bristol within yᵉ Province of yᵉ Massachusets Bay in New England Gentleman for & in Consideration of yᵉ Sum of Six pounds Curraᵗ money of New England to me in hand at & before yᵉ Ensealing and Delivery hereof well & Truely paid by Ichabod Plaisted of Berwick in yᵉ County of York within yᵉ Province aforesᵈ Esqʳ yᵉ recᵗ whercof I do hereby Acknowledge Have given granted Sold released & Confirmed and by these presents do give grant

Sell release & Confirm to ye s^d Ichabod Plaisted his heirs & Assignes forever all ye Right Title Interest use property claime & Demand whatsoever which I ye s^d John Rogers Ever had or now have or at any Time hereafter of right ought to have of in and unto a piece or parcell of Land Now in ye Possession of s^d Ichabod Plaisted being by Estimation About Three Acres be it more or Less being next to ye Salmonfalls mills & is buted & bounded as followeth Viz^t on ye Southeasterly Side of it with ye highway that Comes down to ye Salmonfall Mills & on ye East End of it with ye Country highway being in breadth at the Easterly End Eighty one foot to a marked post & from thence to run down Towards ye river to ye Uper end of ye Logg fence & from thence by ye Logg fence down to ye Salmonfalls river the westerly end whereof being bounded with ye s^d river To Have And To Hold ye s^d piece or parcel of Land with ye Appur̃^{ces} to him ye s^d Ichabod Plaisted his heirs & Assignes to his & their only proper use benefit & behoofe forever And I ye s^d John Rogers for me my heirs Ex^{rs} & Adm^{rs} do Covenant grant & agree to & with ye s^d Ichabod Plaisted his heirs & Assignes to Warrant & Defend ye s^d Bargained & granted pmisses & Appur̃^{ces} to ye s^d Ichabod Plaisted his heirs & assignes forever against y^e Lawfull Claimes & demands of all psons whomsoever Claiming by from or und^r me In Witness whereof I y^e s^d John Rogers have hereunto Set my hand & Seal this Tweny Ninth day of Octob^r 1714. Annoq, RR^s Georgii Nunc Magna Brittainia &c^t Primo

Signed Scaled & Delivered   John Rogers ($_{Seal}^a$)
  in y^e psence of us : The words
  [Gentleman] being first
  interlined between y^e Third
  & fourth lines on y^e other Side
  John Ballantine jun^r
  Benjamin Rolfe

Recieved y^e day & year within written of y^e within Named Ichabod Plaisted Esqr y^e Sum̃ of Six pounds in full of y^e purchase Consideration within Mentioned   p John Rogers
    Suffolk sc/ Boston Octob^r 29th 1714

John Rogers The Subscrib^r of ye within written Instruments psonally Appearing Acknowledged ye same to be his Act & deed   Before me A Davenport Just pac^s

Recorded According to ye Original Feb^{ry} 4th 1715/6.
                 p Jos. Ham̃ond Reg^r

Book VIII, Fol. 135.

[135] This writing Witnesseth that I Nicholas Shapleigh of Kittery in New England Merchant for & in Consideration of ye vallue of Three hundred pounds Starling to me in hand paid ye rec^t whereof I do hereby Acknowledge and therewith to be fully Satisfied & do for my Selfe my heirs Ex^{rs} & Adm^{rs} firmly Clearly & Absolutely give grant bargaine Sell Aliene Enfeoffe Convey Assign & make over unto Cap^{tn} Walter Barfoot now resident in Dover in New England afores^d his heirs & Assignes all ye full & whole right of & in my warehouse which is now in my possession & is Scittuate on a point of Land on ye Eastw^d Side of Piscattaqua river mouth Comonly Called and known by ye Name of ye warehouse point Together with a Tract of Land near Adjacent & thereto Adjoyning Containing Twenty pole or rod or there about in length upon a Southwest & by west line runing from ye way that lyes by ye South end of Robert Wadleys fence to a Certaine point of rocks that lyes by ye river Side butting with ye warehouse So down to Low water mark & Seven pole in breadth or thereabo runing upon a west & by north line from ye s^d South Corner of Robert Wadleys fence down to Low water mark upon a Straight line into ye Cove within ye s^d Warehouse point & is bounded by a ridge of rocks Lying by ye Side of ye s^d Robert Wadleys fence all which s^d Land and warehouse with all & Singular of ye Appurtenances thereunto belonging with their & Every of their priviledges Imunitys whatsoever he ye s^d Walter Barfoot is to Have & To Hold to him & his heirs forever free & clear Acquitted and discharged of & from all former and other Bargaines Sales Joyntures Dowryes Titles Troubles mortgages Alienations & Incumbrances w^{t}soever had made or done by me ye afores^d Nicholas Shapleigh or by any other p^{r}son or psons from by or und^r mee & I ye s^d Nicholas Shapleigh do for my Selfe my heirs Ex^{rs} & Adm^{rs} Covena^t promiss & grant to & with ye s^d Walter Barfoot his heirs & Assignes that he ye s^d Walter Barfoot his heirs & Assiges Shall peaceably & Quietly Have Hold Occupie possess & Enjoy all ye fore Demised pmisses & Every part & parcell thereof with their & Every of their Appurtenances without ye Lawfull Let Trouble Mollestation or hinderence of me ye s^d Nicholas Shapleigh or of any other pson or psons Laying claime or pretending to have Interest in or unto any of ye afore Demised pmisses or to Any part or parcell thereof & that I shall & will Save Secure Defend & keep harmless him ye s^d Walter Barfoot his heirs and Assignes from all & Every Such claime or pretence of Interest as afores^d/ And Lastly I ye s^d Nicholas Shapleigh do for my Selfe my heirs Ex^{rs}

and Adm^rs Covena^t promiss & Agree to & with ye s^d Walter Barfoot his heirs and Assignes that I ye s^d Nicholas Shapleigh Shall & will from time to Time and at all times hereafter be ready upon ye reasonable request & Demand of him ye s^d Walter Barfoot his heirs & Assigns to give & make unto him or them any other further or better Assurence of in or unto ye Afore Demised premisses or unto any part thereof as Shall by those Learned & Experienced in ye Law thought & Adjudged to be most Necessary & requisite & Expedient and for pformence of all & Singular of ye pmisses before Mentioned I ye s^d Nicholas Shapleigh do bind & Ingage my Selfe my heirs Ex^rs & Adm^rs in ye Vallueable Sum of Six hundred pounds Starling unto him ye s^d Walter Barfoot his heirs Ex^rs Adm^rs & Assignes./ In Witness whereof I have hereunto Set my hand & Seal this 24th day of Decemb^r in ye year of our Lord one Thousand Six hundred Sixty one Two Anno Domini 1662   Nicholas Shapleigh (Seal)
Signed Sealed & Delivered
 In psence of
 Thomas Kimball
 Ralph Hall
 Maj^r Nicholas Shapleigh Acknowledged this Instrum^t to be his Act & Deed : 24° Sep^t 1669.
               Before me Elias Stileman Comission^r
We und^r written do Testify that Maj^r Nicholas Shapleigh did give Quiet and peaceable possession unto Cap^tn Walter Barefoot by Turfe and Twigg of & unto ye warehouse & ground granted & Mentioned in this Bill of Sale above mentioned ye 21st of April 1663
 In p^rsence of
 Thomas Kimbal
 Robert Wadleigh
 Recorded According to ye Original Aug^st 18th 1715
               p Jos Hamond Reg^r//

To All People to whom these presents Shall come Greeting Viz^t Know Yee that I Edward Beal of york in ye County of york within her Maj^tys Province of ye Massachusets Bay in New England marriner for & in ConSideration of ye Sum of Twenty one pounds five Shillings in good & Lawfull money of ye Province afores^d to me in hand before ye Ensealing hereof well & Truely paid by Wm Pepperrell of Kittery in ye County & Province afores^d Merch^t The rec^t whereof I do hereby Acknowledge & my Selfe therewith fully Satisfied &

BOOK VIII, FOL. 136.

Contented & thereof & of Every part & parcell thereof do Exonerate Acquitt & discharge ye s^d Wm Pepperrell his heirs Ex^rs Adm^rs for ever by these psents Have given granted bargained Sold Aliened Conveyed & Confirmed & by these presents do freely fully & Absolutely give grant Bargaine Sell Aliene Convey & Confirm unto him ye s^d Wm Pepperrell his heirs & Assigns for ever one Messuage or Tract of upland & meadow Scittuate Lying & being in york afores^d Containing by Estimation Twenty one Acres & one Quarter of An Acre be it more or Less. butted & bounded began Next to Mr Pepperrells bounds a heap of Stones Two poles upon ye upland Thence East halfe a point Southerly fifteen poles to Another heap of Stones by ye river Side Towards s^d Beals house & thence South Southwest a Little Southwardly one hundred & Thirty Two poles to a white birch Tree Standing by Mr Raynes his bounds Mark^t on four sides As Also Mark^t in s^d Tree ⚯ Thence Northwest by s^d Raynses bounds Thirty poles to s^d Pepperrells own bounds a Smal beach Tree Mark^t on four sides So by s^d Pepperrells bounds to ye heap of Stones first above Mentioned To Have & To Hold ye s^d granted & bargained pmisses with all ye Timb^r Trees woods water & water Courses with all ye Appurtenances priviledges & Comoditys to ye Same belonging or in any wise Appurtaining to him ye s^d Wm Pepperrell his heirs & Assigns forever to his & their only propper use benefit and behalfe forever And I ye s^d Edward Beal for me my heirs Ex^rs Adm^rs do Covenant promiss & grant to & with ye s^d Wm Pepperrell his heirs & Assignes that before ye Ensealing hereof I am ye True Sole & Lawfull [136] Owner of ye above bargained premisses & Am Lawfully Siez^d & possest of ye Same in mine own propper right as a good perfect & Absolute Estate of Inheritance in fee Simple & have in my Selfe good right full power & Lawfull Authority to grant bargaine Sell Convey & Confirm s^d bargained premisses in maner as aboves^d & that ye s^d Wm Pepperrell his heirs and Assignes Shall & may from Time to Time & at all Times forever hereafter by force & Vertue of these presents Lawfully peaceably & Quietly have hold use Occupy possess & Enjoy ye s^d Demised & bargained pmisses with ye Appurtenances free & Clear & freely & clearly Acquitted Exonerated and discharged of from all & all maner of former & other gifts grants bargains Sales Leases Mortgages Wills Entails Joyntures dowrys Judgm^ts Executions Incumbrances & Extents./ Furthermore I ye s^d Edwd Beal for my Selfe my heirs Ex^rs Adm^rs do Covenant & Engage ye above demised premisses to him ye s^d William Pepperrell his heirs & Assignes against y^e

Lawfull Claims & demands of Any pson or psons whatsoever forever hereafter to Warra^t Secure & Defend. And Elizabeth Beal ye wife of me ye s^d Edwd Beal doth by these p^{r}sents freely willingly give Yield up & Surrend^r all her right of Dowry & Power of Thirds of in & unto ye above demised premisses unto him ye s^d Wm Pepperrell his heirs & Assignes In Witness whereof I have hereunto Set my hand & Seal the Sixth day of March in ye Twelfth year of ye reign of Our Soveraign Lady Anne by ye Grace of God Queen of Great Brittaine ffrance & Ireland and in ye year of our Lord One Thousand Seven hundred & Thirteen fourteen

It is further to be understood before Signing & Sealing of this Instrum^t That Whereas there is an Interlining in y^e fifteenth Line in these words (By y^e river side Towards s^d Beals house) was before y^e Signing Sealing & Delivering of this Instrum^t Edward Beale ($_{seal}^a$)

Signed Sealed & Delivered   Eliz^a Beal her mark ($_{seal}^a$)
In y^e psence of
William Fernald jun^r

The mark ʃ of
Samuel Hutchins
Mirram Pepperrell
York ss Jan^{ry} 3^d 1715/6

The above named Edwd Beal Acknowledged y^e Above written Instrum^t to be his free Act & Deed./

Before Charles ffrost J peace
Recorded According to y^e Original Jan^{ry} 3^d 1715/6

p Jos Hamond Reg^r

These Presents Witness that I Nathaniel Thomas of Marshfield in ye County of Plymouth Gent for a good & Valluable Consideration me thereunto moveing have Given granted & Confirmed & by these p^{r}sents for me & my heirs do freely fully & absolutely give grant & Confirm unto William Pepperrell of Kittery in ye County of york Esqr a drift or Cartway over my Land at Kittery point in ye Township of Kittery afores^d from ye way which Leads from s^d Pepperrells house to ye Publick meeting house to ye Eastermost Corner of ye Land ye s^d Pepperrell purchased of Mrs Hutchinson So as may be Least prejudicial to my other lands there not hereby granting y^e Soyle of y^e s^d Way To Have and To Hold y^e s^d Cart or drift way to be laid as afores^d to him y^e s^d William Pepperrell & his heirs./ In

Witness whereof I have hereunto Set my hand & Seal y⁰ Twenty Seaventh day of May Annoq Dom̄ 1712/

Signed Sealed & Delivered   Nathaniel Thomas ($^a_{Seal}$)
  In psence of us
  Joseph Otis
  Thomas Allen
  May yᵉ 29ᵗʰ 1712./

Nathaniel Thomas above named Acknowledged yᵉ Above written Instrument to be his Act & Deed./
     Before me./   Joseph Otis Justˢ of peace
Recorded According to yᵉ Original Janʳʸ 3ᵈ 1715/6./
         p Jos Ham̄ond Regʳ

  To All People to whom these presents Shall William Fry of the Town of Kittery in yᵉ Province of Maine In New England Sendeth Greeting Know Yee that I the Said William Fry for and in Consideration of the Sum̄ of forty Pounds Currant Money to me in hand before the Ensealing and Delivery of these presents well and truly paid by Phillip Pike of the Town of Portsm⁰ in yᵉ Province of New Hampshʳ in Newengland Taylor yᵉ receipt whereof I do hereby acknowledge and my Self therewith fully Satisfied and Contented and thereof and of Every part and pʳcell thereof do Exonerate acquit and Discharge yᵉ Said Phillip Pike his heirs Executors Administrators for Ever by these Presents Have Given granted bargained Sold aliened Enfeoffed, conveyed and Confirmed And by these psents Do freely fully and absolutely give grant Bargain Sell Alien Enfeoff Convey and Confirm unto him the Said Phillip Pike his heirs and assigns foreuʳ one peice Lot or pcell of Land containing about ten acres be it more or Less: Scituate lying & being at yᵉ mouth of Sturgeon Creek in yᵉ Township of Kittery Aforesᵈ Being butted & bounded as followeth: Viz^tt: part of it being marsh & Thatch Sturgeon Creek is on the North Side of yᵉ Land of Reinold Jinkins on yᵉ South Side Dover River on yᵉ west Side It being Comonly Called Frys Point Together with all the Marshes fflats Thatch Banks orchards gardens Trees Woods or fences that are on the Same Together with all Preveledges & Aptenances to yᵉ [137] Same belonging or in any wise apertaining Always Excepting & Reserving a burying Place of three Rod Long & Two Rod Wide fronting on Dover River with free Egres & Regress to & from it as ocasion Requires To have and To hold all the above Granted & bargained premisses with all yᵉ previledge & appurtenances to yᵉ Same belonging or in any wise appertaining (Except what is before Excepted to be to him the Said Phillip Pike his heirs and assignes forever to his and their only proper use benifit & behoof forever and I ye s^d William Fry for me my heirs Execut^rs & Admin^rs do covenant promise & grant to & with ye s^d Phillip Pike his heirs and assigns y^t before the Ensealing hereof I am ye True Sole and Lawfull owner of ye above granted and bargained p^rmises and have in my Self good right full pow^r and Lawfull authority to grant bargaine Sell Convey & Confirm s^d granted and bargained p^rmises in mañer as aboves^d and that ye s^d Phillip Pike his heirs and assignes Shall and may from time to time and at all times forev^r hereafter by force and vertue of these p^rsents Lawfully peaceably and Quiately have hold use occupy possess and Injoy all ye above granted and bargained premises with all the previledges & Comoditys & appurtenances free & Clear & freely & Clearly acquitted & Discharged from all and all maner of former and other gifts Grants bargaines Sales Leases Mortgages Wills Entailes Joynters Dowries Judgm^ts Executions Extents and from all other Troubles Charges or Incumbrances whatsoever

Furthermore I ye s^d William Fry for my Self my heirs Execut^rs and administrat^rs Do Covenant & Ingage ye above Demised premises to him ye s^d Phillip Pike his Heirs and assignes against the Lawfull claimes and Demands of any person or persons w^tsoever forever Hereafter to warrant Secure and Defend Also Hannah the wife of me the s^d Wm Fry doth by these presents Freely and willingly give Yeald up and Surrend^r all of her right of dowry and Power of thirds of in and unto ye above granted and bargained premises unto him y^e s^d Phillip Pike his heirs and assignes forever: In Witness whereof they y^e s^d William Fry & Hannah his wife have hereunty Set their hands and Seals this fourth Day of aprill In y^e year of our Lord one Thousand Seven Hundred and Thirteen — 1713/   William Fry (^a_Seal)
Sealed & delivered   the mark of——
 In the presence of us   Hannah Fry (^a_Seal)
William Brook
Jeremiah Wheelwriah
James Jeffry

Province of New Hampsh^r aprill the 4 : 1713/.

William Fry and Hannah His wife Personally Appearing before me the Subscriber one of Her Maj^tys Councill and Justices of y^e Peace for s^d Province Acknowledged y^e above Instrument to be their ffree act and Deed

Jno Wentworth

Recorded According to ye Original Jan^ry 7° 1715/

p Jos. Hañond Reg^r

Book VIII, Fol. 138.

This Indenture made ye Sixth Day of Octob^r Anno Domini One Thousand Seven Hundred fifteen and in ye Second year of ye Reign of our Soveraign Lord George King of England &c^t Between William Peirce of york in the County of york in his Maj^tys Province of ye Massachusets Bay in New England yeoman of ye one party & Mr Nathaniel Raynes of ye Same Town Gentleman of ye other party Witnesseth that ye s^d William Pearce for and in Consideration of ye Sum of Nine pounds Eight Shillings Currant money of New England to him in hand paid before the Ensealing & Delivery of these presents by Mr Nath^ll Raynes afores^d ye Receipt whereof to full Sattisfaction he ye Said William Peirce Doth by these presents acknowledge & thereof & of every part thereof for him Self his Heirs Execut^rs & administrat^rs Doth acquit Exonerate & Discharge ye s^d Nath^ll Rayns his Heirs Executors & administrators every of them forever by these presents and for Divers good Causes and Considerations him thereunto moving he ye s^d William Peirce hath given granted bargained Sold Aliened Enfeoffed Conveyed & Confirmed & by these presents Doth [138] Fully Freelly Clearly and absolutely give grant bargain Sell aliene Enfeoffe convey and Confirm unto ye s^d Nath^ll Raynes his heirs and assignes forever a certaine Tract of Land by Estimation Ten acres be it more or Less Sittuated within this Town of york upon ye neck of Land where ye s^d Bale now Liveth on ye southwest Side of york River and upon the North West or West Side of a Lott of Land Given by s^d Beal to his Son in Law Joshua Knapp the bounds are as followeth Viz^t begining by ye River Side Adjoyning to s^d Knaps bounds and runs by s^d Knaps bounds South Eighty four poles & then runs west Twenty poles to a great Hemlock Tree markt on four Sides then runs North to ye aboves^d River and So is bounded by s^d River to ye place first began at ye s^d Bale only doth Except a way of Two poles Wide for a previledge to pass and Repass to ye neck of Land next to ye Sea together wth Two Cows & orchards Houses Barnes on s^d Land and all Such rights Liberties & Imunities profits previledges Commodities Emmolum^ts and Appurtenances as in any kind Appertain thereunto with the Reversions and Remainders thereof & all ye Estate right interest Title Inheritance property possession claime & Demand w^tsoever of him ye s^d Wm Peirce of in and to the Same and of every part thereof To have and To hold all ye above granted pmises with all and Singularly ye Appurtenances — thereof unto ye s^d Nath^ll Raynes his heirs & assignes To his and their own Sole & proper use benefit & behoof from henceforth & forev^r

Book VIII, Fol. 138.

And ye s^d Wm Pearce for him self his heirs Execut^rs Admin^rs Doth hereby Covenant promise grant & agree to and with ye s^d Nath^ll Raynes his heirs & Assignes in manner & form Following (that is to Say) That at ye time of the Ensealing & Delivery of these presents he ye s^d William Pearce is ye true Sole & Lawfull owner of all ye afores^d bargained premises & Stands Lawfully Seized thereof in his own proper right & good perfect & in DefenSable Estate of Inheritance in Fee Simple having in him Self full power good right & Lawfull Authority to Sell & Dispose of ye Same in maner as afores^d & that ye s^d Nathan^ll Raynes his heirs & assignes Shall & may henceforth forever Lawfully peaceably & quietly Have Hold use Occupy and possess & Injoy ye above granted premisses with ye appurtenances thereof free & Clear & Clearly acquitted & Discharged of & from all & all manner of former & other Gifts grants bargaines Sales Leases Mortgages joyntures Dowries Judgm^ts Executions Entailes forfitures & of & & from all other Titles Troubles Charges & Incumbrances whatsoev^r had Made Committed Done or Suffered to be Done by ye s^d Wm Pearce his heirs or assignes at any time or times before ye Ensealing & Delivery hereof & further ye s^d William Peirce Doth hereby Covenant promise bind & Oblige him self his heirs Executors & administrators from henceforth and ever hereafter to Warrant & Defend all ye above granted pmises & ye appurtenances thereof unto ye Said Nath^ll Raynes his Heirs & assignes against ye Lawfull Claims & Demands of all & Every person & parsons Whomsoever and at any time or times hereafter on demand and pass Such further & Ample assurances & Confirmation of ye premisses unto ye s^d Nathan^ll Raynes his Heirs & assignes forever as in Law or Equity can be reasonably Devised advised or Required

Provided always & these presents are upon Conditions never ye Less that if ye above named Wm Peirce his Heirs Execut^rs administrat^rs Shall & Do well and truly pay or Cause to be paid unto ye afore named Nath^ll Raynes or his Certain Attorney heirs Execut^rs Admin^rs or assignes at york afores^d in ye present Currant money of ye afores^d Province as it Now passeth the Sum of Nine pounds Eight Shillings at or before ye Sixth Day of Octob^r next Ensueing wch will be in ye year of our Lord one Thousand Seven hundred Sixteen just one year after ye Date of This Instrument without fraud Coven or further Delay that then this present InStrum^t Deed of bargain & Sale & Every Clause & Article therein Contained Shall cease Determine be null

York decemr the 26: 1722 then and before Reserved of William Pearce Nine Pounds and Eight Shillings being with ye Lawfull Intrest in full for this deed of mortgage from s^d pearce to me Nathaniell Raynes
Witness Abra^m Preble Reg^r

void & of non Effect but if Default happen to be made in ye afores^d paym^t Contrary to ye true Intent thereof then to abide remain in full force Strength and virtue to all intent and purposes in ye Law Whatsoever

In Witness whereof ye s^d Wm Peirce hath hereunto Set his hand & Seal ye Day & year first above written

Signed Sealed & Delivered   W^m: Pearce (Seal)
   In Presents of
   Joseph Harris
   Sam^{ll} Donnel Junr
   Nathan^{ll} Freeman
     York ss : Octob^r 5th 1715/

William Pearce above named acknowledged ye above written Instrum^t to be his free act & Deed
         Before John Wheelwright Jus: pes
Recorded According to ye Original Jan^{ry} 3^d 1715/
           p Jos. Hamond Reg^r

[139] Whereas there is a Controversie between John Morell Junr and Richd Chick both of ye Town of Kittery in ye County of york Yeoman relateing to ye bounds & possession of their Lands & marsh or meadow Lying on ye North Side of Sturgeon Creek at or near a place Called ye round about marsh or Jinkins his marsh in Kittery afores^d for ye Issuing of which Controversie they ye s^d Morrell & Chick have refer^d them selves to ye Determination award & Arbitram^t of Cap^{tn} John: Heard & Joseph Hamond of s^d Kittery Gent whose Award Shall be a finall Issue of Said Controversie Now Know all men by these presents that Wee ye s^d John Morrell & Richd Chick Do by these psents bind & oblige our Selves our heirs Execut^{rs} & Administrat^{rs} in ye penall Sum of fifty pounds Current money of New England to Stand to & abide by ye award & Arbitram^t of ye s^d John Heard & Joseph Hamond wch s^d Sum of fifty pounds Shall be recovered without Chancery by ye party observ^t of ye party Delinquent in ye pmises In Witness whereof ye s^d John Morrell & Richard Chick have hereunto Set their hands & Seals the 27th Day of Sep^{tr} Annoq Domini: 1715/

Signed Sealed & Delivered   John Morrell (Seal)
   In presents of   Richard Chick (Seal)
   Nicholas Morrell
   Peter Wittum
Recorded According to ye Original Sep^t 27th 1715./
           p Jos. Hamond Reg^r

Kittery y{e} 27{th} of Sep{tr} 1715/

Wee y{e} Subscribers being Chosen and appointed by John Morrell Jun{r} & Richard Chick of Kittery in y{e} County of york to arbitrate & Decide a Controversie between them relating to y{e} bounds & possession of Their Lands marsh or meadow Lying on y{e} North Side of Sturgeon Creek at or near a place Called y{e} round about marsh or Jenkens his marsh As by a Certain bond und{r} their hands & Seals bereing Even Date with these presents Doth at Large appear we haveing accordingly mett on The place heard y{e} pleas & Debates of both partyes & Seen their Titles & Evidences Doe upon Deliberate Consideration of all Curcumstances Judge it meet & Just that the bounds between them Do begin at a red Oak Tree being in y{e} Line between Sam{ll} Smals Land & s{d} Rich{d} Chicks Land from thence Extending towards y{e} Creek within one rod of high water mark & thence by y{e} Creek Side Straight to a Small young Oak Tree marked & from s{d} oak to Extend Southeast Nearest to a Single pine & thence to Continue y{e} Same Course untill it Comes within one rod of highwater mark as afores{d} and So by y{e} Creek as it runs one rod from high water mark to a place Call{d} Grinums Gut and that all y{e} Land marsh & Thatch ground Lying with out s{d} Line or bound Adjoyning to s{d} Creek Do forever hereafter remain y{e} proper Estate of y{e} s{d} John Morrell Jun{r} his heirs & assignes forever & y{e} Land on y{e} Contrary Side unto s{d} Richd Chick and to his heirs & assignes forev{r} And further wee do Allow y{e} s{d} Rich{d} Chick y{e} priviledge of passing to & from Sturgeon Creek with his Teeam &c{t} w{ch} Landing place Shall be Joyning to Sam{ll} Smalls bounds by y{e} red Oak Tree first above mentioned y{e} s{d} Chick Keeping up y{e} fence So that s{d} Morrell may have no Damage y{r} by Witness our hands & Seals y{e} Day & year above written

John Heard (Seal{a})
Jos: Hamond (Seal{a})

Recorded According to y{e} Original Sep{t} 27{th} 1715./
p Jos. Hamond Reg{r}

To All People unto whom these presents Shall Come Jn{o} ffrost of New Castle in y{e} province of New Hampshier marrin{r} Send Greeting Know Yee y{t} I y{e} s{d} John ffrost for & in Consideration of y{e} Sum of Twelve pounds to me in hand or Secured to be paid by two bills bareing Even Date with this by Rich{d} Chick of Kittery in y{e} County of york in y{e} Province of y{e} Massachusets Bay in New England have given granted and Confirmed & by these presents for my Self my heirs Do fully freely & Clearly give grant Convey & Confirm unto y[e] s[d] [140] Richard Chick his heirs & assignes forever all that my Right title & Interest that I now have or ever had unto two Certain peaces of Sallt marsh Scittuate Lying & being on Sturgeon Creek in y[e] town of Kittery afores[d] as p the two Deeds from James Emery and Stephen Jenkins to my father Charles ffrost Esq[r] Dec[d] & by his will to me as Referance there unto may be had To have and To hold all and Singular y[e] aboves[d] pmises with all there appurtenances unto him y[e] s[d] Richard Chick his heirs Executors Administrators & assignes forever In Witness whereof I y[e] s[d] Jn[o] ffrost have hereunto Set my hand and Seal y[e] 28th day of January 1708/9 and in y[e] 8th year of her Maj[ts] Reign

Signed Sealed & Deliv[d]   Jn[o] ffrost (Seal)
In y[e] presents of us
Charles ffrost
Richard Alten

         York ss/ Kittery may 28th 1714

The above named John ffrost acknowledged the above Instrum[t] to be his free act & Deed
         Before me Charles ffrost J peace
Recorded According to y[e] Original Sep[t] 27th 1715./
         p Jos. Hamond Reg[r]

To All People to whom these presents Shall Come Greeting Know ye that I James Tanner of wells in the County of York in the province of the Massachusets Bay in New England for & in Consideration of y[e] Sum of Thirty pounds money to me in hand paid before the Ensealing hereof by Thomas Perkins of Greenland In y[e] province of New Hampsh[r] receipt whereof I doe hereby acknowledge & my Selfe therew[th] fully Satisfied & contented and thereof and of every part & parcell thereof doe Exonerate Acquit & Discharge the s[d] Thomas Perkins his Heirs Execut[rs] Administrators for Ever by these presents Have given granted Bargained Sold Aliened conveyed & Confirmed unto him y[e] s[d] Perkins His Heirs Executors Administrators or assignes for Ever all my right and Title of Lands that is Lying & being in y[e] Eastward part of New England Comonly Called and Known by the name of North Yarmouth or Royalls River (that is to Say the one third part of all the Lands of Jn[o] Royall Dec[d] in North Yarmouth Now In the possession of y[e] s[d] James Tanner To Have and To Hold y[e] s[d] Granted and

Book VIII, Fol. 140.

Bargained pmisses with all y⁰ Appurtenanᶜˢ priviledges to the Same belonging or in any wise appertⁿᵍ to him yᵉ sᵈ Thomas Perkins his Heirs & assignes forever And I yᵉ sᵈ James Tanner for me my heirs Executʳˢ Administrators Doe covenant and grant to and with yᵉ sᵈ Thomas Perkins his heirs and assigns that before the ensealing hereof I am the true Sole & Lawfull owner of yᵉ sᵈ Lands as aforesᵈ and am Lawfully Seized & possessed of the Same in my own proper Right as a good Estate of Inheritance in Fee Simple and Have in my Selfe good Right full power and Lawfull Authority to give grant Bargain Sell Convey & Confirm sᵈ Bargained pʳmisses in manner as aforesᵈ And that yᵉ sᵈ Thomas Perkins his Heirs and assignes Shall & may from time & at all times for Ever hereafter by force and virtue of of these presents Lawfully peaceably & Quietly Have hold Use & occupy possess & Enjoy yᵉ sᵈ Demised & Bargained premisses wᵗʰ the Appurtenances free & Clearly & freely Acquitted Exonerated & Discharged of from all & all Manner of former Gifts grants bargains Sales Leases Wills Entailes Joyntures Dowries Judgments Executions & Extents Furthermore yᵉ sᵈ James Tanner for my Selfe my Heirs Executors Administrators Doth Covenant & Ingage yᵉ above Demised pʳmisses to him yᵉ sᵈ Thomas Perkins his Heirs & assignes against the Lawfull Claims or Demands of any pʳson or pʳsons whatsoever forever Hereafter to Warrant Secure & Defend : and Phebe Tanner yᵉ Wife of me yᵉ sᵈ James Tanner Doth by these pʳsents freely and willingly give Yeald up & Surrender all her Right of Dowry & power of thirds of yᵉ above Demissed premisses unto him the said Thom Perkins His Heirs & assignes In Witness whereof the partys to these pʳsents Have Interchangably Set their hands & Seals this first Day of Octobʳ Annoq, Domini 1714 & in the first year of yᵉ Reign of our Soveraign Lord George the first of Great Brittaine france & Ireland King &cᵗ Enterlined between yᵉ ninth & tenth line before acknowledged   James Tanner (ₛₑₐₗᵃ)
Signed Sealed & Delivered   Phebe Tanner (ₛₑₐₗᵃ)
  In yᵉ presents of us
  James March
  Barachias Farnaum
  Nathaniel Farnaum

James Tanner appeared before me The Subscriber & acknowledged yᵉ above Instrument to be his free act Deed this 10ᵗʰ day of January 1714/   John Plaisted Jus pes

Recorded with yᵉ records of Deeds &cᵗ According to yᵉ Original April 7º 1715   p Jos. Hamond Regʳ

Book VIII, Fol. 141.

[141] To All People to whom these presents Shall Come Lemuel Gowen of Boston in ye County of Suffolk wthin his Maj^{tys} Province of ye Massachusets Bay in New England Mercha^t & Sarah his wife Sends Greeting &c^t Know Yee that the Said Lemuel Gowen & Sarah his wife for and in Consideration of the Sum of one Hundred pounds Currant money of New England to them in hand before ye Ensealing & Delivery of these presents well and Truly paid or Secured in ye Law to be paid by Abraham Morrell Blacksmith William Tetherly & Samuel Tetherly Shipwright all of ye Town of Kittery in ye County of york in ye province of ye Massachusets Bay in New England afores^d The receipt whereof ye s^d Lemuel Gowen & Sarah his wife Do by these presents Acknowledge & themselves therewith fully satisfied Contented & paid Have given granted bargained sold Alicned released enfeoffed & Confirmed and by These presents Do freely fully & Absolutely give grant bargaine Sell release Assigne Enfeoffe Convey Deliver and Confirm unto ye s^d Abraham Morrell William Tetherly & Samuel Tetherly their Heirs and assignes forever all Those their Certain Tracts of parcells of Land Scittuate Lying & being within ye Townrship of Kittery afore Said Containing Two Hundred Acrebe ye Same more or Less According to ye Meets & boundarys hereafter in this Instrument Mentioned & Expressed Viz^t/ One Hundred acres parcell thereof was purchased of James Gowen bounded as followeth begining on ye East Side os Stoney brook which runs out of York pond a Little to ye South of york highway & runs from s^d brook Two hundred rods East in Length and Eighty six rods in breadth North and South as p s^d Deed from s^d James Gowen on Record in ye County of york referrence being thereunto had may more at Large appear Thirty Acres or There abouts other parcell thereof being an Addition to ye s^d hundred acres granted to s^d Lem^{ll} Gowen by ye Town of Kittery May ye Tenth 1703/ About forty Acres other parcell thereof Lying on ye west Side of a Hill Known by ye Name of third hill which was Laid out and Measured unto William Gowen ye father of ye s^d Lemuel Gowen on ye 31st of December 1674/ being One hundred fifty six poles in Length North North west & Forty poles in breadth East North East bounded East with James Heards land North with Israel Hodsdens land west with John Bradys land South with york way as by ye return thereof under ye Surveyrs hand on record in s^d Town of Kittery at Large Doth Appear Thirty Acres other parcell thereof was granted unto s^d Lemuel Gowen May ye Tenth 1703/ and Laid out & measured unto him June ye 19th 1703 bounded

as by ye surveyers return on record in Kittery aforesaid At Large doth Appear/ Together with all ye Trees Timb^r woods und^r woods waters waters water Courses Swamps Meadows meadow grounds rights Members profits priviledges Comoditys Advantages heriditaments & appurtenances whatsoever upon belonging or in any wise appertaining unto ye s^d granted Tracts and parcells of Land or any part or parcell thereof & the revercōn & revercōns remaind^r & remainders rents Issues and profits thereof And all ye Estate Right Title Interest Inheritance use property Possession Claime & Demand w'soever of them ye s^d Lemuel Gowen & Sarah his wife their Heirs Executors administrators of in and to the Same To Have & To Hold ye s^d several Tracts of Land & Every part & parcell thereof and all & Singular ye premisses & Appurtenances herein before granted bargained & sold unto ye s^d Abra^m Mořell Wm Tethery & Samuel Tetherly As Tennants in Comon to be Equally Divided between them their heirs & assignes to their & Each of their only proper use benefit & behoofe forever/ And ye s^d Lemuel Gowen & Sarah his wife for themselves their Heirs Executors & Administrators Do hereby Covenant grant & Agree to & with ye s^d Abra^m Morrell William Tetherly & Samuel Tetherly their Heirs and assignes in manner following/ (That is to Say) That they ye s^d Lemuel Gowen & Sarah his wife at & untill ye Ensealing & Delivery of these presents are ye True & Lawfull owners of ye s^d Tracts of Land & pmisses & Stands Lawfully Seiz^d thereof in their own proper right as a good perfect and Absolute Estate of Inheritance in fee Simple without any Manner of Condition revercon or Limitation of Use or Uses w'soever So as to Alter change Defeat or make voyd ye same and have full power good right and Lawfull Authority to grant sell & Assure ye s^d Land & pmisses in manner as afores^d and That ye Same are free and clear & Clearly Acquitted & Discharged of and from all former and other gifts grants bargains sales Leases Mortgages [142] Wills Entayles Judgments Executions Titles Troubles charges & Incumbrances whatsoever And further that they ye s^d Lemuel Gowen & Sarah his wife their heirs Executors & administrators Shall & Will Warrant & Defend ye s^d Tracts of Land & premisses hereinbefore bargained & sold unto ye s^d Abra^m Morrell William Tetherly & Samuel Tetherly their heirs & assignes forever against ye Lawfull Claimes & Demands of all & Every pson or psons w'soever In Witness whereof y^e S^d Lemuel Gowen & Sarah his wife have hereunto Set their hands & Seales The Thirteenth Day of Novemb^r Adnoq Domini One Thousa^d seven hundred &

Book VIII, Fol. 142.

ffifteen 1715/ Annoq, RR^s Georgii Magna Brittannia &c^t
Secundo/   Lem^{ll} Gowen ($_{Seal}^{a}$)
Signed Sealed & Delivered   Sarah Gowen ($_{Seal}^{a}$)
 In presents of us
     John Banks
 Witnesses John De Graue
    Suffolk ss/ Boston Nov^{er} 30th 1715

Mr Lemuel Gowen and Sarah his wife parsonally appearing Acknowledged this Instrument to be their free act And Deed   Before me   Penn Townsend Jus pes
Recorded According to y^e Original Decr 24th 1715./
            p Jos. Hamond Reg^r

This Indenture made ye Twentyeth Day of January In ye year of our Lord seventeen hundred & fifteen Annoq, RR^s Georgii Magna Brittannia &c^t Secundo/ Between Abraham Morrell William Tetherly & Samuel Tetherly all of ye Town of Kittery in the County of York within his Maj^{tys} Province of ye Massachusets Bay in New England Witnesseth that whereas ye s^d Abra^m Morrell William Tetherly & Samuel Tetherly are & do now Stand Seized and Possessed as Tennants in Comon of & in Sundry Tracts and pcells of Land & priviledges Thereunto belonging which they Lately purchased of Lemuel Gowen of Boston Merch^t as by a Certain Deed of Sale und^r ye s^d Gowens hand & seal bearing Date ye Thirteenth Day of Novemb^r 1715/ reference being thereunto had More at Large Doth appear which Lands are scittuate in Kittery afores^d Lying and being as followeth Viz^t one hundred & Thirty acres or thereabouts parcell thereof Lyes on ye Eastward Side of Stoney brook Extending to york line being Eighty six rods in breadth North & South forty acres other parcell thereof Lying on ye west Side of a hill known by ye Name of Third hill ye bounds whereof are set forth in ye s^d Deed Thirty acres other parcell thereof was granted unto ye s^d Lemuel Gowen by thes^d Town of Kittery May the Tenth 1703 ye bounds whereof are set forth in ye Surveyers return on record in s^d Town./ Now to ye End a perpetual Division be made between ye aboves^d partys of & in all ye aboves^d Several Tracts and parcells of Land &c^t It is Covenanted concluded & agreed by & between ye partys to these presents in manner following (That is to Say that ye s^d William Tetherly & Sam^{ll} Tetherly for themselves their heirs Execut^{rs} & Adm^{rs} Covenant & agree that ye s^d Abraham Morrell his heirs & assignes Shall from hence

Book VIII, Fol. 143.

forth have Hold & peaceably Enjoy in severalty forever to his own proper Use and behoofe all ye aboves^d Two Tracts or parcells of Land Viz^t ye forty acres at Third hill and ye Thirty acres granted to Lemuel Gowen as aboves^d with the appurtenances & priviledges thereunto belonging & That ye s^d W^m & Samuel Tetherly nor their heirs Shall from hence forth claime or Demand any right Title or Interest in or to ye Same or any part thereof but that ye s^d William Tetherly & Samuel Tetherly shall at all Times for ever hereafter from all actions rights and Demands thereof be Utterly Excluded and for ever Debarred by these presents./ And the Said Abraham Morrell for himself his heirs Execut^{rs} & Adm^{rs} doth Covenant and agree that ye s^d William Tetherly & Samuel Tetherly their heirs and assignes Shall from hence forth Have Hold and peaceably Enjoy in severalty forever to their own proper Use and behoof all ye above mentioned Tract of Land between Stoney brook & york line Containing One hundred & Thirty acres with ye appurtenances and priviledges thereunto belonging & that ye s^d Abraham Morrell nor his heirs &c^t Shall from henceforth claime or Demand any right Title or Interest in or to ye Same or any part y^r of but that ye s^d Abraham Morrell Shall at all times for ever hereafter from all actions rights & Demands thereof be Uterly Excluded and forever debared by these presents./ It is further agreed between ye partys aboves^d that ye s^d Abra^m Morrell has free Liberty to Cutt One Hundred Trees on ye Eastw^d Side of Stoney brook and that ye s^d William & Sam^{ll} Tetherly have Liberty to Cutt & Carry of Twenty Trees on ye forty acres at Third hill And further it is Agreed that if there be any priviledge for ye building a Mill or Mills on any of the Said parcells of Land the Said partys are to have Equal Shears in ye Stream being at proportionable and Equal Charge in building and maintaining the Same from time to time In Witness whereof the party's to these presents have hereunto Set Their hands and seals the day & Date first above written   Abraham Morrell (seal^a)
Signed Sealed & Delivered [143] William Tetherly (seal^a)
   In presence of us   Samuel Tetherly (seal^a)
Jos Hamond
Dorcas Hamond
            York ss/ Kittery march 1 1715/6
The above named Abra^m Morrell William Tetherly & Samuel Tetherly acknowledged the above written Instrument to be their free act & Deed
                  Before me   Charles ffrost J peace
Recorded According to ye Original March 12th 1715/6
                  p Jos. Hamond Reg^r

Book VIII, Fol. 143.

To All Christian People to whom this p'sent writing Shall Come Know yee that Wee Peter Abbot Thomas Abbot & John Abbot Sons to Walter Abbot dec'd of Kittery in y'e Province of Maine for diverse good Causes & Considerations me thereunto moveing but more in Especial for that it was y'e mind & will of our deceased father aboves'd to give & dispose to his daughter Sarah then wife to M'r Thomas Wills a Tract of Land lying in Kittery near the place known to be called by y'e name of Crooked lane with a house and out houseing fenceing wood trees standing & und'r wood with all y'e Appurtenances thereunto belonging for diverse Causes & in Consideration that whereas Yet there was never a deed of Gift given by our father Walter Abbot to his daughter Sarah Concerning this Land & houseing aboves'd wee whose names above mentioned do wholly & freely give & dispose According as it was y'e mind & will of our father aboves'd all that part and parcell of Land & houseing aboves'd to M'r Thomas Wills his heirs that is to Say Two thirds to his y'e s'd Thomas Wills's Son Thomas & y'e other third to Sarah his daughter to them & their heirs forever freely & firmly to hold Enjoy & possess without y'e Let hinderence Mollestation of us whose names are above Mentioned our heirs Adm'rs or Assignes but in Case Either of these heirs Either Son or daughter Should die without Issue this whole Estate aboves'd to fall to y'e Surviveing p'ty and for y'e True pformance of y'e Same we have hereunto Interchangeably Set & Affixed our hands & Seals y'e day & date Mentioned Dated this 30th of January in y'e year 1688./ Peter Abbot (a Seal)
Signed Sealed & Delivered Thomas Abbot (a Seal)
  In y'e p'rsence of us
Leonard Drown & Eliz'a his wife

by her E·D mark

Leonard Drown within Named made Oath before me y'e Subscrib'r that he saw y'e within Named Peter & Thomas Abbot Sign Seal & Deliv'r y'e within Instrum't as their free Act & Deed and that their Brother John Abbot was Consenting to y'e Same as also s'd Drowns wife Signed as a witness at y'e Same time./ Dated in Portsm'o this 2'd of Sep't 1712 John Plaisted of his Maj'tys Council & Just peace
Recorded According to y'e Original Jan'ry 30th 1715/6
                    p Jos. Hamond Reg'r

To All Christian People to whom these p'rsents Shall Come Greeting Know yee that I Richard Gowell of Kittery in y'e

County of york in her Maj^tys Province of ye Massachusets Bay in New England Yeoman for ye Natural Love I have & do bear unto my welbeloved Son William Gowell and in Consideration thereof have given granted & forever Set over unto him & his heirs Lawfully begotten of his body. And do by these presents give grant Convey Aliene Set over & Confirm unto him ye s^d William Gowell & his heirs Lawfully begotten of his body forever Ten Acres of Land being part of Twenty Acres of Land that I reserved out of my Son Richard Gowells deed of gift bareing date 10th day of June 1710 may more At Large Appear referrence thereunto being had three Acres a part thereof is that Tract of Land that I purchased of Ensign Richd King be it more or Less & fronts ye great Cove & bolt Cove & Joyns to my other Lands & ye Lands of John Soper Together with ye barn that Stands on s^d Land with all ye Orchard & Trees of other Kind that Stand on ye s^d Tract of Land he ye s^d William Gowell to Allow his brother Richard Gowell Liberty to go through ye pmisses in ye winter to the Landing & to Land & to Lay wood or other things at ye s^d Landing & to pass or repass with his Teem for that purpose./ & ye other Seven Acres of Land Lyes at ye Northeast end of my Land or outer end thereof Together with all ye Timber wood or under wood Standing or Lying on s^d Land withall ye priviledges & Appurtenances thereunto belonging unto ye s^d Two Tracts of land To Have & To Hold all ye s^d Two Tracts of Land unto ye sole & only use benefit & behoofe of him ye s^d William Gowell & his heirs Lawfully begotten of his body forever to possess & Enjoy ye Same Imediately after ye decease of me ye s^d Richard Gowell & my wife his mother & not before/ ye peaceable possession thereof to Warrant & Defend against all psons w^tsoever Laying a Lawfull Claime thereunto In Witness whereof I have hereunto Set my hand & Seale this fourteenth day of Septemb^r in ye year of our Ld One Thousand Seven hundred and fourteen./

Signed & Sealed & Delivered   Richard Gowell (Seal)
   In ye presence of us ye Subscrib^rs   his mark
   John Tompson
        her
   Martha X Gowell
       mark

These p^rsents witness that I Richard Gowell Junr do Consent to & ratifie all that my father hath done by Vertue of this Above deed of Gift to my brother William Gowell Witness my hand & Seal this 14th day of Septr 1714

      her   Richd Gowell jun^r (Seal)
   Martha X Gowell
       mark
   John Tompson

BOOK VIII, FOL. 144.

York sc March 21ˢᵗ 1714/5
The within Named Richᵈ Gowell Acknowledged yᵉ within written Instrumᵗ to be his free Act & deed & Richᵈ Gowell Junʳ within Named also Appearing & Acknowledged yᵉ within written postscript to be his free Act & Deed
before me/ Charles ffrost J peace
Recorded According to yᵉ Original Septʳ 14ᵗʰ 1715./
p Jos. Hamond Regʳ

[144] At a Legal Town meeting held at Kittery May 24ᵗʰ 1699. Granted to Richard Gowell his heirs or assignes forever Ten acres of land if he can find it Clear of former grants
 A True Coppy as appears of record in Kittery Town book./ Examᵈ p Jos. Hamond Cler
 Know All men by these presents that I Richard Gowell of Kittery in yᵉ County of York in yᵉ Province of yᵉ Massachusets bay for a valluable Sum of money to me in hand well & truely paid by John Tompson of yᵉ same Kittery Have given granted Assigned made over & Confirmed unto yᵉ sᵈ John Tompson his heirs & Assignes for ever all my right Title and Interest of in & unto yᵉ above grant of Ten Acres of land To Have and To Hold yᵉ Same to him yᵉ sᵈ John Tompson his heirs &cᵗ without any Mollestation let or hinderence of or by me yᵉ sᵈ Richard Gowell my heirs or Assignes or by Any other pson or psons from by or undʳ me In Witness whereof I have hereunto Set my hand & Seal this Eighteenth day of Decembʳ Anno Dm 1710./
Signed Sealed & Delivered
 In yᵉ psence of us Richard ✝ Gowell (ₛₑₐₗᵃ)
Wᵐ Pepperrell Junʳ mark
Jacob Remick
York sc May 9ᵗʰ 1715
 The above named Richard Gowell psonally Appearing before me yᵉ Subscribʳ one of his Majᵗʸˢ Justices of yᵉ peace for sᵈ County York Acknowledged this Instrumᵗ to be his Act & Deed Before me Charles ffrost
 Recorded According to yᵉ Original Septʳ 14ᵗʰ 1715./
p Jos. Hamond Regʳ

 Know All men by these psents that I Clement Hughs of rtsm° in yᵉ Province of New Hampshʳ in New England

Merch^t have & do by these psents for my Selfe my heirs Ex^{rs} & Adm^{rs} fully remise release & for ever Quit claime Exonerate & discharge my brother in law John Tompson of Kittery in ye County of York in ye Province of ye Massachusets Bay in New Engl^d afores^d weaver his heirs Ex^{rs} & Adm^{rs} all & all maner of Suits Actōn Cause or Causes of Acton Acco^{ts} reconings Trespasses Strifes Variences Quarrells Controversies Debts dues Claims & Demands whatsoever of him ye s^d John Tompson from ye begining of ye world to ye date of these psents referring to ye Estate of our father John Tompson Late of Kittery afores^d dec^d In Testimony whereof I do hereunto Set my hand & Affix my Seale this Eighth day of March in ye Eleventh year of ye reign of our Soveraign Lady Anne of Great Brittaine &c^t Queen Annoq Domini 1711/2   Clem^t Hughs (a Seal)
Signed Sealed & Delivered
  In ye p^{r}sence of us
  James Libbey
  Nich^o Hastier
  Joshua Remick
    Pro N : Hamp^r
Mr Clement Hughs Acknowledged this above Instrum^t to be his Act & Deed this 8th of Septr 1715
            Before me   Theo : Atkinson J peace
Recorded According to ye Original Septr 14th 1715./
                 p Jos. Hamond Reg^r

At a Legal Town Meeting held at Kittery May 10th 1703
  Granted unto Joseph Couch fifty Acres of Land to him & his heirs forev^r to be laid out clear of former grants
               Attests Jos. Hamond Cler^d

Know All men by these psents that I Joseph Couch of Kittery in ye County of York in ye Province of ye Massachusets Bay in New England for a Valluable Sum of money to me in hand well & Truely paid by John Tompson of ye Same Kittery Have given granted Assigned made over & Confirmed unto ye s^d John Tompson his heirs & Assigns for ever All my right Title & Interest of in & to Eleven Acres of ye aboves^d Grant of Land To have & To hold ye same to him ye s^d John Tompson his heirs &c^t without any Mollestation let or hinderance from by or und^r me y^e s^d Joseph Couch my heirs or Assignes In Witness where-

of I have hereunto Set my hand & Seale this fifteenth day of April Anno Domini One Thousand Seven hundred & Twelve 1712 :/   Joseph Couch (seal)
Signed Sealed & Delivered
  In y^e psence of us
  Jos. Hamond

  Katherine $\times$ Couch
    her / mark

These psents Witness that I Roger Couch do Consent to Confirm & ratify all that my father has done by Vertue of this above written deed in referrence to y^e Above^{sd} Eleven Acres of Grant of Land that he Sold to y^e aboves^d Tompson as Witness my hand & Seal this 28th of Octob^r 1714./

    Wm Pepperrell jun^r his R mark
  Witness Jos Simpson   Roger Couch (seal)

York sc/ 28th day of Octob^r 1714   This day Roger Couch psonally Appeared before me ye Subscriber one of his Maj^{tys} Justices for ye County afores^d & Acknowledged that he gave his free Consent to what his father has here within mentioned & Acted   Wm Pepperrell Js peace

York sc/ At an Inferio^r Court of Comon pleas held by Adjournm^t at york Novemb^r ye 16th 1714 Mr Joseph Hamond psonally Appearing made Oath that he Saw ye within Named Joseph Couch Sign Seal & Deliver ye within Instrum^t as his Act & Deed and that himselfe with Katherine Couch Signed ye same as witnesses   Attests John Wheelwright

Recorded According to ye Original Septr 14th 1715/
       p Jos: Hamond Reg^r

Know All men by these presents that I Sam^{ll} Tompson of Portsm^o in ye Province of New Hampsh^r in New England house Carpenter have & do by these presents for my Selfe my heirs Ex^{rs} & Adm^{rs} fully remise release & for ever Quit claime Exonerate & Discharge my brother John Tompson of Kittery in ye County of York in ye Province of ye Massachusets bay in New England afores^d Weaver his Ex^{rs} & Adm^{rs} all & all [145] Maner of Suits Actions Cause or Causes of Actions Acco^{ts} reconings Trespasses Strifes Variences Quarrells Controvercies debts dues Claims & Demands whatsoever of him ye s^d John Tompson from ye begining of ye world to ye date of these presents referring to ye Estate of our father John Tompson Late of Kittery afores^d dec^d or any other reconing Acco^t or dealing which

heretofore have been between us of what nature of kind so ever In Testimony whereof I do hereunto Set my hand & Affix my Seale this 26th day of Novembr in ye Eleventh year of ye reign of our Soveraign Lady Anne of Great Brittaine &ct Queen Anno Dom 1712   Samuel Tompson (${}_{Seale}^{a}$)
Signed Sealed & Delivered
  In ye psence of us
  John Jones
  Thomas Knight

Thomas Knight psonally Appearing before me ye Subscribr one of his Majtys Justices of peace At Portsmo in ye Province of New Hampshr in New England & membr of Councill within ye same this 23d Augst 1715 & made Oath that he Saw Samll Tompson Sign Seal & Deliver ye Above Instrumt as his Act & that John Jones did at Same Time Sign with him as witness

John Jones Also made Oath at same Time that he did Also Sign as a Witness & that to ye best of his remembrence Samll Tompson did Sign & Seal ye sd Instrumt
                        Samll Penhallow
Recorded According to ye Original Sept 14th 1715./
                        p Jos. Hamond Regr

Know All men by these presents that I Joshua Remich of Kittery in ye County of York in ye Province of ye Massachusets bay for a Valluable Sum of Money to me in hand well & truely paid by John Tompson of ye Same Kittery Have given granted Assigned made Over & Confirmed unto ye sd John Tompson his heirs & Assigns for ever all my right Title and Interest of in & unto Six Acres & a halfe of Grant for land which is part of a grant of Twenty Acres granted to me by ye Town of Kittery May 24th 1699 To have & To hold ye same to him ye sd John Tompson his heirs & Assigns forever without any Mollestation let or hinderence of or by me ye sd Joshua Remich my heirs or Assignes or by Any other pson or psons from by or undr me

In Witness whereof I have hereunto Set my hand & Seal this 20th day of Decembr Anno Dom. 1714.
Signed Sealed & Delivered   Joshua Remich (${}_{Seal}^{a}$)
  In ye psence of us
  Jacob Remich
  Peter Staple

Book VIII, Fol. 145.

York sc/ March y'e Twenty first day 1714/5
The above Named Joshua Remich psonally Appeared before me y'e Subscrib'r one of his Maj'tys Justices for y'e County afores'd & Acknowledged this Instrum't to be his Act & deed
Charles ffrost
Recorded According to y'e Original Sept'r 14'th 1715/
p Jos Hamond Reg'r

Know All men by these presents that I Anne Jeffry Relict And Administratrix of Thomas Crockitt Late of y'e Town of Kittery Deceased with the ffree Consent of my husband Digory Jeffry & y'e more in order to fullfill y'e mind of my Late Husband Thomas Crockett afores'd Have given granted & Confirmed unto my Son In Law William Roberts and Anne his Now wife & doe by these presents Give grant & Confirm all that Tract of Land Lying & being on that Neck of Land Called Crockets Neck Near unto y'e Homestead of y'e s'd Crockett & is bounded Southward with a Little Creek & Land of John Parrott & of Lands of my Deceased Son Ephraim Crockett Northward Eastward and westward it being y'e homestead of y'e s'd Roberts with an adition of Land Six acres to his whome bounds Layed there unto by my free Consent and ord'r & Likewise by y'e free Consent of my sons Hugh & Joseph Crockett & my Daughter in Law Anne Crockett & was bounded and Laid out by y'e Town Surveyer To Have and To Hold all y'e aboves'd Tract of Land unto y'e s'd William Roberts And Anne his wife to them and their heirs for Ever and furthermore I y'e afores'd Anne Jeffry Doe Covenant to & with y'e s'd William Roberts that I am y'e true & proper owner of y'e given and granted premisses at y'e time of y'e makeing of this Instrument & Doe by these psents bind my Selfe my heirs Ex'rs & adminitrators To y'e s'd W'm Roberts his heirs or assignes y'e Peaceable & Quiet possession thereof to maintain against all persons Laying Lawfull Claime thereunto Witness my hand and seal this Twenty second day of June one Thousand Six hundred ninty five

In presents of us
Nicholas Tucker

y'e Sign of
Anne A Jeffry (seal)

y'e Sign of
Joseph ⌶ Crockett

W'm : : : Godsoe
y'e 21 June 1695/

Book VIII, Fol. 146.

Anne Jeffry Came & acknowledged this within Instrum^t to be her act & deed to her son in Law William Roberts before me William Pepperrell J peace

The six acres within mentioned to ye home bounds which was aded to ye home Lot was Enter Lin^d after Signing & Sealing of this Instrument & was Enter lin^d by ye Desier of Both partys by me Wm Pepperrell Jus : pes

Recorded According to ye Original March 12th 1715/6/
 p Jos. Hamond Reg^r

[146] Know All men by these present that I Samuel Spinney of Kittery in ye County of york in New England in Consideration of ye Naturcall Love I have and bear unto my son John Spinney Have given granted Aliened Set over & for Ever Confirm unto him his heirs & Assignes for Ever a certaine Tract of Land Containing fifteen acres being a part of that Tract of Land that I Bought of my broth^r John Shepard as appears by his Deed of Sale Referance thereunto being had may more at Large appear Together with ye one halfe of ye wood Standing or growing on s^d Land & is bounded at ye East End with ye roade that goes to york ferry and on North side with ffrancis pettegrews Land & on ye South and west with my own Land To Have and To Hold all ye s^d Tract of Land unto him ye s^d John Spinney his heirs or assignes for Ever all wayes provided & To be understood that ye s^d John Spinney is here by these presents prohibited from selling ye s^d Lands & premisses To any other person or persons Except his own Brother & that it Shall be Lawfull for ye s^d John Spinney or his heirs To Take use occupy & Possess ye s^d Land & pmisses and Every part thereof unto their own proper Use benefit & behoof for Ever against me ye s^d Samuel Spinney or my heirs or any other person by my procurement the peaceable possession y^r of To Warrant & for ever Defend against all persons Laying a Lawfull Claim thereunto In Witness where of I have hereunto Sett my hand and seal this second Day of March 1713/4 and in ye Twelfth year of her Majestyes

Reign Anne by ye Grace of God Queen of great Brittaine
ffrance & Ireland   Samuel Spinney (seal)
Signed Sealed & Delivered
  In presence of us
  the Subscribers
  Under written
  John Shepard
  Wm- Godsoe

  James ✝ Godsoe

  his mark
York ss : March 12 1715/6
The above named Samuel Spinney acknowledged tha
above written Instrument to be his free act & Deed
                  before Charles ffrost J. peace
Recorded According to ye Original March 12th 1715/6

                          p Jos. Hamond Reg^r

Know All men by these presents that I Jacob Smith of Kittery in ye County of york within his Maj^tys Province of the Massachusets Bay in New England & Prissilla my wife for Divers good Causes & Considerations us thereunto Moveing have remised released & for ever Quitt Claimed and by these presents for our selves & our heirs do fully clearly & absolutely remise release and for ever Quitt Claime unto John Rogers of ye Same Kittery in ye County & Province afores^d in his full & peaceable possession & Siezen & to his heirs & Assignes forever all Such right Estate Title Interest & demand whatsoever as we ye s^d Jacob Smith and Prissilla Smith had or ought to have in or to all or any part of ye Estate reall or personal of Richard Rogers our father Late of Kittery afores^d dece^d by any way or means whatsoever To Have and To Hold all ye Estate unto ye s^d John Rogers his heirs & assignes to ye only use & behoof of ye s^d John Rogers his heirs & assignes for Ever so that neither wee ye s^d Jacob & Prissilla nor our heirs nor any other pson or p^rsons for us or them or in our Or their Names or in ye Name right or stead of any of them shall or will by any way or means hereafter have Claime Challeng or demand any Estate right Title or Interest of in or to ye pmisses or any part or parcell thereof But from all & Every action right Estate Title Interest & Demand of in or to ye pmisses or any part or parcell thereof they & Every of them shall be uterly Excluded & for ever Debarred by these presents

In Witness whereof wee ye s^d Jacob Smith & Prissilla Smith have hereunto set our hands & seals this Twelfth day of march in ye Second year of ye Reign of our Soveraign Lord George of Great Brittaine &c^t King Annoque Domini 1715/6   Jacob Smith (Seal)

Signed Sealed & Delivered   her
In the presence of us   Prissilla ◯ Smith (Seal)
Jos: Hamond   mark
John: Tompson

York ss/ Jacob Smith & Prissilla his wife psonally appearing acknowledged ye above Instrum^t to be their act & Deed March 12th 1715/6   Before Charles ffrost J peace

Recorded According to ye Original March 12th 1715/
                          p Jos. Hamond Reg^r

Know All men by these psents that I Thomas Hoar jun^r of ye Parish of S^{tt} Mary Church in ye County of Devon in ye Kingdom of England Marrin^r and held bound & firmly Obliged unto Richard Gowell of Kittery in ye Province of Maine in New England his heirs Ex^{rs} Adm^{rs} or Assignes in ye full Sum of fforty pounds Curra^t money of New England for ye payment whereof I bind my selfe my heirs Ex^{rs} & Adm^{rs} firmly by these psents. Dated in Portsm^o New Engl^d this Twenty Third of Decemb^r Annoq Domini 1698 and in ye Tenth year of ye Reign of his Maj^{ty} King William Over Engl^d Scotland ffrance & Ireland Defend^r of ye faith &c^t

The Condition of this above obligation is such that if ye Above bounden Thomas Hoar his heirs Ex^{rs} Adm^{rs} or Assigns shall well & Truely pay or cause to be paid unto ye above Named Rich^d [147] Gowell his heirs Ex^{rs} Adm^{rs} or Assignes ye full Sum of fifteen pounds Curra^t money of England in ye NewfoundLand on or before ye Twentyeth day of Augst Next Ensveing ye Date hereof or Twenty pounds Curra^t money of New England At on or before y^e Thirtyeth day of October next Ensueing y^e date here of in Town of Portsm^o in New England or At y^e Dwelling house of s^d Gowell in Kittery afores^d then y^e above Obligation to

be Voyd & of Non Effect Else to remaine in full power force & Vertue   Thomas Hoar ($_{Seal}^{a}$)
Signed Sealed & Delivered
  In y^e psence of
  Eliz^a Harvey
       Sign of
    Jno ⟊ French
  Hen : Penney
          Province of New Hampsh^r March 30th 1716
Eliz^a Harvey psonally Appearing made Oath that shee Saw Thomas Hoar Sign & Seal y^e above Instrum^t & that John French & Henry Penney was then psent & Sign ed as witnesses./   Richd Gerrish Jus^ts Peace
  Recorded According to ye Original April 6th 1716.
                    p Jos. Hamond Reg^r

       To All Christian People to whom this psent deed of Sale Shall Come Greeting Know Ye that I Jonathan Downing of Newington in the Province of New Hampsh^r in New England Carpenter & Eliz^a his wife and Mary Nelson of ye Town & Province afores^d singlewoman for & in Consideration of ye Sum of Sixty five pounds Curant money of New England to them in hand before ye Ensealing hereof well & Truly paid by John Lydston of Kittery in ye Province of Maine in New England afores^d Shipwright The rec^t whereof we do hereby Acknowledge and our selves therewith fully Satisfied & Contented & thereof & of Every part and parcell thereof do Acquitt & Discharge ye s^d John Lydston his heirs Ex^rs Adm^rs for ever by these presents do freely fully & Absolutely give grant bargaine Sell Aliene Convey and Confirm unto him ye s^d John Lydston his heirs & Assignes forever one Messuage or Tract of land Containing by Estimation Thirty Acres be it more or Less Scittuate Lying & being in ye Town of Kittery & is butted & bounded As followeth Viz^t on ye South with ye Land of ye Afores^d Lydston on ye North with ye Land of Joseph Hill dec^d & west on ye river & with ye land of Richard King on ye East To Have & To Hold ye s^d Granted & bargained pmisses with all ye Appurtenances priviledges & Comodityes to ye same belonging or in any wise Appurtaining to him ye s^d John Lydston his heirs Ex^rs Adm^rs & Assignes for ever ye priviledges & Appurtenances not being before particularly Specified is as followeth As Orchards housing barns Easm^ts watercourses &c^t & ye afores^d Jonathan Downing Eliz^a his wife & Mary Nel-

BOOK VIII, FOL. 147.

son do for them & Every of themselves & Every of their heirs Ex[rs] Adm[rs] or assignes do Covena[t] promiss & Engage y[e] Above granted & bargained premisses against y[e] Lawfull claims & Demands of any Maner of person or persons whatsoever from by or under us y[e] afores[d] Jon[a] & Eliz[a] Downing & Mary Nelson for ever to Warrant & Defend unto him y[e] s[d] John Lydston his heirs & Assignes and that it shall & may be Lawfull for y[e] s[d] John Lydston his heirs & Assignes to enter upon & Take possession of y[e] afores[d] granted & bargained premisses So Soon as it shall properly fall unto them the Afores[d] Jon[a] Downing Eliz[a] his wife & Mary Nelson which will be on y[e] Death of their Grandmother Mary Nelson widow who is now the possessor of y[e] s[d] pmisses./ In Witness & Testimony to y[e] Truth and faithfulness of this Instrum[t] of Sale y[e] Afores[d] Jon[a] Downing and Eliz[a] his wife & Mary Nelson all & Each of them have to this present Intrum[t] Set their hands & Seals this fifth day of Aprill in y[e] second year of our Soveraign Lord George of Great Brittaine ffrance & Ireland King Defend[r] of y[e] faith Annoq[,] Domini one Thousand Seven hundred & sixteen 1716

An Adition or postscript to this deed recorded in this book ffolio 236 | Att[r] J Hamond Reg[r]

Mem[o] The words Enterlined between y[e] Two last lines but one./ in y[e] Second year of Our/ were before Signing & Sealing./   Jonathan Downing (a Seal)
Signed Sealed & Delivered   The mark of
   In psence of   Eliz[a] X Downing (a Seal)
Jacob Remich
Richard Downing   Mary Nelson (a Seal)
George Walton

        Pro New Hampsh[r] April y[e] 6th 1716.
Jon[a] Downing Eliz[a] Downing & Mary Nelson psonaly Appearing Acknowledged this within Instrum[t] in writing to be their free Act & Deed Before me/
        Richard Gerrish Just[s] peace
Recorded According to y[e] Original April : 6th 1716./
        p Jos. Hamond Reg[r]

Know all men by these presents that whereas I George Brawn Sold unto John Tidy & Whittum all y[e] Land above y[e] way that Leads from Sturgeon Creek to John Tideys as an Instrum[t] bearing Date with this makes Mention I y[e] aboves[d] Brawn Do Likewise give & Yeald up all my right

Title & Interest in all yᵉ Claims that ever I had on yᵉ Lower side of yᵉ above Mentioned way or Ever are to have to my father George Brawn & Sarah Brawn his wife upon this Condition that my father nor Mother do never Mollist yᵉ aforesᵈ Tidey nor Whittum by any Claime or Thirds or any other Claime whatsoever & upon these Conditions above Mentioned I yᵉ sᵈ Brawn Do give up all my right Title & Claim unto my aforesᵈ father & Mother & to there heirs & assignes forever To Have & To Hold to them their heirs & assignes peaceably to Enjoy yᵉ Same without Mollistation of or by me yᵉ sᵈ George Brawn my heirs Execʳ Admʳˢ or assignes & In Witness Whereof I have hereunto Set my hand & Seal this Twenteth day of March annoque Domini 1714/

Signᵈ & Sealᵈ & Delivered
in yᵉ presence of us
Nicholas Morrell
Peter wittum
John Brawn

George ⨉ Brawn (ₛₑₐₗ)
   his mark

Mary ₿ Brawn (ₛₑₐₗ)
   mark

[148] York ss/ Kittery March 24ᵗʰ 1713/4
The : within : Subscribed-George : Brawn ; & : mary. Brawn : appearing Acknowledged : yᵉ : within written : Instrumᵗ : to : be : their : free : act & : Deed : Before : me
        Charles : ffrost : J : peace
Recorded According to yᵉ Original ffebʳʸ 18ᵗʰ 1715/6
        p Jos. Hammond Regʳ

To All Christiane People to whom these Presents Shall or may come Greeting Know Ye that I Daniel Moulton now Resident At Portsmouth in the Province of New Hampshʳ in New England Marriner for Divers good causes & Consideration me hereunto moving have Granted Surrendered Remised Released and forever Quit claimed and by these Prsents Do for me my heirs Executʳˢ & Administrators Grant Surrender Remise Release & for ever Quit claim unto my Loving Brother Jeremiah Moulton of York in yᵉ County of York in yᵉ Province of yᵉ Massachusets bay in New england & to his heirs & assignes for ever all my Right Title Interest use Property Reversion claim Benefit & Demand whatsoever of in & to all yᵉ Lands Tenements Heredittaments & other Estate whatsoever both Reall & personall Lying & being in the Township of york aforesᵈ and of late belonging to my father Joseph Moulton Late of yᵉ aforesᵈ Town & County Deceased. To Have & To Hold all my sᵈ Right Title

Book VIII, Fol. 148.

Interest use & other ye before granted pmisses Unto the s^d Jeremiah Moulton his heirs & Assigns for ever to ye sole & only proper use & behoof of him ye s^d Jeremiah Moulton his Executors & Assignes for ever & I ye s^d Dan^{ll} Moulton for my self my heirs Executors & Adm^{rs} Do Covenant promiss & grant to & with ye s^d Jeremiah Moulton his heirs Executors & Administrators that he ye s^d Jeremiah Moulton his heirs & assignes Shall & may from time to time & at all Times for Ever hereafter peaceably & Quietly Have Hold occupy possess & enjoy all & Singular ye before Released premises without any Let Suit Trouble or Interuption whatsoever of or by me ye s^d Daniel Moulton my heirs Executors adm^{rs} or assignes or of or by any other person or persons w^{t}soever Laying any Lawfull Claime thereto from by or und^r me In Testimony w^{r}of I have hereunto Set my hand & Seal this Twenty Second day of Feb^{ry} Anno Domini 1715 Annoq, Regni Georgii Regis Secundo   Dan^{ll} Moulton ($_{seal}^a$)
Signed Sealed & Delivered
  In presents of us
  Sam^{ll} Penhallow
  Benj^a Gambling
  Province of New Hampsh^r 22^d Feb^{ry} 1715 Daniel Moulton personally appearing before me the Subscriber one of his Maj^{tys} Justices of y^e peace for s^d province acknowledged y^e aforegoing Instrument to be his Volluntary act & Deed
            Sam^{ll} Penhallow
  Recorded According to ye Original April 5th 1716/
            p Jos. Hamond Reg^r

To All People to whom this deed of sale shall Come Nathaniel Webber of Boston in ye County of Suffolk in New England Sawyer Sendeth Greeting./ Know Ye that whereas my father Thomas Webber formerly of Kenebeck Husbandman & my Mother Mary Webber did by Vertue of an Indian deed to my s^d ffather dated — and a deed of Gift from Uncle John Parker to my s^d Mother dated did possess & Enjoy a Certaine Tract of land being & lying on Smal point neck in ye late Province of Maine Now ye County of York in ye province of ye Massachusets Bay in New England./ bounded Northerly with Winegance Creek or John Leightons' plantation Easterly with ye river of Sagadehock or Kenebeck running down s^d river four Miles in Length or thereabouts./ Southerly with John Parkers plantation & westerly with Casco bay as p s^d deeds on record may more fully Appear

Book VIII, Fol. 149.

And did Inhabit & Improve ye Same till driven Thence by ye Indian Warr Since which they are both deceased Intestate whereby According to ye Laws of this Province One Seventh part of ye s^d lands dos descend unto ·& of right belong to me Now Know Ye that I ye s^d Nathl Webber for & in Consideration of ye Sum of Ten pounds Curra^t money of New England to me in hand well & Truely paid before ye Ensealing & Delivery of these presents by John Wentworth of Portsmouth in ye Province of New Hampshire Esqr Thomas Hutchinson Adam Winthrop David Jeffries Oliver Noyes Esq^{rs} Stephen Minot John Ruck & John Watts Gen^t All of Boston afores^d and for other good Causes Especially to promote ye settling a fishing Town Thereabouts have given granted Sold Enfeoffed & Confirmed & do by these presents freely & fully give grant Sell Enfeoffe & Confirm unto ye s^d John Wentworth Thomas Hutchinson Adam [149] Winthrop David Jeffries Oliver Noyes Stephen Minot John Ruck & John Watts their heirs Ex^{rs} Adm^{rs} & Assigns one Seventh part of ye s^d Tract of land butted & bounded as afores^d to me of right belonging as heir to my s^d father & Mother Together with with all wood Trees uplands Meadows waters water Courses priviledges & Appurtenances Thereunto in any wise belonging To Have & To Hold ye s^d Seventh part of s^d land with all priviledges & Appur^{ces} Thereunto to them ye s^d John Wentorth Thomas Hutchinson Adam Winthrop David Jeffries Oliver Noyes Stephen Minot John Ruck & John Watts their heirs & Assignes forever free & clear of all claimes & Demands of me ye s^d Nathaniel Webber my heirs Ex^{rs} or Adm^{rs} or any person or persons claiming by from or under me and free & clear from all former & other Sales Titles Mortgages & Incumbrances w^{t}soever Excepting One Mortgage made Jan^{ry} 1676/7 of s^d Land by my s^d father Thomas Webber to John Dalin or Assignes for Thirty Eight pounds Nine Shillings & Ten pence whereof Sixteen pounds Twelve shillings and Two pence was long Since paid./ In Witness whereof I have hereunto Set my hand & Seal in Boston afores^d this fourteenth day of ffeb^{ry} Anno Domini Seventeen hundred & fifteen /6 in y^e Second year of y^e reign of King George Over Great Brittaine &c^t with y^e reserve of One hundred Acres of Land to be laid out if I shall Se Cause to Settle it within four years by my selfe or heirs   Nathaniel Webber ($^a_{Seal}$)
Signed Sealed & D^d
  In psence of
  John Penhallow
  Edmund Mountfort
  Suffolk sc March 14: 1715/6

Book VIII, Fol. 149.

Nath[l] Webber Appeared this day before me y[e] Subscrib[r] & Acknowledged y[e] Aboue Instrum[t] to be his Act & Deed
Before me W[m] Harris Jus[t] Peace
Recorded According to y[e] Original May y[e] 1[st] 1716.

p Jos: Hamond Reg[r]

To All People to whom this deed of Sale shall Come Na[t]han Webber of Boston in y[e] County of Suffolk in New England Marriner only Son and heir of John Webber late of Boston Marriner Sendeth Greeting Know Ye that whereas my Grandfather Thomas Webber formerly of Kenebeck river husbandman and my Grandmother Mary Webber did by vertue of an Indian deed to my s[d] Grandfather dated and a deed of Gift from my Great Uncle John Parker to my s[d] Grandmother dated did possess & Enjoy a Certaine Tract of Land being & Lying on Small point Neck in y[e] late Province of Maine now y[e] County of York in y[e] Province of y[e] Massachusets Bay in New England bounded Northerly with Winegance Creek or John Leightons plantation Easterly with y[e] river of Sagadahock or Kenebeck runing down s[d] river four miles in length or Thereabouts Southerly with John Parkers plantation & westerly with Cascos Bay as p s[d] deeds on record may more fully Appear & did Inhabit & Improve y[e] same until driven thence by y[e] Indian Warr & both died Siezed of y[e] Same in their own right Intestate & whereby According to y[e] Laws of This Province giving to y[e] Eldest Son a double Share of y[e] land of Intestate Estates & whereas y[e] s[d] Thomas Webber & Mary Webber had five Sons & one daughter at y[e] Time of their decease So that Two full Seventh parts of s[d] land does descend unto & of right belong to me As heir of y[e] Eldest Son Now Know Ye that I y[e] s[d] Nathan Webber for & in Consideration of y[e] Sum of Ten pounds Curra[t] money of New England to me in hand well & Truely paid before y[e] Ensealing & Delivery of these presents by John Wentworth of Portsm[o] in y[e] Province of New Hampsh[r] Esq[r] Thomas Hutchinson Adam Winthrop David Jeffries Oliver Noyes Esq[rs] Stephen Minot John Ruck & Jn[o] Watts Gentlemen all of Boston afores[d] & for other good Causes & Considerations Especially to promote y[e] Settling a fishing Town thereabouts have given granted bargained Sold Aliened Enfeoffed & Confirmed & do by these psents freely & fully give grant bargaine Sell Enfeoffe & Confirm unto y[e] s[d] John Wentworth

Book VIII, Fol. 150.

Thomas Hutchinson Adam Winthrop David Jeffries Oliver Noyes Stephen Minot John Ruk & John Watts their heirs Ex^{rs} Adm^{rs} & Assignes Two full Seven parts of ye s^d Tract of land butted & bounded as afores^d to me of right belonging as heir to my father John Webber Eldest Son & heir to my Grandfather & Grandmother afores^d Together with all woods Trees uplands Meadows waters water Courses priviledges & Appur^{ces} Thereunto in any wise belonging or Appurtaining To Have & To Hold ye s^d Two full Seven parts of s^d land with all priviledges & Appurtenances thereunto to them ye s^d John Wentworth Thomas Hutchinson Adam Winthrop David Jeffries Oliver Noyes Stephen Minot John Ruck & John Watts their heirs & Assignes forever free & Clear of all Claims & demands of me s^d Nathan Webber my heirs Ex^{rs} or Adm^{rs} or any pson or psons Claiming by from or under me or my father John Webber free & Clear from all former & other Sales Titles Mortgages whatsoever Except a Mortgage to John Dalin made 1676/7 for Thirty Eight pounds Nine shillings & Ten pence : whereof Sixteen [**150**] pounds Twelve Shillings & Two pence was long Since paid./ In Witness hereof I have hereunto Set my hand & Seal in Boston afores^d the Twenty first day of ffeb^{ry} Anno Domini Seventeen hundred and fifteen/6. in ye Second year of ye reign of King George Over Great Brittaine &c^t/

Signed Sealed & Delivered   Nathan Webber ✝ (Seal)
In psence of us   his mark
John Penhallow
Edmund Mountfort

This is to Certify that I Abigail Newman of Boston in ye County of Suffolk in New England Widow Only daughter of John Webber dec^d Eldest son of Thomas Webber formrerly of Kenebeck husbandman for and in Consideration of Three pounds to me in hand paid before ye Ensealing & Delivery of These presents do hereby Quit claime to my part of ye lands At Smal point Neck Over against Arrowsick Iland As discribed in ye aboves^d deed formerly possessed by my s^d Grandfather Thomas Webber & descending from him to my Brother Nathan Webber & Me his only Children and do hereby for my Selfe my heirs Ex^{rs} & Adm^{rs} make Over grant confirm & Convey whatsoever right or share I have or ought to have in s^d lands to Aboves^d John Wentworth Esqr & his partners mentioned in s^d deed To Have & To Hold to them their heirs Ex^{rs} Adm^{rs} & Assignes in fee forever As Witness my hand & Seal hereunto Set This Twenty first day of ffeb^{ry} Anno: Domi Seventeen hundred

Book VIII, Fol. 150.

& fifteen/6 in ye second year of ye reign of King George Over Great Brittaine &c^t
Signed Sealed & D^d Abigail ᗢᖴ Newman (seal)
In psence of   her / mark
John Penhallow
Edmund Mountfort
    Suffolk sc./ The day & year above Mentioned ye Above named Nathan Webber & Abigail Newman psonally Appearing before me ye Subscrib^r one of his Maj^{tys} Justices of ye peace for ye County afores^d Acknowledged ye aboves^d Instrument to be their Act & Deed./
                       Anthony Stoddard Jus pac^s
Recorded Accorded to ye Original May 1st 1716./
                       p Jos. Hamond Reg^r

    To All People to whom this deed of Sale shall Come James Webber of Boston in ye County of Middlesex in New England Marriner Sendeth Greeting Know ye that Whereas my father Thomas Webber formerly of Kenebeck husbandman & my mother Mary Webber did by Vertue of An Indian deed to my s^d father dated   & a deed of Gift from my Uncle John Parker to my s^d Mother dated   possess & Enjoy a Certain Tract of Land being & lying on Smal point Neck in ye late Province of Maine now in ye County of York in ye Province of ye Massachusets Bay in New England bounded Northerly with Winegance creek or John Leightons plantation Easterly with ye river of Sagadahock or Kenebeck runing down s^d river over against Arrowsick Island four Miles in Length or thereabouts Southerly with John Parkers plantation & Westerly with Casco Bay as p s^d deeds on record may more fully Appear & did Inhabit & Improve ye same Till driven thence by ye Indian Warr Since which they are both deceased Intestate whereby According to ye Laws of this Province One Seventh part of s^d lands dos descend unto & of right belong to me./ Now Know Yee that I ye s^d James Webber for & in Consideration of ye Sum of Ten pounds Currant money of New England to me in hand well & Truely paid before ye Ensealing & Delivery of these presents by John Wentworth of Portsm^o in ye Province of New Hampsh^r Esqr Thomas Hutchinson Adam Winthrop David Jeffies Oliver Noyes Esq^{rs} Stephen Minot John Ruck & John Watts Gent All of Boston afores^d & for other good Causes & Considerations Especially to promote the Setling a fishing Town Thereabouts have given granted Sold Enfeoffed and Confirmed & do by these presents freely & fully give grant Sell Enfeoffe & Confirm unto ye s^d John Wentworth Thos Hutchinson Adam Winthrop David Jeffries Oliver Noyes Steph^x Minot John Ruck & John Watts their heirs Ex^{rs} Adm^{rs} & Assigns ye afore mentioned One Seventh parts of ye s^d Tract of land butted & bounded as afores^d to me of right belonging as heir to my s^d father & Mother & Also one Seventh part more of s^d land wch I bought of my brother Saml Webber Together with all woods Trees uplands Meadows Waters Watercourses priviledges & Appur^{ces} Thereunto./ to them ye s^d John Wentworth Thos Hutchinson Adam Winthrop David Jeffries Oliver Noyes Stephen Minot John Ruck & John Watts To Have & To Hold to them their heirs & Assignes for ever ye s^d Two Seventh parts of s^d Land wth all ye priviledges & Appurtenances thereunto belonging free & Clear of all claims & demands of me ye s^d James Webber my heirs Ex^{rs} or Adm^{rs} & of my brother Saml Webber his heirs Ex^{rs} or Adm^{rs} or any person or persons Claiming by from or under us [151] Or them and free & Clear from all former & other Sales Titles Mortgages or Incumbrances whatsoever Excepting one Mortgage made Jan^{ry} 1676/7. of s^d land by my s^d father Thomas Webber to John Dalin or Assigns for Thirty Eight pounds Nine shillings & Ten pence whereof Sixteen pounds Twelve shillings & 2^d was long Since paid./ In Witness w^{r}of I have hereunto Set my hand & Seal in Boston afores^d this Nineteenth day of March Anno Dom^i Seventeen hundred & fifteen/6 in the Second year of y^e reign of King George Over Great Brittaine &c^a Reserving One hundred Acres of Land butting on y^e river to me & my heirs

Signed Seal^d & Dd   James Webber ($_{Seal}^a$)
 In presence of
John Penhallow
Buttalph Belknap
    Suffolk ss/ Boston March 19th 1715/6
Mr James Webber this day Acknowledged the above Instrum^t to be his Act & deed Before me./
        Anthony Stoddard Jus Pac^s
Recorded According to y^e Original May 1st 1716./
       p Jos Hamond Regist^r

Know All men by these presents that I John Whiple of Ipswich in ye County of Essex in New England Maltster in Consideration of Sixty pounds to me in hand paid & Secured

to be paid by John Leighton of Kittery in y[e] County of York in New England Carpenter./ do bargaine and sell unto s[d] John Leighton all my Interest in a Lot of fifty Acres of Land granted to my wife y[e] 29th ffebruary 1671 as may more fully Appear by y[e] record in Kittery Town book of records & all my Interest in a grant of land to William Leighton of Thirteen Acres of Land in Kittery in Crooked lane Next unto Richard Abbots As by grant may more fully Appear. To Have and To Hold y[e] Same to him & his heirs forever According to grant And Moreover y[e] s[d] Whipple doth hereby Covenant promiss and grant to y[e] s[d] Leighton forever hereafter peaceably & Quietly to have hold Occupy & Enjoy to him & their use & uses y[e] Afores[d] grants as bounded & do Warrant y[e] Sale thereof to be free & Clear from all psons whatsoever laying Any Lawfull Claime thereto from by or und[r] me y[e] s[d] Whipple my heirs Ex[rs] Adm[rs] or Assignes for ever./ In Witness whereof I y[e] s[d] Whipple have Set to my hand & Seal this Twenty fifth of Octob[r] Seventeen hundred & fifteen   John Whipple (Seal[a])
Signed Seal[d] & D[d]   Katherine Whipple (Seal[a])
In presence of
John Appleton
Anna Woodbery
  Essex ss/ Ipsw[ch] Nov[r] 21st 1715
Then y[e] Aboves[d] John Whipple & Katherine his wife Acknowledged this Instrum[t] to be their free Act & Deed./
    Before John Appleton J P[ce]
Recorded According to y[e] Original April y[e] 7th 1716.
    p Jos. Hamond Reg[r]

County of York/
  To the Marshal of y[e] County of York or his Dep[ty]
In his Maj[tys] Name you are required to Levie of y[e] goods Cattle or Chattells of Abra[m] Corbet to y[e] vallue of fifty Six pounds Eighteen Shillings & 6[d] whereof Six pounds 8[s] 6[d] is to be paid in money or goods At money price & 3/6[d] for y[e] Execution to Satisfie ffrances Smal for a Judgm[t] granted him at a Court holden at Wells July 2 1672 for this County whereof fayle you not to make a True return und[r] Yo[r] hand. Dated this 9[th] July 1672 p Curia͡ Edw[d] Rishworth Recor
  This Execution was Levied upon Abra[m] Corbets house & land as it was shewed me w[r]by the Constable did Attach it According to y[e] Teno[r] of y[e] Execution & Possession given

to ffrancis Smal by me Nath¹ Maysterson Marshall Dated 7
73 which Land is not that Measured out by me to ffran : Small

The Aprisem^t of this land Levied upon by this Execution was Apprised by Christopher Mitchell & Jere : Gutteridge upon their Oaths being in ye whole 57^l. 2^s : 0^d So much as was to Satisfy ye Execution in kind fifty pounds 10^s to be delivered in land as Aprised at 6/ p Acre & 6^l 12^s 0^d at 4/ p acre whereunto ye Marshalls my own Charge is to be Added which is forty Shillings

         Nath¹ Maysterson Marshall

Vera Coppy of this Execution within written & of the Marshalls return thereof & of his Attest of ye Apprisal of ye land Extended upon Transcrib^d out of ye Original this 14th July 74.   p Edwd Rishworth Record^r

Recorded According to ye Coppy As Above this 12th of May 1716   p Jos. Hamond Reg^r

We the under written being Chosen by ye Marshal of ye County of York to prise & Tract ot land Adjoyning to ye land that was lately Cap^{tn} Richd Lockwood & lyeth along ye river Side Towards ye house that Rice Thomas dwelleth in & that was form^{rly} prised by Christopher Mitchell & Jeremiah Guttridge As ye land of Mr Corbet for ye use of ffrancis Small & now Execution Levied on it for ye use of George Munjoy which land was presented unto us by ye Marshal Wee not Agreeing as to ye Vallue of ye land Cap^{tn} John Wincoll being chosen Umpire was Aprised at fourteen Shillings p Acre being a proportion in ye woods as is by ye water Side and were Sworn before Cap^{tn} John Wincoll As Witness our hands this 14th July 1674./ & ye house prised at Twenty Shilling   Walter Gendle

        Digery Jeffry D mark
        John Wincoll

Recorded According to ye Original May 12th 1716
        p Jos. Hamond Reg^r

Book VIII, Fol. 151.

[151] Know All men by these p^rsents whom it doth Concern that we Christopher Mitchel & Jeremiah Gutridge being desired by ye Marshal of York & ffrancis Smal to Apprise a parcell of Land as they Said belong to Mr Abra^m Corbet for ffrancis Small which wee did Apprise At Six Shillings p Acre & ye Cost that was money At four shillings and is ye land that was Attached and ye Execution Levied on by ye Marshal for ffrancis Small which Land lyeth Along ye river Against M^r ffryers Island lying between ye Late land of Cap^{tn} Lockwood & ye Steping Stones & what was in breadth by ye water Side to run back in ye woods a proportion is ye Intent of our Aprisal as witness our hands./
     Jeremiah Gudridge

    Christoph^r Mitchel (his mark

Christopher Mitchell & Jere Goodridge Owned ye above written with their hands to it to be their Act & Deed this 15th day of July 1674./ Before me John Wincoll Associate

Recorded According to ye Original May 12th 1716.
       p Jos Hamond Reg^r

This Execution was levied on ye house & land of ffrancis Small that was formerly Delivered ffrancis Smal by Execution as the land of Mr Abraham Corbet & delivered Mr George Munjoy containing 200 acres and two : prized by Diggery Jeffery & Walter Gendall on Oath & Capt Jno Wincoll & laid out by said Wincoll & was prized att 14 shillings p Acre containing 202 Acres is a hundred thirty five pound 17^s shillings & : 5£ 11^s & charges & laid it out as atest my hand this : 16th July 1674

Book VIII, Fol. 151.

```
           S k by W & N & by E  227 pole
      ┌─ ─ ─ ─ ─ ─ ─ ─ ─ ─ ─ ─ ─ ─ ─ ─ ─┐
      │                                 │
      │                                 │
   E  │        Cont⁴ 222 Acres)         │  The Creek runing to Braveboat harbr
   by │                                 │
   S &│                                 │
   W  │                                 │
   & by│                                │
   N   │      (Recorded According to y⁵ │
   168 │       Original May 12th 1716./ │
   pole│       p Jos. Hamond Regr       │
      │                                 │
      └─ ─ ─ ─ ─ ─ ─ ─ ─ ─ ─ ─ ─ ─ ─ ─ ─┘
              N by E: & S. b. W  197 pole
              Lockwoods line
```

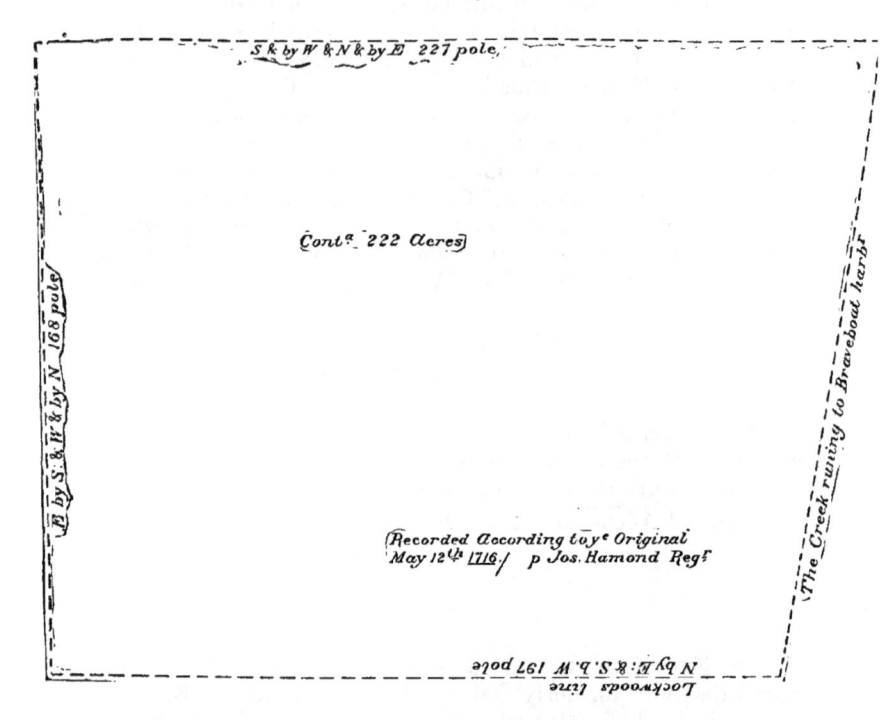

To All People before whom this deed of Sale Shall Come Greeting Now Know Ye that I James Oare of Wells in y⁵ County of york in this their Maj⁽ᵗʸˢ⁾ Teritory & Dominion of y⁶ Province of y⁶ Massachusets Bay in New England Logyer for & in Consideration of y⁸ Sum one hundred & forty pounds Starling to me well & Truely paid in hand by Jonathan Corwin Esq⁽ʳ⁾ of y⁶ Town of Salem in y⁸ County of Essex and Province afores⁽ᵈ⁾ Merch⁽ᵗ⁾ y⁶ rec⁽ᵗ⁾ whereof I do by these presents Acknowledge & Every part & parcell thereof & therewith to be fully Satisfied Contented & paid & of Every part & parcell thereof do fully freely & Absolutely Acquit Exonerate & discharge y⁸ s⁽ᵈ⁾ Corwin his heirs Ex⁽ʳˢ⁾ Adm⁽ʳˢ⁾ & assignes forever by these presents have granted bargained & Sold and do by these presents further give grant bargaine Sell Aliene Enfeoffe & Confirm unto y⁶ afores⁽ᵈ⁾ Jonathan Corwin Esq⁽ʳ⁾ a Certaine Tract of upland & Meadow land Containing by Estimation Two hundred Acres be it So much little more or Less and it is Scituate in y⁸ Township of Wells afores⁽ᵈ⁾ At a place Called Mousam it being Cape porpus river falls & it is butted & bounded as followeth Viz^t The land of ye s^d Carwin Northwesterly ye Land Lying down the river by ye highway one hundred & fifty poles & then ye line runs E. N. E by Several Marked Trees So farr as Seting of upon a Square it makes ye afores^d Sum̃ of Two hundred Acres & at ye North Easterly End it buts upon ye Com̃on lands of ye s^d Town of Wells All which Tract of Land afores^d was granted to me ye s^d James Oare & Henry Brown & Laid out by their Com̃ittee as by ye records of ye s^d Town will plainly Appear. Also this Tract of land Contains one Dwelling house & barn fields & fences with ye right of Trees & Timber like Trees wood brush & herbage Stones water and water Courses to him ye s^d Jonathan Corwin Esqr his heirs Ex^{rs} Adm^{rs} & Assignes forever To have & To hold ye above granted premises with Every part & parcell thereof with all ye rights of houses fences Cultures Improvem^{ts} Trees & Timber like Trees wood & underwood Standing lying or growing upon ye Same or that Ever Shall grow upon it ye grass & herbage Also ye Stones water & water Courses with all other ye right Title priviledges profits & Advantages thereunto belonging or in any wise appurtaining to him ye s^d Jon^a Corwin his heirs Ex^{rs} Adm^{rs} & Assigns forever to his & their own only proper use benefit & behoofe farthermore I ye s^d James Oare do for my Self my heirs Ex^{rs} Adm^{rs} & Assigus Covenat promiss & grant to & with ye s^d Jon^a Corwin Esqr him his heirs Ex^{rs} Adm^{rs} & Assignes that I am at ye Insigning of this Instrum^t ye true & rightfull owner of ye premisses & therefore have good right full power & Lawfull Authority to make Sale thereof [**152**] And that ye s^d Jonathan Corwin his heirs or Assignes shall or may at All Times & from time to time forever hereafter peaceably & Quietly have hold Occupie possess & Enjoy y^r Same in as full & Ample maner as I my Selfe did or might have done without ye Lawfull Suite Let hinderence Mollestation Eviction Ejection of me or any from by or under me Warrantizing ye Same from all former gifts grants Sales Leases Joyntures Dowryes Mortgages Attachm^{ts} Judgm^{ts} or Executions formerly had made or done granted of or by me At any time & from any other pson or pson or psons Lawfully claiming or haveing Any right Title or Interest therein or any part thereof and that ye above granted premisses may Continue & remaine a good True Absolute Sure Indefeazable Title of Inheritance in fee Simple unto ye s^d Jon^a Carwin Esqr his heirs Ex^{rs} Adm^{rs} and Assignes forever I y^e s^d James Oare have hereunto Set my hand & Affixed my Seal this Eighth day of Sept Annoq, Domini Sixteen hundred Ninety

BOOK VIII, FOL. 152.

Two Annoq Regni Regis & Regina Guillielmi & Maria Anglia &c^t Quarto/ Signed Sealed & D^d The mark of James Oare ✗ ($^a_{Seal}$)
In presence of
Saml Wheelwright
Joseph Storer
James Convers
 Sep^t y^e 8th 1692./ Then Appeared before me One of their Maj^{tys} Justices of y^e peace for y^e County of York James Oare of Wells & Acknowledged this Above written Instrum^t to be his Voluntary Act & Deed./ Saml Wheelwright
 Recorded According to ye Original May 9th 1716./
       p Jos. Hamond Reg^r

 To All Christian People to whom this present Deed of Sale May Come or Doth Concern Joseph Simpson of New Castle and Hannah his wife) of of The Province of New Hampsh^r in New England Sendeth Greeting Know Ye : that ye s^d Joseph & Hannah for & in Consideration of a Certain Sum of money to them in hand Paid or other wise Settisfactory Secured : to be paid By Thomas Addams of York in ye County of york of ye Province of ye Massachusets Bay in New England Have given granted Bargained Sold allinated Enfeoffed & Conveyed & Doth by these Presents Give Grant bargaine Sell Allinate Enfeoffe & Convey & fully freely & Absolutely Make over & Confirm unto ye Said Thomas A Certain Peace or Parcell of upland Swampy Land & Meadow Ground Containing by Estamation Twenty Four Acres Be it More of Quantity or Less ye which Land & Swampy ground Lyeth between Two Lots of ye s^d Thomas on ye Southwest Side of ye high Way that Leads to york Corn Mills & is Bounded as followeth Viz Begining att a white oak Stake Near By Samuel Bragdons fence that is at ye head of Bass Creek wch s^d Stake Stand a Little South West from a White Rock & runs from thence North East Northwardly by ye bounds of s^d Thomasis houss Lot Ninety four Poles or perch to a Small beach tree Markt on four Sides which s^d Beach tree is ye Southward Corner Bound Marked Tree of Daniel Simpsons Land he Bought of his Brother Joseph Simpson above Named and runs from s^d Beach Tree by s^d Danils bounds forty Six poles or Perch Northwestward to a bove s^d Thomas Addamsis bound of a Peace of Swampy Land their and Runs by s^d bounds Ninety four poles Southwest a Little Southwardly and then on a

Book VIII, Fol. 153.

straight line to ye Stake & White Roak first above Mentioned Together with all ye Rights Bennifits Priviledges & Advantages thereunto belonging both of upland Swampy Land & Meadow ground with all ye rights of Wood und^r Wood Timb^r & Timb^r Trees standing Lying or belonging unto s^d Tract of Land Swamp or Meadow ground or any Part or parcell thereof or any wise at any Time redownding to ye Same unto ye s^d Thomas Addams his heirs Ex^{rs} Adm^{rs} & Assignes as a Sure Estate in fee Simple forever./ To have & To hold Quietly to possess and Injoy Moreover the Said Joseph and Hannah Doth for them selves their Heirs Executors & administrators Covenant Ingage & Promiss to and with the a bove s^d Thomas his Heirs Executors administrat^{rs} and assignes ye aboves^d Land Swampy Land & Meadow ground to be free & Clear from all former Gifts Grants Bargaines Sales Rents Rates Mortgages Dowrys Leases Intailments or any other Incumbermt^s Whatso Ever as also from all future Claims Challingis Suits at Law or any Interuption whatsoever to be had or Cominsed by them the s^d Joseph or Hannah their Heirs Executors administrators or assignes & ye s^d Joseph & Hannah Proceeding the Date of this Instrument to quit all Claimes unto the aboves^d Land Swampy Land and Meadow ground & doe oblige them selves their Heirs Ex^{rs} & Adm^{rs} as they do Warrantize ye s^d Land & premisses unto ye s^d Thomas his heirs Execut^{rs} Adm^{rs} & assigns to Defend ye Same agst All & Such person or persons that Shall upon grounds of Law lay any claime unto ye s^d Land Swampy land or Meadow ground or any part or parcell thereof In Witness hereof the aboves^d Joseph Simpson & |Hannah his wife have hereunto put their hands & Seals this third day of June in y^e year of [**153**] Our Lord one Thousand Seaven hundred & Eight and in y^e Seaventh year of y^e reign of our Soveraign Lady Anne Queen of Great Brittaine &c^t   Joseph Simpson ($_{Seal}^{a}$)
Signed Sealed & Delivered ($_{Seal}^{a}$)
In y^e psence of us Witnesses
Daniel Simpson
Abra^m Preble Junr

York sc/ York Novemb^r y^e 9th 1708
Joseph Simpson Acknowledged y^e Above written Instrum^t to be his Act & Deed Before me Abrã Preble Justice peace
Recorded According to y^e Original May 8th 1716.

p Jos Hamond Reg^r

BOOK VIII, FOL. 153.

To All Christian People to whom this present deed of sale may Come or doth Concern Johnson Harmon & Mary his wife of York in ye County of york of ye Province of ye Massachusets Bay in New England Sendeth Greeting./ Know Yee that ye s^d Johnson & Mary for & in Consideration of a Certain Sum of money to them in hand paid or other wayes Satisfactorily Secured to be paid by Hezekiah Adams of s^d York in ye Afore named Province of ye Massachusets Bay./ Have given granted bargained Sold Alienated Enfeoffed & Confirmed & do by these presents give grant Burgaine Sell Enfeoffe & Confirm & fully freely and Absolutely Make Over unto ye s^d Hezekiah A Certaine piece of land both upland & Swampy land & Meadow ground Containing by Estimation Ten acres be it more or Less lying & being within ye Township or precinct of s^d York & is butted & bounded as followeth on ye Southwest End by the Town way that leads from ye head of Bass creek to Rowland Youngs on ye Southeast Side or Southward Corner is a pine Tree mark^t on four Sides being ye westward Corner of a lot of land of Thomas Adams^{es} & runs from thence by above named path Northwest westwardly Twenty pole in breadth to ye Land of John Parker & is bounded by s^d Parkers Land as his fence now Stands Near on a northeast line Eighty pole to ye land now in ye possession of Cap^{tn} Lewis Bane & is in breadth by s^d Banes fence Twenty poles and thence is bounded on a Southwestward line by ye land or fence of s^d Thomas Adams to ye Tree first above Mentioned Together wth all ye rights benefits priviledges & Advantages thereunto belonging both of land Meadow ground Swampy land Spring or Springs brookes of Water wood or und^r wood Timber Timber trees Standing lying being or remaining on s^d land Meadow ground Swampy land or any part thereof unto him ye s^d Hezekiah Adams his heirs Ex^{rs} Adm^{rs} & Assigns./ To Have & To Hold & Quietly & peaceably to possess Occupy & Enjoy ye s^d land Meadow ground & Swampy ground with all its priviledges as a Sure Estate in fee Simple forever & further ye s^d Johnson Harmon & Mary his wife do for themselves Their heirs Ex^{rs} & Adm^{rs} Covenant Ingage & promiss to & wth ye aboves^d Hezekiah Adams his heirs Ex^{rs} Adm^{rs} & Assigns ye Aboves^d Land Meadow ground & Swampy land with all its priviledges to be free and clear from all former gifts grants Sales Mortgages rents rates Dowryes and Incumberm^{ts} whatsoever as also from all future Claimes Challenges Lawsuits or any Interuptions whatsoever & ye s^d Johnson & Mary do unto & with ye s^d Hezekiah his heirs Ex^{rs} Adm^{rs} & Assignes Oblige themselves their heirs Ex^{rs} &

Book VIII, Fol. 154.

Adm^{rs} to warrantise & defend ye aboves^d Land Meadow ground & Swampy land against all person or persons that Shall by Title of Law Ever after ye date of this deed disturb or Interrupt ye s^d Hezekiah his heirs Ex^{rs} Adm^{rs} or Assignes And ye s^d Johnson & Mary do by these presents for themselves their heirs Ex^{rs} & Adm^{rs} fully discharge their whole Sole right & Title to s^d land & all its priviledges forever after ye date hereof untill which time they do Avouch themselves ye proper owners of it and Every part thereof In Witness of these presents thes^d Johnson Harmon & Mary his wife have hereunto Set their hands & Seals this Twenty third day of July in ye year of our Lord One Thousand Seaven hundred and Nine And in ye Eighth year of her Majt^{ys} Reign over Great Brittain &c^t Johnson Harmon (seal)
Signed Sealed & Delivered   Mary Harmon (seal)
  In ye psence of
Samuel Clark
Abra^m Preble Junr
York sc/ Augst ye 8th 1709 :/ Johnson Harmon & Mary his wife psonally Appeared & Acknowledged ye above written deed of Sale to be their Act & Deed./
                Before me   Abrã Preble Just^s peace
Recorded According to ye Originall May ye 8th 1716./
                              p Jos Hamond Reg^r

  To All People to whom this present deed of Sale Shall Come Eliab Littlefield of Manchester in ye County of Essex in his Maj^{tys} Province of ye Massachusets Bay in New England husbandman Sendeth Greeting Know Yee that ye s^d Eliab Littlefield for & in Consideration of ye Sum of Twenty one pounds lawfull money to him in hand paid At & before ye Ensealing & delivery of these presents by George Jacobs of Wells in ye County of york & province afores^d the rec^t whereof ye s^d Littlefield doth hereby Acknowledge & Every part & parcell thereof & doth Acquit Exonerate & discharge ye s^d George Jacobs his heirs & Assigns forever by these presents. Have Given granted bargained Sold Aliened Enfeoffed & Confirmed and by these presents do fully freely Clearly & Absolutely give [154] Grant bargaine Sell Alien Enfeoffe & Confirm unto him ye s^d George Jacobs his heirs Ex^{rs} Adm^{rs} & Assignes forever Six Acres of Marsh which marsh formerly belonged to John Littlefield Deceased & Lyes in ye Township of s^d Wells & bounded on ye west Side

BOOK VIII, FOL. 154.

by Crosses point & on the North East Side by a ditch runing into ye back Creek & on ye Southwest by Zachariah Goodale & from thence to ye first begining. Together with all & Single ye rights priviledges & Apurtenances thereunto belonging or in any wise Appurtaining to Every part & parcell thereof To Have & To Hold ye s^d Six acres of Marsh to ye s^d George Jacobs & his heirs & Assignes to his & their own proper use benefit & behoofe forever./ And ye s^d Eliab Littlefield for himselfe his heirs Ex^rs Adm^rs & Assignes in maner as followeth./ That is To Say that At ye Time of this present bargaine & Sale & untill ye Ensealing & delivery of these presents he ye s^d Littlefield is ye True Sole and Lawfull owner & doth Stand Leagally possessed of ye Same in a perfect Estate of Inheritance in fee Simple & that I the s^d Littlefield have full power & Lawfull Authority to make Sale of ye Same./ And ye s^d George Jacobs his heirs Ex^rs Adm^rs & Assigns Shall peaceably & Quietly Have Hold use Occupie possess & Enjoy ye Above Mentioned pmisses And further ye afores^d Eliab Littlefield his heirs Ex^rs & Adm^rs Shall & will from Time hence forth & forever hereafter Warrant & Defend ye Above bargained pmisses unto him ye s^d George Jacobs his heirs Ex^rs Adm^rs & Assignes forever against ye Lawfull claims & Demands of all & Every pson whatsoever In Witness whereof The above Named Eliab Littlefield have hereunto Set my hand & Seal this Twenty day of June One Thousand Seaven hundred & fifteen./

Signed Sealed & Delivered
  In ye presents of us   Eliab (his mark) Littlefield (a Seal)
  John Kingsbury
  Nicholas Morrell
  John Sayward
  York sc/

Eliab Littlefield psonally Appeared before me this 18th day of Jan^ry 1715/6 & Acknowledged this above writen Instrum^t or deed of Sale to be his free Act & Deed

                         John Wheelwright Just^s peace

Recorded According to ye Original April 3^d 1716./

                         p Jos. Hamond Reg^r

Know All men by these presents that I William Child of Berwick in ye County of york in ye Province of Massachusets Bay in New England Mason for & in Consideration of ye Sum of five pounds in Curra^t money of ye Province afores^d to me in hand well & Truely paid by Bial Hambleton

Book VIII, Fol. 154.

of ye Same Town County & Province afores^d husbandman the rec^t whereof I do hereby Acknowledged & my Selfe therewith Satisfied Contented & paid Have given granted bargained Sold Aliened Assigned Enfeoffed Set over & Confirmed And do by these presents give grant bargaine Sell Aliene Assign Enfeoffe Set over & Confirm unto Him ye s^d Bial Hambleton his heirs & Assigns forever a Certaine piece or parcell of Land Scittuate Lying & being in Berwick afores^d Containing Two acres & four pole Viz^t Eighteen rod or pole upon Each Side being Square bounded by ye highway that goes to Humphreys pond So Called on ye Northwest Southerly upon ye Land formerly Called broughtons & on all ye other parts upon Lands of s^d Childs Opposite to Land of Walter Allen To have & To hold ye s^d Two Acres & four poles as bounded with all ye rights profits priviledges & appurtenances unto ye same belonging or in any wise Appurtaining to ye only propper use & behoofe of him ye s^d Bial Hambleton his heirs & Assignes forever free & clear of all other & former gifts grants bargains Sales Mortgages Judgm^{ts} Executions & all other Incumbrances whatsoever & I ye s^d William Child At & before ye Ensealing & Delivery hereof am ye Lawfull owner of ye hereby granted and bargained premisses & have good right full power & Lawfull Authority to grant bargaine Sell & Convey ye Same as afores^d & that it Shall & may be Lawfull to & for ye s^d Bial Hambleton his heirs & Assigns to have hold use Occupy possess & Enjoy ye Same Quietly & peaceably from henceforth & forever without any reclaim Challenge or demand from me ye s^d William Child my heirs Ex^{rs} or Adm^{rs} and I do hereby further bind & Oblige my Selfe & them to Warrant Acquit & Defend him ye s^d Bial Hambleton his heirs Ex^{rs} Adm^{rs} or Assigns in y^e Quiet and peaceable possession thereof against all other person or persons Laying Legall claime thereunto or any part thereof from henceforth & forever./ In Witness whereof I y^e s^d William Child have hereunto Set my hand & seal y^e first day of Septemb^r Annoq$_h$ Domini 1715

Signed Sealed & D^d William   his   Child (Seal)
In y^e psence of   mark
John Croade
Deberoh Croade
John Belcher

             York sc/ Kittery Septr 20. 1715./

William Child above named Acknowledged the above written Instrum^t to be his free act & deed And Eliz^a y^e wife

Book VIII, Fol. 155.

of ye Child Also Appearing and Surrendered up all her right of Dower to ye above bargained Premisses./
      Before Charles ffrost J. peace
Recorded According to ye Original May ye 8th 1716./
        p Jos Hamond Reg^r

To All People to whom these p^{r}sents shall Come Thomas Allen of ye Town of Kittery in ye County of York in New England Shipwright Sendeth Greeting./ Know Y^e that ye s^d Thomas Allen for ye Consideration of ye Sum of One hundred fifty Six pounds due to John Wentworth & One hundred & Seaventeen pounds due unto Mary Martyn in all Two hundred Seaventy three pounds Curra^t money of N England to him in hand before ye Ensealing & Delivery hereof well & Truely paid by John [155] Wentworth Esqr of ye Town of Portsm^o in New Hampsh^r in New England Merch^t And Mary Martyn of ye Same place widow Shopkeeper the rec^t whereof ye s^d Thomas Allen doth hereby Acknowledge and himselfe therewith fully Satisfied & Contented & thereof & of Every part & parcell thereof do Exonerate thes^d John Wentworth & Mary Martyn their heirs Ex^{rs} Adm^{rs} & Assigns forever by these presents Have given granted bargained Sold Aliened Enfeoffed Conveyed & Confirmed & by these presents do freely fully clearly & Absolutely give grant bargaine Sell Aliene Enfeoffe Convey & Confirm unto ye s^d John Wentworth & Mary Martyn their heirs & Assigns forever a Certaine Dwelling house & land Scittuate Lying & being within ye Township of Kittery afores^d being Butted & bounded as followeth Viz^{tt} One Acre of it At a place called Kittery point & fronting on Piscattaqua river as ye Same was bought of Nathl Thomas of Marshfield in ye County of Plym^o in New England Gent^l as Appears by his deed to s^d Thomas Allen bareing date ye 16th day of May: 1710 referrence to s^d deed being had will more large Appear & Also Seven Acres of land s^d Allen bought of Ebenezer More & s^d Eben^r More bought it of Saml Penhallow Esqr and s^d Saml Penhallow bought it of Benjamin Woodbridge of ye Town of Medford in ye County of Middlesex in New England as by s^d Woodbridges deed to s^d Saml Penhallow bareing date ye 2^d day of Novemb^r 1706 will plaine Appear referrence to s^d deed being had Together with all ye priviledges & Appurtenances to ye s^d parcells of Land belonging or in any wise Appurtaining unto them ye s^d John Wentworth & Mary Martyn their heirs

& Assignes forever To have & To Hold all & Singular ye S^d house Dwelling house out houses Orchards gardens fences buildings yard on Either of ye aboves^d parcells of land & All & Singular ye both of ye aboves^d parcells of butted & & bounds as by ye deeds recited by their dates Together with all profits priviledges & Appurtenances whatsoever to ye s^d house or houses & parcells of Land belonging or in any wise Appurtaining to them ye s^d John Wentworth and Mary Mary Martyn their heirs & Assigns forever to ye only proper use benefit & behoofe forever of them ye s^d John Wentworth and Mary Martyn their heirs & Assigns forever free & Clear & Clearly Acquitted & Discharged of & from all & all maner of form^r and other gifts grants bargains Sales Titles Troubles & Incumbrances whatsoever And that I ye s^d Thomas Allen & my heirs to them ye s^d John Wentworth & Mary Martyn their heirs & Assigns shall and will Warrant & forever defend ye Same from & against all Lawfull Claims & demands whatsoever./ Provided Alwayes Nevertheless and it is ye True Intent & Meaning of these presents and of the partyes hereunto & So hereby declare to be that if ye s^d Thomas Allen his heirs Ex^{rs} or Adm^{rs} or Any of them do in discharge of this deed of Mortgage well and Truely pay or Cause to be paid unto ye s^d John Wentworth & Mary Martyn their heirs Ex^{rs} Adm^{rs} or Assigns ye s^d Sum of Two hundred Seaventy Three pounds Like Currant Money with due Interest for ye Same & all Charges that may Arise Concerning ye pmisses at or before ye Tenth day of May wch will be in ye year of our Lord One Thousand Seven hundred and Twenty Two At ye Dwelling house of ye s^d John Wentworth in Portsm^o afores^d That then & from thenceforth this present deed & bargaine & sale & Every Clause Covenant & thing therein Contained Shall Cease determin & be utterly Voyd frustrate & of Non Effect to all Intents & purposes whatsoever as if ye Same had never been made anything herein Contained to ye Contrary thereof in Any wise Notwithstanding but if Default Shall happen to be made in ye paym^t of ye s^d Sum of Two hundred Seaventy Three pounds Like Curra^t money./ One hundred fifty Six pounds thereof due to ye s^d John Wentworth & one hundred & Seaventeen pounds to Mary Martyn with ye Interest & Charges as afore or any part thereof at ye daytime & place before mentioned & Expressed that then it shall be lawfull Imediately after Such default shall be made to & for ye s^d John Wentworth & Mary Martyn their heirs Ex^{rs} Adm^{rs} or Assigns into & upon all & Singu-

[margin: This Deed &^{c} is Assigned & made Over to William Pepperrell Esqr Lib^o-23 fo^{lo} 19.—]

lar yᵉ before granted & bargained pmisses with yᵉ Priviledges & Appurtenances & Every part & parcell thereof wholly to Enter & yᵉ Same from thenceforth peaceably & Quietly to have hold Occupy possess & Enjoy & to have take & receive yᵉ rents Issues & profits thereof to them & their own proper use & uses for ever an Estate of fee Simple./ In Witness whereof yᵉ sᵈ Thomas Allen hath hereunto Set his hand & Seal this Eighteenth day of May Anno Domˣ One Thousand Seaven hundred & Sixteen./ 1716./ Thomas Allen (ₛₑₐₗᵃ)
Signed Sealed & Delivered
  In presence of us
  Thomas Phipps
  Benjᵃ Akerman
  Province of New Hampshʳ Thomas Allen Appeared before yᵉ Subscribʳ this 17ᵗʰ day of May 1716. & Ackdowledged yᵉ Above & foregoing Instrumᵗ in writing to be his Volluntary Act & Deed./   M. Hunking Justˢ peace
  Recorded According to yᵉ Original June 18ᵗʰ 1716
                        p Jos Hamond Regʳ

  Whereas I William Phillips Now resident in Saco did buy of Capᵗⁿ Bryan Pendleton a Certain Neck of Land below Saco river & Extending it Selfe to yᵉ Mill Together with Wood Island Gibbons Island and a Certaine Tract of Land up Saco river Comonly known by yᵉ Name of West point and formerly in possession of John West and Cow Island Together with Certain Cattle both Cows Sheep & goats as more at large do Appear in a deed of Sale under the hand of yᵉ sᵈ Pendleton dated 2ᵈ day May 1661./
  Now These are to Certify whom it may Concern that I yᵉ sᵈ William Phillips Together with my wife Bridget Phillips have and do redeliver up and give Quiet & peaceable possession of yᵉ aforesᵈ Neck of land with yᵉ houses thereon Extending to yᵉ Mill wood Island Gibons Island & yᵉ Tract of land in Saco river Some [156] Time in yᵉ possession of John West with Cow Island both Meadow & upland Together with Two Steers of Three years old & Vantage Two Steers of Two years old Six Cows Two Calves four Steers of one year old Three hiefers of one year old & Vantage with all yᵉ Goats at Wood Island all which aforesᵈ pʳmisses we yᵉ sᵈ Wᵐ & Bridget Phillips do fully Surrendʳ & give Quiet possession of to sᵈ Bryan Pendleton his heirs and Assigns for ever Together with forty Sheep & their Increase

Book VIII, Fol. 156.

& do by these presents Ingage that Neither our Selves or Either of us Nor any other und[r] us Shall Never Mollest disturb or disquiet y[e] aboves[d] Pendleton his heirs or Assigns for ever as Witness w[r] of we Set our hands & Seals 2 day May 1664./   Will[m] Phillips (seal[a])
Witness   Francis Littlefield Sen[r]   Bridget Phillips (seal[a])
          Walt[r] Pennel
This Instrum[t] Owned Before me./
                                   Francis Hook Comission[r]
Recorded According to y[e] Original May 26th 1716.
                                   p Jos. Hamond Regist[r]

To All People to whom this psent writing shall come I John Tinney of Kittery in y[e] County of York in his Maj[tys] Province of y[e] Massachusets Bay in New England husbandman Send Greeting Know y[e] that I y[e] s[d] John Tinney as well for & in Consideration of y[e] Natural Affection and fatherly love which I have & bare unto my welbeloved Son William Mitchell and Daughter Eliz[a] Mitchell wife of s[d] W[m] Mitchell of Kittery afores[d] as also for diverse other good Causes & Considerations me at this present Especially moveing have given & granted & by these presents do give grant & Confirm unto y[e] s[d] William Mitchell and Elizabeth his wife & her heirs Lawfully begotten of her body for ever One Messuage or Tract of Land & marsh Scittuate lying and being in Black point Joyning upon a river Called Spurwink where y[e] s[d] John Tinney formerly possessed & Lived on And furthermore y[e] s[d] John Tinney does by these presents give as afores[d] all his right Title to All y[e] Land which does now belong to y[e] s[d] Tinney lying Near y[e] s[d] river Called Spurwink To have & To hold y[e] s[d] granted & bargained premisses with all y[e] Appurtenances priviledges & Comodityes to y[e] Same belonging or in Any wise Appurtaining to him y[e] s[d] W[m] And Eliz[a] Mitchell & her heirs Lawfully begotten of her own body forever to his & their own proper use benefit & behalfe for ever. freely & Quietly without any Matter of Challenge Claime or demand of me y[e] s[d] John Tinney or of Any other pson or psons whatsoever for me in my Name by my Cause means or procurem[t] or without any money or other thing therefore to be Yielded paid or done unto me y[e] s[d] John Tinney my heirs Ex[rs] Adm[rs] or Assigns. And I y[e] s[d] John Tinney all & Singular y[e] afores[d] land & Marsh with all y[e] priviledges & Appurtenances to y[e] Same

belonging to Warrant yͤ sᵈ Wᵐ & Elizᵃ Mitchell & her heirs as aforesᵈ to yͤ use aforesᵈ against all people do Warrant & forever Defend by these pʳsents./ In Witness whereof I have hereunto Set my hand & Seal this Twenty Second day of August in yͤ Second year of our Soveraign Lord George by yͤ grace of God King of Great Brittaine ffrance & Ireland and in yͤ year of our Lord One Thousand Seven hundred & fifteen./   John Tinney (ₛₑₐₗᵃ)
Signed Sealed & Delivered.
 In yͤ presence of
 Tho : ffry
 Dorrothy Pepperrell
 Margery Pepperrell
 28 of March : 1716
Then John Tinney psonally Appeared before me and did Acknowledge this above Instrument to be his free Act & Deed./   Wᵐ Pepperrell J. peace
Recorded According to yͤ Original April 9⁰ 1716
                          p Jos : Harmon Regʳ

Know All men by these presents that I William Godsoe of Kittery in yͤ County of York in New England for a Valluable Consideration to me in hand paid by ffrancis Pettegrew of yͤ Same place Yeoman have given granted bargained & Sold And do by these presents for my Selfe and my heirs bargaine Sell Enfeoffe and for ever Confirm unto yͤ sᵈ ffrancis Pettegrew his heirs & Assigns forever a Small Tract of Land Containing by Estimation about Three Quarters of an Acre as it is now fenced in by yͤ sᵈ ffrancis Pettegrew & is bounded westward by his own Land and Southward by yͤ New road going to York & Northward with yͤ Land of Richard Rogers the fence as it now Stands bounds yͤ sᵈ Tract To have & To hold yͤ sᵈ Tract of land Together with all priviledges & Appurtenances thereto belonging or in any wise Appurtaining thereunto unto yͤ sᵈ Francis Pettegrew his heirs & Assigns forever against me yͤ sᵈ Wᵘᵐ Godsoe or any of my heirs or any other pson or psons by my procuremᵗ The peaceable possession thereof to Warrant And forever Defend against all psons Laying a Lawfull Claime thereunto In Witness whereof I have hereunto Set my hand & Seal this first day of June in yͤ year of our Lord one Thousand Seaven hundred & Sixteen 1716.

And in yᵉ Second year of yᵉ reign of our Soveraign Lord King George./ William Godsoe (seal)
Signed & Sealed in yᵉ
psence of us yᵉ Subscribʳˢ

Wᵐ {his mark} Jones

Danˡ {his mark} Jones

Pro: New Hampshʳ/
Mʳ Wᵐ Godsoe psonally Appeared before me yᵉ Subscribʳ one of his Majᵗʸˢ Justices of yᵉ peace & Acknowledged yᵉ above Instrumᵗ to be his Volluntary Act & Deed At New Castle June yᵉ 2ᵈ 1716   John Frost

Recorded According to yᵉ Original June 20ᵗʰ 1716./
                                p. Jos: Hamond Regʳ

[157] To All People to whom this present deed or Instrumᵗ in writing Shall Come Know Ye that I Mary Hunking of Portsmouth in yᵉ Province of New Hampshʳ Widow for & in Consideration of yᵉ Sum of Thirty pounds Currat money of New England aforesᵈ to me in hand At & before yᵉ Ensealing & Delivery of these presents well & Truely paid or Secured in yᵉ Law to be paid by Nathaniel ffernald of Kittery in yᵉ County of York within his Majᵗʸˢ Province of yᵉ Massachusets Bay in New England Yeoman yᵉ recᵗ whereof I do hereby acknowledge & my Selfe therewith to be fully Satisfied Contented & paid have given granted bargained Sold Aliened released Enfeoffed & Confirmed & by these presents do freely fully & Absolutely give grant bargaine Sell release Assigne Enfeoffe Convey deliver & Confirm unto yᵉ sᵈ Nathˡ ffernald his heirs & Assignes for ever all that my Certain Lot or Tract of Land Scittuate Lying & being within yᵉ Township of Kittery aforesᵈ Containing forty Acres of Land which sᵈ forty acres was granted unto me by the Town of Kittery on yᵉ Twenty eighth day of July 1679 and lies at yᵉ NorthEast End of Capᵗⁿ John Leightons Seaventy Acres being Sixty poles in breadth Northwest & by North & one hundred & Seaven pole in length North East & by East which lot or Tract of land was laid out & bounded on yᵉ Twelfth day of June Sixteen hundred Ninety four as by yᵉ return thereof under yᵉ Surveyers hand on rec-

Book VIII, Fol. 157.

ord in the Town of Kittery reference being thereunto had may more amply & At Large Appear Together with all y[e] Trees Timber woods underwoods waters water Courses Swamps Meadows Meadows Meadow grounds rights Memb[rs] profits priviledges Comoditys Advantages Heriditaments and Appurtenances whatsoever upon belonging or in any wise Appurtaining unto y[e] s[d] Granted lot or Tract of land or any part or parcell thereof & y[e] reverson and reversons remaind[r] & remaind[rs] rents Issues & profits thereof And All y[e] Estate right Title Interest Inheritance use property possession Claime & Demand w[t]soever of me y[e] s[d] Mary Hunking my heirs Ex[rs] & Adm[rs] of in & to the Same To have & To hold y[e] s[d] Lot or Tract of land & Every part and parcell thereof & all & Singular y[e] pmisses & Appurtenances herein before granted bargained & Sold unto him y[e] s[d] Nath[l] ffernald his heirs & Assigns to his & their own Sole & proper use benefit & behoofe for ever And I y[e] s[d] Mary Hunking for my Selfe my heirs Ex[rs] & Adm[rs] do Covena[t] grant & Agree to & with y[e] s[d] Nath[l] ffernald his heirs & Assigns in Maner following that is to Say that I y[e] s[d] Mary Hunking at & untill y[e] Ensealing & Delivery of these psents am y[e] True & Lawfull owner of y[e] s[d] Lot or Tract of land & pmisses and Stand Lawfully Siezed thereof in my own proper right as a good perfect & Absolute Estate of Inheritance in fee Simple w[th]out any Maner of Condition reverson or Limitation of use or uses whatsoever So as to Alter change defeat or make Voyd y[e] Same & have full power good right & Lawfull Authority to grant Sell and assure y[e] s[d] land & pmisses in Manner as afores[d] & that y[e] Same are free & Clear & Clearly Acquitted & discharged of and from all former and other gifts grants bargains Sales Leases Mortgages Wills Entails Judgm[ts] Executions Titles Troubles Charges & Incumbrances whatsoever & further that I y[e] s[d] Mary Hunking my heirs Ex[rs] & Adm[rs] Shall & will Warrant & Defend y[e] s[d] lot or Tract of land & premisses herein before granted bargained & Sold unto y[e] s[d] Nath[l] ffernald his heirs & Assigns for ever against y[e] Lawfull Claims & Demands of all & Every pson & psons whatsoever=In Witness whereof I y[e] s[d] Mary Hunking have hereunto Set my hand & Seal this Twenty first day of January in y[e] Second Year of y[e] reign of our Soveraign Lord George of Great Brittaine &c[t] King Annoq, Domini Seventen hundred & fifteen Sixteen 1715/6

Signed Sealed & Delivered   Mary Hunking (Seal[a])
  In psence of us   Mary Hunking (Seal[a])
  Amos ffernald
  Jeremiah Calef

BOOK VIII, FOL. 158.

Province of New Hampshire—
Mrs Mary Hunking Exectrix to ye Last will & Testm^t of Mr John Hunking Dec^d & Mary ye Daughter of s^d Hunking psonally Appearing before me ye Subscrib^r this 29th day of March 1716 and Acknowledged ye Above Instrum^t in writing to be their Volluntary Act & Deed./

p John Wentworth Jus^{ts} Peace

Recorded According to ye Original May 7° 1716.

p Jos. Hammond Reg^r

To All People to whom these presents shall Come Know Yee that I: John Tompson of Berwich in ye County of York & within his Majestys Province of ye Massachusets Bay in New England Labourer for & in Consideration of a Valluable Sum to me in hand well & Truely paid at ye Ensealing & Delivery of these presents by Benjamin Libbey of ye Town County & Province afores^d ye rec^t whereof I Acknowledge to my full Content & Satisfaction & do hereby Acquit & Discharge ye s^d Benj^a Libbey his heirs & Assignes forever by these presents have fully freely Clearly & Absolutely given granted bargained Sold Aliened Enfeoffed & Confirmed unto ye s^d Benjamin Libbey & to his heirs Ex^{rs} Adm^{rs} & Assignes forever ye one halfe of Twenty one acres of Land granted to me ye s^d John Tompson by ye Town of Kittery March ye Twentyeth Sixteen hundred Seaventy Eight Together with all & Singular ye wayes profits Priviledges rights Comoditys & Appurtenances thereunto belonging To have & To hold ye halfe of ye s^d grant of land & all other of ye above granted & bargain^d premisses with their Appurtenances unto him ye s^d Benjamin Libey & to his heirs Ex^{rs} Adm^{rs} & Assignes for ever & ye s^d Benj^a Libby his heirs & Assigns shall & may from henceforth & forever hereafter Lawfully peaceably & Quietly have hold use Ocupie Possess & Enjoy ye s^d Land with all ye rights & Priviledges as afores^d without the Let hinderence Interruption or denial of me ye s^d John Tompsom [158] My heirs Ex^{rs} or Adm^{rs} ye Premisses being free from all former grants Conveyances & Intanglements And Further I ye s^d John Tompson my heirs Ex^{rs} & Adm^{rs} will for ever hereafter Warrant and defend all ye above granted and bargained premisses to him ye s^d Benj^a Libbey his heirs or Assignes from by or und^r me my heirs Ex^{rs} or Adm^{rs} In Witness whereof I have hereunto Set my hand & Seal June y^e Thirtyeth Anno Domini Seventeen

Book VIII, Fol. 158.

hundred & Sixteen & in y^e second year of his Majesty King George his reign over Great Brittaine &c^t./
Signed Sealed & Delivered   John Thompson (${}^a_{Seal}$)
 In presence of
Elisha Plaisted
John Stocklenes
York sc/ June 3th 1716./
John Tompson psonally appeared before me y^e Subscrib^r one of his Maj^tys Justices of y^e Peace for y^e County of York & Acknowledged y^e Above written Instrum^t to be his Volluntary Act & deed./
      Elisha Plaisted Just^s peace
Recorded According to ye Original June 30th 1716./
       p Jos Hamond Reg^r

To All People to whom this present deed or Instrum^t in writing shall Come Know Y^e that I Daniel Stone of Berwick in ye County of York within his Majestyes Province of the Massachusets Bay in New England Cordwainer for and in Consideration of ye sum of Eleven pounds Curra^t money of New Engl^d to me in hand at and before ye Ensealing & Delivery of these presents well and Truely paid by Benjamin Libbey of Berwick in ye County & Province afores^d husbandman ye rec^t whereof I do hereby Acknowledge & my Selfe therewith fully Satisfied Conteuted & paid Have given granted bargained and Sold and by these presents for my Selfe my heirs Ex^rs and Adm^rs do give grant Bargaine Sell Aliene Enfeoffe Convey & Confirm unto him ye s^d Benjamin Libbey his heirs and Assigns for ever a Certain Tract or parcell of land Containing Thirty Acres being ye Moiety or halfe part of Sixty acres of Land laid out unto Daniel Stone Senr dec^d by vertue of Two grants of ye Town of Kittery one of which grants bares date March ye 20th 1678/9. The other granted him may ye 10th 1703. and which Together with Twenty Acres Laid out to Jonathan Stone in one Intire piece makes Eighty Acres in ye Whole Scittuate in ye Township of Berwick afores^d and begins about Sixteen pole North and by West from Mr John Croads Northeast Corner bounds then East by North Eighty poles then South by East one hundred and Sixty poles then West by South Eighty poles to Mr Croads bounds and is bounded on ye West Side by Mr John Croads land and the other three Sides with reputed Comons as p ye Survey^r return on record in Kittery Appears

Book VIII, Fol. 158.

which s^d Thirty acres of Land was given and bequeathed unto me by my father Daniel Stone dec^d as p his last Will & Testam^t refference being thereunto had more at large it doth Appear To have & To hold ye s^d Thirty of Land with all & Singular ye premisses & Appurtenances thereunto belonging or in any wise Appurtaining unto him ye s^d Benj^a Libbey his heirs & Assignes for ever to his & their own propper use Benefit and behoofe for ever more And further I ye s^d Daniel Stone for my Selfe my heirs Ex^{rs} and Adm^{rs} to & with him ye s^d Benj^a Libbey his heirs and Assigns do Covenant in maner following That is to Say that at & untill ye Ensealing & Delivery of these psents I am ye true Sole & Lawfull owner of the above bargained Land & pmisses & have in my Selfe full power good right & Lawfull Authority ye Same to Convey as afores^d and that ye same & Every part thereof is free and Clear & Clearly Acquitted and Discharged of and from all & all maner of former & other gifts grants bargains Sales Leases Mortgages and all other Incumbrances whatsoever./ And I ye s^d Daniel Stone for my selfe my heirs Ex^{rs} & Adm^{rs} shall & will Warra^t and Defend ye Title of ye Thirty acres of land & premisses herein before granted bargained and Sold unto y^e s^d Benjamin Libbey his heirs and Assigns for ever against y^e Lawfull Claims & Demands of all & Every psons and psons Whatsoever./ In Witness whereof I y^e s^d Daniel Stone have hereunto Set my hand & Seal this Eighteenth day of July Annoq$_e$ Domini Seventeen hundred & Sixteen

Annoq$_e$ R^{i}R^s Georgii Magna Brittania &c^t Secundo
Signed Sealed & Delivered   Daniel Stone ($_{Seal}^a$)
 In the psence of
 Joseph Woodsum
 Nathaniel Gubtail
     York sc Berwick July 18th 1716.
 Daniel Stone above named psonally Appearing Acknowledged y^e above written Instrum^t to be his Volluntary Act & Deed   Coram Elisha Plaisted Jus^t p
 Recorded According to y^e Original July 21st 1716/
               p Jos. Hamond Reg^r

This Indenture made ye Seventh of Decemb^r in ye year of our Lord God One Thousand Six hundred Sixty & five between Allexand^r Thoyts of ye river of Kenebeck of ye one part & Richard Patteshal of Boston in New England and Humphrey Davie & Robert Patteshall of Boston in New

England Merchants of yᵉ other part Witnesseth that the sᵈ Allexandʳ Thoyts for & in Consideration of yᵉ Sum of Three hundred & fourteen pounds & five Shillings which he yᵉ sᵈ Allexander doth Acknowledge to have recᵈ by These presents & himselfe to be fully Satisfied & paid hath by these presents given granted bargained Sold and Confirmed And doth by these presents give grant bargaine Sell & Confirm unto yᵉ sᵈ Humphʳˢ Davie Robert Pateshal & Richard Pateshall their heirs & Assignes for ever all that part & parcell of land lying & being Situate in Kenebeck river in yᵉ Province of Maine yᵉ uper part yᵉ bounds begining at yᵉ Cove which is yᵉ lower bounds of a Tract of Land given & granted unto Mʳ Robert Gutch & So to run downward along by yᵉ water Side to yᵉ river Comonly known & Called by yᵉ Name of Winnigunseck with all & Singular its Marshes Meadows pastures feedings woods & underwoods Also wᵗʰ yᵉ Dwelling house of yᵉ sᵈ Allexandʳ Thoyts. Together with all barns Stables out houses buildings & Edefices to yᵉ sᵈ house & land or to any part or parcell of it belonging also with all its rights Members Jurisdictions & Appurtenᶜᵉˢ Together with all deeds writings Interest [159] Use Possession propperty Claim & Demand whatsoever also with four Cows Two Oxen & one bull of him yᵉ sᵈ Allexander Thoyts in or to yᵉ Same or any part or parcell of it To have & To hold yᵉ sᵈ lands Cattle houses & all & Singular yᵉ premises hereby granted bargained & Sold with their & Every of their Members & Appurtenances to yᵉ sᵈ Humphry Davie Robert Pateshal & Richard Pateshal their heirs & Assignes forever against him yᵉ sᵈ Allexandʳ Thoyts his heirs & Assigns and all & Every person & persons whatsoever Lawfully Claiming by from or under him them or any of them Shall & will forever defend by these presents And theˢᵈ Allexander Thoyts for himselfe his heirs Executʳˢ & Admʳˢ do Covenant promiss grant & Agree to & with yᵉ sᵈ Humpʳʸ Davie &cᵗ in maner & form following That is To Say theˢᵈ Humphry Davie Robert Pateshall and Richard Pateshall at yᵉ Time of yᵉ Ensealing & Delivery of these presents are in a good pure perfect & Absolute Estate of Inheritance of all & Singular yᵉ yᵉ before granted premisses & Every part thereof Shall be fully Vested and Setled in & upon yᵉ sᵈ Humphry Davie Robert Patteshall & Richard Pateshall According to yᵉ True meaning of these pʳsents And that yᵉ sᵈ Humphry Davie Richᵈ Pateshall & Robert Pateshall & Every of them Shall from time to time & forever be defended by yᵉ sᵈ Allexander Thoyts his heirs Exʳˢ & Admʳˢ of & from all maner of other & former gifts grants bargains sales Leases Mortgages Titles Troubles

Book VIII, Fol. 159.

Charges demands & Incumbrances whatsoever had made Comitted Suffered Omitted or done by ye s^d Allexander Thoyts his heirs Execut^{rs} or Adm^{rs} or by any other pson or psons whatsoever Lawfully claiming by from or und^r him them or any of them his or their Means act or procurem^t In Witness whereunto ye s^d Allexand^r Thoyts hath hereunto put his hand & Seal this Seventh day of Decemb^r One thousand Six hundred Sixty & five & in ye Seventeenth year of the reign of our Soveraign Lord King Charles ye Second

Whereas there is a parcell of marsh lying & being on ye South Side of Winniganseek river Vallued at Sixty pounds which s^d Sum of Sixty pounds ye afores^d Allexand^r Thoyts doth Acknowledge to have rec^d by these presents that if ye s^d Alexander doth make good ye s^d Marsh unto Humphry Davie Robert Patteshall & Richard Patteshall then ye s^d Allexand^r to keep & detaine ye s^d Sum of Sixty pounds already rec^d by him or Else to repay & Allow thes^d Sum of Sixty pounds back again to ye s^d Humphry Davie Robert Pateshall & Richard Pateshall their heirs or Assignes

Signed Sealed & Delivered

   In psence of   Allexander his mark Thoyts (Seal)
      Nich^o Reynalls
Witnesses Edwd Pryor
      Thomas Stevens

There being a True Coppy of ye within written deed Delivered to Mr Humphry Davie Wee whose names are under written do Acknowledge for ourselves our heirs Ex^{rs} Adm^{rs} or Assignes to & with Mr Humph^{ry} Davie his heirs Ex^{rs} Adm^{rs} or Assigns that Thes^d Davie is halfe Interested and owner of ye land & Cattle &c^t within Mentioned & ye halfe belongeth to our Selves as Witness our hands this 24th of May 1668./   Richd Peteshall

Witness
Edwd Peteshall
Recorded According to ye Original July 25th 1716
                    p Jos. Hamond Reg^r

Mrs Anne Hodsden the daughter of Mr Allexand^r Thoyts being Sixty Six years of Age Testifieth that her father Mr Allexander Thoyts of ye river Kennebeck Lived at Winegance against Arrowsick Island and that ye uper part of his land lay as far up ye river as ye uper end of Arowsick Island and ye Lower bounds butted upon ye river Called Winegansed river & that her father Mr Allexander Thoyts had dealings with Mr Richard Patteshall in Partnership with Mr Humphry Davie of Boston and that ye s^d Richard Patteshall agoing up ye river in his Sloop Came too at my fathers Meadow by Winegansed river and Attached his Cattle there and then Came up to my fathers house & Attached it also ye Land barn & Cattle there which So Angered my father that he resolved he Should keep them altho he had great Quantity of furrs and Skins Sufficient for ought I know to discharge ye Debt and thereupon they drew ye Deed of Sale of houses Barns Lands which I Very well remember was done and knew Edward Pryor & Thomas Stevens Two of ye Witnesses to ye Deed of Sale and that my father Moved of that place Some time after up ye river to ye best of my remembrance my s^d father Lived at this place Eight or nine years before ye s^d Richd Patishall Attached his houses & Lands &c^t./

Boston July 10th 1716

Anne A Hodsdon
her mark

Mrs Anne Hodsden then psonally Appeared before us whose names are hereunto Subscribed and made Oath to ye Trueth of ye above written Deposition and Certifie that ye words Edward Pryor and Thomas Stevens were Interlined in ye above written deposition before the Takeing thereof./

Edw. Bromfield   Just^d pac
Tho: Newton   Quom Unus

Recorded According to ye Original July 25th 1716

p Jos. Hamond Reg^r

Be it known unto all men by these p^{r}sents that Thomas Clark & Thomas Lake of Boston in New Engl^d Merch^{ts} for diverse good Causes hereunto moveing & n Special out of their good will to Allexand^r Thwaits of Kenebeck in New England his wife and Children do hereby Absolutely give & grant Alienate & Confirm unto ye Children of ye s^d Allexand^r Thwaits and Anne his wife to Say Elizabeth Anne John Rebecca Allexand^r Lydia Jonathan Mary & Margriet Thwaits a Certaine Tract of land lying & being of ye Western Side of Kenebeck river & against a small Island Called Kitts Island about a mile below Meaumkeg begining at a Certaine Smal brook about forty poles to ye Northward of a round hill a little above ye s^d Kitts Island and So down ye river Southward to a Certaine brook comeing into ye river against ye lower end of ye Sandy flats in ye Midle of ye river being Estimated near about a mile from ye first named brook and So running into ye lands four miles holding ye Same breadth as is between y{e} s{d} Two brooks And in Case y{e} s{d} land do not take in y{e} Meadow which y{e} s{d} Allexander is now Mowing that then [**160**] Thes{d} Thomas Clark & Lake also grants unto y{e} afores{d} Nine Children threscore acres of y{e} s{d} Meadow if there be So much there To have & To hold to y{e} aforementioned Nine Children of y{e} s{d} Allexander Thwaits and Anne his wife to them & Either of them their heirs Ex{rs} & Adm{rs} in Equall proportions from y{e} Day of y{e} Date untill y{e} Setling of Twelve famillys thereabouts or y{e} granting of a Township y{e} one halfe of y{e} Same for ever and y{e} other halfe to be Yielded up to such inhabitants or Township for Incoragom{t} of their Setleing there provided that it do not intrench upon any Land that shall be Improved before that time And it is hereby declared that y{e} s{d} Allexander Thwaite And Anne his wife have Liberty to Improve y{e} s{d} land dureing their Natural lives or Either of them for y{e} Education and bringing up y{e} s{d} Children providing that what building fenceing or other Improvem{t} he y{e} s{d} Allexand{r} or Anne his wife shall make upon y{e} s{d} land be kept and left in good and Sufficient repair And at y{e} decease of y{e} s{d} Allexand{r} & Anne his wife y{e} s{d} land & whatsoever houses or other Improvem{t} shall be made be Equally divided unto y{e} s{d} Nine Children their heirs Ex{rs} & Adm{rs} alwayes provided that they nor any of them their heirs Adm{rs} or Assigns Trade with y{e} Natives for moose bever or other furrs And in Testimony that y{e} s{d} Thomas Clark & Thomas Lake for themselves their heirs Ex{rs} and Adm{rs} have given and granted y{e} aforementioned land & Meadow with all their Title & Interest therein and Liberty & priviledge thereunto belonging unto y{e} s{d} Nine Children their heirs Ex{rs} & Adm{rs} As afore mentioned they have put to their hands & Seals y{e} Tenth day of Aug{st} in y{e} year of our Lord 1668. And in y{e} Twentyeth year of the reign of our Soveraign Lord Charles y{e} Second King of England Scotland france & Irel{d} Defend{r} of y{e} faith &c{t}

Signed Sealed & Delivered & y{e} word Westward Interlined in y{e} thirteenth line in y{e} psence of
Richard Collecott
Richard Pugsley
Sylvanus Davis
Hen: Frencham/

Thomas Clark for three Eights (a Seal)
Thomas Lake for three Eights (a Seal)
and Two Eights for Capt{n} Allen and M{t} Nichalson according to the Trust Comited to me to act for them as for my Selfe

Recorded According to y{e} Original June 11{th} 1716

p Jos. Hamond Reg{r}

BOOK VIII, FOL. 160.

Know All men by these presents that I Thomas Abbet of Berwick in y{e} County of York and within his Maj{tys} Province of y{e} Massachusets Bay in New England Labourer for & in Consideration of y{e} Sum of Thirty & Six pounds Curra{t} money to me in hand paid at & before y{e} Ensealing & Delivery of these psents to my Acceptation & Ample Satisfaction have without any dispute Controversie or further tho,t Absolutely Sold Aliened Confirmed and do by these psents Assuredly give grant bargaine & make Sale to John Abbet and his heirs Execut{rs} & Assignes of whom I rec{d} s{d} money Acquitting his heirs therefrom & Every of them their part a grant of Land Scittuate Lying & being in y{e} Township of s{d} Berwick Containing Sixty Acres being a grant granted to M{r} Thomas Abbet dec{d} y{e} Eighteenth of Decemb{r} 1669 by York path & fifty Acres being an Addition to y{e} above granted./ Granted to him s{d} Thomas Abbet dec{d} y{e} Thirteenth day of Aprill one Thousand Six hundred & Seventy & one y{e} full of which Amounts to One hundred & Ten Acres runing a mile in length from y{e} Brow of y{e} rocky hill at Slutts Corner East Southeast to John Taylers marsh & fifty Six pole in breadth bounded on y{e} Northwest on land of M{r} Fox on y{e} East with John Taylers Marsh & Comon land and on y{e} South & west by y{e} Comon lands Together with all & Singular all y{e} rights profits priviledges & Appurtenances thereunto belonging or in any maner of kind Appurtaining To Have & To hold all y{e} above granted & bargained premisses with their Appurtenances unto him y{e} s{d} John Abbet & to his heirs Ex{rs} Adm{rs} & Assignes to his & their Universal use Occupication Improvem{t} & Ireversable possession declareing y{e} pmisses Acquitted from all former grants bargains Sales Leases Mortgages Titles Troubles dowrys Thirds Executions Claims & demands Executions Judgm{ts} or Controversies in Law And further I y{e} s{d} Thomas Abbet my heirs Execut{rs} & Adm{rs} shall & will from hence forth & forever hereafter Warrant & defend all y{e} above granted & bargained pmisses with their Appurtenances unto him y{e} s{d} John Abbet his heirs & Assignes against y{e} Lawfull claimes & demands of all persons whatsoever As Witness my hand & Seale Dated Berwick Decemb{r} y{e} Sixteenth Anno Domini Seventeen hundred & fourteen in y{e} first year of his Maj{tys} reign Over Great Brittain
Signed Sealed & Delivered   Thomas X Abbet (Seal)
  In y{e} presence of us   his mark   a
  Joseph Woodsum
  John Bradstreet
  Note that s{d} Thomas Abbet Shall have firewood of s{d} Land

dureing his Naturall Life uninteruptedly./ Entred before Subscription
 Berwick July 24th 1716
Thomas Abbet psonally Appear^d before me ye Subscrib^r and Acknowledged this within written Instrum^t for to be his Volluntary Act & Deed./ Elisha Plaisted Just. p
 Recorded According to ye Original Aug^st 2^d 1716./
p Jos. Hamond Reg^r

Know All men by these presents that I John Woodman of York in ye County of York in ye Province of ye Massachusets Bay in New Engl^d yeoman have recieved full Satisfaction for ye within written deed of Mortgage & have remised released and forever Quitted Claime to the Land therein Expressed and by these presents do for me my heirs Execut^rs & Adm^rs & Every of us clearly & Absolutely remise release & forever Quit Claime unto Saml Spinney of Kittery his heirs Execut^rs Adm^rs & Assignes all my right Title & Interest to the Land Contained in ye within written deed of Mortgage & Also [161] from all & all maner of Actions Suits debts dutys bonds bills Acco^ts and demands whatsoever which I have had or may have Against ye s^d Saml Spinney for or by reason of any Matter Cause or thing whatsoever from ye begining of ye world to ye day of ye Date of these p^rsents Witness my hand & Seal this Eighteenth day of June Anno Domini 1716./ John Woodman (Seal a)
Signed Sealed & Delivered
 In ye psence of us
 John Newmarch
 John Adams
 Rich^d R Rogers   (his mark)
York sc July 4th 1716.
John Woodman above named Acknowledged ye above written Instrum^t to be his free Act & Deed
Before John Weeelwright Just^ce Peace
Recorded According to ye Original July 16 : 1716./
p Jos. Hamond Reg^r
The deed of Mortgage to which this Instrum^t has reference is recorded in this book folio 29th
Attests J : Hamond Reg^r

Book VIII, Fol. 161.

To All People to whom this present deed of Sale Shall Come Susanah Seacomb of Boston in y[e] Province of y[e] Massachusets Bay in New England Single woman Sendeth Greeting Know Yee that I y[e] sd Susannah Seacomb as Trustee to the Estate Lands and Chattles of my Late Hon[d] ffather m[r] Richard Seacomb Late of Casco Bay in y[e] Eastern parts of New England Dec[d]/ Empowered by his last will & Testament as Trustee to Sell Dispose and Convey all y[e] Lands & Chattles of my sd ffather or Late in his Tenure & Occupation at Casco Bay aforesd for the Bringing up of Noah & Richard Seacomb his two Sons as by sd will now on Record at Salem in y[e] Province aforesd reference thereunto being had may appear/ for and in Consideration of the Sum of Fourteen Pounds in Currant money of New England to me in hand well & Truly p[d] at & before the ensealing hereof by John Rogers of Boston aforesd Gent the receipt whereof I Doe hereby acknowledge which has been by me expended towards bringing sd Children up & my Selfe therewith fully satisfied contented & paid & thereof & from every part thereof do acquit and fully Discharge the sd John Rogers his Heirs & assignes forever by these p[r]sents: Have given granted bargained Sold Alliened Conveyed & Confirmed & by these p[r]sents Doe fully freely & absolutely give grant bargaine Sell Alliene Convey & Confirm unto him the sd John Rogers his Heirs Executors' administrators & Assignes all That y[e] Lands Late in y[e] tenure & Occupation of my sd ffather in Casco Bay aforesd being butted & bounded by Sundry Deeds and writings from the former proprietors unto y[e] sd Rich[d] Seacomb & are as followeth (Viz[t]) ffifty acres of Land & Ten acres of Marsh bought of John Clean as by his Deed Dated Nov[r] 20th 1657 Also one Island Containing one Hundred acres by a Town grant on record also all y[e] Lands in y[e] Town of Casco aforesd as by a Town grant and all and Singular the other Tracts Lotts farms or Islands that Shall or may be found belonging to me as Trustee aforesd Together with all wayes Easm[ts] woods Trees mineralls floods Rivers & Appurtenances to y[e] sd Lands & all & Every of them belonging or In any wise appertaining & all Deeds writings & Evidences Relating unto or Testifying of y[e] Same & every part thereof To Have & To Hold all & Singular the above granted & Sold p[r]mises and their appurtenances unto him the sd John Rogers his Heirs & assignes forever & and to his & their Sole & propper use & behoofe from henceforth forever and y[e] s[d] Susannah Seacomb doth for herselfe her heirs Ex[rs] & Adm[rs] Cov-

enant promise & grant to & with the s^d John Rogers his heirs & assignes that the p^rmises before bargained & their appurtenances are at & before the Ensealing hereof free & Clear acquitted & Discharged of & from all & all maner of former & other gifts grants bargains Sales titles troubles acts allienations Joynters Dowers wills entailes or Incumbrances what soever & that I have as Trustee afores^d in my Selfe full power good right & Lawfull Authority the p^rmisses and every of them to give grant bargaine Sell aliene Convey & Confirm unto him ye s^d John Rogers his heirs & assigns as aforesd & that he ye s^d John Rogers his heirs & assignes Shall & may from time to time & at all times forever hereafter Have Hold use emprove occupy possess and enjoy ye Same & every of them with their appurtenances free & Clear without any Lawfull lett hinderence Mollestation or disturbance had made or done or sufered to be done by me the s^d Susanah Seacomb or from any other person from by or under me And that I ye s^d Susanah Seacomb Shall & will Warrent and Defend the the Sale of ye pmisses unto him ye s^d John Rogers his heirs & Assignes against my Selfe and Every other person Lawfully claiming any right thereto or Interest therein forever by these presents./ And that I ye s^d Susannah Seacomb my heirs Ex^rs & Adm^rs shall & will do any other further thing or things that may be for ye better Secureing & more Sure makeing ye p^rmisses unto him ye s^d John Rogers his heirs & assignes in Maner as afores^d/ In Witness whereof I ye s^d Susannah Seacomb have hereunto Set my hand & Seal the Twenty fifth day of June Anno Dom: One Thousand Six hundred & Ninety Eight in ye Tenth year of ye reign of our Soveraign Lord William King of Great Brittain france & Ireland &c^t   Susannah Seacomb (a Seal)
Signed Sealed & Delivered
In ye psence of us
Matt: Paulling
Sarah Knight
1698
    Boston June 26th 1698:
Susannah Seacomb psonally Appearing before me ye Subscrib^r One of his Maj^tys Councill for ye Province of ye Massachusets Bay & Justice of peace within ye Same & Owened this Instrum^t to be her Volluntary Act & Deed   Jno Saffin
Recorded According to ye Original June 9th 1716/
        p Jos. Hamond Reg^r

Book VIII, Fol. 162.

[162] To All People to whom this present Deed of Sale Shall Come John Haughton of Roxbury in ye Province of the Massachusets Bay in New England Shipwright Sendeth Greeting Know Yee that I ye s^d John Haughton for and in Consideration of the full & Just Sum̃ of Ten Pounds in Currant money of New England to mee in hand well & Truly paid by John Rogers of Boston in the Province of the Massa-Bay afores^d Gent- the Recait of which Sum̃ : I Doe hereby acknowledge & my Selfe therewith to be fully satisfied Contended & paid and thereof & from every part & parcell thereof I ye s^d John Haughton and Ruth my wife Doe for us our heirs Execut^{rs} & Admin^{rs} Acquit Exonerate & fully Discharge him ye s^d John Rogers his heirs Executors & administrators firmly by these p^{r}sents Have given granted Bargained Sould Alliened enfeoffed conveyed & Confirmed and by these p^{r}sents Doe for us the s^d John Haughton and Ruth my wife our heirs Executors & administrat^{rs} fully freely and absolutely give grant Bargaine Sell alliene enfeoffe Convey & Confirme unto him ye s^d John Rogers his heirs & assignes all that our Tract of Land Lying and being Scittuate in Falmouth in Casco Bay in New England aforesd̃ which Land I bought of John Greason as by a Deed bearing Date the Twelfth Day of this Instant Septemb^r may more fully appear and sd̃ Tract of Land is by Estimation Fourscore & Ten Acres be the same more or Less being butted and bounded Easterly on Psumscutt River Southerly upon a brook Westerly upon the Land of John Brown Late of Casco aforesd̃ Dec^d Northerly upon ye Land of Robert Nickolls or however otherwise bounded or reputed to be bounded To Have and To Hold the sd̃ Tract of Land so Measureing & butted & bounded as aforesd̃ Together with all ye wayes Easements Imunityes Timber woods Timber trees waters water Courses or ruñs of water mines Minerals and all and Singular the proffits priviledges & appurtenances to ye sd̃ Tract of Land bellonging or in any wise appurtaining unto him ye s^d John Rogers his heirs & assignes and to his & their Sole and proper use Benifit & behoofe from henceforth & forevermore And Wee the s^d John Haughton & Ruth my wife Doe Covenant promise & grant to & with him the sd̃ John Rogers his heirs Executors Administrators & assignes That at ye time of the ensealing & Delivery of these p^{r}sents the sd̃ Tract of Land and every part & parcell thereof is free & Clear acquitted & Discharged of & from all & all manner of former and other gifts grants bargains Sales Joyntures Dowers Wills Entails Deeds Mortgages Judgments Executions & of & from all other Incumbrances what-

soever And that Wee or one of us are ye true right & proper owner of y^t premiss & every part y^r of And have in our Selves full power good right and Lawfull authority ye Same to give grant bargaine Sell & Convey as as afores^d And that he the s^d John Rogers his heirs and assignes shall and may from time to time & at all times for ever hereafter have hold use Improve Occupie possess and enjoy ye before granted & bargained p^{r}mises & their Appurtenances and every of them without any Lawfull Lett hinderance Mollestation Deniall claime or Demand of us ye s^d John Haughton & Ruth my wife our heirs Executors Administrators or Assignes And that Wee ye s^d John Haughton and Ruth my wife Shall & will from time to time & at all times for ever hereafter Shall & will warran^t & Defend ye Sale of the p^{r}mises unto him ye s^d John Rogers his heirs & assignes against our Selves & Every other person Lawfully pretending any right thereto or interest in the same or any part thereof for ever by these p^{r}sents & that Wee will make any other further act or thing that may be for ye better confirming & more sure makeing the p^{r}remises & ye Sale thereof as aforeS^d unto him ye s^d John Rogers his heirs and assignes according to the Laws of this province : In Witness whereof we ye sd John Haughton & Ruth my wife have hereunto Set our hands & Seals y^e three and Twenteth day of Septemb^r Ann^o Dom : One Thousand Six Hundred & Ninety Eight in y^e Tenth year of the Reign of Our Soveraign Lord William the Third over England Scotland France & Ireland King Defender of the faith &c^t/ 1698/ John Haughton ($_{Seal}^a$)

Signed Sealed and Delivered
   In the Presents of us   Ruth ⦿ Haughton ($_{Seal}^a$)
   Timothy Prout   mark
   Sarah Knight
   16 :98

Boston in the County of Suffolk Sept^{er} 23 : 1698 The Subscriber personally appearing before me the Subscriber one his Maj^{tys} Justices of peace for the County aboves^d and acknowledged this Instrum^t to bee their voluntary act and Deed   Timothy Prout

Recorded According to ye Original June 9° 1716./
                                            p Jos Hamond Reg^r

To All People to whom this present Deed of Sale Shall come James Corbin of woodstok in the Cuonty of Suffolk within the Province of the Massachusets Bay in New England Mason which sd James was the Kinsman and now is the only heir att Law of Robert Corbin Late of Casco Bay in the Eastern parts of New England Dec^d Sendeth Greeting Know Yee That I ye sd James Corbin for & in Consideration of ye sum of ten pounds of Currant Silver money of New England to me in hand well & Trully [163] paid att and before the Ensealing and Delivery hereof by John Rogers of Boston in the County aforesd Gent the receipt Whereof I Do hereby acknowledge and my Self therewith fully Satisfied and paid and thereof and of Every part and parcell thereof Do acquit and fully Discharge the sd John Rogers his heirs Execut^{rs} and Administrators and assignes for Ever by these p^{r}sents Have given granted bargained and Sold allimened Conveyed & Confirmed and by these presents Doe fully freely & absolutely give grant bargaine Sell Alliene convey & Confirm unto him the Said John Rogers his heirs Execut^{rs} administrat^{rs} and assignes All that the Lands Late in the Tenure or occupation of Robert Corbin and whereon ye s^d Robert Corbins Late Dwelling house and Orchard Stood on Casco Bay aforesd & all & Singular other Tract or Tracts of Land Meadow Marshes Island or Islands Massuages or Tenements whatsoever Devided or undivided that Shall or may be found belonging unto me ye s^d James Corbin as heir at Law to Robert Corbin aforesd which s^d Lands are butted & bounded by Sundrey Deeds & writings from the former Proprietors unto the sd Robert Corbin & Contain in Quantity about one Hundred acres more or Less Together with all wayes Easem^{ts} Woods Trees Rivers and appurtenances whatsoever to ye s^d Lands and all & every of them belonging or in any wise appertaining And all Deeds Writeings & Evedences relateing unto or Testifying of ye same & Every part thereof: To have and to hold all & Singular the above granted Sold p^{r}mises and their Appurtenances unto him the said John Rogers his heirs & Assignes forever and to his and their Sole use benifit & behoof from henceforth and forever by these presents And I ye s^d James Corbin for my Self my heirs Executors & administrators Do Covenant promise and grant to & with the s^d John Rogers his heirs & assignes that ye before bargained p^{r}mises & their appurtenances are att & before the Ensealing & Delivery free and Clear acquited & Discharged of & from all and all mañer of former and other gifts grants bargaines Sales Titele Troubles acts allienations Joyntures Dowers wills Entailes

or Incumbrances whatsoever And that I have in my Selfe as heir afores^d full power good Right & Lawfull authority to give grant bargain aliene Convey & Confirm ye p'mises & Every of them with their appurtenances unto him the sd John Rogers his heirs & assignes as afores^d/ And that he the Said John Rogers his heirs & assignes Shall and may from time to time and att all times forever hereafter have hold use Emprove occupie posses & Injoy the Same & Every of them with their appurtenances free & Clear without any Lawfull Lett hindrance: Molestation or Disturbance had made or Done or Suffered to be done by me ye s^d James Corbin or by Any other pson by or under me And I the sd James Corbin the aforementioned bargained premises & Every part & parcell thereof unto him ye sd John Rogers his heirs & assigns against my Selfe my heirs Executors & administrat^{rs} and Every other person Claimeing any Right thereto or Interest therein Shall & will warrant & forever Defend by these Presents: And I ye s^d James Corbin my heirs Executors and administrat^{rs} Shall and will make Signe Seal & Deliver or otherwise duely execute any other and further act or Deed for the more Effectual Secureing the p^{r}mises unto him ye s^d John Rogers his heirs & assignes as by him or his Councill Learned in ye Law Shall be devised Advised or required In Witness whereof I have hereunto Set my hand & Seal the twentieth day of octob^r Annoq, Dom 1698/ Annoq, RR^s Gulielmi 3ii Angla &c^t Decimo/   James Corbin (Seal)
Signed Sealed & Delivered
 In presents of us
 Joseph Marion
 Edward Weaver
  Boston Octob^r 24th 1698/

The above named James Corbin psonally appearing before me ye Subscrib^r one of his Majesties Councill for ye province of ye Massachusets Bay and Justice of peace in ye Same acknowledged ye above written Instrum^t to be his free & volluntary act & Deed   Penn Townsend

Recorded According to ye Original June 9° 1716.

        p Jos Hamond Reg^r

To All People to whom these presents Shall Come I Richard Secomb of Portsm^o in ye Colony of Rode island & Providence plantation in New England Weaver Sendeth

Greeting Know ye that I yᵉ sᵈ Richᵈ Secomb for & in Consideration of yᵉ full & Just sum of Eight & twenty pounds Currant money of New England to me in hand paid before Signing & Sealing of these pʳsents by mʳ John Rogers of Swanzy in yᵉ County of bristoll in yᵉ province of yᵉ Massachusets Bay in New England [164] Yeoman Have remised released and for ever Quit Claimed & by these presents Doe for me my heirs & assignes and Every of us freely Clearly & absolutely remise releas and for ever quit Claime unto yᵉ sᵈ John Rogers his heirs Executors administratʳˢ & assignes for Ever all yᵉ Estate Right Title Interest Possession Reversion Claime & Demand whatsoever wᶜʰ I yᵉ sᵈ Richard Seacomb now have may might or ought to have or wᶜʰ I or my heirs at any time hereafter Shall or may have might or ought to have by virtue of yᵉ Last will & Testamᵗ of my Honᵈ father Richᵈ Seacomb Decᵈ unto Certain tracts & parcells of Land marshes & Islands Lying & being in yᵉ Eastwᵈ parts of yᵉ aforesᵈ province att Casco Bay & places adiacent as by anchant grants Deeds & other writings may more Largly appear & also all & all mañer of actions Suites Debts Duties bonds bills writings Obligatory Reckonings accounts & Demands whatsoever which I yᵉ sᵈ Richᵈ Seacomb now have or for ever may have by vertue of sᵈ will Ratifying alowing & Confirming a Deed of sale given to yᵉ sᵈ John Rogers by my Sister Susanᵃ Seacomb Executrix to the aforesᵈ will : To have and To hold yᵉ sᵈ Lands marshes & Islands Debts Duties bonds bills Writeings Reckonings accounts & Demands whatsoever unto yᵉ sᵈ John Rogers his heirs & assignes to his & their one proper use & behoof for ever So as neither I yᵉ sᵈ Richard Seacomb nor my heirs Shall or may at any time hereafter ask Claime Challeng or Demand any Right Title Interest Claime or Demand whatsoever of in or to yᵉ pmises before mentioned or of in or to any part or parcell thereof but yʳ of & yʳ from Shall be uterly Debared & for ever Secluded by these pʳsents & I yᵉ sᵈ Richᵈ Seacomb & my heirs yᵉ sᵈ Lands & all & Singular other yᵉ pʳmises above mentioned unto yᵉ sᵈ John Rogers his heirs & assignes to yᵉ use & behoof aforesᵈ against me yᵉ sᵈ Richard Seacomb & my heirs or any other person or persons whatsoever Claimeing yᵉ Same or any part thereof will warrant & for ever Defend by these pʳsents/ In Witness whereof I yᵉ sᵈ Richard Seacomb have hereunto Set my hand & Seal this Eleventh Day of January in yᵉ first year of yᵉ Reign of George King of Great Brittain &cᵗ and in yᵉ year of our

Book VIII, Fol. 164.

Lord one Thousand Seven hundred & fourteen or fifteen
1714 or 15/   Richard Secomb ($_{Seal}^a$)
Signed Sealed & Delivered
 In y^e presence of us
 Nathaniel Searts
 Sarah Stearts
  Bristoll ss/
 The above named Richd Seacomb personally appearing before me y^e Subscrib^r Did acknowledge this above written Instrum^t to be his free act and Deed In Little Compton y^e 17th day of Jan^ry in y^e first year of his maj^tys Reign annoq Domini 1714/5/ Thos Church Jus ps
 Recorded According to ye Original June 9° 1716./
        p Jos Hamond Reg^r

 This Bill of Sale made this fourteenth Day of agust in ye year of our Lord god one thousand Six hundred Eighty & five & in ye first year of ye Reign of our Soveraign Lord James ye Second by ye grace of god king of England Scotland france & Ireland Defender of the faith Between Thos Cloice & Susanah his wife of falmouth in Casco Bay in New England husbandman of ye one party & Richd Seacomb of ye above s^d falmo^th Gent-man of ye other party Witneseth— that I Tho: Cloice & Susan^a my wife have for Divers valluable Considerations & Six pounds in money to be paid to me in poork at three pence ye pound & beef in ye price as money before ye Ensealing & Delivery hereof have demised granted bargained & Sold & Do by this present bill of Sale Demise Set over & Sell unto ye abovesd Richard Seacomb all my Right Title & Interest in that farm where my father in Law George Lewis Lived & Dyed which he gave to his three youngest Daughters Containing fifty acres or thereabouts bounded on ye Northern Side by Nathaniel walles To have & To hold to him his heirs Executors Administrators and assignes with all priviledges & appurtenances what Ever : Except that part of ye fresh marsh which Doth belong to me and I ye s^d Thos Cloice & Susan^a my wife Do further Covenant & agree to & with ye aboves^d Richd Seacomb for us our heirs executors administrators & assignes that he ye s^d Richd Seacomb his heirs Execut^rs administrators & assignes Shall from time to time & all times hereafter quietly & peaceably Enjoy ye Same without any Let hinderence or Molestation whatsoever by me my heirs Executors administrators or assignes and from any other person or persons whatsoever Claimeing any right Title or Interest by any former Deed or Bill of Sale or other Conveyance whatever & I Thos Cloice & Susan : my wife Doe Covenant & agree to & with Richd Seacomb for us our heirs Execut^{rs} admin^{rs} & assignes that it Shall be Lawfull for ye s^d Richd Seacomb his heirs Execut^{rs} administrat^{rs} and assignes to require Either of us to Seal to any bill of Sale or Deed whatever for the beter Confirmation of ye s^d Estate as any Learned Councill Shall think fit it being within ye term of Seven years & at ye proper Cost of ye s^d Richd Seacomb In Witness here of ye partyes above mentioned have Enterchangeably Set their hands & Seals the Day & year a bove Written/

Souled & Delivered   Thomas Cloice (Seal)

  in ye presence of us
[165] Thomas Bailey   ye mark of Susan : ℰ Cloice (Seal)
John : Jordan

Thomas Cloice & his wife appeared before me & owned this bill of Sale to be their act and Deed unto m^r Richd Seacomb this 7th of Septm^r 1685./ before me

      Anthoney Brackett Comission^r

Recorded According to ye Original June 9° 1716

       p Jos Hammond Reg^r

Know All men by these presents that I Jothan Lewis of Greenland in ye province of New hampsh^r by & with y^e Consent of my wife mary Lewis y^e Daughter of George Lewis of Casco Bay Dec^d for & in Consideratin of y^e full Sum of fifteen pounds in boards in hand recieved & Secured before y^e Ensealing & Delivery of these p^{r}sents well & Truely payd & Secured to be paid y^e receipt whereof y^e s$\bar{d}$ Lewis & mary his wife Doe acknowledge and them selves fully Satisfied Content & paid & thereof and of Every part and penney thereof Doth acquit & Discharge m^r Richard Seacomb of Casco Bay his heirs Executors administrators & assignes for ever by these p^{r}sents as also for Divers Causes & Considerations us there unto moving have given granted bargained & Sold & by these presents Doe give grant bargaine Sell Deliver & Confirm unto ye afore s^d Richd Seacomb his heirs & assignes forever all That tract or parcell of Land being by Eastemation about Thirty acres Lying & being in Casco Bay bounded upon ye westward Side by a Creek & upon ye Eastward by ye Land of one Nathan^{ll} walles & is part of that Land George Lewis Lived upon & Dyed there which s^d Land is part of mary Lewis ye wife of Jotham aboves^d & Hannah her Sister the wife of James Darlin fell. To them for their portion with all profits priviledges & appurtenances thereunto belonging Together with all Timber trees woods under woods being growing Standing or Lying on s^d Land To Have and To Hold ye here before granted & bargained p^{r}misses & Every part & parcell thereof unto ye s^d Richd Seacomb his heirs Execut^{rs} admin^{rs} & assignes forever and s^d Lewis and mary his wife both for them Selves & in behalfe of there Sister Hannah above named their heirs Execu^{rs} admistrators & assignes Doth Covenant promis & grant to & with sd Richd Seacomb his heirs Executors administrat^{rs} & assignes & to & wth Every one of them by these presents that all and Singular ye sd p^{r}mises with all profits benefits & advantages in and by these presents given & granted bargained and Sold at ye time of ye Ensealing & Delivery hereof are & be and at all times hereafter Shall be remaine & Continue Clearly acquitted Exonerated Discharged & kept Harmless from all & all manner of former bargaines Sales gifts grants Leases Charges Dowrey title trouble & Incumbrances whatsoever made Committed Suffered or Done or to be had made Committed Suffered or Done by s^d Jotham Lewes & hannah ye wife of James Darlin & s^d Darlin their heirs Executors administrators or assignes or by any of them or by any other person whatsoever Claimeing any right thereto from by or under him them or any of them as also to Save & Keep harmless s^d Seacomb from any Claim Phillip Lewis may pretend: unto by any Right from y^e aboves^d George Lewis In Witness whereof we have hereunto Set our hands & Seales this 30th day of August 1686

Signed Sealed & Delivery   Jotham Lewis ($_{Seal}^a$)
  In Presents of   y^e mark of
  Anthony Clarrian
  John Pickerin Senr Mary ⟋⟋ Lewis ($_{Seal}^a$)
                       y^e wife of Jothan Lewis

Portsmouth in y^e Province of New hampsh^r the 13th of Septemb^r 1686 then Came before me Jotham Lewis & mary his wife & acknowledged the above written to be their act & Deed   before me John Hincks of y^e Councell
Recorded According to y^e Original June 9° 1716 :/
                       p Jos. Hammond Reg^r

To All Christian People to whom this present writting Shall Come Greeting Know Yee that I John Greason of

Boston In New England Seaman for & in Consideration of a good and valluable Sum of ten pounds of good Currant & Lawfull money of New England to me well and truly in hand paid by John Haughton of Roxbury in ye County of Suffolk in New England afores^d ye receipt whereof I Doe by these presents acknowledge and therewith to be fully Satisfied & Contented have granted bargained and Sold Alliened Enfeoffed & Confirmed And by these presents Doe fully Clearly & absolutely grant bargaine And Sell alliene Enfeoffe & Confirm unto him ye s^d John Haughton his heirs Execut^rs Administrat^rs & assignes a Certaine Tract or p^rcell of Land formerly ye Lands of Robert Greason Father of ye s^d John Greason Lying & being in falm^o a^t Casco Bay in New England afore Said/ To have and To hold the above granted & bargained Tract or Tracts of Land with all ye priviledges and appurtenances to ye Same appertaining or in any wise belonging unto him ye s^d John Haughton his heirs Execut^rs Administrators & assignes for Ever to his and [**166**] their only proper use and behoofe and I ye s^d John Greason for for me my heirs Execut^rs administrators and assignes Doe Covenant and promise to and with the said John Haughton his heirs Executors administrators and assignes That I the said John Greason now am and at ye Ensealing hereof Shall Stand and be rightly Sole seazed of & in ye above granted bargained premises in an Endefeasable Estate of Inheritance in fee Simple & that I have good right full power and Lawfull authority to grant bargaine assigne Set over & Confirm ye same unto him ye s^d John Haughton his heirs Executors administrat^rs and assignes in manner as is aboves^d for ever & that ye s^d John Haughton his heirs Executors administrators & assignes them & Either of them Shall and may at all times and from time to time for Ever hereafter peaceably & Quietly have hold occupie Possess & Enjoy ye premises in & by these p^rsents granted bargained & Sold & Every part & parcell thereof with all ye priviledges & appurtenances to ye Same appertaining or in any wise belonging without the Let hindrance Deniall or Contradiction of me ye s^d John Greason my heirs Executors administrat^rs or assignes or of any other person or persons whatsoever or whosoever Lawfully Claimeing & haveing any right Title or Interest therein or in any part or parcell thereof from by or under us or of any or Either of us or by any other Lawfull wayes or meanes Whatsoever In Witness whereof I have hereunto Set my hand and Seal the twelfth day of Septemb[r] in y[e] year of our Lord One Thousand Six hundr[d] Ninety Eight

Signed Sealed and Delivered   John Greeson (a Seal)
  In Presence of
         mark
   Will: \W/ Phillips
      mark
   Jn[o] —+— Shine

Before Signing & Sealing it is agreed upon that in y[e] Second Line four words Should be rehearsed out & Likewise in y[e] 22[d] Line being a mistake Greason being writting for Haughton which is one word by reason of a mistake y[e] parties here Concernd Doe also agree that it Should be Rehearsed out

Boston Septemb[r] y[e] 24th 1698 then william Philps & John Shine parsonally appeared before me y[e] Subscriber one of his Maj[tys] Justices for y[e] County of Suffolk & made Oath that they ware both of them present & Saw John Greason Signe Seal & Deliver this Instrum[t] and that they Set their hands thereto as Witnesses   Timothy Prout

Recorded According to y[e] Original June 9th 1716
                          p Jos. Hamond Reg[r]

  · The Deposition of Nath[l] Wallis Aged fifty Two years or thereabouts Testifyeth and Saith that some time before y[e] first Indian Warr began I being at George Lewis his house s[d] Lewis shewed me his Will w[ch] he had made Concerning y[e] Disposeing of his Estate to his Children and this Deponant being there heard s[d] Lewis[s] will read and there was in y[e] will that his Two sons was to have Twelve pence apiece but for his land he had given to his three youngest daughters and all his goods & s[d] Wallis Asked s[d] Lewis why he gave his land to his daughters s[d] Lewis replyed he had given his Sons Enough Already and further Saith not

Taken upon Oath this 9° July 1683.
            Before Antho. Bracket Comission[r]

Recorded According to y[e] Original June 9° 1716.
                         p Jos : Hamond. Reg[r]

Granted Likewise to m[r] Rich Seacomb An Island Northwest from Jewells Island Comonly Called by y[e] name of

Book VIII, Fol. 167.

Hogg Island Containing fourscore or a hundred Acres More or Less

This is a True Coppy Taken out of ye records p me
Antho: Brackett Clerk
June 9º 1716
Recorded According to ye Coppy Aboves^d/
p Jos. Haṁond Reg^r

The Testimony of Mr John Phillips of Boston Aged 77 years or thereabouts Saith that Robert Corbin of Casco Bay & Clement Corbin of Muddy river have been Several Times at my house and I have heard ye s^d Robert Own ye s^d Clement Corbin to be his Cousin and Call him so many Times when they were Together.

Boston 28 : 8 : 1681. Sworn by m^r John Phillips Before us
Tho. Danforth Dep^t Govr
J Dudley Assista^t . . .
Recorded According to ye Original June ye 9th 1716.
p Jos. Haṁond Reg^r

The Testimony of Jabish Buckminster Aged 37 or there abouts Saith that I have been many Times in Company with Robert Corbin of Casco Bay And ye s^d Robert did frequently Inquire of me for his Cousin Clement Corbin of Muddy river & how he did and bid me remember his love unto him from time to time

Sworn by Jabez Buckminster 28 : 8 : 1681 Before us
Tho Danforth Dep^{ty} Govr
J Dudley Assista^t
Recorded According to ye Original June 9º 1716
p Jos. Haṁond Reg^r

[167] To All People to whom this Deed of Sale Shall Come Sam^{ll} Holman of Scittuate in ye County of Plymouth Laborer & Hannah Holman of Boston in ye County of Suffolk in New England Spinster Send Greeting Know Y^e that whereas Richard Callacot of Boston afores^d Mercht & Thomazin his wife Did by deed dated April ye Tenth 1684 Convey to our uncle Thomas Holman & our father Saml Holman

in Equall Halves One Moiety of a Tract of Land lying & being on y[e] west side of Kenebeck river in the province of Maine bounded as followeth Viz[t] from y[e] place where the dwelling house of Allexander Thwaits Stood down y[e] s[d] Kenebeck river to y[e] Lower part of a point of land Called Abbacadusset point Takeing in y[e] whole point of s[d] land and from s[d] point to run on a Straight line into y[e] Maine land four miles inward from y[e] afores[d] river & Also from y[e] s[d] place where s[d] dwelling house Stood to run upon a Straight line into y[e] Maine land four miles inward from y[e] s[d] river & So from y[e] s[d] river to Extend four miles into y[e] maine land all y[e] whole length of y[e] s[d] Tract of land from y[e] afores[d] place where y[e] house Stood to the utmost & Lowest part of y[e] afores[d] point or any part thereof and also One Moiety or halfe part of Two Islands & land lying in Kenebeck river afores[d] Near unto y[e] place where y[e] Afores[d] dwelling house Stood lying near Southeast from y[e] Same Comonly known by y[e] name of Swan Alley which s[d] Moiety is to begin from y[e] Lowermost part of y[e] furthest of s[d] Islands & So to Extend from thence to y[e] Middle of a Certaine Cove there as p s[d] deed may Appear which land above mentioned our s[d] father Sam[l] Holman haveing never in his lifetime Alienated deceased Intestate leaveing behind him one Son & Two daughters whereby Two fourth parts of his share or Interest dos Acrue and descend to his Son Sam[l] & One fourth part to his daughter Hannah Now Known Y[e] that we y[e] s[d] Sam[l] Holman & Hannah Holman for & in Consideration of nine pounds Currant money of New England to us in hand well & Truely paid by John Wentworth of Portsm[o] in y[e] Province of New Hampsh[r] Esq[r] Thomas Hutchinson Adam Winthrope David Jeffries Olliver Noyes Esq[rs] Stephen Minot John Ruck & John Watts Gent all of Boston afores[d] & in Consideration that y[e] above Mentioned Tract of Land is wholly Comprised & Included within a pattent now Claimed & possessed by the above named Wentworth and partners have for us our heirs Ex[rs] & Adm[rs] freely & fully given Granted Sold Enfeoffed & Confirmed and do by these presents frely and fully give grant Sell Enfeoffe & Confirm unto y[e] s[d] John Wentworth Thomas Hutchinson Adam Winthrop David Jeffries Oliver Noyes Stephen Minot John Ruck & John Watts all our right share Title & Interest in y[e] Lands afore mentioned being Three fourth parts of our s[d] fathers share According to s[d] deed Together with Three fourth parts of all y[e] Trees woods underwoods Swamps Meadows lands Waters water courses rivers fishings fowlings and all priviledges & Apurtenances to y[e] Same or any part thereof belonging To Have & To Hold y[e] s[d] Three

Book VIII, Fol. 167.

fourth parts of our s^d fathers share with ye priviledges & Appurtenances to them The Said Wentworth & partners above named their heirs & Assignes for ever free & clear & clearly acquitted & discharged of & from all former and other Gifts grants Sales Titles Troubles Mortgages & Incumbrances whatsoever./ In Witness whereof We have hereunto Set our hands and Seals in Boston afores^d this Twenty Second day of May Anno Dom^l Seventeen hundred & Sixteen in ye Second year of ye reign of King George Over Great Brittaine &c^t   Samuel Holman (Seal)

Signed Sealed & D^d
  In presence of
Edmund Mountfort
Buttalph Belknap

Hannah ⸱ her mark ⸱ Holman (Seal)

Boston May 22^d 1716 psonally Appeared before me ye Subscrib^r Saml Holman and Hannah Holman & Acknowledged the within deed of Sale to be their Act & deed./

Coram me Wm Harris Just^s Pac^s

Recorded According to ye Original Septr 10th 1716.

p Jos. Hamond Reg^r

To All People to whom these presents shall come James Berry of Boston in ye County of Suffolk in New England Labourer & Rachell his wife Send Greeting Know Y^e that whereas ye s^d Rachell was formerly possessed of the Severall Tracts of Land hereafter mentioned within the Province of Maine & Continued Siezed thereof till driven thence by the Indian Warr Viz^t one Tract bounded Easterly by Small point harbour and by a Small river runing Northerly out of ye Sea Towards Smal point harbour and by a line drawn from s^d river over to smal point harbour Near ye place where ye house of John Drake former husband of s^d Rachell once Stood bounded Southerly by ye Maine Sea Westerly by Casco Bay Northerly by Small point harbour Including all ye land within those bounds which Tract ye s^d Rachell bought before her Marriage above forty years ago of Blind Joan Great Agumagus & Sheepscot John Indians proprietors thereof Also a Tract of land bounded Northerly upon land of Robert Edmunds runing thence to lookout hill and fronting Easterly about One Quarter of A mile upon Atkins^s Bay & runing backward to Crooked Tree along by Spruce Swamp for a mile or thereabouts which Tract was granted and given to ye s^d Rachell above forty years Since by Grigery Mudge who built upon ye Same Also Another Tract

Called Smal point neck or ye parcell of upland & Marsh lying between ye Two Smal rivers that run from the Maine Sea to ye westward of Seguin Island Northerly into the land being bounded Easterly & Northerly by Land formerly belonging to Thomas Atkins & Lately Sold to Thomas Hutchinson Esqr & partners Southerly with ye Maine Sea & Westerly with ye land formerly belonging to John Drake but lately also Sold to s^d Hutchinson & partners which Tract was many years Since Possessed before ye Indian Warrs by John Hanson and by him left to ye s^d John Drake and aboves^d Rachell his wife [168] Now Know ye that ye above mentioned James Berry & Rachell his wife for & in Consideration of ye Sum̄ of Nine pounds Ten Shillings Curra^t money of New England to them in hand well & Truely paid before ye Ensealing & Delivery of these presents by John Wentworth of Portsmouth in ye Province of New Hampsh^r Esqr Thomas Hutchinson Adam Winthrop David Jeffries Oliver Noyes & John Watts Esq^rs Stephen Minot and John Ruck Gent all of Boston afores^d & for other good Causes & Considerations them thereunto moveing have given granted Sold Aliened Enfeoffed & Confirmed and do by these presents for themselves their heirs Executors & Administrat^rs fully freely & Absolutely give grant Sell Aliene Enfeoffe & Confirm to ye s^d John Wentworth Thom^s Hutchinson Addam Winthrop David Jeffries Oliver Noyes John Watts Stephen Minot & John Ruck ye Three Several Tracts of land above mentioned Together with all & Singular ye uplands Meadows Trees woods underwoods Mines Quarries Minerals waters water courses coves ponds Harbo^rs beaches flats priviledges & Appurtenances whatsoever to ye s^d Tracts of land or any of them now or heretofore belonging or any wayes Appurtaining. To have & To hold ye above mentioned Tracts of land with ye Appurtenances to ye above mentioned John Wentworth Thomas Hutchinson Adam Winthrop David Jeffries Oliver Noyes John Watts Stephen Minot and John Ruck to them their heirs Ex^rs Adm^rs & Assignes for ever free and Clear and Clearly Acquitted & discharged of & from all & all maner of former & other gifts grants bargaines Sales Titles Troubles demands Mortgages and Incumbrances forever./ and further ye s^d James Berry and Rachell his wife by these presents freely & fully resign and Quitclaim unto ye aboves^d Wentworth & partners ye Thirds or right of Dower of ye s^d Rachell to a Tract of land Adjoyning to the premisses formerly possessed & built upon & Inhabited by ye s^d John Drake and Rachell his wife and Lately Sold by Peter Soulard of Boston & Martha his wife daughter of ye s^d John & Rachell Drake to ye aboves^d Wentworth & partners As p s^d deed ye fourth day of April last referrence thereto being had will Appear./ In testimony of their Consent to & Confirmation of ye premisses ye s^d James Berry & Rachell his wife have hereunto Set their hands & Seals in Boston afores^d this Twentieth day of July Anno Dom^i Seventeen hundred and Sixteen in y^e Second year of the reign of King George Over Great Brittaine &c^t

Signed Sealed & dd
  In presence of
Stephen Minot Junr
Wm Taylor

The mark of
James ✝ Berry (Seal^a)
The mark of
Rachell ✗ Berry (Seal^a)

Suffolk sc/ Boston N E July 20° 1716 =
James Berry & Rachell Berry psonally Appeared before me y^e Subscrib^r & Acknowledged y^e Above written Instrum^t to be their Act & Deed   Grove Hirst J paces
Recorded According to y^e Original Septr 10th 1716/.

                               p Jos. Hamond Reg^r

    To All People to whom this Deed of Sale shall come Peter Soullard of Boston in ye County of Suffolk in New England Labourer & Martha his wife Send Greeting Know ye that whereas John Drake the father of ye s^d Martha did more than forty years Since purchase of John Hanson a Tract of land bordering upon Smal point harbour & Casco Bay in ye Province of Maine and did build upon Inhabit and for Several years Improve the Same till driven thence by ye Indian Warr at which Time his house & therein ye Deed for s^d land were Consumed to Ashes by ye Enemy./ Since which ye s^d John Drake is deceased Intestate leaveing one only child Martha now ye wife of ye s^d Peter Soullard whereby ye right Title Interest & propriety in ye s^d Land is devolved on the s^d Martha./ Now Know Y^e that ye s^d Peter Sullard & Martha his wife for and in Consideration of ye Sum of fifteen pounds Current money of New England to them in hand well & Truely paid before the Ensealing & Delivery of these presents by John Wentworth of Portsmouth in ye Province of New Hampsh^r Esqr Thomas Hutchinson Adam Winthrop David Jeffries Oliver Noyes Esqr Stephen Minot John Ruck & John Watts Gent all of Boston afores^d ye rec^t whereof they do hereby Acknowledge have for them their heirs Ex^{rs} & Adm^{rs} given granted Sold Enfeoffed & Confirmed & do by these presents fully freely & Absolutely give grant Sell

Enfeoffe and Confirm to ye s^d John Wentworth Thomas Hutchinson Adam Winthrop David Jeffries Oliver Noyes Stephen Minot John Wats all that Tract of land above mentioned begining at ye South East part of Small point harbour and runing upon a line Easterly to a Smal river that Comes out of ye Sea then Tending away North Northeasterly for a mile & halfe or thereabouts. Then on a return Westerly to Casco Bay So as to Include five hundred acres of upland besides all ye meadow lying on the Westerly Side of ye above mentioned river with whatsoever right or Interrest ye s^d Martha now hath or ought to have to ye lands there in right of her s^d Father To have & To Hold ye aboves^d tract of land with all woods Trees uplands Meadows waters water Courses priviledges & Appurtenances w^{t}soever to ye Same or any part thereof belonging or in any wise Appurtaining to them ye s^d John Wentworth Thomas Hutchinson Adam Winthrop David Jeffries Oliver Noyes Stephen Minot John Ruck & John Watts their heirs & Assignes for ever to be holden in Severalty & not by right of Survivership free & Clear of all claims & Demands from them ye s^d Peter & Martha Soullard or any pson by from or und^r them & free & Clear of all former & other gifts grants deeds Sales Mortgages Titles Troubles and Incumbrences whatsoever./ In Witness Whereof ye s^d Peter & Martha have hereunto Set their hands & Seals in Boston afores^d this fourth day of Aprill Anno Dom^i Seventeen hundred & Sixteen in ye Second year of ye reign of King George Over Great Brittaine &c^t

Signed Sealed & D^d Peter Soullard (Seal)
   In presence of
   Andrew Ruck   Martha ✝ Soullard (Seal)
   Abigail Ruck   mark

[169] Boston April 14th 1716 The above Subscribers Peter Soullard & Martha his wife personally Appearing before me Acknowledged this Instrum^t to be their act & Deed.
                  Elisha Hutchinson Jus^t Peace
Recorded According to ye Original Sep^t 10th 1716./
                      p Jos. Hamond Reg^r

To All People to whom this Deed of Sale Shall Come Elizabeth Davis of Beverly in ye County of Essex Widdow Sam^{ll} Clark of Marblehead in ye County afores^d Blacksmith and Anne his wife Sam^{ll} Gurney of Little Compton in ye County of Bristol Husbandman & Sarah his wife George

Book VIII, Fol. 169.

Pike of mendom in y[e] County of Suffolk Husbandman & Hester his wife James Berry of Boston in y[e] County afores[d] Labourer & Rachall his wife Thomas Washborn of Bridgwater in y[e] County of Bristoll Husbandman & Abigail his wife John Haskins of Scittuate in y[e] County of Plymouth Husbandman & Ruth his wife Send Greeting Know Yee that whereas Thomas Atkins formerly of Kenebeck Husbandman and Father of all the Females above Mentioned Did above Sixty Years Since purchas of the Indians a Large Tract of Land in y[e] Province of Maine in New England Lying between the River of Sagadehock or Kenebeck & Casco Bay & Did build upon Improve & Possess the Same Tell Driven thence by y[e] Indian Warr & Did when y[e] war was over return to his s[d] Land & Dy there Intestate Leaveing behind him no Son but Tenn Daughters whereby according to y[e] Laws of this Province y[e] s[d] Tract of Land Dos Decend & of right Equally bellong unto y[e] s[d] Ten Daughters Now Know Yee that the s[d] Elizabeth Davis Sam[ll] & Anne Clark Sam[ll] & Sarah Gurney George & Hester Pike Thomas & Abigail Washburn John and Ruth Haskins in Consideration of y[e] Sum of Thirty Pounds Currant Money of New England to them y[e] s[d] Daughters in hand well & Truly paid (that is to Say) five Pounds for Each Daughters Share & y[e] s[d] James & Rachall Berry for Ten pounds to them paid for her Share & y[e] Share of her Sister Rebecca Hall Living at Tarpolin Cove which Share they Doe hereby Dispose of and Oblige themselves within four months to procure Her y[e] s[d] Halls Confirmation of: Have given granted Sold Enfeoffed & Confirmed & Do by these presents Each for themselves Severally give grant Sell Enfeoffe & Confirme unto John Wintworth of Portsmouth in y[e] Province of New Hampsh[r] Esq[r] Thomas Hutchinson Adam Winthrop David Jeffrees & Oliver Noyes Esq[r] Stephen Minot John Ruck & John Watts Gen[t] all of Boston afores[d] their Heirs Execut[rs] Administrators & assignes one Tenth Part & y[e] s[d] James & Rachall Berry Two Tenth parts that is in the whole Eight Tenth parts of y[e] s[d] Tract of Land being Butted & bounded as follows Viz[t] fronting Easterly upon a Small Bay Called or known by the name of Atkins,s Bay Southerly bounded by a Creek Coming out of y[e] Sea & runing between this Land & Sagadehock point or Hunniwells Plantation bounded Southerly by y[e] Sea and Westerly by a river Coming out of y[e] Sea parting it from Small point runing at first Northwesterly or thereabouts & then turning away NorthEasterly runing up to y[e] head of y[e] Marshes where it bounds upon Land formerly belonging to John Hanson &

from thence runing into yᵉ Woods about five or Six miles by Computation up to yᵉ End of a fresh Meadow and from thence upon a Return to yᵉ head of a marsh Lying upon Long Cove which runs into atkins,s Bay parting it from Land of Robert Edmunds Together wᵗʰ all Woods Trees uplands Meadows Waters water Courses priviledges and appurtenances thereunto belonging or in any wise appertaining To Have and to Hold yᵉ sd Eight Tenth parts of yᵉ Land aforesᵈ or of whatsoeuer Land Did of right belong to their sᵈ Father Thomas Atkins with all priviledges & appurtenances thereunto to them yᵉ sᵈ John Wintworth Thomas Hutchinson Adam Winthrop David Jeffres Oliver Noyes Stephen Minot John Ruck & John Watts to be holden of them in Severalty & not by right of SurvivourShip to them their heirs & assignes for ever free & Clear of all Claimes and Demands of them yᵉ sᵈ Elizᵃ Davis Samˡˡ & Anne Clark Samˡˡ & Sarah Gurney George & Hester Pike Thomas & Abigail Washburn John & Ruth Haskins James & Rachal Berry & Rebecca Hall or Either of them their or Either of their heirs Execut'ˢ or Adm'ˢ or any person or persons claiming by from or under them or any of them and free & Clear from all former & other gifts grants Sales Titles Troubles Mortgages & Incumbrances wᵗsoever In Witness whereof we have hereunto Set our hands and Seales in Boston aforesᵈ this Second Day of aprill Anno Dom Seventeen hundred & Sixteen in yᵉ Second year of yᵉ Reign of King George over Great Brittaine &cᵗ

Signed Sealed & Delivered by yᵉ nine persons one other Side
In Presence of
The Interm't between yᵉ Twentieth & Twenty first Lines of yᵉ first page being first made
John Penhallow
Edmund Mountfort

Elizᵃ ⊬ her mark Davis (ₛₑₐₗᵃ)
                widdow
Hester ⌇ her mark Pike (ₛₑₐₗᵃ)
Thomas Washurn (ₛₑₐₗᵃ)
Abigail ✝ her mark Washburn (ₛₑₐₗᵃ)
James ✗ ≡ his mark Berry (ₛₑₐₗᵃ)
Rachal ✗ her mark Berry (ₛₑₐₗᵃ).
Ruth ⌐ her mark Haskins (ₛₑₐₗᵃ)
Elizᵃ ✝ her mark Davis (ₛₑₐₗᵃ)

Sarah ✗ her mark Gurney (ₛₑₐₗᵃ)
(Seal)
(Seal)
(Seal)
(Seal)

Book VIII, Fol. 170.

Suffolk ss/ Boston aprill 2ᵈ 1716/
Eliz* Davis appeared before me G: Hirst Hester Pike widdow appearᵈ before me   G : Hirst
    Suffolk ss/
Thomas Washburn & abigail his wife G: Hirst James Berry & Rachel his wife appeared before me & acknowledged yᵉ above Instrumᵗ to be their act & deed aprill 26ᵗʰ 1716/   W Harris Justice Pece

Ruth Haskins aprill 27ᵗʰ W Harrisˢ/
Eliz* Davis for anne Clarkes right may 4 1716 G Hirst
Sarah Gurney May 11ᵗʰ 1716 W Harrisˢ

[170] Marblehead May 3ᵈ 1716 Anne Clark gives up all her right & Title in her fathers Estate to her Sister Eliz* Davis As Witness my hand   Anne ✝ Clark mark
    Witness
    George Nickols

Situate this 25ᵗʰ of Aprill 1716/ These may Certifie all whome it may Concern that John Haskins of Situate Doe give unto my wife Ruth Haskins all my right & Interest in Thomas Atkins Estate Witness my hand
          The mark of ✝ John Haskins

Received the Sum of five pounds in full of my tenth part of yᵉ within Deed & yᵉ Sum of five pounds for my Sister Susanna Green her 10ᵗʰ part wᶜʰ I promiss to procure her Confirmation this 2ᵈ of Aprill 1716/
    of Oliver Noice Esqʳ
                        her
                     Eliz* ⌐⌐ Davis
                        mark

Recᵈ of Oliver Noice Esqʳ yᵉ Sum of five pounds in full of my 10ᵗʰ part of yᵉ within Deed my husband being Dead this 11ᵗʰ of aprill 1716/
                        her
                  Hester ⌐ Pike
                        mark

Received of Oliver Noyce Esqʳ of five pounds in full of my 10ᵗʰ part of yᵉ within Deed my husband Consenting thereto Boston aprill 27ᵗʰ 1716/
                       her
                  Ruth ⌐ Haskins
                      mark

Book VIII, Fol. 170.

Received of Oliver Noyes Esqr five pounds in full for my 10th part of ye within Deed this 27th aprill 1716/

Rachal ✗ Berry
her mark

Boston May 4th 1716 Rec^d of Oliver Noyes Esqr five pounds in full for ye tenth part of ye within Land belonging formerly to my Sister Anne Clark wch She has given to me as p her Deed annext hereunto

Elizabeth —✝— Davis
her mark

Boston may Tenth 1716. Rec^d of Oliver Noyes Esqr five pounds in full for my right of ye within mentioned Deed

Sarah —/— Gurney
her mark

A True Coppy of ye foregoing Deed of Sale Together wth ye Several Quit Claims & receipts above written being on ye Backside of s^d deed & Annexed thereunto is here recorded According to ye Originals Septemb^r ye 10th 1716./

p Jos Hammond Reg^r

This Indenture made this Twenty Eighth day of June anno Domini one thousand Seven hundred and Sixteen In the Second Year of ye Reign of our Soveragn Lord George King of great Brittain &c^t Between Samuel Spinney of Kittery in ye County of York in the Province of the Massachusets Bay in New England Yeoman on the one part and John Dennett of the Same place Carpenter on the other part Witnesseth That I the Said Samuel Spinney for and in Consideration of the Sum of Fifty pounds in Currant money of this Province to me in hand well and truly paid before the Ensealing hereof by the above said John Dennet the receipt whereof I do hereby acknowledge and my Selfe therewith to be fully Satisfied Contented and thereof and Every part and parcell thereof Do Exonerate acquit and Discharge the said John Dennet his heirs Executors & admin^r for ever by these presents Have given granted bargained Sold Allened enfeoffed Conveyed and Confirmed And by these Presents do fully freely & absolutely give grant bargaine Sell alliene

Book VIII, Fol. 171.

enfeoffe convey and confirm unto him the said John Dennet his heirs Executors adm⁽ʳˢ⁾ and assignes for ever a certaine tract or parcell of Land Scituate Lying and being in yᵉ Township of Kittery afores⁽ᵈ⁾ Containing Twenty five acres butted & bounded on the Northernend by the land of the said John Dennet and on the Eastern side by the Land of the s⁽ᵈ⁾ Sam⁽ˡˡ⁾ Spinney and Nathaniel Kane and on the western Side by yᵉ Land of the Said Dennet and to run Southerly the Same breadth that it is on yᵉ Northern end towards the Land of Thomas Woorster untill Twenty five acres are compleated; Together with all the rights profits priviledges and appurtenances as in any kind appertaine thereunto To have and To hold the said Granted and bargained Premises with all the appurtenan⁽ᶜˢ⁾ Priviledges and Commodities to the Same belonging or in any wise appertaining to him the said John Dennet his heirs Execut⁽ʳˢ⁾ adm⁽ʳˢ⁾ and assigns for ever to his and their own proper use benifit and behoof for ever And I the Said Sam⁽ˡˡ⁾ Spinney for me my heirs Executors and adminis⁽ʳˢ⁾ do covenant Promise and grant to and with yᵉ Said John Dennet his Heirs Execut⁽ʳˢ⁾ administrators and assignes that before the ensealing hereof I am the true Sole and Lawfull owner of yᵉ above bargained Premises and am Lawfully Seized and Possessed of the Same in my own proper Right as a good parfect and absolute estate of Inheritance in Fee Simple And have in my Selfe good Right full power & Lawfull authority to grant Bargaine Sell Convey and Confirm Said bargained premises in manner as afores⁽ᵈ⁾ and that the Said John Dennet his heirs Executors adm⁽ʳˢ⁾ and assignes Shall and may from time to time and at all Times for ever hereafter by force and virtue of these presents Lawfully peaceably and Quietly have hold use occupie possess and Injoy the said Demised and bargained premises with the appurtenances free and Clear and freely and Clearly acquitted Exonerated and Discharged of and from all and all manner of [171] Former and other gifts grants bargaines Sales Leases Mortgages Wills Entails Joyntures Dowries Judgments Executions Incumbrances & Extents w⁽ʰ⁾soever Furthermore I yᵉ s⁽ᵈ⁾ Samuel Spinney for my Selfe my heirs Execut⁽ʳˢ⁾ and adm⁽ʳˢ⁾ Do Covenant and promise at and upon the Reasonable Requst (and at yᵉ proper Cost & Charges in the Law) of yᵉ s⁽ᵈ⁾ John Dennet his heirs Executors Admin⁽ʳˢ⁾ or Assignes to make do preform and Execute any further or other Lawfull and reasonable Act or acts Thing or Things Device or Devices in yᵉ Law: need full or requisite

York March yᵉ 30ᵗʰ 1723 Receaved of Samuel Spinney fifty Pounds Money with yᵉ Interest in full of this deed of Mortgage and I do hereby acquit and absolutely discharge the Same in Every Part and Parçell thereof witness my hand John Dennet Witnes Abraᵐ Preble Regʳ

for the more perfect assureance Seteling and Sure makeing of the premises as afore said provided nevertheless and it is the true intent and meaning of grantor and grantee in these presents anything herein contained to the Contrary notwithstanding that if the above named Samuel Spinney his heirs Executors Adm^{rs} or assignes Do well and Truly pay or Cause to be be paid to ye s^d John Dennet his heirs Executors Adm^{rs} or assignes in good Current money of the afore said Province the Sum of fifty pounds before or at or upon ye Twenty Eighth day of June In the year of our Lord one Thousand Seven hundred twenty and Two and also annually and Every year pay or Cause to be paid ye Lawfull Interest of ye above mentioned Sum without fraud Coven or further Delay that then this above written Deed Indenture or Obligation and Every Clause and article therein Contained Shall cease be null void & of none effect but if Default happen to be made in ye afore sd paym^t Contrary to ye true Intent hereof then to abide & remaine in full force Strength & virtue to all Intents and purposes in ye Law w^{t}soever In Witness whereof I have hereunto Set my hand and Seal ye Day and year first above written memorand^m ye word year was Enterlined before Signing   Samuel Spinney (Seal)
Signed Sealed and Delivered
  In Presence of us   Margret /y/ Spinney (Seal)
  John Newmarch   mark
  John Newmarch Tert^r
      her
  Margret W Hammon
     mark
York ss/ July 18th 1716
  The within named Samuel Spinney and margret his wife psonally appearing Acknowledged ye within Instrum^t to be their free act and Deed   before abra^m Preble Jus: pes
  Recorded According to ye Original July 23^d 1716
                      p Jos: Hamond Reg^r

  To All People to whom these Presents shall come Greeting Know ye That I Sam^{ll} Spinney of Kittery in the County of york within his Majesties Province of the Massachusets Bay in New England Yeoman for & in Consideration of ye Sum of Two pounds and Ten Shillings an acre to me in hand paid well and truly before the ensealing and Delivery hereof by John Dennet of the Same place Carpenter ye Receipt whereof I do hereby acknowledge and my Selfe there-

with fully Satisfied & paid and thereof and Every part And
parcel thereof do exonerate acquit & Discharge ye s^d John
his Heirs Executors & admin^{rs} forever by these Presents
Have given granted bargained Sold Aliened Conveyed &
Confirmed and by these Present do fully freely & absolutely
give grant bargaine Sell aliene Convey & Confirm unto him
ye s^d John Dennet his heirs & assignes for ever a certaine
tract or parcel of Land Scituate & Lying in ye Township of
Kittery afores^d Containing by estimation five acres & an
half be it more or less butted & bounded on ye western
Side Twenty four poles and on ye northern End thirty Seven
poles by ye Land of ye s^d John Dennet & on the Eastern
Side Twenty four poles & Southern end thirty Seven poles
by ye Land of the above Said Spinney To Have & To hold
the said granted & bargained Premises with all the appurtenances priviledges and commodities to the Same belonging
or in any wise appertaining to him thes^d John Dennet his
heirs Executors Adm^{rs} and assignes for ever To his & their
only proper use benefit & behoof for ever And I ye s^d Samuel Spiñey for me my Heirs Execut^{rs} And Adm^{rs} do Covenant promise and grant to & with ye s^d John Dennet his
heirs Execut^{rs} Adm^{rs} and And assignes that before ye ensealing
hereof I am the True Sole & Lawfull owner of ye above
bargained & Sold premises and am lawfully Seized & possessed of the Same in mine own proper right as a good perfect & absolute Estate of Inheritance in Fee Simple and
have in my Self good right full power & Lawfull Authority
to grant bargain Sell Convey & Confirm Said bargained
Premises in manner as aboves^d And that ye s^d John Dennet
his heirs Execut^{rs} Admin^{rs} & Assignes Shall & may from
time to time and at all Times forever hereafter by force &
virtue of these psents Lawfully peaceably & Quietly have
hold use occupy possess & enjoy ye s^d Demised & bargained
pmises with ye appurtenances free & Clear & freely & clearly acquitted exonerated & Discharged of and from all & all
mañer of former or other gifts grants bargaines Sales leases
Mortgages wills Entailes Jonters Dowries Judgm^{ts} executions & Incumbrances w^{t}soever Furthermore I ye s^d Samuel
Spinney for my Selfe my heirs Executors & Adm^{rs} do Covenant & Ingage ye above Demised pmises and every part
thereof to him ye s^d John Dennet his heirs Executors Adm^{rs}
& assignes against the Lawfull claimes or Demands or of
any person or persons whatsoever forever hereafter to warrant Secure & Defend In Witness whereof I ye s^d Samuel
Spinney have hereunto Set my hand & Seal the Twenty
Eighth day of June In y^e Year of our Lord One Thousand

BOOK VIII, FOL. 172.

Seven hundred & Sixteen Annoq, RR^s Georgii Magna Brittania &c^t Secundo
Signed Sealed & Delivered
In the presence of
John Newmarch
John Newmarch tert^r
Margriet /|/) Hammon
  mark

Samuel Spinney ($_{Seal}^{a}$)
  her
Margriet ᧚ Spinney ($_{Seal}^{a}$)
  mark

York ss/ July 18th 1716

The within Named Sam^{ll} Spinney and Margriet his wife psonally Appearing acknowledged y^e within Instrument to be their free act & Deed   before Abra^m Preble Jus Pes

Recorded According to y^e Original July 23^d 1716.

        p Jos Ham̃ond Reg^r

[172] Know All men by these Presents that I Samuel Spinney of Kittery in the County of york in ye Province of the Massachusets Bay in New England Yeoman for & in Consideration of my Son John Spinney of ye aforesaid place his giving Granting & Confirming unto me my heirs & assignes forever that fifteen acres of Land which I formerly gave: him as by a deed of gift baring date ye Second day of March 1713/14/ may appear for wch land he hath Delivered to me a Deed bearing even Date wth these presents which is to my full Content & Satisfaction Have given granted Set over aliened Enfeoffed & Confirmed & by these presents Do give grant & forever: Confirm unto my aboves^d Son John Spinney his heirs & assignes a certaine Tract of land Containing fifteen acres Scituate & being in ye Township of Kittery and is part of That Tract of Land which I bought of Thomas Bice formerly of Kittery Dec^d and by a Deed bareing Date January ye 4th day 1689/90/ may appear & is bounded on ye northern Side & western end by my own land & on the Eastern End by Thomas Weathers dece^d his land & on ye southern Side by ye Land of John Shapleigh Dece^d excepting & reserving to my Self Two poles next to s^d Shapleighs Land for a highway for me Together with all the Timber & wood Standing or lying on ye s^d Land & all other appurtenances & Priviledges unto ye s^d fifteen acres of Land belonging To have & to hold ye s^d granted & Demised with all the Comodities to the Same belonging to him ye s^d John Spinney his heirs & assignes forever To his and their only proper use benefit & behoof forever And I ye s^d Samuel

Spinney do for me my heirs Execut[rs] & Adm[rs] Covenant & grant to & wth y[e] s[d] John Spinney his heirs & assignes that by force & virtue of these Presents y[e] s[d] John Spinney his heirs & assignes Shall & may from time to time & at all times have hold use & enjoy lawfully & peaceably forever hereafter y[e] s[d] Premised Premises w[th] y[e] appurtenances fre & Clear & freely & Clearly acquitted & Discharged of & from all & all manner of former or other gifts grants Sales Mortgages & Incumbrances w[t]soever had made or Done by me before the Ensealing & Delivery hereof and also forever to warrant & Defend y[e] aboves[d] Demised & granted premises to him y[e] s[d] John Spinney his heirs & assignes against y[e] lawfull claimes or Demands of any person or persons for ever And Margret Spinney y[e] wife of y[e] s[d] Sam[ll] Spinney doth by these presents freely yeald up all her right of Dowry & power of thirds in & to y[e] above demised pmises unto y[e] s[d] Jn[o] Spinney his heirs & assignes In Witness whereof we have hereunto Set our hands & Seals this twenty third day of July Anno Domini one Thousand Seven hundred & Sixteen Annoq RR[s] Georgii Magna Brittania &c[t] Secundo/ y[e] word pmises was Enterlined before Signing

Signed Sealed & Delivered   Samuel Spinney (a Seal)
  In y[e] presence of
  John Newmarch   Margriet (her M mark) Spinney (a Seal)

Rich[d] (his mark) Rogers
John Newmarch tert[r]
August 1st day 1716

Samuel Spinney did parsonally appear & did acknowledge this wth in written Instrum[t] to be his free act & deed before me
                      W[m] Pepperrell Js pes
Recorded According to y[e] Original Sept[r] 13 : 1716./
                      p Jos. Hamond Reg[r]

To All whom these presents shall come I John Brande of York in New England husbandman Send Greeting Know Yee that I y[e] s[d] John Brande for & in Consideration of y[e] love I bare unto Mary Pulman of york afores[d] y[e] Daughter of Jesper Pulman and more Especially for & in Consideration of y[e] love that my mother bare unto y[e] s[d] John Pulman uncle unto y[e] s[d] Mary Pulman have for my Selfe my heirs Ex[rs] Adm[rs] and Assignes given granted delivered & Confirmed & by these presents do fully freely & absolutely give grant deliver & Confirm unto ye s^d Mary Pulman her heirs Ex^rs Adm^rs & assigns So much land as ye ware house now that is builded Stands on & three foot more Towards my Orchard on ye backside of ye s^d house which lyeth by ye water Side in ye river of York Adjoyning near to my Orchard with ye Priviledges thereunto belonging To have & To hold ye s^d land & priviledges hereby given & Confirmed to ye s^d Mary Pulman her heirs Execut^rs Adm^rs & assigns as her & their own proper Estate for ever & to her & their own propper use & behoofe for ever more./ And I ye s^d John Brande do also promiss that ye s^d Mary Pulman her heirs Ex^rs Adm^rs & Assignes or any of them Shall & Lawfully may from Time to Time & at all Times hereafter peaceably & Quietly have hold use & Enjoy ye s^d land & priviledge hereby freely given without any maner of let Suit Trouble Eviction Ejection Mollestation disturbence Challenge claime denial or demand whatsoever of or by me ye s^d John Brand my heirs Ex^rs Adm^rs & Assigns or any of them or by any other pson or psons whatsoever Lawfully Claiming or to Claime from by or und^r me my Act or Title

In Witness whereof I have hereunto put my hand & Seal this 19th of Octob^r 1689./
Signed Sealed & Delivered   John (his mark) Brand (a Seal)
In p^rsence of

Sarah (her mark) Penwill
John Penwill
Recorded According to ye Original July 3^d 1716./
                  p Jos. Hamond Reg^r

To All People to whom these presents shall Come Francis Raynes of york in ye County of York in his Maj^tys Province of the Massachusets Bay in New England Shipwright Sends Greeting./ Know ye that I ye s^d Francis Raynes for & in Consideration of ye Sum of ffifty pounds in Curra^t money of ye Province afores^d to me in hand before ye Ensealing hereof well & Truely paid by Nathan Raynes of york afores^d Shipwright the rec^t whereof I do hereby acknowledge & thereof & of Every part & parcell thereof do Exonerate Acquit & discharge ye s^d Nathan Raynes his heirs & Assignes for ever have given granted bargained Sold Aliened Conveyed & Confirmed and do by these presents freely fully & Absolutely give grant Bargaine Sell Aliene Convey & Confirm unto him ye s^d Nathan Raynes his heirs & Assignes for ever One Messuage or Tract of upland & Meadow lying in York Containing by Estimation One hundred Seaventeen Acres & a halfe [173] More or less which is Just One halfe of ye lot of land which our father Nathaniel Raynes was possessed of butted & bounded as followeth on ye southwest by ye marsh of Brave boat harbour begining at a forked white oak on a point of upland a Little below s^d Brave boat harbour bridge which s^d Tree is now fallen on ye ground which was formerly a Southward Corner of a lot of Three hundred acres of Land granted to Cap^{tn} Raynes & runs Southeast One hundred & Sixty poles to a white birch mark^t four square Thence East northeast one hundred and nineteen poles to a heap of Stones & thence Northwest One hundred and Sixty poles & then West Southwest to ye point of upland began at with One halfe of ye Marsh belonging to ye afores^d lot of land with all ye Timber Trees woods houses Orchards water & water & water Courses whatsoever To have & To hold ye s^d granted & bargained premisses with all ye Appurtenances priviledges & Comoditys to ye Same belonging or in any ways Appurtaining to him ye s^d Nathan Raynes his heirs & Assignes for ever to his & their only proper use benefit & behoofe for ever more So that Neither I ye s^d Francis Raynes my heirs or Assignes nor any other person or persons by from or und^r me them or any of them Shall or will by any Means hereafter have claime Challenge or demand any Estate right Title or Interest of in or to all or any part of ye s^d Granted & released premisses but of & from Every Acc͞on of right Estate Title Interest claime & demand of in & to the premisses & Every part & parcell thereof I my Selfe & Every of them Shall be Utterly Excluded & for ever debarred by these psents.. And further I ye s^d Francis Raynes for my Selfe my heirs Ex^{rs} Admin^{rs} do hereby Covenant grant and agree ye Above granted and released premisses with ye Appurtenances & Every part thereof unto ye s^d Nathan Raynes his heirs & Assignes against ye lawfull Claims & demands of all & Every person & persons Any wayes Claiming or demanding ye Same or any part thereof by from or under me for ever hereafter to Warrant & Defend. In Witness whereof I have hereunto Set my hand & seal this Second day of August in y^e first year of y^e reign of Our Soveraign King George by y^e grace of god King of Great Brittaine France

& Irel[d] and in y[e] year of Our Lord One Thousand Seven hundred & fifteen

Signed Sealed & Delivered   Francis Raynes ($_{\text{Seal}}^{\text{a}}$)
In y[e] presence of
Edward Beale
Daniel Simpson
Jeremiah Moulton jun[r]
York sc. York may y[e] 9th 1716

Francis Raynes psonally appeared before me y[e] Subscriber & Acknowledged y[e] above written deed of Sale to be his free Act & Deed   Abra Preble Just[s] pe[o]

Recorded According to y[e] Original July y[e] 3[d] 1716./
       p Jos Hamond Reg[r]

To All Christian People to whom this present deed of Sale may Come Elihue Parsons of York in y[e] County of York in y[e] Province of y[e] Massachusets Bay in New Englond housecarpenter Sendeth Greeting Know yee y[e] s[d] Elihue Parsons for & in Consideration of Seven pounds & Ten shillings money to him in hand well & truely paid by Jabez Blackledg of y[e] same York labourer the paym[t] whereof y[e] s[d] Elihue doth for himselfe his heirs & Assignes to be fully Satisfied and Contented for y[e] premisses hereafter Specified the which y[e] s[d] Elihue hath Given granted bargained & Sold Aliened Enfeoffed & Conveyed and doth by these presents give grant bargaine Sell Aliene Enfeoffe & Convey & fully freely & Absolutely make Over & Confirm unto y[e] s[d] Jabez Blackledg & to his heirs & assignes forever One Tennement piece parcell or Tract of upland & Swampy land Containing five Acres more or less within y[e] Township of s[d] york being Scittuated upon y[e] Southwest Side of s[d] York river upon y[e] Southeast Side of Ebenezer Blasdels house lot & is butted & bounded as followeth Viz[t] begining at a Smal hemlock tree Standing near a Cove of Salt marsh by s[d] York river which s[d] hemlock tree is marked on four Sides being a late bound marked tree between y[e] s[d] Elihue Parsons & y[e] s[d] Ebenezer Blasdel & runs from thence nine poles & Six foot to White oak Stake marked on four Sides drove down in y[e] head of s[d] Marsh cove and runs from thence Southwest Ninty & Six poles to a white oak Stake marked on four Sides and from thence northwest Nine poles & Six foot to aboves[d] Ebenezer Blasdels bounds and from thence by s[d] Blasdells bounds North East to y[e] hemlock tree first or above mentioned Together wth all y[e] rights priviledges Appurtenances & Advantages thereunto belonging both of land **Timber** trees wood under wood standing Laying or being on s^d land or priviledge or priviledges or any wayes at any Time redownding to ye Same or any part or parcell thereof unto him ye s^d Jabez Blackledg his heirs & Assignes for ever To have & to hold & Quietly & peaceably to Possess Occupy & Enjoy as a Sure Estate in fee Simple More Over ye s^d Elihue Parsons doth for himselfe his heirs Ex^{rs} & Adm^{rs} to & with ye s^d Jabez Blackledge his heirs & Assignes Ingage ye above bargained premisses with all its priviledges to be free & clear from all former gifts grants bargains Sales rents rates Dowryes Mortgages Executions or other Incumberm^{ts} whatsoever as also from all future Claims Challenges Arests or any other Interuptions whatsoever to be had or Comenced by him ye s^d Elihue Parsons his heirs Ex^{rs} Adm^{rs} or assignes or any other person or persons whatsoever upon Grounds or Title of Law hereafter upon any part or Parragraph of this Instrum^t and that proceeding of ye date hereof thes^d Elihue will warrantize & Defend ye Same [174] In Witness hereof ye s^d Elihue Parsons hath hereunto Set his hand & Seal this fifteenth day of March in y^e year of our Lord: One Thousand Seven hundred & fifteen. 16. And in y^e Second year of y^e Reign of Our Soveraign Lord George King of Great Brittaine &c^t

The words more or less was before Signing Interlined
Signed Sealed & Delivered   Elihue Parsons (${}^a_{Seal}$)
In presence of
Samuel Preble
David 'V' Thomas
   mark
York sc April y^e 6th 1716./

The within Named Elihue Parsons psonally appeared before me Abra^m Preble Esquire one of his Maj^{tys} Justices of y^e peace for this County of York & Acknowledged this with Instrum^t to be his free Act & Deed./
                     Abra^m Preble J Peace
Recorded According to ye Original July 3^d 1716.

                     p Jos. Hamond Reg^r.

To All Christian People to whom these present deed of Sale may Come Messu^{rs} Peter Nowell Samuel Came Daniel Simpson & Richard Milbery Selectmen of ye Town of York in ye County of york in the Province of Maine in New Eng-

Book VIII, Fol. 174.

land Send Greeting. Know Yee that y² s^d Peter Samuel Daniel & Richard by ye Power Given to them by ye s^d Town of York for & in Consideration of fifty five pounds money to them in hand paid by William Grow of s^d York Cordwainer ye rec^t whereof ye s^d Peter Samuel Daniel & Richard do Acknowledge in behalfe of s^d Town of York to be fully Satisfied & paid and do by these presents Acquit Exonerate & discharge ye s^d Wm Grow his heirs & Assignes for ever of all & Every part of ye Premisses hereafter Set forth ye which ye s^d Selectmen have in ye behalfe of s^d Town of York given granted bargained Sold Aliened Enfeoffed & made over and do by these presents give grant bargaine Sell Aliene Enfeoffe & make over unto ye s^d Wm Grow his heirs & Assignes forever a dwelling house & One Acre and fifty Six pole of upland within this Town of s^d York Scittuated upon a Creek known by ye Name of ye Meeting house Creek upon ye Southwest of ye Old meeting house or ruins thereof the which is now in ye Possession of Nicholas Sewall of s^d York which s^d land is butted & bounded As followeth Viz^t begining at a heap of Stones about four rods or poles from ye westward Corner of s^d Old meeting house which s^d heap of Stones is ye westward Corner bound mark of a Small parcell of land now in ye possession of ye s^d Nicholas Sewal and runs from s^d heap of Stones Southwest to ye s^d Meeting house Creek Sixteen poles as also from s^d heap of Stones East Southeast fifteen poles by ye Land of s^d Nicholas Sewall to a white oak Stake driven into ye ground by ye land now in ye possession of ye widdow Johnson & So is bounded by s^d Johnson to a great Stake near ye East End of aboves^d house & on ye Southwest of s^d lot is bounded by s^d Meeting house Creek the house being ye house built for ye Parsonage Together with all ye rights priviledges & Advantages thereunto belonging or Appurtaining to ye Same or any part or parcell thereof or any wise at any Time redownding to ye same unto him ye s^d Wm Grow his heirs & Assigns for ever To have & To hold and Quietly & peaceably to possess Occupie & Enjoy ye s^d Premisses with all its Priviledges as a Sure Estate in fee Simple forever after the date hereof from by or und^r them ye s^d Selectmen or their Successsors or any person or persons whatsoever Proceeding ye date hereof And they ye Selectmen above Named do in ye behalfe of s^d Town of York Promiss unto ye s^d Wm Grow his heirs & Assignes to Warrantize & Secure ye Same unto ye s^d Grow his heirs & Assignes in all Lawfull points whatsoever./ In Witness hereof ye s^d Peter Nowell Samuell Came Daniel Simpson Richard Milbery have hereunto Set their hands & Seals this

Book VIII, Fol. 175.

Eighth day of March One Thousand Seven hundred & fourteen in ye first year of ye reign of our Soveraign Lord George King of Great Brittaine &c^t

Signed Sealed & Delivered   Peter Nowell (seal)
  In presence of   Saml Came (seal)
  Johnson Harmon   Daniel Simpson (seal)
  Caleb Preble   Richd Milbery (seal)
  Abra^m Preble

Mr Peter Nowell Mr Sam^ll Came Mr Richd Milbery & Mr Daniel Simpson Came before me this 8 day of March 1714/5 And Acknowledged this within written deed of Sale to be their Act & deed   Before me   Lewis Bane Just^s peace

Recorded According to ye Original Septr 17th 1716./

                    p Jos: Hamond Reg^r

To All People to whom these p^rsents Shall Come Greeting Know yee that I Peter Nowell of York in ye County of York in ye Province of the Massachusets bay in New England Yeoman for & in Consideration of a parcell of Land as shall appear by a deed of Sale ye rec^t thereof I do hereby Acknowledge my selfe therewith fully Satisfied & Contented & thereof & of Every part & parcell thereof do do Exonerate Acquit & discharge ye s^d John Linscot his heirs Ex^rs Adm^rs for ever by these p^rsents have given granted bargained & by these presents do fully & Absolutely give grant bargain Sell Aliene Convey & Confirm unto him ye s^d John Linscot his heirs & Assignes for ever One Messuage or Tract of Land Containing forty Acres which was granted to s^d Nowell by ye Town of York which land lyeth between ye partings of york river on ye Southwest side of a lot of m^r Edward Johnsons at birch hill begining at ye west Corner of s^d Johnsons land at a white Oak [175] Marked on four Sides which is ye Corner bounds of s^d Johnsons land and runs from thence S^o west Eighty poles or perch to a red Oak marked on four Sides & from thence S^o East Eighty poles or perch to a great pine Tree marked on four Sides and thence North East to Aboves^d Johnsons bounds & So by s^d bounds to the place where we begun To have & To hold ye s^d Granted & bargained premisses with all ye appurtenances priviledges & Comodityes to ye Same belonging or in any wise appurtaining to him ye s^d John Linscot his heirs & Assignes for ever to his & their own propper use bennefit & behoofe for ever And I ye s^d Peter Nowell for me my heirs Ex^rs Adm^rs do Covenant promiss & grant to & with ye s^d John Linscot his

Book VIII, Fol. 175.

heirs & Assignes that before y⁰ Ensealing hereof I am y⁰ True Sole & Lawfull Owner of y⁰ Above bargained premisses And Am Lawfully Siez^d & possess^d of y⁰ Same in my own propper right as a good perfect and Absolute Estate of Inheritance in fee Simple And have in my Selfe good right full power & Lawfull Authority to grant bargaine Sell Convey & Confirm s^d bargained premisses in Mann^r as aboves^d And that y⁰ s^d John Linscot his heirs & Assignes shall and may from Time to Time & at all times for ever hereafter by force & vertue of these presents Lawfully peaceably & Quietly have hold use Occupy Possess & Enjoy y⁰ s^d Demised & bargained premisses with y⁰ Appurtenances free & Clear & freely & Clearly Acquitted Exonerated & discharged of from all & all maner of form^r and other gifts grants bargaines Sales Leases Mortgages wills Entails Joyntures Dowries Judm^ts Executions Incumbrances w^tsoever furthermore I y⁰ s^d Peter Nowell for my Selfe my heirs Execut^rs Adm^rs do Covenant & Ingage y⁰ above demised premisses to him y⁰ s^d John Linscot his heirs & Assignes against y⁰ Lawfull Claims or demands of Any pson or psons whatsoever for ever hereafter to warrant secure & Defend./ In Witness whereof I have hereunto Set my hand & Seal y⁰ Eighteenth day of Septr in y⁰ year of our Lord god Seventeen hundred fourteen./   Peter Nowell (Seal)
Signed Sealed & Delivered   Sarah Nowell (Seal)
  In presence
  James Smith
  Joseph Smith
       his
  Henry ✕ Browcen
     mark
July 3^d 1715/ York sc: York in y⁰ County of york Mr Peter Nowell & his wife psonally appeared before me y⁰ Subscriber & Acknowledged this Instrum^t to be his Act & deed   Before me Lewis Bane Just^s of peace
Recorded According to y⁰ Originall Septr 29th 1716.
                    p Jos Hammond Reg^r

Know All men by these presents that I y⁰ within named Ebenezer Pemberton for & in Consideration of y⁰ Sum of One hundred and fifty pounds within Mentioned & y⁰ Lawfull Interest thereon Ariseing to y⁰ day of y⁰ Date hereof to me in hand paid by the within Named Peter Nowell y⁰ receipt whereof to full Content & Satisfaction I hereby Acknowl-

edge have remised released & Quit Claimed & by these presents for me my heirs Ex^{rs} Adm^{rs} & Assignes to remise release & forever Quitclaim unto ye s^d Peter Nowell his heirs Ex^{rs} Adm^{rs} & Assignes As well ye proviso or Condition Contained & Comprised in ye within written Instrum^t or deed of Mortgage as also all & all maner of Suits Cause & Causes of Actions & Suits for or Concerning y^e same In Witness whereof I y^e s^d Ebenez^r Pemberton have hereunto Set my hand & seal the Thirteenth day of Septr 1716./
Annoq, R^i R^{is} Georgii Mag Brittania &c^t Tertio./
Sealed & Delivered   Eben^r Pemberton ($_{Seal}^{a}$)
  In y^e presence of
Nathl Williams
Rebekah Briggs
Suffolk ss Boston Sep^t 13 : 1716./

The above named Ebenezer Pemberton psonally appearing Acknowledge the Above written Instrum^t to be his free Act & deed   Before me Edw : Bromfield J peace
Memorandum./   The Deed of Mortgage to which this Instrum^t has referrence is recorded in this book folio 67 :
                              Att^r Jos Hamond Reg
Recorded According to ye Original Sep^{tr} 20th 1716/
                                p Jos : Harmon Reg^r

To All Christian People &c. Know ye that I Thomas Averell of Capenuduck in ye County of york in ye Province of Maine in New England Planter divers good Causes & Considerations me thereunto moveing & more Especially for a Valluable Sum in hand already paid or well Secured to be paid Have given granted bargained Sold Aliened Enfeoffed and Confirmed and by these presents do give grant bargaine Sell Aliene Enfeoffe and Confirm unto m^r Francis Littlefield Senr of ye Town of Wells in ye Province of Maine a Certaine Tract of Land Comonly known by ye name of Tatnack Lying & being Scittuate about Six miles from ye Town of Wells Containing by Estimation Two hundred Acres be it more or less Together with Six acres of fresh meadow Lying and being about a Quarter of a mile from ye place where my house Once Stood in Three Parcells haveing an Oak Tree Marked Against Each parcell To have & To hold ye afores^d land & meadow with all ye Appurtenances & priviledges thereto Appurtaining to ye s^d ffrancis Littlefield his heirs & Assignes forever without Any let hinderence or Mollestation from any person or persons whatSoever laying claime there-

Book VIII, Fol. 176.

to And I s^d Averell do hereby [176] Oblige and bind my Selfe And Assignes & heirs to Defend y^e premisses In Witness whereof I have hereto Set my hand & Seal this 10th day of October 1689./ Thomas Averell ($_{Seale}^{a}$)
Read Signed Sealed and
 Delivered in y^e presence of us
  The mark of

Mary /\/D Davis
 The mark of

Jony ,—: Dannel

Its hereby provided & to be understood that y^e afores^d ffrancis Littlefield from y^e time of the Date hereof Shall pay whatever rents are due to y^e lord proprietor from s^d Land this also Inserted before Signing & Sealing

Thomas Averell Came before me this 26th of Octob^r 1689: and did Acknowledge ye Above writing to be his act & deed
 John Davis Dep^{ty} Presid^t
Recorded According to ye Original Octob^r ye 1st 1716./
 p Jos. Hamond Regist^r

To All Christian People to whom this present writing shall Come Know ye that I ffrancis Littlefield of Wells in ye County of york in ye Province of Maine in New England planter for diverse good Considerations me thereunto moveing and more Especially for a Valluable Sum in hand paid or well Secured to be paid have given granted bargained Sold Aliened Enfeoffed and Confirmed & by these presents do give grant bargaine Sell Enfeoffe and Confirm unto Nathl Rust Senr in in ye Town of Ipswich in ye County of Essex in New England Glovier a Certaine Tract of Land Adjoining to ye head of my own lot being an hundred Acres runing ye whole bredth of my own Lot in width & in length west northwest as my own lot runs To have & To hold ye afores^d land with all ye priviledges and Appurtenances thereunto belonging to ye s^d Nathl Rust his heirs and Assignes for ever without any Let hinderence Mollestation or Trouble from any pson or psons whatsoever laying claime thereto Either by right of Dowry or any other way whatsoever & for y^e Confirmation hereof I y^e s^d Littlefield do hereby Oblige & bind my Selfe my heirs Ex^{rs} Adm^{rs} & Assignes to Defend the premisses./

Book VIII, Fol. 176.

In Witness w{r}of I have hereunto Set my hand & Seal this 30{th} day of Octob{r} 1689.   F{r} : Littlefield ($_{Seal}^{a}$)
      Tho: Jacobs
Witness
      Nath{l} Rust Jun{r}
   ffrancis Littlefield did appear before me Octob{r} y{e} 30{th} 1689 & did Acknowledge this Instrum{t} Above written to be his Act & Deed.   Before me   Sam{l} Appleton Assista{t}
   Furthermore y{e} Aboves{d} Francis Littlefield doth Ingage by y{e} Aboves{d} pmisses that if in Case y{e} aboves{d} Rust Se Cause hereafter to Change y{e} Above Specified land for an hundred Acres Adjoining to that which was Called Thomas Averells land Comonly Called by y{e} name of Tatnack that then y{e} s{d} Littlefield Shall upon y{e} Surrendering up of this deed give him a firm deed of an hundred Acres at that place According to y{e} Aboves{d} Nath{l} Rusts mind./
    Tho: Jacobs   F{r} Littlefield ($_{Seale}^{a}$)
Nath{l} Rust Jun{r}
Francis Littlefield did acknowledge this Instrum{t} above written Novemb{r} y{e} 30{th} 1689.
          Before me   Sam{l} Appleton Ass{t}.
Recorded According to y{e} Original Octob{r} y{e} 1{st} 1716.
                p Jos. Hamond Reg{r}

   To All Christian People to whom this present writing Shall Come Know ye that I Francis Littlefield of Wells in y{e} County of York in y{e} Province of Maine in New Engl{d} planter for diverse good Causes & Considerations me there unto moveing & more Especially for a valluable Sum in hand already paid or well Secured to be paid have given granted bargained Sold Aliened Enfeoffed & Confirmed and by these presents do give grant bargaine Sell Aliene Enfeoffe & Confirm unto Nathaniel Rust Sen{r} in y{e} Town of Ipswich in y{e} County of Essex in New England Glovier a Certaine Tract of land Comonly known by the name of Tatnack Lying & being Scittuate about Six miles from y{e} Town of Wells Containing by Estimation Two hundred Acres be it more or less Together with Six acres of fresh meadow Lying & being about a Quarter of a mile from y{e} Aboves{d} place where Thomas Averells house of Capenudock in y{e} County of york once Stood which Meadow being in Three parcells haveing an Oak Tree marked against Each parcell To have & To Hold y{e} afores{d} land & meadow with all y{e} priviledges and

Book VIII, Fol. 177.

Appurtenances thereunto belonging to ye s^d Nathl Rust his heirs & Assignes forever without any let hinderence Mollestation or Trouble from any person or persons whatsoever laying claime thereto Either by right of Dower or any other way whatsoever And for y^e Confirmation hereaf. I y^e s^d Littlefield do hereby oblige & bind my Selfe my heirs Ex^{rs} Adm^{rs} & assignes to Defend y^e premisses

In Witness whereof I have hereunto Set my hand & Seal this 30th day of Octob^r 1689./   Fran^s Littlefield (s$_{eal}^a$)
     William Hubbard
Witness
     Nathl Rust Junr

Francis Littlefield did appear before me and did Acknowledge this Instrum^t above written to be his Act & deed before me Octob^r y^e 30th 1689   Saml Appleton Assista^t

Recorded According to y^e Original Octob^r y^e 1st 1716./
                                p Jos. Hamond Reg^r

This Indenture made ye thirteenth day of Septr Anno Domini One Thousand Seven hundred & Sixteen Annoque Regni Regis Georgii Tertio./ Between John Nelson of Long Island within ye Township of Boston in ye County of Suffolk & Province of ye Massachusets Bay in New England Esqr Sole Executor & Devisee of & in ye Last Will & Testament of Sylvanus Davis Late of Hull in ye County & Province afores^d Merch^t Dec^d on ye One part. And Thomas Hutchinson of Boston afores^d Esqr John Wentworth of Portsmouth in ye Province of New Hampsh^r Esqr Adam Winthrop David Jeffries & Oliver Noyes Esq^{rs} Stephen Minot John Ruck & John Watts Gent all of Boston afores^d on ye other part Witnesseth that ye s^d John Nelson for & in Consideration of ye Sum of forty pounds Lawfull money of New England to him in hand well & Truely paid at & before ye Delivery hereof by ye s^d Thomas Hutchinson John Wentworth Adam Winthrop David Jeffries Oliver Noyes Stephen Minot John Ruck & John Watts ye rec^t whereof to full Content & Satisfaction ye s^d John Nelson hereby Acknowlegeth [177] Hath given granted bargained Sold Aliened Enfeoffed released Conveyed and Confirmed and by these presents Doth fully freely clearly & Absolutely give grant Bargaine Sell Aliene Enfeoffe release Convey & Confirm unto ye s^d Thomas Hutchinson John Wentworth Adam Winthrop David Jeffries Oliver Noyes Stephen Minot John Ruck & John Watts their heirs & assignes forever The Severall Tracts or parcells of Lands.

Book VIII. Fol. 177.

hereafter Mentioned (That is to Say) All that Certain Tract or parcell of upland and Meadow Lying Scittuate on y[e] westward Side of Kenebeck river upon y[e] Neck of land known by y[e] name of Small point y[e] Southward bounds whereof begins at a run or brook of water about halfe a mile to y[e] Southward of y[e] house late of y[e] s[d] Sylvanus Davis At a great hemlock Tree Mark[t] & up y[e] s[d] run or brook to y[e] Southward Side of a Spruce Swamp and from thence to y[e] Southward End of Two fresh Meadows lying to y[e] westward or west Southerly from y[e] s[d] house with Mark[t] Trees from y[e] afores[d] hemlock tree to y[e] Southward End of y[e] afores[d] fresh Meadows Suposed to be about a mile in breadth up & down y[e] river & So holding y[e] Same breadth Across y[e] s[d] Neck of Land Over to Casco Bay also a parcell of Meadow land Containing about fifteen Acres lying on y[e] Eastward side of Casco Bay to y[e] Northwest from Small point About Two Leagues Called or known by y[e] name of Davis[s] harbour Also a Small piece of Meadow land or Salt Marish lying wth in Small point harbour Containing by Estimation about Ten acres granted to y[e] s[d] Sylvanus Davis by y[e] Selectmen of y[e] Town of harwich and afterwards Confirmed to him by S[r] Edmund Andros Kn[t] Then Governo[r] of this Province It being a round Marsh within y[e] Small Salt water falls that run out of s[d] Marsh about halfe a mile within y[e] harbours Mouth within Two little Islands which s[d] Three Several Tracts or parcells of land & Meadow are lying Scittuate within y[e] County of york formerly Called y[e] Province of Maine Also an Island Called & known by y[e] name of Great Stage Island Lying upon y[e] Eastward side of y[e] Mouth of Kenebeck at Sackedahoc Also a Tract of land Containing by Estimation about two hundred acres more or less on y[e] East side of Kenebeck riv[r] Over against Swan Island purchased by y[e] s[d] Sylvanus Davis of y[e] Indian Sagamores as Appears by a good deed dated the Twenty Second day of August 1671./ Also a Tract of land lying up in & about a place Called & known by y[e] name of Oyester river in Dameris Scoty river Containing five hundred Acres more or less bounded as follows Viz[t] on a neck of land lying above y[e] Salt water falls on y[e] westward Side of a Smal river Called Oyester river which runs up into y[e] woods Nearest North East being y[e] Eastward side of y[e] s[d] Neck and the westward bounds of y[e] s[d] Neck of Land is the Salt pond or Bay which y[e] great fresh falls fall into./ upon y[e] Southward End of y[e] s[d] Neck Stands a white pine Tree & a white Oak being both Mark[t] part of y[e] bark Chopt off & from s[d] Southward point over y[e] Cove of s[d] Salt pond Nearest North & by west halfe a point Westerly To A Small green point of land whereon Stands a red oak & a white Oak Tree both markt ye bark Cutt So that ye s^d five hundred acres of land lyes betwixt Oyester river on ye Eastward Side and the Salt pond or bay on ye westward side Nearest ye Courses afores^d & to run back into ye bounds According to ye s^d Courses from ye Southward End of s^d Neck untill five hundred Acres be up or Compleated + And Also a Tract of land lying Eastward of Masconks begining at Madoamok point up to ye falls of Magesemanussuck & runing two miles above ye Same and in breadth One mile on Each Side ye river which land ye s^d Sylvanus Davis by & with ye Consent of Sr William Phipps Kn^t & Governour of this province for that time being Purchased of Madokowando Sagamore of Penobscot And Edgeremet Sagamore of Kenebeck by a good deed dated ye Tenth of May 1694 Also ye priviledge of Sixty feet of Land in front at highwater mark & So to Low water mark upon ye westward Side of ye fishing Island at Sacadahock granted to s^d Davis by ye Principle Inhabitants of New Town Anno 1681./ or however otherwise ye afores^d Tracts or parcells of land or any of them are or may be described or reputed to be bounded./ Together with all and Singullar ye houseing Outhouses warehouses barns Edefices buildings & fences Errected or Standing upon any part of ye s^d lands woods underwoods Copps Trees rocks mines miueralls ponds rivers Creeks Bayes rights Comodityes profits priviledges members & Appurtenances whatsoever to ye Same or any part thereof belonging or therewith now or heretofore used Ocupied or Enjoyed And all ye Estate right Title & Interest of him ye s^d John Nelson of & in ye s^d granted premisses & ye reversions & remainders thereof./+ Of all which Severall Tracts or parcells of Lands & premisses afore given granted and Sold Thes^d Sylvanus Davis dyed Seiz^d in fee and in & by his last will & Testam^t duely proved Aproved & Allowed dated ye Eighth day of April Anno Domini 1703./ Gave & Devised ye same being ye residuary part of his real Estate unto him ye s^d John Nelson To have & To hold ye Severall Tracts pieces or parcells of land, Land before mentioned with ye dwelling houses Out houses barns Edefices and fences Standing thereon and all other ye herein before given and granted premisses unto them ye s^d Thomas Hutchison John Wentworth Adam Winthrop David Jeffries Oliver Noyes Stephen Minot John Ruck & John Watts their heirs & Assignes for ever in Severalty that So No Advantage may be had or Claimed by right of Survivorship to their Sole propper use benefit & behoofe from henceforth & forever-

more./ And yᵉ sᵈ John Nelson doth Avouch himselfe to be yᵉ right full owner of yᵉ sᵈ granted premisses haveing full power to grant Sell & dispose thereof in Maner as aforesᵈ yᵉ same being free & Clear of & from all prior & other gifts grants bargains Sales Leases Mortgages Joyntures Dowers Titles Charges Incumbrances Claimes & Demands whatsoever And yᵉ sᵈ John Nelson for himselfe his heirs Exʳˢ & Admʳˢ [178] Doth hereby Covenant & grant to & with yᵉ sᵈ Thomas Hutchinson John Wentworth Adam Winthrop David Jeffries Oliver Noyes Stephen Minot John Ruck & John Watts their heirs and assignes to Warrant & Defend yᵉ sᵈ Tracts and parcells of Lands & premisses afore granted with their Appurtenances unto them forever in Severalty as aforesᵈ agˢᵗ all other pʳsons whomsoever Claiming any right Title or Interest therein by from or undʳ him yᵉ sᵈ John Nelson his heirs or assignes In Witness whereof yᵉ sᵈ John Nelson hath hereunto put his hand & Seal the day & year first herein before written   Jnᵒ Nelson (ₛₑₐₗᵃ)
Signed Sealed & Delivered
  In presence of us
  Edmund Mountfort
  Buttalph Belknap
    Suffolk sc/ Boston Sepᵗ 15ᵗʰ 1716.
The within Named John Nelson Acknowledged yᵉ Afore written Instrumᵗ to be his free act & deed./
          Before me   E Lyde J peace
Recorded According to yᵉ Original Septʳ 21ˢᵗ 1716.
            p Jos. Hammond Regʳ

Whereas We the Subscribers Thomas Hutchinson John Wentworth Adam Winthrop David Jeffries Oliver Noyes John Watts Stephen Minot & John Ruck have Joyntly purchased of Severall persons a large Tract of Land in yᵉ Eastern parts of this Province of yᵉ Massachusets Bay in New England & Obtainᵈ a Confirmation of yᵉ Same from the General Court as p reference to our Deeds & yᵉ sᵈ Confirmation upon record will more at Large Appear and haveing made a good progress Towards Settlemᵗ there do now find it Necessary and of Advantage to us that Some Considerable part of Our sᵈ purchase Should as Soon as may be./ be Assigned to Each partner for yᵉ better Improvemᵗ thereof to be henceforth held in Severalty by him his heirs & Assignes for ever :/ In Order whereunto we have thought it Equal & Expedient to Covenant and agree And do by these pʳsents

for us our heirs Execut^{rs} & Administrat^{rs} Covenant and agree to & with Each other That whensoever any Island Tract or parcell of land Shall be Appropriated to any of us a grant as Short & Concise as may be describing ye quantity boundaryes or Scittuation thereof shall be made to ye s^d partner & Signed & Sealed by ye other partners or the Maj^r part of us (The whole being notified & Entered in our book of records ye performance whereof shall make unto ye s^d party his heirs or Assignes a good & Sufficient Title to ye Tract or parcell of Land So granted for ever free & Clear of all claims & demands of us Our heirs Ex^{rs} & Adm^{rs}./ And if it shall So happen that any other person or persons shall lay claime to ye whole or any part of any Island Tract or parcell of land Appropriated as afores^d In every Such case we Oblige ourselves our heirs &c^t Either to Compound Joyntly if need be with ye person or persons So laying claime or otherwise to defend & Secure ye Same in course of law at our joynt & Comon charge unto our s^d Grantee his heirs &c^t or in failure thereof that we will forthwth Appropriate or Assign unto him His heirs &c^t an Equivolent for ye land So recovered from him in Some other part of Our purchase./ To the true performence w^{r}of we do by these presents respectively bind ourselves Our heirs Execut^{rs} & Adm^{rs} As Witness Our hands & Seals Dated in Boston in New England this fourth day of Septr Anno Domini Seventeen hundred & Sixteen in ye third year of ye reign of King George Over Great Brittaine &c^t Thos Hutchinson (Seal)
Signed Sealed & Dd John Wentworth (Seal)
  In presence of Adam Winthrop (Seal)
  The under written being first David Jeffries (Seal)
    agreed on that in Case of ye Oliver Noyes (Seal)
    Death of any of us before the J: Watts (Seal)
    Severall divisions of our pur- Stephen Minot (Seal)
    chase are made it shall then be John Ruck (Seal)
    in ye power of ye Majo^r part
of ye Survivors to Order from Time to Time any further divisions that shall be thought necessary haveing a due regard to ye Interest of ye Deceased
  Edward Winslow
  John Gerrish
  Suffolk sc. Boston Septr 28th 1716/ The within Named Thomas Hutchinson Adam Winthrop & John Watts Esq^{rs} & David Jeffries Esqr & on ye Twelfth day of Octob^r John Wentworth Esqr & m^r John Ruck & on ye Thirteenth Oliver Noyes Esqr and m^r Stephen Minot psonally appeared &

Book VIII, Fol, 179.

Each of them Acknowledged ye within Instrum^t to be their Act & deed　　Before me　　Edwd Hutchinson Just^s p s
Recorded According to ye Original Octob^r 20th 1716./
　　　　　　　　　　　p Jos. Hamond Reg^r

Wee the Subscribers Thomas Hutchinson John Wentworth David Jeffries Oliver Noyes & John Watts Esq^{rs} Stephen Minot & John Ruck Gent^r Proprietors of Lands between Kenebeck & AmbroScoggen rivers & Casco bay have Granted & Assigned & do by these presents for us our heirs Ex^{rs} & Adm^{rs} Grant & Assign unto our partner Adam Winthrop of Boston in ye County of Suffolk in New England Esqr in Fee a Large Island Comonly called or known by the name of Swan Island Lying in Merrymeeting Bay in ye County of York begining or bounded on ye Northeast end at ye mouth of Kenebec river & runing down Southwesterly near to Abbacadusset point To have & To hold as s^d Winthrops part or Share of One first Division of Our purchase to him ye s^d Adam Winthrop his heirs and Assignes for ever free & Clear from all demands of us or Either of us our or Either of Our heirs Ex^{rs} or Adm^{rs} & to be Defended by us against all persons whomsoever According to our agreem^t on record As Witness our hands & Seals hereunto Set [179] In Boston afores^d this Tenth day of Septr Anno Domⁱ Seventeen hundred & Sixteen in ye Third of ye reign of King George Over Great Brittaine &c^t　　Thos Hutchinson (seal)
Signed Sealed & Dd　　　　　　John Wentworth (seal)
　In presence of us　　　　　　David Jeffries (seal)
　Edward Winslow　　　　　　Oliver Noyes (seal)
　John Gerrish　　　　　　　　Stephen Minot (seal)
　　　　　　　　　　　　　　　John Ruck (seal)
　　　　　　　　　　　　　　　J. Watts (seal)

Suffolk sc/ Boston Sep^{tr} 28th 1716
　　The within named Thom^s Hutchinson & John Watts Esq^{rs} & David Jeffries Esqr & the Twelfth day of Octob^r John Wentworth Esqr & m^r John Ruck & on ye Thirteenth Oliver Noyes Esqr & Mr Stephen Minot psonally Appeared & Each of them Acknowledge ye within Instrum^t to be their Act & Deed　　　　　Before me　Edwd Hutchinson Just^s Ps
Recorded According to ye Original Octob^r 20th 1716./
　　　　　　　　　　　p. Jos. Hamond Reg^r

　　This Indenture made ye 19th day of may Annoq, Domⁱ 1713 between William Wilson of ye Town of Kittery in ye province of Maine housecarpenter of ye one part And Andrew Lewis of ye Same place Carpenter of ye other part Witnesseth that ye s^d Wm Wilson for and in Consideration of ye Sum of Twenty Shillings Curra^t money to him in hand before ye Ensealing & Delivery of these presents well and Truely paid by ye s^d Andrew Lewis the rec^t whereof I do hereby Acknowledge and thereof & of Every part & parcell thereof doth Acquit Exonerate & Discharge ye s^d Andrew Lewis his heirs Ex^{rs} Adm^{rs} & Assignes & Every of them for ever by these presents hath given granted bargained Sold Aliened Conveyed & Confirmed and by these presents do fully freely clearly & Absolutely give grant bargaine Sell Aliene Enfeoffe Convey & Confirm unto ye s^d Andrew Lewis his heirs & Assignes for ever all his right Title Interest Claime property Challenge & demand whatsoever of in & to Seventeen Acres of Land in ye Town of Kittery afores^d It being part of a fifty Acre grant Granted to William Lewis his heirs & Assignes forever At a Legal Town meeting at Kittery May ye tenth 1703./ & Sold by s^d Wm Lewis to ye aboves^d Wm Wilson Together with all priviledges Comodityes & Appur^{ces} to the belonging or in any wise Appurtaining To have & To hold ye s^d right Estate Title claime property Challenge & demand whatsoever and all & Singular ye Other & before granted & bargained premisses priviledges & Appurten^{ces} unto ye s^d Andrew Lewis his heirs & Assigns for ever and that without ye least let hurt Trouble denial or Mollestation of me ye s^d Wm Wilson my heirs Ex^{rs} or Adm^{rs} or any of them or of any other person or persons whatsoever Lawfully claiming by from or und^r him them or any of them. In Witness whereof ye s^d Wm Wilson hath hereunto Set his hand and Seal ye day & year first above written 1713.

Signed Sealed & Delivered   W^m (his mark) Wilson (Seal)
  In presence of us
  Joseph Maxfield
  Joseph Gunnison
    23 July 1714./

Then Wm Wilson personally appeared before me ye subscrib^r one of her Maj^{tys} Justices for s^d County of york & did acknowledge this within written Instrum^t to be his free act & deed.   Wm Pepperrell

Recorded According to ye Original Septr 17th 1716./
             p Jos. Hammond Reg^r

Know All men by these presents that I Peter Lewis Junr of Kittery in the County of York Shipwright for a valluable Consideration to me in hand paid by my brother Andrew

Book VIII, Fol. 179.

Lewis of y⁶ Same place Yeoman have given granted bargained & Sold And do by these presents give grant bargaine & Sell a Smal Tract of land Containing one Acre and a halfe & Twenty Eight pole and lyes at or near y⁶ head of the land that was mʳ Withersˢ unto my sᵈ Brother Andrew Lewis his heirs & Assignes for ever & Takes its begining at a post in the fence a little above sᵈ Andrew Lewisˢ house & runs from sᵈ post South Sixteen pole to a heap of Stones & from thence East Twenty four pole to a Stake & from thence Northwest Twenty Two pole and from that Extent Nine pole to y⁶ first Station at y⁶ aforesᵈ post To have & To hold y⁶ sᵈ Tract of Land as it is bounded & Set forth unto him y⁶ sᵈ Andrew Lewis his heirs & Assignes for ever Against me y⁶ sᵈ Peter Lewis & my heirs for ever y⁶ peaceable possession thereof to Warrant & Defend against all persons whatsoever laying a lawfull claime thereunto In Witness whereof I have hereunto Set my hand & Seal this Second day of June One Thousand Seven hundred & Thirteen 1713./

Signed & Sealed in y⁶
  presence of us y⁶ Subscribʳˢ   Peter Lewis [his mark] (Seal)
Joseph Gunnison
Wᵐ Pepperrell junʳ
Francis Winkley

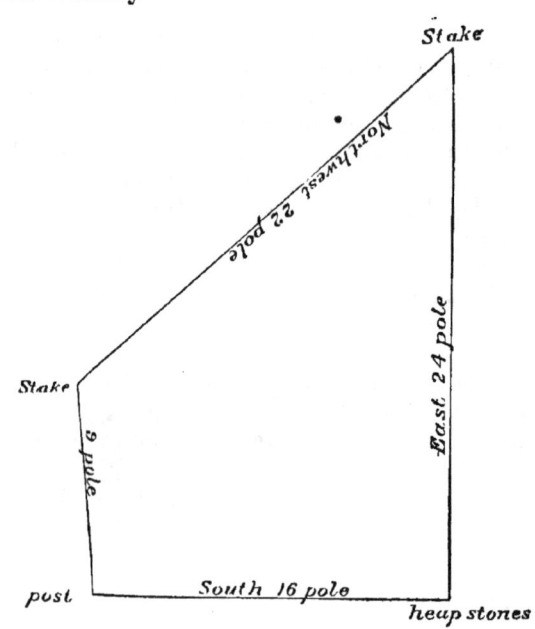

A True Figur of y⁶ abovesᵈ land laid out by me
                                            Wᵘ Godsoe Surveyʳ

Kittery may 14th 1714. This day Peter Lewis personally Appeared before me the Subscriber one of her Maj^tys Justices for ye County of york and acknowledged this above written deed or Obligation to be his free act & Deed./
        Wm Pepperrell..
Recorded According to ye Original Septr 17th 1716
      p Jos. Hamond Reg^r

[180] To All Christian People to whom this presents Deed of Sale Shall Come Know ye that I George Fenix of ye Town of Kittery in ye County of york in province of Maine in New England yeoman & Hannah my wife Sendeth Greeting Know ye that I George Fenix & Hannah my wife for & in Consideration of Ten pounds in Currant money to me in hand at & before ye Ensealing & Delivery of these presents paid by Saml Hutchins of Kittery in ye County of York in province of Maine in New England yeoman well & Truely paid The rec^t whereof I do hereby acknowledge & our Selves therewith fully Satisfied & Contented whereof & of Every part & do Acquit Exonerate & Discharge ye s^d Saml Hutchins his heirs Ex^rs Adm^rs & Every of them by these presents Have Given granted Sold Alien^d Enfeoffed & Confirmed & by these presents do fully freely Clearly and Absolutely give grant bargaine Sell Set over & Confirm unto ye s^d Saml Hutchins his heirs Ex^rs Adm^rs or Assignes all that Tract of land of Ten Acres be it more or Less bounded as followeth bound. upon ye land formerly Enoch Hutchins^s & upon ye land of Rowland Williams Now dec^d & upon ye South side of Rowland Williams & bounds upon a piece of Marsh formerly belonging to ye Mendums runing along be the Side of ye Marsh by ye Courses as may Appear by record referrence thereunto being laid out to ye s^d George Fennex in ye year 1713. by m^r William Godsoe Survey^r for ye Town of Kittery by Vertue of a Town grant granted to Wm Lewis of Kittery as may Appear by record purchased by William Willson & from s^d Wilson to George Feñix as may appear by record being had Together with all ye land Trees fences wood unted wood & all Appurtenances thereunto belonging To have & To hold all ye aboves^d land as they are Set forth & Every part and member thereof unto ye only Sole use of him ye s^d Saml Hutchins his heirs Ex^rs Adm^rs or Assigns forevermore against ye s^d George Fennix or his heirs Ex^rs Adm^rs or Assigns or anethy other under them what Sum ever and furthermore I ye s^d George Fennix

Book VIII, Fol. 180.

for my Selfe & my heirs Ex^{rs} Adm^{rs} to & with ye s^d Saml Hutchins his heirs or assignes Covena^t to & with ye s^d Hutchins that ye premisses are Clear from all Incumbrances what Sumever and as I ye s^d George Fennix Obligeth himselfe and his heirs Ex^{rs} Adm^{rs} to defend all ye s^d Land as here discribed against all persons what Sumever laying any lawfull claime thereunto & that this deed of Sale Shall Stand in full force & vertue as a firm & Lawfull deed of Sale in all points in Law Nothing Except^d In Witness who have hereunto Set our hands and Seals this the Seventh day of March One Thousand Seven hundred & fourteen Anno Domini 1713/14./

Signed Sealed & Delivered   George Fennix   his   (Seal)
  In presence of us   mark
  Wm Fernald Junr
  Wm Pepperrell Junr

This 7th day of March 1713/4./ Then George Fennix personally appeared before me the Subscriber One of her Maj^{tys} Justices for York Acknowledged this above Instrum^t to be his free act & Deed./   Wm Pepperrell Js peace

Recorded According to ye Original Septr 24th 1716./

                      p Jos: Hamond Reg^r

Know All men by these presents that I Eliab Littlefield of Manchester in ye County of Essex in New England Miller for & in Consideration of a valluable Sum of One hundred & Thirty pounds money part in hand paid & ye rest Secured to be paid me by bonds und^r ye hand and Seal of Thomas Perkins Junr of Topsfield in ye County afores^d weaver which is to my full Satisfaction & Contentm^t have bargained and Sold & do by these presents freely fully & Absolutely give grant bargaine Sell Aliene Assigne & Set over to ye s^d Thomas Perkins his heirs & Assignes forever a Certaine Tract of land & Marsh Scittuate at Capeporpoise in ye province of Maine Containing about Two hundred Acres more or Less It being all that my land & Marsh which I have on ye northeast side of Cape porpoise river which place was formerly John Barrots & was formerly Called Barrots place or farm bounded at ye Northwest Corner with Barrots falls where s^d Barrots mill formerly Stood thence bounded on ye river as ye river runs till it Comes to the Creek Comonly Called Millers Creek & thence by s^d Creek till it Comes to a rock Comonly Called Princes rock & from s^d rock to run Over to ye falls first mentioned To have & To hold s^d

Two hundred Acres of Land & Marsh Together with ye priviledges for a mill at ye falls where s^d Barrots mill formerly Stood with all other priviledges & rights in Com̃ons or undivided lands. Appurtenances of wood Timber rocks Mines wayes Easm^{ts} watering places water Courses & all other profits to & Every part thereof belonging to him ye s^d Thomas Perkins his heirs Ex^{rs} Adm^{rs} & Assignes as an Estate of Inheritance in fee Simple forever./ And further I ye s^d Eliab Littlefield do hereby Warrantize this Sale & avouch ye Premisses to be free from all former Gifts grants bargains Sales Judgm^{ts} Executions Dowers Thirds Entailes & all other Intanglem^{ts} whatsoever & that he ye s^d Thomas Perkins his heirs Ex^{rs} Adm^{rs} or assignes Shall forever hereafter peaceably & quietly have hold use Occupy Possess & Enjoy ye Same with all ye priviledges thereof without any Let or Interruption of me my heirs Ex^{rs} or Adm^{rs} or any other person whatsoever laying legall claime thereunto To all above written I have Set my hand & Seal this Twenty Sixth day of Decemb^r Anno Dom^i Seventeen hundred & fifteen The words rights in Com̃ons or undivided lands were Interlined before Signing & Sealing./

Signed Sealed & Delivered
  In presence of us   Eliab his mark Littlefield (Seal)
      Samuel Leach
Witnesses
        William Reding

Essex sc/ Salem Decemb^r 29th 1715

Then Eliab Littlefield ye within Conveyor psonally Appeared & Acknowledged ye within Instrum^t to be his Voluntary act & Deed.   Coram Steph Sewall Jus^t peace

Recorded According to ye Original Augst 15th 1716./
                      p Jos. Ham̃ond Reg^r

[181] To All People to whom these presents Shall Come Greeting Know ye that I Samuel Spinney of Kittery in ye County of york within his Maj^{tys} province of ye Massachusets Bay in New England Yeoman for & in Consideration of Two pounds & Ten Shillings an Acre to me in hand before ye Ensealing hereof well & Truely paid by Richard Rogers of ye Same place afores^d Cooper the rec^t weereof I do hereby Acknowledge & my Selfe therewith fully Satisfied and Contented & thereof & of Every part & parcell thereof do Exonerate Acquit & Discharge ye s^d Richard Rogers his heirs Ex^{rs} & Adm^{rs} by these presents for ever have given granted

bargained Sold Aliened Conveyed & Confirmed & by these presents do fully freely & Absolutely give grant bargaine Sell Aliene Convey & Confirm unto him ye s^d Richard Rogers his heirs & Assignes for ever a Certaine Tract or parcell of land Scittuate lying & being in ye Township of Kittery afores^d on ye western Side of ye river Called Spruce Creek Containing by Estimation Twenty Two Acres Butted & bounded on ye Eastern End with ye land formerly m^r Thomas Withers dec^d Thirty Two poles & halfe & then runing between ye land I formerly purchased of Thomas Rice dec^d and ye land Claimed by Francis Pettigrew untill ye s^d Twenty Two Acres are accomplished Together with all Such rights profits priviledges & Appurtenances as in any kind Appurtaine thereunto with all ye Estate right Title Interest Claime & Demand w^{t}soever of me ye s^d Saml Spinney of in & to ye Same & Every part thereof To have and To hold all ye above granted & bargained premises with all ye Appurtenances & Comodityes to ye Same belonging or in any wise Appurtaining to him ye s^d Richard Rogers his heirs & Assignes for ever to his & their only propper use benefit & behoofe from henceforth for ever And I ye s^d Saml Spinney for me my heirs Ex^{rs} & Adm^{rs} do Covenant promiss & grant to & with ye s^d Richard Rogers his heirs Ex^{rs} Adm^{rs} & Assignes that before ye Ensealing & delivery hereof I am ye True Sole & Lawfull owner of ye above bargained premisses & am Lawfully Siezed & possessed of ye Same in mine own propper right as a good perfect & Absolute Estate of Inheritance in Fee Simple and have in my Selfe good right full power & lawfull Authority to grant bargaine Sell Convey & Confirm s^d bargained premisses in maner as aboves^d And that ye s^d Richard Rogers his heirs Ex^{rs} Adm^{rs} & Assignes Shall & may from time to Time & At all Times forever hereafter by force & Vertue of these presents lawfully peaceably & quietly have hold use Occupie possess & Enjoy ye s^d Demised & bargained premisses with ye Appurtenances free & clear & freely and Clearly Acquitted & Discharged of & from all & all maner of former & other gifts grants bargaines Sales leases Mortgages Entailes Joyntures Dowries Judgm^{ts} Executions Extents & Incumbrances whatsoever had made Comitted done or Suffered to be done by me ye s^d Saml Spinney or any other person or persons by my procurem^t at any time or times before ye Ensealing & Delivery hereof Furthermore I ye s^d Saml Spinney for my Selfe my heirs Ex^{rs} and Adm^{rs} do Covenant promiss & Ingage ye above demised p^{r}misses to him ye s^d Richard Rogers his heirs Ex^{rs} Adm^{rs} & Assignes against The Lawfull Claims of any person or persons whatsoever for ever hereafter to Warrant Secure & Defend. And Margaret ye wife of me ye s^d Saml Spinney doth fully & freely give & yield up unto ye s^d Ric^d Rogers his heirs & Assignes all her right & Title of Dower & Interest of in or to ye Premisses respectively for ever by these presents In Witness whereof we have hereunto Set Our hands & Seals this Twenty fourth day of July Anno Domini One Thousand Seven hundred & Sixteen/ Annoq, R^ni R^is Georgii Magna BrittAnia &c^t Secundo./

Signed Sealed & Delivered   Samuel Spinney (Seal)
   In ye presence of
   John Newmarch   Margaret *her M mark* Spinney (Seal)
   John Newmarch Tert^r

John *his Y mark* Spinney

The 1st of August 1716./

Saml Spinney did personally Appear & did Acknowledge this above written Instrum^t to be his free Act & deed
             Before me./   Wm Pepperrell Js Peace
Recorded Accorded to ye Original Septr 25th 1716.

                   p Jos. Hammond Reg^r

To All Christian People to whom this present Deed of Sale may Come Mr Saml Donnell & Alice his wife of york in ye County of York in province of the Massachusets Bay in New England Sendeth Greeting Know ye that the s^d Samuel & Alice for & in Consideration of forty & Eight pounds money to them ye s^d Samuel & Alice Truely paid by Mr Peter Nowell of ye Same York the rec^t whereof they do therewith Acknowledge themselves therewith fully Satisfied & paid & do hereby Acquit Exonerate & discharg ye s^d Peter Nowell & his heirs & Assignes forever of ye paym^t of Every part of ye premisses hereafter Set forth & Specified the which ye s^d Samuel & Alice have given granted bargained Sold Aliened Enfeoffed & made over And do by these presents give grant bargaine Sell Aliene Enfeoffe & make Over & fully freely and Absolutely Convey & Confirm unto ye s^d Peter Nowell & his heirs & Assignes forever One Certain piece parcell Tract or Tenement of Land & Meadow ground or Swampy land lying & being within ye Township of s^d York & is Scittuated upon ye bell marsh brook or Northwest branch of s^d York river being by Estimation Eighty & Two Acres be it more or less & is butted & bounded as fol-

loweth Viz^t begining at a great maple Standing on the Northwest side of s^d bell marsh brook on ye Northeast of Arthur Bragdons land there./ And runs from s^d Maple tree which is marked on four Sides East North east Eighty Two poles or Perch upon a Square to a Small pine Tree Marked four Sides and from thence North Northwest one hundred & fifty Two poles to a red oak Tree mark^t on four Sides & runs from thence South Southwest Eighty Two poles to red oak Tree Mark^t on four Sides & thence South Southeast to ye Maple Tree began at being part of a grant of Ninety Acres of land given by [182] The Town of York unto Henry Donnell late of s^d York deceased June ye 17th 1685./ As by York Town book may Appear Together with all ye rights & priviledges Appurtenances & Advantages thereunto belonging or any wayes at any time Appurtaining or redounding unto s^d land or priviledges or any part or parcell thereof unto ye s^d Peter Nowell his heirs & Assignes forever To have & To hold & quietly and peaceably to Occupy possess & Enjoy as a Sure Estate in Fee Simple Moreover ye s^d Samuel Donnell & Alice his wife doth for themselves their heirs Ex^{rs} & Adm^{rs} to & with ye s^d Peter Nowell his heirs & Assigns Covenant Ingage & promiss ye above bargained premisses with all its priviledges to be free & Clear from all former gifts grants bargains Sales rents rates Mortgages & all other Incumberm^{ts} whatsoever as also from all future Claimes Challenges writts Executions Law Suits or any other Interruptions whatsoever to be had or Comenced by them their heirs Ex^{rs} Adm^{rs} or Assignes or any other person or persons whatsoever after ye date hereof that henceforth they do warrantize & will Defend y Same./ In Witness hereof the s^d m^r Samuel Donnell & Alice his wife have hereunto Set their hands & Seals this Ninteenth day of Septr in ye year of Our lord One Thousand Seven hundred & Sixteen 1716./   Samuel Donnell (seal)
Signed Sealed & Delivered   Alice Donnell (seal)
   In presence of
   Francis Raynes
   Charles White.
     York sc/
York Septr ye 19th 1716./ m^r Saml Donnell & m^{rs} Alice Donnell within Named psonally Appeared before me ye Subscrib^r one of his Maj^{tys} Justices of ye peace for s^d County & Acknowledged this within written Instrum^t to be their free act & Deed./   Abra^m Preble
   Recorded According to ye Original Sep^{tr} 20th 1716./
          p Jos. Hamond Reg^r

Book VIII, Fol. 182.

To All Christian People to whom this present Deed of Sale may Come Henry Brookin of york in ye province of ye Massachusets Bay in New Engl^d Sendeth Greeting Know Y^e that ye s^d Henry for & in Consideration of fourteen pounds money to him in hand paid by m^r Peter Nowell of s^d York hath given granted bargained Sold Aliened Enfeoffed & Conveyed & doth by these presents give grant bargaine Sell Aliene Enfeoffe & Covey and fully freely & Absolutely Confirm & make Over unto ye s^d Nowell One Certaine Tract of land Containing Thirty Acres lying & being within ye Township of s^d York & is Scittuated upon ye Northwest Side of the bell marsh brook ye which s^d Thirty Acres of land was granted unto Wm Shaw At a Town meeting in s^d York March ye 29 : 1699 and laid out to s^d Shaw March ye 6th 1699/700 as p York Town record or Town book may Appear & Sold by s^d Will Shaw unto aboves^d Henry Brookin as p a deed referrence thereunto being had may appear and is bounded as followeth Viz^t begining at a white Oak Tree marked on four Sides Standing in ye Eastward Corner of Phillip Welches land & runs North Northwest One hundred and Sixty poles to Another white oak Tree marked on four Sides Then East northeast Thirty two poles to Another white Oak marked on four Sides & from thence South Southeast to ye Aboves^d bell Marsh brook & So is bounded by s^d brook unto ye white oak Tree first above Mentioned Together with all ye rights priviledges Appurtenances & Advantages belonging to s^d Thirty acres of land or any part or parcell thereof or whatever hereafter may redownd to ye Same or any part or parcell of it unto him ye s^d Peter Nowell his heirs & Assignes forever To have & To hold and quietly & peaceably to Occupy possess & Enjoy as a Sure Estate in Fee Simple moreover ye s^d Henry Brookin doth Ingage for himselfe his heirs Ex^{rs} & Adm^{rs} to & with ye s^d Nowell his heirs and Assignes ye above bargained premisses with all ye priviledges thereunto belonging are free & Clear from all former gifts grants bargaines Sales rents rates Dowryes Mortgage deed Executions Lawsuits or any other Incumberm^{ts} whatsoever as also from all future Claimes Chalenges Arrests or any other Interruptions whatsoever to be had or Comenced by him ye s^d Henry his heirs Ex^{rs} Adm^{rs} or Assignes or any other person or persons upon Grounds proseeding this date And for ever hereafter ye s^d Henry doth Oblige himselfe his heirs Ex^{rs} & Adm^{rs} to Warrantize & defend ye above premisses./ In Witness hereof ye s^d Henry Brookin hath hereunto Set his hand & Seal this Nineteenth day of Septr in ye year of Our Lord One Thousand Seven hundred

BOOK VIII, FOL. 183.

& Sixteen & in ye Third year of ye reign of Our Soveraign Lord George King of Great Brittaine &c^t/
Signed Sealed
  In presence of   Henry X Brookin (Seal)
  Francis Raynes   his mark
  Charles White
  Eben^r Williams
    York sc/
York Septr ye 19th 1716. Henry Brookin psonally Appear^d & Acknowled this within written Instrum^t to be his free act & Deed   Before me Abra^m Preble Jus^t peace
Recorded According to ye Original Septr 20th 1716.

                               p Jos: Hamond Reg^r

To All Christian People to whom this present Deed of Sale may Come or Concern Phillip Welch & Elizabeth his wife of York in ye County of York in ye Province of ye Massachusets Bay in New England Sendeth Greeting Know Y^e the s^d Phillip & Elizabeth for & in Consideration of fifteen pounds money to them in hand paid faithfully and Truely by Cap^{tn} Peter Nowell of Afores^d york have given granted bargained sold Aliened Enfeoffed & made over and doth by these presents give grant bargaine Sell Aliene Enfeoffe & make Over & fully freely & Absolutely Convey & Confirm unto ye s^d Nowell & his heirs & Assignes for ever One Certaine Tract piece or parcel of land Containing Thirty Acres lying & being within y^c Township of s^d york and is Scittuated upon ye Northwest Side of a brook known by ye name of ye bell marsh brook ye which s^d land was granted unto ye s^d Phillip Welch & his wife [183] At a Town Meeting in s^d York March ye 16^{tn} 1698 & is butted and bounded as followeth vizt begining at three Small birch Trees Standing the northwest Side of ye aboves^d bell marsh brook & So runing up s^d brook Joyning thereunto Thirty two poles to a white oak Tree marked four Sides and from thence North Northwest One hundred & Sixty poles to another white oak Tree marked on four Sides and from thence west northwest Thirty Two poles to a pitch pine Tree marked on four Sides & from thence to ye Three birches began at Together with all ye rights priviledges Appurtenances & Advantages thereunto belonging or any wayes Appurtaining both of wood und^r wood Standing lying or remaining upon s^d land or any

part or parcell thereof unto him ye s^d Peter Nowell his heirs & Assignes for ever To have & To hold and Quietly & peaceably to possess occupie & Enjoy as a Sure Estate in fee Simple and ye s^d Phillip Welch & Eliz^a his wife doth Vouchsafe themselves ye True rightfull and proper Owners of ye above Specified & bargained premisses untill ye Sealing & Delivery of this Instrum^t & have in themselves full power & Lawfull Authority to make Sale thereof & Moreover ye s^d Phillip Welch & his wife Eliz^a doth for themselves their heirs Ex^{rs} & Adm^{rs} to & with ye s^d Peter Nowell his heirs & Assignes Covena^t Ingage & promiss ye aboves^d lands with all its priviledges to be free and clear from all former grants gifts bargaines Sales Mortgages Law suits or any other Incumbrances whatsoever As also from all future Claimes Challenges Executions widdows thirds or any other Incumbrances whatsoever to be had or Comenced by him ye s^d Phillip Welch or his wife their heirs Ex^{rs} Adm^{rs} or Assignes or any other person or persons whatsoever after ye date hereof ye aboves^d Phillip Welch & Eliz^a his wife have hereunto Set their hands & Seals this Twenty fifth day of Septr in ye year of Our Lord God One Thousand Seven hundred Sixteen & in the Third year of ye reign of Our Soveraign Lord George by ye grace of God King Great Brittaine &c^t/
Signed Sealed & Delivered
  In presence   Phillip ⟨his mark⟩ Welch (Seal)
  Sam^{ll} Came
  Charles White
                            Elizabeth ⟨her mark⟩ Welch (Seal)

York Septr ye 25th 1716. This day rec^d of Captn Peter Nowell Ten pounds money & five pounds in Goods in full of ye within Mentioned Land.
                    p me Phillip ⟨his mark⟩ Welch

York sc/ York Septr ye 25 : 1716./ The Above Named Phillip Welch and Elizabeth Welch psonally Appeared & Acknowledged ye above written Instrum^t to be their free Act & Deed   Before me   Abra^m Preble Jus^t peace
Recorded According to ye Original Octob^r 3^d 1716./
                    p Jos: Hamond Reg^r

To All to whom this present Deed of Gift may Come or Concern m^r Samuel Webber & Deberoh his wife of York in ye County of York in New England Sendeth Greeting Know ye that Saml & Deberoh Divers good Causes & Considerations them thereunto moveing but more Especially for & in Consideration of ye good will & Natural & real Affection they have & do Continually bear unto Two of their welbeloved Sons Namely Thomas & Benj^a Webber have given granted bargained Aliened Enfeoffed & Conveyed & doth by these presents give grant bargaine Aliene Enfeoffe & Convey & fully freely & Absolutely make Over & Confirm unto ye s^d Thomas Webber & Benjamin Webber forty Acres of upland & Swampy Land Scittuated lying & being upon ye North-East Side of Cape Nedick river in s^d york & is butted & bounded as followeth Viz^t by ye land former granted unto John Smith Senr of s^d York Deceased & now in ye possession of Some of his children upon the South East Side and by s^d Cape nedick river upon ye Southwest of s^d land and other wayes bounded by marked trees being on both Sides of one branch of s^d Capenudick river Comonly Called ye back river as p ye returns of ye Laying out s^d Land may more at Large Appear only ye s^d Sam^{ll} Webber doth reserve to himselfe halfe an acre of land at ye old mill pond & Conveniency for laying loggs or bords or both where there is Errected a Saw mill at aboves^d back river & Conveniency of a way through s^d land as he may have Accasion or any from by or und^r him Together with all ye rights priviledges Appurtenances & Advantages thereunto belonging or any wayes at any time redounding unto ye same or any part or parcell thereof only what is above Excepted unto ye s^d Thomas & Benjamin in Joynt & Equall Copartnership To have & To hold & Quietly & peaceably to possess & Enjoy as a Sure Estate in fee Simple both them their heirs & assignes for ever & that ye s^d Saml & Deberoh do hereby proceeding ye date hereof Acquit & Discharge ye Same According to ye Above Instrum^t & will Warrantize & defend ye Same from by or und^r them their heirs & Assignes In Witness hereof ye aboves^d Saml Webber & Deberoh his wife have hereunto Set their hands & Seals this Eighteenth day of Aprill in ye year of Our Lord One Thousand Seven hundred & fourteen in ye first year of ye reign of Our Lord George King of Great Brittaine &c^t./   Samuel Webber (seal)

Signed Sealed & Delivered
   In ye presence of
   Lydia Storer her mark

   Deborah Webber Junr
      mark

Deberoh Webber (seal)
   mark

Book VIII, Fol. 184.

York sc./ At an Inferio^r Court of Comon pleas holden at york Octob^r 2^d 1716. Lydia Storer & Deberoh Webber Junr made Oath that they Saw m^r Saml Webber dec^d & Deberoh his wife Sign Seall & Deliver this Instrum^t as their Act & Deed & that they Set their hands as Witnesses thereunto
Attest^r J. Hamond Clerk
Recorded According to ye Original Octob^r 2^d 1716.
p Jos Hamond Reg^r

[184] To All Christian People to whom these presents may Come William Shaw of York in ye County of york in ye Province of ye Massachusets bay in New England Sendeth Greeting./ Know Y^e that ye s^d William Shaw for & in Consideration of a Certain Sum of money to him in hand well & truely paid by Henry Brookin of said york ye rec^t whereof ye s^d Wm Shaw doth Acknowledge himselfe therewith fully Satisfied & paid & doth by these presents Exonerate & discharge ye s^d Brookin his heirs Ex^{rs} & Adm^{rs} forever for a Certaine piece or parcell of land which ye s^d William Shaw hath given granted bargained Sold Aliened Enfeoffed & Conveyed & doth by these presents give grant bargaine Sell Aliene Enfeoffe Convey & fully freely & Absolutely make Over & Confirm unto ye s^d Henry Brookin his heirs & Assignes as aboves^d a Certaine piece or parcell of upland & Swampy land Scittuated lying and being within ye Township of York & is by Estimation Thirty Acres be it more or Less which s^d Thirty Acres of Land lyeth on ye westward side of ye bell marsh brook & is bounded as followeth Viz^t begining at a white Oak Tree Standing on ye Eastward Corner of Phillip Welch his lot mark^t on four Sides and runs from thence North North west One hundred & Sixty poles to Another white Oak Tree markt on four Sides then runs East North East Thirty & Two poles to a white oak mark^t on four Sides then South South East to ye brook aboves^d & is bounded by s^d brook to ye white oak Tree first above Mentioned./ Together with all ye rights priviledges & Advantages thereunto belonging or Appurtaining unto ye aboves^d land or any part or parcell thereof or any wise at any time redounding to ye Same both of land Swampy land wood under wood Standing lying or remaining on s^d land with all other priviledges whatsoever unto ye s^d Henry his heirs & Assignes To have & To hold & Quietly & peaceably to possess ye aboves^d land and all its priviledges as A Sure Estate in fee Simple for ever More over ye s^d W^m doth for himselfe his heirs Ex^{rs} &

Adm^rs Ingage Covena^t Ingage & promiss to & with ye s^d Henry his heirs & Assignes ye aboves^d land with all its priviledges to be free & Clear from all former InCumbern^ts whatsoever as also from all future Lawfull Claims Challenges or Interruptions to be had or Comenced by him ye s^d William his heirs Ex^rs Adm^rs or Assignes or any other person or persons whatsoever after ye date hereof And ye s^d William doth bind himselfe his heirs Ex^rs & Adm^rs to Warrantize & Defend ye aboves^d premisses with all its priviledges In Witness hereof ye aboves^d William Shaw hath hereunto put his hand & Seal this first day of July in ye year of Our Lord One Thous^d Seven hundred & Twelve./ William Shaw (Seal)
Signed Sealed & Delivered
  In ye presence of   her
  Joseph Trumball   Ann *A* Shaw
  Abra^m Preble Junr   mark

May 22^d 1713./ William Shaw above Named personally Appeared & Acknowledged ye Above written deed of Sale to be his Act & Deed: Before me Abra^m Preble Jus^t peace

  Recorded According to ye Original Octob^r 3^d 1716./

                              p Jos: Hamond Reg^r

  To All Christian People to whom these presents Shall Come Greeting Know Ye that I Francis Raynes of York in ye County of york in the Province of ye Massachusets Bay in New England Shipwright for and in Consideration of ye Sum of Twenty five pounds to me in hand before ye Ensealing hereof well & Truely paid by Henry Brookin of ye above place County & province ye rec^t whereof I do hereby Acknowledge & my Selfe therewith fully Satisfied & Contented & thereof & of Every part & parcell thereof do Exonerate Acquit & discharge ye s^d Henry Brookin his heirs Ex^rs Adm^rs forever by these presents Have given granted bargained Sold Aliened Conveyed & Confirmed And by these presents do freely fully & Absolutely give grant bargaine Sell Aliene Convey & Confirm unto him ye s^d Henry Brookin his heirs & Assignes forever One Messuage or Tract of Land Scituate Lying & being in York in ye s^d County Containing by Estimation Twenty Acres be it more or less butted & bounded Viz^t Begining at a birch Tree which was marked on four Sides So runing west & by South forty poles along by ye road then wee marked a beach Tree from thence we run South Southwest fifty Eight poles untill we Came to a maple Tree marked on four Sides which was ye head bounds going to John Mores from thence we run Twenty Seaven & halfe poles East South East marking Trees in ye Line Till we Come to a pine Tree which we Marked on four sides then we run North East Eighty Eight poles marking Trees as we went in ye Line untill we Come to a Corner near Samuel Winch^{es} bounds from thence we run up Northwest Twenty poles marking Trees untill we Came to ye beach tree where we began by ye Country road till ye s^d Twenty Acres was Compleated To have & To hold ye s^d granted & bargained pmisses with all ye Appurtenances priviledges & Comodityes to ye Same belonging or in any wayes Appurtaining to him ye s^d Henry Brookin his heirs & Assignes for ever to his & their only propper use benefit & behoofe for ever & I ye s^d Francis Raynes for me my heirs Ex^{rs} Adm^{rs} do Covenant promiss & grant to & with ye s^d Henry Brookin his heirs & Assignes that before the Ensealing hereof I am ye True Sole & Lawfull owner of ye above bargained premisses & am Lawfully Siezed & possessed of ye same in my own propper right as a good perfect and Absolute Estate of Inheritance in Fee Simple & have in my Selfe good right full power & Lawfull Authority to grant & bargaine Sell Convey & Confirm s^d bargained premisses in maner as above s^d And that ye s^d Francis Raynes his heirs & Assignes Shall & may from Time to Time & at all times for ever hereafter by force & Vertue of These presents Lawfully peaceably & quietly have hold use Occupie possess & Enjoy ye s^d Demised & bargained premisses with the Appurtenances free & Clear & freely & Clearly Acquitted Exonerated & Discharged of from all & all maner of former & other gifts grants bargains Sales Leases Mortgages Wills Entailes Joyntures [185] Dowries Judgments Executions Incumbrances & Extents Furthermore I ye s^d Francis Raynes for my Selfe my heirs Ex^{rs} Adm^{rs} do Covenant & Ingage ye above demised premisses to him ye s^d Henry Brookin his heirs and Assignes against ye Lawfull Claims or demands of Any person or persons whatsoever forever hereafter to Warrant Secure & Defend In Witness whereof I ye s^d Francis Raynes have hereunto Set my hand and Seal this fourteenth day of April in ye year of Our Lord God Seventeen hundred & Sixteen./

It is to be understood before ye Signing Sealing & Delivery hereof that ye fifteenth line & Sixteenth line in ye above Instrum^t was Interlined Seven & halfe & ye word Eight

Signed Sealed & Delivered   Francis Raynes (Seal)
  In presence of
Natha^{ll} Raynes
Natha^{ll} Freeman

Book VIII, Fol. 185.

York sc/ York April ye 14th 1716 m^r Francis Raynes personally Appeared before me ye Subscrib^r one of his Maj^{tys} Justices of the peace within s^d County of York & Acknowledged this above written to be his free Act & Deed
         Abra^m Preble
Recorded According to ye Original Octob^r 3^d 1716.
        p Jos. Hamond Reg^r

Know All Men by these presents that I Moses Spencer of Berwick in ye County of York in ye Massachusets Bay in New England husbandman for & in Consideration of five pounds Ten Shillings Curra^t money of New England to me in hand paid or Secured to be paid by Samuel Bracket of ye Same Town & County Labourer ye rec^t whereof I Acknowledge & my Selfe therewith fully Content and paid Have given granted bargained Sold Enfeoffed & Confirmed and by these presents do for my Selfe my heirs Ex^{rs} & Adm^{rs} Give grant bargaine Sell Enfeoffe & Confirm unto ye s^d Saml Bracket his heirs & Assignes & Certaine Tract of land Scittuate lying & being in Berwick afores^d being part of ye land s^d Spencer Now lives upon Containing by Estimation Six Acres be it more or Less being Sixteen pole in breadth Southwest & by South & to Extend in length According to that breadth fore mentioned Viz^t Sixteen pole as far as s^d Spencers own land runs on a South East & by East line bounded Southwest by Benj^a Nasons land Northwest by Richard Lords land on ye Northeast by s^d Spencers land & on ye South East by East by land which James Warren Claimes Together with all priviledges & Appurtenances to ye s^d Tract belonging or in any wayes Appurtaining Together with good & Sufficient highway to ye Country road by Richard Lords to go from s^d Brackets to s^d Spencers house to So to ye Country road he ye s^d Bracket maintaining a good & Sufficient fence on One Side of ye highway from his house to ye Country road as far as s^d Spencers land reaches that way & s^d Spencer Maintaining ye other side To have & To hold ye aboves^d Tract of land with ye Appurtenances & ye highway for Egress & regress to ye s^d Bracket his heirs & Assignes for ever as a good & Sure Estate in fee Simple And ye s^d Moses Spencer doth for himselfe his heirs & Ex^{rs} Adm^{rs} Covena^t promiss grant & agree to & with ye s^d Saml Bracket his heirs & Assignes that he ye s^d Moses Spencer at ye Time of ye Ensealing & Delivery of these presents hath good right & Lawfull Authority to bargaine & Sell The

Book VIII, Fol. 185.

Same in maner afores⁴ And that yᵉ sᵈ Sam¹ Bracket his heirs & Assignes & Every of them Shall & may for ever hereafter Quietly have hold & Enjoy yᵉ before hereby demised premises without any disturbence or Interruption of yᵉ sᵈ Moses Spencer his heirs or Assignes or of Any other person or persons whatsoever & Clear & free from all & all manner of former gifts grants bargains Sales Mortgages Joyntures Dowers & all Incumbrances whatsoever And yᵉ sᵈ Moses Spencer for himselfe his heirs Exʳˢ & Admʳˢ doth Covenant to & with the sᵈ Bracket to Defend yᵉ sᵈ Bracket his heirs & Assignes in yᵉ quiet & peaceable possess. of yᵉ aforesᵈ Tract of land & yᵉ Appurtenances In Witness whereof yᵉ sᵈ Moses Spencer hath hereunto Set his hand & Seal this Twenty third day of March in yᵉ Second year of yᵉ reign of King George Over Great Brittaine &cᵗ in yᵉ year of our Lord God One Thousand Seven hundred & fifteen Sixteen

Memorandum before Sealing yᵉ words [be it] between yᵉ fourteenth and fifteenth lines on yᵉ first page from yᵉ top were Interlined   Moses Spencer (Seal)
Signed Sealed & Delivered
   In yᵉ presence of us
   Jeremiah Wise
   Daniel Goodin
            The mark
William. ⋀ .Newton
         of
York sc/ March 23. 1715/6 Moses Spencer & Elizᵃ his wife psonally Appeared before me yᵉ Subscribʳ one of his Majᵗʸˢ Justices of yᵉ peace for sᵈ County & Acknowledged yᵉ above Instrumᵗ in writing to be their Volluntary Act & deed She giveing up her Thirds or right of Dower at yᵉ Same Time to yᵉ premisses./   Coram me Elisha Plaisted Justˢ
Recorded According to yᵉ Original May 10ᵗʰ 1716./
                              p Jos: Hammond Regʳ

To All People unto whom these presents Shall Come. Samuel Walker of Piscattaqua in New Jersey in America Gent Sends Greeting Know Yᵉ that I yᵉ sᵈ Sam¹ Walker for & in Consideration of yᵉ Sum of Two hundred & fifty pounds in good Bills of Credit of yᵉ Province of the Massachusets Bay in New England to me in hand well & Truely paid at & before yᵉ Delivery hereof by William Pepperrell Junʳ of of Kittery in yᵉ County of York Merchᵗ yᵉ recᵗ whereof I Acknowledge Have given granted bargained & sold and by these presents do give grant bargaine Sell Convey & Confirm unto y[e] s[d] W[m] Pepperrell Jun[r] his heirs & Assignes for ever all my right Estate Title Interest propperty Claime & Demand whatsoever of in & to All that Certaine Tract or parcell of land Scittuate lying & being in Saco within y[e] late province of Maine now known by y[e] County of York in New England Afores[d] Containing by Estimation Six Thousand Acres More or Less Two full third parts whereof of right belongs to me y[e] s[d] Samuel Walker the whole being bounded with a brook Southeasterly Comonly Called Nicholas brook Northeasterly with Two miles from y[e] Great river Northwesterly with y[e] Extent of Three miles & An halfe & Eighteen poles above the Saco Mill falls & Southwest with y[e] great river as Also All my right Title & Interest being Two thirds of & in y[e] herbage Comonage for Timber & all other things Standing lying & growing upon [186] four Thousand five hundred Acres more of Land lying upon y[e] North East Side of y[e] land aboves[d] Together with all & Singular y[e] Profits priviledges Edefices buildings fences waters water Courses ponds Mines Mineralls Emollum[ts] & Appurtenances whatsoever to y[e] s[d] Granted premisses belonging or in any wise Appurtaining & y[e] reversion & reversions remaind[r] & remainders thereof To have & To hold Two full third parts of & in y[e] s[d] Tract or parcell of land Containing Six Thousand Acres more or Less & all other y[e] herein before given & granted premisses with y[e] Members and Appur[ces] thereof unto him y[e] s[d] William Pepperrell his heirs & Assignes for ever And I y[e] s[d] Sam[l] Walker for my Selfe my heirs Ex[rs] & Adm[rs] do Covena[t] promiss grant & Agree with y[e] s[d] W[m] Pepperrell his heirs & Assignes by these presents in Maner following./ That is to Say./ that at & untill y[e] Delivery hereof I am y[e] True Sole & Lawfull Owner of all y[e] Above given & granted land & premisses & Stand Siezed thereof in fee haveing in my Selfe full power to give grant Sell & Dispose of y[e] Same in Manner as Afores[d] y[e] s[d] Granted premises now being free & Clear of & from all former & other gifts grants bargaines Sales Titles Troubles Joyntures or power of Thirds of my present wife Mortgages Incumbrances Wills Judgm[ts] Executions Extents Claimes and Demands whatsoever./ & further I y[e] s[d] Sam[l] Walker do Covena[t] and Grant for my Selfe my heirs Ex[rs] & Adm[rs] to Warrant And defend y[e] s[d] Given granted & bargained land & premises with the Appur[ces] & Every part thereof unto him y[e] s[d] W[m] Pepperrell his heirs & Assignes for ever Against y[e] Lawfull Claimes & demands of all & Every other person & persons whomsoever. In Witness whereof I y[e] s[d] Sam[l] Walker have

hereunto Set my hand and Seal y^e Twenty Sixth day of Octob^r Anno Domini One Thousand Seven hundred & Sixteen Annoq RR^s Georgii Tertio./   Saml Walker (s^a_eal)
Signed Sealed & Delivered
  In presence of us
  Andrew Tyler
  Mary Checkley
  Rec^d y^e day & year above written of Wm Pepperrell Junr The Sum of Two hundred & fifty pounds in full for y^e afore granted premisses   p me Saml Walker
  Suffolk sc/ Boston Octob^r 26th 1716./
  Then y^e Above Named Saml Walker Acknowledged the afore going Instrum^t to be his free Act & deed
              Before me./ Saml Checkley Just^s peace
Recorded According to ye Original Novr 15th 1716./
                    p Jos: Hamond Reg^r

  Know All men by these presents that I Samuel Walker of Piscattaqua in New Jersey in Amerrica Gent am holden & Stand firmly bound & Obliged unto Wm Pepperrell Junr of Kittery in ye County of york Merch^t in ye full Sum of One hundred & fifty pounds Lafull money of New England to be paid unto him ye s^d Wm Pepperrell his Ex^rs Adm^rs or Assigns to ye True paym^t whereof I my Selfe my heirs Ex^rs & Adm^rs firmly by these presents Sealed with my Seal Dated ye 26th day of Octob^r Anno Dom: 1716
  The Condition of this Obligation is Such that Whereas ye above bounden Saml Walker has Sold s^d Wm Pepperrell a Certaine Tract of land lying & being in Saco As Appears p a deed of Sale under ye s^d Saml Walkers hand & Seal bareing Even date with ye above Obligation which Land was purchased of Benj^a Blackman by ye s^d Saml Walkers father & Sampson Sheafe & ye s^d Sampson Sheafe Sold his Third part to s^d Walker & ye s^d Saml Walker do promiss and Ingage in ye aboves^d Sum that his now wife Shall not lay any Claime for her thirds or any other part but y^e s^d Wm Pepperrell Shall Enjoy Two thirds of y^e whole Tract of land & Appurtenances As Mentioned in s^d deed in peaceable & Quiet possession that then this above bond to be Voyd or Else to remaine in full force Strength & Vertue   Saml Walker (s^a_eal)
Signed Sealed & Delivered
  In presence of
  Andrew Tyler
  Mary Checkley
  Suffolk sc Boston Octob^r y^e 26th 1716

Book VIII, Fol. 187.

Mr Saml Walker personally Appeared & Acknowledged y^e Instrum^t on y^e Other Side to be his Act & deed.
　　　　　　Before me./　Saml Checkley Jus^t : of peace
Recorded According to　ye Original Novr 5th 1716./
　　　　　　　　　　　p Jos. Hamond Reg^r

　　To All People to whom these presents Shall Come Ephraim Savage Gent : Sole Adm^rs of ye goods Chattells rights & Credits of Richard Wharton late of Boston in ye County of Suffolk within ye Province of ye Massachusets Bay in New Engl^d Esqr dec^d Sendeth Greeting./ Whereas ye Estate of ye s^d Richard Wharton proved Insolvent not being Sufficient to pay & Satisfie his Just debts ye s^d Adm^r upon Aplication made to ye Superio^r Court of Judicature was by them fully Impowered as ye Law in Such Case made provides & directs to make Sale of ye dec^ds lands & real Estate to Inable him to pay & discharge ye Just debts Owing by ye dec^d in proportion So far as ye Estate Would Extend, And whereas Amongst other Creditors ye s^d dec^d was Justly Indebted by bond to ye Deacons of ye first Church in Boston for ye use of ye poor of ye s^d Church the principle Sum of Eight pounds Money besides ye Interest thereof from ye Seventh day of Decr in ye year 1686./ Know Y^e that I ye s^d Ephraim Savage Adm^r as afores^d for ye Consideration afore Expressed & for & Toward paym^t of ye s^d debt Owing to ye first Church in Boston in proportion So far as ye s^d Estate will Extend by Vertue of ye Power & Authority to me granted as afores^d by ye Superio^r Court of Judicature [187] Have given granted bargained Sold released Enfeoffed & Confirmed and by these presents do give grant Bargaine Sell release Enfeoffe Convey & Confirm to John Marion Josiah Tay & Thomas Hubbart present Deacons of ye s^d first Church in Boston their Successors in ye s^d Office & Assignes in Trust to & for ye use of ye poor of ye s^d first Church all that Certaine Tract of Six hundred & fifty Acres of land being Scittuate on ye westermost Side of a Certaine Island Called Great Chebeage Al^s recompence Island in Casco bay within ye late Province of Maine also three hundred & fifty Acres more of land Scittuate in Casco Bay afores^d at the westermost End of Maquoit begining at ye mouth of Puggy Muggy river to run Eight score poles East & by South to ye Eastermost end of a great rock on ye edge of the shoare & from thence North Three hundred & fifty poles to a great Spruce tree Mark^t on four Sides & Stands on a hill in a

Spruce Swamp & from thence west Eight Score poles which afores^d Tracts or parcells of land are parcell of the Estate of ye said Richard Wharton whereof he died Siezed being Taken up & laid out to him by A Comittee Appointed by ye General Court in ye year 1683 in Satisfaction of a grant made to him by ye s^d Genl Court of ye Late Massachusets Collony in ye Latter End of ye year Eighty Two of One Thousand Acres of land in ye Province of Maine Either upon any free Island or place upon ye Maine to him his heirs & Assigns forever as by ye records of ye s^d Court relation thereto being had doth & may More fully Appear And all ye Estate right Title Interest use propperty possession Claime & demand of ye s^d Richd Wharton & his heirs of in & to ye afores^d Several Tracts or parcells of land with ye members & Appurtenances thereof To have & To hold ye s^d Two Several Tracts or parcells of Six hundred & fifty & Three hundred and fifty Acres of land Lying Scittuate & Discribed as afores^d with the Members & Appur^{ces} thereof to ye s^d John Marion Josiah Tay and Thomas Hubbart present Deacons of y^e s^d first Church in Boston their Successors & Assigns to & for y^e use of y^e poor of y^e s^d first Church for Ever./ In Witness whereof y^e within Named Ephraim Savage hath hereto Set his hand & Seal the fifteenth day of May—Anno Dom : 1713./ Annoq$_e$ RR^s Anna Magna Brittania &c^t Duodecimo   Ephraim Savage ($_{Seal}^{a}$)
Signed Sealed & Delivered
  In y^e presence of us
  John Gibbon
  Jos Marion
  Upon y^e day of y^e date above written Rec^d of y^e Deacons of y^e first Church in Boston y^e within Mentioned bond for y^e principle Debt of Eighty pounds over & Above y^e Interest grown due thereupon : the purchase Consideration
                              p Ephraim Savage
     Suffolk sc/ Boston may 15th 1713./
  The above Named Ephraim Savage p^{r}sonally Appearing Acknowledged ye Above & within written Instrum^t
                    Before me Js^a Addington J Pac^s
  Recorded According to ye Original Novemb^r 10th 1716./
                        p Jos. Hamond Reg^r

  To All People unto whom these presents Shall Come John Prichard of Boston in ye County of Suffolk in New England Joyner and Shop keeper & Sarah his wife Send Greeting

Book VIII, Fol. 187.

Know Y^e that I ye s^d John Prichard by and with the free Consent of Sarah my s^d wife Testifyed by her Executing of these presents) for & in Consideration of the Sum of One Hundred Seventy nine pounds Six Shillings to me in hand at & before the Delivery hereof paid by Phillip Burger of Boston afores^d Merchant the receipt whereof I acknowledge have given granted bargained Sold Conveyed & Confirmed and by these Presents Do give grant bargain Sell Convey & Confirm unto ye s^d Phillip Burger his heirs & Assignes for ever The Three Several Tracts or Parcells of Land hereafter mentioned Scittuate lying & being within the bounds of the Township of York (That is to Say) A Certaine Tract or Percell of land Containing by Estamation One Hundred thirty two Acres more or less butted & bounded Easterly by land of Allexander Maxwell And One Mackinime Southerly by york River to a Cove Comonly called Coats's Cove & Extending from ye s^d River Northerly as Other Lots in ye s^d Town of York Adjoyning to ye s^d River Do run untill the afores^d Quantity of one Hundred and Thirty two acres be Compleated Also another Tract of Land Containing about Twenty Acres more or less (which was formerly Estate of Samuel Webber of York) Begining at a heep of Stones by the side of the Highway Adjoining to the Land that was Edward Rishworth on ye Southwest Side and So runing One Hundred & Eight rods upon a northeast Line And from thence Thirty & Two rods upon A Northwest line & from thence Ninety & Six Rods upon a Southwest line & from thence Twenty rods upon A Southeast line & from thence Twelve rods upon A Southwest line to the heap of Stones by the way Side where the bounds first began And Also all that Tract of Land which was heretofore the Estate of Eliakim Hutchinson Esqr Containing by Estimation Thirty[80] five Acres more or less & which he Sold & Conveyed to Nathaniel Harris of York Afores^d Yeoman by a good Deed of Sale wherein the Same is particularly bounded & described Together wth all & Singular the Edifices Buildings rights Commodityes trees woods underwoods profits priviledges Members and appur^{ces} to ye s^d Tracts or parcels of Land or any parcell thereof belonging And the Reversions And Remainders thereof All which granted Lands and premises were for a valluable Consideration Sold and Conveyed unto me ye s^d John Prichard by ye within named Nathaniel Harris in & by these Severall Deeds for ye Same As by ye s^d Deeds or ye Record thereof will plainly appear To have & To hold ye s^d three Several Tracts or parcels of Land with ye housing Edifices & buildings thereon standing and all other the above given & granted premises with their appurtenances unto him ye s^d Phillip Burger his heirs & assignes for ever to his & their Sole proper [188] use and behoof for ever more And I the Said John Prichard Do Avouch my selfe at & untill the delivery hereof to be the true Sole & Lawfull Owner of all the afore granted pmisses Haveing in my Selfe full power & Lawfull Authority to grant sell and Dispose thereof in manner as afores^d the Same being Free & Clear & Clearly Exonerated & Discharded of and from all former and other gifts grants bargains Sales leases releases Mortgages Joyntures Dowers Judgments Executions titles troubles Charges and Incumbrances whatsoever And I ye s^d John Prichard for my Selfe my Heirs Execut^{rs} & Administrators Do Covena^t grant and Agree to & with the s^d Phillip Burger his Heirs & assignes by these presents to Warrant & Defend the s^d given & granted Lands & premisses with their appur^{ces} unto him & Them for ever against the lawfull Claims & Demands of all Persons whomsoever Provided alwayes & these presents are upon this Condition Never : theless any thing above Contained to the Contrary notwithStanding That if thes^d John Prichard his heirs Execut^{rs} or Admin^{rs} Shall & Do well and Truely Pay or Cause to be paid unto ye s^d Phillip Burger his Executors Administrators or assignes the Sum of One Hundred Seventy nine pounds Six Shillings in good Bills of Credit on the province of ye Massachusets Bay or Currant Silver money of new england in manner following that is to Say Fifty nine pounds fifteen Shillings & four pence thereof on or before the twenty Seventh of July next Fifty nine pounds fifteen Shillings & four pence more thereof on or before the Twenty Seventh Day of Novemb^r next Ensuing & the remaining Sum of Fifty nine pounds fifteen Shillings and four pence on or before the Twenty Seventh day of March which will be in the year of Our Lord One Thousand Seven Hundred & Seventeen without fraud Coven or futher delay Then this Deed of Sale or Mortgage to be void & of none Effect But in Default thereof to remain in full force & vertue In Witness whereof the s^d John Prichard & Sarah my wife have hereunto put our hand & Seals this Twenty Seventh day of March Anno Domini 1716 Annoq, RR^s Georgii Secundo   John Prichard (Seal)

Signed Sealed & Delivered   the mark of
  In presence of us
  Thomas Phillip   Sarah ✗ Prichard (Seal)
  Jo Hearne

Received the Day & year above written of Phillip Burger the Mortgagee the Sum of One Hundred Seventy nine

Book VIII, Fol. 189.

pounds Six Shillings being ye full Consideration mentioned in ye afore going Deed   p me John Prichard

Suffolk ss/ Boston March 1716/
The above named John Prichard & Sarah his wife appeared before me & acknowledged the fore going Instrum^t to be their free Act & & Deed   Jus^t Pac^s

Suffolk ss/ Boston aprill 11 : 1716/
Sarah Prichard Appeared before me the Subscrib^r one of his Maj^tys Justices of the peace fores^d County of Suffolk & acknowledged the fore going Instrum^t to be his free act & Deed & on ye Day following being ye Twelfth Instant John Prichard Acknowledged the Afores^d Instrument to be his act & Deed   Before me Elisha Cook Jus^t peace
Recorded According to ye Original Novr 10th 1716.

p Jos. Hamond Reg^r

Whereas there hath been a Controversie between Mrs Mary Plaisted of york in ye County of york in New England Adm^r to the Estate of m^r John Sayward formerly of s^d york dec^d on ye one part & John Sayward Son of ye S^d John Sayward dec^d on ye other part relateing to the Settlem^t & Distribution of ye Estate of ye s^d John Sayward dec^d And relateing to ye s^d Administrat^x her acco^t of Administration on s^d Estate for ye Issueing of s^d Controversie & putting a final End and Period to any further Differance relateing to the pmisses they ye s^d Mary Plaisted & John Sayward have referred themselves to ye Determination award & arbitram^t Decision & Judgm^t of Collo^l John Wheelwright & Cap^tn Joseph Hill of wells Collo^ll Wm Pepperrell Maj^r Charles ffrost & m^r Joseph Hamond of Kittery & m^r Samuel Came & m^r James Grant of york all within ye County of york afores^d to Consider of ye s^d Account and to Ad to or Deminish ye Same & rectify all defects which in their Judgm^t Shall be found therein & we do likewise by these presents for our Selves our heirs Execut^rs & adm^rs Give unto ye said Abitrators or any five of them our full & whole [189] Strength power & authority in all respects whatsoever relateing to ye premisses to act as we our Selves Could or might do in our own psons/ and further we do by these presents for us our heirs Execut^rs & administrat^rs Bind & oblige our Selves in ye Penall Sum of five Hundred pounds Currant money of New England to Stand to & Abide by y^e

Book VIII, Fol. 189.

Determination award finall End Decision & Judgm^t of ye s^d Arbitrat^{rs} or any five of them as afores^d which s^d Sum of five hundred pounds Shall be recovered wthout Chancery by ye party Observent of ye party fayling in ye pmisses Always Provided that ye s^d Arbitrat^{rs} Give in their award in writting under their hands & Seals Some Time before y^e Last day of Jan^{ry} next In Witness whereof we y^e Said Mary Plaisted & John Sayward have hereunto Set our hands & Seals this Eighth day of Octob^r Seventeen Hundred & Sixteen Annoq, RR^s Georgii Magna Brittania &c^t Tertio

Signed Sealed & Delivered   Mary Plaisted ($_{Seal}^a$)
   In y^e Presence of us   John Sayward ($_{Seal}^a$)
   William Brasey
   Jonathan Bane

York ss/ york octob^r the 8th 1716/ mr^s Mary Plaisted & m^r John Sayward Personally appeared and acknowledged this within Instrum^t to be their free act and Deed

           before me Abra^m Preble Jus : pes
Recorded According to y^e Original Jan^{ry} 3^d 1716.

                   p Jos. Hamond Reg^r

Whereas there has been a Controversie between Mr Mary Plaisteed of york in ye County of york in New England Administratrix to ye Estate of m^r John Sayward formerly of s^d york Dec^d on ye one part & John Sayward Son of s^d John Sayward Dec^d on ye other part relateing to ye Settlem^t & Distribution of s^d Estate & relating to her Acc^t of administration &c^t as by a Certain bond or Instrum^t in Writing und^r their hands & Seals bearing Date ye Eighth Day of octob^r Seventeen hundred & Sixteen in which bond or Instrum^t they have referred ye Decision & Determination to us ye Subscribers

Accordingly Weė met at ye house of Mrs Mary Plaisted aboves^d in York where both partyes Appeared & haveing produced their Titles Acco^t &c^t Speak to ye Subject Matter of ye pmises We viewed their Several papers & Acco^t & Muturely Considered The Same with their Several pleas & argum^t relating to the premisses have Awarded as followeth Viz^t Whereas ye s^d m^{rs} Mary Plaisted has Lately Errected a New Dwelling house on part of that thirty four acres of Land which ye s^d John Sayward Dec^d purchased of Mr Ed^{wd} Rishworth bounded Southeast by ye new mill Creek So Called Southwest by ye Land of Thos Moulton dec^d or ye highway wch Leads to y^e

Grismill Northwest by yᵉ Cuntrey road & Northeast by sᵈ County road & yᵉ Land of Mathew Astine And in Consideration of Sundrey Expences She has been at do Award & Decree that yᵉ sᵈ Dwelling house with yᵉ barn & One acre of Land Adjoyning to it bounded with yᵉ highway Northwestwᵈ & Northeastwᵈ Extending Southwest from yᵉ North Corner of sᵈ Land Twenty Two poles Thence Southeast Twelve poles & Thence back Northward to yᵉ road four rods SouthEast from yᵉ sᵈ North Corner be held & Enjoyed by yᵉ sᵈ Mary Plaisted as her own proper Estate in fee Simple to her & her heirs for ever & that yᵉ remaindʳ of sᵈ Tract of Land be held & Enjoyed by yᵉ sᵈ John Sayward as his own proper Estate in fee Simple to him his heirs for ever Excepting one Third part thereof which is to be in yᵉ hands & under yᵉ Improvemᵗ of yᵉ sᵈ Mʳˢ Mary Plaisted dureing her Natural life which is Set out & bounded as follows from yᵉ west Corner by yᵉ highway Thirty four poles to yᵉ North Corner thence Southeast by yᵉ Country road Twenty four poles to a heap of Stones thence South & by west to yᵉ Southward Side of sᵈ Sayward bounds We do further award & Decree that all other yᵉ Lands and Estate of yᵉ sᵈ John Sayward decᵈ be Improved as abovesᵈ Two third parts thereof to yᵉ sᵈ John Sayward & one third to yᵉ sᵈ Mary Plaisted Dureing her natural Life and afterward yᵉ whole to yᵉ sᵈ John Sayward & his heirs forever

and Whereas yᵉ sᵈ John Saward has purchased yᵉ right of his Sisters Susanna & Hannah Sayward yᵉ Share of Esther & mary Sayward Now in Cannada remaines to them if Demanded We Award & Decree that yᵉ sᵈ John Sayward Shall within one year from yᵉ Date hereof pay unto his mother Mʳˢ Mary Plaisted yᵉ Sum of Thirteen pounds & Ten shillings Provided She Give bond with good Security to refund & pay back to yᵉ sᵈ John Sayward yᵉ sᵈ Sum of Thirteen pounds if ever yᵉ sᵈ Esther & Mary Come to Demand it or any part thereof or any part of yᵉ Estate of yᵉ sᵈ John Sayward Decᵈ [**190**] We further Order Award & Decree that all accoᵗˢ of Administration & all other Accoᵗˢ whatsoever Shall be hereby ballanced between yᵉ sᵈ Mary Plaisted & John Sayward which has heretofore been made by Either of them relateing to yᵉ sᵈ Estate & that they Shall not Mollest or Trouble Each other for or Concerning any matter or thing relateing to sᵈ Estate or yᵉ Settlemᵗ thereof from yᵉ begining to yᵉ Day of the Date hereof/ And that yᵉ Charges of this Arbitration & all things Touching yᵉ same be Equally born by yᵉ sᵈ Mary Plaisted & John Sayward In Witness whereof We have hereunto Set our hands & Seals this third Day of January in yᵉ Third

BOOK VIII, FOL. 190.

year of ye Reign of Our Soveraign Lord George of Great Brittaine &c^t King Annoq, Domini Seventeen hundred & Sixteen

       John Wheelwright (Seal)
     Joseph: Hill (Seal)
     Joseph: Hamond (Seal)
     Samuel Came: (Seal)
     James: Grant: (Seal)

Recorded According to ye Original Jan^ry 3^d 1716./

       p Jos: Hamond Reg^r

Linscot
To
Came

To All People to whom these Presents Shall Come Greeting Know Y^e that I John Linscot in ye County of york In ye Province of ye Massachusets Bay In New England Yeoman for & in Consideration of the Sum of Thirty five pounds in hand paid by Sam^ll Came the receipt thereof I Do hereby Acknowledge my Selfe therewith fully Satisfied and Contented & y^r of & of Every part & parcell thereof Do Exonerate acqnit & Discharge ye s^d Samuel Came his heirs Executors Administrators for ever by these presents Have given granted bargained & by these presents do fully & absolutely give grant bargain Sell Alliene Convey & Confirm unto him ye s^d Sam^ll Came his heirs and Assignes for ever One Messuage or Tract of Land Containing forty Acres which was granted to Mr Peter Nowel by ye Town of york which Land Lyeth between the partings of York River on ye South west Side of a lott of m^r Edward Johnsons at Burch Hill begining at the west Corner of s^d Johnsons land at a white Oak Marked on four Sides which is ye Corner Bounds of s^d Johnsons Land and runs from thence South West Eighty poles or pearch to a Red Oak marked on four Sides & from thence Southeast Eighty poles or perch to a great pine tree Marked on four Sides & thence North East to above s^d Johnsons bounds & So by Said bounds to the place where we began To Have & to Hold ye S^d Granted & bargained premisses with all the Appurtenances priviledges & Comodities to the Same belonging or in any wise Appartaining to him the Said Sam^ll Came his heirs & Assignes for ever to his & their own proper use bennifit & behoofe forever & I ye s^d John Lynscot for me my heirs Executors Administrat^rs Do Covenant promiss & Grant to & with the s^d Sam^ll Came his heirs & And assignes that before the Enseafing hereof I am the true Sole & Lawfull owner of the above bargained premises & am

Lawfully Seized, & possessed of yᵉ Same in my own proper right as a good perfect & Absolute Estate of Inheritance In Fee Simple & have in my Self good right full power & Lawfull Authority to grant bargain Sell Convey and Confirm Said Bargained premisses in manner as above Said & that yᵉ sᵈ Samuel Came his heirs & Assignes Shall & may from time to time & at all times for ever hereafter by force & virtue of these presents Lawfully peaceably & quietly have hold use occupie possess & Enjoy yᵉ sᵈ Demised & bargained premisses with yᵉ Appurtenances free & Clear & freely & Clearly Acquitted Exonerated & Discharged of from all & all manner of former & other Gifts Grants bargaines Sales Leases Mortgages Wills Entailes Joyntures Dowries Judgmᵗˢ Executions Incumbrances what so ever Furthermore I yᵉ sᵈ John Lynscot for my Self my heirs Executʳˢ Admʳˢ Do Covenᵗ & Engage yᵉ above Demised pmisses to him yᵉ sᵈ Samuel Came his heirs & assignes against the Lawfull Claimes or Demands of any person or persons Whatsoever for ever hereafter to warrant Secure & Defend In Witness whereof I have hereunto Set my hand & Seal thirteen day of Aprill in the year of Our Lord God One Thousand Seven hundred & Sixteen   John ⱭⱭ Lynscot (seal)

Signed Sealed & Delivered
In Presence
Joseph Moulton
James Allen
nathˡˡ Freeman

    York ss/ Januᵃ 1ˢᵗ 1716/17

The above named John Lynscot Personally appeared & acknowledged this above written to be his act & Deed

        Before me Abramᵐ Preble Jus Pes

Recorded According to yᵉ Original Janʳʸ 1ˢᵗ 1716/7

        p Jos Hamond Regʳ

---

[191] To All Christian People to whom these Presents Shall Come Greeting Know Yᵉ that I Arthur Bragdon Senʳ in yᵉ Town of york & in Said County in the Province of Massachusets Bay in New England Farmer for & in Consideration of yᵉ Sum of Ten pounds in good & Lawfull money of yᵉ Province afore sᵈ To me in hand before the Ensealing hereof well and truly paid by Elexander Junkins of sᵈ place County & Province aforesᵈ Farmer the Receipt whereof I Do hereby Acknowledge & my Self therewith fully Satisfied & Contented and thereof and of every part and parcell there-

Book VIII, Fol. 191.

of Do Exonerate acquit and Discharge the Said Alex^a Junkins his Heirs Executors adm^{rs} for ever by these Presents have Given & Granted Bargained Sold aliened Conveyed and Confirmed and by these Presents Do Freely Fully & Absolutely Give Grants Bargains Sales Aliene Convey and Confirm unto him the Said Alex^a Junkins his Heirs and assignes for ever One Messuage or or Tracts of Marsh Two Acres Scittuated Lying and being in york in the County afores^d Butted & bounded Westerly by the River & Northwest by a piece of Marsh of Alexand^r Junkins Easterly by a piece of Marsh of Leiu^t Jos^a Bankes Northerly by a Gutter that runs through Curtices Marsh To Have and to Hold ye s^d Granted & Bargained pmisses with all the appurtenances Priviledges & Commodities to ye Same belonging or in any ways appertaining To him ye s^d Alex^a Junkins his heirs & Assignes for ever To his & their only proper use Benefit & Behalfe for ever And I ye s^d Arthur Bragdon for me my heirs Execut^{rs} Admin^{rs} Do Covenant Promise and grant to & with the Said Alex^a Junkins his heirs & Assignes that before the Ensealing hereof I am the True Sole & Lawfull owner of ye above Bargained Premises & am Lawfully Seized & Possessed of ye Same in mine own proper right as a good perfect & absolute Estate of Inheritance in Fee Simple & have in my Selfe Good right Full power & Lawfull Authority to grant Bargaine Sell Convey & Confirm s^d bargained premisses in manner as above s^d & that ye s^d Alex^a Junkins his heirs & Assignes Shall & may from time to time and At all times for ever hereafter by Force & virtue of these Presents Lawfully & peaceably & Quietly Have hold use Occupy Possess & Enjoy the Said Demised & bargained Premises with ye Appurtenances ffree & Clear & freely & Clearly acquitted Exonerated & Discharged of from all & all maner of former & other Gifts Grants Bargaines Sales Leases Mortgages Wills Entailes Joyntures Dowries Judgments Executions Incubrances & Extents furthermore I ye s^d Arther Bragdon for my Self my heirs Execut^{rs} Adm^{rs} Do Covenant & Engage ye above Demissed Premisses to him ye s^d Alex^a Junkins his heirs & Assignes Against ye Lawfull Claims or Demands of any person or persons whatsoever for ever hereafter to warrant Secure & Defend In Witness whereof I have hereunto Set my hand & Seal ye Tenth day of may in ye year of our Lord God One Thousand Seven hundred & Eleven

Signed Sealed & Delivered   Arthur Bragdon (a Seal)
 In Presence   mark
 James Bayley   Sarah ⨯ Bragdon
 Nath^{ll} Freeman

Book VIII, Fol. 192.

York ss/ Jan^r 1st 1716/ Arthur Bragdon above Named parsonally appearing Acknowledged ye above Instrum^t to be his act & Deed   Before me   Abra^m Preble Jus pes
Recorded According to ye Original Jan^ry 1st 1716/7
p Jos. Harmon Reg^r

To All Christian People to whom this Present Deed of Sale May Come or Concern Job : Young and Thos Hayns of york in ye County of York in ye Province of ye Massachusets Bay in New England Sendeth Greeting Know Y^e that the Said Job : and Thomas for & in Consideration of a Certain Sum of money to them & Each of them in hand paid or otherwise Sattisfactorily Secured to be paid by Allexand^r Junkins and Jos^e Junkins both of afores^d York the Said Job : & Thos have given granted bargained Sold Alienated Enfeoffed & Confirmed & Do by [192] these presents give Grant Bargain Sell Allienate Enffeofe & Confirm & fully freely & Absolutely make over unto the Said Allex^n & Joseph A Certain Peace or peaces or Persels of Marsh or Meadow Ground Containing by Eastimation four acres be it more or Less the which Marsh or Meadow Ground is within the Township or precincts of ye Town of Kittery in the County of York abobe named which Marsh or Meadow Ground is : Known by ye name of Youngs^s Marsh being a Part of a percel of Marsh formerly belonging to Rowland Young of York Dec^d who was ye father of Afores^d Job young & father of ye wife of ye s^d Thomas Haynes the which Marsh is Lying and being upon ye head of ye South West Branch of afores^d York River upon both Sides of brook or Stream whereon m^r Cutts & Insign Leighton have Lately Erected & built a Sawmill & is bounded as followeth Viz^t on the Southward Side of Said brook or Creek is bounded by the Marsh of Rowland Young being a Pine Tree Marked by ye woods & So by a fence to s^d Creek Side and their is a Stake Drove Down into the Marsh & on ye North ward Side is bounded by a Point of upland Caled the Stacking Neck or by afores^d Rowland Youngs Marsh and the other bounds is the woods or upland Round to ye Pine Tree above mentioned Together with all the Rights Priviledges & Advantages thereunto belonging both of Thatch grass & whatsoever Priviledge may hereafter redownd to the Same or any Part or parcel thereof unto the s^d Allexand^r Junkins & Joseph Junkins their heirs Executors Adm^rs & Assignes as a Sure Estate in fee Simple for ever To Have and To Hold, & Quietly & peaceably

Book VIII, Fol. 192.

to possess Occupy & Enjoy the Same More over the Said Job: & Tho[s] Do for them Selves their heirs Execut[rs] and Admin[rs] to & with y[e] s[d] Allexand[r] & Joseph their heirs Execut[rs] Adm[rs] & Assignes Covena[t] Engage & Promise y[e] above said Marsh & Meadow Ground with all its Priviledges to be free & Clear from all former Gifts grants bargains Sales Rents Rates Dowries Mortgages Leases or any Incumberm[ts] whatsoever as also from all future Claims Challenges Demands or Interruptions to be had or Comminced by them the Said Tho[s] or Job: their heirs Execut[rs] Admin[rs] or assignes or any other Person or Persons upon grounds of Law but for ever after the Date of this Instrum[t] y[e] s[d] Job: & Tho[s] Do Oblige themselves their heirs Execut[rs] & Adm[rs] that they will for ever Warra[t] & Defend the aboves[d] Premisses with all its Priviledges unto y[e] s[d] Allexand[r] Junkins & Joseph Junking theirs heirs Execut[rs] & Assignes fully & absolutely as is above Specified in Every part & particular In Witness hereof y[e] above said Job: Young & Thomas Haynes have hereto Set their hands & seales this third Day of January in y[e] year our Lord One Thousand Seved hundred & Nine and in the Eighth year of the Reign of our Soverain Lady Anne Queen of Great Brittaine &c[t]

Signed Sealed & Delivered
In the presence of us   Job: his Y   Young (Seal[a])
Daniel Black   Witnesses   mark
Abra[m] Preble jun[r]
    Thomas Haynes (Seal[a])
    her
    Sarah S Young
    mark

Job Young & Tho[s] Haynes above Named personally appeared & acknowledged the above Written Deed of Sale to be their act and Deed This 5th day of January 1709/10/
          Before me Abra[m] Preble Jus: pes
Recorded According to y[e] Original Jan[ry] 1st 1716/7
              p Jos. Hamond Reg[r]

To All People to whom this Present Deed of Sale Shall Come I Daniel Dill Jun[r] of York In y[e] County of York in y[e] Province of the Massachusets Bay in New England farmer send Greeting Know Y[e] that for & in Consideration of y[e] Sum of Twelve pounds Currant money of New England To me in hand well & Truly paid at & before the Ensealing & Delivery of these presents by Allexand[r] Junkins of york In ye County & province aboves^d ye Receipt whereof I Do hereby acknowledge & my Selfe therewith to be fully Contented & paid & thereof & of & from Every part & parcell thereof for me ye s^d Daniel Dill jun^r my heirs Executors Administrators & Assignes Do Exonerate [193] Acquit and fully Discharge him ye s^d Allexand^r Junkins his heirs Executors Adm^rs & Assignes by these presents for ever I ye s^d Daniel Dill have given granted bargained Sold Aliened Enffeoffe Convey & Confirm unto him ye s^d Junkins his heirs & Assignes a piece or parcell of Land Lying & being Scittuate in ye Township of York above Scotland Garrison at ye head of ye Land formerly known by ye name of Clarks farm & Now ye Land of Peter Nowells & is bounded as followeth begining at a White Oak Marked on four Sides Standing about 6 poles Northwest from ffrosts bounds at ye head of ye land formerly Cornhutch Johnsons Land & running Northwest Sixty poles to a Small White oak Marked then North ye East Eighty poles to a White oak Marked then South ye East Sixty poles to A Hemlock marked & then Southwest to ye oak first mentioned with an Addition at ye head It all make Thirty Seven Acres this Land Thus bounded or Otherwise reputed to be bounded Is ye Land that was Laid out to s^d Dill In 1700/ for which he had a grant in ye year 1699/ Together with all ye profits priviledges & appurtenances to ye s^d Land belonging or other wise appertaining with all ye Timber Stones wood w^tsoever To have and To hold ye Said peice & parcel of Land wth all ye Rights Titles Interests Clames Demands which I ye s^d Dan^ll Dill Now have or in time past have had or which I my heirs Execut^rs Adm^rs or Assignes In time To Come may might Should or in any wise ought to have of in or to ye above granted premisses or any part thereof to him ye s^d Allexand^r Junkins his heirs Execut^rs Adm^rs & Assignes for ever & to his & their Sole & Proper use benefit & behooffe & I ye s^d Dan^ll Dill for me my heirs Executors Adm^rs & Assignes Do Covena^t & Promise & grant to & with him ye s^d Junkins his heirs & Assignes that at & before ye Ensealing & Delivery hereof I am ye true right & propper owner of ye above granted premisses & that I have in my Self full power good right the Same to grant & Confirm unto him ye s^d Allexand^r Junkins his heirs & Assignes as Aboves^d & that It Shall & may be Lawfull for ye s^d Junkins his heirs & Assignes ye aboves^d premisses & Every part thereof at all times for ever after To have hold use Improve possess & Injoy Lawfully & Peaceably without any Lawfull Let or Disturbance of or by me or any person or persons from by or under me or my procurem^t & that ye Sale thereof

& Every part thereof against my Selfe my heirs Executors Adm^{rs} & Assignes & against all other parsons Lawfully Claiming ye Same or any part thereof Excepting the Seven acres at ye head granted as addition which Land I Will Warra'ise & Defend against my Selfe my heirs Executors Adm^{rs} & Assignes & against all other Persons as far as my right & Title is good for ye better Confirming & more Sure makeing of ye premises unto ye s^d Allexander Junkins his heirs Execut^{rs} Adm^{rs} & Assignes According to ye Laws of this Province In Witness whereof I ye aboves^d Dan^{ll} Dill have hereunto Set my hand & Seal this first day of Aprell In ye year of our Lord Christ One Thousand Seven hundred & Eight
Signed Sealed Delivered
  In Presence of us   Dan^{ll} [his mark] Dill (a Seal)
  Arthur Bragdon jun^r
  Arthur Bragdon Senr
                               Eliz^a [her mark] Dill

Dan^{ll} Dill aboves^d personally appeared before me the Subscrib^s this 11 day of June 1708/ & acknowledged the above written To be his act and Deed Before me
                         Abra^m Preble jus pes
Recorded According to ye Original Jan^{ry} 1st 1716/7./
                         p Jos Hamond Reg^r

To All Christian People to whom this Present Deed of Sale may Come or Consern Jos: Young jun^r of York In ye County of York in the Province of ye Massachusets Bay in New England Sendeth Greeting Know Ye That for & in Consideration of a Certain Summ of money to him in hand paid or other ways Secured to be paid by Allexand^r Junkins of afores^d York at the Signing of this Instrum^{ts} Have given Granted bargained Sold Alinated Enfeoffed & Confirmed & Do by these presents give grant gargain Sell Alinate Enfeoffe & Confirm & fully freely & absolutely Make over & Confirm unto [194] The Said Allexand^r A Certain Peace or parcel of Salt Marsh & Thatch Ground or banks which is by Estimation two Acres be it more or Less the which is Sittuated Within the TownShip of aboves^d York upon ye North West Branch of s^d York river & is bounded as followeth Viz^t on the North West & ye South East Sides is bounded by ye Marsh of Arthur Bragdon Senr & on the North East Side is bounded by a Small Creek and on the South West by ye Southwest Side bounded by y^e

aboves^d Branch of York River With ye Thatch bank runing to Insign Banckes Marsh Together with all the Rights Bennefits Priviledges & advantages that Doth belong to s^d Marsh and Thatch Ground or any Wise at any time Redowning to ye Same or any part thereof unto him the Said Allexand^r Junkins his heirs Execut^{rs} Adm^{rs} & assignes To Have and To Hold & Quietly & Peaceably to Possess Occupy & Enjoy as a Sure Estate in fee Simple & ye above Said Joseph Young Doth for him Self his heirs Execut^{rs} Adm^{rs} to & with the Said Allexander Junkins his heirs Execut^{rs} Adm^{rs} and assignes Doth Covena^t Ingage & Promise the aboves^d Marsh & Thatch Ground to be fre & Clear from all former grants Gifts Mortgages Sales rents Rates Leases & from all Incumberm^{ts} whatsoever as also from all future Claims Challenges Disturbances Suits or Demands to be had or Comminced by him his heirs Ex^{rs} Adm^{rs} or Assignes or from any other Person or Persons w^{t}soever upon grounds Proceeding the Date of this Instrumt for ever To Warranties by these Presents & Defend ye Same In Witness hereof ye s^d Joseph Young jun^r hath hereto Set his hand & Seal this Twenty first Day of August in ye year of our Lord One Thousand Seven hundred & Seven & in ye Sixth year of ye Reign of our Soveraign Lady Anne Queen of Great Brittaine &c^t

Signed Sealed & Delivered   Joseph Young jun^r (a Seal)
   In ye Presence of
   Joseph Sayward
   Micom Mackentire

Joseph young aboves^d personally appear^d before me ye Subscriber this 17th Day of Octob^r 1707/ & acknowledged ye above Written Deed of Sale to he his Act and Deed
                     Abra^m Preble Justice Peace
Recorded According to ye Original Jan^{ry} 1st 1716/7/
                     p Jos Hamond Reg^r

    To All Christian People to whom this present Deed of Sale may Concern Dan^{ll} Mackintire of York in ye County of York of the Province of the Massachusets Bay in New England Sendeth Greeting Know ye that ye s^d Daniel for & in Consideration of a Certaine Sum of Money to him in hand Well & Truly Paid by Allexand^r Junkins & Joseph Junkins of s^d york the receipt whereof he ye s^d Dan^{ll} Doth hereby acknowledg him Selfe: therewith fully Satisfied & Contented for Every part & Parcel thereof Do Exonerat & Discharge ye s^d Allexand^r & Joseph their heirs Execut^{rs} & adm^{rs} for

ever by these presents Have given granted bargained Sold
Alliened Enfeoffed & Confirmed and by these Presents Do
freely fully & absolutely give grant bargaine Sell Aliene
Enfeoffe Convey & Confirm unto them the Said Allexand^r &
Joseph their heirs & Assignes for ever A Certain Peace or
Parcel of Swamp Land (within this Township of york) Containing Twenty acres by Estimation be it more or Less Near
to the Land that was Daniel Livingstones Late of york
Deceased at ye head of bascove Brook or how ever otherwise bounded or reputed to be bounded being the land or
Swamp marsh formerly Sould by Mathew Astine & Eliz^a
Addams unto Joanna Liveingstone Together with all the
rights Priviledges Profits advantages or appurtenances unto
the s^d Land or Swamp Marsh belonging or appertaining or unto
any part or parcell thereof or any Wise at any thimes Redowning to ye same unto ye s^d Allexand^r & Joseph their
heirs & Assignes for ever To Have & To Hold and, Quiately
& Peaceably to possess Occupy & Injoy the same as a Sure
Estate In fee Simple to them ye s^d Allexand^r & Joseph their
heirs & Assignes for Their own behalf & own proper use &
benefit for ever & the Said Dan^{ll} Doth for him Self his
heirs Execut^{rs} & Adm^{rs} Covena^t Promise & grant to & with
the s^d Allexand^r & Joseph their heirs & Assignes that before
the Ensealing hereof that he ye s^d Dan^{ll} is ye true Sole &
Proper owner of the above bargained Premises & is Lawfully Seized & Possessed of ye same in his own proper
Right as a good Perfect & absolute Estate of Inheritance
[195] In ffee Simple & hath in him Self good Lawfull Right
& full Power & Authority to give grant Sell & Convey and
Confirm the Said bargained Premises in manner as afores^d &
that the s^d Allexand^r & Joseph their heirs & Assignes Shall
& may from time to time and at all times for ever hereafter
by force & virtue of these Presents Lawfully & Peaceably
Occupy & Injoy the above Demised & bargained Premises
with all Its Priviledges free & Clear & ffreely & Clearly
Acquitted and Exonerated & Discharged of & from all Manner of former & other gifts grants bargains Sales Leases
Mortgages Wills Intails Joynturs Dowries or any other Incumberments or Interruptions Whatsoever & further More
the Said Daniel Doth for him Self his heirs Executors &
Adm^{rs} Doth Covena^t and Ingage the above Demised Premises
to them ye s^d Allexand^r Junkins & Joseph Junkins their
heirs & Assigns against ye Lawfull Claims & Demands of
any person or persons Whatsoever hereafter to warrant to
Save & Defend In Witness hereof the s^d Dan^{ll} Mackintire
Hath Set his hand & Seal This Twenty first day of March

Book VIII, Fol. 195.

In ye year of our Lord One Thousand Seven Hundred & Ten Eleven & in ye Tenth year of ye Reign of Our Soveraign Lady Anne Queen of Great Brittain &c^t
Signed Sealed & Delivered   Daniel Mackintire (a Seal)
   In Presence of us
   Joseph Young
   Sam^ll Bragdon
   Abram Preble jun^r
   March 23 : 1710/11
Dan^ll Mackintire above Named parsonally Appeared And Acknowledged the above Written Deed of Sale to be His act & Deed   Before me   Abra^m Preble Js ps
Recorded According to ye Original Jan^ry 1st /716/7/
                 p Jos : Hamond Reg^r

To All Christian People to whom this Deed of Sale May Come or concern Daniel Mackintire of york in y^a County of york in ye Province of the Massachusets Bay in New England Sendeth Greeting Know ye the Said Daniel for and in Consideration of Four pound Money to him in hand Well & Truly Paid Py Allexand^r Junkins of s^d york hath given granted bargained Sold Alliened Enfeoffed and made over and Doth by these Presents give grant barguin Sell Alliene Enfeoffe and make over unto the Said Allexand^r Junkins & his heirs & Assignes One peice or parcell or Tract of Fresh Marsh Containing five Acres Scituate & Lying within ye Township of York Afores^d abonte A mile Distance from a Place Called ye bell marsh Joyning to ye Marsh Called Micom Mackintizs Marsh Southwestward as p a Deed given by the aboves^d Allexander to s^d Daniel bearing Date Septemb^r the 23^d 1709 Referance thereunto being had may more at Large Appear together with all the Profits Priviledges advantages & appurtenances to ye Same belonging or in any wise appertaining To have & To hold the S^d Peace or Parcel of Marsh with all its Priviledges with all rights Titles Claimes & Demands which Daniel Now hath Ever had or ought to have unto ye s^d Marsh or any Pert or Parcell thereof unto him ye s^d Allexand^r Junkins his heirs & Assignes for ever & More over ye s^d Daniel Doth for him Self his heirs Executors & Adm^rs to and with ye s^d Allexand^r his heirs & Assigns Covena^t Ingage & Promise the above bargained Premises with all its Priviledges to be free & Clear from all former gifts grants bargains Sales Rents rates Mortgages or any other Incumberm^ts Whatsoever As also from all future

Claimes Challenges Arrests Law Suits Executions or any Other Interruptions to be had or Comiuced by him ye s^d Daniel his heirs or Assignes or any other Person or Persons whatsoever & hereby ye s^d Daniel Doth Oblige him Self his heirs Excu^{rs} and adm^{rs} to Warranties & Defend the above bargained and Demised Premisses unto ye s^d Allexander Junkins & his heirs & assignes In Witness hereof y^e s^d Daniel Mackint^r hath hereunto Set his hand & Seal this Seventeenth Day of Decemb^r in y^e year of our Lord One Thousand Seven hundred & Sixteen & in y^e third year of the Reign of our Soveraign Lord George King Over Great Brittain &c^t Dan^{ll} Mackintire ($^{\,a}_{seal}$)
Signed Sealed & Delivered
  In Presence of us
  John Burrell
    y^e mark of   Witnesses

  Job / Young

Joshua Linscott
    York ss/ york Decemb^r 17th 1716
  Dan^{ll} Mackintire parsonally appeared before the Subscrib^r one of his Maj^{tys} Justices of y^e Peace for s^d County & Acknowledged the above written Instrum^t to be his free act & Deed   Abra^m Preble
  Recorded According to ye Original Jan^{ry} 1st 1716/7./
                                   p Jos. Hamond Reg^r

  [196] This Indenture made this Sixth Day of February One Thousand Seven Hundred and Twelve 13th In ye Twelfth year of ye Reign off our Soveraign Lady Queen Anne of great Brittain &c^t between Joseph Dearing of Kittery in ye County of york in New England Shipwright and Mary his wife on ye One Party & Andrew Pepperrell in ye Province of New HampShier Marriner of ye other Party Witnesseth That the Said Joseph Dearing and Mary His Said Wife ffor & in Consideration off ye Sum off ffive pound ffive Shillings Money off New England to them in hand at & before the Ensealing & Delivery off the presents well & Truly paid and Secured in ye Law to be by ye s^d Andrew Pepperrell the receipt whereof To full Content and Satisfaction they Doe hereby Acknowledge & thereof Do acquitt ye s^d And^w Pepperrell

Book VIII, Fol. 196.

his heirs Execut[rs] Adm[rs] and assignes & Every of them ffor Ever by these presents have given granted bargained Sold Conveyed & Conffirmed by these Presents Doe freely fully Absolutely give grant bargaine Sell Convey & Confirm unto y[e] s[d] And[w] Pepperrell his heirs Assignes ffor ever all that Third part off his Peice or Parcell off Land & Swamp at Scittua[t] Lying & being in the Town off Kittery Near Spruce Creek which Land Was formerly granted to John Bray dec[d] as p Return from under y[e] Surveyrs hand for fifty Acres only Eighteen Acres & Quarter was Eroniously Laid out on S[d] Emerys Land but Ten & half Acres is my Third part Clear of all Incumbrances & is butted & bounded Northerly by Land of s[d] Andrew Pepperrell & Southerly Westerly & Easterly by Land of S[d] Pepperrells Together with all & Singular y[e] Wood Trees Underwood Stones waters water Courses & all y[e] other Rights Profits Priviledges thereunto belonging or in any wise appertaining To Have & To hold y[e] S[d] Peice or parcell off upland & Swamp with all y[e] above mentioned pmises to be granted & bargained unto y[e] S[d] Andrew Pepperrell his heirs & assignes to his & Their only proper use benifit & behoof ffor ever & y[e] s[d] Joseph Dearing & Mary his wife ffor them Selves their heirs Execut[rs] Adm[rs] do Covenant Promise grant & agree to & with y[e] s[d] Andrew Pepperrell his heirs Execut[rs] Adm[rs] & Assignes by these presents In manner following (that is to Say that at the time of this bargaine & Sale & untill y[e] Ensealing & Delivery of these Presents they have in them Selves good right full power & Lawfull Authority to grant bargaine ffor Sell Convey y[e] Same In manner as aboves[d] being free & Clear from all former gifts grants bargains Titles Troubles Incumbrances w[t]soever and will Warrant & Defend y[e] Same unto y[e] s[d] Andrew Pepperrell his heirs & assignes for ever against y[e] Lawfull Claimes & Demands of all & Every Person & Persons & Lastly will doe or Cause to be done any other act or Acts for y[e] further Conffirmation & more Sure makeing of y[e] Above bargained premises : as by his or their Councell Learned In y[e] Law Shall be Reasonably Advised Devised or Required In Witness whereof y[e] s[d] Joseph Dearing & Mary his s[d] Wife have hereunto Set their hands & Seals this Sixth Day of ffebruary : 1712/3   Jos : Dearing (Seal[a])
Signed Sealed & Delivered   Mary Dearing (Seal[a])
  In Presents off us
  W[m] Pepperrell
  Hannah Vearin

Book VIII, Fol. 197.

The 25 July /1713/ Then Joseph Dearing & Mary his wife Parsonally appeared before me ye Subscrib^r & acknowledged the wthin Written Instrum^t to be their free act & Deed/
Wm Pepperell Js pes
Recorded According to ye Original Decr 13th 1716./
p Jos: Hamond Reg^r

To All Christian People to whom these Presents Shall Come Andrew Lewis of Kittery in ye County of York within his Maj^{tys} Province of ye Massachusets Bay in New England Yeoman Sends Greeting Know Yee that ye S^d Andrew Lewis for and in Consideration of a Certain Sum of money to him in hand paid before ye Ensealing & Delivery of these Presents by John ffrost of New Castle within his Maj^{tys} Province of New Hampsh^r marriner the Rec^t whereof to full Content and Satisfaction he ye s^d Andrew Lewis Doth by These Presents acknowledge and thereof & of Every part & Parcell thereof for him self his heirs Executors & Adm^{rs} Doth acquit Exonerate & Discharge the s^d John ffrost his heirs Execut^{rs} & adm^{rs} & every of them for ever by these presents & for Divers other Good Causes & Considerations him hereunto moving he ye S^d Andrew Lewis hath given granted bargained Sold Aliened Enfeoffed Conveyed & Confirmed & by these presents Doth fully freely Clearly & absolutely give grant bargaine Sell Aliene Enfeoffe Convey & Confirm unto [**197**] The Said John ffrost his heirs & assignes for Ever all his part or Portion or proportion of in or unto the Comon or undivided Lands within ye Townships of Kittery & Barwick as ye Same hath been heretofore Stated & proportioned or how Ever otherwise the Same may hereafter be Stated or proportioned Together with all Such Rights Liberties Imunities profits Priviledges Comodities Emoluments & appurtenances as in any Kind appertaines thereunto with ye Revertions & Remainders thereof & all the Estates Rite Title Interest Inheritances property Possession Claim & Demand w^tsoever of him ye s^d Andrew Lewis of in & to the Same & Every part y^r of To have and To hold all & Singular ye above granted pmisses with all the Appurtenances thereof unto ye S^d Jno ffrost his heirs & Assignes to his & Their own Sole & proper use benefit & behoof from hence forth & for ever and that ye s^d John ffrost his heirs Execut^{rs} or Assignes Shall act & have ye Voice of ye s^d Andrew Lewis in ye ordering Settleing & Divideing of S^d Comon Right as he ye S^d andrew Lewis might himself have had or

Done before ye Sale thereof and ye s^d Andrew Lewis doth hereby Covena^t promiss bind & oblige himself his heirs Execut^{rs} and admin^{rs} from hence forth & for ever hereafter to Warrant and Defend all ye above Granted premisses & ye appurtenances thereof unto ye Said Jno ffrost his heirs & assignes against ye Lawfull Claims & Demands of all & Every parson or parsons whom So ever & at any Time or Times hereafter on demand to give & Pass Such further and ample assurance & Confirmation of ye Premisses unto ye s^d John ffrost his heirs & Assignes for ever as in Law or Equity Can be Reasonably Devised Advised or Required In Witness whereof ye S^d Andrew Lewis hath hereunto Set his hand & Seal the Twenty Third Day of May in ye year of our Lord One Thousand Seven Hundred & fifteen & in ye first year of ye Reign of our Soveraign Lord George King of great Brittain France and Ireland Defender of ye faith &c^t

Signed Sealed & Delivered   Andrew Lewis (a Seal)
  In the Presence of us   (a Seal)
  Mark Langdon
  Ruth Phillips
  Christian Hixon

York ss/ Andrew Lewis personally appeared before me ye Subscriber one of his Maj^{tys} Justices of Peace and acknowledged the above Instrum^t to be his act and Deed Dated at Kittery March/ 24th 1715/6   Wm Pepperrell Js Pes

Recorded According to ye Original Decr 10th 1716

                               p Jos : Hamond Reg^r

To All People to whom these Presents Shall Come Greeting &c^t Know ye that I Abra^m Preble of york in ye County of york within his Mait^{is} Province of ye Massachusets Bay in New England Gent^r for & in Consideration of ye Sum of fifty pounds in & passable money of ye Province afores^d to me in hand before ye Ensealing hereof well & Truly paid by John Sayword in ye Town & County afores^d Yeoman ye Receipt w^rof I Do hereby acknowledge & my Selfe therewith fully Satisfied & Contented & thereof & Every part & parcel thereof Do Exonerate Acquit & Discharge the Said John Sayword his heirs Execut^{rs} Adm^{rs} for ever by these Presents have given granted Sold Alliened Conveyed & Confirmed & by these Presents Do freely fully & absolutely give grant bargain Sell Aliene Convey & Confirm unto him ye s^d John Sayword his heirs & assignes for ever all that part of the Estate of Mr John Sayword Late dec^d which properly belongeth to me or to my wife) Late dec^d namely Susanna ye Daughter of ye afores^d Mr Sayword or to his heirs Either in Possession or in Reversion that is to Say the Sixth part of ye afores^d Estate Together with all ye Rights Priviledges & Comodities to ye Same belonging or in any wayes appertaining with all ye Rights Priviledges & advantages that ever Did belong to me ye afores^d Abra^m Preble or to my Late wife Namely Susanna or to her heirs or ever here after Shall belong to me or my wifes hereafter ye Death of Mrs Mary Plaisted ye late widow Relict & Administrat^{rx} of ye Deceased above Said or other wayes by ye Death of any of ye Relation or any other wayes or means or manner whatsoever Doth of Right belong to me or to my wife or to her heirs or ever did in ye Estate of ye above Said Sayword both Real & personall to have & to hold ye s^d granted & bargained pmises with all ye appurtenances priviledges & Comodities to the Same belonging or in any ways awas appertaining to him ye s^d John Sayword his heirs & assignes for ever to his & their only proper use benefit & behalf forever and I ye s^d Abra^m Preble for my Self heirs Execut^{rs} Adm^{rs} Do Covenant promise & grant to & with ye s^d John Sayword his heirs Execut^{rs} adm^{rs} & assignes against all manner of persons Shall & will warrant & forever Defend by these presents the above granted Premisses and at any Time or Times hereafter on Demand to give & pass Such further & ample assureance & Confirmation of ye premises unto y^e [198] Said John Sayword his heirs & assignes for Ever as in Law or Equity Can reasonably Devised Advised or required./ In Witness whereof ye s^d Abra^m Preble hath hereunto Set his hand & Seal ye Twenty Third Day of Octob^r in ye year of our Lord 1716/ & in ye Second year of ye Reign of our Soveraign Lord George of great Brittain &c^t King./ it is to be und^r Stood before Signing that ye aboves^d Abra^m Preble &c Stands Obliged to make good to aboves^d John Sayword &c only the one Sixth Part of aboves^d Estate now to be divided to & among Said Children & afterward as aboves^d as S^d Saywords Estate Shall appear   Abra^m Preble (a Seal)

Signed Sealed & Delivered
  In Presents of
  James Webber
  Joseph Banks
  Jonathan Bane

Book VIII, Fol. 198.

York ss/ January 2d 1716
The within Named Abraham Preble psonally appearing Acknowledged this Instrum[t] to be his act and Deed
Before me John Wheelwright Js pes
Recorded According to y[e] Original Jan[ry] 3[d] 1716/7
p Jos. Hamond Reg[r]

Know all men by these Presents that I John Ball of Spruce Creek in y[e] Township of Kittery within his Majt[ys] Province of the Massachusets Bay in New England Yeoman for & in Consideration of y[e] full & Just Sum of Thirty Shillings in good Lawfull money to me in hand paid by John ffrost of New Castle in New Hampsh[r] marrin[r] the receipt whereof I do by these Presents Acknowledge have given granted & Do by these Presents give grant bargain & Sell unto the Said John ffrost & his heirs Executors Adm[rs] & Assignes all That my Right Title & Interest I have or may or ever had in or unto any Comon Right or undivided Lands within the Township of Kittery & barwick with all & Singular y[e] Priviledges & Appurtenances thereunto belonging or in any wise appertaining To Have and To Hold all y[e] s[d] Comon Right free & Clearly Acquited & Discharged from all other former gifts grants Mortgages & Incumbrances whatsoever In Confirmation of which I Do by these Presents Oblige my Selfe my heirs Execut[rs] & Adm[rs] to warrant & Defend y[e] s[d] pmisses against y[e] Lawfull Claims of all & Every person w[t]soever as Witness my hand & Seal at N Castls y[e] 21[st] Day of may /1715/ & in y[e] first year of his Majt[ys] Reign

Signed Sealed & Delivered In y[e]
In y[e] Presents of
Ebenez[r] Emones
Benj[a] Hutchins his mark
Eliz[a] Lewis her mark

John his B Ball mark (Seal[a])

Province New hampsh[r] 22 June 1716
m[r] John Baull Acknowledged y[e] above Instrum[t] to be his act & Deed before   Theo Atkinson J Peace
Recorded Accorded to y[e] Original Dec[r] 10th 1716.
p Jos. Hamond Reg[r]

John Wheelwright Aged fifty three years or thereabouts Testifieth that about Thirty four or five years past I ye Deponant wrought with Mr John Sayward dec^d in ye meeting house in York upon Setting up the Gallerys and Stairs and ye s^d Sayward did Some work on ye Lower Seats in s^d Meeting house & did finish or near finish ye Galleryes & Stairs in ye time I wrought with s^d Sayward & Set up ye pillars that Supported ye s^d Gallerys

Sworn in Court in perpetuam Rei Memoriam./ Jan^{ry} 29th 1716/7   p Jos Hamond Clerk

Recorded According to ye Original Jan^{ry} 29th 1716/7
        p Jos. Hamond Reg^r

The Testimony of Lewis Bane of full age Testifieth & Saith that About Thirty five years past that he Saw Mr John Sayward dec^d About building ye Galleryes & other repairing ye Old meeting house in York the Gallerys were built & house repaired to ye best of my knowledge According to an Instrum^t that was made between ye Selectmen of york & Mr John Sayward bareing date ye year 1680 & further saith not

Sworn in Court in perpetuam Rei Memoriam Jan^{ry} 29th 1716/7
       p Jos. Hamond Clerk

Recorded According to ye Original Jan^{ry} 29th 1716/7
       p Jos Hamond Reg^r

The Deposition of Thomas Adams of full age Testifieth & Saith that I this Deponant Thirty five years past or thereabouts did Se John Sayward dec^d at work upon ye Gallerys in ye Old meeting house in york & upon ye Seats below in ye s^d house and that s^d Sayward did finish s^d Gallerys & Seats & further Saith Not

Sworn in Court in perpetuam Rei Memoriam Jan^{ry} 29th 1716/7   p Jos. Hamond Clerk

Recorded According to ye Original Jar^{ry} 29th 1716/7/
       p Jos. Hamond Reg^r

The Deposition of Joseph Banks of full age Testifieth & Saith that he this Deponant about Thirty five years Since did se John Sayward dec^d at work in ye Old meeting house

BOOK VIII, FOL. 199.

in york upon y[e] Gallerys and Seats in s[d] house & Several other particulars Mentioned in Articles of Agreement between y[e] Town of York & s[d] Sayward bareing date y[e] 10th of Dec[r] 1680./ & that y[e] s[d] Several pieces of Work were done & finished./

Sworn in Court in perpetuam Rei Memoriam Jan[ry] 29th 1716/7   p Jos. Hamond Clerk

Recorded According to y[e] Original Jan[ry] 29th 1716/7
                               p Jos. Hamond Reg[r]

These Presents Testifie that I John Davis Sen[r] late of Capeporpus in y[e] County of York Blacksmith for & in Consideration of y[e] Sum of Twenty Six pounds Ten Shillings in Curran[t] pay of New England in hand paid me before y[e] ensealing hereof by William Palmer of Kittery in y[e] Same County Yeoman the receipt whereof I do hereby Acknowledge and my selfe to be therewith fully Satisfied Contented & paid and do for me my heirs Ex[rs] & Adm[rs] & for Every of them for ever Exonerate Release Acquit & discharge him y[e] s[d] W[m] Palmer his heirs Ex[rs] Adm[rs] & Assignes of & from y[e] s[d] Sum & of Every part parcell & penney [199] Thereof Have by & with y[e] Consent of Katherine my wife & my Son John Davis given granted bargained Sold Aliened Enfeoffed Conveyed Assigned and Set over And by these presents do give grant Bargaine Sell Aliene Enfeoff Convey Assign & Set over unto y[e] s[d] William Palmer & to his heirs Ex[rs] Adm[rs] & Assignes all my right Title & Interest unto that my halfe part of a Certaine Neck of land Scittuate & being in Capeporpus afores[d] Commonly Called & known by y[e] Name of Batsons Neck with all y[e] halfe part of Marsh Adjoyning to it as it is now Severed & divided by Several Marked trees through y[e] s[d] neck of land formery in y[e] possession Tenure & Occupation of John Elson and now or late in y[e] possession Tenure or Occupation of my Selfe the other halfe part of y[e] s[d] neck of land & Marsh now & late belonging to and in y[e] Tenure possession & Occupation of fferdinando Coft or his Assigns Together with a Certaine parcell of land Comonly Called & known by y[e] Name of y[e] Grass plot Near Adjoyning together whether laid out or no as also unto and in all Lands whether upland or Marsh in y[e] s[d] Town of Capeporpus which I have at any time bought and have not as yet disposed of wth all & Every dwelling house & out houseing or any part of all y[e] premisses before bargained & Sold with all y[e] rights priviledges & Imunityes Timber and Timber

Trees woods & underwoods therewith formerly used or thereunto belonging or Appurtaining as Appurtenances To have & To hold ye s^d halfe Neck of land Marsh Town grants bought lands Garden plot &c^t before Mentioned unto him ye s^d Wm Palmer his heirs Ex^{rs} Adm^{rs} or Assignes for ever. And ye s^d John Davis for himselfe his heirs Ex^{rs} and Adm^{rs} & for Every of them doth Covenant promiss & grant to & with the s^d Wm Palmer his heirs Ex^{rs} Adm^{rs} & Assignes & to & — Every of them by these presents that at ye present & before the Ensealing hereof he Standeth Siezed & possessed of all ye above mentioned bargained premisses in a good Estate of fee Simple and that he hath not formerly done or Suffered to be done Any Act or thing which may hinder or Impeach ye right Title or Interest of him ye s^d Wm Palmer his heirs Ex^{rs} Adm^{rs} or Assignes unto All or any part or parcell of y^e Above bargained premisses but that y^e s^d Wm Palmer his heirs Ex^{rs} Adm^{rs} or Assignes or any of them Shall and may At All Times for ever hereafter peaceably & Quietly have hold Occupie possess & Enjoy all y^e before mentioned Bargained & Sold p$_r$misses & Every part & parcell thereof free & discharged of & from all maner of form^r gifts grants Mortgages Sales Extents Judgm^{ts} Executions Dowers or Title of Dowers & without y^e Lawfull let Trouble Mollestation or denial of him y^e s^d John Davis his heirs Ex^{rs} or Adm^{rs} or any of them And ye s^d John Davis for himselfe his heirs Ex^{rs} & Adm^{rs} and for Every of them doth further Covenant promiss & grant to & with ye s^d Wm Palmer his heirs Execut^{rs} Adm^{rs} & assignes & to & with Every of them that he & they Shall and will at all times hereafter well & Sufficiently defend ye Title thereof unto him ye s^d Wm Palmer his heirs Ex^{rs} Adm^{rs} or Assignes Against All p^{r}sons Whatsoever./ In Witness whereof ye s^d John Davis hath hereunto Set his hand & Seal Dated in Portsmouth this Tenth day of Jan^{ry} Anno Domini One Thousand Six hundred Seaventy & five & in ye Twenty Seaventh year of ye Reign of our Soveraign Lord Charles ye Second King of England Scotland ffrance & Ireland Defend^r of the faith &c^t 1675/

Signed Sealed & Delivered wth John Davis Senr (Seal)
ye words Same in ye 3^d line   (Seal)
Interlined before ye Enseal-   his
ling./ Assignes in ye 6th line./   John : P : Davis jun^r (Seal)
Sales in ye 31st line./ with in
ye 35 line by Jno Davis Senr mark
John Fernel
John Persons
Richd Stileman Scr

Book VIII, Fol. 199.

Signed Sealed & Delivered by John Davis Jun[r] w[th] the Interlines as above in p[r]sence of us
  Jn[o] Parsons. Rich[d] Stileman Scr:
  Gr[t] Island y[e] 21[st] ffeb[ry] 1675 John Davis Sen[r] & John Davis Jun[r] Came & Acknowledged this Instrum[t] to be their free Act & Deed./
      before me Elias Stileman Comission[r]
Recorded According to y[e] Original Feb[ry] 6[th] 1716/7
       p Jos. Hamond Reg[r]

  To All People to whom this present deed of Sale Shall Come Timothy Waymouth of Kittery in y[e] County of York and within her M[a]j[tys] Province of y[e] Massachusets Bay in New England husbandman Sendeth Greeting Know y[e] that y[e] s[d] Timothy Waymouth for & in Consideration of y[e] Sum of fifty pounds to him in hand well & truely paid at y[e] Ensealing and y[e] Delivery of these presents by Elizabeth Hubord Widdow Woman & Phillip Hubord Marrin[r] both of Berwick in y[e] County & province afores[d] the rec[t] whereof y[e] s[d] Timothy Waymouth doth hereby Acknowledge to his full Content & Satisfaction and doth Acquit Exonerate & discharge y[e] s[d] Elizabeth & Phillip Hubord & their heirs Execut[rs] and Adm[rs] forever of every part & parcell thereof. And Hath by these presents freely clearly & Absolutely given granted bargained Sold Aliened Enfeoffed & Confirmed unto y[e] s[d] Eliz[a] Hubord & Phillip Hubord & to their heirs Ex[rs] Adm[rs] & Assignes all his homestead Scituate lying & being in s[d] Berwick Containing fifty Acres be y[e] Same more or Less bounded Southwest on Mast Cove Northwest on Land of William Hearl Eastwardly on Land of Jonathan Nason & North on Land of Thomas Grely Together with all & Singular y[e] dwelling house barn Stable Orchard thereon also y[e] wayes profits priviledges rights Comodityes hereditaments & Appurtenances & whatsoever thereunto belongeth or in any kind or mañer Appertaining To have & To hold y[e] s[d] homestead houseing Orchard & all y[e] Above Granted & bargained premisses with their Appurtenances unto them y[e] s[d] Eliz[a] Hubord & Phillip Hubord & to their heirs Ex[rs] Adm[rs] & Assignes to his & their own only proper use benefit & behoofe for ever and y[e] s[d] Timothy Waymouth for himselfe his heirs Ex[rs] & Adm[rs] doth Covena[t] promiss & Agree to & with y[e] s[d] Elizabeth Hubord & Phillip Hubord their heirs Ex[rs] Adm[rs] & Assigns in maner & form following That is to Say that at y[e] time of this present bargaine & Sale & untill y[e]

Ensealing & delivery of these presents is y⁰ True Sole & Lawfull owner & doth Stand Legally possessed of y⁰ Same in a perfect Estate of Inheritance in fee Simple without any Mañer of Condition reservation or Limitation of use or uses whatsoever whereby to Alter change or make Voyd this present deed of Sale haveing in him selfe full power good right & Lawfull Authority to give grant bargaine Sell and Assure yᵉ same in maner and form as afores⁴ & yᵉ sᵈ Elizabeth Hubord & Phillip Hubord their heirs Exʳˢ Admʳˢ & Assignes from henceforth & for ever hereafter Shall & may Lawfully peaceably & Quietly have hold use Occupie possess and uninteruptedly Enjoy all yᵉ above granted & bargained premisses yᵉ Same being frely & Clearly Acquitted Exonerated & discharged of & from all former & other gifts grants Bargains Sales Leases Mortgages Executions Judgmᵗˢ Thirds Dowries Joyntures rights Titles Troubles charges Claimes & demands whatsoever./ And further yᵉ sᵈ Timothy Waymouth his heirs Exʳˢ & Admʳˢ shall & will from henceforth Warrant & defend all yᵉ above granted & bargained premisses unto them yᵉ sᵈ Elizᵃ Hubord & Phillip Hubord & to their heirs Exʳˢ Admʳˢ & Assignes for ever hereafter agˢᵗ yᵉ Lawfull claims & demands of all & Every person whatsoever In Witness whereof he hath hereunto Set his hand & seal in Berwick afores⁴ March yᵉ Twelfth Anno Domini Seventeed hundred & Thirteen 14 in yᵉ Thirteenth year of yᵉ reign of our Soveraign Lady Queen Anne Over Great Brittaine   Tim⁰ Waymouth (Seal)

Signed Sealed & Delivered
   In presents of us
   John Gowen
   Nathˡ Tarbox
   John Bradstreet
      York sc/ Berwᵏ Janʳʸ yᵉ 28ᵗʰ 1716/7./

Then Appeared before me Elisha Plaisted Justice of peace Tim⁰ Waymouth & Acknowledged this Instrumᵗ to be his Act & deed./   Elisha Plaisted Justˢ peace
   Recorded According to yᵉ Original Febʳʸ 13ᵗʰ 1716/7/
                 p Jos Hammond Regʳ

[200] To All People to whom this present Assignmᵗ of this deed of sale shall Come Elizᵃ Hubord of Berwick in yᵉ County of York Widdow Woman and Phillip Hubord of yᵉ sᵈ Town & County within his Majᵗʸˢ Province of yᵉ Massachusets Bay in New England Marriner sendeth Greeting

Book VIII, Fol. 200.

Know Yee that ye sd Eliza Hubord & Phillip Hubord doth hereby Assigne this within written deed of sale to Joseph Hodsden & John Hooper of ye sd Town County & Province and to their heirs Exrs Admrs & to their Assignes for ever for & in Consideration of ye vallue recd for ye within deed of Sale & for all & for Every part and parcell thereof of all ye within houses lands Orchards out houses & all rights priviledges & Appurtenances within Mentioned to Joseph Hodsden and John Hooper & their heirs & Assignes for ever the rect whereof sd Eliza Hubord & Phillip Hubord doth hereby Acknowledge to their full Content and Satisfaction And do Acquit & discharge ye sd Joseph Hodsden & John Hooper & their heirs Exrs & Admrs for ever of Every part & parcell thereof And Will Warrant ye within mentioned premisses & defend ye Same against ye Lawfull Claims of All prsons whatsoever and wheresoever & will give any further Assurence or Asurences to ym and to their heirs Exrs Admrs or Assignes As ye Learned in ye law may Advise or devise & we ye sd Eliza Hubord & Phillip Hubord further doth Covenat Bargaine & agree with with ye sd Joseph Hodsden & John Hooper and their heirs Exrs Admrs & Assignes that we have in our selves good right full power & Lawfull Authority to sell & Alienate & Assign over the Same free & Clearly Acquitted of all former gifts grants bargains or sales Leases Mortgages Executions Judgmts thirds dowries Joyntures rights Troubles Charges Claimes & demands whatsoever & they shall from henceforth & forever hereafter peaceably & Quietly Occupy and Enjoy ye Same without any Let or hinderence of or from Either of us or our heirs Exrs Admrs for ever./ In Witness hereof we have hereunto Set our hands & Seals this Twenty Eighth day of Janry in ye third year of his Matys reign George King Over Great Brittaine &ct Annoq, Domini 1716./

Signed Sealed & Delivered   Elizabeth X Hubord (Seale)
In ye presents of us   mark
Elisha Plaisted   Phillip Hubord (Seal)
Jonathan Stone

     York sc/ Berwick Janry 28th 1716/7

Then Appeared before me Elisha Plaisted one of his Majtys Justices for ye sd County and Acknowledged ye above written Instrumt Eliza Hubord & Phillip Hubord for to be their Act & deed   Elisha Plaisted Juss peace

   Recorded According to ye Original Febry 13th 1716/7
                    p Jos. Hamond Regr

Book VIII, Fol. 200.

Know all men by these Presents that I Richard Gowell of Kittery in ye County of york In New England yeoman In Consideration of ye Natureal love I have & Doe bear unto my well beloved Son Richard Gowell Have given Granted Set over & for Ever Confirmed unto him the Said Richd Gowell and his heirs Lawfully begotton of his body after my Decease and the Decease of my Now wife his Mother All that my Dwelling house & Lands whereon I Now Dwell with all ye out houseing & orchards & Gardens meadows fields & Pastures belonging thereunto Excepting & Reserveing unto my own use or disposeing out of ye Premisses Twenty acres of Land To dispose of According to my Pleasure also I give unto my s^d Son after my Decease & my wife all my Stock of Cattle with my Implements for ye Carrying on of my husbandtry Together with all Timber & wood & und^r wood Standing on ye aboves^d Lands or Laying on ye Same or any wayes appertaining unto ye Premisses Together with all ye appurtenances & ye Priviledges wayes out lets & Easem^{ts} Landing & Convenances w^{t}soever All wayes Provided & to be un^{r}Stood that If it Shall Please God that I Should dec^{es} before my Now wife that my s^d Son Shall Enjoy & Possess to his own use the one halfe of all ye above Given & granted premisses & my beloved Now wife to possess & Enjoy ye other halfe to her own use & benefit (provided She remaine a Widdow) Dureing her Natural life To have & To hold all ye above Said houses & Lands & houseing (Except what is above Excepted out of ye premisses) unto ye only & Sole use of him ye s^d Richard Gowell & his heirs Lawfully begotten of his body in Lawfull Matterimony Together with all & Singular the Orchards gardens meadows fields & pastures with ye Stock of Cattle of w^t Kind so ev^r as is above Exprest without the Lett of or hindrance of any person or persons w^{t}soever Immediately after ye deceas of me ye s^d Richd Gowell and my Now wife his mother & furthermore I ye s^d Richd Gowell doe for my Selfe & my heirs Covenant to & with my s^d Son Richd Gowell & his heirs that ye Premisses are free from all Incumbrances by me made & that I am ye True & Lawfull owner thereof & have within in Selfe full power to give & Dispose of ye Same ye Peaceable Possession thereof To Warrant & for ever defend against all persons Laying a Lawfull Claim thereunto In Witness whereof I

Book VIII, Fol. 201.

have hereunto Set my hand & Seal this Tenth Day of June one Thousand Seven Hundred & Ten./ 1710/

Signed & Sealed in y[e] Presence
  of us the Subsbribers
William Godsoe
  ye mark of
Eliz[a] E Surplice

the mark of
Richard ⚲ Gowell (a Seal)

York ss/ Jan[ry] 26 : 1713/14

y[e] above named Richard Gowell appearing & acknowledged y[e] Above written Instrum[t] to be his free act & Deed/
                  Jura[t] Cor Charles ffrost Js ps

And furthermore I doe by these presents oblige my Son Rich[d] Gowell to pay unto Each of his Sisters ten Shillings in money on demand after y[e] s[d] Deceas of me y[e] s[d] Rich[d] Gowell & my wife

Recorded According to y[e] Original Feb[ry] 5th 1716/7
                          p Jos. Hamond Reg[r]

[201] Know All men by these Presents than I John Stover of y[e] Town of Saco in y[e] Province of main In New england for divers good Causes & Considerations thereunto me Moveing & more Espetially for the Just Sum of Twenty three pounds ten Shillings In money and good Currant Pay to me in hand paid by Thomas Wise Now Resident in y[e] Town of York in y[e] fores[d] Province of maine Fisherman Wherewith I doe Acknowledge my Selfe to be fully Contented & Satisfied & Doe for my Selfe my heirs Executors and Administrators or Assignes for ever Acquitt & Discharge y[e] s[d] Tho[s] Wise from whom I received y[e] Sum afores[d] from Every part & percell thereof have given granted Sold Enfeoffed and Confirmed & Doe by these psents give grant Sell Enfeoffe & Confirm unto the above Named Tho[s] Wise his heirs Execut[rs] Adm[rs] and Assignes A Certaine Tract of Land Lying on y[e] South Side of York River formerly Called by y[e] name of Gorgana Alies York bounded from y[e] Cove Opposite to y[e] house formerly Known by y[e] Name of Rich[d] Ormisbys house & y[e] afores[d] Cove being Called by y[e] Name of y[e] Little Cove up to y[t] Land Called Eddy point & Soe back into y[e] Countrey South South West untill Twelve Acres of Land be fully Ended & Compleated there being a Small Strip of Marsh above half an Acre be it more or Less Included within y[e] Afores[d] bounds To have & To hold y[e]

above named & bounded Tract of Land upland & Meadow with all ye profits priviledges Commons Imunities & Liberties of wood Timber & all other appurtenances belonging to ye s^d Land or to them any ways appertaining from me my heirs Execut^rs Adm^rs & assignes unto ye Afores^d Thos Wise his heirs Execut^rs Adm^rs & assigned for ever & further I ye s^d John Stover doe Covena^t & agree with ye s^d Thos Wise that ye Land afores^d is free & Clear from all Claims bargains Sals Mortgages Titles & Incumbrances whatsoever & Doe by these p^rsents warrant & Defend ye Same from me my heirs Ex^rs Adm^rs & assigns unto ye s^d Thos Wise his heirs Executors adm^rs or assignes for ever from all persons w^tsoever pretending any Claim Title or Interest by from or und^r me or any by my procurem^t In Witness thereunto I have hereto Affixed my hand & Seal this 2^d Second day of July 1684/ All This being done by y^e Consent of my wife Anne Stover

Signed Sealed & Delivered   the mark of
In y^e Presence of us   John ✝ Stover (s^a_eal)
ffrancis Jonson
John Penwill

John Stover Came before me this 2^d day of July & Acknowledged y^e aboves^d Instrument to be his own Act & deed   Before me./   John Davis Dep^ty Presid^t

The s^d Stover owned Delivery & Siezen

Recorded According to y^e Original Feb^ry 5th 1716/7

                 p Jos : Hamond Reg^r

To All Christian People to whom these presents Shall Come Nicho^s Moorey of ffreetown in the County of Bristol in ye Province of Massachusets Bay in New England Yeoman) Sendeth Greeting &c^t Know ye that ye s^d Nicholas Moorey for & in Consideration of ye Sum of Sixty pounds Current money of This province to him in hand paid by James Tylor of Bradford in ye County of Essex in ye aboves^d Province husbandman The receipt whereof the s^d Nichol^s Moorey Doth hereby acknowledge & himselfe therewith ffully Satisfied Contented and paid & thereof & of Every part & parcell thereof Doth hereby fully & Absolutely Exonerate acquit & Discharge the s^d James Tyler his heirs Ex^rs & adm^rs forever hath given grated bargained Sold made over & Delivered unto & by these presents Doth give grant bargain Sell make over Confirm & Deliver unto him ye s^d James Tyler & to his heirs & assignes for ever the one halfe

Book VIII, Fol. 202.

part of ye right or propriety which ye s^d Nicholas Moorey Claimes or Challengeth in ye Township of Capeporpois in ye County of york in ye aboves^d province the which propriety of ye s^d Mooreys was Originally Joseph Boles Griffin Montagues and Morgen Howells with fifty acres of Salt meadow &c^t Therein Contained be it more or Less the which ye s^d Nicholas Moorey bought of Samuel Snow of Boston (Cordwainer) the full one halfe Shear both Divided & undivided butted & bounded as may appear on the records of ye County of york & as formerly Sold to Joseph Bayley To have & To hold the one half part of ye Land & rights which ye s^d Nicholas Moorey Claims in ye Township of Capeporpois in ye County of york booth Divided & undivided & also fifty acres of Salt meadow be it more or Less butted & bounded as aboves^d to him ye s^d James Tyler & to his heirs & assignes for ever Moreover I ye s^d Nicholas Moorey do hereby for my Selfe my heirs Executors & adm^{rs} Covenant promise & grant to & with ye s^d James Tyler his heirs & assignes that he ye s^d Nicholas Moorey is ye true & proper owner of ye aboves^d Land & meadow & Rights as aboves^d both divided & undivided & all the members & appurtenances of ye Same & that he hath in himself good right full power & Lawfull authority the above granted premisses with ye appurtenances there of In his own name to give : grant bargain Sell make over & assure ye Same as above Spezcified and that it Shall be for ever hereafter free & Lawfull to & for ye James Tyler & his heirs & assignes To have & To hold & peaceably and Quietly to possess & Enjoy & Improve ye aboves^d One half of ye Interest or propriety that ye s^d Nicholas Moorey holds or Claims in ye s^d Township of Capeporpois both Divided & undivided and also fifty Acres of Salt meadow as aboves^d be ye Same more or Less with all & Singular the members & appurtenances thereof with all priviledges and benefits thereunto belonging & profits there from arising with all the Estate right Title Interest & Demand of him ye Nicholas Moorey his heirs Executors & adm^{rs} to ye premisses & to Every part thereof for ever and by him ye s^d Nicholas Moorey his heirs Executors & adm^{rs} well and Sufficiently Saved & kept harmless and Indemnified of & from all and all manner of former & other Gifts grants bargains Sales [202] Mortgages Leases Joyntures Judgments Dowers Executions recognisances Charges Troubles Suits at Law & Incumbrances whatsoever that may arise by any person or persons Laying any Lawfull Claim y^r unto for ever In Witness hereof I s^d Nicholas Moorey have hereunto Set my hand & Seal this fourteenth Day of Decemb^r

Annoque Domini One Thousand Seven hundred & Sixteen
In ye Third year of ye Reign of our Soveraign Lord George
of great Brittain ffrance and Ireland King Defender of y^e
faith &c^t Nicholas Moorey (a Seal)
Signed Sealed & Delivered
  In ye Presence of us
  John Wilbore
  Abigail Hodges
  In Taunton In Bristol County Dec^{er} ye 14th 1716

The above Named Nicho^s Moorey did personally appear before me ye Subscriber & Acknowledge this Instrum^t To be his free voluntary act & Deed/
            Before me Henry Hodges Justice
Recorded According to ye Original Feb^{ry} 20th 1716/7
                    p Jos. Hamond Reg^r

Know all men by These presents that I Nicholas Moorey of freetown in ye County of Bristol in ye Province of ye Massachusets Bay in New England yeoman am holden & Stand firmly bound & obliged unto James Tyler of Bradford in ye County of Essex & Province aboves^d husbandman In ye Sum of one hundred pounds Currant money of this Province to be paid to y^e s^d James Tyler his Certain Attorney Executors or adm^{rs} to y^e which payment well & Truly to be made I s^d Nicholas Morey Do bind my Self my heirs Ex^{rs} & Adm^{rs} firmly by these presents Sealled with my Seale Dated in Taunton this fourteenth Day of Decem^{er} annoq$_{,}$ Domini 1716/ In y^e Third year of his Maj^{tys} Reign The Condition of this Obligation is Such that if y^e above bounded Nicholas Moorey his heirs Execut^{rs} or adm^{rs} or any them Shall will from time to time & at all times for ever hereafter Save harmless & Indempnified y^e s^d James Tyler his heirs Executors and adm^r & assignes of & from all & all manner of Loss Trouble damage molestation or Disquietment or Charge which ye s^d James Tyler his heirs or assignes may or Shall meet with all from any person or persons whatsoever that Shall or Lay any Just Claime or Challange to any part or parcel of ye Land or Meadow or Right in Land Divided or undivided in ye Township of Capeporpois in ye County of york which ye s^d Nicholas Moorey Sold to ye s^d James Tyler as may appear by one deed of Sale und^r ye hand & Seal of ye s^d Nicholas

Book VIII, Fol. 202.

Moorey bearing Evedate with these presents then ye above written Obligation to be null void & of none Effect or Els to Stand & remain in full force Strength & virtue
Signed Sealed & Delivered   Nicholas Moorey (seal)
  In ye presence of us
  John Wilbore
  Abigail Hodges
In Taunton In Bristol County Decemb^r ye 14th 1716 the above Named Nicholas Moorey acknowledged this Instrum^t to be his free act & Deed   before me   Henry Hodges Justice
Recorded According to ye Original Feb^ry 20th 1716/7./
                        p Jos. Hamond Reg^r

This Indenture made this Sixth Day of aprill one Thousand Seven Hundred fifteen & in ye first year of ye Reign of our Soveraign Lord George by ye Grace of God King of England &c^t Between Tim^o Wamouth of Kittery in ye County of York in the Massachusets bay in New england on ye one part & Samuel Hodsden of ye Town & County afores^d on ye other part Witnesseth that I ye s^d Timothy waymouth of Divers good Causes & Considerations me thereunto moveing Have given granted Bargained Sold Aliened Conveyed & Confirmed & by these presents Do freely fully & Absolutely give grant bargaine Sell Aliene Convey & Confirm unto him ye s^d Samuel Hodsden his heirs & Assignes for ever one Messuage or Tract of Land Scittuate Lying & being in Kittery in ye County afores^d Containing by Estimation Twenty acres of upland Lying near to mast Cove & it is bounded on ye west Side by Edwd Waymouths Lott by marked trees & on South Side by fresh brook of water and it is bounded on ye North Side by Thomas Etheringtons   Lott & Several marked trees bounded on ye East Side or head of this Lott by a Lott given to Jeremiah Hodsden as may & Doth appear by Several marked trees to ye s^d purpose be it more or Less To have & To hold ye s^d granted & bargained premisses with all ye appurtenances Priviledges & Commodities to ye Same belonging or in any wise appertaining to him ye s^d Samuel Hodsden his heirs & assignes for ever to his & their own proper use benefit & behoofe for ever & I ye s^d Tim^o Waymouth for me my heirs Execut^rs adm^rs Do Covenant

Book VIII, Fol. 203.

Promise & grant to & with y⁰ sᵈ Samuel Hodsden his heirs & Assignes that before y⁰ Ensealing hereof I am y⁰ True Sole & Lawfull owner of y⁰ above bargained premisses & am Lawfully & fully Seized & possessed of y⁰ Same in my own proper Right as a good perfect & absolute Estate of Inheritance in fee Simple & have in my Self good Right full power & Lawfull Authority To grant bargain Sell Convey & Confirm sᵈ bargained pmisses in manner as abovesᵈ & that y⁰ sᵈ Samuel Hodsden his heirs & assignes Shall & may from time to time & at all times for ever hereafter by force & virtue of these presents Lawfully Peaceably & Quietly have hold use occupy Possess & Enjoy y⁰ sᵈ Demised & bargained premisses with y⁰ appurtenances free & Clear & freely & Clearly Acquitted Exonerated & Discharged of & from all & all manner of former & other gifts grants bargains Sales Leases Mortgages wills Entails Joyntures Dowries or power of Thirds Judgments Executions Incumbrances & Extents the intent & meaning of this above Obligation is Such that If y⁰ abovesᵈ Tim⁰ Waymouth Do Well & Truly pay or Caus to be paid unto Richard Scamon of Dover in y⁰ Province of Newhampshʳ y⁰ full & Just Sum of Thirty Six pound Sixteen Shillings of Lawfull & passable money of New england at y⁰ time of a bill which y⁰ afore Said Tim⁰ Waymouth & Samˡˡ Hodsden gave & was bound, Joyntly & Severally to y⁰ aforesᵈ Richard Scamon & if y⁰ [**203**] Aforesᵈ Timothy Waymouth Do Pay y⁰ aforesᵈ Sum att y⁰ times as y⁰ aforesᵈ bill Specifies then this above written Deed or Obligation & Every Clause & Article therein Contained Shall be null void & of none Effect or Els Shall abide in full force & virtue In Confirmation hereof I have hereunto Set my hand & Seal the Day & year above written

Signed Sealed & Delivered   Timothy Waymouth (ₛₑₐ)

In y⁰ presence of us
Benjᵃ Peirce
Edwᵈ Whitehouse

     York ss/ May 23 1716

The above named Tim⁰ Waymouth acknowledged y⁰ above written Instrumᵗ to be his free act & Deed

                               Before Charles ffrost J peace

Recorded According to y⁰ Original Janʳʸ 29ᵗʰ 1716/7/
                           p Jos. Hamond Regʳ

[Marginal note: Recᵈ of Timothy Waymouth yᵉ full Sum mentioned in this Instrumᵗ & I do Acquit & Discharge him of yᵉ Same this 17ᵗʰ ffebʳʸ 1717/ Samuel Hodsden]

Book VIII, Fol. 203.

This present writing Witnesseth that I Rice Howell of Gorgeaña in ye province of Maine in New England doth by these presents for diverse good Causes & Considerations me Especially hereunto moveing have fully freely & Absolutely Given granted Sold Assigned & Set over unto m^r Abraham Preble of Gorgeaña afores^d a Certaine Tract of land or ground lying on ye South Side of this river of Gorgeaña being bounded from ye Cove lying Opposite to ye house formerly known by ye name of Richard Ormsbys house and ye afores^d Cove being Called by ye Name of Little Cove up to that point of land Called Eddy point & So into ye Country South Southwest untill Twelve Acres of land or ground are fullfilled & Accomplished & Compleat And ye which Land ye s^d m^r Abraham Preble Afores^d To have & To hold to him & to his heirs Ex^rs Adm^rs & Assignes for ever in as full Ample and benneficial Mañer & form as I Rice Howell have or did Enjoy ye Same In Witness whereof I have hereunto Set my hand & Seal dated ye Seventeenth day of Feb^ry Anno Dom: 1651./

Signed Sealed & Delivered   the mark of
In ye presence of us   Rice ⊢⊣ Howell (Seale^a)
Henry Norton
    The mark of
Rich^d   R·B   Burges

Recorded According to ye Original Feb^ry 5th 1716/7
           p Jos: Hammond Reg^r

To All Christian People to whom these presents Shall Come Samuell ffuller of Salem in ye County of Essex within his Maj^tys Province of ye Massachusets Bay in New England husbandman Sends Greeting./ Know Y^e that ye s^d Saml ffuller for & in Consideration of ye Sum of fifty pounds passable money of New England to him in hand paid before the Ensealing & Delivery of these presents by Stephen Harding of Wells in ye County of York & province of Maine Blacksmith ye rec^t whereof to full Content & Satisfaction he ye s^d Saml ffuller doth by these presents Acknowledge & thereof & of Every part thereof for him selfe his heirs Ex^rs & Adm^rs doth Acquit Exonerate & discharge ye s^d Stephen Harding his heirs Ex^rs & Adm^rs Every of them for ever by these presents & for Diverse other good Causes & Considerations him hereunto moveing he ye s^d Saml ffuller hath given granted

Book VIII, Fol. 203.

bargained sold Aliened Enfeoffed Conveyed & Confirmed & by these presents doth fully freely Clearly and Absolutely give grant bargain Sell Aliene Enfeoffe Convey & Confirm unto ye s^d Stephen Harding his heirs & Assignes for ever the one halfe of a Certaine Tract of Land Containing Six hundred Acres of upland Marsh Meadow & Swamp be it more or be it Less Scittuate lying & being in Wells afores^d Butted & bounded as followeth bounded on ye Eastwardly upon Kenebunk river westwardly by pond Marsh on ye northwest Side of pond Marsh Northwardly by bucklins line Southwardly by ye Sea./ Together with all Such rights Libertyes Imunityes profits priviledges Comodityes Imollum^{ts} & Appurtenances as in any kind Appurtaine thereunto with ye reversions & remainders thereof And All ye Estate right Title Interest Inheritance property possession Claime & Demand whatsoever & of him ye s^d Saml ffuller of in & to ye Same & Every part thereof To have & To hold all ye above granted premisses with all & Singular ye Appur^{ces} thereof unto ye s^d Stephen Harding his heirs & Assignes to his & their own Sole & proper use benefit & behoofe from henceforth for ever & ye s^d Saml ffuller for him selfe his heirs Ex^{rs} & Adm^{rs} doth hereby Covenant promiss grant & agree to & with ye s^d Stephen Harding his heirs & Assigns in maner & form following./ That Is To Say) that at ye time of ye Ensealing & delivery of these presents he ye s^d Saml ffuller is ye True Sole & Lawfull owner of all ye above bargained premisses & Stands lawfully Siezed thereof his own proper right of a good perfect & Indefeazable Estate of Inheritance in fee Simple haveing in himselfe full power good right & Lawfull Authority to Sell & dispose of ye Same in maner as afores^d & that ye s^d Stephen Harding his heirs and Assignes Shall & may henceforth for ever lawfully peaceably and Quietly have hold use Occupy possess & Enjoy ye above granted premisses with ye Appurtenances thereof free & Clear & Clearly Acquitted & discharged of & from all & all maner of former & other gifts grants bargains Sales Leases Mortgages Joyntures Dowers Judgm^{ts} Executions Entailes forfeitures & of & from all other Titles troubles Charges & Incumbrances whatsoever had made Comitted done or Suffered to done by ye s^d Saml ffuller his heirs or Assignes at any time or times before ye Ensealing & Delivery hereof And further ye s^d Saml ffuller doth hereby Covenant promiss bind & Oblige himselfe his heirs Ex^{rs} & adm^{rs} from henceforth & for ever hereafter to Warrant & defend all ye Above granted premisses & ye Appurtenances thereof unto ye s^d Stephen Harding his heirs & Assignes against ye Lawfull Claims &

demands of all & Every person or persons whomsoever & at any Time or times hereafter on demand to give & pass Such further & Ample Assurence & Confirmation of ye premisses unto ye s^d Stephen Harding his heirs & Assignes for ever as in Law or Equity Can be reasonably devised Advised or required In Witness whereof ye s^d Saml ffuller & Mary his wife in Testimoney of her full Consent & free relinquishm^t of all her right of Dowry and power of thirds in ye premisses have Mutually Set to their [**204**] hands & Seals this fifteenth day of March One Thousand Seven hundred and Seventeen and in ye third year of his Maj^{tys} Reign

Signed Sealed & Delivered

In presence of us
Joseph Upton
Joseph Upton jun^r
Shubael his ✗ Sterns
    mark

Samuel his ✗ ffuller (a Seal)
Mary ffuller mark (a Seal)

Essex Ipswich March 16th 1716
Then ye Aboves^d Saml Fuller p^{r}sonally Appear^d & Acknowledged this Instrum^t to be his free Act & Deed
    Before John Appleton Jus Ps.
Recorded According to ye Original March ye 18th 1716/7.
    p Jos. Hammond Reg^r

To All People unto whom these presents Shall Come Henry Wright of Boston in ye County of Suffolk in New England Housewright Sendeth Greeting./ Know Y^e that I ye s^d Henry Wright for & in Consideration of ye Sum of four pounds in Province Bills to me in hand well & Truely paid to full Content & Satisfaction before ye Ensealing & Delivery of these presents by Ichabod Plaisted of Portsmouth in ye County of New Hampshire Gentleman./ do by these presents give grant Sell make Over and Confirm unto ye s^d Ichabod Plaisted & to his heirs & Assignes for Ever a Certaining or being fifty Acres Lying or being in the Town of Kittery on Piscataqua river in ye County of York Afores^d To Have & To Hold ye s^d fifty Acres of Land unto ye s^d Ichabod Plaisted & to his heirs & Assignes to his & their own proper use benefit and behoofe from this time forth & for ever./ And further I ye s^d Henry Wright do At ye Ensealing & delivery of these presents Avouch my Selfe to be ye Lawfull owner of ye s^d fifty Acres of Land being free & clear & Clearly Acquitted & discharged of & from all maner of former Gifts grants bargaines Sales Titles Troubles charges or Incumbrances

BOOK VIII. FOL. 204.

whatsoever haveing in my Selfe full power & Authority to dispose of ye Same as in maner Above Expressed And further I ye s^d Henry Wright do by these presents Covenant promiss bind & Oblige my Selfe my heirs Ex^{rs} Adm^{rs} unto ye s^d Ichabod Plaisted & to his heirs & Assignes that We will for ever hereafter Warrant and defend ye s^d fifty Acres & Land Against all ye Lawfull Claims and demands of Any person or persons Whatsoever that shall At any time hereafter Lay Any Lawfull Claime to ye same In Witness whereof I have hereunto Set my hand & Seale in Boston afores^d this Twenty Seventh day of Jan^{ry} Anno Domini one Thousand Seven hundred & Twelve./

Signed Sealed & Delivered   Henry —P— (The mark of) Wright (a seal)
  In presence of us
  John Green
  Edward Rawson

      Suffolk sc/ Boston Jan^{ry} 27th 1712/3
Henry Wright personally Appeared and Acknowledged this Instrum^t to be his Act & Deed
                Before me John Clark Jus^t peace
Recorded According to ye Original March 19th 1716/7./
                    p Jos: Hammond Reg^r

Know all men by These Present That I Joseph Tucker of Kittery in ye County of York and Province of ye Massachusets Bay In New England Yeoman for And In Consideration of Forty Eight pound to me in hand Already paid To Full Content and Satisfaction Doe give grant bargaine Sell Alliene & Deliver and have by These psents freely Clearly & Absolutely given granted bargained Sold Alienated and Delivered & for Set over unto my Honnoured mother Jane Tucker Relict To my Honoured ffather Nicholas Tucker Dec^d his heirs Ex^{rs} Adm^{rs} And Assignes for Ever fifteen Acres of Land which was to me given by will by my Honoured father before mentioned Lying & being in ye Township of Kittery in manner and form bounded as followeth on The Northern Side by my Broth^r William Tuckers Land and on The Eastern by John ffrinks land & on ye Southern Side by The land y^t was Phillip Carpenters Dec^d & on ye River Called Spruce Creek Together wth all appurtenances or Priviledges w^{t}soever belonging or appertaining thereunto of what Kind so ever To Have and To Hold ye aboves^d fifteen Acres of Land be it more or Less Together With all ye appurtenances & priviledges y^t unto belonging

unto y⁰ only And Sole use use benefit & behoof of her y⁰ afores⁴ Jane Tucker her heirs Exʳˢ Admʳˢ & Assignes for ever As her & Their own propper Estate In Fee Simple without any Condition or Limmittation wᵗsoever and that it Shall be Law full for yᵉ sᵈ Jane Tucker or her heirs Exʳˢ &cᵗ of yᵉ abovesᵈ Land to Take use Possess Occupy & Improve yᵉ Abovesᵈ Tract of Land from Time to Time and at all Times hereafter wᵗʰ out any Lett Hindrance or other Lawfull molestation from me yᵉ sᵈ Joseph Tucker or any other person or persons by procuremᵗ yᵉ Peaceable possession thereof forever hereafter to Warrant & maintaine against all persons Laying any Lawfull Claim right Title or Interest yʳ unto In Witness wʳ of I have Set to my hand & Seal this 7ᵗʰ Day of march 1716/7//   Joseph Tucker (ₛₑₐₗᵃ)
Signed Sealed & Delivered
 · In Presence of us
   Ebenezer Moore
   John Ingersoll
   Euegene Lynch
         York sc/ March 8ᵗʰ 1716/7
Joseph Tucker within Named Acknowledged yᵉ wᵗʰin written Instrumᵗ to be his free act & Deed
                before Charles ffrost J Peace
Recorded According to yᵉ Original April 13ᵗʰ 1717./
                p Jos. Ham̃ond Regʳ

To All People to whom these presents Shall Come Greeting: Know Ye that I Daniel Paul of Kittery in yᵉ County of York within his Majᵗʸˢ Province of yᵉ Massachusets Bay in New England Shipwright for and in Consideration of Twenty Acres Land Sold Conveyed & by way of Exchange made by James Fernald of yᵉ Same place Yeoman & a Conveyance of yᵉ Same bareing date with these [205] Presents which Twenty Acres of land lyes in yᵉ Township of York and is part of or one Moiety of that forty acres of land that yᵉ sᵈ James ffernald purchased in partnership with me yᵉ sᵈ Daniel Paul of John Morrell of Kittery Bricklayer in yᵉ year of our Lord One thousand Seven hundred & Ten Eleven as by yᵉ records thereof may more at large Appear in yᵉ records of yᵉ County of York refferrence thereunto being had and in Consideration of yᵉ abovesᵈ Twenty Acres of land Conveyed unto me yᵉ sᵈ Daniel Paul by yᵉ sᵈ James Fernald abovesᵈ Have given granted bargained & Sold by way of Exchange unto yᵉ sᵈ James Fernald his heirs & Assignes for ever a

Certaine Tract of land in Kittery at ye head of his Lot that lyes in ye great cove Vulgarly called Spinneys Creek & is in Length East & west forty poles & in breadth North & South Twenty one poles & is bounded on ye North with Sopers lot & on South & East with ye lands of ye s^d James Fernald West with ye land of s^d Paul./ Together with all Appurtenances and priviledges that do Any wayes Appurtaine unto ye s^d Tract of land To Have & To Hold ye granted & bargained premisses aboves^d with all ye Appurtenances priviledges & Comodityes to ye Same belonging or in any wayes Appurtaining to him ye s^d James Fernald his heirs & Assignes for ever to his & their only propper use benefit & behalfe for ever more./ And I ye s^d Daniel Paul for me my heirs Ex^{rs} Adm^{rs} do Covenant promiss & grant to & with ye s^d James Fernald his heirs & Assignes that before ye Ensealing hereof I am ye True Sole & Lawfull Owner of the above bargained premisses & am Lawfully Siezed of & possessed of ye same in my own proper right. And have in my Selfe good right full power & Lawfull Authority to grant & dispose of ye premisses as aboves^d And that ye s^d James Fernald his heirs & Assignes shall & may from time to time & at all times for ever hereafter by force & vertue of these presents Lawfully peaceably and Quietly Have hold use Occupie possess & Enjoy ye s^d demised and bargained premisses with the Appurtenances free & Clearly Acquitted from all & all maner of former & other gifts grants bargaines Sales leases Mortgages Entailes Joyntures Dowers Judgm^{ts} Executious Incumbrances & Extents Furthermore I ye s^d Daniel Paul for my Selfe my heirs do Covena^t & Engage ye above demised premisses to him ye s^d James Fernald his heirs & Assignes against ye Lawfull Claimes & Demands of Any person or persons what So ever for ever hereafter to Warrant Secure & Defend In Witness whereof I have hereunto Set my hand & Seal this Thirtyeth day of March One Thousand Seven hundred & Seventeen 1717

Signed Sealed & Delivered   Daniel Paul (Se^{a}al)
  In ye presence of us ye Subscrib^{rs}
  Withers Berry
  Wm Godsoe
  Katherine Surplis
    York sc/ March 29th 1717./

This day Daniel Paul psonally Appeared before me ye Subscrib^r one of his Maj^{tys} Justices of ye peace for s^d County & Acknowledged this above Instrum^t to be his free Act & Deed   Wm Pepperrell
  Recorded According to ye Original April 1st 1717./
                        p Jos. Hamond Reg^r

Book VIII, Fol. 205.

To All Christian People to whom these presents may Come Greeting Know Ye that I John Libbey of Portsmouth in ye Province of New Hampsh^r in New England formery of Scarbrough in ye Province of Maine Miller for & in Consideration of a Valluable Sum of money in hand paid me by my Son Daniel Libbey Now of Portsm^o afores^d the rec^t whereof I do by these presents Acknowledge & my Selfe to be fully Satisfied therewith & thereof & of Every part & parcell thereof do Acquit Exonerate & discharge him ye s^d Daniel Libbey his heirs Ex^{rs} Adm^{rs} firmly by these presents Have given granted bargained & sold & by these presents do give grant bargaine & Sell Aliene Enfeoffe & Confirm unto him ye s^d Daniel Libbey a Certaine Tract of Land Lying & being at black point Al^s Scarbrough in ye County formerly Called ye Province of maine in New England which tract of land I bought of m^r Josh^a Scottow of ye s^d place & is butted & bounded as followeth Viz^t on ye East of my father John Libbeys field in part bounded therewith & with Marked trees Westerly & Northerly with ye line of Scottows Pattent with Scottows Land Easterly & with a small Swamp bordering on Scottows Marsh Southerly to run from ye Southwest Corner of my s^d father Libbeys garden fence upon a Straight line unto Scottows fence upon ye top of ye hill toward ye East Together with Six Acres of Marsh land lying next to ye Clay pitts bordering upon black point river near oposite to Sarah Mills house ye land afores^d without ye Six Acres of Marsh being fifty Acres as I bought it of m^r Josh^a Scottow dec^d as by his bill of Sale under his hand bareing date ye first day of august 1668./ may more at Large Appear As likewise fifty acres more of land Adjoyning to my house which was granted unto me ye 14th Octob^r 1671./ by ye selectmen of Scarbrough together with an other parcell of Land lying in Scarbrough Alias Black point given me by ye select Selectmen of ye s^d town as may further Appear by a grant und^r their hands bareing Date ye 5th day of ffeb^{ry} (84) Signed by Robert Elliot Richard Hunnewell & Wm Burrage Selectmen being bounded as follows Viz^t begining & Joing to Mathew Libbys on ye East Side & So runing forty pole on an East line to a great hemlock marked on two sides from thence upon a South line fourscore pole ye whole being Twenty Acres or thereabouts Together with all ye right Claime or Interest which I have or ought to have to Any other Lands or possessions in ye Town of Scarbrough Al^s Black point Excepting & reserving my right to those lands which formerly belonged to my father John Libbey of ye s^d place dec^d all ye above Mentioned & Specified Tracts of land with all ye priviledges & Appurtenances to ye same Appurtaining with all my right to all or any other tract or tracts Excepting & reserving what is above Excepted I grant Bargaine & Sell to my Son Daniel Libbey of Portsm^o afores^d To have & To Hold to him his heirs & Assignes for ever & I the Aboves^d John Libbey do for me my heirs Ex^{rs} Adm^{rs} Covenan^t promiss & grant to & with my Son Daniel Libbey that I have good right & Lawfull Authority to grant bargaine & Sell ye above granted premisses & that at ye time of ye sealing and delivery of this present Bill of Sale I am ye True & Lawfull own^r [206] of the Lands above granted And that I ye aboves^d John Libbey or my heirs Ex^{rs} Adm^{rs} will maintaine & Defend ye same to him & his heirs & assignes for Ever and that he ye Aboves^d Daniel Libby & his heirs Ex^{rs} Adm^{rs} or assignes Shall and may at all Times for ever hereafter Quietly & peaceably Have hold Occupie possess & Enjoy ye above granted premisses without ye lawfull let Contratiction or denial of me ye Aboves^d John Libbey or of my heirs Ex^{rs} Adm^{rs} or Assignes or any other person Whatsoever Claiming or haveing Any right title or Interest in ye same or to Any part thereof by from or und^r me or by any other Lawfull wayes or Means Whatsoever./ In Testimoney of ye truth of ye above written Covenants I ye aboves^d John Libbey have hereunto Set my hand & Affixed my Seal this Nineteenth day of January in ye fourth year of ye Reign of our Soveraign Lady Anne Annoq, Domini 1705/

The words (To Have & To Hold between ye Eighteenth & Nineteenth lines were Interlined before Sealing./

Signed Sealed & Delivered   John Libbey ✝ his mark (Seal)
In presence of us
John Cutt
Eleaner Phipps
Thos Phipps

Pro New Hampsh^r/ John Libby personally Appeared & Acknowledged ye Above Instrum^t to be his free & Volluntary Act & Deed this 1st of April 1707./

Coram Thos Phipps J^s Pac^s
Recorded According to ye Original April 30th 1717./
p Jos Hammond Reg^r

We whose Names are here und^r written to give & grant to John Libby Junr 50 Acres of land Adjoyning to his

Book VIII, Fol. 206.

house 8ᵇʳ 14ᵗʰ 1671 provided it be No bodys Legal right afore./
       Richard Foxell
       Giles Barge
       John Teenny
       Sa : Okmans
       Hen : Williams
Recorded According to yᵉ Original April the 30ᵗʰ 1717./
      p Jos : Hamond Regʳ

Febʳʸ yᵉ 5ᵗʰ 84 : We yᵉ selectmen of Scarbrough whose Names are here undʳ written do give & grant unto John Libbey A parcell of land begining & Joyning to Mathew Libbeys on yᵉ East side & So runing forty poles upon An East line to a great hemlock Marked on two sides from thence upon a South line four score poles We do give & grant this parcell of land with all yᵉ priviledges thereunto belonging being Twenty Acres or thereabouts

    Robert   ℞   Elliot his mark

    Richᵈ   R   Hunewell his mark

    Wᵐ Burrage Selectmen
This Instrumᵗ was recorded in yᵉ town book by me
       Wᵐ Burrage Clerk
Recorded According to yᵉ Original April yᵉ 30ᵗʰ 1717./
      p Jos Hamond Regʳ

Know All men by these presents that I Wᵐ Hook Senʳ of Salisbury in yᵉ County of Essex in yᵉ province of yᵉ Massachusets Bay in New England yeoman for & in Consideration of that Natural Love & Affection which I have & do bear to my Sons Humphrey Hook of Almsbury in yᵉ County aforesᵈ & Jacob Hook of Salisbury aforesᵈ & also in Consideration of a former deed of gift made to my sᵈ Sons which is since lost not being fully Executed have given granted bargained Sold Aliened Enfeoffed Conveyed & Confirmed & do by these presents fully freely & Absolutely give grant bargaine Sell Alienate Enfeoffe Convey & Confirm unto my sᵈ Sons Humphrey & Jacob Hook their heirs & Assignes for ever Sundry Lotts Tracts & parcells of land & Meadow Lying & being in yᵉ Township of York in yᵉ province of Maine formerly So Called & now in ye County of York in ye province of ye Massachusets Bay in New England that is to Say a Certaine piece or parcell of land & Meadow of about five hundred Acres more or Less Containing ye one Moiety or Halfe part of Hookes farm So Called Scittuate on ye Northerly Side of York river At Scotland So Called To Have & To Hold with Meets Butts & bounds as formerly granted & Laid out & Also A Certaine parcell of land Scittuate on ye Sea Side being by Estimation fourscore rods wide & about one Mile & An halfe long begining at one mile & an halfe distance from ye Mouth of York river & So runing Northeasterly Towards Capeneck unto ye Extent of my father Hookes grant being by Estimation Two hundred & fifty Acres more or less & Also all that tract & parcell of Land Comonly Called & known by ye Name of Cape nedduck as it was formerly granted to my s^d father m^r Wm Hooke dec^d by Letters pattents & furthermore One thousand Acres more of land wthin ye s^d Township of York out of ye grants & pattents formerly made to my s^d father m^r Wm Hooke dec^d To Have & To Hold all & Singular ye above demised & granted premisses with all ye rights priviledges Comodityes & Appurtenances of what kind & Nature So ever to Each & Every of them belonging or in any wise Appurtaining to them ye s^d Humphrey & Jacob Hook their heirs & Assignes for ever in Even proportion to be Equally divided between them & to their only proper use benefit & behoofe as a good sure & perfect Estate of Inheritance in fee Simple for ever & I ye s^d William Hook Senr do by these presents for my Selfe my heirs Ex^{rs} & Adm^{rs} Covena^t promiss & grant to & with my s^d Sons Humphrey Hook & Jacob Hook their & Each of their heirs & Assignes in maner & form following that is to Say) that I have good right & full power to grant & Confirm all & Singular ye above granted & demised premisses in maner as above s^d & that it may & Shall be Lawfull for my s^d Sons Humph^{ry} & Jacob their heirs & Assignes by Vertue of these presents At any time hereafter to Claime demand Ask Challenge Enter upon Sue for recover receive divide or Improve & for ever hereafter To Have Hold use Occupy possess & Enjoy any all & Singular ye above granted & Demised premisses & Every part & parcell thereof lawfully peaceably & Quietly & free & Clear of & from all other & former gifts grants bargains Sales Mortgages Entailes Dowries Judgm^{ts} [**207**] Executions Charges troubles titles Claims Mollestations & Incumbrances whatsoever by me had made or done or by my means privity or procurem^t And that I ye s^d Wm Hook my heirs Ex^{rs} & Adm^{rs} shall &

will for ever hereafter Warra^t Secure Maintaine & Defend all & Singular ye Above granted & bargained premisses with ye Appurtenances unto my s^d Sons Humphrey & Jacob Hook their heirs & Assignes for ever in maner as is above Express^t Against all y^e Lawfull Claims & Demands of any person or persons whatsoever./ Witness my hand & Seal this first day of May Anno Domini 1717./ Annoq RR^s Georgii Magna Brittania &c^t Tertio./ Memorand^x that y^e word (means) was Interlined before Sealing   William Hook ($_\text{Seal}^\text{a}$) Signed Sealed & Delivered

 In presence of us
Wm Bradbury
John Stevens Junr
C: Cushing

 Mr Wm Hook Senr personally Appeared before me y^e Subscrib^r one of his Ma^tys Justices of y^e peace for y^e County of Essex this Second day of May 1717./ & Acknowledged this Above written Instrum^t to be his Volluntary Act & deed./
           Thomas Noyes
Recorded According to ye Original May ye 3^d 1717./
         p Jos: Hammond Reg^r

 To All People to whom these presents Shall Come John Harmon Benj^a Stone John Kingsbury Jonathan Young Jonathan Bane Samuel Bragdon Joseph Holt John Stagpole all of York in ye County of york in ye Province of ye Massachusets Bay in New England Sendeth Greeting Know ye that ye s^d John Harmon Benj^a Stone & Comp^a for & in Consideration of ye Sum of Two hundred & Twenty pounds in Curra^t mony of ye aboves^d Province to them in hand paid before ye Ensealing hereof well & Truely paid by William Moodey of Newbery in ye County of Essex in New England Gentleman ye rec^t whereof We hereby Acknowledge & thereof & of Every part & parcell thereof do Exonerate Acquit and discharge ye s^d Wm Moodey his heirs & Assignes for ever Have given granted bargained Sold remised released Conveyed & Confirmed and by these presents do fully freely & Absolutely give grant bargaine Sell release Transfer Convey & Confirm s^d Wm Moodey & to his heirs & Assignes for ever all ye right Title Claime or demand whatsoever which We ye s^d John Harmon Benj^a Stone &c^t Ever had now have or which we our heirs Ex^rs Adm^rs in time to Come may might Should or in any wise ought to have of in or to All that land that lyeth between Thomas Adams & ye land form-

erly Thomas Besons According to a grant given by ye Town At a Legall Town Meeting in York March 8th 1714/5 & a grant bareing date March 13th 1715/6 which was granted to John Harmon Benj^a Stone & Comp^a Above Mentioned which grant Appears in York towh book the first grant aboves^d in page 276, ye Second grant in above in page 285 To Have & To Hold ye s^d granted & released premisses & Every part thereof to him ye s^d Wm Moodey & to his heirs & Assignes for ever To his & their only proper use benefit & behoofe for ever more So that Neither We ye s^d John Harmon Benj^a Stone & Comp^a our heirs or assignes or any other person or persons by from under us them or any of them Shall or Will by Any means hereafter Have Claime Challenge or demand any right Title or Interest of in or to all or any part of ye s^d granted & released premisses but of & from all & Every Action of right Title Interest Claime & Demand of in & to ye premisses & every part & parcell thereof we our Selves & Every of them shall be utterly Excluded & for ever debarred by these presents./ & further We ye s^d John Harmon Benj^a Stone & Comp^a for our Selves our heirs Ex^{rs} Adm^{rs} do hereby Covena^t grant & agree ye Above granted & released premises with ye Appurtenances & Every part thereof unto ye s^d Wm Moodey their heirs & Assigns against ye Lawfull Claims & demands of all & Every person & persons any wayes Claiming or demanding ye Same or any part thereof by from or under us for ever hereafter to Warrant & Defend./ In Witness whereof We have hereunto Set our hands & Seals this Sixth day of May Anno Domini Seventeen hundred Seventeen   John Harmon (Seal)
Signed Sealed & Delivered   Benj^a Stone (Seal)
   In presence   John Kingsbery (Seal)
   Lewis Bane   Jonathan Young (Seal)
   Nath^{ll} ffreeman   Jonathan Bane (Seal)
                             Samuel Bragdon (Seal)
                             Joseph Hoult (Seal)
                             John Stagpole (Seal)
       York ss in york May ye 6th 1717.
John Harmon Benj^a Stone John Kingsbery Jon^a Young Jon^a Bane Samuel Bragdon & Joseph Hoult Each for themselves & John Harmon & Benj^a Stone in behalfe of John Stagpole p power of Attorney personally Appeared And Acknowledged this above Instrum^t to be their free Act & deed   Before me Abra^m Preble Just^s peace
  Recorded According to ye Original May 7th 1717./
                  p Jos: Hamond Reg^r

Book VIII, Fol. 208.

To All People to whom these presents Shall Come John Stevens Coper Jane his wife formerly Jane Smith Widow James Grant Marrin^r & Johnana his Wife all of Boston y^e. County of Suffolk in New Engl^d which s^d Jane & Johanna are Two of ye Daughters of James Ingles late of s^d Boston Marrin^r dec^d Send Greeting Whereas ye s^d James Ingles in & by his last will & Testam^t Dated ye Second day of ffeb^{ry} Anno Domini 1702/3. Duely proved Approved & Allowed Among other things gave & devised to his Daughters Johana Grant & Jane Smith Each of them one fifth part of all his lands & houses as by ye s^d Will more plainly Appears & Whereas ye s^d James Ingles dyed Siezed in his own right in fee of a Considerable real Estate Consisting of [**208**] Houseing lands & Mills lying within ye County of York formerly Called ye province of Maine Two fifth parts whereof of right belong to ye s^d Jane Stevens & Johana Grant Pursua^t to ye s^d Will Now Know ye that We ye s^d John & Jane Stevens James & Johana Grant in Consideration of Ten shillings paid by John Smith of Boston afores^d Marrin^r Son of me ye s^d Jane & Nephew of me ye s^d Johana But more Especially for & in Consideration of ye Natural Love good Will & Affection which we have and bear unto ye s^d John Smith Have given & granted and by these presents to give grant Enfeoffe release & Confirm unto ye s^d John Smith All ye Share propperty Inheritance Claime & demand w^{t}soever wch We ye s^d John & Jane Stevens James & Johana Grant or Either of us ever had now have or at any time hereafter Can pretend to have or Claime by Vertue of ye Will of ye s^d James Ingles or otherwise howsoever of in and to all Such Lands Tenem^{ts} heriditam^{ts} Mills & real Estate w^r of he dyed Siezed Scittuate within ye County of York in ye late province of Maine Together with ye profits priviledges & Appur^{ces} thereof To Have & To Hold ye s^d Given granted & released premisses with ye Appur^{ces} & Every part thereof unto ye s^d John Smith his heirs & Assignes to his and their only Sole & propper use bennefit & behoofe for ever freely peaceably & Quietly without any Maner of Condition redemption or revocation in any wise so that of & from all maner of right Estate Title Interest reclaime Challenge or demand what soever to be by us or Either or any of us Our or Either of our heirs Ex^{rs} Adm^{rs} or Assignes at any time hereafter had or Claimed of in or to ye s^d given & granted premisses or any part thereof We & Each & Every of us & them shall & Will be debarred & forever Excluded by force & Vertue of these presents In Witness whereof We have hereunto put our hands & Seals this Twenty first day of Decemb^r Anno Dom-

ini one thousand Seven hundred & Sixteen Annoq Rⁱ Rˢ
Georgii Tertio   John Stevens (seal)
Signed Sealed & Delivered   Jane Stevens (seal)
  In presence of us   James Grant (seal)
  Joseph Buckley   Joanna Grant (seal)
  Phⁱⁱⁱ Barger
  Samˡ Wainwright
Suffolk sc/ Boston Decʳ 1ˢᵗ 1716.

John Stevens & Jane his Wife James Grant & Joaña his wife Acknowledged the Afore going Instrumᵗ to be their free Act & deed   Before me   John Clark Just Pacˢ
Recorded According to yᵉ Original May 14ᵗʰ 1717./
                            p Jos. Hamond Regʳ

To all People To whom This pʳsent Writing Shall Come Greeting I Joseph Shaw of late Boston in yᵉ County of Suffolk but now of yᵉ Town of Haverill in yᵉ County of Essex in yᵉ Province of yᵉ Massachusets Bay in New England House Carpenter for & in Consideration of yᵉ Sum of Ten Pounds Curᵗ money of New England already to me in hand pᵈ before yᵉ Signing Sealing & Delivery hereof well and Truely made in Equal Share by John Hutchins yeoman Samˡ Palmer yeoman Benjamin Thurston House Carpenter of yᵉ Town of Bradford & Abraham Rideout of yᵉ Town of Haverill Scrivener all of yᵉ County of Essex aforesᵈ yᵉ receipt whereof I do hereby acknowledge & thereof & of Every part & parcell thereof I Do hereby Acquit Enonerate & for Ever Discharge them & Each of them yᵉ sᵈ John Hutchins Samuel Palmer Benjamin Thurston & Abraᵐ Rideout & Each of their heirs Executors Admʳˢ & assignes for ever by these pʳsents Hath Given Granted Bargained Sold Alienated Enfeoffed Conveyed & Confirmed & by these pʳsents Doth fully freely & absolutely Give grant Bargaine Sell Aliene Enfeoffe Convey & Confirm unto them yᵉ sᵈ John Hutchins Samˡˡ Palmer Benjᵃ Thurston & abrᵐ Rideout in Equal Share & Division both in Quantity & Quallity all & Singular & every part & parcel of my right title property Claime & Demand of in & to a Certaine Tract or parcel of Land Lying being & Scittuate at Saggadi:Hock in yᵉ Province of maine in New England aforesᵈ at yᵉ Northern Side of a place there Comonly Called & known by yᵉ name of yᵉ mill Pool being butted & bounded as followeth Vizᵗ begining at a Great Rock at yᵉ upper End of Thomas Atkins his field & Close & from thence to yᵉ Steping Stones & from thence upon a Straight line to yᵉ head of all yᵉ marshes as far as yᵉ Salt water runeth at Small point side as yᵉ Same was first purchased by John Pritchett of Thoˢ atkins ot sᵈ Saccadi : Hock planter And Partickularly mentioned in a Deed of Salle undʳ yᵉ hand & Seal of yᵉ sᵈ Thoˢ Atkins bearing date yᵉ Sixteenth Day of Aprill Anno Dom : 1660 and afterwards bought by or belonged unto Henry Emms of Boston Paker & Sold by sᵈ Emms unto my father Joseph Shaw formerly of sᵈ Boston Cooper Deceased as by yᵉ deed of Sale undʳ yᵉ hands & Seals of sᵈ Henry Emms & Elizᵃ his wife bareing Date yᵉ 26ᵗʰ day of march in yᵉ year 1688 will more fully appear : Together wᵗʰ all Lands meadows Marshes Rivers fishings fowling Creeks Coves Beaches flats woods undʳ woods Swamps profits Priviledges Comodities heriditaments & appurtenances wˢoever To yᵉ sᵈ Tract of Land belonging or in any wise appertaining To Have and To Hold yᵉ sᵈ Tract of Land & Every part & Parcels Thereof So butted & bounded as aforesᵈ unto them and Each of them in Equall Share for Quantity & Quallity to yᵉ sᵈ John Hutchins Samˡˡ Palmer Benjᵃ Thurston & Abrᵐ Rideout Their & Each of there heirs & assignes for Ever peaceably & Quietly to have hold Occupy Possess and Enjoy all my Right & Title of in & to yᵉ Same and to warrant & Defend my sᵈ right & Title to them as an Absolute Estate of Inheritance in fee Simple to them their heirs & assignes for ever free & Clear from all other Salles & Incumbʳᶜᵉˢ by me made

[209] In Witness whereof I have hereunto Set my hand and Affixed my Seal in sᵈ Haverhill on yᵉ Seventh Day of February in yᵉ year of our Lord One Thousand Seven Hundred & Sixteen/ 17   Joseph Shaw (ₛₑₐₗᵃ)
Signed Sealed & Delivered
In Presence of us
Andrew Mitchell
James Jarvis
Daniel Davis

    Essex sc/ Haverhill Aprill yᵉ 8ᵗʰ 1717
Then Joseph Shaw personally appearing Acknowledged This Instrument to be his act & Deed before me John White
        Justice of the Peace
Recorded According to yᵉ Original May 22ᵈ 1717
      p Jos: Hamond Regʳ

To All Christian People to whom these Presents Shall Come Greeting Know yᵉ that Charles ffrost of Kittery in yᵉ

County of york within ye Province of ye Massachusets Bay In New England Esqr for Divers good Causes & Considerations him moveing hath remised, Released & for ever quit Claimed & by these p^rsents for himself his heirs Execut^rs & Adm^rs Doth fully Clearly & absolutely remise release & forever quit Claime unto Wm Moodey of Newbury in ye County of Essex in ye Province afores^d & to his heirs Execut^rs Adm^rs & assignes for ever all Such right Estate title Interest & Demand w^tsoever as he ye s^d Charles ffrost had or ought to have of in or to all that Tract of Land Containing three hundred & Seventy Acres in ye whole being three hundred & fifty acres of upland & about twenty acres of Grassey Swamp be it more or Less Scittuate Lying & being in ye Township of york in ye County of york afores^d on ye Southwest Side of york River adjoyning to that Tract of Land which formerly was Thomas Besons on ye Southermost Side thereof which s^d Three Hundred & Seventy acres of Land ye s^d Charles ffrost bought & purchased of Abigail Fryer of New Castle in ye Province of New hampsh^r Relict widow & Executrix to ye last will & Testam^t of Joshua Fryer Late of New Castle Afores^d marriner dec^d./ and now ye wife of ye s^d Wm Moodey/ as by her deed or Instrum^t In writing bareing Date ye Twenty Third day of august One Thousand Seven hundred & Ten referance thereunto being had will more at Large appear To Have & To Hold ye s^d Three Hundred & Seventy acres of Land to him ye s^d William Moodey his heirs & assignes for ever So That ye s^d Charles ffrost nor his heirs or any other person or persons for him or them Shall or will by any ways or means by any Act or Deed of ye s^d Charles ffrost from This Day forward have Clame Challeng or Demand any Estate right Title or Interest of in or to ye premisses or any part or parcell y^rof but from and all and Every Action right Estate Title Interest & Demand of in or to ye pmisses or any part or parcel thereof They and Every of them Shall utterly be Excluded & barred for ever by these p^rsents In Witness w^r of the s^d Charles ffrost Hath hereunto Sett his hand & Seal y^e Tenth Day of may in y^e Third year of his Maj^tys Reign Anno Dom 1717

Signed Sealed & Delivered   Charles ffrost ($_{Seal}^{a}$)
  In Presence of us
  Jeremiah Wise
  John Belcher

            York sc/ Kittery may 16: 1717

  Maj^or Charles ffrost Personally appeared before me y^e Subscrib^r one of his Maj^tys Justices of y^e peace for s^d

Book VIII, Fol. 210.

County & Acknowledged y{e} above Written Deed or Instrum{t} to be his act & Deed and at y{e} Same Time Jane his Wife Did also give up all her Wright of Dower or Thirds Contained therein w{ch} otherwise She might have had   John Wheelwright

  Recorded According to y{e} Original May : 16 : 1717./
         p Jos. Hamond Reg{r}

	£ : s : d
William Dixey is to pay me for the house & Land I bought of George Newman	23 : 5 : 0
I have paid Tho Walford for him	3 : 10 : 0
I am to pay Tho Jones for him	1 : 07 : 0
	28 02 : 0
	23 : 00 : 00
Rec{d} of this. By 81 bushells of Corn	5 : 2 : 0

  at 4/6{d} p bs{l}   18 : 5 : 0
  & by Samuel allowed him for that   4 : 15 : 0
  he had not Some Corn for his use   £23 : 0 : 0 Rests due

  Whereas p y{e} Acco{t} above it Appeareth that I Samuel Maverick have made W{m} Dixey D{r} for 23{l} : 5{s} for a house & Land w{ch} I bought of George Newman as by an Assignation under his hand bareing date the Last of Octob{r} 1634./ Appeareth which Assignation is in y{e} hands of W{m} Dixey. Now Know all men that I Sam{l} Maverick do hereby make over all my Interest in y{e} s{d} house & Land unto W{m} Dixey his heirs or assignes he paying me on y{e} Last of Sept{r} Next if demanded five pounds 2/ Starling or as Soon After as it Shall be demanded by Sam{l} Maverick or his Assignes & in Case y{e} s{d} W{m} Dixey Shall Mislike y{e} afores{d} Bargaine on y{e} Last of Sept{r} Next then Sam{l} Maverick doth hereby promiss to take y{e} house & Land againe & to repay him y{e} afores{d} 23{l} 5/ y{e} afores{d} 5{l} 2{s} due to Sam{l} Maverick being deducted [210] And y{e} house & fence in Such repair as he found it in & for True performence hereof We bind our selves our heirs or Adm{rs} In Witness whereof we have Interchangeably hereto Set our hands this 13{th} of Jan{ry} 1636.

  Witness Edw{d} Godfrey   Samuel Maverick
   The mark ⟨A⟩ of
   Arthur Bragdon
   Recorded According to y{e} Original April y{e} 3{d} 1717./
        p Jos. Hamond Reg{r}

Book VIII, Fol. 210.

To All Christian People to whom these presents may Come or Concern Job Curtis of York in y[e] County of York in y[e] Province of Maine in New Engl[d] Cordwain[r] & Bithiah his wife Sendeth Greeting./ Know Y[e] that s[d] Job and Bithiah for & in Consideration of a new house to be built &c[t] According to y[e] Dementions of this date./ Have given granted bargained Sold Aliened Enfeoffed & made over and doth by these presents give grant bargaine Sell Aliene Enfeoffe & make over & fully frely & Absolutely Convey & Confirm unto Cap[tn] Lawis Bane & Job Banks of s[d] York in Equal Copartnership Also Quantity & Quallity one Certaine piece parcel or parcells of upland Meadow land Containing fifty Acres be it more or Less being y[e] one Quarter part of a Lot of land laid out by the Selectmen of Afores[d] York July y[e] 2[d] 1667./ unto Richard Bankes Thomas Curtis Sam[l] Twisden & Abra[m] Preble in Copartnership as p York Town book reference thereunto being had may Appear the whole Containing Two hundred Acres & Yet undivided As Also y[e] Quarter part of a fall mill with one Saw & y[e] one Quarter part of the Stream & Dam thereunto belonging y[e] which s[d] land &c[t] is Scittuated Lying & being within y[e] Township of s[d] York at a place well known by y[e] Name of Scittuate plains which butts and bounds are Set forth in aboves[d] York Town book. Together with all y[e] rights priviledges Advantages Imolluments & Appurtenances thereunto belonging or any wayes at any time redownding unto the aboves[d] Quarter part of s[d] Two hundred Acres of land & Mill & dam & Stream As Also y[e] Meadow land wood under wood Timber Timber Timber Trees Standing lying & remaining thereon unto them y[e] s[d] Cap[tn] Lewis Bane & Job Bankes & unto their heirs & Assignes for ever To have & To hold & Quietly & peaceably to possess Ocupie & Enjoy as a Sure Estate in fee Simple Morever y[e] s[d] Job Curtis & Bithiah his wife doth for themselves their heirs Execut[rs] & Adm[rs] to & with y[e] s[d] Cap[tn] Bane & Job Bankes Covena[t] Ingage & promiss y[e] above bargained premisses with all its priviledges to be fre & Clear from all former gifts grants Bargaines Sales rents rates Mortgages dowryes & all other Incumberm[t] whatsoever As Also from all future Claimes Challenges Arests Lawsuits or any other Inturruptions upon grounds of Law whatsoever proceeding y[e] Date hereof Avouching themselves to be y[e] only true Owners thereof unto or till y[e] Sealing of this deed or Instrum[t] and that they have good right & Authority to Sell as is above Express[t] & that they will henceforth Defend & Warrantise y[e] Same In Witness hereof y[e] s[d] Job & Bithiah his wife hath hereunto Set their hands &

BOOK VIII, FOL. 210.

Seals this thirtyeth day of April in y{e} year of our Lord One Thousand Seven hundred & Seventeen & in the third year of y{e} reign of our Soveraign Lord King George Over Great Brittaine &c{t}

Signed Sealed & Delivered   Job <u>his</u> Curtis (seal)
  In y{e} presence of us   mark
  Sam{l} Bankes
  Abra{m} Preble   Bithiah <u>her</u> Curtis (seal)
             mark

York sc/ April y{e} 30{th} 1717./ The above Named Job Curtis & Bithiah his wife p{r}sonally Appeared & Acknowledged y{e} above written Instrum{t} to be their free Act & Deed
       Before me   Abra{m} Preble Just{s} peace
Recorded According to y{e} Original May 16{th} 1717./
          p Jos : Hamond Reg{r}

   To All People to whom this present Deed of Sale Shall Come Timothy Wentworth of Berwick in y{e} County of York & within his Maj{tys} Province of the Massachusets Bay in New England yeoman Sendeth Greeting Know Ye that y{e} s{d} Timothy Wentworth for & in Consideration of Twenty pounds Currant money in New England to him in hand Well & Truely paid At y{e} Ensealing & Delivery of these presents by James Smith of York in y{e} County & Province afores{d} Blacksmith the rec{t} whereof he Acknowledges & owns himselfe fully satisfied Contented & paid And doth Acquit Exonerate & finally discharge y{e} s{d} James Smith his heirs Ex{rs} & Adm{rs} by these presents hath fully frely clearly & Absolutely given granted bargained Sold Aliened Enfeoffed & Confirmed unto y{e} s{d} James Smith & to his heirs Ex{rs} Adm{rs} & Assignes Twenty Acres of Land Scittuate Lying & being in y{e} Township of Berwick Namely Ten Acres at y{e} uper End of his Sixty Acre lot bounded Northeast & by North on John Keyes land y{e} other Ten acres being an Additional grant to s{d} Wentworth & is bounded on y{e} Comons & y{e} Sixty Acre Lot or however otherwayes bounded or reputed to be bounded Together with all & Singular y{e} wayes profits priviledges rights propertyes Comodityes heriditaments & Appurtenances thereunto belonging. To Have & To Hold y{e} s{d} Twenty Acres of land & all other y{e} above granted & bargained premisses with their Appurten{ces} thereunto belonging unto him y{e} s{d} James Smith & to his heirs Ex{rs} Adm{rs} & Assignes to his & their only proper use benefit and behoofe forever And yᵉ sᵈ James Smith his heirs Exʳˢ Admʳˢ & Assignes Shall & may from henceforth & for ever hereafter [211] Lawfully peaceably & Quietly have hold use Occupie possess & Enjoy all yᵉ above granted & bargained premisses frely & Clearly Acquited Exonerated & discharged of & from all maner of former & other gifts grants bargains sales leases Mortgages thirds Dowries Joyntures Executions claimes & Demands whatsoever & further yᵉ sᵈ Timothy Wintworth his heirs Exʳˢ & Admʳˢ shall & will from henceforth & forever hereafter Warraᵗ & Defend all yᵉ Above granted & bargained premisses with their Appurtenances unto yᵉ sᵈ James Smith & to his heirs Exʳˢ Admʳˢ & Assignes for ever frely & Clearly Against yᵉ Lawfull Claims & demands of All & Every person whatsoever

In Witness whereof he hath hereunto Set his hand & Seal & Sarah his wife In Testimony of Acquitting of her right of thirds to sᵈ premisses yᵉ Eighth of June Anno Domini Seventeen hundred and fifteen & in yᵉ first year of his Majesty King George his Reign Over Great Brittaine./
Signed Sealed & Delivered
  In yᵉ presence of us   his ⚹ mark
  Joseph Pray   Timothy Wentworth (a Seal)
  John Bradstreet
                                 her ⚹ mark
                             Sarah Wentworth (seale)

Note that yᵉ sᵈ Wintworth & his heirs for ever shall have a highway of Two rod wide through yᵉ sᵈ Twenty Acres to the Comons next his own land & sᵈ Keys./

this Entred before Signing Sealing & Delivery The highway to run yᵉ length way of sᵈ 20 Acres & no otherwayes yᵉ sᵈ Ten Acres of land of yᵉ Additional to Joyn to yᵉ sᵈ Ten Acres out of yᵉ sᵈ Sixty Acre Lott

York ss June yᵉ 8ᵗʰ 1715. At Berwick./ Then Timothy Wentworth and Sarah his wife made their Appearance before me the Subscriber one of his Majᵗʸˢ Justices of yᵉ peace for sᵈ County & Acknowledged yᵉ Above written Instrumᵗ to be their Volluntary Act & Deed   Ichabod Plaisted

Recorded According to yᵉ Original May. 16ᵗʰ 1717/
                           p Jos: Hammond Regʳ

To All People to whom these presents Shall Come Greeting Now Know ye that I Samuel Littlefield of Wells in yᵉ County of York in yᵉ province of yᵉ Massachusets Bay in New England Planter for & in Consideration of yᵉ full &

Just Sum of fifteen pounds in good Currant Money of New England to me in hand paid by Stephen Harding of ye Town afores^d Blacksmith as well as for other good & Lawfull Causes & Considerations me thereunto Moveing have given & granted & do by these p^{r}sents fully clearly & Absolutely give grant bargaine Sell Alienate Enfeoff & make over & Confirm to Stephen Harding afores^d a Certaine Tract of Land Containing Thirty Acres lying & being in ye Township Of Wells bounded as followeth Viz^t Easterly by land formerly belonging to John Butland & now in possession of Stephen Harding Southerly by ye Sea Westerly by land I lately Sold to James Carr Junr & Isaac Chase of Newbury which Westerly bounds begin at ye Eastermost end of a Smal Cove of Sands next Adjoyning to ye great Hill & from S^d Cove to run up into ye woods on a north line untill ye aboves^d Thirty acres be Compleated which aboves^d thirty Acres of land was Granted by ye Comissioners & Selectmen of Wells to ffrancis Littlefield & Anthony Littlefield by a grant und^r their hands bareing date Novr 27th 1653./ the which thirty Acres : of land bounded as afores^d I the aboves^d Samuel Littlefield for my Selfe my heirs Ex^{rs} Adm^{rs} do Confirmed & Set over to Stephen Harding afores^d his heirs Ex^{rs} Adm^{rs} or Assignes To Have & To Hold Together with all & Singular ye priviledges rights & Appurtenances thereto belonging or any wise Appurtaining as a free & Clear Estate in fee Simple for ever & I ye aboves^d Saml Littlefield do for my Selfe my heirs Ex^{rs} & Adm^{rs} Covenant & promiss to & with ye aboves^d Stephen Harding & his heirs Ex^{rs} Adm^{rs} or Assignes that I am at ye time of ye Ensealing hereof ye True & rightfull owner & proprietor of ye above granted premisses and that I have full power good right & Lawfull Authority to Sell and dispose of ye same as afores^d Moreover do Affirm & promiss the Same to be free & Clear & fully Clearly & Absolutely Acquitted and Discharged of & from all other & former gifts grants bargains Sales Dowries Mortgages or Incumbrance whatsoever Furthermore to Warrant Secure & Defend ye same as aboves^d from all or any person or persons whatso ever laying any Legall Claime thereto to which & Each Article as above Expressed I ye aboves^d Saml Littlefield do bind my selfe my heirs Ex^{rs} & Adm^{rs} to ye afores^d Stephen Harding his heirs Ex^{rs} Adm^{rs} or assignes./ In Witness whereof I y^e aboves^d Saml Littlefield have hereto Set my hand & Seal this Twentyeth day of May Anno Domini 1717./ And in the third year of y^e reign of our Soveraign Lord George by y^e grace of God of

Great Brittaine ffrance & Ireland King Defend[r] of y[e] ffaith &c[t]   Samuel Littlefield ($_{Seal}^{a}$)
Signed Sealed & Delivered
In presence of us   Frances her ✗ mark Littlefield ($_{Seal}^{a}$)
Nicholas Cole
Thomas Wells

Mary her ff mark Cole

York ss/ The within written Sam[l] Littlefield and Frances his wife personally Appeared before me the Subscrib[r] one of his Maj[tys] Justices of y[e] peace for s[d] County & Acknowledged y[e] within written Instrum[t] to be their free Act & Deed Also y[e] s[d] Frances did at y[e] Same Time give up her right of Dower or thirds herein Contained   John Wheelwright

Recorded According to y[e] Original June 26th 1717.

p Jos: Hamond Reg[r]

[212] To All People to whom these presents shall Come Greeting &c[t] Know Ye that I Joseph Sevey of y[e] Town of Portsm[o] in her Maj[tys] Province of y[e] New Hampsh[r] in New England husbandman for & in Consideration of y[e] Sum of Thirty five pounds money to me in hand well & Truely paid by Dominicus Jordan of Kittery in y[e] County of York in her Maj[tys] Province of y[e] Massachusets Bay in New England Carpenter y[e] rec[t] whereof I do hereby Acknowledge and my selfe therewith fully Satisfied & Contented and thereof & of Every part & parcell thereof do Acquit & discharge y[e] s[d] Dominicus Jordan his heirs Ex[rs] & Adm[rs] for ever by these presents have given granted bargained sold Aliened Conveyed & Confirmed & by these presents do fully frely & Absolutely give grant Bargaine Sell Aliene Convey & Confirm unto him y[e] s[d] Dominicus Jordan his heirs & Assignes for ever one Certaine parcell & neck of Land Lying & being in y[e] Township of Kittery afores[d] w[ch] Neck of Land Containing by Estimation five Acres be y[e] same More or Less with Two Acres thereunto Joyning which Neck being bounded upon y[e] Southard Side with y[e] Creek going into Braveboat harb[r] and upon y[e] North Side of y[e] Cove going into m[r] Roger Dearings building Yard & upon y[e] Eastw[d] side bounded with y[e] Creek which goes between y[e] Neck & y[e] Land formerly Called Lockwoods land & upon y[e] Northside with Two Acres belonging to y[e] Neck which is

bounded by y'e land which was formerly Accounted Maj'r Nicholas Shapleighs & now in y'e possession of M'r Roger Dearing & lying near y'e highway & by y'e house of m'r Robert Mitchell which Neck & Two Acres of Land was formerly in y'e possession of John Pierce dec'd & after y'e Decease of John Pierce was in y'e Possession of Joseph Pierce his Son as will at Large Appear by an Inventory Taken & recorded To have & To hold y'e s'd granted & bargained premisses with all y'e Appurtenances priviledges & Comodityes to y'e same belonging or any wise Appurtaining to him y'e s'd Dominicus Jordan his heirs & Assignes for ever to his & their only proper use bennefit & behoofe & I y'e s'd Joseph Sevey for me my heirs Ex'rs & Adm'rs do Covena't promiss & grant to & with y'e s'd Dominicus Jordan his heirs & Assignes that before y'e Ensealing hereof I am y'e True sole & Lawfull owner of y'e above bargained premisses and have in my selfe good right full power & Lawfull Authority to grant bargaine Sell Convey and Confirm s'd bargained premisses in Manner as aboves'd & that y'e s'd Dominicus Jordan his heirs & Assignes Shall & may from time to time and at all times for ever hereafter by force & vertue of these presents Lawfully peaceably & Quietly have hold use Occupy possess and Injoy y'e s'd Demised & bargained premisses with their Appurten'ces free & Clear & Clearly Acquitted & Discharged of & from all & all maner of former & other gifts grants Bargaines Sales Titles Troubles & Incumbrances whatsoever./ Furthermore I y'e s'd Joseph Sevey for my Selfe my heirs Ex'rs & Adm'rs do Covena't & Ingage y'e above demised premisses Especially y'e Neck of land to him y'e s'd Dominicus Jordan his heirs & Assignes against y'e Lawfull Claims or Demands of any person or persons what Soever but it is to be understood that I y'e s'd Joseph Sevey do not oblige my selfe to make good y'e forementioned Two Acres of Land which Lyes upon y'e North side of y'e neck between y'e Neck & highway which is part in y'e possession of Robert Mitchell Except I Can get it out of his hands by a fair Tryal at the Charge & y'e Cost of y'e s'd Dominicus Jordan but as for y'e Neck of Land five Acres More or Less I do Covenant & Ingage to Defend against person or persons whatsoever for ever hereafter to Warrant Secure & Defend And Hannah Sevey Wife of Me Joseph Sevey doth by these presents freely and Willingly give Yield up & Surrend'r all her right of Dowry and power of thirds of in & unto y'e above Demised premisses unto him y'e s'd Dominicus Jordan his heirs & Assignes for ever./ In Witness whereof Wee have hereunto Sett our

hands & Seals yᵉ Eighth day of Aprill Annoq Domini One Thousand Seven hundred & Twelve./
Signed Sealed
   In presence of   Joseph his X mark Sevey (Seal)
   Benjamin Sevey
   John Pickerin   (ᵃ Seal)
   Willᵐ Pepperrell junʳ
York sc Kittery in yᵉ Province of Main
Aprill yᵉ 8ᵗʰ 1712./ Joseph Sevey Appeared before me yᵉ Subscribʳ & Acknowledged yᵉ above deed to be his free Act: & Deed & promissed his now wife should Sign to yᵉ same./
                         Wᵐ Pepperrell Just peace.
Recorded According to yᵉ Original June 2ᵗʰ9 1717./
                         p Jos. Hamond Regʳ

Know All men by these presents that I Colº Samˡ Browne of Salem in yᵉ County of Essex in yᵉ Province of yᵉ Massaachusets Bay in New Englᵈ Esqʳ for & in Consideration of yᵉ Sum of One hundred & Twenty pounds Curraᵗ Money of New England or Province Bills of Credit to him in hand paid by Samˡ Harmon of Wells in yᵉ County of York in yᵉ sᵈ Province husbandman yᵉ recᵗ whereof he yᵉ sᵈ Samˡ Brown doth Acknowledge & thereof doth Acquit & for ever discharge yᵉ sᵈ Samˡ Harmon his heirs & Assignes for ever by these presents hath granted bargained Sold Aliened Enfeoffed Conveyed & Confirmed & by these pʳsents doth grant Bargaine Sell Aliene Enfeoffe Convey & Confirm unto yᵉ sᵈ Samˡ Harmon his heirs and Assigns for ever a Certaine farm with a dwelling house & orchard lying on Ogunquit side Containing One hundred Acres As Appears by Wells Town records granted to Nathˡ Masters Anno 1666 & Also fifty Acres more granted to yᵉ sᵈ Nathˡ Masters by yᵉ sᵈ Town Anno 1669. to Containe thirty poles in breadth & to run up into the [213] Country as other Lots do Also a Certain parcell of Salt Marsh Creek & thatch bankes Lying near yᵉ harbours mouth bounded as followeth vizᵗ yᵉ uper End of sᵈ Marsh by a parcell of Marsh belonging to Joseph Littlefield & So to run down to yᵉ harbours Mouth & lying between Two parcells of Marsh Lately belonging to mʳ Thomas Wells sᵈ Marsh in yᵉ Middle being Eighteen poles or thereabouts in breadth yᵉ whole parcell of Marsh Creek & thatch bankes Containing five Acres or more bounded by yᵉ sᵈ Joseph Littlefield At one End & So between yᵉ sᵈ mʳ Wells Marsh down to yᵉ river Called Webhant river also an Island of thatch being in ye s^d Town of Wells butting on ye river & bounded on ye Northeast side & southwest side by Marsh formerly Ezekiel Knights And Also Ten Acres of fresh Meadow Comonly Called by ye Name of Masters^s Meadow ground./ All which houseing lands Thatch bank Marsh and Meadow are Scittuated Lying & being in ye Town of Wells afores^d being more fully butted bounded & discribed in an Instrum^t of Conveyence made duely Executed & recorded from Nathl Masters to ye afore Named Col^o Saml Brown Esqr bareing date ye 7th of Septr Anno Domini 1715./ referrence being thereunto had may more at large Appear./ To have & To hold ye s^d farm dwelling house orchard Meadow Marshes Creeks & thatch banks & Every part & parcell thereof Together with all ye fences rights Comons priviledges & Appurtenances w^{t}soev^r to all or any of them belonging or in any wise Appurtaining to ye s^d Saml Harmon his heirs & Assigns As fully & Absolutely to All Intents and purposes whatsoever As ye s^d Saml Brown might or Could have done by force & Vertue of the Conveyence from y^e s^d Masters afores^d before this Instrum^t was made./ In Witness & for Confirmation hereof he y^e s^d Saml Brown Esqr hath hereunto Set his hand & Seal this fourteenth day of Septr Anno Regni Regis Georgii Nunc Magna Brittania &c Tertio Annoq, Domini 1716. Sam^{ll} Browne ($_{Seal}^a$)

Signed Sealed & Delivered
  In y^e presence of us
  Ric^h Newcombe
  Mehitable Sewall
      Essex sc/ Salem Sep^t 15th 1716
Then Col^o Saml Browne Esqr psonally Appearing Acknowledged y^e foregoing Instrum^t to be his volluntary Act & Deed   Coram Stephen Sewall Just peace
Recorded According to ye Original June 4th 1717./
                p Jos : Harmon Reg^r

To All People to whom these presents Shall Come Greeting./ Know Y^e that I George Buckling of ye Town of Wells in ye County of York in his Maj^{tys} Province ye Massachusets Bay Millman &c^t for & in Consideration of ye sum of Six pounds Bills of Credit of ye s^d Province to me Secured to be paid by James Wiggins of ye same Town & place Milman have given granted & bargained Sold Conveyed and Confirmed & by these presents do freely fully & Absolutely give grant bargain Sell Convey & fully Confirm unto him ye s^d

James Wiggins his heirs & Assignes for ever my Whole right & Title to a Tract of Land which was given to John Clayce by ye Inhabitants of ye Town of Wells at a Legall Town meeting the s^d Land Scittuate Lying & being in ye aboves^d Town & Adjoyning to Nathaniel Clayces^{es} land at Egunquick Together with a parcell of salt marsh which was given ye aboves^d John Clayce by Thomas Mills./ Likewise all ye right & Title of land & Marsh that I Ever had or Obtained by Mary my wife To have & To hold ye s^d granted & bargained premisses with all priviledges of Marsh to ye same belonging or in any wise appurtaining to him ye s^d George Buckling his heirs & Assignes For ever & I George Buckling for me my heirs Ex^{rs} & Adm^{rs} do Covena^t & Engage the above Demised premisses to him ye s^d James Wiggins his heirs & Assignes against ye Lawfull Claims or demands of any pson or persons whatsoever forever hereafter to Warra^t Secure and Defend./ And Mary Buckling ye wife of me ye s^d George Buckling doth by these presents freely Willingly give Yield up and Surrender all her right of Dowry & power of thirds of in & unto the above demised premisses unto him ye s^d James Wiggins his heirs & Assignes./ In Witness whereof we have Each of us set our hands & seals Dated ye Sixteenth day of May in ye Third year of King George^{es} Reign in ye year of our Lord One Thousand Seven hundred & Seventeen

Signed Sealed & Delivered   George ⨯ Buckling (seal)
In ye presence of   his mark
Dependence Littlefield
Hannah Littlefield   Mary ⨯ Buckling (seal)
Ric^d Martin

May 20th 1717./ The within Named George Buckling & Mary his wife personally Appeared Before me John Wheelwright Esqr & Acknowledged ye within Mentioned to be their Act & Deed   John Wheelwright Just peace

Recorded According to ye Original July 4th 1717.

p Jos: Hammond Reg^r

To All People to whom these presents shall Come Greeting Know Y^e that I William Tucker of Kittery in ye County of York in her Maj^{tys} Province of ye Massachusets Bay in New England Shipwright for & in Consideration of ye sum of Thirteen pounds to me in hand before ye Ensealing hereof Well & Truely paid by John Walker of Kittery afores^d Shipwright ye rec^t whereof I do hereby Acknowledge & my

Selfe therewith fully & Contentedly Satisfied & thereof & Every part thereof do Exonerate Acquit & discharge ye s^d John Walker his heirs Ex^{rs} Adm^{rs} for ever by these presents have given granted bargained sold Aliened Conveyed & Confirmed & by these presents do freely fully & Absolutely give grant bargaine Sell Aliene Convey & Confirm [214] Unto him ye s^d John Walker his heirs & Assigns for ever one Acre of land Scittuate lying & being on Kittery point in the Township of Kittery on ye Eastern side of Spruce Creek & on ye Northern Side of George Berrys Two Acres of land which was by s^d Berry Purchased from Nathaniel Thomas of ye County of Plymouth in ye Massachusets Province Esqr which s^d Acre of Land is to Extend from ye bank Eight rod in Width from s^d Berryes line & Twenty rod in Length by a Northwest & by West Course Including ye land below ye bank to Low water Mark & to Extend One rod higher at ye head for ye highway At ye bank if any there be To Have & To Hold ye s^d granted & bargained premisses with all ye Appurtenances priviledges & Comoditityes to ye Same belonging or in any wise Appurtaining to him ye s^d John Walker his heirs & Assigns for ever to his & their own proper use bennefit & behoofe for ever & I ye s^d Wm Tucker for me my heirs Ex^{rs} Adm^{rs} do Covenant promiss & grant to & with ye s^d John Walker his heirs & Assigns that before ye Ensealing hereof I am ye True sole & Lawfull owner of ye Above bargained premisses and am Lawfully siezed & possessed of ye same in my own propper right as a good perfect & Absolute Estate of Inheritance in fee Simple & have in my selfe good right full power & Lawfull Authority to grant bargaine Sell Convey & Confirm s^d Bargained premisses in maner as aboves^d And that ye s^d John Walker his heirs & Assignes shall & may from time to time & At all times for ever hereafter by force & vertue of these presents Lawfully peaceably & Quietly have hold use Occupie possess & Enjoy ye s^d Demised & bargained premisses with ye Appurtenances free & Clear & frely & Clearly Acquitted Exonerated & Discharged of from all & all maner of former and other gifts grants bargains sales Leases Mortgages Wills Entails Joyntures Dowries Judgm^{ts} Executions Incumbrances & Extents

Furthermore I ye s^d Wm Tucker for my selfe my heirs Ex^{rs} Adm^{rs} do Covenant & Ingage ye above demised premisses to him ye s^d John Walker his heirs & Assignes against ye Lawfull Claims or demands of any person or persons whatsoever forever hereafter to Warrant Secure & Defend./ And Alice Tucker ye wife of me ye s^d Wm Tucker doth by these presents freely Willingly give Yield up & Surrender all her

right of Dowry & power of thirds of in & unto ye above demised premisses unto ye s^d John Walker his heirs & Assignes In Witness whereof I have hereunto Set my hand & seal this first day of June in y^e third year of y^e reign of our Soveraign Lord George of Great Brittaine ffrance & Ireland &c^t & in y^e year of our Lord One Thousand Seven hundred & seventeen./   William Tucker (${}_{\text{Seal}}^{\text{a}}$)
Signed Sealed & Delivered   her
  In y^e presence of   Alice $\mathcal{A}$ Tucker (${}_{\text{Seal}}^{\text{a}}$)
Wm Pepperrell Junr   mark
Eugene Lynch   The word [Shipwright] Interlined between y^e 3^d & 4th line before signing & sealing

    York sc June 1st day Anno Domini 1717
  This day Wm Tucker & Alice his wife both psonally Appeared before Me y^e Subscriber One of his Maj^tys Justices of y^e peace for s^d County & Acknowledged this within Instrum^t to be their free Act & Deed./   Wm Pepperrell
  Recorded According to ye Original June 22^d 1717./
                        p Jos Hamond Reg^r

  To All Christian People to whom these presents shall Come I Nicholas Tucker of Kittery in ye County of York in his Maj^tys Province of ye Massachusets Bay in New England Sendeth Greeting./ Know Y^e that I ye s^d Nicholas Tucker for & in Consideration of ye Natural love I have for & do bear unto my Welboleved Son William Tucker of ye same place Have given and granted & do by these presents freely clearly & Absolutely give grant & for ever Set over unto him ye s^d William Tucker & his heirs Ex^rs Adm^rs or Assignes forever Two third parts of my land whereon I Now live & possess Containing by Estimation thirty Acres of Land lying next to Mr Mores Land or on ye Northwest side of my Land Together with all ye Appurtenances & priviledges whatsoever belonging unto the s^d Land or Appurtaining thereunto of What Kind soever To have & To hold all ye aboves^d thirty Acres of land or Two third parts of my land be it more or Less together with all ye Appurtenances & priviledges thereunto belonging unto ye only & sole use bennefit & behoofe of him ye s^d Wm Tucker & his heirs Ex^rs Adm^rs or Assignes for ever more as his & their own propper Estate in fee simple without any Maner of Condition or Limitation whatsoever And that it shall be Lawfull for the s^d William Tucker his heirs Ex^rs Adm^rs or

Book VIII, Fol. 215.

Assignes as above^d to take use possess Occupie & Improve all ye aboves^d tract of Land from time to time & At All times hereafter without and Let hinderence or other Lawfull Mollestation from me ye s^d Nicholas Tucker or any other person by procurement the peaceable possession thereof forever hereafter to Warrant & Maintaine against all persons Laying a Lawfull claime thereunto In Witness whereof I have set to my hand & seale this Twenty fifth day of Decemb^r One Thousand Seven hundred & Sixteen./ 1716

Signed Sealed & Delivered   Nicholas Tucker ($^a_{Seal}$)
  In y^e p^{r}sence of us y^e Subscribers
  Ebenezer More
  George Frink
  Gowen Wilson
     York sc/

At an Inferio^r Court of Comon pleas holden at York April y^e 2^d 1717.

Ebenezer More & George ffrink psonally Appearing made Oath that they were present & Saw the within Named Nicholas Tucker sign seal & Deliver the within Instrum^t in writing as his Act & deed unto which they Set their hands as Witnesses   Att^r Jos. Hamond Clerk

Recorded According to ye Original April 3^d 1717.
                      p Jos: Hamond Reg^r

To All People to whom these presents shall Come Greeting Know Y^e that I Henry Barter of Kittery in ye County of York within his Maj^{tys} Province of ye Massachusets Bay in New England Yeoman for & in Consideration of ye Sum of Eighty Nine pounds Six shillings in good & Lawfull money of ye Province afores^d to me in hand before the Ensealing hereof Well & Truely paid One halfe by Ebenezer More of Kittery in ye County afores^d shipwright the other halfe paid by John Norton formerly of Hampton Now of Kittery Afores^d Joyner [215] The receipt whereof I do hereby Acknowledge & my Selfe therewith fully Satisfied & Contented & thereof & of Every part & parcell thereof do Exonerate acquit and discharge ye s^d Ebenezer More & John Norton their heirs Ex^{rs} Adm^{rs} for ever by these presents Have given granted bargained Sold Aliened Conveyed & Confirmed & by these presents do freely fully & Absolutely give grant bargaine Sell Aliene Convey & Confirm unto them ye s^d Ebenezer More & John Norton their heirs Ex^{rs} Adm^{rs} & Assignes for ever One Messuage or Tract of land and Meadow Scittuate

Book VIII, Fol. 215.

lying & being in Kittery in ye County afores^d Containing by Estimation Twenty Seven Acres three quarters of One Acre and Twenty Six pole be it more or Less butted & bounded by the land formerly Nicholas Tuckers by a North East line & Cap^{tn} Thomas with an North & by East line & a Creek of water which is all that tract of land and Meadow which I ye s^d Henry Barter Purchased of Thomas Hooper as will at large Appear p ye s^d Hoopers deed to s^d Barter with all Trees wood fences Water & Water Courses to it belonging or in ways Appurtaining To have & To hold ye aboves^d granted & bargained premisses with all ye Appurtenances priviledges & Comodityes to ye same belonging or in any ways Appurtaining to them ye s^d Ebenezer More and John Norton their heirs & Assigns for ever to his & their only propper use benefit & behalfe for ever/ And I ye s^d Henry Barter for me my heirs Ex^{rs} Adm^{rs} do Covena^t promis & Grant to & wth ye s^d Eben^r More & John Norton their heirs & Assignes that before ye Ensealing here of I am ye True Sole & Lawfull owner of ye above bargained premisses & am Lawfully Siezed & possessed of ye same in mine own propper right as a good perfect & Absolute Estate of Inheritance in fee Simple & have in my Selfe good right full power & Lawfull Authority to grant bargaine Sell Convey & Confirm s^d bargained premisses in maner as aboves^d & that ye s^d Eben^r More & John Norton their heirs & Assignes shall & may from time to time & at all times forever hereafter by force & vertue of these presents Lawfully peaceably & quietly have hold use Occupie possess & Enjoy ye s^d Demised & bargained premisses with ye Appurtenances free & Clear & freely & Clearly Acquitted Exonerated & discharged of from all & all maner of former & other gifts grants bargains sales or Incumbrances whatsoever Furthermore I ye s^d Henry Barter for my selfe my heirs Ex^{rs} Adm^{rs} do Covenant & Ingage ye Above demised premisses to them ye s^d Eben^r More & John Norton their heirs & Assignes agst ye Lawfull Claimes or demands of Any p^rson or persons whatsoever for ever hereafter to Warrant Secure & defend./ And Sarah Barter wife of me ye s^d Henry Barter doth by these presents freely Willingly give Yield up and Surrender all her right of Dowry & power of thirds of in & unto ye Above demised premisses unto them ye s^d Eben^r More & John Norton their heirs & Assignes./ In Witness whereof I have hereunto Set my hand & Seal this Twentyth day of ffeb^{ry} in the third year of ye reign of our Soveraign Lord George by ye grace of God King of

Book VIII, Fol. 215.

Great Brittaine ffrance & Ireland & In ye year of our Lord one Thousand Seven hundred & Sixteen Seventeen./

Signed Sealed & Delivered   Henry Barter (a Seal)
In ye presence of
Thomas Jenkins   Sarah } her Barter (a Seal)
Nathan^l Ingersoll   mark
Wm Pepperrell jun^r

York sc/ Apr^l 1st day Anno : 1717

This day Henry Barter & his wife Sarah Barter both psonally Appeared before me ye Subscrib^r One of his Maj^tys Justices of ye peace for s^d County & Acknowledged this w^thin Instrum^t to be his free Act & Deed./   Wm Pepperrell

Recorded According to ye Original Apr^l 2^d 1717./

p Jos. Hamond Reg^r

To All People to whom these presents shall Come Greeting Know Y^e that John Gowen of Kittery in ye County of York within his Maj^tys Province of ye Massachusets Bay in New England Marrin^r for & in Consideration of ye sum of One hundred & fifty pounds in money of ye Province afores^d to me in hand before the Ensealing hereof well & Truely paid by Thomas Weed of Amesbury in ye County of Essex in ye Province afores^d Weaver the rect whereof I do hereby Acknowledge & my selfe therewith fully Satisfied & Contented & thereof and of Every part thereof do Acquit & discharge ye s^d Thomas Weed his heirs Ex^rs & Adm^rs forever by these presents Have given granted bargained sold Aliened Conveyed & Confirmed & by these presents do freely fully & Absolutely give grant bargaine sell Aliene Convey & Confirm unto him ye s^d Thomas Weed his heirs & Assignes for ever one Messuage : or Tract of Land Scittuate lying & being in Kittery in ye County afores^d Containing by Estimation Twenty Acres be it more or less butted & bounded on ye North side by Nicholas Gowens Land & on ye East by the Country road as it is staked out & on ye South by David Sayer as formerly bounded to a Little Tree in a Gutter by Broughtons Swamp So Called & from s^d Tree to run Northwest by North to our first station which is a stake standing by s^d Gutter near a Stoney bridge & So to A Tree Marked & Stakes to ye Countrey road afores^d To have & To hold ye s^d granted premisses with all ye Appurtenances priviledges & Comodityes to ye same belonging or in any wayes Appurtaining to him ye s^d Thomas Weed his heirs & Assigns forever to his & their only proper use benefit & behalfe for ever

Book VIII, Fol. 216.

& I ye s^d John Gowen for me my heirs Ex^{rs} Adm^{rs} do Covena^t promiss & grant to & with ye s^d Thomas Weed his heirs & Assignes that before ye Ensealing hereof I am ye True Sole & Lawfull owner of ye Above bargained premisses & am Lawfully Siezed & possessed of ye Same in mine own proper right as a good perfect & Absolute Estate of Inheritance in fee Simple & have in my Selfe good right full power & Lawfull Authority to grant bargaine Sell Convey & Confirm s^d premisses in maner as afores^d & that ye s^d Thomas Weed his heirs & Assignes shall & may from time to time & At all Times for ever hereafter by force & vertue of these presents Lawfully peaceably & Quietly have hold use Occupy possess & Enjoy ye s^d Premisses with ye Appurtenances free & Clear & freely & Clearly Acquitted Exonerated & discharged of from all & all manner of former & other gifts grants bargains Sales leases Mortgages Wills Entails Joyntures Dowryes Judgm^{ts} Exections Incubrances & Extents./ Furthermore I ye s^d John Gowen for my selfe my heirs Ex^{rs} Adm^{rs} do Covena^t & Engage ye above demised premisses to him ye s^d Thomas Weed his heirs & Assignes Against ye Lawfull Claims or demands of any person or persons whatsoever for ever here after to Warrant Secure & Defend & Mercy Gowen ye wife of me ye s^d John Gowen doth by these presents freely willingly give Yield up and Surrender all her right of Dowry & power of thirds of in & unto ye Above demised premisses unto him ye s^d Thomas Weed his heirs & Assignes In Witness whereof I have hereunto Set my hand & seal ye fifteenth day of June in ye third of ye reign [216] Of Our Soveraign Lord George by the grace of God King of Great Brittaine ffrance & Ireland and in y^e year of our Lord One Thousand Seven hundred & Seventeen./ It is to be undersood that I reserve to my Selfe a burying place Two rods & halfe Square where my son George was buryed in y^e southeast Corner of s^d land./   John Gowen ($_{Seal}^a$)
Signed Sealed & Delivered   Mercy Gowen ($_{Seal}^a$)
   In y^e presence of
   Charles Frost.
   Daniel Emery
   Jane Frost.
      York sc June 15th 1717

John Gowen & Mercy Gowen above Named Acknowledged y^e Above written Instrum^t to be their free Act & Deed./   Before   Charles ffrost J peace
Recorded According to y^e Original July 1st 1717.
           p Jos. Hamond Reg^r

Book VIII, Fol. 216.

To All People to whom this present Deed of Sale or Instrum^t in writing Shall Come Nicholas Morrell of Kittery in ye County of York within his Maj^{tys} Province of ye Massachusetts Bay in New England Bricklayer Sends Greeting./ Know ye that I ye s^d Nicholas Morrell for & in Consideration of ye Sum of Eight pounds Curra^t money of New England to me in hand well & Truely paid by Adryan ffry of Kittery in the County & Province afores^d Glaser have given granted bargained Sold released Enfeoffed & Confirmed & by these presents for my Selfe my heirs Ex^{rs} & Adm^{rs} do freely Clearly & Absolutely give grant bargaine Sell release Assign Enfeoffe Convey & Confirm unto him ye s^d Adryan ffry his heirs & Assignes for ever One Acre of Land Scittuate Lying and being in Kittery afores^d At ye Southermost Corner of s^d Morrells field or that was his Now in ye possession of James Davis bounded on ye Southeast Side by ye Land of Samuel Hill to Extend from ye highway which Leads from Kittery Mill dam to Cold harbour NorthEast and by East in ye line dividing between s^d Morrell & Hills Land Twenty Six pole & Twelve foot & by ye s^d road or highway Twenty one pole & thence on a direct line to ye Extent afores^d Twenty Six poles & Twelve foot Lying in form of a Tryangle Also a Tract of land ye west Side of ye highway aforesd So down to ye river begining on ye South Side with a Tract of land I ye s^d Morrell Lately Sold to John Coal of Kittery Afores^d Containing three quarters of An Acre More or Less as p his deed und^r my hand referrence being thereunto had may more At Large Appeare being Seven poles & Ten foot by ye highway to Extend West Northwest three poles to ye river then west by South to Low water Mark which lines is to be ye bounds between ye Afores^d ffry & Coal./ thence to Extend by ye highway Northerly to ye North End of s^d ffryes now dwelling house by ye road afores^d Twenty five foot to run down to ye river on a West Course to ye river then halfe A point Northerly to Low water mark wch Tracts is part of that Land which ye s^d Morrell purchased of Richard Estis late of Kittery Afores^d Together with all ye priviledges And Appurtenances thereunto belonging whatsoever thereunto belonging of Water Courses may Appears upon or belonging thereunto ye above granted & bargained premisser or Any part or parcell thereof and ye reversion & reversions remainder & remainders rents Issues or any profits thereof & all ye Estate right Interest Inheritance use propperty possession Claime & Demand whatsoever of me ye s^d Nich^o Morrell my heirs Ex^{rs} Adm^{rs} & Assigns of in or to ye same Except as before Excepted To Have & To Hold ye s^d Several

Tracts of Land & Every part thereof & all & Singular ye premisses & Appurtenances herein before granted bargained & Sold unto him ye s^d Adryan ffry his heirs & Assignes to his & their own proper use benefit and behoofe for ever And I ye s^d Nicholas Morrell for my Selfe my heirs Ex^{rs} & Adm^{rs} do hereby Covenant grant & agree to & with ye s^d Adrian ffry his heirs & Assignes in Maner following (That is to say) that I ye s^d Nicholas Morrill At & until ye Ensealing & delivery of these presents am ye True & Lawfull owner of ye premisses herein before granted & Stand Lawfully Siezed thereof in my own proper right as a good perfect & Absolute Estate of Inheritance in fee Simple without any maner of Condition or Limitation of use or uses whatsoever so As to Alter change defeat or make Voyd ye same & have in my Selfe power good right & Lawfull Authority to grant Sell & Assure ye s^d land & premisses in Maner as afores^d & that ye same are free & clear & Clearly Acquitted & Discharged of & from all & all maner of former & other gifts grants bargains sales Leases Mortgages Wills Entails Judgm^{ts} Executions Titles Troubles Charges & Incumbrances whatsoever & I ye s^d Nicholas Morrell my heirs Ex^{rs} & Adm^{rs} to him ye s^d Adrian ffry his heirs & Assigns Shall & will Warrant & Defend ye same./ In Witness whereof I have hereunto Set my hand & Affixed my seal this Sixteenth day of Aprill in ye third year of ye reign of our Soveraign Lord Gorge by ye grace of God King of Great Brittaine ffrance & Irel^d & in ye year of our Lord One Thousand Seven hundred & Seventeen./   Nicholas Morrell (a seal)

Signed Sealed & Delivered
  In ye presence of us
  Samuel Smaley
  Elizabeth Smaley
  John Morrell
             York sc April 22^d 1717./

Nicholas Morrell above Named Acknowledged the within writen Instrum^t to be his free Act & Deed & Sarah the wife of ye s^d Nicholas Morrell Appeared & Quitted her right of Dower to ye pmisses within Named./
               Before Charles ffrost J. Peace
Recorded According to ye Original May 13th 1717./
                     p Jos. Hamond Reg^r

To All Christian People to whom this present deed of Sale shall Come Greeting./ Know Ye that I Adryan ffry of

Kittery in ye Province of ye Massachusets Bay in New England Glaser for & in Consideration of ye sum of fifty Eight pounds of Curra^t money of New England to me well & Truely paid by Michael Kenard of Portsmouth in ye Province of New Hampshire Cooper ye rect whereof I do [217] Hereby Acknowledge & my Selfe therewith fully Satisfied & Contented and thereof & of Every part & parcell thereof do Acquit & discharge ye s^d Michaell Kenard his heirs Ex^rs Adm^rs for ever by these presents do fully freely and Absolutely give grant bargaine Sell Aliene Convey & Confirm unto him ye s^d Michael Kenard his heirs & assignes for ever one Messuage or tract of Land Lying in Two parcell Scittuate lying & being in ye Town of Kittery afores^d with all ye buildings thereon as dwelling house Shop out houseing & fences which s^d parcells of Land I bought of Nicholas Morrell of Kittery & is bounded on Either side as is Set forth in a deed or Conveyance which I had of s^d Nicholas Morrell for s^d Land bareing Date ye Sixteenth day of April in ye year one thousand Seven hundred & Seventeen referrence being had thereunto To Have & To Hold ye aboves^d Granted & bargained premisses with all ye Appurtenances priviledges & Comodityes thereunto belonging or Appertaining to him ye s^d Michael Kenard his heirs Ex^rs Adm^rs & Assignes forever unto him ye s^d Michael Kenard & his heirs and Assignes to their proper use & behoofe forever./ And I ye s^d Adryan Fry do for my Selfe my heirs Ex^rs Adm^rs & Assignes do Covenant promiss & Ingage ye Above granted & bargained premisses Against all persons whatsoever Shall & Will Warrant And defend unto ye s^d Michael Kenard his heirs Ex^rs Adm^rs & Assignes for ever In Witness whereof I have hereunto Set my hand & Seal this thirteenth day of May in ye third year of ye reign of our Soveraign Lord George of Great Brittaine ffrance & Ireland King Defend^r of ye faith Annoq, Domini One Thousand Seven hundred & Seventeen
Signed Sealed & Delivered   Adryan Fry (seal)
In presence of
John Lydston
Jacob Remich
William Tetherly

York sc Kittery May 16, 1717

Adryan ffry Above Named Acknowledged ye Above written Instrum^t to be his free Act & Deed & Mercy ye wife of the above Named ffry Also Quitted her right of Dower to ye premisses./   Before Charles ffrost J. peace
Recorded According to ye Original May 16th 1717./
                    p Jos. Hamond Reg^r

Book VIII, Fol. 217.

This Indenture made ye third day of Augst Anno Domini One Thousand Six hundred Eighty Eight Annoq̧ Rⁱ R^s Jacobi Nunc Anglia &c^a Secundo Quarto./ Between Vines Ellacot of North Yarmouth in Casco Bay within ye Province of Maine in his Maj^{tys} Teritory & Dominion of New England Yeoman & rebecca his wife on ye one part & William Stoughton of Dorchester in ye County of Suffolk within ye Territory afores^d Esqr of ye other part. Witnesseth that ye s^d Vines Ellacot & Rebecca his wife for & in Consideration of ye Sum̃ of Two hundred & Sixty pounds in Currant money of New England to them in hand at & before the Ensealing & Delivery of these presents Well & Truely paid by ye s^d William Stoughton the receipt whereof they do Acknowledge & of & from ye Same & Every part & parcell thereof do fully Acquit exonerate & discharge ye s^d William Stoughton his heirs Ex^{rs} Adm^{rs} & Assignes for ever by these presents have given granted bargained Sold Enfeoffed & Confirmed & by these pnt^s do give grant bargaine Sell Enfeoffe & Confirm unto ye s^d William Stoughton his heirs Ex^{rs} Adm^{rs} & Assignes for ever to ye use hereafter named All that their Island Comonly Called & known by ye Name of Hogg Island formerly Cousens Island Lying Scittuate in Casco Bay & within the Township of North Yarmouth afores^d As it is Invironed & Compassed about with ye Sea or Salt water all ye upland & Meadow ground upon the s^d Hogg Island Containing thirteen hundred forty Six acres Little more or Less Together with all houses Edefices Buildings Barns Stables out houseing wood trees Timber fences Stones rights Members hereditaments feedings fishing fouling hunting profits priviledges and Appurtenances whatsoever thereunto belonging or in Any wise Appurtaining with Eighteen head of Neat Cattle Thirty Swine Ploughs Sled utencills & Implements of husbandry & Improvem^{ts} whatsoever upon ye s^d Island./ Also All ye Estate right Title Dower Interest use property possession Claime & demand whatsoever of ye s^d Vines Ellacott & Rebecca his wife & of Either of them of in & unto ye same & ye Revertion & Revertions Remainder & remainders thereof with all Deeds grants pattents writings Evidences Escripts & miniments relating thereunto to be delivered up fair & uncancelled To have & to hold ye s^d Island Com̃only called & known by ye Name of hogg Island formerly Cousens Island all ye Land as well upland as Meadow ground Containing thirteen hundred forty Six acres little more or less houses Edefices buildings fences Stones wood timber Stock Improvements rights members heriditaments profits priviledges Memb^{rs} Accomodations & Appurtenances thereunto belonging & all other ye premisses with ye revertion & revertions remainder & remainders thereof unto ye s^d William Stoughton his heirs Ex^{rs} Adm^{rs} & assignes for ever to ye only proper use benefit & behoofe of the Honourable ye Governo^r & Company of ye Corporation in London for ye propagation of ye Gospel to ye Indians in New England & other places Adjacent in America & the Assignes for ever./ And ye s^d Vines Elacott for himselfe & Rebecca his wife his heirs Ex^{rs} & Adm^{rs} doth Covenant promiss grant & agree to & with ye s^d William Stoughton his heirs Ex^{rs} Adm^{rs} & Assignes in maner following that is to Say that at ye Time of this bargaine & Sale & untill ye Ensealing & Executing of these prs^s he s^d Vines Ellacott is ye true Sole & Lawfull owner and Stands Lawfully Seised in his own proper right of all ye above granted Island Lands & other ye premisses in a good Sure perfect & firm Estate in fee & hath in himselfe full power good right & Lawfull Authority to grant bargaine Sell & Confirm ye same unto ye s^d William Stoughton his heirs Ex^{rs} Adm^{rs} & Assignes in maner as afores^d & that ye s^d William Stoughton his heirs Ex^{rs} Adm^{rs} and Assignes by force & vertue of these prs^{ts} shall & may from Time to time & at all times for ever Lawfully peaceably and Quietly & peaceably have hold use Occupie possess & Enjoy all ye afore mentioned to be granted & bargained premisses wth ye rights member profits & Appurtenances thereof to ye use [218] Afore expres^t free & Clear & Clearly Acquitted Exonerated & discharged of & from all & all maner of former & other gifts grants bargaines Sales Leases Mortgages Joyntures dowers Judgments Extents Executions Titles Troubles claims Incumbrances rents charges & demands whatsoever Yielding & paying only unto our Soveraign Lord ye King his heirs & Successors for ever ye Sum of Ten Shillings in Currant money of New England p annum on ye five & Twentyeth day of March Yearly to be paid at ye fort in Boston According to ye Direction of his Majestyes patent granted of ye premisses unto ye s^d Vines Ellacott./ And the s^d Vines Ellacott for himselfe his heirs Ex^{rs} & Adm^{rs} doth further Covena^t promiss grant & Agree to & with ye before named named William Stoughton his heirs Ex^{rs} Adm^{rs} & Assignes at all time & times for ever to warrant & defend all ye within bargained & granted premisses with their Appur^{ces} unto him ye s^d William Stoughton his heirs Ex^{rs} Adm^{rs} & Assignes to ye use above Express^t Against ye Lawfull Claims & demands of all & Every person & persons whomsoever and at & upon ye Lawfull & reasonable request or demand of ye s^d William Stoughton his heirs Ex^{rs} Adm^{rs} or Assignes to do

Book VIII, Fol. 218.

Execute & perform any other & further Lawfull & reasonable Act & Acts device and devices in ye Law for ye better Confirmation & more Sure making of ye s^d bargained premisses unto ye s^d Wm Stoughton his heirs Ex^{rs} Adm^{rs} & Assignes for ever According to y^e True Intent & meaning of these presents as by his or their Councill Learned in y^e Law Shall be devised Advised or required./ In Witness whereof y^e s^d Vines Ellacott & Rebecca his wife have hereunto put their hands & Seals the day & year first above written./   Vines Ellacott ($_{Seal}^a$)
Signed Sealed & D^d by Vines Ellacott
 In presence of
 Samuel Maxfield
 John Trescott
    his
 W^m /M\ Royal
   mark

Suffolk sc Anno R^{i}R^s Georgii Tertio At an Inferio^r Court of Comon pleas begun & held at Boston for & within y^e County of Suffolk on y^e first Tuseday of July being y^e Second day of y^e s^d Month Annoq$_{,}$ Domini 1717

John Trescott & Wm Royal Two of y^e Witnesses to the within written Instrument psonally Appearing Made Oath that they Saw y^e within Named Vines Ellacott Sign Seal & Deliver y^e within written Instrum^t as his Act & Deed unto which they y^e Deponants Set to their Names As Witnesses of y^e Execution thereof At y^e same time./
     Attest^r John Ballantine Clerk
Recorded Accorded to y^e Original July 6th 1717./

         p Jos. Hamond Reg^r

This Indenture made y^e third day of August Anno Dm one Thousand Six hundred Eighty & Eight Annoq$_{,}$ RR^s Jabobi Nunc Anglia &c^a Secundi Quarto Between William Stoughton of Dorchester in y^e County of Suffolk within his Majestyes Territory & Dominion of New England Esqr on y^e one part & Vines Ellacott of North Yarmouth in y^e Province Of Maine within y^e Territory afores^d Yeoman of y^e other part Witnesseth that ye s^d William Stoughton for & under ye Annual rents payments & Covenants hereafter in these presents Expressed & reserved hath Demised Set & to farm Letten & by these presents doth demise Set & to farm Let unto ye s^d Vines Ellacott his Ex^{rs} Adm^{rs} & Assignes who hath Accordingly hired of him s^d Wm Stoughton all that his

Book VIII, Fol. 218.

Island Comonly Called & known by y[e] Name of hogg Island formerly Cousens[s] Island Lying Scittuate in Casco Bay within y[e] Township of North Yarmouth afores[d] All y[e] Lands as well upland as Meadow Containing Thirteen hundred & forty Six Acres Little more or Less houses Edifices buildings Improvem[ts] Stock Utensells & Implem[ts] of husbandry thereupon rights members profits priviledges and Appur[ces] thereto belonging for & Dureing y[e] Space or Tern of Two full years from y[e] day of the date hereof thence next Ensueing which s[d] Demised premisses were sold & Conveyed unto the s[d] William Stoughton by him y[e] s[d] Vines Ellacott by deed Indented bareing date Even with these prst[s] unto y[e] use therein Exprest he s[d] Vines Ellacott his Ex[rs] Adm[rs] or Assignes Yielding & paying therefore unto y[e] s[d] W[m] Stoughton his heirs Ex[rs] Adm[rs] or Assignes at or in y[e] Now dwelling house of s[d] W[m] Stoughton Scittuate in Dorchester aboves[d] unto y[e] use of the Honourable y[e] Governour & Company of y[e] Corporation in London for y[e] propagation of the Gospel to y[e] Indians in New England & other places Adjacent in America or their Assigns y[e] full & Just Sum of Twenty pounds & Sixteen shillings p Annum of & in y[e] present Currant money of New England Coyne or in good Sivill Pillar & Maxeco pieces of Eight At y[e] rate of Six shillings p piece Each peice of Eight to weigh full Seventeen peney weight upon y[e] third day of August Yearly & in Every Year of s[d] term Also well & Truely paying unto our Soveraign Lord y[e] King his heirs & Successors the sum of Ten shillings in Curra[t] money of New England p Annum upon Each five & Twentyeth day of March to be paid at y[e] Fort in Boston According to y[e] direction of his Maj[tys] patent Granted of y[e] s[d] Demised premisses./ And if it hapen to be a default or failure in paym[t] of y[e] s[d] rents or Sums of Money or Either of them in whole or in part After y[e] Expiration of y[e] respective dayes afore Limited wherein the same Ought to be paid or Either of them that then & from henceforth it shall & may be Lawfull & free to & for y[e] s[d] W[m] Stoughton his heirs Ex[rs] Adm[rs] & Assignes into & upon all y[e] Afore Demised premisses to Enter and Quiet & peaceable possession & Seisen thereof to take have & keep for ever & from & out thence utterly to Amove Expell & Eject him s[d] Vines Ellacott his Ex[rs] Adm[rs] or assignes Any thing afore written Notwithstanding & y[e] s[d] Vines Ellacott for himselfe his heirs Ex[rs] Adm[rs] & Assignes doth Covena[t] promiss grant & agree at y[e] full Expiration or other determination of this present demise peaceably & Quietly to Yield Surrender & deliver up unto y[e] s[d] W[m] Stoughton his heirs Ex[rs] Adm[rs] or Assignes

all ye within demised Island Comonly Called hogg Island Lands & other ye premisses with ye houses buildings & fences thereupon in [**219**] Good Tenantable Condition & repair./ And he s^d Wm Stoughton for him Selfe his heirs Ex^rs Adm^rs & Assignes doth hereby Covenant promiss grant & agree to & with ye s^d Vines Ellacott his heirs Ex^rs Adm^rs & Assignes that in Case ye s^d Vines Ellacott his heirs Ex^rs Adm^rs or Assignes Shall & do well and truely pay ye s^d Yearly rents in maner & time as is afore Exprest and Likewise at or before ye full Expiration of ye Term of this demise and do well & truely pay or Cause to be paid unto ye s^d Wm Stoughton his heirs Ex^rs Adm^rs or Assignes at or in his now Dwelling house Scittuate in Dorchester to ye use above Mentioned over & above ye s^d Annual rent ye full & Just Sum of Two hundred & Sixty pounds principal in ye present Curra^t money of New England Coine or in pieces of Eight of ye Quallity rate & weight aboves^d then & in Such Case ye s^d Wm Soughton his heirs Ex^rs Adm^rs or Assignes upon rec^t of all ye s^d paym^ts shall & will at ye Cost & Charges in ye Law of ye s^d Vines Ellicott his heirs Ex^rs Adm^rs or Assignes release and forever Quit claime unto ye s^d Vines Ellacott his heirs & Assignes forever all Estate right title use Interest property Trust Claime & whatsoever of him ye s^d Wm Soughton his heirs Ex^rs Adm^rs or Assignes of in & unto all ye within mentioned to be demised premisses & Every part & parcell thereof & also deliver up unto him or them all deeds Instrum^ts & writings in ye hands or Custody of ye s^d Wm Soughton his heirs Ex^rs Adm^rs or Assignes relating thereunto./ In Witness whereof ye s^d partys to these prst^s have Interchangeably Set their hand & Seals ye day & year first within written./
Signed Sealed & Delivered   Vines Ellacott (a Seal)
  In presence of

William W Ryall (his mark)
John Trescott
Samuel Maxfield
  Suffolk sc/ Anno RR^s Georgii Tertio
At an Inferio^r Court of Comons pleas begun & held at Boston for & within ye County of Suffolk on ye first Tuesday of July being the Second day of ye s^d Month Annoq, Dom 1717 William Royall & John Trescott two of ye witnesses to ye Afore written Instrum^t personally Appearing made Oath that they Saw ye Afore named Vines Ellacott Sign Seal & Deliver ye Same as his Act & Deed unto which

BOOK VIII, FOL. 219.

they ye Deponants Subscribed their Names as Witnesses of ye Execution thereof. At ye Same time.
      Attest^r John Ballantine Clerk
Recorded According to ye Original July: 6th 1717./
        p Jos. Hamond Reg^r

 To All People to whom these presents Shall Come Know Y^e that I Wm Pepperrell Junr of Kittery in ye County of york Mercha^t do by these presents give grant Bargaine & Sell all my right & Title which I have or ought to have to ye within mentioned Tract of land to him ye s^d Thomas Huff his heirs & Assignes for ever & that I Will by these presents Warra^t & Defend ye s^d Land from any person or persons laying any Claime thereunto from by or und^r me or any of my heirs Ex^{rs} Adm^{rs} In Witness whereof I have hereunto Set my hand And Seal this Twenty Sixth day of March Anno Dom^i 1717
   Henry Barter   Wm Pepperrell Junr (a Seal)
Witness Eben More
   Jos C Crocket
    mark
 York sc./ March 26th day 1717. This day William Pepperrell Junr psonally Appeared before me the Subscriber one of his Maj^{tys} Justices of ye peace for s^d County & Acknowledged this above Instrum^t to be his free Act & Deed./
        Wm Pepperrell
Recorded According to ye Original April 2^d 1717
       p Jos. Hamond Reg^r
 Memorandum this above Instrument was Indorsed on ye Back side of a Deed of Sale from Thomas Huff to Wm Pepperrell above Named bareing date ye 10th day of March 1714/15 which Instrum^t or deed is recorded in this Book folio. 81./   Att^r Jos. Hamond Reg^r

 To All People to whom these presents Shal Come Greeting Know Y^e that I Thomas Huff of Capeporpoise in ye County of York within his Maj^{tys} Province of ye Massachusetts Bay in New England housecarpenter for & in Consideration of ye Sum of Sixty five pounds Curra^t money of Afores^d to me in hand before ye Ensealing hereof well & Truely paid by Henry Barter of Kittery in ye County afores^d Yeoman ye rec^t whereof I do hereby Acknowledge & my Selfe therewith fully Satisfied & Contented & thereof & of Every part & parcell thereof do Exonerate Acquit & discharge ye s^d Henry Barter his heirs Ex^rs Adm^rs for ever by these presents Have given granted Sold Aliened Conveyed & Confirmed & by these presents do freely fully & Absolutely give grant Bargaine Sell Alliene Convey & Confirm unto him ye s^d Henry Barter his heirs and Assignes one Messuage or Tract of upland & Meadow Scituate Lying & being in Kittery in ye County afores^d Containing by Estimation Eighteen Acres & one halfe of an Acre be it more or Less which is ye Land where I formerly dwelt & lyes between Henry Barters & Joseph Crockets dec^d formerly their dwelling houses which is all that tract of Land which was given me ye s^d Thomas Huff by my father in Law Aaron Ferriss formerly of Kittery now dec^d Except one acre & one halfe of an acre which I have already given to m^r Ebenezer Emons & his heirs for ever as will more at large Appear p a deed of gift from s^d Aaron Ferris to me ye s^d Thomas Huff Together with all ye houses barns Orchards Timber Trees wood water & water Courses whatsoever To Have & To hold ye s^d granted & bargained premisses with all ye Appur^ces priviledges & Comoditys to ye same belonging or in Any wayes Appurtaining to him ye s^d Henry Barter his heirs & Assignes for ever to his & their only proper use benefit & behalfe for ever & I ye s^d Thomas Huff for me my heirs Ex^rs Adm^rs do Covena^t promiss & grant to & with ye s^d Henry Barter his heirs & Assignes that before ye Ensealing hereof I am ye True Sole & Lawfull owner of ye above bargained Premisses & am Lawfully Siez^d & posses^d of ye same in mine own propper right as a good perfect & Absolute Estate of Inheritance in fee Simple & have in my Selfe good right full power & Lawfull Authority to grant bargaine Sell Convey & Confirm s^d bargained premisses in Manner as aboves^d & that ye s^d Henry Barter his heirs & Assignes shall & may from Time to Time & at all Times for ever here after by force & vertue of these presents Lawfully [**220**] Peaceably & Quietly have hold use Occupie possess & Enjoy ye s^d Demised and bargained premisses with ye Appurtenances free & Clear & freely & Clearly Acquitted Exonerated & Discharged of from all & all maner of former & other gifts grants bargaines Sales Mortgages Wills Entails Joyntures Dowryes Judgm^ts Executions Incumbrances & Extents./ Furthermore I ye s^d Thomas Huff for my Selfe my heirs Ex^rs Adm^rs do Covenant & Ingage ye above demised premisses to him ye s^d Henry Barter his heirs & Assignes Against ye Lawfull Claimes or demands of Any person or persons whatsoever for ever hereafter to Warrant Secure and Defend./ And Sarah Huff wife of me yᵉ sᵈ Thomas Huff doth by these pʳsents freely willingly give Yield up & Surrender all her right of Dowry & power of thirds of in & unto yᵉ Aboves demised premisses unto him yᵉ sᵈ Henry Barter his heirs & Assignes./ In Witness whereof I have hereunto Set my hand & Seal the Twenty Seventh day of March in yᵉ third year of yᵉ Reign of our Soveraign King George by yᵉ grace of God King of Great Brittaine france & Ireland Anno Domini One Thousand Seven hundred & Seventeen

Signed Sealed & Delivered   Thomas Huffe (ₛₑₐₗ ᵃ)
  In yᵉ presence of   ——— (ₛₑₐₗ ᵃ)
  Eben : More
  Jos C Crocket
     mark
  Wᵐ Pepperrell Junʳ

    York sc/ March 27ᵗʰ 1717./

This day Thomas Huff psonally Appeared before me yᵉ Subscriber one of his Majᵗʸˢ Justices of yᵉ peace for sᵈ County & Acknowledged this above writen deed or Obligation to be his free Act & Deed   Wᵐ Pepperrell Js Peace

  Recorded According to yᵉ Original April 2ᵈ 1717./
                          p Jos. Hamond Regʳ

Know All men by these presents that I Fluellin Sometimes resideing at Saco Indian for & in Consideration of Satisfaction./ have & by these presents do sell all my land from Saco Pattent bounds Southward beyond Capeporpus river for breadth & from yᵉ head of Wells & Capeporpus Township heds up into the Countrey to his furthest Extent with all yᵉ Appurtenances & priviledges whatever Excepting four miles Square Sold to bush Sanders & Turbat to Lieut Wᵐ Phillips of Boston in yᵉ County of Suffolk his heirs & Assignes forever To have & To hold & peaceably to Enjoy from any other Indians as Witness my hand this thirtieth day of March in yᵉ year of Our Lord. 1661./

Subscribed & Delivered wᵗʰ the   his
  words Appurtenances yʳ of   Fluellin V mark
  In yᵉ presence of us
    Richard R·F Foxell
        his mark
    Har: Symonds
    John Alden

Book VIII, Fol. 220.

Fluellins Extent above mentioned was Intended to Captⁿ Sundayes rocks As is Inserted in Rogomocks deed written by me   John Alden
   Recorded According to ye Original July 31st 1717./
                                  p Jos Hamond Reg^r

   Know All men by these presents that I Hombinowitt Alias John Rogomock Indian of Saco in ye County of Yorkshire for and in Consideration of Satisfaction Already rec^d in hand have & by these presents do Absolutely give grant Assign & Sell & Confirm unto Lieu^t William Phillips of Boston in ye County of Suffolk in New England that all my right Title Interest & Claime of & to all my lands lying on ye west side of Saco river from ye Salmonfalls to Cap^{tn} Sundays rocks & So upward in ye Countrey to his furthest Extent with all ye Liberty priviledges & Appurten^{ces} thereto in any wise belonging or Appurtaining to him y^e s^d Lieu^t Wm Phillips his heirs & Assignes and to his & their use forever As Witness my hand and Seal this Nine & Twentyeth day of August 1660./

Signed Sealed & Delivered In y^e presence of us   The mark of   Hombinowitt
Ezbon Sanford   Alias m^r John Rogomock
The mark of   ($^a_{Seal}$)
W^m /M\ Cannon
John Alden

   Memorandum that y^e within Specified was Taken possession of by Lieu^t John pich of Newbery in New England from the within Mentioned Rogomock in the presence of Arcules Woodman & Ju^o Presse both of Turfe & Twigg y^e Seventh of Sep^t in y^e year 1660 for y^e use of Lieu^t Wm Phillips
   Recorded According to ye Original July 31st 1717./
                                  p Jos. Hamond Reg^r

   To All People unto whom these presents Shall Come Thomas Goodwill of Boston in ye County of Suffolk in ye Province of the Massachusets Bay in New England Shipwright Sendeth Greeting./ Know Ye that I ye s^d Thomas Goodwin with ye Assent & Consent of Rebeca my wife for

& in Consideration of y[e] Sum of Two hundred & Thirty pounds in good bills of Credit of y[e] Province of y[e] Massachusets Bay afores[d] to me in hand well & Truely paid at & before y[e] delivery hereof by William Pepperrell Jun[r] of Kittery in y[e] County of York Mercha[t] the rec[t] whereof I Acknowledge Have given granted bargained & Sold & by these presents do give grant bargaine & Sell Convey & Confirm unto y[e] s[d] W[m] Pepperrell Jun[r] his heirs & Assignes forever all my right Estate Title Inheritance Interest propriety Claime & demand whatsoever of in & to One full third part & all my remaining right of a Certaine Tract or parcell of Land Scituate & lying & being in Saco within y[e] late province of Maine now Known by y[e] County of York in New England afores[d] which s[d] Tract of Land Benj[a] Blackman formerly bought of John Bonighton and James Gibbons butted & bounded as by their Respective deeds dated y[e] Twelfth day of Decemb[r] in y[e] year of our Lord One Thousand Six hundred & Eighty three that of John Bonighton being on y[e] East side of Saco river bounded by a Small brook Northward which parts his Pattent division from y[e] Division of James Gibbons./ Westward with y[e] s[d] river Eastward with Two miles distant from y[e] river Southward with a Small brook to y[e] Northward of Nicholas his house./ And that of Gibbons a Tract of Land Lying & being upon [**221**] The s[d] river of Saco begining at a Smal run on y[e] North of M[r] Bonightons old plantation Extending its Selfe up y[e] s[d] river three miles & a halfe & Eighteen poles & back from y[e] river Two miles being y[e] whole Second Division of Pattent land laid out to him by s[d] James as by s[d] Deeds are Specified as also all my right Title & Interest being one third part of & in y[e] herbage Commonage for timber & all other things Standing Lying & growing upon s[d] land Together with all & Singular y[e] profits & priviledges Edifices buildings fences waters water courses ponns mines Mineralls Imolluments & Appurtenances whatsoever to y[e] s[d] granted premisses belonging & Appurtaining & y[e] reversōn & reversōns remaind[r] and remainders thereof To have & To hold One full third part & my remaining right of & to & in y[e] s[d] tract or parcell of Land butted & bounded as afores[d] & all other y[e] therein before given & granted premisses with y[e] Members and Appurtenances thereof unto him y[e] s[d] W[m] Pepperrell his heirs And Assignes for ever./ And I y[e] s[d] Thomas Goodwill for my Selfe my heirs Ex[rs] & Adm[rs] do Covena[t] promiss grant & Agree to & with y[e] s[d] W[m] Pepperrell his heirs & Assignes by these presents in Maner following that is to Say that at & untill y[e] Delivery hereof I am y[e] True sole & Lawfull

owner of all yᵉ Above & before given & granted Land & premisses & Stand Siezed there of in fee haveing in my Selfe full power to give grant Sell & Dispose of yᵉ same in Manner as aforesᵈ yᵉ sᵈ granted premisses Now being free & Clear of & from all former & other gifts grants bargaines Sales Titles troubles Joyntures or power of thirds of my present wife Mortgages Incumbrances Wills Judgmᵗˢ Executions Extents Claimes & demands whatsoever. And further I yᵉ sᵈ Thomas Goodwill do Covenant & grant for my Selfe & my heirs Exʳˢ & Admʳˢ to Warratᵗ & Defend yᵉ sᵈ given granted & bargained land & premisses with yᵉ Appurtenances & Every part thereof unto him yᵉ sᵈ Wᵐ Pepperrell his heirs & Assignes for ever agˢᵗ yᵉ Lawfull Claimes & Demands of All & Every other person & pʳsons Claiming from by or under me or from by or under yᵉ before Named Benjamin Blackman./ In Witness whereof I yᵉ sᵈ Thomas Goodwill & Rebecca my wife have hereunto Set our hands and Seals this Eighteenth day of May Anno Domini one Thousand Seven hundred & Seventeen Annoq̇ RRˢ Georgii Tertio./
Signed Sealed & Delivered   Thomas Goodwill (ˢᵉᵃˡ)
  In pʳsence of us   Rebecca Goodwill (ˢᵉᵃˡ)
John Adames
Ebenezer Kimbal

Recievᵈ yᵉ day & Year above written of Wᵐ Pepperrell Junʳ yᵉ Sum of Two hundred & thirty pounds in full for yᵉ afore granted premisses./   Thomas Goodwill

Suffolk sc Boston May yᵉ 18ᵗʰ 1717. The above Named Thomas and Rebecca Goodwill Acknowledged yᵉ afore going Instrumᵗ to be their Act & Deed
            Before me   Samˡ Checkley Justˢ of peace
Recorded According to yᵉ Original June yᵉ 8ᵗʰ 1717.
               p Jos. Hamond Regʳ

Know All men by these presents that I Capᵗⁿ Sunday Alias Meeksombe Indian of Newichewanack & Sometimes of Saco river for diverse good Causes & Considerations Already to me in hand well & Truly paid by Majʳ Wᵐ Phillips of Saco for which I do Acknowledge my selfe fully Satisfied Contented & paid have given granted bargained & sold Aliened Enfeoffed & Confirmed & do by these presents give grant bargaine Sell Aliene Enfeoffe & Confirm unto Majʳ Wᵐ Phillips three hills of Rocks with woods Meadow and all Appurtenances thereunto belonging Lying & being Scittuate above Saco falls about thirty five or forty Miles more or Less up into the Country To have & To hold his heirs Ex^{rs} Adm^{rs} or Assigns for ever freely & Clearly Acquitted Exonerated & discharged from all maner of Deeds sales Conveyances Mortgages Ingagem^{ts} or Incumbrances whatsoever Also I ye s^d Cap^{tn} Sunday do by these presents for me my heirs Ex^{rs} Adm^{rs} & Assignes do Warrant to Defend & Save & keep harmless ye s^d Maj^r Wm Phillips his heirs Ex^{rs} Adm^{rs} or assignes from all maner of persons that shall Lay any Claime or pretend to Claime any right Title or Interest unto ye s^d rocks hills land Meadow. woods or ye Appurtenances thereunto belonging of ye performence of ye premisses I have Subscribed hereunto my hand & Affixed my Seal this Twentieth & Second day of June in ye year of our Lord One Thousand Six hundred Sixty & four

Signed Sealed & Delivered In ye pressence of us Meeksombe Als Cap^{tn} Sunday
Nathl Phillips
John Spencer his mark
Denis ? Dryland
his mark
Sarah Harmon

Recorded According to ye Original July 31st 1717/
p Jos. Hamond Reg^r

To All People to whom these presents Shall Come Greeting &c^a Know ye that I Obadiah Read of Boston in ye County of Suffolk within her Maj^{tys} Province of New England for & in Consideration of ye Sum of Ten pounds money to me in hand at or before ye Ensealing hereof & forty pounds to be paid me within four years after ye Ensealing of this deed which paym^t well & Truely to be paid by James Boston of Wells ye rec^t whereof I do hereby Acknowledge & my Selfe therewith fully Satisfied & Contented and thereof & of Every part & parcell thereof do Exonerate Acquitt & discharge ye s^d James Boston his heirs Ex^{rs} Adm^{rs} for ever by these presents do freely fully & Absolutely give grant bargaine Sell Aliene Convey & Confirm unto him ye s^d James Boston his heirs & Assignes for ever one Messuage or tract of land Scittuate lying & being in wells in ye County of York Containing by Estimation Fou hundred & fifty acres of upland

& Swamp with wood & Timber be it more or Less Buted & bounded buting on ye highway being Ninety poles [**222**] in Breadth & So runing into ye woods till ye same be Compleated have Robert Hilton on One Side & Jos^h Storer on ye other To have & To hold ye s^d granted & bargained premisses with all ye Appurtenances priviledges & Comodityes to ye same belonging or in any wise Appurtaining to him ye s^d James Boston his heirs & Assigns for ever to his & their only propper use bennefit & behoofe for ever & I ye s^d Obadiah Read for me my heirs Ex^{rs} Adm^{rs} do Covena^t promiss & grant to & with ye s^d James Boston his heirs & Assignes that afore ye Ensealing hereof I am ye True Sole & Lawfull owner of the above bargained premisses & am Lawfully Siez^d & possessed of ye Same in my own proper right as a good perfect & Absolute Estate of Inheritance in fee Simple & have in my Selfe good right full power & Lawfull Authority to grant bargaine Sell Convey & Confirm s^d bargained premisses in Manner as above s^d & that ye s^d James Boston his heirs & Assignes Shall & may from time to Time and at all Times for ever hereafter by force & vertue of these p.n^{ts} Lawfully peaceably & Quietly have hold use Occupy possess & Enjoy ye s^d Demised & bargained premisses with ye Appurtenances free & Clear & freely & Clearly Acquitted Exonerated & discharged of from all and All Manner of former & other gifts grants & bargaines Sales Leases Mortgages Wills Entailes Joyntures Dowryes Judgm^{ts} Executions Incumbrances & Extents./ Furthermore I ye s^d Obadiah Read for my Selfe my heirs Ex^{rs} Adm^{rs} do Covenant & Ingage ye above demised premisses to him ye s^d James Boston his heirs & Assignes against ye Lawfull Claims or demands of Any person or persons whatsoever hereafter to Warrant Secure & Defend So far as my deeds hath Need./ Elizabeth ye wife of me ye s^d Obadiah Read doth by these presents freely Willingly give Yield up & Surrender all her right of Dowry & power of thirds of in & unto ye above demised premisses unto ye s^d James Boston his heirs & Assignes. In Witness whereof we have Set our hands & Seals this Twenty fourth day of May One Thousand Seven hundred & Ten

As Witness These   Obadiah Read (a Seal)
  James Emmes   Elizabeth Read (a Seal)
  John Goffe Senr
  Ezra : Whitmarsh

Book VIII, Fol. 222.

Suffolk sc/ Boston May y[e] 24[th] 1710 —
Obadiah Read & Eliz[a] his wife p[r]sonally Appeared and Acknowledged this Instrum[t] to be their Volluntary Act & Deed   Before me   John Clark Jus[t] peace
Recorded According to y[e] Original July 3[d] 1717./
p Jos: Hamond Reg[r]

To All Christian People to whom this deed of Sale Shall Come Abra[m] Morrell of y[e] Town of Kittery in y[e] County of York within his Maj[tys] Province of y[e] Massachusets Bay in New England Blacksmith Sendeth Greeting Now Know Ye that I y[e] Aforenamed Abraham Morrell together with y[e] free Consent of Phebe my present wife for divers Causes & good Considerations me thereunto moveing & more Especially for & in Consideration of the Sum of Ninety Six pounds in Cura[t] money of New England to me in hand paid before y[e] Ensealing & Delivery of these presents by Nicholas Harford of y[e] Town of Dover in y[e] Province of New Hampshire in New England afores[d] shopkeeper the rec[t] thereof I do Acknowledge & my Selfe therewith to be fully Satisfied Contented & paid & of Every part parcell & peney thereof I do Exonerate Acquit & forever discharge y[e] afores[d] Nicholas Harford him his heirs Ex[rs] Adm[rs] & by these presents have freely fully Clearly & Absolutely given granted bargained & Sold & by these presents do freely Clearly & Absolutely give grant bargaine Sell Enfeoffe Aliene Assigne Assure Set over Convey & Confirm unto y[e] afores[d] Nicholas Harford & his heirs Ex[rs] Adm[rs] & Assignes for ever Two Certaine Lotts or parcells of Land Scituate lying & being in Kittery town afores[d] Containing Twenty Seven Acres & halfe of land bounded as followeth y[e] first lot Containing five acres Adjoyning to y[e] afores[d] Abra[m] Morrells Land on y[e] North & on y[e] East by y[e] highway & on y[e] South by Samuel Hills land & on y[e] west by Dover river being Sixty four poles in Length East from y[e] river to y[e] highway & in breadth from afores[d] Abra[m] Morrells land South till five Acres be fully Acomplished y[e] Second Lot Containing Twenty Two Acres & halfe bounded as followeth begining at y[e] East end of Sam[l] Hills home lot fifteen poles in breadth North & South from thence it runs Eighty Two poles East y[e] same breadth

Book VIII, Fol. 223.

[sidenote: The Land Contained in this Deed is Assigned & Made over to Nath^{ll} Chapman by Nicholas Harford & is recorded in Lib^r 9 Folio 54 Attest^t Jos. Hamond Reg^r]

by John Morrells Land & then it Extends North in breadth thirty three poles more to a highway of three poles wide between ye s^d Land & W^m ffryes land then East by ye afores^d highway unto the highway that Leads to Kittery road then upon a South line to Thomas Muzeets land & then upon a west line forty rods & then it Extends in breadth upon a South line about Twenty Seven poles & then upon a west line bareing ye same breadth till Twenty Two Acres & halfe be fully Accomplished./ All which s^d two lots or parcells of land Containing Twenty Seven Acres & halfe as they are Set forth in ye above written deed of Sale Together with all fences & fenceing Stuff & all fruit trees Timber trees & all Such rights Libertyes profits priviledges Appurtenances as in any kind Appurtaine with ye reversions & remainders thereof And all ye Estate right Title Interest to Each & Every of them belonging or any ways Appurtaining Shall before & to ye whole & Sole use benefitt of him ye afores^d Nicholas Harford To have and To hold all & Singular ye above bargained Two Lotts of land with all ye priviledges & Appurtenances thereunto belonging as above Mentioned unto ye Afores^d Nicholas Harford & his heirs Ex^{rs} Adm^{rs} & Assignes forever without any Mollestation Let Suit or denial of any person or persons [223] Whatsoever And I ye afores^d Abraham Morrell do for my Selfe my heirs Ex^{rs} Adm^{rs} Covena^t & promiss to & with ye afores^d Nicholas Harford him his heirs Ex^{rs} Adm^{rs} & Assignes that I have in my Selfe good right full power & Lawfull Authority in & to ye afore bargained premisses to Sell & dispose of & that ye same & Every part thereof are free & Clear and freely & Clearly Exonerated Acquit & discharged of & from all former & other gifts grants bargains Sales leases Wills Entailes Mortgages Judgm^{ts} Executions powers of thirds & all other Incumbrances of what Nature or kind Soever whereby ye Afores^d Nicholas Harford himselfe his heirs Ex^{rs} Adm^{rs} or Assignes or any or Either of them shall or may at any time hereafter any wayes be Mollested or Ejected out of ye afore bargained premisses or any part thereof by Any person or persons whatsoever And further I ye afores^d Abra^m Morrell do Covena^t Oblige & bind my Selfe my heirs Ex^{rs} & Adm^{rs} firmly by these presents that ye afore bargained premisses & Every part & parcell thereof with ye priviledges & Appurten^{ces} to Each & Every of them belonging or any wayes Appurtaining as they are Set forth in this foregoing Deed of Sale to Warrant & forever defend unto ye afores^d

Book VIII, Fol. 223.

Nicholas Harford & to his heirs Ex^{rs} Adm^{rs} & Assigns Against all & Every person & persons whatsoever as a full free and Stable Estate of Inheritance in fee Simple unto him ye afores^d Nicholas Harford & to his heirs Ex^{rs} & Assignes forever more In Confirmation thereof I have hereunto Set my hand & Seal this Twelfth day of ffeb^{ry} in y^e first year of y^e reign of our Soveraign Lord George by y^e Grace of God of Great Brittaine ffrance & Irel^d King & Anno Dom 1714/5

Signed Sealed & Delivered   Abraham Morrell ($_{Seal}^{a}$)
& the possession given
In presence of us   Phebe her Morrell ($_{Seal}^{a}$)
Francis Allen   mark
James Davis

York sc Novr 2^d 1715./ The above named Abra^m Morrell Acknowledged y^e above written Instrum^t to be his free Act & deed   Before   Charles ffrost J peace

Recorded According to y^e Original July 20th 1717./
                          p Jos. Hamond Reg^r

The Deposition of Samuel Bray & Jon^a Preble of full age Testifieth & Saith that being Imployed in ye year 1716. in ye Month of May to help Captn Peter Nowell in ye building of a Saw mill & Gristmill in a Creek at Arowsick Island for m^r Edwd Hutchinson & m^r John Watts as we are Informed we proceeded in ye work till ye Mills were both raised the flood gate made & ready to hang ye Sawmills going Gears put in the Aprons laid & we know that the runing Gears for ye most part were ready for ye Grist Mill and as far as we understood Could not proceed any further for want of ye Dam and furth Saith Not

Sworn before us ye 3^d July 1717./ in perpetuam Rei Memoriam   Abra^m Preble   Justices
                 Elisha Plaisted   Quoram unus
Recorded According to ye Original July 3^d 1717
                          p Jos. Hamond Reg^r

To All Christian People to whom these presents shall Come I Job Curtis of York in ye County of York in ye Province of ye Massachusets Bay in New England planter Send Greeting./ Know Y^e that I ye s^d Job Curtis for & in Consideration of that Good will Conjugal love & Dear affection which I have & do bear unto Bethiah Mastin of y° Same Town County and Province Viz^t York of ye Massachusets & in Consideration of a Contract of Marriage between s^d Job Curtis & Bethiah Mastin as also for divers other good & Lawfull Considerations me thereunto moveing Have Given & granted & do by these presents freely Clearly & Most heartily give & grant unto ye s^d Bethiah Mastin all my home place on which I now live lying in York afores^d between ye land of Caleb Preble & ye Land of Joseph Bankes runing below ye highway to ye Land of John Parker & ye land of Thomas Adams & runing above ye highway over ye Little river to ye rockey grounds Together with ye Dwelling house & barn now Standing on s^d home place I do likewise give & grant unto Bethiah Mastin aboves^d all that my thirty acre grant as it was laid out to me partly at ye head of my home place & partly at ye head of Daniel Simpsons Land I do likewise give & grant unto ye s^d Bethiah Mastin all that my three acres of Salt marsh which lyeth on ye westerly Side of ye Southwest branch of York river between ye Marsh formerly Alexander Maxells And ye Marsh formerly Benj^a Donnells now in ye Improvem^t of Joseph Holt To have & To hold all ye above granted premises with all maner of rights priviledges & Appurtenances thereunto belonging to her ye s^d Bethiah Mastin her heirs Ex^{rs} Adm^{rs} & Assignes as her & their proper Estate & Inheritance without any Lett or Mollestation for ever./ I do also give unto ye s^d Bethiah Mastin Two Cows & Six sheep or what shall be Equivolent to her satisfaction out of my Stock./ The Condition of this present deed of Gift is Such that if Bethiah Mastin aboves^d Shall die before Job Curtis aboves^d then all above written is to be Voyd & of Non Effect But if ye s^d Job Curtis shall die & Leave s^d Bethiah Mastin a widdow then this present Instrum^t to remaine in full force

In Witness whereof I have hereunto Set my hand & Seal this 13th day of March in y^e third year of y^e reign of our Soveraign Lord George of Great Brittaine &^{a} King Defender of y^e faith Annoq, Domini 1716/7./ The mark of
Signed Sealed & Delivered
  In presence of   Job   Curtis (s$^a_{eal}$)
  Samuel Moodey
  Richard Milbery
  Hannah Moodey

York sc./ April y^e 30th 1717. Job Curtis within Named personally Appeared & Acknowledged this within written

Book VIII, Fol. 224.

Instrument to be his free Act & Deed Before me Abra^m Preble Just peace
Recorded According to y^e Original July 27th 1717./
p Jos. Hamond Reg^r

Know All men by these presents that we Samuel Penhallow & Sam^ll Keais of Portsmouth in ye Province of New Hampshire in New Engl^d for & in Consideration of ye Sum of Seventy pounds Curra^t money of New England to us in hand paid by George Jaffrey of Portsm^o in s^d Province Esqr before ye Signing & Sealing hereof Have [**224**] Bargained & Sold and by these presents do bargaine Sell Aliene Enfeoffe Convey Confirm & make over unto ye s^d George Jaffrey Esqr his heirs Execut^rs Admin^rs & Assignes One halfe of Withers^es Island Comonly So Called to Say ye Lower halfe as is layd by Dodavah Curtis & our selves with the one halfe bennefit of ye Cove & all maner of priviledges & Appurten^ces thereunto belonging either from ye Maine river or back river wch s^d halfe of ye afores^p Island was formerly given by Mr Thomas Withers unto Thomas Rice his wife daughter of ye s^d Withers as Appears by a Certaine deed bareing date July 24 1671 and after that Sold by s^d Rice & his wife unto Cap^tn Thomas Daniel ye 15th of May 1681. and then Willed by ye Executrix of ye s^d Daniel unto ye s^d Samuel Penhallow & Samuel Keais To have and To hold ye afores^d halfe of ye s^d Island with all ye priviledges rights & propertyes thereunto belonging from us ye s^d Samuel Penhallow & Samuel Keais our heirs Ex^rs & Adm^rs unto him ye s^d George Jaffrey Esqr his heirs & Assignes for ever as freely fully & Absolutely without any Maner of reserve as it was Willed us by Mrs Bridget Graffort who was relict unto y^e s^d Cap^tn Daniel, hereby Warranting & Defending y^e same from all Maner of persons whatsoever from by or under us. In Testimony whereof we have hereunto Set our hands & Affixed our Seals this thirteenth day of Aug^st 1716./

Signed Sealed & Delivered   Samuel Penhallow ($^a_{Seal}$)
   In y^e presence of   Samuel Keais ($^a_{Seal}$)
   Wm Fairweather
   Thomas Ayres
   Mary Gerrish
Province of New Hampshire
Saml Penhallow Esqr & Mr Saml Keais psonally Appearing before The Subscriber this 5th day of Jan^ry 1716/7 &

Book VIII, Fol. 224.

Acknowledged y^e Above Instrum^t in Writing to be their Voluntary Acts & Deeds./   J Wentworth Jus^t Peace
Recorded According to ye Original May 7th 1717./
                   p Jos. Hamond Reg^r

To All Christian People to whom these presents shall Come Elisha Kelly of Smuttinose in ye County of York within ye Province of the Massachusets Bay in New England fisherman & Susaña his wife Sends Greeting Know Ye that ye s^d Elisha Kelley & Susaña his wife for & in Consideration of ye sum Two hundred & five pounds Curra^t money of New England in hand paid by Stephen Minot of Boston in ye County of Suffolk Junr otherwise Called Stephen Minot of Boston afors^d Merch^t have given granted bargained Sold Aliened & Confirmed & do by these presents Give grant bargaine Sell Aliene & Confirm unto ye s^d Stephen Minot his heirs Ex^rs Adm^rs & Assignes for ever a Certaine Messuage & Tennem^t Lying & being on Smuttynose afores^d Containing Three Acres more or Less with all & Singular the houses out houses ware houses Stages Stage rooms flakes & flake rooms thereunto belonging or in any wise Appurtaining which is ye Tennem^t whereon ye s^d Kelley Now dwells being bounded on ye Northwest by ye Sea on ye Southwest by Thomas Manering & on ye Northeast by ye Land of Mr Francis Wainwright dec^d And also a Tract of land on Starr Island in ye Province of New Hampsh^r Containing Six Acres More or Less lying on ye Southeast & East by ye land of John Salter & Richd Yetton with all ye Priviledges of Stages & Stage rooms flakes & flake rooms Appurtaining thereunto & also all ye right & Title which ye s^d Kelley hath or ought to have on hogg Island in ye County of York afores^d & all other ye rights or Titles which ye s^d Elisha Kelley holds or ought to hold by a deed of Gift from his father Roger Kelley Late of Smuttynose afores^d Esqr dec^d bareing date y^e   day of   To have & To hold to him ye s^d Stephen Minot his heirs Ex^rs Adm^rs & Assignes for evermore & ye s^d Elisha Kelley & Susana his wife do hereby Covena^t & agree that ye premisses aboves^d is free & Clear and freely & Clearly Acquitted Exonerated & discharged of & from all former gifts grants bargaines Sales Mortgages Titles Troubles or Incumbrances whatsoever & that they have in themselves good right full power & Lawfull Authority the Same to Sell & Dispose of in Mauer as afores^d & that ye s^d Elisha Kelley & Susana his wife their heirs Ex^rs & Adm^rs will forever hereafter Warrant

& Defend yᵉ above granted premisses & yᵉ Appur.ᶜᵉˢ against yᵉ Lawfull Claims of all & Every person or persons whatsoever to him yᵉ sᵈ Stephen Minot his heirs Exʳˢ Admʳˢ & Assigns for ever./ The Condition of yᵉ above deed or Mortgage is Such that if yᵉ above named Elisha Kelley his heirs Exʳˢ or Admʳˢ do well & truely pay or Cause to be paid unto yᵉ above named Stephen Minot his heirs Exʳˢ Admʳˢ or Assignes the full & Just Sum̄ of Two hundred & five pounds Curraᵗ money of New England or bills of Credit to yᵉ vallue thereof At or before yᵉ first day of June which will be in yᵉ year of our Lord One Thousand Seven hundred and Nineteen without fraud Coven or further delay that then the above deed or Mortgage to be Voyd & of Non Effect but on default of payment as aforesᵈ to Abide & remaine in full force Strength & Vertue. In Testimoney whereof yᵉ sᵈ Elisha & Susaña Kelley have hereunto Set their hands & Seals yᵉ Twenty first day of June in yᵉ third year of his Majᵗʸˢ reign Anno. Dom : 1717.   Elisha Kelley (ᵃ Seal)
Signed Sealed & Delivered   Susana Kelley (ᵃ Seal)
  In presence of us
  Charles ffrost
  Daniel Greenough
  Mary Kelley
York sc/ June 21ˢᵗ 1717 : Elisha Kelley & Susaña Kelley above named Acknowledged yᵉ above written Instrumᵗ to be their free act & Deed./   Before   Charles ffrost J Peace
  Recorded According to yᵉ Original July 12ᵗʰ 1717./

                              p Jos. Ham̄ond Regʳ

[225] Know All men by these presents that I Richard Rice of Kittery in the County of York in yᵉ Province of yᵉ Massachusets Bay in New England yeoman do for a valluable Sum of money to me in hand paid by Benjamin Libbey of Berwick in yᵉ aforesᵈ Province yeoman the receipt whereof I do hereby Acknowledge./ Alienate Sell & make over unto yᵉ sᵈ Benjamin Libbey his heirs & Assignes forever all yᵉ right Title Interest & Claime that I have unto a Thirty acre grant of Land which is part of a forty acre grant granted to me by the Town of Kittery at a Publick Town meeting May 10ᵗʰ 1703 as by yᵉ records of yᵉ sᵈ Town may more at Large Appear referrence thereunto being had To have & To hold yᵉ sᵈ Thirty acre grant wᵗʰ all yᵉ priviledges & Appurtenances thereunto belonging from me yᵉ sᵈ Richard Rice my heirs &

Book VIII, Fol. 225.

Assignes unto him ye s^d Benjamin Libbey his heirs & Assignes for ever./ In Witness whereof I have hereunto Set my hand & Seal this Twenty first day of July Anno Domini One Thousand Seven hundred & Sixteen Annoq, RⁱR^s Georgii Magna Brittania &c^t Secundo.   Richd Rice (s_{ea}^al)
Signed Sealed & Delivered
 In ye presence of
 John Newmarch
 John Newmarch Tert^r
York sc/ Kittery Decr 10th 1716./ Richard Rice psonally Appearing before me ye Subscrib^r Acknowledged ye Above Instrum^t in writing to be his Volluntary Act & Deed
                              Elisha Plaisted Jus^t peace
Recorded According to ye Original July ye 1st 1717./
                      p Jos. Hamond Reg^r

This Indenture made ye first day of August 1668 & in ye 20th year of the Reign of our Soveraign Lord Charles ye ii^d Between Joshua Scottow of Boston on ye One part & John Libbey Junr of Blackpoint on the other part Witnesseth that ye s^d Joshua Scottow for himselfe heirs Ex^{rs} Adm^{rs} & Assigns doth give grant & Confirm unto ye s^d John Libby and his heirs for ever under ye Conditions & Limitations herein Expressed and Specified fifty acres of upland lying & Abutting on ye East of his father Libbys field in part bounded therewith & with Marked Trees Westerly & Northerly with ye lines of Scottows pattent with Scottows Land Easterly and with a Small Swamp bordering upon Scottows Marsh Southerly to run from the Southwest Corner of s^d Libeyes garden fence upon a Straight line unto Scottows fence upon ye Top of ye hill Towards ye East Together with Six acres of Marsh land lying next to ye Clay pitts bordering upon blackpoint river Near Oposite to Sarah Mills^s house To have & To hold ye s^d fifty Six Acres to him ye s^d John Libby his heirs Ex^{rs} Adm^{rs} & assignes forever Yielding & paying yearly Two days work for ever at Such Time or times as it Shall be Lawfully demanded & Also forever to repair & maintaine all that fence belonging to s^d Scottows Marsh both that Set up by s^d Libby &c^t and before his house & Land & that before his fathers Land Joyning to Wm Sheldon & Likewise to fence in & forever to maintaine & keep in repair ye fence Needful for ye Salt marsh bordering upon his father Libbys Marsh and was by y^es^d Scottow purchased of Christop^r Elkins late dec^d and of Wm Burrage formerly belonging & Granted by Henry Jocelyn Esqr unto ye Late John Burrage & for not performence of ye premisses it Shall be Lawfull for ye s^d Scottow his heirs or assignes to Enter upon ye s^d land & distreine & ye distress So Taken to Carry to Apprize by two Sworn men & pay himselfe his heirs or Assignes ye s^d due & Charge vallueing Each day at three Shillings money & to deliver ye overpluss of ye distress unto ye owner thereof the s^d Libby is to have liberty of free Comonage on that Side of pine Creek & also there to Cutt down & make use of Any Timber or trees for ye maintaining & Setting up of ye s^d fence & fences It is also agreed that if ye s^d land shall be Left unimployed or deserted so as that there shall not be found Quickstock or household Implem^{ts} to Satisfie for ye s^d rent and Charges of Setting up & repairing ye s^d fence and fences aboves^d that then it shall & may be lawfull for ye s^d Scottows his heirs & Assignes to reenter & possess himselfe or themselves of ye s^d Land & without any Suit or Tryall At Law any thing herein Expressed Notwithstanding & that it shall be Lawfull for ye s^d Scottow his heirs or Assignes to pass through any part of it to fetch his hay out of his Marshes if Need shall require In Confirmation of y^e premisses According to y^e Conditions & Limitations above Expressed the partyes above named have Interchangeably Signed & Sealed./ the words [fence Needfull for y^e] Interlined before Signing & Sealing & also Setting up &] being Interlined   Joshua Scottow ($_{Seal}^a$)

Read Signed Sealed & Delivered In y^e presence of us y^e Subscrib^{rs} it being antidated by Consent of both partyes y^e rent runing from that time It is agreed by both partyes that y^e Two due dayes above Expressed in this Covena^t are to be remitted Intirely & that y^e fence above Expressed is to be Sufficient Against Great Cattle & to be a three raile fence & that Jno Libby is to have Liberty to Cutt for maintainence of ye fences in any part of Scottows Comon Land. Dated ye 19th June 1675

Henry Williams
Joseph Oliver

This Agreem^t of fifty acres is to be understood with John Libbey Senr owning ye Land in his possession on ye Easter side of his old plantation for fifty Acres

Cap^{tn} Joshua Scottow Appeared before me this 19th October 1685 & Acknowledged this Instrum^t to be his Act & Deed   Edwd Tyng Just peace

Recorded According to ye Original May ye 1st 1717./

p Jos: Hamond Reg^r

Book VIII, Fol. 226.

To All Christian People to whom these presents may Come or doth Concern Robert Gray of York in y[e] County of york in y[e] Province of the Massachusets Bay in New England Labourer & Elizabeth his wife for & in Consideration of Sixty Acres of upland & a third part of a Saw mill with one Saw & priviledge in a Stream of water whereon s[d] Mill Standeth with a Small dwelling house &c[t] within y[e] Township of s[d] York upon y[e] Northeast Side of y[e] river Called Capenedick river as p a deed of y[e] date of these presents given by Benjamin Webber of s[d] York unto y[e] s[d] [**226**] Robert Gray the s[d] Gray & his wife hath given granted bargained Sold Aliened Enfeoffed & made over and doth by these give grant Bargaine Sell Aliene Enfeoffe & make over unto y[e] s[d] Benjamin Webber and his heirs & Assignes for ever Two Certaine pieces parcells Tennem[ts] or tracts of Land lying & being within y[e] Township of s[d] York and is Scittuate upon y[e] Southwest Side of s[d] york river upon y[e] Northwest Side of y[e] Creek Comonly Called y[e] old mill Creek./ the whole two Tracts or parcells of Land Containing Sixty Six Acres Viz[t] That tract or parcell whereon s[d] Robert Gray Now Liveth is forty & Two Acres butting upon y[e] Marsh of s[d] Mill creek & runeth up s[d] York river Northwest bounded by y[e] Land of Andrew Grover upon y[e] Southwest side & y[e] Land of Elihue parsons upon y[e] Northeast side & y[e] other Twenty four Acres lyeth near y[e] head of a Cove Called y[e] long Cove Also bounded by y[e] Land of Andrew Grover & Elihue Parsons on y[e] Northeast & Southwest as above s[d] other Lot or tract of land is & on y[e] head or Northwest by y[e] Land of Ebenezer Blasdell or is otherwise reputed to be bounded as p An Instrum[t] of Division Some years Ago made between James Allen Mathew Grover Andrew Grove Elihue Parsons & s[d] Robert Gray being had s[d] bounds may At Large Appear Together with all y[e] rights priviledges & Appurten[ces] thereunto belonging both of house or housen land Meadow ground buildings fences Timber trees wood underwood Standing lying remaining or belonging unto above s[d] tracts of land or any part or parcell thereof or that may hereafter redownd unto y[e] Same unto him y[e] s[d] Benjamin Webber & to his heirs and Assignes forever To have & To hold & Quietly to possess Occupy & and Enjoy as a sure Estate in fee Simple Moreover y[e] s[d] Robert Gray doth for himselfe his heirs & Admin[rs] to & with y[e] s[d] Benj[a] Webber his heirs & Assignes Covenant Ingage & promiss the Above bargained premisses with all its priviledges to be free & Clear from all former gifts grants Bargaines Sales rents Mortgages or any

other Incumberments whatsoever as also from all future Claims Challenges Arrests Law suits or any other Interruptions whatsoever/ to be had or Comenced by him ye s^d Robert his heirs Ex^{rs} Adm^{rs} or any other person or persons upon Grounds of Law or Title proceeding ye date hereof he doth Warrantize & will defend ye same./ In Witness hereof ye s^d Robert Gray & Elizabeth his wife have hereto Set their hands & Seals this thirteenth day of July in ye year of our Lord 1717. And in ye third year of the Reign of our Soveraign Lord George King of Great Brittaine &c^t
Signed Sealed & Delivered
   In psence of   Robert 2 Gray (a seal)
   Nathl Freeman
   Abra^m Preble   Elizabeth Gray ꝛ (a seal)
   York sc/
Robert Gray personally Appeared Before me Abra^m Preble Esqr one of his Maj^{tys} Justices of ye peace for ye Aboves^d County & Acknowledged ye within written to be his free Act & deed./   Abra^m Preble
   Recorded According to ye Original Augst 9th 1717./
               p Jos. Hamond Reg^r

Know All men by these presents that I Harlackenden Symonds of Ipswich Gentleman within ye Jurisdiction of ye Massachusets for a Valluable Sum had & rec^d of James Barnand of Watertown in ye Jurisdiction afores^d Hath given granted bargained Sold Enfeoffed & Confirmed & do p these presents for my Selfe heirs Ex^{rs} and Assignes give grant bargaine Sell Enfeoffe & Confirm unto James Barnard afores^d one hundred Acres of Land Lying Scittuate and being above ye Township of Wells of ye East Side of ye river Called Capeporpus river & ye Sea & ye Township of Wells being on ye South Side & to Lye Adjacent to ye Land of m^r Daniel Epps I ye s^d Harlackenden Symonds do pass over ye aboves^d Land unto the afores^d James Barnard According to ye right & Title wch I ye s^d Harlackinden Symond hath derived from my brother Epps And further I ye afores^d Harlackinden Symonds do grant and Allow ye afores^d James Barnard to take ye afores^d parcell of Land out of Either Side or end of ye parcell of Land that I bought of my Brother m^r Daniel Epps Provided that he ye s^d James Barnard Shall not Exceed to take above an Eighth part of ye Meadow that

Book VIII, Fol. 227.

is in y^e tract of Land wch I bought of my brother Mr Daniel Epps And to y^e Confirmation of y^e afores^d premisses I bind me my heirs Ex^rs Adm^rs & Assignes In Witness whereof I have hereunto Set my hand & Seal this 16th day of January in y^e year of our Lord 1662./ Harlackenden Symonds ($_{Seal}^{a}$)
Signed Sealed & Deliv^rd
 In y^e presence of
Joseph Taynter

Willm & Bray

This Deed Acknowledged by Mr Harlackenden Symonds Jan^ry 1662./   Ri : Billingham Dep^ty Govr

Recorded According to y^e Original May 27 1717./

                    p Jos Hamond Reg^r

To All Christian People to whom these presents Shall Come Greeting Know Ye that I Joseph Jacobs Phillip & Susanna ffowler all of Ipswich being Grandchildren unto m^r William Symones formerly of Wells in ye County York dec^d in New England for & in Consideration of the valluable Sum of Seventy & five pounds in Currant Bills of Cridit of the Province of ye Massachusets Bay in New England to us in hand paid by Symonds Epps of Ipswich in New England Gent before ye Sealing and Delivery of these presents the rec^t whereof we do Acknowledge & our Selves therewith fully Satisfied Contented & paid Have given granted bargained & Sold Aliened Assigned Enfeoffed Set over & Confirmed and do by these presents firmly Clearly & absolutely give grant bargaine Sell Enfeoffe Set over and Confirm unto ye s^d Symonds Epps his heirs Ex^rs Adm^rs [227] And Assignes for Ever one Quarter or forth part of a farm in Wells in ye County of York that was our Grandfathers m^r William Symonds aboves^d dec^d the whole farm Containing by Estimation about three hundred Acres be the Same more or Less of upland Marsh & Meadow ground the aboves^d Quarter part fell to ye s^d Joseph Jacobs & his Sister Susana ffowler from their aboves^d Grandfather Symonds Together

with all yᵉ wood Timber profits priviledges & Appurtenances that doth in any wise belong or Appurtaine unto yᵉ sᵈ farm To have & To hold yᵉ abovesᵈ parcell of Land with all yᵉ profits priviledges & Appurtenances in any wise thereunto belonging unto him yᵉ sᵈ Symonds Epps his heirs Exʳˢ Admʳˢ & Assignes & to their only proper use & benefit forever./ And we yᵉ sᵈ Joseph Jacobs Phillip ffowler & Susana ffowler do Covenant promiss & agree to & wᵗʰ yᵉ sᵈ Symonds Epps that we have full power & good right to Sell yᵉ abovesᵈ lands & it may & shall be Lawfull for sᵈ Epps to use Occupy possess & Enjoy yᵉ Same for ever promissing to Warrant & Defend his Title thereunto from all persons Legall Claime./ In Witness of all & Singular yᵉ premisses we have hereunto Set our hands & Seals this Seventeenth day of July Anno Domini One Thousand Seven hundred & Seventeen And in yᵉ Third year of his Majestyes Reign./   Joseph Jacob (ˢᵉᵃˡ)
Signed Sealed & Delivered   Phillip ffowler (ˢᵉᵃˡ)
  In presence of us   Susaña ffowler (ˢᵉᵃˡ)
Robert Lord
Samuel Lord

memorⁿ It is to be understood that yᵉ bounds of sᵈ land bought is by yᵉ Sea Wall yᵉ Little river Gooches Land & near Nannys farm

Essex sc/ Ipswich July yᵉ 17ᵗʰ 1717.
Mʳ Joseph Jocobs Mʳ Phillip ffowler & Susaña his wife psonally Appeared & Acknowledged this Instrumᵗ to be their free Act & Deed./ Before Samˡ Appleton Just peace
Recorded According to yᵉ Original Augˢᵗ 9° 1717/.
                                p Jos. Hamond Regʳ

Know All men by these presents that I Daniel Epps of Salem in yᵉ County of Essex in yᵉ Province of yᵉ Massuchets Bay in New England Gent Have Constituted & Ordained my Trusty & welbeloved Brother Majoʳ Symonds Epps of Ipswich in yᵉ County aforesᵈ Gent my True & Lawfull Attorney for me & to my use to Sell & dispose of All yᵉ upland Marish & Meadow which any wayes belongs to me which my Honᵈ ffather Daniel Epps of Ipswich Esqʳ dyed possessed of Vizᵗ all beyond Piscataqua river in yᵉ County of York in yᵉ Province of Maine in New England ratifying and Confirming what my sᵈ Attorney shall do in or about yᵉ premisses as if I my Selfe had done it./ In Witness where-

Book VIII, Fol. 227.

of I have hereunto Set my hand & Seal this Decemb[r] 15[th] Anno Domini 1716. & in y[e] 3[d] year of his Majestyes Reign./
Signed Sealed & Deliver[d]   Daniel Epps (${}^a_{Seal}$)
  In p[r]sence of us
  Edward Evelith
  Ruth Epps./
Daniel Epps psonaly Appeared Dec[r] 15[th] 1716 and Acknowledged y[e] above written Instrument to be his Act & Deed   Before me./   Jos Wolcot Just peace
Recorded According to y[e] Original Aug[st] 9° 1717./
                             p Jos. Hamond Reg[r]

    This Indenture made y[e] Sixteenth day of April Anno Domini Seventeen hundred and Sixteen in y[e] Second year of y[e] reign of our Soveraign Lord George by y[e] grace of God of Great Brittaine ffrance & Ireland King Defender of y[e] faith &c[t] Between Daniel Paul of Kittery in y[e] County of York within his Maj[tys] Province of y[e] Massachusets Bay in New England Shipwright of y[e] one part & John Dennet of y[e] Same Town County & Province Yeoman of y[e] other part Witnesseth that y[e] s[d] Daniel Paul for & in Consideration of y[e] Sum of Sixteen pounds in good & Lawfull Publick Bills of Credit of y[e] Province aboves[d] to him in hand at & before y[e] Ensealing & Delivery hereof well & truely paid by y[e] s[d] John Dennet the receipt whereof he hereby Acknowledgeth and himselfe therewith fully Satisfied & Contented & thereof doth Acquit & Discharge y[e] s[d] John Dennett his heirs & Assignes for ever hath Given granted bargained Sold released Enfeoffed Conveyed & Confirmed & by these presents doth give grant bargaine Sell release Enfeoffe Convey & Confirm unto y[e] s[d] John Dennet his heirs & Assignes for ever all that his Lott or Tract of Land Scittuate Lying & being in y[e] Towship of Kittery afores[d] bounded westward by Spinneys Creek So Called Southward with y[e] land of James Fernald & Northward with y[e] Land of John Soper dec[d] or y[e] highway & runing back into y[e] wood between y[e] s[d] two Lotts untill Twenty Acres be Compleated it being formerly y[e] Lands & possession of his father Stephen Paul late of s[d] Kittery dec[d] According as y[e] Same was Laid out & bounded to him as more at Large Appears on record in y[e] Town of Kittery afores[d] reference thereunto being had Together with all & Singular y[e] woods Trees underwoods fences profits priviledges heriditaments & Appurtenances whatSoever unto y[e] s[d] Tract or lot of land belonging or in any wise Appurtaining

BOOK VIII, FOL. 228.

with ye reversions & remainders thereof & all ye Estate right Title Dower Interest Inheritance use property possession Claime & Demand whatsoever of ye s^d Daniel Paul of in & to ye s^d granted premisses & Every part & parcell thereof./ To have & To hold ye s^d lott or tract of land & all other ye premisses afores^d unto ye s^d John Dennet his heirs & Assignes to his & their only propper use benefit & behoofe forever./ Provided Alwayes & upon Condition Nevertheless that if ye s^d Daniel Paul his heirs Ex^rs or Adm^rs Shall & do well & Truely pay or Cause to be paid unto ye s^d John Dennet his heirs Ex^rs Adm^rs or assignes ye full & Just Sum of fifteen pounds in good & Lawfull publick bills of Credit on ye Province afores^d wth Lawfull Interest for ye Same in Like good & Lawfull bills of publick Credit at on or before ye Sixteenth day of Aprill which will be in ye year of Our Lord Seventeen hundred & Eighteen which payment of Principle & Interest is to be made in time as before Limitted without fraud or delay then this present deed & Every grant and Article therein Contained shall Cease determine be voyd and of Non Effect but if Default happen to be made in ye s^d payment in [228] Maner as afores^d then to Abide & remaine in full force Strength & Vertue./ And ye s^d Daniel Paul for himselfe his heirs Ex^rs & Adm^rs doth by these presents Covenat grant & Agree to & with ye s^d John Dennet his heirs Ex^rs Adm^rs and Assignes from time to time & At all times forever to Warrant & defend all ye s^d Tract or parcell of Land with other ye premisses & Appurtenances unto him ye s^d John Dennet his heirs & Assignes Against ye Lawfull Claimes & demands of all & Every person & persons./ whomsoever & that ye s^d bargained premisses at ye time of ye Ensealing and Executing of these presents are free & Clear & fully Acquitted & discharged of & from all former & other gifts grants bargaines Sales Mortgages Titles troubles charges & Incumbrances whatsoever In Witness whereof ye s^d Daniel Paul hath hereunto Set his hand and Seal the day and year first above written./
Signed Sealed & Delivered   Daniel Paul (Seal)
  In ye presence of us
  Jos. Hamond
  Hannah Hamond

York February 4. 1730 Then received of Mr Daniel Paul the within named Mortgager the full of Principle and Interest due on the within mortgage in full discharge of the Same

p me James his (mark) Fernald Assignee of ye within named Mr John Dennet

Witness Jos: Moody Reg^r

BOOK VIII, FOL. 228.

York sc/ July 31st 1717./ this day Daniel Paul psonally Appeared before me ye Subscriber one of his Majesties Justices of ye peace for ye County afores^d & Acknowledged this foregoing Instrum^t to be his free Act & Deed
Wm Pepperrell
Recorded According to ye Original Augst 19th 1717./
p Jos. Hamond Reg^r

Know All by these presents that I John Dennet of Kittery in ye County of York within his Ma^{tys} Province of ye Massachusets Bay in New England Yeoman do by these presents Assigne Set over & Convey unto my welbeloved kinsman James ffernald of ye Same place yeoman all my right Title Interest Claime & Demand that I Now have or May hereafter have in ye within Specified Indenture Containing Twenty Acres of Land reference to ye s^d Indenture being had may More At Large Appear to have & to hold y^e s^d Twenty Acres of Land with all y^e Appurtenances & priviledges thereunto belonging unto y^e only & Sole use benefit & behoofe of him y^e s^d James ffernald his heirs & Assignes for ever In Witness whereof I have hereunto Set my hand & Seal this 30th March 1717./   John Dennet($_{Seal}^a$)
Signed & Sealed & Delivered
 In y^e presence of us y^e Subscribers
Mary Dennet
  The mark of
Sarah 🜚 Hooper
York sc/ July 31st 1717. This day John Dennet psonally Appeared before me y^e Subscrib^r one of his Maj^{tys} Justices of y^e peace for the County afores^d Acknowledged this above Instrum^t to be his free Act & deed./   Wm Pepperrell
Recorded According to ye Original Assignm^t As it Stands Indorsed on ye backside of ye foregoing deed of Mortgage Augst 19 : 1717.   p Jos. Hamond Reg^r

To All People to whom these presents shall Come Greeting./ Know ye that I Ebenezer More of Kittery in ye County of York within his Majesties Province of ye Massachusets Bay in New England Shipwright & John Norton formerly of Hampton Now of ye Town & County afores^d Joyner for

Book VIII, Fol. 228.

& in Consideration of ye Sum of Eighty Nine pounds Six Shillings in good and Lawfull money of ye Province afores^d to us in hand before ye Ensealing hereof well & truely paid by Henry Barter of ye s^d Town & County Yeoman the rec^t whereof we do hereby Acknowledge & our selves therewith fully Satisfied & Contented & thereof & of Every part & parcell thereof do Exonerate Acquit & discharge ye s^d Henry Barter his heirs Ex^rs Adm^rs for ever by these presents have given granted bargained & Sold & by these presents do freely fully & Absolutely give grant hargaine Sell Aliene Convey & Confirm unto him ye s^d Henry Barter his heirs & Assignes forever one Mussuage or Tract of land & Meadow Scittuate Lying & being in Kittery Afores^d Containing by Estimation Twenty Seven Acres three quarters of An Acre & Twenty Six pole be it more or less lying between Nich^o Tuckers & Crockets Neck which is all that Tract of Land wch we ye s^d More & Norton purchased of s^d Henry Barter As will Appear p ye s^d Barters deed to us ye s^d More & Norton bareing date ye Twenty^th day of this present Month with all trees wood fences water & water Courses to it belonging or in any ways Appurtaining To have & To hold ye s^d granted & bargained premisses with all ye appurtenances priviledges & Comodity to ye Same belonging or in Any ways Appurtaining to him ye s^d Henry Barter his heirs & Assignes forever to his & their only proper use benefit & behalfe for ever & we ye s^d Ebenezer More & John Norton for our Selves our heirs Ex^rs Adm^rs do Covena^t promiss & grant to & wth ye s^d Henry Barter his heirs & Assignes that before ye Ensealing hereof we are ye True Sole & Lawfull owners of ye above bargained premisses & are Lawfully Siez^d & possessed of ye same in our own right as a good perfect & Absolute Estate of Inheritance in fee Simple & have in our selves good right full power & Lawfull Authority to grant bargaine Sell Convey & Confirm s^d bargained premisses in Maner as aboves^d & that ye s^d Henry Barter his heirs & Assignes Shall & may from time to time & at all times for ever hereafter by force & vertue of these presents Lawfully peaceably & Quietly have hold use Occupy possess and Enjoy ye above demised premisses with ye Appurtenances free & Clear & Clearly Acquitted Exonerated & discharged of from all & all maner of former & other gifts grants bargains Sales or Incumbrances whatsoever./ Provided Nevertheless & it is ye true Intent & meaning of ye Grantor & Grantee in these p^rsents any thing herein Con-

tained to yᵉ Contrary Notwithstanding that if yᵉ above Named Ebenezer More & John Norton or Either of them or their heirs Exʳˢ Admʳˢ or Assignes do well & truely pay unto yᵉ above Named Henry Barter his heirs Exʳˢ Admʳˢ or assignes yᵉ above Mentioned Sum of money wᵗʰ Lawfull Interest from this date at or before yᵉ Last day of May in yᵉ year of our Lord one Thousᵈ Seven hundred & Nineteen Then this above written Obligation Shall be utterly Voyd & of Non Effect or Else shall abide in full force & Vertue Sealed wᵗʰ my Seal Dated in Kittery this Twenty fifth day of ffebʳʸ in yᵉ third year of yᵉ reign of our Soveraign Lord George by yᵉ grace of God King of Great Brittaine ffrance & Irelᵈ & in yᵉ year of our Lord One Thousand Seven hundred & Sixteen Seventeen   Ebenezer More (Seal ᵃ)
Signed Sealed & Delivered   John Norton (Seal ᵃ)
In yᵉ presence of
Thomas Jenkins
Nathaniel Ingersol
Wᵐ Pepperrell Junʳ
York sc/ April 1ˢᵗ day Anno: 1717./
This day Ebenʳ More & John Norton both psonally Appeared before me yᵉ Subscribʳ one of his Majᵗʸˢ Justices of yᵉ peace for sᵈ County & Acknowledged this above Instrumᵗ to be his free Act & Deed./   Wᵐ Pepperrell
Recorded According to yᵉ Original Augˢᵗ 21ᵗˢ 1717./
p Jos. Harmon Regʳ

This Mortgage is Discharged by yᵉ within Named Henry Barter in Libᵉ X folio 86 Attʳ J Hamond Regʳ

[229] To All Christian People to whom this presents shall Come Know Ye that I John Heard of Kittery in yᵉ County of York in his Majᵗʸˢ Province of yᵉ Massachusets Bay in New England Yeoman with yᵉ Consent of Jane my wife for & in Consideration of a Valluable Sum of Money to me in hand paid by John Morrell Junʳ of sᵈ Kittery./ have granted & Sold & do by this presents grant bargaine Sell Alienate pass over & Confirm unto sᵈ John Morrell his heirs or Assignes for ever a Tract of Swampy ground lying East from Sturgeon Creek & being bounded on yᵉ East end with Marked trees & on both Sides with yᵉ upland & So to run west to the Extent of yᵉ Swamp being Twenty Acres more or Less which Swampy ground was granted to my father James Heard by yᵉ Town of Kittery October yᵉ Twenty first 1668./ To have & To hold all & Singular yᵉ sᵈ Swampy

ground with all priviledges & Appurtenances thereunto belonging of Timber trees wood underwood water water Courses. &. I y[e] s[d] John Heard do for my Selfe my heirs Ex[rs] Adm[rs] Covena[t] & promiss to & with y[e] aboves[d] John Morrell his heirs Ex[rs] Adm[rs] or Assignes that I have in my Selfe good right full power & Lawfull Authority to Sell y[e] Mmentioned premisses & that it is free & clear from all other gifts grants Leases Mortgages Wills Intailments Judgments Executions power of thirds or any Lawfull claime of any pson & that I Will Save harmless warra[t] & defend as by these presents In Witness hereunto I have Set to my hand & Seals this Ninth day of January Annoq, Domini One thousand Seven hundred and Sixteen Seventeen & in y[e] third year of y[e] reign of our Soveraign Lord George of Great Brittaine ffrance & Ireland King Defend[r] of y[e] faith &c[t]

Signed Sealed & Delivered   John Heard (a Seal)
 In presence of us   her
 John Gowen   Jane X Heard (a Seal)
 Nathan Bartlett   mark
 Daniel Emery

 York sc/ March: 9: 1716/7./
Capt[n] John Heard Acknowledged y[e] within written Instrum[t] to be his free Act & Deed.
      Before   Charles ffrost J. Peace
Recorded According to y[e] Original March 25th 1717./
          p Jos. Hamond Reg[r]

 Know All men by these presents that I William Robinson of GeorgeTown on Arrowsick Island in America am holden & Stand firmly bound and Obliged unto John Cookson of Boston in y[e] County of Suffolk in New England Gunsmith in y[e] full Sum of five hundred pounds to be paid unto y[e] s[d] John Cookson his Ex[rs] Adm[rs] & Assignes to y[e] true paym[t] whereof I bind my Selfe my heirs Ex[rs] & Adm[rs] firmly by these presence and as a Colateral & further Security for y[e] s[d] Paym[t] I y[e] s[d] W[m] Robinson have & hereby to give grant bargaine Sell Convey And Confirm unto y[e] s[d] John Cookson One Quarter part of a Certain Tract of Land lying between Shepscoat Bay & Damaris Scotty river Called by y[e] Indians the Wineganse which is a Carrying place between y[e] s[d] bay and y[e] s[d] river bounded as follows. Two miles up y[e] river afores[d] & two Miles up Shepscoat Bay Side both upon one & y[e] Same point of y[e] Compass with y[e] other & So a Straight line to be run there from ye river to ye s^d Bay with ye point of Land from ye Wineganse or Carrying place down Toward ye Sea & ye Island Called Agguahega or DamerisScotty Island with a Quarter part of All ye Islands with all ye Island Adjoyning & Lying Southerly from ye s^d Neck of Land with all Such rights Libertys Profits priviledges Comodityes & Appurtenances as belong thereunto which s^d granted premisses I bought of John Bland of George Town afores Yeoman as by his deed dated ye fifteenth day of March last will Appear./ & One hundred Acres more of Land in George Town afores^d with ye house & Saw mill & ye Appurtenances thereto belonging Now in my Possession & Two Cows Two Yearlings & their Increase & a horse./ To have & To hold ye s^d Lands & Chattells & all other ye premisses Afore given & granted unto him ye s^d John Cookson his heirs Ex^{rs} Adm^{rs} & Assignes for ever & I ye s^d Wm Robinson do Avouch my Self to be ye true Sole & Lawfull owner of ye s^d Granted Lands & premisses & have full power to Sell & Dispose thereof in Manner as afores^d ye same being free & Clear of & from all maner of Incumbrances w^{t}soever And I ye s^d Wm Robinson do hereby Covenant & grant for my Selfe my heirs Ex^{rs} & Adm^{rs} to & with ye s^d John Cookson his heirs & Assignes by these presents to Warrant & Defend ye s^d Given and Granted Lands & premisses unto him & them for ever Agst ye Lawfull Claims & Demands of All persons whomsoever./ Sealed with my Seal./ Dated ye Eleventh day of April Anno Domini 1717 & in the third year of his Majesties reign

Discharged Lib^o 12 Fol^o 164

The Condition of ye afore written bond & deed of Sale is Such that Whereas ye s^d Wm Robinson & John Cookson have Entred into Certaine Articles of Agreem^t or partnership referring to their Carrying on a Joynt Trade or dealing with ye Eastern Indians from Boston to George Town afores^d as will fully Appear by ye s^d Articles und^r ye hands of ye s^d John Cookson & Wm Robinson Dated ye Eighth day of Aprill Curra^t relation thereto being had: Now if ye s^d Wm Robinson his heirs Ex^{rs} & Adm^{rs} Shall & do in all respects perform fulfill & keep his part of ye s^d Agreem^t According to ye True Intent & meaning thereof And further shall render a Just & True Acco^t of all his Transactions buying Selling dealing respecting their Joynt Trade And also pay or Cause to be paid unto him ye s^d John Cookson his Ex^{rs} Adm^{rs} or Assignes what & So much as shall upon Adjustm^t of Such Acco^{ts} from time to Time be found or Appear due to him ye s^d Cookson for or upon Acco^t of ye s^d partnership or Joynt Trade when & As often as ye s^d [230] William

Robinson his Ex^{rs} &c Shall be thereunto required and and demanded without fraud Collusion or delay./ Then the aforegoing Deed of Sale & writing Obligatory to be voyd & of Non Effect but in Default thereof or any part thereof to Abide & remaine in full force & vertue to all Intents & purposes in y^e Law whatsoever./ William Robinson ($_{Seal}^{a}$)
Signed Sealed & Delivered
  In presence of us
  William Ward
  Samuel Tyley Junr
  Suffolk sc/
  Boston April 11th 1717
Wm Robinson Acknowledged y^e Afore written Instrum^t to be his Act & Deed   Before me./ Samuel Keeling J : Pacis
Recorded According to y^e Original July 27th 1717./
$\qquad\qquad\qquad\qquad\qquad$ p Jos. Hamond Reg^r

To all People to whom these Presents Shall Come I John Ball of Kittery in y^e County of York in y^e Province of y^e Massachusets Bay in New England yeoman Do Send Greeting Know ye that I y^e s^d John Ball for & in Consideration of my Son in Law Francis Pettigrew of the Same Town County & Province Husbandman he his heirs Execut^{rs} or administrators providing for me and my wife Joanna Sufficient maintainance and attendance or Nursing dureing ye Term of our Natureal Lives as also for & in Consideration of that Love good will & Affection which I have & do bear towards my s^d Son in Law & his wife Eliz^a my Daughter have given & granted and by these Presents Do freely Clearly and absolutely give and grant after mine & my wifes Decease unto ye s^d Frances Pettegrew his heirs Execut^{rs} Administrators or assignes all that Tract or parcel of Land whereon I now dwell and am in ye Possession of Scittuate Lying and being in ye Township of Kittery Containing by Estimation Twenty two acres be it more or Less and is bounded on ye Eastern end by ye River Commonly Callen Spruce Creek and on ye Northern Side by a branch of ye above s^d Creek on the Southern Side by ye Land of m^r William Godsoe and on ye western end by ye Land of ye s^d Godsoe & John Sheppard and also all the Houseing & fences that Shall then be upon ye s^d Lands & also all my goods & Chattels of Every Sort whatsoever & wheresoever they may be found after ye Decease of me & my wife : To have and to hold all and Singular the s^d given & granted Premises with all the Appurtenances priviledges and Commodities to ye Same belonging or in any wise appertaining to him ye s^d Frances Pettegrew his heirs Executors administrators and assignes for ever To his and Their only proper use benefit & behoof for ever after our Decease In Witness whereof I the Said John Ball and Joanna my wife have hereunto Set our hands & Seals this Sixth day of June in ye year of our Lord one thousand Seven hundred & Seventeen Annoq̄ Regni Regis Georgii Magnee Britannice &c Tertio

Signed Sealed & Delivered
  In ye Presents of   John ⊕ Ball (a Seal)
  John Newmarch   his mark
  William Godsoe
          his   Joanna ✗ Ball (a Seal)
  William ⊕ Beal   her mark
       mark
June 8th day 1717

Then John Ball personally appeared before me one of his Maj^{tys} Justices for ye County of york & Did acknowledge this Instrument to be his free act & Deed   Wm Pepperrell

Recorded According to ye Original July 1st 1717./
                        p Jos. Ham̄ond Reg^r

To All People to whom these Presents Shall Come Greeting Know ye That I Nicholas Shapleigh of Kittery in ye County of York within his Maj^{tys} Province of the Massachusets Bay in New England Gentleman for and in consideration of Eighteen Pounds 16^s of money to me in hand paid honestly and Truly before the Ensealing & Delivery hereof by Richd Rice of ye Town County & Province afores^d the receipt w^{r}of I do hereby acknowledge and my Self therewith fully Sattisfyed Contented and there of and of Every part & Parcell thereof do Exonerate acquit & discharged the s^d Richard Rice his heirs Executors & Adm^{rs} for ever by these presents Have given granted bargained Sold Aliened Enfeoffed Conveyed & Confirmed and by these Presents do freely fully & absolutely give grant bargain Sell Aliene Enfeoffe Convey and Confirm unto him the Said Richard Rice his heirs & Assignes for ever a Certain Tract or parcell of Land Scittuate Lying and being in ye Town Ship of Kittery afores^d Containing by Estimation Eleven Acres & Three Quarters be it more or Less butted & bounded on ye Eastern end by m^r Wm Godsoes & Walter Denifords Land on y^e

Southern Side & Western End by John Newmarches Land Sixty four poles & half West one half point Northerly to s^d Rices land and by Stephen Eastwickes Land or Shapleigh on ye Northern Side by ye s^d Richard Rices Land or however otherwise bounded or reputed to be bounded Together with all the profits priviledges and appurtenances whatsoever to ye s^d Land belonging or in any wise appertaining To : have and to Hold The Said bargained and granted Premises with all ye Emoluments Commodities Appurtenances and Priviledges to ye Same belonging or in any wise appertaining to him ye S^d Richard Rice his heirs Execut^{rs} Administrators and assignes forever To his and Their only proper use, benefit and behoof forever And I ye s^d Nicholas Shapleigh for me my Heirs Executors Administrat^{rs} Covena^t Promise and grant to & with the s^d Richard Rice his heirs Executors Administrators and assignes that before the ensealing hereof I am the True Sole & Lawfull owner of ye above bargained Premisses & their appurtenances and am Lawfully Seized & Possessed of ye Same in mine own proper right as a good perfect and absolute estate of Inheritance in Fee Simple and have in my Self good right full Power and Lawfull Authority To grant bargaine Sell Convey and Confirm s^d bargained Premisses in manner as aboves^d and that ye s^d Richd Rice his heirs Executors adm^{rs} and assigns Shall And may from Time To Time and at all Times for ever hereafter by force & virtue of these Presents Lawfully peaceably & Quietly have hold use occupy possess & Enjoy the s^d Demised & bargained Premisses with ye appurtenances free & Clear and freely and Clearly acquitted Exonerated & Discharged of & from all & all manner of former or other gifts grants bargains sales Leases Dowries Judgments Joyntures Mortgages Executions & Incumbrances whatsoever Furthermore I ye s^d Nicholas Shapleigh for my Self my Heirs Execut^{rs} Adm^{rs} do Covena^t & Ingage the above demised Premises to him ye s^d Richard Rice his heirs Execut^{rs} Adm^{rs} and assignes against ye Lawfull Claims or Demands of any person or persons whatsoever forever hereafter [231] To Warrant Secure and Defend In Witness whereof I have hereunto Set my hand and Seal this 10th day of may in ye first year of the Reign of our Soveraign Lord George of Great Brittaine &c King And in the Year of our Lord one Thousand Seven hundred & fifteen The words (Sixty four poles & half west one half point Northerly to s^d Rices Land between y^e fourteenth & fifteenth

Book VIII, Fol. 231.

Line ware Enterlined before Signing And That word or Shapleigh   Nicholas Shapleigh ($^a_{Seal}$)
Signed Sealed & Delivered
 In The Presence of
 Jonathan Mendum
 Paul Wentworth
 Peter Staple
    York ss/ Kittery may 17. 1717
  Mr Nicholas Shapleigh within named acknowledged y^e within written Instrument to be his free act and Deed
                Before Charles ffrost J. Peace.
 Recorded According to the Original May 23^d 1717./
                    p Jos. Hamond Reg^r

Know All men by these presents that I James Emery of Berwick in The County of York in The Province of Massachusets Bay in New England Husbandman for and in Consideration of ye Sum of forty pounds Currant money of ye Province afores^d To me in hand well & Truely paid by my Son James Emery Junr the receipt whereof I Do hereby acknowledge and my Self therewith fully Satisfied contented & paid Have given granted bargained Sold Aliened Enfeoffed Set over & Confirmed and do by these Presents give grant bargaine Sell Aliene Assigne Enfeoffe Set over & Confirm unto him my s^d Son James Emery his heirs & assignes for ever Four Acres & half of Salt marsh Scittuate Lying & being at winter harbour being ye Middle part bounded with ye river on ye Northeast Pendleton Fletchers marsh with ye Ditch on ye Southwest Rebeca Hitchcocks on ye Southeast and ye wood Lands on ye Northwest: Also Eight acres and half more of Salt marsh on Casco Side in ye middle part of s^d marsh bounded at ye Southwst End with ye south East & by South Line between ye Rock in ye Corner of ye wood Land and ye great rock on ye Sea wall on ye South East with ye Sea wall on ye North East with wood Land and Phineas Hulls marsh and on ye Northwst with wood Land Also one Third part of one hundred and Seventy four Acres of wood Land begining at ye Sea at ye middle neck by ye head of ye great pond & from thence Northwest into ye woods one Hundred & Six poles North west by walter Pennewells line & Then Southwest Down to ye river that Divides Capeporpas & Saco & from thence to ye marsh Till It Comes to ye Sea wall Also one Third part of ye house Lott of m^r Hitchcocks ye Third part being five acres bounded with Land John Ab-

BOOK VIII, FOL. 231.

bott on y[e] Southwest a Little ——— on y[e] South East and winter Harbour on y[e] west and all y[e] other parts are bounded with Arthur Warmstalls Land Also one Third part more of Rebeca Hitchcocks Right y[e] Third part being four acres & one Third Salt marsh Together with all & Singular y[e] priviledges and Appurtenances unto y[e] Severall parcells of Land & marsh above mentioned & in any wise appertaining To Have and & Hold y[e] Same as butted & bounded with all & Singular y[e] benefits profits & Priviledges thereof to him y[e] s[d] James Emery Jun[r] his heirs & assigns for ever to y[e] only proper use & behoof of him y[e] s[d] James Emery Jun[r] his heirs & assignes for ever free & Clear & Clearly acquitted of & from all other & former gifts grants bargains Sales Titles Troubles Charges & Incumbrances w[t]soever and that I y[e] s[d] James Emery Sen[r] & my heirs to him y[e] s[d] James Emery Jun[r] his heirs and assignes Shall & Will Warrant & for ever Confirn y[e] Same In Witness whereof I y[e] s[d] James Emery Sen[r] have hereunto Set my hand & Seal y[e] 14[th] Day of octob[r] Annoq, Domini one Thousand Seven hundred & fourteen
1714/   James Emery ($_\text{Seal}^\text{a}$)

Signed Sealed & Delivered
  In y[e] Presence of
    Richard Tozar
    John Croade

York ss/ James Emery psonally appeared and acknowledged y[e] above written Instrum[t] To be his act & Deed Barwick Octob[r] 14th 1714   Before me Ichabod Plaisted J. P.

Recorded According to y[e] Original April 29th 1717./
                         p Jos. Hamond Reg[r]

Know all men by theses presents That I James Emery Jun[r] of Barwick In y[e] County of york and within his Maj[tys] Province of y[e] Massachusets Bay in New England husbandman for & In y[e] Consideration of Twenty three pounds Currant money of New England to me in hand well & Truly paid att y[e] Enscaling and Delivery of These presents by William Dyer of y[e] Town County & Province afores[d] husbandman y[e] receipt whereof I acknowledge and my Self fully Satisfied Contented and paid and have absolutely given granted bargained Sold Aliened Enfeoffed Set over & Confirmed unto y[e] s[d] William Dyer and to his heirs Executors adm[rs] and assignes for ever y[e] one half of y[e] following Salt marsh & upland both for Quantity & Quallity all Lying &

being at Winter Harbour vizt The half of four acres & half of Salt marsh being ye middle part bounded with ye river on ye North East Pendleton Fletchers marsh with ye Ditch on ye Southwest Rebecca Hitchcocks on ye SouthEast and ye wood land on ye Northwest Also ye half of Eight Acres & half of Salt marsh on Saco Side in ye middle part of s^d Marsh bounded at ye Southwest End with ye South East & by South Line between ye rock in ye Corner of ye wood Land & ye Great rock on ye Sea wall on ye South East with ye Sea wall on ye North East with wood Land & Phineas Hulls marsh and on ye Northwest with wood land Also ye half of a Third part of one hundred & Twenty four acres of wood land begining at ye Sea at ye middle neck by ye head of ye great pond and from thence north west unto ye woods one hundred & Six poles Northwest by Walter Pennnewells Line and Then Southwest Down to ye river y^t Divides Capeporpas & Saco and from thence to ye marsh Till it comes to y^e [232] Sea wall Also ye half of one Third part of ye house Lott of Mr Richd Hitchcock ye Third part being five acres bounded with land of John Abbots on ye Southwest a little part on ye South East & winter Harbour on ye West and all ye other parts are bounded with arthor Wormstalls Land Also ye half of one Third part more of Rebecca Hitchcocks right ye Third part being four acres and one Third Salt marsh Together with all and Singular ye wayes profits priviledges rights Comodities and appurtenances to Each & Every part & Parcell of marsh and upland above mentioned In any wise appertaining To Have & To Hold the half of ye above granted and bargained marsh and upland with all ye appurtenances thereunto belonging profits and priviledges unto him ye s^d William Dyer & to his heirs Executors adm^{rs} & Assignes to his & Their own onely proper use benifitt & behoof forever & ye s^d James Emery for him Self his heirs Executors & adm^{rs} Doth Covenant promise & Agree with ye s^d William Dyer his heirs Executors adm^{rs} and Assignes in manner & form following That is to Say That I ye s^d James Emery am ye True Sole & Lawfull owner and Stand Lawfully possest of ye Same In a perfect Estate of Inheritance without any manner of Condition reservation or Limitation of use or uses whatsoever And ye s^d William Dyer his heirs Executors administrators and assignes Shall & may from hence forth & for ever hereafter Lawfully peaceably and Quietly have hold Occupie possess & Enjoy all ye above granted & bargained premisses with Their appurtenances freely & Clearly Acquitted Exonerated and Discharged of & from all former gifts grants bargains Sales Leases Thirds Dowries mortgages

Titles Troubles Charges & Incumbrances whatsoever And Further I ye s^d James Emery my heirs Executors & Adm^{rs} Shall & will from henceforth & for ever hereafter warrant & Defend all ye above granted and bargained premisses with their appurtenances unto him ye s^d William Dyer and to his heirs Execut^{rs} & adm^{rs} and assignes forever Against ye Lawfull Claims & Demands of all and Every person w^{t}soever In Witness whereof I have hereunto Set my hand and Seal Dated y^e Twenty Third Day of may Anno Domini Seventeen hundred & Seventeen & in y^e Third year of the reign of his Majesty King over Great Brittaine &c (the words may And third Interlined before Signing & Sealing
Signed Sealed & Delivered   James Emery ($_{Seal}^a$)
 In presence of us
 Daniel Wadlien
 John Bradstreet
 York sc May y^e 24th 1717./
 Then James Emery Junr made his appearence before me y^e Subscrib^r one of his Maj^{tys} Justices of y^e peace & Acknowledged y^e Above written to be his Volluntary Act & Deed   Elisha Plaisted Jus^t peace
 Recorded According to ye Original July 17th 1717./
         p Jos. Hamond Reg^r

 Know All men by these presents that I William Hook Junr of Salisbury in ye County of Essex in ye Province of ye Massachusets Bay in New England Yeoman for Divers good Causes & Considerations me hereunto Moveing have remised released & for ever Quit claimed And do by these presents for my Selfe my heirs Ex^{rs} & Adm^{rs} fully freely & Absolutely remise release and for ever Quitt claim unto my Honoured father m^r Wm Hook of Salisbury afores^d his heirs & Assignes all Such right title Estate part portion Devidend Interest Inheritance claime & Demand whatsoever which I ye s^d Wm Hooke Junr Ever had now have or hereafter may Could Should or Ought to have or make of in or to any grants Pattents Lotts house Lots farms Town rights or Comon rights Tract or tracts & parcells of land Marsh or Meadow whatsoever within ye Township of York in ye County of York in ye Province afores^d by Vertue of a Deed of Gift made & given to me by my s^d ffather Wm Hook under his hand & Seal of Certain Lands & rights in ye s^d Township of York as is therein more fully Exprest bareing Date Aprill 23^d 1717

& yᵉ postscript Adition So Called unto sᵈ deed dated may the third 1717./ in yᵉ third year of his Majᵗʸˢ reign Inrolled in yᵉ records for yᵉ County of Essex aforesᵈ Lib : 28 : Folᵒ 274 or any other former deed or deeds To have & To hold all & Singular yᵉ sᵈ remised & released premisses unto yᵉ sᵈ Wᵐ Hooke Senʳ his heirs & Assignes & to his & their only proper use & behoofe for ever So that Neither I yᵉ sᵈ Wᵐ Hooke Junʳ Nor my heirs Nor any other person or persons in our Name right or Stead Shall nor will by any Way Nor Means hereafter have claime Challenge or demand any Estate right Title or Interest of in or to yᵉ premisses or any part or parcell thereof but thereof & therefrom shall be utterly Excluded & for ever Debarred by these presents And I yᵉ sᵈ Wᵐ Hooke Junʳ my heirs Exʳˢ and Admʳˢ Shall & will for ever hereafter Warrant Secure & Defend all & Singular yᵉ above remised premisses unto yᵉ sᵈ William Hooke Senʳ his heirs & Assignes against all yᵉ Lawfull Claims & Demands of Any person or persons whatsoever from by & under me & Mine Witness my hand & Seal this 28ᵗʰ day of Augˢᵗ Anno Domini 1717./ Annoq̨ RⁱRˢ Georgii Magna Brittania &c Quarto

   Memorandˣ that yᵉ words Any other former deed or deeds were Interlined before Sealing · William Hooke Junʳ (ₛₑₐₗᵃ) Signed Sealed & Delivered

   In presence of us
Caleb Cushing
Solomoˣ Shepard

   Mʳ Wᵐ Hooke Junʳ personally Appeared before me yᵉ Subscribʳ & Acknowledged his hand & Seal & yᵉ above written Instrumᵗ to be his Voluntary Act & Deed. Dated this 28ᵗʰ of Augˢᵗ 1717   Henry Sumerby Justice of yᵉ peace

   Recorded According to yᵉ Original Septʳ yᵉ 5ᵗʰ 1717./

                      p Jos : Hamond Regʳ

Know All men by these presents that We Humphry Hooke of Silisbury and Jacob Hooke of Salisbury in yᵉ County of Essex in yᵉ Province of the Massachusets Bay in New England for diverse good Causes & Considerations us hereunto Moveing have remised released & for ever Quitt claimed & do by these presents for our Selves our heirs Exʳˢ & Admʳˢ [233] fully freely & Absolutely remise release & for ever Quit claime unto our Honᵈ ffather Mʳ William Hooke of Salisbury aforesᵈ his heirs & Assigns all Such right Title

Book VIII, Fol. 233.

Estate Interest part portion Inheritance Devidend claime & demand whatsoever which we ye s^d Humphry & Jacob Ever had Now have or hereafter may could should or Ought to have or make of in & to any grants pattents Lots farm or farms Divisions Comon rights tracts or parcells of Land Marsh or Meadow whatsoever within ye Township of York formerly in ye Province of Maine now in ye County of York in ye Province of ye Massachusets Bay in New England by Vertue of a deed of Gift made & Given to us ye s^d Humphry & Jacob by our s^d father Wm Hook under his hand and Seal of Certain Lands & rights ye s^d Township of York bareing Date ye first day of May Anno Domini 1717. Annoq RR^s Georgii Magna Brittania. &c^t. Tertio./ recorded in ye Publick records for ye County of York Lib : 8th folio 207 or by Vertue of any other deed or deeds of ye premisses formerly made to us by our s^d father Wm Hook To have & To hold all and Singular ye s^d remised & released premisses unto ye s^d Wm Hook his heirs & Assignes & to his & their only proper use benefit & behoofe for ever So that Neither We ye s^d Humphrey & Jacob Nor Either of us Nor our heirs Nor Either of our heirs Ex^{rs} or Adm^{rs} Nor any other p^{r}son or p^{r}sons in our Name right or Stead or in ye Name right or Stead of Any of us Shall nor will by any way or Means hereafter have claime Challange nor demand any right Title Estate or Interest of in & to ye premisses or any part or parcell thereof but thereof & there from Shall be utterly Excluded & for ever Debarred by these presents And We ye s^d Humphry & Jacob our heirs Ex^{rs} and Adm^{rs} shall & will for ever hereafter Warrant Secure and Defend all & Singular ye above remised premisses unto ye s^d Wm Hook his heirs & Assigns Against all ye Lawfull Claims & Demands of Any p^{r}son or p^{r}sons whatsoever from by & under us or ours Witness Our hands & Seals this 28th day of Augst Anno Domini 1717 Annoq Regni Regis Georgii Magna Brittania &c^t Quarto

 Memorand^x that ye words of ye premisses were once Interlined before Sealing   Humphry Hook (a Seal)
Signed Sealed & Delivered   Jacob Hook (a Seal)
 In p^{r}sence of us
  Solomo^x Shepard
  Caleb Cushing
 Cap^{tn} Humphry Hook & m^r Jacob Hook p^{r}sonally Appeared before me ye Subscriber & both of them did Acknowl-

edge their hands & Seals & y̍ within written Instrumt to be their Volluntary Act & Deed. Dated this 28th of Augst 1717.

Henry Sumerby Justce of ye peace

Recorded According to ye Original Sept 5th 1717./

p Jos. Hamond Regr

Be It known unto All men by these p^rsents that I John Cousins of Westgostuggo in ye Province of Maine husbandman for & in Consideration of that love favour and friendship Maintainence Dwelling & Entertainmt that I have already received hereto fore of Mary Sayward of ye Town of York Widdow and for & in Consideration that ye sd Mary Sayward by her deed under her hand & Seale hath Covenanted promissed & Agreed with me ye sd John Cousins for to Take Care of me & provide for me both food & rayment Lodging & Attendence with all other things Convenient & Necessary for a man of my Age Degree & Quallity & Consistent with the Abillity of ye sd Mary Sayward her heirs Exrs & Admrs dureing my Natural Life both & as well in sickness as in health as Also for Divers other good Causes & Considerations in that former recited deed More At Large Specified Have & by these presents do give grant Enfeoff demise Trans ferr Set over & Confirm unto ye sd Mary Sayward her heirs Exrs Admrs & Assignes all that barn now standing upon a Certaine Tract of Land called or known by ye Indian Name Susqussugg or Cousines place Lying & being in Casco in ye Province of Maine aforesd Together with ye ruins of that Mansion or Dwelling house whereunto ye sd barn did formerly belong Together with all ye upland & Marsh unto ye sd barn & ruined house now or heretofore belonging & which ye sd Cousins heretofore for ye space of forty years or More formerly past Occupied possessed & Injoyed which Tract of Land aforesd is by Estimation three hundred Acres be it more or Less & Lyeth near unto a Tract of Land now or of late in ye possession of One mr Wm Ryall bounded with a hill Called herock hill on ye Southeast or thereabouts & on ye Northwest by ye North river that runs to Certaine falls Called Susgussugg or ye Little river & ye other bounds are the Comons And Also for ye aforesd Consideration I ye sd John Cousins do give grant Enfeoffe Set over & Confirm unto ye sd Mary Sayward her heirs Exrs Admrs & Assignes all that Moiety or halfendeal of that Island Comonly Called or known by ye Name of hog Island or otherwise Cousins his Island Lying & being in ye Midst of Casco Bay or thereabouts y⁰ other part or Moiety of sᵈ Island I yᵉ sᵈ John Cousins granted unto Richard Bray formerly by Deed or writing under my hand with all & Every the Apurtenances thereunto belonging Either to the barn three hundred Acres of Land upland & Marsh & Also yᵉ sᵈ halfendeal of yᵉ sᵈ Island & Every part & parcell thereof with their & Every of their Appurtenances in as large & Ample mañer to all Constructions as I yᵉ sᵈ John Cousins Can or may give grant demise Sell or Confirm yᵉ Same to all Constructions Intents & purposes To have & to hold yᵉ sᵈ Barn ruined house & yᵉ foresᵈ three hundred Acres of land So Esteemed upland & Marsh & Also yᵉ sᵈ halfendeal of yᵉ sᵈ Island with all their & Every of their Appurtenances priviledges respectively as all woods under woods Timbʳ water water Courses profits Issues Easemtᵗ Emolumˢ & Comoditys thereunto yᵉ sᵈ premisses or any part thereof Belonging or in Any wise Appurtaining & all yᵉ right Title [234] Interest & possession that I yᵉ sᵈ John Cousins formerly had now have or hereafter ought to have by Vertue of Any deed grant writing or Manuscript from One Richard Vines Gent or any other pʳson whatSoever to her yᵉ sᵈ Mary Sayward her heirs Exʳˢ Admʳˢ & Assignes for ever and I yᵉ sᵈ John Cousins do hereby Acknowledge that yᵉ sᵈ barn ruined house and Lands and also yᵉ Moiety of yᵉ Island aforesᵈ with their & Every of their Appurtenances as before Mentioned are properly my own: in fee Simple & have full power to give grant & Sell yᵉ Same at yᵉ day of yᵉ Date hereof./ And further I yᵉ sᵈ John Cousins for me my heirs Exʳˢ and Admʳˢ & Assignes & for Every & Either of them do hereby Covenant promiss & grant to & with yᵉ sᵈ Mary Sayward her heirs Exʳˢ Admʳˢ & Assignes & to & with Every & Either of them that she yᵉ sᵈ Mary Sayward her heirs Exʳˢ Admʳˢ or Assignes, or Either of them Shall from time to time & at all times hereafter for ever Quietly and peaceably have hold Occupy possess & Enjoy all & Every of the premisses herein and above Mentioned without yᵉ Let disturbence Mollestation or denial or putting out of him yᵉ sᵈ John Cousins his heirs Exʳˢ Admʳˢ or Assignes or of Any other person or persons by his or their Means Consent or procuremᵗ And against any person or persons lawfully Claiming yᵉ sᵈ Estate or Any part or parcell thereof In Witness whereof I yᵉ sᵈ John Cousins have hereunto Set my hand & Seal Even yᵉ fourth day of Aprill in yᵉ One & Thirtieth year of yᵉ reign of Our Soveraign Lord Charles the Second by the grace of God of England Scotland ffrance & Ireland King Defend[r] of y[e] faith &c[t] And in y[e] year of our Lord God 1679./

Sealed & Delivered in
  y[e] presence of us whose
  Names are Subscribed
    The mark of
Charles ⟨ ⟩ Martine
Samuel Webbar
William Wormwood

The mark of
John ⟨⟩ Cousins ([a Seal])

John Cousins Came before me this 26th day of June 1682./ And Acknowledged this Instrum[t] to be his free Act & Deed unto Mary Sayward her heirs Ex[rs] Adm[rs] & Assignes forever./   Edw[d] Rishworth Just peace
Recorded According to y[e] Original Aug[st] y[e] 8th 1717./
                         p Jos. Hamond Reg[r]

To All Christian People to whom this may Come or Concern M[rs] Hannah Preble of York in y[e] County of York in y[e] Province of y[e] Massachusets Bay in New England Widdow Sendeth Greeting./ Know Ye y[e] s[d] Hannah Diverse good Causes & Considerations her thereunto Moveing & More Especially y[e] Natural Affection & True Love she hath & doth alwayes bear unto her Natural & Welbeloved Son Jonathan Preble of s[d] York hath given granted bargained Assigned Aliened Enfeoffed & made over and doth by these presents give grant bargaine Quitclaime Assigne Aliene Enfeoffe & Make over & fully freely & Absolutely Convey & Confirm unto her son y[e] s[d] Jonathan Preble & unto his heirs & Assignes for ever her whole right Title & Interest Shee hath or Ever ought to have unto that Estate of Land & Marsh that M[rs] Mary Sayward the Mother of y[e] s[d] Hannah Late of s[d] York dec[d] purchased or bought of John Cousins of Casco Bay as p a deed from s[d] Cousins unto y[e] s[d] Mary Sayward bareing date y[e] fourth day of April in the year One Thousand Six hundred Seventy Nine referrence thereunto being had may At Large Appear which s[d] Land or Lands & Meadows or Marsh Salt & fresh is Lying & being within y[e] boundaries of s[d] Casco Bay afore Mentioned as p afores[d] deed or writing doth appear as afores[d] which s[d] Lands & Marsh or Estate hath Never yet been Divided between y[e] Children of y[e] s[d] dec[d] unto him y[e] s[d] Jonathan Preble Together with all y[e] rights Titles Interests Emollum[ts] & Ap-

purtenances thereunto belonging or Appurtaining or any wayes redownding unto ye same or any part or parcell thereof that doth Now or Ever hereafter belong unto ye s^d Hannah Preble of any part share or portion of that Estate of John Cousins^{es} before Mentioned unto him ye s^d Jonathan As afores^d To have & To hold And Quietly & peaceably to possess & Enjoy as a Sure Estate in ffee Simple both for him ye s^d Jonathan & his heirs & Assignes forever More over ye s^d Mrs Hannah Preble doth for her selfe her heirs Ex^{rs} & Adm^{rs} to & with her s^d Son Jonathan Covena^t Ingage & promiss her part of aboves^d Premisses to be free & Clear from all former gifts grants bargains Sales Mortgages or any other Incumberm^{ts} whatsoever as also from all future Claimes Challenges or any Interruptions whatsoever Proceeding ye Date hereof to be had or Commenced by her ye s^d Hannah her heirs Ex^{rs} Adm^{rs} or Assignes & she will warrantise & Defend ye Same from all persons from by & under her./ In Witness hereof y^e s^d Mrs Hannah Preble hath hereunto Set her hand & Seal this Seventh day of Augst in y^e year of Our Lord One thousand Seven hundred and Seventeen and in y^e fourth year of y^e reign of our Soveraign Lord George King of Great Brittaine &c^t/   Hannah Preble ($_{Seal}^{a}$)
Signed Sealed & Delivered
  In y^e presence of
  Lewis Bane
  Caleb Preble
    York sc/ York August y^e 8th 1717

Mrs Hannah Preble psonally Appeared before me y^e Subscriber one of his Maj^{tys} Justices of y^e peace for s^d County & Acknowledged this above written Instrum^t to be her free Act & Deed   Abra^m Preble
  Recorded According to ye Original Augst ye 8th 1717./
                     p Jos. Hamond Reg^r

To All People to whom these presents shall Come Joseph Sayward of York in ye County of York within his Maj^{tys} Province of ye Massachusests Bay in New England Milwright Sendeth Greeting./ Know Ye that I ye that I ye s^d Joseph Sayward for & in Consideration of ye Sum of Twelve pounds in Curra^t money of ye aboves^d Province to me in hand before the [235] Ensealing hereof well & truely paid by Jonathan Preble of ye aboves^d Town County & Province Milwright ye rec^t whereof I do hereby Acknowledge & thereof & of

Every part & parcell thereof do Exonerate Acquit and Discharge ye s^d Jon^a Preble his heirs & Assignes forever Have given granted bargained Sold remised released Conveyed & Confirmed and by these presents do fully freely & Absolutely give grant bargaine Sell remise release Transferr Convey & Confirm unto ye s^d Jonathan Preble & to his heirs & Assignes for ever x All ye Estate right Title Interest Inheritance use property Possession Claime & Demand whatsoever which I ye s^d Sayward Ever had now have or which I ye s^d Sayward my heirs Ex^rs or Adm^rs in time to Come may might or Ought to have of in or to all that tract of or parcell or parcells of Land & Marsh Marshes or Marshes that was given by a deed to my Grandmother Mary Sayward Late of s^d York dec^d (belonging to s^d York in her day) by John Cousins of Westgostuggo in ye Province of Maine within Casco Bay Since in York dec^d bareing date ye fourth day of Aprill in ye year of our Lord One thousand Six hundred Seventy Nine As I ye s^d Joseph Sayward Stand related unto ye Estate of my s^d Grandmother ye s^d Mary Sayward dec^d being ye Only Son & Child now Surviving of Jonathan Sayward ye Son of s^d Mary Sayward dec^d my part of s^d Cousins^es Estate being by Computation ye One fifth part of s^d land & Marsh Mentioned in s^d deed ye which s^d Land & Marsh is Scittuated within the boundaryes of Casco bay afore Mentioned both of ye Island & Maine Land and Salt & fresh Marsh Mentioned in afores^d deed ye which s^d Land and Marsh before Mentioned Still being undivided unto him ye s^d Jonathan Preble To have & To hold ye s^d granted & released premisses & Every part thereof to him ye s^d Jon^a Preble & to his heirs and Assignes for ever to his & their only propper use benefit & behoofe forevermore so that Neither I ye s^d Joseph Sayward my heirs or Assignes Nor any other p^rson or p^rsons by from or under me them or any of them shall or will by any Means hereafter have Claime Challenge or demand Any Estate right Title or Interest of in or to All or any part of ye s^d granted & released premisses but of & from all & Every Action of right Estate Title Interest Claime and demand of in & to ye premisses & Every part & parcell thereof I my Selfe & Every of them shall be utterly Excluded & forever debarred by these p^rsents And further I ye s^d Joseph Sayward for my Selfe my heirs Ex^rs Adm^rs do hereby Covenant grant & Agree ye Above granted & released premisses wth ye Appurtenances & Every part thereof unto ye s^d Jon^a Preble his heirs & Assignes Against ye Lawfull Claimes & Demands of All & Every p^rson & p^rsons Any ways claiming or demanding ye Same or any part

thereof by from or under me for ever hereafter to Warrant & Defend./ In Witness whereof I have hereunto Set my hand & Seal ye Eighteenth day of July Anno Domini One Thousand Seven hundred Seventeen and in ye third year of ye reign of George by ye Grace of God King of Great Brittaine &c   Joseph Sayward (a Seal)
Signed Sealed & Delivered
  In ye presence of
  Daniel Simpson
  Caleb Preble
  Nathl Freeman
      York sc July 18th 1717
  Joseph Sayward personally Appeared before me Abra^m Preble Esqr One of his Maj^{tys} Justices of ye peace & Acknowledged ye Above Instrum^t to be his free Act & Deed
                                    Abra^m Preble
  Recorded According to ye Original Augst ye 8th 1717./
                        p Jos: Hamond Reg^r

To All People to whom these presents shall Come John Sayward of York in the County of York within his Maj^{tys} Province of ye Massachusets Bay in New England Yeoman Sendeth Greeting Know Y^e that I ye s^d John Sayward for & in Consideration of ye Sum of five pounds in Curra^t money of ye aboves^d Province to me in hand before ye Ensealing hereof Well & Truely paid by Jonathan Preble of ye aboves^d Town County & Province Milwright the rec^t whereof I do hereby Acknowledge and thereof & of Every part and parcell thereof do Exonerate Acquit & discharge ye s^d Jon^a Preble his heirs & Assignes for ever Have given granted bargained Sold remised released Conveyed & Confirmed & by these presents do fully freely & Absolutely give grant bargaine Sell remise release Transferr Convey & Confirm unto ye s^d Jon^a Preble & unto his heirs & Assignes for ever all ye Estate right Title Interest Inheritance use property possession Claime & Demand whatsoever which I ye s^d Sayward Ever had now have or which I ye s^d Sayward my heirs Ex^{rs} or Adm^{rs} in time to Come may Might or Ought to have of in or to all that tract or parcell or parcells of Land & Marsh Marshes that was given by a deed to my Grandmother Mary Sayward Late of s^d York dec^d belonging to s^d York in her day by John Cousins of Westgostuggo in ye Province of Maine within Casco Bay Since in York dec^d bareing date ye fourth day of Aprill in ye year of our Lord One Thousand

Book VIII, Fol. 235.

Six hundred Seventy Nine As I ye s^d John Sayward Stand related unto ye Estate of my s^d Grandmother ye s^d Mary Sayward dec^d being ye Only Son now Surviveing of John Sayward ye Son of sd Mary Sayward dec^d my part of s^d Cousins^{es} Estate being by Computation ye One   of s^d land & Marsh Mentioned in s^d Deed ye which s^d Land & Marsh is Scittuated within ye boundarys of Casco Bay afore Mentioned both of ye Island & Maine Land & Salt & fresh Marsh Mentioned in afores^d deed ye which s^d lands & Marsh before Mentioned Still being undivided unto him ye s^d Jon^a Preble To have & To hold ye s^d granted & released premisses & Every part thereof to him ye s^d Jon^a Preble & to his heirs & Assignes forever to his & their only proper use benefit & behoofe forevermore So that Neither I ye s^d John Sayward my heirs & Assignes Nor any other person or persons by from or under me them or Any of them Shall or will by Any Means hereafter have Claime Challenge or to Any Estate right Title or Interest of in or to all or any part of ye s^d granted & releas^d premisses but of & from all & Every part Action of right Estate Title Interest Claims & demands of in & to ye premisses & Every part & parcell thereof I my Selfe & Every of them Shall be utterly Excluded & for ever debarred by these presents./ And further I ye s^d John Sayward for my Selfe my heirs Ex^{rs} Adm^{rs} do hereby Covena^t grant & Agree ye Above granted & released premisses with ye Appurtenances & Every part thereof unto ye s^d Jon^a Preble his heirs & Assigns Against ye Lawfull Claims & demands of all & Every person and persons Any wayes Claiming or demanding ye Same or any part thereof by from or under me for ever hereafter to Warrant & Defend In Witness whereof I have hereunto Set my hand & Seal y^e Eighteenth day of July Anno Domini One thousand Seven hundred Seventeen And in y^e third Year of y^e reign of George by y^e grace of God King of Great Brittaine &c

Signed Sealed & Delivered   John Sayward ($_{Seal}^a$)

In presence
Daniel Simpson
Saml Bray
Nathl Freeman
York sc/ July 18th 1717.

John Sayward p^{r}sonally Appeared before me Abra^m Preble Esqr one of his Maj^{tys} Justices of y^e peace for s^d County & Acknowledged y^e above Instrum^t to be his free Act & Deed./
          Abra^m Preble

Recorded According to ye Original Augst 8th 1717./
          p Jos. Hamond Reg^r

[236] Know All men by these presents that I Sam¹ Hill of Kittery in the County of York within y{e} Province of y{e} Massachusets Bay in New England Jun{r} who lately Marryed y{e} within Named Mary Nelson do by these presents for my Selfe my heirs Ex{rs} & Adm{rs} Confirm Ratify & Allow y{e} Sale of y{e} premisses within Expressed According to y{e} Tenour thereof Made by y{e} s{d} Mary Nelson./ In Witness whereof I have hereunto Set my hand & Seal the 20{th} day of July in y{e} third year of his Maj{tys} Reign Anno Domini 1717./

Signed Sealed & Delivered   Sam{ll} Hill Jun{r} (Seal)

In presence of us
Charles ffrost
Sarah X Brawn (her mark)
Sarah ffrost

York sc/ July 20{th} 1717

Sam¹ Hill Jun{r} above Named Acknowledged y{e} above written Postscript to be his free Act & Deed./

     Before Charles ffrost J: peace

Recorded According to y{e} Original Sept{r} 17{th} 1717./

     p Jos. Hamond Reg{r}

memor{x} The deed unto which y{e} above postscript has a reference is recorded in this book Folio 147./

     Att{r} Jos. Hamond Reg{r}

To All Christian People to whom this present Deed of Sale Shall Come Greeting./ Know Ye that I Diamond Sergent of y{e} Town of York in y{e} Province of Maine in New England Tayler & Elizabeth my wife Send Greeting Know ye that I y{e} s{d} Diamond Sergent for & in Consideration of Sixty five pounds of Curra{t} money of New England to me in hand paid before the Enseuling & Delivery of these presents by James Webber Once of Yarmouth Now resident in Kittery Cordwainer well and Truely paid the rec{t} whereof I do hereby Acknowledge & our selves therewith fully Satisfied & Contented thereof & of Every part thereof do Acquit & discharge y{e} s{d} James Webber his heirs Ex{rs} Adm{rs} and Assignes & Every of them for ever by these presents have given granted bargained Sold and do by these presents Absolutely give grant Bargaine & Sell all that house &

Tract of Land Lying in the Township of Kittery in ye County of York At or in a place Called Crooked lane Near Adjacent to Mr Robert Cutts Dwelling house unto ye s^d James Webber his heirs Ex^{rs} Adm^{rs} or Assignes for ever the s^d Dwelling house & Land Containing about three parts of An Acre of Land be it more or Less being ye Late homestead of ye s^d Sergent afores^d & is Now in ye Occupation of Samuel Seward and is that Tract of Land which was Conveyed to Sergent by Nicholas ffrost of Portsm^o as p deed Appears upon record referrence thereunto being had Together with all ye gardens backsides wharfe & Landing Wells fenceing highwayes Easm^{ts} Appurtenances & priviledges whatsoever belonging to ye s^d house & land To have & To hold All ye s^d house & Land as they are hereby Set forth & discribed & Every part & Member thereof unto ye only & Sole use of him ye s^d James Webber his heirs Ex^{rs} Adm^{rs} or Assignes forever more against him ye s^d Diamond Sergent his heirs Ex^{rs} Adm^{rs} or any other under us whatsoever and furthermore I ye s^d Diamond Sergent do for my Selfe my heirs Covena^t to & with ye s^d James Webber his heirs Ex^{rs} Adm^{rs} or Assignes that the premisses are free from all Incumbrances whatsoever as Sales gifts grants Joyntures Dowries Leases Quit rents reversions or remainders And that I ye s^d Diamond Sergent have full power & Lawfull Authority to Sell & dispose of ye same the peaceable and Quiet possession thereof to Warrant & forever defend against all persons whatsoever Laying a Lawfull Claime thereunto & that it shall be Lawfull for ye s^d Webber to Improve & Occupy ye same forever hereafter As Witness we have Set to Our hands & Seal this ye 19th day of August One Thousand Seven hundred & Seventeen in ye 5 year of his Maj^{tys} reign George of England Scotland & Irel^d

Signed Sealed & Delivered   Diamond Sergent (Seal)
  In presence of us   Elizabeth Sergent (Seal)
  Hercules Fernald
  Richard Long
    York sc/ Augst 30th 1717

Diamond Sergent personally Appeared before me one of his Maj^{tys} Justices of peace for County of York./ Acknowledged this Instrum^t to be his free Act & Deed./
                                        Lewis Bane
Recorded Accorded to ye Original Sep^{tr} 9th 1717./
                              p Jos. Hamond Reg^r

Book VIII, Fol. 237.

The Deposition of Martha Lord Aged about Seventy Seven years Testifieth and Saith that She very well remembers m^r Tuckers living at Great Works after m^r Leader Left ye place which was upwards of Sixty years agon And further this Depona^t Saith that m^r Rogers Plaisted dweld at ye Same place fifty Seven years agone or thereabouts and he & his Sons have Mostly been in Possession Ever since And further Saith that ye now Town of Berwick from Sturgeon Creek up to Toziars above Salmon falls hath been Inhabited above Sixty years./ & further Saith not

York sc/ Berwick Septr 19th 1717./ Sworn in Perpetuam rei Memoriam   Before   John Wheelwright   J peace
Charles ffrost   & Quorum
Recorded According to ye Original Sep^t 20th 1717./

p Jos. Hamond Reg^r

James Emery Aged Eighty Seven years Testifieth that ye bridge Called & known by ye Name of fagoty Bridge was in ye brook Neare where John Tompsons house Now Standeth in ye road which formerly Led to york in ye Now road to Wells from Berwick & that there was No other bridg known by that Name as he knoweth of on that brook for more than Sixty years./ Taken upon Oath this 19th of Sep^t 1717. in Perpetua^x rei memor^x Before Jno Wheelwright   Just peace
Charles ffrost   & Quorum
Recorded According to ye Original Sep^t 26th 1717/

p Jos : Hamond Reg^r

[237] The Deposition of John Nason Aged Seventy Seven years or thereabouts Testifieth & Saith that he very well remembers that m^r Richard Laader lived in ye Now Town of Berwick at a place Called ye great Workes & had a dwelling house there & a Sawmill on ye falls Called Assabumbedock falls and was in the possession & Improved ye mill house & ye Land in s^d place/ And Afterwards which is Now Above Sixty years agone Left ye house Mill & land in ye possession of the Hutchinsons and Mr Edward Rishworth And is Now in y^e possession of John Plaisted Esqr and his Son Elisha Plaisted Esqr & Mrs Mary Hill./ In Testimony of what is

BOOK VIII, FOL. 237.

above written I have hereunto Set my hand y^e 19th day of Sep^t Anno Domini 1717./
            his
         John /\$/ Nason
           mark
York sc/ Berwick Septr 19 : 1717./ Jurat in Perpetuam rei Memoriam   Cor: Nobis   Jno Wheelwright   J peace
        Charles ffrost   & Quorum
Recorded According to y^e Original Septr 20th 1717./
       p Jos. Hamond Reg^r

York sc Berwick Septr 19th 1717. James Emery Aged About Eighty Seven years & Anne Tompson Aged About Eighty five years made Oath to ye Truth of ye within Affidavit of John Nason
 Sworn in Perpetuam rei Memoria^x
     Before   Jno Wheelwright   J. peace
        Charles ffrost   & Quorum
Recorded According to ye Original Septr 20th 1717
       p Jos. Hamond Reg^r

 The Deposition of Henry Wright of full age Testifieth & Saith that m^r Roger Plaisted dec^d with whom I lived & Served Ten years which Service Ended Sundry years before his decease was at that time in ye possession of all ye Meadows Called Tadnock Marshes I this Depona^t did Mow & Make hay in s^d Meadows for ye above s^d Plaisted many years & never was Mollested Neither then Nor Since as Ever I heard of or knew by Any Town or private person in all my life and further I this Depona^t do Testifie that ye above s^d Plaisted was in possession of ye Meadow Called by ye Name of ye New Marsh Lying South & by west about a mile & halfe from s^d Tadnock According to my best Judgment which Meadow lyeth upon a brook all along Near a Mile on s^d Brook from ye river side which river is known by ye Name of the Great Works river with all ye points & pieces of Meadow on s^d river from Wm Piles his brook So Called to ye Lower points Near to ye Walnut points on s^d river & I this depona^t have for above fifty years Since helpt to mow & make hay at all those places above Mentioned for y^e person above Named   and his Sons have been in Quiet possession without any Interuption that Ever I heard of or knew to this day & further Saith Not

Henry $\overset{\text{his}}{\wedge}$ Wright
mark

Boston March 14th 1714/5 Jurat in Perpetuam rei Memoria^x Cor: Nobis   Penn Townsend   J. peace
Saml Lynde   & Quoru^x

Dover in New Hampsh^r 25th April 1715.

Walter Allen Came before us y^e Subscrib^r & made Oath to y^e Truth of y^e Deposition of Henry Wright on y^e Other side y^e day & year above written   Richd Waldron   Justices
Jno Plaisted   peace

Recorded According to ye Original Sep^t 20th 1717

p Jos: Hammond Reg^r

To All Christian People to whom these presents Shall Come Samuel Littlefield of Wells Sends Greeting./ Now Know Ye that I Saml Littlefied of Wells in ye County of York Province of ye Massachusets Bay in New England Planter for & in Consideration of the Sum of Thirty one pounds in good & Currant money of New England in hand paid & Secured to be paid to me by ffrancis Sawyer of ye Town & County afores^d & other good & Lawfull Considerations me thereunto moveing have given & granted and do by these presents give grant bargaine Sell Alienate Enfeoffe make over & Confirm unto ffrancis Sawyer afores^d One Quarter part of Kenebunk falls to build a mill or mills which was granted to Edmund Littlefield & to Joseph Littlefield by ye Town of Wells and Capeporpoise to build a mill or mills with all priviledges of ye Stream the grants do Specify & Also Cutting of Timber on Each Side ye river with ye priviledges & Appurtenances belonging to s^d Mill./ that is to Say for Laying of bords & Timber on Each side ye river Sufficient for One years Sawing Yearly for ever & a Tract of Land begining ye foot leveing four rods on ye river Joyning on Moses Littlefield on ye South being 60 pole in breadth runing Towards ye Mill falls on ye Southeast Side runing to Saml Littlefields head Line being thirty Eight Acres At Least a hay way Excepted three rods wide through this Land for ye use of ye Mill & Also five acres of Marsh bounded on ye East Side of Capeporpoise river Alias Mousum on ye North side of a Little hill known by the Name of Clay hill & So bounded where ye s^d Sawyer Sees good to take it most for his Conveniency in ye s^d Saml Lit-

tlefields Marsh And ye s^d ffrancis Sawyer is to pay ye Annual rent to ye Town According to ye Agreem^t on ye Town grant And ye s^d ffrancis Sawyer promisses to ye s^d Saml Littlefield that if he Sees good to Dispose of ye above granted premisses that ye s^d Saml Littlefield Shall have ye first refusal of it./ I ye Aboves^d Samuel Littlefield do make Over & Sell unto ye s^d ffrancis Sawyer To have & To hold from me my heirs Ex^{rs} Adm^{rs} &Assignes unto him his heirs Ex^{rs} Adm^{rs} or Assignes Together with all & Singular ye premisses rights & Appurten^{ces} thereunto belonging or any wayes Appurtaining As a free & Clear Estate in fee Simple for ever. And I ye aboves^d Saml Littlefield for me my heirs Ex^{rs} Adm^{rs} do Covena^t promiss to & with ffrancis Sawyer aboves^d his heirs Ex^{rs} Adm^{rs} or assignes that I am ye true Owner & possessor of ye Aboves^d premisses & have full power right & Authority to Sell & Dispose of ye Same and do affirm & promiss it Every part & parcell of it to be free & Clear & fully Clearly & Absolutely Acquitted & Discharged of & from all other & former gifts & grants bargains Alienations Mortgages Dowryes Sales or Incumbrances w^{t}soever and that I Will Warrant & Defend ye Same from all or any person whatsoever Laying any legal claime thereto. In Witness whereof I ye Aboves^d Saml Littlefield have hereunto put my hand & Seal this Tenth day of December in ye year of our Lord 1716./ And in ye reign of Our Soveraign Lord George King of Great Brittaine Defend^r of ye faith. The Enterlining ye being 60 rods in breadth runing towards ye Mill falls was before Signing & Sealing & Delivery of these presents
Signed Sealed & Delivered   Saml Littlefield (Seal)
  In p^{r}sence of us   her
  Saml Emery   ffrancis X Littlefield (Seal)
  David Littlefield   mark
  David Littlefield

[238] York sc/ Wells May 14 : 1717 :/ The within Named Saml Littlefield and ffrancis his wife p^{r}sonally Appeared before me ye Subscriber one of his Maj^{tys} Justices of ye peace for s^d County & Acknowledged this Instrum^t to be their Act & Deed./ And ye s^d ffrancis did at ye Same time give up all her right of Dower or thirds which otherwise she might have had thereunto./   John Wheelwright

Recorded According to ye Original Septr 10th 1717./
                            p Jos. Hamond Reg^r

Book VIII, Fol. 238.

Eight hundred Acres of Land at least lying near ye Township of Wells and Capeporpus Viz^t on ye North Side thereof part of a great parcell of Land About four or Six mile Square which was formerly Sold by Sosowen ye father & Confirmed by ffewellin ye Son both Sagamores unto Peter Turbut John Sanders & John Bush & by them Sold unto Harlackinden Symonds./ at ye Instance & request of m^r Wm Walker Agent for m^r Samuel Greenwood Edward Martyn and Benj^a Bromsden ye s^d Eight hundred Acres of Land is Surveyed and Laid out to ye s^d Saml Greenwood Edward Martyn & Benj^a Bromsden as followeth that is to Say ye foot line begining at ye North East Side of Mousham river formerly Called Capeporpus river where is a Mark^t Tree between ye river & ye Top of ye hill & So running up a northeast line upon ye head line of ye Township of Wells One Mile unto a pitch pine tree mark^t on four Sides Near a Small Swamp on ye Southwest Side of ye s^d pitch pine Tree & then runing from ye s^d Northeast Corner Tree or pitch pine Tree upon a West Northwest point of ye Compass & So Along by Severall Trees Mark^t & So runing over ye Top of a high rockey hill Near a mile distance from ye s^d Corner or pitch pine Tree & then by Markt Trees and to Continue ye s^d West Northwest line till ye s^d Eight hundred Acres of land be Compleated./ And ye s^d Tract is bounded by ye s^d Mousham or Capeporpus river on ye Southwest Side & on ye Northeast Side by ye s^d West North west point into ye Countrey until ye s^d Eight hundred Acres of Land be Compleated./ The s^d Tract of Eight hundred Acres of Land Layd out this Twenty Seventh day of Septr anno Dm : 1717

By us Joseph Hill Survey^{rs} living
Saml Wheelwright in Wells

Recorded According to ye Original Septr 29th 1717./

p Jos. Hamond Reg^r

To All People to whom these Presents Shall Come Abraham Morrell of Kittery in ye County of york within his Maj^{tys} Province of ye Massachusets Bay in New England Blacksmith Sendeth Greeting Know ye that ye s^d Abraham Morrell for & in Consideration of ye Sum of Twenty four pounds Currant money of New England to him in hand paid before ye Ensealing & Delivery of These Presents by David Sawyer of Kittery in ye County & Province afores^d husbandman ye receipt whereof he ye s^d Abraham Morrell doth by these Presents Ackdowledge & himself there with fully

BOOK VIII, FOL. 238.

Satisfied Contented & paid & thereof doth Acquit & Discharge y[e] Said David Sawyer his heirs Execut[rs] & Administrators forever by these present Have given granted bargained Sold Aliened Assigned Set over & Confirmed unto y[e] s[d] David Sawyer his heirs & assignes forever all That Certaine Tract or parcell of Land Containing Thirty Acres Scittuate Lying & being in y[e] Township of Berwick in y[e] County afores[d] & is That Thirty acres of Land which was Measured & Laid out unto Lemuel Gowen y[e] Nineteenth Day of June 1703 by virtue of a grant from y[e] Town of Kittery unto s[d] Lemuel Gowen bareing Date y[e] Tenth Day of may 1703/ Bounded as followeth Viz[t] begining at a white Oak by a Drean of water that runs unto Whites marsh So Called & on y[e] South SouthEast of moses Spences land & runs in Length Eastnorth East over a Little hill SoThrough y[e] Swamp one hundred & Sixty rods to a Little white oak & as p mark[t] on four Sides Then it goes South SouthEast through y[e] Swamp to a Small Maple mark[t] on four Sides Then it goes west Southwest one hundred & Sixty rods to a white oak mark[t] on four Sides Then north northwest Thirty rods to y[e] first begining To have & To hold y[e] s[d] Thirty acres of land butted & bounded as afores[d] with all and Singular y[e] benefits profits & priviledges thereof unto y[e] s[d] David Sawyer his heirs & assignes To his & Their only proper use benefit & behoof forever And y[e] s[d] Abraham Morrell for himSelfe his heirs Executors & adm[rs] Doth hereby Covenant grant & agree to & with y[e] s[d] David Sawyer his heirs & assignes in manner following (That is to Say) that he y[e] s[d] Abra[m] Morrell at & untill y[e] Ensealing & Delivery of these presents is y[e] True & Lawfull owner of y[e] s[d] Thirty acres of Land & premisses & Stands Lawfully Seized thereof in his own proper right as a good perfect & Absolute Estate of Inheritance in fee Simple without any manner of Condition reverson or Limitation of use or uses whatsoever So as to alter Change Defeat or make void y[e] Same & have full power good right and Lawfull authority to grant Sell & assure y[e] s[d] Land & Premisses in manner as afores[d] And That y[e] Same are free & Clear Acquitted & Discharged of & from all former & other gifts grants Barguines Sales Leases Mortgages Wills Entailes Judgm[ts] Executions Titles Troubles Charges & Incumbrances w[t]soever & further That he y[e] s[d] Abra[m] Morrell his heirs Ex[rs] & Adm[rs] Shall & will warrant & Defend y[e] s[d] Tract of Thirty acres of Land & pmises herein before bargained & Sold unto y[e] s[d] David Sawyer his heirs & Assignes forever Against y[e] Lawfull Claims & Demands of all & Every person & persons whatsoever & Phebee y[e] wife of y[e] s^d Abra^m Morrell Doth also by these presents freely & Willingly give Yeald up & Surrender all her right of Dower & power of Thirds of in & unto ye above Demised pmisses unto him ye s^d David Sawyer his heirs [239] and Assignes for ever In Witness whereof ye s^d Abraham Morrell & Phebee his s^d wife have hereunto Set their hands & Seals ye Twenty fifth day of Septemb^r Anno Domini Seventeen hundred & SevenTeen Annoq, Regni Regis Georgii Magna Brittania &c^t Quarto   Abraham Morrell (a Seal)

Signed Sealed & Delivered   her
  In the Presence of us   Phebee + Morrell (a Seal)
    his   mark
  Moses /7/ Hanscom
    mark
  Samuel Hanscom
  Jos: Hamond
   York ss/ Septr 29th 1717/
  The above Named Abraham Morrell & Phebee his wife personally appearing Acknowledged ye foregoing Deed or Instrum^t in writing to be Their Act & Deed
        Coram : Jos : Hamond J peace
  Recorded According to ye Original Sep^{tr} 29th 1717 :
          p Jos Hamond Reg^r

  This Indenture made This fourteenth Day of February Anno Domini One thousand Seven hundred & Sixteen Seventeen & in ye third year of ye reign of Our Soveraign Lord George King of Great Brittaine &c^t Between Samuell Spinney of Kittery in ye County of York within his Maj^{tys} Province of ye Massachusets Bay in New England Yeoman on ye one part & John Addams of ye Same place Shipwright of ye other part Witnesseth that ye s^d Saml Spinney for and in Consideration of ye Sum of Sixty four pounds of Good Curat^t Money of this Province to him in hand paid by ye Afores^d John Addams ye rec^t whereof he doth hereby Acknowledge & for diverse other good Causes & Considerations him thereunto moveing Hath given granted bargained Sold Conveyed & Confirmed & by these presents doth fully freely & Absolutely give grant bargaine Sell Convey & Confirm unto him ye s^d John Addams his heirs & Assigns for ever a Certaine Tract or parcell of Land Scittuate & being in ye Township of Kittery afores^d Containing Thirty Two Acres butted and bounded as followeth (That is to Say) on ye western End by ye Cove of Water Comonly Called & known by ye Name of

Spinneys Cove & on ye Northern Side by John Dennets Land and runing up from ye water Side by ye s^d Dennets Land ye Length of ye s^d Dennets home Lot & to be of An Equall breadth at ye water Side and at ye uper End So many rods as shall Compleat ye Number of Thirty Two Acres afores^d To Have & To Hold ye s^d granted & bargain^d premisses with all ye Appurtenances & priviledges & Comodityes to ye Same belonging or in any wise Appurtaining to him ye s^d John Addams his heirs & Assignes for ever to his & their own propper use benefit & behoofe for ever & ye s^d Saml Spinney for himselfe his heirs Ex^{rs} Adm^{rs} & Assignes doth Covenant promiss & grant to & with ye s^d John Addams his heirs Ex^{rs} Adm^{rs} & Assignes that before ye Ensealing hereof he is ye True Sole & Lawfull owner of ye above bargained premisses & is fully Siezed & possessed of ye Same in his own propper right as a good perfect & Absolute Estate of Inheritance in fee Simple & hath in himselfe good right full power & Lawfull Authority to grant bargaine Sell Convey and Confirm s^d bargained premisses in mañer as afores^d & that ye s^d John Addams his heirs Ex^{rs} Adm^{rs} & Assignes Shall & may from Time to time & at all times for ever hereafter by force & vertue of these presents have hold use occupy possess & Enjoy Lawfully Quietly and peaceably ye s^d Demised & bargained premisses free & Clear & freely & Clearly Acquitted Exonerated & Discharged of & from all & all maner of former & other gifts grants bargains Sales Leases Mortgages Wills Entails Joyntures Dowries Judgm^{ts} Executions Extents & Incumbrance whatsoever./ Furthermore ye s^d Samuel Spinney for himselfe his heirs Ex^{rs} & Adm^{rs} doth Covena^t & Promiss at & upon ye reasonable request of ye s^d John Addams his heirs Ex^{rs} Adm^{rs} & Assignes to make do perform & Execute any further or other Lawfull & reasonable act or acts thing or things device or devices in ye Law Needfull or requisite for ye more perfect Assurence Setling & Sure makeing of ye premisses as afores^d Provided Nevertheless & it is ye True Intent & meaning of Grantor & Grantee in these presents any thing Contained herein to the Contrary Notwithstanding that if ye above Named Saml Spinney his heirs Ex^{rs} Adm^{rs} or Assignes do well and truely pay or Cause to be paid unto ye above named John Addams or his Certaine Attorney heirs Ex^{rs} Adm^{rs} or assignes in good Curra^t money of New England ye full Sum of Sixty four pounds with ye Lawfull Interest thereof at or upon ye fourteenth day of ffebruary in ye year of our Lord Twenty & Two./ three this this above written deed or Obligation & Every Clause & Article therein Contained shall Cease be null Voyd & of Non Effect./ But if Default happen to be made in y^e afores^d paym^t Contrary to y^e True Intent hereof then to abide & remaine in full Strength force & vertue to all Intents and purposes in y^e Law whatsoever. In Witness whereof the s^d Saml Spinney hath hereunto Set his hand Seal y^e day & year first above written   Samuel Spinney ($_{Seal}^{a}$)

Signed Sealed & Delivered
 In y^e presence of us
 John Newmarch
 Nath^ll Fernald
    his
 John ✝ Spinney
   mark

York ss/ Septr 16th 1717.
Samuel Spinney y^e Mortgager psonally appearing Acknowledged the foregoing Instrum^t to be his Volluntary Act & Deed./   Before Jos: Hamond J: Peace
Recorded According to ye Original Septr 16° 1717./
        p Jos. Hamond Reg^r

[Margin: March 2^d 1720|| I Rec^d of Sam Spinney ye Mortgager ye Mortgager Sixty four pounds with ye Interest thereof And I Do hereby Discharge him from ye Same | John Addams]

[240] This Indenture made ye Twentyeth day of Decemb^r in ye Year of our Lord One Thousand Six hundred & Ninety & in ye Second year of ye Reign of Our most Gracious Soveraign Lord & Lady William & Mary by ye Grace of God of England Scotland ffrance & Ireland King & Queen Defenders of ye faith &c^a between Thomas Danforth of Cambridge in ye County of Middlesex in New England Esqr of ye One part & ffrancis ffoxcroft of Boston in ye County of Suffolk in New England afores^d Merch^t of ye other part Witnesseth that ye s^d Thomas Danforth for & in Consideration of ye Natural Love & Affection which he hath & beareth towards ye s^d ffrancis Foxcroft his Son in Law & for diverse other good Causes & Considerations him thereunto Moving he ye s^d Thomas Danforth hath given granted bargained Sold Aliened Enfeoffed released Delivered & Confirmed & by these presents doth give grant Bargaine Sell Aliene Enfeoffe release Deliver and Confirm unto ye s^d ffrancis ffoxcroft in his Actual Possession & Seizen Now being of ye Lands Tenem^ts heriditam^ts & premisses herein hereAfter granted & released or Mentioned to be granted & released by vertue of One Indenture of Bargaine & Sale for Twelve months to him thereof Made by ye s^d Thomas Danforth bare-

ing date y[e] day Next before y[e] Date of these presents for y[e] Considerations therein Mentioned and by force & Vertue of y[e] Statute for Transferring of Uses of Lands & Tenem[ts] into Possession./ & to his heirs & Assignes forever all that Certaine Island Tract or parcell of Land Meadow or pasture Called or known by y[e] Name of Chebisco Dego Lying & being in Casco Bay in y[e] Province of Maine in New England afores[d] in full According to y[e] grant made of y[e] s[d] Island by y[e] Governo[r] & Company of y[e] Massachusets Collony in New England afores[d] to y[e] s[d] Thomas Danforth & Samuell Nowell Esq[rs] under y[e] Seal of y[e] afores[d] Collony bareing date y[e] Twenty Sixth day of May one Thousand Six hundred Eighty & five as by y[e] s[d] Grant relation being thereunto had more fully & at Large doth & May Appear./ Together with all & Singular y[e] pastures feedings Trees Woods underwoods Swamps Marshes Meadows Arrable Lands wayes Waters water Courses fishings fouling Easments Comons Comon of Pasture passages Stones Beaches fflats wharfes profits priviledges rights Libertys Jurisdictions Imunitys Comoditys heriditaments Imollum[ts] & Appurtenances whatsoever to y[e] s[d] Island Land & premisses or any part or parcell thereof belonging or in any wise Appurtaining or therewith now or at any time heretofore usually Set Let used Occupied or Enjoyed or reputed Taken or known as part parcell or Memb[r] thereof or of any part thereof & y[e] reversion & reversions remainder & remainders rents Issues & profits whatsoever of All & Singular y[e] s[d] hereby granted premisses and all y[e] Estate right Title Interest use possession property Claime & Demand whatsoever of him y[e] s[d] Thomas Danforth of in & to y[e] afore bargained premisses with their & Every of their Appurtenances & Every part & parcell thereof And also all Deeds writings Evidences Charters grants Leases Escripts & Minuments whatsoever Touching & Concerning y[e] s[d] hereby granted & released premisses or any part thereof (Except and Alwayes reserved out of this present Bargaine to y[e] s[d] Thomas Danforth his heirs & Assignes One thousand Acres of Land in & upon y[e] s[d] Island At any time or times hereafter to be laid out upon Some part of y[e] outside of y[e] s[d] Island next y[e] water in Such necks or Skirts as y[e] s[d] Thomas Danforth Shall order or appoint not Exeeding in above Two Distinct parts or places nor upon any parts or places that Shall hereafter be Improved Tilled or cleared upon y[e] s[d] Island by y[e] s[d] ffrancis ffoxcroft his heirs or Assignes before the laying out of the Same To Have & To Hold the Afores[d] hereby granted & released Island land & premisses with their & Every of their appurtenances & Every part &

parcell thereof Except before Excepted unto ye s^d ffrancis ffoxcroft his heirs & Assignes forever to ye only Sole proper use benefit & behoofe of him ye s^d ffrancis ffoxcroft his heirs & Assignes forevermore And ye s^d Thomas Danforth doth hereby grant for himselfe & his heirs that he & they ye before hereby granted & released premisses with their & Every of their Appurtenances (Except before Excepted) unto ye s^d ffrancis ffoxcroft his heirs & Assignes forever against him ye s^d Thomas Danforth & his heirs & Assignes Shall and will Warrant uphold & forever Defend by these presents & ye s^d Thomas Danforth for himselfe his heirs Ex^{rs} & Adm^{rs} doth Covenant pomiss & Grant to & with ye s^d ffrancis ffoxcroft his heirs Ex^{rs} & Adm^{rs} & Every of them by these presents in maner & form following That Is To Say) that he ye s^d Thomas Danforth for & Notwithstanding any act matter or thing Comitted or Suffered by him to ye Contrary is At & untill ye Time of thensealing & Delivery of these presents Lawfully Siezed of & in ye before hereby granted & released premisses with their & Every of their Appurtenances of An Absolute and Indefeazible Estate of Inheritance in fee Simple And for and Notwithstanding any Such Matter Act or thing as afores^d hath good right full power & Lawfull & Absolute Authority to give grant bargaine Sell Aliene Enfeoffe release Deliver & Confirm all & Singular ye s^d hereby Granted & released pmisses with their & Every of their Appurtenances Except before Excepted unto ye s^d ffrancis ffoxcroft his heirs & Assignes forever in maner & form afores^d According to ye True Intent & Meaning of these presents And that it Shall & may be Lawfull to & for ye s^d ffrancis ffoxcroft his heirs & Assigns & Every of them Lawfully peaceably & Quietly to Enter into and upon have hold use occupy possess & Enjoy ye afores^d granted and released premisses with their & Every of their Appurtenances Except before Excepted in maner & form afores^d & to have recieve & take ye rents Issues & profits of ye afores^d premisses & Every part & parcell thereof Except before Excepted without ye Lawfull or Equitable Let Suit Trouble denial disturbence Expulson Evicion Ejection Interuption hinderence or Mollestation whatsoever of him y^e s^d Thomas Danforth his heirs or assignes or any of them In Witness whereof y^e afores^d partys to these presents have Interchangeably hereunto Set their hands & Seals y^e day & year first above written/   Thomas Danforth ($_{Seal}^{a}$)

[241] Signed Sealed & Delivered
  In y^e presence of us
  Ephraim Savage
  Anthony Checkley Junr

Book VIII, Fol. 241.

April Primo 1701./ At an Inferio[r] Court of Com̃on pleas holden at Boston for y[e] County of Suffolk./ The above Named Ephraim Savage & Anthony Checkley Jun[r] made Oath that they were present & did Se y[e] within Named Thomas Danforth Sign Seal & Deliver y[e] within written Instrum[t] as his act & Deed unto which y[e] Depona[ts] Subscribed their Names as Witnesses./
      Attest[r] Addington Davenport Cler
Recorded According to y[e] Original Octob[r] 21st 1717./
          p Jos. Ham̃ond Reg[r]

  This Indenture made y[e] Second day of July Anno Domini one thousand Six hundred Ninty & Seven in y[e] Ninth year of the Reign of our Soveraign Lord King William y[e] third Over England &c[t] Between George Turfrey of Boston in y[e] County of Suffolk within his Maj[tys] Province of y[e] Massachusets Bay in New England Merch[t] of y[e] one part: and ffrancis ffoxcroft of Boston afores[d] Merch[t] of y[e] other part Witnesseth Whereas Maj[r] W[m] Phillips Late of Boston afores[d] formerly of Saco in y[e] Province of Maine in New England afores[d] Gent[r] dec[d] in & by his last will & Testament made in y[e] month of ffebruary Anno D[m]: 1682 and Executed y[e] Twenty ninth day of Sept[r] 1683./ Amongst Divers other Legacyes did therein give & bequeath unto his wife Bridget Phillips his Eldest Son Sam[l] Phillips & youngest Son W[m] Phillips & to their heirs & Assignes for ever in Equall proportions three quarter parts of a Certaine parcell of Land & three Quarter parts of y[e] Saw mill build thereon which Land Lyeth on Saco river in the Province of Maine in New England afores[d] begining at a brook Called Davids brook & from thence runs four Miles up y[e] river of Saco and from y[e] s[d] river of Saco runs four miles into y[e] Country with all y[e] Priviledges & Appurtenances thereunto belonging Except only about Twenty or thirty acres of s[d] Land which s[d] W[m] Phillips Sold unto William ffrost & Timber Sold unto his Son in Law John Alden as by deed is Exprest the other fourth part which makes up y[e] wholle he formerly Sold to M[r] W[m] Tayler for m[r] Ham̃an formerly of ffyall also in & by y[e] s[d] Will did give & bequeath unto them an Island Called Cow Island Lying and being in Saco river afores[d] Together with one halfe part of another Island Called Bonightons Island Lying on Saco river afores[d] purchased of s[d] W[m] Phillips dec[d] of John Bonighton Sen[r] and whereas y[e] s[d] Samuell Phillips of Boston

Margin: Geo. Turfrey to F. Foxcroft.

afores^d Victular by Indenture of bargaine and Sale under his hand & Seal bareing date ye fifth day of June Anno Dom. 1691./ for ye Consideration therein Mentioned did give grant bargaine Sell Aliene Enfeoffe Convey & Confirm unto the above Named George Turfrey his heirs & Assignes for ever all ye Estate right Title Interest Inheritance property possession reversion Claime & Demand whatsoever that ye s^d Samuel Phillips then or before that time ever had or which he his heirs may might Should or ought to have & Claime of in & to all & Singular ye Lands Islands & mills therein before mentioned & Express ed with the Tenem^{ts} thereon being one Quarter part of ye Same Scittuate Lying & being on Saco river in ye Province of Maine afores^d Together with all & Singular ye pastures feedings Trees woods underwoods Swamps Marshes Meadows Arrable Lands wayes waters water Courses Mill dams Mill ponds Headweares utencills and going mill Geares fishings fowlings huntings Easments Comons Comon of Pasture passages Stones beaches flats wharfes profits priviledges rights Libertys Imunitys Comodityes & Appurtenances whatsoever to ye s^d one Quart^r part belonging or in any kind Appurtaining by force & vertue of ye s^d Last Will & Testament or how so ever otherwise without any prejudice to ye right & Interest of his mother Mrs Bridget Phillip & brother Wm Phillips or either of them therein as by ye s^d recited Indenture of bargaine & Sale referrence Whereto being had More fully May Appear Now This Indenture further Witnesseth that ye s^d George Turfrey for & in Consideration of ye Sum of forty pounds Curra^t Money of New Engla^d to him in hand well & Truely paid before ye Ensealing & Delivery of these presents by ye s^d ffrancis ffoxcroft ye rec^t whereof to full Content & Satisfaction he ye s^d Saml Phillips doth hereby Acknowledge & thereof & of Every part & parcell thereof doth Acquit Exonerate & Discharge ye s^d ffrancis ffoxcroft his heirs Ex^{rs} Adm^{rs} & Assignes & Every of them for ever by these presents Hath given granted bargained Sold Aliened enfeoffed Conveyed & Confirmed & by these presents doth fully freely Clearly and Absolutely give grant bargaine Sell Aliene Enfeoffe Convey & Confirm unto ye s^d ffrancis ffoxcroft his heirs & Assigns for ever all ye Estate right Title Interest Inheritance use possession reversion remainder property Claime & Demand whatsoever which ye s^d George Turfrey Ever had Now hath or which he his heirs or Assignes may might Should or in any wise ought to have or Claime of in & to One full Moiety or halfe part of the afore mentioned Quarter part of ye above Mentioned Lands Islands & Mills & Tenements thereon

Scittuate Lying & being on Saco river in y[e] Province of Maine afores[d] Together with all & Singular y[e] pastures feedings trees wood underwoods Swamps Marshes Meadows Arable Lands wayes waters watercourses Milldams ponds headweares Utencills Mill gears fishings fowlings huntings Easements Comons Comon of Pasture passages Stones beaches fflats Marshes profits priviledges rights Libertys Imunitys Comoditys & Appurtenances whatsoever to y[e] s[d] One Moiety or halfe part of y[e] s[d] Quarter part of y[e] s[d] Lands Islands Mills & Tenem[ts] belonging or in any wise Appurtaining or therewith Now or heretofore used Occupied or Enjoyed Excepted reputed Taken or known as part parcell or member thereof To have & To hold all & Singular y[e] above granted & bargained premisses with their Appurtenances & Every part & parcell thereof unto y[e] s[d] ffrancis ffoxcroft his heirs & Assigns for ever to his & their own Sole & proper use benefit & behoofe forevermore./ And y[e] s[d] George Turfrey for himselfe his heirs Ex[rs] & Adm[rs]/ doth Covenant Promiss grant & agree to & with y[e] s[d] ffrancis ffoxcroft his heirs & Assignes by these presents in maner following That is to Say that y[e] s[d] George Turfrey for & Notwithstanding any Act Matter or thing Comitted or Suffered to be done by him at y[e] Time of y[e] Ensealing & Delivery of these presents is y[e] True Sole & Lawfull owner & Stand Lawfully Siezed of & in all y[e] afore bargained [242] Premisses with their & Every of their Appur[ces] of a good perfect & Indefeazible Estate of Inheritance in fee Simple And for & notwithstanding any Such Act Matter or thing as afores[d] hath full power good right & Absolute Authority to grant bargaine Sell Convey & Assure y[e] Same in Maner & forme as afores[d] & that it Shall & may be Lawfull to & for y[e] s[d] ffrancis ffoxcroft his heirs & Assignes & Every of them Lawfully peaceably & Quietly to Enter into & upon have hold use Occupy possess & Enjoy y[e] above granted & bargained premisses with y[e] Appurtenances & have recieve & Take y[e] rents Issues & profits thereof without y[e] Lawfull & Equitable Let Suit Trouble Denial Mollestation Disturbence Expultion Eviction Ejection Interruption or Mollestation whatsoever of him y[e] s[d] George Turfrey his heirs or Assignes or of Any other by his or their Means or procurem[t] And that y[e] s[d] George Turfrey y[e] grantor hath not done or Suffered to be done Any Matter Act or thing whereby y[e] above granted premisses is or may be Any wayes Charged or Incumbred in Estate Title or charge or other Incumbrance whatsoever./ And Lastly that y[e] s[d] George Turfrey his heirs Ex[rs] Shall & will from henceforth & for ever hereafter Warra[t] & Defend the above granted &

bargained premisses with their Appurtenances & Every part thereof unto ye s^d ffrancis ffoxcroft his heirs & Assignes for ever against y^e Lawfull Claims & Demands of all & Every p^rson & p^rsons whomsoever from by or und^r him them or any of them In Witness whereof the s^d George Turfrey party to these presents hath hereunto Set his hand & Seal y^e day & year first above written   George Turfrey (s^a_eal)
Signed Sealed & Delivered
  In p^rsence of us
  Joshua Winsor
  Eliezer Moodey Ser.
    Suffolk sc/ Boston July 5th 1697
  The within named George Turfrey psonally Appearing before me y^e Subscriber one of his Maj^tys Justices of y^e peace within y^e County afores^d Acknowledged the within written Instrum^t to be his ffree & Volluntary Act & Deed
                          Jer: Dum̃or
  Recorded According to ye Original Octob^r 21st 1717./
                          p Jos. Ham̃ond Reg^r

Seal

            The Governo^rur and Company of the
          Massachusets Bay in New England./ To
          all to whom these presents Shall Come
          Send Greeting./ Know ye that in pursu-
          ance of an order or Grant of ye s^d Gov-
          ernour & Company At a General Court
          held at Boston ye Seventh day of May
          Sixteen hundred Eighty & four and of a
          further order or Grant of ye s^d Governo^r
S: Bradstreet Govr & Comp^a At a General Court held at Boston May ye Sixth One Thousand Six hundred Eighty & five as an Explanation of ye Law Title Conveyances Deeds & writings as an Addition thereunto the Governo^r & Comp^a of ye Massachusets Bay in New England Afores^d Have given granted & Confirmed & by these presents for them & their Successo^rs for ever do give grant & Confirm unto the Dep^ty Governo^r Thomas Danforth Esqr President of ye Province of Maine & to Samuel Nowell Esqr for their Great pains & good Service done by order of this Court in ye Expedition & Several Journeys to Casco for which no recomepence hath been made them) An Island Called Chebisco Dego in Casco bay in ye Province of Maine Provided they take the s^d Island in full Satisfaction for all Survice done referring to the Settlement of ye Province of Maine To have & To hold

ye s^d Island Land & premisses with their & Every of their rights Priviledges Jurisdictions heriditaments & Appurtenances./ And ye reversion and reversions remainder & remainders thereof & of Every part and parcell thereof unto & to ye only use & behoofe of them ye s^d Thomas Danforth & Samuel Nowell & to their heirs & Assignes forever./ In Witness whereof We ye s^d Governo^r & Company have Caused ye Comon Seale of ye Corporation to be Affixed to these presents the Twenty Sixth day of May in ye year of our Lord One Thousand Six hundred Eighty & five

Recorded According to the Original Octr 21st 1717./

p Jos. Hamond Reg^r

To All Christians to whom this Deed of Sale may Come Caleb Preble of York in ye County of York in ye Province of ye Massachusets Bay in New Engl^d yeoman Sendeth Greeting./ Know Ye ye s^d Caleb Preble for & in Considerations of Seventy pounds money to him in hand paid or otherwise Satisfactoraly Secured to be paid by James Brown & Joseph Brown of Newbery in ye County of Essex in s^d Province afores^d yeoman at ye rec^t thereof ye s^d Caleb Preble doth acknowledge himselfe therewith fully Satisfied paid and Contented & doth hereby Acquitt & Discharge ye s^d James & Joseph Brown their heirs Ex^{rs} & Adm^{rs} forever for & of all ye Premisses hereafter Named & Set forth ye which ye s^d Caleb Preble hath given granted bargained Sold Aliened Enfeoffed & made over & doth by these presents give grant bargaine Sell Aliene Enfeoffe & make over & fully freely & Absolutely Convey & make over & Confirm unto ye s^d James & Joseph Brown & their heirs & Assignes forever the one Quarter part of all that land & Marsh & Meadow Ground which belongeth unto ye rights & Interests of m^r Richard Comins & his wife lying & being upon ye Eastward Side of Saco river in ye Township of Saco in ye County afores^d it being part of ye Pattent granted unto m^r Thomas Lewis & Mr Richd Bonighton by ye R^t Honble President & Councill for New England Viz^d ye Quarter part of all ye Land & Marsh given or Sold by ye afores^d Mr Richd Bonighton unto his Daughter Eliz^a the wife of Richd Comins & her heirs as it was Asserted & afterwards Divided to her daughters husband John Harmon & Phillip ffoxwell for their part of ye Pattent bounded from Thomas Rogers his Garden by ye Sea runing Two miles & fifty rods Northwest & So North East to ye line of ye Pattent Next unto Blue point which is y^e

first Division & Also one [243] Halfe of yᵉ Land in yᵉ Second Division Two miles Square as is Exprest in yᵉ Division yᵉ one halfe of these Divisions Laid out to yᵉ sᵈ Harmon & Foxell & yᵉ Quarter part of all yᵉ aboveˢᵈ Sold by mʳ Joseph Bankes & Elizabeth his wife unto yᵉ sᵈ Caleb Preble as p a deed bareing Date yᵉ Second day of Augˢᵗ Last past referrence hereunto being had may at Large Appear unto them yᵉ sᵈ James Brown & Joseph Brown and their heirs & Assignes forever Together with all yᵗ rights royaltys priviledges Appurtenances & Advantages belonging unto yᵉ above bargained premisses or any part or parcell thereof unto them yᵉ sᵈ James & Joseph and their heirs & Assignes as abouesᵈ To have & To hold & Quietly & peaceably to Possess & Enjoy as a Sure Estate in fee Simple Moreover yᵉ sᵈ Caleb Preble doth for himselfe his heirs Exʳˢ & Admʳˢ to & with yᵉ sᵈ James & Joseph Brown their heirs and Assignes Covenant Ingage & promiss yᵉ above bargained premisses with all its priviledges to be free & Clear from all former Gifts grants bargains Sales rents rates Dowryes Mortgages Widows thirds or any other Incumbrances whatsoever as also from all future Claimes Challenges Lawsuits or any other Interuptions whatsoever proceeding yᵉ Date hereof to be had or Comenced by him yᵉ sᵈ Caleb his heirs Admʳˢ or Assignes or Any person or persons upon any Grounds or Title whatsoever./ And from henceforth yᵉ sᵈ Caleb Preble doth Warrantize yᵉ above bargained premisses & will Defend yᵉ Same In Witness hereof yᵉ sᵈ Caleb Preble hath hereunto Set his hand & Seale this thirteenth day of September in yᵉ year of our Lord 1717./ And in yᵉ fourth year of yᵉ reign of our Soveraign Lord George King of Great Brittaine &cᵗ/

Signed Sealed & Delivered   Caleb Preble (a Seale)

In presents of
Joseph Banks
Jeremiah Moulton
Nathˡ Freeman

York ss./ York Sepᵗ 13ᵗʰ 1717.

Caleb Preble pʳsonally Appeared before me the Subscriber & Acknowledged yᵉ Above Instrumᵗ to be his free Act & Deed   Abraᵐ Preble Just. peace

Recorded According to yᵉ Original Octobʳ 24ᵗʰ 1717./

       p Jos. Hamond Regʳ

To All Christian People to whom this Deed of Sale may Come or Concern Abraham Preble Samˡ Came Richard Milbery & Joseph Sayward Selectmen of & for ye Town of York in ye County of York in ye Province of ye Massachusets Bay in New England by vertue of a Town Vote bareing Date March ye 8th 1714/5 as p York Town book page ye 275 doth appear ye s^d Selectmen Send Greeting Know ye ye s^d Selectmen for & in ye behalfe of ye s^d Town of York for & in Consideration of five pounds money to them in had paid otherwise Secured to be paid for ye use of s^d Town of York by Daniel Simpson of s^d York Have given granted bargained Sold Aliened Enfeoffed & made over & do by these presents give grant bargaine Sell Aliene Enfeoffe & make over & fully freely and Absolutely Convey & Confirm unto ye s^d Daniel Simpson & his heirs And Assignes one Certaine piece parcell or Tract of upland & Swampy Land Containing five acres lying & being within ye Township of s^d York & is Scittuated between ye Land of Ebenezer Cobourne & ye Land of the s^d Daniel Simpson Near about halfe a mile North East from the highway that Leads from ye Meeting house in s^d York to ye Corn Mill being part of An Island in a Swamp known by ye Name of ye Graey Swamp & part of s^d Swamp & is bounded as followeth Viz^t begining at a hemlock tree mark^t on four Sides Standing Eight poles Northwest from s^d Coborns bounds upon aboves^d Island & runs from thence Northwest Seventeen poles to aboves^d Daniel Simpsons bounds and from thence Southwest halfe a point South fifty three poles & from thence Southeast to a great Spruce tree Marked on four Sides which is Ten poles distance from s^d Simpsons bounds & s^d Tree is distance from s^d Coborns bounds four poles and is bounded from thence on a Straight Line to ye hemlock Tree first above Mentioned Together with all ye rights priviledges Appurtenances & Advantages thereunto belonging or any ways at any time redownding to ye same or any part or parcell thereof unto him ye s^d Daniel Simpson his heirs & assignes for ever To have & To hold & Quietly & peaceably to possess Occupie & Enjoy as a Sure Estate in Fee Simple./ Moreover ye s^d Selectmen in behalfe of s^d Town of York do Covena^t Ingage & promiss to & with ye s^d Daniel Simpson ye above bargained premisses with all its Privilidges unto ye s^d Simpson his heirs & Assignes As above Specified According to this s^d Town of York its Title & Interest therein According to ye aboves^d power granted to ye s^d Selectmen do Warrantize & will Defend ye Same, In Witness hereof in behalfe of this Town of York ye Above Named Abra^m Preble Saml Came Richd Milbery & Joseph Sayward have hereunto Set to their hands & Seals this Ninth day of March in y^e year of our Lord One thousand Seven

hundred & fifteen & in y^e Second year of y^e reign of our Soveraign Lord George King of Great Brittaine &c
Signed Sealed & Delivered   Abra^m Preble
  In p^rsence of us Witnesses   Saml Came   (^a_Seal)
  Lewis Bane   Richd Milbery
  Ebenezer Coborn   Joseph Sayward
  Nathl Freeman

York ss/ York Aug^st 27th 1717./ Abra^m Preble Saml Came Richd Milbery personally Appeared before me y^e Subscrib^r and Acknowledged y^e above Instrum^t to be y^e free Act & deed According to y^e power given them by ye Town of York   Lewis Bane Just^s

Recorded According to ye Original Octob^r 2^d 1717./

p Jos: Hamond Reg^r

[244] Know All men by these presents that I Richard Tucker do Authorize Mr Robert Jordan to make use of land Adjoyning to ye falls of Casco river above Mrs Mackworths and there to Erect & build a Saw mill or mills as he Shall Se Expedient not takeing above one hundred acres of land to his use In Witness of these presents I have Subscribed my hand this 11th of Septr 1657   Richard Tucker

  Witness Richd Walron
        Robt Patteshal

York 5 : 5ta : 59 m^r Richd Tucker being present in Court Confessed this to be his act   Tho: Danforth

Vera Copia Transcribed out of ye Original

p Edw: Rishworth Record^r

Recorded According to ye Coppy as aboves^d Novr ye 7th 1717   p Jos Hamond Reg^r

Be it Known to all men by these presents that I Robert Jordan do freely Acquit & Discharge Mr John Phillips from all demand or demands in what respect or respects whatsoever from ye begining of the world to this present 28th day of July 1658./ In Witness I have Subscribed my Name on reservation ye s^d Mr Phillips doth & Shall Acquit deliv^r and possess ye s^d Jordan to & in ye proper & Singular Interest he hath or ought to have or may be Supōsed to have to all his rights in Lands Cattle or Chattells whatsoever./ further I do Ingage hereby to discharge & acquitt ye s^d Mr John Phillips

from all demands may be made by Rob[t] Hethersay in point of Covenant in respect to a Saw mill to be Errected at Casco river falls this is Mutually Subscribed unto by us
Witness   James Parker   Robert Jordan
          George Lewis ✗ Signed   John Phillips I P
          ffrancis Small   Signed
Vera Copia Transcribed out of y[e] Original & Compared./
          p Edw Rishworth Record[r]
Recorded According to y[e] Coppy as above Nov[r] 7th 1717./
          p Jos. Hamond Reg[r]

To the Inhabitants of Casco Bay Love presented
Whereas Yo[r] Neighb[r] Robert Jordan & others out of prencity to the publick good & for y[e] reconciling of trade in these parts have Indeavered & Assayed to Errect a Sawmill at their great Charges all or y[e] most whereof hetherto hath Come to remediless damage through Some obstructions & a death put upon s[d] work & design the s[d] Jordan doth to you hereby declare that as he resolveth he in himselfe hath a right & priviledge to & in y[e] place for y[e] Errection of Such a work but in Such Case as it Shall be made duely & Legally Appear y[e] s[d] right & priviledge to be Invalid[d] then y[e] s[d] Jordan hath a right & Priviledge there by y[e] Consent & Allowence of m[r] Richard Tucker under his hand to Such right he pretendeth to or may have there Also y[e] s[d] Jordan by Vertue of a Covena[t] made wth John Phillips hath a right & priviledge to & in y[e] s[d] place for Errection of y[e] s[d] Mill in referrence to y[e] pretention of a right there from M[r] Cleve by Vertue of a Contract with him all which being not Now to be disputed./ Thes[d] Jordan desireth of you in regard of y[e] present disolation we Stand in that you would as you Se Cause And reason by yo[r] Subscription Declare whether y[e] s[d] Jordan may have or hath yo[r] free Consent & Allowence to go on & perfect y[e] s[d] work & fall Timb[r] for y[e] work & Effects thereof with other Conveniences in peacefull manner without Violence or Opposition rendering himselfe willingly Satisfactory to Such person or persons in future who Can or shall Justly make it Appear they are or have been unduely Injured by his So doing or otherwise that you would declare yo[r] reasonable Exception

Book VIII, Fol. 244.

June 18th Presented by me Robert Jordan & Interlined
1658 before Subscription
          Consented to by us

Robert Corbin	Wm Ryall
Tho Greinely — his mark	Jane Mackworth ⨍ her mark
John Sares	Tho: Morrice his mark ⨯
Tho: Hains	James Andrews
Francis Neale	Gyles Roberts his mark R
Michael Mitton	
Nathl Wallis	Richd Martyn his mark X
Nich^o White ⨗ his mark	Sampson Penley
	Joseph Phippen
The mark of	The mark ⨯ of
John Wallis	Tho: Stanford

Vera Copia Transcribed out of ye Original & Compared this 15th Augst 1659.   p Edw: Rishworth Record^r
Recorded According to ye Coppy as above Novr 7th 1717./
                                         p J. Hamond Reg^r

We whose Names are under written do Affirm by our Subscriptions that on ye 29th day of July we Saw Mr John Phillip Deliver over to Robert Jordan one Cow in part of ye whole rights & Interest he had in his Lands goods Cattle & Chattells as Singularly propper unto ye s^d Jordan his heirs Ex^{rs} Adm^{rs} or assignes Against him his heirs Ex^{rs} Adm^{rs} or Assignes./ In Testimony to this Truth m^r John Phillip with us Doth Subscribe
    James Pecker   John I: P Phillips Signed
    Geo. Lewis Signed E
    Francis Smale
Vera Copia Transcribed out of ye Original
                         p Edw: Rishworth Record^r
Recorded According to ye Coppy as above Novr 7th 1717./
                                 p Jos. Hamond Reg^r

Book VIII, Fol. 245.

We have According to our Lord Proprietors Comand Viewed ye Land in Difference between m^r Trelawney & m^r Cleves and We find that which Cleves & ye Jury Tooke for Casco river to be but a Creek into which we Saw but one Little brook to run but ye other wch m^r Trelawney Takes for Casco : river to be ye river it hath its Issue out of a great pond Named Sabadock the river is of a reasonable Depth & breadth by ye relation of ye Antient Inhabitants & Natives Ever to have been Called Casco river thus Much have we Certified the Lord of ye Province to whose Determination we have referred it Tho : Gorges
  Richd Vines
  Henry Jocelin

This is a True Coppy of y Certificate that m^r Gorges m^r Vines & have Sent to m^r Trelawney Attested by m^r Hen : Jocelin his oath Taken in Court./ Edw : Rishworth Record^r

Vera Copia Transcrib^d out of ye Original & Compared this 13^d Augst 52 p Edw Rishworth Record^r

Recorded According to ye Coppy as above Novr 7th 1717
  p Jos. Hamond Reg^r

[245] The Deposition of Roger Willine Aged about 20 one or Twenty 2 years Agone he helped to row up ye river which runeth by Mrs Jane Mackworths to ye falls Called Casco falls m^r Richd Vines m^r Arthur Mackworth m^r Jno Winter m^r Henry Abilie with divers others whom he hath forgotten where he Saw Mr Richard Vines Deliver unto m^r Jno Winter possession of ye Land and falls there by Turfe & Twigg./ This Deposition was Taken ye 7th day of Decemb^r 1658./ Before me./ Francis Neale Commission^r Sworn in ye presence of
  Isaac Walker.

Vera Copia Transcribed out of ye Original & Compared
  p Edw : Rishworth Record^r

Recorded According to ye Coppy as above. Novemb^r 7th 1717 p Jos. Hamond Reg^r

These presents Shall Witness that I George Cleve of Casco in New England Gentleman do hereby freely & fully give unto my Son in Law Michael Mitton of Casco afores^d all my right & Interest in that Tract of land Lying in Casco Bay granted unto me by Colonel Allexander Rigby Esqr and now in ye Possession of me ye s^d George Cleve & other of my Tenants to be from henceforth ye only & proper Lands of him ye s^d Michael Mitton & his heirs for ever According to ye Tenor Expressed in ye s^d Grant to me from ye s^d Allexander Rigby Together with all ye houses and Buildings to me belonging in & upon ye s^d Tract of Land./ Also I do hereby fully & freely give unto ye s^d Michael Mitton all my Utencills of household stuff in & about ye house & buildings as well wthin door as without Together with all my Cattle as well Cows & Calves & Steers & Swine Young & old as also all other Cattle or goods of any Sort or kind whatsoever for & in Consideration of a Suñ of Money to me in hand paid before ye Sealing & Delivery hereof as also for & in Consideration that he ye s^d Michael Mitton Shall at all Time & Times hereafter Maintaine & provide for me ye s^d George Cleve & for Joan my Now wife good & Sufficient Meat & drink Apparrell & Lodging and Physick & all other Necessarys for ye reliefe of this fraile life for both of us & ye Longest Liver of both of us as well as for other Considerations me hereunto moveing as well ye Marriage of my daughter as other wayes all which hath Moved me to make this firm Deed of Gift unto my s^d Son in Law Michael Mitton Written with my own hand & Sealed with my Seal & Livery & Siezen given of ye full & peaceable possession of ye s^d Lands and possession of ye s^d Cattle & goods by Delivering into his hands in part of all ye rest one Bay Gelding & a ring of Gold in Lieu & part of all ye rest of ye Cattle & goods therein Specified Dated this 24th day of ffebruary: 1650./././   George Cleve & a Seale

Witness

       his mark

Thomas Harkine

Eliz^a Mitton

Anna   Mitton

Wm Tilly

Recorded According to ye Original Novr ye 7th 1717./

        p Jos. Hañond Reg^r

Know All men by these presents that I Michael Mitton of ye Town of ffalmouth in ye County of York Gent, Do by these presents make over give Sell Grant & Confirm unto Robert Jordan Gent his heirs Ex^{rs} & Assignes fforever all y^e

right Title Interest I have might have or ought to have to any Land or Lands within ye Town of falmouth to ye only proper use of ye afores^d Robert Jordan of ye Town of ffalmouth in ye County of York his heirs Ex^rs & Assignes forever against me my heirs Ex^rs & Assignes for ever for & in Consideration that ye s^d Robert Jordan ye day of ye Date of theses presents hath Confirmed unto me ye Afores^d Michael Mitton my heirs & Assignes forever all & Severally ye Grants of lands I have recieved from my father in Law m^r George Cleve or any other person unto which ye afores^d m^r Jordan hath Affixed his ffirm they were Attested before him./ In Witness w^r of I ye s^d Michael Mitton have hereunto Set my hand & Seal this Twenty fifth day of August 1660./

Signed Sealed & Delivered   Michael Mitton   (their Seal)
In ye presence of us   her
George Munjoy   Elizabeth E Mitton
ffrancis Neale   mark
John Guye
Acknowledged by Elizabeth Mitton Before me
                             ffrancis Neale Comission^r
Recorded According to ye Original Novr 7th 1717
                     p Jos. Hamond Reg^r

Sr Edmund Andros Kn^t Captn Genl & Govern^r in Chief of his Majestyes Territory and Dominion of Stow England To Mr Phillip Welles Surveyor or any of the Deputy Surveyors Whereas Dominicus Jordan of Spurwink in ye Province of Main hath by his Petiõn Set forth that Robert Jordan his Late father Dece^d Did by his last will and Testament bequeath unto him One thousand Acres of Land besides Meadow thereto belonging lyeing upon the River of Spurwinck afore Said & that by vertue Thereof he hath possessed the Same for ye Space of Tenne years Past and hath built and improved a Considerable Parte thereof & Settled five or Six tennants thereon praying his Majestyes Confirmæon for ye Same I Doe therefore hereby Requier and authorize you to Survey & Lay out for the s^d Diminicus Jordan the Said one Thousand Acres of Land & Meadow thereto belonging and to make a platt or draft there of and the Same to Return into ye Secryes Office at Boston that a pattent may be granted to him accordingly & for So Doing This shall be your warrant Given under my hand and Seales at Boston the Eighteenth day of January in the third

Year of his Majestyes Reign/ Annoq, Domi 1687 By his
Excell command E : Andros
John West D Secr̃y
Capt Richard Clemants pray lay out ye above Express^d
land & make returne thereof to me
                                Phillip Wells Survey^r
Recorded According to ye Original Novr 7th 1717
                        p Jos. Hañiond Reg^r

[246] To all People to whom these presents Shall Come
Greeting &c^t Know Y^e that I William Rogers of Kittery in
the County of York in his Maj^{tys} Province of ye Massachusets Bay in New England Husbandman for & in Consideration of a valluable Sum of money to me in hand before y^e
Ensealing hereof well & Truely paid by Stephen Tobey of
ye Same Town County and Province afores^d Shipwright the
Rec^t whereof I do hereby acknowledge & my Self therewith
fully Satisfied & Contented & thereof & of Every part and
parcell thereof do Exonerate Acquit & Discharge ye s^d Stephen
Tobey his heirs Ex^{rs} & Adm^{rs} for ever by These presents
Have given Granted bargained Sold Aliened Convey^d &
Confirmed & by these presents Do freely Fully & Absolutely give grant Bargaine Sell Aliene Convey & Confirm
unto him ye s^d Stephen Tobey his heirs & assignes for ever
One Moiety or half part of a Certain Tract of Land Scitt-
tuate Lying & being in Kittery in the County of York Con-
taining Seventy Acres According as ye Same was Laid out &
bounded unto me by ye Surveyer or Survey^{rs} for ye Town of
Kittery Viz^t forty acres whereof Laid out by Nicholas
Gowen Surv^y January ye 22^d 1702/3 begining at ye Southeast Corner of a lot that was laid out to Trustram Haridon
Adjoyning to York bounds & is bounded by Said Lot on y^e
North & is in Length East and west One hundred & Eighteen poles and in breadth North & South fifty five poles/
Thirty Acres ye remaining part of Said tract was Laid out
by John Gowen Survey^r March 20th 1702/3 begining at the
Line that Divides Kittery & york Next to my own Land
afore Mentioned & To run by s^d Line South /Easterly) Sixty
poles then west Northerly by John ffrosts land Ninety Two
poles then North to my own land fifty : poles then East by
my s^d land Ninety two Poles to ye first begining as by y^e
Several Survey^{rs} returns on Record in ye Town of Kittery
reference being thereunto had To have & To Hold ye s^d
Moiety or half part of ye s^d Tract of Seventy Acres of Land

BOOK VIII, FOL. 246.

with all y⁰ Appurtenances Priviledges & Commodityes to y⁰ Same belonging or in any wise Appurtaining to him y⁰ s⁴ Stephen Tobey his heirs and Assigns for Ever to his & their only proper use benefit and behoofe for ever/ And I y⁰ s⁴ William Rogers for me my heirs Exʳˢ & Admʳˢ do Covenant promiss & grant to & with y⁰ s⁴ Stephen Tobey his heirs & Assignes that before y⁰ Ensealing hereof I am the True Sole and Lawfull Owner of the above bargained premisses and am Lawfully Siezed & Possessed of y⁰ Same in my own proper right as a good perfect & Absolute Estate of Inheritance In fee Simple & Have in my Self good Right full power & Lawfull Authority to Grant bargaine Sell Convey and Confirm s⁴ bargained premisses in Manner as aboves⁴ and that y⁰ s⁴ Stephen Tobey his Heirs & assignes shall And may from time to time and at all Times for ever hereafter by force & vertue of these presents Lawfully Peaceably & Quietly have Hold use Occupy possess & Enjoy y⁰ s⁴ Demised & bargained premisses with y⁰ Appurtenances free & Clear & frely & Clearly acquitted Exonerated and discharged of & from all and all manner of former or other Gifts Grants bargaines Sales Leases Mortgages Wills Entailes Joyntures dowries Judgmᵗˢ Executions & Incumbrances Whatsoever the peaceable possession Thereof and Every part and parcell thereof Against my Self my Heirs Exʳˢ and Admʳˢ and against all other persons Claiming y⁰ Same from by or under me them or any of them I Will forever Save harmless Warraᵗ & Defend by These presents/ In Witness whereof I y⁰ s⁴ William Rogers with mary my Wife have hereunto Set our hands & Seals this Sixteenth Day of Septʳ anno Domini One Thousand Seven Hundred and Seventeen/ Annque Regni Regis Georgii Magna Brittania &cᵗ Quarto

Signed Sealed & Delivered
In the Presence of us   William 𝒲, his mark Rogers (ₛₑₐₗ)

Samuel Hill
Richard Gowell Junʳ   Mary ⊂ her mark Rogers (ₛₑₐₗ)

York sc Sept 16ᵗʰ 1717

William Rogers & mary his wife personally appearing Acknowledged y⁰ fore foregoing Instrumᵗ in writing to be their free act & Deed   Before Joseph Hammond J Peace
Recorded According to y⁰ Original Novʳ y⁰ 1ˢᵗ 1717./·

p Jos. Harmon Regʳ

Book VIII, Fol. 247.

Mrs Mary Weare Aged Eighty three years or there abouts Testifieth & Saith that She well rememb^{rs} m^r Henry Saywards building ye Meeting house at York which was about fifty years ago and that he was to have Land for building s^d house & that her husband Peter Weare dec^d was About that time a Lot layer & was Improved by ye Neighborhood often to Lay out land in ye Town of York

York sc/ York Novr 23^d 1717. Jurat in Perpetuam Rei Memoriam   Cor̃. Nobis   Abra^m Preble   Justices
                     Jos. Ham̃ond   Quoram

Recorded According to ye Original Novr 23^d 1717./
                     p J : Ham̃ond Reg^r

Mr Saml Donnell Aged Seaventy Years or thereabouts Testifieth & Saith that for ye most part of ye time this Sixty years past he hath dwelt in ye Town of York and that he well remembers that about fifty years Since m^r Henry Sayward did build A Meeting house in s^d York for ye Publick worship of God and that he hath Several times Seen ye s^d Henry Sayward & his men at work in building ye s^d Meeting house which house is yet Standing in ye Town of york

York sc/ York Novr 22^d 1717. Jurat in Perpetuam Rei Memoriam   Cor̃ Nobis   Abra^m Preble   Justices
                     Jos. Ham̃ond   Quoram

Recorded According to ye Original Novr 23^d 1717./
                     p Jos. Hamond Reg^r

[247] Abraham Tilton Aged Seaventy & Two years or thereabouts Testifieth and Saith that forty years agoe or thereabouts he hired a farm of m^r Samuel Wheelwright in Wells at ye Easterly end of ye Town & was all that Tract of Land Lying between ye land then of John Wells on ye N Easterly Side & ye land of James Gooch on ye S. Westerly Side & So up into ye woods as other Lots then run with a Certaine Quantity of Marsh All which Land & Marsh he ye s^d Tilton hired of s^d m^r Samuel Wheelwright & Lived on ye Same by his order & in his right for about Two years in which Time he ye s^d Tilton built a house & Saw Mill on s^d land & after ye Expiration of ye Time he agreed for ye s^d Tilton resigned all ye s^d Tract of Land or farm with ye s^d house & Mill Standing on the Same unto ye s^d Samuel Wheelwrights Custody & possession againe And further Saith that

Book VIII, Fol. 247.

he ye s^d Tilton paid his rent According to his Agreem^t unto ye s^d m^r Saml Wheelwright for his use

Essex sc/ Ipswich Octob^r 8th 1714. Then Abraham Tilton of Ipswich p^rsonally Appeared & made Oath to ye Truth of ye Aboves^d Evidence to Ly in perpetuam rei Memoriam
  Taken Before John Appleton Quo. Unus
         Saml Appleton J. Ps

Recorded According to ye Original wch Came Sealed to my hand Octr 2^d 1717   p Jos. Hamond Reg^r

To All Christian People to whom these presents may Come or do Concern Hannah Smith Now Widdow Late wife of Joseph Smith Late of York dec^d but formerly wife of Timothy Hodsden Also of s^d York dec^d of York York in ye County of York in ye Province of Maine in New England Sendeth Greeting Know Ye that ye s^d Hannah Smith for & in Consideration of Thirty pounds money to her well & truely in hand paid or otherwayes Sattisfactoraly Secured to be paid by Andrew Toothacre of s^d York ye rec^t whereof ye s^d Hannah doth Acquit release discharge & relece ye s^d Andrew Toothacre his heirs & Assignes forever./ And have given granted bargained & Sold Alienated Enfeoffed & made over and doth by these presents give grant bargaine Sell Aliene Enfeoffe & make over and fully freely & Absolutely Ingage & Confirm unto ye s^d Andrew Toothacre his heirs and Assignes a Certaine piece or parcell of Land lying & being within ye Township or prescinct of s^d York and is Scittuated on the Southwest Side of s^d York river being by Estimation Thirty Acres More or Less butting in breadth by s^d York river thirty & Two poles between ye head of ye Long Cove & ye land Now in ye Possession of Josiah Maine & is butted & bounded as followeth Viz^t begining at a beach Tree Standing by s^d York river on ye East Side of s^d Maines Land which was formerly m^r Edward Rishworths Which was marked on four Sides & So by ye river last thirty & Two poles or perch to a maple Tree Marked on four Sides and from s^d beach & Maple Southwest on both Sides to a freshet brook that runs into ye old mill Creek Together with all ye rights bennefits priviledges Appurtenances & Advantages thereunto belonging both of wood und^r wood Timb^r Timber Trees Standing Lying or remaining thereon or any other priviledge belonging thereunto or any ways at any time redownding to ye Same or any part or parcell thereof unto him ye s^d Andrew Toothacre his heirs & Assignes forever To have & To hold & Quietly & peaceably to Possess Occupy & Enjoy Moreover ye s^d Hannah doth for herselfe her heirs Ex^{rs} & Adm^{rs} Covena^t Ingage & promiss to & with ye s^d Andrew his heirs & Assignes ye aboves^d premisses with all its priviledges to be free & Clear from all Sorts or Maner of Incumberments whatsoever & forever after ye Date hereof ye s^d Hannah doth Warrantise & will Save harmless & Defend ye s^d Andrew in all ye aboves^d land & priviledges as is Set forth in Every particular above Mentioned./ In Witness hereof ye aboves^d Hannah Smith hath hereunto Set her hand & Seal this fourth day of December in ye year of our Lord one Thousand Seven hundred & thirteen in ye Twelfth year of her Maj^{tys} reign &c^t

Signed Sealed & Delivered   Hannah her H mark Smith (her Seal)
In presence of
Lewis Bane
Samuel Came
Abra^m Preble

York ss/ Decr ye 7th 1713./ Hannah Smith p^{r}sonally Appeared before me one of her Maj^{tys} Justices of ye peace in ye County of York & Acknowledged ye above written to be her act and Deed./ Before me Abra^m Preble Justice a peace

Recorded According to ye Original Decr 4th 1717./

p Jos. Hamond Reg^r

To All People unto whom this present Deed of Sale Shall Come Jacob Perkins of york in ye County in york in ye Province of the Massachusets Bay in New England Cooper Know ye that ye s^d Jacob Perkins for & in Consideration of ye Sum of four hundred pounds Passable money in New England unto him in hand At & before ye Ensealing & Delivery of these presents Well & Truely paid by James Carr of Newberry Junr in ye County of Essex in New England afores^d Cordwainer ye rec^t of which Sum to full Content & Satisfaction I ye s^d Jacob Perkins do hereby Acknowledge & thereof & from every part & parcell thereof ye s^d James Carr his Ex^{rs} Adm^{rs} & Assignes he do Acquitt Exonerate & fully discharge for ever by these presents Have granted bargained Sold Aliened Set over Conveyed & Confirmed & by these presents do fully freely Clearly & Absolutely Grant bargaine Sell Aliene Set over Convey & Confirm unto ye s^d Carr his heirs Ex^{rs} Adm^{rs} & Assignes for ever a piece of upland

& Meadow ground Scittuated on y⁶ Southwest Side of Cape Nedick river in yᵉ Township of York where Now yᵉ sᵈ Perkins now Liveth Containing by Estimation Seventy Acres be it [248] More or Less Sixty Acres whereof was Sold to sᵈ Perkins by Hannah Green & her Children by a deed bareing Date yᵉ 20ᵗʰ of March 1708 reference thereunto being had may more at large Appear the other Ten acres given to sᵈ Perkins by yᵉ Town of York March 17ᵗʰ 1713/4 as p̄ his return in york Town book may Appear and is butted & bounded as followeth./ on yᵉ North East Side of Aforesᵈ Cape nedick river & on yᵉ Southeast by yᵉ Land of Dependence Stover & on yᵉ Northwest & Southwest by yᵉ Land of John Woodbridge with a Small parcell of Marsh on yᵉ Southwest Side of Capenedick river as is Set forth in afore Sited deéd to sᵈ Perkins sᵈ Land being in Length from sᵈ river Next to sᵈ Woodbridges land One hundred Seventy Six pole as will Appear more at Large in sᵈ Perkins⁹ aforesᵈ deed & return with one Dwelling house & barn Standing on sᵈ Land Together with Six oxen three Cows Ten Swine Nine Sheep One Mare four yearlings & three Calves & yᵉ whole of hay or Corn upon sᵈ Land with all yᵉ other Matterials for yᵉ husbandry./ Together with all & Singular yᵉ Trees woods underwoods rivers Coves Creeks pools ponds Mines Minerals housen Edifices fences rights Members profits priviledges wayes Easemᵗˢ Emollumᵗˢ profits & Appurtenances whatsoever unto yᵉ sᵈ upland and Marsh & Each & Every of them belonging & in any wise Appurtaining & therewith now or heretofore as part parcell or Member thereof known used Accepted Taken Occupied & Enjoyed by yᵉ sᵈ Jacob Perkins & all the right Title use Inheritance Possession Claime & Demand wᵗsoever of him yᵉ sᵈ Jacob Perkins his heirs Exʳˢ & Admʳˢ of in & to yᵉ Same upland and Marsh & Every part & parcell thereof with yᵉ Appurtenances thereof and yᵉ reversion & reversions remainder & remainders thereof & of Every part thereof To have & To hold yᵉ aforesᵈ land & Marsh herein before granted & described as aforesᵈ Together with all & Singular yᵉ herein before granted premisses with yᵉ Appurtenances thereof & of Every part & parcell thereof unto yᵉ sᵈ James Carr his heirs Exʳˢ Admʳˢ & Assignes unto his & their own Sole & propper use benefit and behoofe for ever Absolutely without any Mannered of Condition redemption or revocation in any wise & yᵉ sᵈ Jacob Perkins at yᵉ Time of yᵉ Ensealing & Delivery of these presents do Avouch himSelfe to be yᵉ True Sole & Lawfull owner of all & Singular yᵉ premisses as herein before granted bargained & Sold & Stand Lawfully Siezᵈ in and of yᵉ Same as an Absolute

Book VIII, Fol. 248.

Estate of Inheritance in fee Simple and that I have in my my Self full power good right & Lawfull Authority ye Same & Every part & parcell thereof to grant Sell & Assure in Maner as afores^d/ And Also that at ye Time of this present grant bargaine & Sale & unto ye Sealing & Delivery of these presents ye upland & Marsh herein before granted with ye Appurtenances thereof & of Every part & parcell thereof is & are free Clear & Clearly Acquitted Exonerated and fully Discharged of & from all & all maner of former & other gifts grants bargaines Sales Leases releases Mortgages Joyntures Dowries Judgm^{ts} Executions Acts Alienations Charges & Incumbrances whatsoever & further I ye s^d Jacob Perkins do hereby bind & Oblige my Selfe my heirs & Each of their heirs respectively all And Singular ye herein before premisses with ye Appurtenances thereof & of Every part & parcell thereof unto ye s^d James Carr his heirs Ex^{rs} Adm^{rs} Assignes & Every of them against ye Lawfull Claimes & Demands of all & Every p^{r}son & p^{r}sons whomsoever to Warra^t & forever defend by these presents & Also to make & pass any other further Legall Act & act thing & things Device and Instrum^{ts} in ye Law whatsoever as shall by ye s^d James Carr his heirs Ex^{rs} Adm^{rs} or Assignes At his & their Cost & Charges be required and desired for ye further Assurence Sure making ye premisses unto him & them./ Also Anna his wife of ye s^d Jacob Perkins do hereby release & Set over unto ye s^d James Carr all her right of Dowry & thirds in ye premisses and have also Sealed & Executed these presents./ In Witness whereof ye s^d Jacob Perkins & Anna his wife have hereunto Set their hands & Seals this Twenty third day of Octob^r Anno Domini One Thousand Seven hundred & Seventeen In ye fourth year of his Maj^{tys} Reign George by the Grace of God King Great Brittaine &c^t

It is to be understood before ye Ensealing & Delivery of this p^{r}sent deed of Sale that ye Twenty first line downward is Interlined & halfe of ye Twenty Second ye whole Twenty third and part of ye Twenty fourth Lines are rased out./   Jacob Perkins (a Seal)
Signed Sealed & Delivered   (a Seal)
  In p^{r}sence of us
          mark
Josiah   Black
Samuel Marston
Nath^{ll} Freeman

BOOK VIII, FOL. 249.

York sc/ Octob{r} 23{d} 1717./ The above Named Jacob Perkins p{r}sonally Appeared & Acknowledged y{e} Above & within written Instrum{t} to be his free Act & Deed.
     Before me/ Abra{m} Preble Jus{t} peace
Recorded According to y{e} Original Oct{r} 28{th} 1717.
       p Jos. Hamond Reg{r}

 Know All men by these presents that Samuel Sibley of Salem in y{e} County of Essex house carpenter & Sarah his wife one of y{e} Daughters of John Wells Late of y{e} Town of Wells in y{e} County of York all in y{e} Province of y{e} Massachusets Bay in New England for & in Consideration of y{e} Sum of Twelve pounds to them y{e} s{d} Sam{l} Sibley & Sarah Sibley well & Truely paid by their brother Thomas Wells of y{e} s{d} Town of Wells husbandman y{e} rec{t} whereof they hereby Acknowledge & themselves therewith fully Satisfied Contented & paid have bargained & Sold and do by these presents give grant Sell Enfeoffe Set over & forever Confirm unto y{e} s{d} Thomas Wells his heirs Ex{rs} & Adm{rs} & Assignes all that part Share portion or proportion that is any wayes due Appurtaining or belonging unto y{e} s{d} Sam{l} & Sarah of y{e} Estate of their s{d} father John Wells before named dec{d} that is to Say all her right Share part or proportion in any Lands Meadows Marshes or other grounds Either divided or hereafter to be divided Scittuate Lying & being in y{e} Township of Wells afores{d} To have & To hold all y{e} s{d} right & Interest with all y{e} priviledges rights Comonages Imunitys priviledges [249] And Appurtenances thereunto belonging unto him y{e} said Thomas Wells his heirs & Assignes for ever to his & their own proper use benefit & behoofe as an Estate of Inheritance for ever In Witness whereof y{e} s{d} Sam{l} & Sarah have hereunto Set their hands & Seals y{e} 13{th} day of January 1703/4/   Samuel Sibley (Seal)
Signed Sealed & Delivered Sarah Sibley (Seal)
 In presence of us
 John Sibley
 Joseph Cooke
  Essex sc/
 Sam{l} Sibley & Sarah Sibly p{r}sonally Appeared this 24{th} Jan{ry} 170¾ before me the Subscrib{r} being one of her Maj{tys} Justices for s{d} County & Acknowledged y{e} within written

Book VIII, Fol. 249.

Instrum^t to be their Act & Deed./ And Sarah his wife freely Surrendered up her right of Dower to ye Same./

Jonathan Corwin

Recorded According to ye Original Octob^r 1st 1717./

p Jos. Hamond Reg^r

To All Christian People to whom these presents Shall Come James Tyler of Bradford in ye County of Essex in ye Province of ye Massachusets Bay in New England husbandman Sendeth Greeting & know ye that ye s^d James Tyler for & in Consideration of ye Sum of Thirty pounds Curra^t money of this province to him in hand paid by Jabish Dorman of Boxford in the County & Province aboves^d husbandman the rec^t whereof ye s^d James Tyler doth hereby Acknowledge & himSelfe therewith fully Satisfied Contented & paid./ And thereof & of Every part & parcell thereof doth hereby Absolutely Exonerate Acquit & discharge ye s^d Jabish Dorman his heirs Ex^{rs} & Adm^{rs} forever hath given granted bargaine Sell make over & Deliver unto him ye s^d Jabish Dorman & to his heirs & Assigns forever ye one halfe part of ye right or propriety which ye s^d James Tyler Claims or Challengeth in ye Township of Capeporpoise in the County of York in ye aboves^d Province ye which property ye s^d Tyler purchased of m^r Nicholas Moorey of ffreetown in ye County of Bristoll in ye Province of ye Massachusets Bay in New England Yeoman which was Originally Joseph Bolls^s Griffith Montagues and Morgan Howells and also halfe my right in fifty acres of Salt Meadow therein Contained be it more or Less which ye s^d Tyler purchased of ye s^d Nicholas Moorey which was formerly Samuel Snows of Boston Cordwainer the full halfe part of my Share both divided & undivided butted & bounded as may Appear on ye records of ye County of York And as formerly Sold to Joseph Bayley To have & To hold ye one halfe part of ye land & rights which I ye s^d James Tyler Claims in ye Township of Capeporpoise in ye County of York by Vertue of a deed of Sale which may Appear und^r ye hand & Seal of ye aboves^d Nicholas Moorey bareing date ye fourteenth day of Decemb^r in ye year One Thousand Seven hundred & Sixteen butted & bounded as afores^d to him ye s^d Jabish Dorman & to his heirs & Assignes forever./ Moreover I ye s^d James Tyler do hereby for my Selfe & my heirs Ex^{rs} & Adm^{rs} Covena^t and Promiss & grant to & with ye s^d Jabish Dorman & his heirs & Assignes that he ye James Tyler is ye True & proper owner of ye aboves^d land & Meadow

& rights as aboves^d both divided & undivided and all ye Memb^{rs} & Appurtenances of ye Same and that he hath in himselfe good full power and Lawfull Authority ye aboves^d Granted premisses with the Appurtenances thereof in his own name to give grant bargaine Sell make over & Assure ye Same as above Specified & that it Shall for ever hereafter free and Lawfull for ye s^d Jabish Dorman & his heirs and Assignes to have & to hold & peaceably & Quietly to possess Enjoy & Improve ye aboves^d one halfe of ye Interest or propriety that the s^d James Tyler holds or Claims in ye Township of Capeporpoise both Divided & undivided & also halfe my right in ye afores^d fifty acres of Salt Meadow be ye Same more or Less with all & Singular ye Members & purtenances thereof with all priviledges & benefits thereunto belonging & profits therefrom Ariseing with all ye Estates rights Titles Interest demand of him ye s^d James Tyler his heirs Ex^{rs} and Adm^{rs} to ye premisses & to Every part forever and by him ye s^d James Tyler his heirs Ex^{rs} & Adm^{rs} well & Sufficiently Saved & kept harmless & Indempnified of & from all & all maner of former & other gifts Grants bargains Sales Mortgages Leases Joyntures Judgm^{ts} Dowrys Executions recogniscences Charges Troubles Suits at Law & Incumbrances whatsoever that may Arise by any p^{r}son or persons Laying any Lawfull Claime thereunto forever./ In Witness hereof I y^e s^d James Tyler have hereunto Set my hand & Seal y^e Eleventh day of January in y^e year One Thousand Seven hundred & Sixteen Annoq$_s$ Domini 1716 And in y^e third year of y^e reign of our Soveraign Lord George of Great Brittaine ffrance & Ireland King Defender of y^e faith &c^t.   James Tyler (s$_{eal}^a$)
Signed Sealed & Delivered
 In presence of us
 Edmond Chadwick
 John Griffing
 John Lane

The words (halfe my right in) Entred between y^e Seventeenth & Eighteenth lines are Allowed by me./   James Tyler.
 Josh: Hardy:
 Jno Griffing
York sc/ James Tyler personally Appeared before me y^e Subscriber one of his Maj^{tys} Justices of ye peace for s^d County & Acknowledged ye above written Instrum^t to be his Act & Deed this 23^d day of Feb^{ry} 1716/7
                    John Wheelwright
Recorded According to ye Original Decr 7th 1717./
              p Jos. Hamond Reg^r

Know All men by these presents that We Ezra Rolfe & Sarah his wife & Martha Jackson Sister to s^d Rolfes wife all of Bradford in ye County of Essex in New England We for & in Consideration of fifteen pounds to us in hand paid or Sufficient Security given for ye paym^t of it to our Satisfaction we have therefore Sold and do by these presents Confirm and make over unto James Tyler of ye Same Town & County all our right & Interest in a parcel of Land & meadow & Marsh lying between Black point river & Saco river in ye province of Maine We do as aboves^d make over all our right & Interest of ye aboves^d Premisses which fell to our father John Jackson dec^d which did belong unto [250] Our Grandfather Jackson dec^d from whom our s^d father derived his right./ Is to be understood we make over all our right unto ye s^d James Tyler his heirs Ex^{rs} Adm^{rs} & Assignes forever To have & To hold our share in that land and Meadow as aboves^d in ye place Specified with all Trees woods water Courses priviledges & Appurtenances thereunto belonging also all our right if any appear to be in any more Land & Meadow which was our Grandfathers lying further Eastward./ We do further for our selves heirs Ex^{rs} & Adm^{rs} Covenant & promiss that it Shall be Lawfull for him his heirs Ex^{rs} Adm^{rs} & Assignes to have use Occupy possess & Enjoy all ye aboves^d premisses without any Disturbence or hinderence from us or any from by or und^r us./ for ye Clear understanding of what is above written this is Added that we do not oblige our Selves to Defend the Title of these premisses as aboves^d but against any who may pretend right from by or under us for ye Confirmation of all above written We have Set to our hands & Seals./ Dated ffeb^{ry} 14th Anno 1716/7

The words [And Meadows] Interlined before Signing & Sealing

Signed Sealed & Delivered
In ye presence of
Saml Palmer
Saml Tenny

Ezra Rolfe (Seal)
Sarah Rolfe her mark ◯ (Seal)
Martha Jackson her mark ⋎ (Seal)

Essex sc/ Haverhill Septr ye Sixteenth day 1717. Then Ezra Rolfe & Sarah Rolfe his wife & Martha Jackson all p^{r}sonally Appearing Acknowledged this Instrum^t within written to be their free & Volluntary Act & Deed./

Before me./ John White Justice of ye peace

Recorded According to ye Original Octob^r 7th 1717./

p Jos. Hamond Reg^r

Book VIII, Fol. 250.

To All Christian People to whom this present deed of Sale Shall Come or doth Concern James Alling of York in y[e] County of York in y[e] Province of y[e] Massachusets Bay in New England Sendeth Greeting Know y[e] that y[e] s[d] James Alling for & in Consideration of y[e] Sum of   pounds money to him in hand well & Truely paid by m[r] Sam[l] Came of s[d] York y[e] rec[t] thereof y[e] s[d] James Alling doth Acknowledge himselfe therew[th] to be fully Satisfied paid & Contented & doth hereby for himselfe his heirs Assignes Acquit Exonerate & fully discharge y[e] s[d] Sam[l] Came his heirs Ex[rs] & Adm[rs] of all & Every part of y[e] premisses hereafter Set forth and Expressed the which y[e] s[d] James Alling hath Given granted bargained Sold Aliened Enfeoffed & Conveyed & doth by these presents give grant bargaine Sell Aliene Enfeoffe & Convey & fully freely & Absolutely make over and Confirm unto y[e] s[d] Sam[l] Came and to his heirs & Assignes for ever One Certain piece parcell or Tract of land Containing Seventeen Acres & fifty poles be it more or Less lying & being within y[e] Township of s[d] York & is Scittuate upon y[e] South Side of y[e] Southwest branch of s[d] York river butting upon y[e] Marsh reputed to Thomas Cards Marsh y[e] which is part of a grant of Twenty Acres of Land given by the Town of York afores[d] to s[d] Alling At a Town meeting in s[d] York May y[e] Twelfth day in y[e] year of our Lord One Thousand Six hundred and Ninety & nine as p York Town Book may Appear and Laid out to s[d] James Alling March y[e] first in y[e] year 1702/3 & is butted & bounded as followeth viz[t] begining at a white oak Tree markt four Sides Standing by s[d] Thomas Cards Marsh and runs from thence South Southeast Seventy Six poles to an Aps Tree Mark[t] on four Sides and runs from thence South & by East One hundred & fifty pole to y[e] dividing line between York & Kittery and is in breadth Twelve poles & runs from thence North & by west One hundred & fifty poles & then North Northwest Seventy Six poles and there is bounded by a white birch Tree Marked on four Sides Standing by aboves[d] Thomas Cards marsh & is bounded by s[d] Marsh Twelve poles to y[e] white oak first above mentioned Together with all y[e] Priviledges Emollum[ts] Titles rights grants returns & Advantages thereunto belonging or Appurtaining or that may hereafter belong or redownd unto y[e] Same or any part or parcell thereof unto him y[e] s[d] Sam[l] Came & his heirs & Assignes for ever To have & To hold & Quietly & peaceably to Possess Occupy & Enjoy as a Sure Estate in fee Simple Moreover y[e] s[d] James Allen doth for himselfe his heirs Ex[rs] & Adm[rs] to & with y[e] s[d] Sam[l] Came his heirs & Assignes Covena[t] Ingage and Promiss y[e] above

bargained premisses to be free & Clear from all former gifts grants bargaines Sales rents rates dowryes widdows thirds Entailes Mortgages or any other Incumberments w^{t}soever and Also from all future Claimes Challenges Claims Arrests Law suits or any other Incumberments whatsoever to be had or Comenced by him ye s^d James Alling his heirs Ex^{rs} Adm^{rs} or Assignes or any other person or persons whatsoever Proceeding ye Date hereof & he ye s^d James Alling doth hereby promiss to Defend & will & doth Warrantize ye Same./ In Witness hereof ye s^d James Alling hath hereunto Set his hand & Seal this Twenty third day of August in ye year of our Lord One Thousand Seven hundred & Seventeen And in ye fourth year of ye reign of our Soveraign Ld George King of Great Brittaine &c^t/ James Allen (a Seal)
Signed Sealed & Delivered
In ye presence of us Witnesses
Peter Nowell
Arthur Bragdon
Nathl Freeman

York sc/ York Augst ye 27th 1717.
James Allen personally Appeared & Acknowledged this above written Instrum^t to be his free Act & Deed./
Before me Abra^m Preble Just peace
Recorded According to ye Original Octob^r 2^d 1717./
p Jos. Hamond Reg^r

To All People to whom these presents Shall Come Jonathan Littlefield of Wells & Samuel Hill of Charlestown Send Greeting Now Know ye that whereas I Saml Hill aboves^d did Some time Since Sell to Jonathan Littlefield aboves^d a Tract of land & Meadow in wells given me by ye Last will & Testam^t of my uncle Joseph Cross deceased & ye Conveyance not Appearing nor yet Compleated According as ye Law Directs We ye aboves^d Jonathan Littlefield of Wells in ye County of york in ye province of ye Massachusets Bay in New England And Saml Hill of Charlestown in in ye County of Suffolk Province afores^d Divers good & Lawfull Causes us thereunto Moveing [251] Especially for & in Consideration of ye Sum of forty Six pounds good Curra^t money of New England to aboves^d Samuel Hill in hand paid by David & Jonathan Littlefiel of Wells to full Satisfaction Have given & granted and do by these presents fully & Clearly give grant bargaine Sell Enfeoffe & Set over

Book VIII, Fol. 251.

to David Littlefield of Wells in y[e] County of york Province afores[d] all that Tract of land & Marsh which was made over from Sam[l] Hill to Jonathan Littlefield in y[e] forementioned Conveyance which is Supposed to be lost Viz[t] a Certain Tract of upland & meadow Lying & being in y[e] Township of Wells Containing y[e] Quantity of Two hundred Acres be it more or Less being on y[e] Northeast Side of land now Improved by & in possession of Daniel Sawyer Twenty poles in breadth to y[e] Northeastward of s[d] Land of Daniel Sawyer & that breadth down to Webhaunt river & up into y[e] Country as other lots run all this to be in y[e] present possession of David Littlefield Aboves[d] & after y[e] decease of Mary Widdow relict of Joseph Cross and now wife of Nicholas Morey then y[e] s[d] David Littlefield is to have and Enjoy all that parcell of land & marsh which lyes between y[e] aforementioned Twenty poles & y[e] next brook Comonly Called Cross[es] brook and to run as y[e] s[d] brook runs down to Webhant river both upland & Marsh below y[e] highway and from y[e]s[d] highway upward to run as y[e] other lots run that Joyn thereto All which land & Meadow & Every part & parcell thereof We the aboves[d] Jonathan Littlefield & Sam[l] Hill do for our selves our heirs Ex[rs] Adm[rs] Confirm & Set over & David Littlefield afores[d] dureing his Natural life and at his Decease to his heirs of his own body and to them their heirs Execut[rs] Adm[rs] or Assignes Together with all & Singular y[e] priviledges rights & Appurtenances thereof to have & To hold as a free & Clear Estate in fee Simple forever./ And we y[e] aboves[d] Jon[a] Littlefield and Sam[l] Hill do for our selves our heirs respectively Affirm and promiss that it & Every part & parcell thereof is free and Clear and fully & Clearly & Absolutely Acquitted & Discharged of & from all other and former Gifts grants bargains Sales Dowryes Mortgages or Incumbrances whatsoever Except what is before Excepted And that they are y[e] True & rightfull owners of s[d] land According as before Expressed & that we have full power right & Authority to Sell & dispose of y[e] Same as above Expressed./ Moreover that we do by these presents Warra[t] and will Defend y[e] same from all or any p[r]son or p[r]sons in by from or under us or our heirs Ex[rs] Adm[rs] or assignes respectively In Witness whereof We y[e] aboves[d] Sam[l] Hill & Jonathan Littlefield have hereunto put our hands & Seals this fourth day of May in the year of our L[d] one Thousand Seven hundred & thirteen and the Twelfth year of

Book VIII, Fol. 251.

yᵉ reign of our Soveraign Lady Anne by yᵉ grace of God of Great Brittaine ffrance and Ireland Queen./
Signed Sealed & Delivered   Jonathan Littlefield (ₛₑₐₗ ᵃ)
    In presence of us   Samuel Hill (ₛₑₐₗ ᵃ)
    Nicholas Cole
    Daniel Simpson
    Abigail Littlefield
      York sc/
Jonathan Littlefield and Samˡ Hill pʳsonally Appeared before me yᵉ Subscribʳ one of her Majᵗʸˢ Justices of yᵉ peace for sᵈ County & freely Acknowledged yᵉ above Instrumᵗ or deed of Sale with their hands & Seals Affixed thereunto to be their Volluntary Act & Deed this 6ᵗʰ day of may 1713
                             John Wheelwright
Recorded According to yᵉ Original Octobʳ 23ᵈ 1717./
                             p Jos. Hamond Regʳ

To All Christian People to whom these presents Shall Come Samuel Littlefield Sendeth Greeting Now Know yᵉ that I Samˡ Littlefield of Wells in yᵉ County of York Province of yᵉ Massachusets Bay in New England planter for & in Consideration of yᵉ Sum of fifteen pounds in good & Lawfull money of New England in hand paid or Secured to be paid to me by David Littlefield of yᵉ Town & County aforesᵈ & other good & Lawfull Considerations me thereunto Moveing Have given granted and do by these presents give grant bargaine Sell Alienate Enfeoffe make over & Confirm unto David Littlefield aforesᵈ One Quarter part of yᵉ sᵈ falls at Kenebunk which was granted to my father Edmund Littlefield & Joseph Littlefield decᵈ by yᵉ Town of Wells & Capeporpoise for yᵉ building of a Saw mill or mills also yᵉ Priviledg of Laying of Timber & bords on both sides yᵉ river & with yᵉ priviledges of yᵉ Stream that yᵉ grants do Specifie as to yᵉ Transportation of Timbʳ both up Stream & Down with yᵉ priviledges of Cutting Timber on both sids yᵉ river for yᵉ use of yᵉ Mill also a hey way on both sides yᵉ river to hall Timbʳ for yᵉ use of yᵉ Mill & Also all yᵉ rest of yᵉ partners have yᵉ Same priviledge to Occupy yᵉ Same hey way & yᵉ sᵈ David Littlefield is to pay yᵉ Annuall rent to yᵉ Town According to yᵉ Agreemᵗ upon yᵉ Town grant & it is Also Agreed that if yᵉ sᵈ David Littlefield Sees good to dispose of yᵉ abovesᵈ pʳmisses he is to give me yᵉ first refusal of it./ I yᵉ above Said Samˡ Littlefield do make over and Sell unto David Littlefield aforesᵈ To have & To hold from me

Book VIII, Fol. 252.

my heirs Ex^{rs} Adm^{rs} or assignes unto him his his heirs Ex^{rs} Adm^{rs} or Assignes Together with all & Singular Priviledges rights & Appurtenances thereunto belonging or any wise Appurtaining as a free & Clear Estate in fee Simple forever & I ye aboves^d Samuel Littlefield for me my heirs Ex^{rs} Adm^{rs} do Covena^t and promiss to & with David Littlefield aboves^d his heirs Ex^{rs} Adm^{rs} & Assignes that I am ye True owner & possessor of ye aboves^d premisses & have full power right & right & Authority to Sell & dispose of the Same & do Affirm & promiss it & Every part & parcell to be free and Clear and fully Clearly & Absolutely Acquitted & discharged of and from all other and former gifts grants bargains Alienations Mortgages Dowryes Sales or Incumbrances whatsoever and that I Will Warrant and Defend ye Same from all or any p^{r}son or p^{r}sons whatsoever laying any Legall Claime thereto./ In Witness w^{r}of I ye Aboves^d Samuel Littlefield have hereunto put my hand & Seal ye Tenth day of Decemb^r in ye third year of ye reign of our Soveraign Lord George by ye Grace of God King of Great Brittaine Defend^r of ye faith Anno Dom 1716./

Signed Sealed & Delivered   Saml Littlefield (Seal)
  In presence of
  Francis Sawyer   Frances X Littlefield (Seal)
  Saml Emery   her mark
  W^m ⟨his mark⟩ Tayler

   York sc/ Wells may 14 : 1717

The within named Samuel Littlefield & Frances his wife p^{r}sonally Appeared before me ye Subscrib^r one of his Maj^{tys} Justices of ye peace for s^d County & Acknowledged this Instrum^t to be their Act & Deed & ye s^d Frances did at ye Same time give up: all her right of Dower or thirds which otherwise She might have had thereunto   John Wheelwright

Recorded According to ye Original Octob^r 23^d 1717./
                                     p Jos. Hamond Reg^r

[252] To All People to whom these presents shall Come Greeting./ Now Know Y^e that I Nathaniel Clark of Wells in ye County of York in ye Province of the Massachusets Bay in New England Cordwain^r for & in Consideration of ye Natural Love And Affection that I have & Do bear to my Son Nathl Clark of Wells afores^d Have given and granded and do by these presents give grant Enfeoffe Confirm & Set over to my Son Nathl Clark afores^d a Certain parcell of Land Lying

Book VIII, Fol. 252.

& being in ye Township of Wells bounded as followeth Southwest by land of Thomas Wells Northwest by ye Little river NorthEast by land Claimed by Lewis Allen & Nicholas Cole Southeast by a red Oak marked on three Sides & three Nails driven into the three Spots and from thence to run over on a Southwest line to Thomas Wells his land only retaining Two rod on ye Northeast Side of s^d granted land ye whole length thereof for a way for my Selfe and Successors./ As Also I give & grant to him Two Acres of Salt Marsh in ye Town of Wells Adjoyning to Thomas Wells his Marsh on the further branch of Little river & Also I grant & give to him one hundred Acres of Land & five Acres of Meadow granted to me by ye Town of Wells in March 1713/4 All which parcells of Land Marsh & Meadow bounded as afores^d I ye aboves^d Nathl Clark do give & Set over to my Son Nathl Clark to him his heirs Ex^{rs} Adm^{rs} & Assigns Together with all ye priviledges rights & Appurtenances thereto belonging or any wise Appurtaining To have & To hold as a free and Clear Estate in fee Simple for ever only it is Provided that if my Son Nathl Clark Should Incline to Sell ye above granted that his brother or bretherin Shall have ye refusal thereof./ giving as an other will give for ye Same./ And I ye aboves^d Nathl Clark do Covenant & promiss to & with my Son Nathaniel Clark afores^d that I am ye rightfull owner of ye above granted premisses & have full power to give & dispose of ye Same as afores^d and that ye premisses are free & Clear & fully & Clearly Acquitted & Discharged of & from all other and former gifts grants bargaines Sales Mortgages or Incumbrances whatsoever. Moreover that I will Warrant and defend ye Same from all or any p^{r}son or p^{r}sons whatsoever Laying any Legall Claime thereunto in by from or und^r me my heirs Ex^{rs} Adm^{rs} or Assignes. In Witness whereof I ye aboves^d Nathaniel Clark have hereto put my hand & Seal this fourth day of May Anno Domini one Thousand Seven hundred & fifteen & in ye first year of ye reign of our Soveraign Ld George by ye Grace of God of Great Brittaine ffrance & Ireland King Defender of ye faith &c^t

The length of ye above granted land on ye Northeast Side from ye Little river to ye red oak bounds at ye Southeast End of ye above granted land is one hundred Ninety & Eight rods or poles./ this addition aboves^d is Inserted before ye Signing & Sealing hereof./   Nathaniel Clark (a Seal)

Signed Sealed & Delivered
     In presence of us   Patience Clark (her mark) (a Seal)
     Abigail Lane
     Abigail Parsons
     Saml Emery

BOOK VIII, FOL. 252.

York sc/ May 19th 1715./
Then Nath¹ Clark & Patience his wife Appeared & Acknowledged yᵉ within written Instrumᵗ to be their Act & deed And Patience yᵉ wife of Nath¹ Clark resigned up her right of Dowry or thirds
    Before me John Wheelwright Just peace
Recorded According to yᵉ Original Octobʳ 28th 1717./
       p Jos. Hamond Regʳ

To All Christian People to whom these presents Shall Come Greeting Know Yᵉ that Symonds Epes & Mary his wife of Ipswich in yᵉ County of Essex in the Province of yᵉ Massachusets Bay in New England Gent for & in Consideration of a Valluable Sum of One hundred & Sixty pounds to us in hand paid by Nath¹ Clark Junʳ of Wells in yᵉ County of York in New England husbandman before yᵉ Ensealing & Delivery of these presents yᵉ recᵗ whereof we do Acknowledge and our selves therewith fully Satisfied Contented & paid have given granted bargained & Sold Aliened Assigned Enfeoffed Set over and Confirmed and do by these presents firmly clearly & absolutely give grant bargaine Sell Enfeoffe Set over & Confirm unto yᵉ sᵈ Nath¹ Clark his heirs Exʳˢ Admʳˢ & Assignes for ever one halfe part of a farm in Wells in yᵉ County of york that was our Grandfathers mʳ Wᵐ Symondsᵉˢ formerly of Wells decᵈ yᵉ whole farm Containing by Estimation about three hundred Acres of upland Marsh & Meadow ground be yᵉ same More or Less bounded Southerly & Northwesterly upon Gooches land & upon yᵉ Seawall & Little river Southeasterly & Northeasterly Together with all yᵉ wood Timbʳ profits priviledges and Appurtenances that doth in Any wise belong or Appurtaine unto the halfe part of abovesᵈ farm Excepting Six acres of Salt Marsh where sᵈ Epes shall Choose which he doth reserve for his own use and his heirs for ever & a way to Convey that: that may grow thereon through sᵈ farm To have & To hold yᵉ abovesᵈ parcell of Land with all yⁿ profits priviledges and Appurtenances in any wise thereunto belonging unto him yᵉ sᵈ Nath¹ Clark his heirs Exʳˢ Admʳˢ & Assigns and to their only proper use forever & we yᵉ sᵈ Symonds Epes & Mary my wife do Covenaᵗ promiss and agree to & with yᵉ sᵈ Nath¹ Clark that we have full power & good right to Sell yᵉ abovesᵈ Lands and it Shall & may be Lawfull for sᵈ Clark to use Occupy possess & Enjoy yᵉ Same for ever promissing to warrant & Defend his Title thereto from all pʳsons Legall Claime

Book VIII, Fol. 253.

In Witness of all & Singular ye premisses we have hereunto Set our hands and Seals this fifth day of August in ye year of our Lord One Thousd Seven hundred & Seventeen & in ye third year of his Majtys Reign   Symonds Epes (a Seal)
Signed Sealed & Delivered   Mary Epes (a Seal)
  In presence of us
    The mark of
  Jonathan 𝒮𝒪 Piper

Mary Watson
  Essex ss/ Ipswich Augst 6th 1717 Majr Symonds Epes & Mr Mary his wife personally Appeared & Acknowledged this Instrumt to be their free Act & Deed./
                    Before Saml Appleton Just peace
  Recorded According to ye Original Octobr 28th 1717./
                          p Jos. Hamond Regr

  To All Christian People to whom these presents Shall Come John Banks and Joseph Bankes of york in ye County of york in ye Province of ye Massachusets Bay in New England planters Send Greeting Know ye that ye sd John Bankes & Joseph Bankes for & in Consideration of ye Sum of fifty pounds Currat money of New England to us in hand paid before ye Ensealing & Delivery of these presents by Richard Milbery of York in yorkshire aforesd planter ye rect whereof to full Content & Satisfaction they ye sd John & Joseph Bankes do by these prsents Acknowledge & thereof & of Every part thereof for themselves their heirs Exrs & Admrs do Acquit Exonerate & discharge ye sd Richard Milbery his heirs Executrs & Admrs every of them for ever by these presents & for divers other good Causes & Considerations them thereunto Moveing they ye sd [253] John Bankes & Joseph Bankes have given granted bargained Sold Aliened Enfeoffed Conveyed & Confirmed & by these presents do fully freely clearly and Absolutely give grant bargaine Sell Aliene Enfeoffe Convey & Confirm unto ye sd Richd Milbery his heirs and Assignes forever ye whole of our Two thirds of a Certaine Tract of Land Containing by Estimation forty Acres be it more or Less lying on mr Dumers Neck in york aforesd butting on ye Sea and bounded on all ye other Sides by sd Milberys Land which Two thirds of sd Land or farm was given to us by Captn Job Alcock Late of Portsmouth decd as may Appear by his last will & Testamt & has been for Some years Last past in ye Possession of Richd Milbery

Book VIII, Fol. 253.

afors^d as. Tennant to s^d Alcock Together with all Such rights Libertys Imunitys profits priviledges Comoditys Imolluments & Appurtenances as in any kind Appertaine there unto with ye reversions & remainders thereof & all ye Estate right Title Interest Inheritance propperty possession Claime & Demand of them ye s^d John Bankes & Joseph Banks of in & to ye Same & Every part thereof To have & To hold all ye above granted premisses with all & Singular ye Appurtenances thereof unto ye s^d Richd Milbery his heirs and Assignes to his & their own sole & propper use benefit & behoofe from henceforth for ever & ye s^d John Bankes & Joseph Bankes for themselves their heirs Execut^{rs} & Adm^{rs} do hereby Covena^t promiss grant & agree to & with ye s^d Richard Milbery his heirs & Assigns in maner & form following that is to Say that at ye Time of ye Ensealing & Delivery of these presents they ye s^d John Bankes & Joseph Bankes are ye True Sole & Lawfull owners of all ye afore bargained premisses Viz^t ye whole two thirds of s^d Tract of Land or farm above described & do Stand Lawfully Siezed thereof in their own proper right of a good perfect & Indefeazable Estate of Inheritance in ye Condition Expressed in ye last will & Testament of Cap^{tn} Job Alcock aboves^d haveing in themselves full power good right and Lawfull Authority to Sell & Dispose of ye s^d Two thirds of Aboves^d farm in maner as afores^d & that ye s^d Richard Milbery his heirs & Assigns Shall & may henceforth forever Lawfully peaceably & Quietly have hold use Occupy possess & Enjoy ye above granted premisses with the Appurtenances thereof free & Clear & Cleanly Acquitted & discharged of and from all & all maner of former & other gifts grants bargains Sales Leases Mortgages Joyntures Dowers Judgm^{ts} Executions Entails forfeitures and of & from all other Titles troubles Charges & Incumbrances whatsoever had made done or Suffered to be done by ye s^d John & Jos^{ph} Bankes or either of them their heirs or Assignes or any of them at any time or times before ye Delivery hereof And further ye s^d John Bankes and Joseph Bankes do hereby bind & Oblige themselves their heirs Ex^{rs} & Adm^{rs} from henceforth & forever hereafter to Warra^t & Defend all ye above granted premisses & ye Appurtenances thereof unto ye s^d Richard Milbery his heirs & Assignes against ye Lawfull Claims & Demands of all & Every person or persons whomsoever and at any time or times hereafter on demand to give & pass Such further & Ample Assurance & Confirmation of ye premisses unto ye s^d Richard Milbery his heirs & Assignes forever as in Law or Equity Can be reasonably devised Advised or required./ In Wit-

ness whereof y⁰ sᵈ John Bankes & Joseph Bankes have hereunto Set their hands & Seals yᵉ Tenth day of March in yᵉ year of our Lord 1714/5 & in yᵉ first year of our Soveraign Lord Georges reign over Great Brittaine &cᵗ
Signed Sealed & Delivered   John Bankes (₍ₛₑₐₗ₎ᵃ)
   In presence of   Joseph Bankes (₍ₛₑₐₗ₎ᵃ)
Samˡ Moodey
Thomas Sewall
Benjᵃ Plumer
York sc/ York march yᵉ 22ᵈ 1715./ Joseph Bankes & his wife John Bankes & his wife yᵉ above named pʳsonally Appeared before me yᵉ Subscribʳ one of his Majᵗʸˢ Justices of yᵉ peace in yᵉ County aforesᵈ & Acknowledged yᵉ above written Instrumᵗ to be their act & Deed   Lewis Bane
Recorded According to yᵉ Original Octobʳ 2ᵈ 1717.
                              p Jos. Hamond Regʳ

To All Christian People to whom this present deed of Sale Shall Come John Snell of Portsmouth in yᵉ Province of New Hampshire in N: E. Cooper doth with Elizabeth his wife Send Greeting Know yᵉ that we yᵉ sᵈ John & Elizabeth Snell in Consideration of thirty pounds Curraᵗ money of N. E. to us in hand paid before the Ensealing & Delivery of these presents by Richard Milbery of york in yᵉ Province of Main in N. E. Planter the recᵗ whereof to full Satisfaction We yᵉ sᵈ John & Elizabeth Snell do hereby Acknowledge for which with divers other good & Lawfull reasons & Considerations us thereunto Moveing we yᵉ sᵈ John & Elizabeth Snell have for ourselves our heirs Executʳˢ & Admʳˢ Given granted bargained Sold Conveyed & Confirmed unto yᵉ sᵈ Richard Milbery his heirs Exʳˢ Admʳˢ & Assignes To have & To hold use & Enjoy to them & their heirs for ever a Certaine piece or parcell of Salt Marsh Containing by Estimation Three Acres be it More or Less Scittuate lying & being in yᵉ S. W. branch of york river in yᵉ Province of Maine aforesᵈ bounded on yᵉ Easterly side by yᵉ Marsh formerly John Parkers now in yᵉ Improvemᵗ of Ebenʳ Blazdell on yᵉ N Westerly Side by yᵉ land of John Macintire & on yᵉ S. West & S. Easterly Sides by yᵉ sᵈ Milberys own Marsh which Marsh with all rights priviledges & Appurtenances thereunto in any wise belonging yᵉ sᵈ John & Elizabeth Snell do by these presents fully clearly & Absolutely give grant bargaine Sell make over Enffeoffe Convey & Confirm unto yᵉ sᵈ Richard Milbery his heirs and Assignes for ever without any maner of Let or

Mollestation from us yᵉ sᵈ John Snell or Elizabeth his wife or any from by or under Either of us./ And we yᵉ sᵈ John & Elizabeth Snell do further grant Agree Covenᵗ & promiss for ourselves our heirs Exʳˢ & admʳˢ to & with yᵉ sᵈ Richard Milbery his heirs & assignes to Warrant and Defend all yᵉ above bargained premisses to sᵈ Milbery & his heirs & from all persons whatsoever laying any Just or Lawfull Claime thereunto As Also to pass at any Time Such further & more Ample Conveyance & Assurance as may or can reasonably in yᵉ Law be devised Advised or required. In Witness whereof we the said John & Hannah Snell have hereunto Set our hands & Seals this   day of February in yᵉ Second year of yᵉ reign of our Soveraign Lord George of Great Brittaine &cᵗ King Annoq, Doˣ 1715   Jnᵒ Snell (ₛₑᵢₗᵃ)
Signed Sealed & Delivered
  In presence of
  John Pickerin
  Samuel Came
  Mʳ John Snell as by his hand & Seal personally Appeared before me yᵉ Subscribʳ & Acknowledged yᵉ above Instrumᵗ to be his free Act & Deed this 22ᵈ of February 1715/6
                John Plaisted Just peace
  Recorded According to yᵉ Original Octobʳ yᵉ 2ᵈ 1717./
              p Jos. Hamond Regʳ

[254] These Presents Witnesseth that Whereas I Richard Bonighton Son & heir to Mʳ John Bonighton decᵈ have bargained & Sold unto Lieuᵗ Peter Weare of Hampton yᵉ Sum of Sixscore Acres of Land lying & being on yᵉ Northerly or Northeasterly of Saco river in yᵉ Pattent granted to his Honoured Grandfather Mʳ Richard Bonighton & Thomas Lewis as by Deed bareing Date yᵉ Sixteenth day of Novembʳ One Thousand Seven hundred & Thirteen may fully Appear./ I yᵉ sᵈ Richard Bonighton do by these presents Constitute & Appoint Mʳ Humphrey Scamon & Mʳ Peter Nowell of York in yᵉ Province of Maine or either of them to be my True & Lawfull Attorneys or Attorney to Measure out bound and Deliver & put yᵉ sᵈ Weare in possession of yᵉ land Sold to sᵈ Weare According as it Appears in sᵈ Deed & whatsoever my sᵈ Attorneys or Attorney Shal do in sᵈ Case I hold it Stable & good firm to all Intents & purposes as if I were present my Selfe & did it in my own pʳson In Witness & Confirmation hereof I hereunto Set my hand and Affix my Seal this Sixteenth day of Novʳ One thousand Seven hun-

dred & thirteenth & in y⁰ Twelfth year of her Majᵗʸˢ Reign Queen Anne over Great Brittaine France & Ireland Queen Defend' of y⁰ faith &c'/ The mark & Seal of
Witness Signed Sealed & Richard Bonighton (seal)
Delivered in y⁰ presence
of us
Nath¹ Weare Jun'
Thomas Waite
Daniel Weare
Hampton in New Hampsh'/ Richᵈ Bonighton personally Appeared this Seventeenth day of Novemb' 1713./ And Acknowledged this above writing & Letter of Attorney to be his free & Volluntary Act & Deed./ Before me
Nath¹ Weare Justice of peace
Recorded According to y⁰ Original Octob' 31ˢᵗ 1717./
p Jos. Hamond Reg'

By Vertue of y⁰ Power given unto me by a letter of Attorney from Richard Bonighton Cordwain' Son & heir to M' John Bonighton I have Laid out to Peter Weare One hundred Acres of upland & Twenty Acres of Marsh or Meadow as followeth toʷ from a Little white oak by Saco rivers Side at y⁰ mouth of Bonightons Creek I measured Six score rods up Saco river to a white oak marked by y⁰ rivers side & from thence Eight score rods near Northeast to a white Oak marked on four Sides & from thence near Southeast fourscore rods to a pitch pine marked & from thence to y⁰ place where I began./ And Twenty Acres of Marsh or Meadow Lying on Goose fair brook Joyning to m' James Gibinsᵉˢ Division line of y⁰ Pattent on y⁰ East & So from upland to upland up y⁰ brook westward till y⁰ Twenty acres are Compleated and finished./ And put y⁰ sᵈ Peter Weare in Possession of sᵈ Land and Marsh or Meadow as above bounded According to his Deed of Sale bareing Date y⁰ Sixteenth day of Novemb' One thousand Seven hundred & thirteen./ As Witness my hand & Seal this 25ᵗʰ day of October Anno Domini 1717./ & in y⁰ 4ᵗʰ year of our Soveraign King George his reign over Great Brittaine./
Humphrey Scammon
Recorded According to y⁰ Original Oct' 31ˢᵗ 1717./
p Jos. Hamond Reg'

To All Christian People to whom these p'sents may Concern or Come Thomas Addams of York in y⁰ County of york in ye Province of ye Massachusets in New England Yeoman Sendeth Greeting Know ye that ye s^d Thomas for & in good Consideration Especially the Natural love & Dear Affection that he hath & doth bear unto his Dutyfull Son Saml Addams hath freely & voluntaryly given granted Aliened Enfeoffed & Confirmed & doth by these presents give grant Aliene Enfeoffe Convey make over & Absolutely Confirm unto ye s^d Saml & his heirs forever a Certaine piece Tract or parcell of Land Lying & being within ye Township of s^d york Scittuated upon ye Southwest Side of s^d York river & is by Estimation fifty Acres be it More or Less & is a part of s^d Thomas Addams^{es} land lying on ye s^d Southwest Side of York river between ye land of Lieu^t Charles ffrost & ye land of William Pepperrell Esqr & ye s^d Saml Addams^{es} Land now given is Next to & Adjoyning unto ye s^d Pepperrells Land which is upon the South East Side thereof & Joyning to s^d York river upon ye Northeast End or front thereof & runs from s^d Pepperrells bounds by s^d river Northwest Twenty three poles to a white Oak Stake Mark^t four Square & a heap of Stones about s^d Stake & runs from thence Southwest One hundred & Sixty poles through s^d Thomas Addams^{es} home Lot as it is Termed & So though ye midle of ye Additional Grant of Land to Kittery bounds & is bounded by s^d Kittery & York bounds or Dividing line between s^d Kittery & York Southeast to s^d Pepperrells bounds & from thence it runs Northeast by s^d Pepperrells line down to s^d river Together wth all ye rights priviledges & Advantages belonging unto s^d Land both upland Swampy Land Orchard wood under wood Standing lying & being on s^d Land unto ye s^d Saml Addams & his heirs forever To have & To hold & Quietly & peaceably to Possess Occupy and Enjoy ye same as a Sure Estate only ye s^d Thomas Addams doth reserve for his own proper use the priviledge of ye Orchard dureing his Natural life as Also Liberty to Cut firewood & Timber and Liberty to Carry off ye Same from time to time & at all times dureing his life as Accasion may be & No otherwayes In Witness hereof ye s^d Thomas Adams hath hereto Set his hand & Seal this fifteenth day of Novemb^r in ye year of our Lord One Thousand Seven hundred & Eleven

Signed Sealed & delivered   Thomas [his mark] Addams (a Seal)
  In presence of us Witnesses
    James Lowel
    Joseph Wright   Hannah [her mark] Addams (a Seal).

Book VIII, Fol. 255.

Thomas Addams aboves^d and Hannah Addams his wife personally Appeared & Acknowledged the Above written deed of gift to be their Act & Deed this fourth day of Feb^{ry} 1711/2 Before me Abra̅ Preble Just pea^{ce} Recorded According to ye Original Decr 24th 1717./

p Jos. Ham̅ond Reg^r

Know All men by these presents that We Paul Williams & Joanna Williams Relict of John Gaskin dec^d & Edward Walker & Deliverence Walker his wife & Elizabeth Gaskin Daughters of ye s^d Gaskin afores^d all of us of Kittery in ye County of York in New England for & in Consideration of ye Sum of fifteen pounds in Curra^t money [**255**] Of New England to us in hand paid by Nicholas Weeks of ye Same place Shipwright the rec^t thereof we do Acknowledge and our selves therewith fully Contented and paid & do by these presents Acquitt ye s^d Nicholas Weeks & his heirs for ever for ye same And for ye Consideration aboves^d We ye s^d Paul Williams Joanna Williams Edward Walker Deliverence Walker Elizabeth Gaskin have given granted bargained & Sold And do by these presents frely fully & Absolutely give grant Bargaine Sell & for ever Set over unto ye s^d Nicholas Weekes his heirs & Assigns for ever all that Tract of Land Containing Ten Acres lying in ye Township of Kittery in ye County of york afores^d and lyes at ye Northeast end of ye Late m^r John Holes home Lot in ye Town and County aboves^d & is forty pole Square and is that tract of land that m^r John Hole Sold & Delivered ye possession of unto ye s^d John Gaskin deceas^d who Some time Lived thereon & Improved ye Same by building & fencing & Planting Together with all ye Timber wood or underwood Standing or Laying on s^d land with all ye Appurtenances & priviledges thereunto belonging or in any wise Appurtaining unto ye s^d Ten Acres of land as it is Set forth & bounded in An Instrum^t und^r ye hand & Seal of Mrs Elizabeth Hole bareing date ye Second day of May One Thousand Six hundred & Ninety as She was an Attorney to her husband Mr John Hole referrence thereunto being had may more at Large Appear To have & To hold all ye s^d Ten acres of land & Every part thereof unto the only & Sole use benefit & behoofe of him y^e s^d Nicholas Weekes his heirs & Assigns for ever./ & furthermore we y^e s^d Paul Williams Joanna Williams Edward Walker Deliverence Walker Elizabeth Gaskins do for our Selves & our heirs Covenant to & with y^e s^d Nicholas Weekes his heirs & Assignes for ever that y$_e$

premisses aboves^d Are free & Clear from All Incumbrances whatsoever as Sales gifts Mortgages Dowrys or Joyntures and that we are y^e True & proper owners thereof & have within ourselves full power & Lawfull Authority to Sell & dispose of y^e Same the peaceable possession thereof to Warrant & forever defend Against all p^rsons whatsoever Laying a lawfull Claime thereunto In Witness whereof We have hereunto Set our hands & Seals this Eighteenth day of May One thousand Seven hundred & fourteen

Signed Sealed & Delivered in the p^rsence of us ye Subscribers
Jonathan Kene
Mary : H : Williams
her mark
William Godsoe

The mark of
Paul P. W. Williams (Seal)
the mark of
Joanna ● Williams (Seal)
Edward Walker (Seal)
The mark of
Elizabeth E Gaskin (Seal)
(Seal)

6 of July : 1717./ Then Joanna Williams & Elizabeth Gaskin p^rsonally Appeared before me & did Acknowledge this Above Instrum^t to be their free Act & Deed
Wm Pepperrell Just peace

York sc/ Berwick Decr 7th 1717./ The within Mentioned Edward Walker psonally Appearing before me ye Subscriber one of his Maj^tys Justices of ye peace Acknowledged ye within written Instrum^t to be his Act & Deed./
Saml Plaisted

Recorded According to ye Original Decr 7th 1717/
p Jos. Hamond Reg^r

Know All men by these p^rsents that I Christian Remick of ye Town of Kittery in ye province of Maine do for diverse good Considerations me moveing thereunto but more Especially ye fatherly Affection & Tender Care & love that I bare unto my beloved Son Jacob Remick do by these presents freely grant and give unto him my beloved Son afores^d & to his Lawfull heirs forever & Certaine Tract & parcell of Land Containing Twenty Acres Scittuate & Lying in ye afores^d town of Kittery in ye Province of Maine on ye East Side of ye Great Cove that runs up behind Thomas Spinneys at ye head of ye afores^d Jacob Remicks own and Peter Dixons land fifty three pole broad Southeast & by South and Sixty pole Long North East & by East bounded with s^d Christian Remicks land on ye Northwest & Richard Gowells land on ye Southeast & John Morrells Land on ye Northeast ye afores^d parcell of Land thus butted & bounded Contains Twenty acres To have & To hold ye aboves^d land with all ye priviledges & Appurtenances thereunto belonging to him & his heirs forever as afores^d without any let or Mollestation by me or any und^r me unto which Daly Gift I do hereby freely & Volluntaryly give & Grant as aboves^d unto my Son Jacob as aboves^d forever unto which Deed of Gift I do hereunto freely Set my hand & Seal this Sixteenth day of October Anno Dom 1686./   Christian Remick ($^a_{Seal}$)

Signed Sealed & Delivered
  In y^e Presence of us
  Benjamin Islington
  James Phillips
Christian Remick Came before me this 9th of March 1686 & Acknowledge this Above deed or writing to be his Act & deed   Before John Hinckes of the Councill
  Recorded According to y^e Original Decr 18th 1717./
           p Jos. Hamond Reg^r/

To All People to whom these p^{r}sents Shall Come Jacob Remick of Kittery in ye County of york Shipwright Sendeth Greeting Know ye that I ye s^d Jacob Remick for & in Consideration of ye Natural love & Affection which I have & do bear unto my welbeloved Son Samuel Remick of ye afores^d Town of Kittery have given granted made over & Confirmed unto him ye s^d Saml Remick my Son his heirs Ex^{rs} & Assignes Ten acres of Land Scittuate Lying & being in ye Township of Kittery at ye East End of my land it being Sixty pole northeast & by East & Twenty Six pole & a halfe Northwest & by North bounded with John ffernalds Land on ye East & Joshua Remicks land on ye North & Richd Gowells Land on ye South with all ye Timb^r wood Standing & Lying on ye s^d Land with all ye Priviledges & Appurtenances thereunto belonging or any wise Appurtaining unto ye above granted premisses unto my Son Samuel Remick his heirs Ex^{rs} & Assignes To have & To hold ye s^d Land unto ye use & only benefit of him ye s^d Saml Remick his heirs Ex^{rs} & Assignes forever to possess & Enjoy ye Same ye peaceable & Quiet possession thereof to warrant & defend Against all persons Claiming ye Same from by or under me In Witness whereof I y^e s^d Jacob Remick have

Book VIII, Fol. 256.

hereunto Set my hand & Seal this Eighteenth day of Decr in y^e fourth year of y^e reign of his Soveraign Maj^{tys} of Brittaine King George & in y^e year of our Lord one Thousand Seven hundred & Seventeen   Jacob Remick (${}^a_{Seal}$)
Signed Sealed & Delivered
  In presence of us
    Thomas Cole
    Hannah Hamond
  York sc/ Decr 18th 1717. Jacob Remick above Named p^{r}sonally Appearing Acknowledged the Above Instrum^t in writing to be his free Act & Deed
                     Before   Jos. Hamond J. peace
Recorded According to ye Original Decr 18th 1717
                    p Jos. Hamond Reg^r

[256] To All Christian People to whom these presents Shall Come I Abell Hamilton of ye Town of Kittery in ye County of York in her Maj^{tys} Province of ye Massachusets Bay in New England husbandman & Deberoth my wife Sendeth Greeting for & in Consideration of a valluable Sum of money to us in hand paid by Roger Plaisted of ye Town afores^d Batchelor ye rec^t whereof we do Acknowledge our selves to be fully Satisfied & therewith Contented for every part given granted Bargained Sold Alienated Enfeoffed & Confirm And do by these presents for our Selves our heirs Ex^{rs} Adm^{rs} & Assignes forever Absolutely fully and freely give grant bargaine Sell Alienate Enfeoffe Assign pass over & Confirm a Certaine parcell or Tract of Land being & Scittuate in ye Township of Kittery afores^d And at a place in s^d Town Called Salmon falls being by Estimation Seven Acres more or Less as it is herein bounded Lying on ye Southwest Side of the highway that leads from Salmonfall brook to John Keys house Adjoyning to s^d highway and bounded on ye Northwest Side with ye Land of Cap^{tn} Ichabod Plaisted & on ye highway Takeing its breadth from s^d Plaisteds land Twenty Two poles and from thence runing Southwst and by South forty poles and from thence on ye line South East & by East to Richard Tozars land & by s^d Tozers land to Salmonfall river & is bounded on ye Southwest by South by s^d river To have & To hold ye above granted premises with all & Singular ye priviledges and Appurtenances thereunto belonging to him ye s^d Roger Plaisted & to his heirs Ex^{rs} Adm^{rs} & Assignes forever freely & Clearly Exonerated & discharged from all former Deeds Wills Leases

Book VIII, Fol. 256.

Mortgages Dowrys or any other Incumbrances whatSoever had made done or Suffered to be done by me y̌e s̄d Abel Hamilton or Deberoh my wife whereby y̌e s̄d Roger Plaisted his heirs Exrs Admrs and Assignes or Either them may be in any wayes Mollested or disturbed in their Quiet & peaceable Injoymt & Improvemt of ye above granted premisses or any part or parcell thereof & further I ye s̄d Abel Hamilton firmly by these presents do bind my Selfe my heirs Executrs Admrs & Assignes unto ye Aforesd Roger Plaisted & to his heirs Exrs Admrs and Assignes for ever to Save them harmless & to Warrat & Defend ye Title of ye above granted premisses Against any person or persons whatsoever that may or shall hereafter claime or Challenge any Lawfull right or propriety to ye above granted premisses or any part thereof In Witness hereof I ye foresd Abel Hamilton & Deberoh my wife have hereunto Set our hands & Seals this fourth day of Octobr Anno Domi One Thousand Seven hundred & Nine & in ye Eighth year of her Matys Reign Anne by ye grace of over great Brittaine france & Ireland Queen Defender of the faith &ca

Signed Sealed & Delivered   Abel (his mark) Hamilton (a Seal)
   In the presence of
      Gabriel Hamilton
us James Frost Witnesses Deberoh (her X mark) Hamilton (a Seal)
      James Warren

York sc Berwick June 2d 1710

Abel Hamilton & Deberoh his wife personally Appearing before me ye Subscriber one of her Majtys Justices in sd County & Acknowledged ye above Instrumt to be their free Act & Deed./   Ichabod Plaisted J : peace

Recorded According to ye Original Octobr 22d 1717./

p Js Hamond Regr

Know All men by these presents that I Ephraim Joy of Berwick in the County of York in ye Province of ye Massachusets Bay in New England Carpenter for & in Consideration of ye Sum of Eight pounds Currant money of ye province aforesd to me in hand well & Truely paid by Roger Plaisted of ye Same town County & Province aforesd Gent the rect whereof I do hereby Acknowledge And my Selfe therewith fully Sattisfied & paid Have bargained Sold Aliened Assigned Enfcoffed Set over & Confirmed & do by these presents bargaine Sell Aliene Assign Enfeoffe Set over & Confirm unto ye s̄d Roger Plaisted his heirs & Assignes for ever a certaine piece or parcell of land Containing Seven acres & halfe being ye One halfe of fifteen Acres p^{rt} of a grant of forty Acres given s^d Joy by ye Town of Kittery ye 24th May 1699./ begining at ye head of William Grants ten Acres that lyeth on Crambery Meadow brook ye afores^d ten acres being ye Northwest bounds & Extends Southeast & by South forty nine poles & Southwest by South fifty Nine poles which is ye length of ye aboves^d fifteen Acres as Appears by ye return of Nicholas Gowen Survey^r ye 25th of August 1701./ To have & To hold ye halfe of ye fifteen acres which is Seven Acres & halfe as afores^d bounded as afores^d to him ye s^d Roger Plaisted his heirs & Assignes forever free & Clear & freely & Clearly Acquitted & discharged from all former & other gifts grants bargaines Sales & all other In- cumbrances whatsoever & that it shall & may be Lawfull to & for ye s^d Roger Plaisted his heirs & Assignes to have hold use Occupy Possess & Enjoy ye Same & Every part thereof from henceforth forever without any Mollestation or Inter- ruption from me ye s^d Ephraim Joy my heirs Ex^{rs} or Adm^{rs} & from all other person or persons laying legal Claime thereto Shall & will Warrant & for ever Defend y^e same./ In Witness whereof I have hereunto Set my hand & Seal the 5th day April 1714./

Signed Sealed & Delivered
In y^e Presence of
Sylvanus Nock
Biel Hamilton

Ephraim $\times$ Joy (seal) *his mark*

Sarah $\times$ Joy *her mark*

York ss/ Ephraim Joy Appeared & Acknowledged y^e above written Instrum^t to be his act & deed & Sarah his wife relinquished her right of Dower or thirds in y^e lands aboves^d at Berwick y^e 4th day April 1714.

Before me./ Ichabod Plaisted J peace
Recorded Accorded to y^e Original Octob^r 22^d 1717./

p Jos. Hammond Reg^r

This Indenture mad ye Thirtyeth day of Novemb^r Anno Domini 1717 Annoq R^{is} Georgii Nunc Magna Brittania &c^a Quarto Between Samuel Scadlock of Marble head in ye County of Essex in his Maj^{tys} Province of ye Massachusets Bay in New England of ye One party and Cyprian Southack of Boston in ye County of Suffolk in Province afores^d Gent of ye Other party Witnesseth That ye s^d Saml Scadlock for & in Consideration of ye Sum of Ninty pounds & Eighteen shillings Currant money of New England or good Bills of Credit of ye Province afores^d to him in hand well & truely paid before ye Ensealing & Delivery of these presents by him ye s^d Cyprian Southack ye rec^t whereof he hereby Acknowledge & himselfe therewith fully Satisfied Contented & paid Have given granted bargained Sold Aliened Set over & Confirm^d unto ye s^d Cyprian Southack & doth by these presents give [257] Grant bargaine Sell Aliene Set over & Confirm unto ye s^d Cyprian Southack his heirs Ex^rs Adm^rs & Assigns for ever Two third parts of a farm Scittuate Lying & being in ye Township of Capeporpus in Saco in ye Province of Maine in New England afores^d lying at a place Called Little river within Timber Island butted & bounded as follows Viz^t on ye Southeast with ye river on ye Southwest with land of Grigery Jeffords on ye Northwest with Wast lands & on ye Northeast with land formerly of m^r Pembleton or however otherwise bounded or reputed to be bounded Together with all Such rights Titles profits priviledges Comoditys and Appurtenances as in any kind Appurtaine thereunto with ye reversions & remainders thereof And all ye right Title Interest Claime & demand whatsoever of him ye s^d Saml Scadlock in & to ye Same & Every part thereof To have & To hold./ All ye above bargained premisses with all & Singular ye Appurtenances thereof unto him ye s^d Cyprian Southack his heirs Ex^rs Adm^rs & Assigns to his & their Sole use benefit & behoofe for ever./ And ye s^d Samuel Scadlock for himselfe his heirs Ex^rs & Adm^rs doth hereby promiss grant & Agree to & with ye s^d Cyprian Southack his heirs Ex^rs Adm^rs & Assigns in maner following Viz^t that At ye time of ye Ensealing & Delivery of these presents he ye s^d Saml Scadlock is ye True Sole & Lawfull owner of ye Afore Bargained p^rmisses and has in himselfe good right full power & Lawfull Authority to Sell & dispose of ye same in maner as aboves^d & that ye s^d Cyprian Southack his heirs & Assignes shall & May henceforth for ever peaceably & Quietly have hold use Occupy possess & Enjoy ye above demised premisses Together with ye Appurtenances free & Clear and Clearly Acquitted & Discharged of & from all & all maner of former gifts grants bargains Sales Mortgages Titles troubles & Incumbrances whatsoever./ And further ye s^d Saml Scadlock doth hereby bind and Oblige himselfe his heirs Ex^rs & Adm^rs from henceforth & for ever to Warrant & Defend all ye above granted premisses & Appurtenances thereof unto ye s^d Cyprian Southack his heirs & Assigns Against the Legal Claimes & Demands of all & Every person or persons whomsoev^r Provided Alwayes and these presents are

Book VIII, Fol. 257.

upon Condition Nevertheless that if ye Above Named Saml Scadlock his heirs Ex^rs or Adm^rs shall & do well & truely pay or Cause to be paid unto ye aforenamed Cyprian Southack or his Certaine Attorney heirs Ex^rs Adm^rs or assignes ye full & Just Sum of Ninety pounds Eighteen shillings Curra^t money of NewEngland or in good bills of Credit of ye Province of ye Massachusets Bay afores^d at on or before ye first day of Decr which will be Anno Dom^i 1720./ without fraud Coven or further delay that this present deed of Mortgage to be voyd & of None Effect or upon Default hereof to Stand & remaine in full force Strength & Vertue to all Intents & purposes in ye Law whatsoever./ In Witness & for Confirmation of all afore writen I have hereunto Set my hand & Affixed my Seal ye day & year first above written

Signed Sealed & D^d   his mark
   In p^rsence of us   Samuel ʔ Scadlock (Seal)
   Saml Harris
   Benj^a Marston jun^r

Essex ss./ Marblehead Novr 30th 1717./ then Samuel Scadlock afore Named in ye premisses personally Appeared And Acknowledged the before written Instrum^t to be his Volluntary Act & Deed./

           Before me Nathl Norden Just peace
Recorded According to ye Original Decr 17th 1717./
                   p Jos. Hamond Reg^r

To All People to whom this present Deed or Instrument in writing shall Come Know Ye that I Roger Dearing of Kittery in ye County of York within her Maj^tys Province of ye Massachusets Bay in NewEngland Shipwright for & in Consideration of ye Natural love & Affection wch I bear Towards my Welbeloved Son & Daughter William Racklift & Martha his wife of Kittery in ye County of York & Province afores^d Have given & granted & by these presents do give & grant unto him ye s^d Wm Racklift & Martha his wife & to ye heirs Lawfully begotton of her body forever a Certaine piece or parcell of land Scittuate lying & being within ye Township of Kittery afores^d Containing by Estimation three Quarters of an acre of land be it more or Less being a garden Spot & yard with a Cellar & a well in it which s^d piece or parcell of land was Delivered to me by Execution upon a Judgment of Court obtain^d Against Henry Greenland on ye 2^d day of July 1672 & lyes at a place Called Kittery point fronting & Abbutting on Piscattaqua river on ye Southwest & is that Tract of land whereon ye s^d Wm Racklift hath built & Now Dwells To have & To hold ye s^d piece or parcell of land with all & Singular ye priviledges & Appurtenances thereunto belonging or in any wise Appartaining unto them ye s^d Wm Racklift & Martha his s^d wife & to their heirs as aboves^d forever more & I ye s^d Roger Dearing for my Selfe my heirs Ex^{rs} & Adm^{rs} to & with ye s^d Wm Racklift & Martha his wife & their heirs as aboves^d do Covenant & Ingage bind & Oblige my Selfe to Warra^t & Defend ye Title of ye above granted premisses with the Appurtenances Against my Selfe my heirs Ex^{rs} &c^a & Against all & Every person & persons lawfully Claiming y^e same or any part thereof./ In Witness whereof I have hereunto Set my hand & Seal this Tenth day of March Anno Domini 1713/4 Seventeen hundred & thirteen or fourteen

Annoq, Regni Anna Regina Decimo Tertio
Signed Sealed & Delivered   Roger Dearing ($^a_{Seal}$)
In presence of us
Hannah Hamond
Joseph Hamond jun^r
    York sc/ Kittery Novr 29th 1717
Roger Dearing above Named p'sonally Appearing Acnowledged y^e above Instrum^t in writing to be his Act & Deed   Coram. Jos. Hamond J. peace
Recorded According to y^e Original Novr 29th 1717/
                         p Jos. Hamond Reg^r

Know All men by these p^{r}sents that I Walter Allen of Berwick in ye County of York in ye Province of ye Massachusets Bay in NewEngl^d planter for & in Consideration of ye Sum of Seventeen pounds Curra^t money of ye Province afores^d to me in hand well & Truely paid by Ichabod Plaisted of ye same town County & Province afores^d Esqr the rec^t whereof I ye s^d Walter Allen do hereby Acknowledge & my Selfe therewith fully Satisfied Contented & paid have given granted bargained Sold Aliened Assigned Enfeoffed Set over & Confirmed & do by these presents give grant bargaine Sell [258] Aliene Assign Enfeoffe Set over & Confirm unto him ye s^d Ichabod Plaisted his heirs & Assignes forever a Certaine tract of land Scittuate lying & being in Berwick afores^d Viz^t a grant of Sixty Acres Next Humphry Chadborns lot of a hundred Acres on ye South Side ye pond by a South west & by South line an hundred rods & ye breadth Eighty five South east and by East there being Allowance given for a highway of Six rods broad through it (Excepting Ten Acres to Jonathan Stimson To have & To hold ye s^d Sixty Acres land as its laid out as by ye return thereof Appears Excepting as before Excepted to Jonathan Stimson unto him ye s^d Ichabod Plaisted his heirs & Assignes forever with all & Singular ye benefits profits priviledges thereof to him ye s^d Ichabod Plaisted his heirs & Assignes forever to ye Only Sole use & behoofe of him ye s^d Ichabod Plaisted his heirs & Assignes forever free & Clear & Clearly Acquitted of and from all other & former gifts grants bargains Sales titles Troubles Charges & Incumbrances whatsoever And that I ye s^d Walter Allen and my heirs to him ye s^d Ichabod Plaisted his heirs & Assigns Shall & will Warrant & forever Confirm ye same In Witness whereof I ye s^d Walter Allen have hereunto Set my hand & Seal ye 22^d day of Septemb^r Annoq, Domini One Thousand Seven hundred & fourteen 1714./

Signed Sealed & Delivered   Walter Allen (seal)

In ye presence of

Thomas T.H Holms (his mark)

John Croade

    Berwick 23^d day July : 1717

The Above written Walter Allen personally Appeared before me One of his Maj^{tys} Justices of ye peace & Acknowledged that ye above written was his Act & Deed./

                                                Elisha Plaisted

Recorded According to ye Original Decr 17th 1717./

                                                     p Jos. Hamond Reg^r

Know All men by these p^{r}sents that I William Pepperrell of Kittery in the County of York in N. England Merch^t for ye Consideration of forty Eight pounds money to me in hand paid before ye Ensealing hereof as likewise for one halfe of a Sawmill biult & house at Saco in ye County afores^d by Nathaniel Weare of Hampton in ye Province of New Hampshire in N. Engl^d Milwright ye rec^t whereof I do hereby Acknowledge & thereof fully Satisfied & Contented Have by these presents given granted bargained & Sold & do by these presents fully freely & Absolutely give grant bargaine and Sell unto s^d Nathaniel Weare his heirs & Assignes forever one Quarter part of a Certaine Tract or parcell of land Lying & being in Saco afores^d Containing by Estimation Six thousand Acres be ye Same more or Less which land s^d Pepperrell Purchased of Sam¹ Walker of Piscattaqua in N: York & Thomas Goodwill of Boston in yᵉ Province of the Massachusets Bay in N England as will more fully Appear as p Deeds under their hands Now on record being bounded with a brook Southeasterly Comonly called Nicholsᵉˢ brook Northeasterly with Two Miles from yᵉ great river & Northwesterly with yᵉ Extent of three Miles & one halfe & Eighteen poles above yᵉ Saco Mill falls and Southwesterly with yᵉ great river as also One Quarter part of in & to yᵉ Herbage Comonage for Timber & all other things Standing And growing upon four thousand And five hundred Acres more of land or thereabouts lying upon yᵉ Northwest Side of yᵉ Land abovesᵈ Together with one Quarter part of all yᵉ Priviledges Comoditys & Appurtenances to yᵉ Same belonging or in any wayes Appurtaining to him yᵉ sᵈ Nath¹ Weare his heirs & Assignes for ever To have & To hold all yᵉ above granted & bargained premisses to him yᵉ sᵈ Nath¹ Weare his heirs & Assignes for ever./ ffurthermore I yᵉ sᵈ William Pepperrell do by these pʳsents promiss & grant to & with yᵉ sᵈ Nath¹ Weare his heirs Exʳˢ Admʳˢ & Assignes that they Shall & may from time to time & at all times by force and Vertue of these presents Lawfully peaceably & Quietly have hold use Occupy possess & Enjoy all yᵉ aforesᵈ Demissed premisses I yᵉ sᵈ Wᵐ Pepperrell do by presents firmly bind my Selfe my heirs Exʳˢ & Admʳˢ to Warraᵗ Secure & Defend yᵉ sᵈ Nath¹ Weare from any pson or psons Claiming thereunto from by or undʳ me or any of my heirs Exʳˢ Admʳˢ or Assignes./ In Testimony whereof I have hereunto Set my hand & Seal this Second day of Decembʳ Anno Domini One Thousand Seven hundred & Seventeen./   Wᵐ Pepperrell junʳ (ₛₑₐₗ ᵃ)

Signed Sealed & Delivered
 In Presence of
 Geo: Jackson
 Humphrey Scamon

York ss Decʳ 17ᵗʰ 1717./ This day Wᵐ Pepperrell Junʳ pʳsonally Appeared before me yᵉ Subscriber one of his Majᵗʸˢ Justices of yᵉ peace for yᵉ County aforesᵈ & Acknowledged this foregoing Instrumᵗ to be his free Act & Deed
           Wᵐ Pepperrell

Recorded According to yᵉ Original Decʳ 19ᵗʰ 1717./
       p Jos. Hamond Regʳ

Know All men by these presents that I William Pepperrell of Kittery in the County of York in NEngland Merchᵗ for & in Consideration of ye Sum of One hundred & Thirty one pounds money to me in hand paid before ye Ensealing hereof as likewise for Assisting in building A Sawmill & house At Saco in ye County afores^d by Humphrey Scamon Junr of Saco afores^d Marrin^r the rec^t whereof I do hereby Acknowledge & thereof fully Satisfied & Contented have by these presents given granted bargained & Sold & do by these presents fully freely & Absolutely give grant bargaine & Sell unto s^d Humphrey Scamon his heirs & Assigns forever one Quarter part of a Certain Tract of land lying & being in Saco Afores^d Containing by Estimation Six thousand Acres be ye Same more or less which land s^d Pepperrell purchased of Saml Walker of Piscataqua in N: York & Thomas Goodwill of Boston in ye Province of ye Massachusets Bay in N: England as will more fully Appear as p Deeds und^r their hands Now on record being bounded with a brook Southeasterly Comonly Called Nichols^{es} brook./ Northeasterly with Two Miles from ye great river & Northwesterly with ye Extent of three Miles one halfe & Eighteen poles above ye Saco Mill falls & Southwesterly with ye great river As also one Quarter part of in & to ye Herbage Comonage for Timber & all other things Standing & growing upon four thousand five hundred Acres more of land or thereabouts lying upon ye Northwest Side of ye Land aboves^d Together with [259] One Quarter part of all ye priviledges Comoditys & Appurtenances to ye same belonging or in any wayes Appurtaining To have & To hold all ye above granted & bargained premisses to him ye s^d Humphrey Scamon his heirs & Assignes forever. Furthermore I ye s^d Wm Pepperrell do by these presents promiss & grant to & with ye s^d Humphrey Scamon his heirs Ex^{rs} Adm^{rs} & Assigns that they shall & may from time to time & at all times forever hereafter by force & Vertue of these p^{r}sents Lawfully peaceably & Quietly have hold use Occupy possess & Enjoy all ye afores^d granted and bargained premisses./ I ye s^d Wm Pepperrell do by these presents firmly bind my Selfe my heirs Ex^{rs} & Adm^{rs} to Warra^t Secure & Defend ye s^d Humphrey Scamon his heirs & Assignes from any person or p^{r}sons Claiming thereunto from by or und^r me or any of my heirs Ex^{rs} Adm^{rs} or Assigns./ In Testimony whereof I have hereunto Set my hand & seale this Second day of Decemb^r Anno Domini One thousand Seven hundred & Seventeen./

Signed Sealed & Delivered   Wm Pepperrell jun^r ($_{Seal}^a$)
  In p^{r}sence of
  Geo: Jackson
  Nathl Weare

Book VIII, Fol. 259.

York sc/ Decr 17th 1717./ this day Wm Pepperrell Junr p'sonally Appeared before me y^e Subscrib^r one of his Maj^{tys} Justices of y^e peace for y^e County afores^d & Acknowledged this above Instrum^t with what on y^e other side to be his free Act & Deed   Wm Pepperrell
Recorded According to ye Original Decr 19th 1717./
                p Jos. Hamond Reg^r

Articles of Agreement made Concluded & Agreed upon this Sixteenth day of Decr Anno Domi One thousand Seven hundred & Seventeen Between Wm Pepperrell jun^r of Kittery in ye County of York in N: England Merch^t and Humphrey Scamon Junr of Saco in ye County afores^d Marrin^r & Nathaniel Weare Junr of Hampton in ye Province of N: Hampshire Milwright./ Whereas ye s^d Pepperrell hath bought & purchased of Saml Walker of Piscataqua at N: York & of Thomas Goodwill of Boston in ye Province of ye Massachusets Bay in N: England which land is by Estimation Six thousand Acres as by Deeds will fully Appear Scittuate lying & being at Saco afores^d at ye falls known by ye Name of Blackmans falls & has Sold one Quarter part of s^d Purchase to s^d Humphrey Scamon & one Quarter part to s^d Nathl Weare And they have built a Sawmill at s^d falls And for ye further proceeding & Quiet Managem^t of ye same We ye aboves^d Pepperrell Scamon & Weare do for our selves our heirs Ex^{rs} & Adm^{rs} Covena^t promiss & Engage to & with Each other that our Agreem^t and Articles which are as followeth do stand & remaine good & firm to us & our heirs Ex^{rs} Adm^{rs} & Assigns for ever Viz^t./

First the mill floom Stage & all ye priviledges & Appurtenances belonging to s^d Mill to be one halfe Pepperrells one Quarter Scamons & one Quarter Wears with ye profits & priviledges belonging to ye same

Secondly We reserve for ye partners as afores^d ye benefit of s^d falls for building of Mill or Mills or Dam or any thing as they shall Se fit & a piece of Land for laying of Timber building on or what Shall be thought Needfull for ye Improvement of s^d Mill or mills Which land is bounded as followeth with ye river from ye Mill falls up to ye first brook & So along by ye brook to a maple tree Mark^t at ye first turn of ye brook./ from thence Southeast Sixteen rod to a white pine mark^t from thence Twelve rod to a white birch Mark^t from thence South & by west to ye river & So to s^d falls & likewise ye house that we have built Already for ye use of y^e

partners According to their right afores^d Pepperrell One halfe ye other Two partners a quarter a piece./ We have likewise Agreed & Divided part of ye s^d tract of Land about one hundred & Sixty Acres reserving wayes & landings which are as followeth for ye use of ye afores^d partners without Stoppage or hinderence a Convenient way from ye mill or land reserved for ye use of ye mill to ye brook that did part Bonightons land from Gibbons ye way to go by ye river side as likewise a Conven^t Landing there as likewise a way of Two rods wide from ye mill Towards ye Sea or rivers mouth where that way now goeth or Near thereabouts if So Conven^t & from that way between the s^d Pepperrell & Scamons Division of Land a way of four rod wide near where Bonightons house formerly Stood down to ye river Eight rod from ye river to a pitch pine & to run Southeast and Northwest Across ye point which is reserved for a Landing Thes^d Wm Pepperrells land is bounded with a white pine afores^d on ye Southwest Corner Runing Northeast One hundred & Sixty rod to a red or black oak Mark^t & from thence Southeast Eighty rod to a white pine & from thence Southwest to a Stake Near Bonightons old Seller which is One hundred & Sixty rod from thence ye Same Course to ye river & by ye river Northwest to ye afores^d reserved land & So bounded on y^t land to ye pine first Mentioned./ Thes^d Humphrey Scamons land is bounded Northwest by Pepperrells land ye way & landing afores^d Excepted between Pepperrell & Scamon to ye white pine which was Pepperrells Corner bounds & then forty rods Southeast to a maple from thence Southwest to a maple by ye river & So by ye river to s^d landing place afore mentioned./ The s^d Nathl Weares land is bounded by Scamons land from ye Maple last Mentioned One hundred & Sixty rod to a maple afores^d & then forty rods Southeast to a white Oak & from thence Southwest to a great rock by the Mouth of a Small Creek & So by ye river to ye first Maple./ We ye afores^d partners have agreed to Lay out One hundred & Sixty Acres of Land more on ye northwest of this Division up ye river to be laid out after ye Same Maner as this first is So he that had ye Lowest down ye river Shall have ye Lowest in the Next Division successively./ We further Agree that All ye rest of ye s^d land by in Comon for ye use of all ye partners at present Alwayes reserving & agreeing that if there be any place that may be found in ye whole Tract of land which may be beneficiall for a mill or mills it shall be to ye benefit of ye whole partners or Else if any one of ye partners desire to Come to a Division it shall be divided According to proportion within three Months after demand made and So Each

to Enjoy his own Quietly [260] By himselfe And in Confirmation of all & Every particular & Article above Mentioned we ye s^d Pepperrell Scamon & Weare do bind our Selves our heirs Ex^rs & Adm^rs to Stand to & abide by as a firm & Sure Agreem^t for ever All afores^d written./ In Testimony whereof We have hereunto Set our hands & Seals ye day & year first written   Wm Pepperrell jun^r (Seal^a)
Signed Sealed & Delivered   Humphrey Scamon jun^r (seal^a)
In p^rsence of   Nathl Weare (Seal^a)
Geo: Jackson
Jno Watkins
York ss Decr 1 7th day 1717./ This day Nathl Weare jun^r Humphrey Scamon jun^r & Wm Pepperrell Junr all p^rsonally Appeared before me ye Subscrib^r One of his Maj^tys Justices of ye peace for s^d County and Acknowledged ye above Instrum^t with what on ye other Sides to be their free Act & Deed./   Wm Pepperrell
Recorded According to ye Original Decr 19th 1717./
p Jos. Hamond Reg^r

Know All men by these presents that I Bial Hamilton of Kittery in ye Parrish of Berwick in ye County of York in ye Province of ye Massachusets Bay in New England Planter for & in Consideration of ye Sum of Six pounds in Currant money of ye Province afores^d to me in hand well & Truely paid by John Fall of Kittery in ye parrish County & Province afores^d Planter the rec^t whereof I ye s^d Bial Hamilton do hereby Acknowledge & my Selfe therewith fully Satisfied Contented & paid have given granted bargained Sold Aliened Assigned Enfeoffed Set over & Confirmed & do by these presents give grant Bargaine Sell Aliene Assign Enfeoffe Set over And Confirm unto him ye s^d John Fall his heirs & Assignes forever five Acres of land being part of a fifty acre grant granted to Ephraim Joy by ye Town of Kittery May tenth Seventeen hundred & three and by him Conveyed to me s^d Bial Hamilton & it begins at Timothy Wentworths North Corner bounds then Northwest & by North forty poles then Southwest & by west forty poles then Southeast & by South forty poles then Northeast & by East forty poles to our first Station Viz^t Ten Acres being Contained in s^d bounds in Equal shares between Joseph Pray & me ye s^d Hamilton the one halfe of wch being five acres bounded as Afores^d I do hereby Convey unto him ye s^d John Fall his heirs & Assigns forever To have & To hold ye Same with all & Singular ye benefits profits priviledges and Appurtenances thereto belonging to him yᵉ sᵈ John Fall his heirs & Assignes forever free & Clear & Clearly Acquitted of & from all other & former gifts grants bargaines Sales Titles troubles charges & Incumbrances whatsoever and that I yᵉ sᵈ Bial Hamilton & my heirs to him yᵉ sᵈ John Fall his heirs and Assignes Shall & will Warrant & forever Confirm yᵉ Same In Witness whereof I yᵉ sᵈ Bial Hamilton have hereunto Set my hand & Seal yᵉ 18ᵗʰ day of May Annoq̧ Domini 1713./

Signed Sealed & Delivered   Bial Hamilton (ₛ𝑒ₐₗᵃ)
  In yᵉ presence of   Mary Hamilton (ₛ𝑒ₐₗᵃ)
John Leighton
John Smith

May 20 : 1713. Bial Hamilton & Mary his wife Acknowledged yᵉ above Instrumᵗ to be their Act & deed
          Before me   Ichabod Plaisted Jusᵗ of peace
Recorded According to the Original May 13ᵗʰ 1717./
                    p Jos. Hammond Regʳ

This Indenture made the Twenty fourth day of August in yᵉ year One Thousand Seven hundred & Eleven Between William Godsoe of Kittery in yᵉ County of York in New England on yᵉ One part & Richard Rice of yᵉ Same place as he is an Assignee of his father Mʳ Thomas Rice & also As he is an Assignee & Attorney of & for mʳˢ Sarah Shapleigh & Mʳ Nicholas Shapleigh both of yᵉ same place as they are Administratʳˢ unto the Estate of Mʳ John Shapleigh decᵈ on yᵉ other part Witnesseth that yᵉ sᵈ Wᵐ Godsoe for Divers considerations hereafter in these pʳsents Exprest doth for himselfe his heirs Exʳˢ & Admʳˢ give grant bargaine & Sell & forever Set over unto yᵉ sᵈ Richard Rice his heirs & Assignes forever One Yoak of red or brindle Young Oxen Together with all & Every yᵉ Severall parcells or Tracts of Land lying in yᵉ Township of Kittery aforesᵈ that did belong unto yᵉ Estate of yᵉ late Mʳ Thomas Withers and undisposed of by him in his life time or by Jane yᵉ late wife of sᵈ Wᵐ Godsoe as she was Executrix to yᵉ Last Will & Testamᵗ of yᵉ sᵈ Thomas Withers decᵈ Excepting & reserving out of yᵉ sᵈ premisses or lands Twenty Two Acres At pine point & yᵉ Advantage or priviledge of Exchange with yᵉ Town of Kittery for yᵉ Same true refferrence thereunto being had As may More at large Appear To have & To have & To hold yᵉ sᵈ Yoak of Oxen & Several Tracts of Land Together with all their Appurtenances & priviledges thereunto belonging or in any wise Appurtaining thereunto Except what was above Excepted out of ye Aboves^d lands or premisses unto ye Only & sole use of him ye s^d Richard Rice his heirs or Assigns forever Against him ye s^d Godsoe his heirs Ex^{rs} or Adm^{rs} or any other p'son Claiming from by or under him./ And ye s^d Richard Rice on ye other part doth for himselfe & his heirs & in ye behalfe of his aboves^d father & his heirs & in ye behalfe of Mrs Sarah Shapleigh & Nicholas Shapleigh & their heirs Ex^{rs} or Adm^{rs} as they are Adm^{rs} to ye Estate of ye Above Named And for ye Considerations above Named Do by these presents give grant bargaine Sell & forever Set over unto ye above Named Wm Godsoe his heirs & Assignes forever all that their right Title claime or demand in or to Twenty two Acres of land At a place Called pine point fronting Spruce creek in ye Town of Kittery with all ye benefits & priviledges & Advantages whatsoever may Any ways Accrew thereby by Way of Exchange with ye Town of Kittery to be taken Next to Mr Withers his grant of One hundred pole back into ye Woods from Spruce Creek & on ye west Side thereof Next oak point as will more At large Appear reference thereunto being had Together with all ye Appurtenances & priviledges belonging to s^d Land or Exchange therefor unto ye Only & Sole use of him ye s^d Wm Godsoe his heirs or Assignes forever To have & To hold all ye aboves^d lands & Exchange herein. above Exprest unto ye Only & Sole use benefit & behoofe of him ye s^d Wm Godsoe his heirs & Assignes forever against them ye s^d Richard Rice or Thomas Rice Sarah Shapleigh Nicholas Shapleigh or any of their heirs Ex^{rs} or Adm^{rs} or any other p'son that shall Claime from by or und^r ye s^d Richd Rice Thomas Rice Sarah Shapleigh & Nich^o Shapleigh or their heirs forever more./ And for ye Consideration aboves^d I ye s^d Richd Rice do hereby Ingage & promiss both for himselfe & his s^d father Thomas Rice & in ye behalfe of ye s^d Sarah Shapleigh & Nicholas Shapleigh as he is an Assigee & an Attorney for them that Neither of them or their heirs Ex^{rs} or Adm^{rs} Shall Mollest [261] Or Disturb Any person in their Quiet Possession who have Taken Alienations or deeds of s^d Godsoe or Jane his late wife Executrix as aboves^d of Mr Thomas Withers./ In Witness hereof both partys have Set to their hands & Seals ye Day & year first above written

Wm Godsoe (a Seal)
Richd Rice (a Seale)

These presents Witness that we ye above Named Sarah Shapleigh & Nich^o Shapleigh do by these presents Allow ratify & Confirm all that our Attorney hath hereby done in

our name & by our Authority Witness our hands & Seals yᵉ Date abovesᵈ
Signed & Sealed in yᵉ pʳsence of us
The Sign of
Margriet ℳ Cox
The Sign of
Sarah ✗ Rankin
Charles Frost

Sarah ⌠ her mark Shapleigh (ₛₑₐₗ ᵃ)
Nicholas Shapleigh (ₛₑₐₗ ᵃ)

York ss Kittery March 10ᵗʰ 1711/2./ The within Named Sarah Shapleigh Nicholas Shapleigh Wᵐ Godsoe & Richᵈ Rice pʳsonally Appearing before me the Subscribʳ one of her Majᵗʸˢ Justices of yᵉ peace for sᵈ County of York Acknowledged yᵉ within Instrumᵗ to be their free Act & Deed./
John Hill

Recorded According to yᵉ Original May 24ᵗʰ 1717./
p Jos. Hamond Regʳ

This Indenture made yᵉ Thirtieth day of Augˢᵗ in yᵉ year of our Lord Seventeen hundred & Seventeen Annoq̃ Regni Regis Georgii Magna Brittania &cᵃ Quarto./ Between John Morrell Senʳ of Kittery in yᵉ County of York bricklayer of yᵉ one part and Nicholas Morrell of yᵉ Same Town & County Eldest Son of yᵉ sᵈ John Morrell of yᵉ other part Witnesseth/ Whereas yᵉ sᵈ John Morrell by one Certaine deed or Instrumᵗ in writing under his hand and Seal bareing date yᵉ twenty Ninth day of March in yᵉ year of our Lord One Thousand Six hundred Ninety & two did give & grant unto his sᵈ Son Nicholas Morrell his heirs &cᵗ all his farm which he then lived upon with yᵉ houses & buildings Erected & Standing thereon to be Enjoyed & Possessed by yᵉ sᵈ Nichᵒ Morrell Imediately after yᵉ decease of yᵉ sᵈ John Morrell & his wife then being as by sᵈ deed or Instrumᵗ in writing more fully & at large Appears./ Now this Indenture further Witnesseth that yᵉ sᵈ John Morrell for & in Consideration of yᵉ Several Articles Mentioned in an Obligation under the hand & Seal of yᵉ sᵈ Nicholas Morrell bareing even date with these pʳsents to be Complyed with & performᵈ by him yᵉ sᵈ Nichᵒ Morrell his heirs and Successors dureing yᵉ Natural life of yᵉ sᵈ Jonn Morrell./ hath given granted bargained Sold & made over unto yᵉ sᵈ Nicholas Morrell his heirs and Assignes for ever All yᵉ right title Interest Claime & demand wᶜʰ he hath in that tract of land whereon he now Dwelleth with ye houses buildings fences Edefices Orchards gardens &c^a thereon lying Scittuate in the Township of Kittery afores^d At a place Called Cold harbo^r Containing by Estimation One hundred Acres be ye Same more or Less/ Together with Two Oxen Six Cows Sixteen Ews one ram Two Cattle of Two years old & two Calves with all ye priviledges & Appurtenances to ye Above Mentioned premisses or all or any of them belonging with ye Carts Sleds plows chains & all other Implem^{ts} of husbandry belonging to or used on s^d farm of what kind or Nature So ever To have & To hold unto him ye s^d Nich^o Morrell his heirs & Assignes for ever to his & their only proper use benefit & behoofe from henceforth & forever As fully & Absolutely to all Intents & purposes whatsoever as ye s^d John Morrell Could have Injoyed ye Same before the Ensealing & Delivery of these presents. In witness whereof ye s^d John Morrell hath hereunto Set his hand & Seal ye day & year above written./

Signed Sealed & Delivered   John his mark Morrell (Seal)
In ye Presence of us
John Dennet
Nicholas Weekes
Jos. Hamond

York sc/ Sep^t 21st 1717

John Morrell within Named personally Appearing Acknowledged ye within Deed or Instrum^t in writing to be his Volluntary Act & deed   Coram. Jos. Hamond J. peace

Recorded According to ye Original Septr 21st 1717./

                                 p Jos Hamond Reg^r

At a Legal Town Meeting holden in York March 17th 1711/12./ Voted that ye Land formerly Laid out to m^r Henry Sawyard on ye Southwest Side of York river June ye 25th 1667 shall run Southwest from s^d river According as ye other Lots of Land run Charles ffrost Esqr of full age Testifieth that he was at ye Town meeting with in Expressed And At his Desire the vote within written was Offered to the Inhabitants who Voted ye Same by a great Majority in ye Affirmative he Observing there was but five hands in the Negative after which he ye Depona^t went to ye Town Clerk of york for a Coppy who told him he was Directed by ye Moderater Not to record s^d Vote./ But gave him y^e Minute book out of which he took y^e Coppy on the other side

Book VIII, Fol. 262.

York sc/ Jan^{ry} 8th 1717./ Jura^t in Perpetuam Rei Memorian   Cor^x Nobis   Jos. Hamond : Just^s Quor^x Unus
Saml Plaisted : Just Peace
Recorded According to y^e Original Jan^{ry} 8th 1717
$$\overline{8}$$
p Jos Hamond Reg^r

Priscilla Johnson of York Aged About Eighty years Testifieth & Saith that Mr William Hook deceased had Servants wch dwellt upon & Mannaged the farm now in Controversie between Coll^o Elisha Hutchinson & m^r William Hook Called Scotland in york & there kept a Stock of Cattle upon his farm Improveing both Meadow & upland for his Stock & use and Several Times while m^r Hookes Servants lived there I had been at ye farm in ye house with ye Serv^{ts} all was for the use of m^r Wm Hook Dec^d and that ye s^d m^r Hook did at ye same time live in york and had two Sons born there Humphrey Hook & Wm Hook And it is about Sixty years agoe more or Less. Mrs Priscilla Johnson Came this 12th day of August 1699 made oath to y^e above Written before me   Saml Donnell Just peace
Recorded According to y^e Original January 8th 1717.
$$\overline{8}$$
p Jos Hamond Reg^r

The Deposition of John Eaton Aged about forty Eight years who Saith & Testifieth that being Imployed by Mr Wm Hook of Salisbury about four & Twenty years ago to go to york in y^e Province of Maine to Mow a piece of Meadow [262] And So to make it to hay which Meadow y^e s^d Hook told me this s^d Depona^t that it was part of a farm of ye s^d Hookes And I this Depona^t did goe Along with ye s^d Hook to s^d york & did Cutt ye s^d Meadow & make ye hay & Sold it for ye s^d Hookes benefits & did quietly Improve y^e,; s^d Meadow without any Let Trouble or Mollestation of any person but Severall Inhabitants of ye s^d town of york Said it was m^r Hookes propper Estate or Land & further Saith Not :/ Dated y^e 3^d day of July 1694./ Essex This day John Eaton Appeared & made Oath to his above written Testimony At Salisbury Before Robert Pike Esqr one of their Maj^{tys} Justices afores^d County & one of y^e Councill
Recorded According to y^e Original Jan^{ry} 8th 1717—
$$\overline{8}$$
p Jos. Hamond Reg^r

Book VIII, Fol. 262.

This is to Testify unto whom it may Concern that I Henry Blasdell many years agoe liveing at Aguamenticus Now Called york at which time Mr Wm Hook lived at y^e Same place and m^r Hook hired me to keep goats for him upon his Land Called Cape nedock Neck And I do remember he had one Son born there which was Wm Hook after which ye s^d Wm Hook went for England being a pritty big lad & afterwards returned Againe to New England And afterwards lived upon his fathers farm & Since have Sene him Severall Times & is ye Same man who Now Lives here at Salisbury./ Henry Blasdell Henry Blasdell Above Named & Subscribed p^{r}sonally Appeared before me at my house in Salisbury October ye 18th 1700 and made Oath to ye Truth of all above written
     Before me Robt Pike Justice of ye peace
Recorded According to ye Original January 8th 1717.
             8
         p Jos. Hamond Reg^r

 This it to Testify unto whom it may Concern that I Thomas Bradbury many years Ago Lived At Accomenticus now Called york At which time Mr William Hooke lived At ye Same place & was Marryed and while I was there resident he had two Sons born (i e) Humphrey & William after which ye s^d W^m went with his mother for England being a pritty bigg lad and afterwards return^d Againe to New England & Came to his mother who then lived at Boston And I being then with his mother At Boston She told me her Son W^m was Come home I then Saw with her At Boston being ye Same man who now lives here At Salisbury
          p me Tho Bradbury
 I Mary Bradbury ye wife of s^d Tho: Bradbury went to Se Mrs Hook the wife of Mr Wm Hooke when she was Newly brought to bed of her Son W^m whom I then Suckled And this is that William Hooke which now lives at Salisbury./
         The mark
      of Mary *MB* Badbury

Mr Thomas Bradbury & Mrs Mary Bradbury his wife p^{r}sonally Appeared before me at my house in Salisbury & made Oath to their Testimony above written & Subscribed ye twenty Sixth day of June Anno Domini 1694 in ye Sixth year of their Maj^{tys} reign./ Robt Pike one of their Maj^{tys} Justices of ye peace in ye County of Essex & of ye Councill
 Recorded According to ye Original Jan^{ry} 8th 1717.
             8
         p Jos. Hamond Reg^r

BOOK VIII, FOL. 262.

This Indenture made y[e] Twenty Sixth day of Aug[st] Anno Domini one thousand Seven hundred & Twelve in y[e] Eleventh year of y[e] reign of our Soveraign Lady Anne of Great Brittaine ffrance & Ireland Queen Defender of the faith &[ca] Between Edward Bromfield of Boston in y[e] County of Suffolk within y[e] Province of y[e] Massachusets Bay in New England Merchant Attorney of Jacob Cole Rector of y[e] Parrish of Swyre & Vicar of Toller Fratrum & Winford Eagle in y[e] County of Dorset only Surviving Son & heir At Law of George Cole Late of the Burough of Dorchester in the County of Dorset within y[e] Kingdom of Great Brittain Merch[t] Deceased of y[e] One part & Ichabod Plaisted of Kittery in y[e] County of York and Province afores[d] Esq[r] on y[e] other part Witnesseth that y[e] s[d] Edward Bromfield in his Capacity afores[d] by Vertue of a power of Attorney from y[e] s[d] Jacob Cole Duely proved & of record in y[e] Publick Notarys Office for & in Consideration of forty three pounds Seven Shillings in good & Lawfull Bills of Credit of y[e] province afores[d] to him in hand at & before y[e] Ensealing hereof well & Truely paid for Acco[t] & to y[e] use of y[e] s[d] Jacob Cole by y[e] s[d] Ichabod Plaisted the rec[t] whereof to y[e] use afores[d] y[e] s[d] Edward Bromfield doth hereby Acknowledge & thereof Doth Acquit & Discharge the Said Ichabod Plaisted his heirs Ex[rs] Adm[rs] & Assignes for ever Hath given granted bargained Sold released Enfeoffed Conveyed & Confirmed and by these presents doth fully & Absolutely give grant Bargaine Sell release Enfeoffe Convey & Confirm unto y[e] s[d] Ichabod his heirs & Assignes forever All that y[e] s[d] Jacob Coles one Sixth part the whole in Six Equall parts to be Divided of & in a Certaine Tract or Tracts of land Lying Scittuate in Kittery afores[d] betwixt Quamphegon & Salmonfalls & y[e] falls at Quamphegon & y[e] Mill or Mills Standing thereon & right of all other Lands in Kittery Afores[d] below y[e] s[d] falls Adjoyning to Sturgeon Creek which y[e] s[d] George Cole in his Lifetime purchased of Thomas Broughton of Boston afores[d] Merch[t] & Mary his wife Now Descended to y[e] s[d] Jacob Cole and held by him in Comon & undivided however butted & bounded & be y[e] Quantity & Contents thereof More or Less Together with one Sixth part of All & Singular y[e] woods timb[r] Trees under woods herbage feedings Stones ponds rivers Streams Waters Watercourses rights Members profits priviledges & Appurtenances thereon & thereunto belonging Also all y[e] Estate right Title Interest Inheritance use property possession Claime & Demand of y[e] s[d] Jacob Cole of in & to y[e] s[d] land & premisses with y[e] revercon & revercons remainder & remainders thereof To have & To hold One Sixth part of y[e]

BOOK VIII, FOL. 263.

s^d tract or tracts of land & of All other ye granted premisses with the rights Members & Apurten^{ces} thereof to ye s^d Ichabod Plaisted his heirs & Assignes to his & their only proper use benefit & behoofe forever And ye s^d Edward Bromfield doth hereby Covenant grant & Agree to & with ye s^d Ichabod Plaisted his heirs & Assignes that he ye s^d Edward Bromfield is Lawfully & Sufficiently Impowred by ye s^d Jacob Cole to grant bargaine Sell Alienate dispose & Convey ye s^d land & premisses as afores^d and to Warra^t & Defend ye Same unto ye s^d Ichabod Plaisted his heirs & Assignes forever Against ye s^d Jacob Cole & all & Every other p^{r}son or persons from by or under him In Witness whereof ye s^d Edward Bromfield hath hereunto Set his hand & Seal the Day & year first above written   Edw: Bromfield (a/Seal)

[263] Signed Sealed & Delivered
In ye presence of us
James Maxwell
Jos. Marion

Rec^d on ye day of ye Date within written of the within Named Ichabod Plaisted the Sum of forty three pounds Seven Shillings in good & Lawfull Publick Bills of Credit in full of ye purchase Consideration within Mentioned

p Edw Bromfield

Suffolk sc/ Boston Augst 26th 1712./ The within Named Edw Bromfield p^{r}sonally Appearing Acknowledged ye within written Instrum^t to be his Act & Deed Before me./

Is^a Addington J : P

Recorded According to ye Original Decr 17th 1717./

p Jos. Hamond Reg^r

Articles of Agreement Inden: & made Concluded & fully agreed upon the Twelfth of April in ye year of our Lord One thousand Seven hundred and Seventeen And in ye third year of ye Reign of our Soveraign Ld George by ye grace of God King of Great Brittaine ffrance & Ireland Defender of the faith Between Mr Joshua Downing & Mr Samuel Hill and W^m ffry & ye relict of Mr Joseph Hill All of ye County of York Yeoman in his Maj^{tys} Province of ye Massachusets Bay in New England./ Witnesseth that Whereas there has been a difference between us about a Certain tract of Land by us bought in Joynt Tenancy that We have Divided what Land of our purchase that was not before these presents Divided or Sold by us or our predecessors that Lyeth on ye North Side of m^r Shapleighs land of which we derived our

Book VIII, Fol. 263.

title from ye heirs of Mr Antipas Maverick as more plainly may Appear by record Devided by John Gowen by ye request of us as wee Shewed him ye bounds there being thirty Acres & Seventy & One rods A piece for Each of us four Each mans bounds as followeth To the Son of Joseph Hill dec^d his thirty Acres & Seventy pole bounded as followeth from a little beach tree that Stands in ye way that from ye way that goes from Kittery road to Cold harb^r and as it goes to Kittery Mill which tree is ye head bounds of Mr Dennets Land then Southwest halfe a point west forty poles and thence athwart Joseph Hills former Lot Southeast halfe a point South forty Two poles to Mr Shapleighs line to a Certaine red oak Marked on four Sides which Tree was an old Mark^t tree in s^d Shapleighs line and Divides ye afores^d Hill & Mr Downing in this Division And from that Oak to a beach between s^d Hill & Mr Downing to ye beach at our first begining./ the Course is Northwest by North three Degrees Northerly as may Appear by Marked Trees this is ye Lower End of Mr Downings Land./ Then Mr Downings land runs by m^r Shapleighs afores^d line North East by East An hundred & one poles to ye way that goes to ye ferry at Cold harbour thence Northwest by North Twenty one poles to a Stake Stuck in ye way Side which Stake is ye head bounds between Mr Downings part and Mr Saml Hill Sen^{rs} part Containing his thirty Acres & Seventy poles then ye Dividing between them goes back to our first begining at ye Little beach by Marked trees One hundred & Seven poles west three degrees Southerly there being left out of ye whole Division twelve feet on Each side of ye hundred & Seven poles for a way to the Mill at Kittery and ye way At horsidown to Cold harbour ferry as it is Allowed in our Division goes quite above Mr Downings land and s^d Saml Hills land four poles wide to W^m ffrys land & is m^r Samuel Hills part of this Division Takes its begining at ye Stake afore Mentioned & runs by m^r Downings & ye highway to ye little beach at our first. One hundred & Seven poles thence Northwest halfe a point North forty four poles on ye head of m^r Dennets & thence East & by North one hundred & four poles to ye ferry way afores^d then by ye way to ye Stake at ye begining fifty five poles South East & by South Containing thirty Acres & Seventy poles Clear of ye road./ W^m ffry his part of this Division takes its begining in his own field by ye Side of ye fores^d way in ye East & by North line & runs Southeast by South Seventy Eight pole to m^r Shapleighs line then Northeast by East till it Strikes Kittery way that goes from Sturgeon Creek to Kittery Eighty Eight poles thence by ye Side of ye s^d road Twenty

Eight poles to a beach tree Standing in ye East & by North line and thence runs back to his first begining west & by South One hundred & thirteen poles Containing thirty acres & Seventy poles./ to this Division as Agreed by us whose names are hereunder written as witness our hands this Sixteenth day of April One thousen Seventeenth hundr^d And in ye third year of his Maj^{tys} reign Annoq Domini 1717./

Nathan Bartlet   Joshua Downing
Nicholas Shapleigh   Saml Hill
   W^m ffry

Province New Hampsh^r April ye 16th 1717./ The p^{r}sons above Mentioned to wit Joshua Downing Saml Hill & W^m ffry all personally Appeared & Acknowledged ye within Instrum^t to be their Act & Deed   before me
   James Davis Justice of peace
Recorded According to ye Original April 19th 1717./
   p Jos. Hamond Reg^r

Know All men by these presents that I Nicholas Morrell of Kittery in ye County of york in his Maj^{tys} Province of ye Massachusets Bay in New England bricklayer am holden and Stand firmly bound & Obliged unto my honoured father John Morrell of ye same town County and Province afores^d in ye full & Just Sum of fifty pounds Currant money of New England afores^d or his Certaine Attorney on demand to the which paym^t well & Truely to be made unto ye s^d John Morrell &c^t I bind my Selfe my heirs Ex^{rs} & Adm^{rs} ffirmly by these presents Sealed with my Seal./ Dated ye thirtieth day of August Anno: Domini Seventeen hundred & Seventeen Annoq Regni Regis Georgii Magna Brittania &c^a Quarto

The Condition of this Obligation is Such that if ye above bounden Nicholas Morrell his heirs Ex^{rs} Adm^{rs} or assignes do well & Truely Yield render [264] And pay or Cause to be paid unto ye s^d John Morrell or his Certaine Attorney ye whole produce of five Acres of Tillage land to be planted and Sowed of s^d land whereon s^d John Morrell now Dwells and s^d Nicholas to have five Acres to himselfe with one halfe ye fruit & Cyder also halfe ye Increase produce & profit which ye s^d Nicholas Morrell Shall raise & made of Six Cows Sixteen Ews one ram Two Cattle of Two years old and two Calves All which premisses are Mentioned & Expressed in a deed or Instrum^t in writing under the hand & Seal of ye s^d John Morrell bareing Even date with these presents And to be paid unto ye s^d John Morrell Yearly & Every Year in y^e

Specie ye premisses Shall produce or otherwise to his Satisfaction Dureing his Natural Life the time to Comence from y^e Twentieth day of Septemb^r Next without fraud or further delay That then this present Obligation to Cease Determin be Voyd & of Non Effect but on default thereof to Abide & remaine in full force Strength And Vertue to all Intents Constructions & purposes in y^e Law w^{t}soever   Nicho^s Morrell ($_{Seal}^{\ a}$)
Signed Sealed & Delivered
  In presence of us
  John Dennet
  Nicholas Weekes
  York sc/ Septr 21st 1717./ Nicholas Morrell personaly Appearing Acknowledged the Above Obligation or Instrum^t in writing to be his free Act & Deed./
                    Coram Jos. Hamond J. peace
Recorded According to ye Original Sep^t 21st 1717.
                           p Jos. Hamond Reg^r

  To All Christian People to whom this present Deed of Gift Shall Come I John Fennicke of Kittery in ye County of York in ye province of ye Massachusets Bay in New England Yeoman & Deberoh my wife Send Greeting. Know Y^e that for & in Consideration of ye Sum of Eight pounds in Curra^t money of New England to me well & truely paid at & before ye Ensealing and Delivery of these presents by Hezekiah Elwell of ye Same town County & Province afores^d fisherman the rec^t whereof I do hereby Acknowledge & my Selfe therewith to be fully Satisfied & paid & of & from every part & parcell thereof do Acquitt & Discharge fully ye s^d Hezekiah Elwell his heirs Ex^{rs} Adm^{rs} & Assigns by these presents forever but more Especially in Consideration of ye Love good will & Natural Affection which I have & do bare towards ye s^d Hezekiah Elwell my Son in Law & my daughter Elizabeth his wife Have given granted And by these presents do freely clearly & Absolutely give & grant unto ye s^d Hezekiah Elwell & Elizabeth his wife and to their heirs Lawfully begotten of her body a Certain tract or parcell of land Containing Twelve Acres be it more or Less which land is Scittuate lying & being in the Township of Kittery on ye western Side of ye place Comonly Called by the name of Spruce Creek at ye head of broad Cove in ye s^d Creek & is butted & bounded on ye Eastern end by ye Afores^d Cove on ye western end by ye road that goes to York on ye Southern side by the land of Walter Denniford & on y^e

Northern side by ye land of Mr Godsoe/ Tother with all ye Severall benefits priviledges & Appurtenances to ye s^d land belonging or in any wise Appurtaining To have & To hold ye s^d tract of land with all its Appurtenances with all ye Estate right Title Claime and demand which I ye s^d John Fennicke now have or in time Past have had or which I my heirs Ex^rs Adm^rs or Assignes may might Should or in any wise ought to have in time to Come of in or to the Above given & granted premisses or Any part thereof to him ye s^d Hezekiah Elwell & Elizabeth his wife and their heirs Lawfully begotten & born of her forever & to ye Sole & proper use benefit & behoofe of ye s^d Hezekiah Elwell & Elizabeth his wife & to their heirs Lawfully begotten & born of her Not to be Sold Alienated or Conveyed Away from their heirs as afores^d forevermore

In Witness whereof I thes^d John Fennicke & Deberoh my wife have hereunto Set our hands & Seals this 15th Jan^ry 1710.

Signed Sealed   John Fennicke (s^a_eal)
In y^e presence of us   y^e mark
Henry Barter   Deberoh ⟨R⟩ Fennick (s^a_eale)

The 15th of Jan^ry 1710./ Then John Fenneck & his wife Deberoh personally Appeared before me the Subscriber one of her Maj^tys Justices for s^d Province And Acknowledged this Instrum^t to be their free Act & Deed

Wm Pepperrell Just. peace

Recorded According to y^e Original Sept 9th 1717./

p Jos. Hammond· Reg^r

To All People to whom these presents shall Come I John Burnum of Ipswich in ye County of Essex in ye Province of the Massachusets Bay in New England America Send Greeting Know Ye that I ye s^d John Burnum for divers good Causes & Considerations me thereunto Moveing but Especialy for & in Consideration of a valuable Sum in hand paid & by me recieved of Hugh Pike of Newbury in ye County afores^d to my full Satisfaction & Content & I do Accordingly for my Selfe my heirs Ex^rs and Adm^rs Acquit Exonerrte & discharge ye s^d Hugh Pike his heirs Ex^rs & Adm^rs by these presents Have given granted bargained & Sold Enfeoffed & Confirmed & do by these presents fully freely

Book VIII, Fol. 265.

clearly & Absolutely give grant bargaine Sell Enfeoffe & Confirm unto ye s^d Hugh Pike three hundred Acres of Land being part of a Tract of land which my Selfe & Diverse others as Joynt purchasers purchased of Mr Harlackinden Symonds of Ipswich in ye County afores^d which s^d tract of Land is Six miles in Length & four Miles in breadth known by ye Name of Cocks Hall in ye County of yorkshire in ye Province of Maine & is bounded As followeth Viz^t./ At ye Southeast end partly upon ye line of ye Township of Wells partly upon ye line of ye line of ye Township of Capeporpoise & on ye Northeast Side partly bounded by ye Line of ye land formerly Maj^r Wm Phillips his land and partly upon ye Comon land & on ye Northwest end ye s^d land is bounded on ye Comon land & bounded on ye Southwest Side with ye land of ye s^d Symonds as by a deed of Sale und^r ye hand & Seal of ye s^d Mr Harlackenden Symonds bareing date June 12th Anno Dom 1688 and by him Acknowledged June 22^d 1688 before John Usher Esqr & Entred with ye records of ye County of york Octob^r 12th 1693 in folio 84 more at large may Appear & I ye s^d John Burnum for my Selfe my heirs Ex^{rs} & Adm^{rs} do Covena^t and Promiss to & with ye s^d Hugh Pike his heirs Ex^{rs} Adm^{rs} & Assignes that ye s^d three hundred Acres of land & Every part & parcell thereof is [265] ffree & clear and freely & clearly Exonerated discharged & Acquitted of & from all former gifts grants bargains Sales Alienations Charges Mortgages Dowers Joyntures Extents Judgments Executions & all other Incumbrances whatsoever and I ye s^d John Burnum for my Selfe my heirs Ex^{rs} & Adm^{rs} do and Shall from time to time & at all times Warrantize & maintaine ye s^d bargained premisses with all & Singular ye Appurtenances & priviledges & Comodityes to ye s^d three hundred Acres of land herein mentioned belonging as namely ye Trees woods underwoods Standing or lying upon ye s^d Land with all meadows Swamps waters waterCourses Mines or Mineralls in or upon ye s^d land whatsoever or wheresoever it be from all maner of persons whatsoever claiming or pretending to have any Just & Lawfull right & title or Interest to ye s^d bargained premisses & every part & parcell thereof To have & To hold ye s^d bargained p^{r}misses every part & parcell thereof to him ye s^d Hugh Pike his heirs his Ex^{rs} Adm^{rs} and Assigns forever In Witness & Confirmtion of All ye above written I ye s^d John Burnum have hereunto Set my hand & Seal this fifteenth day of June Anno Dom Sixteen hundred ninety &

BOOK VIII, FOL. 265.

four Annoque Regni Regis et Regina Gullielmi et Maria
Nunc Anglia &c[t] Sexto   John Burnum jun[r] (Seal)
Signed Sealed & Deliver[d]
by John Burnum to
Hugh Pike in p[r]sence of us
Jacob Tappin
Joseph Little
John Burnum jun[r] Appeared y[e] Tenth day of July: 1694 in y[e] Sixth year of their Maj[tys] reign and Acknowledged y[e] above written Instrument to be his Act & Deed before me Daniel Pierce one of their Maj[tys] Justices of y[e] peace
Recorded According to y[e] Original Octob[r] 29th 1717./
p Jos: Hamond Reg[r]

Know All men by these presents that I James Pitman of Portsm[o] in y[e] Province of New Hampsh[r] Marriner in his own right & as Attorney to Joseph Pitman for Divers good Causes me thereunto Moving particularly for & in Consideration of y[e] Sum of Twenty five pounds Eighteen Shillings & Nine pence to me in hand paid before y[e] Ensealing of these presents y[e] rec[t] whereof I do hereby Acknowledge Have given granted bargained Sold Enfeoffed & Confirmed and by these presents do give grant bargaine Sell Aliene Enfeoffe & Confirm unto Oliver Noyes of Boston in y[e] County of Suffolk in y[e] Province of y[e] Massachusets Bay Esq[r] all that my Certaine Tract or parcell of land Lying & being in y[e] bounds of James Town on y[e] point of Land Comonly Called & known by y[e] Name of Pemaquid point Near to Kings Bridge on y[e] South Side of y[e] Same Containing by Estimation One hundred & four Acres begining at y[e] Sea Side at a Spruce tree that is marked & from thence Extending East Southeast by y[e] head of y[e] Salt Marsh Sixty four poles to a Spruce Tree Marked on four Sides & from thence South Southwest Two hundred & Sixty pole to a Spruce tree Marked on four Sides in y[e] woods and from thence West Northwest Sixty four pole to a Spruce tree Marked near unto y[e] Sea Side on a point of Land & from thence North Northeast Two hundred & Sixty pole to y[e] place where began with Twenty Acres of Meadow Lying Convenient to be laid out or of Marsh To have & To hold y[e] s[d] One hundred & four Acres of upland & Twenty Acres of Meadow unto y[e] s[d] Oliver Noyes his heirs & Assignes to y[e] Sole & only proper use benefit & behoofe of y[e] s[d] Oliver Noyes his heirs & Assignes forever & y[e] s[d] James Pitman doth Affirm himselfe to have full power

Book VIII, Fol. 265.

& Authority to Dispose of said as descendant of James Pittman who Died Siezed in fee of s^d land and as Attorney to his Brothers./ And ye s^d Oliver Noyes doth Covenant & promiss that if ye s^d James Pitman doth pay unto Oliver Noyes ye Sum of Twenty Six pounds within ye Space of Two years Next After ye Date of these presents that he will by Deed reconvey ye s^d lands otherwise to remaine forever y^e fee of y^e s^d Oliver Noyes to him & his heirs forever./ In Witness hereof I have hereunto Set my hand & Seale this Twenty fourth of Decemb^r Seventeen hundred & Seventeen & in y^e fourth year of his Maj^{tys} Reign
In presence of us y^e Interlination
  between y^e 2^d & third line be-   James $\overset{mark}{,}$ Pitman ($_{Seal}^a$)
  fore Signing
  Paul Gerrish
  Richd Cutt

James Pitman p^{r}sonally Appeared before me y^e Subscrib^r one of his Maj^{tys} Justices of peace At Portsm^o in y^e Province of New Hampsh^r in New England this 24th Decr 1717 & Acknowledged y^e above Instrum^t to be his act & Deed./
                          Saml Penhallow
Recorded According to ye Original Jan^{ry} 4th 1717./
                          p Jos. Hamond Reg^r

To All Christian People to whom these presents shall Come Greeting Know ye that I Daniel Emery Now resident in Kittery in ye County of York in ye Province of ye Massachusets Bay in New Engl^d Mason for & in Consideration of fifty pounds to me in hand paid by Job Emery my Brother of Berwick in ye County & Province above mentioned ye rec^{ts} whereof I own my Selfe Satisfied Contented & paid & of Every part & parcell thereof Do Acquitt and forever discharge Have given granted bargained & Sold & do by these presents give grant bargaine Sell release Alienate Enfeoffe pass over and Confirm unto Job Emery afores^d All my right Title Interest property Claime or Demand in or to a Certaine piece or parcell of Land Scittuate & in ye Township of Kittery & bounded as followeth Viz^t on ye East by Commons on rockey hill & on ye North by Moses Goodins land and on ye west by James Emerys Land & on ye South by Nathan Lords land & it Contains forty Acres more or Less as it Appears by Deed of Sale from our father the one halfe of ye above mentioned Land being my own proper right I now make Over as aboves^d to my brother Job Emery To have &

To hold y² halfe of y² afores⁴ Tract Together with all & Singular y² Appurtenances priviledges & Comodityes of Woods Timber Trees under woods Waters Water Courses to him y² s⁴ Job Emery his heirs & Assignes forever without Let Interuption or Mollestation of me y² s⁴ Daniel Emery or any other p'son or persons by from or under me or by my procurem' my heirs or Assignes forever & for Confirmation of y² premisses I y² s⁴ Daniel Emery hereunto Set my hand & Seall this Twelfth day of March One thousand Seven hundred & thirteen fourteen 1713/4 & in y² thirteenth year of her Maj^{tys} reign of Great Brittain &

Signed Seal⁴ & D⁴   Daniel Emery ($_{Seal}^a$)
  in p'sence of us
  John Gowen
  John Belcher
  John Gowen Jun'

  York ss./ Kittery March 12th 1713/4

The above Named Daniel Emery p'sonally Appearing Acknowledged y² above written Instrum' to be his free Act & deed   Before me Charles ffrost J peace

Recorded According to y² Original Augst 1st 1717./

          p Jos. Hamond Reg'

[266] Know All men by these presents that I Joseph Woodsum of Berwick in y² County of York in New England Tayler do Own & Acknowledge my Selfe to Stand & be Justly Indebted unto Job Emery of y² Same Town & County in y² full & Just Sum of One hundred pounds Curra' passable money of New England and all y² lands Chattells & other Matterialls for which Sum & other things Mentioned I bind my Selfe my heirs Ex^{rs} Adm^{rs} & Assignes unto him y² s⁴ Job Emery his heirs Ex^{rs} Adm^{rs} or Assignes as given und' my hand & Seale this Second day of July in y² year of our Lord 1717./

The Condition of y² above Obligation is Such that if y² above bounden Joseph Woodsom his heirs Ex^{rs} Adm^{rs} or Assignes do pay or Cause to be paid unto Abigail Abbot of y² Same town & County her heirs Ex^{rs} Adm^{rs} or Assignes the Sum of Two Shillings & Sixpence p week Currant money of New England Dureing y² Courts pleasure then y² above Obligation to be Voyd or of Non Effect otherwayes to Stand be & remaine in full force & Vertue./

Signed Sealed & Deliver⁴   Joseph Woodsum ($_{Seal}^a$)
  In presence
  Thomas Knight
  Nath¹ ffreeman

Book VIII, Fol. 266.

York sc July 2ᵈ 1717 the Above Named Joseph Woodsum
Acknowledged yᵉ Above written Instrumᵗ to be his free Act
& Deed   Before Elisha Plaisted Just peace
Recorded According to yᵉ Original Augˢᵗ 1ˢᵗ 1717
                    p Jos. Hamond Regʳ

To All People to whom these presents Shall Come Samuel
Hill of Charlestown Sends Greeting./ Now Know yᵉ that I
Samˡ Hill of Charlestown in yᵉ County of Middlesex in yᵉ
Province of yᵉ Massachusets Bay in New England Marriner
for & in Consideration of yᵉ full & Just Sum of fifty pounds
in good Curraᵗ money of New England to me Secured to be
paid by Mʳ Andrew Brown of Winter harbour in yᵉ County
of York in yᵉ Province aforesᵈ Have given & granted & do
by these presents give grant bargaine Sell Alienate Enfeoffe
make over & Confirm unto Andrew Brown aforesᵈ a Certain
Tract of Land Lying & being in yᵉ Township of Cape Porpoise Containing One hundred Acres it being partly Vizᵗ
Sixty Acres yᵉ Antient Seat of Richard Young of Cape porpoise decᵈ which Sixty Acres was given him by yᵉ Town of
Capeporpoise & partly Vizᵗ yᵉ other forty Acres a Tract of
Land Sold by Henry Hetherly to Richard Young & bounded
by Richᵈ Youngs field & from thence runing down yᵉ Little
river Next to Capeporpoise unto a pine Tree by a great rock
Near yᵉ Water Side below yᵉ foot of yᵉ falls as Also yᵉ priviledge of yᵉ Stream on that side Vizᵗ on yᵉ Easterly side of
yᵉ Little river Excepting yᵉ Lower falls which is Now in
Controversie./ The Easterly bounds of yᵉ aforesᵈ forty Acres
is from yᵉ pine tree before Mentioned to run upon a nornor-
west line till it Meet with yᵉ abovesᵈ Antient Inheritance of
Richᵈ Young As Also thirteen Acres of Salt Marsh Seven
Acres whereof lyeth a place Comonly Called Princes rock &
yᵉ other Six acres of sᵈ Marsh Lying & being up towards
Millers & yᵉ opening of yᵉ pines yᵉ sᵈ thirteen Acres of
Meadow being formerly given to William Randal by yᵉ town
of Capeporpoise yᵉ which hundred Acres of land & priviledges & yᵉ Stream & Meadow as before Expressed I yᵉ
Abovesᵈ Samˡ Hill For my Selfe my heirs Exʳˢ & Admʳˢ do
Confirm & Set Over to Andrew Brown aforesᵈ to him his
heirs Exʳˢ Admʳˢ or assignes Together with all & Singular yᵉ
priviledges rights & Appurtenances thereto belonging or any
wise Appurtaining To have & To hold as a free & clear Estate of Inheritance in fee Simple forever./ And I yᵉ abovesᵈ
Samˡ Hill do for my Selfe my heirs Exʳˢ & Admʳˢ Covenant

& promiss to & with yᵉ aboveˢᵈ Andrew Brown & his heirs Exʳˢ Admʳˢ or Assignes that I am at the Ensealing hereof yᵉ true & rightfull owner of yᵉ above granted premisses & that I have full power right & Authority to sell & dispose thereof As Above Expressed./ Moreover that yᵉ premisses & Every part & parcell thereof is free & clear & fully & Clearly Acquitted & discharged of & from all other & former gifts grants bargaines Sales Mortgages or Incumbrances whatsoever Furthermore I yᵉ sᵈ I yᵉ abovesᵈ Saml do for my heirs Exʳˢ & Admʳˢ Covenaᵗ & promiss hereby unto yᵉ Abovesᵈ Andrew Brown or his heirs Exʳˢ Admʳˢ or Assignes to Warraᵗ & defend yᵉ Above recited premisses from all or any pʳson or persons whatsoever Laying Any Legal claim thereto or any part or parcell .thereof./ And Elizᵃ Hill yᵉ wife of me yᵉ abovesᵈ Samˡ Hill doth by these presents give up & Surrender fully & freely all her right of Dowry or power of thirds of in or unto yᵉ above bargained premisses. In Witness whereof yᵉ abovesᵈ Samˡ Hill & Elizabeth his wife have hereunto Set their hands & Seals this Twenty fourth day of Augˢᵗ Anno Domˡ 1717 in yᵉ fourth year of yᵉ reign of our Soveraign Lord George by yᵉ grace of God of Great Brittaine ffrance & Ireland King &cᵃ   Samˡ Hill (ₛₑₐₗᵃ)
Signed Sealed & Delivered   (ₛₑₐₗᵃ)

In presence of us
Samˡ Emery
Mary Emery

York sc/ Wells Augˢᵗ 24ᵗʰ 1717/

Samˡ Hill pʳsonally Appeared before me and Acknowledged this above written deed or Instrumᵗ to be his Act & deed./   John Wheelwright Just peace

Recorded According to yᵉ Original Febʳʸ 15ᵗʰ 1717/8./
     p Jos. Hamond Regʳ

Know All men by these presents that I Samˡ Scadlock formerly of Capeporpus at a place known by yᵉ Province of Maine Now of Marblehead in yᵉ County of Essex within yᵉ Province of yᵉ Massachusets Bay in New England fisherman for & in Consideraçon of that good will & Natural Affection which I have & do bear unto my Son & Daughter Bezaliel Gatchel of Marble head in yᵉ County of Essex fisherman & Susanna his wife my Natural Daughter and for divers other good and Lawfull Consideraçons me thereunto Moveing Have given granted bargained Enfeoffed Sold & Conveyed & do by these presents give grant Convey Confirm

Book VIII, Fol. 267.

Enfeoff & Set over unto ye s^d Bezaliel Gatchell & Susanna Gatchell One Third part for Quantity & Quallity of all that houseing & Land Marshes Meadows Isles Swamps & Low Ground that in any Maner is belonging or Appurtaining to me ye Conveyor Scittuate lying & being [267] in the Eastern parts whether At Capeporpus or At ye Small river or Elsewhare Particularly One full third part for quantity & quallity of that tract of upland & Meadow which my father William Scadlock dec^d purchased of Wm Phillips as by Deed bareing date ye 19th day of Augst 1661 and slso a Third part of all other lands that is any wayes belonging to me lying betwixt Casco bay and Piscattaqua river./ To have & To hold a full third part of all ye houseing lands Marshes & Meadows afores^d with a third part of all ye Timb^r wood rocks Stones Mines Mineralls Waters rivers brookes Springs WaterCourses Standing runing lying or being thereon or any part thereof or belonging or Appurtaining thereto with all ye rights priviledges & Appurtenances thereof unto them ye s^d Bezaliel Gatchell & Susanna his wife their heirs and Assignes forever to their own proper use & behoofe as an Estate in fee without Any Let hinderence Mollestation or disturbence from me ye s^d Saml Scadlock my heirs Ex^{rs} Adm^{rs} or Assignes or any Else from by or under me./ In Witness whereof I have hereunto Affixt my hand and Seal ye 3^d day of Octob^r Anno R^{i}R^s Georgii Nunc Magna Brittainia &c^a Quarto Annoq, Dom̃ 1717./

Signed Sealed & Delivered
In p^{r}sence of us
Joseph Hillard
R^{ch} Newcombe

The mark of
Saml ⊃ Scadlock (seale ^{a}.)
Anne Scadlock

Essex sc/ Salem Octob^r 3^d 1717

Then Saml Scadlock & Anne Scadlock Acknowledged this Instrum^t to be their Act & Deed Coram Stephen Sewal js peace

Recorded According to ye Original Feb^{ry} 19th 1717/8./

p Jos. Hamond Reg^r.

To All People unto whom this present Deed & Sale shall Come We Sarah Shapleigh Widow & relict of John Shapleigh late of Kittery in ye County of York in ye Province of ye Massachusets Bay in New England Dec^d And Nicholas Shapleigh Son of ye Aboves^d John Shapleigh dec^d Adm^{rs} to the Estate of ye aboves^d John Shapleigh Late of Kittery dec^d Send Greeting Know ye that for & in Consideration of ye sum of thirty pounds in Curra^t Money of New England to us well & Truely paid at & before the Ensealing & Delivery of these p^rsents by Mr William Godsoe of ye afores^d town County & Province Yeoman ye rec^t whereof we do hereby Acknowledge and ourselves therewith to be fully Satisfied & paid & of & from Every part & parcell thereof for us our heirs Ex^rs & Adm^rs do Exonerate & Acquit ye s^d Godsoe his heirs Ex^rs Adm^rs & Assignes by these p^rsents forever have given granted bargained sold released Enfeoffed delivered & Confirmed and by these p^rsents do for ourselves our heirs Ex^rs & Adm^rs give grant bargaine Sell release Enfeoffe Deliver & Confirm unto ye s^d Wm Godsoe his heirs & Assignes a Certaine Tract of Land lying & being in the Township of Kittery afores^d between ye Places Comonly Called Crooked lane & Spruce creek Containing by Estimation fifteen Acres or there abouts & is bounded by ye road that goes to york on ye Eastern side on ye Southern side by ye Land of Walter Deniford on ye western side by the land of ye afores^d John Shapleigh dec^d & on ye Northern side by ye land of ye aboves^d Wm Godsoe Together with all ye Severall beñefits priviledges & Appurtenances to ye s^d Land belonging or in any wise Appurtaining To have & To hold ye s^d tract of land with all ye Priviledges unto ye s^d William Godsoe his heirs & Assignes & to ye only use benefit & behoofe of him ye s^d William Godsoe his heirs & Assignes forever And we ye s^d Sarah Shapleigh and Nicholas Shapleigh do for our selves our heirs Ex^rs Adm^rs & Assignes hereby Covena^t Promiss & Grant to & with ye s^d Wm Godsoe his heirs Ex^rs Adm^rs & Assignes that at & before ye Ensealing and Delivery hereof we are ye right & proper owners of ye above bargained & Sold p^rmisses and are Lawfully possest thereof and have good right & Lawfull Authority in our own Names ye Same to sell & Convey as aboves^d & that ye Same is free & Clear from all former & other gifts sales Mortgages Dowries Troubles and Incumbrances whatsoever & that ye sale thereof & Every part thereof Against Against our selves our heirs Ex^rs & Adm^rs & Against all other p^rsons whatsoever lawfully claiming & Demanding ye Same unto ye s^d Wm Godsoe his heirs & Assignes shall & will Warra^t & by these p^rsents for Ever Defend./ In Witness whereof together with y^e Delivery of the bargained & Sold p^rmisses we have hereunto Set our hands & Seals this thirteenth day of Aug^st in y^e Tenth year of y^e reign of our Soveraign Lady

Anne Over great Brittaine &c^t Queen Anno$_q$ Domini One thousand Seven hundred & Eleven

Signed Sealed & Delivered
In y^e p^rsence of us
John Newmarch
Mary Newmarch
Richd Rice

Sarah S̄ (her mark) Shapleigh (seal)
Nicholas Shapleigh (mark) (seal)

John Godsoe Ŧ (his mark)

Benj^a Welch

Kittery Octob^r 22 : 1711./ Mr Nich^o Shapleigh psonally Appeared before me ye Subscrib^rs one of her Maj^tys Justices of peace & Acknowledged this Instrum^t to be his Act & Deed   Wm Pepperrell

Recorded According to ye Original March 20th 1717/8/
    p Jos. Hamond Reg^r

To All People to whom this p^rsent Deed of Sale shall Come Thomas Allen of Kittery in ye County of york in New England shipwright Sendeth Greeting Know ye that I ye s^d Thomas Allen for & in Consideration of ye Sum of Two hundred pounds Curra^t money of New England to me in hand well & Truely paid before ye Delivery & Ensealing of these p^rsents by Joseph Crocket of s^d Town & County husbandman ye rec^t whereof I do hereby Acknowledge to full Content & Satisfaction & thereof & of Every part thereof do Acquit Exonerate & Discharge ye s^d Joseph Crocket his heirs Ex^rs & Adm^rs forever by these p^rsents have given granted bargained & sold & by these presents do fully freely & Absolutely give grant bargaine Sell Aliene Enfeoffe Set over & Confirm unto ye s^d Joseph Crocket his heirs & Assignes for ever All ye Estate right Title Interest use possession reversion remainder Property claime & Demand whatsoever which I ye s^d Thomas Allen have or had or that I my heirs or Assigns or any of us At any time or times hereafter shall have may Might should or ought to have or Claime of in & to one third part of a Certaine Tract or parcell of Land & Meadow Lying & being in Kittery afores^d Sold unto me s^d Thomas Allen by Coll^o Nathl Thomas As Appears p deed und^r s^d Thomas^es hand & Seal Bareing Date . . . 1712 to me ye s^d Thomas Allen Roger Dearing & Ebenez^r More for ye whole tract [268] of ye aboves^d land whereof One third was Sold to me ye s^d Thomas Allen by ye s^d Coll^o Nathl Thomas

Together with all my right & Interest of in & to One third part of ye afores^d land Together with one third part of All ye Timb^r priviledges to it belonging or in Any wayes Appurtaining as it was mine To have & To hold all ye above granted premisses with their Appurtenances & Every part & parcell thereof unto ye s^d Jos Crocket his heirs & Assignes for ever & further that I ye s^d Thomas Allen my heirs Ex^{rs} & Adm^{rs} shall & will from henceforth forever hereafter Warrant & Defend ye above & within granted premisses with ye Appurten^{ces} thereof unto ye s^d Joseph Crocket his heirs & Assignes against all and Every p^{r}son or p^{r}sons whomsoever Any wayes Lawfully claiming or demanding ye Same or any part thereof by from or under me my heirs or Assignes./ In Witness whereof I ye s^d Thomas Allen have hereuto Set my hand & Seal the Second day of February Anno Domini one Thousand Seven hundred & Sixteen./

Signed Sealed & Delivered   Thomas Allen (a Seal)

   In ye p^{r}sence of
               his
   John Barton   X
               mark

        his
   Henry   Barter jun^r
      mark

Wm Pepperrell Junr

   York sc/ 2^d day of ffeb^{ry} Anno 1716

This day Thomas Allen psonally Appeared before me ye Subscriber one of his Maj^{tys} Justices of Peace for s^d County & Acknowledged this above & that on ye otherside to be his free Act & Deed./   Wm Pepperrell

Recorded According to ye Original March 3^d 1717/8/

                        p Jos. Hamond Reg^r

   To All People to whom these presents Shall Come Greeting Now Know Ye that I Joseph Storer of Wells in ye County of York in ye Province of ye Massachusets Bay in New England for & in Consideration of ye full & Just Sum of forty pounds in good & Lawfull money of New England to me in hand paid in part & partly well Secured to be paid to me ye aboves^d Joseph Storer by Moses Stephens of ye Town & County afores^d Carpenter Have given & granted and do by these p^{r}sents fully clearly & Absolutely give grant

Book VIII, Fol. 268.

bargaine Sell Alienate Enfeoffe Make over & Confirm unto Moses Stephens Afores^d a Certaine tract of Land Lying & being in ye Township of Wells Containing one hundred Acres bounded as followeth Viz^t Northeasterly by Land of Mr Jonathan Hammond Southeasterly by ye Country road or highway Southwesterly by land Called Reeds land Now in ye Tenure & Occupation of James Baston and Northwesterly by ye Comon or highway at ye head of ye lots. It being Land formerly belonging to my brother Saml Storer dec^d and Conveyed to me by deed under hand & Seal of Lydia Storer Widow relict to Saml Storer dec^d ye which land bounded & Estimated as afores^d I ye aboves^d Joseph Storer do for my selfe my heirs Ex^{rs} Adm^{rs} Confirm & Set over to Moses Stephens afores^d his heirs Ex^{rs} Adm^{rs} or Assignes To have & To hold together with all and Singular ye priviledges rights & Appurtenances thereto belonging or Any wayes Appurtaining as a free & Clear Estate in Fee Simple forever & I ye Afores^d Joseph Storer do for my Selfe my heirs Ex^{rs} & Adm^{rs} Covena^t & promiss to & with ye afores^d Moses Stephens his Heirs Ex^{rs} Adm^{rs} & Assignes that I am at ye time of Ensealing hereof the True & rightfull owner of ye above granted premisses & that I have full power good right & Lawfull Authority to dispose of ye same as aboves^d and that it is free & clear & fully clearly & Absolutely Acquitted & Discharged of & from all other & former gifts grants bargains Sales Dowries Alienations Mortgages Intrusions or Incumbrances whatsoever Furthermore I ye s^d Joseph Storer for my Selfe my heirs Ex^{rs} & Adm^{rs} do Covena^t & promiss & Engage ye above demised premisses to him ye s^d Moses Stephens his heirs Ex^{rs} Adm^{rs} & Assigns against ye Lawfull Claims & Demands of Any p^{r}son or p^{r}sons whatsoever forever hereafter to Warra^t Secure & Defend./ And Hannah Storer ye wife of me ye s^d Joseph Storer doth by these p^{r}sents freely willingly give Yield up & Surrender all her right of Dowry & power of thirds of in & unto ye Above demised premisses unto him ye s^d Moses Stephens his heirs & Assignes./ In Witness whereof I the Aboves^d Joseph Storer & Hannah my wife have hereto Set our hands & Seals the fifteenth day of May Anno : Domini One thousand Seven hundred & Sixteen And in y^e Second year of y^e reign of our Soveraign Lord George by y^e grace of God of Great Brittaine &c^t King./   Joseph Storer ($^a_{Seal}$)

Signed Sealed & Delivered   Hannah Storer ($^a_{Seal}$)
  In presence of us
  Joseph Hill
  Joseph Littlefield
  Saml Emery

Book VIII, Fol. 268.

York sc/ Joseph Storer & Hannah his wife Appeared before me & Acknowledged y^e Above written Instrum^t to be their Act & Deed this fifteenth day of May 1716./

John Wheelwright Just peace
Recorded According to ye Original Jan^{ry} 7th 1717/8/
p Jos. Hamond Reg^r

Finis.

INDEX.

INDEX OF

Date.	Grantor.	Grantee.	Instrument.
1714, Dec. 16	ABBET, Thomas	John Abbet	Deed
1688, Jan. 30	ABBOT, Peter, and Thomas Abbot	Thomas Wills	Deed
	ABBOT, Thomas, see Peter Abbot		
1720, Mar. 2	ADDAMS, John	Samuel Spinney	Discharge
1711, Nov. 15	ADDAMS, Thomas et ux.	Samuel Addams	Deed
171$\frac{2}{3}$, Feb. 17	ALLEN, Francis, and Reinold Jenkins	Each other	Deed of Exchange
1717, Aug. 23	ALLEN, James	Samuel Came	Deed
1701, Oct. 14	ALLEN, Samuel	John Usher	Mortgage
1716, Feb. 2	ALLEN, Thomas	Joseph Crocket	Deed
1716, May 18	ALLEN, Thomas	John Wentworth & Mary Martyn	Mortgage
1716, Feb. 2	ALLEN, Walter	Ichabod Plaisted	Deed

GRANTORS.

Folio.	Description.
160	110 acres, a mile in length from brow of Rocky hill at Slut's corner, east, then southeast to John Taylor's marsh, 56 poles in breadth, reserving right to firewood, in *Berwick*.
143	House and land at Crooked lane, in *Kittery*.
239	Of the mortgage recorded folio 239.
254	50 acres on southwest side of York river, in *York*.
6	15 acres near Dover river and Sturgeon creek, in exchange for two small tracts near Dover river, in *Kittery*.
250	17 acres and 50 poles on south side of southwest branch of York river, part of a town grant, in *York*.
1	Territory from middle of Naumkeag river, around Cape Ann, to Piscataqua harbor, thence to head of Newichewannock river, thence northwest until the distance from Piscataqua harbor equals 60 miles; also up Naumkeag river, with the southern half of Isles of Shoals; the whole called New Hampshire; also 10,000 acres southeast of Sagadahoc river, called Masonia; also beginning at the entrance of Newichewannock river and to the head thereof, containing in breadth 3 miles, all the length.
267	A third part of a certain tract bought of Nathaniel Thomas, in *Kittery*.
154	1 acre; also 7 acres bought of Ebenezer More, in *Kittery*.
257	A grant of 60 acres, excepting 10 acres, next Humphrey Chadbourne's lot, in *Berwick*.

Index of Grantors.

Date.	Grantor.	Grantee.	Instrument.
1723, June 20	Austine, Matthew et ux.	William Pepperrell	Deed
1689, Oct. 10	Averell, Thomas	Francis Littlefield	Deed
1703, July 3	Bailey, Joseph	Nicholas Morey	Levy on Execution
1703, July 3	Bailey, Joseph	Nicholas Morey	Levy on Execution
1715, May 21	Ball, John	John Frost	Deed
1717, June 6	Ball, John et ux.	Francis Pettigrew	Deed
	Bane, Jonathan, see John Harmon		
1714, Oct. 11	Bane, Lewis	Jonathan Bane	Deed
1715, Oct. 5	Bane, Lewis	James Smith	Discharge
171$\frac{4}{5}$, Mar. 10	Banks, John et ux. and Joseph Banks et ux.	Richard Milbury	Deed
17$\frac{13}{14}$, Feb. 22	Banks, Joseph et ux.	Peter Weare, Richard Milbury and Peter Nowell	Deed
	Banks, Joseph, see John Banks		
1713, May 28	Barter, Henry	William Pepperrell, junior	Mortgage
17$\frac{18}{19}$, Feb. 20	Barter, Henry et ux.	Ebenezer More & John Norton	Deed
1711, Jan. 18	Beal, Arthur	William Pearse et ux.	Deed

Index of Grantors. 5

Folio.	Description.
20	A third part of a certain grant bought of Nathaniel Thomas, in *Kittery*.
175	200 acres, called Tatnack (Totnucke), six miles from town of Wells; also 6 acres, in *Wells*.
125	100 acres at Cape Porpoise.
125	140 acres at Cape Porpoise.
198	All right, title and interest he may have in common and undivided lands, in *Berwick* and *Kittery*.
230	22 acres, bounded east by Spruce creek, north by branch of said creek, south by William Godsoe's land, west by said Godsoe's and John Sheppard's land, with house, goods and chattels, in *Kittery*.
90	30 acres on the northeast side of highway leading from the meeting-house to the corn-mill, in *York*.
127	Of the mortgage recorded folio 14.
252	Two-thirds of a 40 acre tract on Dummer's neck, in *York*.
30	One-half of all their lands and marsh on northeast side of Saco river, in *Saco*.
42	16 acres and 40 acres on Crocket's neck, in *Kittery*.
214	27¾ acres bought of Thomas Hooper, in *Kittery*.
103	10 acres on the southwest side of York river, in *York*.

Book VIII.   42

Index of Grantors.

Date.	Grantor.	Grantee.	Instrument.
17$\frac{13}{14}$, Mar. 6	BEAL, Edward et ux.	William Pepperrell	Deed
1714, Dec. 23	BEAL, Edward et ux.	William Pepperrell	Mortgage
1716, July 20	BERRY, James et ux.	John Wentworth and Thomas Hutchinson Adam Winthrop David Jeffries Oliver Noyes John Watts Stephen Minot John Ruck	Deed
	BERRY, James, see Elizabeth Davis		
1709, Aug. 24	BLACK, Daniel et ux.	Peter Nowell	Deed
	BLAGDON, Hannah, see Mary Blagdon		
1713, Oct. 25	BLAGDON, Mary, and Hannah Blagdon Nicholas Follet et ux.	Lewis Bane	Deed
1678, Oct. 25	BOLLS, Joseph	Elizabeth Lock	Deed
1713, June 1	BOLLS, Samuel	Samuel Hammond	Deed
1713, Nov. 16	BONIGHTON, Richard	Peter Weare	Deed
1713, Nov. 16	BONIGHTON, Richard	Humphrey Scammon and Peter Nowell	Power att'y
1675, Oct. 8	BOOTH, Simon et ux.	Bryan Pendleton	Deed
1710, Nov. 28	BRACEY, William et ux.	Daniel Junkins	Deed

Index of Grantors.

Folio.	Description.
135	21¼ acres next to said Pepperrell's land, in *York*.
69	200 acres, bounded northwest by William Pepperrell's land, northeast by the river, southwest by Mr. Rayne's land, southeast by the sea; also all his land on the south side of York river, in *York*.
167	Tract bounded east by Small Point harbor, bought of the Indians; tract bounded north by Robert Edmund's land, running thence to Lookout hill, fronting a quarter of a mile Atkins' bay; tract called Small Point neck; also a right of dower to land formerly possessed by John Drake, in *Casco Bay*.
30	2 acres northeast side of Hull's creek, in *York*.
15	15 acres on New Mill creek, in *York*.
46	A tract of upland and 10 acres of marsh at the Three Mile brook, in *Wells*.
119	300 acres, with 10 acres of marsh, town grant, in *Wells*.
8	120 acres on northeast side of Saco river, also all his right in Bonighton's or Indian island, in *Saco*.
254	To measure and deliver 120 acres northeast of Saco river, to Capt. Peter Weare, in *Saco*.
88	Tract of upland and marsh, with buildings, at Winter Harbor [now Biddeford].
36	20 acres on the southwest side of York river; also 20 acres formerly John Pierce's, in *York*.

Index of Grantors.

Date.	Grantor.	Grantee.	Instrument.
1715, May 13	Bracket, Samuel et ux.	Richard Toziar	Deed
1714, Jan. 7	Bradstreet, John	Mary Spencer	Mortgage
1710, Dec. 12	Bragdon, Arthur	Peter Nowell	Deed
1711, May 10	Bragdon, Arthur et ux.	Alexander Junkins	Deed
1714, Nov. 16	Bragdon, Joseph	John Woodbridge	Deed and Receipt
	Bragdon, Samuel, see John Harmon		
1689, Oct. 19	Brand, John	Mary Pulman	Deed
1714, Mar. 20	Brawn, George et ux.	George Brawn, senior, et ux.	Deed
1716, Sept. 19	Brookin, Henry	Peter Nowell	Deed
1716, Sept. 14	Brown, Samuel	Samuel Harmon	Deed
1717, May 16	Buckling, George et ux.	James Wiggin	Deed
1694, June 15	Burnum, John, junior	Hugh Pike	Deed
1714, Jan. 4	Burrell, John et ux.	Samuel Came	Deed
1713, July 29	Calef, Jeremiah et ux.	James Chadbourne	Deed
1712, Dec. 10	Came, Samuel	Robert Oliver	Deed
1714, Apr. 21	Chadbourne, James et ux.	Charles Frost	Deed

Folio.	Description.
93	20 acres, part of a town grant to Isaac Botts, in *Berwick*.
75	1½ acres, bounded northwest by the Great Works river, with shop and appurtenances, in *Berwick*.
33	37 acres near Bell marsh, in *York*.
191	2 acres of marsh, bounded west by the river, northwest by said Junkins' land, east by Lieutenant Banks' land, in *York*.
114	20 acre town grant, in *York*.
172	So much land as the ware-house stands on, and 3 feet more, on York river, adjoining said Brand's orchard, in *York*.
147	Land on the lower side of way that leads from Sturgeon creek to John Tidy's, in *Kittery*.
182	30 acres on northwest side of Bell Marsh brook, in *York*.
212	A farm of 100 acres, with dwellinghouse; also 50 acres, both town grants to Nathaniel Masters; 5 acres of marsh bounded by land of Joseph Littlefields, Mr. Wells and Webhannet river; also an island thatch on the river, and 10 acres known as Master's meadow, in *Wells*.
213	A tract, town grant to John Clayce. at Orgunquit; also a marsh given by Thomas Mills to John Clayce; likewise all right to any land he may have through his wife, in *Wells*.
264	300 acres, part of a tract purchased with others of Harlakinden Symonds, in *Coxhall* [now Lyman].
65	Marsh and thatch banks on the southeast side of Bass cove, in *York*.
47	Two tracts of land near Sturgeon creek, in *Kittery*.
18	20 acres on the northwest branch of York river, in *York*.
71	3 acres, part of said Chadbourne's farm, in *Kittery*.

Index of Grantors.

Date.	Grantor.	Grantee.	Instrument.
1686, May 17	CHAMPERNOWN, Francis et ux.	John Billin	Deed
1714, Mar. 27	CHAPMAN, John et ux.	Abraham Morrell	Deed
	CHICK, Richard, see John Morrell		
1715, Sept. 1	CHILD, William et ux.	Bial Hambleton	Deed
1716, May 3	CLARK, Anne	Elizabeth Davis	Release
1715, May 4	CLARK, Nathaniel et ux.	Nathaniel Clark, junior	Deed
1668, Aug. 10	CLARK, Thomas, and Thomas Lake	Children of Alexander Thoyts	Deed
1701, Mar. 14	CLARK, Thomas, estate of, by Elisha Hutchinson and Elizabeth Hutchinson, executrix	Nathaniel Harris	Deed
1650, Feb. 24	CLEVE [Cleaves] George	Michael Mitten	Deed
1685, Aug. 14	CLOICE, Thomas et ux.	Richard Seacomb	Deed
	COCKS, James, see Anne Spiller		
1715, June 23	COFFIN, James	His daughters	Assignm'nt
1712, Aug. 26	COLE, Jacob, by Edward Bromfield, attorney	Ichabod Plaisted	Deed
1711, Mar. 27	COLE, John	Francis Allen	Deed
1712, Sept. 6	COLE, John	Nath'l Ramsdell	Deed

Index of Grantors.

Folio.	Description.
17	20 acres northwest of Champernown's Island, in *Kittery*.
25	22½ acres, at the east end of Samuel Hill's home-lot, in *Kittery*.
154	2 acres and 4 poles, bounded northwest by road to Humphrey's pond, south by land formerly called Broughton's, on other sides by said Child's land, in *Berwick*.
170	All her right and title to Thomas Atkins' estate.
252	A tract bounded by Thomas Wells', Nicholas Cole's, Lewis Allen's land and Little river; 2 acres of marsh adjoining Thomas Wells' on Little river; also a town grant of 105 acres, in *Wells*.
159	A certain tract on the west side of Kennebec river, against *Kitts island*.
95	132 acres bounded by Alexander Maxwell's and Micum Mackentire's land, also by York river, in *York*.
245	A tract granted him by Alexander Rigby, together with houses, buildings, cattle and household utensils, in *Casco bay*.
164	All his right in a farm belonging formerly to George Lewis, in *Falmouth*.
122	His interest in patent of Cape Neddick, in *York*.
262	One-sixth in common of lands, fall and mills at Quamphegan falls, in *Berwick*.
5	30 acre town grant by and in *Kittery*.
14	Town grant of 30 acres, in *York*.

Index of Grantors.

Date.	Grantor.	Grantee.	Instrument.
	COOPER, John, see Martha Lord		
1673, ——	CORBET, Abraham	Francis Small	Levy on Execution
1698, Oct. 20	CORBIN, James	John Rogers	Deed
1712, Apr. 15	COUCH, Joseph	John Tompson	Deed
1714, Oct. 28	COUCH, Roger	John Tompson	Confirmation
1679, Apr. 4	COUSINS, John	Mary Saywood	Deed
1714, Jan. 24	CROADE, John et ux.	Nathan Lord, sr.	Deed
1714, June 17	CROADE, John	Joseph Wood	Deed
1715, Apr. 13	CROADE, John	Joseph Boynton	Mortgage
1715, Dec. 12	CROADE, John	Joseph Boynton	Deed
1713, —— 26	CROCKET, Richard et ux.	Henry Barter	Deed
	CROCKET, Thomas, estate of, by Anne Jeffry, administratrix	William Roberts et ux.	Deed
1713, Dec. 12	CURTIS, Dodevah	Benj. Berry and Withers Berry	Deed
171⁶⁄₉, Mar. 13	CURTIS, Job	Bethiah Mastin	Deed
1717, Apr. 30	CURTIS, Job et ux.	Lewis Bane and Job Banks	Deed

Index of Grantors. 13

Folio.	Description.
151	202 acres along the Piscataqua river, in *Kittery*.
162	100 acres, with dwelling-house, in *Casco bay*.
144	11 acres, part of a town grant, by and in *Kittery*.
144	Of the above deed.
233	300 acres near a tract formerly in possession of William Ryall, in Casco; also one-half of Cousin's (Hog island), in *Casco bay*.
73	27 acres, part of 50 acres bequeathed Moses Spencer by William Spencer, in *Berwick*.
94	4 acres foot of Rocky hill, in *Berwick*.
87	Dwelling-house; all his right in saw-mill on Worster's river; 3 acres on east end of Cock's pond; also all his interest on north side of said pond, all in *Berwick*.
131	The deed or mortgage recorded in folio 87.
62	40 acres, bounded west by Spruce creek, north by Tucker's creek and known as Crockett's neck, in *Kittery*.
145	Tract called Crockett's neck, also 6 acres adjoining home-lot, in *Kittery*.
22	Land, house and saw-mill, purchased of Sarah Shapleigh and Nicholas Shapleigh, in *Kittery*.
223	His home place between Caleb Preble's and Joseph Banks' land, together with dwelling-house and barn; likewise 30 acres at the head of his home place and Daniel Simpson's land; 3 acres of marsh on the west side of southwest branch of York river; also 2 cows, 6 sheep, or their equivalent, in *York*.
210	50 acres, one-quarter of mill and stream at Scituate plains, in *York*.

Index of Grantors.

Date.	Grantor.	Grantee.	Instrument.
	Cutt, John, see John Leighton		
1690, Dec. 20	Danforth, Thomas	Francis Foxcroft	Deed
1716, Apr. 2	Davis, Elizabeth, and Hester Pike Thomas Washburn et ux. James Berry et ux. Ruth Haskins Sarah Gurney	John Wentworth and Thomas Hutchinson Adam Winthrop David Jeffries Oliver Noyes Stephen Minot John Ruck John Watts	Deed and Receipt
	Davis, John jr., see John Davis senior		
1675, Jan. 10	Davis, John senior, and John Davis junior	William Palmer	Deed
1716, Sept. 13	Davis, Sylvanus, estate of, by John Nelson, executor	Thomas Hutchinson and John Wentworth Adam Winthrop David Jeffries Oliver Noyes Stephen Minot John Ruck John Watts	Deed
171⅔, Feb. 6	Dearing, Joseph et ux.	Andrew Pepperrell	Deed
1711, Apr. 4	Dearing, Roger	Richard Mitchell	Assignm'nt of Mortgage
17¾, Feb. 5	Dearing, Roger	Roger Couch	Deed
171¾, Mar. 10	Dearing, Roger	William Racklift et ux.	Deed
1717, Mar. 30	Dennet, John	James Fernald	Assignm'nt

INDEX OF GRANTORS. 15

Folio.	Description.
240	All of Sebascodegan island, except 1000 acres, in *Casco bay*.
169	Eight-tenths of a tract between the Kennebec river and Casco bay, formerly possessed by their father, Thomas Atkins, deceased.
198	One-half of a neck of land called Batson's neck ; also one-half of marsh and lot adjoining, called the Grass plot, together with other lands and dwelling-house, in *Cape Porpoise*.
176	A tract on the west side of Kennebec river, called Small Point ; 15 acres east side of Casco bay, called Davis' harbor ; 10 acres at Small Point harbor ; also Great Stage island, on east side of the mouth of the Kennebec river ; 200 acres on east side of Kennebec river, purchased from the Indians ; 500 acres near Oyster river, in Damariscotta river ; also a tract east of Masconks, purchased of the Indians, together with buildings, fences, etc.
196	10½ acres near Spruce creek, in *Kittery*.
45	Houses and lands in Kittery, recorded in folio 45.
19	3 acres, with houses and barns, also 1 acre of marsh at Brave-boat harbor, in *Kittery*.
257	¾ of an acre at Kittery point, in *Kittery*.
228	Of mortgage recorded in folio 227.

Index of Grantors.

Date.	Grantor.	Grantee.	Instrument.
1723, Mar. 30	DENNET, John	Samuel Spinney	Discharge
1698, Jan. 15	DERING, Henry	Roger Dearing	Mortgage
1708, Apr. 1	DILL, Daniel et ux.	Alexander Junkins	Deed
	DIXEY, William, see Samuel Maverick		
1685, Jan. 2	DONNEL, Henry	John Stover	Deed
1716, Sept. 19	DONNELL, Samuel et ux.	Peter Nowell	Deed
	DOROTHY, John, see Anne Spiller		
1716, Apr. 5	DOWNING, Jonathan et ux., and Mary Nelson	John Lydston	Deed
1717, Apr. 16	DOWNING, Joshua et ux., and Samuel Hill William Fry	Each other	Division
1714, Nov. 17	DOWNING, Joshua et ux.	James Fernald	Deed
1713, June 9	DUMMER, Jeremiah	Abraham Preble, junior	Deed and Receipt
1688, Aug. 3	ELLACOT, Vines	William Stoughton	Lease and Agreement to convey
1688, Aug. 3	ELLACOT, Vines	William Stoughton	Deed
1712, Mar. 4	ELLIOT, Robert	Samuel Penhallow	Assignmn't
1713, Dec. 4	ELLIOT, Robert	Benjamin Hilton	Deed
1713, Feb. 18	ELLIOT, Robert	Hannah Cole	Deed
171¾, Mar. 12	EMERY, Daniel	Job Emery	Deed

Index of Grantors.

Folio.	Description.
170	Of mortgage recorded in folio 170.
45	Houses and land, in *Kittery*.
192	37 acres above Scotland garrison, in *York*.
1	A parcel of land at the Long sands; also all the Barberry marsh, on east side of the great island in said marsh, in *York*.
181	82 acres on northwest branch of York river, in *York*.
147	30 acres, bounded south by said Lydston's land, north by Joseph Hill's land, west by the river, east by Richard King's land, in *Kittery*.
263	Of tract on north side of Mr. Shapleigh's land, in *Kittery*.
59	40 acre town grant, by and in *Kittery*.
3	14 acres at a place called the Ridge of land; 2 acres of swamp near Paimer's cove, in *York*.
218	Hog island, formerly Cousin's island, with buildings, barns, etc., in North Yarmouth, *Casco bay*.
217	Same as above.
1	Of mortgage recorded in Book VI, 165.
39	26 acres on southwest side of York river, in *York*.
40	26 acres on southwest side of York river, in *York*.
265	20 acres, bounded by commons, Rocky hill and land of Moses Goodwin, James Emery and Nathan Lord, in *Kittery*.

Index of Grantors.

Date.	Grantor.	Grantee.	Instrument.
	EMERY. Daniel, see James Emery		
17$\frac{13}{14}$, Mar. 12	EMERY, James, and Daniel Emery	John Morrell, jr.	Deed
1713, Apr. 21	EMERY, James	Bial Hambleton	Deed
1714, Oct. 14	EMERY, James	James Emery, jr.	Deed
1717, May 23	EMERY, James	William Dyer	Deed
17$\frac{13}{14}$, Mar. 12	EMERY, Job	Daniel Emery	Deed
1716, Dec. 15	EPPS, Daniel	Symond Epps	Power of Attorney
1717, Aug. 5	EPPS [Epes], Symond et ux.	Nathaniel Clark, junior	Deed
———	FALMOUTH, Proprs. of	Richard Seacomb	Grant
1710, Jan. 15	FENNICK, John et ux.	Hezekiah Elwell et ux.	Deed
1714, Aug. 2	FENNICK, John	Charles Frost	Deed
1714, Mar. 7	FENNIX, George	Samuel Hutchins	Deed
1711, Dec. 7	FERNALD, James	Nicholas Morrell	Deed
1730, Feb. 4	FERNALD, James	Daniel Paul	Discharge
1708, Feb. 14	FERRIS, Aaron et ux.	Thomas Huff	Deed

Folio.	Description.
23	Quitclaim to 200 acres on south side of Sturgeon creek, in *Kittery*.
36	One-third of 18 acres part of a 40 acre town grant to William Grant, in [*Berwick*] *Kittery*.
231	4½ acres of marsh, bounded northeast by river, southwest by Pendleton Fletcher's marsh, southeast by Rebecca Hitchcock's marsh, northwest by woodlands; 8½ acres of marsh on Saco side in middle part of said marsh; also one-third of 174 acres of woodland, beginning at the sea, in Winter Harbor [now Biddeford]; also 5 acres, part of Mr. Hitchcock's house-lot; also a third part more of Rebecca Hitchcock's right in marsh.
231	One half of land bought of his father, James Emery, senior, in *Winter Harbor* [now Biddeford].
52	100 acres near York pond, reserving 20 acres, in *Kittery*.
227	To sell land beyond Piscataqua river.
252	One-half of farm, formerly William Symonds', deceased, in *Wells*.
166	An island northwest from Jewell's island, called Hog island, in *Casco bay*.
264	12 acres on west side of Spruce creek, at the head of Broad cove, in *Kittery*.
71	All his part in common and undivided lands, in *Berwick* and *Kittery*.
180	10 acres, town grant to William Lewis, in *Kittery*.
94	20 acres part of a town grant, in *Kittery*.
227	Of the mortgage recorded folio 227.
12	Land and buildings at Spruce creek; also quarter part of a sloop, in *Kittery*.

Date.	Grantor.	Grantee.	Instrument.
1661, Mar. 30	FLUELLIN, Indian	William Phillips	Deed
1712, Sept. 29	FOLLET, John	Diamond Sargent	Deed
	FOLLET, Nicholas, see Mary Blagdon		
	FOWLER, Philip, see Joseph Jacob		
1714, Nov. 10	FREEMAN, Nathaniel	John Woodbridge	Deed
1710, May 23	FRINK, John et ux.	William Briar	Deed
1715, Mar. 14	FRINK, John	Charles Frost	Deed
171$\frac{2}{3}$, Feb. 16	FROST, Charles	Peter Nowell	Receipt
1717, May 10	FROST, Charles et ux.	William Moodey	Deed
1717, June 12	FROST, Charles	John Gowen	Discharge
	FROST, Charles, see John Leighton		
	FROST, Charles, see Josiah Maine		
170$\frac{3}{8}$, Jan. 28	FROST, John	Richard Chick	Deed
	FROST, John, see John Leighton		
1713, June 20	FROST, Nicholas et ux.	Samuel Skillin	Deed
1713, Nov. 7	FROST, William	Samuel Emery	Deed
	FROST, William, see Martha Lord		
1717, May 13	FRY, Adrian et ux.	Michael Kenard	Deed

INDEX OF GRANTORS. 21

Folio.	Description.
220	From Saco patent bounds south beyond Cape Porpoise river for breadth, and from the head of Wells and Cape Porpoise township up into the country, except four square miles sold Bush, Sanders and Turbut.
55	50 acre town grant by and in *Kittery*.
113	20 acre town grant by and in *York*.
74	25 acres at Spruce creek, in *Kittery*.
127	All his part in common and undivided lands, in *Kittery* and *Berwick*.
88	For £33:10, judgment of court against Capt. Harmon.
209	370 acres on southwest side of York river, in *York*.
76	Of mortgage recorded in folio 76.
139	2 parcels of marsh on Sturgeon creek, in *Kittery*.
7	One-quarter of a tract on east side of Spruce creek, in *Kittery*.
13	110 acre town grant by and in *Wells*.
216	2 parcels of land, with dwelling house and buildings, bought of Nicholas Morrell, in *Kittery*.

BOOK VIII. 43

Index of Grantors.

Date.	Grantor.	Grantee.	Instrument.
1713, Apr. 4	FRY, William et ux.	Philip Pike	Deed
	FRY, William, see Joshua Downing		
1817, Mar. 15	FULLER, Samuel et ux.	Stephen Harding	Deed
17$\frac{4}{5}$, Feb. 28	GAGE, Edmund et ux.	Ebenezer More	Deed
	GASKINS, Sarah, see Elizabeth Davis		
1638, June 2	GODFREY, Edward	William Hooke	Lease
1638, June 27	GODFREY, Edward	Humphrey Hooke and William Hooke Thomas Hooke Giles Eldredge	Receipt
1711, Aug. 24	GODSOE, William, and Richard Rice	Each other	Deed of Exchange
1716, June 1	GODSOE, William	Francis Pettegrew	Deed
1711, May 21	GOOCH, James et ux.	Joseph Hill	Deed
1717, May 18	GOODWILL, Thomas et ux.	William Pepperrell, junior	Deed
1713, May 20	GOODWIN, Thomas et ux.	Daniel Goodwin	Deed
1638, May 4	GORGES, Sir Ferdinando	Edward Godfrey and Oliver Godfrey Richard Row	Deed
1710, June 10	GOWELL, Richard	Richard Gowell, junior	Deed

Index of Grantors.

Folio.	Description.
136	10 acres, except a burying-place, at the mouth of Sturgeon creek, in *Kittery*.
203	One-half of 600 acres, bounded east by Kennebunk river, west by Pond marsh, north by Bucklin's line, south by the sea, in *Wells*.
84	22 acres of upland and 3 acres of marsh, with dwelling house and barn, northwest side of Brave-boat harbor, in *Kittery*.
121	Lands northwest of Cape Neddick creek, in *York*.
122	For their part of the charge in procuring grant for Cape Neddick, in *York*.
260	One yoke of oxen and several tracts of land, belonging to the estate of Thomas Withers, deceased (except 22 acres), in exchange for 22 acres at Pine Point, fronting Spruce creek, in *Kittery*.
156	¾ of an acre, bounded west by his own land, south by road to York, north by Richard Roger's land, in *Kittery*.
9	One-quarter part part of saw-mill and privilege of stream, on Merryland river, in *Wells*.
220	One-third of a tract bought by Benjamin Blackman of John Bonighton and James Gibbons, in *Saco*.
34	Several parcels of land near Slut's corner, in *Berwick*.
120	1500 acres on northwest side of Cape Neddick creek, in *York*.
200	Dwelling house and all land, except 20 acres, in *Kittery*.

Index of Grantors.

Date.	Grantor.	Grantee.	Instrument.
1710, Dec. 18	GOWELL, Richard	John Tompson	Deed
1714, Sept. 14	GOWELL, Richard	William Gowell	Deed
1714, Sept. 14	GOWELL, Richard, jr.	William Gowell	Confirmation
	GOWELL, Richard, jr., see Moses Worster		
	GOWELL, Richard, see Moses Worster		
1714, June 1	GOWEN, John et ux.	John Frost	Deed
17$\frac{4}{5}$, Feb. 10	GOWEN, John et ux.	Charles Frost	Mortgage
1717, June 15	GOWEN, John et ux.	Thomas Weed	Deed
1715, Nov. 13	GOWEN, Lemuel et ux.	Abraham Morrell and William Tetherly, Samuel Tetherly	Deed
1710, June 1	GRANT, Alexander	Bial Hambleton	Deed
	GRANT, James, see John Stevens		
1717, July 3	GRAY, Robert et ux.	Benj. Webber	Deed
17$\frac{3}{4}$, Mar. 13	GREELY, Thomas et ux.	Timothy Waymouth	Deed
1688, Sept. 12	GREESON, John	John Houghton	Deed
1706, Nov. 5	GUDRIG, Isaac, estate of, by Margaret Adams, administratrix	Philip Carpenter	Deed
1715, Apr. 25	GUNNISON, Elihu	Charles Frost	Deed
	GURNEY, Sarah, see Elizabeth Davis		

Index of Grantors.

Folio.	Description.
144	10 acre town grant, by and in *Kittery*.
143	10 acres, 3 acres purchased of Richard King, 7 acres at northeast end of said Richard Gowell's land, in *Kittery*.
143	Of above deed.
64	50 acre town grant, in *Berwick*.
76	108 acres, the farm where said John Gowen dwells, in *Kittery*.
215	20 acres, bounded north by Nicholas Gowen's land, east by road, south by David Sawyer's land, reserving burying place, in *Kittery*.
141	100 acres purchased of James Gowen; two 30 acre town grants; also 40 acres on west side of Third hill, in *Kittery*.
35	8 acres and 20 rods on Love's brook, in *Berwick*.
225	2 tracts of 66 acres, on southwest side of York river and northwest side of Old Mill creek, in *York*.
25	20 acres near Mast cove; 61 acres bounded by Israel Hodsden's land and commons, in *Kittery*.
165	A tract belonging formerly to his father, Robert Greeson, in *Falmouth*.
43	10 acres between the lands of Nicholas Tucker and Henry Barter, in *Kittery*.
128	His part in the common and undivided ands, in *Kittery* and *Berwick*.

Index of Grantors.

Date.	Grantor.	Grantee.	Instrument.
1714, Aug. 3	Haley, William et ux.	Andrew Haley	Deed
	Ham, Samuel, see Moses Worster		
1709, Oct. 4	Hamilton, Abel et ux.	Roger Plaisted	Deed
1713, May 18	Hamilton, Bial	John Fall	Deed
	Hammond, Joseph, see John Leighton		
17$\frac{12}{13}$, Feb. 13	Hanscom, Job	Thomas Hanscom	Deed
17$\frac{12}{13}$, Feb. 17	Hanscom, Moses	Thomas Hanscom	Deed
	Hanscom, Tobias, see Martha Lord		
1714, Nov. 2	Harmon, John	John Woodbridge	Deed and Receipt
1717, May 6	Harmon, John and Benjamin Stone John Kingsbury Jonathan Young Jonathan Bane Samuel Bragdon Joseph Hoult John Stagpole	William Moodey	Deed
1709, July 23	Harmon, Johnson et ux.	Hezekiah Adams	Deed
1712, Aug. 10	Harmon, Johnson	Samuel Came	Deed
1714, Apr. 27	Harmon, Johnson	Samuel Came	Deed

Folio.	Description.
54	30 acre town grant by and in *Kittery*.
256	7 acres on highway from Salmon Falls brook to John Key's house, in *Kittery* [*Berwick*].
260	5 acres, part of a town grant to Ephraim Joy, in *Kittery* [*Berwick*].
22	All his right and title to houses and lands of his father, Thomas Hanscom, deceased, in *Kittery*.
22	All his right and title to houses and lands of his father, Thomas Hanscom, deceased, in *Kittery*.
114	Two 20 acre town grants, in *York*.
207	A town grant between Thomas Adams' and Thomas Beeson's land, in *York*.
153	10 acres, bounded southwest by town way from Bass creek to Rowland Young's, in *York*.
11	63 acres on northeast side of cove of marsh belonging to the ministry of York, in *York*.
50	50 acres between two branches of York river, at the Partings, in *York*.

Index of Grantors.

Date.	Grantor.	Grantee.	Instrument.
17$\frac{1}{2}$, Jan. 15	HARMON, Johnson	Peter Nowell	Mortgage
1697, June 8	HARRIS, John	Jonathan Woodman	Deed
1714, Mar. 2	HARRIS, Nathaniel	John Prichard	Deed
1715, May 10	HARRIS, Nathaniel	John Prichard	Deed
1715, May 10	HARRIS, Nathaniel	John Prichard	Deed
1715, May 12	HARRIS, Nathaniel	John Prichard	Deed
1716, Apr. 25	HASKINS, John	Ruth Haskins	Release
	HASKINS, Ruth, see Elizabeth Davis		
1698, Sept. 23	HAUGHTON, John et ux.	John Rogers	Deed
	HAYNES, Thomas, see Job Young		
17$\frac{9}{10}$, Mar. 2	HEARD, John, and Nicholas Morrell	Each other	Deed of Exchange
1711, Dec. 17	HEARD, John	Nicholas Morrell	Deed
17$\frac{3}{4}$, Feb. 27	HEARD, John et ux.	Nathan Bartlet	Deed
17$\frac{1}{2}$, Jan. 9	HEARD, John et ux.	John Morrell, jr.	Deed
	HILL, John, see John Plaisted		
1709, Sept. 21	HILL, Samuel	John Frink	Deed
1717, Aug. 24	HILL, Samuel	Andrew Brown	Deed

Index of Grantors.

Folio.	Description.
91	8 acres of marsh; 10 or 12 acres of upland between two branches of York river, in *York*.
99	200 acres bought of Harlakinden Symonds, in *Coxhall* [now Lyman].
97	50 acres, part of a tract bought of Harlikinden Symonds, in *Coxhall* [now Lyman].
97	132 acres, bounded by Alexander Maxwell's, Micum Mackentire's land and York river; also a tract with buildings, bought of Samuel Webber, in *York*.
98	35 acres bought of Eliakim Hutchinson, in *York*.
98	20 acres bought of Samuel Webber, in *York*.
170	His right and interest in Thomas Atkins' estate.
162	90 acres, bounded east by Presumpscot river, south by a brook, west by land of John Brown, north by land of Robert Nichols, in *Falmouth*.
82	A tract beginning at the highway from Sturgeon creek bridge to the cedars joining Nicholas Frost's land; in exchange for a tract bounded northwest by road from Sturgeon creek bridge to Newichewannock, in *Kittery*.
79	30 acres granted his grandfather, John Heard, by town of *Kittery*.
47	2 lots out of his homestead land, in *Kittery*.
229	20 acres east of Sturgeon creek, in *Kittery*.
74	50 acres at Spruce creek in *Kittery*.
266	100 acres at *Cape Porpoise*.

Index of Grantors.

Date.	Grantor.	Grantee.	Instrument.
	Hill, Samuel, see Jonathan Littlefield		
	Hill, Samuel, see Joshua Downing		
1717, July 20	Hill, Samuel, junior	John Lydston	Confirmation
1698, Dec. 23	Hoar, Thomas	Richard Gowell	Bond
1717, Feb. 17	Hodsden, Samuel	Timothy Waymouth	Discharge
	Holman, Hannah, see Samuel Holman		
1716, May 22	Holman, Samuel, and Hannah Holman	John Wentworth and Thomas Hutchinson Adam Winthrop David Jeffries Oliver Noyes Stephen Minot John Ruck John Watts	Deed
1660, Aug. 29	Hombinowitt, alias John Rogomock	William Phillips	Deed
1717, Aug. 28	Hook, Humphrey, and Jacob Hook	William Hook	Deed
	Hook, Jacob, see Humphrey Hook		
1693, Feb. 2	Hook, William	James Coffin	Assignment
1717, May 1	Hook, William	Humphrey Hook and Jacob Hook	Deed
1717, Aug. 28	Hook, William, junior	William Hook	Deed

Folio.	Description.
236	Of deed recorded in folio 147.
146	To secure payment of £40.
202	Of the mortgage recorded folio 202.
167	Their interest in a tract of land on west side of Kennebec river; also two islands in said river.
220	All his lands west of the Saco river from Salmon Falls to Capt. Sunday's rocks, and twenty miles up into the country.
232	All their right in lands by a deed from their father, said William Hook, in *York*.
122	His interest in patent at Cape Neddick, in *York*.
206	500 acres, one-half of Hook's farm, on north side of York river, at Scotland, 250 acres on the seaside; also that tract called Cape Neddick, granted his father, William Hook, deceased; and 1000 acres more out of the grants and patents to his father, William Hook, in *York*.
232	All his right to lands by a deed from his father, said William Hook, in *York*.

Index of Grantors.

Date.	Grantor.	Grantee.	Instrument.
	Hoult, Joseph, see John Harmon		
1651, Feb. 17	Howell, Rice	Abraham Preble	Deed
1716, Jan. 28	Hubord, Elizabeth, and Philip Hubord	Joseph Hodsden & John Hooper	Deed
	Hubord, Philip, see Elizabeth Hubord		
17$\frac{14}{15}$, Mar. 10	Huff, Thomas	William Pepperrell, junior	Deed
1716, Dec. 15	Huff, Thomas	Samuel Penhallow	Mortgage
1717, Mar. 27	Huff, Thomas	Henry Barter	Deed
17$\frac{11}{12}$, Mar. 8	Hughs, Clement	John Tompson	Release
171$\frac{6}{7}$, Jan. 21	Hunking, Mary, and Mary Hunking, jr.	Nathaniel Fernald	Deed
	Hunking, Mary, junior, see Mary Hunking		
17$\frac{13}{14}$, Jan. 11	Hutchins, Jonathan	Benjamin Hutchins	Deed
1714, June 29	Hutchins, Samuel	Benjamin Hutchins	Deed
1703, Apr. 24	Hutchinson, Eliakim et ux.	Nathaniel Harris	Deed
1707, July 8	Hutchinson, Eliakim	James Plaisted	Assignment
1716, Sept. 4	Hutchinson, Thomas, and John Wentworth Adam Winthrop David Jeffries Oilver Noyes, John Watts, Stephen Minot John Ruck	Each other	Agreement

Folio.	Description.
203	12 acres on south side of Gorgeana (York) river, in *York*.
200	Land and buildings bought of Timothy Waymouth, in *Berwick*.
80	18 acres between Henry Barter's and Joseph Crocket's lands, in *Kittery*.
81	All his interest in lands, houses and stock conveyed to him by Aaron Ferris, in *Kittery*.
219	18½ acres between Henry Barter's and Joseph Crocket's lands, in *Kittery*.
144	Relating to estate of John Tompson, deceased, in *Kittery*.
157	40 acre town grant, by and in *Kittery*.
49	All his right in land near the head of Eastern creek, in *Kittery*.
49	Same as above.
96	25 acres, on which stood the late Edward Rishworth's house; also 10 acres at Burnt Plain, in *York*.
66	Land and cattle, in *York*.
178	That considerable part of their purchase of lands be assigned to each partner.

Date.	Grantor.	Grantee.	Instrument.
1716, Sept. 10	HUTCHINSON, Thomas, and John Wentworth David Jeffries Oliver Noyes Stephen Minot John Ruck John Watts	Adam Winthrop	Deed
1714, May 20	INGERSOL, Elisha	John Chapman	Deed
1715, Mar. 14	INGERSOL, John	Elisha Ingersol and John Chapman	Deed
1715, Mar. 14	INGERSOL, John	Charles Frost	Deed
1715, May 19	INGERSOL, John	Nathaniel Ingersol	Deed
	JACKSON, Martha, see Ezra Rolfe		
1717, July 17	JACOB, Joseph, and Philip Fowler et ux.	Symond Epps	Deed
	JEFFRIES, David, see Thomas Hutchinson		
	JENKINS, Reinold, see Francis Allen		
1703, June 2	JENKINS, Stephen, and Anne Kincaid	Reinold Jenkins	Deed
1658, July 28	JORDAN, Robert, and John Phillips	Each other	Conditional Release
1714, Apr. 5	JOY, Ephraim et ux.	Roger Plaisted	Deed
	KEAIS, Samuel, see Samuel Penhallow		
1715, Apr. 11	KELLEY, Elisha et ux.	John Ellis	Mortgage
1717, June 21	KELLEY, Elisha et ux.	Stephen Minot	Mortgage

INDEX OF GRANTORS.   35

Folio.	Description.
178	Swan island, in *Merrymeeting bay*.
46	31½ acres on east side of Spruce creek, in *Kittery*.
79	All his land, except a parcel bought of George Montjoy, in *Falmouth*.
128	All his part in common and undivided lands, in *Berwick* and *Kittery*.
94	36 acres on east side of Spruce creek, in *Kittery*.
226	One-quarter of farm, formerly William Symond's, deceased, in *Wells*.
6	14 acres at Cold Harbor, in *Kittery*.
244	Relating to lands, cattle, chattels; also saw-mill to be erected at Casco River falls.
256	7½ acres, part of a town grant, in *Kittery*.
111	Land and dwelling-house at Crooked lane, in *Kittery*.
224	3 acres on Smutty-nose island; 6 acres on Starr island, with buildings, etc., Isles of Shoals; also all his right in Hog island, *Casco bay*.

INDEX OF GRANTORS.

Date.	Grantor.	Grantee.	Instrument.
	KENE, Nathaniel, see Samuel Spinney		
	KINCAID, Anne, see Stephen Jenkins		
	KINGSBURY, John, see John Harmon		
1699, May 24	KITTERY, Town of	James Fernald	Grant
1699, May 24	KITTERY, Town of	Richard Gowell	Grant
1703, May 10	KITTERY, Town of	John Follet	Grant
1703, May 10	KITTERY, Town of	Joseph Couch	Grant
	LAKE, Thomas, see Thomas Clark		
1713, Nov. 23	LEIGHTON, John, and Charles Frost Robert Cutt Joseph Hammond John Frost	Each other	Division Deed
1715, May 23	LEWIS, Andrew	John Frost	Deed
1686, Aug. 30	LEWIS, Jotham et ux.	Richard Seacomb	Deed
1713, June 2	LEWIS, Peter	Andrew Lewis	Deed
1705, Jan. 19	LIBBEY, John	Daniel Libbey	Deed
1713, Nov. 1	LIBBEY, John, senior	John Libbey	Deed
1714, Sept. 18	LINSCOT, John	Peter Nowell	Deed
1716, Apr. 13	LINSCOT, John	Samuel Came	Deed

Folio.	Description.
94	30 acres, to be clear of other grants.
144	10 acres, to be clear of other grants.
55	50 acres of land.
144	50 acres, to be clear of other grants.
20	30 acres on Piscataqua river; 5 acres on Sturgeon creek; 34½ acres northeast from the head of Major Clark's and Joshua Downing's land; 30 acres near the highway from Sturgeon creek to Spruce creek; 60 acres bounded by land of John Frost, Robert Knight and Katherine Leighton, in *Kittery*.
196	All his portion in common and undivided lands, in *Berwick* and *Kittery*.
165	30 acres, part of that land belonging to George Lewis, deceased, in *Casco bay*.
179	1½ acres and 28 poles at the head of land formerly Mr. Wither's, in *Kittery*.
205	50 acres, bought of Joshua Scottow; 6 acres of marsh on Black Point river; 50 acres and 10 acres, two town grants; together with any right to other lands, reserving lands which belonged to his father, John Libbey, deceased, in *Scarborough*.
13	A tract, farm and marsh, at Black Point, *Scarborough*.
107	31½ acres at Birch hill, in *York*.
190	40 acres between the Partings of York river, *York*.

Index of Grantors.

Date.	Grantor.	Grantee.	Instrument.
1701, Aug. 7	LITTLEFIELD, Dan'l et ux.	Daniel Junkins	Deed
1715, June 20	LITTLEFIELD, Eliab	George Jacobs	Deed
1715, Dec. 26	LITTLEFIELD, Eliab	Thomas Perkins, junior	Deed
1689, Oct. 30	LITTLEFIELD, Francis	Nathaniel Rust, senior	Deed
1689, Oct. 30	LITTLEFIELD, Francis	Nathaniel Rust, senior	Deed
1713, May 4	LITTLEFIELD, Jonathan, and Samuel Hill	David Littlefield	Deed
	LITTLEFIELD, Moses, see Martha Lord		
1716, Dec. 10	LITTLEFIELD, Sam'l et ux.	David Littlefield	Deed
1716, Dec. 10	LITTLEFIELD, Sam'l et ux.	Francis Sawyer	Deed
1717, May 20	LITTLEFIELD, Sam'l et ux.	Stephen Harding	Deed
	LORD, Benjamin, see Martha Lord		
170$\frac{4}{5}$, Mar. 22	LORD, Martha, and Nathan Lord Benjamin Lord John Cooper Tobias Hanson William Frost Moses Littlefield	William Lord	Deed
1712, Aug. 11	LORD, Martha, and Benjamin Lord	Richard Lord	Deed
	LORD, Nathan, see Martha Lord		
17$\frac{19}{20}$, Mar. 21	MACKENTIER, Daniel	Alexander Junkins and Joseph Junkins	Deed

Index of Grantors. 39

Folio.	Description.
39	2 acres of marsh on southwest branch of York river, in *York*.
153	6 acres, formerly John Littlefield's, deceased, in *Wells*.
180	200 acres northeast side of Cape Porpoise river, in *Cape Porpoise*.
176	200 acres, called Tatnack; also 6 acres of meadow, in *Wells*.
176	100 acres adjoining his own lot, in *Wells*.
250	200 acres on northeast side of Daniel Sawyer's land; also a parcel of land between said land and Cross' brook, in *Wells*.
251	One-quarter part of falls, at *Kennebunk*.
237	One-quarter part of Kennebunk falls and 30 acres; also 5 acres of marsh bounded by Mousam river and Clay hill, in *Wells*.
211	30 acres, town grant to Anthony and Francis Littlefield, in *Wells*.
54	40 acres, with house and barn, adjoining said William Lord's land; also cattle and goods, in *Kittery*.
117	5 acres near White's marsh, in *Berwick*.
194	20 acres near the land of Daniel Livingstone, deceased, at the head of Bass Cove brook, in *York*.

Date.	Grantor.	Grantee.	Instrument.
1713, Mar. 16	MACKENTIER, Daniel	John Mackentier	Deed
1715, June 27	MACKENTIER, Daniel, and Micum Mackentier	John Newmarch	Deed
1716, Dec. 17	MACKENTIER, Daniel	Alexander Junkins	Deed
1714, May 24	MACKENTIER, John	Micum Mackentier	Deed
	MACKENTIER, Micum, see Daniel Mackentier		
1715, Feb. 28	MAINE, Josiah, and Charles Frost	Each other	Deed of Exchange
1685, May 26	MASSACHUSETTS, Gov. and Company of	Thomas Danforth and Samuel Nowell	Deed
1715, Sept. 7	MASTERS, Nathaniel, estate of, by Nathaniel Masters, administrator	Samuel Brown	Deed
1636, Jan. 13	MAVERICK, Samuel, and William Dixey	Each other	Agreement for Sale
1664, June 22	MEEKSOMBE, alias Capt. Sunday, Indian	William Phillips	Deed
1713, Apr. 14	MENDUM, Jonathan et ux.	Samuel Skillin	Deed
1713, Apr. 13	MENDUM, Nathaniel et ux.	Samuel Skillin	Deed
1715, June 13	MERRYFIELD, William et ux.	Thomas Cole	Deed
	MINOT, Stephen, see Thomas Hutchinson		
1660, Aug. 25	MITTON, Michael et ux.	Robert Jordan	Deed

Index of Grantors.

Folio.	Description.
38	17 acres on west side of York river, in *York*.
104	30 acres on southwest side of southwest branch of York river, in *York*.
195	5 acres, a mile from Bell marsh and adjoining Micum Mackentier's marsh, in *York*.
89	40 acres, except 3 acres, on southwest side of York river, in *York*.
129	A parcel of land adjoining said Micum's land, in exchange for 1 acre at the northeast corner of land formerly Edward Rishworth's, in *York*.
242	Sebascodegan island, in *Casco bay*.
109	Farm of 100 acres on Ogunquit side; also 50 acre town grant; 8 acres of marsh near harbor's mouth; also an island of thatch and 10 acres, called Master's meadow, in *Wells*.
209	For house and land.
221	A tract above Saco falls, about 35 or 40 miles up into the country.
28	One-half of a tract on Spruce creek, in *Kittery*.
6	One-quarter of a tract on east side of Spruce creek, in *Kittery*.
124	One-sixth of marsh at Newichewannock, in *Berwick*.
245	All lands granted him by George Cleve, or any other person, in *Falmouth*.

Index of Grantors.

Date.	Grantor.	Grantee.	Instrument.
1716, Dec. 14	Moorey, Nicholas	James Tyler	Deed
1716, Dec. 14	Moorey, Nicholas	James Tyler	Bond
17$\frac{19}{20}$, Feb. 25	More, Ebenezer, and John Norton	Henry Barter	Mortgage
171$\frac{4}{5}$, Feb. 12	Morrell, Abraham et ux.	Nicholas Harford	Deed
1715, Jan. 20	Morrell, Abraham, and William Tetherly Samuel Tetherly	Each other	Division
1717, Sept. 25	Morrell, Abraham et ux.	David Sawyer	Deed
1710, June 19	Morrell, John, junior	John Tidy	Deed
1715, Sept. 27	Morrell, John, and Richard Chick	Each other	Arbitration and Award
1717, Aug. 30	Morrell, John	Nicholas Morrell	Deed
171$\frac{4}{5}$, Mar. 7	Morrell, Nicholas et ux.	James Davis	Deed
17$\frac{14}{15}$, Mar. 10	Morrell, Nicholas et ux.	Nathan Bartlett	Deed
1717, Apr. 16	Morrell, Nicholas	Adrian Fry	Deed
1717, Aug. 13	Morrell, Nicholas	John Morrell	Bond
	Morrell, Nicholas, see John Heard		
1715, Feb. 22	Moulton, Daniel	Jeremiah Moulton	Deed

Index of Grantors. 43

Folio.	Description.
201	One-half of land and rights which said Moorey claims; also 50 acres bought of Samuel Snow, in *Cape Porpoise*.
202	To warrant above premises.
228	27¾ acres and 26 poles between Nicholas Tucker's land and Crocket's neck, in *Kittery*.
222	5 acres adjoining said Morrell's land on the north, highway on the east, Samuel Morrell's land on the south, Dover river on the west; also 22½ acres at the east end of Samuel Hill's home lot, in *Kittery*.
142	Of land purchased of Lemuel Gowen, in *Kittery*.
258	30 acre town grant to Lemuel Gowen by town of Kittery, in *Berwick*.
107	30 acres on north side of Sturgeon creek, in *Kittery*.
139	Establishing division line between their lands, on north side of Sturgeon creek in *Kittery*.
261	100 acres at Cold harbor, with house, buildings, cattle and implements of husbandry, in *Kittery*.
78	35 acres, part of the land purchased of Richard Estes; also a highway from the river, in *Kittery*.
83	4 acres on north side of Sturgeon creek, in *Kittery*.
216	1 acre, southwest corner of a field in possession of James Davis; also ¾ of an acre; both tracts part of land purchased of Richard Estes, in *Kittery*.
263	Conditioned to pay the produce of 5 acres of tillage land; also one-half the increase, produce and profit of a certain number of cattle.
148	All his right and title to estate, both real and personal, of Joseph Moulton, deceased, in *York*.

Date.	Grantor.	Grantee.	Instrument.
1714, Dec. 17	MOULTON, Jeremiah et ux.	Joseph Moulton	Deed
1675, May 1	MUNJOY, George	John Ingersol	Deed
17$\frac{1}{3}$, Feb. 28	NASON, Baker et ux.	John Hooper	Deed
1713, June 25	NASON, Benjamin	Richard Lord	Deed
	NELSON, Mary, see Jonathan Downing		
171$\frac{5}{6}$, Feb. 21	NEWMAN, Abigail	John Wentworth and Thomas Hutchinson Adam Winthrop David Jeffries Oliver Noyes Stephen Minot John Ruck John Watts	Deed
1714, July 6	NORTON, George et ux.	John Woodbridge et ux.	Deed
	NORTON, John, see Ebenezer More		
1714, Sept. 18	NOWELL, Peter et ux.	John Linscot	Deed
1714, Dec. 27	NOWELL, Peter et ux.	Ebenezer Pemberton	Mortgage
1716, Apr. 20	NOWELL, Peter	Alexander Thompson	Discharge
1718, May 23	NOWELL, Peter	Johnson Harmon	Discharge
	NOYES, Oliver, see Thomas Hutchinson		
1692, Sept. 8	OARE, James	Jonathan Corwin	Deed

Index of Grantors.

Folio.	Description.
68	A tract on northwest side New Mill creek, in *York*.
86	A tract at Capisic, in *Falmouth*.
101	6 acres, beginning at the north corner of Benjamin Nason's land, in *Berwick*.
117	2¼ acres on south side of town highway, in *Berwick*.
150	Her part in lands at Small Point neck, formerly possessed by Thomas Webber.
112	Several parcels of land, in *York*.
174	40 acre town grant, between the Partings of York river, in *York*.
66	130 acres, bounded south by York river, at Scotland, in *York*.
6	Of mortgage recorded in folio 67.
91	Of mortgage recorded in folio 91.
151	200 acres, with dwelling-house and barn, at Mousam, in *Wells*.

Index of Grantors.

Date.	Grantor.	Grantee.	Instrument.
1714, Nov. 9	Otis, Job et ux.	William Thomas	Deed
1715, July 7	Otis, Joseph	Joseph Boynton	Deed
1688, Apr. 20	Parker, John et ux.	Thomas Kimble	Deed
17¼, Mar. 15	Parsons, Elihu	Jabez Blackledge	Deed
17¼, Mar. 1	Parsons, John	Elihu Parsons	Deed
1629, May 17	Passaconaway, and Runaawitt Wahangnonawitt Rowles, Indian Sagamores	John Wheelwright Augustine Storer Thomas Wight William Wentworth Thomas Levit	Conditional Deed
1716, Apr. 16	Paul, Daniel	John Dennet	Mortgage
1717, Mar. 30	Paul, Daniel	James Fernald	Deed
	Paul, John, see John Skriggin		
	Paul, John, see John Thompson		
1715, Oct. 6	Pearce, William	Nathan'l Raynes	Mortgage
1715, June 29	Pearse (Pearce), William et ux.	Joseph Harris	Mortgage
1716, Sept. 13	Pemberton, Ebenezer	Peter Nowell	Discharge
1681, June 22	Pendleton, Elinor, and James Pendleton	Pendleton Fletcher	Confirmation
	Pendleton, James, see Elinor Pendleton		
17¼, Mar. 10	Penhallow, Samuel	William Pepperrell, junior	Assignm'nt of Mortgage

Index of Grantors.

Folio.	Description.
106	300 acres bought of Nathaniel and Gilbert Winslow; also 20 or 30 acres more, in *Casco bay.*
100	Dwelling house, in *Berwick.*
24	A tract on Kennebec river.
173	5 acres on southwest side of York river, in *York.*
100	22 acres between Daniel Simpson's and John Preble's land, in *York.*
16	Tract of main land bounded by the Piscataqua river and Merrimac river; also the Isles of Shoals.
227	20 acres on Spinney's creek, in *Kittery.*
204	A tract near Spinney's creek, in *Kittery.*
137	10 acres on southwest side of York river, with buildings and two cows, reserving a way 2 poles wide, in *York.*
105	10 acres on southwest side of York river, in *York.*
175	Of mortgage recorded in folio 67.
88	Of their share in land in deed recorded folio 88.
81	All his right in mortgage from Thomas Huff.

Index of Grantors.

Date.	Grantor.	Grantee.	Instrument.
1716, Aug. 13	PENHALLOW, Samuel, and Samuel Keais	George Jaffrey	Deed
1713, June 6	PEPPERRELL, William	William Pepperrell, junior	Deed
1718, Apr. 2	PEPPERRELL, William	Edward Beal	Discharge
1717, Mar. 26	PEPPERRELL, William, junior	Thomas Huff	Deed
1717, Dec. 2	PEPPERRELL, William, junior	Nathaniel Weare	Deed
1717, Dec. 2	PEPPERRELL, William, junior	Humphrey Scamon, junior	Deed
1717, Dec. 16	PEPPERRELL, William, junior, and Humphrey Scamon, junior, Nathaniel Weare	Each other	Agreement and Division
1717, Oct. 23	PERKINS, Jacob	James Carr	Deed
	PHILLIPS, John, see Robert Jordan		
1664, May 2	PHILLIPS, William et ux.	Bryan Pendleton	Deed
1712, Oct. 17	PICKERIN, John	John Sayward	Deed
1713, Aug. 27	PICKERIN, John	Ebenezer Blasdel and Ralph Farnum	Deed

INDEX OF GRANTORS.

Folio.	Description.
223	One-half of Wither's island, in *Kittery*.
41	60 acre town grant, and 45 acres adjoining the land bought of Joseph Crocket; also a town grant upon the land known as Farmoth, and 30 acres purchased of Edmund Gosse, in Kittery; also a tract purchased of Mary Hooke, and 95 acres north of Richard Mitchell's, in *York*.
69	Of mortgage recorded in folio 69.
219	Refers to deed recorded in folio 81.
258	One-quarter of 6,000 acres, bought of Samuel Walker and Thomas Goodwill; also one-quarter part of timber on 4,500 acres northeast of abovesaid land, in *Saco*.
258	One-quarter of 6,000 acres bought of Samuel Walker and Thomas Goodwill; also one quarter part of timber on 4,500 acres northeast of abovesaid land, in *Saco*.
259	In regard to land and saw-mill, in *Saco*.
247	70 acres, with dwelling-house and barn, on southwest side of Cape Neddick river; also cattle, sheep, swine, horse, hay and corn.
155	A neck of land below Saco river; also Wood island, Gibbon's island, Cow island and a tract called West point on Saco river, in *Saco*.
111	2 acres on north side of Mill creek, in *York*.
116	A parcel of land on southwest side of York river, in *York*.

Index of Grantors.

Date.	Grantor.	Grantee.	Instrument.
	PIKE, Hester, see Elizabeth Davis		
1717, Dec. 24	PITMAN, James	Oliver Noyes	Mortgage
	PLAISTED, Elizabeth, see Olive Wincoll		
	PLAISTED, Ichabod, see Olive Wincoll		
	PLAISTED, James, see Olive Wincoll		
1706, July 3	PLAISTED, James et ux.	Ichabod Plaisted	Deed
1702, Dec. —	PLAISTED, John et ux., and John Hill et ux.	Abraham Lord	Deed
	PLAISTED, John, see Olive Wincoll		
1716, Oct. 8	PLAISTED, Mary, and John Saywood	Each other	Arbitration and Award
	PLAISTED, Mehitable, see Olive Wincoll		
	PLAISTED, William, see Olive Wincoll		
	PRAY, Joseph, see Richard Toziar		
1716, Oct. 23	PREBLE, Abraham	John Saywood	Deed
1710, June 20	PREBLE, Abraham, jr.	Joseph Weare	Deed
1714, May 24	PREBLE, Abraham, jr.	Nath'l Donnell	Deed
1717, Sept. 13	PREBLE, Caleb	James Brown and Joseph Brown	Deed

INDEX OF GRANTORS. 51

Folio.	Description.
265	124 acres at Pemaquid point, in *Jamestown*.
132	All his land belonging to him from the estate of his father, Roger Plaisted, deceased, in *Kittery*.
52	29 acres, part of land purchased of Eliakim Hutchinson, in *Kittery*.
188	In regard to the estate of John Saywood, deceased.
197	One-sixth part of the estate of John Saywood, deceased, both real and personal.
4	2 acres at the head of Burnt plain, in *York*.
90	3 acres near a cove formerly known as Palmer's cove, in *York*.
242	One-quarter of that land belonging formerly to Richard Comins, on east side of Saco river, part of patent to Bonighton and Lewis.

Date.	Grantor.	Grantee.	Instrument.
1717, Aug. 7	PREBLE, Hannah	Jonathan Preble	Deed
17$\frac{13}{14}$, Jan. 12	RAMSDELL, Nathaniel	Peter Nowell	Deed
17$\frac{13}{14}$, Feb. 16	RAMSDELL, Nathaniel	Caleb Preble	Deed
17$\frac{12}{13}$, Jan. 21	RANDOL, Richard	Richard Randol and William Randol	Deed
1715, Apr. 15	RAYNES, Francis	John Woodman	Mortgage
1715, Aug. 2	RAYNES, Francis	Nathan Raynes	Deed
1716, Apr. 14	RAYNES, Francis	Henry Brookin	Deed
1715, July 19	RAYNES, Nathaniel, and John Woodman	Each other	Arbitration and Award
1722, Dec. 27	RAYNES, Nathaniel	William Pearce	Discharge
1710, May 24	READ, Obadiah et ux.	James Boston	Deed
1714, Oct. 25	REED, John	John Wentworth	Deed
1686, Oct. 16	REMICK, Christian	Jacob Remick	Deed
1717, Dec. 18	REMICK, Jacob	Samuel Remick	Deed
1714, Dec. 20	REMICH (Remick), Joshua	John Tompson	Deed
1716, July 21	RICE, Richard	Benjamin Libbey	Deed
	RICE, Richard, see William Godsoe		
1705, Dec. 29	RICE, Thomas, junior	Thomas Rice, sr.	Deed

Index of Grantors. 53

Folio.	Description.
234	Her share in land which her mother, Mary Saywood, bought of John Cousins, in *Casco bay*.
110	One-quarter of one-half of marsh bought of Arthur Bragdon, senior, near Agamenticus hill, in *York*.
115	A parcel of marsh northwest of Agamenticus hill, in *York*.
63	30 acre town grant, in *Kittery*.
103	5 acres at Brave-boat harbor, in *York*.
172	117 acres formerly possessed by his father, Nathaniel Raynes, in *York*.
184	20 acres near John More's and Samuel Winch's bounds, in *York*.
131	Relating to a tract of land at Brave-boat harbor, in York; also certain debts and dues.
138	Of mortgage recorded in folio 137.
221	450 acres bounded by Robert Hilton's, Josiah Storer's lands and highway, in *Wells*.
130	50 acres on Salmon Falls river, in Berwick; also an addition granted by town of *Kittery*.
255	20 acres on east side of cove behind Thomas Spinney's land, in *Kittery*
255	10 acres bounded by John Fernald's, Joshua Remick's and Richard Gowell's land, in *Kittery*.
145	6½ acres, part of a town grant, in *Kittery*.
225	30 acres, part of a town grant, in *Kittery*.
12	10 acres at the southwest end of his 30 acre lot, in *Kittery*.

Index of Grantors.

Date.	Grantor.	Grantee.	Instrument.
1668, Oct. 9	Rishworth, Edward	Richard Hutchinson	Mortgage
1715, Aug. 30	Roberts, William, estate of	William Pepperrell	Levy on Execution
1717, Apr. 11	Robinson, William	John Cookson	Bond and Mortgage
1714, Oct. 29	Rogers, John	Ichabod Plaisted	Deed
1717, Sept. 16	Rogers, William et ux.	Stephen Tobey	Deed
	Rogomock, John, see Hombinowitt		
171$\frac{6}{7}$, Feb. 14	Rolfe, Ezra et ux., and Martha Jackson	James Tyler	Deed
	Ruck, John, see Thomas Hutchinson		
	Runaawitt, see Passaconaway		
1717, Aug. 19	Sargent (Sergent), Diamond et ux.	James Webber	Deed
1707, May 21	Sargent, Edward	Ichabod Plaisted	Deed
171$\frac{4}{5}$, Jan. 6	Savage, Ephraim et ux.	John Butler et ux.	Deed
170$\frac{4}{5}$, Mar. 22	Sawyer, William et ux.	Francis Sawyer	Deed
1712, May 1	Sayward, Hannah	John Sayward	Deed
1717, July 18	Sayward, John	Jonathan Preble	Deed
	Sayward, John, see Mary Plaisted		

INDEX OF GRANTORS.

Folio.	Description.
65	70 acres next Thomas Moulton's and Nathaniel Maysterson's lands; also a meadow on northwest side of Old Mill creek, and two thirds of all his cattle, in *York*.
126	14 acres, with dwelling house, in *Kittery*.
229	One-quarter of a tract between Sheepscot bay and Damariscotta river; also Damariscotta island, with one-quarter part of all adjacent islands; also 100 acres in Georgetown, with house, saw-mill, cattle and horse.
134	3 acres next Salmon Falls mills, in *Berwick*.
246	35 acres near York bounds, in *Kittery*.
249	Meadow and marsh between Black Point river and Saco river.
236	¾ of an acre with house, near Crooked lane, in *Kittery*.
133	180 acres at Salmon Falls, in *Berwick*.
122	1,000 acres at a place called Whigby, on the Kennebec river.
10	A tract of land and one-quarter of saw-mill, in *Wells*.
110	All her right, title and interest in estate of John Saywood, deceased, in *York*.
235	All his right and title to land bought by Mary Saywood of John Cousins, in *Casco bay*.

Index of Grantors.

Date.	Grantor.	Grantee.	Instrument.
1717, July 18	SAYWOOD, Joseph	Jonathan Preble	Deed
1717, Oct. 3	SCADLOCK, Samuel et ux.	Bezaleel Gatchell et ux.	Deed
1717, Nov. 30	SCADLOCK, Samuel	Cyprian Southack	Mortgage
	SCAMON, Humphrey, jr., see William Pepperrell		
1671, Oct. 14	SCARBOROUGH, Town of	John Libbey	Grant
1684, Feb. 5	SCARBOROUGH, Town of	John Libbey	Grant
1668, Aug. 1	SCOTTOW, Joshua	John Libbey	Conditional Deed
1698, June 25	SEACOMB, Richard, estate of, by Susannah Seacomb, trustee	John Rogers	Deed
17$\frac{1}{4}$$\frac{2}{3}$, Jan. 11	SEACOMB, Richard	John Rogers	Deed
1712, Apr. 8	SEVEY, Joseph	Dominicus Jordan	Deed
1711, Aug. 13	SHAPLEIGH, John, estate of, by Nicholas Shapleigh and Sarah Shapleigh, administrators	William Godsoe	Deed
166$\frac{1}{2}$, Dec. 24	SHAPLEIGH, Nicholas	Walter Barfoot	Deed
1711, Aug. 24	SHAPLEIGH, Nicholas and Sarah Shapleigh	William Godsoe and Richard Rice	Confirmation
1715, May 10	SHAPLEIGH, Nicholas	Richard Rice	Deed

Index of Grantors. 57

Folio.	Description.
234	All his right and title to land bought by Mary Saywood of John Cousins, in *Casco bay*.
266	One-third of upland and meadow which his father, William Scadlock, deceased, bought of William Phillips, in Cape Porpoise; also a third part of all lands belonging to him between Casco bay and Piscataqua river.
256	Two-thirds of a farm at Little river, in *Cape Porpoise*.
206	50 acres, to be clear of other grants.
206	20 acres adjoining Matthew Libbey's land.
225	50 acres east of said Libbey's father's field, and 6 acres of marsh next the Clay pit, in *Scarborough*.
161	50 acres; 10 acres of marsh bought of John Clean; an island of 100 acres; also any other land belonging to said estate, in *Casco bay*.
163	Confirming previous deed given by Susannah Seacomb, executrix.
212	A neck of land containing 5 acres, and 2 acres adjoining, formerly in possession of John Pearce, deceased, in *Kittery*.
267	15 acres, between Crooked lane and Spruce creek, in *Kittery*.
135	A tract of land with warehouse, on Piscataqua river.
261	Of deed of exchange, recorded in folio 261.
230	11¾ acres, bounded east by William Godsoe's and Walter Deniford's land, south and west by John Newmarch's land, north by said Rice's land, in *Kittery*.

Index of Grantors.

Date.	Grantor.	Grantee.	Instrument.
	SHAPLEIGH, Sarah. see Nicholas Shapleigh		
1716, Feb. 7	SHAW, Joseph	John Huchins & Samuel Palmer Benj. Thurston Abraham Rideout	Deed
17$\frac{08}{10}$, Mar. 1	SHAW, William et ux.	Peter Nowell	Deed
1712, July 1	SHAW, William et ux.	Henry Brooken	Deed
170$\frac{3}{4}$, Jan. 13	SIBLEY, Samuel et ux.	Thomas Wells	Deed
1708, June 3	SIMPSON, Joseph	Thomas Adams	Deed
17$\frac{13}{14}$, Mar. 6	SKILLION, Samuel	William Pepperrell, jr.	Mortgage
1714, July 1	SKILLION, Samuel	William Wilson	Deed
1714, Dec. 6	SKRIGGIN, John, and John Paul	Each other	Arbitration and Award
1674, July 15	SMALL, Francis	George Munjoy	Levy on Execution
1713, Dec. 4	SMITH, Hannah	Andrew Toothacre	Deed
17$\frac{14}{18}$, Mar. 12	SMITH, Jacob et ux.	John Rogers	Quitclaim Deed
1712, ——	SMITH, James	Daniel Junkins	Deed
1713, Sept. 16	SMITH, James	Lewis Bane	Mortgage
1715, May 23	SMITH, James et ux.	Peter Nowell	Deed

INDEX OF GRANTORS. 59

Folio.	Description.
208	A tract north of the Mill pool, in *Sagadahoc*.
31	20 acres on York river, in *York*.
184	30 acres on the west side of Bell marsh brook, in *York*.
248	All their share in lands belonging to the estate of their father, John Wells, deceased, in *Wells*.
152	24 acres on southwest side of highway leading to York corn mills, in *York*.
42	80 acres on Spruce creek, in *Kittery*.
61	30 acres, part of a town grant, in *Kittery*.
63	Relating to the estate of Stephen Paul, deceased.
151	202 acres on Piscataqua river, in *Kittery*.
247	30 acres on York river, between Long cove and land of Josiah Maine, in *York*.
146	To estate, real or personal, of Richard Rogers, deceased, in *Kittery*.
38	12 acres on south side of Bass cove marsh, in *York*.
14	80 acres, with house and barn, bounded northwest by William Shaw's land, southwest by road to Newichewannock, southeast by Daniel Junkins' land, northeast by town commons, in *York*.
108	46 acres, bounded southwest by the way from York to Berwick, northwest by land formerly Job Alcock's, southeast by land formerly Robert Jenkins', northeast by town commons, in *York*.

Index of Grantors.

Date.	Grantor.	Grantee.	Instrument.
1715, Apr. 4	SNELL, John et ux.	Richard Milberry	Deed
1715, Feb. —	SNELL, John	Richard Milberry	Deed
1716, Apr. 4	SOULLARD, Peter et ux.	John Wentworth and Thomas Hutchinson Adam Winthrop David Jeffries Oliver Noyes Stephen Minot John Ruck John Watts	Deed
17$\frac{1}{2}$, Jan. 22	SPENCER, Humphrey et ux.	Daniel Goodwin, senior	Deed
1714, Jan. 7	SPENCER, Mary	John Bradstreet	Deed
17$\frac{9}{10}$, Jan. 23	SPENCER, Moses et ux.	John Croade	Deed
1713, Mar. 30	SPENCER, Moses	Richard Lord	Deed
17$\frac{5}{8}$, Mar. 23	SPENCER, Moses et ux.	Samuel Brackett	Deed
1713, Oct. 26	SPILLER, Anne, and James Cocks et ux. John Dorothy et ux.	Diamond Sargent	Deed
17$\frac{3}{4}$, Mar. 1	SPINNEY, Samuel	John Woodman	Mortgage
17$\frac{3}{4}$, Mar. 2	SPINNEY, Samuel	John Spinney	Deed
1714, May 7	SPINNEY, Samuel, and Nathaniel Kisne	Each other	Agreement
1716, June 28	SPINNEY, Samuel et ux.	John Dennet	Mortgage

INDEX OF GRANTORS. 61

Folio.	Description.
93	50 acres on Mr. Dummer's neck of land, in *York*.
253	3 acres on southwest branch of York river, in *York*.
168	500 acres, beginning at the southeast part of Small Point harbor, formerly possessed by John Drake, deceased, in *Casco bay*.
33	1 acre at a place called the Outlet, in *Berwick*.
75	1½ acres bounded northwest by Great Works river, in *Berwick*.
73	27 acres, part of 50 acres bequeathed him by William Spencer, in *Berwick*.
118	6 acres at the east end of Francis Herlow's land; 12 acres beginning at Benjamin Nason's land, in *Berwick* [*Kittery*].
185	6 acres, bounded by Benjamin Nason's, Richard Lord's, James Warren's and said Spencer's land, in *Berwick*.
11	40 acres, bounded northeast by York line, in *Kittery*.
29	Land with houses and buildings, in *Kittery*.
146	15 acres bought of John Shepard, in *Kittery*.
55	Establishing division line between their lands, near Spruce creek, in *Kittery*.
170	25 acres, bounded north and west by land of said John Dennet, east by land of Nathaniel Kisne and said Samuel Spinney, in *Kittery*.

Date.	Grantor.	Grantee.	Instrument.
1716, June 28	SPINNEY, Samuel et ux.	John Dennet	Deed
1716, July 23	SPINNEY, Samuel et ux.	John Spinney	Deed
1716, July 24	SPINNEY, Samuel et ux.	Richard Rogers	Deed
171⅙, Feb. 14	SPINNEY, Samuel et ux.	John Addams	Mortgage
1715, Mar. 21	SPINNEY, Thomas et ux.	James Fernald	Deed
	STAGPOLE, John, see John Harmon		
1716, Dec. 21	STEVENS, John et ux., and James Grant et ux.	John Smith	Deed
1714, Dec. 25	STIMPSON, Richard	Samuel Emery	Deed
	STONE, Benjamin, see John Harmon		
1716, July 18	STONE, Daniel	Benjamin Libbey	Deed
1716, May 15	STORER, Joseph et ux.	Moses Stephens	Deed
1714, Nov. 15	STOVER, George et ux.	John Stover	Deed
1684, July 2	STOVER, John	Thomas Wise	Deed
	SUNDAY, Capt., alias Meeksombe, see Meeksombe		
1662, Jan. 16	SYMONDS, Harlakinden	James Barnard	Deed
1714, Oct. 1	TANNER, James et ux.	Thomas Perkins	Deed
	TETHERLY, Samuel, see Abraham Morrell		

Folio.	Description.
171	5½ acres bounded on the north and west by said John Dennet's land, east and south by said Samuel Spinney's land, in *Kittery*.
172	15 acres, part of that tract bought of Thomas Bice, reserving 2 poles for highway, in *Kittery*.
181	22 acres on west side of Spruce creek, in *Kittery*.
239	32 acres, bounded by Spinney's cove and John Dennet's land, in *Kittery*.
84	2 acres, bounded south by James Fernald's land, east by a brook, west by John Spinney's land, in *Kittery*.
207	Their share in the estate of James Ingles, deceased.
88	110 acres, granted William Venney by town of *Wells*.
158	30 acres, part of a town grant, in *Berwick*.
268	100 acres, belonging formerly to his brother, Samuel Storer, in *Wells*.
60	His right and title in house and land on southwest side Cape Neddick river, in *York*.
201	12 acres on south side York river, in *York*.
226	100 acres on east side of Cape Porpoise river.
140	Land on Royall's river, in *North Yarmouth*.

Index of Grantors.

Date.	Grantor.	Grantee.	Instrument.
	Tetherly, William, see Abraham Morrell		
1712, May 27	Thomas, Nathaniel	William Pepperrell	Deed
1714, Nov. 6	Thompson, Alexander et ux.	William Rogers	Deed
17$\frac{4}{5}$, Jan. 3	Thompson [Tompson], Alexander	Peter Nowell	Mortgage
171$\frac{4}{5}$, Jan. 22	Thompson, John et ux.	Thomas Fernald	Deed
1707, Oct. 6	Thompson [Tompson], John, and John Paul	Thomas Knight	Deed
1716, June 30	Thompson, John	Benjamin Libbey	Deed
1665, Dec. 7	Thoyts, Alexander	Richard Pateshall Robert Pateshall Humphrey Davie	Deed
1715, Aug. 22	Tinney, John	William Mitchell et ux.	Deed
1712, Nov. 26	Tompson, Samuel	John Tompson	Release
17$\frac{2}{3}$, Jan. 21	Toziar, Richard	Richard Randol and William Randol	Deed
1715, Mar. 29	Toziar, Richard, and Joseph Pray	Each other	Division
17$\frac{4}{5}$, Mar. 7	Tucker, Joseph	Jane Tucker	Deed
1716, Dec. 25	Tucker, Nicholas	William Tucker	Deed
1657, Sept. 11	Tucker, Richard	Robert Jordan	License
1717, June 1	Tucker, William et ux.	John Walker	Deed

Index of Grantors.

Folio.	Description.
136	A cartway over his land at Kittery point, in *Kittery*.
61	20 acre town grant near Spruce creek road, in *Kittery*.
67	40 or 50 acres that Benjamin Curtis bought of Master Everet, in *York*.
85	10¼ acre town grant by and in *Kittery*.
61	5½ acres adjoining their house-lots, in *Kittery*.
157	One-half of a 21 acre town grant, in *Kittery*.
158	A tract on the Kennebec river, beginning at a cove, the lower bounds of Robert Gutch's land, so to run along the water side to Winnegance [Winnegansick] river, also cattle, house, barn, etc.; also a marsh on the south side of Winnegance river.
156	A tract at Black Point; also all his land near Spurwink river, in *Scarborough*.
144	Referring to estate of John Tompson, deceased.
64	10 acres, part of a 100 acre town grant, by and in *Kittery*.
92	Establishing division lines between their lands above Salmon Falls, in *Berwick*.
204	15 acres, bounded north by William Tucker's land, east by John Frink's land, south by land formerly Philip Carpenter's and Spruce creek, in *Kittery*.
214	30 acres, next to Mr. Moore's land, in *Kittery*.
244	To use land adjoining the falls of Casco river and erect saw-mill or mills.
213	1 acre on Kittery point, in *Kittery*.

Index of Grantors.

Date.	Grantor.	Grantee.	Instrument.
1697, July 2	TURFREY, George	Francis Foxcroft	Deed
1716, Jan. 11	TYLER, James	Jabez Dorman	Deed
1709, Sept. 10	WADLEY, William	John Croade	Deed
	WAHANGNONAWITT, see Passaconaway		
	WALKER, Edward, see Paul Williams		
1713, Sept. 17	WALKER, Richard	John Harris	Deed
1716, Oct. 26	WALKER, Samuel	William Pepperrell, junior	Deed and Receipt
1716, Oct. 26	WALKER, Samuel	William Pepperrell, junior	Bond
	WASHBURN, Thomas, see Elizabeth Davis		
	WATTS, John, see Thomas Hutchinson		
17$\frac{1\,3}{1\,4}$, Mar. 12	WAYMOUTH, Timothy	Elizabeth Hubbard and Philip Hubbard	Deed
1715, Apr. 6	WAYMOUTH, Timothy	Samuel Hodsden	Mortgage
1715, June 3	WAYMOUTH, Timothy et ux.	John Frost	Deed
1710, June 10	WEARE, Joseph	Abraham Preble, junior	Deed
1708, Nov. 26	WEARE, Mary	Peter Nowell and Hopewell Weare	Deed

Index of Grantors. 67

Folio.	Description.
241	One-eighth in common of saw-mill and tract of sixteen square miles on Saco river, except 20 acres and timber sold; also one-eighth of Cow island, and one-sixteenth of Boniton's island, in *Saco*.
249	One-half his right in lands bought of Nicholas Moorey, also 25 acres bought of said Moorey, in *Cape Porpoise*.
86	His right in a stream running out of William Cock's pond, with 1 acre of land, in *Berwick*.
4	300 acres on east side of Cape Porpoise river, in *Coxhall* [now Lyman].
185	Two-thirds of 6,000 acres one ast side of Saco river; also two-thirds of adjoining tract, in *Saco*.
186	In £52 that his wife shall not claim her thirds or any other part of land conveyed to said Pepperrell.
199	50 acres with dwelling house, bounded southwest by Mast cove, northwest by William Hearl's land, east by Jonathan Nason's land, north by Thomas Greely's land, in *Berwick*.
202	20 acres near Mast cove, in *Berwick*.
104	54 acres on Neguttaquid river, in *Berwick*.
1	¼ acre on York river, in *York*.
32	8 acres salt marsh on northwest branch of York river, in *York*.

Index of Grantors.

Date.	Grantor.	Grantee.	Instrument.
	WEARE, Nathaniel, see William Pepperrell		
17$\frac{18}{19}$, Mar. 19	WEBBER, James	John Wentworth and Thomas Hutchinson Adam Winthrop David Jeffries Oliver Noyes Stephen Minot John Ruck John Watts	Deed
171$\frac{5}{8}$, Feb. 21	WEBBER, Nathan	John Wentworth and Thomas Hutchinson Adam Winthrop David Jeffries Oliver Noyes Stephen Minot John Ruck John Watts	Deed
171$\frac{8}{8}$, Feb. 14	WEBBER, Nathaniel	John Wentworth and Thomas Hutchinson Adam Winthrop David Jeffries Oliver Noyes Stephen Minot John Ruck John Watts	Deed
1714, Apr. 18	WEBBER, Samuel et ux.	Thomas Webber and Benjamin Webber	Deed
1714, Apr. 1	WEBBER, Samuel et ux.	Richard Milbury (Milberry)	Deed
1714, June 24	WEBBER, Samuel et ux.	Richard Milbury (Milberry)	Deed
1716, Sept. 25	WELCH, Philip et ux.	Peter Nowell	Deed and Receipt

Index of Grantors. 69

Folio.	Description.
150	Two-sevenths of a tract at Small Point neck, reserving 100 acres.
149	Two-sevenths of a tract at Small Point neck.
148	One-seventh of a tract at Small Point neck, reserving 100 acres.
183	40 acres, on northeast side of Cape Neddick river, reserving ½ acre, in *York*.
51	16 acres on northeast side of Little river, in *York*.
50	One-quarter of saw-mill and 1 acre of land, known as Cape Neddick mill, in *York*.
182	30 acre town grant on northwest side of Bell marsh brook, in *York*.

Book VIII. 46

Index of Grantors.

Date.	Grantor.	Grantee.	Instrument.
	WENTWORTH, John, see Thomas Hutchinson		
1710, Nov. 22	WENTWORTH, Timothy et ux.	Nicholas Morrell	Deed
1715, June 8	WENTWORTH, Timothy et ux.	James Smith	Deed
1713, May 15	WHARTON, Richard, estate of, by Ephraim Savage, administrator	John Marion and Josiah Tay Thomas Hubbart and successors, deacons of the First church, Boston	Deed and Receipt
1714, Nov. 5	WHARTON, Richard, estate of, by Ephraim Savage administrator	Thomas Hutchinson and John Wentworth Adam Winthrop John Watts David Jeffries Stephen Minot Oliver Noyes John Ruck	Deed
1715, Oct. 25	WHIPPLE, John et ux.	John Leighton	Deed
1687, Oct. 22	WHITE, Richard	John More	Deed
1692, Sept. 27	WHITE, Richard	Henry Dering	Deed
1715, Nov. 1	WHITNEY, Nathaniel et ux.	Joseph Harris	Deed
	WILLIAMS, Joanna, see Paul Williams		
1714, May 18	WILLIAMS, Paul, and Joanna Williams Edward Walker Elizabeth Gaskin	Nicholas Weeks	Deed

Index of Grantors. 71

Folio.	Description.
70	One-half his interest in a water-course, saw-mill and land, on Worster's river, in *Berwick*.
210	10 acres at the upper end of his 60 acre lot, 10 acres bounded by said 60 acres and commons; reserving a highway, in *Berwick*.
186	650 acres on Great Chebeague island; 350 acres at the west end of Maquoit, in *Casco bay*.
56	A tract called Pejepscot [Brunswick], bought of the estate of Thomas Purchase; Merriconeag neck and Sebascodegan island, in Casco bay; also the land granted Richard Wharton, five miles above Androscoggin falls.
151	His interest in a 50 acre town grant; also in a grant given William Leighton, at Crooked lane, in *Kittery*.
116	30 acre town grant at Brave-boat harbor, in *York*.
44	90 acres beginning at bridge at the head of Brave-boat harbor, in *Kittery*.
126	A tract and marsh, called Sunken marsh, on southwest side of York river, in *York*.
254	10 acres at the northeast end of the late John Hole's home lot, in *Kittery*.

Index of Grantors.

Date.	Grantor.	Grantee.	Instrument.
171⅔, Feb. 26	WILSON, Hannah	Ebenezer More	Deed
1713, May 19	WILSON, William	Andrew Lewis	Deed
1709, Mar. 26	WINCOLL, John et ux.	John Smith	Deed
1712, July 29	WINCOLL, John et ux.	Nathan Lord and Richard Lord	Deed
1682, Sept. 16	WINCOLL, Olive et ux., and William Plaisted James Plaisted John Plaisted Ichabod Plaisted Elizabeth Plaisted Mehitable Plaisted	Each other	Agreement
1703, May 3	WINSLOW, Gilbert	Job Otis	Deed
1702, Feb. 17	WINSLOW, Nathaniel et ux.	Job Otis	Deed
	WINTHROP, Adam, see Thomas Hutchinson		
1685, Dec. 6	WISE, Thomas et ux.	Isaac Guturidge	Deed
17¼, Feb. 28	WOOD, Joseph	John Hooper	Deed
1716, June 18	WOODMAN, John	Samuel Spinney	Discharge
1726, Apr. 6	WOODMAN, John	Francis Raynes	Discharge
	WOODMAN, John, see Nathaniel Raynes		
1717, July 2	WOODSUM, Joseph	Job Emery	Bond
1713, July 22	WORSTER [Woster], Moses, and Richard Gowell Richard Gowel, jr. Samuel Ham	Each other	Division

Folio.	Description.
85	One-quarter of saw-mill on east side of Spruce creek, in *Kittery*.
179	17 acres, part of a 50 acre town grant to William Lewis, in *Kittery*.
77	90 acres, part of a town grant to John Wincoll, deceased, and George Veazy, in *Berwick*.
118	65 acres, bounded south by highway and Wilcock's pond, east by Thomas Spencer's land, north by Great Works river, west by land laid out for the ministry, in *Berwick*.
132	In regard to lands, cattle and chattels belonging to the estate of Roger Plaisted, deceased.
27	One-half of 300 acres, also one-half of 20 or 30 acres on Arisicket [Harraseket] river, in *Casco bay*.
26	Same as above.
132	A tract on south side of river, in *York* [*Gorgeana*].
102	3½ acres bought of John Croade, in *Berwick*.
160	Of mortgage recorded in folio 29.
103	Of mortgage recordeded folio 103.
266	Conditioned to pay Abigail Abbot 2s. 6d. per week.
18	Fixing division line between their lands at Spinney's creek, in *Kittery*.

Index of Grantors.

Date.	Grantor.	Grantee.	Instrument.
17$\frac{13}{14}$, Feb. 24	Worster [Woster], Moses	Thomas Worster	Deed
17$\frac{14}{15}$, Mar. 21	Worster [Woster], Moses	Thomas Worster	Deed
1712, Jan. 27	Wright, Henry	Ichabod Plaisted	Deed
1714, Mar. 8	York, Town of	William Grow	Deed
17$\frac{14}{15}$, Feb. 15	York, Town of	Nicholas Sewall	Deed
1715, Mar. 9	York, Town of	Daniel Simpson	Deed
1709, Jan. 3	Young, Job et ux., and Thomas Haynes	Alexander Junkins and Joseph Junkins	Deed
	Young, Jonathan, see John Harmon		
1707, Aug. 21	Young, Joseph, junior	Alexander Junkins	Deed
1715, May 16	Young, Katherine et ux.	Thomas Cole	Deed

Folio.	Description.
23	A tract of land, household goods, cattle and all other personal estate, in *Berwick*.
82	Remaining part of 200 acres, bought of John Wincoll, also of two grants of land and of saw-mill on Worsters river, in *Kittery* [*Berwick*].
204	50 acres on Piscataqua river, in *Kittery*.
174	1 acre, with dwelling-house, on Meeting-house creek, in *York*.
123	2 acres and 14 poles of land, in *York*.
243	5 acres between Ebenezer Coburn's and said Simpson's land, in *York*.
191	4 acres, called Young's marsh, at the head of the southwest branch of York river, in *Kittery*.
193	2 acres on northwest branch of York river, in *York*.
123	One-sixth of meadow and marsh at Newichewannock, in *Berwick*.

INDEX OF

Date.	Grantee.	Grantor.	Instrument.
1714, Dec. 16	ABBET, John	Thomas Abbet	Deed
1709, July 23	ADAMS, Hezekiah	Johnson Harmon et ux.	Deed
1708, June 3	ADAMS, Thomas	Joseph Simpson	Deed
17$\frac{16}{17}$, Feb. 14	ADDAMS, John	Samuel Spinney et ux.	Mortgage
1711, Nov. 15	ADDAMS, Samuel	Thomas Addams et ux.	Deed
171$\frac{2}{3}$, Feb. 17	ALLEN, Francis, and Reinold Jenkins	Each other	Deed of Exchange
1711, Mar. 27	ALLEN, Francis	John Cole	Deed
1714, Oct. 11	BANE, Jonathan	Lewis Bane	Deed
1713, Oct. 25	BANE, Lewis	Mary Blagdon and Hannah Blagdon, Nicholas Follet et ux.	Deed
1713, Sept. 16	BANE, Lewis	James Smith	Mortgage
1717, Apr. 30	BANE, Lewis, and Job Banks	Job Curtis et ux.	Deed

GRANTEES.

Folio.	Description.
160	110 acres, a mile in length from brow of Rocky hill at Slut's corner, east, then southeast to John Taylor's marsh, 56 poles in breadth, reserving right to firewood, in *Berwick*.
153	10 acres, bounded southwest by town way from Bass creek to Rowland Young's, in *York*.
152	24 acres on southwest side of highway leading to York corn mills, in *York*.
239	32 acres, bounded by Spinney's cove and John Dennet's land, in *Kittery*.
254	50 acres on southwest side of York river, in *York*.
6	15 acres near Dover river and Sturgeon creek, in exchange for two small tracts near Dover river, in *Kittery*.
5	30 acre town grant by and in *Kittery*.
90	30 acres on the northeast side of highway leading from the meeting-house to the corn-mill, in *York*.
15	15 acres on New Mill creek, in *York*.
14	80 acres, with house and barn, bounded northwest by William Shaw's land, southwest by road to Newichewannock, southeast by Daniel Junkins' land, northeast by town commons, in *York*.
210	50 acres, one-quarter of mill and stream at Scituate plains, in *York*.

Index of Grantees.

Date.	Grantee.	Grantor.	Instrument.
	BANKS, Job, see Lewis Bane		
166½, Dec. 24	BARFOOT, Walter	Nicholas Shapleigh	Deed
1662, Jan. 16	BARNARD, James	Harlakinden Symonds	Deed
1713, —— 26	BARTER, Henry	Richard Crocket et ux.	Deed
1717, Mar. 27	BARTER, Henry	Thomas Huff	Deed
17$\frac{1}{9}$, Feb. 25	BARTER, Henry	Ebenezer More and John Norton	Mortgage
17$\frac{3}{4}$, Feb. 27	BARTLET, Nathan	John Heard et ux.	Deed
17$\frac{4}{5}$, Mar. 10	BARTLET, Nathan	Nicholas Morrell et ux.	Deed
1718, Apr. 2	BEAL, Edward	William Pepperrell	Discharge
1713, Dec. 12	BERRY, Benjamin, and Withers Berry	Dodevah Curtis	Deed
	BERRY, Withers, see Benjamin Berry		
1686, May 17	BILLIN, John	Francis Champernown et ux.	Deed
17$\frac{5}{8}$, Mar. 15	BLACKLEDGE, Jabez	Elihu Parsons	Deed
1713, Aug. 27	BLASDEL, Ebenezer, and Ralph Farnum	John Pickerin	Deed

Index of Grantees. 79

Folio.	Description.
135	A tract of land with warehouse, on Piscataqua river.
226	100 acres on east side of Cape Porpoise river.
62	40 acres, bounded west by Spruce creek, north by Tucker's creek and known as Crockett's neck, in *Kittery*.
219	18½ acres between Henry Barter's and Joseph Crocket's lands, in *Kittery*.
228	27¾ acres and 26 poles between Nicholas Tucker's land and Crocket's neck, in *Kittery*.
47	2 lots out of his homestead land, in *Kittery*.
83	4 acres on north side of Sturgeon creek, in *Kittery*.
69	Of mortgage recorded in folio 69.
22	Land, house and saw-mill, purchased of Sarah Shapleigh and Nicholas Shapleigh, in *Kittery*.
17	20 acres northwest of Champernown's Island, in *Kittery*.
173	5 acres on southwest side of York river, in *York*.
116	A parcel of land on southwest side of York river, in *York*.

Index of Grantees.

Date.	Grantee.	Grantor.	Instrument.
1710, May 24	BOSTON, James	Obadiah Read et ux.	Deed
1715, Apr. 13	BOYNTON, Joseph	John Croade	Mortgage
1715, Dec. 12	BOYNTON, Joseph	John Croade	Deed
1715, July 7	BOYNTON, Joseph	Joseph Otis	Deed
17$\frac{1}{8}$, Mar. 23	BRACKETT, Samuel	Moses Spencer et ux.	Deed
1714, Jan. 7	BRADSTREET, John	Mary Spencer	Deed
1714, Mar. 20	BRAWN, George, senior, et ux.	George Brawn et ux.	Deed
1710, May 23	BRIAR, William	John Frink et ux.	Deed
1716, Apr. 14	BROOKIN, Henry	Francis Raynes	Deed
1712, July 1	BROOKIN, Henry	William Shaw et ux.	Deed
1717, Aug. 24	BROWN, Andrew	Samuel Hill	Deed
1717, Sept. 13	BROWN, James, and Joseph Brown	Caleb Preble	Deed
	BROWN, Joseph, see James Brown		
1715, Sept. 7	BROWN, Samuel	Nath'l Masters, estate of, by Nath'l Masters, administrator	Deed
17$\frac{1}{8}$, Jan. 6	BUTLER, John et ux.	Ephraim Savage et ux.	Deed

INDEX OF GRANTEES. 81

Folio.	Description.
221	450 acres bounded by Robert Hilton's, Josiah Storer's lands and highway, in *Wells*.
87	Dwelling-house; all his right in saw-mill on Worster's river; 3 acres on east end of Cock's pond; also all his interest on north side of said pond, all in *Berwick*.
131	The deed or mortgage recorded in folio 87.
100	Dwelling house, in *Berwick*.
185	6 acres, bounded by Benjamin Nason's, Richard Lord's, James Warren's and said Spencer's land, in *Berwick*.
75	1½ acres bounded northwest by Great Works river, in *Berwick*.
147	Land on the lower side of way that leads from Sturgeon creek to John Tidy's, in *Kittery*.
74	25 acres at Spruce creek, in *Kittery*.
184	20 acres near John More's and Samuel Winch's bounds, in *York*.
184	30 acres on the west side of Bell marsh brook, in *York*.
266	100 acres at *Cape Porpoise*.
242	One-quarter of that land belonging formerly to Richard Comins, on east side of Saco river, part of patent to Bonighton and Lewis.
109	Farm of 100 acres on Ogunquit side; also 50 acre town grant; 8 acres of marsh near harbor's mouth; also an island of thatch and 10 acres, called Master's meadow, in *Wells*.
122	1,000 acres at a place called Whigby, on the Kennebec river.

Index of Grantees.

Date.	Grantee.	Grantor.	Instrument.
1717, Aug. 23	CAME, Samuel	James Allen	Deed
1714, Jan. 4	CAME, Samuel	John Burrell et ux.	Deed
1710, Aug. 10	CAME, Samuel	Johnson Harmon	Deed
1714, Apr. 27	CAME, Samuel	Johnson Harmon	Deed
1716, Apr. 13	CAME, Samuel	John Linscot	Deed
1706, Nov. 5	CARPENTER, Philip	Isaac Gudrig, estate of, by Margaret Adams, administratrix	Deed
1717, Oct. 23	CARR, James	Jacob Perkins	Deed
1713, July 29	CHADBOURNE, James	Jeremiah Calef et ux.	Deed
1714, May 20	CHAPMAN, John	Elisha Ingersol	Deed
	CHAPMAN, John, see Elisha Ingersol		
170$\frac{8}{9}$, Jan. 8	CHICK, Richard	John Frost	Deed
	CHICK, Richard, see John Morrell		
1715, May 4	CLARK, Nathaniel jr.	Nathaniel Clark et ux.	Deed
1717, Aug. 5	CLARK, Nathaniel jr.	Epps [Epes], Symond et ux.	Deed
1693, Feb. 2	COFFIN, James	William Hook	Assignment

INDEX OF GRANTEES.

Folio.	Description.
250	17 acres and 50 poles on south side of southwest branch of York river, part of a town grant, in *York*.
65	Marsh and thatch banks on the southeast side of Bass cove, in *York*.
11	63 acres on northeast side of cove of marsh belonging to the ministry of York, in *York*.
50	50 acres between two branches of York river, at the Partings, in *York*.
190	40 acres between the Partings of York river, *York*.
43	10 acres between the lands of Nicholas Tucker and Henry Barter, in *Kittery*.
247	70 acres, with dwelling-house and barn, on southwest side of Cape Neddick river; also cattle, sheep, swine, horse, hay and corn.
47	Two tracts of land near Sturgeon creek, in *Kittery*.
46	31½ acres on east side of Spruce creek, in *Kittery*.
139	2 parcels of marsh on Sturgeon creek, in *Kittery*.
252	A tract bounded by Thomas Wells', Nicholas Cole's, Lewis Allen's land and Little river; 2 acres of marsh adjoining Thomas Wells' on Little river; also a town grant of 105 acres, in *Wells*.
252	One-half of farm, formerly William Symonds', deceased, in *Wells*.
122	His interest in patent at Cape Neddick, in *York*.

Index of Grantees.

Date.	Grantee.	Grantor.	Instrument.
1715, June 23	COFFIN, James, Daughters of	James Coffin	Assignm't
1713, Feb. 18	COLE, Hannah	Robert Elliot	Deed
1715, June 13	COLE, Thomas	William Merryfield et ux.	Deed
1715, May 16	COLE, Thomas	Katherine Young et ux.	Deed
1717, Apr. 11	COOKSON, John	William Robinson	Bond and Mortgage
1692, Sept. 8	CORWIN, Jonathan	James Oare	Deed
1703, May 10	COUCH, Joseph	Town of Kittery	Grant
17$\frac{13}{14}$, Feb. 5	COUCH, Roger	Roger Dearing	Deed
17$\frac{19}{10}$, Jan. 23	CROADE, John	Moses Spencer et ux.	Deed
1709, Sept. 10	CROADE, John	William Wadley	Deed
1716, Feb. 2	CROCKET, Joseph	Thomas Allen	Deed
	CUTT, Robert, see John Leighton		
1713, Nov. 23	CUTT, Robert, and John Leighton Charles Frost Joseph Hammond John Frost	Each other	Division Deed
1685, May 26	DANFORTH, Thomas, and Samuel Nowell	Gov. of Massachusetts and Company	Deed

INDEX OF GRANTEES.

Folio.	Description.
122	His interest in patent of Cape Neddick, in *York*.
40	26 acres on southwest side of York river, in *York*.
124	One-sixth of marsh at Newichewannock, in *Berwick*.
123	One-sixth of meadow and marsh at Newichewannock, in *Berwick*.
229	One-quarter of a tract between Sheepscot bay and Damariscotta river; also Damariscotta island, with one-quarter part of all adjacent islands; also 100 acres in Georgetown, with house, saw-mill, cattle and horse.
151	200 acres, with dwelling-house and barn, at Mousam, in *Wells*.
144	50 acres, to be clear of other grants.
19	3 acres, with houses and barns, also 1 acre of marsh at Brave-boat harbor, in *Kittery*.
73	27 acres, part of 50 acres bequeathed him by William Spencer, in *Berwick*.
86	His right in a stream running out of William Cock's pond, with 1 acre of land, in *Berwick*.
267	A third part of a certain tract bought of Nathaniel Thomas, in *Kittery*.
20	30 acres on Piscataqua river; 5 acres on Sturgeon creek; $34\frac{1}{2}$ acres northeast from the head of Major Clark's and Joshua Downing's land; 30 acres near the highway from Sturgeon creek to Spruce creek; 60 acres bounded by land of John Frost, Robert Knight and Katherine Leighton, in *Kittery*.
242	Sebascodegan island, in *Casco bay*.

Index of Grantees.

Date.	Grantee.	Grantor.	Instrument.
	DAVIE, Humphrey, see Richard Pateshall		
1716, May 3	DAVIS, Elizabeth	Anne Clark	Release
171$\frac{4}{5}$, Mar. 7	DAVIS, James	Nicholas Morrell et ux.	Deed
1698, Jan. 15	DEARING, Roger	Henry Dering	Mortgage
1716, Apr. 16	DENNET, John	Daniel Paul	Mortgage
1716, June 28	DENNET, John	Samuel Spinney et ux.	Mortgage
1716, June 28	DENNET, John	Samuel Spinney et ux.	Deed
1692, Sept. 27	DERING, Henry	Richard White	Deed
	DIXEY, William, see Samuel Maverick		
1714, May 24	DONNELL, Nathaniel	Abraham Preble, junior	Deed
1716, Jan. 11	DORMAN, Jabez	James Tyler	Deed
1717, Apr. 16	DOWNING, Joshua et ux., and Samuel Hill William Fry	Each other	Division
1717, May 23	DYER, William	James Emery	Deed
	ELDRIDGE, Giles, see Humphrey Hooke		
1715, Apr. 11	ELLIS, John	Elisha Kelley et ux.	Mortgage

INDEX OF GRANTEES. 87

Folio.	Description.
170	All her right and title to Thomas Atkins' estate.
78	35 acres, part of the land purchased of Richard Estes; also a highway from the river, in *Kittery*.
45	Houses and land, in *Kittery*.
227	20 acres on Spinney's creek, in *Kittery*.
170	25 acres, bounded north and west by land of said John Dennet, east by land of Nathaniel Kane and said Samuel Spinney, in *Kittery*.
171	5½ acres bounded on the north and west by said John Dennet's land, east and south by said Samuel Spinney's land, in *Kittery*.
44	90 acres beginning at bridge at the head of Brave-boat harbor, in *Kittery*.
90	3 acres near a cove formerly known as Palmer's cove, in *York*.
249	One-half his right in lands bought of Nicholas Moorey, also 25 acres bought of said Moorey, in *Cape Porpoise*.
263	Of tract on north side of Mr. Shapleigh's land, in *Kittery*.
231	One half of land bought of his father, James Emery, senior, in *Winter Harbor* [now Biddeford].
111	Land and dwelling-house at Crooked lane, in *Kittery*.

Index of Grantees.

Date.	Grantee.	Grantor.	Instrument.
1710, Jan. 15	ELWELL, Hezekiah et ux.	John Fennick et ux.	Deed
17$\frac{13}{14}$, Mar. 12	EMERY, Daniel	Job Emery	Deed
1714, Oct. 14	EMERY, James, jr.	James Emery	Deed
171$\frac{3}{4}$, Mar. 12	EMERY, Job	Daniel Emery	Deed
1717, July 2	EMERY, Job	Joseph Woodsum	Bond
1713, Nov. 7	EMERY, Samuel	William Frost	Deed
1714, Dec. 25	EMERY, Samuel	Richard Stimpson	Deed
1716, Dec. 15	EPPS, Symond	Daniel Epps	Power of Attorney
1717, July 17	EPPS, Symond	Joseph Jacob and Philip Fowler et ux.	Deed
1713, May 18	FALL, John	Bial Hamilton	Deed
	FARNUM, Ralph, see Ebenezer Blasdel		
1717, Mar. 30	FERNALD, James	John Dennet	Assignm't
1714, Nov. 17	FERNALD, James	Joshua Downing et ux.	Deed
1699, May. 24	FERNALD, James	Town of Kittery	Grant
1717, Mar. 30	FERNALD, James	Daniel Paul	Deed
1715, Mar. 21	FERNALD, James	Thomas Spinney et ux.	Deed

Folio.	Description.
264	12 acres on west side of Spruce creek, at the head of Broad cove, in *Kittery*.
52	100 acres near York pond, reserving 20 acres, in *Kittery*.
231	4½ acres of marsh, bounded northeast by river, southwest by Pendleton Fletcher's marsh, southeast by Rebecca Hitchcock's marsh, northwest by woodlands; 8½ acres of marsh on Saco side in middle part of said marsh; also one-third of 174 acres of woodland, beginning at the sea, in Winter Harbor [now Biddeford]; also 5 acres, part of Mr. Hitchcock's house-lot; also a third part more of Rebecca Hitchcock's right in marsh.
265	20 acres, bounded by commons, Rocky hill and land of Moses Goodwin, James Emery and Nathan Lord, in *Kittery*.
266	Conditioned to pay Abigail Abbott 2s. 6d. per week.
13	110 acre town grant by and in *Wells*.
88	110 acres, granted William Venney by town of *Wells*.
227	To sell land beyond Piscataqua river.
226	One-quarter of farm, formerly William Symond's, deceased, in *Wells*.
260	5 acres, part of a town grant to Ephraim Joy, in *Kittery* [*Berwick*].
228	Of mortgage recorded in folio 227.
59	40 acre town grant, by and in *Kittery*.
94	30 acres, to be clear of other grants.
204	A tract near Spinney's creek, in *Kittery*.
84	2 acres, bounded south by James Fernald's land, east by a brook, west by John Spinney's land, in *Kittery*.

Index of Grantees.

Date.	Grantee.	Grantor.	Instrument.
171⅞, Jan. 21	FERNALD, Nathaniel	Mary Hunking and Mary Hunking jr.	Deed
171⅞, Jan. 22	FERNALD, Thomas	John Thompson et ux.	Deed
1681, June 22	FLETCHER, Pendleton	Elinor Pendleton and James Pendleton	Confirmation
1703, May 10	FOLLET, John	Town of Kittery	Grant
1690, Dec. 20	FOXCROFT, Francis	Thomas Danforth	Deed
1697, July 2	FOXCROFT, Francis	George Turfrey	Deed
1709, Sept. 21	FRINK, John	Samuel Hill	Deed
1714, Apr. 21	FROST, Charles	James Chadbourne et ux.	Deed
1714, Aug. 2	FROST, Charles	John Fennick	Deed
1715, Mar. 14	FROST, Charles	John Frink	Deed
17¼⅘, Feb. 10	FROST, Charles	John Gowen et ux.	Mortgage
1715, Apr. 25	FROST, Charles	Elihu Gunnison	Deed
1715, Mar. 14	FROST, Charles	John Ingersol	Deed
	FROST, Charles, see John Leighton		
	FROST, Charles, see Josiah Maine		

Index of Grantees.

Folio.	Description.
157	40 acre town grant, by and in *Kittery*.
85	10¼ acre town grant by and in *Kittery*.
88	Of their share in land in deed recorded folio 88.
55	50 acres of land.
240	All of Sebascodegan island, except 1000 acres, in *Casco bay*.
241	One-eighth in common of saw-mill and tract of sixteen square miles on Saco river, except 20 acres and timber sold; also one-eighth of Cow island, and one-sixteenth of Boniton's island, in *Saco*.
74	50 acres at Spruce creek in *Kittery*.
71	3 acres, part of said Chadbourne's farm, in *Kittery*.
71	All his part in common and undivided lands, in *Berwick* and *Kittery*.
127	All his part in common and undivided lands, in *Kittery* and *Berwick*.
76	108 acres, the farm where said John Gowen dwells, in *Kittery*.
128	His part in the common and undivided lands, in *Kittery* and *Berwick*.
128	All his part in common and undivided lands, in *Berwick* and *Kittery*.

Index of Grantees.

Date.	Grantee.	Grantor.	Instrument.
1715, May 21	Frost, John	John Ball	Deed
1714, June 1	Frost, John	John Gowen et ux.	Deed
	Frost, John, see John Leighton		
1715, May 23	Frost, John	Andrew Lewis	Deed
1715, June 3	Frost, John	Timothy Waymouth et ux.	Deed
1717, Apr. 16	Fry, Adrian	Nicholas Morrell	Deed
	Fry, William, see Joshua Downing		
1717, Oct. 3	Gatchell, Bezaleel et ux.	Samuel Scadlock et ux.	Deed
1638, May 4	Godfrey, Edward, and Oliver Godfrey Richard Row	Sir Ferdinando Gorges	Deed
	Godfrey, Oliver, see Edward Godfrey		
1711, Aug. 24	Godsoe, William, and Richard Rice	Each other	Deed of Exchange
1711, Aug. 13	Godsoe, William	John Shapleigh, estate of, by Nicholas Shapleigh and Sarah Shapleigh, administrators	Deed

INDEX OF GRANTEES. 93

Folio.	Description.
198	All right, title and interest he may have in common and undivided lands, in *Berwick* and *Kittery*.
64	50 acre town grant, in *Berwick*.
196	All his portion in common and undivided lands, in *Berwick* and *Kittery*.
104	54 acres on Neguttaquid river, in *Berwick*.
216	1 acre, southwest corner of a field in possession of James Davis; also ¾ of an acre; both tracts part of land purchased of Richard Estes, in *Kittery*.
266	One-third of upland and meadow which his father, William Scadlock, deceased, bought of William Phillips, in Cape Porpoise; also a third part of all lands belonging to him between Casco bay and Piscataqua river.
120	1500 acres on northwest side of Cape Neddick creek, in *York*.
260	One yoke of oxen and several tracts of land, belonging to the estate of Thomas Withers, deceased (except 22 acres), in exchange for 22 acres at Pine Point, fronting Spruce creek, in *Kittery*.
267	15 acres, between Crooked lane and Spruce creek, in *Kittery*.

Index of Grantees.

Date.	Grantee.	Grantor.	Instrument.
1711, Aug. 24	Godsoe, William, and Richard Rice	Nicholas Shapleigh and Sarah Shapleigh	Confirmation
17½, Jan. 22	Goodwin, Daniel, senior	Humphrey Spencer et ux.	Deed
1713, May 20	Goodwin, Daniel	Thomas Goodwin et ux.	Deed
1710, June 10	Gowell, Richard, jr.	Richard Gowell	Deed
	Gowell, Richard, jr., see Moses Worster		
1698, Dec. 23	Gowell, Richard	Thomas Hoar	Bond
1699, May 24	Gowell, Richard	Town of Kittery	Grant
	Gowell, Richard, see Moses Worster		
1714, Sept. 14	Gowell, William	Richard Gowell	Deed
1714, Sept. 14	Gowell, William	Richard Gowell, junior	Confirmation
1717, June 12	Gowen, John	Charles Frost	Discharge
1714, Mar. 8	Grow, William	Town of York	Deed
1685, Dec. 6	Guturidge, Isaac	Thomas Wise et ux.	Deed
1714, Aug. 3	Haley, Andrew	William Haley et ux.	Deed
	Ham, Samuel, see Moses Worster		
1715, Sept. 1	Hambleton, Bial	William Child et ux.	Deed
1713, Apr. 21	Hambleton, Bial	James Emery	Deed

INDEX OF GRANTEES. 95

Folio.	Description.
261	Of deed of exchange, recorded in folio 261.
33	1 acre at a place called the Outlet, in *Berwick*.
34	Several parcels of land near Slut's corner, in *Berwick*.
200	Dwelling house and all land, except 20 acres, in *Kittery*.
146	To secure payment of £40.
144	10 acres, to be clear of other grants.
143	10 acres, 3 acres purchased of Richard King, 7 acres at northeast end of said Richard Gowell's land, in *Kittery*.
143	Of above deed.
76	Of mortgage recorded in folio 76.
174	1 acre, with dwelling-house, on Meeting-house creek, in *York*.
132	A tract on south side of river, in *York* [*Gorgeanna*].
54	30 acre town grant by and in *Kittery*.
154	2 acres and 4 poles, bounded northwest by road to Humphrey's pond, south by land formerly called Broughton's, on other sides by said Child's land, in *Berwick*.
36	One-third of 18 acres, part of a 40 acre town grant to William Grant, in [*Berwick*] *Kittery*.

Index of Grantees.

Date.	Grantee.	Grantor.	Instrument.
1710, June 1	HAMBLETON, Bial	Alexander Grant	Deed
	HAMMOND, Joseph, see John Leighton		
1713, June 1	HAMMOND, Samuel	Samuel Bolls	Deed
17$\frac{12}{13}$, Feb. 13	HANSCOM, Thomas	Job Hanscom	Deed
17$\frac{12}{13}$, Feb. 17	HANSCOM, Thomas	Moses Hanscom	Deed
1717, Mar. 15	HARDING, Stephen	Samuel Fuller et ux.	Deed
1717, May 20	HARDING, Stephen	Samuel Littlefield et ux.	Deed
171$\frac{2}{3}$, Feb. 12	HARFORD, Nicholas	Abraham Morrell et ux.	Deed
1718, May 23	HARMON, Johnson	Peter Nowell	Discharge
1716, Sept. 14	HARMON, Samuel	Samuel Brown	Deed
1713, Sept. 17	HARRIS, John	Richard Walker	Deed
1715, June 29	HARRIS, Joseph	William Pearse (Pearce) et ux.	Mortgage
1715, Nov. 1	HARRIS, Joseph	Nathaniel Whitney et ux.	Deed

Index of Grantees. 97

Folio.	Description.
35	8 acres and 20 rods on Love's brook, in *Berwick*.
119	300 acres, with 10 acres of marsh, town grant, in *Wells*.
22	All his right and title to houses and lands of his father, Thomas Hanscom, deceased, in *Kittery*.
22	All his right and title to houses and lands of his father, Thomas Hanscom, deceased, in *Kittery*.
203	One-half of 600 acres, bounded east by Kennebunk river, west by Pond marsh, north by Bucklin's line, south by the sea, in *Wells*.
211	30 acres, town grant to Anthony and Francis Littlefield, in *Wells*.
222	5 acres adjoining said Morrell's land on the north, highway on the east, Samuel Morrell's land on the south, Dover river on the west; also 22½ acres at the east end of Samuel Hill's home lot, in *Kittery*.
91	Of mortgage recorded in folio 91.
212	A farm of 100 acres, with dwellinghouse; also 50 acres, both town grants to Nathaniel Masters; 5 acres of marsh bounded by land of Joseph Littlefields, Mr. Wells and Webhannet river; also an island thatch on the river, and 10 acres known as Master's meadow, in *Wells*.
4	300 acres on east side of Cape Porpoise river, in *Coxhall* [now Lyman].
105	10 acres on southwest side of York river, in *York*.
126	A tract and marsh, called Sunken marsh, on southwest side of York river, in *York*.

Index of Grantees.

Date.	Grantee.	Grantor.	Instrument.
1701, Mar. 14	HARRIS, Nathaniel	Thomas Clark, estate of, by Elisha Hutchinson and Elizabeth Hutchinson, executrix	Deed
1703, Apr. 14	HARRIS, Nathaniel	Eliakim Hutchinson et ux.	Deed
1716, Apr. 25	HASKINS, Ruth	John Haskins	Release
17$\frac{9}{10}$, Mar. 2	HEARD, John, and Nicholas Morrell	Each other	Deed of Exchange
1711, May 21	HILL, Joseph	James Gooch et ux.	Deed
	HILL, Samuel, see Joshua Downing		
1713, Dec. 4	HILTON, Benjamin	Robert Elliot	Deed
1716, Jan. 28	HODSDEN, Joseph, and John Hooper	Elizabeth Hubord and Philip Hubord	Deed
1715, Apr. 6	HODSDEN, Samuel	Timothy Waymouth	Mortgage
1638, June 27	HOOKE, Humphrey, and William Hooke Thomas Hooke Giles Eldredge	Edward Godfrey	Receipt
1717, May 1	HOOKE [Hook], Humphrey, and Jacob Hook	William Hook	Deed
	HOOK, Jacob, see Humphrey Hook		
	HOOKE, Thomas, see Humphrey Hook		

Index of Grantees.   99

Folio.	Description.
95	132 acres bounded by Alexander Maxwell's and Micum Mackentire's land, also by York river, in *York*.
96	25 acres, on which stood the late Edward Rishworth's house; also 10 acres at Burnt Plain, in *York*.
170	His right and interest in Thomas Atkins' estate.
82	A tract beginning at the highway from Sturgeon creek bridge to the cedars joining Nicholas Frost's land; in exchange for a tract bounded northwest by road from Sturgeon creek bridge to Newichewannock, in *Kittery*.
9	One-quarter part of saw-mill and privilege of stream, on Merryland river, in *Wells*.
39	26 acres on southwest side of York river, in *York*.
200	Land and buildings bought of Timothy Waymouth, in *Berwick*.
202	20 acres near Mast cove, in *Berwick*.
122	For their part of the charge in procuring grant for Cape Neddick, in *York*.
206	500 acres, one-half of Hook's farm, on north side of York river, at Scotland, 250 acres on the seaside; also that tract called Cape Neddick, granted his father, William Hook, deceased; and 1000 acres more out of the grants and patents to his father, William Hook, in *York*.

Index of Grantees.

Date.	Grantee.	Grantor.	Instrument.
1638, June 2	Hook [Hooke], William	Edward Godfrey	Lease
1717, Aug. 28	Hook [Hooke], William	Humphrey Hook and Jacob Hook	Deed
1717, Aug. 28	Hook [Hooke], William	William Hook, junior	Deed
	Hook [Hooke], William, see Humphrey Hooke		
17$\frac{14}{15}$, Feb. 28	Hooper, John	Baker Nason et ux.	Deed
17$\frac{14}{15}$, Feb. 28	Hooper, John	Joseph Wood	Deed
	Hooper, John, see Joseph Hodsden		
1688, Sept. 12	Houghton, John	John Greeson	Deed
17$\frac{13}{14}$, Mar. 12	Hubbard, Elizabeth, and Philip Hubbard	Timothy Waymouth	Deed
	Hubbard, Philip, see Elizabeth Hubbard		
	Hubbart, Thomas, see John Marion		
1708, Feb. 14	Huff, Thomas	Aaron Ferris et ux.	Deed
1717, Mar. 26	Huff, Thomas	William Pepperrell, junior	Deed
17$\frac{13}{14}$, Jan. 11	Hutchins, Benjamin	Jonathan Hutchins	Deed
1714, June 29	Hutchins, Benjamin	Samuel Hutchins	Deed

Index of Grantees.

Folio.	Description.
121	Lands northwest of Cape Neddick creek, in *York*.
232	All their right in lands by a deed from their father, said William Hook, in *York*.
232	All his right to lands by a deed from his father, said William Hook, in *York*.
101	6 acres, beginning at the north corner of Benjamin Nason's land, in *Berwick*.
102	3½ acres bought of John Croade, in *Berwick*.
165	A tract belonging formerly to his father, Robert Greeson, in *Falmouth*.
199	50 acres with dwelling house, bounded southwest by Mast cove, northwest by William Hearl's land, east by Jonathan Nason's land, north by Thomas Greely's land, in *Berwick*.
12	Land and buildings at Spruce creek; also quarter part of a sloop, in *Kittery*.
219	Refers to deed recorded in folio 81.
49	All his right in land near the head of Eastern creek, in *Kittery*.
49	Same as above.

Book VIII.   48

Date.	Grantee.	Grantor.	Instrument.
1716, Feb. 7	HUTCHINS, John, and Samuel Palmer Benjamin Thurston Abraham Rideout	Joseph Shaw	Deed
1714, Mar. 7	HUTCHINS, Samuel	George Fennix	Deed
1668, Oct. 9	HUTCHINSON, Richard	Edward Rishworth	Mortgage
1716, Sept. 13	HUTCHINSON, Thomas, and John Wentworth Adam Winthrop David Jeffries Oliver Noyes Stephen Minot John Ruck John Watts	Sylvanus Davis, estate of, by John Nelson, executor	Deed
1716, Sept. 4	HUTCHINSON, Thomas, and John Wentworth Adam Winthrop David Jeffries Oliver Noyes Stephen Minot John Ruck John Watts	Each other	Agreement
1714, Nov. 5	HUTCHINSON, Thomas, and John Wentworth Adam Winthrop David Jeffries Oliver Noyes Stephen Minot John Ruck John Watts	Richard Wharton, estate of, by Ephraim Savage, administrator	Deed
	HUTCHINSON, Thomas, see John Wentworth		
1715, Mar. 14	INGERSOL, Elisha, and John Chapman	John Ingersol	Deed
1675, May 1	INGERSOL, John	George Munjoy	Deed
1715, May 19	INGERSOL, Nathaniel	John Ingersol	Deed

Folio.	Description.
208	A tract north of the Mill pool, in *Sagadahoc*.
180	10 acres, town grant to William Lewis, in *Kittery*.
65	70 acres next Thomas Moulton's and Nathaniel Maysterson's lands; also a meadow on northwest side of Old Mill creek, and two thirds of all his cattle, in *York*.
176	A tract on the west side of Kennebec river, called Small Point; 15 acres east side of Casco bay, called Davis' harbor; 10 acres at Small Point harbor; also Great Stage island, on east side of the mouth of the Kennebec river; 200 acres on east side of Kennebec river, purchased from the Indians; 500 acres near Oyster river, in Damariscotta river; also a tract east of Masconks, purchased of the Indians, together with buildings, fences, etc.
178	That considerable part of their purchase of lands be assigned to each partner.
56	A tract called Prejepscot [Brunswick], bought of the estate of Thomas Purchase; Merriconeig neck and Sebascodegan island, in Casco bay; also the land granted Richard Wharton five miles above Androscoggin falls.
79	All his land, except a parcel bought of George Montjoy, in *Falmouth*.
86	A tract at Capisic, in *Falmouth*.
94	36 acres on east side of Spruce creek, in *Kittery*.

Index of Grantees.

Date.	Grantee.	Grantor.	Instrument.
1715, June 20	Jacobs, George	Eliab Littlefield	Deed
1716, Aug. 13	Jaffrey, George	Sam'l Penhallow and Samuel Keais	Deed
	Jeffries, David, see Thomas Hutchinson		
	Jeffries, David, see John Wentworth		
1703, June 2	Jenkins, Reinold	Stephen Jenkins and Anne Kincaid	Deed
	Jenkins, Reinold, see Frances Allen		
1712, Apr. 8	Jordan, Dominicus	Joseph Sevey	Deed
1660, Aug. 25	Jordan, Robert	Michael Mitton et ux.	Deed
1657, Sept. 11	Jordan, Robert	Richard Tucker	License
1658, July 28	Jordan, Robert, and John Phillips	Each other	Conditional Release
17$\frac{10}{11}$, Mar. 21	Junkins, Alexander, and Joseph Junkins	Daniel Mackentier	Deed
1709, Jan. 2	Junkins, Alexander, and Joseph Junkins	Job Young et ux. and Thomas Haynes	Deed
1710, Nov. 28	Junkins, Daniel	William Bracey et ux.	Deed
1701, Aug. 7	Junkins, Daniel	Daniel Littlefield et ux.	Deed
1712,——	Junkins, Daniel	James Smith	Deed

INDEX OF GRANTEES. 105

Folio.	Description.
153	6 acres, formerly John Littlefield's, deceased, in *Wells*.
223	One-half of Wither's island, in *Kittery*.
6	14 acres at Cold Harbor, in *Kittery*.
212	A neck of land containing 5 acres, and 2 acres adjoining, formerly in possession of John Pearce, deceased, in *Kittery*.
245	All lands granted him by George Cleve, or any other person, in *Falmouth*.
244	To use land adjoining the falls of Casco river and erect saw-mill or mills.
244	Relating to lands, cattle, chattels; also saw-mill to be erected at Casco river falls.
194	20 acres near the land of Daniel Livingstone, deceased, at the head of Bass cove brook, in *York*.
191	4 acres, called Young's marsh, at the head of the southwest branch of York river, in *Kittery*.
36	20 acres on the southwest side of York river; also 20 acres formerly John Pierce's, in *York*.
39	2 acres of marsh on southwest branch of York river, in *York*.
38	12 acres on south side of Bass cove marsh, in *York*.

Date.	Grantee.	Grantor.	Instrument.
	JUNKINS, Joseph, see Alexander Junkins		
1717, May 13	KENARD, Michael	Adrian Fry et ux.	Deed
	KENE, Nathaniel, see Samuel Spinney		
1688, Apr. 20	KIMBLE, Thomas	John Parker et ux.	Deed
1707, Oct. 6	KNIGHT, Thomas	John Thompson [Tompson], and John Paul	Deed
1713, Nov. 12	LEIGHTON, John, and Charles Frost Robert Cutt Joseph Hammond John Frost	Each other	Division Deed
1715, Oct. 25	LEIGHTON, John	John Whipple et ux.	Deed
	LEVIT, Thomas, see John Wheelwright		
1713, June 2	LEWIS, Andrew	Peter Lewis	Deed
1713, May 19	LEWIS, Andrew	William Wilson	Deed
1716, July 21	LIBBEY, Benjamin	Richard Rice	Deed
1716, July 18	LIBBEY, Benjamin	Daniel Stone	Deed
1716, June 30	LIBBEY, Benjamin	John Thompson	Deed
1705, Jan. 19	LIBBEY, Daniel	John Libbey	Deed

Folio.	Description.
216	2 parcels of land, with dwelling house and buildings, bought of Nicholas Morrell, in *Kittery*.
24	A tract on Kennebec river.
61	5½ acres adjoining their house-lots, in *Kittery*.
20	30 acres on Piscataqua river; 5 acres on Sturgeon creek; 34½ acres northeast from the head of Major Clark's and Joshua Downing's land; 30 acres near the highway from Sturgeon creek to Spruce creek; 60 acres bounded by land of John Frost, Robert Knight and Katherine Leighton, in *Kittery*.
151	His interest in a 50 acre town grant; also in a grant given William Leighton, at Crooked lane, in *Kittery*.
179	1½ acres and 28 poles at the head of land formerly Mr. Wither's, in *Kittery*.
179	17 acres, part of a 50 acre town grant to William Lewis, in *Kittery*.
225	30 acres, part of a town grant, in *Kittery*.
158	30 acres, part of a town grant, in *Berwick*.
157	One-half of a 21 acre town grant, in *Kittery*.
205	50 acres, bought of Joshua Scottow; 6 acres of marsh on Black Point river; 50 acres and 10 acres, two town grants; together with any right to other lands, reserving lands which belonged to his father, John Libbey, deceased, in *Scarborough*.

Index of Grantees.

Date.	Grantee.	Grantor.	Instrument.
1713, Nov. 1	LIBBEY, John	John Libbey, senior	Deed
1671, Oct. 14	LIBBEY, John	Town of Scarborough	Grant
1684, Feb. 5	LIBBEY, John	Town of Scarborough	Grant
1668, Aug. 1	LIBBEY, John	Joshua Scottow	Conditional Deed
1714, Sept. 18	LINSCOT, John	Peter Nowell et ux.	Deed
1713, May 4	LITTLEFIELD, David	Jonathan Littlefield and Samuel Hill	Deed
1716, Dec. 10	LITTLEFIELD, David	Samuel Littlefield et ux.	Deed
1689, Oct. 10	LITTLEFIELD, Francis	Thomas Averell	Deed
1678, Oct. 25	LOCK, Elizabeth	Joseph Bolls	Deed
1702, Dec. —	LORD, Abraham	John Plaisted et ux. and John Hill et ux.	Deed
1712, July 29	LORD, Nathan, and Richard Lord	John Wincoll et ux.	Deed
1714, Jan. 24	LORD, Nathan, senior	John Croade et ux.	Deed
1712, Aug. 11	LORD, Richard	Martha Lord and Benjamin Lord	Deed
1713, June 25	LORD, Richard	Benjamin Nason	Deed
1713, Mar. 30	LORD, Richard	Moses Spencer	Deed

Folio.	Description.
13	A tract, farm and marsh, at Black Point, *Scarborough*.
206	50 acres, to be clear of other grants.
206	20 acres adjoining Matthew Libbey's land.
225	50 acres east of said Libbey's father's field, and 6 acres of marsh next the Clay pit, in *Scarborough*.
174	40 acre town grant, between the Partings of York river, in *York*.
250	200 acres on northeast side of Daniel Sawyer's land; also a parcel of land between said land and Cross' brook, in *Wells*.
251	One-quarter part of falls, at *Kennebunk*.
175	200 acres, called Tatnack (Totnucke), six miles from town of Wells; also 6 acres, in *Wells*.
46	A tract of upland and 10 acres of marsh at the Three Mile brook, in *Wells*.
52	29 acres, part of land purchased of Eliakim Hutchinson, in *Kittery*.
118	65 acres, bounded south by highway and Wilcock's pond, east by Thomas Spencer's land, north by Great Works river, west by land laid out for the ministry, in *Berwick*.
73	27 acres, part of 50 acres bequeathed Moses Spencer by William Spencer, in *Berwick*.
117	5 acres near White's marsh, in *Berwick*.
117	$2\frac{1}{4}$ acres on south side of town highway, in *Berwick*.
118	6 acres at the east end of Francis Herlow's land; 12 acres beginning at Benjamin Nason's land, in *Berwick* [*Kittery*].

Date.	Grantee.	Grantor.	Instrument.
	LORD, Richard, see Nathan Lord		
170$, Mar. 22	LORD, William	Martha Lord and Nathan Lord Benjamin Lord John Cooper Tobias Hanson William Frost Moses Littlefield	Deed
1716, Apr. 5	LYDSTON, John	Jonathan Downing et ux. and Mary Nelson	Deed
1717, July 20	LYDSTON, John	Samuel Hill, jr.	Confirmation
1713, Mar. 16	MACKENTIER, John	Daniel Mackentier	Deed
1714, May 24	MACKENTIER, Micum	John Mackentier	Deed
1715, Feb. 28	MAINE, Josiah, and Charles Frost	Each other	Deed of Exchange
1713, May 15	MARION, John, and Josiah Tay Thomas Hubbart	Richard Wharton, estate of, by Ephraim Savage, admr.	Deed and Receipt
	MARTYN, Mary, see John Wentworth		
171$, Mar. 13	MASTIN, Bethiah	Job Curtis	Deed
1636, Jan. 13	MAVERICK, Samuel, and William Dixey	Each other	Agreement for Sale

INDEX OF GRANTEES. 111

Folio.	Description.
54	40 acres, with house and barn, adjoining said William Lord's land; also cattle and goods, in *Kittery*.
147	30 acres, bounded south by said Lydston's land, north by Joseph Hill's land, west by the river, east by Richard King's land, in *Kittery*.
236	Of deed recorded in folio 147.
38	17 acres on west side of York river, in *York*.
89	40 acres, except 3 acres, on southwest side of York river, in *York*.
129	A parcel of land adjoining said Micum's land, in exchange for 1 acre at the northeast corner of land formerly Edward Rishworth's, in *York*.
186	650 acres on Great Chebeague island; 350 acres at the west end of Maquoit, in *Casco bay*.
223	His home place between Caleb Preble's and Joseph Banks' land, together with dwelling-house and barn; likewise 30 acres at the head of his home place and Daniel Simpson's land; 3 acres of marsh on the west side of southwest branch of York river; also 2 cows, 6 sheep, or their equivalent, in *York*.
209	For house and land.

Index of Grantees.

Date.	Grantee.	Grantor.	Instrument.
171⅘, Mar. 10	Milbury [Milberry], Richard	John Banks et ux. and Joseph Banks et ux.	Deed
	Milbury [Milberry], Richard, see Peter Weare		
1715, Apr. 4	Milbury [Milberry], Richard	John Snell et ux.	Deed
1715, Feb. —	Milbury [Milberry], Richard	John Snell	Deed
1714, Apr. 1	Milbury [Milberry], Richard	Samuel Webber et ux.	Deed
1714, June 24	Milbury [Milberry], Richard	Samuel Webber et ux.	Deed
1717, June 21	Minot, Stephen	Elisha Kelley et ux.	Mortgage
	Minot, Stephen, see John Wentworth		
	Minot, Stephen, see Thomas Hutchinson		
1711, Apr. 4	Mitchell, Richard	Roger Dearing	Assignm'nt of Mortgage
1715, Aug. 22	Mitchell, William et ux.	John Tinney	Deed
1650, Feb. 24	Mitten, Michael	George Cleve [Cleaves]	Deed

INDEX OF GRANTEES. 113

Folio.	Description.
252	Two-thirds of a 40 acre tract on Dummer's neck, in *York*.
93	50 acres on Mr. Dummer's neck of land, in *York*.
253	3 acres on southwest branch of York river, in *York*.
51	16 acres on northeast side of Little river, in *York*.
50	One-quarter of saw-mill and 1 acre of land, known as Cape Neddick mill, in *York*.
224	3 acres on Smutty-nose island; 6 acres on Starr island, with buildings, etc., also all his right in Hog island, *Isles of Shoals*.
45	Houses and lands in Kittery, recorded in folio 45.
156	A tract at Black Point; also all his land near Spurwink river, in *Scarborough*.
245	A tract granted him by Alexander Rigby, together with houses, buildings, cattle and household utensils, in *Casco bay*.

Index of Grantees.

Date.	Grantee.	Grantor.	Instrument.
1717, May 10	Moodey, William	Charles Frost et ux.	Deed
1717, May 6	Moodey, William	John Harmon and Benjamin Stone John Kingsbury Jonathan Young Jonathan Bane Samuel Bragdon Joseph Hoult John Stagpole	Deed
17$\frac{1}{2}$, Feb. 28	More, Ebenezer	Edmund Gage et ux.	Deed
171$\frac{2}{3}$, Feb. 26	More, Ebenezer	Hannah Wilson	Deed
17$\frac{18}{19}$, Feb. 20	More, Ebenezer and John Norton	Henry Barter et ux.	Deed
1687, Oct. 22	More, John	Richard White	Deed
1703, July 3	Morey, Nicholas	Joseph Bailey	Levy on Execution
1703, July 3	Morey, Nicholas	Joseph Bailey	Levy on Execution
1714, Mar. 27	Morrell, Abraham	John Chapman et ux.	Deed
1715, Nov. 13	Morrell, Abraham, and William Tetherly Samuel Tetherly	Lemuel Gowen et ux.	Deed
1715, Jan. 20	Morrell, Abraham, and William Tetherly Samuel Tetherly	Each other	Division
1715, Sept. 27	Morrell, John, and Richard Chick	Each other	Arbitration and Award
1717, Aug. 13	Morrell, John	Nicholas Morrell	Bond

Index of Grantees. 115

Folio.	Description.
209	370 acres on southwest side of York river, in *York*.
207	A town grant between Thomas Adams' and Thomas Beeson's land, in *York*.
84	22 acres of upland and 3 acres of marsh, with dwelling house and barn, northwest side of Brave-boat harbor, in *Kittery*.
85	One-quarter of saw-mill on east side of Spruce creek, in *Kittery*.
214	27¾ acres bought of Thomas Hooper, in *Kittery*.
116	30 acre town grant at Brave-boat harbor, in *York*.
125	100 acres at Cape Porpoise.
125	140 acres at Cape Porpoise.
25	22½ acres, at the east end of Samuel Hill's home-lot, in *Kittery*.
141	100 acres purchased of James Gowen; two 30 acre town grants; also 40 acres on west side of Third hill, in *Kittery*.
142	Of land purchased of Lemuel Gowen, in *Kittery*.
139	Establishing division line between their lands, on north side of Sturgeon creek, in *Kittery*.
263	Conditioned to pay the produce of 5 acres of tillage land; also one-half the increase, produce and profit of a certain number of cattle.

Index of Grantees.

Date.	Grantee.	Grantor.	Instrument.
171¾, Mar. 12	Morrell, John, junior	James Emery and Daniel Emery	Deed
171⁶⁄₇, Jan. 9	Morrell, John, junior	John Heard et ux.	Deed
1711, Dec. 7	Morrell, Nicholas	James Fernald	Deed
1711, Dec. 17	Morrell, Nicholas	John Heard	Deed
1717, Aug. 30	Morrell, Nicholas	John Morrell	Deed
1710, Nov. 22	Morrell, Nicholas	Timothy Wentworth et ux.	Deed
	Morrell, Nicholas, see John Heard		
1715, Feb. 22	Moulton, Jeremiah	Daniel Moulton	Deed
1714, Dec. 17	Moulton, Joseph	Jeremiah Moulton et ux.	Deed
1674, July 15	Munjoy, George	Francis Small	Levy on Execution
1715, June 27	Newmarch, John	Daniel Mackentier and Micum Mackentier	Deed
	Norton, John, see Ebenezer More		
1709, Aug. 24	Nowell, Peter	Daniel Black et ux.	Deed
1710, Dec. 12	Nowell, Peter	Arthur Bragdon	Deed
1716, Sept. 19	Nowell, Peter	Henry Brookin	Deed
1716, Sept. 19	Nowell, Peter	Samuel Donnell et ux.	Deed

Index of Grantees.   117

Folio.	Description.
23	Quitclaim to 200 acres on south side of Sturgeon creek, in *Kittery*.
229	20 acres east of Sturgeon creek, in *Kittery*.
94	20 acres part of a town grant, in *Kittery*.
79	30 acres granted his grandfather, John Heard, by town of *Kittery*.
261	100 acres at Cold harbor, with house, buildings, cattle and implements of husbandry, in *Kittery*.
70	One-half his interest in a water-course, saw-mill and land, on Worster's river, in *Berwick*.
148	All his right and title to estate, both real and personal, of Joseph Moulton, deceased, in *York*.
68	A tract on northwest side New Mill creek, in *York*.
151	202 acres on Piscataqua river, in *Kittery*.
104	30 acres on southwest side of southwest branch of York river, in *York*.
30	2 acres northeast side of Hull's creek, in *York*.
33	37 acres near Bell marsh, in *York*.
182	30 acres on northwest side of Bell Marsh brook, in *York*.
181	82 acres on northwest branch of York river, in *York*.

Index of Grantees.

Date.	Grantee.	Grantor.	Instrument.
171$\frac{4}{5}$, Feb. 16	Nowell, Peter	Charles Frost	Receipt
17$\frac{14}{15}$, Jan. 15	Nowell, Peter	Johnson Harmon	Mortgage
1714, Sept. 18	Nowell, Peter	John Linscot	Deed
1716, Sept. 13	Nowell, Peter	Ebenezer Pemberton	Discharge
17$\frac{13}{14}$, Jan. 12	Nowell, Peter	Nathaniel Ramsdell	Deed
17$\frac{08}{10}$, Mar. 1	Nowell, Peter	William Shaw et ux.	Deed
1715, May 23	Nowell, Peter	James Smith et ux.	Deed
17$\frac{14}{15}$, Jan. 3	Nowell, Peter	Alex'ndr Thompson [Tompson]	Mortgage
1716, Sept. 25	Nowell, Peter	Philip Welch et ux.	Deed and Receipt
	Nowell, Peter, see Peter Weare		
	Nowell, Peter, see Humphrey Scammon		
1708, Nov. 26	Nowell, Peter, and Hopewell Weare	Mary Weare	Deed
	Nowell, Samuel, see Thomas Danforth		
1717, Dec. 24	Noyes, Oliver	James Pitman	Mortgage
	Noyes, Oliver, see Thomas Hutchinson		
	Noyes, Oliver, see John Wentworth		

Index of Grantees. 119

Folio.	Description.
88	For £33 : 10, judgment of court against Capt. Harmon.
91	8 acres of marsh; 10 or 12 acres of upland between two branches of York river, in *York*.
107	31½ acres at Birch hill, in *York*.
175	Of mortgage recorded in folio 67.
110	One-quarter of one-half of marsh bought of Arthur Bragdon, senior, near Agamenticus hill, in *York*.
31	20 acres on York river, in *York*.
108	46 acres, bounded southwest by the way from York to Berwick, northwest by land formerly Job Alcock's, southeast by land formerly Robert Jenkins', northeast by town commons, in *York*.
67	40 or 50 acres that Benjamin Curtis bought of Master Everet, in *York*.
182	30 acre town grant on northwest side of Bell marsh brook, in *York*.
32	8 acres salt marsh on northwest branch of York river, in *York*.
265	124 acres at Pemaquid point, in *Jamestown*.

Index of Grantees.

Date.	Grantee.	Grantor.	Instrument.
1712, Dec. 10	OLIVER, Robert	Samuel Came	Deed
1703, May 3	OTIS, Job	Gilbert Winslow	Deed
1702, Feb. 17	OTIS, Job	Nathaniel Winslow et ux.	Deed
	PALMER, Samuel, see John Hutchins		
1675, Jan. 10	PALMER, William	John Davis sr., and John Davis jr.	Deed
17$\frac{14}{15}$, Mar. 1	PARSONS, Elihu	John Parsons	Deed
1665, Dec. 7	PATESHALL, Richard, and Robert Pateshall Humphrey Davie	Alexander Thoyts	Deed
	PATESHALL, Robert, see Richard Pateshall		
1730, Feb. 4	PAUL, Daniel	James Fernald	Discharge
	PAUL, John, see John Skriggin		
1722, Dec. 27	PEARCE, William	Nathan'l Raynes	Discharge
1711, Jan. 18	PEARSE, William et ux.	Arthur Beal	Deed
1714, Dec. 27	PEMBERTON, Ebenezer	Peter Nowell et ux.	Mortgage
1675, Oct. 8	PENDLETON, Bryan	Simon Booth et ux.	Deed
1664, May 2	PENDLETON, Bryan	William Phillips et ux.	Deed

INDEX OF GRANTEES. 121

Folio.	Description.
18	20 acres on the northwest branch of York river, in *York*.
27	One-half of 300 acres, also one-half of 20 or 30 acres on Arisicket [Harraseket] river, in *Casco bay*.
26	Same as above.
198	One-half of a neck of land called Batson's neck; also one-half of marsh and lot adjoining, called the Grass plot, together with other lands and dwelling-house, in *Cape Porpoise*.
100	22 acres between Daniel Simpson's and John Preble's land, in *York*.
158	A tract on the Kennebec river, beginning at a cove, the lower bounds of Robert Gutch's land, so to run along the water side to Winnegance [Winnegansick] river, also cattle, house, barn, etc.; also a marsh on the south side of Winnegance river.
227	Of the mortgage recorded folio 227.
138	Of mortgage recorded in folio 137.
103	10 acres on the southwest side of York river, in *York*.
66	130 acres, bounded south by York river, at Scotland, in *York*.
88	Tract of upland and marsh, with buildings, at Winter Harbor [now Biddeford].
155	A neck of land below Saco river; also Wood island, Gibbon's island, Cow island and a tract called West point on Saco river, in *Saco*.

Index of Grantees.

Date.	Grantee.	Grantor.	Instrument.
1712, Mar. 4	Penhallow, Samuel	Robert Elliot	Assignm't
1716, Dec. 15	Penhallow, Samuel	Thomas Huff	Mortgage
171$\frac{2}{3}$, Feb. 6	Pepperrell, Andrew	Joseph Dearing et ux.	Deed
1723, June 20	Pepperrell, William	Matthew Austine et ux.	Deed
17$\frac{13}{14}$, Mar. 6	Pepperrell, William	Edward Beal et ux.	Deed
1714, Dec. 23	Pepperrell, William	Edward Beal et ux.	Mortgage
1715, Aug. 30	Pepperrell, William	William Roberts, estate of	Levy on Execution
1712, May 27	Pepperrell, William	Nathan'l Thomas	Deed
1718, May 28	Pepperrell, William jr.	Henry Barter	Mortgage
1717, May 18	Pepperrell, William jr.	Thomas Goodwill et ux.	Deed
17$\frac{14}{15}$, Mar. 10	Pepperrell, William jr.	Thomas Huff	Deed
17$\frac{14}{15}$, Mar. 10	Pepperrell, William jr.	Samuel Penhallow	Assignm't of Mortgage
1713, June 6	Pepperrell, William jr.	William Pepperrell	Deed
17$\frac{13}{14}$, Mar. 6	Pepperrell, William jr.	Samuel Skillion	Mortgage
1716, Oct. 26	Pepperrell, William jr.	Samuel Walker	Deed and Receipt

INDEX OF GRANTEES. 123

Folio.	Description.
1	Of mortgage recorded in Book VI, 165.
81	All his interest in lands, houses and stock conveyed to him by Aaron Ferris, in *Kittery*.
196	10½ acres near Spruce creek, in *Kittery*.
20	A third part of a certain grant bought of Nathaniel Thomas, in *Kittery*.
135	21¼ acres next to said Pepperrell's land, in *York*.
69	200 acres, bounded northwest by William Pepperrell's land, northeast by the river, southwest by Mr. Rayne's land, southeast by the sea; also all his land on the south side of York river, in *York*.
126	14 acres, with dwelling house, in *Kittery*.
136	A cartway over his land at Kittery point, in *Kittery*.
42	16 acres and 40 acres on Crocket's neck, in *Kittery*.
220	One-third of a tract bought by Benjamin Blackman of John Bonighton and James Gibbons, in *Saco*.
80	18 acres between Henry Barter's and Joseph Crocket's lands, in *Kittery*.
81	All his right in mortgage from Thomas Huff.
41	60 acre town grant, and 45 acres adjoining the land bought of Joseph Crocket; also a town grant upon the land known as Farmoths, and 30 acres purchased of Edmund Gosse, in Kittery; also a tract purchased of Mary Hooke, and 95 acres north of Richard Mitchell's, in *York*.
42	80 acres on Spruce creek, in *Kittery*.
185	Two-thirds of 6,000 acres on east side of Saco river; also two-thirds of adjoining tract, in *Saco*.

INDEX OF GRANTEES.

Date.	Grantee.	Grantor.	Instrument.
1716, Oct. 26	PEPPERRELL, William jr.	Samuel Walker	Bond
1717, Dec. 16	PEPPERRELL, William jr. and Humphrey Scamon junior Nathaniel Weare	Each other	Agreement and Division
1715, Dec. 26	PERKINS, Thomas jr.	Eliab Littlefield	Deed
1714, Oct. 1	PERKINS, Thomas	James Tanner et ux.	Deed
1717, June 6	PETTIGREW[Pettegrew], Francis	John Ball et ux.	Deed
1716, June 1	PETTIGREW[Pettegrew], Francis	William Godsoe	Deed
	PHILLIPS, John, see Robert Jordan		
1661, Mar. 30	PHILLIPS, William	Fluellin, Indian	Deed
1660, Aug. 29	PHILLIPS, William	Hombinowitt, alias John Rogomock	Deed
1664, June 22	PHILLIPS, William	Meeksombe, alias Capt. Sunday, Indian	Deed
1694, June 15	PIKE, Hugh	John Burnum, jr.	Deed
1713, Apr. 4	PIKE, Philip	William Fry et ux.	Deed
	PLAISTED, Elizabeth, see Olive Wincoll		

INDEX OF GRANTEES. 125

Folio.	Description.
186	In £52 that his wife shall not claim her thirds or any other part of land conveyed to said Pepperrell.
259	In regard to land and saw-mill, in *Saco*.
180	200 acres northeast side of Cape Porpoise river, in *Cape Porpoise*.
140	Land on Royall's river, in *North Yarmouth*.
230	22 acres, bounded east by Spruce creek, north by branch of said creek, south by William Godsoe's land, west by said Godsoe's and John Sheppard's land, with house, goods and chattels, in *Kittery*.
156	¾ of an acre, bounded west by his own land, south by road to York, north by Richard Roger's land, in *Kittery*.
220	From Saco patent bounds south beyond Cape Porpoise river for breadth, and from the head of Wells and Cape Porpoise township up into the country, except four square miles sold Bush, Sanders and Turbut.
220	All his lands west of the Saco river from Salmon Falls to Capt. Sunday's rocks, and twenty miles up into the country.
221	A tract above Saco falls, about 35 or 40 miles up into the country.
264	300 acres, part of a tract purchased with others of Harlakinden Symonds, in *Coxhall* [now Lyman].
136	10 acres, except a burying-place, at the mouth of Sturgeon creek, in *Kittery*.

Index of Grantees.

Date.	Grantee.	Grantor.	Instrument.
1716, Feb. 2	Plaisted, Ichabod	Walter Allen	Deed
1712, Aug. 26	Plaisted, Ichabod	Jacob Cole, by Edward Bromfield, attorney	Deed
1706, July 3	Plaisted, Ichabod	James Plaisted et ux.	Deed
1714, Oct. 29	Plaisted, Ichabod	John Rogers	Deed
1707, May 21	Plaisted, Ichabod	Edward Sargent	Deed
1712, Jan. 27	Plaisted, Ichabod	Henry Wright	Deed
	Plaisted, Ichabod, see Olive Wincoll		
1707, July 8	Plaisted, James	Eliakim Hutchinson	Assignment
	Plaisted, James, see Olive Wincoll		
	Plaisted, John, see Olive Wincoll		
1716, Oct. 8	Plaisted, Mary, and John Saywood	Each other	Arbitration and Award
	Plaisted, Mehitable, see Olive Wincoll		
1709, Oct. 4	Plaisted, Roger	Abel Hamilton et ux.	Deed
1714, Apr. 5	Plaisted, Roger	Ephraim Joy et ux.	Deed
	Plaisted, William, see Olive Wincoll		
	Pray, Joseph, see Richard Toziar		

Index of Grantees. 127

Folio.	Description.
257	A grant of 60 acres, excepting 10 acres, next Humphrey Chadbourne's lot, in *Berwick*.
262	One-sixth in common of lands, fall and mills at Quamphegan falls, in *Berwick*.
132	All land belonging to him from the estate of his father, Roger Plaisted, deceased, in *Kittery*.
134	3 acres next Salmon Falls mills, in *Berwick*.
133	180 acres at Salmon Falls, in *Berwick*.
204	50 acres on Piscataqua river, in *Kittery*.
66	Land and cattle, in *York*.
188	In regard to the estate of John Saywood, deceased.
256	7 acres on highway from Salmon Falls brook to John Key's house, in *Kittery* [*Berwick*].
256	7½ acres, part of a town grant, in *Kittery*.

Index of Grantees.

Date.	Grantee.	Grantor.	Instrument.
1651, Feb. 17	PREBLE, Abraham	Rice Howell	Deed
1713, June 9	PREBLE, Abraham jr.	Jeremiah Dummer	Deed and Receipt
1710, June 10	PREBLE, Abraham jr.	Joseph Weare	Deed
17$\frac{3}{4}$, Feb. 16	PREBLE, Caleb	Nathaniel Ramsdell	Deed
1717, Aug. 7	PREBLE, Jonathan	Hannah Preble	Deed
1717, July 18	PREBLE, Jonathan	John Saywood	Deed
1717, July 18	PREBLE, Jonathan	Joseph Saywood	Deed
1714, Mar. 2	PRICHARD, John	Nathaniel Harris	Deed
1715, May 10	PRICHARD, John	Nathaniel Harris	Deed
1715, May 10	PRICHARD, John	Nathaniel Harris	Deed
1715, May 12	PRICHARD, John	Nathaniel Harris	Deed
1689, Oct. 19	PULMAN, Mary	John Brand	Deed
171$\frac{3}{4}$, Mar. 10	RACKLIFT, William et ux.	Roger Dearing	Deed
1712, Sept. 6	RAMSDELL, Nathaniel	John Cole	Deed
17$\frac{2}{3}$, Jan. 21	RANDOL, Richard, and William Randol	Richard Randol	Deed
17$\frac{2}{3}$, Jan. 21	RANDOL, Richard, and William Randol	Richard Toziar	Deed
	RANDOL, William, see Richard Randol		

Folio.	Description.
203	12 acres on south side of Gorgeana [York] river, in *York*.
3	14 acres at a place called the Ridge of land; 2 acres of swamp near Paimer's cove, in *York*.
1	¼ acre on York river, in *York*.
115	A parcel of marsh northwest of Agamenticus hill, in *York*.
234	Her share in land which her mother, Mary Saywood, bought of John Cousins, in *Casco bay*.
235	All his right and title to land bought by Mary Saywood of John Cousins, in *Casco bay*.
234	All his right and title to land bought by Mary Saywood of John Cousins, in *Casco bay*.
97	50 acres, part of a tract bought of Harlakinden Symonds, in *Coxhall* [now Lyman].
97	132 acres, bounded by Alexander Maxwell's, Micum Mackentire's land and York river; also a tract with buildings, bought of Samuel Webber, in *York*.
98	35 acres bought of Eliakim Hutchinson, in *York*.
98	20 acres bought of Samuel Webber, in *York*.
172	So much land as the warehouse stands on, and 3 feet more, on York river, adjoining said Brand's orchard, in *York*.
257	¾ of an acre at Kittery point, in *Kittery*.
14	Town grant of 30 acres, in *York*.
63	30 acre town grant, in *Kittery*.
64	10 acres, part of a 100 acre town grant, by and in *Kittery*.

Date.	Grantee.	Grantor.	Instrument.
1726, Apr. 6	RAYNES, Francis	John Woodman	Discharge
1715, Aug. 2	RAYNES, Nathan	Francis Raynes	Deed
1715, Oct. 6	RAYNES, Nathaniel	William Pearce	Mortgage
1715, July 19	RAYNES, Nathaniel, and John Woodman	Each other	Arbitration and Award
1686, Oct. 16	REMICK, Jacob	Christian Remick	Deed
1717, Dec. 18	REMICK, Samuel	Jacob Remick	Deed
1715, May 10	RICE, Richard	Nicholas Shapleigh	Deed
	RICE, Richard, see William Godsoe		
1705, Dec. 29	Rice, Thomas senior	Thomas Rice jr.	Deed
	RIDEOUT, Abraham, see John Hutchins		
	ROBERTS, William et ux.	Thomas Crocket, estate of, by Anne Jeffry, administratrix	Deed
1698, Oct. 20	ROGERS, John	James Corbin	Deed
1698, Sept. 23	ROGERS, John	John Haughton et ux.	Deed
1698, June 25	ROGERS, John	Richard Seacomb estate of, by Susannah Seacomb, trustee	Deed

Index of Grantees. 131

Folio.	Description.
103	Of mortgage recorded in folio 103.
172	117 acres formerly possessed by his father, Nathaniel Raynes, in *York*.
137	10 acres on southwest side of York river, with buildings and two cows, reserving a way 2 poles wide, in *York*.
131	Relating to a tract of land at Brave-boat harbor, in York; also certain debts and dues.
255	20 acres on east side of cove behind Thomas Spinney's land, in *Kittery*
255	10 acres bounded by John Fernald's, Joshua Remick's and Richard Gowell's land, in *Kittery*.
230	11¾ acres, bounded east by William Godsoe's and Walter Deniford's land, south and west by John Newmarch's land, north by said Rice's land, in *Kittery*.
12	10 acres at the southwest end of his 30 acre lot, in *Kittery*.
145	Tract called Crockett's neck, also 6 acres adjoining home-lot, in *Kittery*.
162	100 acres, with dwelling-house, in *Casco bay*.
162	90 acres, bounded east by Presumpscot river, south by a brook, west by land of John Brown, north by land of Robert Nichols, in *Falmouth*.
161	50 acres; 10 acres of marsh bought of John Clean; an island of 100 acres; also any other land belonging to said estate, in *Casco bay*.

Index of Grantees.

Date.	Grantee.	Grantor.	Instrument.
17¼⅜, Jan. 11	Rogers, John	Richard Seacomb	Deed
17¼⅝, Mar. 12	Rogers, John	Jacob Smith et ux.	Quitclaim Deed
1716, July 24	Rogers, Richard	Samuel Spinney et ux.	Deed
1714, Nov. 6	Rogers, William	Alex'der Thompson et ux.	Deed
	Row, Richard, see Edward Godfrey		
	Ruck, John, see Thomas Hutchinson		
	Ruck, John, see John Wentworth		
1689, Oct. 30	Rust, Nathaniel sr.	Francis Littlefield	Deed
1689, Oct. 30	Rust, Nathaniel sr.	Francis Littlefield	Deed
1712, Sept. 29	Sargent, Diamond	John Follet	Deed
1713, Oct. 26	Sargent, Diamond	Anne Spiller and James Cocks et ux. John Dorothy et ux.	Deed
1717, Sept. 25	Sawyer, David	Abraham Morrell et ux.	Deed
1716, Dec. 10	Sawyer, Francis	Samuel Littlefield et ux.	Deed
170⅔, Mar. 22	Sawyer, Francis	William Sawyer et ux.	Deed
1712, Oct. 17	Sayward [Saywood], John	John Pickerin	Deed

Index of Grantees. 133

Folio.	Description.
163	Confirming previous deed given by Susannah Seacomb, executrix.
146	To estate, real or personal, of Richard Rogers, deceased, in *Kittery*.
181	22 acres on west side of Spruce creek, in *Kittery*.
61	20 acre town grant near Spruce creek road, in *Kittery*.
176	200 acres, called Tatnack; also 6 acres of meadow, in *Wells*.
176	100 acres adjoining his own lot, in *Wells*.
55	50 acre town grant by and in *Kittery*.
11	40 acres, bounded northeast by York line, in *Kittery*.
258	30 acre town grant to Lemuel Gowen by town of Kittery, in *Berwick*.
237	One-quarter part of Kennebunk falls and 30 acres; also 5 acres of marsh bounded by Mousam river and Clay hill, in *Wells*.
10	A tract of land and one-quarter of saw-mill, in *Wells*.
111	2 acres on north side of Mill creek, in *York*.

Book VIII.   50

Date.	Grantee.	Grantor.	Instrument.
1716, Oct. 23	SAYWARD [Saywood], John	Abraham Preble	Deed
1712, May 1	SAYWARD [Saywood], John	Hannah Sayward	Deed
	SAYWARD, John, see Mary Plaisted		
1717, Dec. 2	SCAMON, Humphrey jr.	William Pepperrell junior	Deed
	SCAMON, Humphrey jr., see William Pepperrell		
1713, Nov. 16	SCAMMON, Humphrey, and Peter Nowell	Richard Bonighton	Power of Attorney
1685, Aug. 14	SEACOMB, Richard	Thomas Cloice et ux.	Deed
———	SEACOMB, Richard	Proprietors of Falmouth	Grant
1686, Aug. 30	SEACOMB, Richard	Jotham Lewis et ux.	Deed
17$\frac{1}{5}$, Feb. 15	SEWALL, Nicholas	Town of York	Deed
1715, Mar. 9	SIMPSON, Daniel	Town of York	Deed
1713, June 20	SKILLIN, Samuel	Nicholas Frost et ux.	Deed
1713, Apr. 14	SKILLIN, Samuel	Jonathan Mendum et ux.	Deed
1713, Apr. 13	SKILLIN, Samuel	Nathaniel Mendum et ux.	Deed
1714, Dec. 6	SKRIGGIN, John, and John Paul	Each other	Arbitration and Award

Index of Grantees.

Folio.	Description.
197	One-sixth part of the estate of John Saywood, deceased, both real and personal.
110	All her right, title and interest in estate of John Saywood, deceased, in *York*.
258	One-quarter of 6,000 acres, bought of Samuel Walker and Thomas Goodwill; also one-quarter part of timber on 4,500 acres northeast of abovesaid land, in *Saco*.
254	To measure and deliver 120 acres northeast of Saco river, to Capt. Peter Weare, in *Saco*.
164	All his right in a farm belonging formerly to George Lewis, in *Falmouth*.
166	An island northwest from Jewell's island, called Hog island, in *Casco bay*.
165	30 acres, part of that land belonging to George Lewis, deceased, in *Casco bay*.
123	2 acres and 14 poles of land, in *York*.
243	5 acres between Ebenezer Coburn's and said Simpson's land, in *York*.
7	One-quarter of a tract on east side of Spruce creek, in *Kittery*.
28	One-half of a tract on Spruce creek, in *Kittery*.
6	One-quarter of a tract on east side of Spruce creek, in *Kittery*.
63	Relating to the estate of Stephen Paul, deceased.

Index of Grantees.

Date.	Grantee.	Grantor.	Instrument.
1673, ——	SMALL, Francis	Abraham Corbet	Levy on Execution
1715, Oct. 5	SMITH, James	Lewis Bane	Discharge
1715, June 8	SMITH, James	Timothy Wentworth et ux.	Deed
1716, Dec. 21	SMITH, John	John Stevens et ux. and James Grant et ux.	Deed
1709, Mar. 26	SMITH, John	John Wincoll et ux.	Deed
1717, Nov. 30	SOUTHACK, Cyprian	Samuel Scadlock	Mortgage
1714, Jan. 7	SPENCER, Mary	John Bradstreet	Mortgage
17$\frac{3}{4}$, Mar. 2	SPINNEY, John	Samuel Spinney	Deed
1716, July 23	SPINNEY, John	Samuel Spinney et ux.	Deed
1720, Mar. 2	SPINNEY, Samuel	John Addams	Discharge
1723, Mar. 30	SPINNEY, Samuel	John Dennet	Discharge
1716, June 18	SPINNEY, Samuel	John Woodman	Discharge
1714, May 7	SPINNEY, Samuel, and Nathaniel Kene	Each other	Agreement
1716, May 15	STEPHENS, Moses	Joseph Storer et ux.	Deed
	STORER, Augustine, see John Wheelwright		
1688, Aug. 3	STOUGHTON, William	Vines Ellacot	Lease and Agreement to convey
1688, Aug. 3	STOUGHTON, William	Vines Ellacot	Deed

Folio.	Description.
151	202 acres along the Piscataqua river, in *Kittery*.
127	Of the mortgage recorded folio 14.
210	10 acres at the upper end of his 60 acre lot, 10 acres bounded by said 60 acres and commons; reserving a highway, in *Berwick*.
207	Their share in the estate of James Ingles, deceased.
77	90 acres, part of a town grant to John Wincoll, deceased, and George Veazy, in *Berwick*.
256	Two-thirds of a farm at Little river, in *Cape Porpoise*.
75	1½ acres, bounded northwest by the Great Works river, with shop and appurtenances, in *Berwick*.
146	15 acres bought of John Shepard, in *Kittery*.
172	15 acres, part of that tract bought of Thomas Bice, reserving 2 poles for highway, in *Kittery*.
239	Of the mortgage recorded folio 239.
170	Of mortgage recorded in folio 170.
160	Of mortgage recorded in folio 29.
55	Establishing division line between their lands, near Spruce creek, in *Kittery*.
268	100 acres, belonging formerly to his brother, Samuel Storer, in *Wells*.
218	Hog island, formerly Cousin's island, with buildings, barns, etc., in North Yarmouth, *Casco bay*.
217	Same as above.

138 INDEX OF GRANTEES.

Date.	Grantee.	Grantor.	Instrument.
1685, Jan. 2	STOVER, John	Henry Donnel	Deed
1714, Nov. 15	STOVER, John	George Stover et ux.	Deed
	TAY, Josiah, see John Marion		
	TETHERLY, Samuel, see Abraham Morrell		
	TETHERLY, William, see Abraham Morrell		
1714, Nov. 9	THOMAS, William	Job Otis et ux.	Deed
1716, Apr. 20	THOMPSON, Alexander	Peter Nowell	Discharge
1668, Aug. 10	THOYTS, Alexander, Children of	Thomas Clark and Thomas Lake	Deed
	THURSTON, Benjamin, see John Hutchins		
1710, June 19	TIDY, John	John Morrell jr.	Deed
1717, Sept. 16	TOBEY, Stephen	William Rogers et ux.	Deed
1712, Apr. 15	TOMPSON, John	Joseph Couch	Deed
1714, Oct. 28	TOMPSON, John	Roger Couch	Confirmation
1710, Dec. 18	TOMPSON, John	Richard Gowell	Deed
17½, Mar. 8	TOMPSON, John	Clement Hughs	Release
1714, Dec. 20	TOMPSON, John	Joshua Remich [Remick]	Deed
1712, Nov. 26	TOMPSON, John	Samuel Tompson	Release

Index of Grantees. 139

Folio.	Description.
1	A parcel of land at the Long sands; also all the Barberry marsh, on east side of the great island in said marsh, in *York*.
60	His right and title in house and land on southwest side Cape Neddick river, in *York*.
106	300 acres bought of Nathaniel and Gilbert Winslow; also 20 or 30 acres more, in *Casco bay*.
6	Of mortgage recorded in folio 67.
159	A certain tract on the west side of Kennebec river, against *Kitts island*.
107	30 acres on north side of Sturgeon creek, in *Kittery*.
246	35 acres near York bounds, in *Kittery*.
144	11 acres, part of a town grant, by and in *Kittery*.
144	Of the above deed.
144	10 acre town grant, by and in *Kittery*.
144	Relating to estate of John Tompson, deceased, in *Kittery*.
145	6½ acres, part of a town grant, in *Kittery*.
144	Referring to estate of John Tompson, deceased.

Index of Grantees.

Date.	Grantee.	Grantor.	Instrument.
1713, Dec. 4	Toothacre, Andrew	Hannah Smith	Deed
1715, May 13	Toziar, Richard	Samuel Bracket et ux.	Deed
1715, Mar. 29	Toziar, Richard, and Joseph Pray	Each other	Division
17$\frac{15}{16}$, Mar. 7	Tucker, Jane	Joseph Tucker	Deed
1716, Dec. 25	Tucker, William	Nicholas Tucker	Deed
1716, Dec. 14	Tyler, James	Nicholas Moorey	Deed
1716, Dec. 14	Tyler, James	Nicholas Moorey	Bond
171$\frac{8}{9}$, Feb. 14	Tyler, James	Ezra Rolfe et ux. and Martha Jackson	Deed
1701, Oct. 14	Usher, John	Samuel Allen	Mortgage
1717, June 1	Walker, John	William Tucker et ux.	Deed
	Watts, John, see Thomas Hutchinson		
	Watts, John, see John Wentworth		

Index of Grantees.

Folio.	Description.
247	30 acres on York river, between Long cove and land of Josiah Maine, in *York*.
93	20 acres, part of a town grant to Isaac Botts, in *Berwick*.
92	Establishing division lines between their lands above Salmon Falls, in *Berwick*.
204	15 acres, bounded north by William Tucker's land, east by John Frink's land, south by land formerly Philip Carpenter's and Spruce creek, in *Kittery*.
214	30 acres, next to Mr. Moore's land, in *Kittery*.
201	One-half of land and rights which said Moorey claims; also 50 acres bought of Samuel Snow, in *Cape Porpoise*.
202	To warrant above premises.
249	Meadow and marsh between Black Point river and Saco river.
1	Territory from middle of Naumkeag river, around Cape Ann to Piscataqua harbor, thence to head of Newichewannock river, thence northwest until the distance from Piscataqua harbor equals 60 miles; also up Naumkeag river, with the southern half of Isles of Shoals; the whole called New Hampshire; also 10,000 acres southeast of Sagadahoc river, called Masonia; also beginning at the entrance of Newichewannock river and to the head thereof, containing in breadth 3 miles, all the length.
213	1 acre on Kittery point, in *Kittery*.

Index of Grantees.

Date.	Grantee.	Grantor.	Instrument.
17$\frac{13}{14}$, Mar. 13	WAYMOUTH, Timothy	Thomas Greely et ux.	Deed
1717, Feb. 17	WAYMOUTH, Timothy	Samuel Hodsden	Discharge
	WEARE, Hopewell, see Peter Nowell		
1710, June 20	WEARE, Joseph	Abraham Preble junior	Deed
1717, Dec. 2	WEARE, Nathaniel	William Pepperrell junior	Deed
	WEARE, Nathaniel, see William Pepperrell jr.		
17$\frac{13}{14}$, Feb. 22	WEARE, Peter, and Richard Milbury Peter Nowell	Joseph Banks et ux.	Deed
1713, Nov. 16	WEARE, Peter	Richard Bonighton	Deed
1717, July 3	WEBBER, Benjamin	Robert Gray et ux.	Deed
	WEBBER, Benjamin, see Thomas Webber		
1717, Aug. 19	WEBBER, James	Diamond Sargent [Sergent] et ux.	Deed
1714, Apr: 18	WEBBER, Thomas, and Benjamin Webber	Samuel Webber et ux.	Deed
1717, June 15	WEED, Thomas	John Gowen et ux.	Deed
1714, May 18	WEEKS, Nicholas	Paul Williams and Joanna Williams Edward Walker Elizabeth Gaskin	Deed

Index of Grantees. 143

Folio.	Description.
25	20 acres near Mast cove; 61 acres bounded by Israel Hodsden's land and commons, in *Kittery*.
202	Of the mortgage recorded folio 202.
4	2 acres at the head of Burnt plain, in *York*.
258	One-quarter of 6,000 acres bought of Samuel Walker and Thomas Goodwill; also one quarter part of timber on 4,500 acres northeast of abovesaid land, in *Saco*.
30	One-half of all their lands and marsh on northeast side of Saco river, in *Saco*.
8	120 acres on northeast side of Saco river, also all his right in Bonighton's or Indian island, in *Saco*.
225	2 tracts of 66 acres, on southwest side of York river and northwest side of Old Mill creek, in *York*.
236	¾ of an acre with house, near Crooked lane, in *Kittery*.
183	40 acres, on northeast side of Cape Neddick river, reserving ½ acre, in *York*.
215	20 acres, bounded north by Nicholas Gowen's land, east by road, south by David Sawyer's land, reserving burying place, in *Kittery*.
254	10 acres at the northeast end of the late John Hole's home lot, in *Kittery*.

Date.	Grantee.	Grantor.	Instrument.
170¾, Jan. 13	WELLS, Thomas	Samuel Sibley et ux.	Deed
1714, Oct. 25	WENTWORTH, John	John Reed	Deed
1716, May 18	WENTWORTH, John, and Mary Martyn	Thomas Allen	Mortgage
1716, July 20	WENTWORTH, John, and Thomas Hutchinson Adam Winthrop David Jeffries Oliver Noyes John Watts Stephen Minot John Ruck	James Berry et ux.	Deed
1716, Apr. 2	WENTWORTH, John, and Thomas Hutchinson Adam Winthrop David Jeffries Oliver Noyes John Watts Stephen Minot John Ruck	Elizabeth Davis and Hester Pike Thomas Washburn et ux. James Berry et ux. Ruth Haskins Sarah Gurney	Deed and Receipt
1716, May 22	WENTWORTH, John, and Thomas Hutchinson Adam Winthrop David Jeffries Oliver Noyes John Watts Stephen Minot John Ruck	Samuel Holman and Hannah Holman	Deed
171⅚, Feb. 21	WENTWORTH, John, and Thomas Hutchinson Adam Winthrop David Jeffries Oliver Noyes John Watts Stephen Minot John Ruck	Abigail Newman	Deed

Index of Grantees. 145

Folio.	Description.
248	All their share in lands belonging to the estate of their father, John Wells, deceased, in *Wells*.
130	50 acres on Salmon Falls river, in Berwick; also an addition granted by town of *Kittery*.
154	1 acre; also 7 acres bought of Ebenezer More, in *Kittery*.
167	Tract bounded east by Small Point harbor, bought of the Indians; tract bounded north by Robert Edmund's land, running thence to Lookout hill, fronting a quarter of a mile Atkins' bay; tract called Small Point neck; also a right of dower to land formerly possessed by John Drake, in *Casco Bay*.
169	Eight-tenths of a tract between the Kennebec river and Casco bay, formerly possessed by their father, Thomas Atkins, deceased.
167	Their interest in a tract of land on west side of Kennebec river; also two islands in said river.
150	Her part in lands at Small Point neck, formerly possessed by Thomas Webber.

Index of Grantees.

Date.	Grantee.	Grantor.	Instrument.
1716, Apr. 4	WENTWORTH, John, and Thomas Hutchinson Adam Winthrop David Jeffries Oliver Noyes John Watts Stephen Minot John Ruck	Peter Soullard et ux.	Deed
171$\frac{5}{6}$, Mar. 19	WENTWORTH, John, and Thomas Hutchinson Adam Winthrop David Jeffries Oliver Noyes John Watts Stephen Minot John Ruck	James Webber	Deed
171$\frac{5}{6}$, Feb. 21	WENTWORTH, John, and Thomas Hutchinson Adam Winthrop David Jeffries Oliver Noyes John Watts Stephen Minot John Ruck	Nathan Webber	Deed
171$\frac{5}{6}$, Feb. 14	WENTWORTH, John, and Thomas Hutchinson Adam Winthrop David Jeffries Oliver Noyes John Watts Stephen Minot John Ruck WENTWORTH, John, see Thomas Hutchinson WENTWORTH, William, see John Wheelwright	Nathaniel Webber	Deed

Folio.	Description.
168	500 acres, beginning at the southeast part of Small Point harbor, formerly possessed by John Drake, deceased, in *Casco bay.*
150	Two-sevenths of a tract at Small Point neck, reserving 100 acres.
149	Two-sevenths of a tract at Small Point neck.
148	One-seventh of a tract at Small Point neck, reserving 100 acres.

Date.	Grantee.	Grantor.	Instrument.
1629, May 17	WHEELWRIGHT, John, and Augustine Storer Thomas Wight William Wentworth Thomas Levit	Passaconaway and Runaawitt Wahangnonawitt, Rowles, Indian Sagamores	Conditional Deed
1717, May 16	WIGGIN, James	George Buckling et ux.	Deed
	WIGHT, Thomas, see John Wheelwright		
1688, Jan. 30	WILLS, Thomas	Peter Abbot and Thomas Abbot	Deed
1714, July 1	WILSON, William	Samuel Skillion	Deed
1682, Sept. 16	WINCOLL, Olive, and William Plaisted James Plaisted John Plaisted Ichabod Plaisted Elizabeth Plaisted Mehitable Plaisted	Each other	Agreement
1716, Sept. 10	WINTHROP, Adam	Thomas Hutchinson and John Wentworth David Jeffries Oliver Noyes Stephen Minot John Ruck John Watts	Deed
	WINTHROP, Adam, see Thomas Hutchinson		
	WINTHROP, Adam, see John Wentworth		
1684, July 2	WISE, Thomas	John Stover	Deed
1714, June 17	WOOD, Joseph	John Croade	Deed

Index of Grantees. 149

Folio.	Description.
16	Tract of main land bounded by the Piscataqua river and Merrimac river; also the Isles of Shoals.
213	A tract, town grant to John Clayce. at Orgunquit; also a marsh given by Thomas Mills to John Clayce; likewise all right to any land he may have through his wife, in *Wells*.
143	House and land at Crooked lane, in *Kittery*.
61	30 acres, part of a town grant, in *Kittery*.
132	In regard to lands, cattle and chattels belonging to the estate of Roger Plaisted, deceased.
178	Swan island, in *Merrymeeting bay*.
201	12 acres on south side York river, in *York*.
94	4 acres foot of Rocky hill, in *Berwick*.

Book VIII.   51

Index of Grantees.

Date.	Grantee.	Grantor.	Instrument.
1714, Nov. 16	Woodbridge, John	Joseph Bragdon	Deed and Receipt
1714, Nov. 10	Woodbridge, John et ux.	Nathaniel Freeman	Deed
1714, Nov. 2	Woodbridge, John	John Harmon	Deed and Receipt
1714, July 6	Woodbridge, John et ux.	George Norton et ux.	Deed
1715, Apr. 15	Woodman, John	Francis Raynes	Mortgage
17$\frac{3}{4}$, Mar. 1	Woodman, John	Samuel Spinney	Mortgage
	Woodman, John, see Nathaniel Raynes		
1697, June 8	Woodman, Jonathan	John Harris	Deed
1713, July 22	Worster [Woster], Moses, and Richard Gowell Richard Gowell jr. Samuel Ham	Each other	Division
17$\frac{3}{4}$, Feb. 24	Worster, Thomas	Moses Worster [Woster]	Deed
17$\frac{4}{5}$, Mar. 21	Worster, Thomas	Moses Worster [Woster]	Deed

Index of Grantees.   151

Folio.	Description.
114	20 acre town grant, in *York*.
113	20 acre town grant by and in *York*.
114	Two 20 acre town grants, in *York*.
112	Several parcels of land, in *York*.
103	5 acres at Brave-boat harbor, in *York*.
29	Land with houses and buildings, in *Kittery*.
99	200 acres bought of Harlakinden Symonds, in *Coxhall* [now Lyman].
18	Fixing division line between their lands at Spinney's creek, in *Kittery*.
23	A tract of land, household goods, cattle and all other personal estate, in *Berwick*.
82	Remaining part of 200 acres, bought of John Wincoll, also of two grants of land and of saw-mill on Worster's river, in *Kittery* [*Berwick*].

OMISSIONS IN INDEX OF

Date.	Grantor.	Grantee.	Instrument.
1716, Mar. 27	PRICHARD, John, et ux.	Philip Burger	Mortgage

Date.	Grantee.	Grantor.	Instrument.
1716, Mar. 27	BURGER, Philip	John Prichard	Mortgage
1711, May 10	JUNKINS, Alexander	Arthur Bragdon et ux.	Deed
1708, Apr. 1	JUNKINS, Alexander	Daniel Dill et ux.	Deed
1707, Aug. 21	JUNKINS, Alexander	Joseph Young junior	Deed
1679, Apr. 4	SAYWOOD, Mary	John Cousins	Deed

GRANTORS AND GRANTEES.

Folio.	Description.
187	132 acres on York river; 20 acres belonging formerly to the estate of Samuel Webber; 35 acres bought of Nathaniel Harris, in *York*.

Folio.	Description.
187	132 acres on York river; 20 acres belonging formerly to the estate of Samuel Webber; 35 acres bought of Nathaniel Harris, in *York*.
191	2 acres of marsh, bounded west by the river, northwest by said Junkins' land, east by Lieut. Banks' land, in *York*.
192	37 acres above Scotland garrison, in *York*.
193	2 acres on the northwest branch of York river, in *York*.
233	300 acres near a tract formerly in possession of William Ryall, in Casco; also one-half of Cousins' [Hog island], in *Casco bay*.

INDEX TO OTHER PERSONS.

Abbot,
  Abigail, 266.
  John, 3, 94, 101, 102, 143, 231.
  Richard, 151.
  Thomas, 160.
  Walter, 143.
Abilie, Henry, 245.
Adams, Addams,
  Charles, 23.
  Elizabeth, 194.
  John, 161, 221.
  Mark, 44.
  Philip, 30.
  Samuel, 130, 254.
  Thomas, 30, 153, 198, 207.
Addington,
  Isaac, 3.
  James, 96, 187, 263.
Akerman, Benjamin, 155.
Alcock, Job, 93, 108, 116, 253.
Alden, John, 220, 241.
Allen,
  Captain, 160.
  Francis. 223.
  James, 116, 190, 226.
  Lewis, 252.
  Samuel, 3.
  Thomas, 136.
  Walter, 154, 237.
Almery, Robert, 15.
Alten, Richard, 140.
Andrews, James, 244.
Andros, Sir Edmund, 177, 245.
Appleton, John, 151, 204, 247.
  Samuel, 5, 176, 227, 247, 252.
Atkins, Thomas, 167, 169, 208.
Atkinson, Theodore, 3, 19, 40, 41, 45, 81, 144, 198.
Austin, Austine,
  Matthew, 20, 133, 189, 194.
  Samuel, 46.
Averill, Thomas, 170, 176.
Ayres, Thomas, 224.

Bailey, Thomas, 165.
Baker, Goodman, 46.
Bale, 138.
Ball, Thomas, 70.
Ballantine,
  John, 218, 219.
  John, junior, 134.
Balston, Nathaniel, junior, 6.
Bane,
  Jonathan, 15, 189, 198.
  Lewis, 33, 60, 72, 92, 106, 108, 109, 110, 115, 123, 126, 153, 174, 175, 198, 207, 234, 236, 243, 247, 253.
Banfield, Christopher, 107.

Banks,
  Ensign, 194.
  John, 93, 142.
  Joeeph, 60, 90, 93, 198, 223, 243.
  Lieutenant, 191.
  Richard, 95, 210.
  Samuel, 210.
Bare, John, 100.
Barefoot, W., 116.
Barge, Giles, 206.
Barger, Philip, 208.
Barnes, Henry, 55.
Barrot, John, 180.
Barry, James, 130.
Barter, Henry, 13, 43, 80, 127, 219, 264.
  Henry, junior, 268.
Bartlett, Nathan, 79, 229, 263.
Barton, John, 268.
Baston, James, 268.
Batting, Abraham, 111.
Bayley,
  James, 191.
  Joseph, 201.
Beale,
  Arthur, 105.
  Edward, 173.
  William, 61, 230.
  ——, 138.
Belcher, Beltcher,
  John, 47, 52, 71, 72, 77, 79, 83, 105, 127, 128, 154, 209, 265.
  Samuel, 132.
Belknap, Buttalph, 167, 178.
Beltcher, John, see John Belcher.
Benmore, Philip, 23.
Bennet, Aaron, 113.
Berry,
  George, 214.
  Withers, 205.
Besson, Thomas, 129, 207, 209.
Bethel, Richard, 110.
Bice, Thomas, 172.
Billin, John, 44.
Billingham, R., 226.
Black Bess, 40.
Black,
  Daniel, 4, 192.
  Josiah, 218.
  Sarah, 1, 4.
Blackdon, George, 112.
Blackman, Benjamin, 186, 220.
Blackstone, Abigail, 94.
Bland, John, 229.
Blaney, John, 56, 58.
Blasdel, Blasdell,
  Ebenezer, 173, 253, 256.
  Henry, 262.
Blind, Joan, Indian, 167.

INDEX TO OTHER PERSONS. 155

Boles, Bolls, Joseph, 201, 249.
Bonighton, 259.
  John, 8, 220, 221, 241, 254.
  Richard, 9, 17, 31, 242.
Booth, Mother, 88.
Botts, Isaac, 93.
Boynton,
  John, 87.
  Nathaniel, 97.
Bracey, Bracy, William, 59, 68, 189.
Brackett,
  Anthony, 165, 166.
  Samuel, 87.
Bradbury,
  Mary, 262.
  Thomas, 262.
  William, 207.
Bradstreet,
  John, 35, 73, 94, 107, 160, 199, 211, 231.
  S., 242.
Bragdon,
  Arthur, 31, 38, 69, 110, 115, 181, 195, 210, 250.
  Arthur, junior, 31, 193.
  Arthur, senior, 110, 193, 194.
  Samuel, 152.
  Thomas, 66, 110, 115.
Braun, Brawn,
  John, 147.
  John, senior, 39.
  Sarah, 236.
Bray,
  John, 196, 233.
  Samuel, 223.
  William, 226.
Bready, John, 25, 141.
Breeden, Elizabeth, 127, 128.
Briar, William, 74.
Bridges, Josiah, 33.
Briggs, Rebecca, 175.
Bromfield, Edward, 159, 175.
Bromsdon, Benjamin, 66, 238.
Brooks,
  John, 82.
  William, 137.
Broughton, 154, 215.
  Thomas, 262.
Browcen, Henry, 175.
Brown,
  Henry, 84, 151.
  John, 162.
  Joseph, 15.
Buckley, Joseph, 208.
Bucklin, 203.
Buckminster, Jabez, 166.
Burges, Richard, 203.
Burrage, William, 205, 206, 225.
Burrell, John, 195.
Bush, John, 238.
——, 220.
Buship, John, 72.
Butland, John, 211.
Butler, Peter, 122.

Byfield, Nathaniel, 125, 126.
Calif, Jeremiah, 157.
Came,
  Mr., 91.
  Samuel, 51, 111, 116, 183, 188, 190, 243, 247, 253.
Cannon, William, 220.
Card,
  John, 104.
  Thomas, 90, 114, 250.
Carpenter, Philip, 204.
Carr, James, junior, 211.
Cary,
  John, 125, 126.
  Nathaniel, 14.
Chadborn, Chadbourne,
  Humphrey, 53, 54, 258.
  James, 6, 23, 25, 47.
Chadwick, Edmund, 249.
Champernown, Captain, 17.
Chapman,
  John, 95, 128.
  Nathaniel, 222.
Chase, Isaac, 211.
Checkley,
  Anthony, junior, 241.
  Mary, 186.
  Samuel, 186, 221.
Child, Henry, 54.
Church, Thomas, 164.
Clark, 193.
  John, 55, 58, 97, 98, 99, 204, 208, 222.
  Major, 20.
  Nathaniel, 10.
  Samuel, 153.
Clarrian, Anthony, 165.
Clayce,
  John, 213.
  Nathaniel, 213.
  Thomas, 86.
Clean, John, 161.
Clement, Richard, 245.
Cleve,
  George, 245.
  Mr., 244.
Coburn, Ebenezer, 243.
Cock, William, 86.
Coffin,
  Daniel, 122.
  James, 122.
  Tristram, 122.
Coft, Ferdinand, 199.
Cole, Coal,
  George, 262.
  John, 216.
  Joseph, 14.
  Mary, 211.
  Nicholas, 80, 211, 251, 252.
  Thomas, 255.
  Widow, 40.
Coleman, Eleazer, 62.
Collecott, Richard, 160, 167.
Conley, Abraham, 82.
Convers, James, 152.

Cook, Cooke,
  Elisha, 188.
  Joseph, 249.
Cooper, John, 117.
Copleston, John, 132.
Corbin,
  Clement, 166.
  Robert, 162, 163, 166, 244.
Corwin, Jonathan, 249.
Cosso, Mary, 40.
Cotton, William, junior, 8.
Couch,
  Joseph, 45.
  Katherine, 144.
  Mary, 45.
  Roger, 144.
Cousins, John, 234, 235.
Cox, see also Cock,
  Margart, 261.
  Thomas, 78.
Croade,
  Deborah, 154.
  John, 34, 35, 47, 71, 93, 102, 117, 154, 158, 231, 258.
  Thomas, 73.
Crocket,
  Abraham, 41.
  Elihu, 12.
  Ephraim, 44, 62, 145.
  Hugh, 145.
  Joseph, 41, 48, 80, 104, 145, 219, 220.
  Richard, 42.
  Thomas, 62.
Cross, Joseph, 250.
Cumins, Comins, Richard, 31, 242.
Curtis,
  Benjamin, 67.
  Dodevah, 224.
  Joseph, 23 49, 125, 126, 129.
  Thomas, 210.
Cushing,
  C., 207.
  Caleb, 232, 233.
  John, 100.
  John, junior, 107.
Cutt,
  John, 206.
  Mr., 192.
  Richard, 131, 265.
  Robert, 236
  Sarah, 75, 76.

Dalin, John, 149, 159.
Dane, John, 5.
Danforth, Thomas, 166, 244.
Daniel, Thomas, 224.
Dannel, Jony, 176.
Darlin, James, 165.
Darramkine, Indian, 57.
Davenport,
  A., 134.
  Addington, 4, 241.
Davie, Humphrey, 159.

Davis,
  James, 83, 216, 223, 263.
  John, 1, 3, 176, 201, 264.
  Major, 1.
  Mary, 1, 176.
  Nicholas, 39.
  Sylvanus, 160.
Dearing,
  John, 41.
  Mary, 41.
  Roger, 212, 267.
  Sarah, 81.
De Grane, John, 142.
Deneford,
  Joan, 7.
  Walter, 230, 264, 267.
Dennet,
  John, 18, 94, 239, 261.
  Mary, 228.
  Mr. 263.
Dickingson, John, 100.
Dill, John, 33.
Dixey, William, 209.
Dixon, Peter 255.
Doane, John, 125.
Doer, John, 3.
Domhegon, Indian, 57.
Donnel, Donnell,
  Benjamin, 223.
  Henry, 36, 182.
  Nathaniel, 91.
  Samuel, 90, 108, 126, 246, 261.
  Samuel, junior, 90, 103, 138.
Downing,
  Joshua, 20.
  Richard, 147.
Drake, John, 167, 168.
Drew, John, 97, 98, 99.
Drown,
  Elizabeth, 143.
  Leonard, 143.
Dryland, Denis, 221.
Dudley, J., 166.
Dummer,
  Jeremiah, 9, 12, 90, 242.
  Mr., 93.
  Shubael, 3, 90.
Dunn, Nicholas, 55.

Eastwick, Stephen, 230.
Eaton, John, 261.
Edgermet, Indian Sagamore, 177.
Edmunds, Robert, 167, 169.
Edwards, John, 121.
Eldredge, Giles, 122.
Elenwod, John, 41.
Elkins, Christopher, 225.
Ellingham, 111.
Elliot, Eliot,
  Benjamin, 3.
  Robert, 25, 116, 205, 206.
Elson, John, 199.
Emery, 79.

Index to Other Persons. 157

Emery, continued.
  Anthony, 23.
  Daniel, 21, 61, 64, 65, 76, 85, 105, 130, 216, 229.
  James, 92, 140, 236, 237, 265.
  Mary, 266.
  Samuel, 237, 251, 252, 266, 268.
Emms, Emmes,
  Henry, 208.
  James, 222.
Emons, Ebenezer, 105, 198.
Endle, Richard, 46, 95.
Epps,
  Daniel, 226, 227.
  Ruth, 227.
Erington, Abraham, 24.
Esmons, Henry, 44.
Estes, Richard, 78, 216.
Etherington, Thomas, 25, 202.
Evelith, Edward, 227.
Everet, Master, 67.

Fairweather, William, 224.
Farnum,
  Barachias, 140.
  Nathaniel, 140.
Fellows, William, 131.
Fennick, John, 28.
Fernald,
  Amos, 157.
  Hercules, 236.
  James, 227.
  John, 199, 225.
  Nathaniel, 239.
  William, junior, 136, 180.
Ferris, Aaron, 42, 80, 81, 219.
Finney, Joshua, 54.
Fletcher, Pendleton, 231.
Flewellin, Fluellin, Indian, 238.
Folsom, Peter, 10.
Fox, Mr., 160.
Foxell, Foxwell,
  Philip, 31, 242, 243.
  Richard, 206, 220.
Foy, James, 17, 43, 70.
Freeman,
  Mary, 124.
  Nathaniel, 15, 65, 68, 92, 101, 109, 110, 111, 114, 115, 124, 138, 185, 190, 191, 207, 226, 235, 243, 248, 250, 266.
French,
  John, 147.
  Samuel, 54.
Frencham, Henry, 160.
Frenhawk, Francis, 122.
Frink,
  George, 75, 214.
  John, 204.
Frost, 6.
  Charles, 22, 23, 25, 47, 52, 62, 65, 67, 68, 70, 73, 79, 80, 82, 83, 84, 86, 88, 90, 91, 94, 104, 105, 114, 115, 127, 136, 140, 143, 144, 145, 146, 148, 154, 188, 200, 203, 204, 216, 217, 223, 224, 229, 231, 236, 237, 254, 261, 265.

Frost, continued.
  Charles, junior, 79, 83.
  Dorothy, 29.
  James, 64, 256.
  Jane, 216.
  John, 20, 21, 67, 156, 246.
  Nicholas, 23, 82, 83, 123, 124, 236.
  Nicholas, junior, 20.
  Philip, 31.
  Sarah, 236.
  William, 9, 241.
Fry, Frye,
  Adrian, 25.
  Thomas, 156.
  William, 6, 25, 222.
Fryer,
  Abigail, 71, 209.
  Joshua, 209.
  Mr., 151.
  Nathaniel, 25, 48.
Gach, Edmund, 18.
Gage, Edmund, 19.
Gale, 111.
Gambling, Benjamin, 15, 63, 78, 148.
Gaskell,
  Samuel, 45.
  Samuel, junior, 45.
Gaskin, John, 254.
Gatchell, Samuel, 117.
Gendle, Walter, 151.
Gerrish,
  John, 178, 179.
  Mary, 224.
  Paul, 265.
  Richard, 81, 147.
Gibbons, Gibbins, 259.
  Ambrose, 17.
  James, 220.
  James, senior, 88.
  John, 187.
  Judith, 88.
Gibbs,
  Henry, 106.
  Robert, 55.
Gilden, John, 84.
Goddard, Edward, 4.
Godfrey,
  Edward, 121.
  Oliver, 121.
Godsoe,
  Elizabeth, 22, 59, 84, 103.
  James, 146.
  John, 267.
  Mr., 264.
  William, 5, 12, 18, 22, 41, 48, 59, 61, 62, 84, 103, 131, 145, 146, 179, 180, 200, 205, 230, 255.
Goffe, John, senior, 222.
Gooch, James, 247.
———, 252.
Goodwill, Thomas, 258, 259.
Goodwin, Goodin,
  Daniel, 53, 185.
  Daniel, senior, 34.
  Moses, 265.

158   Index to Other Persons.

Goodwin, Goodin, continued.
  Thomas, 117, 132.
Gorges,
  Theol., 121.
  Tho., 244.
Gosse, Edmund, 41.
Gould, Joseph, 107.
Gowell,
  Martha, 143.
  Richard, 143, 246, 255.
Gowen,
  James, 141.
  John, 26, 52, 79, 199, 229, 246, 263, 265.
  John, jr., 52, 79, 265.
  Lemuel, 142, 238.
  Nicholas, 82, 215, 246, 256.
  William, 141.
Graffort, Bridget, 224.
Grant,
  James, 65, 105, 188, 190.
  Peter, 35, 52.
  William, 36, 64, 256.
Graves, John, 48.
Gray, James, 14, 118.
Greason, Greeson,
  John, 162.
  Robert, 165.
Great Agumague, Indian, 167.
Greely, Thomas, 199.
Green,
  Hannah, 248.
  John, 204.
  Susannah, 170.
Greenland, Henry, 257.
Greenough,
  Daniel, 224.
  John, 58.
Greenwood, Samuel, 238.
Greinely, Thomas, 244.
Griffing, John, 249.
Gross, Thomas, 58.
Grover,
  Andrew, 226.
  Matthew, 226.
Grow, William, 69.
Gunnison,'
  Elihu, 46.
  Joseph, 55, 179.
  Mr., 74.
Gusset, Sattery, 86.
Gutch, Robert, 158.
Gutteridge, Jeremiah, 151.
Guye, John, 245.

Haggatt, Jok., 122.
Haiding, Arthur, 41.
Hains,
  John, 36.
  Thomas, 127, 244.
Haley, Andrew, 7, 8, 28, 43.
Hall,
  James, 13.

Hall, continued.
  Ralph, 135.
Hambleton,
  Abel, 93.
  Biel, 24, 256.
  Gabriel, 256.
Hamlyn, William, 12.
Hammond, Haman,
  Benjamin, 49.
  Dorcas, 143.
  Elizabeth, 39.
  Hannah, 20, 228, 255, 257.
  Jonathan, 10, 39, 59, 268.
  Joseph, 5, 14, 18, 20, 22, 23, 29, 59, 63, 76, 80, 83, 92, 127, 139, 143, 144, 146, 183, 188, 190, 198, 214, 228, 239, 246, 255, 257, 261, 264.
  Joseph, junior, 29.
  Mary, 39.
  Mr., 241.
Hanscom,
  Moses, 239.
  Samuel, 239.
  Thomas, 24, 25.
  Thomas, junior, 25.
Hanson, John, 167, 168, 169.
Haridon, Trustram, 246.
Harkins, Thomas, 245.
Harmon,
  Captain, 88.
  John, 31, 50, 242, 243.
  Johnson, 18, 30, 40, 51, 91, 126, 174.
  Margaret, 171.
  Sarah, 221.
Harris,
  Anne, 12.
  John, 97, 132.
  Joseph, 138.
  Nathaniel, 187.
  Samuel, 257.
  William, 149, 167, 169.
Harvey, Elizabeth, 147.
Hastier, Nicholas, 144.
Hatch, Samuel, 9, 13.
Hathorne, John, 13.
Hayes, Edward, 52.
Hazen, Edward, 45.
Heard,
  Captain, 72.
  James, 141, 229.
  John, 80, 81, 83, 139.
Hearle, William, 199.
Hearne, John, 188.
Heath, Joseph, 32.
Henderson, Howard, 130.
Herlow, Francis, 118.
——, 117.
Heskins, Nicholas, 25, 116.
Hetherly, Henry, 266.
Hethersay, Robert, 244.
Hewes,
  Martha, 47.
  Solomon, 47.

INDEX TO OTHER PERSONS. 159

Hill,
  John, 5, 34, 73. 92, 117, 261.
  Joseph, 13, 147, 188, 190, 238, 263, 268.
  Mary, 237.
  Samuel, 25, 74, 78, 216, 222, 246.
  Samuel, junior, 78.
  William, 74.
Hillard, Joseph, 267.
Hilton,
  Edward, 17.
  Robert, 222.
Hinckes, John, 48, 165, 255.
Hirst, Grove, 168, 169.
Hitchcock,
  Mr., 231.
  Rebecca, 231.
  Richard, 231.
Hixon, Christian, 197.
Hodges,
  Abigail, 202.
  Henry, 202.
Hodsden,
  Anne, 159.
  Benoni, 77.
  Israel, 25, 141,
  Jeremiah, 25, 202.
  Timothy, 247.
Hoitt, John, 107.
Holes,
  Elizabeth, 255.
  John, 255.
Holman,
  Samuel, 167.
  Thomas, 167.
Holms, Thomas, 258.
Holt, Joseph, 223.
Hooke,
  Eleanor, 95.
  Francis, 45, 122, 156.
  Humphrey, 122, 261, 262.
  Mary, 41.
  Thomas, 122.
  William, 122, 206, 261, 262.
Hooper,
  Abigail, 71.
  Sarah, 228.
  Thomas, 215.
Hornibrook, John, 3.
Howells, Morgan, 201, 249.
Hoy, John, 67.
Hubart,
  John, 9.
  Mary, 9.
Hubbard,
  John, 96.
  William, 176.
Huff, Thomas, 81, 219.
Hughs, Clement, 26.
  Thomas, 86.
Hull, Phineas, 231.
Hunking,
  Ala, 1, 116.
  John, 157.
  M., 155.

Hunnewell, Richard, 20, 205.
Hunt, Samuel, 119.
Hutchins,
  Benjamin, 198.
  Enoch, 49, 180.
  Samuel, 136.
Hutchinson, 237.
  Edward, 96, 178, 179, 223.
  Eliakim, 53, 66, 98, 187.
  Elisha, 97, 169, 261.
  Elizabeth, 96.
  Sa., 66.
  Thomas, 167.
  William, 66, 96.

Ingarsoll,
  Elisha, 25, 95.
  John, 46, 204.
  John, junior, 95.
  Nathaniel, 215, 228.
Ingles, James, 207, 208.
Islington, Benjamin, 255.

Jackson, George, 14, 47, 258, 259, 260.
  John, 249.
  Ruth, 125.
Jacobs,
  George, 89.
  Thomas, 176.
Jarvis,
  Daniel, 209.
  James, 209.
Jeffords, Gregory, 257.
Jeffry,
  Digory, 11, 145, 151.
  James, 85, 119, 137.
Jenkins,
  Jabez, 6.
  Reinold, 79, 136.
  Stephen, 140.
  Thomas, 215, 228.
Johnson,
  Cornhutch, 193.
  Edward, 174, 190.
  Francis, 1, 201.
  Priscilla, 261.
  Widow, 174.
Jones,
  Daniel, 156.
  John, 145.
  Larens, 24.
  Thomas, 209.
  William, 59, 156
Jordan,
  Dominicus, 245.
  John, 165.
  Robert, 244, 245.
Joslyn, Henry, 13, 225, 244.
Joy, Ephraim, 260.
Junkins,
  Alexander, 110.
  Daniel, 14.
  Robert, 108.

Index to Other Persons.

Kane, Nathaniel, 170.
Kater, John, 38.
Keeling, Samuel, 230.
Kelly, Kelley,
  Charles, 111.
  Mary, 224.
  Roger, 224.
Kene, Jonathan, 56, 255.
Key, Keyes, John, 210, 256.
Kimbal,
  Caleb, 89.
  Ebenezer, 221.
  Thomas, 135.
Kincaid, David, 6.
King,
  George, 95.
  Richard, 18, 61, 143, 147.
Kingsbury, John, 101, 114, 126, 154.
Knap, Joshua, 103, 105, 138.
Knight,
  Ezekiel, 109, 213.
  Robert, 21.
  Samuel, 37.
  Sarah, 161, 162.
  Thomas, 86, 145, 266.

Lane,
  Abigail, 252.
  John, 133, 249.
Lang, Robert, 85.
Langdon, Mark, 197.
Lawson, Christopher, 122.
Leach, Samuel, 180.
Leader,
  Mr., 236.
  Richard, 237.
Leathe, John, 97, 98, 99.
Leighton,
  Insign, 192.
  John, 53, 148, 149, 150, 157, 260.
  Katherine, 21.
  William, 151.
Lewis,
  George, 164, 165, 166, 244.
  Eliza, 198.
  Philip, 165.
  Thomas, 8, 31, 242.
  William, 179, 180.
Libbey,
  James, 144.
  John, 13, 205.
  Matthew, 205.
Linscot, Joshua, 195.
Little,
  Charles, 28.
  Ephraim, 28.
  Joseph, 265.
Littlefield,
  Abigail, 251.
  Anthony, 211.
  David, 9, 237.
  Dependence, 31, 213.
  Edmund, 237, 251.

Littlefield, continued.
  Eliab, 13 88.
  Francis, 156, 211.
  Hannah, 213.
  John, 154.
  Joseph, 109, 212, 237, 251, 268.
  Moses, 54, 237.
Livingstone,
  Daniel, 194.
  Joanna, 194
Lockwood, Richard, 151.
  ————, 212.
Long, Richard, 236.
Lord,
  Benjamin, 47, 75, 76, 86, 87.
  Martha, 236.
  Nathan, 265.
  Nathan, senior, 117.
  Richard, 34, 185.
  Robert, 227.
  Samuel, 54, 227.
  William, 82, 83, 105.
Love, William, 133.
Lowell, James, 254.
Ludden, James, 100.
Lydston, John, 217.
Lynch, Eugene, 204, 214.
Lynde,
  Benjamin, 110.
  E., 178.
  Joseph, 14.
  Samuel, 237.
Lyon, Henry, 32.
Mackentier, 11.
  Daniel, 37, 66, 89.
  John, 104, 253.
  Micum, 36, 38, 89, 95, 97, 194, 195.
Mackinime, 187.
Mackworth,
  Arthur, 245.
  Jane, 24, 245.
  Mrs., 244.
Madokowando, Indian Sagamore, 177.
Maine, Josiah, 247.
Mallet, Hosea, 24.
Manering, Thomas, 224.
Marion, Joseph, 163, 187, 263.
Marsh, James, 140.
Marston,
  Benjamin, junior, 257.
  Samuel, 248.
Martin, Martyn,
  Charles, 234.
  Edward, 238.
  Richard, 213, 244.
Mason,
  John, 53.
  Robert Tufton, 53.
Master, Nathaniel, 109, 212, 213.
Mathews, Walter, 112.
Maverick,
  Antipas, 263.
  Mr., 78.
  Samuel, 209.

Index to Other Persons.

Maxell, Maxwell,
 Alexander, 66, 95, 97, 187, 223.
 James, 263.
Maxfield,
 Joseph, 179.
 Samuel, 218, 219.
Mayhew, Reliance, 67.
Maysterson, Nathaniel, 66, 151.
Mendum, 180.
 Jonathan, 7, 43, 104, 231.
 Nathaniel, 29.
 Robert, 7, 8, 28.
 Sarah, 75.
Milberry, Richard, 90, 223, 243.
Mills,
 Sarah, 225.
 Thomas, 213.
Minot, Stephen, junior, 168.
Mistonobite, Indian, 17.
Mitchell,
 Andrew, 209.
 Christopher, 17, 18, 151.
 Joseph, 19.
 Richard, 41, 45.
 Robert, 212.
Mitten, Mitton,
 Anna, 245.
 Elizabeth, 245.
 Michael, 244.
Montague, Griffith, Griffin, 201, 249.
Montjoy, Munjoy, George, 79, 245.
 John, 86.
Moody, Moodey,
 Eliezer, 242.
 Hannah, 223.
 Mr., 30.
 Samuel, 106, 123, 223, 253.
Moorey, Nicholas, 249, 251.
More,
 Eben, 219, 220.
 Ebenezer, 155, 204, 214, 267.
 John, 45, 184.
 Mr., 214.
 William, 30.
Morrell,
 John, 6, 25, 29, 205, 216, 222, 285!
 John, junior, 6, 23.
 John, senior, 6.
 Nicholas, 139, 147, 154, 217.
Morris, Morrice,
 John, 65.
 Thomas, 244.
Mosure, John, 26, 27, 106.
Moulton,
 Jeremiah, 18, 96, 243.
 Jeremiah, junior, 173.
 Joseph, 11, 65, 148, 190.
 Thomas, 66, 189.
Mountfort, Edmund, 149, 150, 167, 169, 178.
Mudge. Gregory, 167.
Muggeridge, Morgeridge, John, 55, 62.
Musey, Thomas, 125.
Muzeet, Thomas, 222.

Nash, Joseph, 26, 27, 106.
Nason,
 Baker, 94, 102, 118.
 Benjamin, 101, 118, 185.
 Jonathan, 105, 199.
 John, 237.
 Richard, 117.
 Sarah, 72.
Neal, Neale,
 Francis, 244, 245.
 Katherine, 107.
 Walter, 17.
Nelson, Mary, 236.
Neonongasset, Indian, 57.
Newcombe, Richard, 213, 267.
Newman,
 George, 209.
 John, 113, 132.
Newmarch,
 John, 7, 29, 75, 95, 161, 171, 172, 181, 225, 230, 239, 267.
 John, Third, 171, 172, 181, 225.
 Mary, 267.
Newton,
 Thomas, 159.
 William, 87, 185.
Nichols,
 George, 170.
 Robert, 162.
Nicholson, Mr., 160.
Nimbanewit, Indian, 57.
Nock, Sylvanus, 256.
Norden, Nathaniel, 257.
Norton,
 George, 95.
 Henry, 203.
 Margaret, 95.
Nowell,
 Peter, 11, 52, 88, 115, 190, 193, 223, 250, 254.
 Samuel, 240.
Noyes, Thomas, 122, 207.

Oare, James, 84.
Ockland, Richard, 130.
Okman, Sa., 206.
Oldham, John, 17.
Oliver, Joseph, 225.
Orgure, Andrew, 125.
Ormsbye, Richard, 132, 201, 203.
Otis,
 Joseph, 107, 136.
 Nathaniel, 100.

Packer, Thomas, 92.
Palmer,
 Samuel, 250.
 Thomas, 66.
Parker,
 Abraham, 41.
 James, 244.
 John, 148, 149, 150, 153, 223, 253.
 John, senior, 39.
 William, 119.

Parret, Parrott, John, 145.
———, 42, 62.
Parsons,
  Abigail, 252.
  Elihu, 85, 116, 226.
  Eliza, 45.
  John, 31, 123.
Patteshall, Pateshall,
  Edward, 159.
  Richard, 159.
  Robert, 244.
Paul,
  Margaret, 5.
  Stephen, 63, 227.
Paulling, Matthew, 161.
Pearce, Pierce,
  Benjamin, 203.
  Daniel, 265.
  John, 36, 89, 113, 212.
  Joseph, 212.
  Thomas, 1.
  William, 59.
Pecker, James, 244.
Pendleton, Pembleton,
  Brian, 88.
  Mr., 257.
Penhallow,
  John, 149, 150, 151, 169.
  Lydia, 81.
  Samuel, 3, 7, 8, 15, 59, 94, 145, 148, 155, 265.
  Samuel, junior, 8.
Penley, Sampson, 244.
Pennel,
  John, 24.
  Walter, 156.
Penney, Henry, 147.
Penwell,
  John, 18, 172, 201.
  Sarah, 172.
Pepperrell,
  Dorothy, 43, 81, 156.
  Margery, 156.
  Miriam, 41, 49, 81, 136.
  William 6, 13, 18, 21, 29, 42, 43, 44, 49, 55, 61, 63, 71, 75, 81, 85, 95, 103, 128, 129, 131, 132, 144, 145, 155, 156, 172, 179, 180, 181, 188, 196, 197, 205, 212, 214, 219, 220, 228, 230, 254, 255, 258, 259, 260, 264, 267, 268.
  William, junior, 49, 61, 63, 70, 85, 144, 179, 180, 212, 214, 215, 220, 228, 268.
Persons, John, 199.
Pettegrew, Francis, 146, 181.
Phillips,
  Bridget, 241.
  James, 255.
  John, 86, 166, 244.
  Nathaniel, 221.
  Ruth, 197.
  Samuel, 241.
  Thomas, 188.
  William, 41, 99, 166, 241, 264, 267.

Phippen, 244.
Phipps,
  Eleanor, 206.
  Thomas, 134, 155, 206.
  William, 177.
Pich, John, 220.
Pickerin,
  John, 18, 81, 212, 253.
  John, senior, 165.
Pierce, see Pearce.
Pike,
  Eliza, 19.
  Hugh, 265.
  Robert, 19, 262.
Piles, William, 133, 237.
Piper, Jonathan, 252.
Pitcher, Nathaniel, 107.
Pitman,
  Francis, 6.
  James, 94, 265.
Plaisted,
  Colonel, 92.
  Elisha, 117, 158, 160, 185, 199, 200, 223, 225, 232, 237, 258, 266.
  Ichabod, 10, 12, 20, 24, 35, 36, 47, 53, 54, 64, 71, 87, 92, 93, 94, 102, 107, 118, 211, 231, 256, 260.
  James, 1, 36.
  John, 35, 48, 54, 61, 75, 76, 77, 111, 112, 116, 118, 131, 140, 143, 237, 253.
  Mary, 24, 38, 68, 123, 197.
  Roger, 25, 133, 236, 237.
  Samuel, 255, 261.
Plummer,
  Benjamin, 253.
  John, 131.
Polleys, Mary, 26.
Pope,
  Joanna, 95.
  Sarah, 61.
  Seth, 120.
Pounding, 6.
Pray, Joseph, 38, 92, 93, 211, 260.
Preble,
  Abraham, 1, 4, 11, 14, 15, 19, 30, 31, 32, 33, 37, 38, 48, 50, 51, 52, 60, 69, 90, 91, 92, 103, 111, 114, 115, 127, 133, 153, 170, 171, 173, 174, 182, 183, 184, 185, 189, 190, 191, 192, 193, 194, 195, 207, 210, 223, 226, 234, 235, 243, 246, 247, 248, 250, 254.
  Abraham, junior, 11, 30, 32, 50, 51, 60, 103, 153, 184, 192, 195.
  Caleb, 32, 174, 223, 234, 235.
  Hephzibah, 37.
  John, 91, 100.
  Jonathan, 223.
  Samuel, 174.
Presse, John, 220.
Prichett, John, 208.
Pront, Timothy, 162, 166.
Pryor, Edward, 159.
Pugsley, 160.

INDEX TO OTHER PERSONS. 163

Pulman,
  John, 172.
  Jasper, 172.
Purchase, Thomas, 56, 57, 58.

Rainking, Constant, 31.
Randall, William, 260.
Rankin, Sarah, 261.
Rawson, Edward, 204.
Raynes,
  Captain, 173.
  Francis, 131, 182.
  Mr., 69, 135.
  Nathaniel, 173, 185.
Reding, William, 180.
Reed, John, 268.
——, 129.
Remick, Remich,
  Jacob, 144, 145, 147, 217.
  Joshua, 144, 255.
Reynalls, Nicholas, 159.
Rice,
  Mary, 37.
  Richard, 12, 83. 103, 267.
  Thomas, 37, 61, 181, 224, 260.
Rigby, Alexander, 245.
Rishworth, Edward, 37, 88, 96, 99, 129, 151, 187, 189, 234, 237, 244, 245, 247.
Roberts,
  Ann, 127.
  Giles, 244.
  Love, 64.
Robing, 42, 62.
Robins, Diggery, 61.
Roch, Samuel, 122.
Roe, Richard, 11.
Rogers,
  John, 22.
  Richard, 146, 156, 161, 172.
  Thomas, 31, 242.
Rogomock, Indian, 220.
Rolfe, Benjamin, 134.
Ropes, Benjamin, 13.
Ross,
  John, 25.
  Stephen, 49.
Round, Mark, 38.
Row, Richard, 121.
Royall, Ryall,
  John, 140.
  William, 218, 219, 233, 244.
Ruck,
  Abigail, 168.
  Andrew, 168.
Rust, Nathaniel, junior, 176.
Rutherford, Robert, 119.

Saffin, John, 161.
Sagamores, Indians, 57, 58.
Sanders, John, 125, 238.
——, 220.
Sanderson, William, 112.
Sanford, Ezbon, 220.

Sargent (Sergent),
  Diamond, 42, 63.
  Peter, 96.
Satchfield, William, 121.
Savage, Ephraim, 240.
Sawyer, Sayer,
  Daniel, 251.
  David, 215.
  Francis, 251.
  John, 13.
Saywood,
  Esther, 189.
  Hannah, 189.
  Henry, 15, 129, 246, 261.
  James, 51.
  John, 51, 68, 110, 154, 197, 198, 235.
  Jonathan, 235.
  Joseph, 194, 243.
  Mary, 189, 234, 235.
  Susannah, 189.
Scadlock, William, 267.
Scammon, Humphrey, 254, 258.
Scottow, Joshua, 205.
Seacomb,
  Richard, 164.
  Susannah, 164.
Searts,
  Nathaniel, 164.
  Sarah, 164.
Sentle, Abraham, 94.
Sergent, see Sargent.
Sevey, Benjamin, 212.
Sewall,
  Hannah, 67.
  Mehitable, 213.
  Nicholas, 174.
  Samuel, 40, 44, 67.
  Stephen, 100, 101, 180, 213, 267.
  Thomas, 253.
Seward, Samuel, 236.
Shapleigh,
  John, 6, 57, 58, 172, 260.
  Mr., 263.
  Nicholas, 20, 22, 47, 57, 116, 212, 260, 263.
  Sarah, 22, 260.
Sharp, Samuel, 17.
Shaw,
  Annie, 109.
  Joseph, 208.
  William, 14, 109, 182.
Sheafe, Sampson, 186.
Sheepscot, John, Indian, 167.
Sheldon, William, 225.
Shepherd, Sheppard,
  John, 56, 146, 230.
  Solomon, 232, 233.
Sherman, Daniel, 110.
Shine, John, 166.
Shorey, Samuel, 25.
Sibley, John, 249.
Simpson,
  Daniel, 19, 100, 152, 153, 173, 223, 235, 251.

Simpson, continued.
  Henry, 100.
  Joseph, 43, 49.
Small, Francis, 86, 244.
Smalley,
  Elizabeth, 216.
  Samuel, 77, 216.
Smith,
  Daniel, 132.
  James, 77, 108, 175.
  Joseph, 80, 175, 247.
  Ralph, 125.
  Samuel, 36.
Snell, Elizabeth, 94.
Snow, Samuel, 201.
Soaper, Soper, John, 18, 143, 227.
———, 205.
Sosowen, Indian, 238.
Soulard, Peter, 168.
Spencer,
  John, 221.
  Mary, 35, 73.
  Moses, 34, 73, 238.
  William, 73.
Spinney,
  John, 181, 239.
  Thomas, 255.
Stagpole, John, 126.
Stanford,
  John, 97.
  Thomas, 244.
Staple,
  John, 86.
  Peter, 5, 22, 165, 231.
Sterns, Shubael, 204.
Stevens,
  John, junior, 207.
  Thomas, 122, 159.
Stileman, Styleman,
  Elias, 48, 135, 199.
  Richard, 199.
Stimson, Jonathan, 258.
Stocklenes, John, 158.
Stoddard, Anthony, 150, 151.
Stone,
  Daniel, senior, 158.
  Jonathan, 158, 200.
Storer,
  Joseph, 4, 152.
  Josiah, 222.
  Lydia, 183, 268.
  Samuel, 268.
Story, Charles, 3, 22, 26, 29, 74, 78, 119, 134.
Stover,
  Dependence, 51, 248.
  Sylvester, 60.
Stuart, Stewart, Samuel, 60, 127.
Sumerby, Henry, 232, 233.
Sunday, Captain, Indian, 220.
Surplice,
  Elizabeth, 12, 200.
  Katherine, 205.

Symonds, Simonds,
  Harlakinden, 5, 97, 99, 220, 238, 264.
  William, 226, 227, 252.

Tappin, Jacob, 265.
Tarbox, Nathaniel, 199.
Tareteens, Indians, 16.
Taylor,
  John, 160.
  William, 168, 241, 251.
Taynter, Joseph, 226.
Teeney, John, 206.
Tenny, Samuel, 250.
Tetherly, William, 217.
Thomas,
  Caleb, 27.
  Captain, 215.
  David, 174.
  Elizabeth, 27.
  Nathaniel, 27, 28, 155, 214, 267.
  Rice, 15.
  Sarah, 1.
Thoyts, Alexander, 159, 167.
Tidy, John, 147.
Tilly, William, 245.
Tilton, Abraham, 247.
Tompson,
  Alexander, 18.
  Anne, 237.
  John, 52, 63, 94, 143, 144, 145, 146, 236.
Townsend, Penn, 123, 142, 163, 237.
Toziar, Tozar, Richard, 63, 92, 231, 256.
Trafton, Zacchens, 130.
Trelawney, Mr., 244.
Trescott, John, 218, 219.
Treworgie, James, 25.
Trumball, Joseph, 184.
Tucker,
  Mr., 236.
  Nicholas, 43, 74, 75, 145, 204, 215 228.
  Richard, 43, 244.
  William, 204.
Turbat, ———, 220.
Turbut, Peter, 238.
Tuttle, John, 130.
Twisden, John, 95.
Tyler, Andrew, 85, 186.
  Samuel, junior, 58, 230.
Tyng, Edward, 225.

Upton,
  Joseph, 204.
  Joseph, junior, 204.
Usher, John, 3, 99, 264.

Vaughan,
  George, 14, 17.
  William, 3.
Vearin, Hannah, 196.
Veazy, George, 77.

Index to Other Persons. 165

Venard, John, 41.
Venney, William, 88.
Vering, John, 24.
Vines, Richard, 17, 234, 214, 245.

Wadargascom, Indian, 17.
Wadleigh, Wadley,
  John, 10.
  Robert, 135.
  William, 87.
Wainwright,
  Francis, 87, 224.
  John, 47.
  Samuel, 208.
Waite, Thomas, 9. 254.
Waldron, Richard, 130, 237, 244.
Walker,
  Edward, 87.
  Isaac, 245.
  John, 55, 129.
  William, 238.
Wallis, Walles,
  John, 244.
  Nathaniel, 164, 165, 166, 244.
Walters, William, 50.
Walton, George, 147.
Ward,
  Eleazer, 73.
  William, 230.
Wardlin, Wadlin,
  Daniel, 232.
  William, 35.
Warmstalls, Arthur, 231.
Warren,
  James, 6, 54, 94, 101, 102, 118, 185, 256.
  Margaret, 102.
Warrumbee, Indian, 57.
Watkins, John, 260.
Watson, Mary, 252.
Watts, John, 223.
Way,
  Eleazer, 56, 57, 58.
  George, 56, 57.
Waymouth,
  Edward, 25, 52, 105, 202.
  James, 8.
  Timothy, 65.
Weare,
  Daniel, 9, 254.
  Hopewell, 3.
  Mary, 246.
  Nathaniel, 9, 254, 259.
  Nathaniel, junior, 9, 254.
  Peter, 246, 254.
Weaver, Edward, 163.
Webber,
  Deborah, junior, 183.
  James, 198.
  John, 149, 150.
  Mary, 148, 149, 150.
  Nathan, 150.
  Samuel, 52, 97, 98, 103, 150, 187, 234.
  Thomas, 148, 149, 150, 151.

Weed, Thomas, 76.
Weeden, Indian, 57.
Weeks,
  Joseph, 7, 28, 43.
  Nicholas, 55, 261, 264.
Welch,
  Benjamin, 267.
  Philip, 110, 182, 184.
Wells, Welles,
  John, 247, 248.
  Mr., 213.
  Philip, 245.
  Thomas, 109, 211, 252.
Wentworth,
  J., 224.
  John, 44, 137, 157.
  Paul, 231.
  Samuel, 44, 46.
  Sylvanus, 21.
  Timothy, 35, 260.
West, John, 155, 156, 245.
Wheelwright,
  Jeremiah, 137.
  John, 10, 14, 39, 41, 45, 54, 60, 69, 89, 127, 130, 138, 144, 154, 161, 188, 190, 198, 209, 211, 213, 236, 237, 238, 249, 251, 252.
  Samuel, 152, 238, 247.
White,
  Charles, 182, 183.
  John, 6, 209, 250.
  Nicholas, 244.
Whitehouse, Edward, 203.
Whitmarsh, Ezra, 222.
Whitney, Nathaniel, 40.
Whittum, Peter, 77, 127, 138, 147.
——, 148.
Wiggin,
  James, 44.
  Thomas, 17.
Wihikermet, 57.
Wilbore, John, 202.
Williams,
  Ebenezer, 182.
  Henry, 206, 225.
  Mary, 255.
  Nathaniel, 175.
  Rowland, 180.
  William, 134.
Willine, Roger, 245.
Wilson,
  Gowen, 214.
  Joseph, 85, 101.
  Thomas, 88.
  William, 180.
Wincoll,
  Captain, 37.
  John, 11, 23, 25, 37, 59, 77, 82, 132, 151.
Winch, Samuel, 184.
Winkley, Francis, 179.
Winslow,
  Edward, 178, 179.
  Gilbert, 106.

BOOK VIII.   52

Winslow, continued.
  Nathaniel, 27, 106.
Winsor, Joshua, 242.
Wise, Jeremiah, 34, 71, 92, 93, 185, 209.
Winter, John, 245.
Wiswal, Enoch, 26, 106.
Withers,
  Mr , 37, 179, 180.
  Thomas, 172, 224, 260.
Wolcot, Joseph 227.
Wood, Joseph, 102.
Woodbridge,
  Benjamin. 155.
  John. 90, 248.
Woodbury, Anna, 151.
Woodman,
  Hercules. 220.
  John, 6, 63.
  ———, 172.
Woodsum. Joseph, 158, 160.
Wormwood, Samuel, 234.

Worster,
  Elizabeth, 83.
  Thomas, 170.
  William, 83.
Wright.
  Henry, 237.
  Joseph, 254.

Yeamans,
  Francis, 121, 122.
  Watt, 121.
  William, 122.
Yetton, Richard, 224.
Young.
  Job, 1, 4, 195.
  Joseph, 21, 195.
  Richard, 266.
  Rowland, 153, 192.
  William, 67.

INDEX OF PLACES.

Agamenticus, afterward York, 120, 121, 262.
Allen's island, 3.
America, 1.
Amesbury. Massachusetts, 206.
Androscoggin falls, 57, 58.
  river, 178.

Barnstable county, Mass., 123, 124.
Berwick, 10, 23, 24, 33, 34, 35, 47, 52, 54, 64. 70, 71, 73, 75, 77, 86, 87, 92, 93, 94, 101, 102, 105, 108, 117, 118, 127, 128, 130. 131. 134, 154, 157, 158, 160, 185, 197, 198, 199, 200, 210, 225, 231, 236, 237, 238, 255, 256, 257, 258, 260, 265, 266.
  commons, 64, 77, 93, 94, 102, 133, 158, 210.
  Assabumbedock falls, 237.
  Doubtie's falls, 36.
  Great works, 236, 237.
  Great works river, 75, 118, 237.
  Humphrey's marsh, 35.
  Humphrey's pond, 154.
  Mast cove, 199, 202.
  Mast way, 105.
  Neguttaquid river, 36, 105.
  Newichewannock, 14, 16, 77, 82, 83, 123, 124, 133, 221.
    falls, 16.
    river, 1, 2.
  Quamphegan, 262.
  Rocky hill, 94, 265.
  Salmon falls, 75, 76, 77, 82, 92, 93, 133, 220, 236, 262.
    brook, 256.
    river, 70, 82, 130, 133, 134.
  Slut's corner, 34, 160.
  Unity parish, 93.
  White's marsh, 117, 238.
  William Cock's pond, 86, 87, 118.
  Worster's river, 70, 82.
Beverly, Mass., 169.
Boxford, Mass., 249.
Bradford, Mass., 201, 202, 208, 249.
Bridgewater, Mass., 169.
Bristol, Mass., 121, 125, 126.
Bristol county, Mass., 26, 27, 125, 126, 134, 163, 169, 201, 202.

Cambridge, Mass., 240.
Canada, 189.
Cape Ann, 1.
Cape Cod, 124.

Cape Porpoise, 97, 99, 125, 126, 180, 198, 201, 202, 219, 220, 231, 237, 238, 249, 257. 264, 266, 267
  river, 5, 151, 180, 226, 237.
  Barrot's falls, 180.
  Batson's neck, 199.
  Little river, 257, 266.
  Miller's creek, 180.
  Prince's rock, 180, 266.
  Timber island, 257.
Casco or Casco bay, 24, 26, 27, 57, 106, 148, 161, 162, 163, 165, 166, 167, 168, 169, 177, 178, 217, 233, 234, 235, 242, 244, 245, 267.
  falls, 245.
  river, 244.
  Cousin's island, 166, 217, 218, 233.
  Davis harbor, 177.
  Great Chebeague island, 187.
  Herock hill, 233.
  Jewell's island, 166.
  Maquoit, 57, 187.
  Puggy Muggy river, 187.
  Sebascodegan island, 57, 58, 240, 242.
  Seguin island, 167.
  Small Point harbor, 57, 167, 168.
    neck, 148, 149, 150, 167, 177.
  Susqussugg, 233.
Charlestown, Mass., 1, 3, 10, 14, 250, 266.
Connecticut, 132, see Hartford, New London county, Lyme.

Damariscotta river, 177, 229.
  island, 229.
  Oyster river, 177.
Devon county. England, 146.
Dorchester, England, 56, 262.
Dorchester, Mass., 217, 218.
Dorset county, England, 56, 262.
Dover, N. H., 6, 54, 63, 130, 135, 222, 273.
Dover river, 6, 107, 136, 137, 222.

Eastham, Mass., 123, 124.
England, see Dorchester, Dorset county, Kent county, London, Long Ashton, Seale, Somerset county, St. Mary, parish of, Swyer, Toller Fratrum, Winford Eagle.
Essex county, Mass., 4, 5, 13, 87, 95, 99, 100, 101, 109, 112, 113, 114, 125, 133, 151, 153, 169, 176, 180, 201, 203, 206, 207, 208, 209, 212, 215, 227, 232

INDEX OF PLACES.

Essex county, Mass., continued.
  242, 247, 248, 249, 252, 256, 262, 264, 266.
Exeter, N. H., 7, 10, 28, 62.

Fagoty bridge, 236.
Falmouth, 79, 86, 162, 164, 165, 245.
  Capisic, 86.
    falls, 86.
  Presumpscot river, 162.
Fayal, 241.
Freetown, Mass., 201, 202.

Georgeana, see York.
Georgetown, Mass., 229.
Gloucester, Mass., 132.
Great Island, N. H., 3, 25, 199.
Greenland, N. H., 140, 165.

Hampton, N. H., 8, 9, 30, 214, 228, 254, 258, 259.
Hartford, Conn., 56.
Harwich, 177.
Haverhill, Mass., 208, 209, 250.
Hilton's point, 17.
Hull, Mass., 176.

Ipswich, Mass., 4, 5, 99, 151, 176, 204, 226, 227, 247, 252, 264.
Isles of Shoals, 2, 16, 132.
  Hog island, 224.
  Smutty-nose island, 111, 132, 224.
  Star island, 224.

Jamestown, 265.
  King's bridge, 265.
  Pemaquid point, 265.

Kennebec, 148, 150, 159, 169.
  river, 24, 57, 122, 148, 149, 150, 158, 159, 167, 169, 177, 178.
  Abbacadusset point, 167, 178.
  Arrowsic island, 150, 159, 223, 229.
  Great Stage island, 177.
  Kitt's island, 159.
  Meaumkeag, 159.
  Purchase's bay, 122.
  Purchase's island, 122.
  Swan alley, 167.
  Whigby, alias Whiskeag, 58, 122.
  Winnegance, 159.
    river, 158, 159.
    creek, 148, 149, 150.
Kennebunk, 5.
  river, 203.
  falls, 237, 251.
Kent county, England, 120, 121.
Kittery, 5, 6, 7, 8, 11, 12, 17, 19, 20, 22, 23, 25, 28, 29, 33, 34, 35, 36, 41, 42, 43, 44, 45, 46, 47, 49, 52, 54, 55, 57, 59, 61, 62, 63, 64, 69, 70, 71, 72, 73, 74, 76, 77, 78, 79, 80, 81, 82, 83, 84, 85, 93, 94, 95, 104, 107, 109, 111, 117, 118, 125, 126,

Kittery, continued.
  127, 128, 129, 130, 131, 132, 133, 135, 136, 139, 140, 141, 142, 143, 144, 145, 146, 147, 148, 151, 154, 155, 156, 157, 158, 160, 170, 171, 172, 179, 180, 181, 185, 186, 188, 192, 196, 197, 198, 199, 200, 202, 204, 205, 209, 212, 213, 214, 215, 216, 217, 219, 220, 222, 225, 227, 228, 229, 230, 236, 238, 239, 246, 254, 255, 256, 257, 258, 259, 260, 261, 262, 263, 264, 265, 267.
  commons, 11, 25, 61, 265.
  mill, 263.
  mill dam, 78, 216.
  point, 136, 155, 214, 257.
  road, 61, 222, 263.
  Brave-boat harbor, 19, 44, 84, 212.
  Broad cove, 264.
  Cedars, the, 83.
  Champernown's island, 17, 48.
  Cold harbor, 6, 78, 79, 216, 261, 263.
    ferry, 263.
  Crocket's neck, 42, 145, 228.
  Crooked lane, 111, 143, 151, 236, 267.
  Eastern creek, 49.
  Farmoth, 41.
  Fry's point, 136.
  Great cove, 143, 255.
  Mast cove, 25.
  Pine point, 260.
  Simon's brook, 59.
  Spinney's creek, 18, 205, 227.
    cove, 239.
  Spruce creek, 7, 8, 12, 21, 28, 37, 43, 46, 56, 62, 74, 85, 95, 127, 181, 196, 198, 204, 214, 230, 260, 264, 267.
    road, 61.
  Stony brook, 141, 142.
  Sturgeon creek, 6, 20, 21, 23, 47, 75, 76, 78, 79, 83, 107, 136, 139, 140, 147, 229, 236.
    bridge, 82, 83.
  Third hill, 141, 142.
  Tucker's creek, 62.
  Walton's marsh, 48.
  Wither's island, 223.
  York highway, 141.
    line, 11, 44.
    pond, 52, 141.
  Young's marsh, 192.

Little Compton, R. I., 164, 169.
London, England, 65, 120, 121, 217, 218.
Long Ashton, Somerset county, England, 120, 121.
Long island, Boston, Mass., 176.
Lyme, Conn., 130.
Lynn, Mass., 56.

Madoamok point, 177.
Magesemanussick falls, 177.
Maine, province of, 132.
Manchester, Mass., 109, 112, 113, 153, 180.

Index of Places. 169

Marblehead, Mass., 169, 170, 256, 266.
Marshfield, Mass., 136, 155.
Masonia, 2, 3.
Massachusetts, see Amesbury, Barnstable county, Beverly, Boston, Boxford, Bradford, Bridgewater, Bristol county, Cambridge, Charlestown, Cape Ann, Cape Cod, Dorchester, Eastham, Essex county, Freetown, Gloucester, Hull, Ipswich, Lynn, Long Island, Manchester, Marblehead, Marshfield, Medford, Mendum, Middlesex county, Medford, Newbury, Pembroke, Plymouth county, Rochester, Rowley, Roxbury, Salem, Salisbury, Scituate, Suffolk county, Swansea, Taunton, Topsfield, Watertown, Woodstock.
Medford, Mass., 155.
Mendum, Mass., 169.
Merriconeag neck [Harpswell], 57, 58.
Merrimac river, 16.
Merrymeeting bay, 57, 58.
Middlesex county, 1, 3, 10, 14, 150, 155, 240, 260.
Muddy river, 166.

Naumkeag river, 1, 2.
Newbury, Mass., 47, 99, 100, 112, 113, 114, 122, 125, 133, 207, 209, 211, 220, 242, 247, 264.
New Castle, N. H., 1, 8, 10, 20, 39, 40, 48, 64, 105, 139, 152, 156, 196, 198, 209.
Newfoundland, 147.
New Hampshire, province of, 1; see, also, Dover, Exeter, Great Island, Greenland, Hampton, New Castle, Newington, Portsmouth.
Newington, N. H., 147.
New Jersey, 185, 186.
New Somerset, afterward Maine, province of, 120, 121.
North Yarmouth, 140, 217, 218.
  Arisicket, Harricisecke river, 26, 27, 106.
  Royall's river, 140.

Pejepscot [Brunswick], 56, 58.
Pembroke, Mass., 97.
Penecook, 16.
Penobscot, 177.
Pentucket, 16.
  falls, 16.
Piscataqua (a district), 2, 16, 185, 186, 258, 259; see Kittery.
  harbor, 1.
  river, 1, 3, 16, 17, 20, 42, 48, 62, 135, 155, 204, 227, 257, 267.
Portsmouth, N. H., 1, 3, 6, 8, 13, 15, 25, 47, 52, 56, 74, 77, 81, 93, 111, 116, 118, 136, 143, 144, 146, 147, 148, 149, 150, 155, 157, 165, 167, 168, 169, 176, 199, 204, 205, 212, 217, 223, 236, 253, 265.

Portsmouth, N. H., continued.
  county, 62.
Portsmouth, R. I., 163.

Rhode Island, see Little Compton, Portsmouth.
Rochester, Mass., 119.
Rowley, Mass., 87, 95, 97, 100.
Roxbury, Mass., 162, 165.

Saco, 8, 17, 31, 88, 97, 155, 185, 186, 201, 220, 221, 231, 241, 242, 257, 258, 259.
  river, 8, 31, 155, 220, 221, 241, 242, 249, 254.
  falls in, 221, 258.
  fort, 9.
  sea-wall, 231.
  Blackman's falls, 259.
  Boniton's island, 9, 241.
  Cow island, 155, 156, 241.
  David's brook, 241.
  Gibbon's island, 155.
  Goose-fair brook, 241.
  Great pond, 231.
  Middle neck, 231.
  Nichols brook, 185, 258.
  West point, 155.
  Winter harbor, 88, 231, 266.
  Wood island, 155, 156.
Sagadahoc, 177, 208.
  island, 3.
  point, 169.
  river, 2, 148, 149, 150, 169.
  Atkins bay, 57, 167, 169.
  Long cove, 169.
  Mill pool, 208.
Salem, Mass., 13, 101, 109, 110, 151, 161, 180, 203, 212, 213, 227, 248, 267.
Salisbury, Mass., 122, 206, 232, 233, 261, 262.
Scarborough, 13, 205, 206.
  Black point, 13, 156, 225.
    river, 205, 225, 249.
  Blue point, 242.
  Clay pit, 225.
  Spurwink river, 156, 245.
Scituate, Mass., 26, 27, 100, 106, 167, 169.
Seale, Kent county, England, 120, 121.
Sheepscot bay, 229.
Somerset county, England, 120, 121.
Spruce swamp, 167.
St. Mary, parish of, England, 146.
Suffolk county, Mass , 3, 4, 9, 12, 54, 55, 56, 59, 66, 74, 87, 95, 96, 97, 98, 99, 106, 111, 122, 141, 148, 149, 150, 162, 166, 167, 168, 169, 170, 178, 186, 187, 204, 207, 217, 218, 219, 220, 224, 229, 240, 241, 256, 265.
Swan island, 178.
Swansea, Mass., 26, 27, 134, 163.
Swyre, England, 262.

Tarpolin cove, 169.

170   INDEX OF PLACES.

Taunton, Mass., 125, 202.
Toller Fratrum, England, 262.
Topsfield, Mass., 180.

Watertown, Mass., 226.
Wells, 5, 9, 10, 13, 14, 34, 39, 46, 54, 88, 97, 99, 109. 119, 140, 151, 152, 153, 154, 175, 176, 188, 203, 211, 212, 213, 220, 221, 226, 236, 237, 238, 548, 250, 251, 252, 264, 266, 268.
  Clay hill, 237.
  Cross point, 154, 251.
  Little river, 252.
  Merryland river, 9.
    marsh, 9.
    mills, 13.
  Mousam, or Cape Porpoise river, 151, 237, 238.
  Orgunquit, 109, 212, 213.
  Pond marsh, 119, 203.
  Totnucke, Tatnack, 175, 176, 237.
  Three mile brook, 46.
  Webhannet river, 109, 213, 251.
Westgostuggo, Wescustogo, North Yarmouth, 233, 235.
Winford Eagle, England, 262.
Winnegance, 229.
  creek, 148.
Woodstock, Mass., 162.

Yarmouth, 236.
York, 1, 3, 4, 11, 14, 15, 18, 20, 30, 31, 32, 33, 36, 37, 38, 39, 40, 41, 50, 51, 59, 60, 61, 65, 66, 67, 68, 69, 89, 90, 91, 93, 95, 96, 97, 98, 100, 103, 104, 105, 107, 108, 110, 111, 112, 113, 114, 115, 116, 123, 126, 129, 131, 132, 135, 137, 138, 148, 152, 153, 156, 160, 172, 173, 174, 175, 181, 182, 183, 184, 187, 188, 189, 190, 191, 192, 193, 194, 195, 197, 198, 205, 206, 207, 209, 210, 223, 225, 232, 233, 234, 235, 236, 242, 243, 246, 247, 250, 252, 253, 254, 261, 262, 264.
  called Gorgeana, 132, 201, 203.
  bounds, 246, 254.
  bridge, 108.
  commons, 108.

York, continued.
  ferry, 146.
  river, 1, 10, 18. 31, 32, 36, 38, 39, 40, 50, 59, 66, 69, 89, 91, 95, 97, 103, 104, 105, 111, 116, 126, 129, 138, 172, 173, 174, 181, 187, 190, 192, 194, 201. 206, 209, 223, 226, 247, 250, 253, 254, 261.
  called Gorgeana (York) river, 203.
  Agamenticus hill, 110, 115.
  Barberry marsh, 1, 4.
  Bass cove, 65.
    brook, 194.
    creek, 59, 152, 153.
    marsh, 38.
  Belt marsh, 33, 108, 195.
    brook, 131, 182, 183, 184.
  Birch hill. 107, 174, 190.
  Brave-boat harbor, 103, 116, 131, 173.
    bridge, 173.
  Burnt plain. 4, 96.
  Cape Neddick, 1, 51, 175, 176, 206,
    river, 51, 60, 183, 225, 247, 248.
    creek, 120, 121.
    neck, 262.
  Curtis' cove, 66, 95, 97.
    marsh, 191.
  Dummer's neck, 253.
  Eddy point, 132, 201, 203.
  Frethy's cove, 18.
  Goose cove, 116.
  Hull's creek, 30.
  Kittery bounds, 116, 254.
  Little river, 3. 51.
  Long cove. 226, 247.
  Long sands, 1.
  Meeting-house creek, 174.
  Mill creek, 111.
  Mr. Moody's cove, 30.
  New mill creek, 15, 20, 68, 189.
  Old mill creek, 11, 66, 226, 247.
  Old mill pond, 183.
  Palmer's cove, 3, 90.
  Scituate plains. 210.
  Scotland, 65, 66, 206, 261.
  Scotland garrison, 193.
  Sunken marsh, 126.
  York, county of, 207.

GENERAL INDEX.

Account stated, 25.
Administrators, 43, 56, 58, 109, 188, 189, 197, 267.
Agent, 65.
Assistants of the Government,
  Appleton, Samuel, 176.
  Dudley, J., 166.
Associates, Magistrates,
  Pendleton, Bryan. 88.
  Wheelwright, Samuel, 46.
Attorney, 262.
  letter of, 45.

Berwick. See Index of Places.
  grants recorded, see Index of Grantors under names following:
  Abbet, Thomas. 160.
  Allen, Walter, 257.
  Ball, John, 198.
  Bracket, Samuel, 93.
  Bradstreet. John, 75.
  Child, William, 154.
  Cole, Jacob. 262.
  Croade, John, 73, 87, 94.
  Emery, James, 36.
  Fennicks, John, 7.
  Frink, John, 127.
  Goodwin, Thomas, 34.
  Gowen, John, 64.
  Grant, Alexander, 35.
  Gunnison, Elihu, 128.
  Hambleton, Abel, 256.
  Hambleton, Biel, 260.
  Hubord, Elizabeth, 200.
  Hubord, Philip, 200.
  Ingersol, John, 128.
  Lewis, Andrew, 196.
  Lord, Benjamin, 117.
  Lord, Martha, 117.
  Merryfield, Katherine, 124.
  Morrell, Abraham, 238.
  Nason, Baker, 101.
  Nason, Benjamin, 117.
  Otis, Joseph, 100.
  Reed, John, 130.
  Rogers, John, 134.
  Sargent, Edward, 133.
  Spencer, Humphrey, 33.
  Spencer, Mary, 75.
  Spencer, Moses, 73, 118, 185.
  Stone, Daniel, 158.
  Wadley, William, 86.
  Waymouth, Timothy, 105, 199, 202.
  Wentworth, Timothy, 70, 210.
  Wincoll, John, 77, 118.

Berwick, continued.
  Wood, Joseph, 102.
  Worster, Moses, 23, 82.
  Young, Israel, 123.
  grants referred to,
    town (i e., Kittery) to
      Thomas Abbet, 160.
      Isaac Botts, 93.
      John Gowen, 64.
      Lemuel Gowen. 238.
      Ephraim Joy, 260.
      William Love. 133.
      Richard Nason, 117.
      John Reed, 130.
      Daniel Stone, 158.
      Jonathan Stone, 158.
      George Veazy, 77.
      Edward Waymouth, 105.
      Timothy Wentworth, 210.
  John Abbot to John Hooper, 101.
  Thomas Broughton to George Cole, 262.
  John Croade to Joseph Wood, 102.
  Daniel Goodwin, senior, to Thomas Goodwin, 34.
  Ephraim Joy to Biel Hambleton, 260.
  Benjamin Lord to John Croade, 86, 87.
  Baker Nason to John Hooper, 102.
  Moses Spencer to John Croade, 73.
  William Wadley to John Croade, 87.
  John Wincoll to Moses Worster, 23, 92.

Boston fire, 1676, 24.
Bound trees, see marked trees.
Bridges, 44, 20, 82, 83, 108, 116, 173, 215.
Buildings, houses, etc., 3, 12, 13, 14, 20, 22, 26, 27, 29, 42, 44, 60, 62, 78, 83, 97, 111, 112, 132, 133, 136, 138, 143, 147, 151, 160, 166, 167, 176, 177, 179, 185, 187, 189, 200, 201, 203, 209, 210, 212, 217, 218, 219, 224, 225, 230, 245, 247, 256, 258, 261.
  building yard, 212.
  barns, 6, 14, 18, 19, 20, 54, 85, 138, 147, 151, 158, 159, 177, 189, 199, 217, 219, 223, 233, 248.
  dwelling house, 2, 18, 19, 22, 43, 54, 68, 72, 79, 85, 87, 96, 100, 109, 111, 147, 151, 155, 158, 163, 167, 177, 189, 199, 200, 212, 217, 219, 223, 225, 233, 236, 237, 248.
  homestead, 60.
  mansion, 233.

172   GENERAL INDEX.

Buildings, continued.
  shop, 76, 217.
  stable, 133, 158, 199, 217.
  warehouse, 1, 135, 172, 224.
Burying place, 137, 216.

Cape Porpoise. See Index of Places.
  grants recorded, see Index of Grantors under the names following:
  Bailey, Joseph, 125.
  Davis, John, junior, 198.
  Davis, John, senior, 198.
  Hill, Samuel. 206.
  Littlefield, Eliab, 180.
  Moorey. Nicholas, 201.
  Scadlock, Samuel 256, 266.
  Symonds, Harlakinden, 226.
  Tyler. James, 249.
  grants referred to:
    town to
      William Randall, 266.
      Richard Young, 266.
  Daniel Epps to Harlakinden Symonds, 226.
  Henry Hetherly to Richard Young, 266.
  Nicholas Moorey to Joseph Bailey, 126.
  Nicholas Moorey to James Tyler. 249.
  Andrew Orgures to Joseph Bailey, 125.
  William Phillips to William Scadlock, 267.
  Samuel Snow to Nicholas Moorey, 201.
Cartway, 136.
Casco bay. See Index of Places.
  grants recorded, see Index of Grantors under the names following:
  Berry, James, 167.
  Cleve, George, 245.
  Corbin, James, 162.
  Danforth, Thomas, 240.
  Ellacot, Vines, 217, 218.
  Kelly, Elisha, 224.
  Lewis, Jotham, 165.
  Massachusetts, 242.
  Otis, Job, 106.
  Seacomb, Richard, 164.
  Seacomb, Richard, estate of, 161.
  Soullard, Peter. 168.
  Wharton, Richard, estate of, 56, 187.
  Winslow, Gilbert, 28.
  Winslow, Nathaniel, 27.
  grants referred to:
    town of Casco to Richard Seacomb, 161.
  John Clean to Richard Seacomb, 161.
  John Hanson to John Drake, 167, 168.
  Indians to Rachel Berry, 167.
  Massachusetts, General Court of, to Richard Wharton, 187.
  Massachusetts, Governor and company, to Thomas Danforth, 240.

Casco bay, continued.
  Massachusetts, Governor and company, to Samuel Nowell, 240.
  John Mosure to Joseph Nash, 26, 27.
  Gregory Mudge to Rachel Berry, 167.
  Joseph Nash to Enoch Wiswal, 26, 27, 106.
  Alexander Rigby to George Cleve, 245.
  John Shapleigh to Richard Wharton, 57, 58.
  Gilbert Winslow to Job Otis, 106.
  Nathaniel Winslow to Job Otis, 106.
  Enoch Wiswal to Gilbert Winslow, 27. 106.
  Enoch Wiswal to Nathaniel Winslow, 26, 27, 106.
Certificates, 244.
Clerk of Courts:
  Hammond, Joseph, 14, 127, 183, 198, 214.
  of Bristol county,
    Cary, John, 125, 126.
  of Suffolk county,
    Ballantine, John. 218, 219.
    Davenport. Addington, 241.
Commissioners:
  Bracket. Anthony, 165, 166.
  Hooke, Francis, 156.
  Neale, Francis, 245.
  Stileman, Elias, 135, 199.
Consideration, see also under Pay.
  affection and love, 10, 13, 22, 23, 41, 63, 64, 68, 69, 82, 91, 94, 97, 103, 112, 122, 143, 146, 156, 172, 183, 200, 206, 208, 214, 223, 230, 234, 240, 252, 254, 255, 257. 266.
  contract of marriage, 223.
  good will. 159.
  valuable, 156, 157, 164. 175, 176, 179.
Co-partnership, 51, 183, 210.
Corn mills:
  at Arrowsic island, 223.
  at Saco, 88.
  at York, 91, 152, 189, 243.
Councilors of Massachusetts:
  Lynde, Benjamin, 110.
  Pike, Robert, 262.
  Saffin, John, 161.
  Townsend, Penn, 163.
  Wheelwright, Samuel, 45.
Councilors of New Hampshire:
  Hincks, John, 165, 255.
  Plaisted, John, 48, 144.
  Penhallow, Samuel, 15, 94, 145.
  Wheelwright, John, 137.
Courts,
  held at Wells, 151.
  General, of Massachusetts, 187.
  Inferior Court of Common Pleas,
    held at Boston, 218, 219, 241.
    held at Bristol, 125. 126.
    held at York, 14, 37, 126, 127, 144, 183, 214.
  Superior, 186.
    held at Boston, 57, 58, 74.

General Index. 173

Courts, continued.
  held at Kittery, 109.
Court records of Massachusetts, 187.
Country road, 75, 76, 79, 91, 184.

Deacons of the First Church, Boston, 186, 187.
Depositions:
  Abbot, John, 3.
  Adams, Thomas, 198.
  Alcock, Job, 116.
  Allen, Walter, 237.
  Bane, Lewis, 198
  Banks, Joseph, 198.
  Blasdell, Henry. 262.
  Bradbury, Mary, 262.
  Bradbury, Thomas, 262.
  Bradstreet, John, 35.
  Bray, Samuel, 223.
  Buckminster, Jabez, 166.
  Checkley, Anthony, junior, 241.
  Crocket, Joseph, 48.
  Doer, John. 3.
  Donnell, Samuel, 246.
  Drown, Leonard, 143.
  Eaton, John, 261.
  Elliot, Benjamin, 3.
  Elliot, Robert, 116.
  Emery, James, 236, 237.
  Frost, Charles, 261.
  Gach, Edmund, 18.
  Grant, William, 10.
  Graves, John, 48.
  Hains, William, 37.
  Hall, John, 10.
  Hammond, Joseph. 144.
  Harmon, Johnson, 30.
  Harvey, Elizabeth, 147.
  Hodsden, Anne, 159.
  Jackson, George, 14.
  Johnson, Priscilla, 261.
  Jones, John, 145.
  Knight, Thomas, 145.
  Lord, Martha, 236.
  Nanney, alias Naylor, Katherine, 14.
  Nason, John, 237.
  Phillips, John, 166.
  Phillips, William, 166.
  Preble, Abraham, 14.
  Preble, Abraham, junior, 30.
  Preble, Jonathan, 223.
  Royal, William, 218, 219.
  Savage, Ephraim, 241.
  Shine, John, 165.
  Storer, Lydia, 183.
  Tilton, Abraham, 247.
  Tompson, Anne, 237.
  Trescott, John, 218, 219.
  Wadlin, William, 35.
  Wallis, Nathaniel, 166.
  Walton, Shadrach, 10.
  Weare, Mary, 246.
  Webber, Deborah, junior, 183.
  Wheelwright, John, 198.

Depositions, continued.
  Willine, Roger, 245.
  Wright, Henry, 237.
Deputy Governors:
  Billingham, Ri., 226
  Danforth, Thomas, 166, 242.
Deputy President of Maine:
  Davis, John, 1, 176.
Deputy Sheriff of the county:
  Curtis, Joseph. junior, 125, 126.
Domestic animals:
  bull, 159.
  calves, 54, 156, 245, 248, 264.
  cattle, 12, 22, 23, 54, 66, 132, 151, 155, 159, 200, 217, 245, 261, 264.
  cows, 54, 106, 138, 155, 156, 159, 223, 229, 245, 248, 261, 264.
  ewes, 261, 264.
  goats, 155, 156, 262.
  heifers, 54.
  horses, 229.
  mares, 8, 248.
  oxen, 54, 159, 248, 260, 261.
  sheep, 155, 223, 248.
  steers, 156, 245.
  swine, 217, 245, 248.

English miles, 16.

Falmouth. See Index of Places.
  town clerk, 166.
  grants recorded, see Index of Grantors under the names following:
    Cloice, Thomas, 164.
    Greeson, John, 165.
    Haughton, John, 162.
    Ingersol, John, 279.
    Mitton, Michael, 245.
    Munjoy, George, 86.
    Proprietors of, 166.
  grants referred to:
    George Cleve to Michael Mitton, 245.
    John Greason to John Haughton, 162.
    Sattery Gusset to Francis Small, 86.
    George Munjoy to John Ingersol, 79.
    Francis Small to John Phillips, 86.
Farm, 2, 13, 14, 41, 66, 67, 72, 74, 75, 76, 93, 109, 120, 152, 156, 193, 206, 212, 227, 247, 252, 253, 257, 261.
Feast of the Annunciation of the Blessed Virgin Mary, 120, 121.
Fences, 4, 36, 42, 133, 134, 135, 185, 192, 225.
  to maintain, 225.
Fish, 132.
  flakes, 224.
  flake rooms, 224.
  right reserved by Indians, 16.
  stages, 224.
  sturgeon, 2.
  whale, 2.

General Index.

Furs and skins, 159, 160.
  beaver, 160.
  moose, 160.

Garrison at York, 193.
Georgetown. See Index of Places.
  grants recorded, see Index of Grantors under the name following:
    Robinson, William, 229.
  grants referred to:
    John Bland to William Robinson, 229.
General Court of Massachusetts, 187.
Governor, 17.
  Neale, Walter, 17.
  Vines, Richard, 17.
Governor and Corporation in London, 217, 218.
Governor of the Province of Maine,
  Andros, Sir Edmund, 177.
  Bradstreet, S., 242.
Grants referred to,
  Grantors:
    Abbot, John, 101.
    Adams, Elizabeth, 194.
    Atkins, Thomas, 208.
    Austine, Matthew, 194.
    Baker, Goodman, 46.
    Banks, Joseph, 242.
    Banks, Richard, 95.
    Barter, Henry, 228.
    Beal, Arthur, 103, 105.
    Benmore, Philip, 23.
    Berwick, town of, 210.
    Bice, Thomas, 172.
    Blackman, Benjamin, 186.
    Bland, John, 229.
    Bonighton, John, 220, 221.
    Bonighton, Richard, 31, 242.
    Bragdon, Arthur, 31.
    Bragdon, Arthur, senior, 110.
    Brawn, George, 147.
    Broughton, Thomas, 262.
    Burrage, William, 225.
    Cape Porpoise, town of, 266.
    Casco, town of, 161.
    Child, Henry, 54.
    Clean, John, 161.
    Cleve, George, 245.
    Collicot, Richard, 167.
    Cousins, John, 233, 234, 235.
    Croade, John, 161.
    Crocket, Elihu, 13.
    Crocket, Joseph, 41.
    Dummer, Jeremiah, 90.
    Elkins, Christopher, 225.
    Emery, Anthony, 23.
    Emery, James, 23, 140.
    Emms, Henry, 208.
    Endle, Richard, 46.
    Epps, Daniel, 226.
    Estes, Richard, 78, 216.
    Fernald, James, 205.

Grantors, continued.
  Ferris, Aaron, 80, 81, 219.
  Frost, Nicholas, 236.
  Fry, Adrian, 25.
  Fryer, Joshua, 209.
  General Court of Massachusetts, 187.
  Gibbon, James, 220.
  Goodwill, Thomas, 258.
  Goodwin, Daniel, 34.
  Gorges, Sir Ferdinando, 121.
  Gosse, Edmund, 41.
  Governor and company of Massachusetts, 240.
  Gowen, James, 141.
  Gowen, Lemuel, 142.
  Greason, John, 162.
  Green, Hannah, 248.
  Gusset, Sattery, 86.
  Hanson, John, 168.
  Harmon, Johnson, 18, 40, 126.
  Harris, Nathaniel, 187.
  Heard, John, 83.
  Hetherly, Henry, 266.
  Hill, Samuel, 74.
  Hole, John, 255.
  Hooke, Eleanor, 95.
  Hooke, Mary, 41.
  Hooke, William, 232, 233.
  Hooper, Thomas, 215.
  Hutchinson, Eliakim, 53, 98, 187.
  Hutchinson, Elisha, 97.
  Indians, 148, 149, 150, 167, 169, 177.
  Jenkins, Stephen, 140.
  Jocelyn, Joslyn, Henry, 13, 225.
  Joy, Ephraim, 260.
  Junkins, Alexander, 195.
  Kelley, Roger, 224.
  King, Richard, 143.
  Kittery, town of, 5, 11, 25, 36, 41, 46, 47, 55, 59, 61, 63, 64, 77, 81, 93, 94, 105, 107, 117, 130, 133, 141, 142, 144, 151, 157, 158, 160, 179, 180, 196, 225, 229, 238, 256, 260.
  Lawson, Christopher, 122.
  Lewis, William, 179, 180.
  Littlefield, Samuel, 211.
  Lord, Benjamin, 86, 87.
  Lord, William, 82, 83.
  Mason, Robert Tufton, 53.
  Masters, Nathaniel, 213.
  Mendum, Jonathan, 28, 43.
  Mendum, Robert, 7, 8.
  Mills, Thomas, 213.
  Montjoy, George, 79.
  Moorey, Nicholas, 126, 249.
  More, Ebenezer, 155.
  Morrell, John, 23, 205.
  Morrell, Nicholas, 216, 217.
  Mosure, John, 26, 27, 106.
  Moulton, Jeremiah, 18.
  Mudge, Gregory, 167.
  Nash, Joseph, 26, 27, 106.
  Nason, Baker, 102.

GENERAL INDEX.   175

Grantors, continued.
  New England, President and Council of, 31, 242.
  Norton, George, 95.
  Norton, Margaret, 95.
  Orgures, Andrew, 125.
  Parker, John, 148, 149, 150.
  Pendleton, Bryan, 155.
  Penhallow, Samuel, 155.
  Phillips, William, 241, 267.
  Plaisted, James, 1.
  Raynes, Francis, 131.
  Rice, Thomas, 18, 224.
  Rice, Thomas, senior, 12.
  Rigby, Alexander, 245.
  Rishworth, Edward, 189.
  Scarborough, town of, 205.
  Scottow, Joshua, 205.
  Shapleigh, John, 5°.
  Shapleigh, Nicholas, 22.
  Shapleigh, Sarah, 22.
  Shaw, William, 182.
  Sheafe, Sampson, 186.
  Shepard, John, 146.
  Simpson, Joseph, 152.
  Small, Francis, 86.
  Snow, Samuel, 201.
  Spencer, Moses, 73.
  Storer, Lydia, 268.
  Symands, Harlakinden, 5, 97, 99, 264.
  Thomas, Nathaniel, 155, 214, 267.
  Treworgie, James, 25.
  Tucker, Nicholas, 43.
  Tucker, Richard, 43.
  Twisden, John, 95.
  Venney, William, 88.
  Vines, Richard, 234.
  Wadley, William, 87.
  Walker, Samuel, 258.
  Webber, Samuel, 97, 98, 150.
  Webber, Thomas, 149, 150.
  Wells, town of, 9, 13, 88, 109, 119, 151, 211, 212, 213, 237, 251, 252.
  Whitney, Nathaniel, 126.
  Wilson, William, 180.
  Wincoll, John, 23, 82.
  Winslow, Gilbert, 106.
  Winslow, Nathaniel, 106.
  Wiswal, Enoch, 26, 27, 106.
  Withers, Thomas, 224.
  Woodbridge, Benjamin, 155.
  York, town of, 1, 3, 14, 38, 89, 90, 110, 113, 114, 115, 116, 131, 173, 174, 182, 190, 193, 206, 207, 210, 248, 250.
Grantees:
  Abbet, Thomas, 160.
  Allen, James, 250.
  Allen, Thomas, 155, 267.
  Atkins, Thomas, 160.
  Bailey, Joseph, 125, 126.
  Bane, Jonathan, 207.
  Banks, Richard, 210.

Grantors, continued.
  Barter, Henry, 215.
  Benmore, Philip, 23.
  Berry, George, 214.
  Berry, Richard, 167.
  Blackman, Benjamin, 220.
  Bolls, Joseph, 46.
  Bolls, Samuel, 119.
  Bonighton, Richard, 31, 242.
  Botts, Isaac, 93.
  Bragdon, Arthur, 110, 115.
  Bragdon, Joseph, 114.
  Bragdon, Samuel, 207.
  Bragdon, Thomas, 110, 115.
  Bray, John, 196.
  Bray, Richard, 233.
  Bready, John, 25.
  Brookin, Henry, 182.
  Brown, Henry, 151.
  Brown, Samuel, 213.
  Burnum, John, junior, 264.
  Burrage, John, 225.
  Came, Samuel, 18.
  Carr, James, junior, 211.
  Chadbourne, James, 47.
  Chapman, John, 25.
  Chase, Isaac, 211.
  Clark, Nathaniel, 252.
  Clark, Thomas, 95.
  Clayce, John, 213.
  Cleve, George, 245.
  Cole, George, 262.
  Cole, Coal, John, 5, 216.
  Cole, Joseph, 14.
  Couch, Joseph, 144.
  Cousins, John, 234.
  Croade, John, 73, 86, 87.
  Cumins, Elizabeth, 31, 242.
  Curtis, Dodevah, 22.
  Curtis, Thomas, 2 0.
  Dalin, John, 149, 150.
  Danforth, Thomas, 240.
  Daniel, Thomas, 224.
  Davis, Sylvanus, 177.
  Dearing, Roger, 267.
  Dill, Daniel, 193.
  Donnel, Henry, 1, 182.
  Downing, Joshua, 59.
  Drake, John, 167, 168.
  Dummer, Shubael, 3, 90.
  Emery, James, 23.
  Emons, Ebenezer, 219.
  Fennix, George, 180.
  Fernald, James, 94, 205.
  Ferris, Aaron, 12.
  Freeman, Nathaniel, 113.
  Frink, John, 74.
  Frost, Charles, 140, 209.
  Frost, Philip, 31.
  Frost, William, 9, 13, 241.
  Fry, Adrian, 217.
  Gaskin, John, 255.
  Godfrey, Edward, 121.
  Godfrey, Oliver, 121.

176   GENERAL INDEX.

Grantees, continued.
  Goodwin, Thomas, 34.
  Gowell, Richard, 143, 144.
  Gowen, John, 64.
  Gowen, Lemuel, 141, 142, 238.
  Grant, William, 36.
  Greely, Thomas, 25.
  Gudrig, Isaac, 43.
  Haley, William, 55.
  Haman, Mr., 241.
  Hamilton, Biel, 260.
  Harmon, John, 115, 207.
  Harris, John, 97, 99.
  Harris, Nathaniel, 97, 98, 187.
  Hatch, Samuel, 9.
  Haughton, John, 162.
  Heard, James, 229.
  Heard, John, 80.
  Holman, Samuel, 167.
  Holman, Thomas, 167.
  Hooke, Humphrey, 233.
  Hooke, Jacob, 233.
  Hooke, William, 206.
  Hooke, William, junior, 206.
  Hooper, John, 101, 102.
  Hoult, Joseph, 207.
  Huff, Thomas, 80, 81, 219.
  Hunking, Mary, 157.
  Hutchinson, Eliakim, 53.
  Ingarsol, Elisha, 46.
  Ingarsol, John, 46, 79.
  Joy, Ephraim, 2·6, 260.
  Kelley, Elisha, 224.
  Kingsbury, John, 207.
  Knap, Joshua, 103, 105.
  Leighton, William, 151.
  Lewis, Thomas, 31, 242.
  Lewis, William, 179, 180.
  Libbey, John, 13, 205.
  Littlefield, Anthony, 211.
  Littlefield, David, 9.
  Littlefield, Edmund, 237, 251.
  Littlefield, Francis, 211.
  Littlefield, Joseph, 251.
  Littlefield, Samuel, 237.
  Livingstone, Joanna, 194.
  Lord, Samuel, 54.
  Love, William, 133.
  Mackentier, Daniel, 195.
  Mackentier, Micum, 89.
  Masters, Nathaniel, 109, 212.
  Mendum, Robert, 7, 8.
  Mitton, Michael, 245.
  Moorey, Nicholas, 201.
  More, Ebenezer 155, 228, 267.
  Morrell, Abraham, 142.
  Morrell, John, 23.
  Morrell, John, junior, 23, 107.
  Morrell, Nicholas, 78, 82, 83, 216.
  Nash, Joseph, 26, 27, 106.
  Nason, Richard, 117.
  Norton, John, 228.
  Nowell, Peter, 174, 190.
  Nowell, Samuel, 240.

Grantees, continued.
  Oare, James, 151.
  Otis, Job, 106.
  Paul, Daniel, 205.
  Penhallow, Samuel, 155.
  Pepperrell, William, 41.
  Pepperrell, William, junior, 258.
  Perkins, Jacob, 243.
  Phillips, John, 86.
  Phillips, William, 155, 241.
  Pierce, Pearce, John, 89.
  Pierce, Pearce, William, 105.
  Plaisted, John, 53.
  Pray, Joseph, 38.
  Preble, Abraham, 1, 90, 210.
  Preble, Caleb, 243.
  Prichard, John, 187.
  Prichett, John, 208.
  Purchase, Thomas, estate of, 57 58.
  Ramsdell, Nathaniel, 110.
  Randall, William, 266.
  Randol, Richard, 63.
  Raynes, Captain, 173.
  Raynes, Francis, 131.
  Reed, John, 130.
  Rice, Richard, 225.
  Rice, Thomas, 224.
  Rice, Thomas, junior, 12.
  Robinson, William, 229.
  Roe, Richard, 11, 121.
  Ross, John, 25.
  Sagamores, Indians, 57, 58.
  Sargent, Diamond, 236.
  Savage, Ephraim, 122.
  Saywood, John, 189.
  Saywood, Mary, 234, 235.
  Scadlock, William, 267.
  Scottow, Joshua, 225.
  Seacomb, Richard, 161.
  Shaw, Joseph, 208.
  Shaw, William, 182.
  Sheafe, Sampson, 186.
  Simpson, Daniel, 152.
  Skillion, Samuel, 43, 61.
  Small, Francis, 86.
  Spinney, Samuel, 146, 172, 181.
  Stagpole, John, 126, 207.
  Stanford, John, 97.
  Stimpson, Richard, 88.
  Stone, Benjamin, 207.
  Stone, Daniel, 158.
  Stone, Jonathan, 158.
  Storer, Joseph, 268.
  Symonds, Harlakinden, 226.
  Tetherly, Samuel, 142.
  Tetherly, William, 142.
  Thompson, Alexander, 18, 61.
  Thompson, John, 157.
  Tidy, John, 147.
  Tozier, Richard, 64.
  Tucker, Richard, 43.
  Twisden, Samuel, 210.
  Tyler, James, 249.

General Index. 177

Grantees, continued.
  Veazy, George, 77.
  Way, Elizur, 56, 58.
  Waymouth, Edward, 105.
  Walker, Richard, 5.
  Walker, Samuel, 186.
  Webber, James, 150.
  Webber, Mary, 148, 149, 150.
  Webber, Thomas, 148, 149, 150.
  Weeks, Joseph, 28.
  Wentworth, Timothy, 210.
  Wharton, Richard, 56, 57, 58, 187.
  Whipple, Katherine, 151.
  White, Richard, 116.
  Whitney, Nathaniel, 40, 126.
  Wilson, William, 179, 180.
  Wincoll, John, 77.
  Winslow, Gilbert, 27, 106.
  Winslow, Nathaniel, 26, 27, 106.
  Wiswal, Enoch, 26, 27, 106.
  Wittum, 147.
  Wood, Joseph, 102.
  Woodman, John, 131.
  Worster, Moses, 23, 82.
  Young, Richard, 266.
Grist-mills, see corn-mills.

Highways, 13, 25, 70, 72, 79, 83, 88, 91, 92, 117, 151, 152, 154, 172, 185, 189, 211, 212, 214, 216, 222, 223, 251, 256, 268.
High-water mark, 139, 177.
Home lot, 117, 254.
Houses and appurtenances,
  cellar, 257.
  chimney, 3, 88.
  galleries, 198.
  pillars, 198.
  seats in meeting-house, 198.
  stairs, 198.
  well, 257.
Household goods, supplies, wares, 12, 22, 23, 230, 245.
  movables, 12.
House-lot, 74, 231.
Hunting, liberty of, 16.
Husbandry, appliances and products:
  tools for, 22.
  cart, 87, 261.
  corn, 209, 248.
  grindstone, 54.
  hay, 248.
  implements, 200, 217, 218, 261.
  plow, 261.
  sled, 87, 217, 261.
  team, 139.

Indian enemy, 9.
Indian grants:
  grants recorded, see Index of Grantors under the names following:
  Fluellin, tract above Wells and Cape Porpoise, 220.

Indian grants, continued.
  Hombinowitt, alias John Rogomock, tract west of the Saco river, 220.
  Passaconaway,
  Rowles,
  Runaawitt,
  Wahangnonawitt,
  Sagamores, tract bounded by Piscataqua river and Merrimac river, also Isles of Shoals, 16.
  grants referred to:
  Sosowen to Peter Turbet, John Saunders and John Bush, 238.
  John Bush, John Saunders, Peter Turbet to Harlakinden Symonds 238.
Indian War, 56, 148, 149, 150, 166, 167, 168, 169.
Interest,
  lawful, 103, 138, 175.
  in merchantable fish, 81.
  yearly, 70.
Isles of Shoals. See Index of Places.
  grants recorded, see Index of Grantors under the name following:
  Kelley, Elisha, 224.
  grants referred to:
  Roger Kelley to Elisha Kelley, 224.

Jail, in Kittery, 125.
Jamestown. See Index of Places.
  grants recorded, see Index of Grantors under the name following:
  Pitman, James, 265.
Justices of the Peace:
  Bane, Lewis, 72, 92, 106, 108, 109, 110, 115, 123, 126, 174, 175, 236, 243, 253.
  Donnell, Samuel, 261.
  Freeman, Nathaniel, 124.
  Frost, Charles, 22, 23, 25, 47, 52, 62, 65, 67, 68, 70, 73, 79, 80, 82, 83, 84, 86, 90, 91, 94, 104, 105, 114, 115, 127, 136, 140, 143, 144, 145, 146, 148, 154, 200, 203, 204, 216, 217, 223, 224, 229, 231, 236, 237, 265.
  Hammond, Joseph, 76, 239, 246, 255, 257, 261, 264.
  Hill, John, 5, 34, 73, 117, 261.
  Hooke, Francis, 122.
  Jones, Larens, 24.
  Pepperrell, William, 6, 13, 18, 21, 29, 42, 43, 44, 49, 55, 56, 61, 63, 71, 75, 81, 85, 95, 103, 128, 129, 131, 132, 144, 145, 156, 172, 179, 180, 181, 196, 197, 205, 212, 214, 215, 219, 220, 228, 230, 255, 258, 259, 260, 264, 267, 268.
  Plaisted, Elisha, 157, 160, 185, 199, 200, 223, 225, 232, 258, 266.
  Plaisted, Ichabod, 10, 12, 20, 24, 35, 36, 47, 53, 54, 64, 71, 87, 92, 93, 94, 102, 107, 118, 211, 231, 256, 260.

Justices of the Peace, continued.
  Plaisted, John, 35, 48, 54, 61, 75, 76, 77, 111, 112, 116, 118, 140, 143, 237, 253.
  Plaisted, Samuel, 255.
  Preble, Abraham, 1, 4, 11, 15, 19, 30, 31, 32, 33, 37, 38, 48, 50, 51, 52, 60, 103, 111, 133, 153, 171, 173, 174, 182, 183, 184, 185, 189, 190, 191, 192, 193, 194, 195, 207, 210, 223, 226, 234, 235, 243, 247, 248, 250, 254.
  Rishworth, Edward, 88, 234.
  Tyng, Edward, 225.
  Wheelwright, John, 10, 39, 41, 54, 60, 69, 89, 130, 138, 144, 154, 161, 198, 209, 211, 213, 236, 237, 238, 249, 251, 252, 266, 268.
  Wheelwright, Samuel, 152.
  Wincoll, John, 37.
Justices of the Peace, elsewhere in Massachusetts:
  Addington, Isaac, 3, 96, 263.
  Appleton, John, 151, 204, 247.
  Appleton, Samuel, 5, 227, 247, 252.
  Bromfield, Edward, 159, 175.
  Cary, Nathaniel, 14.
  Checkley, Samuel, 186, 221.
  Clark, John, 55, 59, 97, 98, 99, 204, 208, 222.
  Cook, Elisha, 188.
  Corwin, Jonathan, 249.
  Cushing, John, 100.
  Davenport, Addington, 4, 134.
  Doane, John, 125.
  Dummer, Jeremiah, 9, 12, 242.
  Harris, William, 149, 167.
  Hathorne, John, 13.
  Hirst, Grove, 168.
  Hodges, Henry, 202.
  Hutchinson, Edward, 178, 179.
  Hutchinson, Elisha, 169.
  Keeling, Samuel, 230.
  Lynde, Benjamin, 110.
  Lynde, E., 178.
  Lynde, Joseph, 14.
  Lynde, Samuel, 237.
  Newman, John, 113, 132.
  Norden, Nathaniel, 257.
  Noyes, Thomas, 122, 207.
  Otis, Joseph, 107, 136.
  Palmer, Thomas, 66.
  Pierce, Daniel, 265.
  Pike, Robert, 262.
  Pope, Seth, 120.
  Prout, Timothy, 162, 166.
  Saffin, John, 161.
  Sargent, Peter, 96.
  Sewall, Samuel, 44, 67.
  Sewall, Stephen, 100, 101, 180, 213, 267.
  Stoddard, Anthony, 150, 151.
  Sumerby, Henry, 232, 233.
  Thomas, Nathaniel, 27, 28.
  Townsend, Penn, 123, 142, 163, 237.

Justices of the Peace, elsewhere in Massachusetts, continued.
  Wheelwright, Samuel, 45.
  White, John, 209, 250.
  Wolcot, Joseph, 227.
Justices of the Peace, elsewhere in New Hampshire:
  Atkinson, Theodore, 3, 19, 40, 41, 45, 81, 144, 198.
  Davis, James, 263.
  Frost, John, 131, 156.
  Gerrish, Richard, 81, 147.
  Hunking, Ala., 1, 116.
  Hunking, M., 155.
  Penhallow, Samuel, 7, 8, 15, 59, 94, 145, 148, 265.
  Phipps, Thomas, 134, 206.
  Story, Charles, 3, 22, 26, 29, 74, 78, 119.
  Vaughan, George, 14.
  Waldron, Richard, 130, 237.
  Weare, Nathaniel, 9, 254.
  Wentworth, John, 137, 157.
  Wentworth, J., 224.
  Woodman, John, 6.
Justices of the Peace, elsewhere in Rhode Island:
  Church, Thomas, 164.

Kennebec region. See Index of Places.
  grants recorded, see Index of Grantors under the names following:
  Berry, James, 169.
  Clark, Thomas, 159.
  Davis, Elizabeth, 169.
  Davis, Sylvanus, estate of, 176.
  Haskins, Ruth, 169.
  Holman, Hannah, 167.
  Holman, Samuel, 167.
  Hutchinson, Thomas, ⎫
  Jeffries, David, ⎪
  Wentworth, John, ⎬ Proprs., 178.
  Minot, Stephen, ⎪
  Ruck, John, ⎪
  Watts, John, ⎭
  Lake, Thomas, 159.
  Newman, Abigail, 150.
  Parker, John, 24.
  Pike, Hester, 169.
  Savage, Ephraim, 122.
  Thoyts, Alexander, 158.
  Washburn, Thomas, 169.
  Webber, James, 150.
  Webber, Nathan, 149.
  Webber Nathaniel, 148.
  grants referred to:
    Richard Callacot to Samuel Holman, 167.
    Richard Callacot to Thomas Holman, 167.
    Indians to Thomas Atkins, 169.
    Indians to Sylvanus Davis, 177.
    Indians to Thomas Webber, 148, 149, 150.

General Index.

Kennebec region, continued.
  John Parker to Mary Webber, 148, 149, 150.
  Samuel Webber to James Webber, 150.
  Thomas Webber to John Dalin, 149, 150.
Kittery. See Index of Places.
  meeting-house, 136.
  mill, 6.
  town book, 5, 107, 144, 151.
  or records, 20, 21, 25, 85, 105, 225, 246.
  town clerk, 5, 55, 94, 144.
  town meeting. 55, 94, 144, 179, 225.
  town grants, 55, 94, 144.
  other grants recorded. See Index of Grantors under the names following:
  Abbot, Peter, 143.
  Abbot, Thomas, 143.
  Allen, Francis, 6.
  Allen, Thomas, 154, 267.
  Austine, Matthew, 20.
  Ball, John, 230.
  Barter, Henry, 42, 214.
  Brawn, George, 147.
  Calef, Jeremiah, 47.
  Chadbourne, James, 71.
  Champernown, Francis, 17.
  Chapman, John, 25.
  Cocks, James, 11.
  Cole, John, 5.
  Cooper, John, 54.
  Corbet, Abraham, 151.
  Couch, Joseph, 144.
  Couch, Roger, 144.
  Crocket, Richard, 62.
  Crocket, Thomas, estate of, 145.
  Curtis, Dodevah, 22.
  Cutt, Robert, 20.
  Dearing, Joseph, 196.
  Dearing, Roger, 19, 45, 257.
  Dennet, John, 228.
  Dering, Henry, 45.
  Dorothy, John, 11.
  Downing, Jonathan, 147.
  Downing, Joshua, 59.
  Emery, Daniel, 23, 265.
  Emery, James, 23.
  Emery, Job, 52.
  Fennick, John, 71, 264.
  Fennix, George, 180.
  Fernald, James, 94.
  Ferris, Aaron, 12.
  Follet, John, 55.
  Frink, John, 74, 127.
  Frost, Charles, 20.
  Frost, John, 20, 139.
  Frost, Nicholas, 7.
  Frost, William, 54.
  Fry, Adrian, 216.
  Fry, William, 136.
  Gage, Edmund, 84.

Kittery, continued.
  Gaskin, Elizabeth, 254.
  Godsoe, William, 156, 260.
  Gowell, Richard, 143, 155, 200.
  Gowen, John, 76, 215.
  Gowen, Lemuel, 141.
  Greely, Thomas, 25.
  Gudrig, Isaac, estate of, 43.
  Gunnison, Elihu, 128.
  Haley, William, 54.
  Hammond, Joseph, 20.
  Hanscom, Job, 22.
  Hanscom, Moses, 22.
  Hanson, Tobias, 54.
  Haynes, Thomas, 191.
  Heard, John, 47, 79, 82, 229.
  Hill, John, 52.
  Hill, Samuel, 74.
  Hill, Samuel, junior, 236.
  Huff, Thomas, 80, 81, 219.
  Hunking, Mary, 157.
  Hunking, Mary, junior, 157.
  Hutchins, Jonathan, 49.
  Hutchins, Samuel, 49.
  Ingersol, Elisha, 46.
  Ingersol, John, 94, 128.
  Jenkins, Reinold, 6.
  Jenkins, Stephen, 6.
  Joy, Ephraim, 256.
  Keais, Samuel, 223.
  Kelley, Elisha, 111.
  Kincaid, Anne, 6.
  Lewis, Andrew, 196.
  Lewis, Peter, 179.
  Littlefield, Moses, 54.
  Lord, Benjamin, 54.
  Lord, Martha, 54.
  Lord, Nathan, 54.
  Mendum, Jonathan, 28.
  Mendum, Nathaniel, 6.
  More, Ebenezer, 228.
  Morrell, Abraham, 222.
  Morrell, John, 261.
  Morrell, John, junior, 107.
  Morrell, Nicholas, 78, 82, 83, 216.
  Nelson, Mary, 147.
  Norton, John, 228.
  Paul, Daniel, 204, 227.
  Paul, John, 61.
  Penhallow, Samuel, 223.
  Pepperrell, William, 41.
  Pepperrell, William, junior, 219.
  Plaisted, James, 132.
  Plaisted, John, 52.
  Randol, Richard, 63.
  Remick, Christian, 255.
  Remick, Jacob, 255.
  Remick, Joshua, 145.
  Rice, Richard, 225, 260.
  Rice, Thomas, junior, 12.
  Rogers, William, 246.
  Sargent, Sergent, Diamond, 236.
  Sevey, Joseph, 212.
  Shapleigh, John, estate of, 267.

180 GENERAL INDEX.

Kittery, continued.
Shapleigh, Nicholas, 135.
Skillion, Samuel. 42, 61.
Smith, Jacob, 146.
Spiller, Anne, 11.
Spinney, Samuel, 29, 146, 170, 171, 172, 181, 239.
Spinney, Thomas, 84.
Thomas, Nathaniel, 136.
Thompson, Alexander, 61.
Thompson, John, 61, 85, 157.
Toziar, Richard, 64.
Tucker, Joseph, 204.
Tucker, Nicholas, 214.
Tucker, William, 213.
Walker, Edward, 254.
Whipple, John. 151.
White, Richard, 44.
Williams, Joanna, 254.
Williams, Paul, 254.
Wilson, Hannah, 85.
Wilson, William, 179.
Wright, Henry, 204.
Young, Job, 191.
grants referred to, town to
John, Bray, 196.
John Bready, 25.
James Chadbourne, 47.
John Cole, 5.
Joseph Couch, 144.
Joshua Downing, 59.
James Fernald, 94.
Richard Gowell, 144.
Lemuel Gowen, 141, 142.
William Grant, 36.
William Haley, 55.
James Heard, 229.
John Heard, 80.
Mary Hunking, 157.
John Ingersol, 46.
Ephraim Joy, 256.
William Leighton, 151.
William Lewis, 179, 180.
John Morrell, junior, 107.
William Pepperrell, 41.
Richard Randol, 63.
Richard, Rice, 225.
Richard Roe, 11.
John Ross, 25.
Samuel Skillion, 61.
Alexander Thompson, 61.
John Thompson, 157.
Richard, Toziar, 64.
Katherine Whipple, 151.
Henry Barter to Ebenezer More and John Norton, 228.
Philip Benmore's heirs to John Morrell, 23.
Thomas Bice to Samuel Spinney, 172.
George Brawn to John Tidy and Wittum, 147.
Henry Child to Samuel Lord, 54.
Elihu Crocket to Aaron Ferris, 12.

Kittery, continued·
Joseph Crocket to Wliam Pepperrell, 41.
Anthony Emery to James Emery, 23.
James Emery to Philip Benmore, 23.
James Emery to Charles Frost, 140.
Richard Endle to Elisha Ingersol, 46.
Richard Estes to Nicholas Morrell, 78, 216.
Aaron Ferris to Thomas Huff, 80 81, 219.
Nicholas Frost to Diamond Sargent, 236.
Adrian Fry to John Chapman, 25.
Edmund Gosse to William Pepperrell, 41.
James Gowen to Lemuel Gowen, 141.
Lemuel Gowen to Abraham Morrell, Samuel Tetherly and William Tetherly, 142.
John Heard to Nicholas Morrell, 83.
Samuel Hill to John Frink, 74.
John Holes to John Gaskin, 255.
Thomas Hooper to Henry Barter, 215.
Thomas Huff to Ebenezer Emons, 219.
Eliakim Hutchinson to John Plaisted, 53.
Stephen Jenkins to Charles Frost, 140.
Richard King to Richard Gowell, 143.
William Lewis to William Wilson, 179, 180.
William Lord to Nicholas Morrell, 82, 83.
Robert Tufton Mason to Eliakim Hutchinson, 53.
Jonathan Mendum to William Pepperrell, 43.
Jonathan Mendum to Joseph Weeks, 28.
Robert Mendum to Robert Mendum, 7, 8.
Ebenezer More to Thomas Allen, 155.
John Morrell to John Morrell, jr., 23.
Nicholas Morrell to John Coal, 216.
Nicholas Morrell to Adrian Fry, 217.
Samuel Penhallow to Ebenezer More, 155.
Thomas Rice to Thomas Rice, jr., 12.
Thomas Rice to Samuel Spinney, 181.
Thomas Rice to Thomas Daniel, 224.
Nicholas Shapleigh to Dodevah Curtis, 22.
Sarah Shapleigh to Dodevah Curtis, 22.
John Shepard to Samuel Spinney, 146.
Nathaniel Thomas to Thomas Allen, 155, 267.

GENERAL INDEX. 181

Kittery, continued.
  Nathaniel Thomas to George Berry, 214.
  Nathaniel Thomas to Roger Dearing, 267.
  Nathaniel Thomas to Ebenezer More, 267.
  James Treworgie to Thomas Greely, 25.
  Nicholas Tucker to Richard Tucker, 43.
  Richard Tucker to Isaac Gudrig, 43.
  William Wilson to George Fennix, 180.
  Thomas Withers to Thomas Rice, 224.
  Benjamin Woodbridge to Samuel Penhallow, 155.

Landing place, 139.
Low water mark, 135, 177, 214, 216.
Lygonia, trader for the company of, 17.
Lyman. See Index of Places; also Coxhall.
  grants recorded, see Index of Grantors under the names following:
  Burnum, John, junior, 264.
  Harris, John, 99.
  Harris, Nathaniel, 97.
  Walker, Richard, 4.
  grants referred to:
    Harlakinden Symonds to John Burnum, 264.
    Harlakinden Symonds to John Harris, 97, 99.
    Harlakinden Symonds to Nathaniel Harris, 97.
    Harlakinden Symonds to John Stanford, 97.
    Harlakinden Symonds to Richard Walker, 5.

Maine. See under Associates, Clerk of Courts, Courts, Deputy Presidents, Deputy Governor, Deputy Sheriff, Governor, Justices of the Peace, Marshal of York county, Recorder, Records, Register of Deeds, York county.
Marked trees, 4, 11, 18, 25, 33, 36, 38, 50, 51, 53, 88, 101, 102, 103, 104, 108, 130, 135, 137, 151, 152, 153, 173, 175, 177, 181, 182, 184, 192, 198, 202, 215, 225, 229, 247.
Marshal of York county, 15.
Massachusetts. See under Clerk of Courts, Courts, Councilors, General Court, Justices of the Peace, Recorder, Records.
Mast-way at Berwick, 105.
Meeting-house at Kittery, 136.
Meeting-house at York, 91, 123, 126, 174, 198, 243, 246.

BOOK VIII. 53

Mill at Cape Porpoise, 180.
Mill at Kennebunk falls, 237, 251.
Mill at Kittery, 6.
Mill at Salmon falls, 134.
Mill implements, appurtenances and products:
  crows, 51, 85.
  dam, 51.
  dogs, 51.
  flood-gates, 223.
  gear, 76, 223.
  iron-work, 9, 51, 70.
  saw, 51, 85, 210, 223.
  utensils, 82.
Mines and minerals, 4, 120, 121, 133.
  gold, 2, 120, 121.
  precious stones. 2, 120, 121.
  silver, 2, 120, 121
Ministry, land for the use of, 118.
New England, President and Council for. 31; see also under Secretaries.
New Hampshire. See under Councilors, Justices of the Peace, Proprietors, Recorder, Records.

Occupations:
  agent, 17, 65.
  blacksmith, 14, 25, 141, 169, 198, 203, 210, 211, 222, 238.
  bricklayer, 79, 82, 83, 205, 216, 261, 264.
  carpenter, 25, 80, 94. 101, 109, 144, 147, 151, 170, 171, 173, 179, 208, 212, 219, 248, 268.
  clerk, 13. 66, 88.
  clothier, 75.
  cordwainer, 8, 26, 27, 38, 61, 84, 85, 100, 101, 102, 158, 174, 210, 236, 247, 252.
  factor, 17.
  farmer, 191, 192.
  ferryman, 29.
  fisherman, 14, 24, 42, 62, 111, 201, 264, 266.
  glazier, 216, 217.
  gunsmith, 4.
  housewright, 204.
  husbandman, 4, 22, 34, 49, 52, 62, 70, 93, 96, 117, 118, 119, 148, 149, 150, 153, 154, 156, 158, 164, 169, 172, 185, 199, 201, 203, 212, 231, 233, 238, 246, 248, 249, 252, 268.
  joiner, 7, 97, 98, 105, 112, 113, 114, 126, 187, 214, 228.
  laborer, 35, 73, 86, 94. 114, 157, 160, 167, 168, 169, 173, 185.
  lot-layer, 246.
  malster, 151.
  mariner, 7, 20, 43, 64, 69, 105, 118, 135, 146, 148, 149, 150, 196, 198, 199, 200, 207, 209, 215, 258, 265, 266.
  mason, 154, 265.
  master, 3, 12.

182 GENERAL INDEX.

Occupations, continued.
  merchant, 20, 24, 41, 42, 56, 65, 69, 73, 80, 86, 87, 94, 95, 98, 106, 111, 120, 121, 131, 135, 141, 143, 144, 151, 155, 158, 159, 167, 176, 185, 186, 187, 224, 240, 241, 258, 262.
  miller, 5, 180, 205.
  millwright, 11, 129, 234, 235, 258.
  minister, 3, 14, 16.
  planter, 13, 36, 93, 116, 130, 175, 176, 211, 202, 223, 251, 253, 257, 260.
  rector, 262.
  sawyer, 148.
  school master, 113.
  scrivener, 208.
  servant, 199, 261.
  shipwright, 7, 19, 28, 42, 45, 61, 84, 112, 116, 128, 141, 147, 162, 179, 185, 196, 204, 213, 214, 220, 227, 228, 239, 246, 255, 257, 267.
  shoe maker, 61.
  shopkeeper, 44, 45, 106, 155, 187, 222.
  smith, 108.
  steward, 17.
  surveyor, 5, 11, 25, 41, 64, 85, 105, 107, 129, 142, 145, 157, 158, 179, 180, 196, 238, 246, 256.
  tailor, 55, 136, 236.
  tanner, 25, 47, 83.
  trader, 17.
  vicar, 262.
  vintner, 133.
  weaver, 14, 22, 30, 36, 102, 105, 144, 180, 215.
  yeoman, 1, 3, 4, 5, 6, 10, 20, 22, 23, 25, 26, 27, 29, 30, 33, 36, 39, 46, 47, 49, 55, 59, 60, 61, 66, 67, 68, 71, 73, 74, 76, 77, 78, 79, 82, 84, 85, 87, 95, 97, 98, 104, 108, 110, 117, 123, 125, 127, 128, 129, 130, 133, 137, 139, 143, 156, 157, 160, 164, 170, 171, 172, 174, 179, 180, 181, 190, 196, 197, 198, 200, 201, 204, 206, 208, 210, 214, 225, 227, 228, 229, 230, 232, 235, 239, 242, 254, 263, 264, 267.
Orchards, 14, 19, 20, 26, 42.

Parsonage, at York, 174.
Partners, 167, 168, 260.
Patents to:
  Richard Bonighton and Thomas Lewis, 9, 21, 242, 254.
  Way and Purchase, 172.
  William Hooke, 206.
  Scottow's, 205, 225.
  Purchase's, 122.
  Vines Ellacot's, 218.
  Saco, 220.
Pay:
  annual, 32.
  assisting in building saw-mill and house, 258.
  bills of credit, 66, 67, 185, 188, 212, 213, 220, 226, 262.

Pay, continued.
  beef, 164.
  boards, 165.
  coats, 16, 17.
  current money, 1, 3, 6, 7, 11, 14, 15, 21, 24, 25, 26, 28, 29, 33, 34, 35, 36, 42, 43, 45, 46, 47, 52, 53, 61, 63, 64, 67, 68, 70, 73, 74, 75, 76, 77, 78, 80, 82, 83, 84, 85, 87, 88, 91, 92, 93, 95, 96, 97, 98, 104, 105, 106, 107, 109, 110, 111, 116, 117, 118, 119, 123, 134, 136, 137, 141, 146, 147, 148, 149, 150, 154, 155, 157, 158, 160, 161, 162, 163, 164, 165, 167, 168, 169, 170, 171, 172, 179, 180, 181, 185, 188, 189, 192, 201, 207, 208, 210, 211, 212, 216, 217, 218, 219, 222, 223, 224, 231, 234, 235, 236, 237, 238, 239, 249, 251, 252, 253, 255, 256, 257, 260, 264, 267, 268.
  current pay, 17, 198, 201.
  current silver money, 27.
  fish, 132.
  gun, 8.
  house, 210, 225, 258.
  Indian corn, 17.
  land in exchange, 12, 59, 82, 107, 174, 205, 225.
  lawful public bills, 227.
  maintenance, 12, 94, 230, 233, 245.
  mare, 8.
  money, 1, 5, 6, 8, 11, 14, 18, 19, 30, 31, 39, 40, 44, 50, 51, 54, 61, 62, 71, 84, 88, 89, 90, 94, 101, 102, 114, 115, 117, 118, 126, 127, 128, 132, 140, 144, 145, 152, 153, 164, 173, 174, 180, 182, 184, 191, 193, 195, 196, 201, 205, 215, 225, 229, 231, 242, 243, 246, 247, 248, 250, 256, 266.
  lawful, 13, 20, 25, 38, 69, 80, 85, 93, 100, 103, 110, 110, 111, 112, 123, 133, 135, 153, 165, 176, 186, 191, 198, 202, 214, 228, 251, 268.
  passable, 4, 112, 130, 197, 203, 247, 266.
  pork, 164.
  province bills, 204.
  saw-mill, 225, 258.
  shirts, 16.
  Seville pillars and Mexican pieces, 218.
  victuals, 16.
Pejepscot, afterward Brunswick. See Index of Places.
  grants recorded, see Index of Grantors under the name following:
    Wharton, Richard, estate of, 56.
  grants referred to:
    Thomas Purchase's estate to Richard Wharton, 57, 58.
    Sagamores to Richard Wharton, 57.
    Eleazer Way to Richard Wharton, 56, 58.
Petition to inhabitants of Casco Bay to erect saw-mill, 244.

General Index.   183

Pine trees reserved for masts for the king's ships, 53.
Propagation of the Gospel to the Indians in America, 217, 218.

Recorder, Edward Rishworth, 37, 151, 244, 245.
  of New Hampshire,
    Samuel Penhallow, 3.
    William Vaughan, 3.
Records of Maine, 57.
  of Essex county, Mass., 232.
  of New Hampshire, 3.
Registers of Deeds:
  Hammond, Joseph, 1—268.
  Moodey, Joseph, 103, 228.
  Preble, Abraham, 43, 138, 170.
Rents,
  annual, 217, 218, 251.
  quit rent, 53.
  one pepper corn, 121.
  yearly, 112, 120, 121.
Reservations, 10, 11, 16, 50, 52, 53, 58, 137, 143, 149, 150, 160, 172, 211, 215, 240, 254.
Ring, gold, 245.
Road, 65, 78, 82, 83, 156, 185, 189.

Saco. See Index of Places.
  grants recorded, see Index of Grantors under the names following:
    Banks, Joseph, 30.
    Bonighton, Richard, 8.
    Booth, Simon, 88.
    Emery, James, 231.
    Emery, James, junior, 231.
    Goodwill, Thomas, 220.
    Jackson, Martha, 249.
    Pepperrell, William, junior, 258.
    Phillips, William, 155.
    Preble, Caleb, 242.
    Rolfe, Ezra, 249.
    Turfrey, George, 241.
    Walker, Samuel, 185.
  grants referred to:
    Joseph Banks to Caleb Preble, 248.
    Benjamin Blackman to Sampson Sheafe, 186.
    Benjamin Blackman to Samuel Walker, 186.
    John Bonighton to Benjamin Blackman, 220.
    John Bonighton to William Phillips, 241.
    Richard Bonighton to Elizabeth Comins, 31, 242.
    James Gibbons to Benjamin Blackman, 220.
    Thomas Goodwill to William Pepperrell, junior, 258, 259.
    Bryan Pendleton to William Phillips, 155.
    William Phillips to William Frost, 241.

Saco, grants referred to, continued.
    William Phillips to Mr. Haman, 241.
    President and Council for New England to Thomas Lewis and Richard Bonighton, 31, 242.
    Sampson Sheafe to Samuel Walker, 186.
    Samuel Walker to William Pepperrell, junior, 258, 259.
Sagadahoc region.
  grants recorded, see Index of Grantors under the name following:
    Shaw, Joseph, 208.
  grants referred to:
    Thomas Atkins to John Prichett, 208.
    Henry Emms to Joseph Shaw, 208.
Saw-mills at:
  Arrowsic island, 223.
  Berwick, 70, 82, 87, 237.
  Cape Neddick, 51, 183, 225.
  Casco river, 244.
  Georgetown, 229.
  Kittery, 22, 85, 192.
  Saco, 241, 258, 259.
  Wells, 9, 10.
Scarborough. See Index of Places.
  town book, 206.
  clerk, 206.
  selectmen, 205, 206.
  grants recorded, see Index of Grantors under the names following:
    Libbey, John, 205.
    Libbey, John, senior, 13.
    Scottow, Joshua, 225.
    Tinney, John, 156.
  grants referred to, town to
    John Libbey, 206.
  William Burrage to Joshua Scottow, 225.
  Christopher Elkins to Joshua Scottow, 225.
  Henry Jocelyn to John Burrage, 225.
  Henry Jocelyn, Joslyn, to John Libbey, 13.
  Joshua Scottow to John Libbey, 205.
Secretary of New England,
  West, John, deputy secretary, 345.
Sheriff of the county,
  Preble, Abraham, 127.
Steward of plantation at Hilton's point, 17.
St. Michael's, feast of, 120, 121.

Titles:
  bachelor, 22, 256.
  captain, 1, 5, 14, 17, 18, 23, 37, 48, 52, 59, 72, 82, 87, 88, 91, 92, 93, 100, 108, 111, 116, 123, 127, 135, 139, 151, 153, 155, 157, 173, 182, 210, 214, 245, 253, 256.
  colonel, 41, 92, 97, 131, 188, 212, 245, 261, 267.

184   GENERAL INDEX.

Titles, continued.
  ensign, 143, 192, 194.
  esquire, 1, 3, 5, 21, 41, 48, 52, 53, 56, 71, 72, 76, 90, 99, 109, 116, 125, 126, 127, 128, 129, 131, 133, 134, 136, 140, 148, 149, 150, 151, 155, 167, 168, 169, 170, 176, 186, 187, 212, 217, 218. 223, 224. 225, 226, 227, 235, 240, 242, 245, 254, 257, 261, 262, 264, 265.
  gentleman, 1, 4, 11, 14, 20. 39, 40, 46, 56, 57. 74, 91, 120, 121, 131, 134, 136, 137, 139, 148, 149, 150, 155, 161, 162, 164, 167, 168, 169, 176, 185, 186, 198, 204. 207, 226, 231, 241, 245, 252, 256.
  lieutenant, 8. 30, 36. 220, 254.
  major, 1, 3. 5, 20, 47, 57, 59, 88, 99, 116, 188, 209, 212, 221, 227, 241, 252, 264.
  Mr., 3, 5, 8, 14, 18, 22, 25, 29, 30, 31, 35, 37, 40. 45, 46, 48, 49, 51. 61, 63, 65, 66. 69, 74, 77, 78, 87, 90, 91, 92, 97, 98, 99. 102, 103, 105, 108, 109, 122, 123, 124, 126, 131, 132, 133, 136, 137, 142, 143, 144, 151, 157, 158, 159, 160, 174, 175, 179, 180, 181, 183, 186, 188, 189, 190, 192, 197, 198, 203, 205, 212, 214, 221, 223, 224, 227, 230, 231, 232, 233, 234, 255, 260, 261, 263, 264, 267, 268.
  Mrs., 32, 41, 68, 75, 88, 157, 159, 188, 189, 197, 224, 244, 246, 260, 261.
  reverend, 3, 14.
  spinster, 167.
  widow, 11, 15, 40, 56, 75, 85, 95, 117, 127, 147, 150, 155, 157, 169, 174, 197, 199, 200, 207, 209, 223, 233, 234, 247, 251, 267. 268.
Town, to promote the settling of, 148.
Turf and twig, possession by, 45, 135, 220, 245.

Vessel,
  sloop, 12, 159.

Warrant to surveyors, 245.
Wells. See Index of Places.
  town meeting, 213.
  town records, 109, 151.
  commissioners, 211.
  selectmen, 211.
  grants recorded, see Index of Grantors under the names following:
    Bolls, Joseph, 46.
    Bolls, Samuel, 119.
    Brown, Samuel, 212.
    Buckling, George, 213.
    Clark, Nathaniel, 252.
    Epps, Symond, 252.
    Fowler, Philip, 226.
    Frost, William 13.
    Fuller, Samuel, 203.
    Gooch, James, 9.
    Hill, Samuel, 250.
    Jacob, Joseph, 226.

Wells, continued.
    Littlefield, Eliab, 153.
    Littlefield, Francis, 176.
    Littlefield, Jonathan, 250.
    Littlefield, Samuel, 211, 237, 251.
    Masters, Nathaniel, estate of, 109.
    Oare, James, 151.
    Read, Obadiah, 221.
    Sawyer, William, 10.
    Sibley, Samuel, 248.
    Stimpson, Richard, 88.
    Storer, Joseph, 268.
  grants referred to, town to
    Samuel Bolls, 119.
    Henry Brown, 151.
    Nathaniel Clark, 252.
    John Clayce, 213.
    William Frost, 9, 13.
    Samuel Hatch, 9.
    Anthony Littlefield, 211.
    David Littlefield, 9.
    Edmund Littlefield. 237, 251.
    Francis Littlefield, 211.
    Joseph Littlefield, 251.
    Samuel Littlefield, 237.
    Nathaniel Masters, 109, 212.
    James, Oare, 151.
    William Venney. 88.
    Goodman Baker to Joseph Bolls, 46.
    Peter Folsom to William Sawyer, 10.
    Samuel Littlefield to James Carr, junior, 211.
    Samuel Littlefield to Isaac Chase, 211.
    Nathaniel Masters to Samuel Brown, 213.
    Thomas Mills to John Clayce, 213.
    Lydia Storer to Joseph Storer, 268.
    William Venney to Richard Stimpson, 88.
  Wills referred to:
    Job Alcock, 93, 253.
    Thomas Clark, 95.
    Joseph Cross, 250.
    Sylvanus Davis, 176.
    Joshua Fryer, 209.
    Bridget Graffort, 224.
    John Hunking. 157.
    James Ingles, 207.
    Robert Jordan, 245.
    George Lewis, 166.
    Robert Mendum, 7, 8, 28.
    William Pepperrell, 41.
    William Phillips, 241.
    Richard Seacomb, 161, 164.
    William Spencer, 73.
    Nicholas Tucker, 204.
    Thomas Withers, 260.

Yarmouth, North. See Index of Places.
  grants recorded, see Index of Grantors under the names following:
    Cousins, John, 233.
    Preble, Hannah, 234.

General Index.

Yarmouth, North, continued.
  Saywood, John, 235.
  Saywood. Joseph, 234.
  Tanner, James, 140.
  grants referred to:
    John Cousins to Richard Bray, 233.
    John Cousins to Mary Saywood, 234.
    Richard Vines to John Cousins, 233.
York. See Index of Places.
  town book, 1, 3, 14, 36, 40, 89, 182, 207, 210, 243, 248, 250.
  town clerk, 261.
  town meeting, 1, 89, 113, 114, 115, 183, 207, 250.
  town records, 89, 104, 115, 182.
  town vote, 243.
  meeting house, 174, 243.
  ministry, 11, 30.
  moderator, 261.
  parsonage, 174.
  selectmen, 89, 104, 123, 129, 174, 198, 210, 243.
  town grants, 123, 174, 243.
  other grants recorded, see Index of Grantors under the names following:
    Addams, Thomas, 254.
    Allen, James, 250.
    Bane, Jonathan, 207.
    Bane, Lewis, 90.
    Banks, John, 252.
    Banks, Joseph, 252.
    Beal, Arthur, 103.
    Beal, Edward, 69, 135.
    Black, Daniel, 30.
    Blagdon, Hannah, 15.
    Blagdon, Mary, 15.
    Bracey, William, 36.
    Bragdon, Arthur, 33, 191.
    Bragdon, Joseph, 114.
    Bragdon, Samuel, 207.
    Brand, John, 172.
    Brooken, Henry, 182.
    Burrell, John, 65.
    Came, Samuel, 18.
    Clark, Thomas, estate of, 95.
    Coffin, James, 122.
    Cole, John, 14.
    Curtis, Job, 210, 223.
    Dill, Daniel, 192.
    Donnel, Henry, 1.
    Donnell, Samuel, 181.
    Dummer, Jeremiah, 3.
    Elliot, Robert, 39, 40.
    Follet, Nicholas, 15.
    Freeman, Nathaniel, 113.
    Frost, Charles, 129, 209.
    Godfrey, Edward, 121.
    Gorges, Sir Ferdinando, 120.
    Gray, Robert, 225.
    Harmon, John, 114, 207.
    Harmon, Johnson, 11, 50, 91, 153.

York, continued.
  Harris, Nathaniel, 97, 98.
  Hook, Humphrey, 232.
  Hook, Jacob, 232.
  Hook, William, 206.
  Hook, William, junior, 232.
  Hoult, Joseph, 207.
  Howell, Rice, 208.
  Hutchinson, Eliakim, 96.
  Kingsbury, Benjamin, 207.
  Linscot, John, 107, 190.
  Littlefield, Daniel, 39.
  Mackentier, Daniel, 38, 104, 194, 195.
  Mackentier, John, 89.
  Mackentier, Micum, 59, 104.
  Maine, Josiah, 129.
  Moulton, Daniel, 148.
  Moulton, Jeremiah, 68.
  Norton, George, 112.
  Nowell, Peter, 66, 174.
  Parsons, Elihu, 173.
  Parsons, John, 100.
  Pearce, William, 105, 137.
  Pepperrell, William, 41.
  Perkins, Jacob, 247.
  Pickerin, John, 111, 116.
  Preble, Abraham, 197.
  Preble, Abraham, junior, 4, 90.
  Prichard, John, 187.
  Ramsdell, Nathaniel, 110, 115.
  Raynes, Francis, 103, 172, 184.
  Rishworth, Edward, 65.
  Sayward, Hannah, 110.
  Shaw, William, 31, 184.
  Simpson, Joseph, 152.
  Smith, Hannah, 247.
  Smith, James, 14, 38, 108.
  Snell, John, 93, 253.
  Stagpole, John, 207.
  Stone, Benjamin, 207.
  Stover, George, 60.
  Stover, John, 201.
  Thompson, Alexander, 67.
  Weare, Joseph, 1.
  Weare, Mary, 32.
  Webber, Samuel, 50, 51, 183.
  Welch, Philip, 182.
  White, Richard, 116.
  Whitney, Nathaniel, 126.
  Wise, Thomas, 132.
  Young, Jonathan, 207.
  Young, Joseph, junior, 193.
  grants referred to, town to
    James Allen, 250.
    Richard Banks, Thomas Curtis, Samuel Twisden and Abraham Preble, 210.
    Arthur Bragdon, 110, 115.
    Joseph Bragdon, 114.
    Thomas Bragdon, 110, 115.
    Joseph Cole, 14.
    Daniel Dill, 193.
    Henry Donnel, 1, 182.

York, continued.
    Shubael Dummer, 3, 90.
    Nathaniel Freeman, 113.
    John Harmon, 115.
    John Harmon, Benjamin Stone, Jonathan Young, Jonathan Bane, Samuel Bragdon, Joseph Hoult and John Stagpole, 207.
    William Hooke, 206.
    Micum Mackentier, 89.
    Peter Nowell, 174, 190.
    Jacob Perkins, 248.
    John Pierce, 89.
    Joseph Pray, 38.
    Captain Raynes, 173.
    Francis Raynes, 131.
    William Shaw, 182.
    Richard White, 116.
    Elizabeth Adams and Matthew Austin to Joanna Livingstone, 194.
    Richard Banks to Thomas Clark, 95.
    Arthur Beal to Joshua Knap, 103, 105.
    Arthur Beale to William Pearse, 105.
    Arthur Bragdon to Philip Frost, 31.
    Arthur Bragdon, senior, to Nathaniel Ramsdell, 110.
    Jeremiah Dummer to Abraham Preble, 90.
    James Fernald to Daniel Paul, 205.
    Joshua Fryer, estate of, to Charles Frost, 209.
    Sir Ferdinando Gorges to Edward Godfrey, 121.
    Sir Ferdinando Gorges to Oliver Godfrey, 121.
    Sir Ferdinando Gorges to Richard Row, 121.
    Hannah Green to Jacob Perkins, 248.
    Johnson Harmon to Samuel Came, 18.
    Johnson Harmon to Nathaniel Whitney, 40 126.
    Nathaniel Harris to John Prichard, 187.

York, continued.
    Eleanor Hooke to Thomas Clark, 95.
    Mary Hooke to William Pepperrell, 41.
    William Hooke to Jacob Hooke, 233.
    William Hooke to Humphrey Hooke, 233.
    William Hooke to William Hooke, junior, 232.
    Eliakim Hutchinson to Nathaniel Harris, 98, 187.
    Elisha Hutchinson to Nathaniel Harris, 97.
    Alexander Junkins to Daniel Mackentier, 195.
    John Morrell to James Fernald, 205.
    John Morrell to Daniel Paul, 205.
    Jeremiah Moulton to Alexander Thompson, 18.
    George Norton to Thomas Clark, 95.
    Margaret Norton to Thomas Clark, 95.
    James Plaisted to Abraham Preble, 1.
    Francis Raynes to John Woodman, 131.
    Edward Rishworth to John Saywood, 189.
    William Shaw to Henry Brooken, 182.
    Joseph Simpson to Daniel Simpson, 152.
    John Twisden to Thomas Clark, 95.
    Samuel Webber to Nathaniel Harris, 97, 98.
    Nathaniel Whitney to John Stagpole, 126.
York county. See under Maine.
    ancient files, 17.
    records, 26, 56, 82, 99, 131, 205, 233, 264.
    grants recorded, see Index of Grantors under the names following:
    Grant, James, 207.
    Stevens, John, 207.

CPSIA information can be obtained
at www.ICGtesting.com
Printed in the USA
LVHW081948070521
686793LV00002B/84